W9-AUX-973

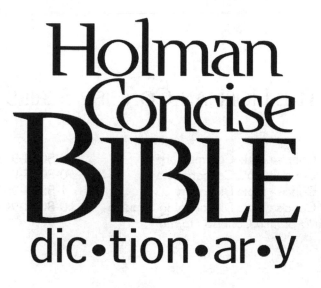

Holman Concise BIBLE dic•tion•ar•y

THE HOLMAN CONCISE SERIES

Holman Concise Bible Commentary   0-8054-9337-9
Holman Concise Bible Concordance   0-8054-9349-2
Holman Concise Bible Dictionary   1-5581-9694-3
Holman Concise Bible Dictionary in Spanish   0-8054-9431-6
Dicconario Bíblico Conciso Holman

BROADMAN & HOLMAN REFERENCE

Holman Concise BIBLE dic•tion•ar•y

OVER 2,800 ENTRIES INCLUDING CONTEMPORARY TOPICS AND ISSUES

BROADMAN
& HOLMAN
PUBLISHERS

NASHVILLE, TENNESSEE

The Concise Holman Bible Dictionary © 1997, 2001
Revised and Reset
by Broadman & Holman Publishers
All rights reserved

Dewey Decimal Classification: 220.3
Subject Heading: BIBLE—DICTIONARIES
Library of Congress Card Catalog Number: 97–22283

Library of Congress Cataloging-in-Publication Data
Concise Holman Bible Dictionary / Trent C. Butler, editor
   p. cm.
   ISBN 1–55819–694–3 (hardcover)
   1.Bible—Dictionaries. 2.Bible—Biography—Dictionaries.
I. Butler, Trent C.
BS440.C62   1997
220.3—DC21

                        97–22283
                        CIP

11 12 13 14 15 10 09 08 07
Q

HOW TO USE THIS DICTIONARY

Most Bible teachers agree that a Bible dictionary is the first reference tool a student of the Bible should acquire.

Having a Bible dictionary and a Bible enable you to begin mining the treasures of the Scriptures. God has inspired each of the books that make up the Bible and made them available to you with the ultimate aim of making you a complete person in Christ.

Bible dictionaries come in all sizes. The *Concise Holman Bible Dictionary* strikes a nice balance between being too brief and providing so much information as to be overwhelming.

The *Concise Holman Bible Dictionary* is comprehensive in range of subjects covered and yet the articles are designed to be used by people who want a first take on a person, place, or concept.

If you are studying a book of the Bible, you may want to turn first to the article that gives a broad stroke overview of that book.

Next, note the words in the passage being studied that you'd like more information on. Chances are you will find one or more articles that provide understanding for those terms.

If you're doing a topical study, you make want to list the words that cluster around that topic and then look up each one. You'll find an article on each of the major doctrines of Christian faith.

One of the uniquenesses of The *Concise Holman Bible Dictionary* among all the dictionaries currently available is the wide range of articles on contemporary issues and concerns.

Many of these issues aren't dealt with by name in the Bible but in the Bible God has given us principles that speak to the subjects about which 21st Century people are concerned. Subjects such as

Abortion	Career Decisions
AIDS	Child Abuse
Animal Rights	Credit Cards
Assisted Suicide	Cremation
Birth Control	Dinosaurs
Birth Defects	Life Support (Artificial)

And many more . . .

Holman Concise BIBLE dic•tion•ar•y

AARON

Moses' brother; Israel's first high priest from priestly tribe of Levi; brother of Miriam. See Ex. 6:16-26. Initiated sacrificial system (Lev. 1-7). Husband of Elisheba; father of: Nadab, Abihu, Eleazar, and Ithamar. First, two died when they offered sacrifices with fire that God had not commanded (Lev. 10:1-2; 16:1-2). Second, two developed priestly lines:

(1) Ithamar through Eli to Abiathar and,

(2) Eleazar to Zadok (1 Sam. 14:3; 22:20; 1 Kings 2:26-27; 1 Chron. 6:50-53).

Aaron started Israel's formal priesthood (Ex. 28–29; Lev. 8–9), offered sacrifices for his own sins (Lev. 16:11) and then for others; served as a symbol or type of the perfect priest (Ps. 110:4, where future king was described as eternal priest; compare Zech. 6:11-15).

Aaron spoke for Moses before Pharaoh and stretched out Moses' staff to bring God's plagues on the land (Ex. 7:9,19). He and Hur helped Moses hold up the staff, the symbol of God's power, so Israel would defeat Amalek (Ex. 17:12). At Sinai, Aaron and his two older sons, Nadab and Abihu, went up mountain with Moses and 70 elders to make the covenant (Ex. 24:9). As Moses delayed on the mountain, the people asked Aaron to "make us gods" (Ex. 32:1). Aaron made a calf and apparently led in its worship. In Num. 12 he and Miriam spoke against Moses' marriage to the Cushite (Ethiopian) woman and jealously murmured against God's selection. Aaron confessed his sin and pleaded for mercy for Miriam. When Korah, Dathan, and Abiram opposed Moses and Aaron, Aaron's intercession stopped the plague (Num. 16). Later, God vindicated Aaron's leadership (Num. 17). At Kadesh, Aaron joined in Moses' sin as they seized God's power for themselves (Num. 20:7-13). Thus Aaron, like Moses, was not allowed to enter the Promised Land.

On Mt. Hor, Aaron died at age 123 (Num. 20:23-28).

AARON'S ROD

Instrument Aaron used to demonstrate to Pharaoh that the God of the Hebrews was Lord. It became a snake when cast down (Ex. 7:8-13), brought about the first three plagues (Ex. 7:19-20; 8:5-7,16-19), and was used to strike the rocks at Horeb and Kadesh to bring forth water (Ex. 17:1-7; Num. 20:7-11). After Korah's rebellion (Num. 16:1-50), Aaron's rod blossomed and bore almonds — God's sign that the house of Aaron should serve Him in the tabernacle, where the rod was placed (Num. 17:1-11; compare Heb. 9:4).

AB

Fifth month in Jewish religious calendar, corresponding to the eleventh month in the Hebrew civic calendar and to parts of July and August.

ABADDON (*to perish*)

Dark side of existence beyond death; parallel with Sheol and death (Job 26:6; 28:22; 31:12; Prov. 15:11; 27:20; Ps. 88:11). KJV and NIV translate Abaddon as "destruction." Hebrew name (Rev. 9:11) of angel of bottomless pit, whose Greek name was Apollyon. See *Hell*.

ABANA or ABANAH (NASB)

Modern Barada River flowing from Mt. Hermon through Damascus in Syria (2 Kings 5:12).

ABARIM

Mountain range in Moab including Mt. Nebo from which Moses viewed the Promised Land (Num. 27:12; 33:47-48; Deut. 32:49; compare Jer. 22:20).

ABBA

Aramaic word for "father" Jesus used to speak of His intimate relationship with God, a relationship others can have through faith (Mark 14:36; Luke 11:1-2; Rom. 8:15; Gal. 4:6-7).

ABEDNEGO

Babylonian name (Dan. 1:7) of Azariah, Hebrew youth conscripted along with Daniel to serve Nebuchadnezzar's court, whom God delivered from the fiery furnace (Dan. 2:48-3:30). See *Meshach.*

ABEL *(breath, vapor, meadow)*

Son of Adam and Eve; first shepherd; first person to worship God correctly (Gen. 4; Heb. 11:4; 12:24); first human to die. Abel's offering was made with a correct attitude and in the proper manner. Jealousy led his brother Cain to kill Abel.

ABEL-BETH-MAACHAH or ABEL-BETH-MAACAH (NASB, NIV, RSV)

Modern Abil el-Oamh, 12 miles north of Lake Huleh near Dan; once part of the Aramean city state of Maachah (2 Sam. 10:6; 20:1-22; 1 Kings 15:20; 2 Kings 15:29). A city with a strong Israelite tradition, known for its wise people.

ABIATHAR *(father of abundance)*

Son of Ahimelech; eleventh high priest in succession from Aaron; survived the slaughter of priests at Nob (1 Sam. 22); became high priest and chief counselor for David (1 Sam. 23:6,9; 30:7; 2 Sam. 2:1; 5:19); shared responsibility with Zadok of taking the ark to Jerusalem (1 Chron. 15:11,12; 2 Sam. 15:24). Faithful to David during Absalom's rebellion (2 Sam. 15), he later supported Adonijah instead of Solomon (1 Kings 1:7). Solomon deposed him from the priesthood and banished him to Anathoth, his home town, fulfilling the prophecy to Eli (1 Sam. 2:31-35). See *Priests; Levites.*

ABIB

Harvest month covering parts of March and April; time of exodus from Egypt (Ex. 13:4) and Passover festival (Ex. 23:15; 34:18; Deut. 16:1);

later called Nisan (Esther 3:7). See *Calendars.*

ABIGAIL *(my father rejoiced)*

(1) Wife of Nabal, and after his death, of David; praised for wisdom in contrast to Nabal. She impressed David with her beauty, humility, praise, and advice (1 Sam. 25:32-33). Nabal died of a heart attack. See 1 Sam. 30:1-18.

(2) Sister of David and the mother of Amasa (1 Chron. 2:16-17), who commanded David's army (2 Sam. 17:25).

ABIHU *(my father is he)*

Second son of Aaron; one of Israel's first priests (Ex. 6:23; 28:1). He saw God (Ex. 24). He and his brother Nadab offered "strange fire" before God (Lev. 10:1-22). See *Priests.*

ABIJAH or ABIJAM *(my Father is Yahweh)*

(1) Second son of Samuel whose crooked acts as judge led Israel to demand a king (1 Sam. 8:2-5).

(2) Son of Jeroboam, first king of the Northern Kingdom. He died according to Ahijah's prophecy (1 Kings 14:1-18).

(3) Son of Rehoboam known for his large family (2 Chron. 13:21); second king of divided Southern Kingdom (915–913); ancestor of Jesus (Matt. 1:7).

(4) Leading priest during the return from Exile (Neh. 12:4); then a priestly house (Neh. 12:17) to which Zechariah, father of John the Baptist, belonged (Luke 1:5).

ABILENE

Mountainous region ruled by the tetrarch Lysanias at start of John the Baptist's ministry (Luke 3:7). Located about 18 miles northwest of Damascus in the Anti-Lebanon range, its capital was Abila. In A.D. 37 Abilene came under the administrative control of Herod Agrippa I. Later it was part of the kingdom of his son, Agrippa II.

ABIMELECH (*my father is king*)

(1) King of Gerar, who took Sarah for himself, thinking she was Abraham's sister rather than his wife (Gen. 20).

(2) Probably the same as *1*, a king who disputed the ownership of a well at Beersheba with Abraham and then made a covenant with him (Gen. 21:22-34).

(3) King of Philistines at Gerar related to or identical with *1*, Isaac lived under his protection and fearfully passed Rebekah, his wife, off as his sister (Gen. 26).

(4) Son of Gideon, the judge of Israel (Judg. 8:31). He seized power after his father's death by murdering his brothers and having himself named king by his relatives at Shechem. This provoked Jotham's famous fable (Judg. 9:7-21).

ABINADAB (*my father is generous*)

(1) Resident oif Kirjath-jearim whose house was resting place of the ark of the covenant for 20 years after Philistines returned it. His son Eleazar served as priest (1 Sam. 7:1-2; 2 Sam. 6:3-4).

(2) Son of Jesse passed over when David was selected as king (1 Sam. 16:8; 17:13).

(3) Son of King Saul killed by Philistines in battle of Mount Gilbo (1 Sam. 31:2).

(4) Solomon's son-in-law and official over Dor, the Mediterranean seaport below Mount Carmel, was the son of Abinadab or Ben-abinadab (1 Kings 4:11).

ABIRAM (*my father is exalted*)

(1) Leader of rebellion against Moses and Aaron, seeking priestly authority. God caused earth to open and swallow the rebels (Num. 16; 26:9-11).

(2) Son of Hiel sacrificed in foundation of rebuilt Jericho, fulfilling Joshua's warning (1 Kings 16:34).

ABISHAG (*my father strayed* or *is a wanderer*)

Young virgin from Shunem brought to David's bed in his last days to keep him warm (1 Kings 1:1-4; 2:17).

ABLUTIONS

Ceremonial washings to make oneself pure before worship. One background for NT baptism. Old Testament washings cleansed from the impurity of an inferior or undesirable condition to prepare for initiation into a higher, more desirable condition (Ex. 29:4; 30:19-21; Lev. 8:6; Lev. 11-15; Deut. 21:1-9). At times ablutions involved a general washing or bathing (Lev. 14:8; 15:5; Num. 19:7-8).

Old Testament teachings give spiritual purity as the goal. Outward washing is only a symbol (Pss. 24:4; 51:7; 73:13; Prov. 30:12; Isa. 1:16; 4:4; Jer. 2:22; 4:14; Ezek. 16:4-9; 36:25-27; Zech. 13:1).

Hebrews 6:2 bids Christians to progress beyond discussion of basic matters, among which are "doctrine of baptisms." Hebrews 9:10 refers to "divers washings" practiced by the Hebrews under the law but no longer necessary because Christ "was once offered to bear the sins of many" (9:28).

The only washing NT commands is baptism (Acts 22:16; 1 Cor. 6:11), which is not effective as a ritual in itself but only as it shows the working of God's Word in the one baptized (Eph. 5:26; see Heb. 10:22).

ABNER (*father is a lamp*)

Saul's uncle and chief military officer (1 Sam. 14:50). At Saul's death, he supported Ish-bosheth, Saul's son (2 Sam. 2:8), until accused of treason for taking one of Saul's concubines (2 Sam. 3:7-8). Abner transferred loyalty to David. In a jealous rage Joab, David's general, killed Abner, who was buried in Hebron (2 Sam. 3). See 1 Sam. 17:55-58; 20:25; 26:5,14-15.

ABODE OF THE DEAD See *Death; Grave; Hades; Hell; Pit; Sheol.*

ABOMINATION, ABOMINATION OF DESOLATION

Something detestable to God, particularly in relation to idolatry; that which becomes odious, despised, or hated as water polluted by dead fish (Ex. 7:18; see 1 Sam. 13:4; Luke 16:15; Rev. 21:27); cannot be accepted in worship or eaten (Lev. 11; see 7:18; Deut. 29:17); worship, cultural, and moral practices that offend such as homosexuality (Lev. 18:22), Egyptians' eating with foreigners (Gen. 43:22), and particularly foreign gods (Ezek. 6:11).

"Abomination of desolation" is a special term in Dan. 9:27; 11:31; 12:11; Matt. 24:15; Mark 13:14; Luke 16:15; Rev. 17:4-5; 21:27. Dan. 9:27; 11:31; and 12:11 give evidence of a heathen idol or altar which would desecrate the holy temple in Jerusalem. It apparently has both a historical reference—apparently the building of an altar of Zeus by Antiochus Epiphanes in Jerusalem in 167 B.C.—and a final eschatological one. Jesus pointed ahead at least to the destruction of Jerusalem by Rome in A.D. 70 and possibly beyond to the end of time.

ABORTION

The Bible places a high value on all human life, including that of the unborn. Biblical teaching declares that life is a sacred, God-given gift (Gen. 1:26-27; 2:7; Deut. 30:15-19; Job 1:21; Ps. 8:5; 1 Cor. 15:26), especially the life of children (Ps. 127:3-5; Luke 18:15-16), and condemns those who take it away (Ex. 20:13; 2 Kings 8:1:13; Amos 1:13). The development of unborn life is controlled by God (Job 31:15; Ps. 139:13-16; Eccl. 11:5; Isa. 44:2; 46:3; 49:5; Jer. 1:5; Luke 1:15; Gal. 1:15). The personhood of the fetus is clearly taught in Ex. 21:22 where the unborn is called a "child" (*yeled*) rather than a "fetus" (*nepel* or *golem*). Hos. 9:11 implies that life begins at conception, while Luke 1:41,44 recognizes the consciousness of an unborn child.

The high value placed on unborn human life in the Bible is consistent with the Mosaic law regarding negligent miscarriage (Ex. 21:22-25). This law can be compared to similar statutes in the Code of Hammurabi (nos. 209-214) in which the punishment exacted for acts of negligence which resulted in a woman's miscarriage was dependent on the legal or social status of the mother, not the personhood (or supposed lack thereof) of her unborn child. Middle Assyrian law no. 53 (12th century B.C.) made a self-induced miscarriage (i.e., an abortion) a capital offense.

ABRAHAM (*father of a multitude*)

First Hebrew patriarch; son of Terah (Gen. 11:27); prime example of faith; "thy friend forever" (2 Chron. 20:7).

God called Abram to migrate from Ur of the Chaldees to Canaan, assuring him that he would father a vast nation. His wife Sarai's beauty attracted the pharaoh when they moved to Egypt during a famine (Gen. 12:10), but God intervened to save her (compare Gen. 20:12). Returning to Palestine, Abram received covenantal assurances from God (Gen. 15; 17). He had a son, Ishmael, with Sarai's handmaid Hagar. Sarai had her long-promised son, Isaac, when Abraham was 100 years old. Ishmael was expelled with his mother Hagar to the wilderness of Paran. God tested Abraham's faith and obedience, commanding him to sacrifice Isaac. God provided an alternative sacrifice, however, saving the boy's life.

In old age, Abraham remarried and had further children, finally dying at 175 years.

God was known subsequently as the God of Abraham (Ex. 3:6). Through him God had revealed His plan for human salvation (Ex. 2:24; compare 32:13; 33:1).

John showed that descent from Abraham did not guarantee salvation (Matt. 3:9; see Luke 19:9; John 8:39; Rom. 9). Foreigners would join him in the kingdom (Matt. 8:11; compare Luke 16:23-30).

For Paul, Abraham was the great example of faith (Rom. 4; Gal. 3). In Hebrews, Abraham provided the model for tithing (Heb. 7) and played a prominent role in the roll call of faith (Heb. 11). James used Abraham to show that justification by faith is proved in works (Jas. 3:21-24).

ABRAHAM'S BOSOM

Place to which the poor man Lazarus was carried by the angels when he died (Luke 16:22-23). At meals to recline in the bosom of the host was considered the highest honor. The poor man was comforted after death by being given the place of closest fellowship with the father of the whole Hebrew nation. See *Heaven.*

ABRAM *(father is exalted)*

Abraham's original name (Gen. 11:26; chgd. in 17:5).

ABSALOM *(father of peace)*

Third son of King David, who rebelled against his father and was murdered by Joab, David's commander (2 Sam. 3:3; 13–19). David's lament over Absalom shows the depth of a father's love over the loss of a son as well as regret for personal failures that led to family and national tragedies.

ABSTINENCE

Voluntary refraining from some action, such as eating certain kinds of foods or drinking alcoholic beverages.

Old Testament examples of abstinence relate to fasting, the sabbath (Ex. 20:8-11), the Nazirite vow (Num. 6), and food laws (Lev. 11; 19:23-25; Deut. 14).The Day of Atonement was the most prominent fast in Israel. Observance of the sabbath and food laws became the distinguishing, if not unique, characteristics of Israelites. See *Nazirite; Sabbath; Vows; Fasting.*

Old Testament forms of abstinence were points of controversy between Jesus and the religious leaders (Mark 2:18–3:6). Jesus emphasized internal motive over external observance (Matt. 6:16-18). Paul established the principle of abstaining from any activity that might

offend or cause another to stumble (Rom. 14; 1 Cor. 8).

ABYSS

Dark abode of the dead (Rom. 10:7). Abaddon rules the Abyss (Rev. 9:11), from which will come the beast of the end time of Revelation (11:7). The beast of the Abyss faces ultimate destruction (Rev. 17:8). Satan will be bound there during the millennium (Rev. 20:1-3). See *Hades; Hell; Sheol.*

ACACIA See *Shittim.*

ACCAD or AKKAD (NIV, NCV, NLT)

Famous city in Mesopotamia ruled by Sargon I about 2350 B.C. (Gen. 10:10); exact location unknown. It gave its name to Akkadian language used by Babylon and Assyria.

ACCENT, GALILEAN

Peculiarity of Peter's speech that showed he was from Galilee (Matt. 26:73; compare Judg. 12:5-6, where a person's speech betrayed his place of origin).

ACCHO or ACCO

Mediterranean seaport north of Mt. Carmel; assigned to tribe of Asher, who could not conquer it (Judg. 1:31). The Greeks renamed Acco, Ptolemais. On his third missionary voyage, Paul spent one day in Ptolemais (Acts 21:7).

ACCOUNTABILITY, AGE OF

That time in the development of a person when he or she can and invariably does sin against God and thus stands in the need of personal redemption through Jesus Christ. The Jews set the arbitrary age of 12 as the year a child assumed adult status in religious matters and had to follow Mosaic law.

Sin is a willful act of rebellion against God on the part of an individual (Rom. 3:9-18). Clearly, an infant or young child is not capable of such a willful act. Salvation is a deliberate act of faith. To exercise this choice, persons must be able to know they are sinners before God, to repent of that rebellious lifestyle, to transfer trust to Jesus as personal Savior and Lord, and to pattern their lives on Christ's example (Rom. 10:9-14). An infant or young child cannot make these distinctions and is not responsible for them.

Each child crosses that boundary of responsibility to God, sins (Rom. 3:23), and stands in need of Christ. Each child will vary in reaching that time.

ACCURSED

Translation of Hebrew *cherem*, technical term in warfare for items captured from the enemy and devoted to God. Devoting battle spoils to a god was practiced by Israel's neighbors (2 Kings 19:11). See *Anathema*; *Blessing and Cursing*.

ACCUSER

Person who claims another is guilty of a crime or a moral offense; Hebrew word is *satan* (compare Ps. 109:6 in various translations). See *Satan*. False accusation called for serious punishment (Deut. 19:15-21). The psalmist prayed for judgment against his accusers (Ps. 109:4,20,29, NASB, NIV, NRSV). False accusers led to Christ's conviction and death (Matt. 27:12). Jewish accusers (Acts 22:30) finally led Paul to appeal to Rome (Acts 25:11). The law of Moses was sufficient to accuse people of sin (John 5:45), but one day accusations will cease (Rev. 12:10).

ACELDAMA (*field of blood*)

Field Judas Iscariot purchased, where he killed himself (Acts 1:19; see Matt. 27:7). See *Judas*.

ACHAIA

Roman province where Gallio was proconsul in the time of Paul the apostle (Acts 18:12,27-28). It included the southern half of ancient Greece, including the Peloponnesus with Sparta, Athens, and Corinth, the administrative center.

ACHAN or ACHAR (*trouble,* 1 Chron. 2:7).

Judahite (Josh. 7:1) whose theft of a portion of the spoil from Jericho brought divine displeasure and military defeat on the Israelite army. He and his family were stoned to death (Josh. 7:25). See *Ai*; *Joshua*; *Accursed*.

ACHAZ

KJV spelling of Ahaz (Matt. 1:9). See *Ahaz*.

ACHISH

(1) King of Gath, a Philistine city, to whom David fled in fear of Saul (1 Sam. 21:10) and whose army David joined while cunningly expanding his influence around Ziklag (1 Sam. 27; 28:1-2; 29:1-11).

(2) King of Gath to whom Shimei went to retrieve his servants but in so doing violated his agreement with Solomon and lost his life (1 Kings 2:36-46).

ACHMETHA or ECBATANA (NASB, NIV, RSV, TEV)

Capital of ancient Median empire, located in the Zagros Mountains in western Iran, on two major roads that lead from the south and west to the city of Tehran (Ezra 6:2); modern Hamadan.

ACHOR (*trouble, affliction,* or *taboo*)

Valley where Achan and his household were stoned to death (Josh. 7:24-26). Later, it formed part of the border of Judah and is subject of promises in Isa. 65:10 and Hos. 2:15.

ACHSHAPH or ACSHAPH (NIV) (*place of sorcery*)

City state which joined Jabin, King of Hazor, in opposing Joshua as he invaded northern Israel (Josh. 11:1); a border city for Asher (Josh. 19:25); probably located near Acco.

ACHZIB or **ACZIB** (NIV) (*deceitful*)

(1) Town in southern Judah, perhaps modern Tel el-Beida near Lachish (Josh. 15:44). Micah 1:14 makes a wordplay using Achzib, literally the houses of deceitfulness will be deceitful.

(2) Border town of Asher (Josh. 19:29) the Israelite tribe could not conquer (Judg. 1:31); may be modern Tel Akhziv, near Acco.

ACRE

Translation of Hebrew *tsemed*, literally a "team" of oxen; land a team can plow in one day (1 Sam. 14:14; Isa. 5:10).

ACROSTIC

Literary device by which each section of a literary work begins with the succeeding letter of the alphabet. Thus in Ps. 119 the first eight verses begin with *aleph*, the first letter of the Hebrew alphabet; the next eight with *beth*, the second letter of the Hebrew alphabet, and the pattern is continued through verses 169-176, where each begin with *taw*, the last letter of the Hebrew alphabet. Other examples in the Bible include Pss. 9; 10; 25; 34; 37; 111; 112; 145; Prov. 31:10-31; Lam. 1; 2; 3; 4. The acrostic style helped people memorize the poem and expressed completeness of subject matter from A to Z.

ACTS OF THE APOSTLES

Fifth book of NT tracing growth of early church; written by Luke. The two books contain 25 percent of the NT, a larger work than the combined letters of Paul.

Acts is the continuing story of Jesus' work through His new body, the church, beginning once He was no longer bound by the limitations of time and space.

In Acts, Luke emphasizes:

(1) *The Holy Spirit.* At Pentecost the Holy Spirit engulfed the believers who became vehicles through whom the good news of Jesus was proclaimed "unto the uttermost part of the earth" (1:8).

(2) *Outcasts and sinners.* The Ethiopian eunuch (8:26-40), Cornelius (ch. 10), and the Philippian jailer (16:22-34) were rejected by Judaism but accepted and redeemed by Christ.

(3) *Women.* They were cut off from the center of Jewish worship, not permitted beyond their own court in the temple and forced to stand behind a partition in the synagogues while men read the Scriptures. Luke drew attention to the conversions and consequent roles of Lydia (16:11-15,40) and Priscilla (18:18-28). He mentioned the conversion of nameless women at various stops on Paul's missionary journey (see 17:4 as one example).

(4) *The piety of Jesus and His followers.* The first few chapters constantly describe the apostles in the temple praying. Paul's ministry was punctuated by the same type of spirituality.

ADAM

City near Jordan River, where waters of Jordan heaped up for Israel to cross (Josh. 3:16); probably Tel ed-Damieh near the Jabbok River.

ADAM AND EVE (*man* and *life*)

First man and woman created by God from whom all other people are descended. They freely chose to introduce sin into human experience (Gen. 1–3). The consequences of Adam and Eve's sin fell not merely upon them but upon the earth as well (Gen. 3:14-19). Their ultimate punishment was being driven from the garden (Gen. 3:22-24). This was also an act of God's mercy, for it kept humanity from living forever in a sinful state and offered the possibility of future redemption.

In the NT, Jesus' genealogy is traced back to Adam (Luke 3:38). Opinion is divided on the earliest occurrence of Adam as a proper name, some preferring Gen. 2:20; others Gen. 4:25; see 5:1a,3,4,5 and 1 Chron. 1:1.

In 2 Cor. 11:3, Eve's gullibility before the serpent is presented as undesirable. In 1 Tim. 2:11-15, women are urged to be silent and subjected to man because Adam was created before Eve and because Eve was deceived into sinning.

Paul twice used the contrast of Christ with Adam to clarify the achievement of Christ for mankind. Rom. 5:12-21 refers to Adam as the type of the One to come, although the contrast is mainly negative. Just as sin entered the world through one man, Adam (5:12), so the act of righteousness of one man, Jesus, leads to acquittal and life for all people (5:18). In 1 Cor. 15, Paul used the Adam-Christ analogy to affirm the resurrection. As by a man came death, so by a Man has come resurrection (15:21). Just as the first Adam became a living being, so the last Adam became a life-giving Spirit (15:45). Adam represented the old humanity with all its failures, while Jesus represented the new humanity as God intended humanity to be from the beginning. Jesus' sacrifice makes entrance into the new humanity possible. See *Humanity.*

ADAMAH (*soil, farmland*)

(1) Earth or cultivated ground from whose dust God formed mankind, forming the wordplay Adam from dust of '*adamah.* (Gen. 2:7; compare 2:19). See *Earth, Land.*

(2) City in Naphtali (Josh. 19:36) near where Jordan River joins the sea of Tiberias, perhaps modern Hagar ed-Damm.

ADAMANT See *Minerals and Metals.*

ADAR

Twelfth month of postexilic Jewish calendar, including parts of February and March. Time of Festival of Purim established in Esther (9:21). See *Calendars; Festivals.*

ADDER See *Animals, Reptiles.*

ADINO (*loving luxury*)

Chief of David's captains who slew 800 men at one time (2 Sam. 23:8). Does not appear in Septuagint or in Hebrew text of the parallel passage (1 Chron. 11:11). Some translators omit it from 2 Sam. 23:8 (NIV, RSV, TEV).

ADMAH (*red soil*)

City connected with Sodom and Gomorrah as border of Canaanite territory (Gen. 10:19), perhaps under southern part of Dead Sea. Its king was defeated along with kings of Sodom and Gomorrah by coalition of four eastern kings (Gen. 14). See Gen. 19:29; Deut. 29:23; Hos. 11:8.

ADMIN

Ancestor of Jesus in older Greek texts of Luke 3:33 but not in Greek texts available to King James translators.

ADMINISTRATION

(1) Spiritual gift God gives to some members to build up the church (1 Cor. 12:28, NASB, NIV, RSV, NKJV; "governments," KJV; "leadership," NRSV, CEV; "get others to work together," NLT; "power to guide," REB). Greek *kubernesis* occurs only here in NT. It describes the ability to lead or hold a position of leadership.

(2) NASB uses "administer justice" to translate Hebrew idioms "to execute justice" (2 Sam. 8:15; 1 Kings 3:28; 1 Chron. 18:14) and "Execute justice" (Jer. 21:12). See 2 Cor. 8:20. In Hebrew the person who "is over the house," NIV calls the "palace administrator" (2 Kings 10:5). The OT seeks to lead people in authority to establish a society in which God's law brings fairness and justice to all people without favoritism and prejudice.

(3) KJV speaks of differences of administrations (1 Cor. 12:5), translating the Greek, *diakoion,* "services" (NIV, RSV) or "ministries" (NASB).

ADONIJAH (*Yah is Lord*)

(1) Fourth son of David (2 Sam. 3:4). In David's old age, Adonijah tried to establish hereditary kingship for the eldest son in Israel but failed (1 Kings 1:5-50). When Solomon became king, Adonijah asked for Abishag, David's nurse, as a wife. Seeing this as kingly aspiration, Solomon responded by having Adonijah put to death (1 Kings 2:13-28). See *David.*

(2) Levite Jehoshaphat sent to teach the people of Judah the book of the law (2 Chron. 8).

(3) Postexilic leader who signed covenant to obey God's law (Neh. 10:16).

ADONIRAM (*the Lord is exalted*)

Spelled *Hadoram* (2 Chron. 10:18); abbreviated to Adoram (1 Kings 12:18). Officer in charge of work gangs Solomon conscripted from Israel (1 Kings 4:6; 5:14). Israel rebelled against making free citizens work and stoned Adoniram to death.

ADONIS (*lord*)

God of vegetation and fertility worshiped in Greece and Syria. REB translates Isa. 17:10 as "your gardens in honour of Adonis." Hebrew term appears only here in the Bible, being related to Hebrew word meaning, "lovely, pleasant, agreeable." Other translations read, "finest plants" (NIV), "pleasant plants" (KJV), "delightful plants" (NASB), "sacred gardens" (TEV), "pleasant plants" (NRSV; NKJV); "imported gravevines" (NLT); "finest flowers to honor a foreign god" (CEV).

ADONI-ZEDEK (*the Lord is righteous* or *the god Zedek is lord*)

King of Jerusalem who gathered coalition of Canaanite kings to fight Gibeon after Joshua made a peace treaty with Gibeon (Josh. 10).

ADOPTION

Legal process by which person assumed parental responsibilities for another person's child as Mordecai did for Esther, his uncle's daughter (Esther 2:15). Bible contains no law showing the process, rights, or responsibilities involved in adoption. The Old Testament examples of Moses (Ex. 2:10) and Esther (Esther 2:7,15) took place in foreign cultures and may reflect those settings more than the Hebrew practice. The Old Testament implies Israel's relationship with God was that of an adopted child (Ex. 4:22; Deut. 14:2; Hos. 11:1; compare Rom. 9:4).

Believers are God's children (Luke 20:36; Rom. 9:26; Gal. 3:26), in a special and intimate relationship with God. Jesus has a unique relationship as the "only begotten Son" (John 1:18; 3:16). "Adoption" is status persons receive from God through the work of God's Spirit, when redeemed by Jesus (Gal. 4:3-7; Eph. 1:3-6). Adoption symbolizes God's love and grace in accepting believers as intimate members of His family. This drives out fear sinners feel in the holy presence and provides power to pray trustingly to God as our "Abba" (Rom. 8:14-16). See *Abba.* The believer has all rights of inheritance and will join Jesus in inheriting eternal life with God, but it does not mean the believer can escape the world's persecution (Rom. 8:17-30).

ADORAIM (*double strength*)

City Rehoboam fortified at modern Durah, 6 miles southwest of Hebron (2 Chron. 11:9). See *Rehoboam.*

ADORAM See *Adoniram.*

ADRAMMELECH (*Adra is king*)

(1) God of the city of Sepharvaim (2 Kings 17:24). His worshipers sacrificed their own children (17:31-33). See *Sepharvaim.*

(2) Murderer of Sennacherib, king of Assyria, during the king's worship in the temple of Nisroch (2 Kings 19:37). One reading of the Hebrew manuscripts describes this Adrammelech as Sennacherib's son (KJV, NIV, NRSV, REB, NLT, CEV). Other manuscripts do not have "his sons" (NASB).

ADRAMYTTIUM or ADRAMYTIAN (NASB)

Seaport near modern Edremit on northwest coast of Turkey in Roman province of Asia. Home port of ship Paul used to sail from Caesarea to Italy to appeal his case to Caesar (Acts 27:2).

ADRIA or ADRIATIC SEA (NASB, NIV)

Sea separating Italy and Greece in which Paul's ship drifted for fourteen days as he sailed toward Rome to appeal his case to Caesar (Acts 27:27); more extensive than modern Adriatic Sea. Apparently Paul drifted nearly 500 miles from Clauda (27:16) to Malta (28:1).

ADRIEL (*God is my help*)

Man from Meholah on the northern River Jordan (1 Sam. 18:19) who married Merab, Saul's daughter after she was promised to David. David gave his five sons to the Gibeonites, who hanged them in revenge for unexplained actions Saul had taken against Gibeon (2 Sam. 21:1-9).

ADULLAM (*sealed off place*)

City five miles south of Beth-shemesh in Judah, probably modern Tell esh-Sheikh Madkur (Gen. 38:1,12; Josh. 12:15; 15:35; 1 Sam. 22:1; 23:13; 2 Chron. 11:7; Neh. 11:30; Mic. 1:15).

ADULTERY

Unfaithfulness in marriage that occurs when one of the marriage partners voluntarily engages in sexual intercourse with a person other than the marriage partner; prohibited by Israel's covenant law (Ex. 20:14). Both the adulterous man and woman were viewed as guilty, and the punishment of death was prescribed for both (Lev. 20:10; see Ps. 51:4). Old Testament prophets used adultery as a metaphor to describe unfaithfulness to God (Jer. 3:6-10; Ezek. 23:27; Hos. 4:11-14).

Jesus taught that adultery has its origins within (Matt. 15:19). Lust is as much a violation of the law's intent as is illicit sexual intercourse (Matt. 5:27-28; compare 1 Cor. 6:9; Gal. 5:19; Jas. 4:4). The NT associates remarriage after divorce and adultery except where unfaithfulness caused the divorce (Matt. 5:32; Mark 10:11-12). The marriage bond is broken by death (Rom. 7:3; 1 Cor. 7:39). Adulterers can be forgiven (John 8:3-11) and be included among God's people (1 Cor. 6:9-11). See *Divorce; Marriage; Adventuress.*

ADUMMIM (*red ones*)

Rocky pass on road descending from Jerusalem to Jericho; modern Tal'at ed-damm; border of Judah and Benjamin (Josh. 15:7; 18:17).

ADVENT

Coming or second coming of Christ; period before Christmas during which Christians prepare for the Christmas season and reflect on the meaning of the coming of Christ. See *Church Year; Second Coming.*

ADVENTURESS

Woman feared for breaking up marriages (RSV). Translated "strange woman" (KJV), "adulterous woman" (Prov. 23:27, NASB), "wayward wife" (NIV; see NCV), "adulteress" (NRSV, NLT), "sinful woman" (CEV) and "immoral women" (TEV; NKJV) in Prov. 2:16; 5:20; 6:24; 7:5; 23:27. Some see an adventuress as living in part by her wits, but largely by sex. Others see her as seeking social advancement or wealth by seduction or other immoral means. They may be women cut off from Israelite society and normal social relationships.

ADVERSARY

Enemy either human or satanic. Psalmists often prayed for deliverance from adversaries (Pss. 38:20; 69:19; 71:13; 81:14; 109:29). The devil is the greatest adversary and must be resisted (1 Pet. 5:8-9).

ADVOCATE

One who intercedes for another; Christ interceding with the Father on behalf of sinners. *Advocate* appears in NLT, NASB in Job 16:19, with the concept in Gen. 18:23-33; Ex. 32:11-14; 1 Sam. 7:8-9; Jer. 14:7-9,13,19-22; Amos 7:2,5-6. Translators often use "Advocate" for Greek *parakletos* (1 John 2:1, a word found elsewhere only in John 14:16,26; 15:26; 16:7 for the Holy Spirit). See *Comforter; Helper; Holy Spirit.*

AENON (*double spring*)

Location where John the Baptist was baptizing while Jesus was baptizing in Judea (John 3:23). Probably in broad open valley called Wadi-Farah, west of the Jordan and northeast of Nablus.

AFFAIRS

The Bible describes several instances of willful sexual activity outside the bounds of marriage, including enticement (Gen. 39:7-18; Prov. 7:6-23; 9:13-18), adultery (2 Sam. 11:2-5; Hos. 3:1; John 4:17-18), incest (Gen. 38:12-26; 2 Sam. 13:1-14; Ezek. 22:11; 1 Cor. 5:1), and the use of a prostitute (Gen. 38:15; Joel 3:3; 1 Cor. 6:13-20).

Marital unfaithfulness is expressly forbidden in Ex. 20:14; Prov. 5:15-20, Matt. 5:27-28 (where voyeurism is equated with adultery), 1 Cor. 6:9,18; 7:1-3; Col. 3:5-6 and 1 Thess. 4:3-5. Immoral behavior falls under the judgment of God (Heb. 13:4). The Bible also portrays some of the consequences which persons involved in sexual immorality—along with members of their families (Gen. 35:22; 2 Sam. 13:21-22) and other innocent parties (2 Sam. 11:6-21; 12:10-14; Job 31:9-10)—must face. These consequences include alienation (1 Cor. 5:1-2), guilt (Ps. 51:1-14), hatred (2 Sam. 13:15,22), public embarrassment (Gen. 38:23-26; 1 Sam. 2:22-24; 2 Sam. 12:11-12; Matt. 1:19), unplanned pregnancy (2 Sam. 11:5), and personal devastation (Prov. 6:27-32; 7:21-27; Rom. 1:26-27).

The prophets used marital unfaithfulness, and particularly prostitution ("playing the harlot"), as a graphic symbol of Israel's spiritual unfaithfulness to God (Isa. 1:21; Jer. 2:20;

3:1-2; Ezek. 16:15-58; Hos. 1–3; Rev. 17:5). However, just as God remains willing to forgive unfaithfulness between spouses (2 Sam. 12:13; John 8:10-11), so He is willing to forgive those who are unfaithful to Him (Hos. 14:4-7).

AFFLICTION

State of being pained or distressed by oppressors. The sources of affliction are:

(1) God's retribution upon disobedience (Lam. 3:32-33; Isa. 30:20; Jer. 30:15);

(2) the natural conditions of life (Gen. 16:11; 29:32; Ps. 25:18; Jas. 1:27);

(3) personal sin (Ps. 107:17; Col. 6:7);

(4) forces of opposition (Isa. 51:21-23); and

(5) evil spirits and/or Satan (1 Sam. 16:14; Job 1:6-12);

(6) persecution because of faithfulness to Christ (2 Cor. 6:4; 1 Thess. 1:6).

God sees and knows our affliction (Gen. 29:32; 31:42; Ex. 3:7; 2 Kings 14:26; Acts 7:34). Affliction is only temporary (2 Cor. 4:17). God can deliver from any affliction (Ex. 3:17).

To endure affliction, Christians: pray to the Lord (Ps. 25:18; Lam. 1:9; Jas. 5:13); comfort others (Jas. 1:27; Phil. 4:14); remain faithful through suffering (2 Cor. 6:4; 1 Tim. 4:5; Jas. 1:2,12; 1 Pet. 4:13); cultivate an attitude of joy (Jas. 1:2); and follow the example of Jesus Christ (1 Pet. 2:19-23).

AFTERBIRTH

The placenta and fetal membranes expelled after delivery. God's judgment made women seek nourishment from the most disgusting sources (Deut. 28:57; compare 2 Kings 6:24-31; Lam. 2:20; 4:10).

AGABUS (*locust*)

Prophet in the Jerusalem church who visited church at Antioch and predicted universal famine that came about ten years later (Acts 11:27-29), leading Antioch church to begin famine relief ministry for church in Jerusalem. At Caesarea, Agabus pre-

Paul would be arrested in Jerusalem (Acts 21:10-11).

AGAG (*fiery one*)

Common title for Amalekite kings (Num. 24:7), particularly one Saul left alive in disobedience to God and Samuel killed (1 Sam. 15:8).

AGAGITE

Descendant of Agag; synonym for Amalekite (Esther 3:1). See *Agag; Amalekite.*

AGAPE See *Love; Lord's Supper.*

AGAR See *Hagar.*

AGATE See *Minerals and Metals.*

AGING

Natural process of humans growing older and, according to the Bible, gaining respect; normal part of the life cycle (Ps. 90:10; Isa. 46:4) bringing physiological changes (1 Kings 14:4; 2 Sam. 19:35; Eccl. 12:1-5; Zech. 8:4), wisdom (Deut. 32:7; Job 12:12), honor (Ex. 20:12; Lev. 19:32; 1 Tim. 5:1-2), and continuing service (Gen. 12–50; Josh. 13:1; 14:10; Ps. 92:14; Joel 2:28; Luke 1-2; 2 Tim. 1:5; Titus 2:2-3). The NT focuses on the responsibility of children or the family of faith to care for dependent or disabled aging persons (Mark 7:1-13; Matt. 15:1-6; 1 Tim. 5:4, 8; Jas. 1:27) and widows (Acts 6:1-7).

Some elderly are foolish (Eccl. 4:13). While aging brings diminishing strength (Eccl. 12:1-8), God's grace and help are ever the same (Isa. 46:4).

AGRAPHA (*unwritten things*)

Words of Jesus not in the four canonical gospels such as Acts 20:35 and 1 Cor. 11:24-25. More are found in Apocryphal writings, Gnostic gospels, the Talmud, Islamic sources, Oxyrhynchus Papyri, and the church fathers. A few agrapha may be authentic, but this is hard to prove.

AGRICULTURE

Art of cultivating the land to grow food; primary occupation in the Bible. Even those who lived in towns usually owned gardens or farms. The religious calendar was mainly based on the agricultural year. See *Festivals.* Primary crops of the Bible include grain, grapes, and olives (Gen. 27:28; Deut. 7:13; Joel 1:10). See *Harvest; Winnowing; Vine; Winepress; Oil.*

AGRIPPA See *Herod.*

AGUE

KJV translation (Lev. 26:16) of Hebrew word meaning "burning with fever." See *Fever.*

AGUR (*hired hand*)

Author of at least part of Prov. 30.

AHAB (*father's brother*)

(1) Seventh king (874–853 B.C.) of Northern Kingdom; son and successor of Omri; married Phoenician princess Jezebel and built her an "ivory house" (1 Kings 22:39); incited God's anger more than any previous Israelite king; enjoyed some political and military success, but suffered from spiritual compromise and failure (1 Kings 16:30-32; 18:4,19; 21). Ahab twice defeated Ben-hadad, the Syrian king, but died in the third battle. An inscription of Shalmanezer III of Assyria says Ahab committed 2,000 chariots and 10,000 men to the Battle of Qarqar (853 B.C.).

Ahab appears to have worshiped Yahweh, God of Israel, along with other gods. He consulted Yahweh's prophets (1 Kings 20:13-14,22,28; 22:8,16), used the divine name to name his children (Ahaziah, Jehoram, and Athaliah), and did not interfere in the execution of the priests of Baal after the contest on Mt. Carmel (1 Kings 18:40). Jezebel's influence overshadowed the prophets, and

Ahab became a prime example of evil (Mic. 6:16).

(2) False prophet living in Babylon who prophesied lies and faced Jeremiah's condemnation (Jer. 29:20-23).

AHASUERUS See *Xerxes; Persia.*

AHAVA

River in Babylon and nearby town where Ezra assembled Jews to return to Jerusalem (Ezra 8:15,21,31).

AHAZ (*he has grasped*)

Evil king of Judah (735–715); son and successor of Jotham and father of Hezekiah; participated in most monstrous of idolatrous practices (2 Kings 16:3,11). Ahaz refused Isaiah's counsel when Rezin, king of Syria, and Pekah, king of Israel, joined forces to attack Jerusalem. He appealed for help to Tiglath-pileser III of Assyria (Isa. 7) and surrendered to Assyrian domination.

AHAZIAH (*Yahweh has grasped*)

(1) Son and successor of Ahab as king of Israel (850–840 B.C.; 1 Kings 22:40); death (2 Kings 1:2-17), fulfilled Elijah's prophecy.

(2) Son and successor of Jehoram as king of Judah (about 842 B.C.; 2 Kings 8:25); died from wounds as he fled from Jehu while visiting King Joram of Israel (2 Kings 9:27).

AHIJAH (*my brother is Yahweh*)

(1) Priest of Eli's family in Shiloh (1 Sam. 14:3–4). He brought the ark of God to Saul (1 Sam. 4:18).

(2) Scribe of Solomon (1 Kings 4:3).

(3) Prophet from Shiloh who tore his clothes in 12 pieces and gave 10 to Jeroboam to signal God's decision to divide the kingdom after Solomon's death (1 Kings 11:29-39). Later the blind prophet announced the end of Jeroboam's reign and of his dynasty (1 Kings 14:1-18; 15:29). See 2 Chron. 9:29.

AHIKAM (*my brother stood up*)

Son of Josiah's scribe Shaphan; father of Gedaliah (2 Kings 25:22-25; Jer. 39:14); took book of law to Huldah to determine God's will (2 Kings 22:8-20); protected Jeremiah (Jer. 26:24).

AHIMAAZ (perhaps *brother of anger* or *my brother is counselor*)

Son of Zadok, David's priest (2 Sam. 15:27); David's secret messenger from the court when Absalom rebelled (2 Sam. 15:36; 7:17; 17:18-21; 18:19-29).

AHIMELECH (*my brother is king*)

See *High Priest.* Chief priest at Nob who gave David and his men bread of the presence (1 Sam. 21:1-15). Jesus used this action to justify breaking worship regulations to meet human need (Matt. 12:1-8) and to show He is Lord of the sabbath. Ahimelech also gave Goliath's gigantic sword to David, resulting in the eventual death of 85 priests by King Saul (1 Sam. 22).

AHINOAM (*my brother is gracious*)

(1) King Saul's wife (1 Sam. 14:50).

(2) Wife of David from Jezreel (1 Sam. 25:43; 27:3; 2 Sam. 2:2-4); mother of Ammon, his first son (2 Sam. 3:2). See 2 Sam. 30:1-20.

AHITHOPHEL (*brother of folly,* if not scribal attempt to hide name including Canaanite god such as Ahibaal)

David's counselor who joined Absalom's revolt against David (2 Sam. 15–17). His counsel was seen as equal to word of God (16:23).

AHITUB (*my brother is good*)

(1) Priest, son of Phinehas; grandson of Eli ministering in Shiloh (1 Sam. 14:3); Ahimelech's father (22:9).

(2) Father of Zadok, the high priest under David and Solomon (2 Sam. 8:17); Ezra's ancestor (Ezra 7:2).

AHLAB (*mountain forest* or *fertile*)

City Asher could not conquer (Judg. 1:31; see Josh. 19:29). Probably Khirbet el-Machalib on Mediterranean 4 miles above Tyre.

AHOLAH See *Oholah*.

AHOLIAB See *Oholiab*.

AHOLIBAH See *Oholibah*.

AHUZZATH (*that grasped* or *property*)

Official present at Philistine covenant of peace with Isaac (Gen. 26:26). Literally "the friend of the king," his office was the closest advisor of the king. Compare KJV, NASB, NIV, REB.

AI (*ruin* or possibly *heap*)

Also spelled Aija, Aiath, and Hai. City 2 miles from Bethel; Abram built altar there (Gen. 12:8; see 13:3); Joshua's leadership threatened there (Josh. 7:1-9); and Achan and his family suffered ruin (Josh. 7:16-26); Joshua made Ai a ruin (Josh. 8:1-29). See Isa. 10:28; Jer. 49:3; Ezra 2:28.

AIDS (Acquired Immunodeficiency Syndrome)

While the Bible does not specifically address AIDS, it does provide principles by which AIDS may be understood and those affected by AIDS may find comfort and hope.

Like all disease, suffering, and death, AIDS is a consequence of the Fall (Gen. 2:17; 3:19b; Rom. 1:27). Unlike most other diseases, however, the HIV virus primarily (though not exclusively) infects persons through acts of irresponsible behavior (Hos. 8:7a; Gal. 6:7-8). The Bible enjoins all followers of Christ to cultivate pure lifestyles (Phil. 4:8; Col. 3:1-7; 2 Pet. 1:5-11), thereby minimizing the risk by which they might become infected by the HIV virus and develop AIDS. Jesus showed compassion to lepers (Mark 1:40-42), social outcasts (Mark 5:1-8; John 4:1-38), and others who were sick and in desperate need (Matt. 9:36; 14:14; Mark 1:32-34) by touching (Matt. 20:34; Mark 1:41) and healing all who came to Him. Paul adjures Christians to express active empathy for those in need (Rom. 12:15; Gal. 6:2), declaring that sufferers are comforted by God through the work of Jesus (2 Cor. 1:3-4). In the same way, those who are affected by AIDS are able to find comfort and hope through the love of God.

AIJALON (*place of the deer*) or **AJALON**

(1) Danite levitical city (Josh. 19:42; 21:24) and nearby valley where moon stood still at Joshua's command (Josh. 10:12); modern Yalo about 14 miles from Jerusalem near the Philistine border, south of Beth-horon. See Judg. 1:34-35; 18:1; 1 Sam. 14:31; 1 Chron. 8:13; 2 Chron. 11:10; 28:16-21.

(2) Elon, a Zebulonite judge, was buried in a northern Aijalon (Judg. 12:12), perhaps Tell et-Butmeh.

AIJELETH SHAHAR (*doe of the dawn*)

Musical direction in title of Ps. 22. May be musical tune.

AJALON

Variant spelling of Aijalon. Spelled Jakan in 1 Chron. 1:42.

AKELDAMA See *Aceldama*.

AKHENATON

Egyptian Pharaoh (1370–1353 B.C.). See *Egypt*.

AKKAD See *Accad*.

AKKADIAN

First known Semitic invaders of Mesopotamia and language they spoke; international language of diplomacy and commerce in the Near East before 1000 B.C.; capital was Akkad (Agade). See Gen. 10:10. Akkadians, under Sargon the Great, conquered Mesopotamia and established world's first true empire (2360–2180 B.C.).

The Semitic language was used in cuneiform inscriptions and documents as early as 2400 B.C. Akkadian dialects may be outlined in three phases: Old Babylonian and Old Assyrian, about 2000–1500 B.C., Middle Babylonian and Middle Assyrian, about 1500–1000 B.C., and Neo-Babylonian, about 1000–100 B.C., and Neo-Assyrian, about 1000–600 B.C.

AKRABBIM (*scorpions*)

"Ascent of Akrabbim" southwest of the Dead Sea forms southern border of Canaan (Num. 34:4; Josh. 15:3; Judg. 1:36); mountain pass on the road southeast of Beersheba, modern Neqb es-Safa.

ALABASTER See *Minerals and Metals*.

ALAMOTH (*upon* or *according to young woman*)

Musical notation apparently signifying a tune for a high voice, a song for a soprano (1 Chron. 15:20; Ps. 46 title).

ALARM

Signal to move or be on the alert. Hebrew is literally a shout, but musical instruments were used (Num. 10:1-10). See Lev. 25:9; Num. 10:5-6; 31:6; Josh. 6; 1 Sam. 4:5; 2 Chron. 13:12; Jer. 4:19; Hos. 5:8; Joel 2:1.

ALDEBARAN

Red star of first magnitude in eye of Taurus; brightest star in Hyades; REB reading for Arcturus.

ALEXANDER THE GREAT

(*Alexander*) King of Macedonia (356–323 B.C.). See *Greece; Intertestamental History and Literature*.

ALEXANDRIA

Capital of Egypt from 330 B.C.; most important center of Judaism outside of Jerusalem; Septuagint was produced; founded by Alexander the Great as an outstanding Greek cultural and academic center with finest library in ancient world, having over 500,000 volumes; designed as Egypt's principal port of the peninsula on western edge of Nile delta. See Acts 6:9; 18:24; 27:6; 28:11.

ALGUM

Rare, unidentified wood Solomon imported from Lebanon for the temple (2 Chron. 2:8; 9:10-11; compare almug, 1 Kings 10:11-12); used for gateways and for musical instruments.

ALIEN

Foreigner living in a community without relatives. People fleeing famine became aliens among the people where they settled (Gen. 26:3; Deut. 18:6; 2 Sam. 4:3; 1 Kings 17:20, "to sojourn" is to be an alien; Isa. 16:4). An alien stood between a person born in the community and a foreigner without any ties to the community. The alien could become a soldier (2 Sam. 1:13), worship God and keep the sabbath (Ex. 23:12; Deut. 31:12), or own house (Gen. 19:9). See Gen. 20:1; 26:3; 32:5; 1 Chron. 22:2; Jer. 7:6; 14:8; 22:3; Ezek. 22:7,29. Israel began history in Egypt as aliens (Ex. 23:9; Deut. 14:21; 24:17-20; 26:12; 27:19; Lev. 17:8,15; 18:26; Num. 9:14). God loves aliens (Deut. 10:19). All people are aliens on earth (Pss. 39:12; 119:19).

ALLEGORY

Means of presenting or interpreting a story by focusing on hidden or symbolic meanings rather than the literal meaning. Allegory arose from the Cynic and Stoic philosophies of the Hellenistic period (400–200 B.C.). None of the OT was written allegorically. Allegorical interpretation of the OT arose among Hellenistic Jews in Alexandria after 200 B.C. Philo, died about A.D. 50, was its most prolific proponent.

Some of Jesus' parables were interpreted as allegories (Matt. 13:24-30,36-43; Mark 4:1-20). Paul employed allegorical interpretations (1 Cor. 5:6-8; 9:8-10; 10:1-11; Gal. 4:21-31), once employing the word *allegory* itself (Gal. 4:24). The Letter to the Hebrews deals allegorically with OT themes like Melchizedek, the OT priesthood, and the tabernacle.

ALLELUIA See *Hallelujah.*

ALLIANCE See *Covenant.*

ALLOTMENT

Land allocation either by God or by lot, especially of Canaan to Israel (Num. 32; Josh. 13–19; compare Ezek. 48) through the lot of the priest (Josh. 14:1-2). See *Tribes of Israel.*

ALMIGHTY

Title of God, translating Hebrew *El Shaddai.* See *Names of God.*

ALMOND

A large, nut-bearing tree and the nuts (fruit) it bears. Specific references in Gen. 30:37; 43:11; Ex. 25:33-34; Num. 17:8; Eccl. 12:5; Jer. 1:11. See *Plants.*

ALMS

Gifts for the poor. Israel's ideal was a time when no one was poor (Deut. 15:4). Every three years the tithe of the produce for the year was to be brought to the towns for the Levites, the aliens in the land, the orphans, and the widows (Deut. 14:28-29).

Although Jesus criticized acts of charity done for the notice of men (Matt. 6:2-3), He expected His disciples to perform such deeds (6:4) and even commanded them (Luke 11:41; 12:33). Alms could refer to a gift donated to the needy (Acts 3:2-3,10) or to acts of charity in general (Acts 9:36; 10:2,4,31; 24:17). Such actions are ultimately performed in behalf of the Lord (Matt. 25:34-45; see Acts 2:44-46; 4:32-35; Rom. 15:25-28; 1 Cor. 16:1-4; 2 Cor. 8–9; Jas. 1:27; 1 John 3:17-18). See *Aliens; Mercy; Hospitality; Stewardship.*

ALMUG See *Algum.*

ALOE See *Plants.*

ALPHA AND OMEGA

First and last letters of Greek alphabet used in Revelation to describe sovereignty and eternal nature of God or Christ (Rev. 1:8,17; 21:6; 22:13).

ALPHAEUS or **ALPHEUS**

(1) Father of apostle called James the Less (Matt. 10:3; Mark 3:18; Luke 6:15; Acts 1:13).

(2) Father of apostle Levi (Mark 2:14). See *Matthew.*

ALTAR

Structure used in worship for presenting sacrifices to God or gods. Altars were used to sacrifice animals, grain, fruit, wine, and incense. See *Sacrifice and Offering.* The simplest altars, and perhaps oldest, were the earthen altars (Ex. 20:24) made of either mud-brick—typical building material in Mesopotamia — or a raised roughly shaped mound of dirt.

The stone altar is mentioned most often in biblical records and is most frequently found in excavations. These could consist of a single large stone (Judg. 6:19-23; 13:19-20; 1 Sam. 14:31-35) or unhewn stones carefully stacked (Ex. 20:25, 1 Kings 18:30-35). Hebrew stone altars were not to have steps (Ex. 20:25-26), probably in part to distinguish them from Canaanite altars. In Ezekiel's vision (chs. 40–48), the altar of the restored temple has three levels and many steps.

The central altar in the court of Solomon's temple was a bronze altar about 30 feet square and 15 feet high (2 Chron. 4:1), the altar of burnt offering. The earlier tabernacle had a similar altar made of acacia (or shittim, KJV) wood overlaid with bronze (Ex. 27:1-2).

More importantly, the horns of the altar were the place where blood from a sacrificial animal was applied for atonement from sin (for example, Ex. 29:12; Lev. 4:7; see Jer. 17:1). Apparently, grasping the horns of the altar was a way of seeking sanctuary or protection when one was charged with a serious offense (1 Kings

1:50-51; 2:28-34; compare Ex. 21:12-14).

A gold altar or altar of incense was located in the inner room of the sanctuary, just outside the holy of holies (1 Kings 7:48-50; compare Ex. 30:1-6). See *High Place.*

New Testament references to altars concern proper worship (Matt 5:23-24) and hypocrisy in worship (Matt. 23:18-20). See Luke 1:11; Rom. 11:3; Heb. 13:10; Jas. 2:21; Rev. 9:13. The theme of the NT is that Jesus Christ is the ultimate sacrifice who puts us right with God.

AL-TASCHITH (KJV) or
ALTASHHETH (NASB)

Word in Psalm title (Pss. 57; 58; 59; 75) transliterated by NASB; KJV but translated, "Do not destroy" by NIV, NRSV, NKJV, NCV, CEV, NLT, REB; may indicate tune to which the people sang the Psalm.

AMALEKITE

Descendant of Amalek, grandson of Esau (Gen. 36:12); nomadic tribe that inhabited the desolate wasteland of the northeast Sinai peninsula and the Negeb; first group to attack the Israelites after the exodus at Rephidim (Ex. 17:8-16; Num. 14:39-45; 24:20; compare Deut. 25:17-19). Because of their atrocities, God commanded Saul to exterminate the Amalekites (1 Sam. 15:2-3). Saul disobeyed, and the Amalekites were not defeated completely until almost 700 B.C. (1 Chron. 4:43).

AMARNA, TELL EL

Site 200 miles south of Cairo on east bank of the Nile River of ancient Egyptian city Akhenaton; in 1888, clay tablets were found containing primarily diplomatic communications between Egypt and Egyptian-controlled territories, including Syria and Palestine. Rulers of small Palestinian city-states including Shechem, Jerusalem, and Megiddo complain of mistreatment by other rulers and ask for Egyptian aid. These letters evidence the political unrest, disunity, and instability of the period prior to the Hebrew conquest. See *Egypt.*

AMASA (*burden* or *bear a burden*)

(1) Captain of Judah's army replacing Joab during Absalom's rebellion against his father David (2 Sam. 17:25).

(2) Leader in tribe of Ephraim who prevented Israel's soldiers from sin (2 Chron. 28:12-14).

AMAW (*his people*)

Home of Balaam (Num. 22:5) on Sajur River near Euphrates, south of Carchemish near Aleppo; variously translated "land of children of his people" (KJV); "his native land" (NIV, NCV, NLT); "among his relatives" (CEV); "land of the sons of his people" (NASB, NKJV); "land of the Amavites" (REB); and "land of Amaw" (NRSV, TEV).

AMAZIAH (*Yahweh is mighty*)

Several people including:

(1) priest at Bethel who sent Amos home, saying he did not have the right to prophesy against King Jeroboam II (789–746 B.C.) in the king's worship place (Amos 7:10-17);

(2) ninth king of Judah, son of Joash and father of Uzziah (797–767 B.C.) who avenged his father's murder in an uncommonly merciful way, only killing the guilty servants, not the servants' children (2 Kings 14:5-6). See 2 Chron. 25.

AMBASSADOR

Representative of one royal court to another. See 2 Chron. 32:31; 35:21; Prov. 13:17; Isa. 30:4; 33:7; 57:9; Ezek. 17:15; Jer. 49:14; Obad. 1; possibly Josh. 9:4 (KJV, NASB, NIV, CEV, NLT, compare NRSV, TEV, REB). Paul saw himself even in prison as an ambassador of the divine King (Eph. 6:20; compare 2 Cor. 5:20).

AMBER

Yellowish or brownish translucent resin that takes a good polish; used by Ezekiel to describe his opening vision (Ezek. 1:4,27; 8:2, KJV, NLT, NRSV); also translated "gleaming bronze"(RSV), "glowing metal"(NASB, NIV, NCV), "brass" (REB), "bronze" (TEV), "polished metal" (CEV). Some think Greek (Septuagint) and Latin (Vulgate) suggest electrum — an amalgam of silver and gold.

AMBUSH

Military tactic hiding troops for surprise attack while carrying on normal battle with other troops (Josh. 8; Judg. 9:25,43-45; 20:29-43; 1 Sam. 15:5; 2 Chron. 13:13; compare Hos. 6:9). Psalmists asked for God's help against wicked persons who sought to ambush them (Pss. 10:8; 59:3; 64:4; compare Prov. 1:11,18; Lam. 4:19). Jeremiah accused his people of spiritual ambush against one another (Jer. 9:8; see 51:12). Paul's nephew saved him from Jewish plans to ambush him (Acts 23:12-33; 25:3).

AMEN

Transliteration of Hebrew word signifying something as certain, sure and valid, truthful and faithful; it shows acceptance of the validity of a curse or an oath (Num. 5:22; Deut. 27:15-26; Jer. 11:5), acceptance of a good message (Jer. 28:6), and joins in a doxology to affirm what has been said or prayed (1 Chron. 16:36; Neh. 8:6; Ps. 106:48). "Amen" may confirm what already is or indicate a hope for something desired. In Jewish prayer, "amen" comes at the end as an affirmative response to a statement or wish made by others, and is so used in the NT epistles (Rom. 1:25; 11:36; 15:33; 1 Cor. 16:24; Gal. 1:5; Eph. 3:21; Phil. 4:20). Paul ended some of his letters with "amen" (1 Thess. 5:28; 2 Thess. 3:18).

Jesus used "amen" at the beginning of a statement to affirm the truth of His own statements (Matt. 5:18; 16:28; Mark 8:12; 11:23; Luke 4:24; 21:32; John 1:51; 5:19), affirming that the kingdom of God is bound up with His own person and emphasizing the authority of what He said. Jesus is called "the Amen" in Revelation 3:14, meaning He Himself is the reliable

and true witness of God. See Isa. 65:16.

AMETHYST See *Minerals and Metals.*

AMMI *(my people)*

Name Hosea gave restored Israel (2:1) in contrast to Lo-ammi (1:9), "not my people," third child of Gomer.

AMMI-NADIB

KJV personal name in Song of Solomon 6:12. Most modern versions express uncertainty here: "my noble people" (NASB, NKJV) or "my people" (NIV), "prince chosen of my people" (REB), "beside my prince" (NRSV, NCV) or "eager for love" (TEV), "on a glorious" (CEV); "with my beloved one" (NLT).

AMMON, AMMONITES

Semitic people related to Israel through Lot (Gen. 19:30-38) living northeast of the Dead Sea in city-state around Rabbah; often battled with the Israelites for possession of fertile Gilead. See Deut. 2:20; 23:3; Judg. 10:6–11:40; 1 Sam. 11; 31:11-13; 2 Sam. 10–12; 23:37; 1 Kings. 11; 1 Chron. 11:39; 2 Chron. 12:13; 20:1; 24:26; 26:8; 27:5; Ezra 9:1; Neh. 2:10,19; 4:3,7; 13:1; Jer. 40:11,14; 41:10,15; 49:1-2; Ezek. 25. Solomon took one or more Ammonite wives and allowed the worship of Milcom, the Ammonite god, in Jerusalem (1 Kings 11:1-8; compare 2 Kings 23:13).

AMNON *(trustworthy, faithful)*

David's first son (2 Sam. 3:2); raped half-sister Tamar, whose brother Absalom avenged this outrage by killing Amnon (2 Sam. 13:1-20).

AMON *(faithful)*

(1) Governor of Samaria when Jehoshaphat was king of Judah; put prophet Micaiah in prison (1 Kings 22:26).

(2) King of Judah (642 B.C.) following his father Manasseh; killed in a pal-

ace revolt (2 Kings 21:19-23). See Matt. 1:10.

(3) Postexilic ancestor of temple staff members (Neh. 7:59), called Ami in Ezra 2:57.

(4) Egyptian god whose worship center at Thebes Jeremiah threatened with divine destruction (Jer. 46:25).

AMORITES (*westerners*)

People who occupied part of the Promised Land and often fought Israel; general name for all the inhabitants of Canaan, as is "Canaanite" (Gen. 15:16; Josh. 24:15; Judg. 6:10; 1 Kings 21:26). They controlled Babylonia (2000-1595 B.C.), their most influential king being Hammurabi (1792–1750). Between 2100 and 1800 they settled in the hill contry of Canaan. See Gen. 14; Num. 13:29; 21:21-35; Deut. 3:8; Josh. 10:1-27; 11:1-15; 12:2; Judg. 1:34-36; 11:19; 1 Kings 9:20,21; 2 Chron. 8:7,8; Pss. 135:10-12; 136:17-22. Amorite culture lay at the root of Jerusalem's decadence (Ezek. 16:3,45); and Amorite idolatry tainted the religion of the Northern and Southern Kingdoms (1 Kings 21:26; 2 Kings 21:11; Amos 2:9-10).

AMOS (*a load*)

Prophet from Judah who ministered in Israel about 750 B.C. A layperson who disclaimed professional status as a prophet (7:14-15), Amos indicted both Judah and Israel, challenging the superficial qualities of religious institutions.

Amos probably began his ministry with God's call in 765 B.C., "two years before the earthquake" (1:1). Under Jeroboam II the Northern Kingdom rivaled Solomon's generation in its stability and economic prosperity (2 Kings 14:23-27). The Southern Kingdom prospered under King Uzziah (Amos 1:1). The social, moral, and religious problems attending that prosperity became the focus for Amos's voice of judgment.

AMOS, BOOK OF

Third book in minor prophets containing collection of prophecies by Amos. Morally, Israel and Judah justified themselves as righteous as shown by God's blessings on them. Rampant luxury and self-indulgence were clearly manifest (see chs. 1; 4; 5; 6; 8). Israel exploited the poor (2:6; 3:10; 4:1; 5:11; 8:4-6), distorted justice, and turned the dynamism of personal religious experience into the superficiality of institutional religion (7:10-17). Opposing these moral and religious evils, Amos hammered his central theme: "But let judgment run down as waters, and righteousness as a mighty stream" (5:24).

Whether in addressing other nations, Israel, or Judah, the prophet condemned those who sin against a universal conscience (1:1–2:3), the revealed law (2:4-5), or God's redeeming love (2:6-16). Amos challenged people to live by covenant standards. His word of judgment was severe for the "first ladies of Samaria" who encouraged the injustice and violence of their husbands (4:1). For individuals superficially and confidently "at ease in Zion, and trust in the mountain of Samaria" (6:1), their only hope was renewal of authentic religious experience leading to a life of justice and righteousness which would overflow the land (5:24). For those who rejected that way, only judgment remained: "Prepare to meet thy God, O Israel!" (4:12).

AMPHIPOLIS (*around the city*)

City near Aegean Gulf between Thessalonica and Philippi. Paul and Silas passed through it on their way to Thessalonica on Paul's second missionary journey (Acts 17:1).

AMRAM (*exalted people*)

Father of Moses, Aaron, and Miriam and grandson of Levi (Ex. 6:18-20), for whom Levitical family was named (Num. 3:27; 1 Chron. 26:23).

AMRAPHEL (Akkadian, *the God Amurru paid back* or *the mouth of God has spoken*)

Otherwise unknown King of Shinar or Babylon who joined coalition to defeat Sodom and Gomorrah. Abraham rescued Lot from them (Gen. 14:1-9).

AMULETS

NASB, NRSV translation of rare Hebrew word for charms, oaths used to describe an ornament women wore (Isa. 3:20). NIV, NLT, NKJV, NCV, REB translate charms; CEV, TEV magic charms; KJV, earrings. See *Charm.*

ANAB (*grape*)

Mountain city in southern Judah from which Joshua eliminated the Anakim (Josh. 11:21); allotted to Judah (Josh. 15:50); modern Khirbet Anab about 15 miles southwest of Hebron. See *Anak, Anakim.*

ANAHARATH (*gorge*)

City on border of Issachar (Josh. 19:19), possibly modern Tell el-Mukharhkhash between Mt. Tabor and the Jordan.

ANAK, ANAKIM (*long-necked* or *strong-necked*), **ANAKITES**

Ancestor and his giant descendants who occupied Canaan, especially Hebron and the hill country (Num. 13:22; Josh. 11:21); part of the Nephilim (Gen. 6:4; Num. 13:33) with remnants lived among the Philistines (Josh. 11:22). Arba was a hero of the Anakim (Josh. 14:15).

ANAM

NASB, TEV reading of 1 Chron. 1:11, interpreting Anam as a place rather than as a tribe or nation. See *Anamim.*

ANAM MELECH (*Anu is king*)

God of the Sepharvites, who occupied part of Israel after the Northern Kingdom was exiled in 721 B.C. Worshipers sacrificed children to this god (2 Kings 17:31).

ANAMIM, ANAMITES

Tribe or nation called "son of Egypt" (Gen. 10:13).

ANANIAS (Greek form of Hebrew *Hananiah, Yahweh has dealt graciously*)

(1) Husband of Sapphira (Acts 5:1-6). They sold private property and falsely claimed to give all the proceeds to the common fund of the early Jerusalem church (Acts 4:32-34). Both were struck dead for having lied to the Holy Spirit (Acts 5:3,10).

(2) Disciple in Damascus who helped Paul after his Damascus Road vision (Acts 9:10-19).

(3) Jewish high priest A.D. 47 to 58 (Acts 23:2; 24:1) and thus president of the Sanhedrin which tried Paul in Jerusalem (Acts 23–24). Anti-Roman Jewish revolutionaries assassinated him at the outbreak of the Jewish revolt (A.D. 66). See *Sadducees; Sanhedrin.*

ANATH

Amorite and Canaanite god. See *Canaan.*

ANATHEMA

Someone or something sacrificed to God for destruction in fulfillment of a vow; possibly technical term in the early church meaning to exclude from church membership. Greek translation of Hebrew *cherem*, the holy war ban imposing destruction of war booty (Lev. 27:28; Deut. 20:10-18). See *Accursed.* Paul invoked the curse on anyone who did not love the Lord (1 Cor. 16:22; compare Rom. 9:3; Gal. 1:8-9). Spiritual gifts, especially ecstatic prophecy, do not cause people to say "Jesus is accursed" (1 Cor. 12:3).

ANATHOTH

Benjaminite city 3 miles northeast of Jerusalem (Josh. 21:18) where King Solomon sent Abiathar after removing him as high priest (1 Kings 2:26-27); home of Jeremiah, who may have been a priest in rejected line of Abiathar (Jer. 1:1). Threatened by the citizens of Anathoth (Jer. 11:21-23), he purchased a field there in obedience to God's word, symbolizing hope after Exile (Jer. 32:6-15). Anathoth was resettled after the Exile (Neh. 7:27; 11:32).

ANCESTORS

People from whom a person is descended; honored in biblical history. Kings traced their lineage to David, and the priests, to Aaron (2 Tim. 1:5; Heb. 11).

ANCESTOR WORSHIP

Adoration or payment of homage to a deceased parent or ancestor; Bible condemns and forbids (Lev. 19:26-32; 20:6,27; Deut. 14:1; 18:10-11; 26:14; Isa. 8:19; 65:4). Several of Israel's neighbors deified ancestors. Ezekiel 43:7-9 may suggest the bodies of Israel's dead kings were being worshiped.

The cult of the dead seeks to manage a relationship with the dead, believing that certain departed spirits must be fed or honored and that they can be channels of information with the spiritual world. Acts of homage, deference, or offerings of food and drink were sometimes required to honor friendly spirits or to placate evil ones. Food, drink, and artifacts buried with the corpse provided for needs in the afterlife. Israelites at times did so (1 Sam. 28). See *Burial; Death; Divination and Magic; Genealogies; Medium.*

ANCHOR

A weight of stone, iron, or lead held on the end of a cable that when submerged in water holds a ship in place (Acts 27:29-30,40). Hebrews 6:19 compares the hope of the gospel to "an anchor of the soul, both sure and steadfast."

ANCIENT OF DAYS

Phrase in Dan. 7 describing the everlasting God; literally, "one advanced in (of) days"; may mean "one who for-

wards time or rules over it." Compare Gen. 24:1; 1 Kings 22:19-20; Job 36:26; Pss. 50:1-6; 55:19; Isa. 26:1-27:1; 44:6; Ezek. 1; Joel 3:2. In ancient Ugaritic literature, the god El is designated as "the father of years."

ANDREW

Disciple of John the Baptist who became one of Jesus' first disciples and led his brother Simon to Jesus (John 1:40-42); fisherman (Matt. 4:18). He questioned Jesus about His prophesy concerning the temple (Mark 13:3). See also John 6:8; Acts 1:13. He is believed to have been killed on an X-shaped cross. See *Disciples, Apostles.*

ANEM (*fountains*)

Levitical city in Issachar (1 Chron. 6:73); modern Jenin or Khirbet Anim. Joshua 21:29 lists the city as En-gannim.

ANGEL

Heavenly messenger who either delivers a message to humans, carries out God's will, praises God, is a member of God's army, or guards God's throne; also called "sons of God," "holy ones," and "heavenly host." The Bible presents no fully delineated angelology. See *Cherub, Cherubim; Host of Heaven; Seraphim; Sons of God.*

Cherubim and seraphim are winged angels, guards, or attendants to the divine throne (Isa. 6:2-6; Ezek. 1:4-28; 10:3-22).

Often angels appear as ordinary men but do things or appear in a fashion clearly nonhuman (Gen. 16:7-11; 19:13,24; Ex. 3:2; Num. 22:23; Judg. 6:21; 13:20; Mark 16:5; John 20:12). Angels are created beings.

Matthew 18:10 and some other passages which assign protective roles to angels imply that a heavenly counterpart represents each person in heaven (for example, Michael, angelic prince over Israel, Dan. 12:1; angels of specific churches in Dan. 10:13; Acts 12:15; Rev. 1:20; 2-3). The term, *guardian angel,* however, is not biblical, and the idea is at best only implied in these passages.

Angels functioned in revealing the will of God and/or announcing key events (Gen. 19:1-22; Ex. 3:2-6; Judg. 2:1-5; 13:2-23; Matt. 1:20-24); ensuring the well-being or survival of God's people (Ex. 14:19–20; 1 Kings 19:1-8; Matt. 4:11; Acts 12:7-11); and enforcing the wrath of God on the wicked among the Jews and the Gentiles (Gen. 19:12-13; 2 Sam. 24:17; 2 Kings 19:35). Hebrews offers a lengthy contrast between Jesus and the angels (Heb. 1:3–2:16).

ANGER See *Wrath.*

ANGLE or ANGLE OF THE WALL See *Turning of the Wall.*

ANIM (*springs*)

City of Judah (Josh. 15:50); modern Khirbet Ghuwein at-Tahta, 11 miles south of Hebron.

ANIMAL RIGHTS

The Bible provides a clear distinction between animals and people. Though both were created by God (Gen. 1:20-30), people alone were made in His image (Gen. 1:27) and have an immortal soul (Gen. 2:7; 1 Pet. 1:9). Adam's naming of the animals (Gen. 2:19-20) signifies his dominion over them (Gen. 1:26-28; Ps. 8:5-8). This dominion was expanded after the Flood when God gave animals to mankind for food (Gen. 9:3).

Even though Jesus said that people are of greater value than animals (Matt. 6:26), this in no way provides license to mistreat them in any way. Because all animals belong to God (Ps. 50:10), they have great intrinsic worth. People are to care for animals and, when using them, treat them with the utmost dignity.

Just as wild animals are cared for by God (Job 38:39-41; Pss. 104:10-30; 147:7-9; Matt. 6:26), so domesticated animals must be treated well by their human owners (Prov. 12:10; 27:23). The Mosaic law stipulates that animals be fed adequately (Ex. 23:11;

Deut. 25:4; compare 1 Cor. 9:9; 1 Tim. 5:18), helped with their loads (Ex. 23:5), not overworked (Ex. 20:10; Deut. 5:14) and treated fairly (Deut. 22:6-7,10). Ezekiel compared Israel's unjust leaders to shepherds who mistreated their sheep (Ezek. 34:1-6), a situation reversed by Jesus the Good Shepherd (John 10:11; compare Luke 15:3-6).

ANIMALS

Living beings God created (Gen. 1:24-26; 2:19-20). Identification of types of animals are not always clear, especially in Old Testament.

Mammals

Any class of higher vertebrates including humans and all other animals that nourish their young with milk secreted by mammary glands and have their skin more or less covered with hair.

Domestic Mammals

Many animals were tamed for use in food production, the military, and transportation.

(1) *Ass or Donkey.* Unclean beast of burden; used by those who traveled in peace; similar to donkeys of today but larger; appear in Mesopotamia (onager) and Egypt 3000 years before Christ; used for riding (Num. 22:21; Judg. 5:10), as a beast of burden (1 Sam. 16:20), and for agricultural work (Deut. 22:10; compare Ezra 2:67). The ass was covered by the sabbath rest regulations, and the firstborn was redeemed (Ex. 13:13). Jesus' choice of an ass for His triumphal entry into Jerusalem symbolized His role as the Prince of Peace (Zech. 9:9; Matt. 21:1-5).

(2) *Camel.* Large, humpbacked, unclean (Lev. 11:4) ruminant (chews cud) of Asia and Africa used to transport burdens or passengers; domesticated before 2000 B.C., able to store several days' supply of water in its stomach; primary mode of transportation for taking goods and people across dry, hot terrain. A young camel can walk 100 miles in a day.

See Gen. 24:35; Job 1:3; Matt. 23:24; Mark 1:6; 10:25; Jer. 2:23; Isa. 60:6.

(3) *Cattle.* Domesticated quadrupeds used as livestock variously called ox, bull, calf, heifer, and cow; commonly refers to all domesticated animals including sheep, goats, and other domesticated animals (Gen. 1:24; John 4:12). Cattle were valued for sacrifices, for food, and as work animals (Deut. 25:4; Luke 14:19).

Bull was sign of great productivity and great strength (Deut. 33:17; Isa. 10:13). In Canaanite religion, the chief of the assembly was called "father bull El."The bull was closely associated with Baal and may have influenced Jeroboam to set up the golden bulls at Bethel and Dan (1 Kings 12:28).The bronze sea in the courtyard of the temple in Jerusalem was resting on the back of 12 bronze bulls.

(4) *Dog.* Scavenger animal that often ran wild; sometimes kept as house pets. In Mark 7:27, Jesus probably was referring to the small dogs that people kept as pets. Some dogs evidently were used to herd sheep (Job 30:1). See below *Wild Mammals, Dog.*

(5) *Donkey.* See *Ass* above.

(6) *Goat.* Hollow-horned ruminant with long, floppy ears, usually covered with long, black hair; sometimes speckled; prominent source of food; probably had long ears and backward-curving horns. The male was used for sacrifices (Lev. 22:27). See *Scapegoat.* The skin was used to make garments, musical instruments, and water bottles; goat hair was woven into fabrics (Ex. 26:7). Sheep and goats grazed in the same pasture, but it was necessary to separate the herds because the male goat was often hostile toward the sheep (Matt. 25:32).

(7) *Horse.* Solid-hoofed animal used for riding, as a war animal, and for transporting goods; not in common use in Israel until the time of David and Solomon; Solomon owned as many as 12,000. They were used to draw chariots (1 Kings 4:26; 10:26). Since the Mosaic law forbade the accu-mulation of horses, Solomon imported horses from Egypt (Deut. 17:16; 2 Chron. 1:16).

(8) *Mule.* Result of crossbreeding a female horse and a male ass; a popular riding animal for royalty (1 Kings 1:33). Since the Mosaic law forbade crossbreeding (Lev. 19:19), the Israelites imported mules (Ezek. 27:14) as war animals, for riding, and for carrying burdens (2 Kings 5:17). They were especially good for moving heavy burdens in mountainous areas.

(9) *Ox.* Large domesticated bovine, extremely valuable as a work animal; often yoked in pairs to do farm work and were used to transport burdens. Permitted as food, they were also offered as sacrifices (Deut. 14:4-6; Lev. 17:3-4). See *Cattle* above; see *Wild Mammals, Ox* below.

(10) *Sheep.* Stocky animal, larger than a goat, but without a beard; primary wealth of pastoral people; prominent in the sacrificial system of Israel; source for food and clothing; often referred to as small cattle. The tail, weighing as much as 15 pounds, was sometimes offered as a sacrifice (Ex. 29:22; Lev. 3:9). Rams' horns were used as trumpets (Josh. 6:4) and as oil containers (1 Sam. 16:1).

(11) *Swine.* Stout-bodied animals with large snout and thick skin; "unclean" (Lev. 11:7; Deut. 14:8; Isa. 65:4; 66:3,17); symbol for baseness and paganism (Matt. 7:6). One who tended swine was barred from the temple.

Wild Mammals

Wild animals provided food and sport and were feared by biblical people:

(1) *Antelope.* Fleet-footed, grass-eating animal with horns; about the size of a donkey with a mane on the underside of its neck that makes it look like a large goat. The pygarg, literally "white rump" (Deut. 14:5, KJV, compare Isa. 51:20) is often considered an antelope. Others (NLT, NRSV, NKJV, NCV, REB, NIV) see the "wild ox" (KJV) of this passage as an antelope.

(2) *Ape.* Large, semierect primate; not native to the Holy Land; some

types were kept as pets; among gifts Hiram sent to Solomon (1 Kings 10:22; 2 Chron. 9:21). See *Baboon*.

(3) *Baboon.* NIV, NCV translation (1 Kings 10:22; 2 Chron. 9:21) based on similarity to Egyptian word. TEV, REB, NKJV translate, "monkeys"; KJV, CEV, NLT, NASB, NRSV, "peacocks" (but see NRSV margin).

(4) *Badger.* Burrowing mammal, largest of the weasel family. Disagreement exists about the translation in Ex. 25:5; 26:14 (badger, KJV; goat, RSV, NLT; sea cows, NIV; dugong, REB; porpoise, NASB; fine leather, TEV, NRSV, NCV). This animal has also been identified as the rock hyrax or coney. See *Coney* below.

(5) *Bat.* Quadruped that nurses its offspring; nocturnal placental flying mammals with forelimbs modified to form wings; listed among unclean birds (Lev. 11:19; Deut. 14:18). Bats live in caves (Isa. 2:20-21).

(6) *Bear.* Large, heavy mammal with long, thick, shaggy hair; eats insects, fruit, and flesh; may grow as high as 6 feet and weigh as much as 500 pounds; ferocious (2 Kings 2:23-24); a threat to vineyards and to herds of sheep and goats (1 Sam. 17:34-35).

(7) *Behemoth.* Large beast in Job 40:15-24; variously identified as an elephant, crocodile (REB), and the water buffalo; most likely hippopotamus (NLT, CEV), large, thick-skinned, amphibious, cud-chewing mammal of the family *Hippopotamidae*.

(8) *Boar.* Male swine; menace to crops (Ps. 80:13). See *Swine* above.

(9) *Chamois.* Small antelope (*rupicapra*) about two feet high; found in mountainous regions. Translated "mountain-sheep" in modern versions (Deut. 14:5).

(10) *Coney.* Unclean wild hare—*Procavia syriaca* also called *Hyrax syriacus*; lives in rocky areas from Dead Sea Valley to Mt. Hermon; design of its feet helps it keep footing on slippery rocks (Lev. 11:5; Deut. 14:7; see Ps. 104:18; Prov. 30:26). See *Badger* above.

(11) *Deer.* Antlered animal with two large and two small hooves. The red deer is probably in Solomon's

daily provisions (1 Kings 4:23). The hart is the male red deer (Ps. 42:1), and the hind, the female (Job 39:1). The fallow deer is a small deer with especially large horns. See Gen. 49:21; Prov. 5:19; Isa. 35:6; Hab. 3:19.

"Doe" refers to the female ibex or mountain goat (Prov. 5:19), the mate of the ibex, *Capra nubiana* or *Capra sinaitica* (Ps. 104:18), or to the female fallow deer (Gen. 49:21; 2 Sam. 22:34; Job 39:1; Pss. 18:33; 29:9; Jer. 14:5; Hab. 3:19; Song of Sol. 2:7; 3:5). The male, *Cervus captrolus*, is the hart or deer of Deut. 12:15,22; 14:5; 15:22; 1 Kings 4:23; Isa. 35:6; Ps. 42:2; Song of Sol. 2:9,17; Lam. 1:6.

(12) *Dog.* Unclean animal; designation for the wicked (Isa. 56:10-11) and the Gentiles (Mark 7:27). See Domestic Mammals, Dog above. Some dogs ran wild in village streets, often in packs (1 Kings 14:11; Pss. 22:16-21; 59:6), but served as watchdogs for herds (Isa. 56:10; Job 30:1) and for the dwellings (Ex. 11:7). Some were trained for hunting (Ps. 22:17,21). Metaphorically, dog was a term of contempt (1 Sam. 17:43; Phil. 3:2; compare Isa. 66:3; 2 Pet. 2:22; Rev. 22:15) and self-abasement (1 Sam. 24:14). "Dog" may refer to a male cult prostitute (Deut. 23:18), though the exact meaning of "dog's wages" is disputed. Jesus used dogs to teach people to be discriminating in whom they chose to teach (Matt. 7:6).

(13) *Dugong.* Aquatic mammal called sea cow; the male has tusklike teeth (reb, Ex. 25:5; 26:14). See Badger.

(14) *Elephant.* Ivory made from their tusks was among the riches Solomon imported (1 Kings 10:22).

(15) *Ferret.* White polecat; KJV translation of Gecko. See below *Reptiles, Gecko*.

(16) *Fox.* Meat-eating, sly, cunning, speedy animal with long, bushy tail; often identified as jackal or wolf rather than fox. See Judg. 15:4; Neh. 4:3; Ps. 63:10; Song of Sol. 2:15; Lam. 5:18; Ezek. 13:4; Matt. 8:20; Luke 9:58; 13:32.

(17) *Gazelle.* Fleet-footed animal noted for its attractive eyes; resem-

bles an antelope but smaller; considered clean by Israel (Deut. 12:15,22 for KJV, "roebuck"; compare Deut. 14:5; 15:22; 2 Sam. 2:18; 1 Kings 4:23; 1 Chron. 12:8; Prov. 6:5; Song of Sol. 2:7,9,17; 3:5; 4:5; 7:3; 8:14; Isa. 13:14).

(18) *Hare.* Long-eared animal; member of rabbit family (*Leporhyidae*), especially those born with open eyes and fur; regarded as unclean (Lev. 11:6; Deut. 14:7).

(19) *Hippopotamus.* See *Behemoth* above.

(20) *Hyena.* Striped, nighttime scavenger that looks like a fox; a repulsive animal in the ancient world; modern translations translate another Hebrew term, "hyena" (Isa. 13:22; 34:14; Jer. 50:39). Egyptians kept them as pets.

(21) *Ibex.* Wild animal resembling a goat; at times identified as wild goat of the Bible (1 Sam. 24:2; Ps. 104:18) or the pygarg of Deut. 14:5. See *Antelope.*

(22) *Jackal.* Noisy, nocturnal scavenger; flesh-eating animal resembling a fox; broader head and shorter nose and ears than fox. See *Fox.* Compare Job 30:29; Ps. 44:20; Isa. 13:22; 34:13; 35:7; 43:20; Jer. 9:10; 10:22; 14:6; 49:33; 51:37; Lam. 4:3; Mic. 1:8; Mal. 1:3. A place they haunt, humans have deserted (Isa. 13:22; Jer. 10:22).

(23) *Jerboa.* Nocturnal, jumping rodent with long hind legs and tail; REB translation of KJV "mouse" (Lev. 11:29).

(24) *Leopard.* Large graceful, fast cat with yellow fur with black spots; one of most dangerous to animals and human beings; common in Palestine, especially in forests of Lebanon. See Song of Sol. 4:8; Isa. 11:6; Dan. 7:6; Hos. 13:7; Rev. 13:2. Some translate Hab. 1:8 as "cheetah."

(25) *Lion.* Large, swift-moving cat with heavy mane; sign of tribe of Judah (Gen. 49:9; Rev. 5:5). Proverbial symbol for strength and daring (Judg. 14:18; Prov. 30:30) with a terrifying roar (Isa. 5:29). Lions seemed to prefer the vegetation of the Jordan valley (Jer. 49:19). See 1 Sam. 17:34-35; Dan. 6:16-23.

(26) *Mole.* Large rodent, gray in color. See Isa. 2:20. In Lev. 11:30 some translate "chameleon" (NIV, NASB, NRSV, REB, NKJV, NLT). Others translate "mole" in Lev. 11:30 (NASB, NEB, NCV, CEV, REB, NKJV, NLT). See *Rodents* below.

(27) *Mouse.* Unclean rodent with pointed snout (Lev. 11:29); apparently feared as carriers of plague (1 Sam. 6:4). See *Rodents* below.

(28) *Ox.* Large beast believed to be ancestor of domestic cattle; symbol of ferocious strength. "Unicorn" (Num. 23:22, KJV) has been identified as a wild ox (NASB, NIV, NRSV, REB, CEV, NKJV, NLT). Compare Num. 24:8; Deut. 33:17; Isa. 34:7; Job 39:9; Pss. 22:21; 29:6; 92:10. See *Cattle* above.

(29) *Porcupine or Hedgehog.* Large rodent with stiff, sharp bristles mixed with hair; NASB, NRSV translation (Isa. 14:23; 34:11; Zeph. 2:14) where Hebrew either refers to the hedgehog (or porcupine) or else to a type of bird (NRSV, NASB, hedgehog; NKJV, NLT, porcupine; NIV, NCV, owl; KJV, bittern; REB, bustard; CEV, wild animals); represents the wild and mysterious world humans do not control.

(30) *Pygarg.* See *Antelope* above.

(31) *Rat.* Large unclean rodent (Lev. 11:29, NIV, TEV, CEV, NCV) eaten by a disobedient people (Isa. 66:17; compare 1 Sam. 6:4-18). Also translated: mouse, KJV, NASB, NRSV, NLT; jerboa, REB. See *Rodents* below.

(32) *Rodents.* Generic term including mice and rats; considered unclean (Lev. 11:29). See 1 Sam. 6:4-18; Isa. 66:17. More than 20 varieties of small rodents live in the Holy Land.

(33) *Weasel.* Small unclean mammal related to mink (Lev. 11:29; compare TEV, REB, NCV, NKJV, CEV, NLT, NASB, mole).

(34) *Whale.* Large aquatic mammal; resembles large fish; KJV translation of terms for sea monster in Ezek. 32:2; Matt. 12:40 which refers to Jonah 1:17, where Hebrew reads "great fish."

(35) *Wolf.* Large wild canine considered primary ancestor of domestic dog; constantly threatened sheep and shepherds and earned a reputation for viciousness (Gen. 49:27; Matt. 7:15; Luke 20:3); stalked prey at night (Jer. 5:6; Zeph. 3:3); used symboli-

cally to describe deceitful and greedy people (Ezek. 22:27; Acts 20:29). John 10:12 describes its method of attack.

Reptiles

Animal that crawls or moves on its belly or on small short legs. Compare translations of grouping of reptiles in Lev. 11:30.

(1) *Adder.* Venomous snake: Gen. 49:17; Pss. 58:4; 91:13; 140:3; Prov. 23:32; NIV in Job 20:16; Isa. 30:6; 59:5. See *Serpent, Viper, Cobra* below.

(2) *Asp.* Venomous snake: Deut. 32:33; Job 20:14,16; Rom. 3:13; often translated, "cobra." Compare Isa. 11:8 in various translations. REB has "asp" for lion in Ps. 91:13. See *Cobra, Serpent, Viper* below.

(3) *Chameleon.* Unclean harmless lizard (*chamaeleo*) that changes color to fit surroundings; unique design of its eyes allows it to look two ways at same time; feeds mostly on insects; lives in trees and bushes; hangs onto branches with its long tail. NRSV, NIV, NKJV, NASB, NLT for KJV "mole" (Lev. 11:30). See *Mole* above; *Crocodile* below. Hebrew word with same spelling but perhaps with different historical derivation in Lev. 11:18; Deut. 14:16 is apparently the barn owl, *Tyto alba.*

(4) *Cobra.* Deadly poisonous snake; loose skin on its neck forms a hood when cobra is excited. NASB, NKJV translation for "asp"; NIV for adder, asp; compare Ps. 91:13; see *Adder; Asp* above.

(5) *Cockatrice.* Legendary serpent; in KJV designates a venomous snake (Isa. 11:8; 14:29; 59:5; Jer. 8:17); probably *Vipera xanthina.* Often "adder" or "viper."

(6) *Crocodile.* Large, thick-skinned, aquatic reptile. NASB, NRSV translation for chameleon. See *Chameleon* above; *Lizard* below.

(7) *Frog.* Web-footed, amphibious animal; see Ex. 8:1-15; Pss. 78; 105.

(8) *Gecko.* Harmless, repulsive-looking wall lizard whose sucking-disc toes enable it to run over walls and ceilings. REB distinguishes three kinds of geckos. KJV, "ferret" (Lev. 11:30).

(9) *Lizard.* Long-bodied reptile distinguished from the snake by two sets of short legs. See Lev. 11:30.

(10) *Serpent.* Generic name translating eight Hebrew words for long-bodied reptiles, specifically snakes such as the adder and viper; continuing symbol of evil and of the evil one (Gen. 3; Ex. 7; Num. 21; Ps. 140:3; Isa. 14:29; 27:1; 2 Cor. 11:3; Rev. 12:9-15; 20:2). At least 33 different species live in Palestine. See *Adder* and *Asp* above; *Viper* below.

(11) *Skink.* Small lizard listed among the unclean animals (Lev. 11:30, NIV). Others translate "sand reptile" (NASB), "snail" (KJV), "sand lizard" (NRSV).

(12) *Snake.* See *Serpent* above.

(13) *Tortoise.* Unclean land turtle (Lev. 11:29, KJV). Others translate "great lizard."

(14) *Viper.* Venomous snake (Job 20:16; Isa. 30:6; 59:5; Acts 28:3; Matt. 3:7; 12:34; 23:33; Luke 3:7). See *Serpent* above. See *Birds; Insects.*

ANISE See *Spices.*

ANKLET

Ornamental rings worn above the ankles; luxury items worn by the women of Jerusalem (Isa. 3:18; compare v. 16).

ANNA *(grace)*

Aged, widowed prophetess who recognized the Messiah when He was brought to temple for dedication (Luke 2:36).

ANNAS *(merciful)*

Son of Seth; priest when John the Baptist began preaching (Luke 3:2); evidently, appointed high priest about A.D. 6 by Quirinius, governor of Syria; deposed in A.D. 15 by Gratus but continued to exercise considerable influence (John 18:13; Acts 4:6).

ANNUNCIATION

Act of announcing or of being announced; angel Gabriel's announcement of Jesus' birth to Mary (Luke 1:26-38).

ANOINT, ANOINTED (Hebrew, *messiach;* Greek, *christos*)

Procedure of rubbing or smearing oneself or another person or thing, usually with (olive) oil, for the purpose of healing, setting apart, or embalming. See Esther 2:12, for cosmetic usage.

Priests and kings were ceremonially anointed as a sign of official appointment to office and as a symbol of God's power upon them.

In the NT *anoint* speaks of daily hair grooming (Matt. 6:17), treating injury or illness (Luke 10:34), and preparing a body for burial (Mark 16:1). Christians see Jesus as God's Anointed One, the Savior (Acts 10:38). The Christian is also anointed by God (2 Cor. 1:21; 1 John 2:27) for ministry.

ANON

Archaic word; "immediately" (Matt. 13:20; Mark 1:30).

ANT See *Insects.*

ANTEDILUVIANS (*before the Deluge*)

Persons living before the Flood (Gen. 4:1,17-24; Gen. 5:1-32; 6-8). The Ancient Near East often attributed cultural achievements to the gods. Scripture emphasizes achievements of human beings created by the one God. See *Flood.*

ANTELOPE See *Animals.*

ANTHROPOLOGY See *Humanity.*

ANTHROPOMORPHISM

Process of applying human characteristics to a god, an animal, or an inanimate object; giving human form to something not inherently human; especially applying human characteristics to God.

Anthropomorphism grew naturally in a faith that viewed God as active and relational. The form of God was preserved in mystery, and His character was revealed rather than conceived.

The inspired writers speak of God's eyes, ears, hands, and feet; but they meticulously avoid letting the descriptions become too tangible and concrete. God walks; smells; sees; shares human emotions, rules, shepherds, and loves.

The Bible's language concerning "image" and "likeness" (Gen. 1:26-27; 5:1-2; 9:6) is the reverse of anthropomorphism. Rather than creating an image of God out of personal experience or imagination, mankind is an image of God. What we are intended to be is most fully reflected in what He is (see 1 John 3:2). See *Image of God.*

The ultimate anthropomorphism is seen in the eternal Word of God becoming flesh and dwelling among us (John 1:14). Jesus took the form (*morphe*) of a slave (Phil. 2:7). Through His sacrifice on the cross He revealed a God of grace whose love knows no boundaries.

ANTICHRIST

Individual (Dan. 7:25; 8:10,13; 11:40) or group of people (Dan. 7:7-28) who oppose God and His purpose (1 John 2:18,22; 4:3; 2 John 7).

Many Jews viewed the arrival of Antiochus Epiphanes IV as the embodiment of these verses. Yet the rule of Antiochus did not meet the full expectations of these Scriptures. Such Roman figures as Pompey and Caligula were identified with the antichrist. See *Abomination, Abomination of Desolation; Intertestamental History.* In later Judaism, the Fourth Kingdom or the collective antichrist was viewed as the Roman Empire (2 Baruch 26-40; 4 Ezra 5:3-4).

In 1 John 2:18, antichrists were human teachers who had left the church. Such antichrists deny the incarnation (1 John 4:3) and Christ's deity (1 John 2:2). In 2 John 7, the antichrists are identified as deceivers who teach that Jesus Christ did not come in the flesh. The concept of antichrist appears as "false Christ" (Matt. 24:24; Mark 13:22), looking to a Roman ruler to once again enter the temple as did Antiochus and Pompey. In Revelation 13:3, the beast from the sea may have looked for a return of Nero.

In 2 Thessalonians 2:1-12, the antichrist figure is armed with satanic power and is fused with Belial, a satanic being. The Roman government restrains its power. In Revelation, the Roman Caesar is the evil force.

Dispensationalists look for a future Roman ruler who will appear during the tribulation and rule over the earth. Amillennialists interpret the term symbolically.

ANTIMONY See *Minerals and Metals*.

ANTINOMIANISM

False teaching that since faith alone is necessary for salvation, one is free from the moral obligations of the law.

ANTIOCH

Two NT cities.

(1) Largest city of Roman empire after Rome in Italy and Alexandria in Egypt; often called Antioch on the Orontes (River) or Antioch of Syria; founded around 300 B.C. by Seleucus Nicator; a bustling seaport; about 20 miles inland from the Mediterranean on the Orontes River, nearly 300 miles north of Jerusalem. Antioch's patron deity was the pagan goddess Tyche or "Fortune."

Persecution of Stephen and others scattered Jewish believers to Cyprus, Cyrene, and Antioch (Acts 11:19) where believers were first called Christians (11:26). Famine relief for the church in Jerusalem was directed and carried out from Antioch. The Holy Spirit led the church at Antioch to set aside Barnabas and Saul for the first organized mission work (13:1-3).

(2) A city in Pisidia in Asia Minor, west of Iconium founded by Seleucus Nicator. Under Roman rule, this city was called Caesarea. Paul preached in a synagogue there on his first missionary journey (Acts 13:14-46; compare 14:19-21; 2 Tim. 3:11).

ANTIOCHUS

Name of 13 rulers of Syria Palestine headquartered in Antioch. See *Daniel; Intertestamental History; Maccabees; Seleucids*.

ANTIPAS

(1) Tetrarch of Galilee when John the Baptist and Jesus began their public ministries (Luke 3:1); ordered John the Baptist beheaded (Matt. 14:3); treated Jesus with scornful contempt (Luke 23:11) prior to the crucifixion, winning the friendship of Pilate.

(2) Martyr of the church of Pergamum (Rev. 2:13).

ANTIPATRIS (*in place of father*)

City Herod the Great built to honor his father Antipater in 9 B.C.; 40 miles from Jerusalem and 25 miles from Caesarea on Via Maris; site of Old Testament Aphek. See Acts 23:31. See *Aphek*.

ANTONIA, TOWER OF

Fortress Herod the Great built near northwest corner of temple about A.D. 6 as his palace residence, barracks for Roman troops, safe deposit for the robe of the high priest, and a central courtyard for public speaking; traditionally considered site of Jesus' trial before Pilate (John 19:13); destroyed in A.D. 66 by Titus. The tower was 75 feet high and was named for Herod's friend, Mark Anthony.

ANXIETY

State of mind wherein one is concerned about something or someone; may range from genuine concern (see Phil. 2:20,28; 2 Cor. 11:28) to obsessions that originate from a distorted perspective of life (Matt. 6:25-34; Mark 4:19; Luke 12:22-31).

APE See *Animals*.

APHARSATHCHITES or APHARSACHITES

Transliteration of Aramaic terms in Ezra 4:9; 5:6; 6:6; in 4:9 may represent provincial officials representing the Persian king; in 5:6 and 6:6 may refer to government investigators or inspectors.

APHARSITES

Transliteration of Aramaic term in Ezra 4:9 variously translated: men from Persia (NIV, NKJV); "Persians" (NRSV, NLT); "secretaries" (NASB); "local leaders" (CEV); "chief officers" (REB).

APHEK (*bed of brook* or *river* or *fortress*)

(1) Modern Tell Ras el Ain near source of Yarkon River in Sharon plain northeast of Joppa; city whose king Joshua defeated (Josh. 12:18); where Philistine armies formed to face Israel (1 Sam. 4:1), resulting in Philistine victory and capture of Israel's ark of the covenant. See 1 Sam. 29. See *Antipatris*.

(2) Northern border city which Joshua did not conquer (Josh. 13:4); may be modern Afqa, 15 miles east of ancient Byblos and 23 miles north of Beirut.

(3) City assigned to Asher (Josh. 19:30) but not conquered (Judg. 1:31); may be modern Tell Kerdanah 3 miles from Haifa and 6 miles southeast of Acco.

(4) City east of Jordan near Sea of Galilee where Benhadad led Syria against Israel about 860 B.C. but met defeat as a prophet predicted (1 Kings 20:26-30). See 2 Kings 13:17.

APHRAH

KJV interpretation of place name in Mic. 1:10; called Beth Ophrah (NIV, NCV); Beth-aphrah (REB, NKJV); Beth-le-aphrah (NASB); Beth Leaphrah (NRSV, TEV, NLT). See *Beth-le-aphrah.*

APIS

Sacred bull worshiped in Memphis, Egypt. NRSV, TEV, CEV, REB divide the words in Jer. 46:15 differently than printed Hebrew text and translates, "Why has Apis fled?" (NRSV) or "Why has your mighty God Apis fallen?"

(TEV). Hebrew text reads, "Why are thy valiant men swept away?" (KJV).

APOCALYPTIC (*to uncover*; figuratively *to disclose, reveal*)

(1) Writings from God that employ symbolic language to tell of a divine intervention soon to take place;

(2) doctrinal system explicit in these writings;

(3) movement(s) that produced the writings and doctrines.

Portions of Joel, Amos, Zechariah, and Isaiah have apocalyptic features, but Daniel is only wholly apocalyptic Old Testament book. The Book of Revelation is called *apokalupsis* in Greek. These writings claim to originate from God; most frequently tell of a divine intervention soon to take place; use sign language or pictorial language which is also parabolic; have an angelic intermediary to explain to the prophet the meaning of the message; and have the prophet make known to others his visions.

Apocalyptic literature encouraged people to be ready for and participate in God's final victory in history. Apocalyptic writing found its correction and true fulfillment in the message of Jesus, and in His living, dying, rising, and in the hope of His appearance.

APOCRYPHA (*things that are hidden*)

Collection of 15 books written between about 200 B.C. and A.D. 100; part of the official Latin Bible, the Vulgate. All 15 apocryphal books except 2 Esdras appear in the Greek translation of the OT, the Septuagint. All except 1 and 2 Esdras and the Prayer of Mannasseh are considered canonical and authoritative by the Roman Catholic Church. From the time of the Reformation, the apocryphal books have been omitted from the canon of the Protestant churches.

First Esdras

Historical book from early first century A.D. paralleling material in last chapters of 2 Chronicles, Ezra, and Nehemiah; covers period from Josiah to the reading of the law by Ezra. The Three Guardsmen Story, 3:1–5:3, the one significant passage not in OT, tells how Zerubbabel was allowed to lead exiles back to Palestine.

First Maccabees

Primary historical source for 180 to 134 B.C.; emphasizes that God worked through Mattathias and his sons to bring deliverance. After introductory verses dealing with Alexander the Great, the book gives the causes for the revolt against the Seleucids and details about Judas and Jonathan. Less attention is given Simon. Brief reference to John Hyrcanus at the close suggests the book was written either late in his life or after his death, probably shortly after 100 B.C.

Second Maccabees

History of early part of revolt against the Seleucids from 180 to 161 B.C.; based on five otherwise unknown volumes by Jason of Cyrene; written shortly after 100 B.C.; not considered as accurate historically as 1 Maccabees. The book clearly teaches a resurrection of the body, at least for the righteous.

Tobit

Historical romance written about 200 B.C.; more concerned to teach lessons than to record history; story of family exiled in Assyria in 721 B.C. The book stresses temple attendance, prayer, paying tithes, giving alms, obeying the law, marrying only within Israel, and separation of Jews from Gentiles. It introduces the concept of a guardian angel.

Judith

Folk novel written between 250 and 150 B.C.; not historically accurate; shows importance of obeying the law. This book places emphasis upon prayer and fasting. Idolatry is denounced, and the God of Israel is glorified. The book includes a strong hatred of pagans and says the end justifies the means.

Additions to Esther

These additions were made between 125 and 75 B.C. Hebrew Esther contains 163 verses; the Greek, 270. Additions are in six different places. The Latin Vulgate places them at the end. Included are the dream of Mordecai, the dream's interpretation, the texts of the letters referred to in 1:22; 3:13; 8:5,10; 9:20,25-30), and the prayers of Esther and Mordecai, providing a religious basis for the book whose original form never mentions God.

Song of the Three Young Men

One of three additions to Daniel made about 100 B.C.; follows 3:23 in Greek text; satisfies curiosity about events in the fiery furnace. Concluding section is a hymn of praise emphasizing that God delivers His people in response to prayer.

Susanna

"Detective story" at the close of Daniel in Septuagint. Two judges sought to become intimate with Susanna. They claimed they had seen her being intimate with a young man. Daniel proved her innocent.

Bel and the Dragon

"Detective story" preceding Susanna in the Septuagint. Daniel proved Bel, a Babylon idol, to be a man-made image. In the second part Daniel killed a dragon, outraging the people. These stories ridicule paganism and the worship of idols.

Wisdom of Solomon

Wisdom collection written about 100 B.C. in Egypt. The first section comforted oppressed Jews and condemned those who had turned from their faith in God. It shows the advantages of wisdom over wickedness. The second section is a hymn of praise to wisdom, identified as a person present with God. The final section shows wisdom as helpful to Israel throughout its history. This writing presents the Greek concept of immortality rather than the biblical teaching of resurrection.

Wisdom of Jesus the Son of Sirach

Wisdom writing also known as Ecclesiasticus; emphasizes importance of the law and obedience to it; written in Hebrew about 180 B.C.; translated into Greek by the author's grandson shortly after 132 B.C. A highly educated, widely traveled, devout Jew combined traditional Jewish wisdom with material from the Greek world. Chapters 44–50 praise the great fathers of Israel, somewhat similar to Hebrews 11. Wisdom is identified with the law.

Baruch

Wisdom collection written shortly before 100 B.C. The first section in prose claims to be a history of the period of Jeremiah and Baruch. The second section in poetry is a praise of wisdom. The final section, also poetic, gives readers hope. Wisdom and law are equated.

Letter of Jeremiah

Attempt to provide the letter mentioned in Jer. 29:1-23 but written shortly before 100 B.C.; often added to Baruch as chapter 6; strongly worded condemnation of idolatry.

Prayer of Manasseh

Devotional writing from before 100 B.C. claiming to be the repentant king's prayer (see 2 Chron. 33:11-13,18-19; compare 2 Kings 21:10-17).

Second Esdras Apocalypse

Written too late to be included in the Septuagint. Chapters 1–2 and 15–16 are Christian writings. Chapters 3–14 are from about 20 B.C. See *Apocalyptic.* It pictures the preexistent Messiah who will remain 400 years and then die. The final section reports that Ezra was inspired to write 94 books: 24, a rewrite of the Old Testament; the other 70 to be given to the wise. See *Pseudepigrapha.*

APOCRYPHA, NEW TESTAMENT

Collective term referring to a large body of religious writings dating to the early Christian centuries; that by form and content, claimed for itself a status and authority equal to Scrip- ture; similar in form to the NT (Gospels, acts, epistles, and apocalypses).

None of the NT Apocrypha (with the possible exception of *The Apocalypse of Peter* and *The Acts of Paul*) has ever been accepted as Scripture.

Some groups accepted apocryphal writings because they built on the universal desire to preserve the memories of the lives and deaths of important NT figures. Apocryphal works were intended to supplement the NT's information about Jesus or the apostles. Heretical groups attempted to gain authority for their own particular views by appealing to apostolic authority. Apocryphal books may be placed in the following categories.

(1) *Apocryphal gospels.* These are further classified into infancy gospels, passion gospels, Jewish-Christian gospels, and gospels from heretical groups.

Infancy Gospels deal with the birth and/or childhood of Jesus, trying to fill in the gaps they believed existed. *The Protoevangelium of James* glorifies Mary, including her miraculous birth, her presentation in the temple, her espousal to Joseph (an old man with children), and the miraculous birth of Jesus. *The Infancy Gospel of Thomas* depicts the boy Jesus using his miraculous powers as a matter of personal convenience such as making 12 sparrows from soft clay, clapping His hands, and the sparrows taking flight.

Others are *The Arabic Gospel of the Infancy, The Armenian Gospel of the Infancy, The Gospel of Pseudo-Matthew, The Latin Infancy Gospel, The Life of John According to Serapion, The Gospel of the Birth of Mary, The Assumption of the Virgin,* and *The History of Joseph the Carpenter.*

Passion Gospels supplement canonical accounts of the crucifixion and resurrection of Jesus. *The Gospel of Peter* is a second-century work that downplays Jesus' humanity, heightens the miraculous, and reduces Pilate's guilt. *The Gospel of Nicodemus* (*Acts of Pilate*) expanded the trial and death of Jesus with witnesses testifying on Jesus' behalf and includes a vivid account of Jesus'"Descent into Hell."

Jewish-Christian Gospels include *The Gospel of the Ebionites*, *The Gospel of Hebrews*, and *The Gospel of the Nazarenes*. *The Gospel of the Hebrews* appears to paraphrase the Gospel of Matthew with a special emphasis on James, the Lord's brother.

Heretical Gospels are mostly Gnostic gospels. See *Gnosticism*. *The Gospel of Truth* contains no references to the words or actions of Jesus. Other heretical gospels include *The Gospel of the Twelve Apostles*; *The Gospels of Philip, Thomas, Matthias, Judas, and Bartholomew*; *The Questions of Mary*; *The Gospel According to Mary*; and gospels attributed to chief heretics such as Cerinthus, Basilides, and Marcion.

Written around A.D. 100, *The Gospel of Thomas* is a collection of 114 secret sayings "which Jesus the living one spoke and Didymus Judas Thomas wrote down." It is one of almost 50 documents discovered in 1945 near Nag Hammadi in Upper Egypt.

(2) *The apocryphal acts*. These are legendary accounts of the journeys and heroics of NT apostles that sought to parallel and supplement *The Book of Acts*. The five major apocryphal acts are stories from between A.D. 100 and 300 named after a "Leucius Charinus" and known as *The Leucian Acts*. Much of what they offer is wildly imaginative, closely akin to a romantic novel (with talking animals and obedient bugs).

The Acts of John (A.D. 150–160) contains miracles and sermons by John of Asia Minor and has a distinct Gnostic orientation. *The Acts of Andrew*, written shortly before A.D. 300, is also distinctly Gnostic. *The Acts of Paul* was written before A.D. 200 by an Asian presbyter "out of love for Paul." He was later defrocked for publishing the writing.

The Acts of Peter, written shortly before A.D. 200, tells of Peter defending the Church from a heretic named Simon Magus by public preaching and later being crucified upside down. Like the other acts, it promotes a life-style of self-denial and withdrawal from society.

The Acts of Thomas, written after A.D. 200, is thought to have originated in Syriac Christianity. It tells how Judas Thomas, "Twin of the Messiah," was given India when the apostles cast lots for the world. Thomas emphasizes virginity.

Other later apocryphal acts include: *The Apostolic History of Abdias, The Fragmentary Story of Andrew, The Ascents of James, The Martyrdom of Matthew, The Preaching of Peter, Slavonic Acts of Peter, The Passion of Paul, Passion of Peter, Passion of Peter and Paul, The Acts of Andrew and Matthias, Andrew and Paul, Paul and Thecla, Barnabas, James the Great, Peter and Andrew, Peter and Paul, Philip*, and *Thaddaeus*.

(3) *The apocryphal epistles*. These are a small group of apocryphal epistles, including many ascribed to Paul. The Epistle of the Apostles from after A.D. 100 is a collection of visions communicating post-resurrection teachings of Christ. The Third Epistle to the Corinthians, also a part of The Acts of Paul, was purported to be Paul's reply to a letter from Corinth. The Latin Epistle to the Laodiceans is a gathering of Pauline phrases probably motivated by Col. 4:16 where Paul makes mention of an "epistle from Laodicea."

Other important apocryphal epistles include *The Correspondence of Christ and Abgar, The Epistle to the Alexandrians, The Epistle of Titus*, of *Peter to James*, of *Peter to Philip*, and of *Mary to Ignatius*.

(4) *The apocryphal apocalypses*. These focus on heaven and hell. The Apocalypse of Peter seems to have enjoyed a degree of canonical status for a time. It presents visions of the resurrected Lord and images of the terror suffered by those in hell. The Apocalypse of Paul is probably motivated by Paul's reference in 2 Cor. 12:2 to a man in Christ being caught up to the third heaven. Other apocalypses include The Apocalypse of James, of Stephen, of Thomas, of the Virgin Mary, and several works discovered at Nag Hammadi. See *Apocalyptic*.

(5) *Other apocryphal works.* These include The Agrapha (a collection of sayings attributed to Jesus), The Preachings of Peter, The Clementine Homilies and Recognitions, The Apocryphon of John, The Apocryphon of James, and certain Gnostic writings such as The Pistis Sophia, The Wisdom of Jesus, and The Books of Jeu.

These writings demonstrate how the NT places a priority on historical fact rather than human fantasy. The NT Apocrypha is usually unreliable historically and always unauthoritative for matters of faith and practice.

APOLLONIA (*belonging to Apollo*)

City in northern Greece or Macedonia on the international highway called Via Egnatia, 30 miles from Amphipolis and 38 miles from Thessalonica. See Acts 17:1.

APOLLOS

Alexandrian Jew who came to Ephesus following Paul's first visit. Able to handle the Old Testament with forcefulness, he lacked a full understanding of God's way, so Priscilla and Aquila instructed him (Acts 18:26). See Acts 18:26-28; 19:1; 1 Cor. 1:12; 3:4-6,22; 16:12; Titus 3:13. See *Aquila and Priscilla*; *Ephesus*; *Corinth*; *Corinthians, 1 and 2.*

APOLLYON (*destroyer*)

Greek name for Abaddon. See *Abaddon.*

APOSTASY (*to stand away from*)

Act of rebelling against, forsaking, abandoning, or falling away from what one has believed. The OT speaks of "falling away" in terms of a person's deserting to a foreign king (2 Kings 25:11; Jer. 37:13-14; 39:9; 52:15). Associated ideas include the concept of religious unfaithfulness: "rebellion" (Josh. 22:22); "cast away" (2 Chron. 29:19); "trespass" (2 Chron. 33:19); and "backslidings" (Jer. 2:19; 8:5). NASB uses "apostasy" in Jer. 8:5 and Hos. 14:4; plural in Jer. 2:19; 5:6; 14:7.

In Acts 21:21, Jews accused Paul of leading Jews outside Palestine to abandon the law of Moses. In 2 Thess. 2:3 Paul taught that apostasy would precede the day of the Lord. See 1 Tim. 4:1. Such apostasy will involve doctrinal deception, moral insensitivity, and ethical wrongdoing.

In the parable of the soils, Jesus spoke of those who believe for a while but "fall away" in time of temptation (Luke 8:13). Hebrews speaks of falling away from the living God because of "an evil heart of unbelief" (3:12). Those who fall away cannot be renewed again to repentance (Heb. 6:6). Yet God is able to keep the believer from falling (Jude 24).

Apostasy is a biblical concept, but its implications have been hotly debated. Some hold that, though true believers may stray, they will never totally fall away. Others affirm that any who fall away were never really saved. Though they may have "believed" for a while, they never experienced regeneration. Still others argue that the biblical warnings against apostasy are real and that believers maintain the freedom, at least potentially, to reject God's salvation. Conviction of sin in itself is evidence that one has not fallen away. Desire for salvation shows one does not have "an evil heart of unbelief."

APOSTLES See *Disciples, Apostles.*

APOSTOLIC COUNCIL

Meeting in Jerusalem at which the apostles and elders of Jerusalem defended the right of Paul and Barnabas to preach the gospel to the Gentiles without forcing converts to obey the Jewish law (Acts 15; compare Lev. 17–18).

APOSTOLIC FATHERS

Early Christian authors believed to have known the apostles but not mentioned in the Bible.

The Didache or Teaching of the Twelve Apostles

Early church manual, in its current form no later than A.D. 100 but possibly much earlier; from Syria; directions concerning baptism, fasting and prayers, the Eucharist, hospitality, worship on the Lord's day, and bishops and deacons with a concluding exhortation.

Epistle of 1 Clement

Third bishop of Rome in A.D. 96 responded to disturbance in church at Corinth and appealed for unity and submission to persons appointed presbyters by the apostles and their successors.

Second Letter of Clement to the Corinthians

Early anonymous sermon about A.D. 140 urging hearers to repent for too great attachment to the "world"; cited authoritative writings; now definitely identified as Gnostic.

Seven Epistles of Ignatius

Bishop of Antioch en route to Rome, where he suffered martyrdom during reign of Trajan (98–117). He wrote the churches of Philadelphia and Smyrna, and Polycarp, Bishop of Smyrna, urged acceptance of episcopal authority, thus suggesting churches of Asia Minor had not yet accepted rule by a single bishop with presbyters and deacons subordinate to him.

Interpretation of the Lord's Oracles

Five-volume work by Papias, bishop of Hierapolis written between A.D. 110 and 120.

Epistle of Polycarp of Smyrna

Cover letter for letters of Ignatius written shortly after A.D. 100; mosaic of quotations from letters of Paul exhorting to true faith and virtue.

The Martyrdom of Polycarp

Oldest account of a martyr's death; recorded soon after it happened in 156; has first use of "catholic" referring to the church; written to strengthen faith under persecution; embellished by miraculous happenings.

The Epistle of Barnabas (so called)

Neither a letter nor a work of Barnabas. This sermon or treatise attempts to prove the Jews misunderstood the Scriptures and did not see Jesus in the Scriptures from the beginning because they interpreted it literally. It includes allegorical exposition.

The Shepherd of Hermas Apocalypse

Argued against people who denied repentance for serious post-baptismal sins such as apostasy, adultery, or murder and said such persons should suffer permanent exclusion.

The Epistle to Diognetus

Attractive apology; perhaps as late as A.D. 200's. The author contrasts the unsatisfying faith of other religions with Christian teachings concerning love and good citizenship.

The Apology of Quadratus

Fragment of defense of Christianity addressed to the Emperor Hadrian; believed to be considerably later than Apostolic Fathers and may be same as *The Epistle to Diognetus.*

As writings that predate the formation of the NT canon, they are invaluable resources for understanding post-apostolic Christianity.

APOTHECARY See *Confection.*

APPEAL TO CAESAR

Right to have one's case heard by the emperor (Acts 25:1-12). By all appearances, Paul based his claim on his Roman citizenship. Some Roman citizens in Africa, however, were refused the right of appeal and were crucified by Galba, the governor of the province. See *Paul.*

APPENDAGE OF THE LIVER See *Caul.*

APPHIA

Christian lady Paul greeted (Philem. 2). Early Christian tradition identified her as Philemon's wife.

APPI FORUM See *Forum of Appius.*

APPIUS See *Forum of Appius.*

APPLE OF THE EYE

English expression referring to the pupil of the eye and therefore something very precious. Three different Hebrew words or phrases are rendered as the apple of the eye:

(1) Deut. 32:10 and Prov. 7:2 literally read "little man"; evidently the reflection of a person in the eye of another;

(2) Psalm 17:8 and Lam. 2:18 (KJV) literally read "the daughter of the eye" with possibly the same significance as 1; and

(3) Zechariah 2:8 literally means "gate." Lamentations 2:18 refers to the pupil of the eye as the source of tears; the other references are metaphorical of something that is precious.

APPLE TREE See *Plants.*

APRON

KJV in Gen. 3:7 for Hebrew word otherwise translated "girdle" (1 Sam. 18:4; 2 Sam. 18:11; 20:8; 1 Kings 2:5; Isa. 3:24). In Acts 19:12 the aprons and handkerchiefs of Paul had healing powers.

AQABA, GULF OF

TEV translation (1 Kings 9:26) to show that the part of the Red Sea meant is the eastern arm below the Dead Sea. See *Elath; Ezion-gaber.*

AQUEDUCTS

Troughs cut out of rock, soil, or pipes made of stone, leather, or bronze used from very early times in the Middle East to transport water from distant places into towns and cities. See 2 Sam. 5:8; 2 Kings 18:17; 20:20; 2 Chron. 32:3-4,30; Isa. 7:3; 22:11; 36:2. The Siloam tunnel was a twisting underground aqueduct that diverted water from the Gihon Spring to the Pool of Siloam (2 Kings 20:20).

AQUILA AND PRISCILLA

Married couple of tentmakers (2 Tim. 4:19) who came from Italy to Corinth (Acts 18:2) after Claudius ordered Jews expelled from Rome (see Rom. 16:3-4). They became Christians and assisted Paul in his ministry, accompanying him to Ephesus (Acts 18:19), instructing Apollos (18:25), having a church in their home, and joining Paul in writing the Corinthians (1 Cor. 16:19). Second Tim. 4:19 may indicate the couple was in Ephesus.

AR (*city*)

Town on northern border of Moab on southern bank of Arnon River (Num. 21:15,28); see Deut. 2:9,18,29; Isa. 15:1.

ARAB (*ambush*)

City in Judean hill country near Hebron (Josh. 15:52). Usually identified with modern er-Rabiyeh.

ARABAH (*dry, infertile area*)

Hebrew noun meaning desert with hot climate and sparse rainfall.

(1) Modern usage refers to rift area 110 miles below Dead Sea to the Gulf of Elath or Aqaba. A copper-mining region, it was guarded by military fortresses to protect valuable trade routes and sea routes connecting to southern Arabia and eastern Africa. See Deut. 2:8; 1 Kings 9:26-27.

(2) Wilderness of Judah; eastern slopes of the mountains of Judah with little rain, deep canyons, and steep cliffs where David hid from Saul (1 Sam. 23:24-25).

(3) Entire Jordan Valley, 70 miles from the Sea of Galilee to the Dead Sea, or more precisely the desert areas above the actual Zor or lushly fertile areas on the immediate shore of the Jordan. See Deut. 3:17 (NRSV, NIV); Josh. 8:14 (TEV, NIV); 11:2, 16; 12:8 (NASB, NIV); 2 Sam. 2:29 (NASB,

NIV); Jer. 39:4 (NASB, NIV); Ezek. 47:8 (NASB, NIV); Zech. 14:10 (NIV).

(4) Sea of the Arabah, the Dead Sea. See NASB, NIV, NRSV of Deut. 3:17; 4:49; Josh. 3:16; 2 Kings 14:25.

(5) Araboth of Moab or plains of Moab, eastern shore of the Dead Sea south of wadi Nimrim. Notice REB translation, "lowlands of Moab." See Num. 22:1; 31:12; 36:13; Deut. 34:1; Josh. 13:32.

(6) Desert area on eastern border of Jordan River from Sea of Galilee to Dead Sea. See Joshua 12:1 (NASB, NIV, NRSV).

(7) Araboth of Jericho or plains of Jericho, area near the Jordan once dominated by city state of Jericho (Josh. 4:13; 5:10; 2 Kings 25:5; Jer. 39:5).

(8) The brook of the Arabah.

ARABIA

Asian peninsula lying between Red Sea on west and Persian Gulf on east incorporating over 1,200,000 square miles; some of the driest climate in the world; home to biblical Arabs; includes all of present-day Saudi Arabia, the two Yemens (San'a' and Aden), Oman, the United Arab Emirates, Qatar, and Kuwait, as well as parts of Iraq, Syria, Jordan, and the Sinai Peninsula. See 1 Kings 10:15; 2 Chron. 9:14; 17:11; 21:16; 22:1; 26:7; Neh. 2:19; 4:7; 6:1; Isa. 13:20; 21:13; Jer. 3:2; 25:24; Ezek. 27:21; Acts 2:11; Gal. 1:17; 4:25.

Most biblical references to Arab peoples or territory are to the northern and western parts of this whole, but sometimes includes both the northern and southern portions.

ARABIM

NASB, REB transliteration of name of waterway (Isa. 15:7). Other translations: "brook of the willows" (KJV); "Ravine of the Poplars" (NIV, NCV); "Valley of Willows" (TEV); "Wadi of the Willows" (NRSV); "Ravine of Willows" (NLT); "Willow Creek" (CEV). Water source may be wadi el-Hesa at southern end of Dead Sea in Moab; 35 miles long; forms border of Edom and Moab; probably same as Brook of Zered (Num. 31:12; Deut. 2:13-14) and dry stream of 2 Kings 3:16,22.

ARABS

People of northwestern parts of Arabia; called "sons of the East"; nomadic herders of sheep and goats, and later, of camels; sometimes *arab* refers to economic status of nomads without geographical or ethnic reference.

Midianites, Ishmaelites, people of Kedar, Amalekites, Dedanites, Temanites, and others were ethnically and linguistically Arab. The Israelites recognized their own blood relationship with the Arabs through Abraham's son Ishmael or his second wife Keturah (Gen. 25).

The inhabitants of southern Arabia, in the mountains fringing the Red Sea and the Indian Ocean, were town-dwellers with a sophisticated system of irrigation and considerable wealth from incenses, spices, gold, silver, precious stones, and trading.

The NT references are to the territory of the Nabatean Arabs, who controlled what is today southern Jordan and the Negeb of Israel; for a time they controlled as far north as Damascus. See Acts 2:11; Gal. 1:17.

ARAD

(1) Canaanite city about 11 miles west southwest of Beersheba (Num. 21:1-3, probably Tel Malhata). Israel renamed devastated city Hormah (See Josh. 12:14; Judg. 1:16-17).

(2) Important fortress for Judah from Solomon's time to Josiah; 17 miles west northwest of Beersheba; not mentioned in Bible. A temple has been found there with architecture much like the biblical tabernacle and temple, including a holy of holies. Even the names of priestly families of Israel have been found here, Pashhur

(Ezra 2:38; 10:22) and Meremoth (Ezra 8:33; Neh. 10:5).

(3) Son of Beriah the Benjamite (1 Chron. 8:15–16).

(4) Canaanite king who attacked Israelites near Mt. Hor and was defeated (Num. 21:1).

ARAM

(1) See *Aramean.*

(2) Original ancestor of Arameans, son of Shem and grandson of Noah (Gen. 10:22-23).

(3) Grandson of Nahor, Abraham's brother (Gen. 22:21).

(4) Asherite (1 Chron. 7:34).

(5) KJV reading of ancestor of Jesus (Luke 3:33).

ARAMAIC

North Semitic language of Arameans; similar to Phoenician and Hebrew; language in which Ezra 4:8–6:18; 7:12-26; Dan. 2:4b–7:28; Jer. 10:11; and 2 words in Gen. 31:47 are written; became international language of commerce and diplomacy in Persian empire and was common language of Jesus' day. See *Aramean.* See 2 Kings 18:26; Mark 5:41; 14:36; 15:34.

Jewish Palestinian Aramaic words and phrases in the NT include *Abba* (father, Mark 14:36); *talitha, qumi* (maiden, arise, Mark 5:41), *lama sabachthani* (Why hast thou forsaken me? Mark 15:34).

ARAMEAN

Loose confederation of towns and settlements in what is now called Syria and parts of Babylon from which Jacob and Abraham came (Deut. 26:5); most important city was Damascus. Arameans lived as independent towns settled by nomads prior to 1000 B.C.

Roughly at start of Israel's monarchy, the Arameans became a potent political force. They seized large portions of Assyrian lands, defeating Tiglath-pileser I and II and Ashur-rabi II. They suffered losses to David (2 Sam. 8:9-10), who married Maacah, daughter of Talmui, king of Geshur.

She bore Absalom (2 Sam. 3:3). See *Assyria; Damascus; Aramaic.*

ARAM-NAHARAIM (*Aram of the two rivers*)

Transliteration in title of Ps. 60 (KJV). See Gen. 24:10; Deut. 23:4; Judg. 3:8; and 1 Chron. 19:6 (NIV). Land between Tigris and Euphrates Rivers.

ARAM-ZOBAH See *Zobah.*

ARARAT

Mountainous region reaching 17,000 feet in western Asia northeast of Lake Van; known as Urartu in sources outside Bible; southeast of the Black Sea and southwest of the Caspian where head waters of Tigris and Euphrates Rivers were found. See Gen. 8:4; 2 Kings 19:37; Isa. 37:38; Jer. 51:27. In Isaiah and 2 Kings KJV reads "Armenia," following Septuagint. People of Ararat identified themselves as "children of Haldi" (the national god) and their land as Biai-nae.

ARAUNAH (possibly Hittite, *freeman, noble*)

Jebusite whose threshing floor David purchased as a site for sacrifice (2 Sam. 24:15-25). (1 Chron. 21:15-30; 2 Chron. 3:1 refer to Araunah as Ornan).

ARBITRATOR See *Mediator.*

ARCH

KJV rendering (Ezek. 40:16-36). KJV translates "porch" elsewhere (for example, 1 Kings 6:3; 7:12,19,21). Other versions translate the word as "porch" (NASB), "portico" and "galleries" (NIV), "vestibule and walls" (NRSV), and "entrance room and galleries" (TEV); "dividing walls" (NLT); "entrance room" (CEV). Aside from 1 Kings 7:6 (where the word describes a covered porch whose roof is supported by columns) the word refers to the entrance room to the main building of the temple just outside the holy place. The entrance was about 30 by 15 feet and 45 feet high (1 Kings

6:2-3; but compare 2 Chron. 3:4). In Ezekiel's vision of the temple, each gate leading into the court of the Gentiles also had a vestibule (40:7-26) as did the gates to the court of the Israelites (40:29-37).

ARCHAEOLOGY AND BIBLICAL STUDY

Study of past based on recovery, examination, and explanation of the material remains of human life, thought, and activity, coordinated with available information concerning the ancient environment. The goal of excavation is to reconstruct, in as far as possible, the total ancient environment of the site.

Biblical archaeology searches for a better understanding of the Bible from sources outside the Bible. The basic affirmations of the Bible — that God is, that He is active in history, and that Jesus is His Son raised from the dead — are not subject to archaeological verification.

Archaeology can help to clarify and illuminate the Bible in many important ways:

(1) *Archaeology and the Biblical Text.* Archaeology, through the recovery of ancient Hebrew and Greek copies of the Scripture, plus the discovery of other old literature written in related languages, has helped scholars to determine a more exact text of the Bible. See *Dead Sea Scrolls; Bible, Texts and Versions.*

(2) *Knowledge of writing has greatly increased.*

(3) *Knowledge of biblical words and meanings have been enhanced.*

(4) *Archaeology has provided locations of many places in the Bible,* including entire kingdoms such as the Hittite empire in Turkey and the ancient city of Ebla at Tell Mardikh in Syria.

(5) *Documents from Assyria, Babylonian, and Egypt have clarified many elements in biblical history.*

(6) *Biblical literature can be better interpreted by comparison with archaeologists' literary discoveries.*

(7) *Other records enlarge our knowledge of biblical characters.*

We learn of Ahab's participation in the battle of Qarqar in 853 B.C. from Shalmaneser III's monument and of Jehu's tribute to Shalmaneser III recorded on the Black Obelisk now in the British Museum. Neither episode is mentioned in the Bible.

(8) *Antecedents of the prophetic movement have been found at Mari and Ebla,* where an occurrence of the Hebrew word equivalent is reported.

(9) *Archaeology breaks down barriers of time and culture.*

Archaeology has uncovered numerous examples of weights and measures, plow points, weapons, tools, jewelry, clay jars, seals, and coins. Ancient art depicts clothing styles, weapons, modes of transportation, methods of warfare, and styles of life. Excavated tombs show burial customs which in themselves reflect beliefs about life and death.

(10) *Archaeological studies have aided with chronology.*

(11) *The Dead Sea Scroll discoveries show Judaism was more complicated than previously suspected.*

ARCHANGEL

The English term archangel is based on a Greek term *archangelos,* which means "chief," or "first angel." The term *archangelos* appears only twice in the Bible. Paul speaks of the voice of the archangel as accompanying the return of Christ to earth (1 Thess. 4:16). The second reference is in Jude 9 which refers to Michael as an archangel who disputed with the devil over Moses' body. Together with Gabriel, Michael fought for Israel against the prince of Persia. In Revelation 12:7, Michael commands the forces of God against the forces of the dragon in a war in heaven.

ARCHELAUS

Son and principal successor of Herod the Great (Matt. 2:22). His brother Herod Antipas also felt entitled to the throne. The brothers appealed to Augustus, who gave Archelaus one half of his father Herod's land and split the remainder between Antipas and Philip. Archelaus interfered in the high priesthood, married against Jewish law, and oppressed the Samaritans and Jews. A revolting populace asked Caesar to denounce Archelaus. In A.D. 6 the Roman government banished him to Gaul and added his territory to Syria.

ARCHER

One who shoots an arrow from a bow to hunt small and large game and in warfare. An archer could pull a 100-pound bow that would shoot an arrow a distance of 300 to 400 yards. See Gen. 49:23-24; 2 Sam. 11:24. See *Arms and Armor.*

ARCHEVITES

Group who protested Zerubbabel's rebuilding of Jerusalem about 537 B.C. (Ezra 4:9). NASB, NIV, NRSV read, "people or men of Erech." See *Erech.*

ARCHI, ARCHITE

Unknown people (Josh. 16:2); a clan of Benjamin or, more likely, remnants of ancient "Canaanite" inhabitants. Their only representative in the Bible was David's Counselor Hushai. See *Hushai.*

ARCHITECTURE IN BIBLICAL PERIOD

Construction, techniques, and materials used in building structures of the Ancient Near East.

The people of the Ancient Near East most often used stone, wood, reeds, and mud. Mud served as mortar and was formed into bricks and then sun dried. Religious or large public buildings used the more expensive lumber that came from cedar, cypress, sandalwood, and olive trees. The sycamore tree served as a less costly lumber. Limestone and basalt were common stones used in construction.

(1) *Public Structures.* Protective walls encircled the city to keep out enemy forces. Retaining walls kept in place any weight that was behind them, were used in agricultural terracing to prevent erosion and create a level place for farming on the sides of hills, and were placed below city walls to stop any erosion of the soil which ultimately might weaken the city walls.

Large public building projects commonly used "headers and stretchers," alternating laying the stones lengthwise and breadthwise to form the wall. Solomon's day featured the casemate wall—two parallel walls with perpendicular walls placed at intervals between the parallel ones. A casemate wall had greater strength than a solid wall and saved material and labor.

The inset-offset wall came into use after the time of Solomon. Each stretch of the wall was placed alternately either slightly ahead or slightly behind the previous section. This allowed the city's defenders to fire at any attackers from three angles: head on and to the right and left of the attackers.

The city gate was the weakest part of the city's defenses. Remains of gates at Megiddo, Gezer, and Hazor show that two square towers flanked the entrance into the gate. The gate complex was composed of three successive chambers or rooms on each side (six chambers in all). A gate separated each pair of chambers, and the six rooms probably served as guardhouses. The approach to the gate from outside the city usually was placed at an angle, forcing any attackers to expose their flanks to the defenders on the city walls and slowing the attackers' pace once inside the walls.

(2) *Private Structures.* Houses in the Old Testament period usually were built around a central courtyard and entered from the street. They often were two stories high with access to the upper story coming from a staircase or a ladder. The walls of the house consisted of mud bricks placed on the stone foundation and subsequently plastered. Floors either were paved with small stones or plaster or were formed from beaten earth. Large wooden beams laid across the walls composed the supporting structure of the roof. Smaller pieces of wood or reeds were placed

in between the beams and then covered with a layer of mud. Rows of columns placed in the house served as supports to the ceiling. Since the roof was flat, people slept on it in the hot seasons and also used it for storage. Sometimes clay or stone pipes that led from the roof to cisterns down below were used to catch rainwater.

The most common type of house — the "four-room" house — consisted of a broadroom at the rear of the house with three parallel rooms coming out from one side of the broadroom. The middle room was a small, unroofed courtyard and served as the entrance to the house. Ovens in the courtyard were constructed with mud bricks and then plastered on the outside. Private and public grain silos were round and dug several feet into the ground; these usually had circular mud brick or stone walls around the silo.

In NT times, Greek and Roman ideas greatly influenced Israelite architecture.

(1) *Public Structures.* Over 20 Roman theaters were built in Palestine and Jordan. At Caesarea, the semicircular auditorium and stage with upper and lower seating sections accommodated 4,500 people. Similar theaters were located at Scythopolis (Beth-Shan), Pella, Gerasa, Petra, Dor, Hippos, and Gadara.

Hippodromes for chariot racing were long, narrow, and straight with curved ends. Gerasa, Caesarea, Scythopolis, Gadara, and Jerusalem had hippodromes.

(2) *Private Structures.* Houses arranged rooms around a courtyard. A stairway on the outside of the house led to the upper stories.

Houses of the rich often had columns placed around a central court that had rooms radiating out from it. Kitchens, cellars, cisterns, and bathing pools may have been located underneath the ground. In Jerusalem, one house covered about 650 square feet, a large house by first-century standards.

ARCTURUS

Constellation of stars God created (Job 9:9; 38:32). Modern translations generally use "Bear" (NASB, NIV, NRSV, NKJV, NLT); TEV, CEV "the (Big) Dipper"; REB, "Aldebaran." Some scholars prefer "the lion."

AREOPAGUS

Site of Paul's speech to the Epicurean and Stoic philosophers of Athens (Acts 17:19); rocky hill about 370 feet high, not far from the Acropolis and the Agora (marketplace); also referred to council that originally met on this hill.

ARETAS (*moral excellence, power*)

Several Arabian kings centered in Petra. First three involved with Hasmoneans. Aretas IV ruled from Petra (9 B.C.–A.D. 40) as a subject of Rome. Herod Antipas married, then divorced Aretas's daughter to marry Herodias (Mark 6:17-18). Aretas joined with a Roman officer to defeat Herod's army in A.D. 36. He apparently had some control over Damascus and sought to arrest Paul after his conversion (2 Cor. 11:32).

ARGOB (*mound of earth*)

(1) Man who either joined Pekah (2 Kings 15:25) in murdering Pekahiah, king of Israel (742–740 B.C.) or was killed by Pekah.

(2) Territory in Bashan in hill country east of Jordan River; famous for its strong cities (Deut. 3:4). Moses gave this land of giants to Manasseh (Deut. 3:13) whose son Jair conquered it (Deut. 3:14) and changed the name to Bashan-havoth-jair.

ARIEL (*God's lion*)

(1) Jewish leader in captivity; Ezra's messenger to the Levites (Ezra 8:16).

(2) Code name for Jerusalem (Isa. 29); apparently the top of the altar on which the priests burned sacrifices.

ARIMATHEA

City of Joseph, who claimed body of Jesus following crucifixion (Matt.

27:57; compare Luke 23:51); may be same as Rama, birthplace of Samuel; modern Rentis, 15 miles east of Jaffa.

ARIOCH (Hurrian, *servant of the moon god*)

(1) King of Ellasar, who joined alliance against Sodom and Gomorrah (Gen. 14).

(2) Commander of bodyguard of King Nebuchadnezzar (Dan. 2:14-25).

ARISTARCHUS (*best ruler*)

Paul's companion caught by the followers of Artemis in Ephesus (Acts 19:29). Apparently the same as Thessalonian who accompanied Paul from Greece to Jerusalem as he returned from third missionary journey (Acts 20:4; see Acts 27:2; Col. 4:10; Philem. 24).

ARK

Boat or water vessel and in particular one built by Noah under God's direction to save Noah, his family, and representatives of all animal life from the flood; became both a symbol of Noah's faith and of God's grace (Gen. 6:14-9:18; Ex. 2:3-5; Matt. 24:38; Luke 17:27; Heb. 11:7; 1 Pet. 3:20).

The shape of the ark was unusual, approximating a giant block about 450 feet long, 75 feet wide, and 45 feet high (Gen. 6:15). The ark had three floors filled with rooms (Gen. 6:14,16), and one window, and one door (Gen. 6:16).

ARK OF BULRUSHES

KJV translation (Ex. 2:3-5); usually read "basket."

ARK OF THE COVENANT

Original container (about 4 feet long, 2½ wide, and 2½ deep) for Ten Commandments; central symbol of God's presence with the people of Israel. Some passages suggest the ark was also regarded as the throne of the invisible deity, or His footstool (Jer. 3:16-17; Ps. 132:7-8). After the conquest, it was variously located at Gilgal, Shechem (Josh. 8:30-35; see Deut. 11:26-32; 27:1-26), or Bethel (Judg. 20:26), and then permanently at Shiloh (1 Sam. 1:9; 3:3). Philistines captured the ark (1 Sam. 4), but God punished their god Dagon and spread bubonic plagues until they returned it (1 Sam. 5:1-6:12; see 6:13-15,19-20). David moved it to his new capital in Jerusalem (1 Sam. 6:21-7:2; 2 Sam. 6). Finally, Solomon built the temple, to house the ark (1 Kings 8; 2 Chron. 5). Jeremiah 3:16-17 may indicate the Babylonians captured or destroyed the ark in 587 B.C. See *Holy of Holies; Mercy Seat; Tabernacle; Temple.*

Hebrews 9:1-10 shows the ark was a part of the old order with external regulations, waiting for the new day of Christ to come with a perfect Sacrifice able to cleanse the human conscience. Revelation 11:19 shows the ark of the covenant will be part of the heavenly temple when it is revealed.

ARKITE

Canaanite clan listed in the table of nations (Gen. 10:17); apparently centered around Arqa, modern Tell Arqa in Syria, 80 miles north of Sidon.

ARM

Upper limb of human body used to symbolize power and strength. See Ex. 6:6; 15:16; Deut. 5:15; Job 35:9; 38:15; 40:9; Pss. 10:15; 44:3.

ARMAGEDDON (*mountain of Megiddo*)

Middle East site of final battle between forces of good and evil (Rev. 16:16) in plain of Esdraelon or Jezreel, a valley 14 by 20 miles in size near the ancient city of Megiddo. King Josiah perished in battle here with Pharaoh-nechoh (2 Kings 23:29-30).

ARMENIA See *Ararat.*

ARMLET

Band or ring worn around the upper arm; Hebrew word translated "chain" (Num. 31:50) and "bracelet" (2 Sam.

1:10); related word is rendered "ornaments of the legs" (Isa. 3:20) in KJV.

ARMS AND ARMOR

Instruments and body coverings for defense and/or protection. The bow and arrow were effective arms from long-range (300–400 yards). Israel had expert archers in men from Benjamin (1 Chron. 8:40; 2 Chron. 17:17; compare 1 Chron. 5:18; 1 Sam. 31:31; 1 Kings 22:34; 2 Kings 9:24; 2 Chron. 35:23). Bows were constructed with single pieces of wood or more effectively with glued layers of wood, horn, sinew, and possibly even with added bronze (2 Sam. 22:35; Job 20:24). The size varied from approximately 3 to 6 feet in length. Arrows were made of wood shafts or reeds, tipped with metal heads. The arrow was guided by feathers, especially from the eagle, vulture, or kite. A leather quiver strapped to the back or hung over the shoulder carried between 20 and 30 of these arrows, or if strapped to a chariot, perhaps as many as 50. Frequently, a leather arm guard was used on the bow arm to protect it from the gut string.

The slingshot (1 Sam. 17:40-50) was for deadly long-range use (Judg. 20:16; 1 Chron. 12:2). A patch of cloth or leather with two braided leather cords on either end would hold a smooth stone. King Uzziah of Judah developed large catapults that projected arrows and stones long-range to defend Jerusalem (2 Chron. 26:15). A javelin is a spear thrown a shorter distance than the archers could arch their arrows or slingers could sling their stones (1 Sam. 17:6; 18:10–11; 19:9–10; 20:33). Usually made of wood or reed, some javelins had a leather cord wrapped around its shaft that caused the released weapon to spin when the cord was retained in the hand, and/or a counterweight fixed on the butt of the shaft. The latter could be sharp enough to stick in the ground and stand the javelin (1 Sam. 26:7) or even used to kill (2 Sam. 2:23). A quiver was used often to aid the soldier in carrying more than one javelin.

Hand-to-hand combat required different weapons. The thrusting spear was longer and heavier than the javelin and could have been thrown if needed (1 Chron. 12:24,34; 2 Chron. 23:9). Front battle lines often featured foot soldiers equipped with rectangular shields carrying spears jutting out beyond the walls of shields and pressing forward at the expense of the enemy front line.

Two types of swords were used: the single edge and the two-edged (Ps. 149:6; Prov. 5:4). The single edge was used most effectively by swinging it and hitting the enemy to lacerate the flesh. The blade could be straight or curved to a great degree. The double-edged sword was most often used for piercing rather than lacerating. A dagger was shorter than the sword (Judg. 3:16-26).

The mace was a war club used to crush the head of an enemy. The heavy metal or stone head of the weapon could be of various shapes: round, oval, or pear-shaped. Its wooden handle would fasten by going through the head like a modern hammer or axe. Use of helmets caused the mace to give way to the piercing edge of the battle ax.

Armor bearers accompanied the military leaders to bring along extra weapons and defensive equipment that would be expended during a battle (arrows, javelins, shields).

Battering rams, as modeled by Ezekiel in his object lesson for the Israelites (Ezek. 4:2), were actually rolled on wheels and had metal ends attached to wooden shafts to withstand collision force with city gates or stone walls.

Defense against all these arms consisted of the shield and armor. Shields were made of wicker, or of leather stretched over wooden frames with handles on the inside. A cross between metal and leather was achieved by attaching metal disks or plates to the leather over a portion of the surface. A round shield used with lighter weapons covered half the body at most (2 Chron. 14:8; Neh. 4:16; 1 Kings 14:25-28). A larger shield was more rectangular and covered nearly, if not all, the body. At times a special shield bearer was employed to carry it (1 Sam. 17:41; 1 Chron. 12:8,34; 2 Chron. 14:8).

Armor covered the body's most vulnerable regions: head and chest. Saul and Goliath wore helmets (1 Sam. 17:5,38; compare 2 Chron. 26:14). The helmet was usually made of leather or metal.

Use of the arrow made a coat of mail (also called a brigandine, Jer. 46:4; 51:3, KJV; or habergeon, 2 Chron. 26:14, KJV) necessary to cover the torso (1 Sam. 17:5; 2 Chron. 26:14; Neh. 4:16; Jer. 46:4; 51:3). Fish scalelike construction of small metal plates sewn to cloth or leather was the breastplate for the ancient soldier. These scales could number as high as 700 to 1000 per "coat." Leg armor (1 Sam. 17:6) was not regularly used.

God is the faithful protector of His people: "a shield unto them that put their trust in him" (Prov. 30:5; compare Gen. 15:1).

ARMY

Nation's military personnel organized for battle. Israel recognized God's anger when God did not go out with their armies (Ps. 44:9).

Armies were organized in different ways. The patriarchs called upon servants and other members of the household (Gen. 14). At times, tribes joined together to take territory (Josh. 1–12; Judg. 1:3; 4:6). Saul first established a standing, professional army in Israel (1 Sam. 13:2), then appointed a professional commander (1 Sam. 17:55). David apparently hired foreign troops loyal to him personally (2 Sam. 9:18; 15:18). Solomon enhanced the foot soldiers with a chariot corps and calvary (1 Kings 10:26). The army was organized into various units with officers over each, but the precise chain of command cannot be determined (2 Chron. 25:5).

ARNON (*rushing river* or *river flooded with berries*)

River forming border of Moab and Amorites (Num. 21:13; compare v. 24; Deut. 3:8; Josh. 3:16; Judg. 11:12-33; see Isa. 16:2; Jer. 8:20); wadi-el-Mojib; near the Dead Sea. The wide river valley rises 1,700 feet to the top of the cliffs above.

AROER (*juniper*)

(1) City on north rim of Arnon Gorge east of Dead Sea, on southern boundary of territory Israel claimed east of the Jordan River (Josh. 13:9; compare v. 16; Num. 32:34; Deut. 3:12); Khirbet Arair, 2½ miles east of the highway along the Arnon River. See Deut. 4:48; Josh. 12:2; Judg. 11:26; 2 Kings 10:33; compare Isa. 17:2; Jer. 48:19). The Moabites had gained control of Aroer under King Mesha, as his inscription on the Moabite Stone witnesses (about 850 B.C.).

(2) City of Gad (Josh. 13:25) near Rabbah, capital of the Ammonites; may be where Jephthah defeated Ammonites (Judg. 11:33).

(3) Town in southern Judah about 12 miles southeast of Beersheba with whose leaders David divided the spoil of battle (1 Sam. 30:28); modern Khirbet Arara. Joshua 15:22 may have originally read Aroer; see 1 Chron. 11:44.

ARPAD or **ARPHAD**

City-state in northern Syria closely identified with Hamath; modern tell Erfad about 25 miles north of Aleppo; see 2 Kings 10:34; 19:13; Isa. 10:5-19; Jer. 49:23.

ART AND AESTHETICS

Making and recognition of objects of beauty. Artistic endeavors go back to God's work in producing the beauty of creation (Gen. 1–2). God gave humans ability to design objects of beauty and grace to make their lives more enjoyable (Gen. 4:21-22).

The Israelites' religious teachings concerning the making and worshiping of idols (Ex. 20:4-6) cast a shadow upon artistic endeavors. God commanded the Israelites to accept the Egyptian artifacts when they left Egypt (Ex. 12:35) and to use artistic skills to build the tabernacle (Ex. 25–27; 35:20-29) with its fancy ark (Ex. 37:7-9; 1 Sam. 4:4), elaborate veils (Ex. 36:35-37), and other furnishings (Ex. 36:9–38:20).

Music and dance became a popularly accepted media for artistic presentation (1 Sam. 18:6; 2 Sam. 6:14; compare Matt. 14:6; 26:30; Mark 6:22; Luke 15:25). Solomon's magnificent temple (1 Kings 5–6; 7:13-51) and other royal edifices (1 Kings 7:1-12) showed Israel had come into its own in artistic endeavors. Even then, foreigners (1 Kings 5:18; 7:13-14) produced most of the intricate wood work on the walls and doors (such as the fancy carvings, applique palmettes, and guilloched borders (1 Kings 6:14-36) as well as the fancy metal work (1 Kings 7:23-50). The Israelites were slowly developing their own craftsmen (1 Kings 5:18). They built fancy public edifices and enhanced the beauty of their own homes (1 Kings 22:39; Jer. 22:14; Ezek. 23:14). This led to their placing more emphasis upon themselves than upon God and His work (Ps. 45:8; Isa. 30:20; Hos. 13:2; Amos 3:15; Hag. 1:4).

ARTAXERXES (Persian *kingdom of righteousness*)

(1) Son of Xerxes I, Artaxerxes I Longimanus or "long-handed," ruled Persia (465 to 424 B.C.) and supported Ezra's work (Ezra 7:6-26). He granted Nehemiah's request to go to Judah (Neh. 2:5-6), making him governor of Judah (Neh. 5:14). He was forced to sign "Peace of Calias" (449) making peace with Greece.

(2) Artaxerxes II Artakshatsu ruled Persia 404 to 359 B.C. Some Bible students identify him as ruler under whom Ezra worked. He gained

power over Greece but lost Egyptian influence.

(3) Artaxerxes III Ochus ruled 358–337 B.C. as a bloody tyrant and gained control of Egypt.

(4) Ruled Persia 337–336 B.C.

ARTEMIS

Greek goddess of the moon who watched over nature for both humans and animals; mother image who gave fertility to humankind; daughter of Zeus and Leto, whose worship Paul's preaching threatened (Acts 19:28).

ARUBBOTH (*smoke hole* or *chimney*)

Provincial headquarters under Solomon where officials administered Sochoh and the land of Hepher (1 Kings 4:10). Modern Arabbah, nine miles north of Samaria.

ARVAD, ARVADITE

Northernmost Phoenician city; provided sailors and soldiers for Tyre (Ezek. 27:8,11); probably rocky island called Ruad today, off the coast of Syria; related to Canaan (Gen. 10:18).

ASA (*doctor* or *healing*)

Son and successor of Abijam as king of Judah (913–873 B.C.; 1 Kings 15:8; Matt. 1:7-8); pious man; removed foreign gods and religious practices, even removing his mother from political power (1 Kings 15:13). The prophet Hanani rebuked him (2 Chron. 16:7) for relying on the king of Syria rather than on God (1 Kings 15:17-20). He also relied on physicians rather than on the Lord (2 Chron. 16:12). See *Israel, History of; Chronology of Biblical Periods.*

ASAPH (*he collected*)

(1) Father of court official under Hezekiah (715–686 B.C.; 2 Kings 18).

(2) Levite musician David appointed to serve in tabernacle until temple was completed (1 Chron. 6:39); father of clan of temple musicians (1 Chron.

9:15; 15:19; 16:37). Their musical service could be called "prophesying" (1 Chron. 25:1-7; compare 2 Chron. 20:14-19; 2 Chron. 29:30). David established tradition of delivering psalms to Asaph for the temple singers to sing (1 Chron. 16:7). Pss. 50, 73–83 are titled "Psalms of Asaph." This may refer to authorship, the singers who used the Psalms in worship, or to a special collection of Psalms. See *Psalms.*

ASCENSION

Act of going to heaven in bodily form from earthly life; experienced by Enoch (Gen. 5:24) and Elijah (2 Kings 2:1-2) but supremely by Jesus Christ (Acts 1:9). The ascension of Jesus concluded the earthly ministry of Jesus, allowing eyewitnesses to see both the risen Christ on earth and the victorious, eternal Christ returning to heaven to minister at the right hand of the Father.

ASCENTS, SONG OF See *Psalms.*

ASH

KJV translation in Isa. 44:14, for word now seen to mean "laurel" or "bay tree." Modern versions read: fir (NASB), pine (NIV, CEV, NCV, NKJV), cedar (NRSV, REB, NLT), laurel tree (TEV).

ASHCHENAZ or **ASHKENAZ** See *Scythians.*

ASHDOD

Northernmost of five principal Philistine cities (Josh. 13:3) allotted to Judah (Josh. 15:46-47), where Philistines defeated Israel and captured ark of the covenant (1 Sam. 4–6), 10 miles north of Ashkelon; 2½ miles east of Mediterranean Sea on Philistine plain.

Some of the Anakim remained there (Josh. 11:22) See *Anak, Anakim.* David subdued the Philistines, implicitly including Ashdod (2 Sam. 5:25; 8:1), but it was not described as under Israel's control until Uzziah (783–742 B.C.) captured it (2 Chron. 26:8). Independent enough to revolt from Sargon II in

711 B.C., the Assyrians subdued them quickly; they remained under Assyrian control until captured by the Egyptian Pharaoh Psammetichus I (664–610) after a 29-year siege as reported by Herodotus. Nebuchadnezzar (604–562 B.C.) captured Ashdod. See Neh. 13:23-24; Isa. 20:1-6; Jer. 25:20; Amos 1:8; Zech. 9:6.

In the Greek period, Ashdod, known as Azotus, was a flourishing city until captured by Israel under Judas Maccabeus, who destroyed altars and images there (1 Macc. 5:68). Jonathan burned the city (1 Macc. 10:84-87). Josephus reported that Pompey separated Ashdod from Israel after his victory (63 B.C.). Gabinius rebuilt the city and joined it to province of Syria. Augustus granted it to Herod the Great. Herod left it to his sister Salome, who willed it to Julia, the wife of Augustus. Its greatness as a city ended with the Roman destruction of A.D. 67.

ASHDOTH-PISGAH See *Pisgah.*

ASHER (*fortune, happiness*)

(1) Eighth son of Jacob, born of Zilpah, the concubine (Gen. 30:13); forefather of tribe of Asher (Gen. 46:17; see 49:20).

(2) Tribe of Asher. See *Tribes of Israel.*

(3) Border town in Manasseh (Josh. 17:7).

ASHERAH

Fertility goddess, mother of Baal, in Syria, Phoenicia, and Canaan; wooden object that represented her. KJV translated Asherah, "*grove*" and "*Ashtaroth.*" Deuteronomy 7:5; 12:3 instructed the Israelites to cut down and burn up the Asherim (plural form of Asherah). Deut. 16:21 prohibited the planting of a tree as an "Asherah." See 1 Kings 15:13; 18:19; 2 Kings 21:7; 23:4; 2 Chron. 15:16. See *Canaan.*

ASHERIM, ASHEROTH

Plural of *Asherah.*

ASHES

Residue from burning associated with sacrifices, mourning, fasting, and divine destruction. Grief, humiliation, and repentance were expressed with ashes on the head or by sitting in ashes. At times ashes remaining from a sacrifice were used for ritual purification.

ASHIMA

Syrian god made and worshiped in Hamath (2 Kings 17:30; compare Amos 8:14) based on Hebrew word for guilt. Hebrew writers may have deliberately written a form of *guilt* instead of the name of a god or goddess. Hamath's goddess may have been Asherah. See *Asherah.* Samaria may have incorporated the god of Hamath into their worship.

ASHKELON

One of five principal Philistine cities; on Mediterranean coast on Via Maris trade route 12 miles north of Gaza and 10 miles south of Ashdod; only Philistine city directly on the seacoast; allotted tribe of Judah; one of largest Palestinian cities. The city revolted from Egypt and was subsequently sacked, perhaps by Ramses II (1282 B.C.) and certainly by Merneptah.

Joshua had not taken Ashkelon (Josh. 13:3), but Judah did (Judg. 1:18). It belonged to the Philistines in the Samson account (Judg. 14:19) and under Saul and David (1 Sam. 6:17; 2 Sam. 1:20). See Amos 1:8; Jer. 25:20; 47:5,7; Zeph. 2:4,7; Zech. 9:5. Ashkelon became a Hellenistic center of culture and learning. Herod the Great had family and friends there, gave the city beautiful buildings, built a palace there, and left the city to his sister, Salome, at his death. The city was attacked by the Jews in the first Roman Revolt (A.D. 66) but survived and was faithful to Rome.

ASHKENAZ See *Scythians.*

ASHTAROTH or ASHTORETH

Plural form of Ashtoreth, Canaanite goddess of fertility, love, and war; daughter of the god El and the goddess Asherah.

(1) Hebrew scribes formed Ashtoreth by replacing vowels of the name Ashtart or Ashteret with vowels from *boshet,* Hebrew for shame, to dishonor the goddess. Greek form is Astarte.

(2) City called Ashtartu or Ashtarot in Bashan in Egyptian documents (after 1800 B.C.); located at modern Tel Ashtarah in Syria about 20 miles east of Sea of Galilee on a major branch of the Via Maris and on the King's Highway.

ASHTEROTH KARNAIM See *Ashtaroth.*

ASHURBANIPAL or OSNAPPAR

Assyria's last great king (668–629 B.C.); son of Esarhaddon; identified in Ezra 4:10 as king of Assyria who captured Susa, Elam, other nations, and settled their citizens in Samaria. His famous library contained more than 20,000 clay tablets, including Assyrian, Sumerian, and Akkadian literature. See *Assyria, History and Religion of.*

ASHURITE or ASHURI (NIV)

Apparently a tribe or clan over which Ish-bosheth, Saul's son, ruled (2 Sam. 2:9). Earliest translations give some evidence the tribe of Asher or the city-state of Geshur is meant. In Ezekiel 27:6, Ashurites made "benches of ivory" (KJV) for Tyre. Most modern translations divide words in Hebrew differently and see a type of wood used: boxwood (NASB), cypress (NIV, REB, NCV), pine (TEV, NRSV, CEV, NLT), cedar (Jerusalem).

ASIA

Roman province in western Asia Minor comprising southwest part of Anatolia; capital was Pergamum, then Ephesus; known for its worship of Artemis (Acts 19:27); location of seven churches of Revelation. See

Acts 2:9; 16:6; 19:10,22; 21:27; 1 Pet. 1:1. See *Rome and Roman Empire*.

ASIA MINOR, CITIES OF

Cities located on Anatolian peninsula (modern-day Turkey) which linked Europe with the Near East. Important to the NT accounts are Alexandria Troas, Assos, Ephesus, Miletus, Patara, Smyrna, Pergamum, Sardis, Thyatira, Philadelphia, Laodicea, Colossae (Colosse, KJV), Attalia, Antioch, Iconium, Lystra, Derbe, and Tarsus.

Coastal Cities

Troas. Described both the northwest region of Asia Minor and its port city. Ten miles south of ancient Troy, Alexandria Troas was founded as a Roman colony under Augustus (27 B.C.–A.D. 14) and served as a primary port for trade passing between Asia Minor and Macedonia. See Acts 16:11; 20:13.

Assos. A bustling port city surrounded by a wall dating to after 400 b.c., Assos featured a temple of Athena high on the acropolis overlooking the harbor.

Ephesus. Served as the primary trading center of all Asia Minor. At the time of Paul, Ephesus was probably the fourth largest city in the world, with a population estimated at 250,000. During the reign of the emperor Hadrian, Ephesus was designated the capital of the Roman province of Asia. Diana's temple there was one of the Seven Wonders of the world, the largest all-marble structure in the Hellenistic world (See Acts 19:34). Turkish town of Seljuk occupies the site of ancient Ephesus.

Miletus. Exercised extensive control over southwestern Anatolia, remaining independent through Lydian rule in the region and withstanding attempted incursions by the Persians until 494 B.C. Once a wealthy port for the wool industry, Miletus had little significance during the NT era (Acts 20:15).

Patara. Was a popular port for ships traveling eastward during the early autumn months when favorable winds made travel to Egypt and the Phoenician coast easier. The harbor sat near the outlet of the Xanthus River and was the main shipping facility of provincial Lydia. See Acts 21.

Smyrna. Surrounded a well-protected harbor on the Aegean coast at the outlet of the Hermus River. During the first century A.D. Smyrna reigned as one of Asia's grandest cities. A large temple dedicated to the Emperor Tiberius boasted the close alliance of the city with the Empire.

Cities of the Interior

Pergamum. Located 15 miles inland overlooking the Caicus River, Pergamum contained the first temple in Asia dedicated to a Roman emperor, Augustus, in 29 B.C. An altar of Zeus may be the "throne of Satan" (Rev. 2:13). The city was well-known as a center of worship for the gods Asklepios, Zeus, Demeter and Persephone, Serapis, Isis, and the cult of the emperor.

Sardis. The greatest city in Lydia, Sardis was the first municipality to mint silver and gold coins. Set in the fertile Hermus valley, Sardis was capital of the wealthy Lydian king Croesus. The city fell to Persian armies in 549 B.C. and to the Romans in 188 B.C. A tremendous earthquake in A.D. 17 struck Sardis a blow from which it never fully recovered.

Philadelphia. Also on the Hermus River, Philadelphia was founded after 200 B.C. and led in worshiping Dionysius. Dangerous tremors followed the terrible earthquake of A.D. 17 for the next 20 years, each one debilitating the city further. John's reference to giving a "new name" (Rev. 3:12) may be a wordplay on the proposed dedication of the city as "Neocaesarea" in honor of aid Tiberius sent.

Laodicea. Lay in the center of the valley where the Meander River joined the Lycus. Situated along the major east-west trade route, it was the chief city of the wealthy province of Phrygia. The city was known for clothes and carpets woven from the rich, glossy black wool raised in the valley. Laodicea served as home to a medical school renowned for production of collyrium, an eye salve. See Rev. 3:14-18.

Colossae. Eleven miles south of Laodicea lay Colossae. As early as 450 B.C., the city was well known as a commercial center, famous for red-dyed wool. The establishment of Laodicea, however, led to the decline of Colassae's prosperity. The church was established by Epaphras during Paul's third missionary journey (Col. 1:7; 4:12-13).

Cities of Eastern Asia Minor

Much of Paul's Asian ministry centered around the provinces of Galatia and Lycaonia. On the first journey, Paul and Barnabas most likely arrived by sea at *Attalia,* a relatively small and unimportant harbor.

Antioch. Northward from the port across Pamphilia, in the province of Galatia (Acts 13:14). Established in 25 B.C. on a much earlier Hellenistic city, Antioch had been renovated by Rome to defend Galatia. A temple to Augustus dominated the central plaza. Wagons bearing Anatolian marble passed through Antioch on their way to ships at Ephesus.

Iconium. Southeast from Antioch is Iconium (Acts 13:51). Located in a fertile, well-watered plain, Iconium supplied large amounts of fruit and grain for the surrounding provinces.

Lystra. Lay 20 miles south of Iconium along the Via Sebaste. The city honored Zeus and Hermes as patron gods (see Acts 14). Timothy was a native of Lystra.

Derbe. Was 60 miles from Lystra at present-day Kerti Huyuk. Derbe was relatively unimportant. Paul's decision to visit the city infers a large Jewish population in the region.

Tarsus of Cilicia. This boyhood home of the Apostle Paul lay on the eastern end of the east-west trade route beginning at Ephesus. The Cydnus River provided Tarsus with an outlet to the Mediterranean Sea, ten miles away. Lumber and linen were the main industries of Tarsus, but the related manufacture of goat's-hair cloth was practiced by many, including Paul. Tarsus also housed a university and school of philosophy.

ASIARCHS

Public patrons and leaders named by cities in the Roman province of Asia. They used their wealth for the public good, especially for supporting worship of the emperor and of Rome. They underwrote expenses of games sponsored in connection with religious festivals. Paul won friends among this elite class (Acts 19:31).

ASKELON See *Ashkelon.*

ASNAPPER

KJV reading (Ezra 4:10) for Asnappar (REB); Osnappar (NASB, NRSV); Ashurbanipal (TEV, NIV, NCV, NLT); Osnapper (NKJV). See *Ashurbanipal.*

ASP See *Animals, Reptiles.*

ASPEN See *Cosmetics; Plants.*

ASS See *Animals.*

ASSASSINS *(dagger men)*

NLT, NRSV, NKJV for Jewish group who attempted to win freedom from the Romans; based on Latin term *Sicarii.* Josephus described them as hiding small daggers in their clothing, which they used in crowded situations to kill their victims. Romans used "Sicarii" to refer to Jews engaged in organized killing of politicians. Paul was mistaken (Acts 21:38) as a leader of 4000 Sicarii. KJV, murderers; REB, TEV, NIV, CEV terrorists; NCV, killers.

ASSAYER

One who tests ore for its silver and gold content. Jeremiah 6:27 (modern translations) describes Jeremiah's calling as an assayer of the people.

ASSEMBLY See *Congregation.*

ASSHUR, ASSHURIM, ASSHURITES

(1) Son of Shem; thus a Semite, as were Hebrews (Gen. 10:22).

(2) Otherwise unknown Arabian tribe (Gen. 25:3); may also be meant in Balaam's oracle (Num. 24:22-24), but reference to Assyria is more likely.

(3) Nation Assyria (Gen. 10:11; Ezek. 27:23; 32:22; Hos. 14:3). See *Assyria.*

ASSISTED SUICIDE

The Bible records several instances of suicide (Abimelech — Judg. 9:54; Samson — Judg. 16:29-30; Saul — 1 Sam. 31:4; Saul's armor-bearer — 1 Sam. 31:5; Ahithophel — 2 Sam. 17:23; Zimri — 1 Kings 16:18 and Judas — Matt. 27:5; compare Acts 16:27). Of these, the deaths of Abimelech and Saul properly fall under the category "assisted suicide." With the possible exception of Samson (whose death may be better termed "martyrdom"), the Bible presents each person who committed suicide as an individual whose behavior is clearly not to be emulated.

While the Bible nowhere specifically prohibits suicide, it does proclaim the sanctity of life (Gen. 1:26-27; 2:7; Ps. 8:5) and assuredly declares that God's people should choose life over death (Deut. 30:15,19). The right to give life and take it away is reserved by God for Himself (Job 1:21; compare Ex. 20:13). Christians are called to steadfastness in the midst of trial (2 Cor. 12:7-10; Phil. 4:11-13; Jas. 1:2-4), but John saw that in the latter days men facing difficulties would instead seek death (Rev. 9:6).

Moses (Num. 11:14-15), Elijah (1 Kings 19:4), Job (Job 6:8-11) and Jonah (Jonah 4:3) each asked God to take their lives, but in every case God refused. Simeon (Luke 2:29) and Paul (2 Cor. 5:2,8; Phil. 1:20-23) longed to be in heaven, yet were content to remain alive, all the while waiting for God to act in His own time. Such instances, while not categorized as "assisted suicide," nevertheless provide ample Biblical evidence that assisted suicide is never the proper choice.

ASSOS See *Asia Minor, Cities of.*

ASSUR See *Assyria.*

ASSURANCE See *Security of the Believer.*

ASSURBANIPAL See *Ashurbanipal.*

ASSYRIA, HISTORY AND RELIGION OF

Nation north of Babylonia along the banks of the Tigris River (Gen. 2:14) in northern Mesopotamia that became large empire, expanding into Palestine (about 855–625 B.C.).

History

Assyria gets its name from Asshur, its first capital, founded about 2000 B.C. Genesis 10:11-12 gives foundation of other Assyrian cities, notably Calah and Nineveh. By 1900 B.C., these cities were vigorously trading as far away as Cappadocia in eastern Asia Minor. An expanded Assyria warred with the famous King Hammurabi of Babylon shortly before breaking up into smaller city states about 1700 B.C.

Tiglath-pileser III (744–727 B.C.), true founder of the Assyrian Empire, changed the administration of conquered territories. Nations close to Assyria were incorporated as provinces. Others were left with native rule, but subject to an Assyrian overseer. Tiglath-pileser also took conquered people into exile to live in lands vacated by other conquered exiles. Compare 2 Kings 17:24. As Tiglath-pileser, also called Pul, arrived on the coast of Phoenicia, Menahem of Israel (2 Kings 15:19) and Rezin of Aram-Damascus brought tribute and became vassals of Assyria. An anti-Assyrian alliance quickly formed. Israel and Aram-Damascus attacked Jerusalem about 735 B.C. in an attempt to replace King Ahaz of Judah with a man loyal to the anti-Assyrian alliance (2 Kings 16:2-6; Isa. 7:1-6) and thus force Judah's participation. Against the protests of Isaiah (Isa. 7:4,16-17; 8:4-8), Ahaz appealed to Tiglath-pileser for assistance (2 Kings 16:7-9). Tiglath-pileser, in response, campaigned against Philistia (734 B.C.), reduced Israel to the area immediately around Samaria (2 Kings 15:29; 733 B.C.), and annexed Aram-Damascus (732 B.C.), deporting the population. Ahaz became an Assyrian vassal (2 Kings 16:10; 2 Chron. 28:16,20-22).

Shalmaneser V (726–722 B.C.) besieged Samaria for three years when Hoshea failed to pay tribute (2 Kings 17:3-5). The city fell to Shalmaneser (2 Kings 17:6; 18:9-12), who apparently died in the same year. His successor, Sargon II (722–705 B.C.), took credit in Assyrian royal inscriptions for deporting 27,290 inhabitants of Samaria.

Sargon countered rebellions in Gaza in 720 B.C. and Ashdod in 712 (Isa. 20:1). Hezekiah of Judah was tempted to join in the Ashdod rebellion, but Isaiah warned against such action (Isa. 18). A rebellious king of Babylon, Merodach-baladan, found support from Elam, Assyria's enemy to the east. Forced to flee Babylon in 710 B.C., Merodach-baladan returned some years later and sent emissaries to Hezekiah in Jerusalem (2 Kings 20:12-19; Isa. 39), apparently as part of a concerted anti-Assyrian revolt.

Sennacherib (704–681 B.C.) faced widespread revolt in southern Mesopotamia led by Merodach-baladan and the Elamites. Hezekiah of Judah led Phoenicia and Palestine in rebellion. Subduing Babylon, Sennacherib then (701 B.C.) reasserted control over the city-states of Phoenicia, sacked Joppa and Ashkelon, and invaded Judah, where Hezekiah had made considerable military preparations (2 Kings 20:20; 2 Chron. 32:1-8,30; Isa. 22:8b-11). Sennacherib's account remarkably supplements the biblical version (2 Kings 18:13–19:36). He claimed to have destroyed 46 walled cities (see 2 Kings 18:13) and to have taken 200,150 captives. Three of Sennacherib's digni-

taries attempted to negotiate the surrender of Jerusalem (2 Kings 18:17-37), but Hezekiah, with Isaiah's encouragement, continued to hold out (2 Kings 19:1-7,20-35). The Assyrian army withdrew, and Hezekiah paid an enormous tribute (2 Kings 18:14-16). The Assyrian account claims a victory over the Egyptian army and mentions Hezekiah's tribute but is rather vague about the end of the campaign. The Bible mentions the approach of the Egyptian army (2 Kings 19:9) and tells of a miraculous defeat of the Assyrians by the angel of the Lord (2 Kings 19:35-36). Sennacherib suffered a major setback, for Hezekiah was the only ruler of the revolt to keep his throne.

Religion

Assyrian religion was essentially the same as Babylonian religion, recognizing thousands of gods with only 20 important in practice.

(1) *The old gods.* Anu, Enlil, and Ea, patron deities of the oldest Sumerian cities, were cosmic gods. After the rise of Babylon, Marduk joined the cosmic deities. Anu of Uruk (biblical Erech; Gen. 10:10), god of the heavens, did not play a very active role. Enlil of Nippur was god of the earth. Ea of Eridu was lord of the subterranean waters and god of craftsmen.

(2) *Astral deities.* Gods associated with heavenly bodies—included the sun-god Shamash, the moon-god Sin, and Ishtar, goddess of the morning and evening star (the Greek: Aphrodite; Roman: Venus). Sin was patron god of Ur and Haran, both associated with Abraham's origins (Gen. 11:31). Ishtar of Nineveh (Canaanite: Astarte/Ashtaroth, Judg. 10:6; 1 Sam. 7:3-4; 1 Kings 11:5), was very popular as the "Queen of Heaven" (Jer. 7:18; 44:17-19,25).

(3) *Younger gods.* Were usually associated with a newer city or none at all. See *Babylon, History and Religion of.*

ASTAROTH See *Ashtaroth.*

ASTARTE See *Ashtoroth.*

ASTROLOGER

Person who "divided the heavens" (literal translation of Hebrew phrase of Isa. 47:13) to determine the future. Babylon's well-educated, professional magicians could not match Daniel and his friends. The "Chaldeans" of Dan. 2:2; 4:7; 5:7,11 may be the nearest reference to astrologers in the book.

ASUPPIM

KJV transliteration (1 Chron. 26:15,17); modern translations read, "storehouse"; "gatehouse" (REB).

ASWAN

NIV, TEV, NLT, NCV, CEV reading in Ezek. 29:10; 30:6 for Syene.

ASYLUM See *Avenger.*

ATAROTH (*crowns*)

(1) Town built up by tribe of Gad (Num. 32:3,34); modern Khirbet Attarus, eight miles northwest of Dibon and eight miles east of Dead Sea.

(2) Village on border of Benjamin and Ephraim (Josh. 16:2,7); may be Khirbet el-Oga in the Jordan Valley.

ATHALIAH (*Yahweh has announced His exalted nature* or *Yahweh is righteous*)

(1) Wife of Jehoram, king of Judah, and mother of Ahaziah, king of Judah; either daughter of Ahab and Jezebel of Israel (2 Kings 8:18) or of Omri, king of Israel (2 Kings 8:26); according to literal reading of text as KJV; interpretation of text extends Hebrew word for daughter to mean female descendant, thus "granddaughter" as in modern translations. She brought the northern court's devotion to Baal to the court of Judah and exercised great influence during her son's one-year reign (1 Kings 8:27-28). At her son's death, she had all male heirs killed and ruled Judah for six years (2 Kings 11:1-4), being the only woman to do so. Jehoiada, the priest, led a revolt, enthroning

Josiah as king and bringing about Athaliah's death (2 Kings 11:5-20).

(2) Son of Jeroham in tribe of Benjamin (1 Chron. 8:26).

(3) Father of Jeshaiah (Ezra 8:7).

ATHENS

Capital of Attica, ancient district of east central Greece, where Paul preached to the Greek philosophers (Acts 17:15-34).

ATONEMENT

Reconciliation; associated with sacrifices to remove effects of sin; in NT refers specifically to reconciliation between God and humans effected by Jesus' death, burial, and resurrection.

In Old Testament, atonement refers to process God established whereby humans can make an offering to God to remove effects of human sin and restore fellowship with God. See *Day of Atonement.* But not only does atonement remove the effects of sin. Atonement enables God to be both just and to pardon sin. Atonement satisfies God's wrath—His eternal opposition to sin while effecting reconciliation with sinners. Jesus Christ takes the punishment required by God's righteous law.

The focal point of God's atoning work is Christ's death on the cross (Rom. 5:10; see John 1:29; Mark 10:45; 14:24).

The relation of the cross to forgiveness of sins (1 Pet. 2:24) was implicit in the earliest Christian preaching (Acts 2:21; 3:6,19; 4:13; 5:31; 8:35; 10:43; compare Rom. 3:25; 1 Cor. 15:3; Gal. 3:13; Eph. 2:13; Heb. 9:28; 10:20). Christ's death was the climax of His perfect obedience. (Phil. 2:8; compare Rom. 5:12-19; Heb. 5:8). His sinless obedience qualified Him to be the perfect Sacrifice for sin (Heb. 6:8-10).

New Testament interprets cross in light of the resurrection. So important is this emphasis that Paul affirms, "If Christ be not raised, your faith is vain; ye are yet in your sins" (1 Cor. 15:17).

The necessity for Christ's atoning work is occasioned by humanity's sinful rebellion (Isa. 59:2). In their unreconciled state, people are God's "enemies" (Rom. 5:10; compare 8:7; Eph. 2:12). No difference exists between Jew and Gentile, "for all have sinned and come short of the glory of God" (Rom. 3:23).

The atonement for sin provided by Christ's death has its origin in divine love (John 3:16; see 1 John 4:9-10). No other reason can explain why "God reconciled us to himself by Jesus Christ" (2 Cor. 5:18; compare Rom. 5:8). Christ died for us because God loves us. Atonement is always seen as a divine gift, never as human achievement. The cross is simultaneously a manifestation of God's will to save and of His wrath against sin.

In His atoning work, Christ is both representative and substitute (2 Cor. 5:21; Gal. 3:13; 1 Pet. 2:24). As representative, Christ acted on behalf of His race (Rom. 5:12-21; 1 Cor. 15:45-49; 2 Cor. 5:17; Eph. 2:14-22).

Substitution means that in Christ, God Himself bears the consequences of human sin. Atonement can be discussed through following images.

(1) *Atonement and ransom*. People are in bondage and cannot free themselves. Jesus paid the ransom price to redeem those in captivity (Mark 10:45; 1 Cor. 6:19-20; compare 7:23; 1 Pet. 1:18-19a).

(2) *Atonement and victory*. Satan has humanity in his power. Christ defeats the devil, and rescues humanity (Matt. 4:1-11; 12:28; Mark 3:27; John 12:31; Col. 2:15; Heb. 2:14-15; 1 John 3:8; compare Luke 10:18).

(3) *Atonement and sacrifice*. Christ's death is a "sacrifice for sins" (Heb. 10:12; compare Eph. 5:2). Christ is identified with the Passover lamb (1 Cor. 5:7), the sacrifice which initiates the New Covenant (Luke 22:20), and the sin offering (Heb. 9:14,25-28). Divine love has assumed the shape of the cross (Gal. 2:20). Through sacrifice, sin is forgiven (Eph. 1:7), and the conscience is cleansed (Heb. 9:14).

(4) *Atonement and glory*. In John's Gospel the whole life and work of Jesus is a revelation of divine glory. This glorification climaxes in Jesus' death on the cross (John 12:23-24; 13:31-32), where He was "lifted up," with the double meaning of "to lift up on a cross" and "to exalt" (John 12:32-33; compare 3:14; 8:28). Divine glory was revealed in the death He died for sins. See *Expiation, Propitiation; Redeem*.

ATONEMENT, DAY OF See *Day of Atonement; Festivals*.

ATTALIA

Seaport on northern Mediterranean coast in Asia Minor where Paul stopped briefly on first missionary journey (Acts 14:25); modern Antalya.

AUGUSTAN COHORT

Roman army unit named after the emperor stationed in Syria from about A.D. 6; given charge of Paul on his way to Rome (Acts 27:1).

AUGUSTUS (*reverend*)

Title Roman Senate gave Emperor Octavian (31 B.C.–A.D. 14) in 27 B.C. He ruled Roman Empire, including Palestine, when Jesus was born and ordered the taxation that brought Joseph and Mary to Bethlehem (Luke 2:1). See *Rome and the Roman Empire*. The title Augustus passed on to Octavian's successors as emperors of Rome. Thus it is applied to Nero in Acts 25:21,25. Note modern translations use "Emperor" or his "Imperial Majesty" (NRSV, REB).

AUTHORITY

Absolute power and freedom of God, the Source of all other authorization or power; used rarely in Old Testament (Gen. 1:28; 3:16; Lev. 19:3; Prov. 29:2; Esther 9:29; Dan. 4:17; 7:13-14).

New Testament consistently teaches "there is no power but of God" (Rom. 13:1; see John 19:11).

The church and its ministry possess genuine religious authority only as they serve the mission of Jesus in faithfulness to the Bible and in building up the church (Matt. 28:18-20). The Christian accepts the truth of Scripture as authoritative by faith, and the command of Scripture as authoritative in obedience, and so demonstrates love for the Lord (John 14:15).

AVA or AVVA

People apparently from Syria, perhaps tell Kafr Ayah on the Orontes River or Elamites from Ama. Assyrians conquered and settled them in Israel to replace Israelites they took into exile (2 Kings 17:24). Their gods' inability to help against the Assyrians could be used to call Jerusalem to surrender (2 Kings 18:34, where Ivvah refers to the same people). Compare 2 Kings 19:13. Avites who made the god Nibhaz (2 Kings 17:31) may refer to these people.

AVEN (*wickedness*)

Noun used in place names to indicate Israel's understanding of the place as site of idol worship:
(1) On or Heliopolis in Egypt (Ezek. 30:17);
(2) major worship centers of Israel such as Bethel and Dan (Hos. 10:8);
(3) valley in place of popularly known names such as Beth-aven for Beth-el (Josh. 7:2; 18:12). See *Beth-aven.*

AVENGER

Person with legal responsibility to protect the rights of an endangered relative, taking life of one who killed a family member (Num. 35:12); receiving restitution for crimes against a deceased relative (Num. 5:7-8), buy-

ing back property lost to the family (Lev. 25:25), redeeming a relative who sold himself into slavery (Lev. 25:48-49), or marrying widow of relative without sons to perpetuate the family (Deut. 25:5-10). Redemption applies to repossessing things consecrated to God (Lev. 27:13-31) or to God's actions for His people (Ex. 6:6; Job 19:25; Ps. 103:4; Isa. 43:1). Ultimately God is the redeemer (Isa. 41:14).

AWE, AWESOME

Emotion combining honor, fear, and respect before someone of superior office or actions; most appropriately applies to God (Job 25:2).

AWL See *Tools.*

AWNING

Deck covering to protect ship's passengers from the sun (Ezek. 27:7); may be similar to covering of Noah's ark (Gen. 8:13) and the tabernacle (Ex. 26:14).

AX, AX HEAD See *Tools.*

AZAZEL See *Scapegoat.*

AZEKAH (*cultivated ground*)

City where Joshua defeated southern coalition of kings led by Adonizedek of Jerusalem (Josh. 10:10); allotted to Judah (Josh. 15:35); located at tell Zakariya 5 ½ miles northeast of Beth Govrin above the Valley of Elah. See 1 Sam. 17:1; 2 Chron. 11:9; Neh. 11:30; Jer. 34:7.

AZOTUS See *Ashdod; Philistines.*

BAAL (*lord, owner, possessor, or husband*)

Personal name and name of lord of Canaanite religion seen in the thunderstorms and worshiped as god who provided fertility.

Compound forms naming persons with authority or who worshiped Baal and locations where Canaanite deities were worshiped, such as Baal-peor (Num. 25:5; Deut. 4:3; Ps. 106:28; Hos. 9:10); Baal-hermon (Judg. 3:3; 1 Chron. 5:23); Baal-gad (Josh. 11:17; 12:7; 13:5). See *Canaan, History and Religion of.*

BAAL-BERITH (*lord of covenant*)

Canaanite deity with temple at Shechem whom the Israelites worshiped following death of Gideon (Judg. 8:33).

BAAL-GAD (*Baal of Gad or lord of Gad*)

Town representing northern limit of Joshua's conquests (Josh. 11:17) in Valley of Lebanon at foot of Mount Hermon; apparently same as Mount Baal-Hermon (Judg. 3:3).

BAAL-HAZOR (*Baal of Hazor*)

Mountainous site where David's son Absalom held celebration of sheep-shearing (2 Sam. 13:23); may be same as Hazor of Neh. 11:33; modern Jebel el-Asur, 5 miles northeast of Bethel.

BAAL-MEON (*lord of the residence or Baal of the residence*)

City Reuben built east of Jordan (Num. 32:36), probably on the tribe's northern border; Khirbet Main, 10 miles southwest of Heshbon and 10 miles east of the Dead Sea; probably same as Beth-baal-meon (Josh. 13:17); Beth-meon (Jer. 48:23). Ezekiel 25:9 pronounces judgment on Moabite Baal-meon about time of Exile in 587.

BAAL-PEOR

Place of worship and name of Moabite, Midianite, and Ammonite deity the Israelites worshiped when they had illicit sexual relations with Moabite women (Num. 25:3); incident became paradigm of sin and divine judgment for later generations of Israelites (Deut. 4:3; Ps. 106:28; Hos. 9:10). See *Moab; Peor.*

BAAL-ZEBUB (*lord of the flies*)

Philistine deity from which Israelite King Ahaziah sought help after injuring himself (2 Kings 1:2). Hebrew writer probably intentionally distorted god's actual name from original Baal-zebul: "Baal, the Prince." Jesus used Beel-zebub, clearly a variation of Baal-zebub, in reference to the prince of demons (Matt. 10:25). See *Baal; Philistines; Satan.*

BAAL-ZEPHON (*lord of the north or Baal of the north*)

(1) Place in Egypt named for Canaanite god near which Israel camped before miracle of crossing the sea (Ex. 14:2,9).

(2) Canaanite god in Ugaritic texts; sanctuary on Jebel el-Aqra 25 miles north of Ugarit. See *Exodus.*

BAALI (*my lord or my Baal*)

Play on words (Hos. 2:16), looking to a day when Israel would no longer worship Baal. Israel, the bride, would refer to Yahweh, her God and husband, as "my man" (Hebrew, *'ishi*) but not as "my lord" (Hebrew, *baali*).

BAASHA

King of Israel (908–886 B.C.) at Tirzah who gained throne by violence, killing his predecessor Nadab (1 Kings 15:27) and exterminating Jeroboam's entire line (15:29). He warred against Asa, king of Judah (1 Kings 15:16). See *Israel; Chronology of Biblical Periods; Tirzah.*

BABBLER

Derogatory term (literally, "seed picker") Epicureans and Stoics used against Paul in Athens (Acts 17:18); writers and thinkers who plagiarized without the ability to understand or properly use what they had taken. Another Greek word *bebelos* (1 Tim. 4:7; 6:20; 2 Tim. 2:16; Heb. 12:16) refers to chatter or babbling talk about worldly things, an activity Christians should avoid.

BABEL (*confusion*)

(1) Hebrew word for Babylon.

(2) City which disobedient descendants of Noah built to "make a name" for themselves, so they would not be scattered over all the earth (Gen. 11:4,9; compare 9:1; 11:4). God confused their language, apparently originating the different human languages.

BABOON See *Animals, Wild.*

BABYLON, HISTORY AND RELIGION OF

City-state in southern Mesopotamia on the river Euphrates, about 50 miles south of modern Baghdad; eventually became large empire that absorbed the nation of Judah and destroyed Jerusalem.

Semitic westerners, or Amorites, established a kingdom shortly after 2000 B.C., period of the Hebrew patriarchs. Hammurabi (1792–1750 B.C.), sixth king of this First Dynasty of Babylon, built a sizable empire, making Babylon the political seat of southern Mesopotamia, the region called Babylonia.

In 851 B.C. the Assyrian king Shalmaneser III made Babylon nominally subject to Assyrian "protection." A series of coups in Babylon prompted the Assyrian Tiglath-pileser III to enter Babylon in 728 B.C. and proclaim himself king under the throne name Pulu (Pul of 2 Kings 15:19; 1 Chron. 5:26). He died the next year. By 721 B.C. the Chaldean Marduk-apal-iddina (Merodach-baladan of the OT) ruled Babylon. With Elamite support he resisted the advances of the Assyrian Sargon II in 720 B.C. Babylon gained momentary independence, but in 710 B.C. Sargon attacked again, forcing Merodach-baladan to flee to Elam. Sargon took the throne of Babylon.

When Sargon died in 705 B.C., Babylon and other nations, including Judah under King Hezekiah, rebelled from Assyrian domination. Merodach-baladan had returned from Elam to Babylon; probably it was in this context that he sent emissaries to Hezekiah (2 Kings 20:12-19; Isa. 39). In 703 B.C. Assyria under Sennacherib defeated Merodach-baladan, who again fled and ultimately died in exile. Another Elamite-sponsored revolt broke out against Assyria. In 689 B.C. Sennacherib destroyed the sacred city of Babylon. His murder, by his own sons (2 Kings 19:37) in 681 B.C., was interpreted by Babylonians as divine judgment for this unthinkable act.

Esarhaddon, Sennacherib's son, immediately began rebuilding Babylon to win the allegiance of the populace. At his death, the crown prince Ashurbanipal ruled over Assyria, while another son ascended the throne of Babylon. In 651 B.C. the Babylonian king rebelled against his brother. Ashurbanipal finally prevailed and was crowned king of a resentful Babylon.

Assyrian domination died with Ashurbanipal in 627 B.C. In 626 B.C. Babylon fell into the hands of a Chaldean chief, Nabopolassar, first king of the Neo-Babylonian Empire. In 612, with the help of the Medes, the Babylonians sacked the Assyrian capital Nineveh. The remnants of the Assyrian army rallied at Haran in north Syria, which was abandoned at the approach of the Babylonians in 610 B.C. Egypt, however, challenged Babylon for the right to inherit Assyria's empire. Pharaoh Necho II, with the last of the Assyrians (2 Kings 23:29-30), failed in 609 to retake Haran. In 605 B.C. Babylonian forces under the crown prince

Nebuchadnezzar routed the Egyptians at the decisive Battle of Carchemish (Jer. 46:2-12).

In 604 and 603 B.C., Nebuchadnezzar II (605–562 B.C.), king of Babylon, campaigned along the Palestinian coast, and Jehoiakim, king of Judah, became an unwilling vassal of Babylon. A Babylonian defeat at the border of Egypt in 601 probably encouraged Jehoiakim to rebel. For two years Judah was harassed by Babylonian vassals (2 Kings 24:1-2). Then, in December of 598 B.C., Nebuchadnezzar marched on Jerusalem. Jehoiakim died that same month, and his son Jehoiachin surrendered the city to the Babylonians on March 16, 597 B.C. Many Judeans, including the royal family, were deported to Babylon (2 Kings 24:6-12). Ultimately released from prison, Jehoiachin was treated as a king in exile (2 Kings 25:27-30; Jer. 52:31-34). Texts excavated in Babylon show that rations were allotted to him and five sons.

Nebuchadnezzar appointed Zedekiah over Judah. Against the protests of Jeremiah, but with promises of Egyptian aid, Zedekiah revolted against Babylon in 589 B.C. In the resultant Babylonian campaign, Judah was ravaged and Jerusalem besieged. An abortive campaign by Pharaoh Hophra gave Jerusalem a short respite, but the attack was renewed (Jer. 37:4-10). The city fell in August of 587 B.C. Zedekiah was captured, Jerusalem burned, and the temple destroyed (Jer. 52:12-14). Many more Judeans were taken to exile in Babylonia (2 Kings 25:1-21; Jer. 52:1-30).

The city of Babylon spanned the Euphrates, surrounded by an 11-mile-long outer wall enclosing suburbs and Nebuchadnezzar's summer palace. The inner wall was wide enough to accommodate two chariots abreast. It could be entered through eight gates, the most famous of which was the northern Ishtar Gate, used in the annual New Year Festival.

Nebuchadnezzar, the greatest Neo-Babylonian king, was the last great ruler of Babylon. He was followed by his son Awel-marduk (561–560 B.C.) —the Evil-Merodach of the OT (2 Kings 25:27-30)—Neriglissar (560–558 B.C.), and Labashi-Marduk (557 B.C.), murdered as a mere child. The last king of Babylon, Nabonidus (556–539 B.C.), seems to have favored the moon god, Sin, over the national god, Marduk. He moved his residence to Tema in the Syro-Arabian Desert for ten years, leaving his son Belshazzar (Dan. 5:1) as regent in Babylon. Nabonidus returned to a divided capital amid a threat from the united Medes and Persians. In 539 B.C. the Persian Cyrus II entered Babylon without a fight. Thus ended Babylon's dominant role in Near Eastern politics.

Babylon remained an important economic center and provincial capital during the period of Persian rule. Alexander the Great began rebuilding Babylon. After Alexander, the city declined economically but remained an important religious center until NT times. The site was deserted by A.D. 200.

In Judeo-Christian thought, Babylon the metropolis, like the Tower of Babel, became symbolic of man's decadence and God's judgment. "Babylon" in Rev. 14:8; 16:19; 17:5; 18:2 and probably in 1 Pet. 5:13 refers to Rome, the city which personified this idea for early Christians.

Babylonian religion is the best-known variant of a complex and highly polytheistic system of belief common throughout Mesopotamia. See *Assyria, History and Religion of* for old gods, astral deities, and young gods.

A number of myths concerning Babylonian gods are known, the most important of which is the *Enuma Elish*, or Creation Epic. This myth showed how Marduk became the leading god through a cosmic struggle. Marduk slew Tiamat (the sea goddess, representative of chaos). From the blood of another slain god, Ea created mankind. Finally, Marduk was exalted and installed in his temple, Esagila.

BACA (*Balsam tree* or *weeping*) Valley in Ps. 84:6 which reflects a poetic play on words describing a person forced to go through a time of weeping who found that God turned tears into a well, providing water.

BACKSLIDING
Israel's faithlessness to God (Isa. 57:17, RSV; Jer. 3:14,22; 8:5; 31:22; 49:4; Hos. 11:7; 14:4). Israel had broken faith with God by serving other gods and by living immoral lives. See *Apostasy.*

BADGER, BADGER SKINS See *Animals.*

BAG
Flexible container that may be closed for holding, storing, or carrying something.
(1) Large bags in which large amounts of money could be carried (2 Kings 5:23; Isa. 3:22; KJV has "crisping pins").
(2) Small bag (purse) used to carry a merchant's weights (Deut. 25:13; Prov. 16:11; Mic. 6:11) or smaller sums of money (Prov. 1:14; Isa. 46:6); may be the same as purse in the NT (Luke 10:4; 12:33; 22:35-36).
(3) Cloth tied up in a bundle (Job 14:17; Prov. 7:20; Hag. 1:6); also translated "bundle" (Gen. 42:35; 1 Sam. 25:29; Song of Sol. 1:13). This type of bag was used to hold money (Gen. 42:35; Prov. 7:20; Hag. 1:6; see 2 Kings 12:10) or something loose such as myrrh (Song of Sol. 1:13). Figuratively, this term speaks of one's sins being bundled up (Job 14:17) and one's life being bundled up and protected by God (1 Sam. 25:29).
(4) The shepherd's bag (KJV "scrip" or "vessel") was used to carry one or more days' supplies; made of animal skins and slung across the shoulder (Gen. 42:25; 1 Sam. 9:7; 1 Sam. 17:40,49). The Hebrew word for shepherd's bag is also translated as "carriage." See *Carriage.*
(5) Large sack used to carry grain (Gen. 42:25,27,35; Josh. 9:4; see Lev. 11:32). Hebrew word is translated as

sackcloth worn during times of mourning or humiliation. See *Sackcloth.*
(6) KJV translation (John 12:6; 13:29) for money box.

BAGGAGE See *Carriage.*

BAGPIPE (NASB)
Translation of musical instrument (Dan. 3:5,10,15); KJV, REB dulcimer; NRSV, drum; NCV, NIV, NLT pipes; NKJV, psaltery; may represent a kettledrum. See *Music, Instruments, Dancing.*

BAHURIM (*young men*)
Benjaminite village on road from Jerusalem to Jericho (2 Sam. 3:16; 16:5; 17:18; 19:16; 1 Kings 2:8-9,36-46; 1 Chron. 11:33); probably Ras et-Tmim, east of Mount Scopus near Jerusalem. 2 Sam. 23:31, lists city as Barhum, due to a copyist's change.

BAJITH (KJV Isa. 15:2)
Interpretation as name of Moabite worship place. Modern translations read "temple" or "shrine."

BAKEMEATS
Old English term for any food a baker prepared (Gen. 40:17, KJV).

BAKER'S STREET
Street in Jerusalem where most, if not all, bakeries were located (Jer. 37:21).

BAKING
Method of cooking in an oven; usually of bread and cakes, main part of the meal (Gen. 19:3; Ex. 12:39; Lev. 26:26; 1 Kings 17:12-13; Isa. 44:15). The bread of the presence (Lev. 24:5) and other offerings (Lev. 2:4-6) were baked. See *Bread; Cooking and Heating; Food.*

BALAAM
Non-Israelite prophet whom Balak, king of Moab, urged to curse invading Israelites for a fee. God refused him permission to curse Israel, but

Balaam journeyed to confer with Balak. Balaam's donkey talked with him (Num. 22:21-30; 2 Pet. 2:16). See Num. 31:8; Deut. 23:3-6; Josh. 13:22. Balaam insisted that God would bless Israel (Num. 23–24) and even spoke of a future star and scepter (Num. 24:17), a prophecy ultimately fulfilled in Jesus. An inscription from about 700 B.C. from Tell Deir Alla east of the Jordan speaks of Balaam as a "seer of the gods."

Peter warned against false teachers who left the straight way and followed the way of Balaam (2 Pet. 2:15; compare Rev. 2:14).

BALAK

King of Moab who sent for Balaam the prophet to pronounce a curse on the Israelites (Num. 22:2).

BALANCES

Instruments consisting of two pans hung on cords attached to a balancing beam used to determine weight, especially in commerce and banking (Lev. 19:36; Job 6:2; Hos. 12:7). Money had to be weighed for every business transaction or purchase (Jer. 32:9-10). Balances could be easily manipulated, especially by having weights that did not measure up to the proper amount or by having two sets of weights, one for buying and one for selling. See Prov. 11:1; 16:11; 20:23; Ezek. 45:9-12; Hos. 12:7; Amos 8:5; Mic. 6:10-11; compare Job 31:6; Ps. 62:9; Prov. 16:11; Isa. 46:6.

BALD LOCUST See *Insects.*

BALDNESS

State of having no hair. Natural baldness is mentioned only in Levitical laws on leprosy (Lev. 13:40-43). Elisha was ridiculed for being bald, but he may have shaved his head to mourn Elijah's departure (2 Kings 2:23; compare Isa. 3:24; 15:2-3; 22:12; Jer. 48:37; Ezek. 29:18). Shaving the head for appearance or in grieving for the dead in ways that imitated pagan customs was prohibited by law for priests (Lev. 21:5; Ezek. 44:20) and laity (Deut. 14:1). Deuteronomy

21:11-12 may refer to a practice of making captives bald, to baldness in mourning, or to a symbol of a change in life-style. See *Grief and Mourning; Leprosy; Hair.*

BALM See *Plants.*

BALM OF GILEAD See *Plants.*

BALSAM See *Cosmetics; Plants.*

BAMAH (*back, high place*) See Ezek. 20:29; *High Place.*

BAMOTH-BAAL (*high places of Baal*)

Site in Moab allotted Reuben (Josh. 13:17); may be modern Gebel Atarus or Khirbet el-Qeiqiyeh. Numbers 22:41 speaks of Bamoth or high places of Baal near the Arnon River. There Balak and Balaam could see all Israel.

BAN See *Accursed; Anathema.*

BAND See *Cohort.*

BANDIT See *Robbery.*

BANGLES See *Anklet.*

BANKING

Occupation designed to provide for the custody, loan, and exchange of money. The first money was bits of metal; coins were struck later. The prototype of paper money may have been leather strips studded with precious metal as a legal medium of exchange. Banking was dated as early as 2000 B.C. in Babylon. By 1500 B.C. banking had spread eastward to sea-traders of Phoenicia on northern coast of Palestine. Banking spread to the Phoenician trade centers by 1000 B.C., including Rome, Athens, Carthage, and Memphis. The earliest banking functions were conducted by religious institutions with priests usually in charge. State or public banks developed in Rome and Athens. Private banks were organized but did not fare so well.

Bankers loaned money with land or persons as collateral, usually charging a minimum of 20 percent interest. OT law protected the poor, forbidding Jews to charge each other interest (Ex. 22:25; Lev. 25:35-38; Deut. 23:19-20; compare Ps. 15:5; Prov. 28:8; Ezek. 18:8,13; 22:12; compare Deut. 23:20). Priests set a standard for the weight of a shekel coin (Num. 3:47). In ancient Israel banking was carried out in transactions between individuals, not as an institution (Neh. 5:1-13). Wealthy individuals loaned money to poor farmers with children, land, and crops as security (5:2-3). Pledges were sometimes required to guarantee a loan (Gen. 38:17), but essential items, like a cloak, could not be kept past nightfall (Deut. 24:12; Amos 2:8). The lender was forbidden to enter the home of the debtor to "fetch his pledge" (Deut. 24:10-11). A man might mortgage his home and fields, pledging his labor as a debt-slave or the labor of his family to satisfy the loan (Neh. 5:1-5; Ps. 119:11). Abuse of this system occurred often enough that the prophets condemned it (Neh. 5:6-13; Ezek. 22:12; compare Prov. 17:18; 22:26).

Jesus' parables of the talents (Matt. 25:14-30) and the pounds (Luke 19:11-27) lend credence to the practice of giving sums to the bankers to invest or to draw interest. Jesus condemned the older custom of burying one's money for safe keeping (Josh. 7:21) as "wicked and slothful" (Matt. 25:25-27).

The temple became a bank, lending money to finance business, construction, and other programs. Pilate raised a storm of protest when he tapped one of the temple funds (Qorban), which was to be used exclusively for religious purposes, to build an aqueduct. After the destruction of the temple in A.D. 70, the Roman emperor Vespasian ordered the continued payment of the tax and its deposit in the temple of Jupiter. See *Money; Moneychangers.*

BANKRUPTCY

Declaring bankruptcy as a legal means of escaping debt was not an option during the biblical period. If a person could not repay his debts, his creditors could seize his property (Neh. 5:3-4; Ps. 109:11) or children (Ex. 21:7-11; 2 Kings 4:1-7; Neh. 5:5; Job 24:9) until sufficient payment was deemed to have been made, or the debtor himself could be sold into slavery (Lev. 25:39-43; compare Prov. 22:7) or imprisoned (Luke 12:58-59).

The regular remission of debts in ancient Israel (Deut. 15:1-3) was never intended to encourage irresponsible borrowing. Rather, the writers of the Bible simply expected that God's people would repay their debts, even if by doing so they would incur great loss (Ex. 22:14; compare Ps. 15:4). Those who did not repay their debts were considered to be wicked (Ps. 37:21) and foolish (compare Luke 14:28-29).

BANNER

Sign carried to give a group a rallying point, usually a flag or a carved figure of an animal, bird, or reptile. It may have been molded from bronze, as was the serpent in Numbers 21:8-9. See Num. 10; Isa. 13:2; 49:22.

BANQUET

Elaborate meal, sometimes called a feast, used in sealing friendships, celebrating victories, and for other joyous occasions (Dan. 5:1; Luke 15:22-24). See *Hospitality.*

Most banquets were held in the evening after the day's work. Usually only men were invited. The women served the food when no servant was present. Those who dined reclined on bedlike seats and lay at right angles to the table (Mark 6:39; Luke 12:37), eating fish, bread, olives, various kinds of vegetables, cheeses, honey, dates, and figs. Beef or lamb was used only by the rich or on special occasions (Mark 14:12; Luke 15:23). Wine was an important part of the feasts. See Matt. 9:9-10; Mark 10:37; 14:1-9; Luke 7:36-50; 14:7-11; 19:1-6; John 2:1-11; 12:1-8; 13:23.

Jesus used the victory feast to refer to the messianic banquet (Matt. 8:11; Luke 13:29). The final victory day is a "marriage supper of the Lamb" of God (Rev. 19:9).

BAPTISM

The immersion or dipping of a believer in water symbolizing the complete renewal and change in the believer's life and testifying to the death, burial, and resurrection of Jesus Christ as the way of salvation. The radical Qumran sect that produced the Dead Sea Scrolls laid great emphasis on purity and purifying rites, normally involving immersion and emphasizing repentance and submission to God's will. Near the time of Jesus, Judaism began emphasizing ritual washings to cleanse from impurity (compare Lev. 16:4,24) and began baptizing Gentile converts, though circumcision still remained the primary entrance rite into Judaism.

John the Baptist immersed repentant sinners (John 1:6,11). John's baptism pointed to the coming of the kingdom of God through the Messiah, who would baptize with the Spirit and with fire (Matt. 3:11).

John also baptized Jesus, who never sinned (Matt. 3:13-17; John 1:13-16). His baptism was to fulfill all righteousness (Matt. 3:15). In this way He was able to identify with sinful mankind and to be a model for others to follow. The main differences between John's baptism and Jesus' baptism lie in the personal commitment to Christ and the coming of the Holy Spirit in Jesus' baptism (John 1:33).

Baptism refers to the suffering and death of Christ (Mark 10:38-39; Luke 12:50; compare Rom. 6:1-7; Col. 2:12). To be baptized is to clothe oneself with Christ (Gal. 3:27, NRSV, NIV). Baptism shows that a person has died to the old way of life and has been raised to a new kind of life—

eternal life in Christ (Matt. 28:19-20; Col. 3:1; 2 Tim. 2:11), pointing to the Christian's resurrection (Rom. 6:1-6).

New Testament baptism is for believers (Acts 2:38; 8:12-13,36-38; Eph. 4:5). Baptism comes after conviction of sin, repentance of sin, confession of Christ as Lord and Savior. To be baptized is to preach a personal testimony through the symbol of baptism.

Baptism occurs once. Rebaptism in the NT seemingly occurred only when a group of people had never received the Holy Spirit (Eph. 4:30; see also Acts 1:4-5; 2:38,41; 8:12-13,36-39).

BAPTISM FOR THE DEAD

A practice Paul mentioned in 1 Cor. 15 where a living believer was baptized on behalf of a dead individual. Paul did not advocate the practice of baptizing for the dead. He pointed to the inconsistency in their thought to convince them of the reality of the resurrection of the dead.

BAPTISM OF FIRE

Jesus' ability to immerse (baptize) people in the presence of God so they are aware of their sins and their need to be cleansed of that sin. To be baptized with the Holy Spirit and fire is to be convicted concerning sin and righteousness and judgment (John 16:8). See Matt. 3:11; Luke 3:16.

BAPTISM OF THE HOLY SPIRIT

Being immersed (baptized) in the presence and being of God (Mark 1:8; John 1:33; 7:37-39; Acts 1:5; 2.3-4,16-21; 10:44; 11:16; see Matt. 3:11; Luke 3:16; compare Joel 2:28-32) and so to be made aware of one's sinfulness and to desire cleansing and purification (John 16:8). One baptized with the Holy Spirit is given the necessary spiritual gifts (Rom. 12:4-8; 1 Cor. 12:1–14:40; Eph. 4:1-16; 1 Tim. 4:16; 1 Pet. 4:10-11), knowledge and guidance (John 14:26; 16:13), and empowered to do works of ministry (Luke 24:49; Acts 1:8) —including witnessing (Acts 1:8; see

John 15:26-27) and working miracles (John 14:12; Acts 3:4-10; 5:12).

BAPTIST See *John (2)*.

BAR

Aramaic translation of Hebrew *ben*, "son of"; often used as a prefix for names of men telling whose sons they were.

BAR-JESUS

Jewish magician and false prophet at Paphos (Acts 13:6), denounced by Paul and struck blind; in Acts 13:8, called Elymas.

BAR-JONA (*son of John*)

Surname of Simon Peter (Matt. 16:17).

BAR-KOCHBA (*son of the star*)

Title Jewish rebels gave to Simeon bar Kosevah, leader of their unsuccessful revolt in A.D. 132–135, designating him as the Messiah (Num. 24:17).

BARABBAS

Murderer and insurrectionist held in custody at the time of the trial of Jesus (Mark 15:17) and set free by Pilate at the crowd's request.

BARAK

Son of Abinoam whom the prophetess Deborah summoned to assume military leadership of the Israelites against Sisera's Canaanite forces (Judg. 4:6).

BARBARIAN

Foreigner, one who did not speak Greek (Acts 28:2,4) or was not a Greek. Paul used the term twice in 1 Cor. 14:11, dealing with unintelligible speech in the church. See Rom. 1:14; Col. 3:11.

BARLEY

Grain for which Palestine was known (Deut. 8:8); food of the poor (Lev. 23:22; Ruth 3:15,17; 2 Sam. 17:28; 2 Kings 4:42; 7:16-18; 2 Chron. 2:10,15; 27:5; Jer. 41:8). Failure of the barley crop was a disaster (Joel 1:11; see Judg. 7:13; Ezek. 4:12; John 6:9,13; 1 Kings 4:28). There was a spring variety (*Hordeum vulgare*) and a winter variety (*Hordeum hexastichon*). See *Plants*.

BARLEY HARVEST

Reaping (Ruth 2:23) began in late April or early May; preceded wheat harvest by two weeks (Ex. 9:31-32); at its beginning first fruits were offered to consecrate harvest (Lev. 23:10).

BARN

Storage place for seed (Hag. 2:19) or grain (Matt. 13:30; see Deut. 28:8; Prov. 3:10; Joel 1:17; Luke 12:18).

BARNABAS (*son of encouragement* —Acts 4:36; linguistically closer, *son of prophecy* or *son of exhortation*)

Levite, native of Cyprus, named Joseph (Joses), before the disciples called him Barnabas; sold his property and gave the proceeds to the Jerusalem church (Acts 4:36-37); introduced Saul of Tarsus to the Jerusalem church (9:26-27). Church chose Barnabas to go to Syrian Antioch and investigate the unrestricted preaching to the Gentiles. He secured Saul as his assistant. They took famine relief to the Jerusalem church (11:19-30). On Paul's first missionary journey, Barnabas at first seems to have been the leader (chs. 13–14). Paul and Barnabas were sent to Jerusalem to try to settle the questions of how Gentiles could be saved and how Jewish Christians could have fellowship with them (15:1-21; compare Gal. 2:1-10). They separated over whether to take John Mark with them again (15:36-41).

In Gal. 2:13 Paul indicated that on one occasion Barnabas wavered on the issue of full acceptance of Gentile Christians. In 1 Cor. 9:6, Paul commended Barnabas for following his (Paul's) practice of supporting himself rather than depending on the churches. Colossians 4:10 simply states that Mark was Barnabas's cousin.

BARREL

KJV translation (1 Kings 17:12-16; 18:33) for"jar"used in carrying water or storing flour. See *Pottery*.

BARREN, BARRENNESS

Woman unable to give birth to children: Sarai (Gen. 11:30), Rebekah (Gen. 25:21), Rachel (Gen. 29:31), Manoah's wife (Judg. 13:2), Hannah (1 Sam. 1:5), and Elizabeth (Luke 1:7,36). Also described as "solitary" (Job 3:7), "desolate" (2 Sam. 13:20; Isa. 49:21; 54:1), or "dead, deadness" (Rom. 4:19). Barrenness was considered a curse from God (Gen. 16:2; 20:18; 1 Sam. 1:5; compare Luke 1:25).

BARTHOLOMEW *(son of Talmai)*

Apostle (Matt. 10:2-4; Mark 3:16-19; Luke 6:14-16; Acts 1:13), always mentioned after Philip. John's account of Philip's call to discipleship is closely related to the call of Nathanael (1:43-51), leading to traditional identification of Bartholomew with Nathanael. See *Nathanael; Disciples, Apostles*.

BARUCH *(blessed)*

Son of Neriah who served as Jeremiah's scribe and friend (Jer. 32:12; 36; 43:3; 45). Jewish tradition attributed many later literary works to Baruch. See *Apocrypha; Jeremiah; Pseudepigrapha*.

BARZILLAI *(made of iron)*

Man from Gilead east of the Jordan who helped David at Mahanaim as he fled from Absalom (1 Sam. 17:27-29; see 19:31-39; 1 Kings 2:7).

BASHAN

Fertile area (Deut. 32:14; Ezek. 39:18); northernmost region of Palestine east of the Jordan River; ruled by King Og in time of Moses (Num. 21:33-35); assigned to Manasseh (Deut. 3:13; Josh. 13:29-31). Principal cities include Edrei, Karnaim, Ashtaroth, and Salecah. See *Palestine*.

BASIN

Used interchangeably with "bowl" for various sizes of wide hollow bowls, cups, and dishes for domestic or more formal purposes (see John 13:5); usually made from pottery but also made of brass (Ex. 27:3), silver (Num. 7:13), and gold (2 Chron. 4:8). One of the largest was used in the sacrificial rituals at the great altar of the temple (Zech. 9:15).

BASKET

Woven containers of various shapes and sizes made of cane, net, or leaves. Baskets were used for carrying food (Gen. 40:16-18), "bird nets" (Amos 8:1-2), harvesting grain (Deut. 26:2; 28:5), carrying heavy burdens such as clay for bricks or even the heads of the 70 sons of Ahab delivered to Jehu (2 Kings 10:7), and a lunch basket (Matt. 14:20; 15:37). Paul used a large basket to escape over the wall of Damascas (Acts 9:25).

BASTARD

Illegitimate child, but not necessarily a child born out of wedlock; could refer to offspring of an incestuous union or of a marriage that was prohibited (Lev. 18:6-20; 20:11-20). Illegitimate children were not permitted to enter the assembly of the Lord (Deut. 23:2). Those who do not have the discipline of the Lord are illegitimate children (Heb. 12:8). In Zech. 9:6 translated as "mongrel" (NRSV, NASB); "half-breeds" (CEV); "foreigners" (NIV, NLT, NCV); "mixed race" (TEV, REB, NKJV).

BATH See *Weights and Measures*.

BATHING

Washing of any kind, usually ritual acts of purification (Ex. 30:19-21; Lev. 14:8). Dry Middle East climate prohibited full bathing except on special occasions (2 Sam. 11:2) or where sufficient water was available (Ex. 2:5; John 9:7). During a time of mourning or fasting, the face and clothes were left unwashed (2 Sam.

12:20), a practice forbidden by Jesus (Matt. 6:17). Lambs were washed at shearing time (Song of Sol. 4:2), babies after birth (Ezek. 16:4), and bodies in preparation for burial (Acts 9:37).

BATHSHEBA (*daughter of abundance*)

Beautiful wife of Uriah the Hittite (2 Sam. 11:3) with whom David had adulterous relationship, leading to his plotting to kill Uriah; David later married Bathsheba (2 Sam. 11:4). She became politically influential as mother of Solomon (1 Kings 1:11–2:19). See *David*.

BATS See *Animals*.

BATTALION See *Cohort*.

BATTERING RAM See *Arms and Armor*.

BATTLE See *Arms and Armor; Army*.

BATTLE-AX See *Arms and Armor*.

BAY

KJV translation in Zech. 6:3,7 as color of horses. Recent interpreters refer to strength of the horses (NIV, NASB, NCV, NKJV); though NRSV reads "gray" (v. 3) and "steeds" (v. 7); REB omits word (v. 3) and emends text (v. 7); CEV has "spotted gray" and omission; TEV, "dappled"; NLT, "gray and powerful."

BAY TREE

KJV translation in Ps. 37:35 for Hebrew, "native" or "indigenous." NRSV, TEV hardly come any closer with "cedar"; nor does NLT with "mighty trees." NASB, NIV, REB, NKJV are closer to Hebrew with "tree in its native soil"; compare CEV, "rich soil"; NCV, "good soil."

BDELLIUM

Translation of word of uncertain meaning (Gen. 2:12; Num. 11:7). Related languages favor identification with a resinous gum that in droplet form may have appearance of a pearl or stone.

BEADS

RSV translation of a term for articles of gold jewelry (Num. 31:50); variously identified as tablets (KJV), armlets, pendants (REB, NRSV), necklaces (TEV, NLT, NIV, NCV, NASB), and breastplates.

BEANS

Leguminous food plant (*Faba vulgaris*); horse or broad bean (2 Sam. 17:28; Ezek. 4:9) sown in autumn and harvested in mid-April just before the barley and wheat. They were cooked green in the pods or after being dried.

BEAR See *Animals*. For constellation, see *Arcturus*.

BEARD

Hair growing on a man's face often excluding the mustache. Near Eastern art depicted Hebrews with full rounded beards in contrast to clean-shaven Romans and Egyptians and to other desert nomads and Palestine residents who often clipped or cut their beards (see Jer. 9:26; 25:23; 49:32; compare Lev. 19:27; 21:5; 2 Sam. 10:4-5; Isa. 7:20; 15:2; 50:6; Jer. 41:5; 48:37; Ezek. 5:1). Hebrew, "beard" also means "old" and was applied to men (Judg. 19:16), slaves (Gen. 24:2), women (Zech. 8:4), and elders (Ex. 19:7).

BEAST

Any animal in distinction from people (Eccl. 3:18-21), reptiles (Gen. 1:24), and sometimes cattle (Gen. 1:30). Beasts were divided into clean and unclean (Lev. 11:1-8), wild and domesticated (Gen. 1:24; 2:20; Ex. 19:13; 22:10; Num. 3:13).

BEATEN GOLD

Thin sheets of gold produced by hammering; used to overlay objects of lesser value such as Solomon's golden shields (1 Kings 10:16-17), tabernacle lampstands (Ex. 25:31, 36;

37:7,22; Num. 8:4), and idols (Isa. 40:19). See *Minerals and Metals.*

BEATEN OIL

Highest grade of olive oil produced by crushing ripe olives in a mortar. See *Oil.*

BEATEN SILVER

Thin sheets of silver produced by hammering and used to overlay objects of lesser value such as the wooden core of an idol (Jer. 10:6-10). See *Minerals and Metals.*

BEATING See *Scourge.*

BEATITUDES

Opening sentences of Jesus' Sermon on the Mount (Matt. 5–7) describing quality of life of a citizen of God's kingdom. Each Beatitude is to be applied and developed in every disciple and carries a strong promise of ultimate good for those who develop the blessed life.

BEAUTIFUL GATE See *Jerusalem; Temple; Gates of Jerusalem.*

BED, BEDROOM

Place to sleep or rest. A bed for the very poor was a mere thin straw mat or cloth pad rolled out on the ground with no more than a stone for a pillow (Gen. 28:10-11; John 5:9) and an outer garment for cover. For the more fortunate poor, a multipurpose, one- room, mud house served as protection from the elements and as a kitchen, work space, and sleeping quarters. For the very few affluent, separate bedrooms had elaborately decorated beds (Esther 1:6; Prov. 7:16-17; Amos 6:4). A bed of iron attracted attention in Deut. 3:11. The bed symbolizes that no secret place is secure from deception (2 Kings 6:12).

BEE See *Insects.*

BEELZEBUB (KJV, NIV) or **BEELZEBUL** (NASB, TEV, NRSV) See *Baal-zebub.*

BEER (*well*)

Frequently occurs in compound constructions of place names: Beer-sheba, "*well of seven.*"

BEERSHEBA (*well of seven*)

Significant patriarchal town in southern Judean wilderness (Gen. 21; 22; 26; 28:10; 46:1-5; see 1 Sam. 8:1-3; Amos 5:5; 8:14; Neh. 11:27,30); important crossroad to Egypt in the geographic center of the dry, semi-desert region known as the Negeb; administrative center of the region settled before 3000 B.C.; southern extreme of Israel, "Dan to Beer-sheba" (2 Sam. 24:2, 1 Kings 4:25; compare 2 Kings 23:8; 2 Chron. 19:4; 30:5). See Josh. 15:28; 19:1,2,9.

BEGINNING AND END See *Alpha and Omega.*

BEHEADING See *Capital Punishment.*

BEHEMOTH See *Animals; Leviathan.*

BEKA See *Weights and Measures.*

BEL See *Apocrypha; Babylon.*

BELIAL

Transliteration of Hebrew term of derision (Deut. 13:13), "useless" or "worthless." KJV interprets as proper name 16 times; modern translations use common noun, "worthless" or "wicked." In Nah. 1:15, where KJV translates, "the wicked," Belial appears to be the name of some specific malevolent power. Paul (2 Cor. 6:15) declared the mutual irreconcilability of Christ and Belial, who appears equated with Satan. Dead Sea Scrolls use Belial for leader of forces of darkness. See *Satan; Antichrist.*

BELIEF, BELIEVE See *Faith.*

BELL

Golden object fastened to the garments of the high priest as a signal or warning of the high priest's movements (Ex. 28:33-35; 39:25-26); also used for horses (Zech. 14:20).

BELLOWS

Instrument that blows air on a fire making it burn hotter (Jer. 6:29; compare Job 20:26; 41:21; Isa. 54:16; Ezek. 22:20-21). See *Assayer*.

BELOVED DISCIPLE

Term in John's Gospel for disciple for whom Jesus had deep feelings; variously identified as Lazarus, an anonymous source or author of the Gospel, an idealized disciple, or John's reference to himself without using his own name. Church tradition and interpretation of biblical evidence appear to point to John.

BELSHAZZAR (*Bel's prince*)

Babylonian king at whose drunken feast God sent a cryptic message of judgment (Dan. 5:1,28,30). Son of Nabonidus, he reigned as coregent with his father (553–539 B.C.). Nabonidus traveled to Arabia and left Belshazzar in control, according to a Babylonian inscription. See *Babylon*.

BEN (*son of*) See *Bar*.

BENAIAH (*Yahweh has built*)

Name of several people including captain of David's professional soldiers (2 Sam. 8:18; 20:23; 1 Chron. 27:5-6) who disarmed an Egyptian and killed him with his own sword (2 Sam. 23:20-23), supported Solomon against Adonijah (1 Kings 1:8-47), and became Solomon's executioner (1 Kings 2:25-46) and army commander (1 Kings 4:4).

BEN-AMMI (*son of my people*)

Son of Lot and his younger daughter after his two daughters despaired of marriage and tricked their father by getting him drunk (Gen. 19:38); original ancestor of Ammonites.

BENCHES

KJV translation for planks of a ship's deck (Ezek. 27:6). See *Ashurite*.

BENEDICTION

Prayer for God's blessing or an affirmation that God's blessing is at hand; most famous is priestly benediction (or Aaronic blessing) in Num. 6:24-25. Most NT epistles close with benedictions as well. See *Blessing and Cursing*.

BENEFACTORS

Honorary title given kings or other prominent people for meritorious achievement or public service; held by some Hellenistic kings of Egypt. In God's kingdom by contrast, members are to devote themselves to humble, obscure, and perhaps menial service (Luke 22:24-27).

BEN-HADAD (*son of* [the god] *Hadad*)

Personal name or royal title of kings of Damascus. See *Damascus; Syria*.

BEN-HINNOM (*son of Hinnom*)

Valley south of Jerusalem serving as northern border of Judah (Josh. 15:8; Neh. 11:30) and southern boundary of Benjamin (Josh. 18:16). Pagan child sacrifices occurred here, some kings of Judah included (Ahaz, 2 Chron. 28:3; Manasseh, 2 Chron. 33:6). Jeremiah announced God's judgment on the valley because of such practices (Jer. 19:1-15; compare 1 Kings 23:10; 2 Kings 16:3; 17:17). The valley would be renamed "valley of slaughter" (Jer. 19:6; compare 32:35). See *Baal; Gehenna; Hell; Jerusalem; Molech*.

BENJAMIN (*son of the right hand* or *son of the south*)

Second son Rachel bore to Jacob; forefather of tribe of Benjamin. See *Tribes of Israel*.

BENJAMIN GATE See *Gates of Jerusalem*.

BERACAH (blessing)

(1) Skilled soldier able to use right or left hand with slingshot and with bow and arrows (1 Chron. 12:3).

(2) Valley near Tekoa where King Jehoshaphat of Judah (873–848 B.C.) and his people blessed God after miraculous victory over Ammon, Moab, and Edom (2 Chron. 20:26); modern wadi Berekut near Khirbet Bereikut.

BEREA (place of many waters)

City in Macedonia 45 miles west of Thessalonica to which Paul escaped after the Jews of Thessalonica rioted (Acts 17:10; see 20:4); modern Verria surrounded by springs in plain below Mount Bermion.

BERITH (covenant) See Baal-berith; Covenant.

BERNICE (gift)

Companion probably in an incestuous relationship with Herod Agrippa II (Acts 25:13); daughter of Herod Agrippa I, born probably about A.D. 28; married first to a person named Marcus, then to her own uncle Herod. Two sons were born from the latter union before Bernice was widowed in A.D. 48. Later she married Polemo, king of Cilicia. Roman historian Tacitus says she was mistress of Roman emperor Titus. See Herod.

BERYL See Jewels, Jewelry; Minerals and Metals.

BESOM

Broom made of twigs (Isa. 14:23, KJV).

BESTIALITY

Sexual intercourse between a human and an animal, punishable by death in OT legal codes (Ex. 22:19; Lev. 20:15-16; see Lev. 18:23; Deut. 27:21). Israel's neighbors practiced bestiality in fertility worship and worship of animal gods.

BETH-ABARA (house of crossing)

KJV and some Greek manuscripts reading for Bethany (John 1:28).

BETH-ANATH (house of Anath)

Fortified city in Naphtali (Josh. 19:38; Judg. 1:33); apparently worship center for Canaanite goddess Anath; may be modern Safed el-Battik, 15 miles east of Tyre.

BETH-ANOTH (house of Anath or house of being heard)

City of Judah (Josh. 15:59); temple to the Canaanite goddess Anath may have been here; may be Khirbet Beit Anun, one and a half miles southeast of Halhul.

BETHANY

Home of Mary, Martha, and Lazarus on Mount of Olives' eastern slope 2 miles southeast of Jerusalem (John 11:18) where Jesus raised Lazarus from the dead (John 11–12), and Mary anointed Jesus at home of Simon the leper (Matt. 26:6; Mark 14:3); site of Christ's ascension (Luke 24:50-53); final stop before Jerusalem just off the main east-west road coming from Jericho.

BETH-ARBEL (house of Arbel)

Sight of infamous battle Hosea used as example of what could happen to Israel (Hos. 10:14); may be Irbid in Gilead, 4 miles northwest of Tiberius. See Shalman.

BETH-AVEN (house of deception or of idolatry)

(1) Border city of Benjamim near Ai east of Bethel (Josh. 7:2; 18:12) and west of Michmash (1 Sam. 13:5); probably tell Maryam less than a mile west of Michmash. See 1 Sam. 14:23.

(2) Hosea (4:15; 5:8; 10:5,8) described Beth-el as house of deception and idolatry instead of house of God.

BETH-DAGON (*house of Dagon*)

Apparently worship place of Philistine god Dagon.

(1) Town in Judah (Josh. 15:41); probably modern Khirbet Dajun on road connecting Ramalleh and Joppa.

(2) Town in Asher (Josh. 19:27); modern Tell Regeb 5 miles southeast of Haifa.

BETH-DIBLATHAIM (*house of the two fig cakes*)

Town in Moab on which Jeremiah prophesied judgment (Jer. 48:22); may be Khirbet et-Tem. About 830 B.C., Mesha, king of Moab, bragged on Moabite Stone that he built the city.

BETH-EDEN (*house of bliss*)

Syrian city-state. See 2 Kings 19:12; Ezek. 27:23; Amos 1:5.

BETHEL (*house of God*)

(1) City at intersection of main north-south road through the hill country and main road from Jericho to the coastal plain with abundant springs, making it fertile and attractive to settlements as early as 3200 B.C.; worship site for patriarchs and Northern Kingdom; modern Beitin. The ark of the covenant was kept in Bethel (Judg. 20:17-28; 21:1-4). There Deborah (Judg. 4:5) and Samuel (1 Sam. 7:16) judged the civil and religious affairs of the Israelites. Jeroboam I made Bethel a religious center of his apostate religion in the Northern Kingdom with a golden calf, non-Levitic priests, and an illegitimate feast (1 Kings 12:29-33).

(2) Apparently a West Semitic god. Many scholars find reference to this deity in Jer. 48:13 or in other passages, especially Gen. 31:13; Amos 5:5.

BETHER (*division*)

(1) Mountain range used as an emotional image in Song of Solomon 2:17. NIV reads, "rugged hills"; NRSV, "cleft mountains"; NCV, "mountain valleys"; CEV, "mountain slopes"; REB, "hills where aromatic spices grow."

(2) Town in Judah according to Greek text of Josh. 15:59, not included in Hebrew; Khirbet el-Yahudi, seven miles southwest of Jerusalem; Bar Kochba's capital.

BETHESDA (*house of mercy*)

Pool in Jerusalem where Jesus healed a man sick for 38 years (John 5:2). Some ancient Greek manuscripts name the place Bethzatha or Bethsaida. See *Healing, Divine.*

BETH-HACCEREM (*house of the vineyard*) or **BETH-HACCHEREM**

City used to signal that enemies approached from the north (Jer. 6:1); postexilic administrative center whose leading official helped Nehemiah repair dung gate (Neh. 3:14); probably modern Ramat Rahel halfway between Jerusalem and Bethlehem. Archaeological excavations show occupation from about 800 B.C. with a grand palace, apparently Jehoiakim's (609–597). See Jer. 22:13-19.

BETH-HAGGAN

Place name (NIV, TEV, NRSV, CEV, NLT, NCV, REB) or common noun (KJV, NASB) meaning "house of the garden." See 2 Kings 9:27; probably modern Jenin, southeast of Tanaach.

BETH-HORON

Twin cities, one higher than the other —Upper and Lower Beth Horon; given Levites; important road here dominates the path to the Shephelah. See Josh. 10:10; 16:3,5; 18:13-14; 21:22; 1 Sam. 13:18; 1 Kings 9:17; 1 Chron. 7:22-24; 2 Chron. 25:13). Upper Beth Horon—1,750 feet above sea level—is modern beit Ur el-Foqa, 5 miles northwest of Gibeon and 10 miles northwest of Jerusalem. Lower Beth Horon, modern beit Ur et-Tahta, is 2 miles to the east and only 1,050 feet above sea level.

BETH-JESHIMOTH (*house of deserts*) or **BETH-JESIMOTH**

Town in Moab where Israel camped just before Moses died and Joshua led them across the Jordan (Num. 33:49; compare Josh. 12:3; Ezek. 25:9; see Josh. 13:20); tell el-Azeme, 12 miles southeast of Jericho.

BETHLEHEM (*house of bread, fighting,* or *Lahamu* [god])

(1) Home and place of anointing of David (1 Sam. 16:1-13; 17:12,15); birth place of Jesus (Matt. 2:1-12; Luke 2:4-20; John 7:43; compare Mic. 5:2) about 5 miles southwest of Jerusalem just off the major road from Jerusalem to the Negeb; Rachel's burial site (Gen. 35:19); first mentioned before 1300 B.C. in the Amarna letters. See Judg. 17:7-13; compare ch. 19; Ruth 1:1-2,19,22; 2:4; 4:11; 2 Sam. 2:32; 23:14,24; 2 Chron. 11:6; Ezra 2:21; Jer. 41:17.

(2) Town in Zebulun, about 7 miles northwest of Nazareth (Josh. 19:15); burial site of Ibzan (Judg. 12:10); modern beit Lahm.

(3) Personal name (1 Chron. 2:51,54).

BETH-PEOR (*house of Peor*)

Reubenite town in whose valley Israel camped as Moses delivered the sermons of the Deuteronomy (Deut. 3:29; see 4:46; Josh. 13:20; Hos. 9:10; compare Num. 25:1-5; Deut. 34:6); modern Khirbet Uyun Musa, 20 miles east of the north end of the Dead Sea.

BETHSAIDA (*house of fish*)

Home of Andrew, Peter, and Philip (John 1:44; 12:21) on northeast side of Sea of Galilee; rebuilt under Philip the tetrarch who named it Julius in honor of the Emperor Augustus's daughter. See Matt. 11:21; Mark 8:22; Luke 9:10; 10:13. Original village may be el-Araj and el-Mesadiyye, while et-Tell would be Herod Philip's city of Bethsaida Julius.

BETH-SHAN or **BETHSHAN** (*house of quiet*) or **BETH-SHEAN**

City, modern Tell el-Husn, above perennial stream of Harod, at crossroad of the Jezreel and Jordan valleys, commanding the routes north-south along the Jordan and east-west from Gilead to the Mediterranean Sea; came under domination of Egypt's 18th dynasty in Late Bronze Age. See Josh. 17:6,16; Judg. 1:27; 1 Sam. 31; 2 Sam. 21:12-14; 1 Kings 4:12; 14:25-28. The city remained abandoned until rebuilt after 300 B.C. and renamed Scythopolis ("city of Scythians"), largest city of the Decapolis (Matt. 4:25; Mark 5:20) and only city of the league west of the Jordan River. It included temples, theater, amphitheater, colonnaded streets, hippodrome, tombs, and many public buildings. Modern village of Beisan preserves ancient city's name.

BETH-SHEMESH (*house of the sun* or *of Shemesh the sun god*)

(1) Town between Mt. Tabor and Jordan River (Josh. 19:22); either el-Abeidiyeh, 2 miles south of Galilee or Khirbet Shemsin, east of Tabor.

(2) Town in Naphtali probably near Beth-anath (Josh. 19:38; Judg. 1:33); unconquered until David; possibly Khirbet er-Ruweisi.

(3) Egyptian town identified with Heliopolis (5 miles northeast of Cairo) by Septuagint of Jer. 43:13.

(4) Town of Dan on southern border with Judah (Josh. 15:10; 19:41) overlooking Sorek Valley about 24 miles west of Jerusalem in strategic "buffer zone" between Philistines and Israelites; modern tell er-Rumeilah. Israel apparently controlled Beth-shemesh about 1050 B.C. when the ark passed through the city returning from the Philistines (1 Sam. 6:13). See 2 Kings 14:11-14; 2 Chron. 25:21-24; 2 Chron. 28:18-19. Israelite city had olive oil, wine, copper, fabric dyeing, and wheat production industries. Nebuchadrezzar destroyed the city (588–587 B.C.).

BETH-TOGARMAH (house of Togarmah)

Place listed in table of nations (Gen. 10:3; compare Ezek. 27:14; 38:6) as son of Gomer and great grandson of Noah. North of Carchemish on an Assyrian trade route, it may be related to modern Gurun between the Halys and Euphrates Rivers.

BETH-ZUR (house of the rock)

City allotted to Judah (Josh. 15:58); Khirbet et-Tubeiqeh, 18 miles southwest of Jerusalem and 4 miles north of Hebron on major highway intersection; one of highest sites above sea level in Palestine. See 2 Chron. 11:7; 12:2; Neh. 3:16. It played a significant role in Maccabean wars.

BETROTHAL

Act of engagement for marriage as binding as marriage (Gen. 19:14; Ex. 22:16; Deut. 22:23-30; 2 Sam. 3:14; Hos. 2:19-20; Matt. 1:18; Luke 1:27; 2:5). Mary and Joseph were betrothed but did not live together until their wedding. Paul used betrothal to explain the ideal relationship, with the church as a chaste virgin being presented to Christ (2 Cor. 11:2).

BEULAH (married)

Symbolic name for Jerusalem (Isa. 62:4) expressing good fortune and closeness of Zion and her sons.

BEVELED WORK

NRSV translation of scrollwork on bronze stands of laver in Solomon's temple (1 Kings 7:29; KJV, "thin work"; NASB, "hanging work"; REB, NIV, "hammered work"; NLT, "wreath decorations"; NKJV, "plaited work"). It was wreathlike in appearance and may have been gold plated.

BEWITCH

KJV for two Greek words. Paul (Gal. 3:1) criticized Galatians captivated by the falsehood of the Judaizers to the point of straying from the gospel. The Greek word has history in magical evil and casting of spells. In Acts 8:9,11 modern versions translate another word: "amazed," "astonish," or "astound."

BEYOND THE JORDAN

Territory on other side of Jordan River; meaning determined by location of speaker; usually points to east side (Transjordan); five times to west side (Gen. 50:10-11; Deut. 3:20,25; 11:30).

BEYOND THE RIVER

Phrase referring to Euphrates River in Mesopotamia. From the perspective of those living in Palestine, it meant east side of the Euphrates River, ancestral home of patriarchs (Josh. 24:3,14-15). From perspective of Persia, "beyond the river" meant west side of the Euphrates River. Darius I named his fifth satraphy "Beyond the River," including Syria and Palestine (Ezra 4:10-20; 5:3,6; 6:6,8,13; 7:21,25; 8:36; Neh. 2:7,9; 3:7).

BEZEK (lightning)

Place where Judah and Simeon defeated Canaanites led by Adonibezek ("lord of Bezek") (Judg. 1:4) and Saul numbered Israelites to deliver Jabesh-gilead (1 Sam. 11:8); Khirbet Salhab about 18 miles from Jabesh-gilead.

BIBLE, FORMATION AND CANON OF

The word "canon" comes from the Latin canon, "norm, list," which is related to the Greek word kanon, "ruler, norm, standard" (Gal. 6:16). It is probably related to Hebrew qaneh, "reed, measuring rod." The Bible is the rule or standard of authority for Christians. The concept of "canon" and process of "canonization" refers to when the books gained the status of "Holy Scripture," the authoritative standard for faith and practice. The term "canon" was probably first used in this sense by Philo of Alexandria (first century A.D.). The Biblical canon is the list of books recognized as authoritative Scripture. The Protestant canon comprises 66 books (39 in the OT and 27 in the NT), but the Roman Catholic and Eastern Orthodox Churches add the 13 books of the Apocrypha to the OT. See *Apocrypha.*

The order of OT books in the Christian canon is based on the Septuagint, the Greek translation of the OT. The Hebrew canon is divided into three sections: the Law or Torah (Genesis–Deuteronomy), the Prophets or Neviim (Former Prophets: Joshua, Judges, 1 & 2 Samuel, 1 & 2 Kings; Latter Prophets: Isaiah, Jeremiah, Ezekiel, and the Book of Twelve), and the Writings or Kethuvim (Psalms, Proverbs, Job, Song of Songs, Ruth, Lamentations, Ecclesiastes, Esther, Ezra-Nehemiah, 1 & 2 Chronicles), with Chronicles being the last book.

The NT begins with the narrative books (Gospels and Acts), followed by the letters or epistles (Pauline and General), and concluding with Revelation. The Pauline letters begin with Romans and end with Philemon; the General letters begin with Hebrews and end with Jude. The letters are arranged on the general basis of size, from longest to shortest. Some NT manuscripts have the letters of James, Peter, John, and Jude before Romans, likely due to the more direct links between Jesus and those men.

The common critical view, which may be traced to Hebert E. Ryle (1892, rev. 1895), is that the three-fold designation of the OT books—Law, Prophets, and Writings—is based on the gradual acceptance of each of these three "collections" as canonical. This is usually tied to the view that Moses did not write the Pentateuch and that the OT historical books would have been compiled after the reign of King Josiah (Judah, 640–609). Recognition of the Law by the fifth century B.C. is based on the fact that the Samaritans, whose canon comprised only the Law, split from the Jews just after the exile. The

canon of the Prophets is thought to have been closed by 200 B.C., explaining why the Prophet Daniel, which critical scholars date in the mid-second century B.C., is found in the Writings in the Hebrew canon. The Writings are usually said to have been set at a meeting of rabbis at Jamnia (Jabneh) sometime between A.D. 70 and 135.

Roger Beckwith (1985), benefiting from the work of Jack P. Lewis (1964), S. Z. Leiman (1976), and others, addressed and refuted many issues raised by the liberal-critical school and concluded that the OT collection could have been settled as early as the fourth century B.C., although it was more probably settled by the second century B.C. For example, the Samaritans' acknowledgment of only the Torah may not be a clue to the canon's history but rather involved a rejection of the previously recognized prophets. Second, the rabbis at Jamnia were concerned not with canonization but with interpretation. Furthermore, the three-fold division of the OT is first mentioned in the prologue to the apocryphal book Ecclesiasticus or Sirach (about 132 B.C.). It is also recognized in Luke 24:44, Josephus (*Against Apion* 1:8), the Dead Sea Scrolls, and Philo. Jesus probably alludes to the OT canon in Matt 23:35 ("So all the righteous blood shed on the earth will be charged to you, from the blood of righteous Abel to the blood of Zechariah, son of Berechiah, whom you murdered between the sanctuary and the altar"; compare 2 Chron. 24:20-22), showing that He was familiar with an OT canon ending with Chronicles. Finally, although the designation of Law, Prophets, and Writings was known and important, Beckwith proved this is not a credible guide to the process of canonization.

When God chose to reveal Himself to His people and to establish a permanent relationship with them, He used the principle of the covenant, a concept familiar from ancient Near Eastern culture. The formation of a covenant commonly involved the creation of a covenant document (Ex. 24:4,7; 34:10,27-28; Deut. 9:9-11,15; 17:18; 27:3,8). Furthermore, the history of the covenant would naturally be reflected in updating that covenant document (Deut. 29:1,21; 31:9,19-22,26; 1 Sam. 10:25; Jer. 30:2; 36:2-6; Hab. 2:2). Therefore with the Mosaic covenant came the Mosaic document, and as each book of the OT was written, its authority as the revealed word of God evoked the immediate embracing of it as sacred and binding upon the emerging Israelite community (Josh. 8:31-35; 23:6). Moses, as the covenant mediator, wrote the Torah under divine leadership (Josh. 1:7; 14:10). The remainder of Scripture, the Former and Latter prophets, the poetry and wisdom literature, and the postexilic books, were likewise accepted immediately as each one was delivered and received into the Israelite community. The closure of this process would have come as the last book was accepted as authoritative and binding (referred to in the Talmud as "defiling the hands," those books that could be read in the synagogue). This may have been Malachi (usually acknowledged as the last prophet) or Chronicles (the last book in the Hebrew canonical order). In any case, what Protestants attest as the 39 books of the OT canon (same as the 22 or 24 books in the Jewish community [e.g., minor prophets were counted as one book; Jeremiah and Lamentations as one; Ezra and Nehemiah as one, etc.]) was settled very close to the time of the last book's writing.

The canonization process for the NT is easier to trace, even though some questions cannot be fully answered. The Pauline Epistles were collected and considered authoritative at least during the first half of the second century, as evidenced by Marcion's canon (ca. A.D. 140) of 10 Pauline Epistles and Luke. The four Gospels became a canonical unit during the second half of the second century, with Irenaeus (A.D. 180) defending the fourfold Gospel canon. By the end of the second century, the core of the NT canon was fixed, with the four Gospels, Acts, 1 Peter, 1 John, and 13 Pauline Epistles all accepted as authoritative texts by the leading churches. Revelation enjoyed early acceptance as well but later, near the middle of the third century, began to be questioned both on content and authorship. Hebrews was debated likewise due to authorship doubts. James, 2 Peter, 2–3 John, and Jude came to be accepted by many churches during the late third century, but they were not fully canonical until the fourth century. The first mention of a 27-book NT canon was made by Athanasius, the bishop of Alexandria, who in his Easter letter of 367, instructed the churches about the NT, listing exactly the 27 books we have. Even at that point, however, some groups such as Syriac churches used a 22-book NT canon (lacking 2 Peter, 2–3 John, Jude, and Revelation) or a 26-book canon (lacking Revelation). However, over time, the 27-book NT canon prevailed in virtually all of the churches.

The early church's task of ascertaining God's will regarding the NT canon was not easy. Marcion promoted a very limited canon in Rome (see above) that represented an extreme reaction against Judaism. He rejected the OT as well as NT writings that were "too Jewish," keeping only Paul and Luke (the only Gentile NT writer). In reaction the church defended the OT and began defining its own NT canon, much broader than Marcion's.

In the late second century Montanism promoted an ongoing "prophetic" voice in the church. This assertion of new revelation caused the church to become more restrictive in defining the canon, limiting the NT to books that could be traced to the apostolic authorship or influence.

As the task continued, the Spirit-led process was guided by

certain standards. For a book to be considered Holy Scripture (canonical), it had to enjoy widespread acceptance among the churches. Regional acceptance was not adequate. Also, criteria were needed to separate later works from those of the first century. Books must date to the apostolic era and be connected to an apostle, whether by authorship or direct association (for example, Mark and Luke were associated with Peter and Paul, respectively). The books also had to prove beneficial to the churches that heard them read. This spiritual dimension was likely paramount. Our NT books were included in the canon because they spoke so strongly to people that they could not be kept out of the canon. Lastly, the books had to be deemed suitable for public reading in the church. Since illiteracy was widespread, the reading of the text in worship was the primary contact with the text for most of the people. Those texts read in worship were heard as the authoritative Word of God. Such texts were on the path of full canonization.

A further stage of canonization occurred during the Reformation. The reformers, echoing Jerome, held that the Jewish OT canon should be followed, and so they accepted only the 39 books of the Hebrew OT, instead of the expanded OT often found in the Septuagint. These additional books (the Apocrypha) were also in the Latin Vulgate, the primary Bible of the Western Church for over 1,000 years prior to the reformation. Bibles for both the Roman Catholic Church and the Orthodox Churches still generally include the Apocrypha, but since Vatican II they have a lesser level of canonicity, being called deuterocanonical. Protestants, while not denying these books are helpful, do not accept them as canonical Holy Scripture.

BIBLE, HERMENEUTICS

Science of interpreting the Bible. To interpret a piece of literature, we must ask at least five questions:

(1) Who was the writer and to whom was he writing?

(2) What was the cultural-historical setting of the writer?

(3) What was the meaning of the words in the writer's day?

(4) What was the intended meaning of the author, and why was he saying it?

(5) What should this mean to me in my situation today?

Some *basic principles* should be observed by the interpreter of the Scriptures. The primary aim of the interpreter is to discover the original meaning of the author who wrote the passage under consideration. Recognition should be given to the human elements the Holy Spirit utilized in giving us God's Word. Preference should be given the interpretation which is clearest and simplest. Only one meaning should be given any passage of Scripture, unless a later passage of Scripture assigns it a second meaning.

Interpretation begins with a *historical task*. The interpreter needs to know as much as possible about the writer and the *cultural-historical setting*. The reader also needs to know who were the *intended recipients*. Words addressed to unbelievers would be interpreted very differently from words addressed to believers. The meaning of a passage might depend upon knowing whether the original audience was Jewish or Gentile.

A *literary task* begins with *translation* of the Scripture from the ancient Hebrew, Aramaic, and Greek into the language best understood by the interpreter. Translation is itself a stage of interpretation. If you cannot translate, you must rely upon good translations of the Bible.

Lexical study consults a lexicon or dictionary to find the meaning key words had for the original writer. In the *grammatical or syntactical* phase, you ask what is signified by the grammatical constructions, the verb forms used, the emphasized elements, the relationships of the words to each other. Good critical commentaries guide you here.

Rhetorical analysis seeks to determine what kind of rhetoric, or language, the ancient writer was using. Here you seek to recognize the various *literary forms* used by the different writers. Prose or poetry? Descriptive narrative; law or prophecy? Figures of speech are incorporated in narrative portions. Such figures of speech must be interpreted in their symbolic sense rather than as literal, descriptive language. Apocalyptic literature employs vivid symbols and fanciful images to convey some message or mystery or prophecy in a veiled, highly imaginative way. See *Apocalyptic.*

The literary *context of a passage* provides gudielines for interpretation. The context may be a paragraph, the whole chapter or even the entire book, in the case of the shorter books of the Bible. Meaning given to a verse without regard to its context is very likely the wrong meaning.

The interpreter must *compare* the meaning given to a passage to what is taught elsewhere in the Scriptures to see if the interpretation "fits" with what the Bible says in other places. We should be careful not to interpret Scripture in such a way that we introduce contradictions into our interpretation of the Bible. The Bible teaches one theme, one message. Within that unity, there is also diversity.

The interpreter has a *personal, spiritual* task. A good interpreter must prayerfully seek the leadership of the Holy Spirit (John 16:12-15; 2 Pet. 1:19-21). Only illumination or divine guidance can lead to correct interpretation.

Finally, the interpreter must seek *application.* Knowing what the Bible said to its original readers and its principles the interpreter must apply the ancient message to our very different life situations.

BIBLE, TEXTS AND VERSIONS

The process of determining and preserving in writing and translations the text of the original documents.

Old Testament Text and Versions

Jewish scribes buried old manuscripts in a storehouse or *genizah* and then destroyed these manuscripts. Hebrew scribes known as Masoretes produced the Masoretic text from A.D. 500 to 1000. Textual scholars use several tools to trace the text behind the Masoretic text. The *Samaritan Pentateuch* is the text of the first five books of the OT preserved among the Samaritans after their separation from Judah about 400 B.C. This text was preserved independently of the Masoretic text even though the oldest copies in existence were not made until after A.D. 1000. Only in a few instances do scholars think the Samaritan Pentateuch preserves readings superior to the Masoretic text.

The Aramaic paraphrases of the OT —the *Targums*—originated because the Jews in the synagogues in the Middle East could not understand the Hebrew Scriptures. As someone read the Hebrew text, an interpreter recited Aramaic paraphrases, that in time became stereotyped. These were written down before Christ (Dead Sea Scrolls contain a fragment of a Targum on Job). Most Targum manuscripts originated A.D. 500 to 1000. The Targums are more of interest for determining Jewish doctrine than for determining the early stages of the OT text.

The *Septuagint*, a Greek translation of the OT made from about 250 to 100 B.C. or shortly thereafter in Alexandria, Egypt, to meet the needs of Greek-speaking Jews and others, preserves some readings (especially in Exodus, Samuel, and Jeremiah) that appear to be superior to the Masoretic text. Some are supported by copies of the Hebrew texts found at Qumran. The two most famous among other Greek translations of the OT are *Aquila* and *Theodotion* from after A.D. 100.

The Dead Sea Scrolls were written before 100 B.C. and are over 1,000 years older than the basic manuscripts of the Masoretic texts. Biblical manuscripts have been found containing fragments or complete copies from every book of the OT except Esther. The scrolls from Qumran do differ from the Masoretic text in some places (1,375 places in Isaiah), but most are insignificant.

Other versions of the OT such as the Syriac, Old Latin, the Latin Vulgate can be used, but none of these yield many significant variants from the Masoretic texts. The careful work of Hebrew scribes preserved the text of the Hebrew Bible for us essentially as it existed in the time before Christ.

New Testament Text and Versions

The NT was preserved at first mostly on perishable papyrus. Only 94 separate fragments of papyrus NT manuscripts are known. Few of them contain more than a part of a single page of text. The original papyrus manuscripts contained only portions of the NT. The earliest of these date shortly after A.D. 100.

The NT circulated from about A.D. 350 as a single volume on great parchment manuscripts also containing Greek OT and other Christian writings such as *1 and 2 Clement*, *The Shepherd of Hermas*, and the *Letter of Barnabas*. Parchment was made from the skins of animals.

Christian writings that quote the Greek NT also furnish evidence for the text of the NT. Some Christian "fathers," however, were very loose in their quotes or quoted from faulty memories.

By A.D. 150 extensive efforts had been made to translate all the Scriptures into the Old Latin and Syriac. From 200 on, translations appeared in various dialects of the Egyptian languages, the languages of Armenia, Georgia, Ethiopia, Arabia, Nubia, and the areas of Europe.

The Latin Vulgate, produced about A.D. 400 by Jerome, became the Bible of the Latin church. Among the Eastern Orthodox, Greek remained the official language of the Scriptures. During the long period from 400 to 1500, most NT Greek manuscripts used the official text of the Orthodox Church, so today most Greek NT manuscripts are of the type designated as Byzantine, Ecclesiastical, Koine, Standard, or Eastern. The earlier and (for most scholars) the most reliable ones are of the Alexandrian (also called Neutral, Egyptian, and African) type. Printers around 1500 had only those of the Byzantine type.

Since then, we have discovered over 5,300 handwritten copies of all or part of the NT. The process of editing and utilizing all of this material in producing the earliest possible text is the task of textual criticism. A major impetus for this work is missionary. Without textual criticism, no modern Bibles in any language would be possible.

BIBLE, THEOLOGY OF

Study of the doctrinal teachings of the Bible.

God is the central character in the Bible. His work to bring redemption to humans is the central theme. The Bible begins by teaching that God created humans and the world in which they live. Humans are responsible to God because they come from God's creative hand. The first man and woman sinned in deliberate rebellion against God, breaking their fellowship with God. Their sin spread to all their descendants, making sinful alienation from God the number one problem of all human beings. The spread of this sin involves the personal, willful act of each of us so that we are all accountable for our sins.

The Bible traces various stages of God's revelation of Himself: the call of Abraham; the establishment of the covenant with the Israelite community as His chosen people; the institution of the sacrificial system, teaching the people the proper way to approach God for forgiveness; the life, death, and resurrection of Jesus as the provision of forgiveness and regeneration for those dead in sin;

the church as the new covenant community, the redeemed people of God on mission for Him in the world; finally, the life to come: in heaven for the redeemed, and in hell for the unregenerate.

God

The OT has four major emphases concerning God.

(1) The unity of God: One and only one God exists and rules this world.

(2) God's holiness is the qualitative difference between God and all else. The holy God must be treated with reverence.

(3) God's sovereign lordship. Since God is Creator and Ruler of all that exists, He must be obeyed at all costs; and all persons must give account to Him.

(4) God is faithful, not fickle and changeable like the gods of the pagans. The NT completes the doctrine of God by sharpening the focus on God as Father and the primacy of God's love.

People

A person is a very special creature of God, made in God's image. God has created a spiritual being, made primarily to live in fellowship with God and act responsibly in maintaining God's creation. Sin corrupted human nature, leaving all people highly susceptible to sin. Except for Jesus Christ, each person who has lived since Adam and Eve has followed in their footsteps, sinning against God.

Redemption

A person's need for redemption has at least five aspects: People must

(1) have their guilt forgiven and removed;

(2) learn responsible obedience;

(3) learn reverence and respect for God;

(4) learn to live by faith;

(5) learn to live for God's purposes, not selfish whims. The Bible is the unfolding story of how God has met each of these needs through the salvation provided through the life, death, and resurrection of Jesus.

Jesus Christ

Jesus Christ is the eternal Son of God who took on human life, living as one Person who was both God and human on this earth. His coming was prophesied in the OT as the coming of a Messiah, a Suffering Servant who would redeem His people. In the NT, His life unfolded as a revelation from God of what God Himself is like. He spoke the ultimate message from God, in clearer, more forceful ways than God had ever spoken by prophet or priest. He died on the cross and was raised the third day as the ultimate fulfillment of the ancient sacrificial system. New Testament writers saw His death as the ultimate expression of God's forgiving love. Jesus' death and resurrection was the way God conquered sin and death.

Holy Spirit

Jesus ascended to the Father to resume His rightful place at the right hand of God. Then the Holy Spirit of God came as the very presence of Jesus, dwelling in each believer. The Holy Spirit, the agent of regeneration, equips each believer for an effective life of service to God in the church and in the world.

Salvation

Salvation comes to the individual upon a response of faith, receiving the free gift of God's grace. Salvation includes the forgiveness of sin and the regeneration of sinful human nature. Salvation issues in a new style of living for the purposes of God in this world under the leadership of God. Salvation, properly understood, should include a life of spiritual growth, ever moving towards the goal of Christlike living.

Church

The church is the new covenant community, the logical outgrowth of the people of God in the OT era. It is the body of Christ, with Christ as the head of the body, His life flowing out into all parts of the body, as He gives direction to it and works through it in the world just as once He worked through His own physical body in the world.

End Time

The Bible points to a time of ultimate fulfillment when God shall complete what He has been doing in this world from the beginning of creation. Jesus will return to this earth, the kingdom of God will be consummated, the dead will be resurrected, and all persons will have continued existence, with the unregenerate spending eternity in hell and believers in Christ spending eternity with God in heaven.

BIER (Literally, *bed*)

Portable litter or bed upon which a body was placed before burial (2 Sam. 3:31; Luke 7:14); comparable to wooden boards used in Muslim funerals to carry bodies today. Asa's bier (2 Chron. 16:14) was a more elaborate type of burial couch, probably placed in the tomb.

BILDAD (*the Lord loved*)

Friend of Job (Job 2:11); a Shuhite who defended traditionalist theological views.

BILHAH (*unworried*)

Handmaid of Rachel (Gen. 29:29) who became Jacob's concubine and mother of Dan and Naphtali (Gen. 29:29; 30:4-7). See *Patriarchs; Tribes of Israel.*

BILL OF DIVORCEMENT See *Divorce.*

BINDING AND LOOSING

Power and means church has to announce that sin was condemned or forgiven. The keys to the kingdom given Peter symbolized locking or unlocking sins and illustrated his authority in binding or loosing (Matt. 16:19). Later (Matt. 18:18), the same power was given to the apostles and the church as a whole. Whatever the church declared to be wrong or right would have been anticipated and rat-ified in heaven by divine sanction. Heaven sets the standard, earth follows heaven's lead. Believers are responsible to have a forgiving spirit and to teach the conditions of forgiveness (Matt. 6:12; John 20:23). The church is to proclaim the way of salvation; those who accept Him are forgiven, but those who reject Him are condemned. Sins have been washed (loosed) by the blood of Jesus (Rev. 1:5).

BIRDS

Warm-blooded, feathered animals with wings. Hebrew term is used collectively to refer to flying creatures or fowls as well as to winged insects (Gen. 1:20–22,26,28,30; 2:19–20). Genesis 6:20 notes the division of birds into species, and Lev. 20:25 categorizes them as clean or unclean. In Lev. 11:13-19 and Deut. 14:12-18 is a list of specific birds that the Hebrews regarded as unclean and therefore not to be eaten. All birds of prey, including eagles, vultures, hawks, and falcons, were classified as unclean.

A second Hebrew term may refer to birds of every kind (Gen. 7:14; Deut. 4:17), but it usually denotes game birds (Ps. 124:7; Prov. 6:5) or the perching birds (passerines, Ps. 102:7; Dan. 4:12).

Two Greek terms are used for birds in general (Matt. 6:26; 8:20; 13:4; Luke 9:58; 12:24; Acts 10:12; 11:6; Rom. 1:23), to describe the completeness of Babylon's destruction (Rev. 18:2), and flesh-eating fowl (Rev. 19:17,21).

The Bible mentions a great number of birds by name. Translators use different English equivalents to refer to the various birds.

Bittern

Any number of small or medium-sized herons (*Botaurus* and related genera) with characteristic booming cry; KJV translation for animal of desolation (Isa. 14:23; 34:11; Zeph. 2:14). See *Animals, Porcupine.*

Bustard See *Animals, Porcupine.*

Buzzard
Large bird of prey feeding on small animals and kin to hawks, vultures, and kites; NASB, NKJV translation in Lev. 11:13; NRSV, NLT translation in Lev. 11:14. See *Glede, Kite, Osprey, Vulture* below.

Chicken, Cock, Hen, Rooster
Strutting, crowing, nesting, brooding bird, *Zarzir motnayim* (Prov. 30:31). Both tame and wild chickens were known in Bible times, but they appear only in Jesus' comparison of His care for Jerusalem to the care of a mother hen for her nestlings. Greek terms are general terms for birds and nestlings (Matt. 23:37; Luke 13:34). All NT references to the cock (except the mention of "cockcrow" in Mark 13:35) relate to Peter's denial of Christ (Mark 14:30).

Carrion vulture See *Vulture* below.

Cormorant
Large seafowl (*Phalacrocorax carbo carbo*) listed among the unclean birds (Lev. 11:17; Deut. 14:17). Other translators call it a fisher-owl (REB, NKJV).

Crane
KJV translation (Isa. 38:14; Jer. 8:7). Modern translations read, "swift" (NIV, NASB); "dove" (CEV, NCV, TEV, REB in Isa. 38:14); or "thrush" (NIV, TEV, NASB in Jer. 8:7).

Cuckow
KJV translation for an unclean bird (Lev. 11:16; Deut. 14:15); also spelled cuckoo. The grouping with carrion-eating or predatory birds would seem to eliminate the cuckoo since it only eats insects. Modern versions read "sea gull" or "long-eared owl" (REB).

Dove, Turtledove
Smaller species of pigeon. See Gen. 8:8-12; Pss. 55:6; 68:13; Song of Sol. 2:14; 5:2; 6:9; Isa. 38:14; 59:11; Jer. 48:28; Ezek. 7:16; Matt. 10:16. The Spirit of God descended like a dove on Jesus after His baptism (Matt. 3:16; Mark 1:10; Luke 3:22; John 1:32). The turtledove played a significant sacrificial role in the Bible (Gen. 15:9; Lev. 1:14; 5:7,11; 12:6; 14:22, 30;

15:14; Luke 2:24). The turtledove signified the arrival of spring (Song of Sol. 2:12; Jer. 8:7).

Eagle
Several large, unclean (Lev. 11:13; Deut. 14:12) birds of prey active in the daytime rather than at night; largest flying bird of Palestine, may reach a wingspread of 8 feet or more; sometimes translated "vulture"; builds great nests of sticks on rocky crags in the mountains (Job 39:27-28; Jer. 49:16). See Ex. 19:4; Deut. 28:49; 32:11; 2 Sam. 1:23; Jer. 4:13; Prov. 23:5; Isa. 40:31. Often used symbolically (Ex. 19:4; Deut. 32:11; Ezek. 1:10; 10:14; Dan. 7:4; Rev. 4:7; 8:13), the eagle represents God's protection and care.

Falcon
Family of hawks (*Falconidae*); unclean birds according to some translations (Lev. 11:14; Deut. 14:13; Job 28:7; Isa. 34:15). See *Kite* below.

Glede
KJV term for unclean bird of prey (Deut. 14:13). Others translate: buzzard (NRSV, NLT); kite (REB); red kite (NIV, NASB, NKJV). Hebrew root suggests bird with keen eyesight, for example a member of the hawk family; may be red kite (*Milvus milvus*).

Gull
Unclean (Lev. 11:16; Deut. 14:15), long- winged, web-footed aquatic bird (family *Laridae*). See *Cuckow* above.

Hawk
Family of unclean birds of prey active in daytime (Lev. 11:16; Deut. 14:15; Job 39:26).

Hen See *Chicken* above.

Heron
Wading birds with long necks and legs (*Areidae*), regarded as unclean (Lev. 11:18; Deut. 14:18). REB reads: "comorant."

Hoopoe
Old World bird of family *Upupidae* having plumed head crest and long, slender, curved bill. Identity of the unclean bird of Lev. 11:19; Deut. 14:18 is disputed: lapwing (KJV); hoo-

poe (modern English translations); water hen (earliest Greek); woodcock (Targum).

Jackdaw

Black and grey bird (*Corvus monedula*) related to but smaller than the common crow (Isa. 34:11; Zeph. 2:14 or in Lev. 11:18, NKJV). Meaning of Hebrew term is obscure. Other identifications include: cormorant; hawk; species of owl; pelican; or wild bird.

Kite

Bird of prey, best described as a scavenger of the *accipitridae* family (hawk), the subfamily of *milvinae* of the genus *milvus;* medium sized with red coloring; considered unclean, not to be eaten (Lev. 11:14; Deut. 14:13), symbol of desolation and doom (Isa. 34:15). See *Falcon, Glede, Hawk* above.

Lapwing

Shore bird (*Vanellus vanellus*) with short bill and crest of feathers on its head (Lev. 11:19; Deut. 14:18, KJV); known for irregular flapping flight and shrill cry. Modern translations read, hoopoe.

Ospray, Osprey

Large, flesh-eating hawk included in lists of unclean birds (Lev. 11:13; Deut. 14:12, KJV, NLT, NRSV; Lev. 11:18, NCV, NIV, REB). Other possibilities include: black vulture (NCV, NIV); bearded vulture (REB); and buzzard (NASB, NKJV).

Ossifrage

Large vultures including bearded vulture, osprey, and giant petrel; unclean bird (Lev. 11:13; Deut. 14:12, KJV). Other translations identify as black vulture (REB) or vulture (NASB, NIV, NRSV).

Ostrich

Largest of birds; unclean (Lev. 11:16; Deut. 14:15); swift, flightless fowl. Job 39:13-18 characterizes the ostrich. See Lam. 4:3. See *Owl* below.

Owl

Bird of prey, order *Strigiformes;* generally nocturnal; unclean. NRSV mentions two species of owl, the little and great owl (Deut. 14:16). KJV adds the owl of the desert (Lev. 11:18; Deut. 14:16) and screech owl (Isa. 34:14). NIV (compare REB) mentions six species: horned owl (Lev. 11:16; Deut. 14:15); screech owl (Lev. 11:16; Deut. 14:15); little owl (Lev. 11:17; Deut. 14:15); great owl; white owl; and desert owl (Lev. 11:18; Deut. 14:16). Owls nesting in ruins are a common image of desolation (Ps. 102:6; Isa. 34:11,15; Zeph. 2:14).

Partridge

Stout-bodied, medium-sized game bird with variegated plumage. See 1 Sam. 26:20; compare Jer. 17:11 in translations.

Pigeon

General term for widely distributed subfamily (*Columbinae*) used for sacrificial offerings and rituals (Lev. 1:14; 5:7,11; 12:6,8; 14:22, 30; compare Luke 2:24). See *Dove* above.

Peacock See *Animals, Wild.*

Pelican

Large, web-footed birds with gigantic bills having expandable pouches attached to the lower jaw. Hebrew in Lev. 11:18; Deut. 14:17 suggests bird that regurgitates its food to feed its young. Other passages (Ps. 102:6; Isa. 34:11; Zeph. 2:14) associate the same Hebrew term with deserted ruins, an unlikely habitat for the pelican. Suggestions include jackdaw (NKJV), owl (NIV, NCV, REB, NRSV), and vulture (RSV).

Quail

Mottled brown migratory game bird smaller than North American bobwhite quails; God used them to provide food for Israel in the wilderness (Ex. 16:13; Num. 11:31-32; Ps. 105:40). Enormous numbers of quail migrate north during the spring after wintering in Africa.

Raven

Unclean, scavenger bird (Lev. 11:15; Deut. 14:14) conspicuous because of its black color (Song of Sol. 5:11); member of crow family; example of God's care for His creation (Job 38:41; Ps. 147:9; Luke 12:24); first bird Noah sent from ark following flood (Gen. 8:7) and bird God sent to sustain Elijah (1 Kings 17:4-6). See Prov. 30:17; Luke 12:24.

Rooster See *Chicken* above.

Sea Gull See *Gull* above.

Sparrow

Member of finch family; Hebrew term carries general meaning "bird" (Ps. 8:8; Ezek. 17:23, NASB, NIV, NRSV); ceremonially clean, sometimes eaten by the poor. Jesus used God's care for the sparrows (Matt. 10:29-31; Luke 12:6-7) as assurance for human beings. See Ps. 84:3; 102:7; Prov. 26:2.

Stork

Large, long-legged, unclean (Lev. 11:19) bird related to heron; known for care they take of their young and for returning each year to the same nesting area. During migration from Africa in winter to Europe in spring, they stop in Palestine. See Job 39:13; Ps. 104:17; Jer. 8:7; Zech. 5:9.

Swallow

Small, long-winged songbird that migrates to Palestine from March until winter. It made nests in the temple (Ps. 84:3) and was often seen with the common sparrow. It was sometimes confused with the swift. See Prov. 26:2; Isa. 38:14; Jer. 8:7.

Swan

Unclean bird (Lev. 11:18; Deut. 14:16, KJV). Others translate: "the desert owl" or "pelican" (NRSV) or "the white owl" (NIV, NASB, NKJV, NCV, NLT).

Swift

Bird similar but unrelated to swallow (Isa. 38:14, NIV; Jer. 8:7, NASB, NIV). Others translate "swallow" (KJV, NRSV). Some commentators think a bulbul or wryneck (REB) is meant; bulbul (*Pycnonotus Reichenovi*) may be best linguistic guess. See *Crane* above.

Thrush

Small songbirds of family *Turdidae* used in NIV, NASB, TEV of Isa. 38:14; Jer. 8:7. See *Crane* above.

Vulture

Several different unclean birds of prey that feed on dead animals (REB, Lev. 11:13-14: giffon-vulture, black vulture, bearded vulture; to which NASB, NKJV add carrion vulture (Lev. 11:18; Deut. 14:17). See Job 15:23; Prov. 30:17; Hos. 8:1; Mic. 1:16; Hab. 1:8; Matt. 24:28; Luke 17:37.

Wryneck

Woodpeckers with peculiar writhing of their necks (*Jynx torquilla* and *Jynx ruficollis*). REB translation in Jer. 8:7. See *Crane* above.

In the Sermon on the Mount, Jesus summarized one of the greatest lessons we can learn from the birds of the air (Matt. 6:25-26).

BIRDS OF ABOMINATION

List of 20 birds not to be consumed by Israelites (Lev. 11:13-19; Deut. 14:12-18); reason for exclusion of these birds is unclear. Suggestions include: association with worship of idols; ate flesh that contained blood; had contact with corpses (Lev. 7:26; 17:13-14; 21:1-4,11; 22:4; Num. 5:2-3; 6:6-11).

BIRTH

Act or process of bringing forth young from the womb. Midwives were often used in the birthing process (Gen. 35:17; 38:28; Ex. 1:15) as were birthstools (Ex. 1:16; see *Birthstool*). The infant's navel cord was cut immediately after birth; the child was cleaned, rubbed with salt, and wrapped in cloths (Ezek. 16:4). Often the child was named at birth (Gen. 21:3; 29:32,35; 30:6-8). The woman was considered ritually unclean for a period of from 40 to 80 days following birth (Lev. 12:1-8; see Luke 2:22).

The birthing process was used figuratively for the relationship of God to His people (Deut. 32:18; compare Job 38:29; Isa. 66:7-9). According to Jesus, it is just as necessary to be born of the Spirit as it is to be born of a woman (John 3:1-7).

BIRTH CONTROL

In response to God's command in the garden of Eden to "be fruitful and multiply, and fill the earth" (Gen. 1:28; compare Gen. 9:1,7), men and women in ancient Israel and Judaea placed a high value on human reproductivity (1 Sam. 1:8; Ps. 127:3-5). Emotional and economic security in ancient Israel was expressed through large families (Ps. 113:9) and protected by legal structures and customs which ensured genealogical continuity (Deut. 25:5-10; Ruth 4:5; Mark 12:18-23). One's personal identity was largely based on kinship and lineage so that a woman who was barren was considered incomplete (Gen. 30:22-23; 1 Sam. 1:5-6). For these reasons, Onan's attempt at birth control was displeasing to both God and his family (Gen. 38:8-10).

Eunuchs were fairly common in the ancient world (e.g., Matt. 19:12; Acts 8:27). Castration was aimed not at birth control but performed for a variety of reasons such as punishment, to mark religious devotion, or to qualify a male for certain jobs which required undistracted loyalty, such as supervising women of the royal household (Esther 1:10-12; 2:3). However, Mosaic law recognized that castration was contrary to the created order and banned castrated persons from religious service (Deut. 23:1). This ban was evidently relaxed by the time of Isaiah (Isa. 56:3-5).

BIRTH DEFECTS

The Bible records four clear cases of birth defects: a man "blind from birth" (John 9:1), a man "crippled from birth" (Acts 3:2), a man "crippled in his feet, who was lame from birth" (Acts 14:8), and a eunuch (male sterility) "born that way" (Matt. 19:12).

A variety of diseases and physical handicaps are mentioned in the Bible with no note as to their origin or cause (e.g., Matt. 9:2; Mark 7:32). Leviticus 21:18-21 lists physical deformities which disqualified a male descendant of Aaron from serving in the sanctuary of the Lord; these include blindness, lameness, disfigurement, dwarfishness, eye defects, and damaged testicles. In many instances such deformities must have been congenital.

The Bible is clear that while the development of a fetus may not be understood by people (Eccl. 11:5), it is both known and guided by God (Job 10:11; 31:15; Ps. 119:73; 139:13-16; Isa. 44:2; 46:3; 49:5; Jer. 1:5; Rom. 8:28). For this reason, every person must be embraced as a whole person in the eyes of God.

BIRTHRIGHT

Special privileges of firstborn male child in a family including a double portion of the estate as an inheritance and the father's major blessing. See Gen. 25:29-34; Deut. 21:15-17.

BIRTHSTOOL

Object on which a woman sat during labor (Ex. 1:16); perhaps of Egyptian origin; same Hebrew word is translated "potter's wheel" (Jer. 18:3).

BISHOP (*inspector, watchman,* or *overseer*)

Ministerial position in church (Acts 20:28; Phil. 1:1; 1 Tim. 3:1-2; Titus 1:7; 1 Pet. 2:25; compare Acts 1:20). Greek word was used for the finance officers of Greek guilds and of the officers Athens sent to its subject-states. Finance officers administered revenues for Greek temples.

Jesus is "the Shepherd and Bishop of your souls" (1 Pet. 2:25). First Timothy 3:1-7 and Titus 1:6-9 give qualifications for a "bishop."

Paul told the Ephesian "elders" (Acts 20:28) the Holy Spirit made them "overseers" "to feed" or "shepherd" (verb related to the noun *pastor*) the church of the Lord. From this, many conclude that in Paul's time "elder," "bishop," and "pastor" were terms used to describe three different functions of the same Christian leader, not three distinct ministerial offices. Ephesus (Acts 20:28) and Philippi (Phil. 1:1) had more than one bishop.

BIT

Metal bar with loops on either end for attaching the reins fastened to the muzzle end of the horse's bridle and inserted in the horse's mouth between the teeth to control the horse (Jas. 1:26; 3:2; see 2 Kings 19:28; Isa. 37:29).

BITHRON (ravine)

Name for ravine or mountain pass (2 Sam. 2:29, KJV, NIV, NKJV) or common noun for "forenoon" (NRSV, TEV, NASB, REB, NLT, CEV, NCV).

BITHYNIA

District in northern Asia Minor (part of modern Turkey). See Acts 16:7; 1 Pet. 1:1.

BITTER HERBS

Herbs eaten with Passover meal (Ex. 12:8; Num. 9:11) symbolizing bitter experiences of slavery in Egypt. Some have suggested that the bitter herbs comprised a salad including lettuce, endive, chicory, and dandelion.

BITTER WATER

Water drunk by a woman suspected of adultery (Num. 5:11-31); combination of holy water and dust from the sanctuary floor. If she were innocent, the water would not harm her, and she would conceive children as a blessing; if guilty, her "thigh would rot" and her "body swell."

BITTERN See Birds.

BITUMEN

Mineral pitch or asphalt (KJV, "slime"; NASB, NIV, "tar pits") found in solid black lumps in the cretaceous limestone on the west bank of the Dead Sea (see Gen. 14:10) and used as a mortar in setting bricks in the buildings and ziggurats in Mesopotamia (see Gen. 11:3) and as a caulking for rafts and basket boats on the Euphrates (see Ex. 2:3; compare Gen. 6:14).

BLACK See Colors.

BLACK PEOPLE, BIBLICAL PERSPECTIVES

Black people in America have a deep affinity for the Bible that has evolved despite the ways the Bible was used from 1620 to 1865 to reinforce attitudes of subservience and servility and to keep the slaves under control.

During the "Great Awakenings" (1740s and 1798–1820), they heard the Bible used to proclaim the good news of salvation. This new life in Christ surpassed anything they had ever known. Some slaves felt the divine call to preach. For those given permission to preach, the Bible became the textbook to learn to read.

Black people memorized stories of deliverance and hope. Embellished, these became daily spiritual substance. Black people identified with the Israelites moving from Egyptian servitude to the Promised Land. They took courage in God's provisions during the wilderness wanderings. The miraculous battles of Joshua, Gideon, Samson, and David inspired them. Black sermonic themes from those days until the 1950s emphasized God's deliverance as illustrated in Daniel and "the Hebrew Boys"; Ezekiel and the Valley of Dry Bones; the messianic passages of the prophets; the miracles of Jesus; His death, burial, and power over death.

God-called men, often denied formal training, heard others read from the Bible and committed those verses to memory. Black preachers became masters at "telling the story." Black people also "sang the story." Bible stories became the substance of spirituals and jubilee songs.

In the 1960s and '70s the quest for Black history and Black pride led to in-depth studies of Bible personalities believed to be black or with African identification. Black people express pride in the rescue of the prophet Jeremiah by Ebedmelech, an Ethiopian (Jer. 38:7-13; 39:15-18). Simon of Cyrene, identified as an African, was considered heroic for helping Jesus carry the cross (Mark 15:21). Black people felt included in the embryonic spread of Christianity when seeing that representatives from African countries were among those upon whom the Holy Spirit fell at Pentecost (Acts 2:5-11,39) and that Christianity did not originally come to Africa through Western missionaries but through people from Pentecost, the influence of the powerful government official whom Philip baptized (Acts 8:26-37), and from the early church fathers—9 of the 18 church fathers being African (Clement, Origen, Tertullian, Cyprian, Dionysius, Athanasius, Didymus, Augustine, and Cyril).

The only Bible passages some black people have difficulty with are those that seem to ignore the problem of slavery as an evil: 1 Cor. 7:20-24; Eph. 6:5-9; Col. 3:22-25; Titus 2:9-10; Philem.; 1 Pet. 2:18-25. These passages have become less objectionable when viewed as an "interim ethic." Paul expected the return of Christ to be so immediate that he gave little place for social change.

In more recent years, the Bible is used more for a practical guide in dealing with issues from a Black perspective. These issues include salvation, moral guidance, ethical behavior, and spiritual nurture.

BLAINS See *Boil.*

BLASPHEMY

Improper action with regard to using God's name; an attitude of disrespect expressed in an act directed against God's character.

Blasphemy involves the actual pronunciation of the name of God with an attitude of disrespect (Lev. 24:14-16; Neh. 9:18,26). Nathan accused David of making a mockery of God's commands and giving an occasion for the enemies of Israel to blaspheme—to misunderstand the true nature of God (2 Sam. 12:14; compare army of the Assyrians, 2 Kings 19:6,22,35-37; Isa. 37:6,23; 52:5-6; Ezek. 35:12-15).

The NT broadens the concept of blasphemy to include actions against Christ and the church as the body of Christ. Jewish leaders regarded

Jesus as a blasphemer (Matt. 26:65; Mark 2:7; 14:64; Luke 22:69) for His claims to forgive sins and be the messiah. The real blasphemers were those who denied the messianic claims of Jesus and rejected His unity with the Father (Mark 15:29; Luke 22:65; 23:39).

Persecutions against Christians are labeled as blasphemous acts (1 Tim. 1:13; 1 Pet. 4:4; Rev. 2:9). Christians must avoid conduct that might give an occasion for blasphemy, especially in the area of attitude and speech (Eph. 4:31; Col. 3:8; 1 Tim. 6:4; Titus 3:2).

Blasphemy is a sin that can be forgiven. However, blasphemy against the Holy Spirit cannot be forgiven (Matt. 12:32; Mark 3:29; Luke 12:10). See *Unpardonable Sin.*

BLASTING

Result of hot east winds which blow across Palestine for days at a time (Deut. 28:22, KJV and RSV; other versions read "blight"), drying up vegetation and ruining crops (Isa. 37:27; see Pss. 90:5-6; 102:3-4; Isa. 40:6-8); one of the great natural calamities (1 Kings 8:37; 2 Chron. 6:28) and a judgment of God upon the disobedient (Deut. 28:22; Amos 4:9; Hag. 2:17).

BLEACH See *Fuller.*

BLEMISH

Condition that disqualifies an animal as a sacrifice (Lev. 22:17-25) or a man from priestly service (Lev. 21:17-24). In the NT, Christ is the perfect sacrifice (without blemish, Heb. 9:14; 1 Pet. 1:19). See Eph. 5:27; Phil. 2:15; 2 Pet. 3:14.

BLESSEDNESS, BLESSING AND CURSING

The act of releasing divine powers which bring to pass the content of the speech of blessing or cursing based on the relationship of the party affected and God. In the relationship humans bless God by praising Him while they ask Him to bring benefits to their lives and remove such from their enemies, seen also as His enemies. Through blessing, God maintains and enriches creation.

Old Testament individuals might bless God (Gen. 9:26; Ex. 18:10; Ruth 4:14; Ps. 68:19). God also blesses men and women (Gen. 12:23; Num. 23:20; Ps. 109:28; Isa. 61:9). Persons might also bless one another (Gen. 27:33; Deut. 7:14; 1 Sam. 25:33), or they might bless things (Deut. 28:4; 1 Sam. 25:33; Prov. 5:18). Normally, however, when used as a verb, the word is in the passive voice ("be blessed"), suggesting only God has the power to bless.

Words of blessing are used as a salutation or greeting, with an invocation of blessing as a stronger greeting than "peace" (Gen. 48:20). Blessings may be used in meeting (Gen. 47:7), departing (Gen. 24:60), by messengers (1 Sam. 25:14), in gratitude (Job 31:20), as a morning salutation (Prov. 27:14), congratulations for prosperity (Gen. 12:3), in homage (2 Sam. 14:22), and in friendliness (2 Sam. 21:3).

The special characteristic of NT blessing is its expression of the religious joy people experience from being certain of salvation and thus of membership in the kingdom of God. Jesus emphasized blessedness in the Beatitudes of the Sermon on the Mount (Matt. 5:3-11) and His congratulations to those who respond positively to the kingdom of God (Matt. 23:39; 24:46; Mark 11:9; Luke 10:23; 14:15).

An extended curse formula in Deuteronomy contrasted blessing and cursing (Deut. 27:15-26; see 28:16-19; Mal. 2:2). Curse could describe persons lightly esteemed (2 Sam. 6:22) or mean "to make contemptible"; hence, to curse persons (Gen. 12:3; Ex. 21:17). The word also means to treat with contempt (2 Sam. 19:44; Isa. 23:9) or to dishonor (Isa. 8:21).

The Lord was the source of all blessing, and people sought in worship to express gratitude for that blessing; indeed, to pray for the continuation of such blessing (Ps. 103:1-2). Central to the covenant

renewal ceremony was the blessing (Deut. 28:3-6). Aaron's benediction both proclaims and petitions the Lord's blessing on the congregation in right relationship with God (Num. 6:24-26).

BLIGHT See *Blasting.*

BLINDNESS

Inability to see; very common in Bible times. The suffering of the blind person was made worse by the common belief that the affliction was due to sin (John 9:1-3).

Blind persons had little opportunity to earn a living and frequently became beggars (Mark 10:46). A blind man was ineligible to become a priest (Lev. 21:18). See Deut. 27:18; Lev. 19:14.

The most common cause was infection. Trachoma was probably prevalent in ancient times. Leprosy could also cause blindness. Almost no effective treatment was available to those who suffered from diseases of the eye and blindness. Jesus frequently healed blind persons (Matt. 9:27-31; 12:22; 20:30-34; Mark 10:46-52; John 9:1-7).

The Bible addresses spiritual blindness as the great human problem (Isa. 42:19; 56:10; Matt. 15:14; 23:16-26). Jesus came to reverse the situation, making it clear who had spiritual sight and who was spiritually blind (John 9:39-41; compare 2 Pet. 1:5-9; Rev. 3:17). People are blinded by the "god of this world" (2 Cor. 4:4; see 1 John 2:11).

BLOOD

Life-providing liquid that flows from the wounded human body; so intimately associated with physical life that Israelites were prohibited from eating blood (Deut. 12:23-24; compare Gen. 9:4-6). A person offering a sacrifice showed that reconciliation with God involved life—the basic element of human existence (Lev. 17:11; see Ex. 12:7,22-23; 24:3).

"Flesh and blood" designates a human being (Matt. 16:17; Gal. 1:6; Eph. 6:12; as sinful in 1 Cor. 15:50).

Eating "blood and flesh" is powerful metaphorical language for sharing in the life that Jesus bestows (John 6:57).

The term *blood of Christ* designates in the NT the atoning death of Christ. Atonement refers to the basis and process by which estranged people become at one with God. At His last Passover, Jesus inaugurated the New Covenant in His blood "shed for many for the remission of sins" (Matt. 26:28; compare Luke 22:20). Jesus died as a sin-bearer that we might live for righteousness and become healed (1 Pet. 2:24). See *Atonement.*

BLOOD, AVENGER OF See *Avenger; Bloodguilt; Cities of Refuge.*

BLOOD, FIELD OF See *Aceldama.*

BLOODGUILT

Guilt usually incurred by killing a person who did not deserve to die (Deut. 19:10; Jer. 26:15; Jonah 1:14), making a person ritually unclean (Num. 35:33-34). Killing in self-defense and execution of criminals were exempted from bloodguilt (Ex. 22:2; Lev. 20:9).

The community shared the guilt of the murderer until the guilty party had paid the penalty of death. No other penalty or sacrifice could substitute for the death of the guilty party, nor was there any need for sacrifice once the murderer had been killed (Num. 35:33; Deut. 21:8-9). See *Avenger.*

Judas incurred bloodguilt by betraying Jesus ("innocent blood," Matt. 27:4). Those who called for the crucifixion accepted the burden of bloodguilt for themselves and their children (Matt. 27:25). Pilate accepted no responsibility for shedding innocent blood (Matt. 27:24).

BLUE See *Colors.*

BOANERGES (*sons of thunder*)

Name Jesus gave to James and John (Mark 3:17); may indicate thunderous temperament these brothers apparently had. See *Disciples, Apostles.*

BOAR See *Animals.*

BOAT See *Ships and Boats.*

BOAZ (*lively*)

(1) Hero of Book of Ruth; wealthy relative of Naomi's husband who married Ruth and became great-grandfather of David (Matt. 1:5; Luke 3:32). See *Ruth.*

(2) Left or north pillar Solomon set up in the temple (1 Kings 7:21) whose function is not known. See *Jachin and Boaz.*

BODY

Visible, material aspect of a person. Body and soul do not form two separate substances; they comprise one individual human in inseparable union (Matt. 6:25).

Humans do not have bodies; they are bodies (compare Gen. 2:24). See *Flesh.*

The Bible then makes basic claims about physical human existence.

(1) The body is our realm of personal evaluation. The body is the place of proper worship (Rom. 12:1), the Temple of the Holy Spirit (1 Cor. 6:19-20), and thus is to be disciplined (1 Cor. 9:27). The inner spiritual life is not to be played off against the outer, physical life (Matt. 6:22; 1 Cor. 6:12-20; 2 Cor. 4:7,10). The goal is not liberation of a "divine" soul from the body but the placing of the body in service for God (2 Cor. 5:10).

(2) Physical love is a gift of the Creator (Gen. 2:23-24; Song of Sol. 1–8). Humans express love with their entire person, not only with their sexual organs. Because the body of the Christian belongs to the Creator, Redeemer, and Holy Spirit, sexual sin is forbidden for the Christian (1 Cor. 6:12-20).

(3) The earthly human stands under the power of sin and of death. All long for redemption (Rom. 7:24; 8:23). Redemption is guaranteed

only by God, who continues to care for the body and soul of humans even after death (Matt. 10:28) and makes the gift of eternal life (Rom. 6:23; see John 1:14; Rom. 7:4). The body will be redeemed through the resurrection of the dead (Rom. 6:5; 8:11; 1 Cor. 15:35-49; 2 Cor. 5:1-10; Phil. 3:21).

(4) Jesus Christ had a physical, earthly body which was crucified in front of the gates of Jerusalem (Mark 15:20-47; Col. 1:22; Heb. 13:11-12). The body of Christ also designates the body of the Crucified One "given for you," with which the church is united in the celebration of the Lord's Supper (Mark 14:24; 1 Cor. 10:16; 11:24).

(5) The church is the body of Christ. See *Body of Christ*.

BODY OF CHRIST

Illustration Paul used to teach how the church is like a living human body with Christ the head exercising authority over the church to guide it (Rom. 12:4-8; Eph. 5:23-32; Col. 1:18). Every believer, like every part of the human body, has individual functions to perform.

All individuals are of equal importance to God, as every body part is important to the body (1 Cor. 12:12-31). When the body suffers, it is an extension of the sufferings of Christ (Col. 1:24); a puffed up (fleshy) mind has lost connection with the Head (Col. 2:16-19).

God calls leaders into His church to equip members to build up the body of Christ (Eph. 4:11-16). Because a believer and Christ are unified as one body and spirit (1 Cor. 6:15-17), sexual immorality is wrong. Members (Eph. 4:25; Col. 3:12-15) are to be kind, tenderhearted, and forgiving to one another. See *Body; Church*.

BOIL

General term for inflamed swellings of the skin; mentioned in connection with blains (KJV; an inflamatory swelling or sore) in the sixth plague on Egypt (Ex. 9:9-10); may be malig-

nant pustule of cutaneous anthrax. Hezekiah's boil (2 Kings 20:7; Isa. 38:21) is identified as a furuncle—localized swelling and inflammation of the skin caused by the infection of a hair follicle that discharges pus and has a central core of dead tissue. The boils suffered by Job (Job 2:7) have been identified with smallpox or with treponematosis (a parasitic infection).

BOLDNESS

Courageous manner of those who preach the gospel (Acts 2:29; 4:13,31; 9:27-29; 13:46; 14:3; 18:26; 19:8; 26:26; 28:31; see 1 Thess. 2:2; Phil. 1:20). Boldness describes the confidence with which Christians can now approach God because of the redeeming work of Christ (2 Cor. 3:4-6,12; Heb. 10:19; 1 John 2:28; 4:17).

BOLLED

KJV translation (Ex. 9:31) for having seed pods. Some see the flax here as either in bud or in blossom.

BOLSTER

KJV translation for "the place where the head is while sleeping" (1 Sam. 19:13,16; 26:7,11,12,16); REB, NRSV, "at his head" (see NIV, NASB).

BOND

Something that restricts freedom, especially chains or other materials used to shackle prisoners or slaves (Judg. 15:14; 1 Kings 14:10; Pss. 107:14; 116:16; Luke 8:29; Philem. 13). Used figuratively to speak of the bonds of wickedness or sin (Isa. 58:6; Luke 13:16; Acts 8:23), of affliction and judgment (Isa. 28:22; 52:2; Jer. 30:8; Nah. 1:13), the authority of kings (Job 12:18; Ps. 2:3), the obligation to keep the covenant (Jer. 2:20; 5:5; see Col. 2:14), the bonds of peace and love (Eph. 4:3; Col. 3:14), and the bonds of an evil woman (Eccl. 7:26).

BONES

Skeletal remains of humans (Gen. 50:25; Ex. 13:19; 1 Sam. 31:13). Metaphorically, "rottenness of bones" signified one whose wife caused shame and confusion (Prov. 12:4; 14:30) or could refer to dejectedness and anticipation of approaching evil (Hab. 3:16). "Shaking of bones" denoted fear (Job 4:14) or sadness (Jer. 23:9). "Burning of the bones" indicated grief and depression (Ps. 102:3; Lam. 1:13; compare Jer. 20:9). "Dryness of bones" meant poor health (Prov. 17:22). "Bone of my bones" may mean having the same nature or being the nearest relation (Gen. 2:23; 2 Sam. 5:1).

BONNET

Conical-shaped cap placed on the head of the priest at the time of investiture; made of fine white linen (Ex. 28:40; 29:9; 39:28; Lev. 8:13). See *Cloth, Clothing.*

BOOK OF LIFE

Heavenly record (Luke 10:20; Heb. 12:23) written by God before the foundation of the world (Rev. 13:8; 17:8) containing the names of those who are destined because of God's grace and their faithfulness to participate in God's heavenly kingdom. Those whose names are in the book have been born into God's family through Jesus Christ (Heb. 12:23; Rev. 13:8); remain faithful in worship of God (Rev. 13:8; 17:8); are untouched by the practice of abomination and falsehood (Rev. 21:27); are faithful through tribulation (Rev. 3:5); and are fellow workers in the work of Jesus Christ (Phil. 4:3). The book of life will be used along with the books of judgment at the final judgment to separate the righteous and the wicked for their respective eternal destinies (Rev. 20:12,15; 21:27).

The OT refers to a record kept by God of those who are a part of His people (Ex. 32:32; Isa. 4:3; Dan. 12:1; Mal. 3:16). As in Revelation (3:5), God can blot out the names of those in the book (Ex. 32:32; Ps. 69:28). In the OT this may simply mean people not in the book die, leaving the list of the living. Those whose names are

written in the book are destined for life in a restored Jerusalem (Isa. 4:3) and deliverance through future judgment (Dan. 12:1). See *Apocalyptic; Book(s); Eschatology.*

BOOK(S)

Scroll; document written on parchment or papyrus and then rolled up; letter (1 Kings 21:8) or longer literary effort (Dan. 9:2). See *Writing; Letter.* Several books are mentioned in the Bible:

Book of the Covenant
Book Moses read from during making of covenant between God and Israel on Mount Sinai (Ex. 24:7; see 2 Kings 23:2,21; 2 Chron. 34:30); included at least material in Ex. 20:23–23:33.

Book of the Law
Document Hilkiah, the high priest, found in the temple under Josiah (2 Kings 22:8). Josiah based his reforms on this book (2 Kings 23).

Book of the Wars of the Lord
Book quoted in Num. 21:14-15 (Num. 21:17-18,27-30 may also come from this book) describing territory God conquered for Israel; probably collection of poems crediting God for the conquest under Moses and Joshua.

Books of Joshua
Joshua wrote one book detailing the allotment of Canaan to the Israelite tribes (Josh. 18:9) and a book similar to the "Book of the Covenant" listed above (Josh. 24:25-26).

Book of Jashar (or Upright)
Book quoted in Joshua's poetic address to the sun and the moon (Josh. 10:12-13) and David's lament for Saul and Jonathan (2 Sam. 1:17-27); probably consisted of poems on important events in Israel's history collected during the time of David or Solomon.

Book of the Acts of Solomon
(1 Kings 11:41) Probably a biographical document that included such stories as Solomon's judgment between the two harlots (1 Kings 3:16-28), his administrative arrange-

ments (1 Kings 4:1-19), and the Queen of Sheba's visit (1 Kings 10:1-13).

Book of the Chronicles of the Kings of Israel

Perhaps a continuous journal compiled by scribes from various sources, but not to be confused with 1 and 2 Chronicles in the Bible; contained more complete information on the reigns of the kings of Israel (1 Kings 14:19; 15:31; 16:5,14,20,27; 22:39; 2 Kings 1:18; 10:34; 13:8,12; 14:15, 28; 15:11, 15,21,26,31).

Book of the Chronicles of the Kings of Judah

Source similar to book of the chronicles of the kings of Israel, not to be confused with 1 and 2 Chronicles in the Bible; contained more complete information on reigns of kings of Judah (1 Kings 14:29; 15:7,23; 22:45; 2 Kings 8:23; 12:19; 14:18; 15:6,36; 16:19; 20:20; 21:17,25; 23:28; 24:5).

Book of the Kings of Israel

(1 Chron. 9:1; 2 Chron. 20:34), the "Book of the Kings of Israel and Judah" (2 Chron. 27:7; 35:27; 36:8), the "Book of the Kings of Judah and Israel" (2 Chron. 16:11; 25:26; 28:26; 32:32), the "Acts of the Kings of Israel" (2 Chron. 33:18), and the "Commentary on the Book of the Kings" (2 Chron. 24:27). These may all be references to the same work, something like a "Midrash of the Kings," containing books of the chronicles of the kings of Israel and Judah listed above or material very similar to them.

Also mentioned in 1 and 2 Chronicles are books of various prophets: the "Book of Samuel the Seer" (1 Chron. 29:29), the "Book of Nathan the prophet" (1 Chron. 29:29; 2 Chron. 9:29), the "Book of Gad the Seer" (1 Chron. 29:29), the "Prophecy of Ahijah the Shilonite" (2 Chron. 9:29), the "Visions of Iddo the Seer against Jeroboam the Son of Nebat" (2 Chron. 9:29), the "Book of Shemaiah the Prophet and Iddo the Seer" (2 Chron. 12:15), the "Story of the Prophet Iddo" (2 Chron. 13:22), the

"Book of Jehu the Son of Hanani" (2 Chron. 20:34), the "Acts of Uzziah" (2 Chron. 26:22; written by Isaiah), the "Vision of Isaiah the Prophet" (2 Chron. 32:32), and the "Saying of the Seers" (2 Chron. 33:19). All of these, except for the last, may have been part of the "Midrash of the Kings."

Various other works are also mentioned in 1 and 2 Chronicles: genealogies of the tribe of Gad (1 Chron. 5:17), the "Chronicles of King David" (1 Chron. 27:24), an untitled work containing the plan for the temple (1 Chron. 28:19), works on the organization of the Levites written by David and Solomon (2 Chron. 35:4), and lamentations for the death of Josiah by Jeremiah and others (2 Chron. 35:25).

Book of the Chronicles

Work which contained genealogies and possibly other historical material (Neh. 7:5; 12:23) but was distinct from 1 and 2 Chronicles.

Books by the Prophets

Isaiah (Isa. 30:8 compare 8:16) and Jeremiah (Jer. 25:13; 30:2; 36; 45:1; 51:60, 63) are said to have written books, perhaps the first stages of the collections of their prophecies we now have.

Book (of Records) of the Chronicles or Book of Memorable Deeds

Royal archives of Persia which contained, among other things, the way in which Mordecai saved the life of King Ahasuerus (Esther 2:20-23; 6:1; 10:2; compare Ezra 4:15).

Book of Remembrance

(Mal. 3:16) Probably same as the Book of Life (see *Book of Life*).

Scripture (Book) of Truth

(Dan. 10:21) Probably same as Book of Life (see *Book of Life*).

BOOT

Soldier's footwear (Isa. 9:5, booted Assyrian warrior; KJV translates rare Hebrew word as "battle"; compare NLT). Assyrian reliefs depict soldiers wearing leather boots laced up to the knee in contrast to sandals worn by

Israelite soldiers. God's Messiah promised full victory even over the more impressively dressed army.

BOOTH

Temporary shelter constructed for cattle (Gen. 33:17) and people (Jonah 4:5), especially for soldiers on the battlefield (2 Sam. 11:11; 1 Kings 20:12,16). Israel after an invasion is compared to a deserted booth in a vineyard (Isa. 1:8; see Job 27:18). The booths at the Feast of Booths were made of twigs woven together (Lev. 23:40-43; Neh. 8:15).

BOOTHS, FEAST OF See *Festivals.*

BOOTY

Things taken by individuals in battle; anything that might be of value or use to the captor, including persons (Num. 31:53; Jer. 15:13; Ezek. 25:7). Booty was taken by individual soldiers whereas spoil was plunder taken by the victor nation as a right of conquest.

BORROW

To accept something, especially money, from another person with intention of returning it at agreed on time. In Hebrew culture borrowing indicated economic hardship, not a strategy for expanding business or household (Neh. 5:1-5; see Lev. 25:35-37).

In Matt. 5:42, Jesus cites generosity "from him that would borrow thee" as one example of an unexpected, unselfish loving response to others' demands and abuses. See *Banking.*

BOSSED, BOSSES

Knobs on the flat surfaces of shields (Job 15:26).

BOTCH

Old English term for boil (Deut. 28:27,35, KJV).

BOTTLE

Vessel for carrying liquids; usually made of animal skins although glass

bottles were known; modern versions read "skin" or "wineskin." See *Containers and Vessels.*

BOTTOMLESS PIT

Literal translation in Rev. 9:1-2,11; 11:7; 17:8; 20:1,3; home of evil, death, and destruction stored up until the sovereign God allowed them temporary power on earth. See *Abyss; Hades; Hell; Sheol.*

BOW AND ARROW See *Arms and Armor.*

BOWELS

Translation in modern versions for intestines and other entrails (Acts 1:18). KJV also used "bowels" for sexual reproductive system (2 Sam. 16:11; Ps. 71:6) and, figuratively, for strong emotions (Job 30:27), especially love (Song of Sol. 5:4) and compassion (Col. 3:12). Both Hebrew and Greek picture entrails as center of human emotions and excitement.

BOWL See *Basin.*

BOX

KJV translation for jar or flask, a container of oil used for anointing (2 Kings 9:1; Mark 14:3).

BOX TREE See *Plants.*

BOZRAH (*inaccessible*)

(1) Ancestral home of Jobab, Edomite king (Gen. 36:33; see Isa. 34:6; Jer. 49:13,22; Amos 1:12); center of shepherds known for woolen garments (see Isa. 63:1); at times capital of Edom; 25 miles southeast of the southern end of the Dead Sea at modern Buseirah. See *Edom.*

(2) Moabite city Jeremiah condemned (Jer. 48:24); may be same as Bezer.

BRACELET

Ornamental band worn by both women and men around the wrist (as distinct from an armlet worn around the upper arm) made mostly of bronze, though examples of iron, silver, glass, and, rarely, gold bracelets have been found. See Gen. 24:22,30,47; Num. 31:50; Isa. 3:19; Ezek. 16:11; 23:42. KJV, TEV and NASB translation for armlet in 2 Sam. 1:10. See *Armlet.*

BRAIDED, BRAIDING

Fixing hair in knots or weaving a wreath into the hair. Good works and spiritual grace are more important than outward appearances (1 Tim. 2:9; 1 Pet. 3:3).

BRAMBLE See *Plants.*

BRANCH

Limb of a tree; lampstands of the tabernacle and temple. Palm branch may stand for nobility, (Isa. 9:14; 19:15). "Being a branch" denotes membership in the people of God (John 15:1-8; Rom. 11:16-21). Spreading branches can symbolize fruitfulness and prosperity (Gen. 49:22; Job 8:16; Ps. 80:11), while withered, burnt, or cut branches symbolize destruction (Job 8:16; Isa. 9:14; Jer. 11:16; Ezek. 15:2)."Branch"or"shoot" is often used as a symbol for a present or coming king of Israel (Isa. 11:1; Jer. 23:5; 33:15; Zech. 3:8; 6:12). See *Messiah.*

BRASEN SERPENT See *Bronze Serpent.*

BRASS See *Minerals and Metals.*

BRAZEN SERPENT See *Bronze Serpent.*

BRAZIER

Portable firepot (NIV) or firepan used for heating a room during cold weather (Jer. 36:22-23; KJV has "hearth"; CEV,"fireplace").

BREAD

Basic food of most people (except nomads and the wealthy) in Bible times; at times translated "food." A coarse meal was ground from wheat (Gen. 30:14) or barley (John 6:9,13). Barley bread was less appetizing but less expensive and therefore common among the poor. See *Cooking and Heating; Mill.* Most bread formed a disk (Judg. 7:13) about one-half inch thick and 12 inches in diameter. Bread was broken or torn, not cut.

Bread was used as an offering to God (Lev. 2:4-10) and symbolized God's presence (Ex. 25:23-30; Lev. 24:5-9). In the NT it symbolizes Jesus Christ Himself (John 6:35), His body (1 Cor. 11:23-24), His kingdom (Luke 14:15), and the unity of His church (1 Cor. 10:17).

BREAD OF THE PRESENCE or SHEWBREAD

Twelve loaves of bread, probably barley or wheat and presumably unleavened, kept always on table set before Holy of Holies as a continual sacrifice and replaced each Sabbath (Ex. 25:30). Old bread was eaten by priests (Lev. 24:5-9). See 1 Sam. 21:4-6; Mark 2:23-28. See *Temple; Tabernacle.*

BREAKFAST See *Food.*

BREASTPIECE or BREASTPLATE

(1) Purselike piece of elaborate embroidery of gold metal, blue, purple, and scarlet yarn, and of fine linen about 9 inches square worn by high priest on his breast as he ministered in the tabernacle or temple; set with 12 stones, each with name of a tribe of Israel engraved on it. It was securely tied to the ephod. See *Ephod.* Inside the breastplate were the Urim and Thummim, worn over the heart (Lev. 8:8; see Ex. 28:15; 28:28-29). See *Urim and Thummim.*

(2) Piece of defensive armor (Eph. 6:14; Isa. 59:17; 1 Thess. 5:8; Rev. 9:9,17). See *Arms and Armor.*

BREATH

Air coming in or out of a living being. Two Hebrew terms are translated "breath," one to refer to the fact of breath in all forms of life, even to God (Gen. 2:7; Job 27:3; 33:4; Dan. 5:23); the other more to the force of breath in the extreme experiences of life, judgment, and death with the expanded meanings—"wind" and "spirit"—relating to one's own will or purpose.

God gave breath to humans in creation (Gen. 2:7; Acts 17:25) and takes breath away at death (Gen. 7:22; Job 34:14). His breath brought the mighty wind at Pentecost (Acts 2:2). Jesus breathed the Holy Spirit on His disciples (John 20:22). Compare Acts 9:1; Rev. 13:15. See *Spirit; Life.*

BREECHES

Priestly garments made of linen covering the thighs for reasons of modesty (Ex. 20:26); worn by high priest on Day of Atonement and by other priests on ceremonial occasions (Ex. 28:42; 39:28; Lev. 6:10; 16:4; Ezek. 44:18).

BRIBERY

Giving something of value with intention of influencing one in the discharge of his or her duties; presents opportunity for perversion of justice (see 1 Sam. 8:3; Prov. 17:23; Isa. 1:23; Mic. 3:11; 7:3); prohibited in the Bible (Ex. 23:8; Deut. 16:19).

BRICK

Building material of clay, molded into rectangular-shaped blocks while moist and hardened by the sun or fire; used to construct walls or pavement. See Gen. 11:3; Ex. 1:14; 5:7-23; 2 Sam. 12:31. Isaiah 65:3 condemned Israel for paganlike practices of offering incense on brick altars.

BRICKKILN

Oven, furnace, or heated enclosure used for processing bricks by burning, firing, or drying.

BRIDE

Female partner in a wedding (Gen. 24:4; 29:15-19; Ezek. 16:8-14; Song of Sol. 1–8); imagery used widely as description of the people of God (Isa. 61:10; 62:5; Jer. 3; 33:10-11; Ezek, 16; Hos. 3). New Testament uses bride imagery of the church and her relationship to Christ (John 3:29; 2 Cor. 11:2; Rev. 19:7-8; 21:2,9; compare 22:17).

BRIDE OF CHRIST See *Bride.*

BRIDE PRICE See *Dowry.*

BRIDLE See *Bit.*

BRIER

Translation of various Hebrew words referring to thorny plants. Used metaphorically of the enemies of Israel (Ezek. 28:24) and of worthless land (Isa. 5:6; 7:23-25; 55:13; compare Mic. 7:4).

BRIGANDINE

KJV in Jer. 46:4; 51:3 for "coat of mail" or "armor." See *Arms and Armor.*

BRIMSTONE

Combustible form of sulphur used as means of divine retribution (Gen. 19:24; Deut. 29:23; Job 18:15; Ps. 11:6; Isa. 30:33; 34:9; Ezek. 38:22; Luke 17:29; Rev. 14:10; 19:20; 20:10; 21:8).

BROAD PLACE

Metaphor for deliverance from danger, anxiety, want, or distress (Job 36:16); also translated "large place" (2 Sam. 22:20; Pss. 18:19; 118:5; Hos. 4:16) or "large room" (Ps. 31:8).

BROAD WALL

Stretch of Jerusalem wall on northwest corner near Gate of Ephraim restored by Nehemiah (Neh. 3:8; 12:38).

BROIDERED

KJV for two Hebrew words with uncertain meaning:

(1) Exodus 28:4,39 suggests: with fringes or hems, checkered (NRSV, NASB, REB), embroidered (NLT, TEV, CEV), skillfully woven (NKJV, NIV, NCV);

(2) Judg. 5:30; 1 Chron. 29:2; Ezek. 16:10, 13,18; 26:16; 27:7,16,24 may mean colorful, embroidered (NRSV, TEV, NCV, NIV), brocade (REB).

BRONZE See *Minerals and Metals.*

BRONZE SERPENT

Figure Moses made and set on a pole in middle of Israelite camp (Num. 21), so Israelites bitten by serpents could express their faith by looking at it and be healed. Hezekiah destroyed this symbol, apparently an object of worship (2 Kings 18:4). Jesus, lifted up on the cross, is God's chosen way to provide spiritual healing for all who have faith (John 3:14). See *Moses; Wilderness; Atonement.*

BROOCH

Jewelry brought by both men and women as offerings (Ex. 35:22, NASB, NRSV, NIV); Hebrew denotes a golden pin (NCV, CEV, "pins"; KJV, "bracelets"; REB, "clasp"; TEV, "decorative pins"; NLT, "medallions"; NKJV, "earrings"). Some recent interpreters think "nose rings" were meant.

BROOM TREE See *Plants.*

BROTHERLY LOVE

Feeling for others leading you to treat others as if they were a part of your family; "to like" another person and to want what is best for that individual; basic word sometimes means "to kiss," to show close friendship (Mark 14:44); never used for the love of God nor for erotic love (Rom. 12:10; 1 Thess. 4:9; Heb. 13:1; 1 Pet. 1:22; 2 Pet. 1:7; compare 1 Pet. 3:8). Israelites were called on to love other people in many relationships: friend to friend (Ps. 38:11; Prov. 10:12); slave and master (Ex. 21:5; Deut. 15:16); neighbors (Lev. 19:18); poor and unfortunate (Prov. 14:21,31); and stranger and foreigner (Lev. 19:34; Deut. 10:19). Often the love relationship between people is in the context of covenant, as with David and Jonathan (1 Sam. 18:1-3).

The church practices brotherly love (1 Thess. 4:9; Rom. 12:10; 13:8-10; 1 Cor. 8:13; Gal. 5:14). For John, brotherly love is a dominant theme. Jesus gave a new commandment "that ye love one another" (John 13:34; see 17:26; 1 John 2:9; 3:10,18,23; 4:8,20; 2 John 6). Epistles connect brotherly love with "hospitality to strangers" (Heb. 13:1-2) and being pure (1 Pet. 1:22; compare 2 Pet. 1:7). See *Love; Hospitality; Ethics.*

BROTHERS

Blood relationship of siblings (Ex. 4:14; Judg. 9:5). Genesis describes sibling rivalry: Cain and Abel (Gen. 4); Jacob and Esau (Gen. 25–28); Joseph and his brothers (Gen. 37–50). In each instance, God favored the younger brother. (See also David among Jesse's sons, 2 Sam. 1:26.) *Brother* also designates physical kinship, political allies, fellow countrymen (Gen. 13:8; 1 Kings 9:13; Luke 3:1; Mark 1:16,19; compare Luke 12:13; 15; 16:28).

Jesus designated as brothers those "which hear the word of God, and do it" (Luke 8:21). Paul addressed the church (male and female) as brothers (1 Cor. 1:10; Phil. 4:1-9; 1 Thess. 1:4).

BROTHERS, JESUS'

Four sons born to Mary and Joseph after Jesus' birth: James, Joses, Juda, and Simon (Mark 6:3; see Matt. 13:55) After the resurrection they joined the disciples in prayer (Acts 1:14). The risen Christ appeared to James, who became the leader of the Jerusalem church (Acts 12:17; 1 Cor. 15:7).

BROWN

KJV for "black" (NASB, NRSV, TEV, REB) or "dark-colored" (NIV) (Gen. 30:32,33,35,40). See *Colors.*

BUCKET

Waterskin for drawing water from a well held open at the top by a stick in the shape of a cross (Num. 24:7; Isa. 40:15).

BUCKLER

Small rounded shield carried in hand or worn on arm. See *Arms and Armor.*

BUGLE

NRSV, NASB, TEV translation (1 Cor. 14:8); elsewhere, "trumpet." See *Music, Instruments, Dancing.*

BUL *(harvest month)*

Eighth month or parts of October and November when Solomon finished building the temple (1 Kings 6:38). See *Calendars; Festivals.*

BULL See *Animals, Cattle; Canaan, History and Religion of.*

BULRUSH

Papyrus reed used to make ark for infant Moses (Ex. 2:3). See *Plants.*

BULWARK

Solid wall-like structure raised for defense, possibly a system of two walls with space between. God's salvation is a bulwark for His people (Isa. 26:1; Ps. 8:2; 1 Tim. 3:15).

BUNDLE See *Bag (3).*

BURGLARY See *Crimes and Punishments.*

BURIAL

Practices connected with honoring dead and placing them in final resting place. Palestine's warm climate and belief the corpse was ritually impure led Israelites to bury their dead as soon as possible, usually within 24 hours of death (Deut. 21:23). To allow a body to decay or be desecrated above ground was highly dishonorable (1 Kings 14:10-14; 2 Kings 9:34-37), and any corpse

found by the wayside was required to be buried (2 Sam. 21:10-14).

The dead were buried in caves, rock-cut tombs, or in the ground. It was desirable to be buried in the family tomb (Gen. 23:19; 25:9; 49:31; 50:13). Wealthy or politically powerful were sometimes buried with lavish accessories, including robes, jewelry, furniture, weapons, and pottery (1 Sam. 28:14; Isa. 14:11; Ezek. 32:27).

Israel practiced cremation only in exceptional cases such as decay following mutilation (1 Sam. 31:12) or the threat of plague. Embalming, apparently an Egyptian practice, is mentioned only in Egyptian setting of Jacob and Joseph (Gen. 50:2-3,26). See *Grief and Mourning.*

BURNING BUSH

Plant God used to attract Moses' attention and demonstrate His presence (Ex. 3:2). See *Moses; Exodus.*

BURNT OFFERINGS See *Sacrifice and Offering.*

BUSHEL See *Weights and Measures.*

BUTLER See *Occupations and Professions.*

BUZZARD See *Birds.*

BYBLOS See *Gebal.*

BYWORD

An object of derision among other peoples; fate of faithless Israel (Deut. 28:37; 1 Kings 9:7; 2 Chron. 7:20; Job 17:6; 30:9; Ps. 44:14).

C

CAB See *Weights and Measures.*

CABIN

KJV (Jer. 37:16) "vault," "cellar," or "prison cell."

CABUL *(fettered or braided)*

(1) Town on northeast border of Asher (Josh. 19:27); may be modern Kabul 9 miles southeast of Acco or nearby Khirbet Ras ez-Zeitun; Josephus's headquarters.

(2) Region in Galilee (probably including 1 above) Solomon gave Hiram, king of Tyre, as payment for materials and services in building the temple and the palace. Hiram did not like them and called them Cabul, "as nothing." Apparently, the "gift" expected a gift in return, according to Near Eastern etiquette, for Hiram gave Solomon 120 talents of gold (1 Kings 9:10-14; compare 2 Chron. 8:2).

CAESAR

Family name of Julius Caesar assumed by following emperors as a title and used as virtual synonym for civil authority. See Matt. 22:15-21. See *Rome and the Roman Empire.*

CAESAR'S HOUSEHOLD

All persons, both slave and free, in the service of the emperor, numbering in thousands. See Phil. 1:13; 4:22.

CAESAREA

Important Mediterranean seaport 23 miles south of Mt. Carmel; known also as Caesarea-on-the-Sea (Maritima), Caesarea Sebaste, Caesarea of Palestine, and Caesarea of Judea. Lack of a natural harbor between Sidon and Egypt led Abdashtart (Greek Straton), a Sidonian king, to build an anchorage about 330 B.C. It became known as Strato's Tower.

Herod built a fine port facility and named the harbor Sebastos (Latin, Augustus). Herod's new city was Hellenistic in design and named Caesarea for Caesar. After Archelaus was removed in A.D. 6 Caesarea became the capital of the province of Judea and the official home of the procurators. A public outbreak resulted in the desecration of the synagogue Knestha d'Meredtha in A.D. 66 which precipitated the Jewish- Roman War. See Acts 8:40; 10; 23:23; 25:1-7; compare Acts 9:30; 18:22; 21:8. Herod Agrippa I died there in his residence (Acts 12:19-23).

CAESAREA PHILIPPI

City near Syria/Palestine border where Jesus asked disciples who they thought He was (Mark 8:27-30); probable sight of the transfiguration (Mark 9:2-8); about 1,150 feet above sea level on triangular plain in upper Jordan Valley along southwestern slopes of Mt. Hermon; near Nahr Banias, one source of the Jordan; modern Banias; one of most lush and beautiful areas in Palestine.

Caesarea Philippi seems to have been a religious center from its earliest days, first for the Canaanite Baal-gad, god of good fortune, and later, the Greek god Pan. Herod the Great built a temple and dedicated it to Emperor Augustus. In 20 B.C., the Romans under Augustus gave the territory to Herod the Great. It passed to his son Philip (4 B.C. to A.D. 34), who rebuilt it into a beautiful place and renamed it Caesarea Philippi, honoring Tiberias Caesar and himself. Herod Agrippa II renamed it Neronias in honor of Nero. After subduing the Jews (A.D. 70), the Romans changed its name back to Paneas.

CAIAPHAS *(rock or depression)*

High priest at time of Jesus' crucifixion (Matt. 26:3); son-in-law of Annas and leader in plot to arrest and execute Jesus. Evidently, he was appointed high priest about A.D. 18 and removed from office about A.D. 36 or 37. See *High Priest.*

CAIN (acquisition)

First son of Adam and Eve (Gen. 4:1). Cain was a farmer, and his brother Abel, a shepherd. God accepted Abel's offering but rejected Cain's. Subsequently, Cain murdered Abel his brother. In punishment, God took from him the ability to till the ground productively and made him a wandering vagabond. God marked him off to protect him from anyone seeking to avenge Abel's murder.

CAKE

Shape of loaf of bread (flat and round).

CALAH

Assyrian capital Nimrod built (Gen. 10:8-12); modern tell Nimrud on east bank of Tigris River where it joins Upper Zab River 20 miles south of Nineveh. Ashurnasirpal II (883–859 B.C.) made it capital of Assyria. See *Assyria, History and Religion of.*

CALAMUS See *Plants.*

CALDRON

Cooking pot of various materials used by different English translations for various Hebrew words (1 Sam. 2:14; 2 Chron. 35:13; Job 41:20; Ezek. 11:3,7,11; Jer. 52:18–19; Mic. 3:3). See *Pottery.*

CALEB (dog), CALEBITE

One of only two spies Moses sent to reconnoiter Canaan who brought back positive report (Num. 13:30). God rewarded him by letting him survive the years of wilderness wandering. At 85 Caleb conquered Hebron (Josh. 14).

CALENDARS

System for ordering time. The Mishna first organized the biblical data into the detailed calendrical system Jews observe today, probably reflecting Jewish practice in Jesus' day. The Bible often dates events by the ancient Jewish festivals.

All the peoples from the Mesopotamian area, as well as the Arabians, the Greeks, and the Romans, began the year in spring. Phoenicians, Canaanites, and Israelites used a fall new year as harvest ended one agricultural cycle and prepared for the next. In the exilic and postexilic periods, the Jews shifted to the spring new year, but since rabbinic times the fall new year has been observed.

The OT reflects a lunar-solar calendar based on observation of heavenly bodies and regulates a sophisticated order of economic and religious activity. The sun's orbit marked the year's beginning, but beginning of months depended on the phases of the moon. The new moon marked the new month. This resulted in some 29-day and some 30-day months and a year of 354¼ days. From the Babylonians, the Hebrews learned to add an extra month every two or three years.

Essenes, known from the Dead Sea Scrolls, created a purely solar calendar with 30-day months that combined mathematical calculation with a special ideology. They added a special day at the end of each three-month period, giving a year of 364 days.

Israel's earliest practice (Ex. 13:4; 23:15; 34:18; 1 Kings 6:1,37-38; 8:3) in naming months was to use the Canaanite month-names, of which four survive in the Bible: Abib (March-April); Ziv (April-May); Ethanim (September-October); and Bul (October-November).

The usual OT practice is to number the months from first to twelfth, first month always in spring, a practice going back to patriarchs from Mesopotamia (Gen. 11:31). Returning exiles brought with them Babylonian names. Judaism retains these Babylonian names: Nisan (Mar.–Apr.); Iyyar (Apr.–May); Sivan (May–June); Tammuz (June–July); Ab (July–Aug.); Elul (Aug.–Sept.); Tishri (Sept.–Oct.); Marcheshvan (Oct.–Nov.); Chishylev (Nov.–Dec.); Tebeth (Dec.–Jan.); Shebat (Jan.–Feb.); Adar (Feb.–Mar.). The intercalated month is called *We-Adar,* "and-Adar."

CAMEL See *Animals.*

CAMEL'S HAIR

Coarse material woven from the hair of a camel's back and hump; finer material was woven with hair taken from underneath the animal. Wearing a hairy mantle was the mark of a prophet (Zech. 13:4; compare 2 Kings 1:8). John the Baptist wore coarse camel's hair (Mark 1:6; compare Matt. 11:8).

CAMP, ENCAMPMENT

Temporary settlement for nomadic and military people. Earliest Israel was group of tribes on the move (Ex. 14:19; 16:13; Num. 2; compare Heb. 13:11,13). In Canaan, "camp" designated a military settlement, whether of Israel (1 Sam. 4:3; 14:21) or of an enemy (2 Kings 7:10). The Hebrew is often rendered "company" (Gen. 32:8,21); "host" (Ex. 14:24); "army" (1 Sam. 17:1). The church is "the camp of the saints" under attack by Satan's forces (Rev. 20:9).

CAMPHIRE   See *Plants, Henna*.

CANA (*nest*)

Town in Galilee where Jesus changed water into wine during a wedding (John 2:1); where nobleman asked Jesus to heal his son (John 4:46); and home of Nathanael (John 21:2); possibly Khirbet Qana 9 miles north of Nazareth.

CANAAN, HISTORY AND RELIGION OF

Territory between the Mediterranean Sea and the Jordan River reaching from the brook of Egypt to the area around Ugarit in Syria or to the Euphrates; land bridge between Mesopotamia and Egypt and between the Mediterranean and the Red Sea. Apparently, Canaan meant different things at different times. Numbers 13:29 limits Canaanites to those who "dwell by the sea and by the coast of Jordan." Compare Josh. 11:3. Israel was aware of the larger "Promised Land" of Canaan (Gen. 15:18; Ex. 23:21; Num. 13:21; Deut. 1:7; 1 Kings 4:21). Israel's basic land reached only from "Dan to Beersheba" (2 Sam. 24:2-8,15; 2 Kings 4:25). At times Israel included land east of Jordan (2 Sam. 24:5-6). At times the land of Gilead was contrasted to the land of Canaan (Josh. 22:9).

History

Term *Canaan* appears to be non-Semitic, possibly Hurrian name. Originally, it may have referred to a merchant class (see Isa. 23:8; Zech. 14:21; compare Hos. 12:7-8; Ezek. 17:4; Zeph. 1:11); geographical Canaan limited to Phoenicia along the seacoast.

The Bible identifies Canaan as son of Ham and grandson of Noah (Gen. 9:18; 10:6) and places it among nations under Egyptian influence (Gen. 10:15-20).

During the Old Kingdom of Egypt (about 2600–2200 B.C.), Egypt's power extended northwards to Ugarit. Also during the Twelfth Dynasty (1990–1790 B.C.), Egypt controlled this area as shown by the Execration Texts.

Amorites invaded Canaan about 2000 B.C. from Mesopotamia. From 1720 until 1570, Hyksos controlled Egypt and sought to dominate Canaan, facing Hurrian and Hittite opposition. Egypt regained its power after 1570 but weakened again about 1400 when small city states in Canaan struggled with one another, as seen in the Amarna Letters. Thus, Israel under Joshua faced no united power but a group of independent city states. After the conquest, the Canaanites and Israelites gradually melded together, becoming united under David's rule.

Religion

Cuneiform tablets from 1400 B.C. to 1200 B.C. discovered at Ugarit provide the best information concerning the thought and religion of the Canaanites prior to Israelite occupation, representing their religious perspectives between 2000 and 1500 B.C. Canaan featured a pantheon of deities, each with clear assignments of responsibilities, but with one god frequently assuming the identity of another.

(1) *El* headed the pantheon as king of the gods. He was creator god and a fertility god, depicted in the form of a bull and resident on Mt. Saphon in the north.

(2) *Athirat* his wife, represented in the OT as *Asherah* with both feminine (*Asheroth*) and masculine (*Asherim*) plurals. Athirat was acknowledged as the mother of 70 deities, a fertility goddess and "creatress of the gods."

(3) *Baal* was the chief god in popular worship. Baal was accessible to the people, not off in the far north. Statues show him with horns to convey the strength and fertility associated with bull imagery.

(4) *Anath* was worshiped by Amorites at Mari around 1750 and apparently had a cult center at Hanat. She was also worshiped in Egypt, especially by Rameses II. In Canaan she was both sister and consort of Baal and goddess of love, the perpetual virgin, and the goddess of warfare who fought for Baal in remarkably cruel and bloodthirsty fashion.

(5) *Mot* was the god of death and sterility, associated with the seasonal cycle of vegetation, the seventh year sabbatical rest of the agricultural land, and personal death. He could rend impotent for a time the regenerative powers of Baal.

(6) *Yam* was called both "Prince River" and "Judge River." He was the chaotic god of the sea, capable of turning cosmos into chaos.

Canaanite worship was tied to procreative sympathetic magic. Sexual union of god and goddess portrayed by priest and priestess assured the fertility of humans, animals, and the larger world of nature. Israel's God forbade such practices, but Israel constantly yielded to the temptations of sympathetic magic, especially in its sexual manifestations.

Israelite names (like Ishbaal, Jerubbaal, and Meribbaal), the architecture of Solomon's temple, the bringing of the gods of Solomon's foreign wives to Jerusalem, and

especially the creating of calves or bulls in the two temples of the north at Bethel and Dan show the continuing influence of Canaanite religion on Israel. See 1 Kings 18–19.

In Canaan the Israelites encountered a people with a proud history and a thriving religion. A long historical process led to the eventual elimination of baalism and other elements of Canaanite religion. Israel's battle with Canaanite religion gave new depth to Israel's faith.

CANALS

Branches of Nile River (Ex. 7:19; 8:5; Isa. 19:6); KJV, "rivers."

CANANAEAN

Identifying phrase for apostle Simon (Mark 3:18 NRSV; KJV renders "Simon the Canaanite"). Other NT scriptures refer to Simon the Zealot (Matt. 10:4; Luke 6:15; Acts 1:13). "Cananaean" is probably Aramaic equivalent of Greek, "zealot" (NIV, REB, NLT, NCV, NASB; note CEV, "eager one"; TEV, "patriot"). See *Disciples, Apostles.*

CANDACE

Title, rather than name, of queen of Ethiopia (Acts 8:27).

CANDLE, CANDLESTICK

KJV translation for "lamp" or "lampstand." Candles were not in use in biblical times. See *Lamps, Lighting, Lampstand.*

CANE See *Plants, Calamus.*

CANKER

Any source of corruption or debasement (2 Tim. 2:17 and Jas. 5:3 KJV). Second Timothy 2:17 deals with gangrene (NASB, REB, NIV, NRSV; note NKJV, NLT, "cancer"; TEV, "open sore that eats away the flesh"; compare CEV), the local death of soft tissues due to loss of blood supply that can spread from infected to uninfected tissue. In James 5:3, the word refers to rust or corrosion.

CANKERWORM

KJV for type of locust (Joel 1:4; 2:25; Nah. 3;15-16). See *Insects, Locust.*

CANNEH

Northern Syrian city; trading partner of Tyre (Ezek. 27:23) known for horses and slaves; probably city called Kannu in Assyrian documents.

CANON See *Bible, Formation and Canon of Old Testament; Bible, Formation and Canon of New Testament.*

CANOPY

Modern versions for pavilion, tent, or covering. See 1 Kings 7:6; Ezek. 41:25; Isa. 4:5; Jer. 43:10. See *Pavilion.*

CANTICLES See *Song of Solomon.*

CAP See *Bonnet.*

CAPERBERRY See *Plants, Fruits.*

CAPERNAUM (*village of Nahum*)

Jesus' base of operations (Matt. 9:1; Mark 1:21; 2:1); home of Peter, Andrew, Matthew, and perhaps James and John; economic center in Galilee with customs station and military installation commanded by a centurion; Tell Hum on the northwest shore of the Sea of Galilee about 2½ miles west of the entrance of the Jordan.

CAPHTOR, CAPHTORIM *or* **CAPHTORITES** See *Philistines; Crete.*

CAPITAL PUNISHMENT

Death penalty legally sanctioned by a society or government for extremely serious offenses.

Offenses Calling for Capital Punishment:

(1) *intentional homicide* (Ex. 21:12; Lev. 24:17; Num. 35:16-21,29-34);

(2) *false witnessing in capital cases* (Deut. 19:16-21);

(3) *idolatry* (Lev. 20:1-5; Deut. 13:2-19; 17:2-7);

(4) *abducting persons for slavery* (Ex. 21:16; Deut. 24:7);

(5) *sexual acts of incest, homosexuality, and bestiality* (Ex. 22:19; Lev. 20:11-17);

(6) *rape* (Deut. 22:23-27), including the girl if she did not cry for help;

(7) *adultery* (Lev. 20:10-12; Deut. 22:22);

(8) *sex relations outside of marriage:*

(a) before marriage, but discovered afterward (Deut. 22:20-21), the woman alone to be executed;

(b) relations with another's betrothed (Deut. 22:23-24), both to be executed;

(c) harlotry of a priest's daughter (Lev. 21:9);

(9) *witchcraft and false claim to prophecy* (Ex. 22:18; Lev. 20:27; Deut. 13:1-5; 18:20; 1 Sam. 28:3,9);

(10) *profaning the sabbath* (Ex. 31:14-17; 35:2; Num. 15:32-36);

(11) *blasphemy* (Lev. 24:14-16,23; 1 Kings 21:13; Matt. 26:65-66);

(12) *cursing or striking one's parents* (Ex. 21:15,17).

Forms of Capital Punishment:

(1) *Stoning* was the usual method in Israel (Ex. 19:13; Lev. 20:27; Deut. 22:24; Josh. 7:25; compare Luke 20:3-6; Acts 7:58). At least two witnesses were needed to verify a charge, and they had to throw the first stones (Deut. 17:6-7; compare John 8:7).

(2) *Burning* was the penalty for incest (Lev. 20:14); harlotry (Gen. 38:24), particularly by a priest's daughter (Lev. 21:9).

(3) *Sword* (Ex. 32:27; Deut. 13:15), *spear* (Num. 25:7ff.), and *shooting by arrow* (Ex. 19:13).

(4) *Beheading* was reserved especially for those who cursed or insulted royalty (2 Sam. 16:9; 2 Kings 6:31-32).

(5) *Crucifixion* was carried out in NT times only by Roman decree and by Roman soldiers (Matt. 27:22-26,33-50; Luke 23:13-33; John 18:28–19:30) for those convicted of political insurrection against Rome. Jewish authorities

under Roman rule were not normally permitted to execute anyone (John 18:31), although rare exceptions are recorded (Acts 5:27-33; 7:57-60; 26:10); whether these were approved by Rome is difficult to say.

CAPITALS See *Chapiter.*

CAPPADOCIA

Roman province in Asia Minor south of Pontus stretching about 300 miles from Galatia eastward toward Armenia, with Cilicia and the Taurus Mountains to the south (Acts 2:9; 1 Pet. 1:1). Although mountainous country, its mostly rural population raised good crops, cattle, and horses. Jews from Cappadocia were in Jerusalem when Peter preached at Pentecost.

CAPTAIN

Officer or leader of some kind. As applied to Christ.

CAPTAIN OF THE TEMPLE

Officer second in authority to high priest responsible for keeping order in temple (Acts 4:1; 5:24,26). Pashhur (Jer. 20:1) and Seraiah (Neh. 11:11) held this office. Plural (Luke 22:4,52) may refer to officers under command of captain of temple.

CAPTIVITY

Israel's Exile in Babylon between 597 B.C. and 538 B.C. See *Exile.*

CARAVAN

Company of travelers (usually merchants) on journey through desert or hostile regions with train of pack animals (see Gen. 37:25; Judg. 5:6; 1 Kings 10:2; Job 6:18-19; Isa. 21:13).

CARBUNCLE See *Minerals and Metals.*

CARCHEMISH *(fort of Chemosh)*

Center of late Hittite kingdom; important city on west bank at bend of Euphrates River; crossing point on international trade route; modern Jerablus, mostly on Turkish side of modern Turkish-Syrian border.

Pharaoh Neco II of Egypt came to Carchemish to save remnants of Assyrian army. He arrived too late to save the Assyrians, perhaps held up by Josiah's unsuccessful challenge at Megiddo (2 Chron. 35:20-24). Nebuchadrezzar defeated Neco at Carchemish, gaining authority over all of western Asia (Jer. 46:2-12).

CAREER DECISIONS

As a rule, during the biblical period sons entered the same line of work as their fathers. Occasionally, however, God chose careers for people, causing them to leave their family occupation in order to serve Him directly (eg. Ex. 3:10; 1 Sam. 16:1-13; 1 Kings 19:19-21; Amos 7:14-15; Mark 1:16-20).

The Bible upholds any line of work that is honest and good (Titus 3:1; compare Gen. 2:15; Neh. 2:18) and does not contradict the gospel (Acts 16:16-18; 19:23-27). All work should be done in the name of Jesus (Col. 3:17) and for the glory of God (1 Cor. 10:31) as if God Himself were the employer (Col. 3:23). This is true whether one works as a bishop, considered by Paul to be a "noble task" (1 Tim. 3:1), or at a job not highly regarded by the world (compare the Egyptian attitude toward shepherding in Gen. 46:34). For this reason, God is more concerned with one's attitude about work than the particular task performed (Eccl. 9:10; Col. 3:23).

God is concerned that each individual's full potential be met. For this reason He guides persons to choose careers (Ps. 73:24) that match their skills and areas of giftedness (compare Ex. 39:43).

CARITES

Term of uncertain meaning (2 Kings 11:4,19; Hebrew text of 2 Sam. 20:23, where "Cherethites" is usually read); perhaps mercenary soldiers recruited from Cilicia by Judah and other countries.

CARMEL, MOUNT

Towering mountain (1,750 feet) where Elijah confronted the prophets of Baal (1 Kings 18:19); near Mediterranean coast between Plains of Acco and Sharon.

CARNAL

Related to fleshly or worldly appetites and desires rather than to godly and spiritual desires. Basic human nature is carnal, sold out to sin and thus living in the realm of death, unable to observe God's spiritual law (Rom. 7:14). See *Body; Flesh*. Even church members can be carnal, being only babes in Christ (1 Cor. 3:1-4). See Heb. 7:16; 9:10; 1 Pet. 2:11.

CARNELIAN See *Minerals and Metals*.

CARPENTER

Trade lifted to a high position of honor by Jesus (Mark 6:3). See *Occupations*.

CARRIAGE

KJV for utensils, baggage, supplies, or anything which can be carried. The term has nothing to do with transportation vehicles. Compare various translations of Judg. 18:21; 1 Sam. 17:22; Isa. 10:28; 46:1; Acts 21:15.

CARRION VULTURE See *Birds, Vulture*.

CASEMENT

Window with lattice work (Judg. 5:28; Prov. 7:6). Archaeologists have found such lattice windows in royal palaces.

CASSIA See *Plants*.

CASTANETS See *Music, Instruments, Dancing*.

CASTAWAY

KJV for battle testing of soldiers, qualifications for office, or testing of metals to make sure they are genuine. Paul used his own example of personal discipline to ensure that his preaching proved true in life as a call to others to do the same (1 Cor. 9:27; compare 2 Cor. 13:5-7; 2 Tim. 3:8; Titus 1:16; Heb. 6:8). He did not want to be cast away as impure metal or disqualified as an unworthy soldier or candidate.

CASTLE

Large, fortified home of the king, often translated palace or citadel (1 Kings 16:18; Amos 6:8; compare 1:4). See *Fortified Cities*.

The basic biblical lesson is that Yahweh is our stronghold, refuge, and fortress (Pss. 18:2; 31:3). Fortress in the NT points to a fortified camp and designated the Roman army barracks or headquarters in Jerusalem (Acts 21:34; 22:24; 23:10). Hebrews invites Christians to be willing to suffer outside the camp, accepting disgrace as did Jesus (Heb. 13:11-13). Compare Rev. 20:9.

CASTOR AND POLLUX

Twin sons of Jupiter or Zeus, who were supposed to watch over sailors; the sign or figurehead of the ship that carried Paul from Malta toward Rome (Acts 28:11).

CATERPILLAR See *Insects*.

CATHOLIC EPISTLES

New Testament letters not attributed to Paul and written to a more general or unidentifiable audience: James; 1 and 2 Peter; 1, 2, and 3 John; Jude.

CATTLE See *Animals*.

CAUDA or CLAUDA

Small island whose name is variously spelled in Greek manuscripts; modern Gavdos, 23 miles southwest of Crete (Acts 27:16).

CAUL

KJV for part of liver that appears to be left over or forms an appendage to the liver: "lobe" (NASB), "covering" (NIV), "best part" (TEV, NCV), "lower part" (CEV), or "appendage" (NRSV) of the liver. See Ex. 29:13. KJV speaks of the "caul of their hearts" (Hos. 13:8) which modern translations render more freely. The Hebrew apparently refers to the chest cavity in which the heart is located. KJV also uses "caul" for a rare Hebrew word (Isa. 3:18) modern linguists take to mean "headbands."

CAULKERS, CAULKING See *Calkers, Calking.*

CAVALRY

An army's mounted soldiers (Ex. 14:9,18,28; Judg. 4; 2 Sam. 8:4). Assyria used cavalry troops as early as 900 B.C. The cavalry provided a line of defense, served as scouts, and chased a defeated army. God would not allow Israel to rely on the wealth and security represented by military horses (Deut. 17:16; Isa. 31:1). Solomon developed a military force featuring horses (1 Kings 4:26; 9:17; 10:26). References to horsemen may all refer to personnel connected with chariots rather than to individual riders or cavalry units.

CAVES

Pits in the cliffs and mountains of Palestine that provided housing and burial sites (Gen. 23:11-16,19; John 11:38) for prehistoric people and on into the Roman period when they also became places of refuge for Jews fleeing Roman persecution. See Josh. 10:16; 1 Sam. 22:1.

CEDAR See *Plants.*

CEDRON See *Kidron Valley.*

CELESTIAL BODIES

Sun, moon, and stars which Paul contrasted with terrestrial or earthly bodies in explaining the difference between the present human body (physical) and the resurrection body (spiritual body, 1 Cor. 15:35-50).

CELIBACY

Abstention by vow from marriage. Jesus said some people have made themselves eunuchs for the sake of the kingdom and that those who were able to should do so (Matt. 19:12). This statement has traditionally been understood as a reference to celibacy (see *Eunuch*). Paul counseled the single to remain so (1 Cor. 7:8; but note 1 Tim. 4:1-3).

CENCHREA or **CENCHREAE**

Eastern port city of Corinth, seven miles east of city on Saronic Gulf (Acts 18:18; Rom. 16:1).

CENSER

Handheld vessel priests used to carry live coals for offering incense before the Lord (Lev. 10:1; Num. 16:17-18; 2 Chron. 26:16-21; Ezek. 8:11-13). Heavenly worship also involved censers and incense (Rev. 8:3-5). See *Tabernacle; Temple.*

CENSUS

Enumeration of a population for the purpose of taxation or for the determination of manpower for war (Ex. 30:13-16; Num. 1; compare 26:2-4). David counted Israel's warriors. Second Sam. 24 says the Lord incited David to carry out the census, and 1 Chron. 21 says that Satan moved David to do so. In both accounts, a pestilence was sent upon Israel because of the census. Ezra 2 accounts for those who came out of exile with Zerubbabel and Nehemiah. A Roman census affected Jesus' birthplace (Luke 2:1-5). See Acts 5:37.

CENTURION

Officer in Roman army, nominally commanding 100 soldiers (Matt. 8:5; Mark 15:39; Acts 27:3). The conversion of the centurion Cornelius marked the beginning of the church's outreach to the Gentile world (Acts 10).

CEPHAS See *Peter.*

CEREAL OFFERINGS See *Sacrifices and Offerings.*

CEREMONIAL LAW

Laws that pertained to the festivals and cultic activities of the Israelites. See *Festivals; Law, Ten Commandments; Sacrifice and Offerings; Worship.*

CERTIFICATE OF DIVORCE See *Family; Divorce.*

CHAFF

Husk and other materials separated from the kernel of grain during the threshing or winnowing process. It blew away in the wind (Hos. 13:3) or was burned up as worthless (Isa. 5:24; Luke 3:17).

CHAINS

English translation of at least eight different Hebrew terms for materials interlaced together into ornamental or restraining objects.

(1) An ornament worn around the neck either signifying investiture in office with political award (Gen. 41:42; Dan. 5:7) or for personal jewelry (Num. 31:50); also worn by animals (Judg. 8:26).

(2) Decorations of gold on high priest's breastplate (Ex. 28:14).

(3) Partition in Solomon's temple (1 Kings 6:21).

(4) Architectural ornaments on temple walls (2 Chron. 3:5,16).

(5) Restraining chains preventing prisoners from escaping (Jer. 39:7; Acts. 28:20). God could loose His minister from chains (Acts 12:7).

CHALCEDONY

Transliteration of Greek name of precious stone in Rev. 21:19. See *Minerals and Metals.*

CHALDEA, CHALDEANS, CHALDEES

Region in central and southeastern Mesopotamia, the land between the lower stretches of the Tigris and Euphrates Rivers; part of modern Iraq close to its border with Iran, and touching upon the head of the Persian Gulf; people who lived there.

After 750 B.C. the Chaldeans emerged as champions of resistance against Assyria. See *Babylon, History and Religion of.*

CHALKSTONE

Soft stone easily crushed; used for describing total destruction of the altar (Isa. 27:9).

CHAMBER

Translation of at least seven Hebrew words for a portion of a house or building. Included are sleeping quarters (2 Kings 6:12); bathroom (Judg. 3:24); private inner room reserved for a bride (Judg. 15:1; Joel 2:16); private, personal cubicle in the temple furnished with benches (1 Sam. 9:22; 2 Kings 23:11); storage rooms (Neh. 12:44); cool upper room on the roof (Judg. 3:20) or over the city gate (2 Sam. 18:33); and the ribs or beams forming side rooms in the temple (1 Kings 7:3). The NT speaks of inner rooms of a house (Matt. 6:6; 24:26; Luke 12:3) or of a storeroom (Luke 12:24). See *Architecture in the Biblical Period.*

CHAMBERING

KJV (Rom. 13:13) for "debauchery" (NRSV, REB), "adultery" (NLT), "be vulgar" (CEV), "lewdness" (NKJV), or "sexual promiscuity" (NASB, NIV).

CHAMBERLAIN

High military or political official whose title is related to Hebrew term meaning "castrated" or "eunuch," but may be actually derived from Accadian term for royal official. See *Eunuch.*

CHAMELEON See *Animals, Reptiles.*

CHAMOIS See *Animals.*

CHAMPAIGN

Open, unenclosed land or plain (Deut. 11:30 KJV). Hebrew has preposition meaning in front of or opposite Gilgal and Arabah. See *Arabah.*

CHAMPION

Mighty one or warrior (1 Sam. 17:51). In 1 Sam. 17:4,23 Hebrew is literally, "the man of the space between;" that is, the man (like Goliath) who fights a single opponent in the space between two armies.

CHANAAN

KJV form of Canaan in Acts 7:11; 13:19.

CHANCELLOR

Title of Persian royal official living in Samaria and helping administer Persian province; not the highest provincial office, that of governor. See Ezra 4:8-9,17.

CHANT See *Music, Instruments, Dancing.*

CHAOS

State of emptiness, waste, desolation, and void.

Chaos is defined by the primeval disorder that preceded God's creative activity. When "darkness was upon the face of the deep," God destroyed the forces of confusion (Gen. 1:2). Throughout Scripture, chaos is personified as the principal opponent of God. In ancient Semitic legends, a terrible chaos-monster was called Rahab (the proud one) or Leviathan (the twisting dragon-creature) or Yam (the roaring sea). See *Rahab; Leviathan.*

The chaos theme is implied, if not used, in the NT depicting God's victory in Christ (Mark 4:35-41, 6:45-52; John 6:16-21; Rev. 21:1).

CHAPITER

KJV translation of architectural term for the 10-foot capital made to stand on top of a pillar (1 Kings 7:16) or the base on which the actual capital is placed. In Ex. 36:38; 38:17,19,28, KJV translates the Hebrew word for "head" as chapiter, while a different Hebrew term is so translated in 2 Chron. 3:15.

CHAPMAN

Old English word for trader (2 Chron. 9:14 KJV). See *Commerce.*

CHARCHEMISH See *Carchemish.*

CHARIOTS

Two-wheeled land vehicles, made of wood and strips of leather, usually drawn by horses and used primarliy as mobile firing platforms in battles; used widely in Mesopotamia before 3000 B.C. and introduced into Canaan and Egypt (Gen. 41:43; 46:29; 50:9) by the Hyksos about 1800–1600 B.C. They were also used for hunting, for transportation of dignitaries (Acts 8:26-38), and in state and religious ceremonies. The Philistines' iron chariots were fortified with plates of metal, making them militarily stronger than those of the Israelites (Judg. 1:19; 4:3,13-17; 1 Sam. 13:5-7). Chariots became an important part of Solomon's army and his commercial affairs (1 Kings 4:26; 9:15-19; 10:28-29). Assyrian records show that Ahab brought 2,000 chariots into the Battle of Qarqar (853 B.C.). See *Arms and Armor.*

CHARITY

KJV for Greek *agape.* NASB, REB use "charity" to translate Greek *ekdidomai,* "to give out," in relation to helping the poor (Luke 11:41; 12:33; Acts 9:36). See *Love; Alms.*

CHARM

(1) Human charm can be deceitful (Prov. 31:30; compare Nah. 3:4), yet the Hebrew term is a characteristic of God's gift of the Spirit (Zech. 12:10; compare Gen. 39:21; Prov. 3:34). Generally, the term means to find favor or acceptance from another person (Gen. 6:8; 33:8), but English translations use *grace* or *favor* rather than "charm" as the translation at these points.

(2) Magic charms sewn as wristbands (Ezek. 13:18, NIV, NKJV, CEV,

NCV, NLT; compare Isa. 3:20); see *Divination and Magic*.

(3) Snake charmers knew "magic words" or "magic acts" to prevent poisonous snakes from harming people (Ps. 58:4-5). The "enchanters" (NASB, NIV, NRSV) are listed among community leaders the prophet condemned (Isa. 3:3; see Jer. 8:17; Eccl. 10:11).

CHARRAN See *Haran*.

CHASTE

Holy purity demanded of God's people with special reference to the sexual purity of women; originally referred to holy purity of deities. See *Clean, Cleanness*.

CHASTEN, CHASTISEMENT

Act of punishment intended to instruct and bring repentance (Jer. 31:18-19) that changes behavior. People fear the experience of God's angry chastisement (Ps. 6:1; 38:1). Still, the Father must correct His children (2 Sam. 7:14; compare Deut. 8:5; 21:18; Prov. 13:24; 19:18). God's chastening leads to healing (Job 5:17-18; compare Prov. 3:11; Heb. 12:5). Such chastisement is God's choice, not that of humans (Hos. 10:10; compare 7:12), showing His love (Rev. 3:19) and leading us away from eternal chastisement (1 Cor. 11:32; compare Deut. 11:2; Ps. 94:12; Heb. 12:10). Chastising seeks to bring blessing (Pss. 94:12; 118:18). The Suffering Servant has borne our chastisement, so we do not have to suffer it (Isa. 53:5).

CHEBAR

River, or more properly a canal, flowing 60 miles from Babylon to Nippur; where Ezekiel had visions (Ezek. 1:1; 3:15; 10:15; 43:3); probably modern Satt-el-nil.

CHEESE

Dairy product forming a basic part of the diet. Three different Hebrew expressions refer to cheese (Job 10:10); "slice of milk" (1 Sam. 17:18); and "curds of the herd" (2 Sam. 17:29).

CHEMOSH (*subdue*)

Deity Moabites worshiped (Num. 21:29). He was expected to provide land for Moab (Judg. 11:24). Solomon erected a sanctuary for Chemosh (1 Kings 11:7). Josiah subsequently defiled the sanctuary (2 Kings 23:13; see Jer. 48:7,13,46). Probably same as Kamish from Ebla (about 2500 B.C.) and divine name in Carchemish.

CHERETHITES, CHERETHIM

People who lived south of or with Philistines (1 Sam. 30:14) either as related tribe or as paid soldiers. Crete may have been their original home. David used some of these soldiers as a personal bodyguard (2 Sam. 8:18; compare Ezek. 25:16; Zeph. 2:5).

CHERITH (*cutting* or *ditch*)

Wadi or brook east of Jordan River; perhaps modern Wadi el-Yubis in northern Gilead. See 1 Kings 17:3.

CHERUB, CHERUBIM

Class of winged angels (Gen. 3:24; Isa. 6:2-6; Ezek. 1:4-28; 10:3-22; Heb.9:5) used for God's cherub throne (1 Sam. 4:4; 2 Sam. 6:2; 22:11; 2 Kings 19:15; 1 Chron. 13:6; 28:18; Pss. 18:10; 80:1; 99:1; Isa. 37:16). See *Angel*.

CHESTNUT See *Plants, Plane Tree*.

CHICKEN See *Birds*.

CHIEF

English translation of at least 13 Hebrew and 4 Greek words designating a leader in political, military, religious, or economic affairs.

CHIEF PRIEST See *Aaron*; *Priests*; *Levites*.

CHILD See *Family*.

CHILD ABUSE

Incidents of child abuse in the Bible usually involve the killing of infants or children. Reported instances of child abuse include the death of Israelite male babies in Egypt (Ex. 1:16-17,22), the male babies of Bethlehem (Matt. 2:16), the sons of Mesha (2 Kings 3:4,27), Ahab (2 Kings 16:3; compare 2 Kings 23:10) and Manasseh (2 Chron. 33:6), and the daughters of Lot (Gen. 19:8) and Jephthah (Judg. 11:30-40). The Bible recognizes that some sinful activity is passed on from generation to generation (Ex. 34:7).

Ezekiel compared the origin of the people of Israel to an abandoned baby (Ezek. 16:4-5) found and cared for by God (Ezek. 16:6-14). The psalmist likened God to a father who "has compassion on his children" (Ps. 103:13), a teaching expanded by Jesus when He declared that God is more caring than even human fathers (Luke 11:11-13).

Jesus' actions in welcoming the little children (Mark 10:13-16) exemplify the care which parents and teachers should bestow on children who are under their protection. Parents are charged to not provoke their children (Eph. 6:4; Col. 3:21), a command that forbids all forms of abuse and neglect. Furthermore, Christians have a responsibility to expose and work to rectify acts which are harmful to others, especially persons who are innocent and helpless (Ps. 82:3-4; Jer. 22:3; Eph. 5:11).

CHILDREN (SONS) OF GOD

Heavenly beings (Gen. 6:1-4; Job 1:6; 2:1; 38:7; Pss. 29:1; 89:6), or more often, those people who acknowledge God as the source and goal of their lives and who enter into a relationship of trust and love with God. All people are potential children of God (John 3:15-16). Jesus was, is, and always shall be the preeminent Child of God.

CHILDREN OF THE EAST See *Kadmonite.*

CHILMAD (*marketplace*)

Trading partner of Tyre in Ezek. 27:23 (Hebrew); Kulmadara, city in Syrian kingdom of Unqi; may be modern tell Jindaris; many Bible students think copyists inadvertently changed text from "all of Media."

CHINNERETH (*harp-shaped*), CHINNEROTH

(1) Sea or lake otherwise called the Sea of Galilee, Lake of Gennesaret, or Sea of Tiberias; eastern border of Canaan (Num. 34:11) and western boundary of Gad (Josh. 13:27).

(2) City of Naphtali (Josh. 19:35) on western edge of Sea of Chinnereth, also called Chinneroth (Josh. 11:2), though this could be a reference to the Sea; modern tell al-Oreimeh.

CHIOS

Island in the Aegean Sea 5 miles off coast of Asia Minor, now called Scio; city of same name (Acts 20:15).

CHISEL See *Tools.*

CHISLEU or CHISLEV See *Calendars;* Neh. 1:1; Zech.7:1.

CHITTIM See *Kittim.*

CHIUN (*the constant, unchanging one*)

Intentional scribal change (Amos 5:26), inserting vowels of *siqquts,* "abomination," for original, Kaiwan, Babylonian god of the stars equivalent to Greek Saturn. NRSV reads "Kaiwan;" NASB, "Kiyyun;" NIV, "pedestal." See *Sakkuth.*

CHOINIX See *Weights and Measures.*

CHOSEN PEOPLE See *Election.*

CHRIST, CHRISTOLOGY (*Anointed one*)

Theological explanation of person and work of Jesus, the Christ. See *Messiah.*

Jesus never overtly claimed to be the Messiah in the sense of announcing an aspiration to be Israel's warrior king. He did claim to be the One in whom the kingdom of God was present (Mark 1:14-15; Luke 11:20; see Matt. 13; Mark 4). His mighty acts in healing the sick and casting out demons were demonstrations of the power and presence of God at work in His ministry (Luke 5:17). His teaching on prayer was based on the awareness He had of God as His Father in an intimate sense, calling him "Abba" (Mark 14:36; Luke 10:21-22; 11:2). See *Abba*. His entire mission heralded the coming of the divine kingdom which was closely tied in with His final journey to Jerusalem (Luke 9:51; 13:32-35) and His sacrifice on the cross (Mark 8:31-32; 9:31; 10:32-34).

Because God's redemption of Israel would take place only by the suffering of the Messiah, Jesus took a reserved and critical attitude to the title "Christ." When Peter confessed "Thou art the Christ" (Mark 8:29), Jesus' response was guarded: not denying it, but distancing Himself from the political and social connotations that a nationalistic Judaism had accepted as commonplace in the expected Deliverer. Even the disciples entertained such a hope (Mark 10:35-45; Luke 24:19-21; Acts 1:6). At the trial, Jesus still maintained a reserve (Matt. 26:63-64; Mark 15:2; Luke 22:67-68). Whatever destiny of suffering and rejection awaited Him, Jesus saw, like Isaiah's servant (52:13–53:12), that God would bring Him out of death to newness of life after He atoned for the sins of the world (Mark 10:45; 14:24; compare Isa. 53:5, 10). Still, He was sentenced to death on the trumped-up charge of claiming to be a messiah for Israel and thus a rival to the emperor (Mark 15:26,32).

The church's first Christological statement was based on the two stages in Jesus' existence: He was the Son of David in His human descent, and since the resurrection He is known as the Son of God with power and alive in the Spirit (Rom. 1:3-4).

This way of seeing Jesus' life and resurrection gave believers a personal relationship with Jesus as a present reality. The first recorded Christian prayer is "Maranatha," "Our Lord, come," addressed to the risen Lord and placing Him on a par with Yahweh, Israel's covenant God (1 Cor. 16:22; Rom. 10:9-13; compare Acts 7:55-56,59) as worthy of worship.

Missionary efforts brought the church into the world of Greek religion in Greco-Roman society. The most relevant title in this religious milieu was "Lord," a title used of gods and goddesses in the mystery religions which were partly oriental, partly Greco-Roman. More significantly, "Lord" was an appellation of honor and divinity that came to be associated with emperor worship and applied to Caesar. Lord, already in use as the name of Yahweh in the Greek OT, now was applied to the exalted Christ. It established a meeting point between Christians and pagans familiar with the deities of their religious world (1 Cor. 8:5-6). Later, "Lord" marked off Christian allegiance to Jesus when the Roman authorities required homage be paid to the emperor as divine (compare Rev. 17:14). See *Lord*.

Hebrews sets out to prove the finality of Christ's revelation as Son of God (1:1-4) and great "high priest" (5:5; 7:1–9:28). John's writings are clearest in their ascription to Jesus of the names *Logos* (Word) and (only) God. (See John 1:1,14,18; 20:28, along with the claims of Jesus registered in the affirmations of "I AM," recalling Ex. 3:14; Isa. 45:5; 46:9; compare John 8:24; 10:30,33.)

John boldly claimed Jesus of Nazareth as Mediator in God's creation (John 1:3,18; 14:6,9; compare Prov. 8) and as preexistent revelation of God. He set the earthly life of Jesus against the backdrop of His eternal Being as one with the Father and the visible glory of the unseen God, thus superseding the law of Moses (John 1:17; compare 5:46-47) and the claims of the Roman emperor (John 20:28: "My Lord and my God").

Even these most explicit statements, along with other teachings in

Paul (Phil. 2:6; Col. 1:15; Titus 2:13; possibly Rom. 9:5) and Hebrews (1:1-4), never compromised the belief in the unity of God, an inheritance the Christians took from their Jewish ancestry as a cardinal element of OT monotheism (belief in one God in a world of many gods). Nor did they lend countenance to the view that Jesus was a rival deity in competition with His Father (John 14:28; 1 Cor. 11:3; Phil. 2:9-11). The worship of the church is properly directed to God who has revealed Himself once-for-all and uniquely in the Son whom He loves (Col. 1:13), and who mirrors the perfect expression of the divine nature (2 Cor. 4:4-6).

The NT never explains how to relate the two sides to Jesus' person—the human and the divine. The Christological debates leading to the Council of Chalcedon in A.D. 451 concluded that Christ's two natures are united in one Person, and this belief has remained the centralist position of the church ever since.

CHRISTIAN

Adherent of Christ; one committed to Christ; follower of Christ. Believers "were called Christians first in Antioch" because their behavior, activity, and speech were like Christ (Acts 11:26; compare Acts 26:28; 1 Pet. 4:16).

CHRISTIAN FESTIVALS See Church Year.

CHRISTMAS

Before A.D. 300, churches in Egypt, Asia Minor, and Antioch observed Epiphany, the manifestation of God to the world, celebrating Christ's baptism, His birth, and the visit of the Magi. Shortly after 300, Christians in Rome began to celebrate the birth of Christ. By 400, most parts of the Christian world observed the new festival.

No evidence remains about the exact date of the birth of Christ. The December 25 date was chosen as much for practical reasons as for theological ones. Throughout the Roman Empire, various festivals were held in conjunction with the winter solstice. In Rome, the "Feast of the Unconquerable Sun" celebrated the beginning of the return of the sun. When Christianity became the religion of the Empire, the church either had to suppress the festivals or transform them. The festival of the sun became a festival of the Son, the Light of the world. See Church Year.

CHRONICLES, BOOKS OF

First and 2 Chronicles are the first two books of a four-book series including Ezra and Nehemiah providing a scribal (priestly) history of Israel from the time of Adam (1 Chron. 1:1) to the rebuilding of the house of God, the walls of Jerusalem, and the restoration of the people in the worship of God according to the law of Moses (Neh. 13:31).

First and 2 Chronicles were originally one book. Septuagint translators divided them into two books after 300 B.C. Chronicles focuses on the most important deeds of that time or indeed of any time—building God's house, the temple in Jerusalem on which God had set His name forever (2 Chron. 7:16). David sought to order the life of Israel around the worship of God (1 Chron. 11:4-9; 16:1; 22:1-2). Solomon, his son, built the temple (2 Chron. 2:1), and Zerubbabel, his son of succeeding generations, rebuilt the temple (Ezra 3:8). The intervening kings of Judah were judged by whether or not they were faithful to God and to His house (compare 2 Chron. 28:1-4 with 29:1-11). The house of God is more than a meeting place; it is also the household of faith—the people of God. In the ultimate sense, we would equate God's house with His kingdom. Accordingly, the writer(s) of Chronicles reminds us that the most important of all deeds are those by which God's kingdom is built in the hearts of people.

The Hebrew Bible places Chronicles as the last book in the OT after even Ezra and Nehemiah. Chronicles doubtless occupied this position in the time of Christ, since He cited Zechariah as the last named prophet who suffered a violent death (2 Chron. 24:20-22; Matt. 23:35; Luke 11:51). The OT thus concludes with God's providential control of history to build (rebuild) His house in Jerusalem. The final admonition of the Hebrew OT is for God's people to go up to Jerusalem and build God's house (2 Chron. 36:23). God's final promise is to bless with His presence those who indeed go up to build (2 Chron. 36:23).

We do not know for sure who wrote Chronicles. Tradition names Ezra the priest and scribe (Ezra 7:1-6). This tradition cannot be proved, but there is no valid objection to it.

The use of sources by the author(s) is obvious (1 Chron. 27:24; 28:19; 29:29; 2 Chron. 24:27; 29:30). See *Books*. Much of the material came from the biblical Books of Samuel and Kings.

Chronicles shows God's control of history to fulfill His desire to dwell among His people in a perfect relationship of holiness (compare Ex. 25:8). God is fulfilling His desire through the Lord Jesus Christ—the Son of David.

God chose a person and a people to build His house. The person is the Messiah. Solomon built the temple in Jerusalem, but the Son who is building and shall build to completion God's true house—and the Son whose reign God will establish forever—is the Lord Jesus Christ (1 Chron. 17:12; Luke 1:31-33; Acts 15:14-16). The people are those of faith whose lineage goes back to Adam through Seth to Shem to Abraham (1 Chron. 1:1,17,28), to whom God made the promise of the seed (the Christ) through whom He would bless all nations (Gen. 12:1-4; 15:4-6; 17:7; 22:16-18; Gal. 3:16). His people are those of Israel and, indeed, of all nations who will put their trust in Him.

God who dwells in holiness must be approached according to the law that God gave to Moses (1 Chron. 15:13). People come to God by way of the altar of sacrifice as ministered by the Levitical priesthood. God in His merciful forgiveness of David revealed the place of the altar of sacrifice to be in Jerusalem at the threshing floor of Ornan (1 Chron. 21:18–22:1).

Chronicles encourages God's people to work together with God and one another to build God's house (see 2 Chron. 36:23). Demonstrated thereby is God's blessing upon those who built and otherwise honored God's house, but God's judgment came upon those who neglected, thwarted the building of, or desecrated the house of God. First and 2 Chronicles challenge God's people of every generation to devote themselves with all their heart to building God's house (2 Chron. 36:23).

CHRONOLOGY OF BIBLICAL PERIOD

When speaking of chronology, one must differentiate between relative and absolute chronology. Absolute chronology is tied to fixed dates—events that are known to have occurred on a specific date (i.e., John F. Kennedy was assassinated on November 22, 1963). Relative chronology places events in their chronological order but without a fixed date (i.e., Jesus was baptized, then tempted, then began His public ministry). Most of the biblical events are dated relatively rather than absolutely. For this reason many chronological charts have differences in specific dates, B.C. or A.D., but generally agree on the relative order of most events.

The primary tool by which absolute dates are provided for ancient Israel is Assyrian chronology, which is established through the use of lists of year names (eponyms) that can be tied to absolute chronology by reference to a solar eclipse known to have occurred in 763 B.C. Two Israelite kings, Jehu and Ahab, are referred to on Assyrian tablets. Thus we know that King Ahab (1 Kings 16–22) fought Shalmaneser III at the Battle of Qarqar and died in

853 B.C. Similarly, we know that King Jehu (2 Kings 9–10) in the first year of his reign paid tribute to the same Assyrian king in 841 B.C. Since the books of Kings give the names and length of reign of all the kings of Judah and Israel, the years of Solomon's reign are known with reasonable accuracy to have been 970 to 930 B.C., David's reign was 1010 to 970 B.C., and Saul's was 1050 to 1010 B.C.

SIGNIFICANT DATES IN OLD TESTAMENT BIBLE HISTORY

	Traditional	Critical
PATRIARCHS		
(Abraham, Isaac, Jacob)	2100–1800	1800–1600
Exodus	1446	1290
Conquest	1400	1250
Judges	1350–1050	1200–1025

Kings of United Israel

	Traditional	Critical
Saul	1050–1010	1025–1005
David	1010–970	1005–965
Solomon	970–931/0	965–925

Kings of the Divided Kingdom

Judah		Israel	
Rehoboam	930–913	Jeroboam	930–909
Abijah (Abijam)	913–910		
Asa	910–869		
		Nadab	909–908
		Baasha	908–886
		Elah	886–885
		(Zimri	885)
		(Tibni	885–880
		Omri	885-874
Jehoshaphat	872–848		
		Ahab	874–853
		Ahaziah	853–852
Jehoram (Joram)	853–841		
		Joram (Jehoram)	852–841
Ahaziah	841		
Athaliah	841–835		
		Jehu	841–814
Joash (Jehoash)	835–796		
		Jehoahaz	814–798
Amaziah	796–767		

SIGNIFICANT DATES IN OLD TESTAMENT BIBLE HISTORY
Kings of the Divided Kingdom

Judah		Israel	
		Jehoash (Joash)	798–782
Uzziah (Azariah)	792–740		
		Jeroboam II	793–753
Jotham	750–732		
		Zechariah	753
		Shallum	752
		Menahem	752–742
Jehoahaz (Ahaz)	735–715		
		Pekahiah	742–740
		Pekah	752–732
		Hoshea	732–722
Hezekiah	729–686		
		Fall of Samaria	722
Manasseh	697–642		
Amon	642–640		
Josiah	640–609		
Jehoahaz II	609		
Jehoiakim	608–598		
Jehoiachin	598–597		
Zedekiah	597–586		

Fall of Judah
Exile and Restoration

Babylonian conquest of Judah, Daniel and other nobles exiled	605
Jehoiachin and thousands exiled to Babylon, including Ezekiel	597
Jerusalem and temple destroyed, Zedekiah and others exiled	587/6
Governor Gedaliah assassinated, many fled to Egypt, taking Jeremiah	582 (?)
Jehoiachin released from prison	562
Persian King Cyrus (559–530) captured Babylon	539
Jewish return to Judah led by Sheshbazzar and Zerubbabel	538
Persian King Cambyses	530–522
Persian King Darius	522–486
Preaching of Haggai and Zechariah, Temple building resumes	520
Temple completed	516/5
Persian King Xerxes/Ahasuerus	486–465
Persian King Artaxerxes	465–424
Ezra's arrival in Judah; wall rebuilding begins?	458
Nehemiah's arrival in Judah; wall completed	445
Nehemiah's temporary absence from Judah	433–431?

Apparent numerical inconsistencies of dates between Kings and Chronicles can be resolved by recognizing (1) such common practices as coregencies (the overlapping reigns of a king and his successor) and rival kings and (2) differences between Israel and Judah in the manner of counting the years of a king's reign. The kings of Judah figured their reign from their first full year as king. A part of a year would be designated as the former king's last year of rule. In Israel a part year was designated as the previous king's last year and the new king's first year. Differences between ancient and modern calendars, for example, often necessitates the giving of alternate dates in the form 931/0 B.C. Furthermore, different methods of harmonizing the dates of biblical kings yield slightly different results. The dates given for the divided kingdom in the chart "Significant Dates in the Old Testament Bible History" are according to the widely used system of Edwin A. Thiele.

Assuming a literal interpretation of 1 Kings 6:1, the exodus occurred in 1446 B.C., and the conquest period lasted about seven years around 1400 B.C. Continuing backwards, based on Exod. 12:40, Jacob's migration to Egypt would have been in 1876 B.C. Data regarding the ages of the patriarchs would place their births at 2006 B.C. for Jacob (Gen. 47:9), 2066 B.C. for Isaac (Gen. 25:26), and 2166 B.C. for Abraham (Gen. 21:5). Because the genealogical lists in Genesis are believed by most to be intentionally incomplete or "open," attempts are usually not made to establish historical dates prior to Abraham.

The last days of the kingdom of Judah involve the kings of Babylon, thus giving an outside source to date Judah's history. These external synchronisms can be used to fix the date of the fall of Jerusalem at around 586 B.C.

The period of exile began with the capture of Jerusalem, the destruction of the temple, and the second deportation of leading citizens in 586 B.C. (An earlier deportation in 597 B.C. had taken King Jehoiachin and his family and many top officials to Babylon.) Ezekiel is a leading prophet among the exiles during this time. Exile ended in 538 B.C. after the capture of Babylon by the Persians under Cyrus in 539 B.C. and Cyrus' edict permitting displaced persons to return to their homelands. The rebuilding of the temple is dated between 520 and 515 B.C. according to dates from Hag. 1:1; Zech. 1:1; and Ezra 4:24; 6:15.

During the Intertestamental Period, Palestine was first under the control of the Persians. Persian rule ended with the conquest of Palestine by Alexander the Great in 333–332 B.C. After the death of Alexander, Palestine fell first under Ptolemaic rule (323–198 B.C.) and then under Seleucid rule (198–164 B.C.). The Jewish revolt led by Judas Maccabeus resulted in the defeat of the Seleucids and the Second Jewish Commonwealth (164–63 B.C.). The temple was reconsecrated in 164 B.C. These events are recorded in the Apocrypha in 1 Maccabees 1–4. The successors to the Maccabees are usually called the Hasmonean rulers. Hasmonean rule ended in 63 B.C. when Pompey occupied Jerusalem and Judea was again under foreign domination.

One might expect that the chronology of the NT would be much more certain than that of the OT. In some respects that is the case but not entirely so. The births of both Jesus (Matt. 2:1) and John the Baptist (Luke 1:5) are set in the reign of Herod the Great. From Josephus we learn that Herod died in the 37th year after the Roman Senate decree named him king (40 B.C.). This would place his death in 4 B.C. Herod's command to kill all the boys in Bethlehem two years old or less (Matt. 2:16) is another clue. The further evidence Luke gives of a census while Cyrenius was governor of Syria presents some difficulty (Luke 2:2). Cyrenius conducted a census while serving as governor in A.D. 6–7, but there is no corroborating historical reference to a census during Herod's reign nor to Cyrenius serving as governor at that time. This simply means that we cannot verify Luke's statement from presently available evidence. Luke may have referred to the census of A.D. 6–7 in Acts 5:37. With Herod's death placed in 4 B.C., Jesus' birth is usually dated between 7 and 5 B.C.

The beginning of John the Baptist's ministry is set in the 15th year of Tiberius (Luke 3:1-2), which was A.D. 28 or 29. Jesus' ministry would then have begun in A.D. 29 or 30 if John's ministry began one to two years before that of Jesus. On the other hand, if Tiberius' reign was considered to have begun when he co-ruled with Augustus, his fifteenth year would be A.D. 26 or 27. This latter date would fit better with Luke's statement that Jesus was about 30 when He began His ministry (Luke 3:23). Jesus' ministry would thus have begun about A.D. 27 or 28. The length of Jesus' ministry is also much debated. None of the four Gospels gives enough details to determine the precise length of the ministry. Lengths of one, two, and three years are most often proposed. John's Gospel mentions three Passover feasts (2:13; 6:4; 11:55). If these are distinct Passovers, they would indicate a ministry of at least a little more than two years.

The Roman historian Tacitus dated Jesus' crucifixion during the reign of Emperor Tiberius (A.D. 14-37) when Pilate was governor of Judea (A.D. 26-37). All the Gospel accounts agree that Jesus died on a Friday, the day before the Sabbath, at the beginning of Passover week. The chronological terms used by John and the Synoptic Gospels are not identical, resulting in disagreement over interpreting and reconciling the two. Nevertheless, it seems that after Jesus and the disciples celebrated the Last Supper on Thursday evening, Jesus was arrested and tried that night as well as the following morning. He was then crucified

the next day, Nisan 14, which fell on a Friday in A.D. 30 and 33. If Jesus' ministry began in A.D. 29 or 30, His crucifixion must have been in A.D. 33. On the other hand, if His ministry began in A.D. 27 or 28, His crucifixion was in A.D. 30.

Dating the events and activities of the apostles is as vexing as dating the events of Jesus' life. There are very few fixed dates. The death of Herod Agrippa I, mentioned in Acts 12:23, occurred in A.D. 44 according to Josephus. Likewise, the edict of Claudius expelling Jews from Rome (Acts 18:2) is usually dated to A.D. 49, and Gallio's term as deputy (Acts 18:12) belongs to A.D. 51–52.

Other events in Acts must be dated relatively, and problems remain. In particular, there is great difficulty in matching the chronology of Acts with the information in the Pauline epistles. However, in general, we can sketch with approximate dates the ministry of Paul as follows:

Conversion, A.D. 33/34
First visit to Jerusalem, A.D. 36
Second visit to Jerusalem, during famine, A.D. 46/47
First missionary journey, A.D. 47–48/49
Conference in Jerusalem, A.D. 49
Second missionary journey, A.D. 49/50–52
Third missionary journey A.D. 53–57
Final visit to Jerusalem, A.D. 57
Reaches Rome, A.D. 60
Further ministry in Asia A.D. 62–63
Return to Rome (execution under Nero) A.D. 64/65

The datable events in the NT all occurred before the fall of Jerusalem and destruction of the temple in A.D. 70..

CHRYSOLITE See *Minerals and Metals.*

CHRYSOPRASE See *Minerals and Metals.*

CHUB See *Libya.*

CHUN

KJV spelling of Cun.

CHURCH

Group of persons professing trust in Jesus Christ, meeting together to worship Him, and seeking to enlist others to become His followers; English translation of Greek *ekklesia*, "called out," commonly used to indicate an assembly of citizens of a Greek city (see Acts 19:32,39). The early Christians perceived themselves as called out by God in Jesus Christ for a special purpose with a privileged status in Jesus Christ (Eph. 2:19).

To link the Old and New Testaments, the first Jewish Christians used a common OT self-designation for the people of God. They understood themselves as the people of the God who had revealed Himself in the OT (Heb. 1:1-2), as the true children of Israel (Rom. 2:28-29) with Abraham as their father (Rom. 4:1-25), and as the people of the New Covenant prophesied in the OT (Heb. 8:1-13). This broad background of meaning in the Greek and OT worlds extends "church" in the NT to a local congregation of called-out Christians, such as the "church of God which is at Corinth" (1 Cor. 1:2), and also to the entire people of God, such as in the affirmation that Christ is "the head over all things to the church, which is his body" (Eph. 1:22-23; compare 4:15-16; 1 Cor. 6:12-20; 12:12-27). See *Body of Christ*.

The church is Christ's bride (Eph. 5:22-31), God's new creation (2 Cor. 5:17), new persons (Eph. 2:14-15), fighters against Satan (Eph. 6:10-20), or bearers of light (Eph. 5:7-9). The church is a fellowship of faith with its members described as the saints (1 Cor. 1:2), the faithful (Col. 1:2), the witnesses (John 15:26-27), or the household of God (1 Pet. 4:17).

The church is devoted to Jesus Christ as Lord. He established the church under His authority (Matt. 16:13-20) and created the foundation for its existence in His redeeming death and demonstration of God's power in His resurrection.

Persons were admitted to the local congregation only upon their placing their trust in Christ as Savior (Acts 3:37-42), openly confessing this (Rom. 10:9-13), and being baptized (Acts 10:44-48; see Matt. 28:18-20).

Church members were called to forgive one another (Col. 3:12-14) and to love one another (Eph. 5:1-2; 1 John 3:16) because God had done this for all of them in Christ. They were to demonstrate the power of Christ's redemption in their own lives (Rom. 12:1–13:7; Gal. 5:19-26; Eph. 4:17-24; Col. 3:12–4:1).

The worship of the early church demonstrated the lordship of Christ and the obligation of Christians to love and to nurture one another (1 Cor. 11:17-22; 14:1-5). Christian worship sought to edify and strengthen the Christians present (1 Cor. 14:26) and challenge pagans to accept Christ (1 Cor. 14:20-25). Excesses were curbed by specific suggestions (1 Cor. 14:26-33a; 1 Tim. 2:1-10) and by the rule that what was done should be appropriate to those committed to a God of peace (1 Cor. 14:33a).

The church lived with an urgency created by the awareness Christ was going to return (1 Thess. 1:9-10) to judge unbelievers (1 Thess. 5:1-10), making witnessing to them an urgent concern. The Lord's Supper was seen as proclaiming "the Lord's death till he come" (1 Cor. 11:26). The return of Christ was to result in glorious joy and the transformation of the Christians—a hope that sustained them in difficult times (2 Thess. 1:5-12).

The church organized itself assuming every member had a gift for service to be used cooperatively for the benefit of all (Rom. 12:1-8; 1 Cor. 12:12-31; 1 Pet. 4:10). The organization of the early churches was not necessarily the same in every locality, depending on size, presence of an apostle, and types of ministry. The guiding principle was that the church was the body of Christ with a mission to accomplish, and the church felt free to respond to the leading of the Holy Spirit in developing a structure that would contribute to its fulfilling its responsibilities (Rom. 12:1-8; 1 Cor. 12:4-11; Eph. 4:11-16).

CHURCH/STATE SEPARATION

There was very little separation between governmental and religious institutions in ancient Israel during OT times. Before the Israelite monarchy, Israel operated under a theocracy; during the monarchy Israel's religious institutions fell under the direct influence of the king (eg., 1 Kings 5–8; 2 Kings 16:10-18; 22:1–23:25). Some prophets, however, acted outside of royal control (eg., 1 Kings 17:1; Amos 7:12-15).

In the NT period individual Christians were subject to the authority of Caesar and his officials, yet local churches, if they remained quiet, were able to function relatively independent of governmental control. As the Christian movement grew in power and influence, the Roman Empire's interests invariably came into contact—and conflict—with those of the church.

God bestows all power, civil (Jer. 27:5-6; Dan. 2:21; John 19:11; Rom. 13:1) and religious. Religious freedom is grounded in the reality of God and the freedom of human conscience to worship Him as is seen fitting. Ultimately, all governmental authorities—and individuals—are subject to God (Rom. 13:4,6), whether a particular state removes religion from civil control or not. It is the responsibility of Christian citizens to obey their governmental authorities (Rom. 13:1-5; 1 Tim. 2:1-2; 1 Pet. 2:13-17) yet promote biblical values in society through all possible spheres of influence.

CHURCH YEAR

Times of worship to celebrate the specifically Christian acts of salvation. The early NT church separated itself from Judaism and its three harvest festivals as the major moments of their religious year (Ex. 23:14-17).

See *Festivals.* Through the years, the church developed Christian festivals: Advent, Christmas, Easter, Epiphany, Holy Week, Lent, and Pentecost along with the Lord's Day on the first day of each week. The major festivals all center on the life of Christ. By A.D. 400, the basic elements of the church calendar were firmly established.

Advent came to be regarded as the beginning of the church year and the half-year between Advent and Pentecost, the period during which all the major festivals occurred, came to be regarded as a time for Christians to concentrate on the life and work of Christ. The rest of the year, from Pentecost to Advent, became a time for concentrating on the teachings of Jesus and the application of those teachings in the lives of Christians.

CILICIA

Geographical area and/or Roman province in southeastern Asia Minor on Mediterranean coast; home to some of the people who opposed Stephen (Acts 6:9). The most important city in Cilicia was Tarsus, Paul's birthplace (Acts 21:39; 22:3; see Acts 15:41; 27:5; Gal. 1:21). By the time of the Council of Jerusalem (Acts 15), Christianity had already penetrated Cilicia.

In the OT the region is called Kue (1 Kings 10:28; 2 Chron. 1:16, RSV, NASB, NIV). See *Paul; Tarsus.*

CINNAMON See *Plants; Spices.*

CINNEROTH See *Chinnereth.*

CIRCUIT

Circular route a person, a geographical feature, or a natural object follows. Samuel went around a circuit of cities to judge Israel (1 Sam. 7:16). The human eye views heaven as a circular vault or dome, where God takes His daily walk (Job 22:14; compare Ps. 19:6; Eccl. 1:6). Jerusalem within its walls represented a circle or circuit, which David repaired (1 Chron. 11:8 NRSV; compare 2 Kings 3:9 NASB; Neh. 12:28 NRSV).

CIRCUMCISION

Act of removing foreskin of the male genital; in ancient Israel, ritually performed on eighth day after birth on children of natives, servants, and aliens (Lev. 9:3). Circumcision was carried out by the father utilizing a flint knife (compare Josh. 5:3).

Israelite practice was founded on the circumcision of Abraham as a sign of the covenant between God and the patriarch (Gen. 17:10). Several Semitic and non-Semitic peoples practiced circumcision according to biblical and other sources: Egyptians, Edomites, Ammonites, Moabites, and the desert-dwelling Arabians (Jer. 9:25-26; compare Ezek. 32:17-32). Philistines, Assyrians, and Babylonians were uncircumcised.

The uncircumcised are those who are insensitive to God's leadership (compare Ex. 6:12; Jer. 6:10). Circumcision of the heart implies total devotion to God (Deut. 10:16; Jer. 4:4).

Controversy arose in the early church (Acts 10–15) as to whether Gentile converts need be circumcised. Paul led the Jerusalem Council to decide circumcision was not essential to Christian faith and fellowship. Circumcision of the heart via repentance and faith were the only requirements (Rom. 4:9-12; Gal. 2:15-21).

CISTERN

Translation of Hebrew term for "hole," "pit," or more often "well"; usually a bottle- or pear-shaped reservoir into which water could drain from a roof, tunnel, or courtyard. The difference between cistern and well often is not apparent. The porous limestone out of which cisterns were dug allowed much of the water put into the cistern to escape. After 1300 B.C., cisterns began to be plastered, which resulted in a more efficient system of water storage. See Gen. 37:20-29; Jer. 14; 38:6; 41:7,9.

CITADEL See *Castle*.

CITIES AND URBAN LIFE

Permanent walled population center that serves as cultural, trade, and government center for surrounding rural and village populations. The oldest city excavated to date is tell es-Sultan, OT Jericho, already a bustling city between 8000 and 7000 B.C. See *Jericho*.

The OT differentiates cities from villages on the presence or absence of a defense wall. Jericho covered less than 10 acres. Nineveh in Assyria, about 715 B.C., covered approximately 1,720 acres or over two and a half square miles. Calah (ancient Nimrud) covered over 875 acres or one and a quarter square miles. Solomon's Jerusalem covered only 33 acres; even at the time of Jesus it covered less than 200 acres. Hazor, in northern Israel, was over 175 acres in area.

Recent population projections suggest that most cities could support 160–200 persons per acre. Thus Shechem might have had a population of 2,000 to 2,500 during the OT period; Jerusalem in Solomon's time could have supported 5,000 to 6,500. Even when Jerusalem expanded in Josiah's time, it would have had no more than 25,000 inhabitants. An inscription found at Ebla in northern Syria and dated to about 2400–2250 B.C. states that Ebla had a population of 250,000. However, it is unclear whether this figure referred to the city, the entire kingdom controlled by Ebla, or was an exaggeration to impress others of the size of Ebla. By A.D. 300, the city of Rome may have had nearly a million inhabitants.

Most of the commercial activity for a region was carried out in the city. Usually, the city was located on the main highway or intersection of highways and trade routes through the area. The major sanctuary or worship place would most frequently be located in the city. Whenever war or invasion threatened, the people of the surrounding villages would flee to the walled city for protection.

The typical Ancient Near Eastern city included the following features:

(1)*Walls* of stone or mud brick, at times quite thick. The rampart at Hazor in northern Israel about 1700 B.C. was almost 50 feet high at places and up to 290 feet thick enclosing over 2 miles. See *Architecture in Biblical Period.*

(2) *Gate:* The most important and most vulnerable part of the wall structure was the gate. Massive guard towers usually flanked the gate. The entrance itself was narrow, usually 12 to 15 feet wide. Two heavy wooden doors could be shut and braced with metal bars at night or in case of attack. The gate complex itself had two or three separate sets of doors through which one had to pass to gain entry to the city. Within the inner gate structure would be four to six guard rooms. The open square was often the site of the marketplace. Also, public buildings often stood near the open square. The city gate also served as the courtroom for the city (Josh. 20:4; Ruth 4:1-6).

(3)*Water supply:* During peaceful times, the water supply could be outside the wall within a reasonable distance from the city. A protected water supply accessible from within the city was necessary to endure a siege during wartime. Many homes had cisterns, especially in the more arid regions. Extensive water tunnel and pool systems were built by cutting through the bedrock of the tell to reach the level of the springs (2 Kings 20:20). The Romans often constructed great aqueducts to bring water from long distances to a city.

(4) *Agricultural land:* The OT speaks of the fields of a city or village (Lev. 25:34; Josh. 21:12; Neh. 11:25,30), and indicates that some of the land was held in common and some was owned by a family or clan. Large cities would not have had enough land surrounding to meet its food needs, so they would depend on the trade of surplus produce from the smaller villages. The villages in turn would depend on the cities for manufactured goods and items of trade from distant areas. Agricultural land was not supposed to be sold out

of the family or clan (Lev. 25:25-28, but see Isa. 5:8).

(5) *Acropolis:* The highest elevation of many cities formed an acropolis or inner citadel and a residence for the aristocracy or royalty. Major shrines or temples were often located on the acropolis.

(6) *Street plan:* Ancient Near Eastern cities usually had a regular street plan. In Babylon, major streets led from the gates into the city center. In the period of the monarchy, Israelite cities regularly had an open court just inside the gate. A circular street led from the court around the perimeter of the city. This circular street gave easy access to all sections of the city, as well as providing the military with quick access to any part of the city wall. Other streets branched off this circular street and led into the center of the city. In the Roman cities, the major road was usually the *cardo*, a wide, flagstone paved highway which ran north-south. The major east-west road was the *decumanus.*

(7) *House plans:* Earliest houses had one main room and courtyard. By the period of the monarchy, the typical Israelite house was a four-room house—an open courtyard with three enclosed rooms. In the courtyard, the family carried out its business as well as the cooking. One of the three rooms would probably house the livestock. The other two rooms would be living areas and storage. Some of these houses have stairs that show the presence of an upper story (1 Kings 17:19,23). The successors to Alexander the Great built many Greek cities in Palestine. Greek culture was the pattern in the Decapolis and other Hellenistic cities.

CITIES OF REFUGE

A safe place to flee for a person who had accidentally killed another. The city provided asylum to the fugitive by sheltering and protecting him until a trial could be held to determine his guilt or innocence. If, in the judgment of the city elders, the death had occurred accidentally and without intent, the man was allowed to stay there without fear of harm or revenge by the dead man's relatives (Josh. 20:2-6; see Ex. 21:12-14; Num. 35:1-34; Deut. 4:41-43; 19:1-13). See *Avenger.*

CITIES OF THE PLAIN

Five cities of Gen. 14—Sodom, Gomorrah, Admah, Zeboiim, and Zoar—thought to be located near the southern end of the Dead Sea. All except Zoar were destroyed for the wickedness of Sodom and Gomorrah (Gen. 19:24-29).

CITIZEN, CITIZENSHIP

Officially recognized status in a political state bringing certain rights and responsibilities as defined by the state. Citizenship rights changed as Roman governments changed. In NT times the definition came in the Julian Law passed near 23 B.C.

Roman citizenship could be gained in several ways: birth to Roman parents, including birth to a Roman woman without regards to identity of the father; retirement from the army; being freed from slavery by a Roman master; buying freedom from slavery; being given citizenship by a Roman general or emperor as an individual or as part of a political unit; purchase of citizenship. Paul was born a citizen, but how his family gained citizenship we do not know.

A citizen became liable for Roman property taxes and municipal taxes, had the right to vote in Rome (though different social classes had different rights at this point), became a member of a Roman tribe, was promised a fair trial without certain forms of harsh punishment, could not be executed without a trial, would not be crucified except by order of the emperor, and upon appeal to Caesar had to be taken to Rome for trial. Paul made use of these rights as he faced opposition and persecution (Acts 16:37; 22:26-28; 25:11).

CITRON

NASB, NIV, NCV, NKJV translation of Greek *thuinos,* scented wood that formed part of the rich international trade (Rev. 18:12). KJV translates, "thyine"; NRSV, "scented"; NLT, "perfumed"; CEV, "sweet-smelling"; TEV, "rare"; REB, "fragrant."

CITY OF CONFUSION (CHAOS)

Name applied to Jerusalem (Isa. 24:10).

CITY OF DAVID

Jerusalem; name given the fortified city of the Jebusites after David captured it (2 Sam. 5:6-10); original reference may have been only to the southeastern hill and the Jebusites' military fortress there. Luke 2:4,11 refers to Bethlehem, the birthplace of David (see John 7:42). See *Jerusalem; Zion.*

CITY OF DESTRUCTION

KJV, NCV, NIV, NASB, NKJV translation following Hebrew of Isa. 19:18; NRSV, TEV, CEV, NLT, REB emends Hebrew to read "city of the sun," taken as reference to Heliopolis.

CITY OF PALM TREES

Jericho or site near Jericho where the Kenites lived (Judg. 1:16; see Deut. 34:3; Judg. 3:13; 2 Chron. 28:15). Some identify the region with Zoar on the south side of the Dead Sea or with Tamar about 20 miles south of the Dead Sea. See *Jericho.*

CITY OF SALT

City allotted to Judah "in the desert" (Josh. 15:62). Archaeological finds do not support an identification with Qumran that some have tried to make.

CITY OF THE SUN See *City of Destruction.*

CITY OF WATERS

City in Ammon, probably part or all of Rabbah, the capital (2 Sam. 12:27).

CIVIL LIBERTIES

Civil liberty is grounded in the biblical teaching that all persons have integrity and worth before God (Gen. 1:26-28; Ps. 8:5-8; Rom. 5:6-8) and that governments are established to maintain order in society (Rom. 13:4). The same Spirit of God who provides liberty from sin and from enslavement to the Mosaic law (2 Cor. 3:17; Gal. 5:1) also provides the power and wisdom by which Christians may live under civil authority (Rom. 13:1-5; 1 Tim. 2:1-2; 1 Pet. 2:13-17).

Christians are enjoined to lead quiet lives (1 Thess. 4:11; 2 Thess. 3:12; 1 Tim. 2:2) and be good citizens (Rom. 13:6-7; 1 Pet. 2:17). Both Jesus and Paul called for the voluntary subordination of personal liberty for the sake of others (Luke 22:26; 1 Cor. 8:9-13; 9:12,15; Eph. 5:21; Phil. 2:4). By so doing, Christians are able to live freely yet responsibly in a pluralistic society (Gal. 5:13-15; 1 Pet. 2:16).

CIVIL RIGHTS

The biblical basis for civil rights is grounded in the impartiality of God (Deut. 10:17-18; Acts 10:34; compare Luke 20:21), in the created order by which all persons are made in the image of God (Gen. 1:27-28; 9:6), and in the redemptive work of Christ (Gal. 3:28).

Mosaic law distinguished between sojourners (non-Israelite residents of the land of Israel) and foreigners (persons who were not resident in Israel). Sojourners were subject to the same laws as were Israelites (Ex. 12:49; Num. 15:15-16; compare Deut. 10:18-19), but the rights of foreigners were somewhat restricted (Ex. 12:43; Deut. 15:3; 17:15; 23:20).

Both the Old and New Testaments acknowledged the practice of slavery in the ancient world and held that the rights of slaves were to be protected to a degree greater than was typically found among neighboring cultures (eg. Ex. 12:44; Lev. 25:39-55).

The NT recognizes the fundamental equality of all who are in Christ (Gal. 3:28) and advocates the voluntary subordination of individual rights for the benefit of others (Luke 22:26; 1 Cor. 8:9-13; Phil. 2:4-8).

CLAN

Kin group more extensive than a family whose boundaries are not always clearly delineated. Each clan was governed by the heads of the families (elders). Several clans formed a tribe, and twelve tribes formed Israel. The clan is sometimes referred to as "division," "kindred," "family," "thousand," or even "tribe." See *Family; Tribes of Israel.*

CLAUDIUS

Roman emperor from A.D. 41 to 54 who made Judea a Roman province in A.D. 44. See *Rome and the Roman Empire.*

CLAUDIUS LYSIAS

Roman army captain who protected Paul from Jews who wanted to assassinate him (Acts 23:26).

CLAY

Basic building and artistic material consisting of various types of dirt or sand combined with water to form a material that could be molded into bricks for building, sculptures, pottery, toys, or writing tablets. A piece of clay marked by a signet ring gave proof of ownership or approval.

CLEAN, CLEANNESS

Personal purity physically and ritually; physically, person who habitually maintains a pattern of personal cleanliness and hygiene; mentally, a pattern of thinking that avoids impure thoughts (Mark 7:15); morally, one who obeys God, a condition sin makes impossible to attain by personal effort. Cleanness was fundamental to the establishing and preservation of holiness in the Israelite community (Lev. 11:43-44). As distinct from all other nations, the Hebrews were provided with specific instructions concerning cleanness and how to recover it when it had been lost through carelessness or disobedience.

God established for the Israelites a special group of laws dealing with clean and unclean animals (Lev. 11:1-47; Deut. 14:1-21) to provide guidance for dietary and other circumstances.

Contact with a dead person (Lev. 5:2; 21:1), a creeping insect or animal (Lev. 22:4-5), the carcass of an animal (Lev. 11:28; Deut. 14:8), or a woman in labor (Lev. 12:4-5) brought about uncleanness, and required ritual purification to remove it. Leprosy was particularly dangerous as a source of uncleanness and required special cleansing rituals (Lev. 14:13) when the sufferer was pronounced cured. Unclean persons transmitted their condition to whatever they touched, so that others who handled such things became unclean also. Even God's sanctuary needed to be cleansed periodically (Lev. 4:6; 16:15-20). See *Discharge.*

To be clean meant a positive demonstration in daily life of God's high moral and ethical qualities of absolute purity, mercy, justice, and grace. Cleanness was a part of the moral stipulations of the law. Thus, murder was both a pollution of the land and a violation of the Decalogue's expressed commands. The killing of the innocent called for a response in justice from the entire Israelite community, based on a principle of blood retribution (Num. 35:33; Deut. 19:10). Grave moral offenses that violated God's law and polluted the nation included adultery (Lev. 18:20) — a capital offense (Lev. 20:10)—and perverted sexual activity which included bestiality, with death as the prescribed punishment (Lev. 20:13).

Ceremonial holiness involved distinguishing between clean and unclean. Moral holiness required the Israelites to behave as a nation separated from the pollutions of contemporary society, and to live upright and righteous lives in obedience to God's laws (Lev. 21:25-26). For the penitent transgressor, a complex system of purificatory rites cleansed from both physical and moral defilement (Lev. 6:28; 8:6; 14:8-9; Num. 8:7; 19:9, 17-18). The law established the principle that blood made atonement for human life (Lev. 17:11), and thus a blood sacrifice involved the highest form of purification (Lev. 14:6, 19-20) or dedication to God (Lev. 8:23-24). Yet even this form of sacrifice was powerless against sins deliberately committed against the spirituality of the covenant (Num. 15:30).

The NT associated cleansing only with the ritual customs of contemporary Judaism. The infant Jesus was presented in the temple for the traditional purification ritual (Lev. 12:2-8; Luke 2:22). Cleansing was a matter of contention between the Pharisees and the disciples of John the Baptist (John 3:25), but Christ obeyed the law in sending healed lepers to the priest for cleansing (Lev. 14:2-32; Matt. 8:4). On other occasions, He asserted His superiority to the ordinances that He would subsequently enrich and fulfill (Matt. 12:8; Mark 2:28; Luke 6:5).

Christ stressed a person's motivation rather than the external or mechanical observance of rules and regulations (Matt. 5:27-28; John 15:2).

Jesus' atoning death as our great High Priest transcended all the Law's cleansing rituals (Heb. 7:27). The blood of Jesus cleanses us from all sin (1 John 1:7). For the Christian the cultic provisions of the OT are nullified. All meats have been declared clean (Mark 7:19; Acts 10:9-16), and the only sacrifices that God requires are those that emerge from a humble and contrite heart (Ps. 51:17). See *Atonement.*

CLOAK

Outer garment. See *Cloth, Clothing.*

CLEOPHAS OR CLOPAS

Relative of one of the Marys who were near the cross during the crucifixion (John 19:25). The Greek text describes him literally as "the of the Clopas" [sic]. The most natural interpretation is: Clopas was the husband of Mary. See *Mary.*

CLOSET

Private room in a dwelling, not a storage place, where Jesus encouraged people to pray (Matt. 6:6; compare Luke 12:3).

CLOTH, CLOTHING

Articles humans use to cover "shameful" body parts (Gen. 3:7-8) and to maintain warmth. The earliest clothing resources were the hides of wild animals (Gen. 3:21).

In the Neolithic period, natural flax fibers were spun and woven into linen fabric.

Cotton seems to have originated in Indus Valley. It was highly prized from Egypt to Babylon for its bright color and soft, yet durable, qualities.

Wool was the most commonly used raw material among the Semitic peoples for felt and other fabrics. Natural wool tones ranged from white to yellow to gray.

Silk was imported from China, then spread to Mesopotamia and eventually to the Mediterranean islands, where the moths were cultivated. *Silk* was generally reserved for royalty and the wealthy.

Hemp and hair (camel's or goat's) produced coarse garments when used alone, but when used with wool, produced rugged quality garments. The fuller would prepare the products for use in garments. Oil, dirt, or other residues were removed by washing the material in an alkaline-based liquid and then repeatedly rinsing with clean water. The material would be left in the sun to dry, bleach, and shrink before final usage (Isa. 7:3).

Raw materials were spun and woven into fabric sections about 6 feet in width and as long as necessary (Ex. 26:1-2,7-8). Three kinds of looms were employed during Bible times: the Egyptian vertical, the Greek vertical, and the horizontal. Primitive warp-weighted vertical looms, using hand-molded clay weights, were prominent even in the Iron II period in Israel. These looms consisted of two uprights, a horizontal beam, and a warp stretched between the beam and a series of loom weights. See Ex. 35:25; 39:3; Prov. 31:13,24.

Predynastic Egyptians (about 3000 B.C.) had begun to master the art of dyeing fabrics. See *Colors.* Dyed textiles were generally reserved for special garments and occasions (see Gen. 37:3-4; Ex. 26:1). Men and women wore *tunics* made of linen or wool hanging from the neck to the knees or ankles with diverse patterns and colors.

Loin cloths or waistcloths of linen (Jer. 13:1) or leather (2 Kings 1:8) were worn by men and used to gird up the tunic for travel. For comfort it could be loosened at night or when resting. Priests were to have their hips and thighs covered (Ex. 28:42) so as not to be exposed when in service to Yahweh.

Cloaks, often referred to as a *mantle* (Deut. 10:18; Ruth 3:3), were outer garments used as night coverings, and thus were not to be loaned (Deut. 24:13; compare John 19:2). Jesus' tunic was probably the garment for which the Roman soldiers cast lots at His death (John 19:23). Long sleeveless external robes of blue or purple fabric were worn by royalty, prophets, and the wealthy (1 Sam. 18:4; Ezra 9:3; Luke 15:22). In times of sorrow or distress, this garment might be torn (Job 1:20). Another kind of outer garment was the *ephod,* usually a special white robe (1 Sam. 2:18).

Women's clothing must have had a noticeable difference since wearing clothes of the opposite sex was strictly forbidden (Deut. 22:5). The undergarments were loose fitting or baggy apparel (Prov. 31:24), and the outer robes were more flowing. Women also wore a headcloth of brightly colored or patterned material that could be used as a wrapped support for carrying loads (Isa. 3:22), a veil (Gen. 24:65; Song of Sol. 5:7), or a hanging protective garment against the hot sun. A long train or veil adorned women of high social stature (Isa. 47:2).

Festive clothing for both men and women was generally made of costly white material, adorned with colorful outer wrappings and headclothes. Gold, silver, or jewels further decorated one's festive attire (2 Sam. 1:24). Priestly dress (Ex. 39:1-31) likewise consisted of only the best fine linen, which was dyed scarlet, indigo, and purple, and of gold ornamentation.

CLOUD

Collection of moisture suspended in the skies over the earth and used by biblical writers to symbolize God's miraculous power and sovereignty as well as His judgment. See Gen. 9:14; Ex. 19:9; 24:15; 40:34; Job 3:5; 7:9; 26:8-9; Isa 44:22; Lam. 2:1; 3:4; Ezek. 30:3,18; 32:7; Joel 2:2; Zeph. 1:15; compare 1 Kings 8:10; Isa. 4:5; Matt. 17:5. From May to September, Palestine has no rain or clouds, but God produced them for His people (1 Sam. 12:17-18; 1 Kings 18:44). The rain cloud promised hope for the crops and thus symbolized grace and life (Prov. 16:15). When Yahweh appears as a Warrior, the clouds are His battle chariots in which He travels (Pss. 68:33; 104:3; Isa. 19:1; compare 1 Sam. 22:10; Isa. 19:1; Nah. 1:3; Rev. 1:7) and from which He shoots down the lightning as arrows (Pss. 18:14; 77:17; Zech. 9:14). A sign of the last days is the coming of the Son of Man on a cloud (Luke 21:27), just as He went into heaven on a cloud (Acts 1:9).

CLOUD, PILLAR OF

Means by which God led Israel through the wilderness with His presence and still hid Himself so they could not see His face (Ex. 13:21-22). God came down to speak to Israel in the cloud during crisis times (Num. 11:25; 12:5). Coming to the tabernacle in the cloud, God spoke to Moses face to face (Ex. 33:11; Num. 14:14). Paul used the protection of the cloud theme to warn Christians that living under God's presence calls for holy living (1 Cor. 10:1-14).

CLOUT

KJV (Jer. 38:11-12) for "tattered clothes, rags."

CLUB See *Arms and Armor.*

CNIDUS

City in southwest Turkey near modern Tekir known for statue of Aphrodite Euploia. Paul's ship passed here on the way to Rome (Acts 27:7).

COAL

Charred wood used for fuel (Lev. 16:12; Isa. 44:12,19). Coals provided heat for refining metal (Ezek. 24:11). Burning coals became a symbol of divine judgment (Ps. 18:13). See *Cooking and Heating.*

COAST

Land bordering a major body of water and used by KJV in obsolete sense of territories, borders, frontiers.

COAT See *Cloth, Clothing.*

COAT OF MAIL See *Arms and Armor.*

COBRA See *Animals.*

COCK See *Birds.*

COCKATRICE See *Animals.*

COCKCROWING

Third watch of the night in the Roman system (Mark 13:35), thus midnight until 3 A.M.

COCKLE See *Plants.*

CODEX

Collection of manuscript pages bound in book form. Biblical codices were handcopied in Greek capital letters on parchment from older manuscripts. Nearly 250 of these manuscripts in codex form, dated from A.D. 300 to A.D. 1100, are preserved. See *Writing.*

COFFER

Old English word for box (1 Sam. 6:8,11,15 KJV).

COHORT

Roman military unit (KJV, "band") with capacity of 1,000 men; 10 cohorts formed a legion (see Matt. 27:27; Mark 15:16). Cornelius (Acts 10:1) apparently commanded a cohort of 100 archers named the *Cohors II Miliaria Italica Civium Romanorum Voluntariorum.* An infantry cohort was stationed in Jerusalem and protected Paul from zealous Jews (Acts 21:31).

COINS

Stamped metal disks issued by a government for trade and valuation. The silver shekel, a weight equaling about four-tenths of an ounce, became the standard measure (Gen. 23:16). A larger measure, the talent, was approximately 75 pounds (see 2 Sam. 12:30; 2 Kings 23:33). "Talent" in NT times probably represented a large sum of money, perhaps $1,000, instead of just a measure of weight (Matt. 18:24; 25:27).

To establish controllable standards, the first coins were minted around 650 B.C. both in Greece and in Lydia of Asia Minor. Excavations in Shechem have uncovered a Greek silver coin dating after 600 B.C. The Bible first mentions money in Ezra 2:69, referring to a Persian gold coin. About 326 B.C., after Alexander overran the Persian Empire, Greek coinage was circulated widely in Palestine. About 110 B.C. the reigning high priest minted in bronze the first real Jewish coins. In accord with the Second Commandment, Jewish coins did not bear the image of any ruler, but they used symbols such as a wreath, a cornucopia, or the seven-branched lampstand of the temple.

The coin most often mentioned in the NT is the *denarion,* a silver coin usually minted in Rome. It carried on one side the image of the emperor (Matt. 22:21), and on the reverse may have been some propaganda symbol.

The denarius was the daily pay for Roman soldiers and the wage of a day laborer in Palestine (Matt. 20:22). In Matt. 26:15, the "thirty" silver shekels Judas received for betraying Jesus may equal the compensation for killing a slave by accident (Ex. 21:32), the shekel having become a specific coin weighing a little less than half an ounce.

A *drachma* was a Greek silver coin (Luke 15:8-9) considered equivalent to the Roman denarius. In 300 B.C., a sheep cost one drachma, but apparently by NT times the drachma was worth much less.

The Greek *didrachma* was worth two drachmas or a Jewish half shekel, the amount of the temple tax paid by every male Jew above 19 (Matt. 17:24).

The coin the poor widow put in the temple treasury (Mark 12:42) was the smallest Greek copper coin (*lepta*), two of which equalled a *quadrans,* smallest Roman copper coins.

COLLAR

Translation of various Hebrew words; may describe:

(1) opening for the head in a garment (Ex. 28:32; Job 30:18; Ps. 133:2);

(2) decorative ornament around the necks of the Midianite kings or their camels (Judg. 8:26; see Prov. 1:9; Song of Sol. 4:9);

(3) stocks or a pillory used to restrain a person (Jer. 29:26); and

(4) shackle of iron placed around the neck of a prisoner (Ps. 105:18).

COLLECTION FOR THE POOR

Money Paul took up from Gentile mission churches in Philippi, Thessalonica, Corinth, and Galatia for the poor of the Jerusalem church (1 Cor. 16:1-4; 2 Cor. 8-9; Rom. 15:25). The offering was evidence that in the Christian family there was neither "Jew nor Greek" (Gal. 3:28).

COLLEGE

KJV (2 Kings 22:14) for "repetition, copy, second," referring to the second district or division of Jerusalem (compare Zeph. 1:10).

COLONY

A town or part of a town the Roman government established to provide land or property for military veterans and the lower class. Only Philippi is described as a colony of Rome (Acts 16:12), though many cities, including Corinth, mentioned in the NT were considered as such. Augustus founded colonies in Antioch (Psidian), Lystra, Troas, and Syracuse. Ptolemais (Acco) and Iconium were Roman colonies, while also in Syria/Palestine, Berytus (Beirut), Heliopolis (Baalbek), and Caesarea became colonies after the time of Jesus. Colonies had autonomous local governments (Acts 16:12-40) and in some cases were exempt from poll and land taxes.

COLORS

In biblical literature, color designations often have general symbolic significance. White may be symbolic of purity or joy; black may symbolize judgment or decay; red may symbolize sin or lifeblood; and purple may be symbolic of luxury and elegance. In apocalyptic literature—Daniel and Revelation—colors are tools to express truths in hidden language: *white* for conquest or victory; *black* for famine or pestilence; *red*, wartime bloodshed; *paleness* (literally "greenish-gray"), death; and *purple*, royalty.

Blue was obtained from Mediterranean mollusks (class of *Gastrohypoda*); the Hebrew word is also translated "purple" (Ezek. 23:6) and "violet" (Jer. 10:9). Blue was considered inferior to royal purple but still a very popular color and was used in the tabernacle (Ex. 25:4; 26:1,4; Num. 4:6-7,9; 15:38), in the temple (2 Chron. 2:7,14; 3:14), and in the clothing of the priests (Ex. 28:5-6,8,15; 39:1).

Natural objects such as milk, leprous skin, and snow are designated white (Gen. 49:12; Lev. 13:3-4; Isa. 1:18) as are the garments of Jesus and angels to indicate the glory of the wearer (Matt. 17:2; 28:3; Acts 1:10).

Black is used to denote the color of physical objects: hair (Lev. 13:31,37; Song of Sol. 5:11), skin (Job 30:30; Song of Sol. 1:5-6; Lam. 4:8), the sky as a sign of rain (1 Kings 18:45), and animals (Gen. 30:32-43; Zech. 6:2,6; Rev. 6:5). "Black" is also used figuratively to describe mourning (Job 30:28; Jer. 4:28; 8:21; 14:2), a visionless day (Mic. 3:6), the abode of the dead (Job 3:5; Jude 13), and the treachery of Job's friends (Job 6:16).

The Bible also mentions green, yellow, vermillion, and gray.

COLOSSE or **COLOSSAE** See *Asia Minor, Cities of.*

COLOSSIANS, LETTER TO THE

Letter from Paul to the church at Colosse; one of the Prison Epistles (along with Ephesians, Philemon, and Philippians). The traditional date and place of writing is A.D. 61 or 62 from Rome. Caesarea in the late 50s and Ephesus in the mid-50s have been suggested as alternatives. The primary purpose of Colossians was to correct false teachings troubling the church.

Philemon and Colossians mention many of the same people and were apparently carried by the same messenger (Col. 4:7-18; Philem. 1, 2, 10, 23, 24).

The book may be divided into two main parts after the typical introduction: polemic against false teachings (1:3–2:23); exhortations to proper Christian living (3:1–4:17). Typical of Paul, a lengthy thanksgiving (1:3-8) and prayer (1:9-14) lead into the body of the letter. Paul thanked God for the faith, hope, and love (1:4-5) that the Colossians had by virtue of their positive response to the gospel. He prayed that they might have a full knowledge and understanding of God's will and live worthy of redeemed saints (1:9-14).

The doctrinal section begins with a description of the grandeur of the preeminent Christ (1:15-20): fully God incarnate (1:15,19), supreme

Lord over all creation (1:15-17), supreme Lord of the church (1:18), and the only Source of reconciliation (1:20).

Paul addressed heresy characterized by:

(1) an inferior view of Christ that did not consider Jesus to be fully divine or perhaps did not accept Him as the sole Source of redemption (1:15-20);

(2) plausible sounding "philosophies" that were antichrist (2:8);

(3) legalistic observance of "traditions," circumcision, and various dietary and festival laws (2:8,11,16,21; 3:11);

(4) worship of angels and lesser spirits (2:8,18);

(5) asceticism, the deprivation or harsh treatment of one's "evil" fleshly body (2:20-23);

(6) claims to possess special insight (perhaps special revelations) which made them (rather than the apostles or the Scriptures) the ultimate source of truth (2:18-19).

The exhortations in chapters 3 and 4 stem from the Christian's new nature and submission to the rule of Christ in every area of one's life (3:9-10,15-17). Rules for the typical first-century household appear in 3:18–4:1, addressing wives and husbands, fathers and children, masters and slaves. Submission to the Lord (3:18,20,22; 4:1), Christian love (3:19), and the prospect of divine judgment (3:24–4:1) must determine the way people treat one another regardless of their social station. Exhortations (4:2-6) and an exchange of greetings (4:7-17) bring the letter to a close.

COLT

Young of various riding animals: camels (Gen. 32:15), donkeys (Gen. 49:11; compare Judg. 10:4; 12:14). See *Animals.*

COMFORTER

KJV for special word for the Holy Spirit in John 14–16 (Greek *parakletos*). See *Advocate; Helper; Holy Spirit.*

COMMANDER See *Chancellor.*

COMMANDMENTS, TEN See *Ten Commandments.*

COMMERCE

Financial interchange and trade including products, places of business, business practices (weights and measures, business law), and the means of transport. The Ancient Near Eastern economy revolved around agriculture, but some manufactured goods were produced and natural resources mined. Farm goods, products, and resources had to be transported to market centers and other countries. Barter and the buying and selling of goods and services held a prominent place in the life of villages and towns.

The irrigated fields of Mesopotamia and Egypt and the terraced hillsides of Palestine produced a variety of agricultural products. Surpluses were transported to regional marketplaces and major cities. Whole grain, meal, flax, nuts, dates, olive oil, fish, and a variety of animal by-products found their way into every home and paid the taxes imposed by the government. Kings like Uzziah (2 Chron. 26:10) had large holdings of land and vast herds that contributed to the overall economy.

Manufactured goods most commonly introduced into national or international commerce included fine pottery, weapons, glassware, jewelry, cosmetics, and dyed cloth. Distinctive styles or fine workmanship created markets for these products and made it worth the costs and hazards of sea and overland transport from village craftsmen to markets.

Ships of Tyre and Tarshish carried iron, tin, and lead, exchanging them for slaves, horses, mules, ivory, and ebony at various ports of call (see Ezek. 27:12-24). Aram or Edom (NIV with footnote) traded "emeralds, purple, embroidered work, fine linen, coral, and rubies" (27:16 NASB), and Judah sent honey, oil, and balm along with wheat as trade goods to

Tyre (Ezek. 27:17). The Phoenicians also supplied their trading partners with wool and cloth dyed purple.

Merchant quarters were established in many trading centers like that at Ugarit, a seaport in northern Syria (1600–1200 B.C.). The economic and political importance of these trading communities is seen in Solomon's construction of storehouse cities in Hamath (2 Chron. 8:4) and in Ahab's negotiations with Ben-Hadad of Syria for the establishment of "market areas in Damascus" (1 Kings 20:34 NIV).

Metropolitan centers, like Babylon and Thebes, had open areas or market squares where commerce took place. The narrow confines of the villages and towns in Palestine restricted commercial activity to shops or booths built into the side of private homes or to the open area around the city gate. The gate of Samaria was a market center where people purchased barley and fine meal (2 Kings 7:18).

Large urban centers, like Jerusalem, had several gates and commercial districts, thus allowing for diversification of commercial activity throughout the city. Jeremiah 18:2 speaks of the Potsherd Gate (author's translation; known as the Dung Gate in Neh. 2:13) and the bakers' street as the principal area of production and supply of bread in Jerusalem (Jer. 37:21). Josephus lists several commercial activities in the city in the Roman period: wool shops, smithies, and the clothes market.

Until the establishment of the monarchy, commercial transactions were governed in each Israelite town by a local standard of exchange. Even these standards were apparently negotiable, however, and sometimes subject to abuse. Thus, Abraham was forced before witnesses in the gate of Hebron to pay an exorbitant rate (400 shekels of silver) for the cave of Machpelah (Gen. 23:16), and Amos condemned those merchants who were "making the ephah small, and the shekel great,

and falsifying the balances by deceit" (8:5).

Until coinage was introduced after 600 B.C., foodstuffs and other goods were obtained through barter in the marketplace or purchased with weights of precious metals (Gen. 33:19; Job 42:11). When minted coinage came into general use during the Hellenistic period (after 200 B.C.), it created a revolution in commerce. See *Coins.* Transactions in accepted coinage, known to bear a definite weight, added to the confidence of the public and eliminated some of the abuses of the marketplace. Coins also facilitated the payment of taxes (Mark 12:15-17) and wages (Matt. 20:2).

From earliest times caravans of traders carried goods throughout the Near East. Palestine, situated on a land bridge between Mesopotamia and Africa, naturally became a center of commercial travel. Groups of Semitic traders, like the Ishmaelites and Midianites (Gen. 37:27-28), used hilltop pathways as well as the Via Maris coastal highway and the King's Highway in Transjordan to move between Mesopotamia and Egypt. Eventually, the introduction of camels and the establishment of caravansaries, inns and rest centers where caravans could rest at night, made it possible for merchants to take a more direct route across the deserts of northern Syria and Arabia. These lucrative trade routes were controlled in the Roman period by the city of Tadmor, the capital of the Palmyran kingdom, and by the Nabateans.

During the monarchy, Israel's trade horizon expanded. Solomon imported vast quantities of luxury and exotic goods (ivory, apes, peacocks, 1 Kings 10:22b) from all over the Near East. He also purchased horses and chariots for his fortress garrisons like those at Gezer, Hazor, and Megiddo (1 Kings 10:26). The nation had no deep water ports on its coastline, so the Gulf of Aqaba became the prime point of entry for goods coming from Africa (spices, precious stones, gold from Ophir, and algum wood). The shipping trade of Israel, as well as many other nations, joined with or was carried by Phoenician merchantmen (1 Kings 10:22). These more experienced sailors could avoid the storms and other hazards that sank many ships in the Mediterranean (2 Chron. 20:37 NIV).

Even in NT times, shipping was restricted to particular routes and seasons (Acts 27:12). The Romans constructed paved roads that facilitated the movement of their armies, as well as people and wagons loaded with goods for sale. Mile markers set up along these roads show how often they were repaired and which emperors took a special interest in the outlying districts of his domain. See *Agriculture; Banking; Economic Life; Marketplace; Transportation and Travel; Weights and Measures.*

COMMUNION

Paul's term describing the nature of the Lord's Supper. See *Fellowship; Lord's Supper.*

COMMUNITY SERVICE

Descriptions of community service recorded in the Bible center primarily on a believer's responsibility to seek the good of others (1 Cor. 10:24; Phil. 2:4). Specific injunctions for community service include the care of the poor (Deut. 15:7-8), orphans and widows (Deut. 14:29; Acts 6:1), sojourners (Lev. 19:10; Deut. 14:29; Heb. 13:2), those who are sick or in prison (Matt. 25:36), the hungry (Isa. 58:7; Matt. 25:35; Jas. 2:15-16) and homeless (Job 31:32; Isa. 58:7), and victims of crime (Luke 10:29-37).

The early church regularly cared for the social and physical needs of its members (Acts 2:45-46; 4:34-37; 6:1-6; 2 Cor. 8:3-4). While it is less clear to what extent the early church met similar needs among persons outside their fellowship, the tenor of Jesus' statements about neighborliness (Luke 10:29-37; compare Luke 4:25-27) suggest that believers also have a responsibility to reach beyond the church and into their communities.

COMPASSION

To feel passion with someone, enter sympathetically into their sorrow and pain, translating at least five Hebrew and eight Greek terms ranging in meaning from to regret, be sorry for, grieve over, or spare someone to what is beautiful, to an emotional cry of hurt, to parental love and devotion, to a feeling of empathy for undeserved suffering, to lamentation and grief for the dead to moderation in emotions and passions. See Ex. 2:6; 2 Sam. 21:7; Neh. 13:22; Job 8:5; Joel 2:18; Jonah 4:10-11; Zech. 12:10; compare Gen. 19:16; 2 Chron. 36:15; Isa. 63:9; Mal. 3:17.

God is the Father and source of compassion (2 Cor. 1:3; Ezek. 20:17; Mark 5:19; Eph. 2:4; 1 Pet. 1:3; Jas. 5:11). God could forbid Israel to have pity (Deut. 7:16) as He refused to have pity on a disobedient people (Ezek. 5:11; Hos. 13:14). God's people should pray for Him to "spare" them (Joel 2:17).

Compassion can be a feeling of pity and devotion to a helpless child, a deep emotional feeling seeking a concrete expression of love (Gen. 43:14; Deut. 13:17), most often with God as subject. Compare Hos. 2:4,23; Zech. 1:16; 10:6.

Compassion is a quality expected of believers (Phil. 2:1; Col. 3:12; 1 Pet. 3:8; compare Heb. 4:15; 10:33-34), a result of being in Christ (Phil. 1:8; for Christ's compassion, see Mark 6:34; 9:22; compare Matt. 9:36; 20:34). The love of God dwells only in those who are compassionate to a person in need (1 John 3:17; compare Matt. 18:27; Luke 10:33; 15:20; Eph. 4:32; 1 Pet. 3:8; Jas. 5:11). In compassion He has provided salvation and forgiveness (Luke 1:78).

CONCUBINE

Secondary wife; generally taken by tribal chiefs, kings, and other wealthy men (Gen. 22:24; 25:6; 1 Chron. 1:32; compare Judg. 8:31; 2 Sam. 3:7; 5:13; 21:11). Solomon took the practice to its extreme, having 300 concubines, in addition to his 700 royal wives

(1 Kings 11:3). Deuteronomy 17:17 forbids kings to take so many wives.

A concubine, whether purchased (Lev. 25:44-46) or won in battle (Num. 31:18), was entitled to some legal protection (Ex. 21:7-12; Deut. 21:10-14). She remained her husband's property. A barren woman might offer her maid to her husband hoping she would conceive (Gen. 16:1ff.; 30:1ff). Monogamous marriage was more common and the biblical pattern (Gen. 2:24; Mark 10:6-9). See *Marriage*; *Slave, Servant*.

CONDEMN

Act of pronouncing someone guilty after weighing the evidence (Ex. 22:9; Deut. 25:1; Matt. 20:18; Mark 14:64; Luke 23:40); making personal judgments of others (Matt. 12:41; Jas. 3:1; Titus 2:8). Corrupt judges "condemn the innocent" (Ps. 94:20-21). God saves the poor man "from those that condemn his soul" (Ps. 109:31). God condemned sin in human nature by sending His own Son (Rom. 8:3). Paul felt that avoiding final condemnation was reason to accept God's chastening (1 Cor. 11:32; compare John 3:17-19; 5:24).

CONDUIT

Water channel or aqueduct in or near Jerusalem channeling water into the city (2 Kings 18:17; 20:20; Isa. 7:3); probably outside the wall northwest of the city beside the highway to Samaria. See *Gihon; Siloam*.

CONEY See *Animals*.

CONFECTION, CONFECTIONER

KJV for salve, ointment, or perfume; one who mixes them; same Hebrew word as KJV, "apothecary"; modern translations, "perfumer" (Ex. 30:25,35; 37:29; 1 Sam. 8:13; Neh. 3:8; Eccl. 10:1). See *Perfume, Perfumers; Occupations and Professions*.

CONFESSION

Admission, declaration, or acknowledgment of sin or of faith, especially in worship. Old Testament confession included ritual acts for sin: the sin (or guilt) offering (Lev. 5:5-6:7) and the scapegoat that represented the removal of sin (16:20-22). Confession of sin may be by a person on behalf of the people as a whole (Neh. 1:6; Dan. 9:20), the collective response of the worshiping congregation (Ezra 10:1; Neh. 9:2-3), or individual acknowledgment of sin by the penitent sinner (Ps. 32:5; Prov. 28:13; see also Pss. 40 and 51).

John's followers were baptized, confessing their sins (Matt. 3:6; Mark 1:6; compare Acts 19:18). God faithfully forgives the sins of those who confess them (1 John 1:9). Believers are to confess sins to one another (5:16), probably within the context of congregational worship. By A.D. 100, routine worship included confession preceding the Lord's Supper for confession of faith. See *Confessions and Credos*.

CONFESSIONS AND CREDOS

Articulate and corporate expressions of the faith in response to the revelatory and saving acts of God. Confession has its primary place in worship and preaching, implying allegiance and commitment, while credo belongs to teaching ministry and refers to doctrine with a note of authority.

The Bible has two types of confessions, the nominal type rooted in the Ten Commandments introduction (the Lord is our God, Ex. 20:2; see also Deut. 5:6; Pss. 3:8; 7:2,4; 10:12; 100:3) and the verbal type (see Deut. 6:21-23; 26:5-9; Pss. 105:8-45; 135; 136) which relates the acts of God.

Joshua 24 is a confession in action with God's mighty acts for Israel (vv. 2-13), Joshua's call to serve the Lord and to put away the strange gods of their fathers (vv. 14-15), people confessing the Lord as their God (vv. 16-17), a recitation of the acts of God for Israel, and a renewed confession (vv. 17-18).

The new element of NT confession was the revelatory acts of God in Jesus, the Christ. Three stages can be distinguished in the church's confessions:

(1) *Life and ministry of Jesus on earth,* confessing Jesus meant to express personal allegiance and commitment to Him and to His cause (Matt. 10:32; Luke 12:8) rather than make a statement about Him.

(2) *After Jesus' resurrection and exaltation,* faith in Christ began to be formulated in one sentence. The most common nominal confession is: Jesus is Lord (Rom. 10:9; 1 Cor. 12:3; Phil. 2:11), conceivably a baptismal confession. Verbal confessions tell the story of Christ in a pointed and condensed form (Phil. 2:5-11; Col. 1:15-20; 1 Tim. 3:16; 1 Pet. 3:18-22; Heb. 1:1-3; compare 1 Cor. 15:3-5) and are related to witnessing.

(3) *In the church's defense against false interpretation,* confessions become primarily doctrinal and credal: Jesus Christ has come in the flesh (1 John 4:2; 2 John 7); Jesus is the Christ (1 John 5:1) or the Son of God (1 John 5:5). Understood together they form the doctrine of Christ (2 John 9).

CONFLICT, INTERPERSONAL

The Bible illustrates, explains and offers solutions for interpersonal conflict.

Among the more notable instances of interpersonal conflict recorded in the Bible are the hostilities between Cain and Abel (Gen. 4:1-16), Abram and Lot (Gen. 13:8-18), Jacob and Esau (Gen. 25–27; 32–33), Jacob and Laban (Gen. 29–31), Saul and David (1 Sam. 18–31), Mary and Martha (Luke 10:38-42), Jesus' disciples (Mark 9:33-37; Luke 22:24-27), Paul and Barnabas (Acts 15:36-41), and the Corinthian believers (1 Cor. 1:10-12; 3:2-4; 11:18).

The root cause of interpersonal conflict is sin (Gal. 5:19-20). James explains that fighting is the result of uncontrolled passions and desires (Jas. 4:1-3). The Book of Proverbs characterizes those who stir up conflict as persons given to anger (Prov. 15:18; 29:22), greed (Prov. 28:25), hate (Prov. 10:12), gossip (Prov. 16:28), and worthless perversions (Prov.

6:12-15). Such conflicts inevitably result in personal destruction (Prov. 6:15), discord (Prov. 6:14), and strife (Prov. 10:12; 16:28). It is no wonder that "the LORD hates...he that soweth discord among brethren" (Prov. 6:16,19).

The Bible places great value on the ability to live at peace with one another (Ps. 34:14; Mark 9:50; Rom. 14:19; 1 Thess. 5:13; Heb. 12:14; 1 Pet. 3:11), in unity (Ps. 133:1), and harmony (Rom. 15:5-6). At the same time, the Bible declares unequivocally that such peace is given only by God (Num. 6:26; John 14:27; 16:33; 2 Cor. 13:11; 2 Thess. 3:16) and lived out only as believers pattern their lifestyles after that of Jesus (Phil. 2:3-8).

CONGREGATION

Assembled people of God as a holy people, bound together by religious devotion to Yahweh rather than by political bonds; may apply to any individual or class collectively such as "the wicked," "the hypocrites"; once used for a herd of bulls (Ps. 68:30) and once for a hive of bees (Judg. 14:8). The congregation of Israel functioned in military, legal, and punishment matters. Every circumcised Israelite was a member. In the NT the congregation is the "called out ones," the church. See *Church.*

CONSCIENCE

Human moral awareness that judges an action right or wrong. The Hebrew "*heart*" refers to conscience in a number of passages, for example, 1 Sam. 24:5; compare 2 Sam. 24:10; Job 27:6; 1 John 3:20-21. "Reins" or "kidneys" sometimes refers to conscience (Ps. 16:7).

In the NT God judges persons by His standards as revealed in Jesus Christ. The "conscience" is a person's painful reaction to a past act that does not meet the standard. A pure conscience is valuable, but Christ is the final standard by which a person is judged. When sensitive and active in judging past acts, the conscience is said to be "good" (Acts 23:1; 1 Tim.

1:5,19; 1 Pet. 3:16,21; Heb. 13:18; compare Acts 24:16). A conscience not active in judging past acts is said to be "weak" (1 Cor. 8:7,10,12) and may be wounded (1 Cor. 8:12). When the conscience is insensitive, it is "seared" (1 Tim. 4:2). The sinful conscience is "defiled" (Titus 1:15) or "evil" (Heb. 10:22).

CONSCIENTIOUS OBJECTORS

While the Bible does not speak directly to the issue of conscientious objectors, it does offer principles which can help an individual determine whether it is proper to invoke the status of conscientious objector in any given situation.

The Bible entreats Christians to be good citizens, and in principle this involves subjection to the governing authorities (Rom. 13:1-7; Titus 3:1; 1 Pet. 2:13-17). As much as it depends on the ability of each individual believer, Christians are commanded to live peaceably with others (Rom. 12:18).

At times Christians find it necessary to disobey the laws of men in order to follow higher standards set by God (Acts 4:19-20; 5:29). Each individual is given a conscience which, when purified by God, helps that person determine a proper course of action within a given set of circumstances (Rom. 14:4; 1 Tim. 1:5, 19; Heb. 13:18; 1 Pet. 3:16). When Shadrach, Meshach and Abednego (Dan. 3:16-18), Daniel (Dan. 6:10-16), the apostles (Acts 5:40-42), and Paul (Acts 25:11) chose to disobey the civil government, they willingly accepted the consequences of their actions.

The issue of a "just war" is complex. While at times God called His people to battle (eg. Josh. 6:2-5; Judg. 1:1-2), the Bible records other instances when war was to be opposed (compare Isa. 7:1-16; 22:8b-11). It is incumbent on every believer to trust God for guidance in each situation.

CONSECRATION

Separated to or belonging to God; holy or sacred; set apart to live according to God's demands and in His service (Ex. 19:6; compare Lev. 19:2; Matt. 23:19). See *Holy*.

CONSERVATISM

Conservatism is a disposition to appreciate, conserve, and foster in the present teachings and values that are rooted in the past. In the Bible, conservatism is most clearly seen in the attitude that Paul took toward faith and Scripture. Paul recognized that he was heir to a body of sacred writings and traditions which must be learned, believed, and carefully taught to others (1 Cor. 11:2; 2 Thess. 2:15; 2 Tim. 1:13-14; 3:14-15; Titus 1:9).

The Pharisees, who placed great stress on observing the traditions of their elders (Mark 7:3-4; compare Deut 6:6-7; Prov. 1:8; 4:1-4), criticized Jesus for His apparent lack of conservatism (Mark 7:5). Jesus' response was to distinguish between human traditions and the words of God (Mark 7:6-13), the latter which, by implication, were intended to enliven men's hearts in a way that mere tradition could not.

CONTAINERS AND VESSELS

Hollow receptacles used to hold dry or liquid substances, ranging from pottery dishes, bowls, urns, and jugs to baskets, metalware, cloth and leather bags, and on to wooden boxes and bowls and glassware of all shapes and sizes. Most common were vessels of clay.

Stoneware was the first to be produced, dating from the Paleolithic (Old Stone) and Epipaleolithic (Middle Stone) Ages (700,000 to 8300 B.C.). The Neolithic (New Stone) and Chalcolithic Ages (8300 to 3100 B.C.) brought larger and deeper stoneware vessels with firing procedures. See *Pottery*.

Metalware has been found in abundance. Palaces and temples often had vessels made of gold or silver; by far the most common material was bronze. Pure copper rarely was used. See *Minerals and Metals; Mines and Mining*.

Wood was used to produce storage boxes and bowls. Boxes were made by nailing together planks, whereas bowls usually were hollowed from single pieces of wood. Glass has a long history in the Middle East. Obsidian (volcanic glass) was brought into Palestine from Anatolia as early as 5000 B.C. Manufactured glass began to appear after 2500 B.C., but vessels made of glass did not appear until about 1500 B.C. Glass containers were made by molding the molten material around a solid core of the desired shape. Highly skilled artisans created pieces that imitated precious stones such as lapis lazuli and turquoise. Only royalty and temples owned glassware. Practically all Palestinian glass was imported from Egypt, whose glass industry reached its zenith between 1400 and 1300 B.C.

Glass drinking bowls became popular in Palestine by 200 B.C. Most originated in Phoenicia. About 50 B.C. came the revolutionary invention of glass blowing. Palestinian artists became famous for their brown glass. Many even began signing their creations—the first known designer products in history. See *Glass; Vessels and Utensils.*

CONTENTMENT

An internal satisfaction which does not demand changes in external circumstances. Food and lodging should be enough for the godly (1 Tim. 6:6-10; compare Matt. 6:34; Heb. 13:15; contrast Luke 12:19). The believer can be content no matter what the outward circumstances (Phil. 4:11-13). Believers are content to know the Father (John 14:8-9) and depend on His grace (2 Cor. 12:9-10; compare 2 Cor. 9:8-11).

CONVERSION

Turning to God; experience of encountering God's reality or purpose and responding in personal faith and commitment (Ps. 19:7; compare 51:13; 85:4; Isa. 1:27; 6:10; Lam. 5:21). Jacob (Gen. 32), Moses, (Ex. 3), and Isaiah (Isa. 6) had life-changing experiences with God. Nebuchadnezzar of Babylon, through a series of unusual circumstances, turned to the King of heaven (Dan. 4:37).

The NT refers only to "the conversion of the Gentiles" (Acts 15:3; compare reference to Isa. 6:10 in Matt. 13:15; Mark 4:12; John 12:40). The way disciples enter the kingdom is to be converted and become as little children (Matt. 18:3; Acts 3:19; compare Luke 22:32; Acts 14:15; 15:19; 26:20; 26:18; compare 1 Thess. 1:9; 2 Cor. 3:16). James encourages us, "that he which converteth the sinner from the error of his way shall save a soul from death" (Jas. 5:20).

Jesus encountered many individuals who then experienced a radical change in their lives: Zacchaeus (Luke 19), woman at the well at Sychar (John 4), sinful woman in Simon's house (Luke 7), and Nicodemus (John 3). In Acts notable conversions include the Ethiopian eunuch (Acts 8), Saul of Tarsus (Acts 9), and Cornelius (Acts 10; compare Acts 2:41; 9:35; 11:21).

In Christian conversion an individual turns from sin and trusts in Jesus Christ for salvation, resulting in an outward change of the mind, emotions, and will (2 Cor. 5:17). Conversion rests on God's sovereign grace and mercy revealed in the cross of Christ (Rom. 5:8). The person accepts Jesus as Lord of life and acknowledges that acceptance to Him. See *Regeneration; Salvation; Faith; Repentance.*

CONVICTION

A sense of guilt and shame leading to repentance. God may be the subject and persons the object (Job 22:4), or a person may be the subject who convicts another person (Ezek. 3:26). Young ministers like Timothy and Titus had the responsibility of "convicting" (rebuking, refuting) those under their charge (1 Tim. 5:20; 2 Tim. 4:2; Titus 1:13; 2:15). Conviction for sin results when the Holy Spirit awakens a person to a sense of guilt and condemnation because of sin and unbelief (John 16:8-11). John the Baptist "convicted" Herod Antipas because of his illicit marriage to Herodias, his brother's wife (Luke 3:19). No one could convict Jesus of sin (John 8:46). See *Sin; Forgiveness; Repentance.*

CONVOCATION, HOLY See *Festivals.*

COOKING AND HEATING

Preparing food through heating it and giving the living environment warmth. In Bible times, the means of heating—open fire—was the means of cooking.

In a bedouin encampment, fire was laid in a hollow scooped out of the ground or on flat stones. The fire was ignited by friction or by firing tinder with sparks (Isa. 50:7,11).

When people moved from tents to houses, fires for cooking were still generally lit out-of-doors in the far corner of the courtyard. Only later were better homes provided with a chimney. A fire was necessary to keep warm, but the only window needed rough curtaining with a blanket. With little space to exit, the smoke blackened the rough ceiling and made the householders choke and splutter. In the monarchy houses of royalty had a form of central heating in which the heat of underfloor fires was ducted underneath paved rooms.

For cooking, large flat stones were put in the hot fire. When the flames had died down, bread dough was placed on the hot stones. Where the fire was placed in a hole in the ground, the dough was actually placed on the hot sides of the depression. Another common method was to invert a shallow pottery bowl over the fire, and place the dough cakes on the bowl's convex surface.

Many years later, the pottery "oven" was invented: a truncated cone placed over the fire. The cakes of bread were then placed on the inside of the cone at the top, away from the flames. Not until Roman times were pottery ovens in use where the firebox was separated from the cooking area by a clay dividing piece.

As communities grew larger, the baker developed his trade. His oven was tunnel shaped. Shelves lined the sides for the dough, and fires were lit on the floor. A housewife could take her own dough to be cooked in the communal oven. Children collected hot embers at the end of the day for kindling fires in their own homes (Hos. 7:4-7). Jeremiah received a bread ration from the local bakery while he was in prison (Jer. 37:21).

A metal baking sheet was sometimes placed over the hot fire and grain put on the metal surface. The grain "popped" and provided what the Bible calls parched corn (1 Sam. 25:18).

The basic food to go with the bread was vegetable soup prepared from beans, green vegetables, and herbs. A large cooking pot was put directly on the fire. The pottage that Jacob gave to Esau was a lentil soup (Gen. 25:30), eaten by forming a scoop with a piece of bread and dipping it in the central pot. Ritual law forbade the mixing of seeds in soups (Lev. 19:19). On special occasions such as the arrival of a guest, meat would be added to the stock.

Most meat was boiled or stewed and was taken either from the herd or in the hunt. Meat was normally roasted only at festivals and very special days such as Passover (Ex. 12:8-9).

Meat was available from the sheep and goats of the flock, but the hunting of wild animals from the jungle in the Jordan Valley was popular. Veal was served to Abraham's guests (Gen. 18:7), while Gideon's guests ate goat meat (Judg. 6:19). Milk, too, was used as a basic cooking ingredient, but it was forbidden to stew a kid in its mother's milk (Ex. 23:19). Milk was drunk for itself and used in preparing other foods. Some milk was fermented to produce yogurt, called "milk" in some translations (Judg. 4:19). Milk was used to make cheese (1 Sam. 17:18) and when placed in a skin bag to be shaken and squeezed by turn, butter was produced. Buttermilk was presumably used but is not mentioned in the Bible.

While in Egypt, Israel became used to food popular in that country —cucumbers, garlic, leeks, onions, and melons (Num. 11:5). Some of these plants were uncooked and were used to eat with bread or as a salad. Others were cooked to give additional flavor to the cooking pot. Herbs were also used to add to the flavor. Salt was collected during the hot season from the shores of the Dead Sea and used for preservation as well as for seasoning. Liberal use was made of dill, cummin (Isa. 28:25-27), coriander, and sugar. Spicy chutneys were also prepared to give added flavor to the food. The *charoseth* used at Passover was a chutney made of dates, figs, raisins, and vinegar.

Olive oil was used both for binding the flour instead of water and for frying (See 1 Kings 17:12). Figs, sycamore figs, pomegranates, and nuts were eaten either raw or stewed.

By NT times, fish was a common addition to the diet. Fish was most commonly grilled over a fire (John 21:9) or salted and eaten later.

Some grapes were dried in the hot sun to become raisins. Most of the grapes were crushed to obtain their juice. See *Wine; Winepress.* Wine was the natural and safest drink because water supplies were often suspect. A housewife sometimes boiled up the juice to make a simple grape jelly or jam, which was spread on bread. This may well be the "honey" in the "land flowing with milk and honey" (Ex. 3:8,17).

COOS

KJV spelling for Cos. See *Cos.*

COPPER See *Minerals and Metals; Mines and Mining.*

CORBAN

Gift particularly designated for the Lord, and so forbidden for any other use (Mark 7:11). Jesus condemned persons who mistakenly and deliberately avoided giving needed care to their parents by declaring as "*corban*" any money or goods that could otherwise be used to provide such care. What began as a religious act of offering eventually functioned as a curse, denying benefit to one's own parents. See *Sacrifice and Offering.*

CORINTH

City in Greece; one of four prominent church centers in NT with Jerusalem, Antioch of Syria, and Ephesus. Paul's first extended ministry was at Corinth, where he remained at least 18 months (Acts 18:1-18). First and Second Corinthians were written to Corinth, and Romans, from Corinth. Prominent Christian leaders associated with Corinth include Aquila, Priscilla, Silas, Timothy, Apollos, and Titus.

Corinth, on southwest end of isthmus that joined southern part of Greek peninsula with mainland to the north, stood on an elevated plain at the foot of Acrocorinth, a rugged hill reaching 1,886 feet above sea level. It was a maritime city between two important seaports: Lechaion on the Gulf of Corinth about 2 miles to the north and Cenchreae on the Saronic Gulf about 6 miles east of Corinth.

Corinthians continued to worship Greek gods with shrines to Apollo, Hermes, Heracles, Athena, and Poseidon. Corinth had a famous temple dedicated to Asclepius, the god of healing, and his daughter Hygieia. The most significant pagan cult in Corinth was the temple of Aphrodite on top of the Acropolis. Even in an age of sexual immorality, Corinth was known for its licentious life-style. Paul began his Corinthian ministry in the synagogue in Corinth.

CORINTHIANS, FIRST LETTER TO THE

Paul's practical letter to the church at Corinth from the city of Ephesus (16:7b-8a). Early in A.D. 50 Paul left Athens and headed for Corinth, where later Silas and Timothy joined him (Acts 18:5). Paul ministered in

Corinth at least 18 months (Acts 18:1-18). He began working with Aquila and Priscilla in tent making. See *Aquilla and Priscilla.* After visiting Jerusalem and Antioch of Syria, Paul returned to Ephesus for a ministry of more than two years (Acts 19:8-10). During Paul's Ephesian ministry a series of disturbing events took place relative to Corinth:

(1) A party spirit arose in Corinth (1 Cor. 1:12-13; 3:3-4).

(2) A series of reports including attacks on Paul (1 Cor. 2:1-10) and problems of immorality (1 Cor. 5:1) came to Paul, some by those of Chloe (1 Cor. 1:11).

(3) Paul wrote a letter (lost unless a portion remains in 2 Cor. 6:14-7:1) warning against fellowship with sexually immoral people (1 Cor. 5:9).

(4) The Corinthians wrote to Paul (1 Cor. 7:1) asking about marriage, fornication, and disorders in public worship.

(5) A delegation (Stephanas, Fortunatus, and Achaicus) came with news from Corinth (1 Cor. 16:17).

(6) Apollos (Acts 18:24-28) quit his work in Corinth and returned to Ephesus, refusing despite Paul's urging to go back to Corinth (1 Cor. 16:12).

(7) Paul sent Timothy to Corinth (1 Cor. 4:17) to heal the problems.

(8) Paul wrote 1 Corinthians from Ephesus (1 Cor. 16:8), expecting them to receive the letter before the arrival of Timothy (1 Cor. 16:10).

Paul wrote 1 Corinthians to give instruction and admonition that would lead to solving the congregation's many problems. Some of these problems may have arisen out of a "super spiritualist" group influenced by incipient Gnostic teachings. All the problems in chapters 1-14 were grounded in egocentric or self-centered attitudes in contrast to self-denying, Christ-centered attitudes. Chapter 15 concerning the resurrection may reflect sincere misconceptions on the part of the Corinthians. Thus Paul contrasted the egocentric life with the Christocentric life, showing the mature Chris-

tian is characterized by giving, not getting.

CORINTHIANS, SECOND LETTER TO THE

Personal, autobiographical letter Paul wrote to church in Corinth between A.D. 55 and 57 from Macedonia. After writing 1 Corinthians, Paul continued his successful ministry at Ephesus (Acts 19:10). Trouble continued to grow worse in Corinth, especially the Corinthians' harsh attacks upon Paul. Divisions within the church and their hostile attacks on Paul denied the essence of the gospel that "God was in Christ, reconciling the world unto himself. . . and hath committed unto us the word of reconciliation" (2 Cor. 5:19).

Timothy returned to Ephesus. Paul made a painful visit to Corinth not recorded in Acts (2 Cor. 2:1-3; 12:14; 13:1-2). Paul also wrote a letter of strong rebuke that he regretted after sending it (2 Cor. 7:8). Later, he rejoiced because the letter provoked them to repentance. Titus probably took this letter (2 Cor. 8:7,16-17), which is not preserved unless it is chapters 10–13 of 2 Corinthians.

After Titus departed for Corinth, Paul left Ephesus with a heavy heart because of Corinth. He expected Titus to meet him at Troas with news of reconciliation. Titus did not meet him. Even though Paul found an open door at Troas, his heart was so heavy that he could not minister (2 Cor. 2:12-13). He went on to Macedonia, where Titus finally met him (2 Cor. 7:6-7) and reported improved conditions at Corinth. In response, Paul wrote 2 Corinthians, promising an early visit to them.

Paul wrote 2 Corinthians to deal with problems within the church and to defend apostolic ministry in general and his apostleship in particular. Second Corinthians teaches that:

(1) God was in Christ reconciling the world to Himself and has given to us a ministry of reconciliation.

(2) True ministry in Christ's name involves both suffering and victory.

(3) Serving Christ means ministering in His name to the total needs of persons.

(4) Leaders in ministry need support and trust from those to whom they minister.

CORNELIUS

Gentile centurion in Roman army who lived at Caesarea and worshiped the one true God (Acts 10:1). He treated the Jews with kindness and generosity. After an angel appeared to him, he sent to Joppa for Simon Peter, who came to him with the message of forgiveness of sins through faith in the crucified and risen Christ. Cornelius' conversion marked the beginning of the church's missionary activity among Gentiles but also raised the question of the possibility of salvation for non-Jews. See *Peter; Acts.*

CORNERSTONE

Stone laid at the corner to bind two walls together and to strengthen them; used as symbol of strength and prominence, often applied to rulers or leaders (Pss. 118:22; 144:12; Isa. 19:13 NIV, REB, NASB; Zech. 10:4). God promised through Isaiah that Zion would be restored, resting on the cornerstone of the renewed faith of Israel (Isa. 28:16; compare Jer. 51:26).

The NT applies Ps. 118:22 and Isa. 28:16 to Christ as the only sure foundation of faith (Matt. 21:42; Mark 12:10; Luke 20:17; compare Acts 4:11; Eph. 2:20-22). First Peter 2:4-8 appeals to the reader to come to the Living Stone (Jesus) the people rejected but who is precious in God's sight (compare Rom. 9:33). Believers are encouraged to become living stones themselves like the Living Stone and be built into a spiritual house (1 Pet. 2:5).

CORPORAL PUNISHMENT

The Bible teaches that corporal punishment can play an important role in correcting misbehavior (Prov. 20:30). Proverbs especially encourages parents to "use the rod" judi-

ciously in child rearing (Prov. 13:24; 22:15; 23:13-14).

Other instances of corporal punishment are noted in the Bible. Gideon beat the men of Succoth with thorns and briers for refusing him help in pursuing the Midianite kings Zebah and Zalmunna (Judg. 8:16). God declared that David's son would be subject to punishment "with floggings inflicted by men" should he do wrong (2 Sam. 7:14), a figurative use of corporal punishment indicating subjection to his enemies. The Mosaic law regulated the severity of a beating as punishment for a crime (Deut. 25:1-3).

The Bible recognizes that corporal punishment, like other forms of discipline, is most effective if received with a willing and submissive spirit. Proverbs 17:10 notes that a fool will not respond to even "more than one hundred lashes."

CORRUPTION

Transient nature of the material world; that is, the world's bent toward change and decay (see especially Rom. 8:21; 1 Cor. 15:42-57; 1 Pet. 1:4); contrasts with the permanent, eternal nature of the resurrection hope.

COS

Island and its chief city between Miletus and Rhodes where Hippocrates founded school of medicine and Paul landed briefly returning from his third missionary journey (Acts 21:1); center for education, trade, wine, purple dye, and ointment; modern Kos.

COSMETICS

Materials used for personal care and beautification by both men and women. Men primarily made use of oil, rubbing it into the hair of the head and the beard (Ps. 133:2; Eccl. 9:8). Women used eye paint, powders, rouge, ointments for the body, and perfumes.

Limestone bowls or palettes about 4 inches in diameter were used to prepare colors for making up the face. Mixing was done with bone spatulas or small pestles.

Small glass vials and small pottery juglets were used as perfume containers and alabaster jars, for ointments. Ivory flasks, cosmetic burners, and perfume boxes (see Isa. 3:20) were common. Women also employed ivory combs, bronze mirrors, hairpins, kohl sticks, unguent spoons, and tweezers. Excavators at Lachish discovered an object that appears to be a curling iron.

Red ocher was used for lip color. White was obtained from lead carbonate. Green eyelid coloring was derived from turquoise or malachite, and black was often made from lead sulphate. Kohl or manganese was used for outlining the eyes. Colors were also produced from ivories, bitumen, and burned woods.

Expert craftsmen made the cosmetics. They imported many of the raw ingredients, especially from India and Arabia. Oils for skin creams were extracted from olives, almonds, gourds, other trees and plants, animal and fish fats. Fragrances came from seeds, plant leaves, fruits, and flowers, especially roses, jasmines, mints, balsams, and cinnamon.

Women used paint to enhance their eyes and to make the eyes appear larger (Jer. 4:30 NASB). Biblical references seem to associate the practice of painting the eyes with women of questionable reputation (2 Kings 9:30; Ezek. 23:40).

Dry powders for eye coloring were stored in pouches, reeds, reedlike tubes of stone, horns, or small jars. The powders were mixed with water or gum and applied to the eyelids with small rods made of ivory, wood, or metal. Egyptian women painted the upper eyelid black and the lower one green. Mesopotamian women preferred yellows and reds. Heavy black lines were traced around the eyes to make them appear more almond shaped.

Creams protected the skin against the heat of the sun and counteracted body odors. Ointments were applied to the head (Matt. 6:17) or to the whole body (Ruth 3:3) as part of hygienic cleansing. They were considered part of the beautification process (Esther 2:12). Anointing one's head with oil was a sign of gladness (Ps. 45:7). In NT times a good host displayed hospitality by anointing guests with ointments (Luke 7:37-50). Ointment was sometimes used to anoint the sick (Jas. 5:14). Perfumed ointments were part of the preparation for burial (Mark 14:8; Luke 23:56).

Perfumes mentioned in the Bible include aloes (Num. 24:6); balm (Ezek. 27:17); cinnamon (Prov. 7:17); frankincense (Isa. 43:23; Matt. 2:11); myrrh (Song of Sol. 5:5; Matt. 2:11); and spikenard (John 12:3). The perfumes were derived from the sap or gum of the tree (frankincense, myrrh), the root (spikenard), or the bark (cinnamon). They were often quite expensive and imported from Arabia (frankincense, myrrh), India (aloes, spikenard), and Ceylon (cinnamon).

The perfumes could be produced as a dry powder and kept in perfume boxes (Isa. 3:20), or as an ointment and kept in alabaster jars, such as the spikenard with which Mary anointed Jesus (John 12:3). They could also be obtained in the natural form as gum or pellets of resin. In this form, they were placed in cosmetic burners and the resin burned. In close or confined quarters, the resulting incense-smoke would act as a fumigation for both the body and the clothes, such as that which seems to be described in the beautification process noted in Esther 2:12.

COUNCIL OF JERUSALEM

Meeting described in Acts 15:6-22 to determine the terms on which Gentile converts to Christianity would be received into the church. Some maintained that all Gentile converts must submit to circumcision and observe the whole of the Mosaic law. Paul and Barnabas contended that imposing such requirements on Gentiles was unreasonable. The Jerusalem council decided that Gentile believers would not be required to become Jewish proselytes, but would be asked to refrain from idolatry, from sexual misconduct, and from eating blood. See *Acts; Paul.*

COUNSELOR

One who analyzes a situation and gives advice to one who has responsibility for making a decision. Israelite kings seem to have employed counselors on a regular basis (see 2 Sam. 16:23; 1 Kings 12:6-14; 1 Chron. 26:14; 27:32,34; 2 Chron. 25:16; Isa. 1:26; 3:3; Mic. 4:9). God is often regarded as a counselor (Pss. 16:7; 32:8; 33:11; 73:24) as is His Messiah (Isa. 9:6; 11:2) and the Holy Spirit (John 14:16,26; 15:26; 16:7). See *Advocate.*

COURT SYSTEMS

Processes for bringing justice and enforcing laws. The head of a family had authority to decide cases within his household without bringing the matter before a professional judge (Gen. 31; 38). The law codes limit his authority in some cases (Num. 5:11-31; Deut. 21:18-21; 22:13-21). Cases involving more than one family were decided by town elders. The elders would serve as witnesses to a transaction (Deut. 25:5-10; Ruth 4:1-12), decide guilt or innocence (Deut. 19; 22:13-21; Josh. 20:1-6), or execute the punishment due the guilty party (Deut. 22:13-21; 25:1-3).

Disputes between tribes were more difficult to resolve, especially when there was no king to execute the law (Judg. 21:25). See *Judg. 19–21.* The function of the so-called "minor judges" (Judg. 10:1-5; 12:8-15) may have been purely judicial or political. Deborah, and later Samuel, were prophets who also decided cases within a limited area (Judg. 4:4-5; 1 Sam. 7:15-17). Moses appointed assistant judges to decide the smaller cases, preserving his energy for difficult ones (Ex. 18:13-26). Local courts referred complex cases to the supreme judges—both priests and secular officials (Deut. 17:2-13; 19:16-19; compare 2 Chron. 19:4-11). This was not an appeals court to

reconsider cases. Appointed by the king, the judges were responsible directly to God (2 Chron. 19:6).

The king possessed limited judicial authority (Deut. 17:18-20). The king did not have the authority to enact new laws or to make arbitrary legal rulings contrary to the prevailing understanding of justice. David was led to convict himself of his crimes against Uriah and his mistreatment of Absalom (2 Sam. 12:1-6; 14:1-24). Unlike Saul, David and Solomon were able to exercise authority to execute or spare persons who represented a threat to their reigns (2 Sam. 1:1-16; 4:1-12; 19:16-23; 21:1-14; 1 Kings 2:19-46). God punished Jezebel and King Ahab for having Naboth executed on trumped-up charges (1 Kings 21–22).

The king was the leading example of a just and honest judge, involved in hearing cases as well as appointing other judges (see 2 Sam. 15:1-6; 1 Kings 3). The relationship of the king's court to the rest of the judicial system is uncertain. See 2 Sam. 14; 1 Kings 3:16-28; 2 Kings 8:1-6.

Priests also possessed judicial authority (Deut. 17:9; 19:17; 2 Chron. 19:8,11) to rule on matters pertaining to the worship of God and the purity of the community. Cult and judicial system were both concerned with removing bloodguilt from the community (Deut. 21:1-9).

Accuser and accused argued their own cases. The burden of proof lay with the defendant. Physical evidence was presented when necessary (Deut. 22:13-21), but proving one's case depended primarily on testimony and persuasive argument. The word of at least two witnesses was required to convict (Deut. 19:15). The system depended on the honesty of witnesses and the integrity of judges (Ex. 18:21; 20:16; 23:1-3,6-9; Lev. 19:15-19; Deut. 16:19-20; 19:16-21; 2 Chron. 19:6-7; compare Isa. 1:21-26; Amos 5:10,12,15; Mic. 7:3). Cases brought by a malicious witness giving false testimony were referred to the central court (Deut. 19:16-21). In some circumstances the accused could submit to an ordeal or an oath to prove his or her innocence (Ex. 22:6-10; Num. 5:11-31; Deut. 21:1-8). Casting lots to discover the guilty party was another extraordinary procedure (Josh. 7; 1 Sam. 14:24-46). The judges were responsible for administering punishment, often with the whole community participating (Deut. 21:21). The court systems could only function well when the community agreed with their decisions and cooperated to enforce them.

COVENANT

Pact, treaty, alliance, or agreement between two parties of equal or of unequal authority; God's covenants with individuals and the nation Israel, finding final fulfillment in the New Covenant in Christ Jesus.

Biblical covenants were built on normal patterns used in economics and politics. Two types of treaties are available for study: those from the Hittite Empire about 1400–1200 B.C. and those from the Assyrian Empire about 850–650 B.C. Neither fits a rigid, unchangeable pattern, but the Hittite treaties between a king and vassal kings or between two kings of equal authority can be described with the following structure:

(1) Royal titles naming and identifying the Hittite king making the treaty.

(2) Historical prologue reviewing in personal terms the past relationships between the two parties to the treaties, emphasizing the gracious acts of the Hittite king.

(3) Treaty stipulations or agreements, often stating first the primary agreement or obligation agreed to by the two parties and then detailing the specific demands or agreements in a longer list.

(4) A clause describing the way the treaty is to be stored and to be read regularly to the citizens affected by it.

(5) List of witnesses to the treaty including the gods and natural phenomena such as mountains, heaven, seas, and the earth.

(6) List of curses and blessings brought on by violating or observing the treaty demands.

The Assyrian treaties often do not have the historical prologue or the blessings. Deuteronomy, Josh. 24, and other OT texts show that Israel was familiar with these treaty forms and used them in their literature. They may also show that Israel used these forms in their worship, renewing regularly the covenant relationship with God. No OT text precisely follows the treaty forms without change, and no text states explicitly that covenant renewal ceremonies formed the center of Israel's worship.

People "cut" a covenant with another person or group of people (Gen. 21:22-34; 26:28). Sacrifices accompanied the covenant making. Jonathan and David cut a covenant of friendship ("covenant of the Lord," 1 Sam. 20:8) in which Jonathan acknowledged David's right to the throne (1 Sam. 18:3; 23:18). The Lord was its witness and guarantee. Abner led the tribes of northern Israel to cut a covenant with David, making David king over the north as well as over southern Judah (2 Sam. 3; compare 5:3; 1 Chron. 11:3). Solomon and Hiram made a covenant of peace that apparently included certain trade agreements (1 Kings 5:12).

King Zedekiah made a covenant "before Yahweh" (Jer. 34:18) with the people of Jerusalem, releasing the Hebrews from slavery (v. 8). A ceremony accompanied this covenant ritual: The two sides cut a calf in two and solemnly paraded between its parts (v. 18). Covenant violation brought condemnation in public worship (Ps. 55:20).

Ezra reformed the restored Jewish community by leading them to make a covenant in God's presence to divorce foreign wives and separate themselves from the children so strongly influenced by the foreign mothers (Ezra 10:3).

Hosea denounced the Northern Kingdom's covenant or vassal treaty with Assyria (Hos. 12:1; compare 7:8-14; 8:9; 10:4; 2 Kings 17:3-4). Such treaties sought to gain military protection from foreign countries rather than relying upon Yahweh, the covenant God. (See Ex. 23:32; 34:12,15; Deut. 7:2; 2 Chron. 23:1; Job 41:4; Ps. 83:4-8; Isa. 33:8).

Israel had a long history of making covenant agreements with foreigners, despite God's warnings not to do so (Josh. 9; compare Judg. 2:2; 1 Sam. 11; compare 1 Kings 15:19; 20:31-35; 2 Chron. 16:3; Isa. 28:15).

In the typical political covenant one party pays for privileges it desires from the other party. Such payment may be enforced by a victorious king or may be offered by a weak king needing help against enemies. Members of such a covenant alliance were called "baals of the covenant" or lords, owners of the covenant (Gen. 14:13), a technical term for allies, or "men of the covenant" (Obad. 7). Covenant treaties carried expectations of humane and moral treatment of other members of the covenant, the covenant being literally a covenant of brothers (Amos 1:9; compare 1 Kings 20:32-33). Breaking covenant conditions meant treason and extreme punishment (Ezek. 17:12-18; compare Amos 1:9). Marriage involved covenant obligations with God as the witness (Mal. 2:14; compare Ezek. 16:8; Hos. 2:19-20).

God's grace in relating to His people by initiating covenants with them is a major theme of the Bible. Noah received God's first covenant (Gen. 9:9-17), a divine oath or promise not to repeat the flood, calling for no human response. The rainbow stands eternally as a sign of God's promise. God established the covenant relationship prior to the flood (Gen. 6:18). Neither "natural" catastrophe nor human sin (compare 6:5; 8:21) can prevent God from maintaining His priority on life.

God made His second covenant with Abraham (Gen. 15:18; 17:2), again with divine promises, not demanding human obedience. God promised to give the land of Canaan to Abraham's descendants. He symbolized this promise through an ancient covenant ceremony (compare Jer. 34), in which animals are cut and covenant participants pass through. Normally, the human covenant partners swear that they will abide by covenant conditions or face the fate of the animals. For Abraham, the rite became a sacrifice to God and a sign of his devotion to the rite even when attacking birds threatened to spoil it. Abraham did not walk through the divided animals. Symbols of God's presence did. God made the oath to keep His promise. Genesis 17 shows the initiation of circumcision as the sign of the covenant. God's covenant promise was extended to include international relations, many descendants, and to be God of the people descended from Abraham forever.

Redemption from Egyptian slavery found its climax in God's covenant with Israel, confessing of God's salvation (Ex. 19:4). The oath or promise came not from God but from the people. They were to "obey my voice indeed, and keep my covenant." Then they would be "a peculiar treasure unto me above all people . . . a kingdom of priests . . . an holy nation" (Ex. 19:5-6). Covenant law was then revealed to God's people as their responsibilities within the covenant relationship. The people accepted this responsibility in a solemn ceremony (Ex. 24:3-8). The covenant with Yahweh meant Israel could make covenants with no other gods (Ex. 23:32). Within the covenant agreement, God included the sabbath covenant, Israel's perpetual promise to observe the seventh day as a day of rest, reflecting God's practice in creation (Ex. 31:16).

Israel refused to take covenant commitment seriously almost from the start (Ex. 32). God renewed the covenant with His people, making explicit His covenant promise to conquer miraculously the land of Canaan promised to Abraham (Ex. 34; note v. 10). Again, covenant with Israel involved Israel's pledge to make no other covenants (34:12,15; Deut. 7:2) and God's commandments as His expectations of a covenant people (Ex. 34:27-28; Deut. 4:13). See *Ten Commandments.*

Israel's sacrificial worship included reminders of the covenant relationship. Salt added to offerings was the "salt of the covenant" (Lev. 2:13; compare Num. 18:19; 2 Chron. 13:5). The bread of the altar also symbolized Israel's everlasting covenant (Lev. 24:8).

Israel apparently celebrated its covenant with ceremonies helping the people identify themselves as the covenant people (Deut. 5:2-3; compare 29:1,12,14-15; Josh 8:30-35; 24:1-28). Israel's ceremonies had some of the same components that Near Eastern covenants or treaties had, particularly blessings for covenant obedience and cursings for disobedience (Ex. 23:25-30; Lev. 26:1-46; Deut. 27:11-26; 28:1-68). After covenant curse or punishment takes effect, God expects the people to confess sin and return to Him (Lev. 26:40; Deut. 4:30-31; 30:1-3). God, on the other side, does not "break my covenant with them: for I am the Lord their God" (Lev. 26:44-45; compare Deut. 7:9,12; Judg. 2:1; Zech. 11:10).

God's covenant with Abraham and with Israel found its special climax in God's covenant with David (2 Sam. 23:5; compare 7:12-16; 2 Chron. 13:5; Pss. 89:3-34; 132:12). Perennial disobedience led to Judah's exile and complaint, "thou hast made void the covenant of thy servant" (Ps. 89:39). Israel's God was the one "who keepest covenant and mercy with thy servants that walk before thee with all their heart" (1 Kings 8:23; 2 Chron. 6:14; Neh. 1:5; 9:32; Ps. 105:8,10; compare Isa. 54:10).

David's son, King Solomon, blazed the trail of covenant breaking, worshiping other gods and setting a model Israel consistently followed through their history (1 Kings 11:11). Even in punishment, God remained faithful, preserving two tribes for the family of David (1 Kings 11:12-13) and protecting the people from enemies (2 Kings 13:23; 2 Chron. 21:7). Occasionally, faithful people gained control and led the people to renew their covenant with God (2 Kings 17:35; 23:3; 2 Chron. 15:12; 29:10; 34:31-32). Eventually, covenant breaking led God to send the Northern Kingdom into eternal exile (2 Kings 17:15-18; 18:11-12). Punishment was not God's final word. He heard His people's cry and "remembered for them his covenant" (Pss. 106:45; 25:10,14; 44:17; 50:5,16; 74:20; 78:10,37; 103:18; 111:5,9; Jer. 11:2-3). God also made a covenant with the priests, acknowledging their obedient and even heroic acts by promising them the office of the priest forever (Num. 25:12-13; Ex. 40:15; compare Deut. 33:8-11). Even the priests proved unfaithful and drew God's anger (Neh. 13:29; Mal. 2:1-9).

God had an "everlasting covenant" with the earth (Isa. 24:5; compare 42:6; 49:8; 59:21; 61:8). Self-evident moral rules of the universe formed God's expectations for all people, but the people of the earth disobeyed these basic rules and thus brought on God's covenant curses (compare Amos 1:1-2:8; Rom. 1).

God extended His covenant with David for the sake of the nations. The entire nation of Israel would fulfill David's role and would bring the nations streaming to Jerusalem to find God's glory (Isa. 55:1-5). God extended His covenant to the outsiders among His own people—eunuchs otherwise forbidden to worship (Isa. 56:3-5; compare Deut. 23:1) and foreigners (Isa. 56:6; compare Deut. 23:2-9).

Hosea condemned Israel for transgressing the covenant (Hos. 6:7; 8:1; 12:1). Still, Hosea pointed forward to a day of hope when God would renew the covenant with Israel (2:18).

Jeremiah claimed Israel had broken the covenant just like those in Moses' day (11:6-10). Jeremiah portrayed God's promise of a New Covenant. Stipulations would not stand on tables of stone as did the old one, but would be deeply nested in the hearts of the people so they would have will and power to obey

(33:31-34; compare 32:40-44; 50:5; Ezek. 16:8,59-63; 20:37). Forgiveness would characterize God's relationship to the New Covenant people. Jeremiah's New Covenant preaching extended to the covenant with David (33:19-26).

Zechariah promised that exiles would return to Jerusalem because God would be true to the covenant of blood He made with Moses (Zech. 9:11; compare Ex. 24). Old Testament covenant language ends in Mal. 3:1 (compare 2:10) with God's announcement that the "messenger of the covenant" will come representing God, proving the covenant relationship is not a thing of the past.

The Qumran community which produced the Dead Sea Scrolls gave new significance to covenant theology. They saw themselves as the people of the new covenant, had strict regulations for applicants for membership, and expected members to obey the OT law as they interpreted it.

The NT transformed *covenant* into "testament," a binding will a person made to ensure proper disposal of goods upon the death of the person making the will (see Gal. 3:15; Heb. 9:17). New Testament gospel fulfilled OT covenant (Luke 1:72; Acts 3:25; compare 7:8; Gal. 3:15-17). Jesus used the Last Supper to interpret His ministry, and particularly His death, as fulfillment of Jeremiah's New Covenant prophecy. In the Last Supper people drank the blood of the New Covenant, remembering His death as the sacrifice for sins (Matt. 26:28; Mark 14:24; Luke 22:20; 1 Cor. 11:25).

Paul was a minister of the New Covenant (2 Cor. 3:6). He asserted that with the coming of Christ and Israel's rejection of Him, God still had a covenant to save Israel (Rom. 11:27; compare 2 Cor. 3:14).

In the NT, only Hebrews makes covenant a central theological theme emphasizing Jesus, the perfect High Priest, providing a new, better, superior covenant (Heb. 7:22; 8:6; compare 8:8,10; 9; 10:16; 12:24; 13:20; 15). If Israel suffered for breaking the Sinai covenant (Heb. 8:9-10), how much more should people expect to suffer if they have "counted the blood of the covenant, wherewith he was sanctified, an unholy thing" (Heb. 10:29).

The two parts of Scripture rest on God's gracious action in redeeming His people and making a covenant with them, showing them the living conditions in the kingdom of God, conditions that also reflect His grace because they are best for the citizens of the kingdom.

COVENANT OF SALT See *Covenant.*

COVERING OF THE LIVER See *Caul.*

COVERING THE HEAD

A disputed worship practice in the church at Corinth (1 Cor. 11:1-16). The Jewish custom was for all women to show modesty and virtue by covering their heads with a veil when they went outside their homes. To appear in a worship service without a veil was unthinkable.

Some of the Corinthian Christian women perhaps understood Paul's emphasis on Christian freedom to mean that they no longer had to observe any of the old Jewish customs—including wearing a veil. The effects of such a change in dress style had been disruptive to the worship services and Christian witness in Corinth. This led Paul to state that a woman should cover her head during the worship service. At the same time, he encouraged the men to follow the Jewish custom of worshiping with uncovered heads.

Paul cited various reasons in 1 Cor. 11:1-16 for his position. He referred to:

(1) the order in creation (v. 3),

(2) social customs of the time (vv. 4-6),

(3) the presence of angels (v. 10),

(4) nature itself (vv. 13-15), and

(5) the common practice in the churches (v. 16). The principle here is that Christians must be sensitive to

the cultures in which they live and not needlessly flout local customs unless there is some moral reason to do so.

COVET, COVETOUS

Inordinate desire to possess what belongs to another, usually tangible things (Ex. 20:17; see Josh. 7:21; Mic. 2:2).

In the NT *covet* could be used in a good sense (1 Cor. 12:39). Another Greek word describes the ruthless self-assertion that the Tenth Commandment forbids (Luke 12:15; Eph. 5:5).

CREATION

The origin of the universe; the universe as the work of God. The God of Israel was the Creator. His creative activities proceeded in orderly and methodical fashion toward the fulfillment of His purpose to create "good heavens" and "a good earth." Genesis 1–11 serves as prologue to God's redemptive purpose in calling Abram (Gen. 12:1-3). Similarly, in Isa. 40–55 concern with God as Creator is in a larger context of concern with God as Redeemer from Babylonian captivity. See Gen. 40:28; 43:7,15; 65:17-18; Job 10:8; 26:7-11; 26:12-13; 38–39.

Genesis 1–2 contain two accounts of creation, the order of man's creation coming at the end in the first and at the beginning in the second. God's creation, "good" as it was (Gen. 1:4,10,12,21,25,31), soon became bad through human rebellion against God. Genesis 11 ends by introducing Terah, the father of Abram, through whom God would bless the world. The link between creation and redemption is clear.

The psalmists' concerns with God as Creator were related to people's place in creation (Ps. 8:3-4), to God's redemptive activity (Pss. 74:17; 95:5), and to praise for the Creator (Pss. 100:3; 104; 24:1-2). One psalmist contrasted creation's perishable nature with the Creator's imperishable nature (Ps. 102:25-27).

The three doxologies in Amos (4:13; 5:8-9; 9:5-6) magnify God the Creator and Controller of creation (compare Eph. 3:9; Acts 14:15). Malachi's reference to God as Creator stresses that one God created all people (Mal. 2:10).

John based God's worthiness to receive "glory and honor and power" on His creative activity (Rev. 4:11). By God's will "all things" existed and were created. Jesus, "The Word," made all things (John 1:3,14; compare Col. 1:16-17; Heb. 1:2). Christians represent God's workmanship "created in Christ Jesus unto good works" (Eph. 2:10).

Both detailed stories of creation in Genesis feature people at center stage. The author of Ps. 8 seemed surprised at the attention the Creator gives to mortal humans formed from the dust (Ps. 8:4), setting them over the rest of creation "a little lower than the angels" (Ps. 8:5-8).

The OT is consistent in its use of the verb "create" (*bara'*). Only God serves as subject of the verb. In Ps. 51:10, "create" (*bara'*) designates a purely physical work, a clean heart, perhaps a transition in using the word. For Isaiah, God "created" "new heavens and a new earth" as well as "Jerusalem" and "her people" (65:17-18). Paul wrote to the Corinthians about being "in Christ" and thereby being "a new creation" (2 Cor. 5:17). "Created in Christ Jesus" is Paul's terminology for spiritual salvation in Eph. 2:10. God alone is the Author of spiritual redemption.

The entrance of human sin has had an adverse effect on creation (Hos. 4:1-3). Paul pictured the whole creation "groaneth and travaileth" under the burden of human sin until it is set free (Rom. 8:21-22). Paul anticipated a day when God would restore the whole creation to its original goodness.

CREATURE

A being with life; the Hebrew phrase in Gen. 2:7, "living soul," refers in all other references to animals and so applies to the similar physical makeup (same matter) rather than the higher relationship with God that is special to humans. God made a covenant with all the creatures of the earth promising never again to destroy the world by a flood (Gen. 9:10,12,15-16). See *Animals*.

CREDIT CARDS

Although credit cards did not exist in the biblical world, credit did, and the Bible speaks strongly against both unwise practices of borrowing and exorbitant interest rates.

The biblical attitude toward borrowing is summarized in Prov. 22:7, which declares that to be a borrower is tantamount to being a lender's slave. Paul taught that it is better to owe no one anything (Rom. 13:8). Nevertheless, the Bible recognizes that some loans are necessary and so counsels against unjust interest rates (Ps. 15:5; Prov. 28:8; Ezek. 18:8, 13). Those who borrow and do not repay are called "wicked" (Ps. 37:21) and will face a day of economic reckoning (Hab. 2:6-7).

The social and economic difficulties incumbent on heavy borrowing were anticipated by the Mosaic law, which commanded that fellow Israelites should not be charged interest on loans (Ex. 22:25; Deut 23:19-20; compare Neh. 5:7-12). This practice runs counter to the modern banking and credit card industries, as does Jesus' maxim to lend without expecting repayment (Luke 6:34).

CREMATION

Cremation is referred to in the OT by the phrase "burning the bones of" (1 Kings 13:2; 2 Kings 23:16, 20; Amos 2:1).

In ancient Israel, death by burning was reserved as a punishment for the worst of criminals (Gen. 38:24; Josh. 7:15, 25; Lev. 20:14; 21:9). Both it and cremation, burning the body after death, were stigmatized as abhorrent by the Israelites. Because burning human bones was considered to be the ultimate desecration of the dead (1 Kings 13:2; 2 Kings 23:16,

20), it was subject to punishment by God (Amos 2:1).

The ancient Greeks cremated bodies after a plague or battle for sanitary reasons, or to prevent their enemies from mutilating the dead. A similar attitude was found among the Israelites, and perhaps explains why the dead bodies of Saul and his sons were burned (1 Sam. 31:12; compare 2 Sam. 21:11-14). Saul's cremation also reflects God's rejection of his ignominious reign. When Amos (6:9-10 NIV) described the burning of bodies after battle, evidently for sanitary reasons, he intended to depict the horrors faced by victims of war.

Early Christians were hesitant to practice cremation because of their understanding that the body was the temple of the Holy Spirit (1 Cor. 6:19), yet recognized that cremation has no effect on the integrity of one's eternal state (Rev. 20:13).

CRETE

Long, narrow, mountainous island south of mainland Greece, running 170 miles east -west but never more than about 35 miles wide; center of Minoan maritime empire named after the legendary King Minos, and associated especially with the famous palaces of Cnossos and Phaestos, that flourished from 2000 to 1500 B.C. This artistically brilliant civilization fell suddenly, perhaps by earthquake followed by conquest, about 1400 B.C., leaving written tablets in the oldest known scripts of Europe, including the undeciphered "Linear A" and the apparently later proto-Greek "Linear B." Minoans of Crete were known to the Egyptians as "Keftiu," which may be the same as biblical "Caphtor," though the biblical term may include a wider reference to coastlands and islands of the Aegean area. The Philistines came to Palestine from Caphtor (Jer. 47:4; Amos 9:7) and may have been part of the widespread migrant "Sea Peoples" rather than Cretans proper.

Cretans were among those listed as present in Jerusalem on the Day of

Pentecost (Acts 2:11), and the gospel may first have reached the island through them.

Paul's route to Rome as a prisoner on a Roman grain ship proceeded south of Crete (Acts 27:8-14).

Paul had left Titus in Crete to exercise pastoral supervision over the churches (Titus 1:5). The character of the people is described in a quotation from a prophet of their own: "Cretians are always liars, evil beasts, slow bellies" (Titus 1:12), words attributed to the Cretan seer Epimenides, who was also credited with having advised the Athenians to set up altars to unknown gods (compare Acts 17:23).

CRIMES AND PUNISHMENTS

System of establishing and enforcing legal norms. Transgression of God's law by one person or group involved the whole community in the guilt, especially in cases of homicide, idolatry, and sexual offenses (see Deut. 19:10; 21:1-9; 2 Kings 24:1-7). When Israel failed to purge the offender and rebellion against God's law from their midst, God punished Israel (Lev. 18:26-28; 26:3-45; Deut. 28).

Israelite law was distinct from the laws of other cultures in several ways. Israel did not consider crimes against property to be capital crimes. Israel observed a system of corporal punishment and/or fines for lesser crimes. Israel restricted the law of retaliation (eye for an eye; *lex talionis*) to the person of the offender. Other cultures permitted the family to be punished for the crimes of the offender. Israel did not observe class differences in the enforcement of the law to the extent that their neighbors did. Nobility and commoner, priest and laypeople were treated equally in theory. However, slaves and sojourners (foreigners) did not have an equal standing with free Israelites—though their treatment in Israel was often better than in surrounding nations. Women did not have equal standing with the men in Israelite culture—especially in regard to marriage and divorce laws and laws pertaining to sexual offenses. Israelites in contrast to surrounding nations could not substitute sacrifices for intentional breaches of the law; sin and guilt offerings were allowed only in cases of unwitting sins (Lev. 4–5).

Israelite law considered some crimes serious enough to warrant capital punishment. See *Capital Punishment*.

Often the OT calls for punishment of being "cut off" from Israel. Some interpret the phrase to mean excommunication or exile from Israel or the community of faith but it seems to signify the pronouncement of the death penalty (Ex. 31:14; Deut. 12:29; 19:1; 2 Sam. 7:9; 1 Kings 11:16; Jer. 7:28; 11:19; Ezek. 14:13, 17, 19, 21; 17:17; 25:7; 29:8; Amos 1:5, 8; 2:3; Obad. 9-10; Nah. 3:15; Zech. 13:8; see Rom. 9:3; 11:22; 1 Cor. 16:22; Gal. 1:6; 5:12). The latter position is accepted in this article. See *Excommunication*.

Crimes of a lesser nature (usually those involving premeditated bodily injury) were punished with some sort of corporal punishment. The law of retaliation (eye for an eye; *lex talionis*) was the operative principle in most cases involving corporal punishment (Ex. 21:23-25; Lev. 24:19-22; Deut. 19:21), restricting vengeance taken on one who inflicted bodily injury. If a person should cause the loss of eye or tooth of his slave, the slave was freed (Ex. 21:26-27).

Corporal punishments also included scourging (Deut. 25:1-3), blinding (Gen. 19:11; 2 Kings 6:18; compare Judg. 16:21; 2 Kings 25:7), plucking out hair (Neh. 13:25; Isa. 50:6), and the sale into slavery of a thief who could not pay the monetary penalties (Ex. 22:1-3; compare Lev. 25:39; 2 Kings 4:1; Neh. 5:5). One text prescribes mutilation (Deut. 25:11-12). Fines were always paid to the injured party (Ex. 21:18-19, 22, 28-32; 22:1-4, 9, 16-17; Lev. 6:1-7; 19:20; Deut. 22:19, 29).

Jesus expanded the prohibition of killing to include anger (Matt. 5:21-26) and the prohibition against adultery to include lust (Matt. 5:27-30). He forbade divorce except on the grounds of unchastity (Matt. 5:31-32). Jesus desired that His disciples waive their rights to reparations (Matt. 5:38-42).

In NT times, Jews seem to have had relative autonomy in matters of their religious law and customs. Even Jewish communities outside Palestine were under the authority of the high priest (Acts 9:1-2) and allowed some measure of autonomy in religious matters (Acts. 18:12-17).

Whether the Jews had authority under the Roman government to impose the death penalty is debated. When Jesus was brought to trial, the Jews' reason for bringing him to Pilate was that they did not have the power to execute criminals (John 18:31). One ancient rabbinic tradition in the Babylonian Talmud (Abodah Zarah 8b) holds that the Jews lost the power to execute criminals for about 40 years. However, incidents in the NT seem to indicate otherwise: statements made at Peter's trial (Acts 5:27-42), the stoning of Stephen (Acts 7:57-60), attempted lynchings (Acts 9:23-24; 14:19; 23:12-15), the authority to kill foreigners caught trespassing in certain areas of the temple (Acts 21:28-31, a practice reported by Josephus, an ancient Jewish historian), and a statement made by Paul (Acts 26:10). Other ancient Jewish records of stonings and burnings indicate that the Jews may have had the authority to impose the death penalty.

The Jews during the period of the NT had the power to impose corporal punishment. This consisted primarily of scourgings (Matt. 10:17; Acts 5:40; 22:19; 2 Cor. 11:24) and excommunication (Luke 6:22; John 9:22; 12:42; 16:2).

The procurator was Rome's legal representative in the provinces. He intervened in local affairs when the public peace and order were threatened (Acts 5:36-37). Roman punishments included crucifixion (usually reserved only for slaves and the lower classes), beheading (see Matt. 14:10; Rev. 20:4), lifetime sentences to work in the mines (that is, kept in bonds; Acts 23:29; 26:31), scourging (Acts 16:22; 22:24), and imprisonment (Acts 16:23-24). See *Appeal to Caesar.*

CROCUS See *Plants.*

CROSS, CRUCIFIXION

Method Romans used to execute Jesus Christ; most painful and degrading form of capital punishment in ancient world. The cross became the means by which Jesus became the atoning sacrifice for the sins of all mankind, thus a symbol for sacrifice of self in discipleship (Rom. 12:1) and the death of self to the world (Mark 8:34).

Originally, a cross was a wooden pointed stake used to build a wall or to erect fortifications around a town. Beginning with the Assyrians and Persians, it began to be used to display the heads of captured foes or of particularly heinous criminals on the palisades above the gateway into a city (1 Sam. 31:9-10). "Hanging" (Esther 2:23; 5:14) may mean impalement (compare Ezra 6:11). According to Jewish law (Deut. 21:22-23), the offenders were "hung on a tree," which meant they were "accursed of God" and outside the covenant people. Such criminals were to be removed from the cross before nightfall lest they "defile the land."

In the west, crucifixion developed into a form of capital punishment, as enemies of the state were impaled on the stake itself. The Greeks and Romans at first reserved the punishment only for slaves, saying it was too barbaric for freeborn or citizens. By Jesus' day, it was used for any enemy of the state, though citizens could only be crucified by direct edict of Caesar. Rome began to use crucifixion more and more as a deterrent to criminal activity; by Jesus' time it was a common sight.

During the intertestamental period, Alexander Janneus crucified 800 Pharisees (76 B.C.), but on the whole the Jews condemned and seldom used the method. Even Herod the Great refused to crucify his enemies. The practice was abolished after the "conversion" of the emperor Constantine to Christianity.

A person crucified in Jesus' day was first of all scourged (beaten with a whip consisting of thongs with pieces of metal or bone attached to the end) or at least flogged until the blood flowed. This was designed to hasten death and lessen the terrible ordeal. After the beating, the victim was forced to bear the cross beam to the execution site to signify that life was already over and to break the will to live. A tablet detailing the crime(s) was often placed around the criminal's neck and then fastened to the cross. At the site the prisoner was often tied (the normal method) or nailed (if a quicker death was desired) to the cross beam. The nail would be driven through the wrist rather than the palm, since the smaller bones of the hand could not support the weight of the body. The beam with the body was then lifted and tied to the already affixed upright pole. Pins or a small wooden block were placed halfway up to provide a seat for the body lest the nails tear open the wounds or the ropes force the arms from their sockets. Finally the feet were tied or nailed to the post.

Death was caused by loss of blood circulation and coronary failure. Especially if the victims were tied, it could take days of hideous pain as the extremities turned slowly gangrenous; so often the soldiers would break the victims' legs with a club, causing massive shock and a quick death. Such deaths were usually done in public places, and the body was left to rot for days, with carrion birds allowed to degrade the corpse further.

Four types of crosses were used:

(1) the Latin cross has the cross beam about two-thirds of the way up the upright pole;

(2) St. Anthony's cross had the beam at the top of the upright pole like a T.

(3) St. Andrew's cross had the shape of the letter X;

(4) the Greek cross had both beams equal in the shape of a plus sign.

Jesus predicted His coming crucifixion many times (Mark 8:31; 9:31; 10:33-34 and parallels; John 3:14; 8:28; 12:32-33). He said His crucifixion

(1) occurred by divine necessity ("must" in Mark 8:31);

(2) brought guilt on both Jews ("delivered") and Romans ("killed") (Mark 9:31);

(3) would lead to His being vindicated by being raised from the dead;

(4) entailed glory (seen in the "lifted up" sayings that imply exaltation in John 3:14; 8:28; 12:32-33).

Mark and Matthew centered upon the horror of putting the Son of God to death. Mark emphasized the messianic meaning. Matthew pointed to Jesus as the royal Messiah who faced His destiny in complete control of the situation. For Matthew the cross inaugurated the last days when the power of death is broken and salvation poured out on all people.

Luke has 2 emphases: Jesus as the archetypal righteous Martyr who forgave His enemies, and the crucifixion as an awesome scene of reverence and worship. In John, the cross becomes His throne, a universal proclamation of Jesus' royal status.

Three major themes are interwoven in NT creedal quotations (Rom 4:25; 6:1-8; 8:32; 1 Cor. 15:3-5; Col. 2:11-12; 1 Tim. 3:16; Heb. 1:3-4; 1 Pet. 1:21; 3:18-22): Jesus' death as our substitute (from Isa. 53:5; compare Mark 10:45; 14:24); Jesus' death and resurrection as fulfilling Scripture; and Jesus' vindication and exaltation by God.

The "preaching of the cross" (1 Cor. 1:18 NASB) is the heart of the gospel. The preaching of the cross is the soul of the church's mission. "Christ crucified" (1 Cor. 1:23; compare 2:2; Gal. 3:1) was the central event in history, the one moment which demonstrated God's control of and involvement in human history. The cross is the basis of our salvation (Rom. 3:24-25; Eph. 2:16; Col. 1:20;

2:14; Acts 2:33-36; 3:19-21; 5:31). See *Atonement.*

Jesus pointed to the cross as a call to complete surrender to God following Jesus even to death (Mark 8:34; 10:38; Matt. 16:24; Luke 9:23; 14:27). Self-centered desires are nailed to the cross (Gal. 5:24), and worldly interests are dead (Gal. 6:14). We are "buried with him" (Rom. 6:1-8, using the imagery of baptism; compare 2 Cor. 5:14-17; Eph. 4:22,24) and then raised to "newness of life" (v. 4). See *Christ, Christology; Justification; Expiation, Propitiation; Redeem, Redemption, Redeemer.*

CROWN

Special headdress worn by royalty and other persons of high merit and honor; probably evolved from the cloth headband or turban worn by a tribal leader; eventually became a metal diadem, with or without ornamentation. See Ex. 28:36-37; 29:6; Lev. 8:9; 2 Sam. 1:10; 12:30. "Crown" was used figuratively, referring to the old man's gray head (Prov. 16:31), a man's virtuous wife (Prov. 12:4), and God's blessings on mankind (Ps. 8:5). Occasionally the word referred to a festive wreath of leaves or flowers (Song of Sol. 3:11).

In the NT, crown usually has a figurative significance (Matt. 27:29; 1 Cor. 9:25; 2 Tim. 4:8; compare 2 Tim. 2:5; Jas. 1:12; Rev. 4:4,10; 12:3; 14:14).

CUP

Drinking vessel of pottery or various metals such as gold, silver, or bronze. See *Vessels and Utensils.* Cup might represent blessings or prosperity for a righteous person (Pss. 16:5; 23:5; 116:13) or portray the totality of divine judgment on the wicked (Pss. 11:6; 75:8; Isa. 51:17, 22; Jer. 25:15; 49:12; 51:7; Ezek. 23:31-34; Rev. 14:10; 16:19; 17:4; 18:6). Jesus voluntarily drank the cup of suffering (Matt. 20:22; 26:39,42; Mark 10:38; 14:36; Luke 22:42; John 18:11). That cup was His death and everything that it involved.

In the Lord's Supper the cup is a symbolic reminder of the atoning death of Jesus (Matt. 26:27-28; Mark 14:23-24; Luke 22:20; 1 Cor. 11:25-26). See *Pottery.*

CUPBEARER See *Occupations and Professions.*

CURSE See *Blessing and Cursing.*

CUSH

(1) Benjaminite about whom psalmist sang (Ps. 7:1).

(2) Son of Ham and grandson of Noah (Gen. 10:8) seen as original ancestor of inhabitants of Cush, the land.

(3) Nation situated south of Egypt with differing boundaries and perhaps including differing dark-skinned tribes (Jer. 13:23) at different periods of history; traditionally translated Ethiopia, following the Septuagint, but Cush was not identical with Ethiopia as presently known. Moses' wife came from Cush (Num. 12:1), probably a woman distinct from Zipporah (Ex. 2:21).

In NT times, several queens of the kingdom of Meroe bore the title Candace. The Ethiopian eunuch to whom Philip explained the gospel was a minister of "Candace queen of the Ethiopians" (Acts 8:27). Candace should be understood as a title rather than a personal name.

CUSHAN-RISHATHAIM (*dark one of double evil*)

King of Aram Naharaim to whom Yahweh gave Israel (Judg. 3:8).

CUTH, CUTHAH

Center of worship of Nergal, god of death in Mesopotamia; tell Ibrahim, about 18 miles northeast of Babylon. See *Nergal.* (See 2 Kings 17:24,30.)

CYMBAL See *Music, Instruments, Dancing.*

CYPRUS

Large island 138 miles east to west and 60 miles north to south in eastern Mediterranean Sea; eclipsed in size only by Sicily and Sardinia. Old Testament Kittim (Isa. 23:1; Jer. 2:10). See *Kittim*. Much of Cyprus is mountainous; the Troodos Mountains (5,900 feet) dominate the western and central sections, while the Kyrenia Mountains (3,100 feet) extend along the northern coast.

Cyprus was the birthplace of Joseph surnamed Barnabas, a Hellenistic Jewish convert who later accompanied Paul (Acts 4:36-37). Persecution associated with Stephen's martyrdom drove Jewish Christians to Cyprus where they preached the gospel to the Jewish community (Acts 11:19-20). In A.D. 46 or 47, Paul with Barnabas and John Mark visited Cyprus on his first missionary journey (Acts 13). The conversion of the deputy, Sergius Paulus, was brought about in part by the blinding of the magician Bar-jesus. John Mark and Barnabas returned to Cyprus after parting company with Paul (Acts 15:39). Later, Paul twice passed by the island on voyages, once on a return to Jerusalem (Acts 21:3) and finally while traveling to Rome (Acts 27:4). See *Kittim*; *Phoenicia*.

CYRENE

Capital city of Roman district of Cyrenaica in northern Africa during NT era; home of Simon who was compelled to carry Jesus' cross (Matt. 27:32). Cyrenaica and Crete formed one province. Simon of Cyrene may have belonged to the rather large population of Greek-speaking Jews who resided in the city.

CYRENIUS See *Quirinius*.

CYRUS

Persian king who permitted Jews to return from exile in 538 B.C.; born about 590 B.C.; third king of Anshan (modern Malyan); became king about 559 B.C.; reared by a shepherd after his grandfather, Astyages, king of Media, ordered that he be killed. Cyrus organized the Persians into an army, revolted against his grandfather and father (Cambyses I), defeated them, and claimed their throne about 550.

Cyrus' decree in 539 B.C. (2 Chron. 36:22-23; Ezra 1:1-4) set free the captives Babylon had taken during its harsh rule, including Jews taken from Jerusalem in 586 B.C. They were allowed to return to rebuild the temple and city. Cyrus restored the valuable treasures of the temple taken during the Exile. Many Jews had done well in Babylon financially and did not want to return to the wastes of Judah. From these people Cyrus exacted a tax to help pay for the trip for those who did wish to rebuild Jerusalem.

Cyrus publicly worshiped the gods of each kingdom he conquered. Thus he won the hearts of his subjects and kept down revolt. He is referred to as Yahweh's shepherd and anointed (Isa. 44:28–45:6). Cyrus was killed while fighting a frontier war with the nomadic Massagetae people. His tomb is in Pasargadae (modern Murghab).

D

DAGON (*little fish* or *dear*)

God of the Philistines; grain or storm god; originally worshiped in Syria and Mesopotamia before 2000 B.C. See *Philistines.*

DALMATIA

Southern part of Illyricum north of Greece and across Adriatic Sea from Italy. See 2 Tim. 4:10.

DAMASCUS, DAMASCENE

Capital of important city-state in Syria with close historical ties to Israel; and one of its citizens; dominant trading and transportation center 2,300 feet above sea level, northeast of Mount Hermon, and about 60 miles east of Sidon. Both major international highways ran through Damascus.

Archaeological excavations indicate settlements from before 3000 B.C. Tablets from the Syrian center of Ebla mention Damascus about 2300 B.C. Abraham chased invading kings north of Damascus to recover Lot, whom they had taken captive (Gen. 14:15). Abraham's servant Eliezer apparently came from Damascus (Gen. 15:2). About 1200 B.C. the Arameans from the nearby desert took control of an independent Damascus.

Soldiers of Damascus attempted to help Hadadezer, king of Zobah—another Syrian city-state—against David. David won and occupied Damascus (2 Sam. 8:5-6). The weakness of Zobah encouraged Rezon to organize a renegade band, much as David had in opposing Saul (1 Sam. 22:2). Rezon became the leader of Syria and headquartered in Damascus (1 Kings 11:23-25). God used him to harass Solomon.

Ben-hadad strengthened Damascus to the point that Asa, king of Judah (910–869), paid him tribute to attack Baasha, king of Israel, and relieve pressure on Judah (1 Kings 15:16-23).

First Kings 20 also features Ben-hadad of Damascus. Ben-hadad ("son of Hadad") was apparently a royal title in Syria, identifying the king of Damascus as a worshiper of the god Hadad. See *Baal; Ben-hadad.*

Elisha helped deliver Samaria when Ben-hadad besieged it (2 Kings 6–7). Elisha also prophesied a change of dynasty in Damascus, naming Hazael its king (2 Kings 8:7-15). At Qarqar in 853 B.C. Ahaziah, king of Judah (841), joined Joram, king of Israel (852–841), in battle against Hazael with Joram being wounded. Jehu took advantage of the wounded king and killed him (2 Kings 8:25–9:26).

Through campaigns in 853, 849, 848, and 845, Shalmaneser III of Assyria severely weakened Damascus, besieging it in 841 and then receiving tribute again in 838. After this, Hazael of Damascus gained influence in Israel, Judah, and Philistia (2 Kings 10:32-33). His son Ben-hadad maintained Damascus' strength (2 Kings 13:3-25). Finally, Jehoash, king of Israel (798–782), regained some cities from Damascus (2 Kings 13:25). Jeroboam II, king of Israel (793–753), gained control of Damascus (2 Kings 14:28). Assyria under Adad-nirari III (810–783), invaded Syria from 805 to 802 and again in 796. About 760 B.C. Amos the prophet condemned Damascus and its kings Hazael and Ben-hadad (Amos 1:3-5).

King Rezin of Damascus joined with Pekah, king of Israel, about 734 B.C. to stop the Assyrians under Tiglath-pileser III (744–727). They tried to force Ahaz of Judah to join them (2 Kings 16:5). Isaiah warned Ahaz not to participate (Isa. 7), saying Assyria would destroy Damascus (Isa. 8:4; compare ch. 17). Ahaz sent money to Tiglath-pileser, asking him to rescue Judah from Israel and Damascus. The Assyrians responded readily and captured Damascus in 732 B.C., exiling its leading people (2 Kings 16:7-9). Damascus had one last influence on Judah; when Ahaz went to Damascus to pay tribute to Tiglath-pileser, he liked the altar he saw there and had a copy made for the Jerusalem temple (2 Kings 16:10-16). Damascus sought to gain independence from Assyria in 727 and 720 but without success. Thus Damascus became a captive state first of the Assyrians, then the Babylonians, Persians, Greeks, Ptolemies, and Seleucids. Finally, Rome gained control of Damascus under Pompey in 64 B.C. Jews began to migrate to Damascus and establish synagogues there. Thus, Saul went to Damascus to determine if any Christian believers were attached to the synagogues so he might persecute them (Acts 9). The Damascus Road became the site of Saul's conversion; and Damascus, the site of his introduction to the church. Paul had to escape from Damascus in a basket to begin his ministry (2 Cor. 11:32). See *Hadad; Syria.*

DAN (*judge*)

(1) First son born to Jacob by Rachel's maid Bilhah (Gen. 30:6). Original ancestor of the tribe of Dan. See *Tribes of Israel; Patriarchs.*

(2) City marking northern boundary of Israel, "from Dan even to Beersheba" (Judg. 20:1); formerly named Laish (Judg. 18:7 or Leshem, Josh. 19:47); modern tell el-Qadi (or tell Dan).

Laish was founded at end of Early Bronze II Age (about 2700 B.C.) and flourished until about 2300 B.C., then remained unoccupied until the Middle Bronze II period (about 2000 B.C.), when a large, well-fortified city was constructed.

Iron Age Laish was rebuilt by local inhabitants shortly before 1200 B.C. but destroyed about 1100 B.C. by the migrating tribe of Dan. Dan has yielded the first inscription with the name David from about 850 B.C., also the first Semitic reference to Israel.

Jeroboam (about 925 B.C.) fortified Dan and Bethel as border fortress/sanctuaries (1 Kings 12:29) with

temples containing golden calf representations of Yahweh. See *Golden Calf; Canaan, History and Religion of.* This city was taken by Ben-hadad of Aram and then recaptured by Jeroboam II before 750 B.C. (2 Kings 14:25). The Israelite city of Dan fell to the Assyrians under Tiglath-pileser III (Pul of OT) about 743 B.C. (2 Kings 15:29). He annexed the city into an Assyrian district. Many Danites were deported to Assyria, Babylon, and Media when Samaria fell to Sargon II in 722 or 721 B.C. (2 Kings 17:6). Foreigners were brought in from Babylon, Aram, and other lands to settle Israel's territory. Josiah of Judah restored the classical borders of Israel "from Dan to Beersheba" after 639 B.C. The partially rebuilt city survived until the onslaught of the Babylonian army of Nebuchadnezzar (about 589 B.C.; compare Jer. 4:14-18).

DANCING

Rhythmic movement to music in celebration and praise; essential part of Israelite life both in and outside worship. There is "a time to mourn, and a time to dance" (Eccl. 3:4).

Biblical dance resembled modern folk dance, performed by both males and females, though apparently not in mixed groups. Both group and individual dances were performed.

Dances celebrated military victories (Ex. 15:20-21; Judg. 11:34; 1 Sam. 18:6; 30:16). Dances were customary at weddings, accompanied with timbrels and other musical instruments (Ps. 45:14-15; Song of Sol. 6:13). Some dances were performed for the sheer entertainment of guests (Matt. 14:6; Mark 6:22). Children played games of "dance" (Job 21:11), often with the accompaniment of a musical instrument (Matt. 11:17; Luke 7:32). The return of a long lost son was cause for celebration and dancing (Luke 15:25). Religious celebration was most often the occasion for dancing (2 Sam. 6:14,16; 1 Chron. 15:29; Pss. 149:3; 150:4). See *Music, Instruments, Dancing.*

DANIEL (*God is judge* or *God's judge*)

(1) Son of David and Abigail, the Carmelitess (1 Chron. 3:1); also called Chileab (2 Sam. 3:3).

(2) Priest in Ithamar lineage (Ezra 8:2; Neh. 10:6) who returned with Ezra.

(3) Daniel (Ezek. 14:14,20; 28:3), spelled differently in Hebrew from all other OT forms, was a storied figure of antiquity mentioned with Noah and Job and famous for wisdom and righteousness. Some interpreters identify this Daniel with the Daniel in the Book of Daniel. Most interpreters place this Daniel at a much earlier date. Some identify the Daniel of Ezekiel with Daniel of Ugaritic literature.

(4) Hero of Book of Daniel; young man of nobility captured by Nebuchadnezzar in 605 B.C. at battle of Carchemish and elevated to high rank in the Babylonian and Persian kingdoms. The Babylonians sought to remove all vestiges of Daniel's nationality and religion; thus, they changed his name to Belteshazzar (Dan. 1:7; 2:26; 4:8-9,18-19; 5:12; 10:1) and trained him in Babylonian arts, letters, and wisdom.

He was active throughout reign of Nebuchadnezzar (604–562 B.C.) and Nabonidus (555–539 B.C.). Daniel became a high Persian governmental official under Cyrus (539–529 B.C.), Cambyses (529–522 B.C.), and Darius I (522–486 B.C.). Daniel was skilled in dream interpretation and political counsel because of his unshakable faith in his God.

DANIEL, BOOK OF

Apocalyptic book among the OT Writings; highest example of OT ethics and the climax of OT teaching about the future of God's people. Daniel combines characteristics of prophecy (Matt. 24:15), wisdom, and apocalyptic writing into a unique type of literature.

Daniel used two languages, Aramaic (2:4*b*–7:28) and Hebrew (1:2–2:4a; 8:1–12:13), plus loan words from Persian and Greek, to write the complex work. The book has two distinctly separate sections (1–6; 7–12): the first told in narrative form about Daniel and his friends with a historical conclusion (6:28) and the second told in form of Daniel's visions.

Daniel's unifying theme teaches that God expects His followers to maintain fidelity in face of threats, wars, legal pronouncements, or changing customs. God promises resurrection reward for the faithful.

Daniel 1:8–6:28 shows how Israelite heroes stood firm in their resolve to stay true to God and their heritage. In six different situations the hero resisted threats or danger of loss of life with no assurance of victory other than faith. Daniel 7:1–12:13 brought these truths to bear on an extremely tense situation. Throughout the book the author focused on the "fourth kingdom," that of a tyrannical despot. Readers faced the choice: believe a ruthless foreign conqueror, or stay true to the faith of the fathers and the God of their history.

DARIUS

(1) King of Persia (522–486 B.C.); successor to Cambyses II; spent early reign putting down revolts in Media, Persia, and Egypt. After solidifying his power in the Middle East, he reconquered the Scythians and Greeks who had rebelled under his predecessor until meeting defeat at Battle of Marathon (490 B.C.). Persia began a gradual regression until finally conquered by Alexander the Great in 331 B.C.

Darius brought a new sense of unity to his empire. The Jews received additional financial aid for finishing the temple in Jerusalem (Ezra 6:8-9).

(2) Darius II Nothus, son of Artaxerxes I, king of Persia (424–405 B.C.); let Jews in Elephantine in Egypt observe Passover; seen as incompetent and unpopular ruler; may be Darius the Persian (Neh. 12:22).

(3) Darius III Codomannus, king of Persia (336–330 B.C.); defeated by Alexander at Issus (333) and at

Gaugemela (331); murdered by conspirators after battle.

(4) Darius the Mede, 62-year-old successor to Belshazzar as king of Babylon (Dan. 5:30–9:27); difficult to identify in Babylonian history; often equated with Gaubaruwa of Gutium who took Babylon for Cyrus and became vice-regent over Mesopotamia or seen as another name for Cyrus.

DATHAN (*fountain* or *warring*) See *Numbers, Book of; Abiram.*

DAVID (*favorite* or *beloved*)

Anointed by Samuel to succeed Saul as king (1 Sam. 15:23,35; 16:1-12); united Israel and Judah; received promise of a royal messiah in his line; ideal king of God's people who ruled from about 1005 to 965 B.C. His musical talent and reputation as a fighter led to his playing the harp for Saul when the evil spirit from God troubled him (16:18). Loving David, Saul made him armor bearer for the king (16:21-22). Faith in God enabled David to defeat the Philistine giant Goliath who threatened Israel (1 Sam. 17).

Saul's son Jonathan became David's closest friend (1 Sam. 18:1; 20); David's victories won the hearts of the people, stirring Saul's jealousy (18:8). Saul tried to kill David, but God's presence repeatedly protected him, while David refused to kill God's anointed (18:10-12; 24:21-22; 27).

David attached himself to Achish, Philistine king of Gath. Achish gave Ziklag to David, who established headquarters there and began destroying Israel's southern neighbors (1 Sam. 27). The other Philistine leaders refused Achish's plan to let David join them in battle against Saul (1 Sam. 29).

David avenged the murder of Saul and sang a lament over the fallen (2 Sam. 1). He moved to Hebron, where the citizens of Judah crowned him king (2 Sam. 2), leading to war with Israel under Saul's son Ishbosheth, whose commanders assassinated him. David did the same to them (2 Sam. 4). The northern tribes then crowned David king at Hebron. He captured Jerusalem and made it his capital and religious center (2 Sam. 6). God through Nathan, the prophet, would not let David build the temple but promised to build a dynasty with eternal dimensions (2 Sam. 7).

David's sin with Bathsheba and Uriah showed his sinful human side (2 Sam. 11). Nathan confronted David with his sin, and David confessed his wrongdoing, professing faith that he would go to be with the child one day. Bathsheba conceived again, bearing Solomon (2 Sam. 12:1-25).

David saw intrigue, sexual sins, and murder rock his own household, resulting in his isolation from and eventual retreat before Absalom. Still, David grieved long and deep when his army killed Absalom (2 Sam. 18:19-33). His census of the people brought God's anger but also revealed the Temple's location (2 Sam. 24). Adonijah sought to inherit his father's throne, but Nathan and Bathsheba worked to ensure Solomon became the next king (1 Kings 1:1–2:12).

David was the role model for Israelite kings (1 Kings 3:14; 9:14; 11:4,6,33,38; 14:8; 15:3,11; 2 Kings 14:3; 16:2; 22:2), the "man of God" (2 Chron. 8:14). God was "the God of David thy father" (2 Kings 20:5). God's covenant with David was the deciding factor as God wrestled with David's disobedient successors on the throne (2 Chron. 21:7). Even as Israel rebuilt the temple, they followed "the ordinance of David king of Israel" (Ezra 3:10).

God's prophets pointed to a future "David" who would restore Israel's fortunes (Isa. 9:7; Jer. 33:20-22; compare Jer. 33:15,17,25-26; Ezek. 34:23-24; 37:24-25; Hos. 3:5; Amos 9:11; Zech. 12:6-10). The NT describes Jesus as Son of God and Son of David from His birth (Matt. 1:1) until His final coming (Rev. 22:16). David took his place in the roll call of faith (Heb. 11:32). This was "David the son of Jesse, a man after mine own heart, which shall fulfill all my will" (Acts 13:22). Recent inscriptions from Dan give first evidence of David outside the Bible.

DAVID, CITY OF

(1) Most ancient part of Jerusalem on its southeast corner representing the city occupied by the Jebusites and conquered by David (2 Sam. 5:7); called Zion; less than 10 acres bordered by Kidron Valley on the east and Tyropoeon Valley on the west. See *Jerusalem; Zion.* Solomon lived there until he built his own palace and temple outside the traditional city of David (1 Kings 3:1).

(2) Luke used "city of David" to refer to Bethlehem, where both David and Jesus were born (Luke 2:4,11).

DAY

Chronological period of varying lengths: time of daylight from sunrise to sunset (Gen. 1:14; 3:8; 8:22; Amos 5:8); 24-hour period (Gen. 1:5; Num. 7:12,18; Hag. 1:15); general expression for "time" without specific limits (Gen. 2:4; Ps. 102:3; Isa. 7:17); period of a specific event (Isa. 9:3; Jer. 32:31; Ezek. 1:28). Zechariah 14:7 even points to a time when all time is daylight, night with its darkness having vanished.

DAY OF ATONEMENT

Tenth day of seventh month of the Jewish calendar (Sept.–Oct.) on which high priest entered the inner sanctuary of the temple to make reconciling sacrifices for the sins of the entire nation (Lev. 16:16-28). The high priest and all other priests were prohibited from entering this most holy place at any other time on pain of death (Lev. 16:2). No other priest could perform duties in the temple during the Day of Atonement ritual (Lev. 16:17). The blood of the goat used as the sin offering was sprinkled like that of the bull to make atonement for the sanctuary (16:15). The mixed blood of the bull and goat were applied to the horns of the altar to make atonement for it (16:18). The

high priest confessed all of the people's sins over the head of the live goat which was led away and then released in the wilderness (16:21-22). The bodies of the bull and goat used in the day's ritual were burnt outside the camp (16:27-28). The Day of Atonement was a solemn day, requiring the only fast designated by the Mosaic law. All work was also prohibited (16:29; 23:27-28).

Hebrews developed images from the Day of Atonement to stress the superiority of Christ's priesthood (8:6; 9:7,11-26; compare 13:11-12). According to one interpretation, Paul alluded to the day's ritual by speaking of Christ as a sin offering (2 Cor. 5:21). See *Atonement.*

DAY OF CHRIST See *Day of the Lord; Judgment Day.*

DAY OF THE LORD

Time when God reveals His sovereignty over human powers and human existence. Lamenatations 2:1 speaks of the day of the Lord's anger in past tense. Joel 1:15 could describe a present disaster as the "day of the Lord."

The OT prophets used a term familiar to their audience, a term by which the audience expected light and salvation (Amos 5:18), but the prophets painted it as a day of darkness and judgment (Isa. 2:10-22; 13:6,9; Joel 1:15; 2:1-11,31; 3:14-15; Amos 5:20; Zeph. 1:7-8,14-18; Mal. 4:5). The OT thus warned sinners among God's people of the danger of trust in traditional religion without commitment to God and to His way of life. Day of the Lord could judge Israel or promise deliverance from evil enemies (Isa. 13:6,9; Ezek. 30:3; Obad. 15).

New Testament writers took up the OT expression to point to Christ's final victory and the final judgment of sinners. In so doing, they used several different expressions: "day of Jesus Christ" (Phil. 1:6,10), "day of our Lord Jesus" (1 Cor. 1:8; 5:5); "day of the Lord" (1 Thess. 5:2); "day of Christ" (Phil. 2:16); "day of judgment"

(1 John 4:17); "the day" (1 Thess. 5:4); "that day" (2 Tim. 1:12); "day of wrath" (Rom. 2:5). People who take a dispensational perspective on Scripture often seek to interpret each of the terms differently, so that the "day of Christ" is a day of blessing equated with the rapture, whereas the day of God is an inclusive term for all the events of end time (2 Pet. 3:12). See *Dispensation*. In this view the day of the Lord includes the great tribulation, the following judgment on the nations, and the time of worldwide blessing under the rule of the Messiah. Bible students who do not take a dispensational viewpoint interpret the several expressions in the NT to refer to one major event: the end time when Christ returns for the final judgment and establishes His eternal kingdom. In either interpretation, the day of the Lord points to the promise that God's eternal sovereignty over all creation and all nations will one day become crystal clear to all creatures.

DAY'S JOURNEY

Customary, though inexact, measure of distance traveled in a day. A Jew's typical day's journey was between 20 and 30 miles, though groups generally traveled only 10 miles per day. See Gen. 30:36; 31:23; Ex. 3:18; 8:27; Deut. 1:2; Luke 2:44.

DEACON, DEACONESS

Church official; servant or minister who waits on tables (Phil. 1:1; 1 Tim. 3:8,12; compare Rom. 16:1). In the NT, the noun is used to refer to ministers of the gospel (Col. 1:23), ministers of Christ (1 Tim. 4:6), servants of God (2 Cor. 6:4), those who follow Jesus (John 12:26), and in other similar ways. No Bible reference explicitly des- cribes the duties of deacons or refers to the origin of the office. Most interpreters believe that deacons, from the beginning, served as assistants of the church leaders. That was clearly the role of deacons after A.D. 100. Deacons of the early church served the needs of the poor, assisted in baptism and the Lord's Supper,

and performed other practical ministerial tasks.

The qualifications of deacons are outlined in 1 Tim. 3:8-13, mirroring those of "bishops." Gifts for teaching, a requirement for "bishops," are not mentioned in the qualifications for deacons. Distributing the elements of the Lord's Supper and, in the early years, serving the *agape* meal were probably important functions of deacons.

Many interpreters believe Acts 6 describes the selection of the first deacons, although the term *diakonos* is not used in the passage and the term *diakonia* ("service" or "ministry") is used only for the work of the Twelve. The seven were set apart for their task in a ceremony in which the apostles "laid their hands on them" (Acts 6:6). This ceremony may reflect the origin of later ordination practice; otherwise, the NT does not mention ordination of deacons.

The list of qualifications in 1 Tim. 3:11 requires that "women" must "likewise" be similar in character to the men. Although this remark may refer to the wives of male deacons (KJV, NIV), it probably should be interpreted as a parenthetical reference to female deacons, or deaconesses (NIV footnote; NASB footnote; NRSV footnote). Romans 16:1 refers to Phebe as a *diakonos* of the church at Cenchrea. Williams New Testament and NLT translate this as "deaconess." NRSV, NLT use "deacon"; NCV, "helper" with note, literally, "deaconess"; REB, "minister." Other translations use "servant." Phebe's role as "helper" and Paul's obvious regard for her work seem to support the conclusion that she functioned as a deacon in her church. Deaconesses are mentioned prominently in Christian writings of the first several centuries. They cared for needy fellow believers, visited the sick, and were especially charged with assisting in the baptism of women converts.

DEAD SEA

Inland lake at the end of the Jordan Valley on the southeastern border of

Canaan with no outlets for water it receives; about 50 miles long and 10 miles wide at its widest point; known in the Bible as Salt Sea, Sea of the Plain, and Eastern Sea. Name "Dead Sea" was applied to it after A.D. 100. The surface of the sea is 1,292 feet below the level of the Mediterranean Sea. At its deepest point the lake is 1,300 feet deep. At its most shallow it is only 10 to 15 feet deep. The Dead Sea's salt content is approximately five times the concentration of the ocean. This makes it one of the world's saltiest seas. No marine life can live there.

DEAD SEA SCROLLS

Inscribed scrolls containing oldest OT texts along with sectarian documents copied between 200 B.C. and A.D. 70 and discovered between 1947 and 1960 in 11 caves on western Dead Sea shore near ruin called khirbet Qumran.

The scrolls comprise three main kinds of literature:

(1) copies of OT books;

(2) non-biblical Jewish books (such as 1 Enoch and Jubilees), probably written by the Essenes;

(3) community's own compositions, including biblical commentaries (for example, on Habakkuk and Nahum), that interpret biblical prophecies as applying to the community and its times; rules of community conduct; and liturgical writings such as prayers and hymns.

The Scrolls show a surprising variety of beliefs. Like other Essenes, they believed that by observing their own interpretation of the Jewish law and by frequent ritual bathing they preserved a faithful remnant. Thus, they were ready for the restoration of the land by God, who would punish the wicked through two messiahs—one priestly, one lay. They had an interest in angels, astrology, and prophetic predictions. Peculiar to Qumran was a dualistic view of the world in which God had appointed an angel of light (one of his names being Melchizedek; see Gen. 14; Heb. 7) and an angel of darkness to govern the

world, all persons being assigned to the realm of one or the other. See *Jewish Parties in the New Testament*.

DEATH

End of life; loss of all vital functions. Death involves all of a person, not separation of a spiritual from a physical self. Israel accepted death with some degree of grace. They found consolation in long life, many children, remembrance of the family name, and burial in the family grave (Gen. 15:15; compare 25:8; 1 Chron. 29:28). Death in the prime of life or without children or without proper burial was understood as a curse. Death and Sheol always represented either a potential or actual threat.

Genesis 2–3 clearly points to sin as the reason humans must experience death (2:17; 3:3; compare Num. 18:22; Prov. 6:12-19; Jer. 31:29-30; Ezek. 18:1-32).

Death is ominous and threatening (Matt. 4:16; 8:23-27; Mark 4:35-41; Luke 1:79; 8:22-25). Jesus vindicated His ministry in the face of John the Baptist's question by revealing His power against the realm of death (Luke 7:22-23). Jesus paradoxically found life through the means of death.

Death has been defeated (1 Cor. 15:26; 2 Tim. 1:8-10). In the future life the dead are not disadvantaged (1 Thess. 4:13-18). Christ is the firstfruits of resurrection from death and gives His Spirit as our firstfruits waiting for final redemption (Rom. 8:23; 1 Cor. 15:20,23). The dead will receive a new resurrection body (1 Cor. 15:35-58). This all means the proper Christian response to death and all of its signs is an indomitable hope (Rom. 8:31-38; 1 Cor. 15:58; 1 Thess. 4:18).

Death is nonetheless an enemy, intimately connected with sin (Rom. 3:23; 5:12-21; compare 6:13; 7:7-25; 8:6-8; Eph. 2:1,5; Col. 2:13). Existence without Christ is death, so conversion to Christ is rebirth (Rom. 6:5-11; Gal. 2:20). Christians should consider themselves dead to sin but alive to God in Christ (Rom. 6:11). How hearers respond to Jesus is a matter of life and death (John 5:24; compare 11:25-26). The doctrine of resurrection affirms that even the realm of the dead belongs to God and that death is overcome only at His gracious command. In Christ we die and are raised as we commit our lives to Him. See *Burial.*

DEATH OF CHRIST See *Cross, Crucifixion; Christ, Christology; Jesus, Life and Ministry of.*

DEATH, SECOND

Final separation from God; spiritual death following physical death (Rev. 20:14; compare 21:8). The second death has no power over those who remain faithful in persecution (2:11), who are martyred (20:6), or for those whose names are written in the book of life (20:15). The alternative is eternal life with God.

DEBIR (*back, behind*)

As a common noun, the Hebrew term refers to the back room of the temple, the holy of holies (1 Kings 6; Ps. 28:2).

(1) King of Eglon who joined in Jerusalem-led coalition against Joshua and lost (Josh. 10:3). See *Eglon.*

(2) Important levitical city in hill country of Judah (Josh. 21:15; compare 10:38; 11:21; 12:13); formerly called Kiriath Sepher (Josh. 15:15; compare Judg. 1:11). Joshua 15:49 uses Kiriath Sannah for Debir. It may have been the most important town south of Hebron.

(3) Town on northern border of Judah (Josh. 15:7); may be Thoghret ed Dabr, the "pass of Debir," 10 miles east of Jerusalem.

(4) Town in Gad east of the Jordan given various spellings in the Hebrew Bible: *Lidebor* (Josh. 13:26); *Lwo Debar* (2 Sam. 9:4-5); *Lo' Debar* (2 Sam. 17:27); *Lo' Dabar* (Amos 6:13); may be modern Umm el-Dabar, 12 miles north of Pella. Other suggested locations are tell el-Chamme or khirbet Chamid.

DEBORAH (*bee*)

(1) Rebekah's nurse who died and was buried near Bethel (Gen. 35:8; 24:59).

(2) Prophetess, judge, and wife of Lapidoth (Judg. 4:4). After Moses, only Samuel filled the same combination of offices: prophet, judge, and military leader. Some scholars believe that Deborah as prophet also composed the victory poem she and Barak sang in Judg. 5.

DEBT, DEBTOR See *Loan.*

DECALOGUE See *Ten Commandments.*

DECAPOLIS (*ten cities*)

Group of Greek cities (Matt. 4:25; Mark 5:20; 7:31) south and east of the Sea of Galilee, originally ten in number established after Alexander the Great's conquests about 333 B.C. but including more cities at a later time. These cities were centers for the spread of Greco-Roman culture and had no great love for the Jews. See *Palestine.*

DECISION, VALLEY OF See *Jehoshapat, Valley of.*

DECREE

Royal order; proclaimed publically by criers (Jonah 3:5-7) designated "heralds" (Dan. 3:4); often throughout the territory of the monarch (1 Sam. 11:7; Ezra 1:1); written and stored in archives for later reference (Ezra 6:1-2). Important decrees include: Cyrus's decree on rebuilding the temple (Ezra 6:3-5); Esther's decree on the celebration of Purim (Esther 9:32); and Caesar Augustus's decree that set the scene for Jesus' birth (Luke 2:1).

As King of the earth, God issues decrees regulating the world of nature (sea, Prov. 8:29; rain, Job 28:26) and humanity (Dan. 4:24). God also decrees the reign of the Messianic King (Ps. 2:7). See Acts 16:4; 1 Cor. 7:37, KJV; Rom. 1:32, NIV, NRSV; Col. 2:14,20, NASB. Any translator using "decree" is interpreting the meaning of a more general Hebrew or Greek term.

DEDAN, DEDANIM, DEDANITE

(1) Original ancestor of Arabian tribe in table of nations (Gen. 10:27). See *Cush.*

(2) Grandson of Abraham; brother of Sheba (Gen. 25:3; compare 10:27).

(3) Arabian tribe centered at al-Alula, 70 miles southwest of Tema and 400 miles from Jerusalem; a station on the caravan road between Tema and Medina; center for incense trade (Isa. 21:13; Jer. 49:8; Ezek. 25:13; 27:15,20; compare Ezek. 38:13).

DEDICATE, DEDICATION

Setting apart or consecrating persons or things to God (or gods), persons, sacred work, or ends. The act is usually accompanied by an announcement of what is being done or intended and by prayer asking for divine approval and blessing. Israel set apart all Israel (Ex. 19:5,6; Deut. 7:6; 14:2); priests (Ex. 29:1-37); the tabernacle altar (Num. 7:10-88), images of pagan deities (Dan. 3:2-3), silver and gold (2 Sam. 8:11), temple (1 Kings 8:63; Ezra 6:16-18), walls of Jerusalem (Neh. 12:27), and private dwellings (Deut. 20:5). The whole church is set apart to God (Eph. 5:26). The individual believer is one of a dedicated, sanctified, consecrated, priestly people; set apart "to offer up spiritual sacrifices, acceptable to God by Jesus Christ" (1 Pet. 2:5).

DEDICATION, FEAST OF

Term for Hanukkah in John 10:22. See *Festivals; Hanukkah.*

DEER See *Animals.*

DEHAVITE

KJV transliteration of Aramaic text in Ezra 4:9. Modern translators read the text as two Aramaic words, *di-hu'*, meaning "that is."

DELILAH (*with long hair hanging down*)

Woman from valley of Sorek loved by Samson (Judg. 16:4); probably a Philistine. She enticed Samson into revealing to her the secret of his great strength and betrayed him to the Philistines. See *Samson; Judge.*

DELIVERANCE

Rescue from danger. In Scripture God gives deliverance (Pss. 18:50; 32:7; 44:4), often through a human agent, in battle (Judg. 15:18; 2 Kings 5:1; 13:17; 1 Chron. 11:14; 2 Chron. 12:7); from famine (Gen. 45:7), from prison (Luke 4:18; Heb. 11:35); and from danger (Acts 7:25; Phil. 1:19). Mordecai warned Esther that if she failed to act out her role as deliverer, God would provide another way (Esther 4:14). KJV also uses "deliverance" to describe the remanent that survives a battle or exile (Ezra 9:13).

DELIVERER

One who rescues from danger (Judg. 3:9,15). Most often God is the Deliverer of His people (2 Sam. 22:2; Pss. 18:2; 40:17; 144:2; Rom. 7:24-25; Col. 1:13; compare Gal. 1:4; 1 Thess. 1:10). Acts 7:35 refers to Moses as a deliverer. Romans 11:26-27 refers to the Messianic King as the Deliverer who will take away Israel's sins.

Job 5:19-26 lists seven ways God delivers. Scripture also speaks of deliverance from sin (Pss. 39:8; 79:9); the way of evil (Prov. 2:12); the power of evil (Matt. 6:13; Gal. 1:4; Col. 1:13); the body of death (Rom. 7:24); the law (Rom. 7:6); and the coming wrath of God (1 Thess. 1:10). Christ brings deliverance by giving Himself for sins.

DEMETRIUS (*belonging to Demeter, Greek goddess of crops*)

(1) Silversmith in Ephesus who incited a riot directed against Paul because he feared that the apostle's preaching would threaten the sale of silver shrines of Diana, the patron goddess of Ephesus (Acts 19:24-41). Demetrius may have been a guild

master in charge of producing small silver copies of Diana's temple with a figure of the goddess inside.

(2) Apparently a convert from the worship of Demeter (3 John 12). He may have carried 3 John to its original readers.

DEMON POSSESSION

Evil demonic spirit's control of individual's personality (Luke 8:2; 13:11,16). The signs of demon possession in the NT include: speechlessness (Matt. 9:33); deafness (Mark 9:25); blindness (Matt. 12:22); fierceness (Matt. 8:28); unusual strength (Mark 5:4); convulsions (Mark 1:26); and foaming at the mouth (Luke 9:39). The cure for demon possession is always faith in the power of Christ.

DENARIUS See *Coins; Economic Life.*

DEPUTY

Official of secondary rank (1 Kings 22:47); KJV for Roman proconsul (Acts 13:7; 18:12; 19:38). See *Proconsul.*

DERBE See *Asia Minor, Cities of.*

DESCENT TO HADES

Phrase taken from Apostles' Creed describing work of the resurrected Christ. First Peter 3:19 says Christ "went and preached unto the spirits in prison." The time may be seen as the days of Noah (v. 20) and thus describe the work of the preexistent Christ or the work of Christ's spirit through Noah. It may be seen as immediately following Christ's resurrection. The content of His preaching may have been judgment; it may have been affirmation of His victory over "angels, and authorities, and powers" (v. 22); it may have been release from Sheol or Hades for saints who preceded Him. The spirits may have been the "sons of God" of Gen. 6:2, the people of Noah's day, the OT sinners, OT people who were true to God, fallen angels, the evil spirits, or demonic powers whom

Jesus contested in His earthly ministry. The prison may have been Sheol or Hades according to OT thinking, a special place of captivity for sinners, a place of punishment for fallen angels, a place of security for such angels where they thought they could escape Christ's power, or a place on the way to heaven where the faithful of old waited to hear the message of Christ's final atoning victory. Whatever the detailed explanation of each of the phrases, the ultimate purpose is to glorify Christ for His completed work of salvation through His death, resurrection, and ascension, showing He has control of all places and powers.

DESERT See *Wilderness.*

DESIRE See *Lust.*

DESIRE OF ALL NATIONS

Phrase Haggai used of a renewed temple (Hag. 2:7). KJV, NIV interpret as prophecy of the coming Messiah. Other translations render the phrase "treasure" (TEV, NRSV, REB, NLT, CEV) or "wealth" (NASB, NCV) of all nations in parallel to the gold and silver of 2:8. Messianic interpretation first appeared in Latin Vulgate, while the treasures would show Yahweh's power to restore glory of His house despite people's poverty.

DESOLATION, ABOMINATION OF See *Abomination of Desolation.*

DESTROYER

Invading army (Isa. 49:17; Jer. 22:7) or supernatural agent of God's judgment (Ex. 12:23; Heb. 11:28), often termed an angel (2 Sam. 24:15-16; 2 Kings 19:35; Ps. 78:49).

DEUTERONOMY, BOOK OF

Fifth book of OT taken from Greek translation meaning "second law." The book consists of Moses' speeches in sermonic style to Israel before they entered the Promised Land.

Deuteronomy 1:1-5 introduces the book, giving the time and place of the addresses. Deuteronomy 1:6–4:40, Moses' first address, recounted Israel's journey from Horeb to Moab and urged Israel to be faithful to Yahweh. Moses set up cities of refuge on the east bank of the Jordan (Deut. 4:41-43). Deuteronomy 4:44–28:68, Moses' second address, taught Israel lessons from the law. These are not laws to be used in the courts to decide legal cases, but instructions for life in the land of Canaan. Moses' third address (Deut. 29:1–30:20) focuses on covenant renewal. Repentance and commitment would assure life and the blessings of God. Rebellion would result in their death as a nation. The concluding chapters present Moses' farewell address (31:1-29); the Song of Moses (31:30–32:52); Moses' blessing (ch. 33), and his death (ch. 34).

The "book of the law," found when Josiah had the temple repaired in his eighteenth year (621 B.C.), has been identified as Deuteronomy since the early church fathers shortly after A.D. 300. Compare Deut. 12 to 2 Kings 23:4-20.

Deuteronomy is a call to repentance, a plea for God's disobedient people to mend their ways and renew the covenant God made with them at Sinai. Moses called for obedience through love to Yahweh, the loving God, who had established the covenant with Israel.

Deuteronomy calls to faith and action in response to God's acts. It stresses the uniqueness of God as the only God without rivals, pointing to worship of any other god as vain, without meaning or hope. It shows the Ten Commandments as the center of the covenant relationship for believers. It holds up love of God as the basic relationship God wants with His people. It calls for total separation from pagan practices and godless lifestyles. It seeks to establish a community at rest, free from internal strife and external war. It calls on God's people to meet the needs of the least privileged members of society. It teaches that commitment leads to

action. It pronounces curses on evildoers who forsake God's covenant and blessings on those faithful to the covenant.

DEVIL, SATAN, EVIL, DEMONIC

Personal spiritual power who leads the forces of evil and opposition to God. *Satan,* a Hebrew common noun meaning "the accuser" or "the adversary," can refer to human adversaries (1 Sam. 29:4; 2 Sam. 19:22; 1 Kings 11:14,23), an angel or messenger of God (Num. 22:22), or a human accuser in a trial (Ps. 109:6, NASB; NIV; NRSV despite a traditional interpretation as Satan, KJV). Hebrew *hassatan* with the definite article, "the," appears as a figure of evil in Job 1:12 and Zech. 3:1-2, apparently representing a title for one of the beings attending the heavenly council rather than a personal name. Here "the satan" or "the accuser" appears as God's agent and minister who seeks to bring charges against individual people before God and the heavenly court. He made a wage with God using Job as the stake. He acted, however, with the express permission of God and kept within the limits that God fixed for him (Job 1:6,12; 2:6). He unsuccessfully accused Joshua, the priest, before God (Zech. 3:1-2). Satan appears without the definite article and is thus certainly a personal name in 1 Chron. 21:1. He provoked David to take a census of Israel. In the parallel passage, God in His anger told David to number Israel (2 Sam. 24:1).

In Gen. 3:1, the subtle serpent coaxed Eve to get her husband to join her in disobeying God. See Gen. 3:14. Revelation 12:9 reveals that the serpent is Satan (see Rev. 20:2).

Judges 9:23 refers to God sending an "evil spirit between Abimelech and the men of Shechem." The "Spirit of the Lord departed from Saul, and an evil spirit from the Lord troubled him" (1 Sam. 16:14). This evil spirit came and went from Saul (1 Sam. 16:23; compare 18:10; 19:9). First Kings 22:21-22 speaks of a "lying spirit" going out from the heavenly council to false prophets. Such language maintains the unique claim of God to be the only God and testifies to His sovereign rule over all earthly activities. It hints at a personal power opposed to God without describing the origin or nature of this power. Satan was evidently perfect in his original state. Pride seems to have been the cause of his fall.

New Testament authors locate the origin of evil in Satan. This recognizes the reality of evil outside and beyond the scope of human will, yet always and finally subordinate to God. Satan abides in hell, which was expressly prepared—apparently by God—for Satan and his angels (Matt. 25:41). Satan rules over the demons, indicating a political power structure (Mark 3:22). Satan has messengers to afflict God's servants (2 Cor. 12:7). He dared ask even the Son of God to worship him (Matt. 4:9). Jesus could call Satan the "ruler of this world" but only as He spoke of Satan's judgment and defeat (John 12:31; 16:11) because he does not have power over Jesus (John 14:30). Thus the devil rules on earth only as people let him. Compare Eph. 2:2; 1 John 5:19. People can escape his power through prayer for deliverance from evil (Matt. 6:13; compare John 17:15). In that case, Satan is limited to being the "prince of the devils" (Matt. 9:34). As such he and his demonic companions have power to cause human illness (Matt. 17:5-18; Luke 13:16). See *Demon Possession*. He could possess Judas, leading him to betray Jesus (Luke 22:3). Those who do not believe and follow Jesus have Satan, not God as their Father (John 8:44; Acts 13:10). Only Satan has been a murderer from the beginning and the father of lies (John 8:44). Compare Acts 5:3. Even one who followed Jesus most closely and recognized His role as Messiah could be called "Satan" for seeking to prevent Jesus from carrying out His role as Suffering Servant (Mark 8:33). Satan constantly tries to snatch God's Word from those who hear it (Matt. 13:19). The church can be commanded to hand an immoral member over to Satan for discipline resulting in final salvation (1 Cor. 5:5; compare 1 Tim. 1:20). Satan constantly seeks to tempt and outwit believers (1 Cor. 7:5; 2 Cor. 2:11; 1 Tim. 3:6-7; 5:15; 2 Tim. 2:26), often pretending to be what he is not (2 Cor. 11:14). He does everything possible to hinder Christian ministry (2 Cor. 12:7; 1 Thess. 2:18). Believers, on the other hand, are warned even in their anger not to give Satan a foothold to tempt them (Eph. 4:27; see 6:11). People can turn from Satan to find forgiveness and salvation (Acts 26:18). The constant use of violence and deceit by Satan requires that believers manifest courage and extreme vigilance (Jas. 4:7; 1 Pet. 5:8-9). The Bible avoids talking of the absolute origin of Satan. It does talk of "angels that sinned" (2 Pet. 2:4; compare Jude 6).

Jesus came into the world to "destroy the works of the devil" (1 John 3:8). The Cross was a decisive victory over Satan and Satan's host (Col. 2:15; see Luke 10:18-19; Heb. 2:14; Rev. 12:9-12). This victory ensured that countless numbers would be delivered from the dominion of darkness and transferred to the kingdom of Christ (Col. 1:13).

Satan and the demonic forces cannot dominate or possess us except by our own consent. Believers will not be tempted beyond our power of resistance (1 Cor. 10:13). The believer has God's armor—the biblical gospel, integrity, peace through Christ, faith in Christ, prayer—as spiritual security (Eph. 6:11-18).

DEW

Moisture from the sea that forms into drops of water on the earth during a cool night; symbol of refreshment (Deut. 32:2; Ps. 133:3); the loving power of God that revives and invigorates (Prov. 19:12); the sudden onset of an enemy (2 Sam. 17:12); brotherly love and harmony (Ps. 133:3); God's revelation (Judg. 6:36-40); and God's blessing (Gen. 27:28).

DIANA See *Artemis.*

DIASPORA

Scattering of Jews from Palestine to other parts of the world over several centuries and the Jews thus scattered; also called "Dispersion." Two major events greatly contributed to the diaspora: Assyria's resettlement of the Northern Kingdom in Assyria in 722 B.C. (2 Kings 17:6) and Babylon's exile of the Southern Kingdom (Judah) in 586 B.C. (2 Kings 25:8-12). Many of these exiles remained permanently in Babylon. Later, wars fought by the Greeks and Romans in Palestine helped scatter more of the Jewish people.

Severe economic conditions in Palestine brought by warfare and heavy foreign taxes further encouraged the diaspora. By NT times, as many Jews lived outside of Palestine as lived in the land. The diaspora helped pave the way for the spread of the gospel.

DIBLAH (*cake of figs*) or **DIBLATH**

Northern border of Israel (Ezek. 6:14). Sometimes changed to *Riblah* on text critical grounds. See *Riblah.*

DIBON (*pining away* or *fence of tubes*) or **DIBON-GAD**

(1) Capital city of Moab captured by Moses (Num. 21:21-31) and controlled by Gad (32:3,34; 33:45-46; Josh. 13:9,17). See Isa. 15:2; compare Jer. 48:18-22. Dibon stood on the northern hill across the valley from modern Dhiban 40 miles south of Amman, Jordan, and 3 miles north of the Arnon River. Nebuchadnezzar destroyed the city in 582 B.C. Nabateans built a temple there during Jesus' childhood. It was apparently abandoned about A.D. 100.

(2) In Nehemiah's day (about 445 B.C.), Jews lived in a Dibon in Judah. This may be the same as Dimonah.

DIETING

For most people of the ancient world, and certainly for the common man, starvation was a constant and very real threat. For this reason, when the biblical writers wanted to describe someone who was blessed, they often said that such persons would eat rich, fat, and sweet foods, or eat in abundance (eg. 2 Sam. 6:19; Neh. 8:10; 9:25; Prov. 24:13; Song of Sol. 5:1; Isa. 7:22; 25:6; Ezek. 16:13; Joel 2:26). Weight loss was something to be avoided.

God created within humanity a wide variety of bodily shapes and sizes. God also created a wide variety of foods for the nourishment and pleasure of people (Gen. 1:29; 9:3). Yet biblical teaching implies that not all foods are equally beneficial for human consumption and that for some people, the desire for certain foods can lead to enslavement (1 Cor. 6:12).

The Book of Proverbs cautions that excessive eating and drinking is the mark of a fool (Prov. 23:20-21; compare Eccl. 5:18; 9:7; 1 Cor. 15:32), and urges bodily restraint (Prov. 23:2; 25:16). The writer of Ecclesiastes noted that one who is blessed "eats at a proper time—for strength and not for drunkenness" (Eccl. 10:17). Daniel and his friends refused the rich foods of Babylon in favor of vegetables and water (Dan. 1:5-16) and were healthier as a result.

New Testament teaching holds that a person's body is the temple of the Holy Spirit (1 Cor. 6:19) and that it must therefore be subdued (1 Cor. 9:27) and cared for in a way that honors God (1 Cor. 6:20). For this reason, excessive eating is contrary to Christian discipline (Phil. 3:19).

DINAH (*justice* or *artistically formed*)

Daughter of Jacob and Leah (Gen. 30:21); sexually assaulted by man named Shechem, who later wished to marry her (Gen. 34). Simeon and Levi, her brothers, took revenge by killing the male residents of the city of Shechem. See *Jacob; Leah; Shechem.*

DINOSAURS

Some interpreters hold that many of the biblical references to Leviathan (Job 41:1-34; Pss. 74:14; 104:26; Isa.

27:1), dragons (Ps. 74:13; Isa. 27:1; 51:9) and the behemoth (Job 40:15-24) preserve early memories of dinosaurs. Most, however, prefer to explain these great monsters in terms of large and terrifying animals known to man today.

The word *Leviathan* (perhaps derived from a verb meaning "to twist") is the proper name of a large sea creature that defies easy zoological classification. Suggestions as to the identity of Leviathan include the crocodile, dolphin, whale, or sea serpent.

The Hebrew word for dragon (*tannîn*), which often refers to serpents (eg., Ex. 7:9; Deut. 32:33; Ps. 91:13), is used generically in Gen. 1:21 for large sea creatures. Other passages mentioning *tannîn* indicate a specific kind of large sea creature (Job 7:12; Ps. 74:13; Isa. 27:1; 51:9) which cannot be identified with certainty.

Behemoth (the plural form of the common Hebrew noun for cattle) occurs as a great monster only in Job 40:15-24. The description in Job suggests a hippopotamus or elephant.

God created all life for His enjoyment and glory, including dinosaurs (compare Ps. 148:7). However, difficulties in interpretation preclude us from knowing to what extent the biblical writers knew about dinosaurs.

DIONYSIUS

Athenian aristocrat converted to Christianity through the preaching of Paul (Acts 17:34); member of Areopagus. See *Areopagus*.

DIOTREPHES (*nurtured by Jove*)

Individual criticized for self-serving ambition evidenced by his rejecting John's authority (3 John 9). See *John, The Letters of*.

DIRECTIONS (GEOGRAPHICAL)

Way people of the Bible oriented themselves within "four corners of the earth" (Isa. 11:12) by facing eastward toward the sunrise. Thus, in front is east (Gen. 29:1; Judg. 6:3,33),

and behind is west (Isa. 9:12), where the sun sets. On the left hand is north, and to the right hand is south.

DISABILITIES AND DEFORMITIES See *Diseases*.

DISAPPOINTMENT

The Bible recognizes the emotional and physical stress which can accompany disappointment and proclaims that hope is always found in God.

Examples of disappointment recorded in the Bible include Samuel (1 Sam. 16:1), the men on the road to Emmaus (Luke 24:17-21), and Paul (1 Thess. 2:17-20). Many of the psalmist's cries reflect the depths of his disappointment in life and, at times, in God Himself (eg., Pss. 39:12-13; 42:5a, 9-11a). Disappointment and discouragement break the spirit (Prov. 15:13), dry up the bones (Prov. 17:22), and can lead to death (Prov. 18:14).

In spite of his circumstances, the psalmist learned to trust in God who, in the end, overcame his disappointment (Pss. 22:5; 40:1; 42:5b). Isaiah saw a day when all who were feeble and fearful would become strengthened (Isa. 35:3-4). In the meantime, Jesus commands that those who are disappointed continue to wait on God, pray, and not lose heart (Luke 18:1; compare Matt. 5:4). Every believer is called to recognize that suffering produces endurance, endurance produces character, and character produces a hope in God that does not disappoint (Rom. 5:3-5).

DISCERNING OF SPIRITS

A gift of the Spirit (1 Cor. 12:10); apparently God-given ability to tell whether a prophetic speech came from God's Spirit or from another source opposed to God.

DISCHARGE

Modern translation term for bodily excretion that rendered one ceremonially unclean (Lev. 15:2-25; Num. 5:2; KJV, "issue").

DISCIPLES (*learners* or *pupils*), **APOSTLES** (*sent on behalf of another*)

Messenger, envoy, or ambassador; divinely appointed, lifetime witness to the saving acts of God, specifically the death and resurrection of Jesus; followers of Jesus Christ, especially the commissioned Twelve who followed Jesus during His earthly ministry.

"*Apostle*" is the title Jesus gave to His closest circle of friends, the Twelve (Luke 6:13). He set them apart to announce the good news of the kingdom (Matt. 10:1-23; Luke 8:1; 9:1-6). After the first Easter, the early church expanded the term to refer to a wider circle of authoritative preachers and witnesses of the resurrected Lord (Acts 14:4,14; Rom. 16:7; 1 Cor. 4:9; 15:5-9; 2 Cor. 11:13; Gal. 1:19; 2:7-9). The criteria employed for replacing Judas among the Twelve (Acts 1:12-22) included being an eyewitness not only of the resurrected Jesus but also of the ministry of Jesus from the days of His baptism by John. Paul and the early church developed a slightly broader application of the term *apostle* that did not demand an eyewitness knowledge of Jesus' ministry. James the brother of Jesus (Matt. 13:55) was certainly no follower of his Brother during His ministry (Mark 3:21,31-35; John 7:3-5). He still became an "apostle" and leader of the Jerusalem church (Acts 15:1-21; Gal. 1:18-19) following his encounter with the resurrected Lord (1 Cor. 15:7). In a similar way, Paul's vision of, and calling by, the resurrected Lord won for him the designation "apostle" (1 Cor. 9:1; 15:8-11; Gal. 1:11–2:10); though this distinction apparently was not conceded by all (2 Cor. 3:1; 12:11-13). We may presume that Barnabas (Acts 14:4,14), Apollos (1 Cor. 4:6-13), and also Andronicus and Junias (Rom. 16:7) were likewise witnesses of the resurrected Lord.

Paul spoke of certain others as "apostles" who likely were not eyewitnesses of the risen Lord (2 Cor. 8:23 NASB and RSV notes; Phil. 2:25);

but such passages are only apparent exceptions, for the helpers in question are called "apostles" (normally translated "representatives" or "messengers") of the churches, clearly suggesting a status different from that of the "apostle of Jesus Christ." The NT office of apostle, by definition, died with its first representatives. The NT certainly speaks of a succession of witnesses to the apostolic tradition (1 Tim. 6:20; 2 Tim. 1:14), so that the gospel they preached—the apostolic theology— has been handed on (the NT itself being the inspired, literary remains of that theology).

"*Disciple*" is related to two OT references (1 Chron. 25:8; Isa. 8:16). In the Greek world, "disciple" normally referred to an adherent of a particular teacher or religious/philosophical school. The disciple's task was to learn, study, and pass along the sayings and teachings of the master. In rabbinic Judaism the term *disciple* referred to one who was committed to the interpretations of Scripture and religious tradition given him by the master or rabbi. In time, the disciple would, likewise, pass on the traditions to others.

In the NT, "disciple" usually refers to disciples of Jesus with other references to disciples of the Pharisees (Matt. 22:16; Mark 2:18), John the Baptist (Mark 2:18; Luke 11:1; John 1:35), and Moses (John 9:28). The Gospels often refer to Jesus as "Rabbi" (Matt. 26:25, 49; Mark 9:5; 10:51; 11:21; John 1:38,49; 3:2,26; 6:25; 20:16, NIV). One can assume that Jesus used traditional rabbinic teaching techniques (question and answer, discussion, memorization) to instruct His disciples. In many respects Jesus differed from the rabbis. He called His disciples to "Follow me" (Luke 5:27). Disciples of the rabbis could select their teachers. Jesus oftentimes demanded extreme levels of personal renunciation (loss of family, property, etc.; Matt. 4:18-22; 10:24-42; Luke 5:27-28; 14:25-27; 18:28-30). He asked for lifelong allegiance (Luke 9:57-62) as the essential means of doing the will of God (Matt. 12:49-50;

John 7:16-18). He taught more as a bearer of divine revelation than a link in the chain of Jewish tradition (Matt. 5:21-48; 7:28-29; Mark 4:10-11).

Jesus gathered a special circle of Twelve disciples, clearly a symbolic representation of the Twelve tribes (Matt. 19:28). He was reestablishing Jewish social identity based on discipleship to Jesus. "*Disciple*" as a reference to the twelve became an exact equivalent to "apostle" in those contexts where the latter word was also restricted to the Twelve (Matt. 10:1-4; Mark 3:16-19; Luke 6:12-16; Acts 1:13,26).

MATTHEW 10:2-4	MARK 3:16-19	LUKE 6:13-16	ACTS 1:13-14
Simon Peter	Simon Peter	Simon Peter	Peter
Andrew	James, son of Zebedee	Andrew	James
James, son of Zebedee	John	James	John
John	Andrew	John	Andrew
Philip	Philip	Philip	Philip
Bartholomew	Bartholomew	Bartholomew	Thomas
Thomas	Matthew	Matthew	Bartholomew
Matthew the publican	Thomas	Thomas	Matthew
James, son of Alphaeus	James, son of Alphaeus	James, son of Alphaeus	James, son of Alphaeus
(Lebbeus) Thaddeus	Thaddaeus	Simon Zelotes	Simon Zealotes
Simon the Canaanite	Simon the Zealot	Judas, brother of James (compare John 14:22)	Judas, brother of James
Judas Iscariot	Judas Iscariot	Judas Iscariot	(Judas Iscariot) Matthias (v. 26)

"*Disciple*" can refer to others besides the Twelve. The verb "follow" became something of a technical term Jesus used to call His disciples, who were then called "followers" (Mark 4:10). These "followers" included a larger company of people from whom He selected the 12 (Mark 3:7-19; Luke 6:13-17). This larger group of disciples/followers included men and women (Luke 8:1-3; 23:49) from all walks of life. Jesus was no doubt especially popular among the socially outcast and religiously despised, but people of wealth and theological training also followed (Luke 8:1-3; 19:1-10; John 3:1-3; 12:42; 19:38-39).

The Twelve were sent out as representatives of Jesus, commissioned to preach the coming of the kingdom, to cast out demons, and to heal diseases (Matt. 10:1,5-15; Mark 6:7-13; Luke 9:1-6). Such tasks were not limited to the Twelve (Luke 10:1-24). Apparently Jesus' disciples first included "a great multitude of disciples" (Luke 6:17). He formed certain smaller and more specifically defined groups within that "great multitude." These smaller groups would include a group of "seventy" (Luke 10:1,17), the "Twelve" (Matt. 11:1; Mark 6:7; Luke 9:1), and perhaps an even smaller, inner group within the Twelve, consisting especially of Peter, James, and John, whose stories of calling are especially highlighted (Matt. 4:18-22; John 1:35-42) and the tradition that John is the "Other"/ "Beloved Disciple" of the Gospel of John (13:23; 19:26; 20:2; 21:20), and who alone accompanied Jesus on certain significant occasions of healing and revelation (Matt. 17:1; Mark 13:3; Luke 8:51). Acts frequently uses "disciple" to refer generally to all those who believe in the risen Lord (6:1-2,7; 9:1,10,19,26,38; 11:26,29). Christ's final commission (Matt. 28:19-20) is to make "disciples," extending the term to all who come to Jesus in faith.

DISCIPLINE

Process by which God taught His people obedience (Deut. 11:2, NIV). Through praise and correction, God led His people, seeking to bring them to maturity where obedience was the rule rather than the exception. The earliest setting for discipline was the family (Deut. 6:20-25).

Prophets repeatedly warned Israel of God's punishing discipline that found extreme realization in the exile of the northern kingdom in 722 B.C. and of the southern kingdom in 586 B.C. The purpose was to create an obedient new covenant remnant.

The Great Commission places the responsibility for disciplining disciples in the hands of the church. The believers are to teach them "to observe all things whatsoever I have commanded you" (Matt. 28:20). "To observe" is much more than simple knowledge. Observance is to live in obedience to the commands of Jesus. Learning and doing what Jesus wants requires a process, a discipline. Churches throughout their history have sought to teach their members the way of the Lord through "church discipline."

Paul admonished the Ephesians to bring their children up "in the nurture and admonition of the Lord" (Eph. 6:4b), avoiding the heavy-handed, physical brutality practiced by their pagan neighbors. Discipline was not to evoke anger from the children (Eph. 6:4a). God treats and disciplines the faithful as beloved sons (Heb. 12:7-10).

DISEASES

Physical and/or mental malfunctions that limit human functions and lessen the quality of life. People living in biblical times had limited means to diagnose and treat illness. The main diagnostic tools were observation and superficial physical examination. Illness was often attributed to sin or to a curse by an enemy. Illness

struck quickly with devastating results. Life expectancy was short.

Ancient Near Eastern literature contains numerous references to physicians and medical practice. A Sumerian physician, Lulu, lived in Mesopotamia about 2700 B.C. A few decades later, a famous Egyptian named Imhotep established a reputation as a physician and priest. The Code of Hammurabi, from about 1750 B.C., contains several laws regulating the practice of medicine and surgery.

The OT has only a few references to physicians. These persons most likely had been trained in Egypt. Physicians were called on to embalm the body of Jacob (Gen. 50:2). King Asa sought medical care from physicians for his diseased feet (2 Chron. 16:12). Some nonmedical references are made to physicians (Jer. 8:22; Job 13:4).

Ancient Hebrew priests were major providers of medical services. They were especially responsible for the diagnosis of diseases that might pose a threat to the community (Lev. 13). Priests in Israel apparently played little role in the actual treatment of ill persons.

Outlying regions of the Roman empire, such as Palestine, apparently had few well-trained doctors, although little information is available concerning professional medical care outside the large cities. The majority of people probably were born and died without ever being treated by a trained physician.

Jesus noted the purpose of a physician is to treat the ill (Matt. 9:12; Mark 2:17; Luke 5:31; compare Luke 4:23). Mark and Luke related the story of a woman whom physicians could not heal (Mark 5:25-34; Luke 8:43-48). Luke was a physician (Col. 4:14). He might have attended the medical school in Tarsus, Paul's hometown. Sites like the Pool of Bethesda (John 5:1-15) and the pool of Siloam (John 9:7) became renowned as places of healing.

Most of the medicine practiced in ancient Palestine and in other outlying parts of the Roman Empire was probably unprofessional. Women, trained by apprenticeship and experience, served as midwives. Some persons became adept at setting broken bones. Families were left to apply their own folk remedies in most cases of illness, perhaps in consultation with someone in the community who had become known for his or her success in the treatment of various ailments. Despite obvious medical limitations, many of the patients recovered; and many of the remedies used were "successful."

The Bible contains little information about the treatment of disease, except through miraculous means. Ancient Babylonian, Egyptian, Greek, and Roman literature gives some information. A Sumerian clay tablet from about 2200 B.C. contains 15 prescriptions. Most medicines were derived from three sources:

(1) different plants;

(2) substances obtained from animals, such as blood, urine, milk, hair, and ground-up shell and bone;

(3) mineral products including salt and bitumen. These medicines were often accompanied by magical rites, incantations, and prayers. Lines were not clearly drawn between religion, superstition, and science.

Ancient people attempted to quarantine afflicted persons and prevent close contact with healthy individuals (Lev. 13). The Hebrew word translated "leprosy" in Lev. 13 is a general term for a number of different skin eruptions. Although true leprosy occurred in ancient times many of the persons brought to the priests undoubtedly suffered from more common bacterial and fungal infections of the skin. The priests had the duty of determining, on the basis of repeated examination, which of these eruptions posed a threat. They had the authority to isolate persons with suspected dangerous diseases from the community.

King Hezekiah (Isa. 38) suffered from a very serious "boil" (v. 21; see same Hebrew word in Job 2:7 and for eruption occurring on men and beasts, Ex. 9:8-11; compare Lev.

13:18-20; Deut. 28:27), almost certainly some type of acute bacterial skin infection. These dangerous infections could cause death. Hezekiah's illness was treated with a poultice of figs (Isa. 38:21), probably applied as a hot compress. Josephus, first-century Jewish historian, said Herod the Great spent his last days at his winter palace in Jericho seeking relief in hot baths from his intense suffering. Physicians bathed him in warm oil.

Medical care frequently used different kinds of salves and ointments (Isa. 1:6; Luke 10:34). Olive oil was used widely, either alone or as an ingredient in ointments. Oil became a symbol of medicine and was used with prayer (Mark 6:13; Jas. 5:14).

Herbs and plant products were among the most popular of ancient medicines, applied to the body as a poultice or taken by mouth. Frankincense and myrrh — gum resins obtained from trees — were commonly used to treat a variety of diseases, although their main use was in perfumes and incense. Some plant remedies may have been harmful, even poisonous (2 Kings 4:39-41). A few may actually have been of some benefit.

Wine was commonly thought to have medicinal value. Wine was used to soothe stomach and intestinal disorders (1 Tim. 5:23) and to treat a variety of other physical problems. Beer was widely used in several medicines, especially by the Babylonians.

"Blemish" meant a deformity or spot (Lev. 21:17-21). A person with a blemish was disqualified from the priesthood. A broken hand or broken foot disqualified one from priesthood (Lev. 21:19). Congenital malformations included extra body parts, such as six toes (2 Sam. 21:20). Dwarfs were barred from priestly duties (Lev. 21:20). Hunchback resulted from injuries to the spine (Lev. 21:20). This deformity often afflicted young girls who typically carried large loads on their shoulders or hips. "Lame" (2 Sam. 4:4) meant a person had limited walking abilities, whether the disability resulted from a birth defect, amputation, or a physical impairment. Blindness (Deut. 28:28) caused from eye infection was common during Bible times. Heat, dust, sunlight, and unclean habits aided the spread of eye diseases, often leading to blindness.

Deafness or dumbness resulted in inability to speak or hear (Mark 7:32). Some cases of deafness were temporary (Luke 1:20). Infirmity is a general term for bodily weakness or disability (John 5:5; 1 Tim. 5:23).

Paralysis (Luke 5:18) often resulted from injuries to the spine. Withered hand and skin (Matt. 12:10) often resulted from the shrinking of the bones, muscles, or both. The result was loss of nerve power or stiffening of the joints.

Mental illness and epilepsy were usually associated with demonic powers. The afflicted person was often isolated, and even abused in some cases. King Saul became mentally unstable and gained some help from music (1 Sam. 16:23). The Babylonian king Nebuchadnezzar became mentally ill (Dan. 4). The king's sanity was restored when he acknowledged the true God.

Sterility was a great burden in biblical times. When Leah suffered a temporary period of sterility, she sent her son, Reuben, to the field to obtain mandrakes. Her barren sister, Rachel, also asked for some of the mandrakes (Gen. 30: 9-24). The root of the mandrake was widely used in the ancient world to promote conception and as a narcotic.

Most babies were born without benefit of a physician. Midwives frequently helped, especially in the case of difficult deliveries (Gen. 35:16-21; 1 Sam. 4:19-22). Babies were often born with mothers seated on a special stool (Ex. 1:16). Many mothers and babies died during childbirth, or in the first few days and weeks after delivery due to infection, blood loss, poor nutrition, and the absence of good medical care. The custom of breast-feeding, fortunately, did help prevent some illness.

King Jehoram died with a painful intestinal disorder (2 Chron. 21:18-20).

King Uzziah died of leprosy (2 Chron. 26:19-23). King Herod Agrippa I died of some kind of parasitic disease (Acts 12:21-23). Ahaziah died following a fall from the upper portion of his home in Samaria (2 Kings 1:2-17). When illness or accident occurred in the ancient world, only limited medical help was available.

The Bible mentions several illnesses accompanied by fever (Matt. 8:14-15; John 4:46-52; Acts 28:8). In Acts 28:8, the man also had dysentery. Most fevers were due to infectious diseases, including malaria. With no effective treatment for any of these infections, death was all too often the outcome. Small children were particularly vulnerable to illness, and the death rate could be high (2 Sam. 12:15-18; 1 Kings 17:17-24; 2 Kings 4:18-37; Luke 7:11-15; 8:40-56; John 4:46-52).

The only surgical procedure mentioned in the Bible is circumcision, done for religious rather than medical reasons and not ordinarily performed by a doctor. Boils were lanced; broken bones were set; arms and legs were amputated. Holes were drilled into skulls to relieve pressure, and stones were removed from the urinary bladder. Teeth were also extracted. Ancient mummies have been found with gold fillings in their teeth. In addition, false teeth, using human or animal teeth, were being prepared by at least 500 B.C.

One of Jesus' major ministries was healing. People flocked to Him, often after having tried all remedies available. Jesus had the power both to forgive sin and to heal (Matt. 9:1-8; compare Mark 2:1-12; Luke 5:17-26).

DISPENSATION

English term commonly used to translate the Greek oikonomia, whose etymology refers to the law or management of a household.

In Eph. 3:2 and 3:9 the dispensation is linked to the mystery of Christ, which Paul says is a revelation from God. The dispensation is hence an arrangement or management in which a responsibility is placed on mankind by God.

When seen in light of the progress of revelation (e.g., John 1:17; Gal. 3–4), the dispensations can be interpreted as taking on added significance. There is progression of revelation as salvation history unfolds. The different ages incorporate different divinely appointed ways of relating to God. These must not be seen as multiple ways of salvation. Salvation is always by grace through faith alone (Rom. 4). The church of the present age has a unique feature of including both Jews and Gentiles in a position of equality that had not been realized before (Eph. 2:11-22). The Mosaic economy as a whole is superseded (see especially Galatians) as was predicted in the OT itself. In 2 Cor. 3:6, Paul mentions himself and his colaborers as ministers of the New Covenant (cp. Luke 22:20). An initial and partial fulfillment of the promises made to Israel in Jer. 31:31-34 and Ezek. 36:22-32 have come to pass in the ministry of the life, death, and resurrection of Jesus Christ. In the future ministry of Christ at His return other remaining aspects of salvation history shall also come to pass. These dispensational arrangements are, therefore, to be seen as both a theology of progressive revelation in relation to time and as a hermeneutical tool for correctly interpreting God's relations to humanity.

Dispensationalism is a system of biblical interpretation that has been prominent in the church since the resurgence of biblical study in the mid 1800s, though its roots go back much further. John Nelson Darby, C. I. Scofield, and Lewis Sperry Chafer were among the most famous advocates of a system of theology and interpretation emphasizing the distinguishable elements within the dispensations. The most characteristic hermeneutical concern for Dispensationalism is the consistent distinction between National Israel and the Church. In the 1950s and '60s the extreme form of the dual nature of God's eternal plan was relaxed somewhat, especially in the writings of Charles Ryrie and John Walvoord. More recently still, reconciliation has begun between some adherents of Dispensationalism and those of nondispensational theology. Particularly significant is the eschatological understanding of the NT with its already/not yet approach to fulfillment of promises made in the OT. Progressive Dispensationalism as advocated by evangelicals such as Craig Blaising, Darrell Bock, and Robert Saucy has emerged as a recent effort to fine-tune the hermeneutical system. This newer approach is closest to nondispensational thinking and could thereby serve as a bridge to unite evangelicals on biblical and theological matters. See *Millennium; Revelation, Book of*

DISPERSION See *Diaspora.*

DIVERSITY

Diversity is a necessary characteristic of human and animal populations (Gen. 10; Acts 17:26-27). Out of His richness God created an unfathomable number of creatures to fill the earth (Gen. 1:11-12, 20-22, 24-25) and respond to Him in praise (Ps. 148).

Although God chose the family of Abraham from among the nations to be His special possession, an ethnically diverse element has always been present in His people (Ex. 12:38; compare Luke 4:25-27). At times Israel responded negatively to diverse populations within their midst, such as when Nehemiah criticized the Jews of Jerusalem for marrying foreign women (Neh. 13:23-30). The issue of diversity became critical during the initial spread of the church to the Gentile world (Acts 10:1-48; 15:1-21) and was resolved on the side of unity in Christ (Gal. 3:28). John saw that the population of heaven will contain persons "of all nations, and kindreds, and people, and tongues" (Rev. 7:9).

God provides a variety of spiritual gifts to equip and empower His church for service in a diverse world (1 Cor. 12:4-31; Eph. 4:11-13).

DIVES

Name sometimes given to rich man (Luke 16:19-31); Latin word for "rich" (Luke 16:19) in Vulgate. The idea that this was the name of the man emerged in medieval times. See *Lazarus*.

DIVIDED KINGDOM

Two political states of Judah and Israel that came into existence shortly after the death of Solomon and survived until fall of Israel in 722 B.C. See *Israel, History of*.

DIVINATION AND MAGIC

Attempt to contact supernatural powers to determine answers to questions hidden to humans and usually involving the future; widely practiced in Ancient Near East, especially among the Babylonians who developed it into a highly respected discipline (Ezek. 21:21). In *hepatoscopy*, divination by liver, specially trained priests observed a sacrifical animal's liver—the seat of life—to determine the future activities of the gods. Livers were carefully divided into zones, each containing its own secrets. Among Irael's neighbors even the gods were subject to the higher power of magic.

Other methods included *augury* (foretelling the future by natural signs, especially the flight of birds), *hydromancy* (divination by mixing liquids; see Gen. 44:5), *casting lots* (Jonah 1:7-8), *astrology* (2 Kings 21:5), and *necromancy* (1 Sam. 28:7-25). God gave Israel's priests the Urim and Thummim (1 Sam. 28:6) to determine His will.

The OT shows even Israel practiced magic (1 Sam. 28:3,7; 2 Kings 9:22; Isa. 2:6; compare Isa. 3:2-3; 2 Chron. 33:6; Jer. 27:9; 29:8). Although varying kinds of divination and magic are reported to have been practiced widely in ancient Israel and among her neighbors (Deut. 18:9-14; 1 Sam. 6:2; Isa. 19:3; Ezek. 21:21; Dan. 2:2), Israel herself was clearly and firmly admonished to have no part in such activities (Lev. 19:26, 31; 20:6,27; Deut. 18:9-14; Ezek. 13:23).

DIVINE FREEDOM

God's self-determining, absolute freedom. God acts according to His own choosing to accomplish His plans and purposes. God has limited His freedom to act according to His nature and to act within the bounds of His creation (Job 34:13; Pss. 115:3; 135:5-6; Isa. 42:21; 45:7; Jer. 18:6; Lam. 3:37-38; Matt. 20:15; Rom. 11:33-36; Eph. 1:11; Heb. 1:12). God's freedom does not mean He authored those things that are imperfect or calculated to bring harm to the person or purposes of His creation (Jas. 1:17).

God's nature is the source of His freedom. He is not one of many gods but reigns as supreme over all (1 Chron. 29:11; Neh. 9:6; Ps. 24:1; Isa. 44:6). He is self-existent and independent within Himself (Ex. 3:14; Deut. 32:40; Jer. 10:10; John 5:26). As absolutely supreme, He is free to act as He wishes. God's power gives Him absolute freedom (1 Chron. 29:12). This enables Him to accomplish anything consistent with His nature (Luke 1:37). God is also Spirit (John 4:24). He is thus totally free of the space or time limitations of this universe (Ps. 139:7-12). God is free to be any place at any time with anybody.

The only influence exerted upon God comes from God's nature, His grace (2 Cor. 8:9), justice (Zeph. 3:5), love (John 3:16), and mercy (Mic. 7:18; Titus 3:5). God's freedom gives humans confidence that God cares for His creatures and works for their good (Rom. 8:28).

DIVINE RETRIBUTION

Process of God's meting out merited requital: punishment for evil or reward for good. Abraham's obedient response to God's call resulted in his being blessed and becoming the mediator of blessing to all the world (Gen. 12:1-3). Israel, if they heard and obeyed God's word, would be blessed (Deut. 6:1-9; compare Matt. 5–7; Mark 10:41; Luke 10:7; John 9:36; Gal. 6:7-8). Banishment from Eden, the flood, and multiplication of languages followed on the heels of sin (Gen. 3–11). Pharaoh and all Egypt incurred God's judgment for not yielding to God's will. Even Israel, because of her failure to place her trust in God, experienced the judgment of exile. Psalms affirm that the same process occurs on an individual level that occurs on the corporate. Job issues a proviso to such a mechanical view of God and suffering in this life. It is dangerous to interpret all suffering as punishment. Humans cannot determine the causes of suffering and should never overlook God's patience, forgiveness, and mercy.

Reward/punishment in this life is a foretaste of what will be experienced at the end of time. The gospel is the standard by which God will reward and punish (Rom. 2:16). Since it is a revelation both of God's faithfulness and of His wrath, gospel preaching enacts the process of end-time judgment and becomes a foretaste of the final reckoning that is to occur on that great and glorious day. See *Eschatology; Eternal Life; Everlasting Punishment.*

DIVINER'S OAK

Place visible from gate of Shechem (Judg. 9:34-37). The tree formed part of a sanctuary. The tree is perhaps that associated with Abraham (Gen. 12:6), Jacob (Gen. 35:4), and Joshua (Josh. 24:26). Compare Deut. 11:30, Judg. 9:6. It may well have played an important role in Canaanite worship at Shechem before Israel took over the ancient worship place. See *Terebinth.*

DIVINITY OF CHRIST See *Christ, Christology; Incarnation; Jesus, Life and Ministry of.*

DIVORCE

Breaking of the marriage covenant. An action contrary to the pattern of "one man, one woman, one lifetime" revealed by God in Gen. 1:27; 2:21-25.

The concept that divorce could constitute sin appeared in Mal. 2:14-16. Malachi stated that marriage represented a covenant between a man and a woman. Further, marriage provided companionship, brought oneness, and promoted a godly seed. The dissolution of marriage for personal benefit represented treacherous behavior before the Lord and is strongly condemned.

Under certain conditions, divorce could occur under OT law (Deut. 24:1-4). Though a wife might abandon her husband, only the husband could seek a divorce. If a husband found "some indecency in her" (NASB), he was allowed, but not required, to write a "certificate of divorce" against his wife. The rejected wife might marry again, but she could not remarry her original husband. The "indecency" has been interpreted either as anything displeasing to the husband or as sexual immorality. The best interpretation is probably that if upon marriage a husband found that his wife had been sexually active during the engagement period (or even before), then he could divorce her. This was an important safeguard since, under OT law, adultery was punishable by death (Lev. 20:10). After the Babylonian captivity of Israel, Ezra (Ezra 10) led the Israelites to "put away all the wives and their children," so as to remove idolatrous foreigners from Israel. Intermarriage with the idolatrous peoples around Israel had been forbidden in Deut. 7:3. Since other foreigners had been accepted into Israel (i.e., Ruth), this may have indicated a refusal to worship the Lord as God on the part of the foreign wives.

The Lord Jesus stated that divorce, except in the case of sexual immorality, would cause complications for remarriage. An improper divorce would make the divorced wife and her future husband adulterers in their relationship (Matt. 5:31-32). In Matt. 19:3-12, Jesus stated that God did not intend for divorce to occur. The Mosaic law allowed for divorce only because of the hardness of Israelite hearts.

In his discussion of the law in Rom. 7:1-3, Paul reaffirmed the principles of the sanctity of marriage, the wrongfulness of divorce, and the potential consequences of remarriage. In 1 Cor. 7:10-16 Paul reiterated the need to preserve the marriage commitment.

Based on Rom. 7:1-3 and 1 Cor. 7:39, Paul believed that divorce was no longer an issue once one's spouse had died. The remaining spouse was free to marry as long as the new marriage was "in the Lord" (1 Cor. 7:39). Therefore, marriage in Scripture represented a sacred bond between one man and one woman for one lifetime. This had ramifications for the leadership qualifications for God's other institution, the church (1 Tim. 3:1-13; Titus 1:5-9). See *Marriage*

DOCTRINE

Basic body of coherent Christian teaching or understanding (2 Tim. 3:16) to be handed on through instruction and proclamation. The heart of doctrine remains a systematic examination of the content of the relationship which God in Christ has entered into with us. Three factors guide a believer in the formulation of Christian doctrines: Scripture, experience, and intellect.

DODANIM

Great grandson of Noah and son of Javan in the table of nations (Gen. 10:4); Rodanim in 1 Chron. 1:7. Dodanim could refer to a land of Danuna, apparently north of Tyre, known from the Amarna letters. They were apparently from the Greek area and may have been Greek speaking. Perhaps they are the inhabitants of Dodona near Epirus.

DOG See *Animals.*

DOOR

Opening for entering or leaving a house, tent, or room. The door was usually made of wood sheeted with metal, though a slab of stone could be used.

"Door" is often used in a figurative sense. "Sin lieth at the door" (Gen. 4:7) means sin is near. The Valley of Achor, a place of trouble (Josh. 7:26), is later promised as "a door of hope" (Hos. 2:15). Jesus called Himself "the door" (John 10:7,9). Faith in Him is the only way to enter the kingdom of God. God gave to the Gentiles "the door of faith," or an opportunity to know Him as Lord (Acts 14:27). Paul constantly sought a "door of service," an occasion for ministry in the name of Christ (1 Cor. 16:9). Jesus stands at the door and knocks (Rev. 3:20), calling all people to Himself.

DOORKEEPER

Person guarding access to an important or restricted place. Temple doorkeeper was an important office. The doorkeepers collected money from the people (2 Kings 22:4). Some Levites were designated doorkeepers (or "gatekeepers") for the ark (1 Chron. 15:23-24). The Persian kings used eunuchs for doorkeepers (Esther 2:21). Women also served this function (John 18:16-17; Acts 12:13).

DOR (*dwelling*)

Canaanite city; modern khirbet el-Burj, 12 miles south of Mount Carmel. Apparently the Tjeker, one of the Sea Peoples, destroyed the city shortly after 1300 B.C. Its king joined the northern coalition against Joshua (Josh. 11:2; 12:23) but met defeat. "*Naphoth Dor,*" or heights of Dor must refer to Mount Carmel since Dor lies on the seacoast. Dor lay in the territory assigned Asher, but the tribe of Manasseh claimed it (Josh. 17:11). The Canaanites maintained political control (Josh. 17:12; Judg. 1:27). Dor served as district headquarters under Solomon (1 Kings 4:11).

DORCAS (*gazelle*)

Christian woman of Joppa known for charitable works (Acts 9:36); also called Tabitha, an Aramaic name. God used Peter to restore her to life.

DOT

REB for Greek "little horn" (Matt. 5:18; compare Luke 16:17); "tittle," KJV; "stroke of a letter or pen," NASB, NRSV, NIV; "comma," CEV; "smallest detail," TEV, NLT; "smallest part of a letter," NCV. The dot is generally held to be a mark distinguishing similarly shaped Hebrew or Aramaic letters. *Iota*, translated "jot" or "smallest letter," is the smallest Greek vowel and is generally taken to refer here to the smallest Hebrew letter, *yodh*. Jesus thus contended that it was easier for heaven and earth to pass away than for the smallest detail of the law to be set aside.

DOTHAN, DOTHAIM

Commercial city of Manasseh, west of Jordan, 11 miles northeast of Samaria, 5 miles southwest of Genin; 13 miles north of Shechem; controlled all traffic going between the hills and the Jezreel Valley; modern Tell Dotha; see Gen. 37:17; 2 Kings 6:13.

DOUGH See *Bread.*

DOVE See *Birds.*

DOWRY

Marriage present that ensured the new wife's financial security against the possibility her husband might forsake her or might die. The husband-to-be or his father paid the dowry or bride price to the bride's father to be kept for the bride. Often the bride received the dowry directly or indirectly through her father. The bride could protest if her father used the dowry for other purposes (Gen. 31:15). See *Marriage; Family.*

DOWNSIZING

The Bible's statements regarding God's providence in times of hardship are directly applicable to personal difficulties which result from corporate and financial downsizing.

The biblical record is ample proof that no one is exempt from trouble (Job 5:7; Ps. 40:12). Job experienced a greater degree of downsizing than perhaps anyone before or since (Job 1:13-19). While Job apparently never understood the reasons for his misfortune (Job 42:1-6), God eventually restored both his wealth and position (Job 42:10-17).

The apostle Paul learned "the secret of being content in any and every situation . . . whether living in plenty or in want" (Phil. 4:11-12). Paul understood that while circumstances are often beyond the control of individuals, nothing is beyond the realm of God, who cares for even the smallest part of His creation (Ps. 24:1; Matt. 6:25-33). For this reason, God answers those who wait for Him (Ps. 40:1).

DOXOLOGY

Brief formula for expressing praise or glory to God containing an ascription of praise to God (usually in third person) and an expression of His infinite nature. Biblical doxologies function as a conclusion to songs (Ex. 15:18), psalms (Ps. 146:10), and prayers (Matt. 6:13), where they possibly served as group responses to solo singing or recitation. Doxologies conclude four of the five divisions of the psalter (Pss. 41:13; 72:19; 89:52; 106:48), with Ps. 150 serving as a sort of doxology to the entire collection. Doxologies also occur at or near the end of several NT books (Rom. 16:27; Phil. 4:20; 1 Tim. 6:16; 2 Tim. 4:18; Heb. 13:21; 1 Pet. 5:11; 2 Pet. 3:18; Jude 25) and figure prominently in the Revelation (1:6; 4:8; 5:13; 7:12).

DRAGON

Mammal inhabiting the desert (Isa. 13:22; 35:7; 43:20; Lam. 4:3); jackal or perhaps wolf (REB). A second Hebrew term has four possible uses:

(1) a large sea creature (Gen. 1:21; Ps. 148:7), possibly a whale (KJV);

(2) a snake (Ex. 7:9-10,12; Deut. 32:33; Ps. 91:13);

(3) a crocodile (Jer. 51:34; Ezek. 29:3; 32:3) as a symbol of Nebuchadnezzar of Babylon or the Egyptian pharaoh;

(4) a mythological sea monster symbolic of forces of chaos and evil in opposition to God's creative and redemptive work (Ps. 74:12-14; Job 7:12; 26:12-13; Isa. 27:1; 51:9-10). Leviathan and Rehab are used as parallel terms. Revelation develops sense 4, clearly identifying the dragon with Satan. The dragon is put under guard (Rev. 20:1-3; see Job 7:12) and later released for final destruction (Rev. 20:7-10; see Isa. 27:1).

DREAMS

Visions seen during sleep. In the Ancient Near Eastern world dreams were the world of the divine and the demonic and often revealed the future or showed the dreamer the right decision to make. People slept in temples or holy places to have a dream to help make decisions. Many of the nations surrounding Israel had religious figures skilled in the interpretation of dreams. They could be consulted at the highest level of government for important decisions. In Egypt and Assyria, these interpreters even developed "dream books" used to interpret the symbols of a dream.

Israel was forbidden to use many of the divining practices of her neighbors, but over a dozen times God revealed something through a dream (see Zech. 10:1-2). Prophecy and the dreaming of dreams were to be tested in the same way (Deut. 13; compare Num. 12:6; 1 Sam. 28:6; Jer. 27:9; Joel 2:28). Some dreams could be wishful thinking (Ps. 126:1; Isa. 29:7,8; compare Jer. 23:28). We can distinguish three types of dreams:

(1) simple message dream apparently did not need interpretation (Matt. 1; 2);

(2) simple symbolic dream with symbols clear enough the dreamer and others could understand it (Gen. 37);

(3) complex symbolic dreams, requiring the interpretive skill of someone with experience or an unusual ability in interpretation (Dan. 2; 4). Even Daniel had dreams with symbolism so complex he had to seek divine interpretation (Dan. 8). Dreams were often used by God to reveal His will, but people cannot rely on dreams to know God's will.

DRESS See *Cloth, Clothing.*

DRINK (beverages)

Water drawn from cisterns (2 Sam. 17:18; Jer. 38:6) or wells (Gen. 29:2; John 4:11) was the primary drink. In times of draught it was necessary to buy water (Deut. 2:28; Lam. 5:4). Milk was also a common beverage, though it was considered a food rather than a drink. "New" or "sweet" wine was likely wine from the first drippings of juice before the grapes had been trodden and had intoxicating effects (Hos. 4:11; Acts 2:13). Sour wine, perhaps vinegar mixed with oil, was a common drink of day laborers (Ruth 2:14; Luke 23:36). Wine was considered a luxury item that could both gladden the heart (Ps. 104:15) or cloud the mind (Isa. 28:7; Hos. 4:11). See *Milk; Water; Wine.*

DROPSY

Edema, a disease with fluid retention and swelling in body cavities and limbs; a symptom of disease of the heart, liver, kidneys, or brain. Thus TEV, NLT, CEV speak of man whose arms and legs were swollen (Luke 14:2).

DRUGS (illegal narcotics)

Several biblical principles address the scourge which results from the use of illegal narcotics.

The Bible's strong counsel against drunkenness (Prov. 20:1; 23:20-21, 29-35; Isa. 28:1, 7-8; Hab. 2:15-16; Gal. 5:16, 21; Eph. 5:18) is clear indication that illegal narcotics, which adversely affect the mind and body to an even greater degree than does alcohol, should be stringently avoided. Like alcohol abuse, drug abuse destroys one's ability to live a reasonable life (Isa. 5:11-12).

The Bible recognizes the compelling reality of temptation to give in to peer pressure, abuse oneself, and shut out one's surroundings (Prov.

31:4-7; Isa. 56:12; 1 Cor. 10:13; 15:33). Peter speaks of the importance of maintaining an alert mind in the face of difficult circumstances (1 Pet. 1:13; 5:8; compare 1 Thess. 5:6). Even on the cross, Jesus refused the drugging effects of wine mixed with gall (Matt. 27:34).

Christians are commanded to honor God with their bodies, which the apostle Paul aptly calls temples of the Holy Spirit (1 Cor. 6:19-20). The Bible teaches the value of self-control (Prov. 25:28; Gal. 5:23) as one means to withstand temptation (1 Cor. 10:13). Ultimately, it is the work of Christ which breaks the cycle of sin and death (Rom. 7:18–8:2).

DRUNKENNESS

State of dizziness, headaches, and vomiting resulting from drinking alcoholic beverages. From Gen. 9:21 on, the Bible describes the shameful state of the drunken person and the shameful actions resulting from the state.

Jesus warned that the cares of life may lead to anxiety and drunkenness (Luke 21:34). Paul repeatedly warned against the dangers of drunkenness (Rom. 13:13; 1 Cor. 5:11; Gal. 5:21; 1 Thess. 5:7). First Timothy 3:3 and Titus 1:7 warn church leaders they must not be drunkards. Drunkenness is a pagan custom, not a Christian one (1 Pet. 4:3). Drunkards are among those who will not "inherit the kingdom of God" (1 Cor. 6:10).

DRUSILLA

Wife of Felix, the Roman governor of Judea; youngest daughter of Herod Agrippa I; Jew who listened to Paul's arguments with her husband (Acts 24:24). See *Herod.*

DUKE See *Chief.*

DUMAH (*silence* or *permanent settlement*)

(1) Son of Ishmael and original ancestor of the Arabian tribe (Gen.

25:14) centered in the Dumah.

(2) City of Judah (Josh. 15:52); probably modern khirbet ed-Dome about 9 miles southwest of Hebron.

DUNG

Excrement of man or beast. An ash heap or rubbish heap was used to convey the haunt of the destitute (1 Sam. 2:8; Luke 14:35). The sacred law required that the dung, along with other parts of the animal, should not be burned on the altar but should be burned outside the camp (Ex. 29:14; Lev. 4:11-12). A major disgrace for a Jew was to have one's carcass treated as dung (2 Kings 9:37; Jer. 8:2). Dung has been used as fertilizer (Luke 13:8; Isa. 25:10) and fuel (Ezek. 4:12-15) for centuries. Paul compared all things he might own as dung compared to his personal knowledge of Christ (Phil. 3:8).

DUST

Loose earth; used in figures of speech for a multitude (Gen. 13:16; Num. 23:10; Isa. 29:5) or an abundance (of flesh, Ps. 78:27; of silver, Job 27:16; of blood, Zeph. 1:17); as a metaphor for death, the grave, or Sheol (Job 10:9; Eccl. 12:7; Dan. 12:2). Dust on a balance is a picture of something insignificant (Isa. 40:15). Human lowliness in relationship with God as well as humanity's close relationship with the rest of creation is expressed in the making of persons from dust .

For Jews to shake dust off their feet was a sign that Gentile territory was unclean. In the NT this action indicates that those who have rejected the gospel have made themselves as Gentiles and must face the judgment of God (Matt. 10:14-15; Acts 13:51).

DWARF

Person of abnormally small size, especially one with abnormal body proportions. The Hebrew word (Lev. 21:20) is used in Gen. 41:3,23 to describe the emaciated cows and shriveled heads of grain. The early

Greek and Latin versions understood the word to mean a type of eye disorder (compare REB).

DWELLING

Place where someone lives, in biblical times either a tent (Gen. 25:27), house (2 Sam. 7:2), or the territory in which one lives (Gen. 36:40,43). The OT repeatedly promises that those who keep the covenant will dwell in safety (Lev. 25:18-19; Zech. 2:10-11). To dwell in a house of clay (Job 4:19) is to possess a mortal body. The heavenly dwelling of 2 Cor. 5:2 is the resurrection body.

References to the dwelling place of God highlight both the imminence and transcendence of God. God draws near to speak, listen, and fellowship (Ex. 25:8; 29:45-46; Num. 35:34; Deut. 33:16; 2 Sam. 7:2; Ezra 7:15; Pss. 9:11; 20:2; 26:8; 43:3; 76:2; 78:60; 132:14; 135:2,21; Matt. 23:21; compare Ezek. 37:27; Rev. 21:3).

God's transcendence appears when God dwells in clouds and thick darkness (1 Kings 8:12), in a high and holy place (Isa. 57:15), or in light (1 Tim. 6:16). Though heaven is spoken of as God's dwelling (1 Kings 8:30, 39, 43,49), even heaven cannot contain God (1 Kings 8:27). The Word become flesh and dwelt among humankind (John 1:14). The church is the dwelling place of God (Eph. 2:22). Christ dwells in believers' hearts (Eph. 3:17). Believers are the temple of God (1 Cor. 3:16); and their bodies, the temple of His Holy Spirit (6:19).

DYEING

The process of coloring materials. The dying process is not mentioned in Scripture, though dyed material is (Ex. 25:4; 36:8,35,37; Judg. 5:30; 2 Chron. 2:7; 3:14). Job 38:14 as emended by some modern translators (NRSV) speaks of "dyeing" the sky. In the NT, Lydia was a seller of purple-dyed goods (Acts 16:14).

The dyeing process involved soaking the material to be dyed in vats of dye, then drying it. This process was repeated until the dyed stuff was the desired color. The process was concluded by soaking in a fixing agent that rendered the cloth colorfast. See *Colors.*

E

EAGLE See *Birds.*

EAR

Physical organ of hearing. Right ears of priests were consecrated with blood (Ex. 29:20; Lev. 8:24). Right ears of lepers were sprinkled with blood and oil as part of their cleansing (Lev. 14:14,17). If a slave volunteered to serve a master for life, the slave's ear was pierced with an awl into the master's doorpost (Ex. 21:6; Deut. 15:17).

Dull, heavy, closed, or uncircumcised ears expressed inattentiveness and disobedience (Isa. 6:10; Jer. 6:10; Acts 7:51). God sometimes uses adversity to open deaf ears (Job 36:15). To awake the ears was to make someone teachable (Isa. 50:4). To uncover or open the ear was to reveal something (Isa. 50:5). The ear exercised judgment (Job 12:11) and understanding (13:1).

EARNEST

(1) Sincerity and intensity of purpose (Rom. 8:19; 1 Cor. 12:31; 2 Cor. 7:7; Heb. 2:1; Jude 3). In the agony of the cross, Christ prayed earnestly (Luke 22:44).

(2) First payment on a purchase that obligates the purchaser to make further payments and secures legal claim to an article or validates a sales contract before the full price is paid; deposit (NIV); pledge (NASB, REB); first installment (NRSV, NLT); guarantee (TEV, NKJV, NCV). See Gen. 38:17. God has given believers the Holy Spirit in their hearts as an earnest or pledge of the salvation to come (2 Cor. 1:22; 5:5; Eph. 1:14).

EARTH, LAND

The whole planet; a limited area of inhabitable territory or a nation; the ground, especially crop land; all representing Hebrew *'erets.* Interpreters and translators must decide from the literary context whether *'erets* means the whole earth, a specific land, or the ground. Naaman, commander of

Syrian army, came to Elisha to be healed of leprosy. His maid is called "the maid that is of the land (*'erets*) of Israel" (2 Kings 5:4; see Jer. 2:6-7). Naaman said of Elisha's God, "I know that there is no God in all the earth (*'erets*), but in Israel" (2 Kings 5:15; compare Jer. 50:1,8,25; 50:23; Hag. 1:10; Zech. 8:12).

The exceedingly good earth is created with the heavens (Gen. 1:1-2,31; compare Job 26:7; 38-41; Isa. 40:28; 42:5; 45:12,18; 48:13). In the OT, the heavenly realm, earthly realm, and subearthly realm (Ezek. 26:15-20; 31:2,14,16,18; 32:18,24; See Job 10:21-22; Ps. 63:9) described the place of God and angels, the place of people now alive, and the place of those who have died.

Land, especially the land of Canaan (Joel 2:18-19), belonged to Yahweh. God was jealous "for His land." He would judge the nations because they had "parted My land" (Joel 3:2; compare Gen. 17:8-9). Those who joined land to land, house to house, field to field (in land monopolies) were condemned (Isa. 5:8-10; compare Amos 6:1,4; Mic. 2:2). To prevent consolidation of land in the hands of a few, Leviticus called for a 50-year jubilee to return property to families (Lev. 25). The Lord of heaven and earth is also the Lord of individual lands. All of the earth as well as specific parts should be used to promote a good life for the inhabitants. People are to give thanks to the One who provided them with the means to achieve such a life.

EARTHQUAKE

Shaking or trembling of the earth due to volcanic activity or, more often, the shifting of the earth's crust. Severe earthquakes produce such side effects as loud rumblings (Ezek. 3:12-13), openings in the earth's crust (Num. 16:32), and fires (Rev. 8:5). Palestine has two to three major quakes a century and two to six minor shocks a year. The major quake centers in Palestine are Upper Galilee—

near Shechem (Nablus)—and near Lydda on the western edge of the Judean mountains. Secondary quake centers are located in the Jordan Valley at Jericho and Tiberias. A memorable earthquake occurred during the reign of Uzziah (Amos 1:1; Zech. 14:5).

Many times God's judgment or visitation is described using the imagery of an earthquake (Ps. 18:7; Isa. 29:6; Nah. 1:5; Rev. 6:12; 8:5; 11:13; 16:18) and is often seen as a sign of the end of time (Matt. 24:7,29). An earthquake is a sign of God's presence or of God's revelation of Himself (1 Kings 19:11-12; Ps. 29:8; Ezek. 38:19-20; Joel 2:10; 3:16; Acts 4:31; Rev. 11:19). At times the whole universe is described as being shaken by God (Isa. 13:13; 24:17-20; Joel 3:16; Hag. 2:6-7; Matt. 24:29; Heb. 12:26-27; Rev. 6:12; 8:5).

Earthquakes could be used by God for good purposes (Acts 16:26). The earth quaked in revulsion at the death of Jesus (Matt. 27:51-54), and the earth quaked to move the stone from Jesus' tomb (Matt. 28:2). Those who love God and are faithful to Him have no need to fear the trembling of the earth (Ps. 46:2-3).

EAST See *Directions (Geographical).*

EAST COUNTRY

Designation for territories lying in the direction of the rising sun. At Gen. 25:6 the reference signifies desert lands more than direction. At 1 Kings 4:30 the wisdom of the East, either of Mesopotamia or of the desert dwelling Arabs, together with the wisdom of Egypt signifies all wisdom. The east country of Ezek. 47:8 lies in the direction of the Dead Sea. The east country and west country of Zech. 8:7 refer to the whole world.

EASTER

Celebration of Jesus' resurrection; oldest Christian festival, except for the weekly Sunday celebration. Since Christ's Passion and resurrection occurred at the time of the Jewish Passover, the first Jewish Christians probably transformed their Passover observance into a celebration of the central events of their new faith and focused on Christ as the paschal Lamb. The celebrations were probably well established in most churches by A.D. 100 and consisted of a vigil beginning on Saturday evening and ending on Sunday morning, including remembrance of Christ's crucifixion as well as the resurrection. Evidence from shortly after A.D. 200 shows the climax of the vigil was the baptism of new Christians and the celebration of the Lord's Supper. By about A.D. 300, most churches divided the original observance, devoting Good Friday to the crucifixion and Easter Sunday to the resurrection. See *Church Year.*

EBAL *(bare)* See *Gerizim and Ebal.*

EBED-MELECH *(servant of the king)*

Ethiopian eunuch in service of King Zedekiah (Jer. 38:7); rescued Jeremiah from cistern imprisonment and received promise in Jer. 39:15-18.

EBENEZER *(stone of help)*

Site near Aphek where Israelites camped before battle against the Philistines (1 Sam. 4:1); probably Izbet Sartah. Here Philistines captured ark of the covenant. After decisive Israelite victory recovering the ark, Samuel erected a monument called Eben-ezer.

EBLA

Major 140-acre ancient site located in Syria about 40 miles south of Aleppo; known today as tell Mardikh; discovery of over 1700 clay tablets in the mid-1970s revealed a major Syrian civilization about 2500 B.C. Excavations have revealed 14 occupation levels at Ebla dating from 2600 B.C. to A.D. 600. Only four levels, dating from 2000–1600 B.C., cover the whole site and indicate the greatest power and prosperity of Ebla. Dating and interpretation of Ebla materials remain a major point of scholarly debate since the major participants in the excavation do not agree. The clay tablets have attracted the most interest at Ebla. They appear to date from about 2350 B.C. They are written in a cuneiform script similar to that used in Mesopotamia. Sumerian was used on a limited scale as well as a new language that has come to be called Eblaite. Many early attempts to draw connections between Ebla and the Bible have proven to be unconvincing. Ebla never occurs in the Bible, and no biblical personalities or events have yet been identified in the Ebla tablets.

Ebla was a major religious center, and over 500 gods are mentioned in the texts. The chief god was Dagon, a vegetation deity associated in the Bible with the Philistines (1 Sam. 5:2). Other gods include Baal, the Canaanite god of fertility, and Kamish (the biblical Chemosh), god of the Moabites (Judg. 11:24). In addition, there is reference to "the god of my father" (compare Gen. 43:23). See *Plants.*

ECBATANA See *Achmetha.*

ECCLESIASTES, BOOK OF

An OT wisdom book like Job and Proverbs. The English title was derived from the Greek Septuagint's translation of the Hebrew, Qohelet (1:1-2,12; 7:27; 12:8-10). Both Qohelet and Ecclesiastes denote one who presides over an assembly, that is, a preacher or teacher.

Traditionally Solomon has been identified as the author of Ecclesiastes, but in modern times many, including a large number of conservative scholars, have followed Martin Luther's lead in assigning the book to the postexilic period (usually between ca. 300–200 B.C.).

In defense of the traditional view, the following evidence has been cited. (1) Both Christian and Jewish tradition (e.g., Talmud) named Solomon as the author. (2) While the text does not state specifically that Solomon wrote the book, in 1:1 the author identifies himself as the "son

of David, king in Jerusalem," and in 1:12 he adds that he was "king over Israel in Jerusalem." Only one son of David, Solomon, ruled over the United Kingdom of Israel (excepting Rehoboam whose brief reign over the 12 tribes and weak character would hardly satisfy the requirements of the text). References in the book to the author's unrivaled wisdom (1:16), opportunities for pleasure (2:3), extensive building programs (2:4-6), and unequaled wealth (2:7-8) all point to Solomon. Like Solomon the writer also penned many proverbs (12:9). (3) Many recent examinations of the language of Ecclesiastes have also supported a pre-exilic date of composition.

Ecclesiastes has been called pessimistic, shocking, unorthodox, and even heretical. For example, certain statements in the book have been interpreted to deny life after death (3:18-21; 9:5-6,10). Yet, in the context of the book, the author is not denying the existence of the human spirit after death but is stating an obvious fact: at death earthly life (life "under the sun") with its joys, sorrows, and opportunities is over. In 12:7 the author explicitly declares that the body "returns to the ground it came from, and the spirit returns to God who gave it" (NIV).

The author of Ecclesiastes has been deemed a pessimist, or even an existentialist. Others have argued he was an apologist who defended faith in God by pointing to the grimness of life without God. However, it may be best to regard the author as a realist. He observed that all persons (both good and bad) experience injustice, grow old, die, and are forgotten. The lives of all human beings are brief. Earthly possessions and mere worldly endeavors are temporary and have no eternal value for believers or nonbelievers. Only what is done for God will endure. Therefore, human beings should live in light of eternity realizing that someday they will give an account to God (12:13-14).

ECONOMIC LIFE

Manner of earning, spending, and distributing material resources in Israel. Success in doing this was determined by the environmental conditions. Adequate rainfall or water sources, arable farm and grazing lands, and the availability of natural resources were the most important of these ecological factors. Once the monarchy was established, the demands of the local and international markets, government stability, and the effects of international politics came into play. Throughout their history the economic life of Israel was at least in part governed by God's laws that concerned the treatment of fellow Israelites in matters of business and charity.

Ancient Palestine's economy was primarily agricultural and not, like Mesopotamia and Egypt, as completely dominated by the concerns of palace or temple. Private ownership of land and private enterprise were the rule, changing somewhat after the establishment of the monarchy when large estates were formed (2 Sam. 9:10) to support the kings and the nobility. The royal bureaucracy attempted to control as much of the country's land and economic activity as possible (1 Kings 4:1-19).

After Assyria and Babylon conquered Israel, the nation's economic efforts (farm production, industry, and trade) were largely controlled by the tribute demands of the dominant empires (2 Kings 18:14-16) and the maintenance of international trade routes. This pattern continued into the NT period when Roman roads speeded trade, but also held the populace in submission. The economy, while relatively stable, was burdened with heavy taxes (Matt. 22:17-21) to support the occupation army and government.

Steppe and desert to the south and east in the Negev and the corresponding areas of the Transjordan mean only dry or irrigation farming was possible. Much of the land was given over to pastoralists guiding their flocks and herds. Well-watered farm lands were found in the Shephelah plateau (between the coastal plain and the hill country) and in the Galilee area of northern Palestine. Rolling hill country dominated the center of the country where agriculture had to be practiced on terraced hillsides and where water conservation and irrigation were necessary to grow crops.

Drought (Gen. 12:10), which destroyed crops (1 Kings 17:1; Jer. 14:1-6), had a ripple effect on the rest of the economy. Some people left the country for the more predictable climate of Egypt (Gen. 46:1-7) or went to areas in Transjordan unaffected by a famine (Ruth 1:1). Economic hardship brought on by climatic extremes also hurt the business of the local potter, tanner, blacksmith, and weaver.

Agriculture in ancient Palestine took three basic forms: grain production (barley and wheat), cultivation of vines and fruit trees, and the care of oleaginous plants (olive, date, and sesame) that provided oil for cooking, lighting, and personal care uses. Most of the energies of the village population were taken up with plowing fields (1 Kings 19:19) and the construction and maintenance of the hillside terraces where vineyards (Isa. 5:1-6; Mark 12:1) and grain were planted. In the hill country, irrigation channels ensured that the terraces were evenly watered by rain and dew.

A man's ownership of land was considered part of a family trust from one generation to the next. Each plot of land was a grant to the household by Yahweh and as such had to be cared for so that it would remain productive (Deut. 14:28-29). Its abundance was the result of hard work (Prov. 24:30-34) and was to be shared with the poor (Deut. 24:19-21). Yahweh's grant of the land was repaid (Num. 18:21-32) through the payment of tithes to the Levites and through sacrifices.

It was strictly against the law to remove the boundary stones (Deut. 19:14; Prov. 22:28). Inheritance laws were well defined. Normally, the oldest son inherited the largest portion of the lands of his father (Deut. 21:17;

Luke 15:31). Land could not be permanently sold outside the family or clan (Lev. 25:8-17; 1 Kings 21:3; compare Isa. 5:8; Mic. 2:2). If a man died without a male heir, his daughters would receive charge of the land (Num. 27:7-8), but they were required to marry within the tribe to ensure it remained a part of the tribal legacy (Num. 36:6-9). A childless man's property passed to his nearest male relative (Num. 27:9-11). The duty of the redeemer, or *go'el,* included the purchase of family lands that had been abandoned (Jer. 32:6-9).

Despite the back-breaking work of harvesting fields with flint-edged sickles (Joel 3:13), the grain and the fruits meant the survival of the village and was cause for celebration (Judg. 21:19). Following the harvest, the threshing floor became the center of economic activity of the village and countryside (Joel 2:24). The village may have had a communal granary, but most kept their grain in home storage pits or private granaries (Matt. 3:12).

Village economies also included the maintenance of small herds of sheep and goats. The flocks were moved to new pastures in the hill country with the coming of the dry summer season (1 Sam. 25:7-8), but this would have required only a few herdsmen (1 Sam. 16:11). Only the shearing of sheep would have involved large numbers of the community (Gen. 31:19; 1 Sam. 25:4; 2 Sam. 13:23-24).

What little industry existed in Israelite villages included the making of bricks and split timbers for house construction, and the weaving of material for clothing. Some households (usually consisting of a group of related families, Judg. 18:22) had the skill to shape cooking utensils and farm tools from clay, stone, and metal. Few, however, had the ability to shape their own weapons, relying in many cases on clubs and ox goads (Judg. 3:31) for protection.

In exceptional cases, village craftsmen may have set up stalls for business where they provided some of the more specialized items, espe-

cially fine pottery, bronze weapons, and gold and silver jewelry. Anything additional could either be done without or obtained in trade with other villages or nations who might possess a particularly fine artisan (1 Sam. 13:20). It is also possible that during a yearly visit to the city (Luke 2:41) to attend a religious festival, the villager could buy wares from the stalls of traders from all over the Near East.

Local trade expanded beyond the sale of surplus commodities and handcrafted items as the villages and towns grew in size. Population growth also increased the needs and appetites for metals (gold, tin, copper, iron), luxury items, and manufactured goods. A network of roads gradually developed to accommodate this economic activity and to tie together the villages and towns throughout the nation. The kings introduced more sophisticated road construction for heavy vehicular traffic and marshaled large numbers of corvée workers (persons who worked in lieu of paying taxes) to construct public works projects (1 Kings 9:15-22). Ezion-geber, a port on the Red Sea, was acquired from the Edomites and serviced a fleet of ships bringing gold from Ophir and rare woods and other luxury items to the royal court (1 Kings 9:26; 10:11-12). Another fleet joined that of Hiram of Tyre in the Mediterranean trade (1 Kings 10:22).

Within the walled cities and towns, most commercial activity occurred within the gate complex or its environs. This would have been the most likely spot for stalls and shops to be set up for business. Legal matters were handled here (Deut. 21:18-19); business contracts could be witnessed (Gen. 23:15-16); and disputes settled (Ruth 4:1-6).

Prices, as always, were determined by the law of supply and demand (2 Kings 6:25; Rev. 6:6), with an extra markup to cover the costs of transport, and, where applicable, manufacturing. Luxury items such as spices and perfumes from Arabia and ivory and rare animals commanded high prices.

Slave labor was an outgrowth of the urbanization of Israel and the constant military campaigns of the kings. The large number of military prisoners joined the levies of forced labor gangs (1 Kings 5:13; 9:20-22) building roads and repairing the walls of the fortresses that guarded the kingdom. Royal estates were managed by stewards (1 Chron. 27:25-31) and worked by large bands of state-owned slaves and a levy of free men (1 Sam. 8:12).

Private individuals did not hold as many slaves as the monarchy or the social elite. Since the laws regarding slaves were quite stringent (Ex. 21:1-11,20,26; Lev. 25:39-46), day laborers were hired by most landowners (Matt. 20:1-5). The leasing of land to tenant farmers was another alternative to the labor problem, but this was not common in Israel until the NT period (Matt. 21:33-41; Mark 12:9).

Israelites could sell their families or themselves into slavery to resolve a debt (Ex. 21:7-11; Lev. 25:39; Matt. 18:25). The law regulated this so that the normal term of slavery or indenture was no more than six years when the slave was to be released and given a portion of the flock and the harvest with which to make a new start (Deut. 15:12-14). Perpetual slavery was only to occur if the Israelite himself chose to remain a slave. This choice might be made because he did not want to be separated from a wife and children acquired during his term of enslavement (Ex. 21:1-6) or because he did not feel he would have a better life on his own (Deut. 15:16). See *Agriculture; Coins; Commerce; Transportation and Travel; Slave, Servant; Weights and Measures.*

ECSTASY

The state of being in a trance, especially a mystic or prophetic trance; out of body state (2 Cor. 12:2-3) or the state of being out of control; associated with bands or schools of proph-

ets (1 Sam. 10:5,9; 19:20; 2 Kings 9:1); often accompanied by music (1 Sam. 10:5; 2 Kings 3:15-16) and rhythmic dance, though the "prophetic frenzy" was brought on by the onrush of the Spirit of God (1 Sam. 10:6,10; 19:20,23) or hand of the Lord (2 Kings 3:15). Prophetic ecstasy could be accompanied by irrational behavior (1 Sam. 19:24; perhaps 21:15) leading prophets to be identified with madmen (2 Kings 9:11; Jer. 29:26; Hos. 9:7). Efforts to control such prophetic expression (Jer. 29:26) were regarded as ill-founded (29:31).

Paul's experience of being caught up into the third heaven or paradise (2 Cor. 12:2-4) is an example of an ecstatic experience. Paul preferred to boast in his weakness than in such spiritual experiences (12:5; 1 Cor. 12:31). The gift of speaking in tongues is thought by some to involve an ecstatic state. See *Prophecy, Prophets.*

ED (*witness*)

Altar that the tribes assigned territory east of the Jordan, built as a witness that Yahweh is God of both the eastern and western tribes. The altar was a symbol and would not be used for burnt offerings (Josh. 22:34).

EDEN

(1) Garden of God; the idyllic place of creation and the region where a garden was placed (Gen. 2:8,10,15; 3:23-24; 4:16). Joel 2:3 compares Judah's condition before its destruction with Eden. In Isa. 51:3 and Ezek. 36:35, Eden illustrates the great prosperity God would bestow on Judah (compare Ezek. 28:13; 31:9,16,18). See *Paradise.*

(2) Levite who cleansed temple under Hezekiah (2 Chron. 29:12) and distributed funds to needy priests (31:15).

(3) City or region in Assyrian province of Thelassar. See *Beth-Eden.*

EDOM (*red* or *ruddy*), EDOMITES

Area southeast and southwest of the Dead Sea, on opposite sides of the

Arabah; largely "wilderness"—semi-desert, not very conducive to agriculture; many of the inhabitants were seminomads. The center of Edomite population, the vicinity of present-day Tafileh and Buseireh, east of the Arabah, is fairly well-watered, cultivable land, and would have boasted numerous villages during OT times. Buseireh is situated on the ruins of ancient Bozrah, the capital of Edom. Most biblical passages pertaining to Edom refer to this center east of the Arabah (Isa. 63:1; Jer. 49:22; Amos 1:11-12). Other passages presuppose the territory west of the Arabah, south of the Judean hill country and separating Judah from the Gulf of Aqaba (Num. 34:3-4; Josh. 15:1-3). In NT times, even the southern end of the Judean hill country (south of approximately Hebron) was known officially as Idumea (Edom).

The "land of Seir" seems to be synonymous with Edom in some passages (Gen. 32:3; 36:8; Judg. 5:4). "Teman" also is used in apposition to Edom in at least one biblical passage (Amos 1:12; compare Job 2:11; Ezek. 25:13), but normally refers to a specific district of Edom and possibly to a town by that name.

The Israelites regarded the Edomites as close relatives, descendants of Esau, Jacob's brother (Gen. 19:30-36; 36; compare Amos 1:11-12). Enmity between Israel and Edom began with Jacob and Esau (when the former stole the latter's birthright) and was exacerbated at the time of the Israelite exodus from Egypt when the Edomites refused the Israelites passage through their land. Much of the conflict came from Edom being a constant threat to Judah's frontier and blocking Judean access to the Gulf of Aqaba.

Both Saul and David conducted warfare with the Edomites (1 Sam. 14:47-48; 2 Sam. 8:13-14). David secured control of the Edomite area west of the Arabah as well as access to the Gulf of Aqaba. Later Hadad of the royal Edomite line returned from Egypt and became an active adversary to Solomon (1 Kings 11:14-22). Conflict and continuing changes in

control of Edom lasted through the monarchy (1 Kings 22:47-50; 2 Kings 8:20-22; 14:22; 16:6; 2 Chron. 25:11-12; 26:1-2; 28:17).

Eventually the Edomites fell under the shadow of the major eastern empires—the Assyrians, Babylonians, Persians, and Greeks. Some scholars hold that the Edomites aided the Babylonians in their attacks on Jerusalem in 597 and 586 B.C., then took advantage of the Judeans in their helpless situation (see Jer. 49:7-22; *Obadiah, Book of*).

By NT times, Nabateans of Arabic origin had established a commercial empire with its center in the formerly Edomite territory east of the Arabah. Their chief city was Petra, and the whole region southeast of the Dead Sea was known as Nabatea. Only the formerly Edomite territory west of the Arabah was still known as Idumea (Edom). Herod the Great was of Idumean ancestry. See *Transjordan; Esau; Nabateans; Petra; Sela.*

EDREI

(1) Royal city of Og, king of Bashan (Josh. 12:4) where invading Israel defeated Og (Num. 21:33-35; Deut. 1:4; 3:10); modern Dera halfway between Damascus and Amman. Clan of Machir in Manasseh laid claim to city (Josh. 13:31).

(2) Fortified city in Naphtali (Josh. 19:37).

EDUCATION IN BIBLE TIMES

Processes, methods, and institutions for training young people to live in biblical lands and times. The primary purpose of education among the Jews was the learning of and obedience to the law of God, the Torah, primarily the first five books of the Bible. The secondary purpose in education was to teach about the practical aspects of everyday life: a trade for the boy; for the girl, care of the house, application of dietary laws, and how to be a good wife.

The home was considered the first and most effective education agency, and parents were considered the first and most effective teachers (Deut.

6:7; compare Gen. 18:19; Prov. 22:6). Parents were to use life's ordinary activities as avenues to teach about God. Primary ways of imparting religious knowledge to children were example, imitation, conversation, and stories. A child could observe his father binding the phylacteries on his arm and head. The natural question: "What are you doing?" could be used to teach the child that it was everyone's duty to "love the Lord thy God with all thine heart, and with all thy soul, and with all thy might" (Deut. 6:5). Timothy is a notable example of a child who had been educated in the Scriptures in the home (2 Tim. 1:5).

When the son reached 12, the Jews believed his education in the Torah was complete enough to help him know the law and keep it. He was then known as a "son of the law." The father would fasten the phylacteries on the arm and forehead of his son.

Girls learned a variety of skills such as weaving, spinning, and treating illnesses. They might also learn to sing and dance and play a musical instrument like a flute or harp. The Jewish people had opportunity to receive religious education from priests and Levites (Lev. 10:10-11; compare 2 Chron. 17:7-9).

The synagogue apparently came into existence during the Babylonian captivity when the Jews were deprived of the services of the temple. They began meeting in small groups for prayer and Scripture reading. When they returned to Israel, the synagogue spread rapidly and developed into an important educational institution housing the elementary school system. Even before Jesus, schools for the young were located in practically every important Jewish community.

The teacher was generally the synagogue "attendant." An assistant was provided if there were more than 25 students. The OT was the subject matter for this instruction. Reading, writing, and arithmetic were also taught. Memorization, drill, and review were used as approaches to teaching.

Boys usually began formal schooling at the "house of the book" at age five. A boy would spend at least a half day, six days a week for about five years, studying at the synagogue. Parents brought their son at daybreak and came for him at midday. While not at school, the boy was usually learning a trade, such as farming or carpentry. If a boy wanted training beyond that given in a synagogue, he would go to a scholarly scribe. Saul of Tarsus received such advanced theological training "at the feet of Gamaliel" in Jerusalem (Acts 22:3).

Jesus is pictured as teaching large crowds (Mark 4:1-2). He was a God-sent teacher who taught with an authority and challenge that held His audiences captive. As risen Lord, Jesus commissioned His followers to carry their evangelism and teaching ministry into all the world (Matt. 28:19-20). Teaching became an important work in the early church in Jerusalem (Acts 2:42; 4:1-2; 5:21,28). Teaching is regarded as a primary function of the pastor (1 Tim. 3:2). Volunteer teachers are also important to the work of the church (Jas. 3:1).

EGLON

(1) Moabite king who oppressed the Israelites for 18 years (Judg. 3:12); finally slain by Benjamite judge Ehud, who ran the obese monarch through with a short sword.

(2) Canaanite city whose king entered an alliance with four other Canaanite rulers against Gibeon (Josh. 10:3; 15:39).

EGYPT

Land in northeastern corner of Africa, home to one of the earliest civilizations, and an important cultural and political influence on ancient Israel. Ancient Egypt was confined to the Nile River valley, a long, narrow ribbon of fertile land (the "black land") surrounded by uninhabitable desert (the "red land"). Egypt proper, from the first cataract of the Nile to the Mediterranean, is some 750 miles long and is separated from Palestine by the Sinai Wilderness. See *Nile River*.

Egypt was relatively isolated by a series of six Nile cataracts on the south and protected on the east and west by the desert. "Two Lands" of Egypt were quite distinct. Upper (southern) Egypt is the arable Nile Valley from the First Cataract to just south of Memphis. Lower (northern) Egypt refers to the broad Delta of the Nile formed from alluvial deposits. The Delta was the entryway to Egypt from the Fertile Crescent across the Sinai.

The numerous Egyptian pharaohs were divided by the ancient historian Manetho into 30 dynasties, a scheme still used for a framework for Egyptian history. The unification of originally separate kingdoms of Upper and Lower Egypt about 3100 B.C. began the Archaic Period (First and Second Dynasties). Egypt's first period of glory, the Third through Sixth Dynasties of the Old Kingdom (2700–2200 B.C.) produced the famous pyramids. Low Nile inundations, the resultant bad harvests, and incursions of Asiatics in the Delta region brought the political chaos of the Seventh through Tenth Dynasties, called the First Intermediate Period (2200–2040 B.C.). Following a civil war, the Eleventh Dynasty reunited Egypt and began the Middle Kingdom (2040–1786 B.C.). Under the able pharaohs of the Twelfth Dynasty, Egypt prospered and conducted extensive trade. Abraham's brief sojourn in Egypt (Gen. 12:10-20) during this period may be understood in light of a tomb painting at Beni Hasan showing visiting Asiatics in Egypt about 1900 B.C.

Under the weak Thirteenth Dynasty, Egypt entered another period of division. Asiatics, mostly Semites like the Hebrews, migrated into the Delta region of Egypt and began to establish independent enclaves, eventually consolidating rule over Lower Egypt. These Asiatic pharaohs were remembered as Hyksos, or "rulers of foreign lands." This period, in which Egypt was divided between Hyksos (Fifteenth and Sixteenth) and native Egyptian (Thirteenth and Seventeenth) dynasties, is known as the Second Intermediate or Hyksos Period (1786–1550 B.C.). Joseph's rise to power (Gen. 41:39-45) may have taken place under a Hyksos pharaoh. See *Hyksos*.

About 1550 B.C., Ahmose I expelled the Hyksos and reunited Egypt, establishing the Eighteenth Dynasty and inaugurating the Egyptian New Kingdom. Successive Eighteenth Dynasty pharaohs created an empire that reached the Euphrates River. Thutmose III (1479–1425 B.C.) won a major victory at Megiddo in Palestine. Amenhotep III (1391–1353 B.C.) ruled over a magnificent empire in peace—thanks to a treaty with Mitanni—and devoted his energies to building projects in Egypt itself.

Amenhotep III's son, Amenhotep IV (1353–1335 B.C.), changed his name to Akhenaton and embarked on a revolutionary reform that promoted worship of the sun disc Aton above all other gods. As Thebes was dominated by the powerful priesthood of Amen-Re, Akhenaton moved the capital over 200 miles north to Akhetaton, modern tell el-Amarna. The Amarna Age, as this period is known, brought innovations in art and literature; but Akhenaton paid little attention to foreign affairs, and the empire suffered. The Amarna Letters, diplomatic correspondence between local rulers in Egypt's sphere of influence and pharaoh's court, illuminate the turbulent situation in Canaan. See *Amarna, tell el*.

Akhenaton's reforms failed. His second successor changed his name from Tutankhaton to Tutankhamen and abandoned the new capital in favor of Thebes. General Horemheb seized the throne and worked vigorously to restore order and erase all trace of the Amarna heresy. Horemheb had no heir and left the throne to his vizier, Ramses I, first king of the Nineteenth Dynasty.

Seti I (1302–1290 B.C.) reestablished Egyptian control in Canaan and campaigned against the Hittites, who had taken Egyptian territory in

North Syria during the Amarna Age. See *Hittites*. He built a new capital in the eastern Delta, near the biblical Land of Goshen. Thebes would remain the national religious and traditional capital.

Ramses II (1290–1224 B.C.) was the most successful Nineteenth Dynasty pharaoh. In 1285, he fought an inconclusive battle against the Hittites at Kadesh-on-the-Orontes in north Syria. In 1270 B.C., a peace treaty recognized the status quo. He embarked on the most massive building program of any Egyptian ruler. The new capital was completed and called Pi- Ramesse ("domain of Ramses"; compare Gen. 47:11), the biblical Ramses (Ex. 1:11).

Merneptah (1224–1214 B.C.) set up a stele in 1220 B.C. commemorating victory over a Libyan invasion and concluding with a poetic account of a campaign in Canaan. It includes the first extrabiblical mention of Israel and the only one in known Egyptian literature. Egypt had a brief period of renewed glory under Ramses III (1195–1164 B.C.) of the Twentieth Dynasty. He defeated an invasion of the Sea Peoples, among whom were the Philistines. The remainder of Twentieth Dynasty rulers, all named Ramses, saw increasingly severe economic and civil difficulties. The New Kingdom and the empire petered out with the last of them in 1070 B.C.

The Late Period (1070–332 B.C.) saw Egypt divided and invaded, but with occasional moments of greatness. While the high priesthood of Amen-Re controlled Thebes, the Twenty-first Dynasty ruled from the east Delta city of Tanis, biblical Zoan (Num. 13:22; Ps. 78:12; Ezek. 30:14; Isa. 19:11; 30:4). A pharaoh, probably of this dynasty (perhaps Siamun), took Gezer in Palestine and gave it to Solomon as his daughter's dowry (1 Kings 3:1; 9:16). Shoshenq I (945–924 B.C.), Shishak of the Bible, founded the Twenty-second Dynasty, briefly united Egypt, and campaigned successfully against the newly divided nations Judah and Israel (1 Kings 14:25; 2 Chron. 12).

Thereafter, Egypt was divided between the Twenty-second through Twenty-fifth Dynasties. "So king of Egypt" (2 Kings 17:4), who encouraged the treachery of Hoshea, certainly belongs to this confused period but cannot be identified with certainty. Egypt was reunited in 715 B.C., when the Ethiopian Twenty-fifth Dynasty succeeded in establishing control over all of Egypt. Taharqa, the biblical Tirhakah, rendered aid to Hezekiah (2 Kings 19:9; Isa. 37:9).

Assyria invaded Egypt in 671 B.C., driving the Ethiopians southward and eventually sacking Thebes (biblical No-Amon; Nah. 3:8) in 664 B.C. Under loose Assyrian sponsorship, the Twenty-sixth Dynasty controlled all of Egypt from Sais in the western Delta. With Assyria's decline, Neco II (610–595 B.C.) opposed the advance of Babylon and exercised brief control over Judah (2 Kings 23:29-35). After a severe defeat at the Battle of Carchemish (605 B.C.), Neco II lost Judah as a vassal (2 Kings 24:1) and was forced to defend her border against Babylon. Pharaoh Hophra (Greek Apries; 589–570 B.C.) supported Judah's rebellion against Babylon, but was unable to provide the promised support (Jer. 37:5-10; 44:30). Despite these setbacks, the Twenty-sixth Dynasty was a period of Egyptian renaissance until the Persian conquest in 525 B.C. Persian rule (Twenty-seventh Dynasty) was interrupted by a period of Egyptian independence under the Twenty-eighth through Thirtieth Dynasties (404–343 B.C.). With Persian reconquest in 343 B.C., pharaonic Egypt had come to an end.

Alexander the Great took Egypt from the Persians in 332 B.C. and founded the great city of Alexandria on the Mediterranean coast. After his death in 323 B.C., Egypt was home to the Hellenistic Ptolemaic Empire until the time of Cleopatra, when it fell to the Romans (30 B.C.). During the NT period, Egypt, under direct rule of the Roman emperors, was the breadbasket of Rome.

Egyptian religion is extremely complex and not totally understood.

Many of the great number of gods were personifications of the enduring natural forces in Egypt, such as the sun, Nile, air, earth. Other gods, like Maat ("truth,""justice"), personified abstract concepts. Still others ruled over states of mankind, like Osiris, god of the underworld. Some of the gods were worshiped in animal form, such as the Apis bull which represented the god Ptah of Memphis.

Many of the principal deities were associated with particular cities or regions, and their position was often a factor of the political situation. Amen, later called Amen-Re, became the chief god of the empire because of the position of Thebes. Theological systems developed around local gods at Hermopolis, Memphis, and Heliopolis. At Memphis, Ptah was seen as the supreme deity who created the other gods by his own word. Dominance was achieved by the system of Heliopolis, home of the sun god Atum, later identified with Ra. This system involved a primordial chaos from which appeared Atum who gave birth to the other gods.

Popular with common people was the Osiris myth. This cycle became the principle of divine kingship. In death, the pharaoh was worshiped as Osiris. As the legitimate heir buried the dead Osiris, the new pharaoh became the living Horus.

The consistent provision of the Nile gave Egyptians, in contrast to Mesopotamians, a generally optimistic outlook on life. This is reflected in their preoccupation with the afterlife, viewed as an ideal continuation of life on earth. In the Old Kingdom, it was the prerogative only of the king, as a god, to enjoy immortality. The common appeal of the Osiris cult was great, however, and in later years any dead person was referred to as "the Osiris so and so."

To assist the dead in the afterlife, magical texts were included in the tomb. In the New Kingdom and later, magical texts known as "The Book of the Dead" were written on papyrus and placed in the coffin. Pictorial vignettes show, among other things,

the deceased at a sort of judgment in which his heart was weighed against truth. This indicates some concept of sin, but afterlife for the Egyptian was not an offer from a gracious god; it was merely an optimistic hope based on observation of his surroundings.

The Bible mentions no Egyptian gods, and Egyptian religion did not significantly influence the Hebrews. An Amarna Age hymn to the Aton has similarities to Ps. 104, but direct borrowing is unlikely. More striking parallels are found in Wisdom literature, as between Prov. 22 and the Egyptian instruction of Amen-em-ope.

EGYPTIAN, THE

Leader who led 4,000 "Assassins" into the wilderness in unsuccessful attempt to capture Jerusalem about A.D. 54. See Acts 21:38.

EHUD (unity, powerful)

(1) Left-handed Benjamite whom the Lord raised up as judge to deliver Israelites from Moabite oppression (Judg. 3:15). By a ruse, he gained access to the Moabite King Eglon and assassinated him. See Judges.

(2) Great grandson of Benjamin and clan leader (1 Chron. 7:10).

(3) Clan leader in Benjamin (1 Chron. 8:6).

EKRON

Northernmost of five major Philistine cities; modern tell Miqne, about 14 miles from the Mediterranean Sea and 10 miles from Ashdod; one of largest sites in Palestine, covering 50 acres.

Ekron was assigned to both Judah (Josh. 15:11,45-46) and Dan (Josh. 19:43). It probably lay on the border between the tribes. Judah captured Ekron along with other parts of the Philistine coast (Judg. 1:18), but Ekron was certainly in Philistine hands when the ark was captured (1 Sam. 5:10; compare 1 Sam. 17:52; 2 Kings 1:2-16).

EL

Generic word for God in Hebrew; synonym for Elohim; name of the high god among the Canaanites. See *Canaan, History and Religion of; Names of God.*

ELAH (*oak, mighty tree,* or *terebinth*) See *Terebinth.*

(1) Clan chief descended from Esau (Gen. 36:41) and thus Edomite.

(2) Valley running east and west just north of Socoh where Saul and his army set up battle lines against the Philistines (1 Sam. 17:2; see 21:9).

(3) King of Israel (886–885 B.C.) killed while he was drunk during rebellion Zimri, his general, led successfully (1 Kings 16:6-14).

(4) Father of Hoshea, who led a revolt and became king of Israel (732–723 B.C., 2 Kings 15:30).

(5) Son of Caleb and father of Kenaz among clans of Judah (1 Chron. 4:15).

(6) Head of clan from Benjamin who settled in Jerusalem after the exile (1 Chron. 9:8).

ELAM

Six men in addition to:

(1) Son of Shem, one of the sons of Noah (Gen. 10:22; 1 Chron. 1:17); may have given his name to region known as Elam.

(2) Region on western edge of ancient Persia, modern Iran. Zagros Mountains lie east and north, while the Persian Gulf is to the south and the Tigris River on the west. Ancient capital of area was Anshan; later, Susa—founded about 4000 B.C. Elamites appear to have invented clay tablets that became standard writing surface. Sargon of Akkad subdued it about 2300 B.C. Soon Elamites sacked Ur and set up Elamite king in Eshnunna. The Elamite presence continued in Babylon until the time of Hammurabi about 1700 B.C. After Hammurabi, Kassites invaded Elam and ruled until about 1200 B.C. The next century was the high point of Elam's power. All of western Iran was theirs. Again the Babylonians brought Elamite power to an end. The Assyrian Ashurbanipal captured Susa in 641 B.C. He may have moved some Elamites to Samaria at that time (Ezra 4:9). As Assyria weakened, Elam and Anshan became part of the kingdom of the Medes. Thus, they participated, with the Babylonians, in the defeat of the Assyrian Empire.

Abraham fought Chedorlaomer, king of Elam, to secure the return of Lot and others (Gen. 14). Isaiah promised God would recover His people from Elam (Isa. 11:11; compare 21:2; 22:6; Jer. 25:25; 49:34-39; Ezek. 32:24). Men from Elam participated in Pentecost. (Acts 2:9). See *Persia; Cyrus; Assyria.*

ELATH (*ram, mighty trees,* or *terebinth*) or **ELOTH** See *Terebinth.*

Port city on northern end of Red Sea marking end of King's Highway and the Way of the Red Sea (Deut. 2:8; 2 Kings 14:22; compare 1 Kings 9:26; 2 Chron. 8:17-18). Archaeologists have usually identified Elath as another name for Ezion-geber and located it at tell el-Kheleifeh. More recent archaeological work has attempted to show that Ezion- geber was the port city on the island of Jezirat Faraun. Elath would then been a mainland base. See *Eziongaber.*

ELDAD (*God loved*)

Along with Medad, one of 70 elders of Israel God selected to help Moses, but the two did not meet at the tabernacle with the others. Still the Spirit came upon Eldad and Medad in the camp, and they prophesied. Joshua attempted to stop them, but Moses prayed that all God's people might have the Spirit (Num. 11:16-29).

ELDER

Tribal leader in Israel and leader of early church; Greek *presbuteros,* transliterated in English as "*presbyter*" and source of "*priest.*"

For early Israel, tribal elders assumed important roles in governing national affairs (Ex. 3:16,18; 24:9-11; Num. 11:16-17). Elders demanded that Samuel appoint a king (1 Sam. 8:4-5), played crucial roles in David's getting and retaining the throne (2 Sam. 3:17; 5:3; 17:15; 19:11-12), and represented the people at the consecration of Solomon's temple of (1 Kings 8:1,3). Deuteronomy makes elders responsible for administering justice, sitting as judges in the city gate (Deut. 22:15), deciding cases affecting family life (Deut. 21:18-21; 22:13-21), and executing decisions (Deut. 19:11-13; 21:1-9).

The "council of elders" was an integral part of the Sanhedrin at Jerusalem. The NT frequently refers to the elders of the Jews, usually in conjunction with chief priests or scribes (Matt. 21:23; Mark 14:43). These elders, apparently members of leading families, had some authority but were not principal leaders in either religious or political affairs. Elders did have leading roles in the government of synagogues.

The earliest Jewish Christian churches, at least the church in Jerusalem, modeled the position of "elder" after the synagogue pattern. Elders apparently served as a decision-making council, even for the whole church (Acts 15; 21:17-26). Paul and Barnabas appointed elders in churches on their missionary journey (Acts 14:23) as spiritual leaders and ministers, not simply a governing council. These elders do not seem to fit the Jewish pattern (Acts 20:28). The context of Titus 1:5-9, the only passage that mentions both elders and bishops, indicates the terms are interchangeable. The elders were the spiritual leaders of the churches (Titus 1:6-9; 1 Tim. 3:1-7). The only specific reference to the ministry of elders is the description (Jas. 5:14-15) of elders praying for and anointing a sick person. None of these passages indicate there was only one elder in each congregation. The reference to laying on of hands in 1 Tim. 4:14, as well as the analogous ceremony in commissioning the seven (Acts 6:6), seems to indicate the church did make formal recognition of their function, or office. With the possible exception of 1 Tim. 4:14, none of the references to such ceremonies imply that the ceremony gave recipients any special status or power.

ELEALEH (*God went up* or *high ground*)

Moabite town that Reuben requested from Moses and strengthened (Num. 32:3,37); modern el-Al, a mile north of Heshbon in a fertile plain. See Isa. 15:4; 16:9; compare Jer. 48:34.

ELEAZAR (*God helps*)

Eight persons including third son of Aaron (Ex. 6:23) and high priest of Israel (Num. 20:28); ancestor of Ezra the scribe (Ezra 7:5); present when Moses commissioned Joshua (Num. 27:22); key figure with Joshua in distributing land to Israelite tribes (Josh. 14:1). Eleazar was buried on a hill belonging to his son Phinehas (Josh. 24:33). See *Aaron; High Priest*.

ELECT LADY

Recipient of John's second letter (2 John 1); sometimes understood to be an individual, but probably reference to a local church congregation whose members would be "children" mentioned in the same verse. "Elect sister" of v. 13 would be another congregation whose members were sending greetings.

ELECTION

God's plan to bring salvation to His people and His world. The doctrine of election is rooted in the particularity of the Judeo-Christian tradition, that is, the conviction that out of all the peoples on earth God has chosen to reveal Himself in a special, unique way to one particular people. This conviction resonates through every layer of OT literature from the early awareness of Israel as "the people of Yahweh" through the Psalms (147:19-20a, "He declares His word to Jacob, His statutes and judgments to

Israel. He has not done this for any nation" [HCSB]; cp. Isa. 14:1; Ezek. 20:5). We can identify five major motifs in the OT portrayal of God's election of Israel. (1) Election is the result of the sovereign initiative of God. (2) The central word in Israel's vocabulary for describing their special relationship with God was "covenant." This covenant was not a contract between equal partners, but a bond established by God's unmerited favor and love. (3) Within the covenanted community God selected certain individuals to fulfill specific functions. (4) Israel's election was never intended to be a pretext for pride but rather an opportunity for service. (5) In the later OT writings, and especially during the intertestamental period, there is a tendency to identify the "elect ones" with the true, faithful "remnant" among the people of God.

Early Christians saw themselves as heirs of Israel's election, "a chosen race, a royal priesthood, a holy nation, a people for His possession" (1 Pet. 2:9 HCSB). Paul treats this theme most extensively, but we should not overlook its central importance for the entire NT. Again, certain individuals are singled out as chosen by God: the 12 apostles (Luke 6:13), Peter (Acts 15:7), Paul (Acts 9:15), and Jesus Himself (Luke 9:35; 23:35).

There are three passages where Paul deals at length with different aspects of the doctrine of election. In the first (Rom. 8:28-39) divine election is presented as the ground and assurance of the Christian's hope. The second passage (Rom. 9–11) is preoccupied with the fact of Israel's rejection of Christ that, in the purpose of God, has become the occasion for the entrance of Gentile believers into the covenant. In the third passage (Eph. 1:1-12) Paul pointed to the Christocentric character of election: God has chosen us "in Christ" before the foundation of the world. We can refer to this statement as the evangelical center of the doctrine of election. Our election is

strictly and solely in Christ. As the eternal Son, He is, along with the Father and the Holy Spirit, the electing God; as the incarnate Mediator between God and humankind, He is the elected One. We should never speak of predestination apart from this central truth.

Paul admonished the Thessalonians to give thanks because of their election (2 Thess. 2:13), while Peter said that we should confirm our "calling and election" (2 Pet. 1:10 HCSB). However, in the history of Christian thought, few teachings have been distorted or more misused. The following questions reveal common misperceptions. (1) Is not election the same thing as fatalism? Predestination does not negate the necessity for human repentance and faith; rather it establishes the possibility of both. God does not relate to human beings as sticks and stones but as free creatures made in His own image. (2) If salvation is based on election, then why preach the gospel? Because God has chosen preaching as the means to awaken faith in the elect (1 Cor. 1:21). We should proclaim the gospel to everyone without exception, knowing that it is only the Holy Spirit who can convict, regenerate, and justify. (3) Does the Bible teach "double predestination," that God has selected some for damnation as well as some for salvation? There are passages (Rom. 9:11-22; 2 Cor. 2:15-16) that portray God as a potter who has molded both vessels of mercy and vessels of destruction. Yet the Bible also teaches that God does not wish any one to perish but for all to be saved (John 3:16; 2 Pet. 3:9). We are not able to understand how everything the Bible says about election fits into a neat logical system. Our business is not to pry into the secret counsel of God but to share the message of salvation with everyone and to be grateful that we have been delivered from darkness into light. Election, then, is neither a steeple from which we look in judgment on others, nor a pillow to sleep on. It is rather a stronghold in time of trial and a confession of praise to God's grace and to His glory.

ELEMENTS, ELEMENTAL SPIRITS

Term from Greek philosophy describing four basic components of the physical world: earth, air, fire, and water but used in NT in ways open to various interpretations. In Heb. 5:12 the term means basic or fundamental principles of Christian belief. At 2 Pet. 3:10,12, most English translations render *elements*, that is, component parts. TEV takes the term with the preceding phrase, thus rendering it heavenly bodies. In Paul (Gal. 4:3,9; Col. 2:8,20), English translations are divided between basic principles or perhaps the four elements (NCV, KJV, NASB, NIV) and elementary spirits or spiritual powers (NRSV, REB, TEV, NLT, TEV, CEV). Others think the reference is to basic Jewish religious observances.

EL-HANAN (*God is gracious*)

Bethlehemite who slew the brother of Goliath (2 Sam. 21:19); Hebrew does not contain the words "the brother of," saying El-hanan killed Goliath. First Chronicles 20:5 indicates El-hanan killed Lahmi, the brother of Goliath (compare 1 Sam. 17:49).

ELI (*high*)

Priest at Shiloh who became custodian of the child Samuel (1 Sam. 1:3; 3); father of Hophni and Phinehas. Eli's death was precipitated by news of the death of his sons and the capture of the ark of God by the Philistines (1 Sam. 4:18).

ELI, ELI, LAMA SABACHTHANI (*My God, my God, why hast thou forsaken me?*)

Jesus' cry on the cross, traditionally known as "fourth word from the cross" (Matt. 27:46; Mark 15:34); quotation from Ps. 22:1. The Markan form, *Eloi*, is closer to Aramaic than Matthew's more Hebraic *Eli*. If Jesus spoke in Hebrew, it would more readily explain the crowd's confusion of "my God" with "Elijah."

Jesus felt deserted as He bore the burden of human sin and suffered the agony of crucifixion. This feeling of His death as a "ransom for many" may, indeed, have obscured for a time His feeling of closeness with the Father, so that even in dying He was tempted as we are. Rather than forsaking the Father in that moment, He cried out to Him in prayer.

ELIAS See *Elijah.*

ELIASHIB (*God repays or leads back*)

The name of seven OT men including the high priest in time of Nehemiah. Eliashib's grandson married a daughter of Sanballat, who strongly opposed Nehemiah's efforts (Neh. 13:28), possibly indicating some tension between Nehemiah and the priestly leaders. He may be the Eliashib whose son had a room in the temple (Ezra 10:6).

ELIHU (*he is God*)

Five OT men including son of Barachel the Buzite who addressed Job (chs. 32–37) after first three friends had finished. See *Job.*

ELIJAH (*my God is Yah*)

Prophet whose work began about 875 B.C. from Tishbe of Gilead in the Northern Kingdom. See 1 Kings 17:1–2 Kings 2:18. In his first miracle (1 Kings 17:1), he said there would be no rain or dew apart from his declaration. Immediately, he retreated to the brook Cherith where he was fed by ravens. At Zarephath he raised the widow's dead son (1 Kings 17:17-24). On Mount Carmel in his greatest public miracle God proved Himself to be the true God over against 450 prophets of Baal and 400 prophets of Asherah (1 Kings 18:19-40) by raining fire from heaven. Elijah next prophesied the drought was soon to end (1 Kings 18:41) after three rainless years. Ahab was told to flee before the storm. Elijah outran his chariot and the storm to arrive at Jezreel.

Elijah also struggled with Baalism represented by Jezebel, daughter of Ethbaal, king of Sidon and Tyre (1 Kings 16:31), and King Ahab's wife. Involvement with Naboth showed the moral superiority of Elijah's faith (1 Kings 21).

Retreating from Jezebel, Elijah came to Mount Horeb. In a small voice, the Lord commanded him to go anoint Hazael king of Syria, Jehu king of Israel, and Elisha as his own successor (1 Kings 19:1-17).

As God prepared to take Elijah, Elisha asked and received (2 Kings 2:1-12) a double portion of Elijah's spirit. Then a chariot and horses of fire separated the two and carried Elijah away in a whirlwind.

Malachi promised God would send Elijah the prophet before the coming "day of the Lord" (Mal. 4:5). John the Baptist was spoken of as the one who would go before Messiah "in the spirit and power" of Elijah (Luke 1:17; compare John 1:21,25; Matt. 16:14; Mark 6:15). Elijah appeared with Moses on the Mount of Transfiguration with Jesus to discuss His "departure" (Matt. 17:4; Mark 9:5; Luke 9:33). Paul illustrated faithfulness with the 7,000 faithful worshipers in Elijah's time (Rom. 11:2-5). The two witnesses in Rev. 11:6 are not identified by name, but their capacity "to shut heaven, that it rain not" leads many to conclude they are Moses and Elijah.

ELIPHAZ (*my god is gold*)

(1) Son of Esau; ancestor of chieftains of several Edomite clans (Gen. 36: 4,15-16).

(2) One of Job's friends from Teman in Edom (Job 2:11).

ELISABETH (*my God is good fortune* or *my God has sworn an oath*)

Mother of John the Baptist; descended from Aaron; barren wife of Zacharias the priest: noteworthy examples of piety and devotion to the Lord (Luke 1:5-6). See John 2; *Annunciation*.

ELISHA (*my God is salvation*)

Israelite prophet who began ministry after Elijah with double portion of Elijah's spirit, about 850 to 800 B.C. (1 Kings 19:15-21; 2 Kings 2-9; 13:14-21). Elisha made bad water wholesome (2 Kings 2:19-22). His reputation soon assumed so sacred an aura that harassment of the prophet merited severe punishment (2 Kings 2:23-24). The prophet used his power to provide a widow with an abundance of valuable oil and saved her children from slavery (2 Kings 4:1-7). He made a poisonous pottage edible (2 Kings 4:38-41), fed a hundred men by multiplying limited resources (2 Kings 4:42-44), and miraculously provided water for thirsting armies (2 Kings 3:13-22). Once he made an iron ax head float (2 Kings 6:5-7). Through him God gave a barren Shunammite woman a son. Later, God's power through Elisha raised the boy from the dead (2 Kings 4:8-37). He healed Naaman the leper (2 Kings 5:1-27). In the war between Syria and Israel, Syrian soldiers were blinded, then made to see. Then, at last, divine intervention totally foiled the Syrian siege of Samaria (2 Kings 6:8–7:20). When a dead man was thrown into Elisha's grave and touched his bones, "he revived, and stood up on his feet" (2 Kings 13:21). Elisha played a major role in Hazael becoming king of Syria (2 Kings 8:7-15) and in the anointing of Jehu as king of Israel (2 Kings 9:1-13).

ELISHAH

All or part of the island of Cyprus, which exported copper and purple cloth (Ezek. 27:7). Others would locate it as Haghio Kyrko in Crete. The Greeks established a colony on Cyprus by about 1500 B.C. This would explain the relationship of Elishah as a son of Javan or the Greeks in the Table of Nations (Gen. 10:4). Compare 1 Chron. 1:7.

ELOI

Greek transliteration of Aramaic *elohi*, "my God." See *Eli, Eli, Lama Sabachthani.*

ELTEKE or ELTEKEH (*place of meeting, place of hearing,* or *plea for rain*)

City in Dan (Josh. 19:44) assigned to the Levites (Josh. 21:23); location uncertain.

ELUL

Sixth month of Hebrew year, name taken over from Accadian; included parts of August and September. See Neh. 6:15; *Calendars.*

EMIM (*frightening ones*), EMITES

Ancient giants or Rephaim (Deut. 2:10-11; compare Gen. 14:5); identified with place in northern Moab, Shaveh Kiriathaim. See *Rephaim.*

EMMANUEL See *Immanuel.*

EMMAUS (*hot baths*)

Village about 7 miles from Jerusalem; destination of two of Jesus' disciples on day of His resurrection (Luke 24:13). See *Resurrection.*

EMPEROR WORSHIP

During the reigns of Nero, Domitian, and other Roman emperors, persecution of Christians was severe because of gross misconceptions regarding the practice of the Christian faith. All the suspected Christian had to do was sprinkle a few sacrificial grains of incense into the eternal flame burning in front of the statue of the emperor. Many Christians gave in. Many did not and were burned alive, killed by lions in the arena, or crucified. The worship of the beast in Rev. 13 speaks of a beast given ruling authority. An image is made of the beast, and all are commanded to worship it (13:4,12,14-15).

EN-EGLAIM (*spring of the two calves*)

Spring near the Dead Sea, where Ezekiel predicted a miracle, the salt waters being made fresh and becoming a paradise for fishing (Ezek. 47:10); apparently Ain Feshcha on western coast of Dead Sea.

EN-GANNIM (*the spring of gardens*)

(1) Town in Shephalah of Judah (Josh. 15:34); modern Beit Jemal, about two miles south of Beth-shemesh or at 'umm Giina one mile southwest of Beth-shemesh.

(2) Levitic town in Issachar (Josh. 19:21; 21:29); modern Jenin west of Beth-shean and about 65 miles north of Jerusalem. Anem (1 Chron. 6:73) is apparently an alternate spelling. The same place may be meant in 2 Kings 9:27 by "Beth Haggan" (NIV, REB, NRSV) or the "garden house" (KJV, NASB).

EN-HADDAH

City in Issachar (Josh. 19:21); apparently el-Hadetheh about 6 miles east of Mount Tabor.

EN-HAKKORE (*spring of the partridge* or *spring of the caller*)

Place where God gave Samson water from the jawbone he had used to kill 1,000 Philistines (Judg. 15:18-19).

EN-HAZOR (*spring of the enclosed village*)

Fortified city in Naphtali (Josh. 19:37); may be khirbet Hazireh, west of Kadesh. Others would locate it southwest of Kedesh on the border joining Naphtali and Asher.

EN-RIMMON (*spring of the pomegranate*)

Town in Judah (Neh. 11:29) where people lived in Nehemiah's day (about 445 B.C.); khirbet er-Ramamin, about two miles south of Lahav. Ain and Rimmon (Remmon) are separate cities in Josh. 15:32; compare 19:7.

EN-ROGEL (*spring of the fuller or spring of the foot*)

Border town between Judah (Josh. 15:7) and Benjamin (Josh. 18:16; see 2 Sam. 17:17; 1 Kings 1:9) near Jerusalem where the Kidron and Hinnom Valleys met at modern Bir Ayyub.

EN-SHEMESH (*spring of the sun*)

Town on border between Judah (Josh. 15:7) and Benjamin (Josh. 18:17); ain el-Hod, "the spring of the apostles," about two miles east of Jerusalem on eastern edge of Bethany.

ENEMY

Adversary, foe, or hater; one who dislikes or hates and seeks to harm another; an individual opponent or a hostile force, either a nation or an army. Enemies of Israel often were considered enemies of God, for Israel was God's nation (Ex. 23:22; compare Amos 1).

Jesus taught us to love our enemies and to seek their good (Matt. 5:43-47; compare Prov. 24:17; 25:21). A person who disobeys divine commands is God's enemy (Rom. 5:10). Job felt that God had become his enemy (Job 13:24). God has made provision for our forgiveness in the life, death, and resurrection of Jesus Christ.

Satan is also called "the enemy" (1 Tim. 5:14-15). The greatest and final enemy is death itself (1 Cor. 15:24), feared by all because of its finality and unknown nature. Jesus has "abolished" death once for all (2 Tim. 1:10). See *Death.*

ENGEDI (*place of the young goat*)

Major, semitropical oasis along the western side of the Dead Sea about 35 miles southeast of Jerusalem; in wilderness district of Judah (Josh. 15:62); source of fine dates, aromatic plants used in perfumes, and medicinal plants (Song of Sol. 1:14); chief source of balsam.

Engedi, also called Hazazon-tamar (2 Chron. 20:2), was inhabited by Amorites in Abraham's time (Gen. 14:7; compare 1 Sam. 23:29; 24; 2 Chron. 20:1-2; Ezek. 47:10).

ENOCH (*dedicated*)

(1) Son of Jared in such close fellowship with God that he was taken up to God without dying (Gen. 5:18; Heb. 11:5; Jude 14); father of Methuselah. The name of Enoch is associated with a large body of ancient extrabiblical literature. See *Genesis; Resurrection; Apocalyptic; Apocrypha; Pseudepigrapha.*

(2) Son of Cain for whom Cain built a city and named it (Gen. 4:17-18).

ENVIRONMENTAL PROTECTION

The earth and its resources belong to God (Lev. 25:23; Job 41:11; Pss. 24:1; 89:11) yet have been entrusted to people (Gen. 1:28-30; 2:15; 9:1-4; compare Deut. 8:7-10). For this reason, people have a sacred responsibility to care for the earth (compare Luke 12:41-48) with the same diligence that God cares for it (Deut. 11:12; Pss. 65:5-13; 104:10-22). Adam's initial activity in the garden of Eden consisted of tilling the ground (Gen. 2:15) and naming the animals (Gen. 2:19-20), thus signalling his active stewardship of creation.

The Mosaic law included statutes which seem to have been aimed specifically at protecting the environment. Among these were injunctions that the land was to lay fallow every seven years (Ex. 23:10-11; Lev. 25:3-7) and that fruit was not to be picked from trees under four years of age (Lev. 19:23-25).

The connection between God's covenant and the land, however, ran much deeper than individual statutes. The Israelites understood that their adherence to the stipulations of God's covenant as a whole had direct consequences for the land. Obedience to God's commands resulted in a land that was blessed; i.e., productive and fertile (Deut. 28:1-6), while disobedience adversely affected the fertility of the land (Gen. 3:17-19; Deut. 11:13-17; 28:1-4,15-18), creating an ecological imbalance (Deut. 29:22-28; Jer. 4:23-28; Hos. 4:2-3).

ENVY

A painful or resentful awareness of another's advantage joined with the desire to possess the same advantage in material goods (Gen. 26:14) or social status (30:1). See Pss. 37:1; 73:3; Prov. 3:31; 24:1,19; Mark 7:22; Gal. 5:26; 1 Pet. 2:1. Envy is a characteristic of humanity in rebellion against God (Rom. 1:29; compare Gal. 5:21; 1 Tim. 6:4; Titus 3:3; Jas. 4:5-6). Envy was the motive leading to the arrest of Jesus (Matt. 27:18; Mark 15:10) and of opposition to the gospel in Acts (Acts 5:17; 13:45; 17:5).

Envy is sometimes a motive for doing good (Eccl. 4:4; Phil. 1:15). See *Jealousy.*

EPAPHRAS (*lovely*)

Christian preacher from Colosse from whom Paul learned of situation of church in Colosse (Col. 1:7); companion of Paul in prison.

EPAPHRODITUS (*favored by Aphrodite or Venus*)

Friend and fellow worker of Paul (Phil. 2:25); delivered gift to Paul from Philippi; became seriously ill while with Paul in prison. Paul sent him back to Philippi, urging the church there to receive him "with all gladness"(Phil. 2:29).

EPHESIANS, LETTER TO THE

Pauline Epistle that best sets out basic concepts of Christian faith; one of four "Imprisonment Epistles." Christianity was introduced to the Asian peninsula early (Acts 13:1–14:28). Paul and Barnabas, during first missionary journey (about A.D. 45–48), established Christianity in Cilicia, Pamphylia, and Phrygia. The newly established religion moved inevitably westward to coast and to flourishing city of Ephesus, city of multiple religions, gods, and goddesses.

At close of second missionary journey (about A.D. 49–52), Paul with Aquila and Priscilla stopped at Ephe-sus. The Ephesians urged Paul to stay there, but he declined (Acts 18:18-21) and sailed to Antioch. He returned to Ephesus for three years (Acts 20:31) during a third missionary journey and experienced the triumph over the challenge of Jewish religious leaders and of Greek goddess Artemis (Roman name: Diana; Acts 19:24).

Interpreters are divided as to the time and place of writing of Ephesians. In all four Imprisonment Epistles, Paul mentioned his imprisonment. Ephesians and Colossians do not mention hope of release. Philippians reflects little anticipation of release. In Philemon, he seemed very confident he would be released; he even urged Philemon to prepare the guest room for him.

Evidence seems to support the opinion that Paul wrote all four Prison Epistles during his imprisonment in Rome about A.D. 61–62 in this order: Ephesians, A.D. 61; Colossians, A.D. 61; Philemon, A.D. 61; Philippians, A.D. 62.

Paul was convinced the religion he proclaimed was the only way of redemption from sin and sonship to God. Paul opposed a Judaism he considered to have become a religion of human attainment, doing the works of the law as a means of being right with God. He offered instead Christianity as a religion of divine provision: salvation by faith in God providing what humans could never attain. That distinction also brought Christianity into conflict with Greek philosophy and with the Greco-Roman nature religions. The Christian view is that the "good life" comes by faith, not by intellectual processes, speculations, and rules of conduct in the integration of personality.

Paul introduced himself as an apostle of Christ Jesus by the will of God. He addressed "the saints which are at Ephesus" (Eph. 1:1), "the faithful in Christ Jesus."

The expression "at Ephesus" is not in the oldest manuscripts of Ephesians, but is in many of the best ones. Its absence has led to speculation that in writing the epistle Paul left a blank space, that he meant the epistle to be a circular one to go to several churches. One manuscript (about A.D. 150) had "at Laodicea" in that place. See Col. 2:1; 4:16 for Paul's reference to his love for the church at Laodicea and his having sent a letter to them.

"Grace be to you, and peace, from God our Father, and from the Lord Jesus Christ" (Eph. 1:2) is in all of Paul's Epistles. Grace is the work of the Father by which salvation from sin comes. Peace is the condition of the believer's heart after grace has done its work.In his theological part (1:13–3:21), Paul centered attention on the plan and propagation of redemption. He began with a song to praise God for what He has done in providing salvation for sinful humanity. This is presented as the work of the Trinity: Father, Son, and Holy Spirit. A refrain "to the praise of the glory of His grace"repeats itself after each section.

Paul turned to thanksgiving to show the blessings of redemption (1:15–2:10). He wanted his readers to know Christ better. Christ's resurrection power can come to persons who were dead in sin but are saved by grace for the good works God has planned for His people.

Paul turned to the language of imperative (2:11–3:21). Through the blood of Christ unity of all races is accomplished. In the cross He brought peace and provided access to God through the one Holy Spirit. All are joined together in Christ's church built on the foundation of the apostles and serving as the residence of the Spirit.This good news is a mystery: a mystery God is calling people to share with other people through His grace, and a mystery that allows all people to approach God in confidence and freedom.

Paul prayed (3:14-21) that Christ may dwell in the believers who will be rooted in love and can grasp the marvelous greatness of that love.

In his ethical part (4:1–6:24), Paul looked at the application of redemption to the church, to personal life, and to domestic life. He sought unity in the Spirit: one body, one Spirit, one

hope, one Lord, one faith, one baptism, one God and Father. Within this unity, Paul celebrated the diversity of individuals within the church, a diversity stemming from the differing gifts Christ gives.

Without faith the individual is devoted to selfish lust and earthly dissipation. The believer becomes like God in holiness, purity, and righteousness; in speaking the truth and building up others. Anger and malice must turn to love, compassion, and forgiveness. This changes one's role at home. Submission to one another becomes the key, a submission motivated by loyalty to Christ and love to the marital partner.That love follows the example of Christ's love for His church. Parents expect honor from children while training children in the Lord's way of love. Similarly, masters and servants respect and help one another.

Paul called his readers to put on God's armor to avoid Satan's temptations.This will lead to a life of prayer for self and for other servants of God. This will lead to concern for and encouragement from other Christians. As usual, Paul concluded his letter with a benediction, praying for peace, love, faith, and grace for his beloved readers.

EPHESUS

Asia Minor center of ministry for Paul and later John. See *Asia Minor, Cities of; Ephesians, Book of; Revelation, Book of; Timothy.*

EPHOD

Simple, linen priestly garment (1 Sam. 14:3; 22:18; compare 2:18; 2 Sam. 6:14); possibly a short skirt, apron, or loin cloth—connected with seeking a word from God (1 Sam. 23:9-12; 30:7-8) and used in a wrong way as an idol (Judg. 8:27; 17:5-6).

EPHPHATHA

Aramaic expression (Mark 7:34) Jesus used in healing a deaf person with a speech impediment; translated,"Be opened."

EPHRAIM (*two fruit land* or *two pasture lands*)

Younger son of Joseph by the Egyptian Asenath, daughter of the priest of On (Gen. 41:52); adopted by his grandfather Jacob and given precedence over his brother Manasseh (Gen. 48:14); progenitor of tribe of Ephraim. See *Tribes of Israel; Patriarchs.*

EPHRAIM, MOUNT *or* **HILL COUNTRY OF**

Hill country belonging to tribe of Ephraim, not one mountain. Cities located there include: Bethel (Judg. 4:5); Gibeah (Josh. 24:33); Ramah (Judg. 4:5); Shamir (10:1); Shechem (Josh. 20:7); Timnath-heres or -serah (Josh. 19:50; Judg. 2:9).

EPHRATAH (*fruitful*), **EPHRATH, EPHRATHAH, EPHRATHITE**

(1) Town near which Jacob buried his wife Rachel (Gen. 35:16-19); home of Jesse, David's father (1 Sam. 16:1; 17:12); near Bethel (v. 16; compare 1 Sam. 10:2; Jer. 31:15); home of coming Messiah (Mic. 5:2; see Ruth 1:2; 4:11).

(2) Caleb's wife (1 Chron. 2:50; spelled Ephrath in 2:19; compare 4:4).

EPHRON (*dusty*)

(1) Hittite who sold cave of Machpelah to Abraham (Gen. 23:8-20; compare 25:9-10; Gen. 49:30-33; 50:13).

(2) Mountain marking tribal border of Judah with Benjamin (Josh. 15:9) located northwest of Jerusalem near Mozah at el-Qastel.

(3) City King Abijah of Judah (913–910 B.C.) took from King Jeroboam of Israel (926– 909 B.C.), according to spelling of Hebrew text (2 Chron. 13:19); earliest Hebrew scribes suggested Ephrain as correct spelling (KJV); apparently identical with Ophrah in Benjamin (Josh. 18:23; 1 Sam. 13:17); located at et-Taiyibeh about 4 miles north of Bethel and 300 feet higher than Jerusalem. City of Ephraim (2 Sam.

13:23; John 11:54) is probably the same city. Some would locate city of Ephraim in lower valley at ain Samieh, on the edge of the desert.

EPICUREANISM

A school of philosophy that emerged in Athens about 300 B.C.; founder is thought to be Epicurus (born 341 B.C. on Greek island of Samos). Paul met Epicureans as he preached about Jesus and the resurrection in Athens (Acts 17:18). Epicurean philosophy centered on search for happiness. Pleasure is the beginning and fulfillment of a happy life. To Epicurus, happiness could only be achieved through tranquillity and a life of contemplation. The goal of Epicureanism was to acquire a trouble-free state of mind, to avoid the pains of the body, and especially mental anguish. Epicurus believed in gods, but he thought they were totally unconcerned with the lives or troubles of mortals.

EPILEPSY

Disorder marked by erratic electrical discharges of the central nervous system resulting in convulsions. In ancient times epilepsy was thought to be triggered by the moon. Many interpreters understand the symptoms of the boy in Mark 9:17-29 as expressions of epilepsy.

EPIPHANY

Appearance or manifestation; festival of Western Christianity observed on January 6, celebrating manifestation of Christ to the Gentiles, the coming of the Magi to see the child Jesus (Matt. 2:1-12). Twelve days between Christmas and Epiphany are often called "Twelve Days of Christmas." Much of Eastern Christianity celebrates Epiphany as the baptism of Jesus, a recognition of His manifestation to humanity as the Son of God (Mark 1:9-11). See *Church Year.*

EPISTLE

Written correspondence. The majority of NT writings are epistles of Paul,

James, Peter, John, and Jude with the anonymous Hebrews. See *Letter.*

ERASTUS (*beloved*)

(1) Disciple Paul sent with Timothy from Ephesus to Macedonia to strengthen churches during third missionary journey (Acts 19:22).

(2) City financial officer of Corinth who joined Paul in greeting the church at Rome (Rom. 16:23).

(3) Disciple who remained at Corinth and was not with Paul when he wrote Timothy (2 Tim. 4:20). He may have been identical with *1* or *2* above.

ERECH

Hebrew transliteration of Akkadian place name: Uruk, one of the oldest Sumerian cities founded before 3100 B.C.; modern Warka, about 120 miles southeast of Babylon and 40 miles northwest of Ur. Genesis' Table of Nations reports that Nimrod included Erech in his kingdom (Gen. 10:10). Ashurbanipal, king of Assyria (668–629 B.C.), exiled "men of Erech" (NASB) to Samaria about 640 B.C. (Ezra 4:9). Gilgamesh, the hero of Akkadian flood stories, appears as king of Erech.

ESARHADDON (*Ashur* [the god] *has given a brother*)

King of Assyria (681–669 B.C.). See 2 Kings 19:36-37; Ezra 4:2; Isa. 19:4; 37:37-38. See *Assyria.*

ESAU

Son of Isaac and Rebecca; elder twin brother of Jacob (Gen. 25:22-26,30; 27:1,11,21-23,32,42; 1 Chron. 1:34); father of the Edomite nation (Gen. 26; Deut. 2:4-29; Mal. 1:2-3). Esau, the extrovert, was a favorite of his father, a hunter providing him with his favorite meats. A famished Esau sold his birthright to Jacob for food (Gen. 25:30-34; see 27:29; Deut. 21:15-17) and then lost the blessing of the eldest son when Rebecca and Jacob deceived him (Gen. 27:1-30). Years later, the two brothers were reconciled (Gen. 33:4-16).

ESCHATOLOGY

Teaching concerning the last things in world history. Chief future events include Jesus' return, the millennium, the last judgment, the final resurrection, and heaven and hell. Early Christianity was rooted in the paradoxical conviction that the last things had "already" occurred, even though they were "not yet" fully completed (1 Cor. 15:20).

For the last century or so, different overall eschatological perspectives have usually been classified according to their viewpoints regarding the millennium—the 1,000-year reign of Christ and His saints (Rev. 20:4-6):

(1) *Premillennialism.* Jesus will return before ("pre-") He establishes a millennial kingdom on this earth. Christ must conquer forces hostile to God then governing the world before He can rule. Towards the end of the millennium, evil will again arise and have to be defeated before God's cosmic rule is perfected. Those who hold the general expectation that Jesus will return before establishing an earthly millennium are called "historic premillennialists." "Dispensational premillennialism" contrasts God's way of working in at least two historical "dispensations": nation of Israel and the church. See *Dispensation.*

(2) *Postmillennialism.* Postmillennialists maintain Christ will return after ("post-") an earthly kingdom is established. The millennium will be simultaneous with an era of ordinary human history. Postmillennialism became popular during evangelical revivals between 1700 and 1900, emphasizing social transformation. Today some socially minded evangelicals are reviving it. They hold that history and society in general have been and will be brought increasingly under Christ's rule, and the kingdom's advance is closely related to that of certain social and religious forces.

(3) *Amillennialism.* Amillennialists interpret all language about a final, earthly realm of peace in a spiritual manner and believe no histori-

cal period called the millennium does or will exist. Amillennialism tends to be individualistic, concentrating on the heavenly destiny of each person rather than on the future of this earth. In the 1800s "amillennialism" was applied increasingly to a more specific eschatology. These amillennialists believed Christ was already reigning in heaven with departed Christians and not through specific ecclesiastical or social movements. These amillennialists expected Jesus to return, conquer His enemies, and to rule over a transformed earth. His perfected rule, however, would be established immediately and not preceded by an interim called the millennium. This specific form of amillennialism, then, is far less individualistic than the general one; it views history before Jesus' return much as does the more general, or "historic,"premillennialism.

People claim the Bible describes five major final events: Jesus' return, defeat of evil, resurrection, judgment, and renewal of the cosmos. Postmillennialists and amillennialists expect them to occur more or less together and to be preceded by a troubled time called the Great Tribulation (Mark 13:19) during which the antichrist will rule. They also anticipate a large-scale conversion of Jews before the end.

Historic premillennialists also expect Israelite conversion and the Great Tribulation to occur before Christ's return. However, they divide each of the other four final events into two phases:

(1) At Jesus' return: antichrist will be defeated, and Satan will be bound (though not wholly destroyed); then "the just" alone shall rise from their graves; they will be judged and rewarded for their good works; and the millennial kingdom will be established.

(2) After the millennium: Satan and all evil will be destroyed; then the "unjust"will rise; they will be judged for their evil works; and the new heavens and new earth will descend (compare Rev. 21).

Dispensational premillennialists distinguish two phases in Jesus' return: the rapture of the church followed by the Tribulation and Israel's conversion and Jesus' return to defeat antichrist, bind Satan, and establish a Judeo-centric millennial kingdom. The resurrection occurs in three phases: at the rapture, all who have died in Christ to that time will be raised; at Jesus' second return, those martyred during the Tribulation will rise; finally, after the millennium, the "unjust"will be resurrected.

Eschatology includes other important topics:

(1) *Universalism.* Most Christians have believed that some people will finally be saved while others will be lost. Some believe in "universalism": everyone will finally be saved. Universalists cite passages emphasizing God's desire that everyone be saved (1 Tim. 2:4; 2 Pet. 3:9) and argue that the scope of salvation becomes continally wider as biblical history advances (Rom. 5:15). They see certain texts directly teaching universalism (1 Cor. 15:22; Rom. 5:18; compare Eph. 1:10; Col. 1:20; 1 Tim. 4:10; 1 John 2:2).

Opponents of universalism point to OT annihilating judgments (Ex. 14:23-28; Josh. 7:24-26; Jer. 51:39-40); Jesus' negative judgments in parables (Matt. 13), and other sayings (Matt 5:29-30; 11:21-24; 23:33). Paul often spoke of future condemnation (Rom. 2:5-9; 2 Cor. 5:10; 1 Thess. 1:10) as do other NT writings (2 Pet. 3:7; Jude 14-15; Rev. 20:11-15).

Universalists find negative judgment incompatible with God's overwhelming love and the dignity of the human person. Opponents of universalism feel that it seriously undercuts the urgency of the call to repentance and the firmness of God's justice and ignores too many biblical texts.

(2) *The nature of hell.* Negative judgment results in consignment to hell. Most Christians have supposed that this will involve eternal conscious torment (Isa. 66:24; Mark 9:48; Rev. 14:9-11). Others have argued such texts should be taken figuratively. For them, such a penalty is

incompatible with God's mercy and disproportionate to all sins that a finite being could commit. Moreover, some find the eternal existence of hell inconsistent with the perfected rule of God over the cosmos. Accordingly, some have proposed that hell consists simply in the annihilation of "the unjust," involving their immediate loss of consciousness. Others have suggested that a gradual annihilation or deterioration of the wicked may be involved. Most evangelical Christians continue to expect a literal hell of torment. See *Hell.*

(3) *The hope of resurrection.* Resurrection has received far less theological discussion than have hell and judgment. Some have questioned whether resurrection is compatible with another notion widely held since the first Christian centuries: immortality of the soul.

Belief in immortality of the soul tends to make one's eschatology spiritualistic and individualistic and ignore bodily resurrection and final judgment; belief in resurrection emphasizes eschatology's physical, historical, and corporate dimensions.

(4) *The intermediate state.* Future resurrection forces the question of the location of the dead until the resurrection. Some teach soul sleep until the resurrection. Some talk of a distinction in eternity and historical time. Others think it best to simply affirm that the dead are somehow "in Christ."

Jesus' contemporaries felt they were living at the end of an "old Age" dominated by forces that opposed God. The early church discovered they lived in a new age, the age of resurrection. Instead of all the righteous being raised, Jesus alone had been, as the "firstfruits" of final harvest (1 Cor. 15:20,23). Those who repented of their sins could receive new life in fellowship with Him. By overcoming death, Jesus had conquered the strongest of those evil forces that oppose God (1 Cor. 15:26,54-57). Since this power had been defeated, no other power in heaven and earth could separate those who participated in Jesus' resurrection from God (Rom. 8:37-39; Eph. 1:18-23;

1 Pet. 3:21-22). The early Christian community discovered that the "new Age" of life and peace had "already" begun among them through the outpouring of God's Spirit. They began to understand that the Spirit, like Jesus, was the "firstfruits" of a new creation (Rom. 8:23), while those who turned to Christ became the firstfruits of a new humanity (Rom. 16:5; Jas. 1:18; Rev. 14:4). Although the powers that dominated the old age had already been defeated, they were "not yet" wholly destroyed. Still the early church's conviction that the new age had broken in imbued them with certainty of victory.

A deeper understanding of the "already- not-yet" life in the new age might help Christians relate more effectively to society at large. Postmillennialists, emphasizing that God's kingdom is already present, have usually been active in society, but have sometimes been unduly optimistic about possibilities for positive social change. Premillennialists, on the other hand, regarding God's kingdom as partially or wholly future, have often recognized the massive scope of evil in the world; but they have sometimes been unduly pessimistic about the value of social involvement. Perhaps a recognition that the "new age" is both present and future and that neither side of this paradox dare be ignored could help the church maximize the strengths of different millennial perspectives without being overcome by the weaknesses of any.

ESDRAELON

Greek translation of Jezreel, indicating low-lying area separating mountains of Galilee from mountains of Samaria; area assigned to Zebulun and Issachar (Josh. 19:10-23), extending from Mediterranean Sea to Jordan River at Beth-Shean. Included are the Valley or Plain of Megiddo in the east and the Valley of Jezreel in the west. Some scholars say the Valley of Jezreel is the name for the entire region, Esdraelon being the western portion, comprised of the

Plain of Accho and the Valley of Megiddo. Esdraelon was a strategically favored place and so often a battleground (Judg. 1:27; 5:19; 1 Sam. 29:1,11; 31:1-7; 2 Kings 9-10; 2 Chron. 35:20-24). See *Armageddon.*

ESDRAS See *Apocrypha.*

ESHCOL (*valley of grapes* or *cluster*)

(1) Valley in Canaan explored by 12 Israelites sent to spy out the land (Num. 13:23).

(2) Brother of Mamre and Aner (Gen. 14:13); Amorite allies of Abram.

ESHTAOL (*asking* [for an oracle]), **ESHTAOLITE** or **ESHTAULITE**

Town in lowlands or Shephelah of Judah (Josh. 15:33); also allotted to Dan (Josh. 19:41); may be modern Irtuf, a mile south of Ishwa. See Judg. 13:25; 16:31; 18:2-11. Its citizens were kin to clan of Caleb and to residents of Kiriath-jearim (1 Chron. 2:53).

ESHTEMOA (*being heard*) or **ESHTEMOH**

(1) Levitic city in Judah (Josh. 15:50; 21:14); modern es-Samu about 8½ miles south-southwest of Hebron and 14 miles northeast of Beersheba. See 1 Sam. 30:28.

(2) Member of clan of Caleb in Judah (1 Chron. 4:17), probably clan father of those who settled Eshtemoa; relation unclear between Eshtemoas in 1 Chron. 4:17, 19.

ESSENES See *Dead Sea Scrolls; Jewish Parties in the New Testament.*

ESTHER (Persian, *Ishtar*)

Heroine of biblical book; Jewish name was Hadassah; Jewish orphan girl raised by her uncle, Mordecai, in Persia. She became queen after Queen Vashti refused to appear at a banquet hosted by her husband, King Ahasuerus. See *Esther, Book of.*

ESTHER, BOOK OF

The book of Esther provides the historical background for the feast of Purim. When Jewish girl Hadassah became queen of Persia, she did not reveal her Jewish identity. Mordecai, her uncle, reported plot against king's life through Esther.

Haman was made prime minister and began to plot against Mordecai and the Jews because they would not pay homage to him. The king issued a decree that all who would not bow down would be killed. Esther learned of the plot and sent for Mordecai. He challenged her with the idea, "Who knoweth whether thou art come to the kingdom for such a time as this?" (Esther 4:14). She entered the king's presence unsummoned, which could have meant death. The king granted her request.

Haman was tricked into honoring Mordecai, his enemy. At a banquet, Esther revealed Haman's plot to destroy her and her people, the Jews. Haman was hanged on the gallows prepared for Mordecai. Mordecai was promoted, and Esther got the king to revoke Haman's decree to destroy the Jews. The Jews killed and destroyed their enemies. The book closes with the institution of the festival of Purim.

Many scholars believe the Book of Esther is a short historical novel or short story sprinkled with historical data and names to make its message more urgent and important, thus comparable to Jesus' parables. Others think it is an attempt to write history with free interspersion of speeches and conversation following the conventions of historical writing of its day. Others insist on the historicity of every detail, pointing to Esther 10:2.

The writer deliberately avoids the name of God. Vengeance is more prominent than devotion. The major theme of the book, persecution returning on the head of those who initiate it, leads through all the details of the story to the final victory, which Purim celebrates.

The book shows the sovereignty of God working in a foreign land to preserve His people. It shows God working through people of unpretentious backgrounds as they prove faithful to Him. It shows ultimate punishment for those who oppose God's people. It calls for celebration of God's deliverance. The book points to justice and indicates that faithfulness to the covenant people is a duty whether it pays or not. Mordecai's insistence that Esther must intervene to save her people is based on the idea that a good Jew must worship and be loyal to the covenant God and to Him alone.

ETAM (*place of birds of prey*)

(1) Rocky crag where Samson camped during his battles with the Philistines (Judg. 15:8-13).

(2) Town in Judah according to earliest Greek translation of the OT but omitted from present Hebrew manuscripts (Josh. 15:59, REB); Khirbet el-Khokh, southwest of Bethlehem. Rehoboam (931–913 B.C.) fortified the city (2 Chron. 11:6; see 10:2; 12:2-4).

(3) Member of Judah; clan father of town of same name associated with Jezreel (1 Chron. 4:3).

(4) Village assigned Simeon (1 Chron. 4:32); may be Aitun, about 11 miles southwest of Hebron.

ETERNAL LIFE

The quality of life including the promise of resurrection that God gives to those who believe in Christ. "Quality of life" involves

(1) life imparted by God;

(2) transformation and renewal of life;

(3) life fully opened to God and centered in Him;

(4) a constant overcoming of sin and moral evil; and

(5) removal of moral evil from the person and from the person's environment.

One trusting in the Son has eternal life; one disobeying the Son has the wrath of God abiding on him (John 3:36; see 3:15-16; 5:24; 6:54). Eternal life is both a present and a future reality (John 5:24; 10:27-28). Since Christ is our life, we must make that life part of us by actively coming to Him and drawing life-giving strength from Him (6:57; compare Matt. 19:16; Mark 10:17-22; Luke 18:18). In Mark 10:29 eternal life refers to an unending future reality.

Eternal life is constantly knowing in personal experience the only genuine God and Jesus Christ whom He sent (John 17:3). In John 12:20-26 Jesus contrasted eternal life with the present life. To be where Christ is means to come into eternal life, a life freed from sin or moral evil.

Eternal life is given by Jesus and the Holy Spirit (Gal. 6:8). Fellowship in life eternal means fellowship with the Triune God.

ETHAN (*long-lived*)

(1) Judah's grandson (compare 1 Chron. 2:6,8).

(2) Man famous for wisdom (1 Kings 4:31). Ezrahite may indicate he was in Canaan before Israel entered, though this is uncertain; associated with Pss. 88; 89 in their titles.

(3) Levite and temple singer (1 Chron. 6:42,44; 15:17) and instrumentalist (1 Chron. 15:19).

ETHICS

Study of good behavior, motivation, and attitude in light of Jesus Christ and biblical revelation. What God is in His character and what He wills in His revelation defines what is right, good, and ethical. God's character gives wholeness, harmony, and consistency to the morality of the Bible. What God required was what He Himself was and is. The heart of every moral command was the call to be holy as God is holy (Lev. 18:5-6, 30; 19:2-4,10,12,14,18,25,31-32,34,36-37). The NT calls us to imitate Christ's humble self-sacrifice (Phil. 2:5-8). The Bible features the grace and love of God, making ethics a living obedience rather than a fearful response.

Three assumptions illustrate how a contemporary ethicist or moral-living individual may be able to base his or her decision on the ethical content of the biblical text:

(1) the Bible's moral statements were meant to be applied to a universal class of peoples, times, and conditions;

(2) Scripture's teaching has a consistency about it so that it presents a common front to the same questions in all its parts and to all cultures past and present;

(3) the Bible purports to direct our action or behavior when it makes a claim or a demand.

Lurking behind each specific biblical injunction can be found a universal principle. From the general principle, a person in a different setting can use the Bible to gain direction in a specific decision.

Biblical ethics are emphatically theistic. They focus on God. To know God was to know how to practice righteousness and justice (Jer. 22:15-16; Prov. 3:5-7). Most significantly, biblical ethics are deeply concerned with the internal response to morality rather than mere outward acts. "The Lord looketh on the heart" (1 Sam. 16:7; see Isa. 1:11-18; Jer. 7:21-23; Hos. 6:6; Mic. 6:6-8).

Scripture's ethical motivation was found in a future orientation. The belief in a future resurrection of the body (Job 19:26-27; Ps. 49:13-15; Isa. 26:19; Dan. 12:2-3) was reason enough to pause before concluding that each act was limited to the situation in which it occurred and bore no consequences for the future: "You ought to live holy and godly lives as you look forward to the day of God and speed its coming" (2 Pet. 3:11-12, NIV).

Biblical ethics are universal. They embrace the same standard of righteousness for every nation and person on earth (Gen. 18:25; compare 13:13; Isa. 13–23; Jer. 45–51; Ezek. 25–32; Dan. 2; 7; Amos 1–2, Obad.; Jonah; and Nah.) and thereby warned of inevitable judgment by God if people do not repent.

The Bible's ethical words could be divided into moral law and positive law. Moral law expressed His character (Ex. 20:1-17; Deut. 5:6-21; Lev. 18-20). Positive law bound men and women for a limited time period. Thus the divine word in the garden of Eden, "but of the tree of the knowledge of good and evil, thou shalt not eat of it" (Gen. 2:17) or our Lord's, "loose him [the colt] and bring him hither" (Luke 19:30) were intended only for the couple in the garden of Eden or the disciples. A study of biblical ethics helps us distinguish between the always valid moral law and the temporary command of positive law.

The moral law is permanent, universal, and equally binding on all men and women in all times. This law is best found in the Ten Commandments. Merely omitting or refraining from doing a forbidden thing is not a moral act. Biblical ethics call for positive participation in life. We must not just refuse to murder, but we must do all in our power to aid the life of our neighbor.

Biblical ethics is based on the complete revelation of the Bible. The Decalogue and its expansions in the Book of the Covenant (Ex. 20:22–23:33); the law of Holiness (Lev. 18–20); and the law of Deuteronomy (Deut. 12–25) join the Sermon on the Mount in Matt. 5–7 and the Sermon on the Plain in Luke 6:17-49 as the foundational texts of the Bible's teaching in the ethical and moral realm.

Jesus gave the greatest summary of ethical instruction (Matt. 22:37-39): love God and love one's neighbor (note the Golden Rule, Matt. 7:12). The best manifestation of this love is a willingness to forgive others (Matt. 6:12-15; 18:21-35; Luke 12:13-34). Love is a fulfillment of the law (Rom. 13:9) because it constrains us to comply with what the law teaches. Love gives willing and cheerful obedience rather than coerced and forced compliance.

The NT sets forth Jesus as the new example of uncompromising obedience to the will and law of God. The

NT is replete with exhortations to live by the words and to walk in the way set forth by Jesus of Nazareth, the Messiah (1 Cor. 11:1; 1 Thess. 1:6; 1 Pet. 2:21-25).

The ethic that Scripture demands and approves has the holiness of the Godhead as its standard and fountainhead, love to God as its impelling motivation, the law of God as found in the Decalogue and Sermon on the Mount as its directing principle, and the glory of God as its governing aim.

ETHIOPIA

Region of Nubia just south of Egypt, from the first cataract of the Nile into the Sudan; modern Ethiopia is further to southeast. Hebrew (and the Egyptian) name for the region was Cush. English translations have generally followed the Septuagint in designating the land as Ethiopia and its inhabitants as Ethiopians. See *Cush.*

ETHIOPIAN EUNUCH

Unnamed official in the court of the queen of Ethiopia (Acts 8:27). See *Cush; Eunuch.* His conversion illustrates the Christian faith transcending national boundaries and perhaps embracing one whose physical mutilation excluded him from full participation in Judaism.

EUNICE (*victorious*)

Mother of Timothy (2 Tim. 1:5) commended by Paul for faith; Jewish woman whose husband was a Gentile. See *Timothy.*

EUNUCH

Male deprived of the testes or external genitals and then title of specific government office (Gen. 37:36; 39:1 refer to a married man), so that any specific usage can refer to one or both definitions. Such were excluded from serving as priests (Lev. 21:20) and from membership in the congregation of Israel (Deut. 23:1). Eunuchs were regarded as especially trustworthy in the Ancient Near East and thus were frequently employed in royal service. The Greek term trans-

lated *eunuch* is literally one in charge of a bed, a reference to the practice of using eunuchs as keepers of harems (compare Esther 2:3,6,15). Isaiah's vision of the messianic era promised the faithful eunuch with a lasting monument and name in the temple, which would be far better than sons or daughters (Isa. 56:4-5). A "eunuch for the sake of the kingdom of heaven" (Matt. 19:12) is likely a metaphor for one choosing single life in order to be more useful in kingdom work. Compare 1 Cor. 7:32-34.

EUODIA (*prosperous journey* or *pleasant fragrance*), or EUODIAS

Female leader in church at Philippi whose disagreement with Syntyche concerned Paul (Phil. 4:2-3); the two were perhaps deacons or hostesses of house churches in their respective homes. Paul commended the women for struggling by his side for the spread of the gospel comparable to Clement and other church leaders.

EUPHRATES AND TIGRIS RIVERS

Two of the greatest rivers of Western Asia. They originate in the Armenian mountains and unite about 90 miles from Persian Gulf to form what is now called the Shatt- al-Arab, which flows into the gulf. In ancient times the Tigris flowed through its own mouth into the gulf. The Euphrates and Tigris were included among the four rivers of Paradise (Gen. 2:14).

The Euphrates was known as "the great river" (Gen. 15:18; Josh. 1:4) or "the river" (Num. 22:5). It formed the northern boundary of the land promised by Yahweh to Israel (Gen. 15:18; Deut. 1:7; see Rev. 9:14; 16:12).

The Euphrates is the longest, largest, and most important river in Western Asia. Many significant cities were located on the Euphrates: Babylon, Mari, and Carchemish.

The Tigris is the site of the major vision of the prophet Daniel (Dan. 10:4). Significant cities on its banks included Nineveh and Asshur. See *Babylon; Nineveh.*

EUTYCHUS (*good fortune*)

Young man who fell asleep listening to Paul preach in Troas (Acts 20:9-10), fell from third floor window sill, and was picked up dead. Paul restored him to life.

EVANGELISM

Active calling of people to respond to the message of grace and commit to God in Jesus Christ. While Israel's influence was primarily national and magnetic in nature, the Bible gives instances of individual and external witness (Dan. 3–6; 2 Kings 5:15-18; Jonah 3:1-10). Though Israel was largely a failure in carrying out her mission, the large number of God-fearers at the beginning of the Christian era show that her magnetic attraction and proselytizing efforts were not entirely unfruitful.

Evangelism is the Spirit-led communication of the gospel of the kingdom in such a way or ways that recipients have a valid opportunity to accept Jesus Christ as Lord and Savior and become responsible members of His church. Luke 8:2-56 shows how Jesus brought the good news. He not only preached, He demonstrated His power over the forces of nature in saving His fearful disciples. He exorcised a demon, healed a poor woman who had hemorrhaged for 12 years, and raised Jairus's daughter from the dead. He brought good news by word and deed. Paul described how his message was used to "win obedience from the Gentiles, by word and deed, by the power of signs and wonders, by the power of the Spirit of God so that I have fully proclaimed the good news of Christ" (Rom. 15:18-19, NRSV).

The biblical mandate remains "to become all things to all men, that I may by all means save some" (1 Cor. 9:22, NASB).

EVE (*life*) See *Adam and Eve.*

EVERLASTING PUNISHMENT

Protracted, continual, and eternal judgment. All "punishment" in the OT is executed within history (e.g.,

plagues, wars, famine, sickness, exile).

The eternal fate of creation and human beings is bound up with gospel preaching and thus with the end-of-time events of Jesus' death, resurrection, and promised return (Heb. 6:2). The opposite of "eternal life"—"everlasting punishment"—is thought of as an "eternal fire," a "second death," or an "eternal destruction."The language paints a picture of endless suffering, loss, doom, and separation from the presence of God. Such end-of-time trauma befalls the evil, angelic powers that oppose God (Matt. 24:41; Jude 6; Rev. 19:3) and those human beings who willfully continue in "sin," a decision that demonstrates solidarity with the evil powers (Matt. 25:46; Mark 3:29; Jude 13; Rev. 14:11). The gospel is a present, historical revelation of end-of-time righteousness and wrath (Rom. 1:16-17). At the time of Jesus' appearance, all evil will be destroyed, and all humans who continued in opposition to God will receive their eternal sentencing (2 Thess. 1:9). See *Eschatology; Hell.*

EVIL

All opposed to God and His purposes or that which, defined from human perspectives, is harmful and nonproductive. Natural evil includes destructive forces in nature ranging from earthquakes and tidal waves to cancer. Moral evil has its source in the choice and action of humans and includes war, crime, cruelty, and slavery.

Moral evil accounts for much of natural evil. The original creation was very good (Gen. 1:31). To be truly human, a person must have the power of choice. God limited Himself in giving people and angels freedom. Humans used freedom in such a way as to bring in evil. Humanity's first sin brought a radical change in the universe: death (Gen. 2:17; 3:2-3,19), anguish in childbearing (3:16), male domination over the wife (v. 16), toilsome labor (v. 17), and thorns and thistles (v. 18). The whole creation has been affected by human sin and is now in bondage to decay (Rom. 8:22). The new heavens and the new earth will have no more suffering (Rev. 21:4). This means evil and suffering are not eternally inevitable but are bound up with the actions of sinful humans.

Back of human revolt stood Satan (Gen. 3; see Rev. 12:9). Satan's appeal stirred within Adam and Eve a desire that led to sin. This means that God did not create evil and sin. He merely provided the options necessary for human freedom. People sinned, and before that, the fallen angels, not God.

God disciplines His people collectively and individually, even through natural evil and pain, to bring them closer to His purposes (Prov. 3:11-12; Jer. 18:1-10; Heb. 2:10; 5:8-9; 12:5-11). This does not mean that all physical evils are the punishment of physical sins.

Human life can develop only in a stable environment. God limited Himself by the establishment of regularity and law. The earthquake, volcano, and storm, which cause human suffering, all belong to nature's regularity. Some so-called natural evil, therefore, can be attributed to the necessary operation of natural uniformities.

Even though evil is because of human revolt and failure, God continues to be active in redeeming people from their self-imposed evil. God deals with evil through judgment and wrath. This judgment can be seen in the OT (Deut. 28:20-21; Isa. 3:11). The wrath of God is not divine vindictiveness, but is dynamic, persistent opposition to sin (Rom. 1:18). A principle of judgment upon, and annulment of, evil operates in history and in individual lives.

God deals with evil through the incarnation, the cross, and the resurrection. God Himself in Jesus Christ became the victim of evil so that there might be victory over evil. Christians can bear suffering for others and assist in God's redemptive purpose (Col. 1:24; Phil. 3:10; 2 Cor. 12:7).

The problem of evil is not completely solved on an intellectual level from our limited human perspective. On the practical and experiential level we can say, "In all these things we are more than conquerors through him that loved us" (Rom. 8:37).

EVIL-MERODACH (*worshiper of Marduk*)

Babylonian king (562–560 B.C.) who treated Jehoiachin, king of Judah, with kindness (2 Kings 25:27); Babylonian name is Amel-Marduk. See *Babylon.*

EXCOMMUNICATION

Practice of temporarily or permanently excluding someone from the church as punishment for sin or apostasy. Excommunication came as a curse from God as punishment for sin (Deut. 27:26; 28:15; Ps. 119:21; Mal. 2:2-9; 4:6). The Jewish community assumed authority to curse on God's behalf (Num. 23:8; Isa. 66:5). Old Testament terms for excommunication mean to be excluded or cut off (Ex. 12:15, 19; Lev. 17:4, 9); to banish, devote, or put to destruction (Ex. 22:19; Lev. 27:28-29; Josh. 6:17), and desolation or thing of horror (2 Kings 22:19; Jer. 25:18). The covenant community protected itself from curse and temptation by distancing covenant-breakers from the community even to the point of executing them.

Christians were frequently subject to expulsion from the synagogue, the worship place of their fathers, as punishment for blasphemy or for straying from the tradition of Moses (Luke 6:22; John 9:22; 12:42; 16:2). The NT churches apparently used excommunication as a means of redemptive discipline. The apostles practiced excommunication based on the binding and loosing authority Jesus gave to them (John 20:23; Matt. 18:18). See *Binding and Loosing.* They excommunicated church members for heresy (Gal. 1:8); for gross, deliberate sin (1 Cor. 5; 2 John 7); and perhaps for falling away from church belief and practice (Heb. 6:4-8). The purpose was to purify the church and to encourage offenders to repent (1 Cor. 5:5-6; 2 Cor. 2:6-10; 2 Thess. 3:15). Punishment ranged in scope from limited ostracism to permanent exclusion and may even have included some form of physical punishment if the church continued synagogue practice (Luke 4:28-30; John 8:2-11; Acts 5:1-5; 7:58). New Testament terms for excommunication include: being delivered to Satan (1 Cor. 5:5; 1 Tim. 1:20); anathema or cursed and cut off from God (Rom. 9:3; 1 Cor. 16:22; Gal. 1:8). See *Apostasy.*

EXERCISE

The Bible speaks only briefly of physical exercise. 1 Tim. 4:8 recognizes the value of bodily training but subordinates it to the greater value of godliness.

Because the human body was created by God, it is incumbent on people to care for their bodies. This is particularly true for Christians, whose bodies are temples of the Holy Spirit (1 Cor. 6:19), which are to be presented to God as living sacrifices (Rom. 12:1). Using the imagery of a runner, the apostle Paul speaks of the need to pommel and subdue his body in order to qualify it for life's race (1 Cor. 9:24-26).

EXHORTATION

Argument (Acts 2:40) or advice intended to incite hearers to action. The ability to exhort or encourage to action is a spiritual gift (Rom. 12:8) sometimes associated with prophets/preachers (Acts 15:32; 1 Cor. 14:3). Elsewhere mutual exhortation is the responsibility of all Christians (Rom. 1:12; 1 Thess. 5:11,14; Heb. 3:13; 10:24-25).

EXILE

Events in which the northern tribes of Israel were taken into captivity by the Assyrians and in which the southern tribes of Judah were taken into captivity by the Babylonians.

The Assyrians and Babylonians introduced the practice of deporting captives into foreign lands. Deportation was generally considered the harshest measure only when other means had failed. Rather than impose deportation, Assyria demanded tribute from nations it threatened to capture. As early as 842 B.C., Jehu, king of Israel, was paying tribute to Shalmaneser, king of Assyria. Not until the reign of Tiglath-pileser (745–727 B.C.) did the Assyrians begin deporting people from the various tribes of Israel (2 Kings 15:29; 1 Chron. 5:26; 17:1-48).

The Assyrians exiled the Israelites into Halah, Gozan, and Media (2 Kings 17:6; 18:11; Obad. 20). The Assyrians brought into Samaria people from Babylon, Cuthah, Ava, Hamath, and Sepharvaim (2 Kings 17:24; Ezra 4:10). Sargon II recorded that 27,290 Israelites were deported. See *Israel, History of.*

There were three deportations of Jews to Babylon: 598 B.C. (2 Kings 24:12-16); 587 B.C. (2 Kings 25:8-21; Jer. 39:8-10; 40:7; 52:12-34); 582 B.C. (Jer. 52:30). After the second deporation, Gedeliah was appointed governor of Judah by the Babylonians, but was assassinated (2 Kings 24:25). The third deportation was a punishment for Gedaliah's assassination.

Life in exile meant life in five different geographical areas: Israel, Judah, Assyria, Babylon, and Egypt. We possess little information about events in any of these areas between 587 B.C. and 538 B.C.

(1) *Israel.* Assyria took the educated, leading people from the Northern Kingdom and replaced them with populations from other countries they had conquered (2 Kings 17:24). They had to send some priests back to the area to teach the people the religious traditions of the God of the land (2 Kings 17:27-28). Such priests probably served a population that contained poor Jewish farmers dominated by foreign leaders. When Babylon took over the area, they established a provincial capital in Samaria. Leaders there joined with other provincial leaders to stop

Zerubbabel and his people from rebuilding the temple (Ezra 4:1-24). Gradually, a mixed population emerged (Ezra 10). Still, a faithful remnant attempted to maintain worship of Yahweh near Shechem, producing eventually the Samaritan community. See *Samaria, Samaritans.*

(2) *Assyria.* Exiles from the Northern Kingdom were scattered through the Assyrian holdings (2 Kings 17:6). Apparently, their small communities, isolated from other Jews, did not allow them to maintain much national identity. We do not know what happened to these people, thus the popular title: "the lost tribes of Israel."

(3) *Judah.* The Babylonians left farmers, in particular, to care for Judah (Jer. 52:16). Some citizens who had fled the country before the Babylonian invasion returned to the land after Jerusalem was destroyed (Jer. 40:12). The Babylonians set up a government that may or may not have been dependent on the provincial government in Samaria. Jews loyal to the Davidic tra- dition assassinated Gedaliah, the governor (2 Kings 25:25). Then many of the people fled to Egypt (2 Kings 25:26; Jer. 43). People remaining in the land continued to worship in the temple ruins and seek God's word of hope (Lamentations). Many were probably not overjoyed to see Jews return from Babylon claiming land and leadership.

(4) *Babylon.* The center of Jewish life shifted to Babylon under such leaders as Ezekiel. Babylon even recognized the royal family of Judah (2 Kings 25:27). Exiled Jews based their calendar on the exile of King Jehoichin in 597 B.C. (Ezek. 1:2; 33:21; 40:1). Jehoiachin's grandson, Zerubbabel, led the first exiles back from Babylon in 538 B.C. (Ezra 2:2; Hag. 1:1). Most of the exiles in Babylon probably followed normal Near Eastern practice and became farmers on land owned by the government. Babylonian documents show that eventually some Jews became suc-

cessful merchants in Babylon. Apparently religious leaders like Ezekiel were able to lead religious meetings (Ezek. 8:1; compare Ezra 8:15-23). Correspondence continued between those in Judah and those in exile (Jer. 29), and Jewish elders gave leadership to the exiles (Jer. 29:1; Ezek. 8:1; 14:1; 20:1). First Chronicles 1–9, Ezra, and Nehemiah show that genealogies and family records became very important points of identity for the exiles. People were economically self-sufficient, some even owning slaves (Ezra 2:65) and having resources to fund the return to Jerusalem (Ezra 1:6; 2:69). Still, many longed for Jerusalem and would not sing the Lord's song in Babylon (Ps. 137). They joined prophets like Ezekiel in looking for a rebuilt temple and a restored Jewish people. They laughed at Babylonian gods as sticks of wood left over from the fire (Isa. 44:9-17; 45:9-10; 46:1-2,6-7; Jer. 1:16; Ezek. 20:29-32). A Babylonian Jewish community was thus established and would exercise strong influence long after Cyrus of Persia permitted Jews to return to Judah. These Jews established their own worship, collected Scriptures, and began interpreting them in the Aramaic paraphrase and explanations that eventually became the Babylonian Talmud, but continued to support Jews in Jerusalem.

(5) *Egypt.* Jews fled Jerusalem for Egypt (2 Kings 25:26) despite God's directions not to (Jer. 42:13–44:30). Many Jews apparently became part of the Egyptian army stationed in northern border fortresses to protect against Babylonian invasion. As such, they may have joined Jews who had come to Egypt earlier. Archaeologists have discovered inscriptions at Elephantine in southern Egypt showing a large Jewish army contingent there. They apparently built a temple and worshiped Yahweh along with other gods. These military communities eventually disappeared, but Jewish influence in Egypt remained. Finally, a large community in Alexandria established itself and pro-

duced the Septuagint, the earliest translation of the Hebrew Bible into Greek.

The Edict of Cyrus in 538 B.C. (2 Chron. 36:22-23; Ezra 1:1-4) released the Jews in Babylon to return to their homeland. Though conditions in the homeland were dismal, many Jews did return. The preaching of Haggai and Zechariah (520–519 B.C.) urged these returning captives to rebuild their temple in Jerusalem. The temple was completed in 515 B.C., the date that traditionally marks the end of the Babylonian exile.

EXODUS

Israel's escape from slavery in Egypt and journey toward the Promised Land under Moses; Israel's most important event historically and theologically. Repeatedly, Yahweh is known and proclaimed as "the one who brought you up from the land of Egypt, out of the house of bondage." Israel remembered the exodus as God's mighty redemptive act. The exodus in the OT was to Israel what the death and resurrection of Christ was to Christians in the NT. Just as Israel commemorated her deliverance from Egyptian bondage in the Feast of Passover, Christians celebrate their redemption from sin in the observance of the Lord's Supper (Luke 22:1-20; 1 Cor. 11:23-26). Israel celebrated the exodus in her creeds (Deut. 26:5-9; 1 Sam. 12:6-8) and in worship (Pss. 78; 105; 106; 114; 135; 136). The prophets taught that election and covenant were closely related to the exodus (Isa. 11:16; Jer. 2:6; 7:22-25; Ezek. 20:6,10; Hos. 2:15; 11:1; Amos 2:10; 3:1; Mic. 6:4; Hag. 2:5).

Exodus 1–15 describes the exodus event. Egyptian sources tell of nomadic people called Habiru entering Egypt from the east fleeing from famine. Evidence from Egypt indicates Egyptians used slave labor in building projects (Ex. 1:11). At one time, the land in Egypt was owned by many landholders; but after the reign of the Hyksos kings the Pharaoh owned most of the land, and the peo-

ple were serfs of the king (Gen. 47:20).

The Bible stresses that the exodus was the work of God. God brought the plagues on Egypt (Ex. 7:1-5) and performed the miracle at the sea (Ex. 15:21). God delivered Israel from bondage because of His covenant with the patriarchs and because He desired to redeem His people (Ex. 6:2-8).

The Bible gives no absolute date for the exodus. First Kings 6:1 dates the beginning of Solomon's temple building in his fourth year (about 960 B.C.) as 480 years after the exodus, which would then be 1440 B.C. (reading 480 literally) during the reign of Amenhotep II (1450–1425 B.C.). Exodus 1:11 says the Israelites in Egypt built the store cities of Pithom and Rameses. The claim that this precludes dating the exodus before 1300 B.C. because the name Rameses was not used in Egypt before then is based on the assumption that we know all about ancient Egypt. It also disregards the evidence of Gen. 47:11 where Goshen is called the "land of Rameses" during the time of Joseph. Some interpret 480 more loosely, perhaps meaning twelve generations. This allows the possibility of a later date for the exodus, perhaps in the 13th century B.C. during the reign of Rameses II (1304–1236 B.C.). See *Wanderings in the Wilderness; Wilderness.*

EXODUS, BOOK OF

Second book of the OT and of the Pentateuch; central book of the OT, reporting God's basic saving act for Israel in the exodus from Egypt, His making of His covenant with the nation destined to be His kingdom of priests, and the building of the tabernacle. See *Pentateuch* for discussion of date and authorship.

Exodus builds on Genesis and its ending with Joseph taking his father's family into Egypt to avoid the harsh sufferings of famine. Exodus begins with the children of Jacob in Egypt under a new pharaoh but seen as feared foreigners instead of welcomed deliverers from famine. Israel thus became slave laborers in Egypt (ch. 1). God delivered the baby Moses from danger, and he grew up in pharaoh's court as son of pharaoh's daughter. Trying to protect one of his own people, he killed an Egyptian. He had to flee to the wilderness of Midian, where he helped seven endangered shepherd girls, one of whom he married. There, God called him at the burning bush of Mount Horeb/Sinai and sent him back to rescue Israel from Egypt (chs. 2–4). A stubborn pharaoh refused to release the Israelites, who griped about Moses. God took this as opportunity to reveal Himself to Israel, to pharaoh, and to the Egyptians through the plagues on Egypt culminating in the death of the eldest sons of all Egypt. This tenth plague became the setting for Israel's central religious celebration, that of Passover and Unleavened Bread in which Israel reenacted the exodus from Egypt and rejoiced at God's supreme act of salvation for His people (chs. 5–13). The miracle of the Red Sea (or perhaps more literally, the Sea of Reeds) became the greatest moment in Israel's history, the moment God created a nation for Himself by delivering them from the strongest military power on earth (ch. 14).

After celebrating the deliverance in song and dance (15:1-21), Israel followed God's leadership into the wilderness. The Israelites cried for the good old days of Egypt, even after God supplied their food and drink needs and after He defeated the Amalekites (15:22–17:15). Moses' father-in-law, Jethro, brought Moses' wife and children back to him in the wilderness and praised God for all that He had done. Jethro advised Moses how to organize a more efficient judicial system (ch. 18). Then Israel came to Sinai, where God called them to become His covenant people, a holy nation to carry out Abraham's mission of blessing the nations. God gave the Ten Commandments and other laws central to the covenant (chs. 19–23), and then confirmed the covenant in a mysterious ceremony (ch. 24). Moses went to the top of the mountain to receive the remainder of God's instructions, especially instructions for building the sacred place of worship, the tabernacle (chs. 24–31). Impatient Israel got Aaron to build an object of worship they could see, so he made the golden calf. The people began worshiping. This angered God, who sent Moses back down to the people. Moses prayed for the people despite their sin, but when he saw the people's sinful actions, he threw the tablets with the law to the ground, breaking them. Moses again went up and prayed for the people. God punished them but did not destroy them as He had threatened. God showed His continued presence in the tent of meeting and in letting His glory pass by Moses (chs. 32–33). God then gave Moses the law on two new tablets of stone and renewed His covenant with the people, providing further basic laws for them. Such intense communication with God brought radiance to Moses' face (ch. 34). Moses then led Israel to celebrate the sabbath and to build the tabernacle (chs. 35–39). Moses set up the tabernacle and established worship in it. God blessed the action with His holy, glorious presence (ch. 40). This provided the sign for Israel's future journeys, following God's cloud and fire.

In the exodus, Israel learned the basic nature of God and His salvation. They also learned the nature of sin, the characteristics of God's leader, the components of worship, the meaning of salvation, and the identity of the people of God.

God revealed His salvation, power, concern, glory, and holy nature. Most of all, He revealed His will to be present among His people and lead them through their daily activities. He showed the way He expected His people to live, a way of holiness, a way of priesthood among the nations guided by the Ten Commandments. Such a life reflected the nature of God Himself (Ex. 34:6-7).

The people worshiped because they had experienced God's salvation. For them salvation meant physical deliverance in military action against a powerful world enemy. It involved following God's instructions and waiting for God's miraculous help. Salvation set up a covenant relationship between God and the people based on God's initiative. See *Covenant.*

EXORCISM

Practice of expelling demons by means of some ritual act. The OT refers to demonic beings but never to exorcisms (Lev. 17:7; Deut. 32:17; Isa. 13:21; 34:14; 2 Chron. 11:15; Ps. 106:37, NRSV). In the NT the demons were earthly powers or spirits allied with Satan. Jesus' power to exorcise is demonstration in the Synoptic Gospels of His power over Satan (Matt. 15:21-28; Mark 1:23-38; 5:1-20; 7:24-30; 9:14-29). Jesus had to silence unclean spirits because they proclaimed Him Son of God (Mark 3:11). His opponents often accused Jesus of being possessed (Mark 3:22; John 7:20; 8:48-49,52; 10:20).

Jesus gave His disciples authority over unclean spirits (Mark 3:14-15; 6:7) that they generally exorcised with success (Mark 6:13), but not always (Mark 9:18). Mark 9:38-41 refers to someone who did exorcisms in the name of Jesus even though he was not a follower of Jesus. Jesus told the disciples not to forbid him. Acts 19:13-16 tells of wandering Jewish exorcists in Ephesus who attempted to exorcise demons in the name of the Jesus but without success.

Contemporary magical papyri describe techniques of exorcism. By contrast, the exorcisms of Jesus mentioned only the technique of prayer (Mark 1:25; 9:25-29). See *Miracles; Divination and Magic; Healing; Demon.*

EXPIATION, PROPITIATION

Terms used by Christian theologians in attempts to define and explain the meaning of Christ's death on the cross as it relates to God and to believers. "Expiation" emphasizes the removal of guilt through payment of a penalty, while "propitiation"

emphasizes the appeasement or averting of God's wrath and justice. Both words show that through Christ's death on the cross for our sins we are reconciled to a God of holy love (Rom. 5:9-11; 2 Cor. 5:18-21; Col. 1:19-23).

In the OT, the note of grace is clearly present. God took the initiative in specifying which sacrifices would be needed.

The NT shows how Jesus fulfilled the OT system of sacrifices and thus replaced it with His own work on the cross. The OT system could not purify the consciences of those who offered them (Heb. 8:7,13; 10:1-4). In their stead, God provided a perfect Sacrifice, that of His own Son. This sacrifice is eternal, not provisional; it is sufficient to cover or expiate all human sin, not just specific sins (Heb. 7:26-28; 9:25-26). He made reconciliation available to all people in all times. Such reconciliation involves a change both in God's attitude toward us and in our attitude toward God. God chose to forgive us before the sacrifice was enacted in history, but His forgiveness could not reach us until this sacrifice took place.

God is both holy and loving. His holiness means that sin cannot be condoned. His love signifies that the sinner can be accepted if the claims of divine holiness are recognized. The atoning sacrifice of Christ both satisfies the demands of His holy law and demonstrates His boundless love. God was not waiting to be appeased (as in the pagan, Greek conception). Rather God provided the sacrificial offering that expiates human sin and makes reconciliation possible. All ritual requirements for sacrifice in the OT are replaced by the sacrifice of the cross (Col. 2:14; Heb. 10:14-18). The only sacrifices now required of the Christian are those of praise and thanksgiving, that take the form of worship in spirit and in truth and the obedience of discipleship (Rom. 12:1; Heb. 13:15-16; 1 Pet. 2:5).

The doctrine of the atonement includes both dimensions: propitiation—averting the wrath of God—

and expiation—taking away or covering over human guilt. A sacrifice was necessary to satisfy the demands of His law, but God Himself provided the Sacrifice out of His incomparable love. See *Atonement; Blood; Christ, Christology; Salvation.*

EYE

The organ of sight. The OT often speaks of the eye where we would speak of the person, reflecting the Hebrew concept of bodily parts as semi-independent entities. The eye can thus approve actions (Job 29:11); be full of adultery (2 Pet. 2:14), desire (Ps. 54:7); or lust (Num. 15:39; 1 John 2:16); despise (Esther 1:17); be dissatisfied (Prov. 27:20; Eccl. 4:8); and dwell on past provocation (Job 17:2). Job even spoke of entering a covenant with his eyes as if they were a second party (31:1). The eyes can be generous to the poor (Prov. 22:9). The eyes can scorn and mock (Prov. 30:17), spare an enemy (1 Sam. 24:10; Isa. 13:18), or wait for a time to sin (Job 24:15). The eyes can offend (Matt. 5:29), that is, cause someone to sin. Jesus' call to pluck out the offending eye is an exaggerated call to let nothing cause one to sin.

The "apple of the eye" is a description of the pupil. Proverbs 7:2 called for making God's law the apple of one's eye, that is, something of value to be guarded (kept) carefully.

God's eye or eyes is a frequent picture of God's providential care (Pss. 32:8; 33:18-19; 2 Chron. 16:9; Prov. 15:3; Jer. 16:17). Apocalyptic pictures involving numerous eyes (Ezek. 1:18; 10:12; Rev. 4:6), likewise, reassure of God's awareness of His people's plight wherever they might be.

EYE OF A NEEDLE See *Needle.*

EZEKIEL (*God will strengthen*)

Prophet and priest during Babylonian exile; son of Buzi (1:3); taken captive to Babylon in 597 B.C. by King Nebuchadnezzar along with King Jehoiachin and 10,000 others (2 Kings 24:14-16). He lived in his own house at Tel-Abib near the river Chebar.

Ezekiel's call came in 593 B.C., the "thirtieth year" (1:1), probably Ezekiel's age (though it has been interpreted as 30 years since the discovery of the law book in 622, 30 years since Jehoiachin's imprisonment, or a system of Babylonian chronology).

Ezekiel was married. His wife died suddenly during the siege of Jerusalem (24:18). Ezekiel continued to preach until at least 571 B.C. (29:17). His ministry can be divided into two phases:

(1) warnings of coming judgment on Judah and Jerusalem (593-587); and

(2) messages of encouragement and hope for the future (587-571). We do not know when or how Ezekiel died.

Ezekiel's personality has been labeled neurotic, paranoid, psychotic, or schizophrenic because of his unusual behavior (for example, lying on one side for 390 days and on the other for 40 days, 4:4-6; shaving off his hair, 5:1-4; and his many visions). Only once was Ezekiel reluctant to obey a command: it would have made him ceremonially unclean (4:14). His objection reflected his priestly training.

Ezekiel lived in a time of international crisis and conflict. Babylonia became the dominant world power. Judah maintained her independence by transferring allegiance to Babylonia but repeatedly found opportunity to rebel. See *Israel, History of.* The last of Judah's kings, Zedekiah (597-587 B.C.), did not heed the warnings of Ezekiel and Jeremiah. He rebelled, and Nebuchadnezzar led an army that besieged Jerusalem for 18 months before the city fell.

Jesus' presentation of Himself as the Good Shepherd in John 10 surely was intended as a contrast to the wicked shepherd in Ezekiel 34. His comparison of Himself to the vine in John 15 may have called to mind the parable of the vine in Ezek. 15. The living creatures in Ezek. 1 reappear in Rev. 4:6-9. The throne of God (Ezek. 1:26-28) is described similarly in Rev. 4:2-3. "Gog, the land of

Magog" (Ezek. 38:2) becomes "Gog and Magog" in Rev. 20:8. The temple vision (Ezek. 40–48) has several parallels in Rev. 21–22. Jesus' frequent reference to Himself as the Son of man is generally considered to have its origin in Dan. 7:13, but He may have appropriated it from the 93 times God addressed Ezekiel as "son of man."

EZEKIEL, BOOK OF

The Book of Ezekiel has been described as an artistic prose masterpiece. The entire book is written in the first person with the exception of 1:2-3. Few other books contain such a rich blend of symbolic actions, visions, figurative speech, and allegories to communicate God's messages. Ezekiel performed at least 11 symbolic acts (3:26-27; 4:1-3,4-8,9-17; 5:1-4; 12:1-16,17-20; 21:6,18-23; 24:15-24; 37:15-23). Visions form the content of 17 of the 48 chapters (1–3; 8–11; 37:1-14; 40–48). Imaginative use of figurative language characterizes Ezekiel (the watchman, 3:17-21; 33:1-9; a refining furnace, 22:17-22; Tyre as a merchant ship, 27:1-36; Pharaoh as a crocodile, 29:2-5). Ezekiel proclaimed many messages by means of allegory (15:1-8; 16:1-63; 17:1-24; 23:1-49; 24:3-14).

God first appeared to Ezekiel in a storm cloud seated on a throne surrounded by cherubim (1:1-28; 10:15). He commissioned Ezekiel to go to the "impudent children and stiffhearted" (2:4) and gave him a scroll to eat (3:1-3), symbolizing his complete identification with God's Word. God addressed him as "watchman" (3:17), a reminder of his responsibility to His people. God imposed silence on him for the next seven and one-half years so that he could not speak unless he had a message from God (3:26-27; 33:21-22).

Ezekiel's ministry began with the performance of a series of symbolic acts, all designed to communicate God's warnings of the coming siege of Jerusalem and the scattering of its people (4:1–5:17). Chapters 8–11 contain an extended vision that took

Ezekiel to Jerusalem, where he saw abominable worship practices in the temple (8:1-18). Ezekiel pronounced woes on the false prophets and prophetesses who were leading the people astray (13:1-23). However, he underlined each individual's personal responsibility before God (18:1-32). God told Ezekiel not to weep when his wife died during the siege of Jerusalem in order to communicate to the people that God's sympathy for His disobedient people was exhausted (24:16-17,22-24).

Ezekiel did not limit his messages to the covenant people. Chapters 25–32 contain a series of messages against the surrounding nations. These messages solemnly warned the covenant people they could not expect to escape punishment if God would also punish nations that did not acknowledge Him.

After Jerusalem fell, Ezekiel changed the emphasis of his messages. The devastated nation needed encouragement, hope for the future. The vision of the valley of dry bones dramatically proclaimed the future resurrection of the nation (37:1-14). The prophecies concerning Gog of the land of Magog gave assurance God would protect His people from their enemies (38:1–39:29).

The closing vision of the restored community announced hope for God's people in the future (40:1–48:35). These chapters are interpreted by some to be a literal description of the temple to be rebuilt after the exile, by some as an allegorical picture of the church, by others as a literal temple to be rebuilt as part of the fulfillment of the dispensational premillennial interpretation of Daniel's seventieth week (Dan. 9:2-27). Others as an example of apocalyptic language to describe God's coming kingdom in understandable terms of the destruction of wickedness and the establishment of a sanctified people in whose midst God would dwell.

Prominent themes of the book include God's presence (1:26-28; 48:35), the sovereign authority of God over all nations' individual responsibility (18:1-32), righteousness (18:5-9), submission to God as the key to blessing (9:4; 16:60-63; 18:30-32; 36:22-38), and hope for the future of the people of God (37-48).

EZION-GABER or **EZION-GEBER** Port city of Edom located on the northern shore of the Gulf of Aqabah (Num. 33:35-36; Deut. 2:8). Solomon utilized this city for shipbuilding purposes. During this time, ships manned by Phoenician sailors sailed from its port to Ophir for gold and other riches (1 Kings 9:26-28; 10:11, 22; 2 Chron. 8:17). See *Commerce; Elath.*

EZRA (*Yahweh helps*)

(1) Family head in Judah (1 Chron. 4:17).

(2) Priest who returned with Zerubbabel (Neh. 12:1,13).

(3) Prince at the dedication of Jerusalem's walls (Neh. 12:32-33).

(4) Chief character in Book of Ezra; priest and scribe descended from Aaron through Phinehas and Zadok (Ezra 7:1-5; 1 Chron. 6:4-14).

EZRA, BOOK OF

Joined with Nehemiah as one book among the writings in Hebrew and Greek OT giving events in restored Jerusalem after the Exile. Each book contains materials found in the other (for example, the list in Ezra 2 is also in Neh. 7). Each book completes the other; Ezra's story is continued in Nehemiah (chs. 8–10). A whole century (538–432 B.C.) would be unknown historically apart from Ezra and Nehemiah. They give the next chapter of the history recorded in Chronicles.

Ezra lived during the reign of Artaxerxes (7:1,7), king of Persia, but which one? Artaxerxes I (Longimanus), 465–425 B.C., or Artaxerxes II (Mnemon), 404–359 B.C.? Biblical order and other evidence support dating Ezra's journey to Jerusalem in 458 B.C. Ezra went to Jerusalem "to seek the law of the LORD, and to do it, and to teach in Israel statutes and

judgments" (7:10). Ezra's teaching was needed to give solidity and strength to the Jewish community struggling against pressures to surrender its ethnic and theological identity.

The Book of Ezra is based on a variety of sources. Jewish tradition is strong that Ezra was the actual author of the entire book, as well as Chronicles and Nehemiah. Vivid details and the use of the first person pronoun permit scholars to speak of the Ezra Memoirs (7:27–9:15).

The book has two major stories, that of Zerubbabel and the group of returnees who rebuilt the temple (chs. 1–6), and that of Ezra (chs. 7–10, completed in Neh. 8–10). Peculiarly, the book names Sheshbazzar (ch. 1) as the leader of the first group to return and not Zerubbabel. See *Sheshbazzar; Zerubbabel.*

Most of the book is written in Hebrew, but two large sections are in Aramaic (Ezra 4:7–6:18; 7:12-26). The Aramaic generally deals with official correspondence between Palestine and Persia.

Extensive lists (2; 8:1-14; 10:18-43) and the Aramiac show that the author was determined to use official documents where possible. Establishing the legitimacy of the Jews was an important objective, and the official documents helped do that. Ezra begins with the story of Sheshbazzar and Zerubbabel and the first Jews to return to Jerusalem from captivity in 538 B.C. Their main objective was to rebuild the temple. Its foundation was laid in 536 B.C. Then there was a long delay. In 520 B.C. Haggai and Zechariah (Ezra 5:1) encouraged the people to finish the project, which they did in 515 B.C. (6:14-16).

Almost 60 years passed before Ezra went to Jerusalem (458 B.C.). He left Persia with a letter from King Artaxerxes giving him unusual power and authority (7:12-26). During a three-day delay, more than 200 "ministers for the house of our God" (8:17) were enlisted. Four months later the group, probably less than 2,000, arrived.

Soon Ezra was informed of the most glaring sin of the Jews: intermarriage with non-Jews, those not in covenant relation with Yahweh (9:2). Ezra was greatly upset (9:3-4). He prayed (9:6-15). In assembly people reached what must have been a heartrending decision:"Let us make a covenant with our God to put away all the wives, and such as are born of them" (10:3). The book concludes with the carrying out of this decision (ch. 10).

Ezra's story reaches its climax in Nehemiah (Neh. 8 10). There he read from "the book of the law of Moses" (Neh. 8:1). A great revival resulted. Ezra's greatest contribution was his teaching, establishing, and implementing "the book of the law of the Lord" (Neh. 9:3) among the Jews.

Ezra believed in the sovereignty of God, who could use a Cyrus, an Artaxerxes, and a Darius to accomplish His purposes. He believed in the faithfulness of God, who brought home as many exiles as He could. He believed in the sacredness and practicality of the Scriptures; he read them to his people and insisted that their teachings be carried out. He was a person of prayer (Ezra 9:5-15; Neh. 9:6-37) and a preacher (Neh. 8:4). He publicly read the Scriptures and helped to interpret them to his congregation (8:8).

Ezra probably saved the Jews from disintegration. His efforts helped guarantee the ethnic and theological continuance of descendants of Abraham.

F

FACE

Front of a person's head. "*Face*" has a variety of meanings: literally, the face of people or animals (Gen. 30:40), seraphim (Isa. 6:2), and the face of Christ (Matt. 17:2); figuratively, the face of the earth (Gen. 1:29), waters (Gen. 1:2), sky (Matt. 16:3), and moon (Job 26:9); theologically, the "presence of God" (Gen. 30:17-23).

In the face, emotions are expressed. The face of the sky expresses the weather, stormy and red, or fair (Matt. 16:2-3). Bowing one's face expresses reverence or awe (Num. 22:31; Luke 5:12) or complete submission (1 Sam. 20:41; Matt. 26:39). When angry or sad, one's countenance (face) will fall (Gen. 4:5; contrast Prov. 15:13). To express displeasure or disgust, the face is averted or "hid" (Ezek. 39:23; Ps. 102:2); to "seek his face" is to desire an audience (Ps. 105:4). To "set my face against" is to express hostility (Jer. 21:10), while turning away the face shows rejection (Ps. 132:10). To "set their faces to" indicates determination (Jer. 42:17; Luke 9:51). The wicked man "hardeneth his face" (Prov. 21:29), and "covered his face with his fatness" (Job 15:27). When in mourning, the face is covered (2 Sam. 19:4).

Because the face reflects the personality and character of person, the word is frequently translated as "person" (Deut. 28:50; 2 Sam. 17:11; 2 Cor. 2:10), or "presence" (Ex. 10:11); even the indefinite "many" (2 Cor. 1:11). "*Face*" is also translated with the phrase "respect persons," (KJV), or "being partial" (RSV), (Deut. 1:17; Prov. 24:23; Matt. 22:16; Gal. 2:6).

Many idioms and phrases also apply to "the face of God." His face shines (Ps. 4:6), indicating good will and blessing. He sets His face against sinners (Lev. 17:10), and hides His face (Ps. 13:1). Sometimes *face* is translated as "presence" (Gen. 4:16; Ex. 33:14; 2 Thess. 1:9). In the tabernacle, the "shewbread" (KJV) or "Bread of the Presence" (NRSV), literally—"bread of the faces"—was a local manifestation of the presence of God. Moses asked to see God's "glory" (Ex. 33:18), but God answered that "thou canst not see my face" (Ex. 33:20). The correlation indicates that in seeing God's face, one would experience His actual presence, and thereby be exposed to God's nature and character. Sinful and nonholy beings cannot survive being in God's holy presence without God's grace or merciful intervention (Ex. 33:17-23). Thus Moses (Ex. 3:6), Elijah (1 Kings 19:13), and the seraphim (Isa. 6:2) hide their faces in God's presence. See *Glory; Shewbread; Presence of God; Eye.*

FAIR HAVENS

Open bay on the southern coast of Crete near the city of Lasea (Acts 27:8-20).

FAIRNESS

Fairness is a prerequisite for wisdom (Prov. 2:9-10) and therefore an important value for life (Ps. 99:4; Prov. 1:2-3). The prophets linked fairness with righteousness (Isa. 11:4; compare Ps. 98:9) and saw that when fairness was lacking, life became tenuous and uncertain (Isa. 59:9-11; Mic. 3:9-12). Biblical persons who exhibited fairness in their words or actions include Jacob (Gen. 31:38-41), Solomon (1 Kings 3:16-27), Jesus (John 7:53-8:11) and the thief on the cross (Luke 23:40-41).

Many injunctions in the Mosaic law are based on the principle of *lex talionis* ("an eye for an eye"). This principle holds that a person's misdeeds were to be punished by actions commensurate with their crime (Ex. 21:23-25; Lev. 24:17-21; Deut. 19:16-21). Later biblical writers understood that reciprocity also attained for behavior which was merely selfish or unwise, but not criminal (Ps. 7:15-16; Prov. 26:27; Matt. 7:2; 2 Cor. 11:15; Gal. 6:7-10).

Biblical injunctions uphold fairness in matters of business (Lev.

19:36; Deut. 25:15; 1 Tim. 5:18), law (Ex. 23:3; Deut. 16:19), speech (Ex. 23:1) and family relationships (e.g., Deut. 21:15-17; Eph. 6:1-9).

God's fairness in his treatment of sin was understood by the biblical writers in different ways. During the early days of ancient Israel, God's fairness was viewed through the concept of corporate solidarity, so that the responsibility for a person's actions carried through to his family (Ex. 34:6-7). By the time of the exile and in the NT, responsibility for sin was seen to be an individual matter (Ezek. 18:10-32) and God's judgment of individuals as individuals was accepted as fair.

FAITH

Trusting commitment of one person to another, particularly of a person to God; central concept of Christianity. One may be called a Christian only if one has faith.

Faith is the acceptance of Christ's lordship (His God-given, absolute authority). It is one's removal from sin and from all other religious allegiances (1 Thess. 1:9). Faith is a personal relationship with God that determines the priorities of one's life. This relationship is one of love built on trust and dependence. We receive it by trusting the saving work of Jesus.

Faith includes a certain amount of "belief" and may denote the content of what is believed. In this sense faith is the conviction that God acted in the history of Israel and "that God was in Christ, reconciling the world unto himself" (2 Cor. 5:19).

In the OT, the concept is named with other words: the "fear of God" (Gen. 20:11; Ps. 111:10; Eccl. 12:13; Mal. 4:2), trust (2 Chron. 20:20; Ps. 4:5; Isa. 26:4), and obedience (Ex. 19:5; 1 Sam. 15:22; Jer. 7:23). Faith is a NT concept that encompasses and enriches these OT concepts. Paul properly took Hab. 2:4 as the center of OT religion. To accept the responsibilities of God's covenant and to trust His word that He alone is God and to commit one's life to His prom-

ises for the present and future—that is faith.

The Greek *pistis* ("faith") and *pisteuo* ("I have faith, trust, believe") have the primary meaning: "trust" or "confidence" in God. Mark 1:15 (NASB) introduces and summarizes the gospel with Jesus' charge to "repent ye and believe in the gospel" (compare Mark 11:22). After healing someone, Jesus often said, "Thy faith hath made thee whole" (Matt. 9:22; Mark 5:34; Luke 7:50; 8:48; compare John 6:29 and 14:1).

Faith is related to salvation (Eph. 2:8-9), sanctification (Acts 26:18), purification (Acts 15:9), justification or imputed righteousness (Rom. 4:5; 5:1; Gal. 3:24), adoption as children of God (Gal. 3:26). Each of these comes by faith. Faith is an attitude toward and relationship with God mediated by Christ Jesus. It is surrender to God's gift of righteousness in Christ rather than seeking to achieve righteousness alone.

Faith is a fruit of the Holy Spirit (Gal. 5:22)—something God creates in a person. "Faith" is also a gift of the Holy Spirit given to some but not to others (1 Cor. 12:8-9). Apparently such special gifts of faith refer to the ability to do great acts for God, what Jesus called moving mountains (Matt. 17:20; 1 Cor. 13:2).

The NT sometimes uses "faith" to designate Christianity itself or that which Christians believe (Acts 6:7; Eph. 4:5; Col. 1:23; 1 Tim. 1:19; Jude 3). To have a right relation with God, it is necessary to "believe" that God is, that God has revealed Himself in Christ, and to accept that God accepts you (Heb. 11:6).

Faith is also Christianity in action: "We walk by faith, not by sight" (2 Cor. 5:7). Faith changes the standards and priorities of life. Similarly, faith is a shield against sin and evil in our lives (Eph. 6:16; 1 Thess. 5:8).

The personal conviction of faith encourages the Christian to continue hoping for the fulfillment of the promises of God. Faith is then meant as a sort of foretaste of the hoped for things (Heb. 11:1).

Faith is what we believe: It is Christianity itself, but primarily it is the relationship we have with God through what Jesus accomplished in His death and resurrection.

FAITHFUL

Steadfast, dedicated, dependable, and worthy of trust. Moses was faithful in all God's household (Num. 12:7; compare 1 Cor. 7:25; Eph. 1:11; Rev. 2:10). The faithful God keeps His covenant, and the faithful people keep His commandments (Deut. 7:9).

God's faithfulness comforts and encourages Christians: "If we confess our sins, he is faithful and just to forgive us our sins, and to cleanse us from all unrighteousness" (1 John 1:9). "God is faithful, who will not suffer you to be tempted above that ye are able" (1 Cor. 10:13). "Faithful is he that calleth you, who also will do it" (1 Thess. 5:24). See *Faith*.

FALL

Traditional name for the first sin of Adam and Eve, that brought judgment upon both nature and humankind. God provided Adam a vocation for fulfillment (Gen. 2:15). The first people had great freedom to take from the goodness of God's creation (2:16), yet their freedom was limited (2:17). The "knowledge of good and evil" (Gen. 3:5,22) was the object and symbol of God's authority, reminding Adam and Eve that their freedom was not absolute but had to be exercised in dependence on God. In prideful rebellion the couple grasped for an absolute self-directing independence. Such absolute dominion belongs only to God. Their ambition affected every dimension of human experience; for example, they claimed the right to decide what was good and evil.

The serpent is identified as Satan the ultimate tempter (1 John 3:8; Rev. 12:9). People cannot blame their sin on demonic temptation (Jas. 1:12-15). The serpent's question distorted or at least extended God's order not to eat of the tree (Gen. 3:1), inviting the woman to treat God and His Word as objects to be considered and evalu-

ated. The serpent painted God as One who sadistically and arbitrarily placed a prohibition before the couple to stifle their enjoyment of the garden.

Humankind's first surrender to temptation began with doubting God's instruction and His loving character. The woman defended God's instruction (Gen. 3:2). She told of God's prohibition of one tree in the middle of the garden. Perhaps anxiety over doubting God's character moved her then to extend the instruction to include touching the tree.

The serpent directly attacked God's character. He declared that the couple would not really die. Instead, he argued that God's motive was to keep the couple from being like God. The couple was unhappy with their freedom as long as they thought more could be had. They sought unrestricted freedom—to be responsible to no one, not even God. The serpent promised that eating would produce equality, not death. The woman saw the fruit was good for food, judged it to be pleasant to the eye, and in her vanity believed it would bring knowledge (Gen. 3:6; compare 1 John 2:16). She ate of the fruit and gave it to Adam who ate as well.

Sin had immediate results in the couple's relationship: the self-first and self-only attitude displayed toward God also affected the way they looked at each other. The mutual trust and intimacy of the one-flesh bond (Gen. 2:24) was ravaged by distrust (3:7).

The couple felt compelled to hide from God. After their sin, shame appropriately marked their relationships both human and divine (Gen. 3:8). God pursued, asking, "Where art thou?" (Gen. 3:9). Sinners finally must speak to God. Adam admitted that God's presence now provoked fear, and human shame provoked hiding (Gen. 3:10).

The man admitted his sin, but only after emphatically reminding God that the woman was instrumental in his partaking. Woman shared equally in the deed, but she quickly blamed the deceiving serpent (Gen. 3:12-13).

Along with shame, blame comes quite naturally to humankind.

God moved immediately to punish. The snake's behavior foreshadowed the reversal of created order and humankind's dominion. Once appealing and crafty, the cursed snake became lower than other animals. The judgment included the strife between snakes and humans. Some believe a fuller meaning of the verse promises Christ's ultimate victory over Satan (Gen. 3:14-15).

The woman's punishment was linked to her distinctive role in the fulfillment of God's command (Gen. 1:28). Her privilege in sharing in God's creative work was frustrated by intense pain. Despite this pain, she would nevertheless desire intimacy with her husband, but her desire would be frustrated by sin. Their mutuality and oneness were displaced by male domination (Gen. 3:16).

Adam's punishment also involved the frustration of his vocation. The fruitful efficiency known prior to the Fall was lost. Even his extreme toil would be frustrated by the cursed earth, that also needed redemption (Isa. 24; Rom. 8:19-23; Col. 1:15-20). Hope ultimately emerged from divine determination to preserve His creation. Grace- giving Yahweh provided clothing for fallen humankind (Gen. 3:20-21).

As a tragic judgment, the sinful pair were driven out of the garden. The serpent's lie concerning death (Gen. 3:4) became visible. Human sin brought death (Gen. 3:19,22).

The NT writers assumed the fallen state of both humans and nature. Both groan for redemption (Rom. 8:19-23). When comparing Adam and Christ, Paul declared that sin and death gained entrance into the world through Adam; sin and death are now common to all people (Rom. 5:12; 6:23). Adam may be pictured as a representative of humankind, all of whom share in his penalty (Rom. 5:19).

FALSE APOSTLES

Designation for Paul's opponents in 2 Cor. 11:13, also designated deceitful workers (11:13) and ministers of Satan (11:15). Such "apostles" preached a "rival Jesus" (likely a lordly, miracle-working "success story"); possessed a different spirit (a self-seeking motivation evidenced by a different lifestyle than Paul's); and believed a different gospel (that disregarded the cross and its corollary of suffering for those who follow Christ). The false apostles appear to have been Jewish Christians (11:22), well trained in speech (11:6), who perhaps claimed "visions and revelations of the Lord" (12:1) as authenticating marks of apostleship. The "false apostles" are characterized as boasting (2 Cor. 10:13-16) according to human standards. Their leadership style was oppressive (11:20). In contrast to Paul, these false apostles relied on the Corinthian Christians for financial support (11:7-11,20; 12:14). Paul countered that suffering for Christ was the mark of true apostleship (11:23). Weakness, not dominating power, reveals God's power (11:30; 12:5,9). If the "super apostles" (11:5; 12:11, NRSV, REB, NIV) are identified with the leaders of the Jerusalem church, they should be distinguished from the false apostles at Corinth. The latter may have claimed the authority of the former.

The false apostles of Rev. 2:2 are characterized as evil men and liars. They should perhaps be identified with the Nicolaitans active at Ephesus (2:6), Pergamos (2:15), and the followers of the "false prophetess" at Thyatira (2:20).

FALSE CHRISTS

Imposters claiming to be the Messiah (Christ in Greek). Jesus associated the appearance of messianic pretenders with the fall of Jerusalem (Matt. 24:23-26; Mark 13:21-22). He warned His followers to be skeptical of those who point to signs and omens to authenticate their false messianic claims. Josephus mentioned several historical figures who might be regarded as false christs:

(1) Theudas, who appeared when Fadus was procurator (A.D. 44–46); he summoned the people to the Jordan River wilderness, promising that he would divide the Jordan like Joshua and begin a new conquest of the land;

(2) various "imposters" during the term of Felix (A.D. 52–59) led crowds into the wilderness with promises of signs and wonders;

(3) an "imposter" during the term of Festus (A.D. 60–62) who promised deliverance and freedom from the miseries of Roman rule for those who would follow him into the wilderness;

(4) Manahem ben Judah (alias "the Galilean"), during the term of Florus (A.D. 64–66), who came to Jerusalem "like a king" and laid seige to the city. These messianic imposters and the barely distinguishable false prophets repeatedly urged the Jewish people to take up armed resistance to Rome or to stay in Jerusalem and fight. In contrast, Jesus urged His disciples to attempt to save themselves by fleeing the city. Some interpreters expect false christs to arise before the future coming of Christ.

FALSE PROPHET

Person who spreads false messages and teachings, claiming to speak God's words.

Hebrew has no word for *false prophet*. All are simply prophets. Yet some do not obey God. They are false. Jeremiah 14:14 describes them: "The prophets prophesy lies in my name: I sent them not, neither have I commanded them, neither spake unto them: they prophesy unto you a false vision and divination, and a thing of nought, and the deceit of their heart" (compare Jer. 23:21-33; Zech. 10:2). False prophets were cast away from God's presence and permanently humiliated (Jer. 7:14-16; 23:39).

Another type of false prophet prophesied on behalf of another god (1 Kings 18:20-39). Israel could not always distinguish between the true and the false prophets (1 Kings 22; Jer. 28). The prophet could only say to

wait and see whose prophecy proves true in history (Deut. 18:22; 1 Kings 22:28; Jer. 29:9). Compare 1 Kings 13.

Jesus cautioned His followers to beware of false prophets who would arise during times of tribulation and in the end times (Matt. 24:11,24; Mark 13:22; see Matt. 7:15-23). He said false prophets are apt to be popular (Luke 6:26).

The apostles instructed believers to be diligent in faith and understanding of Christian teachings in order to discern false prophets when they arise (2 Pet. 1:10; 1:19–2:1; 1 John 4:1). The tests of a prophet are these:

(1) Do their predictions come true (Jer. 28:9)?

(2) Does the prophet have a divine commission (Jer. 29:9)?

(3) Are the prophecies consistent with Scripture (2 Pet. 1:20-21; Rev. 22:18-19)?

(4) Do the people benefit spiritually from the prophet's ministry (Jer. 23:13, 14,32; 1 Pet. 4:11)?

Paul caused a false prophet to be stricken with blindness (Acts 13:6-12). Jesus said false prophets would be cut down and burned like a bad tree (Matt. 7:19; compare 2 Pet. 2:4; Rev. 19:20; 20:10). See *Prophecy, Prophets.*

FALSE WORSHIP

Acts and attitudes that worship, reverence, or give religious honor to any object, person, or entity other than the one true God and impure, improper, or other inappropriate acts directed toward the worship of the true God.

The most consistent problem with false worship seen in the OT is with the nature or fertility deities—Baals and Ashtaroth, Anath, Astarte—the male and female representations of reproduction and growth. Many of the forms of this false worship involved sexual acts. Worship for political reasons was another type of false worship (Zeph. 1:5).

National gods, fertility deities, mystery religions, and emperor worship were serious challenges for the early church. Often the Christian was faced with imperial orders to participate in this kind of false worship. Refusal could bring serious penalties, often execution.

The primary forms of false worship are addressed in the Decalogue (Ex. 20): exclusive loyalty to and worship of Yahweh (v. 3); imageless spiritual worship (v. 4); honor in all of life the God whose name the Hebrews claimed and bore (v. 7).

The Hebrews were guilty of syncretistic or artificially mixed religious practices. The temples Jeroboam built in Bethel and Dan with calves of gold mixed a symbol of Baal with the worship of the God who delivered the Hebrews from their Egyptian bondage (1 Kings 12:28); that was false worship.

False worship includes trusting in military power (Isa. 31:1), trusting in the "works of your hands" (Jer. 25:7), serving God in order to receive physical and material blessings (as Job's friends), and offering unacceptable —tainted or maimed sacrifices—to God instead of the best (Mal. 1:6-8). False worship also occurs when one prays, fasts, or gives alms "before men to be seen of them" instead of sincere devotion to God (Matt. 6:1-18).

Micah 6:8 summarizes true worship: "What doth the Lord require of thee, but to do justly, and to love mercy, and to walk humbly with thy God." Jesus confirmed it: "True worshippers shall worship the Father in spirit and in truth: for the Father seeketh such to worship him. God is a Spirit: and they that worship him must worship him in spirit and in truth" (John 4:23-24). See *Canaan, History and Religion of; Worship.*

FAMILY

A group of persons united by the ties of marriage, blood, or adoption, enabling interaction between members of the household in their respective social roles. God has ordained the family as the foundational institution of human society.

Old Testament The importance of the family unit in Israel is suggested by the fact that about half of the capital crimes were family related, including adultery, homosexuality, incest, persistent disobedience to or violence against one's parents, and rape. The basis for the family unit was the married couple (Gen. 2:4–5:1). From the union of the husband and wife, the family expanded to include the children, and also various relatives such as grandparents, and others.

Along with paternal authority over the family came responsibility to provide for and protect the family. The father was responsible for the religious and moral training of his children (Deut. 6:7,20-25), and before the law he acted as the family priest (Gen. 12:7-8). After establishment of the Levitical priesthood, the father led the family in worship at the sites designated by God with the priests performing the sacrifices (1 Sam. 1). Moral purity was stressed for men and women in Israel with severe penalties for either party when sin occurred (Lev. 18). The father was to give his daughter in marriage (Deut. 22:16) to only an Israelite man, usually one from his own tribe. A daughter found to have been promiscuous before she married was to be stoned on her father's doorstep (Deut. 22:21).

Contrary to the practices of the surrounding nations, wives were not considered property. Though most marriages in the OT were arranged, this does not mean that they were loveless. The Song of Songs extols the joys of physical love between a husband and wife. God is used as an example of the perfect husband who loves His "wife" Israel (Hos. 1–2) and delights to care for her and make her happy.

Mothers gave birth and reared the children, ran the home under her husband's authority, and generally served as her husband's helper (Gen. 2:18; Prov. 31:10-31).

The importance of children in ancient Israel may be inferred from the law of Levirate marriage, which provided for the continuance of the family line (Deut. 25:5-10). They were also the instruments by which the ancient traditions were passed on (Ex. 13:8-9,14). God delights to be praised by children (Ps. 8:2). Children were taught to respect their mothers as well as their fathers (Exod. 20:12; Deut. 5:16; 21:13; 27:16; Prov. 15:20; 23:22,25; 30:17) and to heed their instruction (Prov. 1:8; 6:20). Discipline was one way of showing love to one's children (Prov. 3:11-12; 13:24).

Polygamy (more specifically "polygyny") was one of the abnormal developments of the family in the OT and was first practiced by Lamech, a descendant of Cain. It is never cast in a positive light in Scripture but is a source of rivalry and bickering, as is seen in the lives of Abraham and Jacob (Gen. 16; 29–30). The harems of the kings of Israel are presented as excess that is rebuked in the monarchy (Deut. 17:17). Because of polygamy the kings of Israel were persuaded to worship false gods (1 Kings 11:1-10). The normal family unit in Israel was never polygamous, nor was polygamy widely practiced outside of the monarchy.

Relatives identified as off-limits for marriage (that is, incestuous; see Lev. 18:6-18; 20:11-14,19-21) seem to have been those normally considered members of the "father's house." This included one's father or mother, son or daughter (of whatever generation), sister or brother, uncle or aunt, or a step-relation, half-relation, or in-law, that is, one's father, mother, son, daughter, sister, brother, uncle, or aunt by marriage. The exception was in the case of "Levirate marriage," that is, an unmarried male's marriage to the childless widow of his deceased brother.

New Testament As the family is the basic unit in society and in OT Israel, it was also essential to the life and growth of the early church. The apostolic missionaries sent by Jesus were to focus on households (Matt. 10:11-14), early worship consisted in part of "break[ing] bread from house to house" (Acts 2:36; see also 5:42; 12:12; 20:20), and later churches met regularly in homes (Rom. 16:23; 1

Cor. 16:19; Col. 4:15). Conversions even sometimes happened by household (Acts 10:24,33,44; 16:15,31-34; 18:8; 1 Cor. 1:16). The family also served as a proving ground for church leaders, who should exhibit marital faithfulness, hospitality, competent household management, including wise parenting skills, and having wives "worthy of respect" (1 Tim. 3:2-13; Titus 1:6-9).

In the NT family structure is not discussed as much as the roles and responsibilities of those in the household. The common family unit was a monogamous relationship that included the extended family. By the first century there was a greater measure of independence within the family based upon Roman culture and urban living. Close ties were common between members of the family in Israel.

Jesus reaffirmed the monogamous family and rebuked immorality and divorce during His ministry. He spoke about the indissolubility of the family and that even the civil courts could not break the family bonds (Mark 10:1-12). The responsibility to care for those in the family is seen at the cross where Jesus, though suffering, gave the Apostle John the responsibility to care for His mother (John 19:26-27).

Much of the NT teaching on the family is found in Paul's writings. Household ethics are described in Eph. 5–6 and Col. 3–4. In these texts husbands are responsible for the physical, emotional, religious, and psychological health of wives. A wife's submission is in the marriage context.

Wives are called to be household administrators. As household managers wives are responsible to give the family guidance and direction. Paul states that performing these tasks will inhibit gossiping and other unprofitable activities (1 Tim. 5:14). Thus any decision made within the family without the counsel and guidance of the wife is unwise.

Family roles in the NT also include children, who are commanded to obey their parents (Eph.

6:1-4). Each member of the family has responsibilities. Jesus affirms the importance of children and their importance to Him in Matt. 18:2-14. See *Mother; Marriage; Sex, Biblical Teaching on; Woman; Divorce.*

FAMINE AND DROUGHT

Extreme shortage of food and an excessive dryness of land caused by lack of rain. Drought was the most common cause of famines in the Bible (Gen. 12:10; 26:1; 41:27; Ruth 1:1; 2 Sam. 21:1; 1 Kings 18:2; 2 Kings 4:38; Neh. 5:3; Hag. 1:11). Prophets predicted the coming of droughts and famines (2 Kings 8:1; Isa. 3:1; Jer. 14:12; Acts 11:28). Other natural forces also caused famines: locusts, wind, hail, and mildew (Joel 1:4; Amos 4:9; Hag. 2:17). Enemy oppressors destroyed or confiscated food (Deut. 28:33,51; Isa. 1:7). The siege of cities resulted in famine (2 Kings 6:24-25; 25:2-3). Famines often lasted for years (Gen. 12:10; 41:27; Jer. 14:1-6). During famines, starving people resorted to eating such things as wild vines, heads of animals, garbage, dung, and even human flesh (2 Kings 4:39; 6:25,28; Lam. 4:4-10).

God created the world as a good environment that would normally provide ample water and food for humankind (Gen. 1). The sins of Adam, Eve, and Cain resulted in unfruitfulness of the earth (Gen. 3:17-18; 4:12). When the people obeyed God, the land was productive (Deut. 11:11-14); when they disobeyed, judgment came on the land by drought and famine (Lev. 26:23-26; Deut. 11:16-17; 1 Kings 8:35). Some famines and droughts are the judgment of God (2 Sam. 21:1; 1 Kings 17:1; 2 Kings 8:1; Jer. 14:12; Ezek. 5:12; Amos 4:6), but not all such disasters are connected to divine punishment (Gen. 12:10; 26:1; Ruth 1:1; Acts 11:28). The NT reports that famine will be a part of God's coming judgment of the earth in the last days (Matt. 24:7; Rev. 6:8).

When God sent drought and famine on His people, He sought to bring them to repentance (1 Kings 8:35-36;

Hos. 2:8-23; Amos 4:6-8). God promises that He will protect His faithful ones in times of famine (Job 5:20,22; Pss. 33:18-19; 37:18-19; Prov. 10:3). See *Water.*

FARMER See *Occupations and Professions; Agriculture.*

FASHION

The practice of using clothing to make a statement regarding one's status or position in society was just as prevalent in the biblical world as it is today. However, clothing styles did not change as rapidly in antiquity and so the effort to remain stylish was less hectic.

The exact meanings of many technical terms in the Bible describing specific articles of clothing and accessories remain lost; other terms are more clear. The basic wardrobe in biblical times included a long shirt-like undergarment (the tunic — e.g., John 19:23), an outergarment that could be decorated according to one's status (the robe — e.g., 1 Sam. 18:4), various girdles (loincloths, belts and sashes — e.g., Matt. 3:4; Rev. 1:13), headgear (e.g., 2 Sam. 15:30; Zech. 3:5), footwear (e.g., Ezek. 24:17) and jewelry (e.g., Ex. 32:2; Judg. 8:24-26).

Fine clothing was worn by kings and priests (Ex. 28:1-43; 39:1-31; Matt. 11:8) or others worthy of status (Gen. 37:3; Luke 15:22). Such clothing was a valued commodity (compare Josh. 7:21) and made a precious gift (Gen. 45:22; 2 Kings 5:5; Esther 6:8) but could lead to showiness (Isa. 3:18-26). Believers are instead instructed to clothe themselves modestly so that their true, inward beauty might prevail (1 Tim. 2:9; 1 Pet. 3:3-5).

The outward adornment of clothing was used by the biblical writers to signal the inner spiritual nature of God's people. Once elegantly adorned (Ezek. 16:10-14), Israel sinned and became dressed in filthy rags (Isa. 64:6; Zech. 3:3-4; compare Rev. 3:4). Those who become righteous are clothed in fine white robes (Zech. 3:4-5; Rev. 3:4-5; 7:9,13).

FASTING

Refraining from eating food to know the mind of God, mourn, and/or careless sins (Ezra 8:23; Ps. 69:10; Isa. 58; Zech. 7:5; Joel 2:12).The Bible describes three main forms of fasting:

(1) the normal fast, involving total abstinence from food but not from water (Luke 4:2);

(2) abstinence from both food and water for no more than three days (Ezra 10:6; Esther 4:16; see Acts 9:9);

(3) restriction of diet rather than complete abstinence (Dan. 10:3).

Fasting is to be done as an act before God in the privacy of one's own pursuit of God (Ex. 34:28; 1 Sam. 7:6; 1 Kings 19:8; Matt. 6:17). The early church often fasted in seeking God's will for leadership in the local church (Acts 13:2).

FATE

That which must necessarily happen. The OT speaks of death as the common fate of humankind (Pss. 49:12; 81:15; Eccl. 2:14; 3:19; 9:2-3) and violent death as the destiny of the wicked (Job 15:22; Isa. 65:12; Hos. 9:13). See *Election; Predestination; Providence.*

FATHER See *Family; God.*

FATHERLESS

Person without a male parent, often rendered "orphan" by modern translations; social misfits without one to provide for their material needs and represent their interests in the court (Job 31:21; often mentioned with widows as representatives of the most helpless members of society (Ex. 22:22; Deut. 10:18; Ps. 146:9). Orphans were often forced to beg for food (Ps. 109:9-10).They suffered loss of their homes (Ps. 109:10), land rights (Prov. 23:10), and livestock (Job 24:3). The fatherless were subject to acts of violence (Job 22:9), were treated as property to be gambled for (6:27, TEV, NRSV, NASB, NIV), and were even murdered (Ps. 94:6).

God, however, has a special concern for orphans and widows (Deut. 10:18; Pss. 10:14-18; 146:9; Hos. 14:3), evidenced in the title "a father of the fatherless" (Ps. 68:5). Old Testament Law provided for the material needs of orphans and widows who were to be fed from the third year's tithe (Deut. 14:28-29; 26:12-13), from sheaves left forgotten in the fields (24:19), and from fruit God commanded to be left on the trees and vines (24:20-21). Orphans and widows were to be included in the celebrations of the worshiping community (Deut. 16:11,14). God's people were repeatedly warned not to take advantage of orphans and widows (Ex. 22:22; Deut. 24:17; 27:19; Ps. 82:3; Isa. 1:17). In the NT James defined worship acceptable to God as meeting the needs of orphans and widows (1:27).

FATHER'S HOUSE

Name given to extended family units in the Ancient Near East reflecting a social organization in which a dominant male headed the family. A father's house could designate the clans within a tribe (Ex. 6:14-25) or even an entire tribe (Josh. 22:14). "House of Jacob" (Ex. 19:3; Amos 3:13), "house of Israel" (Ex. 40:38), and "house of Isaac" (Amos 7:16) all refer to the nation *Israel* in terms of a father's house.

In John 2:16, "my father's house" designates the temple that was then equated with Christ's body (2:21).The reference to "my Father's house" with its many dwelling places (14:2) can be explained in two ways. *House* can be understood as a place or as a set of relationships: a household. Already in the psalms, the temple is the house of God where the righteous hope to dwell (23:6; 27:4). It is a short step to the idea of heaven as God's dwelling where there is ample room for the disciples. If *house* is understood as household, the focus is on fellowship with God. In contrast to servants, a son abides in his father's house (John 8:35).

FATHOM

Measure of depth equaling six feet (Acts 27:28). See *Weights and Measures*.

FEAR

Natural feeling of alarm caused by expectation of imminent danger, pain, or disaster; awe and reverence toward a supreme power. Secular fear rises in the normal activities and relationships of life with animals (Gen. 9:2; Amos 3:8); other people (Gen. 26:7); nations (2 Sam. 10:19); wars (Ex. 14:10); enemies (Deut. 2:4); subjugation (Deut. 7:18; 28:10); death (Gen. 32:11); disaster (Zeph. 3:15-16); sudden panic (Prov. 3:25); adversity (Job 6:21), and the unknown (Gen. 19:30). Fear can reflect the limitations of life (Eccl. 12:5) as well as the unforeseen consequences of actions (1 Sam. 3:15).Fear may come from a strong realization of sin and disobedience (Gen. 3:10; 20:8-9). Sin creates estrangement and guilt leading to fear of the day of the Lord (Joel 2:1).

Fear can be regard the young owes to the aged (Job 32:6), honor a child demonstrates toward parents (Lev. 19:3), reverential respect of individuals toward their masters (1 Pet. 2:18) and to persons in positions of responsibility (Rom. 13:7). Fear also can be the sense of concern for individuals (2 Cor. 11:3) as well as the respect for one's husband (1 Pet. 3:2).

Freedom from fear comes as individuals trust in the God who protects (Ps. 23:4) and helps them (Isa. 54:14). Perfect love casts out fear (1 John 4:18; compare 2 Tim. 1:7).

Religious fear is the human response to the presence of God. The reality of God's holiness reveals the vast distinction between humans and God, attracting and repelling at once, and overwhelming a person with a sense of awe and fear. The person responds in reverence and worship, confessing sin and seeking God's will (Isa. 6). The Israelites were exhorted to "serve the Lord with fear" (Ps. 2:11).

Yahweh is a "great and terrible God" (Neh. 1:5; compare Ex. 15:11;

Deut. 28:58; Ps. 99:3).The fear of God is not the dread that comes out of fear of punishment; rather, it is the reverential regard and awe that comes out of recognition and submission to the divine.

Fear protected Israel from taking God for granted or from presuming on His grace. Fear called to covenant obedience (Deut. 10:12-13; compare 6:24-25; 10:20; 13:4). Fear becomes a demand that can be learned (Deut. 17:19). Fear of God was required from every judge (Ex. 18:21) and king (2 Sam. 23:3); even the messianic king would live in the fear of the Lord (Isa. 11:2).To fear God was the beginning of wisdom and thus of the pathway to true life (Prov. 1:7; 9:10; 15:33).

"Fear not" is an invitation to confidence and trust. Without religious connotation, "fear not" expresses comfort and encouragement (Gen. 50:21; Ruth 3:11; Ps. 49:16)."Fear not" in a religious context invites one to trust in God (Gen. 15:1; 26:24; Dan. 10:12,19; Luke 1:13,30).

The "God-fearers" were those who were faithful to God and obeyed His commandments (Job 1:1; Pss. 25:14; 33:18). In the NT "God-fearers" became a technical term for uncircumcised Gentiles who worshiped in the Jewish synagogue.

Paul admonished believers to work out their salvation "with fear and trembling" (Phil. 2:12).The early church grew in number as they lived "in the fear of the Lord" (Acts 9:31). The NT church stands in awe and fear in the presence of a holy God, for fear is "the whole duty of man" (Eccl. 12:13).

FEASTS See *Festivals*.

FELIX

Procurator of Judea when Paul visited Jerusalem and was arrested (Acts 23:24). Antonius Felix became procurator in A.D. 52, succeeding Cumanus. He remained in office until A.D. 60, when the emperor Nero recalled him (Acts 24:27). Acts depicts him as a man who hoped Paul would pay him a bribe (Acts 24:26). Contemporary historians Tacitus and Josephus paint Felix as a brutal, incompetent politician who was finally replaced. See *Paul; Rome and the Roman Empire.*

FELLOWSHIP

Bond of common purpose and devotion that binds Christians together and to Christ. *Koinonia* was Paul's favorite word to describe a believer's relationship with the risen Lord and the benefits of salvation that come through Him. On the basis of faith believers have fellowship with the Son (1 Cor. 1:9), share fellowship in the gospel (1 Cor. 9:23; Phil. 1:5), share a fellowship with the Holy Spirit (2 Cor. 13:14), a most important bond for unity in the life of the church (Phil. 2:1-4).

In the Lord's Supper, the cup is "communion of the blood of Christ," and the bread, "communion of the body of Christ" (1 Cor. 10:16). Such "communion" could not be shared with both Christ and other gods or supernatural beings, so believers do not partake in pagan religious meals, where they would share "fellowship" with evil, supernatural forces, or demons (1 Cor. 10:19-21).

Fellowship with Christ issues in fellowship between believers (1 John 1:3,6-7; 1 Cor. 10:16-17; compare 1 Cor. 11:17-21).

Fellowship with the Lord results in sharing His sufferings (Phil. 2:5-8; 3:10; Col. 1:24; compare Rom. 8:17; 2 Cor. 4:7-12; Phil. 3:10-11; Col. 1:24).

Paul used the term *koinonia* to denote financial contributions he was collecting from Gentile believers to take to Jerusalem for relief of the saints who lived there (Rom. 15:26-27; 2 Cor. 8:4; 9:13). Everyone offered what they were able to offer to benefit others: Jewish Christians, their spiritual blessings; Gentile Christians, their material blessings. Such mutual sharing of one's blessings is a clear and profound expression of Christian fellowship. See *Lord's Supper; Holy Spirit.*

FENCED CITY See *Cities and Urban Life; Fortified Cities.*

FERRET

White European polecat (Lev. 11:30, KJV). See *Animals, Gecko.*

FERTILE CRESCENT

Crescent-shaped arc of alluvial land somewhat isolated by geographical barriers on all sides stretching from the tip of the Persian Gulf to southeastern corner of the Mediterranean Sea; site of rise of civilization. The northeast is bordered by the Zagros Mountains, the north by the Taurus and Amanus ranges. On the west lies the Mediterranean Sea, and the concave southern limit is determined by the vast Syro-Arabian Desert. See *Mesopotamia; Palestine.*

FERTILITY CULT

Religions marked by rites that reenact a myth accounting for the orderly change of the seasons and the earth's fruitfulness. Such myths often involve a great mother-goddess as a symbol of fertility and a male deity, usually her consort but sometimes a son, who like vegetation dies and returns to life again. In Mesopotamia, the divine couple was Ishtar and Tammuz (mourned in Ezek. 8:14); in Egypt, Isis and her son Osiris; in Asia Minor, Cybele and Attis. In Syria, the Ugaritic myths (from before 1200 B.C.) pictured Baal-Hadad, the storm god, as the dying and rising god (compare Zech. 12:11). See *Canaan, History and Religion of.*

Fertility cults attribute the fertility of the cropland and herds to the sexual relations of the divine couple. Sacral sexual intercourse by priests and priestesses or by cult prostitutes was an act of worship or imitative magic intended to emulate the gods and share in their powers of procreation to preserve the earth's fertility (1 Kings 14:23; 15:12; Hos. 4:14). Sacrifices of produce, livestock, and even children (2 Kings 17:31; 23:10) represented giving the god what was most precious in life in an attempt to restore order to the cosmos and ensure fertility. Elijah's struggle with the priests of Baal and Asherah at Mount Carmel is the best-known conflict between worship of Yahweh and a fertility cult (1 Kings 18:17-40).

Israel conceived of the earth's fruitfulness in a way quite unlike that of her neighbors. Israel recognized the one God as the One responsible for rain (1 Kings 18), grain, wine, oil, wool, and flax (Hos. 2:8-9). The Israelites' sacred calendar celebrated the same seasons as their neighbors (barley harvests = feast of unleavened bread; wheat harvests = Pentecost; fruit harvests = booths). Yahweh had no consort; thus fertility was not tied to Yahweh's return to life and sexual functioning. Rather, the ability of plants and animals to reproduce their own kind was rooted in creation (Gen. 1:11-12,22,28). The orderly progression of the seasons was not traced to a primordial battle but was rooted in God's promise to Noah (Gen. 8:22). The fertility of the land was ensured not by ritual reenactment of the sacred marriage but by obedience to the demands of the covenant (Deut. 28:1,3-4,11-12).

In the NT, Diana or Artemis of the Ephesians (Acts 19:35) was a many-breasted fertility goddess. Aphrodite was also associated with fertility. Her temple at Corinth was the home of cult prostitutes responsible for the city's reputation of immorality. (Compare 1 Cor. 6:15-20.) See *Diana; Gods, Pagan; Prostitution; Tammuz; Ugarit.*

FESTIVALS

Regular religious celebrations remembering God's great acts of salvation in the history of His people. The week, with its climax on the seventh day, provided the cyclical basis for much of Israel's worship: as the seventh day was observed, so was the seventh month (that contained four of the national festivals), the seventh year, and the fiftieth year (the year of Jubilee), which followed seven cycles each of seven years. The Feast of Unleavened Bread and the Feast of Tabernacles lasted for seven days each. Each began on the fifteenth of the month—at the end of two cycles of weeks and when the moon was full. Pentecost also was celebrated on the fifteenth of the month and began 50 days after the presentation of the firstfruits, the day following seven times seven weeks.

The seventh day of each week, the sabbath, was listed among the festivals (Lev. 23:1-3). It functioned as a reminder of the Lord's rest at the end of the creation week (Gen. 2:3) and also of the deliverance from slavery in Egypt (Deut. 5:12-25). The sabbath day was observed by strict rest from work from sunset until sunset (Ex. 20:8-11; Neh. 13:15-22). Each person was to remain in place and not engage in travel (Ex. 16:29; Lev. 23:3). Despite such restrictions even as kindling fires (Ex. 35:3) or any work (Ex. 31:14; 35:2), the sabbath was a joyful time (Isa. 58:13-14). See *Sabbath.*

The new moon festival was a monthly celebration characterized by special offerings, great in quantity and quality (Num. 28:11-15), and blowing of trumpets (Num. 10:10; Ps. 81:3). Business ceased (Amos 8:5). New moon and sabbath are often mentioned together (Isa. 1:13; 66:23; Ezek. 45:17; 46:1,3). This festival provided the occasion for King Saul to stage a state banquet and for David's family to offer a special annual sacrifice (1 Sam. 20:5,6,24,29). David's arrangements for the Levites included service on the new moon (1 Chron. 23:31), and the ministry of the prophets was sometimes connected with this occasion (2 Kings 4:23; Isa. 1:13; Ezek. 46:1; Hag.1:1). The new moon of the seventh month apparently received special attention (Lev. 23:24; Num. 29:1-6; Ezra 3:6; Neh. 8:2). New moon festivals were only a shadow of better things to come (Col. 2:16-17; compare Isa. 66:23).

Three annual festivals required the appearance of all males at the sanctuary (Ex. 34:23; Deut. 16:16). During these "feasts to the Lord" (Ex. 12:14; Lev. 23:39,41), free-will offerings were made (Deut. 16:16-17).

The first annual festival—on the fourteenth day (at evening) of the first month (Lev. 23:5)—was Passover, commemorating the final plague on Egypt (Ex. 12:11,21,27,43,48). The uncircumcised and the hired servant were not permitted to eat the sacrifice (Ex. 12:45-49). The Passover was also called the Feast of Unleavened Bread (Ex. 23:15; Deut. 16:16) because only unleavened bread was eaten during the seven days immediately following Passover (Ex. 12:15-20; 13:6-8; Deut. 16:3-8). Unleavened bread was apparently connected to the barley harvest (Lev. 23:4-14). See Josh. 5:10-12; 2 Chron. 30:1,3,13,15 (Hezekiah); and 2 Kings 23:21-23 (Josiah's unique Passover).

During NT times, large crowds gathered in Jerusalem for Passover. Jesus was crucified during the Passover event. He and His disciples ate a Passover meal together on the eve of His death, initiating the Lord's Supper (Luke 22:7,19-20). The NT identifies Christ with the Passover sacrifice (1 Cor. 5:7).

The second annual festival was Pentecost or the Feast of Weeks (Ex. 34:22; Deut. 16:10,16; 2 Chron. 8:13), the Feast of Harvest (Ex. 23:16), and the Day of Firstfruits (Num. 28:26; compare Ex. 23:16; 34:22; Lev. 23:17), celebrated seven weeks, or 50 days, after Passover (Lev. 23:15,16; Deut. 16:9). Celebrating the wheat harvest, Israel praised the Lord as the source of rain and fertility (Jer. 5:24). At this time, people began to bring offerings of firstfruits. It was celebrated as a sabbath with rest from ordinary labors and the calling of a holy convocation (Lev. 23:10-22; Num. 28:26-31). Two lambs were offered. The feast was concluded by the eating of communal meals to which the poor, the stranger, and the Levites were invited. Later tradition associated the Feast of Weeks with the giving of the law at Sinai. In the NT, the Holy Spirit came upon the disciples at Pentecost (Acts 2:1-4).

The Day of Atonement, the third annual festival, came on the tenth day of the seventh month (Tishri–Sept./Oct.) and the fifth day before the feast of tabernacles (Lev. 16:1-34; Num. 29:7-11). Four main elements (Lev. 23:27-32) comprise this most significant feast: a "holy convocation,""humbling their souls" (later explained as fasting and repentance), offerings (Lev. 16; Num. 29:7-11); and the prohibition of labor. See Day of Atonement. According to Heb. 9–10, this ritual is a symbol of the atoning work of Christ, our great High Priest, who did not need to make any sacrifice for Himself but shed His own blood once for all for our sins. Jesus entered heaven itself to appear on our behalf in front of the Father (Heb. 9:11-12).

The fourth annual festival was the Feast of Tabernacles (2 Chron. 8:13; Ezra 3:4; Zech. 14:16), also called the Feast of Ingathering (Ex. 23:16; 34:22), the feast to the Lord (Lev. 23:39; Judg. 21:19), and sometimes simply, "the feast" (1 Kings 8:2; 2 Chron. 5:3; 7:8; Neh. 8:14; Isa. 30:29; Ezek. 45:23,25). Its observance combined the ingathering of the labor of the field (Ex. 23:16), the fruit of the earth (Lev. 23:39), the ingathering of the threshing floor and winepress (Deut. 16:13), and the dwelling in booths (or"tabernacles"), which were to be joyful reminders to Israel (Lev. 23:41; Deut. 16:14). The "booth" in Scripture is not an image of privation and misery; instead it symbolizes protection, preservation, and shelter from heat or storm (Pss. 27:5; 31:20; Isa. 4:6). The rejoicing community included family, servants, widows, orphans, Levites, and sojourners (Deut. 16:13-15).

The seven-day feast began on the fifteenth day of Tishri, the seventh month, five days after the Day of Atonement (Lev. 23:36; Deut. 16:13; Ezek. 45:25). On the first day, booths were constructed from fresh branches of trees (Neh. 8:13-18). Every Israelite was to live in these during the festival to commemorate their fathers living in such booths after the exodus (Lev. 23:40; Neh. 8:15). The dedication of Solomon's temple took place at the feast (1 Kings 8:2). Later additions to the ritual included a libation of water drawn from the pool of Siloam (the probable background for Jesus' comments on "living water," John 7:37-39) and the lighting of huge menorahs (candelabra) at the Court of the Women (the probable background for Jesus' statement, "I am the light of the world," John 8:12).

Modern Rosh Hashanah or Jewish New Year is traced back to the so-called Feast of Trumpets, the sounding of the trumpets on the first day of the seventh month (Tishri) (Lev. 23:24-27; Num. 29:1).

Purim, commemorating deliverance of the Jews from genocide through the efforts of Esther (Esther 9:16-32), derives its name from the "lot" (pur) Haman planned to cast in deciding when he should carry into effect the king's decree for the extermination of the Jews (Esther 9:24). It was celebrated on the fourteenth day of Adar (March) by those in villages and unwalled towns and on the fifteenth day by those in fortified cities (Esther 9:18-19).

The other postexilic holiday was Hanukkah, a festival that began on the twenty-fifth day of Kislev (Dec.) and lasted eight days. Josephus referred to it as the Feast of Lights because a candle was lighted on eight successive days. The festival commemorates the victories of Judas Maccabeus in 167 B.C. and the reinstitution of temple worship after an interruption of three years. John 10:22 calls this feast the feast of dedication.

Each seventh year Israel celebrated a sabbath year for its fields. This involved a rest for the land from all cultivation (Ex. 23:10-11; Lev. 25:2-7; Deut. 15:1-11; 31:10-13). Other names for this festival were "sabbath of rest" (Lev. 25:4), "year of rest" (Lev. 25:5), "year of release" (Deut. 15:9), and "the seventh year" (Deut. 15:9). The sabbatic year, like the year of Jubilee, began on the first day of the month of Tishri (1 Macc. 6:49, 53). Debts were released for all persons, with the exception of foreigners (Deut. 15:1-4). No one was to oppress a poor man. At the Feast of Tabernacles, the law was to be read to the people (Deut. 31:10-13).

The year of Jubilee was also called the "year of liberty" (Lev. 25; Ezek. 46:17). After seven sabbaths of years (49 years), the trumpet was to sound throughout the land; and the year of Jubilee was to be announced (Lev. 25:8-9). The Jubilee year included:

(1) rest for the soil—no sowing, reaping, or gathering from the vine (Lev. 25:11);

(2) reversion of landed property (Lev. 25:10-34; 27:16-24). All property in fields and houses located in villages or unwalled towns that the owner had been forced to sell through poverty and that had not been redeemed was to revert without payment to its original owner or his lawful heirs (exceptions to this are noted in Lev. 25:29-30; 27:17-21);

(3) redemption of slaves. Every Israelite, who through poverty had sold himself to another Israelite or to a foreigner settled in the land and had not been able to redeem himself or had not been redeemed by a kinsman, was to go free with his children (Lev. 25:39-41). The year of Jubilee became a season of the celebration of freedom and grace. See Num. 36:4; Ezek. 46:17. Such laws illuminate the conduct of Naboth and Ahab (1 Kings 21:3-29) and prophetic rebukes (Isa. 5:8; Mic. 2:2).

FESTUS

Successor of Felix as procurator of Judea (Acts 24:27); appointed by Nero in A.D. 60; died in A.D. 62. Paul appealed to Porcius Festus for a trial. See *Paul; Herod; Rome and the Roman Empire.*

FIG, FIG TREE See *Plants.*

FINANCIAL PLANNING

The Bible provides examples of both effective and ineffective financial planning in the face of economic adversity.

Examples of good financial planning include Joseph's preparation for famine in Egypt (Gen. 41:34-36), the servants who wisely invested their master's money (Luke 19:13-19) and the Corinthian believers who laid aside money to help others (1 Cor. 16:1-2; compare 2 Cor. 9:1-5). Proverbs 27:23-27 counsels a shepherd to know well the condition of his flocks so that they will provide for him in the future. Diversification of investments is advised in Ecclesiastes 11:2.

Poor financial planning can be seen in the man who built bigger barns without thought of his impending death (Luke 12:16-21), the man who started to build a tower without the money to complete it (Luke 14:28-30) and the servant who refused to invest his master's money (Luke 19:20-21).

The Bible recognizes that having sound plans helps ensure a successful venture (Prov. 6:6-8; 21:5; 27:23-27; 30:25; Isa. 32:8; 2 Cor. 9:5). A key element in planning is the wise counsel of others (Prov. 13:18; 20:18), especially God, who causes plans to succeed or fail (Ps. 32:8; Prov. 3:6; 16:1-4, 9; Isa. 29:15).

FINANCIAL RESPONSIBILITY

Two maxims underlie the Bible's principles of financial responsibility: the earth and its resources belong to God (Lev. 25:23; Job 41:11; Pss. 24:1; 89:11; Hag. 2:8), and they have been entrusted to people to use wisely (Gen. 1:29-30; 9:1-4).

The overall message of the Bible regarding finances is one of personal thrift combined with generosity toward others. The Bible places a high value on saving money to provide for oneself and others in times of need (Gen. 41:1-57; Prov. 6:6-8; 21:20; Eccl. 11:2; Luke 12:16-21; 1 Cor. 16:2). Because God blesses those who give to others (Deut. 15:10; Ps. 112:5; Prov. 11:25; 22:9; Mal. 3:10; 2 Cor. 9:6-12), the willingness to give generously (Matt. 25:31-46; 2 Cor. 8:3) and without thought of return (Deut. 15:11; 23:19; Ps. 15:5; Matt. 5:42; Luke 6:34; Rom. 11:35) is considered a mark of financial responsibility. Those who save to provide only for themselves, or are unable to save because of extravagant spending, are held to be foolish (Job 20:20-22; Prov. 21:20).

Other marks of financial responsibility include careful financial planning (Prov. 27:23-27), hard work (Prov. 28:19; Eph. 4:28; 2 Thess. 3:10; compare Prov. 24:33-34), diversification of investments (Eccl. 11:2), paying debts when they become due (Prov. 3:27-28), providing for one's family (1 Tim. 5:8), and leaving an inheritance to one's children (Num. 27:7-11; Prov. 13:22; compare Ruth 4:6; Eccl. 5:13-14).

Jesus' stewardship parables speak of financial responsibility as a precursor of greater areas of responsibility in the kingdom of God (Matt. 25:14-30; Luke 16:1-13; 19:11-27).

FIRE

Product of burning that produces heat, light, and flame; invention of fire antedates history. Fire has been from early times the object of worship, often involving child sacrifice as with Israel's neighbors (Lev. 18:21; Deut. 12:31; 2 Chron. 28:3).

God often used fire as an instrument of His power (Gen. 15:17; Ex. 3:2; 13:21-22; 19:18; 24:17; compare Acts 2:3; Rev. 1:14; 2:18). Fire often symbolizes God's holiness and His anger against sin (Isa. 10:17; Heb. 12:29). God uses the fire of experience to test us (Job 23:10). All earthly works will be tested "as by fire" (1 Cor. 3:12-15). The final destiny of God's enemies is the lake of fire (Rev. 19:20; 20:10; compare 2 Pet. 3:7-12).

Fire was to be continually burning on the altar as a visible sign of the continuous worship of God. Fire used for sacred purposes but obtained other than from the altar was "strange fire" (Lev. 10:1-2).

Fire also symbolized God's victories over all enemies (Obad. 18); the Word of God (Jer. 5:14); the Holy Spirit (Isa. 4:4; Acts 2:3); the zeal of the saints (Pss. 39:3; 119:139); angels (Heb. 1:7); lust (Prov. 6:27-28); wickedness (Isa. 9:18); the tongue (Jas. 3:6); and judgment (Jer. 48:45). See *Baptism of Fire; Molech.*

FIREPAN

Bronze (Ex. 27:3) or gold utensil (1 Kings 7:50 KJV, "censers") used to carry live coals from the altar of burnt offering (Ex. 27:3; 38:3), as censers for burning incense (Num. 16:6,17), and as trays for collecting the burnt wicks from the tabernacle lamps (Ex. 25:38; 37:23; KJV, "snuffdishes").

FIRKIN See *Weights and Measures.*

FIRMAMENT

Bright, transport vault or expanse of sky that separates the upper and lower waters (Gen. 1:6-7). One use of "heaven" in the Bible is to refer to the ceiling or canopy of the earth. Heaven in this sense is also referred to as the firmament or sky (Gen. 1:8). Into this expanse God set the sun, moon, and stars (Gen. 1:14-18). It reveals God's handiwork (Pss. 19:1; 150:1; Ezek. 1:22; Dan. 12:3).

The Hebrews visualized the firmament as a rigid, solid dome—a celestial dam for the heavenly waters (Gen. 7:11; 2 Sam. 22:8; Job 26:8; 37:18; Prov. 8:28; Mal. 3:10) punctuated by grilles or sluices, "windows of heaven," through which rain was released. See *Heaven.*

FIRSTBORN

First son born to a couple and required to be specially dedicated to God; represented the prime of human vigor (Gen. 49:3; Ps. 78:51). Every firstborn of Israel, both man and beast, belonged to Yahweh (Ex. 13:2,15; compare 12:12-16). He was presented to the Lord when he was a month old. The father had to buy back the child from the priest at a redemption price not to exceed five shekels (Num. 18:16).

The birthright of a firstborn included a double portion of the estate and leadership of the family. The eldest son customarily cared for his mother until her death, and he also provided for his sisters until their marriage.

The firstborn of a clean animal was brought into the sanctuary on the eighth day after birth (Ex. 22:30) and sacrificed if it were without blemish (Deut. 15:19; Num. 18:17). Apparently, the firstborn of clean animals were not to be used for any work since they belonged to the Lord (Deut. 15:19).

The firstborn of an unclean animal had to be redeemed by an estimation of the priest, with the addition of one-fifth (Lev. 27:27; Num. 18:15; compare Ex. 13:13; 34:20).

Israel was God's "firstborn" (Ex. 4:22; Jer. 31:9) and enjoyed priority status. Within Israel, the tribe of Levi represented the firstborn of the nation (Num. 3:40-41; 8:18). Christ is the "firstborn" of the Father (Heb. 1:6 NIV) "among many brethren" (Rom. 8:29), "firstborn of all creation" (Col. 1:15 NASB), and "firstborn from the dead" (Col. 1:18; Rev. 1:5). See Heb. 12:23. Christian believers, united with and as joint heirs with Christ, enjoy the status of "firstborn" in God's household.

FIRSTFRUITS

Choice examples of a crop harvested first and dedicated to God (Ex. 23:19; 34:26), including grain, wine, and oil, which were used — except for the grain (Lev. 2:14-16)—for the support of the priests (Num. 18:12; Deut. 18:4; compare Deut. 26:1-11; Prov. 3:9). The first sheaf of the new crop of barley was presented as a wave offering before the Lord (Lev. 23:9-14) to acknowledge that all came from God and belonged to Him (Num. 28:26; compare Ex. 23:16; 34:22).

Israel was described as God's "firstfruits" (Jer. 2:3). Christ in His resurrection is the "firstfruits" of those who sleep (1 Cor. 15:20,23). The Holy Spirit is spoken of as "firstfruits" (Rom. 8:23), and believers are also spoken of as "a kind of firstfruits" (Jas. 1:18). The saved remnant within Israel is described as "firstfruits" (Rom. 11:16), as are the 144,000 of the tribulation period (Rev. 14:4). The first converts of an area were designated "firstfruits" (Rom. 16:5; 1 Cor. 16:15).

FISH, FISHING

Animals living in water and breathing through gills; the profession and/or practice of catching fish to supply a family or society's need for food. Fish abounded in the inland waters of Palestine, as well as in the Mediterranean.

Fish were a favorite food and a chief source of protein (Num. 11:5; Neh. 13:16). The primary method of preparing fish was broiling (John 21:9). The law regarded all fish with fins and scales as clean. Water animals that did not have fins and scales were unclean (Lev. 11:9-12). Methods of catching fish included angling with a hook (Job 41:1), harpoons and spears (Job 41:7), use of dragnets (John 21:8), and thrown hand nets (Matt. 4:18). The fish were preserved in salt and brought to Jerusalem where they were sold at a specially named "Fish Gate" in the city.

The Israelites depended largely on foreign trade for their fish (Neh. 13:16). Song of Solomon 7:4 and Isa. 19:10 speak of fishpools and fish ponds, possibly an indication of commercially raised fish or of fish farming.

During NT times, commercial fishing businesses were conducted on the Sea of Galilee by fishermen organized in guilds (Luke 5:7,11; compare John 18:10). They owned their ships, took hirelings into their service, and sometimes formed companies (Mark 1:20; Luke 5:7).

Human helplessness is compared to fish taken in a net (Eccl. 9:12; Hab. 1:14); also a symbol of God's judgment (Ps. 66:11; Ezek. 32:3). Jesus called disciples to be fishers of men (Matt. 4:18-19) and compared the kingdom of heaven to a fish net with many varieties (Matt. 13:47).

FISHHOOK

Curved or bent device of bone or iron used for catching or holding fish (Job 41:1-2; Isa. 19:8; KJV, "angle"; Matt. 17:27). Habakkuk described God's people as helpless fish who would be captured by hooks (1:15) and nets. Amos 4:2 refers to the practice of ancient conquerors of leading captives with hooks through their lips. Compare 2 Chron. 33:11 (NASB, NIV, TEV).

FLAGON

Large, two-handled jar for storing wine (Isa. 22:24, KJV; Ex. 25:29; 37:16; REB, NRSV); cake of raisins, often used as offerings to idols (2 Sam. 6:19; 1 Chron. 16:3; Song of Sol. 2:5; Hos. 3:1, KJV).

FLAX

Plant (Linum usitatissimumro) used to make linen; cultivated by Egyptians before the exodus (Ex. 9:31) and by Canaanites before conquest (Josh. 2:6). Making linen was a common household chore (Prov. 31:13).

FLESH

Skin and/or meat of animals and humans used to represent human dedication to physical desires rather than to obedience to God. Flesh often refers to the muscular part of the body of humans (Gen. 2:21; Job 10:11) and animals (Deut. 14:8; 1 Cor. 15:39). Even dead, a person is still called flesh (1 Sam. 17:44) until body returns as dust to the earth (Eccl. 12:7).

Humans use flesh of animals for food (Gen. 9:3-4; 1 Sam. 2:13,15), while human flesh may be eaten by animals (Gen. 40:19; Rev. 19:17-18). The flesh of animals was used for sacrifice (Ex. 29:31).

"Flesh" can denote the human body in its entirety (Judg. 8:7; 1 Kings 21:27; Eph. 5:29; Heb. 9:13) or a part, especially when referring to the sexual organs (Gen. 17:14; Gal. 6:13; Eph. 2:11; Phil. 3:3; Col. 2:13; compare Lev. 15:2-3,7,19). "All flesh" refers to all of humanity (Joel 2:28; Matt. 24:22; Rom. 3:20; Gal. 2:16) or the human and animal creation (Gen. 6:13,17; 7:16; Lev. 17:14). "Bone of my bones, and flesh of my flesh" (Gen. 2:23; compare 29:14) denotes a kinship between Adam and Eve, who became one flesh (Gen. 2:24; Matt. 19:5; 1 Cor. 6:16; Eph. 5:31).

Paul spoke of his sufferings for Christ as his "flesh" suffering (Col. 1:24). "Flesh" is the created and natural humanity, not automatically sinful, but weak, limited, and temporal and so vulnerable to sin (Gen. 3:5; Matt. 26:41; Mark 14:38).

Those who follow the impulses of the flesh live "after the flesh" (Rom. 8:5). They yield to sinful passions and produce works contrary to God and His law (Rom. 8:5-7; Gal. 5:16-17, 19-21,23-24; compare 1 John 2:16; 1 Pet. 4:2; 2 Pet. 2:10). The fleshly person is unable to discern God's revelation of Himself (Matt. 16:17; Gal. 1:13-24). The flesh serves as a base of operation for sin (Rom. 7:8,11) and thus enslaves a person to sin (Rom. 6:15-23; 7:25). Flesh-driven people are the children of wrath (Eph. 2:3). They cannot inherit the kingdom of God (1 Cor. 6:9-10; Gal. 5:19-21; Eph. 2:11-12; 5:5).

Christ became a flesh-and-blood person (John 1:14; Rom. 8:3; Heb. 4:15) to redeem those in sinful flesh. He did not give in to the desires of the flesh. Believers remain physically "in" the flesh but do not live "according to" the flesh (Gal. 2:20; Phil. 1:22-24), being not in the flesh but in the Spirit (Rom. 8:6-17; Gal. 5:24). See *Body; Image of God.*

FLESH AND SPIRIT

Material substance and immaterial substance. "Flesh" is not an evil concept but a part of the artistry and design of God (Gen. 2:21), part of what God saw as "very good" (Gen. 1:31). Genesis 2:24 suggests the man and his wife would become "one flesh," apparently indicating sexual as well as psychological union.

Still, the Bible frequently contrasts flesh with spirit. Once our first parents had sinned, all subsequent offspring were born with a tendency toward evil that manifests itself particularly in the flesh (Mark 14:38). We are not to fulfill "the lust of the flesh" (1 John 2:16) since "the flesh lusteth against the Spirit" (Gal. 5:17). The walk of obedience to the Holy Spirit, enshrined in the human spirit of

twice-born men, is the only way to avoid allowing the flesh to rule (Gal 5:16). The flesh should never rule the spiritual life of humans. The flesh must be subjugated and made useful to the spiritual purposes and goals of humanity.

Some Christians are carnal Christians (1 Cor. 3:1; compare Rom. 8:7); meaning that while they have been saved, they nevertheless are ruled more by their fleshly desires than by the Spirit. See *Anthropology; Flesh; Spirit.*

FLESH HOOK

Large fork used for handling large pieces of meat, especially at the sacrificial altar. Those in the tabernacle were of brass (Ex. 27:3;38:3); those in the temple of bronze (2 Chron. 4:16) or gold (1 Chron. 28:17).

FLESH POT

Kettle used for cooking meat (Ex. 16:3).

FLOGGING

Punishment by repeated lashes or blows of a whip or rod(s), limited in Bible to 40 blows (Deut. 25:1-3) so that the neighbor who was punished would not be degraded. Children were disciplined with rods (Prov. 23:13-14). Floggings were sometimes inflicted unjustly (Prov. 17:26; Isa. 53:5). Jesus warned His disciples that they would face floggings (Matt. 10:17; beatings, Mark 13:9; compare Acts 5:40; 16:22-23; 2 Cor. 11:24-25). Saul had believers flogged when he persecuted the church (Acts 22:19-20).

FLOOD

Miraculous deluge of water God used to discipline His world made evil through human sin. God is morally outraged by humanity's perversity. His gracious will is to save those in the ark.

God resolved to destroy all living beings (Gen. 6:13) with the exception of righteous Noah and his family (6:9,18). God instructed Noah to make an ark and take his family and seven pairs of every clean species and two of every unclean species of animals, birds, and creeping things, along with provisions for the duration of the flood (6:18-21; 7:1-3). Forty days and and nights of rain covered the earth and destroyed every living creature (7:21-23). Emerging after a year and 10 days, Noah built an altar and sacrificed to God (8:14-20). God blessed Noah and made a covenant that He would never again destroy the earth by flood (8:21; 9:11). He gave the rainbow as a visible sign of that covenant (9:12-17).

The flood demonstrates God's hatred of sin; His patience in dealing with sin; His grace in sparing one family; and His rule over nature and humanity.

FLOUR

Fine-crushed and sifted grain used in making bread (Ex. 29:2; 1 Sam. 28:24). Typically meal, ground course from the whole kernels of grain together with the bran, was used to make bread (Lev. 2:16; 1 Kings 17:12). Most often cereal offerings were of fine flour (Lev. 2:1-2,4-5,7), ground only from the inner kernels of wheat, the best part of the grain (Deut. 32:14). Fine flour was a luxury item (2 Kings 7:1; Ezek. 16:13; Rev. 18:13) such as might be baked as bread for an honored guest (Gen. 18:6; 1 Sam. 28:24).

FLOWERS

Colorful blooms containing a plant's reproductive organs. Flowers grew abundantly in open fields, in crop fields, and in groves of trees around houses during springtime in Palestine. Numerous kinds of wild flowers could be found in the plains and mountains of Palestine. The words "flower" and "flowers" refer to:

(a) colorful blossoms,
(b) towering plants,
(c) open flowers, and
(d) flourishing flowers.

(1) *Almond blossoms* (Gen. 43:11; Ex. 25:33-34; 37:19-20; Num. 17:8; Eccl.

12:5). This tree, a member of the rose family, had beautiful pink blossoms that the Israelites used as models for engravers to adorn the cups of the golden lampstand.

(2) *Bulrush* (Ex. 2:3; Job 8:11; Isa. 18:2; 35:7). Sometimes referred to as "flag," "papyrus" (NIV), "reed" (NASB), or "rush" (NEB). This tall, slender, reedlike plant grew along banks of the Nile River and provided earliest known material for making paper and covering the frames of boats (Isa. 18:2).

(3) *Calamus leaves* (Ex. 30:23; Song of Sol. 4:14; Isa. 43:24; Jer. 6:20; Ezek. 27:19). Sweet- smelling cane or ginger grass apparently imported from India for use in worship (Jer. 6:20). The leaves, when crushed, gave a much-relished ginger smell. The giant reed *Arundo donax* may be meant in 1 Kings 14:15. Compare Job 40:21; Isa. 19:6; 35:7.

(4) *Camphire flowers* (Song of Sol. 1:14; 4:13; 7:13; see REB). Small plant or shrub that bore beautiful cream-colored flowers that hung in clusters like grapes and were highly scented; used for orange dye; sometimes referred to as Henna.

(5) *Caperberry flowers* (Eccl. 12:5). Prickly shrub that produced lovely flowers and small, edible berries as it grew in rocks and walls; supposed to stimulate sexual desires and powers. KJV, NRSV, NIV, TEV translate, "desire" but REB and NASB follow recent Hebrew dictionaries in translating "caperberry."

(6) *Cockle flowers* (Job 31:40). Purplish red flowers of noxious weed called "cockle" or "darnel" (*Lolium tenulentum*) that grew abundantly in Palestinian grain fields. Hebrew name is spelled like Hebrew for "stink"; thus NASB, "stinkweed."

(7) *Crocus* (Song of Sol. 2:1; Isa. 35:1). Spring flowering herb with long yellow floral tube tinged with purple specks or stripes; sometimes translated "rose"; probably the asphodel (REB).

(8) *Fitch* (Isa. 28:25-27, KJV). Nutmeg flower; member of buttercup family; grew wildly in most Mediterranean lands; about two feet high

with bright blue flowers. The pods of the plant were used like pepper. Technically the plant is probably dill (NRSV, NASB, REB, NLT, NCV, CEV) or more precisely black cummin (*Nigella sativa*). NIV translates "caraway."

(9) *Leek* (Num. 11:5). Member of lily family; bulbous biennial plant with broad leaves whose bases were eaten; bulbs were used as seasoning. Israel relished the memory of leeks (*Allium porrum*) from Egypt.

(10) *Lily*. Wide range of flowers; most common was *Lilius candidum*. The lily of Song of Solomon 5:13 was rare variety with bloom similar to a glowing flame. The "lily of the valley" (Song of Sol. 2:1-2,16) is the Easter lily. The lily in Hos. 14:5 is more akin to an iris. The beautiful water lily or lotus was a favorite flower in Egypt and was used to decorate Solomon's temple (1 Kings 7:19,22,26; 2 Chron. 4:5). The "lilies of the field" (Matt. 6:28; Luke 12:27) were probably numerous kinds of colorful spring flowers such as the crown anemone.

(11) *Mandrake* (Gen. 30:14-16; Song of Sol. 7:13). Herb of nightshade family. It had rosettes of large leaves and mauve flowers during winter and fragrant and round yellow fruit during spring; grew in fields and rough ground; considered to give sexual powers and probably can be identified as *Atropa Mandragora*, often used for medicine in ancient times.

(12) *Mint* (Matt. 23:23; Luke 11:42). Aromatic plant with hairy leaves and dense white or pink flowers, probably *jucande olens;* used to flavor food. Jews scattered it on floors of houses and synagogues for sweet smell.

(13) *Myrtle branches* (Neh. 8:15; Isa. 41:19; 55:13; Zech. 1:8-11). *Myrtus communis;* grew on Palestinian hillsides; fragrant evergreen leaves and scented white flowers used as perfumes.

(14) *Pomegranate blossoms* (Ex. 28:33; Num. 13:23; 1 Sam. 14:2; 1 Kings 7:18). *Punica granatum;* dark green leaves with large orange-red blossoms. Decorators carved pomegranates on public buildings. The

fruit symbolized fertility and was used to tan leather and for medicine.

(15) *Rose* (Song of Sol. 2:1; Isa. 35:1). Several varieties belonging to crocus family; not modern "rose" but an asphodel. See *Crocus* above.

(16) *Saffron*. Species of crocus (*Curcuma longa* or *Crocus sativas*). Petals were used to perfume banquet halls; type in Song of Solomon 4:14 may be exotic plant imported from India.

The striking manner in which flowers burst into bloom and then withered illustrated the transient nature of human life (Job 14:2; Ps. 103:15; Isa. 40:6; 1 Pet. 1:24). The flowers of spring (Song of Sol. 2:12) signify renewal. The "fading flower" of Isa. 28:1 represented the downfall of God's disobedient people. God's care for the "lilies of the field" (Matt. 6:28) shows God will take care of His children who need not worry uselessly. The phrase "flower of her age" (1 Cor. 7:36) described a girl reaching womanhood. The rich pass away just as quickly as the period of time for blooming flowers passes away (Jas. 1:10-11).

FOOD

Material used for human nourishment; ingested in two meals daily (see Luke 14:12-13). Breakfast was taken informally soon after getting up and normally consisted of a flat bread cake and a piece of cheese, dried fruit, or olives. Men and boys left for work, eating their breakfast as they went. Mother, daughters, and younger children were kept at home. There was no midday meal as such—although a rest may have been taken for a drink and a piece of fruit when Ruth stopped with the reapers to eat parched corn moistened with wine (Ruth 2:14, NRSV).

Women and children prepared the evening meal on the fire; a vegetable or lentil stew was made in the large cooking pot, herbs and salt being used to add to the flavor. Only on special occasions such as a sacrifice or festival day was any meat added to the stew, and only on very rare occasions was the meat roasted or game or fish eaten.

The pot was placed on a rug on the floor (Gen. 18:8), the whole family sitting round. A blessing or thanksgiving was made, and each member of the family used a piece of bread as a scoop to take up some of the contents of the pot because there was no cutlery. Later in history a table and benches sometimes replaced the rug on the ground (1 Kings 13:20), but the communal pot was still at the center. At the close of the meal, fruit would be eaten, and everything washed down with wine.

Formal meals were always preceded by an invitation (which was politely refused as a matter of course). The host then insisted that people come until the invitations were accepted (Luke 14:16-24). When the guests arrived, their feet were washed by the most humble slaves, and their sandals were removed (John 13:3-11). This protected the carpeted floors from dirt as well as making it more comfortable to sit on one's heels. Heads were anointed with olive oil scented with spices (Luke 7:36-50). Drinking water was then provided. In large houses the special guest moved to the "top table" in a room with a raised floor and would sit on the right-hand side of the host. The second guest would sit on the host's left-hand side (see Luke 14:7-11; 20:46).

One did not so much "sit" at table as recline at table. Couches were drawn up to the tables, head towards the table, and cushions provided so that guests could rest on their left arm and use the right to serve themselves from the table. With this arrangement servants could continue to wash the feet (Luke 7:46). To make conversation, persons had to turn almost on their backs and literally be "on the bosom" of the person to the left (John 13:23-25).

The meal started with a drink of wine diluted with honey. The main dinner had three courses, beautifully arranged on trays. Guests ate with their fingers except when soup, eggs, or shellfish were served. Then spoons were used. Finally, there was a dessert of pastry and fruit. During the meal the host provided entertainment of music, dancing (individual, expressive dances), and readings from poetry and other literature. People of humbler means were able to look in from the darkness outside (Luke 7:37).

Food laws had to be observed at all meals (Lev. 11:1-22; Deut. 9:9; see Ex. 23:19).

FOOD OFFERED TO IDOLS

Something given in worship to a god (1 Cor. 10:28); a cause of controversy in the early church centering on what Christians were permitted to eat. Pagan sacrifices typically consisted of three portions: small part used in the sacrificial ritual; larger portion eaten by the priests or other temple personnel; the largest part retained by the worshiper, either as the main course in a meal served at or near the pagan temple or sold in the local meat market.

Participation in a meal near the pagan temple stands behind the Corinthians' question (1 Cor. 7:1; 8:1) to which Paul responded in 1 Cor. 8. Meat sold at the local marketplace and served for a regular family meal is reflected in Paul's comments in 1 Cor. 10:19–11:1.

Jerusalem council listed "what has been sacrificed to idols" as one thing from which even Gentile Christians were expected to abstain (Acts 15:29; compare 21:25; Rom. 14:1-21; Rev. 2:14,20).

FOOL, FOOLISHNESS, AND FOLLY

Unwise and ungodly people. Persons who do not possess wisdom are called "fools"; their behavior is described as "folly." The religious person chooses wisdom, whereas the nonreligious person opts for folly. Wisdom leads to victory; folly to defeat. Wisdom belongs to those who fear God (Prov. 1:7). The foolish person is the one who is thoughtless, self-centered, and obviously indifferent to God.

"Folly" includes: deliberate sinfulness; simple-mindedness; malicious simple-mindedness; and brutal or subhuman activity. The fool may be the one who is aloof. He "foldeth his hands" (Eccl. 4:5) or follows "worthless pursuits" instead of tending to the farm (Prov. 12:11b, NRSV). He denies God exists (Ps. 14:1). Foolish behavior is characterized by an inability to recognize the true character of God (Job 2:10).

The simple-minded fool is encouraged to change (Prov. 9:4-6), but the fool may be the one who is intentionally perverse. Nabal and Saul represent this kind of intentional and malicious folly toward David (1 Sam. 25:25; 26:21).

A certain kind of wisdom can actually be folly. Wisdom based only on human intellect and experiences without considering God is folly (Matt. 7:26; 25:2-3; Rom. 2:20).

Matthew 23:17 equates folly with blindness. Folly includes thoughtlessness, the pursuit of unbridled aspirations, and a lifestyle characterized by envy, greed, and pride. The incarnation is portrayed as "foolishness," but precisely this kind of perceived "foolishness" is better than worldly wisdom (1 Cor. 1–3). Our understanding of this paradoxical relationship affects the manner in which Christ is proclaimed (1 Cor. 1:18–2:5). We must rely on God's gift and power of proclamation, not on human powers and wisdom. Jesus said,"Whosoever shall say,Thou fool, shall be in danger of hell fire" (Matt. 5:22). See *Wisdom and Wise Men.*

FOOT

Part of the human and animal body used for walking; Scripture refers mainly to the human foot (Ex. 12:11; Acts 14:8) but also to feet of animals (Ezek. 1:7) and, anthropomorphically, to God's feet (Isa. 60:13).

In the ancient world with unpaved roads, feet easily became dirty. Hosts offered to wash their guests' feet (Gen. 18:4), usually done by the lowest servant (John 13:3-14). High honor was paid by anointing another's

feet (Deut. 33:24; Luke 7:46; John 12:3).To remove the shoes was a sign of getting rid of dirt and so indicated holiness in worship (Ex. 3:5). To shake the dust off one's feet meant total rejection of that place (Acts 13:51). Punishment might include binding the feet in stocks (Job 13:27; Acts 16:24). Often "feet" symbolized the whole person (Ps. 119:101; compare Luke 1:79; Acts 5:9; Rom. 3:15).

FOOTMAN

Foot soldiers as distinguished from cavalry (2 Sam. 8:4), soldiers in general (1 Sam. 4:10; 15:4), or men of military age (Ex. 12:37); also a runner who served in the honor guard that ran ahead of the king's chariot (1 Sam. 8:11; 2 Sam. 15:1), the king's guards in general (1 Kings 14:27-28; 2 Kings 10:25), and royal couriers (Esther 3:13,15).

FOOTSTOOL

Piece of furniture for resting the feet, especially for one seated on a throne (2 Chron. 9:18; Jas. 2:3); a symbol for dominion. God is pictured as a King enthroned in heaven with the earth as His footstool (Isa. 66:1; Matt. 5:35). In Ps. 99:5 and Lam. 2:1 God's footstool may be the ark, the temple, or Zion. (Compare Isa. 60:13; Ezek. 43:7.) Only 1 Chron. 28:2 is an unambiguous reference to the ark as a resting place for God's feet.

In Ps. 110:1 God makes the messianic King triumph over His enemies, who are then made His footstool. See Acts 2:34-35; Heb. 1:13; 10:13.

FOOTWASHING

Act necessary for comfort and cleanliness for any who have traveled dusty Palestinian roads with feet shod in sandals. Customarily, a host provided guests with water for washing their own feet. (See Judg. 19:21; Luke 7:44.) Footwashing was regarded as so lowly a task that it could not be required of a Hebrew slave. In this context, the statement of John the Baptist that he was not worthy to untie the sandal (to wash the feet) of the One coming after him (Mark 1:7) indicates great humility. The initiative of the woman who was a "sinner" in washing Jesus' feet (Luke 7:37-50) was more than expected hospitality. Hers was an act of great love that evidenced the forgiveness of her sins (7:47).

By washing His disciples' feet (John 13:4-15) Jesus provided an ethical example of humble, loving service (compare Luke 22:27) and the symbollic command to do for each other what Christ had done for them, that is, lay down His life for them (John 15:13). Thus, Jesus calls us to give our lives in extravagant acts of selfless service.

Washing the feet of other Christians was a qualification for service as a "widow" in the early church (1 Tim. 5:10).

FOREHEAD

Part of the face above the eyes. The emblem of holiness was placed on Aaron's forehead (Ex. 28:38). A mark on the foreheads of those in Jerusalem who mourned for the wickedness of Jerusalem spared them from terrible judgment (Ezek. 9:4; contrast Rev. 13:16-17).

A set forehead indicates opposition, defiance, and rebellion (Jer. 3:3). Hardness of the forehead indicates determination to persevere (Isa. 48:4; Ezek. 3:8-9). The harlot's forehead shows no shame (Jer. 3:3). God made Ezekiel's forehead harder than flint against the foreheads of the people, giving him courage (Ezek. 3:9). The foreheads of the righteous were marked (Rev. 7:3; 9:4; 14:1; 22:4). The apocalyptic woman dressed in purple and scarlet had her name written on her forehead (Rev. 17:5). See *Face.*

FOREIGN AID

The Bible furnishes several examples of financial assistance provided by the government or citizens of one country to citizens of another country in times of economic hardship. The best known instance involved the sale of grain by the government of Egypt "to all the earth" during a prolonged famine in the days of Joseph (Gen. 41:57). Perhaps in response to this event, Moses noted that God's blessing to Israel included the conditional promise that Israel would one day be prosperous enough to lend to other nations rather than having to borrow from them (Deut. 15:6; 28:12).

The NT reports that Christians from Antioch, Macedonia, and Achaia provided financial assistance to believers in Judaea and Jerusalem (Acts 11:27-30; Rom. 15:26; 2 Cor. 8:1-7; 9:1-5).

These examples suggest that Christians should be willing to aid persons who live in other countries in times of need, whether through the church or government.

FOREIGNER See *Alien.*

FOREKNOWLEDGE

Awareness and anticipation of events before they occur. God alone has foreknowledge. Nothing is outside of His knowledge—past, present, or future. Only fools think they can hide their deeds from God (Job. 10:11; 11:4-5; Prov. 15:11; Isa. 29:15-16; compare Ps. 139; Matt. 10:29-31; Heb. 4:13).

Events of history are perceived in faith as the unfolding of God's eternal plans (Gen. 45:4-8; Isa. 14:24-27; 42:9; Jer. 50:45). The life, death, and resurrection of Jesus were the outworking of God's eternal plans to save sinful humanity (Rom. 1:2; compare Matt. 1:22-23; 2:5-6,15; John 19:24) not a chance happening of history (Acts 2:23; 1 Pet. 1:20).

God's foreknowledge of people is not primarily a reference to His intellect, but to His kind will by which He sets people apart to Himself (Jer. 1:5; Rom. 8:29-30; Gal. 1:15-16). To affirm God's foreknowledge is a statement of faith—that God's purpose existed before humankind's response to God (Ps. 139:16). God did not reject the Jewish people whom He foreknew (Rom. 11:2).

Such statements raise the difficult theological question of human freedom. If God already knows in advance who will be saved or elected, does that not eliminate free human will? Does God predestine some people to salvation and others to damnation?

James Arminius (1560–1609), as Origen (185–254) before him, argued that God's foreknowledge of salvation means that God knows in advance what a person's response will be. He elects to salvation in advance those whom He knows will freely accept Christ. This Arminian view is called conditional predestination, being conditioned on God's foreknowledge of the individual's acceptance or rejection of Christ.

The Augustine-Luther-Calvin tradition replies that in the Biblical uses of the term "foreknow" with an explicit object, the object is never *what* is known but *whom* (Acts 26:5; Rom. 8:29; 11:2; 1 Pet. 1:20). And when God is its subject the idea is not so much *knowledge* as *purpose* (Acts 2:23; 1 Pet. 1:1-2). In 1 Pet. 1:20 it is Christ who is foreknown, meaning that His redemptive work was planned "before the foundation of the world." Furthermore, faith, although necessary for salvation, is understood to be a gift of God (Eph. 2:8; Phil. 1:29).

First Peter 1:1-2 declares that the Christian readers being persecuted in Asia Minor were secure in their relationship to God because it was dependent solely on God the Father who had chosen them according to His purposes (foreknowledge), the Holy Spirit who had sanctified them, and Jesus Christ who had cleansed them with His blood. Consequently, the Christian's inheritance is "imperishable, uncorrupted, and unfading" since it is kept under guard in heaven (1:4) and since the continuing faith of the believer is guarded by God's power (1:5). See *Knowledge; Election; Predestination.*

FORERUNNER

A military term for advanced scouts or cavalry that prepared for a full assault. The Christian hope of entering God's presence is guaranteed by Christ, the forerunner having already reached this goal (Heb. 6:20). (Compare the idea of Christ as firstfruits of the dead, 1 Cor. 15:20,23.) A similar idea is expressed in the image of Christ as the pioneer of salvation (Heb. 2:10). Having run ahead on the road of suffering, Christ became the source of salvation that makes our following possible (Heb. 5:8-10).

The OT used the common image of advance agents sent ahead of a king to make arrangements for his travel to picture the mission of a prophetic messenger preparing the way for God's coming (Isa. 40:3; Mal. 3:1). The application of these texts to John by the NT writers (Matt. 11:10; Mark 1:2; Luke 1:76; 7:27) affirm that the coming of Jesus is the coming of God.

FORGIVENESS

An act of God's grace to forget forever and not hold people of faith accountable for sins they confess; to a lesser degree the gracious human act of not holding wrong acts against a person. Forgiveness is the gracious act of God by which believers are put into a right relationship to God and transferred from spiritual death to spiritual life through the sacrifice of Jesus. It is also the ongoing gift of God without which our lives as Christians would be "out of joint" and full of guilt. In terms of a human dimension, forgiveness is that act and attitude toward those who have wronged us that restores relationships and fellowship.

Psalm 51 shows the terrible condition of the unforgiven sinner: unclean (vv. 2,7,10), sinful by his very nature (v. 5), grief and sorrow at being separated from God (vv. 8,11,12), and guilt (v. 14). The primary means of obtaining forgiveness in the OT is through the sacrificial system of the covenant relationship, which God established on Sinai. The bringing of the sacrifice showed the sense of need; the laying of hands on the living sacrifice symbolized identification of the person with the sacrifice, as did the releasing of the life of the animal through the sacrificial slaughter. Emphasis on an unblemished sacrifice stressed the holiness of God contrasted with human sinfulness. The forgiveness of God, channeled through the sacrificial offering, was an act of mercy freely bestowed by God, not purchased by the one bringing the offering.

God's demand for a repentant heart as the basis for forgiveness (see Ps. 51) gained its full expression in the prophets (Isa. 1:10-18; Jer. 7:21-26; Hos. 6:6; Amos 5:21-27). The OT sacrificial system could never give once-for-all forgiveness. It had to be repeated over and over (Heb. 10:1-4).

Jesus is the perfect and final Sacrifice through whom God's forgiveness is mediated to every person (Acts 13:38; Rom. 3:25; Heb. 9:14,28; 10:11-12). Only God can forgive sins; yet Jesus declared that He could do so, and He did (Mark 2:1-12; John 8:2-11). He saw His death as the fulfillment of the OT sacrificial system (Mark 14:24). Forgiveness through the sacrifice of Christ is available for everyone who truly repents (Luke 23:39-43; John 8:2-11).

A firm condition for the receiving of God's forgiveness is the willingness to forgive others (Matt. 6:12,15; 18:12-35; Luke 11:4). Love, not wooden rules, governs forgiveness (Matt. 18:21-22). Jesus powerfully demonstrated this teaching on the cross, as He asked for forgiveness for His executioners (Luke 23:34). See *Cross, Crucifixion; Mercy, Merciful; Redeem, Redemption; Sin; Unpardonable Sin.*

FORNICATION

Various acts of sexual immorality, especially being a harlot or whore; being unfaithful to a marriage commitment (Judg. 19:2).

Normally women are the subject of fornication, but in Num. 25:1 men "began to commit whoredom." Such action was subject to the death penalty (Gen. 38:24; compare Lev. 21:9; Deut. 22:21).

The NT gives fornication at least four dimensions: voluntary sexual intercourse of an unmarried person with someone of the opposite sex (1 Cor. 7:2; 1 Thess. 4:3); synonym for adultery (Matt. 5:32; 19:9; see *Adultery; Divorce);* harlotry and prostitution (Rev. 2:14,20); various forms of unchastity (John 8:41; Acts 15:20; 1 Cor. 5:1).

Jesus went against Jewish tradition and forgave prostitutes and opened the way for them to enter God's kingdom through faith (Matt. 21:31-32; compare Heb. 11:31; Jas. 2:25), though He still regarded fornication as evil (Mark 7:21). Paul extended the use of the Greek term for fornication to cover all sinful sexual activity. A believer must decide to be part of Christ's body or a prostitute's body (1 Cor. 6:12-20). The believer must flee sexual immorality and cleave to Christ, honoring Him with the physical body. Fornication is thus a result of sinful human nature (Gal. 5:19) and unsuitable for God's holy people (Eph. 5:3; 1 Thess. 4:3). The Book of Revelation condemns those guilty to eternal punishment (Rev. 2:21-22).

FORT, FORTIFICATION

Walled structures built for defense against enemy armies. The oldest fortifications in Israel are at Jericho, where a Neolithic stone tower and part of a wall have been dated to 7000 B.C. After 3000 B.C. cities were almost always surrounded by walls. In the time of Solomon, well-dressed ashlars (carefully trimmed limestone blocks) began to be used in the construction of unique fortification systems. These included casemate walls (that is, two parallel stone walls with dividing partitions connecting them) and huge six-chambered gates allowing easy entrance and exit for his chariots. Similar but smaller four-chambered gates were used later in the time of Ahab and Jeroboam II, attached to offsets-insets solid walls. Citadels were often built on the acropolis of the enclosed city. See *Architecture in the Biblical Period; Cities and Urban Life.*

FORTIFIED CITIES

Towns with strong defenses, usually a massive wall structure and inner citadels or strongholds; a major military or administrative center for a region. Location was much more critical than size. See Josh. 19:35-38; 2 Chron. 11:5-12; Jer. 34:6-7. Fortified cities guarded a major highway (Lachish and Hazor), protected mountain passes (Megiddo and Taanach), and served as border fortresses (Arad and Hazor). Troops would be garrisoned in a fortified city. In times of danger, people from the surrounding area would find protection in a fortified city (Jer. 4:5; 8:14).

FORTUNATUS

Corinthian Christian who with Stephanus and Achaicus ministered to Paul at Ephesus (1 Cor. 16:17), perhaps bringing letter from Chloe's household in Corinth and delivering First Corinthians as indicated in the superscription of the Textus Receptus.

FORUM

Open place of a market town or the town itself. The Appii Forum (Acts 28:15) or market town of Appius was located 43 miles to the southeast of Rome on the Appian Way.

FORUM OF APPIUS See *Forum.*

FOUNDATION

That on which a building is built; first layer of structure that provides a stable base for the superstructure. Bedrock was the preferred foundation (Matt. 7:24). The best alternative was a solid platform of close- fitting cut stone (1 Kings 5:17). Modest homes had foundations of rough stone. Generally, building sites were leveled by filling in the foundation trenches with gravel or small stones. The prohibition of laying a foundation for Jericho (Josh. 6:26) was a prohibition of rebuilding the city as a fortified site rather than of inhabiting the place. The splendor of the new Jerusalem is

pictured in its foundation of precious stones (Isa. 54:11; Rev. 21:19).

The OT pictured the earth (dry land) as resting on foundations (2 Sam. 22:16; Pss. 18:15; 82:5). God is pictured as a builder who marked out the foundations (Prov. 8:29) and set the stone (Ps. 104:5). The mountains (Deut. 32:22; Ps. 18:7) and the vault of the heavens (2 Sam. 22:8; Job 26:11) are also pictured as resting on foundations. God's great power is expressed in the images of the earth's foundations trembling (Isa. 24:18) or being exposed (2 Sam. 22:16) before the Almighty. "From the foundations of the earth" means from the time of creation (Isa. 40:21; Matt. 13:35; John 17:24).

Christ's teaching is compared to a rock-solid foundation (Matt. 7:24; Luke 6:48). Foundation serves as a metaphor for the initial preaching of the gospel (Rom. 15:20; Heb. 6:1-2), for the apostles and prophets as the first generation of preachers (Eph. 2:20; compare Rev. 21:14,19), and for Christ as the content of preaching (1 Cor. 3:10-11).

FOUNTAIN

Spring of water flowing from a hole in the earth. Springs are highly prized as water sources and often determine the location of settlements. Thus the frequency of the Hebrew root *En,* meaning spring, in place names: En-dor (Josh. 17:11); En-eglaim (Ezek. 47:10); En-gannim (Josh. 15:34); En-gedi (15:62); En-haddah (19:21); En-hakkore (Judg. 15:19); En-hazor (Josh. 19:37); En-rimmon; (Neh 11:29); En-rogel and En-shemesh (Josh. 15:7); and En-tappuah (17:7). Enaim (Enam, Josh. 15:34) means "two springs." The goodness of Canaan was seen in its abundant water supply (Deut. 8:7).

The OT portrays the earth's dry land resting on foundations over the fountains of the deep (Gen. 7:11). The unleashing of these waters amounted to a return to the chaos before the creation (Gen. 1:1,9). Provisions of spring water is an expression of God's providential care (Ps. 104:10;

Isa. 41:17-18).The blessedness of the end time includes pictures of fountains flowing from the temple (Ezek. 47:1-12; Joel 3:18), Jerusalem (Zech. 14:8), or the throne of God (Rev. 22:1-2) with amazing life-giving powers.

FOWLER

One who traps birds with snares (Pss. 91:3; 124:7); traps (Ps. 141:9; Jer. 5:26-27); ropes (Job 18:10, KJV, "snare"); and nets (Hos. 7:12).

FRANKINCENSE

Ingredient of perfume for most holy place (Ex. 30:34); resinous substance derived from certain trees in the balsam family; gift the Magi presented to Jesus (Matt. 2:11).

FREEDMEN, SYNAGOGUE OF THE

Greek-speaking synagogue in Jerusalem involved in instigating the dispute with Stephen (Acts 6:9; KJV, "Synagogue of the Libertines"); Greek syntax suggests two groups of disputants. The first consisted of the Synagogue of the Freedmen, composed of Cyrenians and Alexandrians (NASB, TEV).This group may have had three parties: the freedmen (freed slaves), the Cyrenians, and Alexandrians. Some early versions have Libyans in place of "libertines," giving three groups of North African Jews. The second party was composed of Greek-speaking Jews of Asia and Cilicia. These may have belonged to the Synagogue of the Freedmen as well (REB). Some have identified the freedmen as the descendants of Pompey's prisoners of war (63 B.C.).

FREEDOM

The ability of a person or group to be and do what they want instead of being controlled by another. People are able to choose their actions and attitudes, their responses to others and to God, but we are not independent of others or God.We do not have the power to do what we want to, whether that be to fulfill the law, love others, or save ourselves.The kind of freedom all persons have is the kind of freedom slaves have.

According to the law, no person is to have complete mastery of another. A person can only be used as a slave for six years. If mistreated during that time, they are to be released. Also, every 50 years, all slaves are to be freed, regardless of how many years of their slavery they have served (Ex. 21:2-11,26-27; Lev. 25:10; Deut. 15:12-18). Whoever is oppressed is viewed as a slave, and God desires that the oppression stop.

Most slaves of the first century were slaves from birth, serving their parents' owners. Few remained slaves for life, being freed when their owners died or after 10 to 20 years of adult service to their owner.They had the opportunity to buy their freedom if they could save or borrow the money their owner charged for freeing them. Before the NT era was over, a large percentage of the free population of the Roman Empire had either been slaves at one time or had parents who were slaves.

The NT depicts all persons as being in slavery—the slavery of sin (John 8:34; Rom. 3:9-12; 2 Pet. 2:19). All people have the opportunity to obtain release from bondage to sin by choosing to follow Christ (Rom. 6:12-14; 10:9-12). The powers of sin and grace are stronger than ourselves (Rom. 7:15-25; see 6:16).When we yield to sin as our master, sin uses the law to deceive us into thinking we are so in control of ourselves that by our own works we can save ourselves by obeying the law. In reality, we do not have the power, or the freedom, to live righteously (Rom. 7:18). Our attempts to fulfill the law by ourselves will simply increase our pride, strengthening sin's control over us. The daily choices we make become more and more consistently obedient to sinful purposes and lead to death.

If we yield to grace, given through Jesus Christ, the Spirit has the power to lead us into life and truth (Rom. 6:19; Eph. 1:11-14). As we continue to live in Christ, He uses His power to mold us more and more into His image (2 Cor. 3:18; Phil. 1:6). Following our every desire is not what freedom is. We are free from our former master: sin; but we are servants. As servants of Christ, we have freedom to disobey our Master and responsibility to direct our actions to fulfill the purposes of Christ (Rom. 6:1,2,15,18,22; 1 Pet. 2:16). See *Election; Slave, Servant.*

FRIEND OF THE KING

Title of a court official (1 Kings 4:5); counselor and companion to the monarch like a Secretary of State.

FRIEND, FRIENDSHIP

Close trusting relationship between two people; simple association (Gen. 38:12; 2 Sam. 15:37) or loving companionship, the most recognizable example being that between David and Saul's son, Jonathan (1 Sam. 18:1,3; 20:17; 2 Sam. 1:26). The OT affirms friendship between God and humans conversing face-to-face (Ex. 33:11; compare Isa. 5:1-7). Abraham was the friend of God (2 Chron. 20:7; Isa. 41:8; Jas. 2:23). Proverbs cautions against dubious friendships and extols the virtues of a true friend (14:20; 17:17-18; 18:24; 19:4, 6; 22:11, 24; 27:6,10,14).

Jesus is described as the "friend of sinners" (Matt. 11:19). He called His disciples "friends" (Luke 12:4; John 15:13-15). The NT highlights the connection between friends and joy (Luke 15:6,9,29), as well as warning of the possibility of friends proving false (Luke 21:16). James warned against friendship with the world (Jas. 4:4). Only in 3 John 14 is "friend" a self-designation for Christians.

FRINGE

Tassels of twisted cords fastened to the four corners of the outer garment, worn by observant Jews as a reminder of covenant obligations (Num. 15:38-39; Deut. 22:12; compare Zech. 8:23). The woman suffering from chronic hemorrhage touched the tassel of Jesus' cloak (Matt. 9:20; Luke 8:44). Though Jesus observed the OT requirement, He criticized those who wore excessively long tassels to call attention to their piety (Matt. 23:5).

FRONTLETS

Objects containing Scripture passages worn on the forehand and between the eyes. Jews followed scriptural commands, literally writing Ex. 13:1-16; Deut. 6:4-9; 11:13-21 on small scrolls, placing these in leather containers and placing these on their forehead and left arm. By NT times, the frontlets were known as phylacteries (Matt. 23:5). Jewish men wore phylacteries during prayer times, except on the sabbath and feast days. Jesus condemned individuals who called attention to themselves by wearing larger than usual phylacteries (Matt. 23:5).

FRUIT

Edible pulp surrounding the seed(s) of many plants: grapes, figs, olives, pomegranates, and apples (perhaps to be identified with apricots or quince). The continuing fruitfulness of Israel's trees was dependent on faithfulness to the covenant (Deut. 28:4,11,18). The first fruit to ripen was offered to God (Ex. 23:16; Neh. 10:35).

The fruit of the womb is a common expression for descendants (Gen. 30:2; Deut. 7:13; Ps. 127:3; Isa. 13:18). Fruit often indicates a thought close to our word *results.* The fruit of the Spirit is the result of the Spirit's workings in the lives of believers (Gal. 5:22-23). Similar is the use of fruit where we would speak of manifestations or expressions: fruits of righteousness (Phil. 1:11; Jas. 3:18), repentance (Matt. 3:8), and light (Eph. 5:9). Jesus cautioned that false prophets could be identified by the fruit they produced (Matt. 7:15-20)—the qualities manifested in their lives. Jesus similarly warned of the necessity of bearing fruit compatible with citizenship in the kingdom of God (Matt. 21:43). Fruit sometimes has the sense of reward (Isa. 3:10; John 4:36; Phil. 4:17). Fruit is also used as a picture for Christian converts (Rom. 1:13; 1 Cor. 16:15).

FRUSTRATION

The Hebrew verb "to frustrate" (from *parar*) means to make ineffective or void, and is used primarily to describe God's response to the plans of people. The Bible declares that God frustrates the plans of those who trust in their own devices or who operate according to their own agendas (Job 5:12; Ps. 33:10; Isa. 44:25), and relates several instances of persons who became frustrated in opposing God. These include Pharaoh (Ex. 8–12), Ahithophel (2 Sam. 17:14,23), Ahab (1 Kings 18:17; 21:1-4), the men of Sanballat and Tobiah (Neh. 4:7,15), and Pilate (John 19:1-16).

Those who strive to follow God often experience frustration in its more general sense of a dissatisfaction arising over unmet expectations. The psalmist cried out in frustration over God's apparent inactivity on his behalf (Ps. 22:1-2; 38:1-22; 39:1-13), and Paul expressed frustration over the lack of faith evident in the Galatian believers (Gal. 3:1-5). Partly in response to such frustrations, Paul learned to be content in every situation (Phil. 4:11-13) and counseled that everything eventually works for good for those who love God and are called according to His purpose (Rom. 8:28). God's promises of comfort extend to those who are frustrated (Isa. 40:1; 1 Cor. 1:3-7), and the spiritual maturity which enables believers to overcome frustration arises from trust in God in the midst of trials (Ps. 22:5; Prov. 3:5-6; Phil. 1:6; Jas. 1:2-4).

FUEL

Materials used to start and maintain a fire: wood (Isa. 44:14-16); charcoal (Jer. 36:22; John 18:18); shrubs (Ps. 120:4); thorn bushes (Eccl. 7:6; Nah. 1:10); grass (Matt. 6:30); weeds (Matt. 13:40); vines (Ezek. 15:4,6); branch trimmings (John 15:6); animal or even human dung (Ezek. 4:12); and the blood-stained clothing of fallen warriors (Isa. 9:5). Oil was used as a fuel for lamps (Matt. 25:3). Coal was not known to the Hebrews.

FULFILL

Observing or meeting requirements; corresponding to what was promised, predicted, or foreshadowed; arrival of times ordained by God. The ethical sense of *fulfill* appears in the OT only in connection with meeting the requirements of a vow (Lev. 22:21; Num. 15:3), never in connection with the law. In the NT, Jesus submitted to John's baptism, identifying Himself with sinful people, in order "to fulfill all righteous" (Matt. 3:15), that is, to meet God's expectation for His life. Jesus described His mission not as coming "to abolish the law or the prophets" but "to fulfill" (Matt. 5:17). The NT repeatedly speaks of love as the fulfilling of the law (Rom. 13:8-10; Gal. 5:14; Jas. 2:8).

The fulfillment of prophecy in the life of Jesus is a major theme in Matthew's Gospel. Isaiah's prophecy (7:14) found fulfillment not only in Christ's virgin birth but also in His nature as "God with us" (Matt. 1:22-23; compare 28:20). Jesus' ministry in both word (Matt. 4:14-17) and deed (8:16-17) fulfilled Scripture (Isa. 9:1-2; 53:4). Jesus' command of secrecy (Matt. 12:16) and His habit of teaching in parables (13:35) likewise fulfilled Scripture (Isa. 42:1-3; Ps. 78:2), as did His humble entry into Jerusalem (Matt. 21:4-5; Zech. 9:9) and His arrest as a bandit (Matt. 26:56). Like Israel, Jesus was God's Son called out of Egypt (Matt. 2:15; Hos. 11:1). The suffering of Israel's mothers (Jer. 31:15) was echoed by the mothers of Bethlehem (Matt. 2:17-18). Both foreshadowed the fate of the Christ child who was spared only to die at a later time.

Luke and Acts are especially interested in Christ's suffering and later glorification as the fulfillment of the expectations of all the OT (Luke 24:25-26,44-47; Acts 3:18; 13:27-41). Jesus interpreted His journey to Jerusalem as a second "exodus"(Luke 9:31), an event that would result in freedom for God's people.

In John, the failure of the people to recognize God at work in Jesus' signs or to accept Jesus' testimony was explained as fulfillment of Scripture (12:37-41; compare Mark 4:11-12). John also viewed details of the Passion story as the fulfillment of Scripture (John 19:24,28; Pss. 22:18; 69:21). Jesus was "the Lamb of God, which taketh away the sin of the world" (1:29), likely a reference to the Passover lamb (John 19:14). Like Bethel (Gen. 28:12), Jesus offered access between heaven and earth (1:51). At Cana, Jesus' gift of wine corresponded to the blessings of God's future (John 2:1-11; Isa. 25:6; Joel 3:18; Amos 9:13; Zech. 9:17). Jesus' body that was to be destroyed and raised was identified with the temple (John 2:19,21). In His being lifted up on the cross (John 3:14), Christ corresponded to the serpent Moses raised in the wilderness (Num. 21:9). In the same way, Christ in giving His life corresponded to the life-giving manna from heaven (John 6:31-32; Ex. 16:15). Time references in John suggest that Jesus gave new meaning to the celebrations of Israel (Passover, 2:13; 6:4; 11:55; Booths, 7:10; Dedication, 10:22).

"All the promises of God in him [Christ] are yea, and in him Amen" (2 Cor. 1:20). Christ was foreshadowed by Adam (Rom. 5:12-21; 1 Cor. 15:22,45-49), by the rock in the wilderness (1 Cor. 10:4), and by the Passover lamb (1 Cor. 5:7). Temporal phrases such as "the time is fulfilled" point to times ordained by God: Christ's ministry (Mark 1:15; Gal. 4:4; Eph. 1:10), Gentile domination of Israel (Luke 21:24), or the appearance of the lawless one (2 Thess. 2:6).

FULLER

One who thickens and shrinks newly shorn wool or newly woven cloth; also one who washes or bleaches clothing. Cleansing was done by treading them on foot or beating clothing with sticks. Clothing was cleansed in a solution of alkali obtained by burning wood to ash. Putrid urine was sometimes used in the process. Due to the foul smell, fullers worked outside the city gates. Biblical references refer to cleansing from sin (Ps. 51:7; Jer. 2:22; 4:14; Mal. 3:2).

FULLNESS

Completeness or totality. Nothing is really complete until it serves the purpose for which God has created it (Ps. 24:1). God "filleth all in all" (Eph. 1:23). This fullness is most clearly expressed in Jesus Christ (Col. 1:19; 2:9) from whom all true believers receive the divine life of fullness (John 1:16; 10:10). It is a life full of joy (John 15:11) and peace despite the tribulations in this world (John 16:33).

FULLNESS OF TIME

God's planned moment for His saving action; the sending of Christ to redeem those born under the law (Gal. 4:4); especially Christ's death as a saving event (John 3:17; Rom. 8:3; 1 John 4:9-10). Fullness of time refers to God's gracious plan from eternity, not so much to world conditions (prevalence of Greek as a common language, Roman roads, or Roman peace) that made rapid spread of the gospel possible.

FURNACE

Device, generally of brick or stone, used to heat materials to high temperatures; not used for central heating but to smelt ore, melt metal for casting, heat metal for forging, fire pottery or bricks, and to make lime. Biblical references to furnaces are mostly figurative for experiences of testing (the Egyptian bondage, Deut. 4:20; 1 Kings 8:51; Jer. 11:4; adversity, Isa. 48:10). The furnace of fire symbolizes divine punishment (Matt. 13:42,50).

FURNITURE

Equipment in a home used for rest, beautification, storage, and work space. Biblical interest in furniture focuses on the sacred furnishings of the tabernacle and the temple (Ex. 25–27; 30; 37–38; 1 Kings 6–7). See *Tabernacle; Temple of Jerusalem.*

G

GABBATHA *(elevation)*

Platform in front of the praetorium or governor's palace in Jerusalem, where Pilate sat in judgment over Jesus (John 19:13).

GABRIEL *(strong man of God)*

Heavenly messenger who brings people a message from the Lord (Dan. 8:15-27; 9:20-27; Luke 1:8-20,26-38). See *Angel.*

GAD *(good fortune)*

(1) See *Tribes of Israel.*

(2) Syrian god known from inscriptions of Phoenicia and Palmyra and used in biblical names such as Baalgad (Josh. 11:17) and Migdal-gad (Josh. 15:37); also apparently meant in Isa. 65:11 where prophet condemned people for setting"a table for fortune"(NASB; Hebrew, Gad).

(3) Prophet who advised David as he fled from Saul (1 Sam. 22:5) and who brought God's options for punishment after David took a census of Israel (2 Sam. 24:11-14; compare 2 Sam. 24:18-19; 1 Chron. 29:29; 2 Chron. 29:25).

GADARA or **GADARENE**

City of Decapolis (Mark 5:1) and its resident. Home of man from whom Jesus expelled demons (Matt. 8:28-34; Mark 5:1-17; Luke 8:26-37). Greek manuscripts alternate among Gadarenes, Gerasenes, and Gergesenes; and appear to favor Gadarenes in Matthew, Gerasenes in Mark and Luke. Gadarene would have to refer to the larger area, not just the city of Gadara. Gergasenes points to the modern city of Kersa on the lake's edge. Gerasene comes from the city of Gerasa about 30 miles southeast of the lake. Gadara has been identified with modern Um Keis, approximately five miles southeast of the Sea of Galilee.

GAIUS *(I am glad, rejoice)*

(1) Macedonian Christian; Paul's traveling companion (Acts 19:29).

(2) Christian from Derbe who accompanied Paul into Asia (Acts 20:4).

(3) Paul's host in Corinth (Rom. 16:23); baptized by Paul (1 Cor. 1:14).

(4) The Christian John loved; recipient of 3 John (3 John 1).

GALATIA *(people of Gaul)*

Roman province in central Asia Minor with changing boundaries. See *Asia Minor.* Celts occupied northern part of Asia Minor, bounded on the north by Pontus and Bithynia, on the east by Tavium and on the west by Pessinus. Galatians lived in open areas, leaving city occupation to their predecessors, the Phrygians. In 25 B.C., Rome made Galatia a province of the empire and extended its borders, adding Lycaonia, Isauria, and Pisidia with Ancyra serving as the governmental center.

Paul visited Galatia (Acts 16:6; 18:23), though his precise route is not clear. Did he visit Phrygian-dominated cities or the true Galatians in the countryside? Was his letter addressed to the original territory in the north or to the Roman province with its southern additions? See *Galatians.* Compare 1 Cor. 16:1; 2 Tim. 4:10, where some manuscripts have Gaul, and 1 Pet. 1:1.

GALATIANS, LETTER TO THE

Paul's letter to the church at Galatia defending his interpretation of the gospel of Christ with a heated defense of justification by faith and freedom in the Spirit. Paul founded the churches of Galatia (Gal. 1:8-9; 4:19). The readers were Gentiles converted from paganism (4:8; 5:2; 6:12), perhaps with some Jewish Christians and proselytes.

Did they live in original northern Galatia? Or only in southern cities the Romans added to the province?

Paul founded churches at Antioch of Pisidia, Iconium, Lystra, and Derbe, cities in the southern part of the Roman province (Acts 13:14– 14:24). Paul visited Lystra and Derbe again (Acts 16:1-6). Paul twice more went through the "region of Phrygia and Galatia" (16:6; 18:23), which could refer to the southern portion of the Roman province or could indicate that Paul went north and founded churches in the territory of Galatia. The southern answer is probably correct since Acts is silent concerning churches in the north, and Paul often used provincial names in addressing letters. See *Galatia.*

Determining the date Paul wrote the epistle involves reconciling Gal. 1:11–2:14 with Acts. Paul mentioned two visits to Jerusalem (Gal. 1:18; 2:1), but Acts recorded five visits (Acts 9:26; 11:27 and 12:25; 15:4; 18:21; 21:17). Probably Galatians 1:18 and Acts 9:26 record Paul's first visit to Jerusalem after his conversion. Paul did not mention the Acts 11:27 and 12:25 visit because he was concerned to relate only his contact with the apostles. This second visit was with the elders, not the Twelve. Acts 15:1-29 and Gal. 2:1-10 are both probably accounts of the Jerusalem Council, in A.D. 49 or 50. After the council, Paul made his second visit to Galatia (Acts 16:1-6), matching the two visits he indicated in the epistle (Gal. 4:13). Then he moved on to Corinth (A.D. 51–52). Perhaps from Corinth he wrote the epistle. See *Apostolic Council.*

Sometime after Paul's last visit (Acts 16:1-6), heretical teachers, who "pervert the gospel" and trouble the churches (Gal. 1:7; 5:10,12), came among the Galatians. These Judaizers claimed to preach the gospel faithfully. They taught that circumcision was necessary for salvation (5:2; 6:12-16), as was obedience to the law of Moses, even the observation of days, months, seasons, and years (4:10). They were acting out of false and selfish motives, those of personal ambition (4:17; 6:13) and offense at the cross of Christ (6:12). They sought to discredit Paul. Paul felt a threat of the Galatians abandoning the gospel in large numbers.

Paul greeted the churches but omitted the praise or thanksgiving that normally followed (1:1-5). Instead, he expressed distress at their fickle faith (1:6-9). He pronounced a curse on those who preached something different from the gospel he had preached to them.

In the major portion of the epistle (1:10–6:10)

(1) Paul defended his qualifications as an apostle against the attacks of the Judaizers (1:10–2:21). Paul closed this section with the main theme of the epistle: Justification (a sinful person coming into a right relationship with God) came not by living bound to the law but by faith in Christ. To be in Christ meant being free from the legal requirements of the law.

(2) Paul supported his thesis of faith alone on three principles: the gift of the Spirit, the promise and faith of Abraham, and the curse of the law (3:1–5:12). The gift of the Spirit came to them through faith, not the law. Abraham received the promise and righteousness by faith 430 years before the law was given. People of faith were true children of Abraham and heirs of the promise. The law could only condemn sinners. Christ removed the curse of the law. The law was given as an interim provision until Christ came. To turn back to the law was to return to slavery. With the coming of Christ, faith and law had become mutually exclusive as ways to approach God.

(3) Paul guarded against abuse of this freedom from the law (5:13–6:10). Christian freedom required the believer to walk by the Spirit, which was contrary to the desires and works of the flesh. Christian freedom must be tempered by Christian love. Paul closed (6:11-18) again urging them not to yield to circumcision and all it represented.

GALBANUM See *Plants.*

GALEED (*pile for witness*)

Place where Jacob and his father-in-law Laban made formal agreement or covenant determining boundary line between their peoples and agreeing not to harm one another (Gen. 31:43-52). Also called Sahadutah and Mizpah. See *Mizpah.*

GALILEAN

Person who lived in Galilee; distinguished by speech from Jews in Jerusalem and Judah (Matt. 26:69; Mark 14:70; compare Acts 2:7). Galileans had a reputation for rebellion and disregard of Jewish law (Acts 5:37), so they could be regarded as sinners (Luke 13:2). Apparently, Pilate had killed some Galileans while they offered the Passover sacrifices in Jerusalem (Luke 13:1). Jesus received a warm welcome from the Galileans, apparently based on an expectation of miracles, not on appreciation for who Jesus was or from faith in Him (John 4:43-54).

GALILEE (*circle* or *region*)

Northern part of Palestine above the hill country of Ephraim and the hill country of Judah (Josh. 20:7); 45-mile stretch between Litani River in Lebanon and Valley of Jezreel in Israel north to south and from Mediterranean Sea to Jordan River, west to east. The Assyrians took the north under Tiglath-pileser in 733 (2 Kings 15:29) and divided it into three districts: the western coast or "the way of the sea" with capital at Dor, Galilee with capital at Megiddo, and beyond Jordan or Gilead (Isa. 9:1).

In time of Jesus, Herod Antipas governed Galilee and Perea. Jesus devoted most of His earthly ministry to Galilee (Matt. 26:69). After the fall of Jerusalem in A.D. 70, Galilee became the major center of Judaism, the Mishnah and Talmud being collected and written there.

GALILEE, SEA OF

Freshwater lake nestled in the hills of northern Palestine with surface nearly 700 feet below level of Mediterranean, some 30 miles west. The nearby hills of Galilee reach an altitude of 1,500 feet above sea level. To the east are the mountains of Gilead with peaks of more than 3,300 feet; to the north are the snow-covered Lebanon mountains. Fed chiefly by the Jordan River, that originates in the foothills of the Lebanon Mountains, the sea of Galilee is 13 miles long north and south and 8 miles wide at its greatest east-west distance. It is subject to sudden and violent storms, usually of short duration. In the OT, this sea is called Chinnereth. See *Chinnereth.* In NT times, it was also called the "lake of Gennesaret" (Luke 5:1). John called it the "sea of Tiberias" (6:1).

In the first century the sea of Galilee was of major commercial significance. Most Galilean roads passed by it, and much travel to and from the east crossed the Jordan rift there. The fishing industry flourished because no other significant freshwater lake existed in the region. Capernaum was a center of that industry. The other lake towns of importance were Bethsaida and Tiberias, a Gentile city constructed by Herod Antipas when Jesus was a young man.

GALL (*herb*)

Bitter, poisonous herb (perhaps *Citrullus colocynthis*), frequently linked with wormwood (Deut. 29:18; Jer. 9:15; 23:15; Lam. 3:19; Amos 6:12) to denote bitterness and tragedy and often associated with unfaithfulness to God, either as a picture of the unfaithful (Deut. 29:18) or as their punishment. On the cross, Jesus was offered sour wine drugged with gall, perhaps opium, which He refused (Matt. 27:34; compare Ps. 69:21). Simon the magician was described as full of the gall of bitterness (Acts 8:23) because he wanted to prostitute the gift of the Holy Spirit.

GALL (*of livers*)

An organ, either the liver or the gallbladder, through which a sword might pass when one was run through (Job 20:25); bile, a sticky, yellow-greenish, alkaline fluid secreted by the liver, that might pour out on the ground when one was disemboweled (Job 16:14); figurative sense (Job 13:26) for bitterness.

GALLIO

Lucius Junius Gallio, deputy or proconsul of Achaia, headquartered in Corinth, where his judgment seat has been discovered; presided over Paul's trial for advocating unlawful religion (Acts 18:12-17). Gallio refused to involve himself in Jewish religious affairs, even ignoring the crowd's beating of Sosthenes, the ruler of the synagogue.

Gallio's name appears on an inscription at Delphi that places Gallio in office in Corinth between A.D. 51 and 53. He was apparently proconsul from May 1, 51, to May 1, 52, though dates a year later are possible. The date gives evidence from outside the Bible for the time Paul was in Corinth and founded the church there.

GALLOWS

Tree used by Persians for execution (Esth. 2:23; 7:9-10; 9:25); perhaps those executed were impaled rather than hung.

GAMALIEL (*God rewards with good*)

(1) Leader of Manasseh, who helped Moses take census (Num. 1:10). Compare 7:54-59.

(2) Highly regarded Pharisee; grandson of the great Rabbi Hillel, member of Sanhedrin (Acts 5:34); Paul's teacher (Acts 22:3). He squelched Sanhedrin's plan to kill the apostles by reminding the members that they might be opposing God. He died about A.D. 52.

(3) Leading Jewish rabbi around 100 A.D.; grandson of 2; credited with many adaptations in Judaism necessitated by destruction of the temple in A.D. 70.

GAMES

Activity done for amusement and fun (2 Sam. 2:14-16; Isa. 11:8; Zech. 8:5); Bible is silent as to the nature of games. Archaeology provides the most valuable information. Over 4,000 years ago, board games with dice were common throughout the Middle East. Game pieces moved from one square to another according to certain rules that are still unknown. Another game commonly referred to as "hounds and jackals" was played throughout the Fertile Crescent.

Playing pieces of varying designs as well as game boards of ivory and stone have been discovered at Samaria, Gezer, Megiddo, and other sites in Palestine. Excavations at Debir (tell beit Mirsim) in Southern Palestine unearthed a limestone board with ten glazed playing pieces and an ivory "die." Boards for a game called "fifty-eight holes" have been found at Megiddo and in Egypt and Mesopotamia as well.

The four Greek Panhellenic games were the largest public sports contests in the Near East. Some believe that Paul was a spectator at the Isthmian games (near Corinth). Among the events were the pentathlon (long-jump, javelin and discus throws, running, and wrestling) and chariot races. All races were run on a long track or stadion with pylons at each end. Runners or charioteers rounded the pylons, racing back and forth instead of circling an oval track. It is evident that the apostle was familiar with athletics (Gal. 2:2; Phil. 3:13-14; 2 Tim. 2:5; 1 Cor. 9:25-27).

Athletes were rubbed with oil and participated without wearing clothing. Competitive spirit was vigorous, and contests were governed by few rules. Prizes for winners of the Panhellenic Games were simple wreaths of olive, wild celery, laurel, and pine. At Rome, one could see basically these same events until wild beasts were introduced into the arena. Sometimes as many as 10,000 gladiators fought at the Roman games. Herod the Great built many amphitheaters in Palestine, including one near Jerusalem where men condemned to death fought with wild animals. Orthodox Jews were repelled by nude athletes and games dedicated to Caesar. Trophies of ornamented wood were considered images and thus forbidden. This and the cruelty of the games makes one understand why devout Jews hated the games.

GANGRENE

Death of soft tissue resulting from problems with blood flow (NASB, NRSV, REB) or an ulcer (canker, KJV; open sore, TEV); used figuratively for false teachings that destroy people who accept them (2 Tim. 2:17).

GANGS

It was not unusual in antiquity for persons who saw themselves as poor, oppressed or disenfranchised to gather themselves together under a charismatic leader and live largely under their own authority, sometimes cooperating with existing authority structures and sometimes opposing them. Whether such groups should be called "gangs," "brigands" or simply "bands of adventurers" depends largely on the particular circumstances involved.

The tendency toward gang formation was greatest in times of weakened centralized authority. Hence Abimelech (Judg. 9:4), Jephthah (Judg. 11:3), men attached to Ishbosheth son of Saul (2 Sam. 4:1-3), Jeroboam (2 Chron. 13:6-7), and even David (1 Sam. 22:2) became commanders of gangs of men who had withdrawn from mainstream society. While David's gang was composed of men who had been oppressed, it is implied, by the economic policies of King Saul (1 Sam. 22:2), the gangs of Abimelech, Jephthah, and Jeroboam consisted of "worthless fellows."

The Bible mentions other instances of gang-like behavior in the rape of the Levite's concubine by the men of Gibeah (Judg. 19:22-26), the attempted rape of Lot's guests by the men of Sodom (Gen. 19:4-11) and the taunting of Elisha by boys (2 Kings 2:23-24).

GARDEN

Plot of ground enclosed or surrounded by walls or hedges on which flowers, vegetables, herbs, fruit, and nut trees were cultivated (Gen. 2:8; 1 Kings 21:2; Esth. 1:5; Isa. 51:3; John 18:1-2). Some were large (Esth. 1:5), the most prominent gardens being royal ones (2 Kings 25:4; Neh. 3:15; Jer. 39:4). Gardeners were employed to tend the more substantial gardens, sowing seed and watering (Deut. 11:10; John 20:15). Orchards or small vineyards were sometimes called gardens. A garden provided food for its owner (Jer. 29:5,28; Amos 9:14) and was a place of beauty where plants were pleasing to the sight (Gen. 2:9). As a guarded and protected place (Song of Sol. 4:12), persons could retreat there for prayer (Matt. 26:36-46), for quiet or solitude (Esth. 7:7). It provided a cool escape from the heat of the day (Gen. 3:8). Friends could meet in gardens (John 18:1-2), or banquets could be served there (Esth. 1:5). It, thus, was often associated with joy and gladness (Isa. 51:3). On the other hand, pagan sacrifices were sometimes offered in gardens (Isa. 65:3; 66:17); and gardens were used as burial sites (2 Kings 21:18,26; John 19:41-42).

The garden of Eden (Gen. 2:8; 3:23-24) was planted by God (2:8) and entrusted to Adam for cultivating and keeping (2:15). Following their sin, Adam and Eve were banished from the garden; but "Eden the garden of God" (Ezek. 28:13) continued as a symbol of blessing and bounty (Ezek. 36:35; Joel 2:3). The "king's garden" in Jerusalem was located near a gate to the city that provided unobserved exit or escape (2 Kings 25:4; Neh. 3:15; Jer. 39:4; 52:7). The "garden" (John 18:1) called Gethsemane (Matt. 26:36; Mark 14:32) was a place where Jesus often met with His disciples (John 18:2); He was betrayed and arrested there.

GATES OF JERUSALEM AND THE TEMPLE

Entrances to Judah's capital and its place of worship. Jerusalem's many gates have varied in number and location with the changing size and orientation of its walls throughout its long history. Persons could enter through an important city gate on the west from Jaffa (Tel Aviv) Road, as they do today. On the east, entrance from the Kidron Valley was made principally through the Sheep Gate (modern Stephen or Lion Gate) in NT times and by a gate south of the modern city walls in OT times. This latter gate may date to the reign of Solomon, being similar to Solomonic gates found at Megiddo, Gezer, and Hazor. Entrance to the temple itself was on its eastern side through the Beautiful Gate (Acts 3:10), near the Golden Gate recently found beneath the city's eastern wall. On the north, the principal gateway (Damascus Gate) opened onto the Damascus Road. Seven gates now allow entrance to the old city of Jerusalem.

The Fish Gate was a northern gate of the second quarter of Jerusalem (Zeph. 1:10) mentioned in connection with fortifications built by Manasseh (2 Chron. 33:14; compare Neh. 3:3; 12:39). The name is perhaps derived from the proximity of the gate to the fish market (compare Neh. 13:16-22). The Fountain Gate was at the southeast corner of the walls of ancient Jerusalem (Neh. 2:14; 3:15; 12:37), probably so named because people brought water from the En-rogel or Gihon springs into the city through this gate. The gate is possibly identical with the "gate between two walls" (2 Kings 25:4; Jer. 39:4; 52:7).

The Ephraim Gate was an entrance to Jerusalem 400 cubits (about 200 yards) from the Corner Gate (2 Kings 14:13). In Nehemiah's time, booths for the celebration of the Feast of Tabernacles were set up in the city square at the Ephraim Gate (Neh. 8:16). The Dung Gate (NASB, refuse; TEV, rubbish) at the southwest corner of the wall was a Jerusalem landmark in Nehemiah's time (Neh. 2:13; 3:13-14; 12:31) and was used for the disposal of garbage that was dumped into the Hinnom Valley below.

The Benjamin Gate (Jer. 37:13; 38:7) is identified by some with Nehemiah's Sheep Gate (Neh. 3:32) or with the Muster Gate (Neh. 3:31). It could indicate the gate that led to tribal territory of Benjamin.

The East Gate refers to three different entrances to Jerusalem or the temple.

(1) KJV refers to the East Gate of Jeru- salem leading to the Hinnom Valley (Jer. 19:2) that lies to the south of the city rather than the east. Modern translations render this phrase "Potsherd Gate." This gate may be identified with the Valley Gate (2 Chron. 26:9; Neh. 2:13,15; 3:13) or perhaps to the Refuse or Dung Gate (Neh. 2:13; 3:13-14; 12:31) located one thousand cubits away.

(2) The East Gate of the outer court of the temple. Since the temple faced east, this gate was the main entrance to the temple complex (Ezek. 47:1; compare 2 Chron. 31:14; Ezek. 10:19; 43:1-2). Only the prince (messianic king) was allowed to enter it (Ezek. 44:1-3).

(3) The East Gate of the inner court of the temple. This gate was closed on the six working days but open on the sabbath (Ezek. 46:1).

The "high gate" is KJV designations for gate of the Jerusalem temple (2 Kings 15:35; 2 Chron. 23:20; 27:3). Most modern translations prefer the designation "Upper Gate." TEV reads "North Gate" or "Main Gate." Its location is not clear, possibly being the same as the Benjamin Gate. Parallel to 2 Chron. 23:20, 2 Kings 11:19 uses "guard" or "herald" as the gate's name, probably reflecting a change of names through history.

The Horse Gate was on the east side of the city wall of Jerusalem near the temple. Jeremiah promised its rebuilding (Jer. 31:40), and the priests under Nehemiah rebuilt it (Neh. 3:28).

The Middle Gate was a city gate of Jerusalem (Jer. 39:3); probably in the middle of the north wall of the preexilic city; possibly identical to the Fish Gate (2 Chron. 33:14; Neh. 3:3; Zeph. 1:10).

The Old Gate, KJV, NASB, NRSV designation for Jerusalem city gate repaired in Nehemiah's time (Neh. 3:6; 12:39). This rendering is doubtful on grammatical grounds (the adjective and noun do not agree). Some interpreters thus propose gate of the old (city). Others take the Hebrew *Jeshanah* as a proper name (NIV, REB, TEV). A village named Jeshanah is located near Bethel. The gate may have pointed in this direction. Still others emend the text to read "Misneh Gate" (Jerusalem Bible). In this case the gate led from the Old City West into the New Quarter (Mishneh). The gate is perhaps identical to the corner gate (2 Kings 14:13).

The Prison Gate, KJV for a gate in Jerusalem (Neh. 12:39): Gate of the Guard or Guardhouse Gate; perhaps identical with Miphkad (Muster) Gate (Neh. 3:31).

GATH (*winepress*)

Name of a number of towns in Palestine connected with wine industry; often used with another name such as Gath-Hepher, Gath-Rimmon, and Moresheth-Gath; principal city among five Philistine city-states (Gath, Ekron, Ashdod, Ashkelon, and Gaza, 1 Sam. 6:17); inhabitants called Gittites (1 Sam. 17:4; 2 Sam. 6:10-11); in Shephelah —band of foothills between coastal plain and central hill country— probably tell es- Safi, 12 miles east of Ashdod.

Gath was a Canaanite city occupied by giant Anakim (Josh. 11:21-22). Joshua and the Israelites apparently did not take Gaza, Gath, and Ashdod (Josh. 11:22). Gath was one of the locations where the Philistines took the ark (1 Sam. 5:8-9) and was the hometown of Goliath (1 Sam. 17:4) and Obed-edom (1 Chron. 13:13). David found sanctuary with Achish (see 1 Kings 2:39), the king of Gath, and perhaps became a vassal of the Philistines (1 Sam. 27:1-7). Eventually, David defeated the Philistines and made Gath an Israelite town (1 Chron. 18:1; see 2 Chron. 11:5-12; 26:6; 2 Kings 12:17). See *Philistines.*

GATH-HEPHER (*winepress on the watering hole*)

City on eastern border of Zebulun (Josh. 19:13); Jonah's home (2 Kings 14:25); modern el-Meshed or nearby khirbet ez-Zurra, three miles northeast of Nazareth.

GAZA (*strong*)

Southernmost town of Philistine city-state system (also included Ashkelon, Ashdod, Ekron, and Gath, 1 Sam. 6:17); on coastal plain about 3 miles inland from Mediterranean Sea; tell Harube in modern Gaza; on major coastal highway that connected Egypt with Ancient Near East; originally occupied by Avvim (Deut. 2:23).

Thutmose III made Gaza a major Egyptian center. Amarna Letters identify Gaza as district headquarters for Egyptian holdings in southern Palestine. Gaza was the major center on southern border of Solomon's kingdom (1 Kings 4:24).

Tiglath-pileser III collected tribute from Gaza about 734 B.C. See 2 Kings 18:8. Sennacherib reinforced his control of Gaza as a vassal in 701 B.C. Pharaoh Neco conquered Gaza about 609 B.C. and made it an Egyptian holding for a few years. Sometime after 605 B.C., Nebuchadnezzar conquered Gaza and made it part of Babylon's empire.

GEBA (*hill*)

Variant Hebrew spelling of Gibeah, with which it is sometimes confused; Levitic city in Benjamin (Josh. 18:24; 21:17); modern Jeba across the wadi Suweinit from Michmash, about five and a half miles north of Jerusalem. See 1 Sam. 13:16-14:18; 1 Kings 15:22; 2 Kings 23:8; 1 Chron. 8:6; Ezra 2:26; Neh. 11:31; 12:29; Isa. 10:29; Zech. 14:10.

GEBAL (*mountain*), GEBALITE

(1) Seaport known to Greeks as Byblos; part of land that remained (Josh. 13:5); modern Dschebel about 25 miles north of Beirut; helped Tyre (Ezek. 27:9). See 1 Kings 5:18. The

fine sarcophagus of King Ahiram found there contained the earliest evidence we have of the Phoenician alphabet. About 900 B.C. Tyre replaced Gebal as the strongest city of Phoenicia.

(2) Member of coalition against Israel (Ps. 83:7); northern part of Arabia near Petra in mountainous country south of Dead Sea.

GECKO See *Animals*.

GEDALIAH (*Yahweh has done great things*)

(1) Man Nebuchadnezzar of Babylon ap- pointed ruler of Judah in 587 B.C. (2 Kings 25:22). Ahikam, his father, was an ally of Jeremiah (Jer. 26:24; 39:14). Fanatically zealous nationalists led by Ishmael murdered him (Jer. 40:1–41:18).

(2) Royal official under King Zedekiah (597–586 B.C.); with group that got king's permission to imprison Jeremiah in cistern (Jer. 38).

(3) Temple singer and prophet who played harp (1 Chron. 25:3) and headed one of 24 divisions of temple servants (1 Chron. 25:9).

(4) An abbreviated form of the Hebrew name is given a priest with a foreign wife under Ezra (Ezra 10:18) and the grandfather of the prophet Zephaniah (Zeph. 1:1).

GEDERAH (*sheepfold* or *stone wall*), **GEDERATHITE**

Village in Shephalah of Judah (Josh. 15:36); modern tell el-Judeireh north of Maraeshah and 10 miles southeast of Lod. Villagers were noted for skill in making pottery (1 Chron. 4:23). The home of one of David's soldiers (1 Chron. 12:4).

GEDEROTH (*walls*)

City in Judah in Shephelah (Josh. 15:41); may be alternate spelling of Gederah or Qatra near Lachish. See 2 Chron. 28:18.

GEHAZI (*valley of vision* or *goggle-eyed*)

Servant of Elisha (2 Kings 4:12) questionable character. He tried to force a grieving woman away from the prophet (2 Kings 4:27). Despite the prophet's commission, he could not restore a child to life (2 Kings 4:31). Later he tried to secure for himself the reward Elisha had refused from Naaman the Syrian and then lied to Elisha (2 Kings 5:20-25). He was stricken with disease of which Naaman had been cured. Gehazi did help widow get her lands restored (2 Kings 8:1-6). See *Elisha.*

GEHENNA (*Valley of whining* or *valley of lamentation*)

Word for hell in intertestamental and NT literature. See *Hinnom.* The valley south of Jerusalem called "the valley of the son of Hinnom" (Josh. 15:8; 18:16; 2 Chron. 33:6; Jer. 32:35), became the place of child sacrifice to foreign gods. In some writings, but not in the Bible, Gehenna was seen as place of temporary judgment for those waiting the final judgment.

The NT uses Gehenna to speak of the place of final judgment (Matt. 5:22, 29; 18:9; Mark 9:43,45,47-48). Only God can commit people to Gehenna and so is the only One worthy of human fear (Matt. 10:28; Luke 12:5). Jesus condemned the Pharisees for making converts but then turning them into sons of Gehenna, that is, people destined for hell (Matt. 23:15,33). James warned people that they could not control their tongues Gehenna had set on fire (Jas. 3:6). See *Hell.*

GELILOTH (*circles* or *regions*) See *Gilgal.*

GENDER EQUALITY

Adam and Eve were created in God's image to be equal in personhood but distinct in gender (Gen. 1:26-27; 5:1-2). The phrase "a helper who is like him" (Gen. 2:18), conveys equality and compatibility on the one hand but also indicates a functional distinction that was part of creation.

Adam and Eve were co-participants in the fall, but Adam as head of the race was the one held responsible by God (Gen. 2:16-17; Ps. 90:3; Rom. 3:18; 5:12,15; 1 Cor. 15:22). The fall introduced distortions into the male-female relationship resulting in marital conflict (Gen. 3:16b).

Redemption in Christ aims to reverse the effects of the fall. Although gender differences remain, all persons — male and female — are one in Christ (Gal. 3:26-28) and participate in unique ways through the work of the Holy Spirit in the life of the church (Acts 2:17-18; 1 Cor. 12:7). The apostle Paul appealed to the order of creation — man first, then woman — to argue for the submission of women to men in certain functions of the church, namely teaching and preaching (1 Tim. 2:11-12; compare 1 Cor. 11:8-9). Husbands have been given headship over their wives in a way analogous to the headship of Christ over the church (Eph. 5:23) and must be motivated in their relationship by agape love (Eph. 5:25).

Women held important positions of authority in both the Old (Ex. 15:20; Judg. 4:4-14; 2 Chron. 34:22-28; Prov. 31:29) and New Testaments (Acts 1:14; Rom. 16:1-3; 1 Cor. 1:11; 16:19; Phil. 4:2). Both men and women exercise leadership in raising and nurturing their children (Ex. 20:12; Prov. 1:8; Eph. 6:1-4).

GENEALOGIES

Records of family lineage that trace the descent of a person, family, or group from an ancestor. (See Gen. 4; Num. 1:19-49; 1 Chron. 1-9; Ezra 8). Genealogies may serve family, political, or religious purposes. In their purposes of legitimation, genealogies describe not only kinship relationships but also geographical, social, economic, religious, and political relationships.

Genealogies may:

(1) demonstrate the relationships and the differences between Israel and other nations (Gen. 10);

(2) demonstrate the unity and coherence of Israel (Ex. 1:1-5) or of all nations (Gen. 10);

(3) build a historical bridge connecting Israel through periods of history for which few narratives are available (1 Chron. 1-9);

(4) reveal a pattern of cycles in world history (Matt. 1:1-17);

(5) describe military functions (Num. 1:5-16);

(6) show a person's or group's right to an office or function (1 Chron. 6; 24-26);

(7) preserve the purity of the nation (see Ezra 10);

(8) assure a sense of national continuity and unity in a period of national despair (1 Chron. 5);

(9) show the movement of history toward God's goal (Gen. 4-5; 11:10-32; 1 Chron. 1-9).

Matthew began his Gospel with a genealogy tracing Jesus' lineage from Abraham through David. Luke also included a genealogy reaching back to Adam and God (3:23-38). Matthew appears to focus on messiahship and Luke on salvation offered to all humankind.

Hebrews 7:3,6 assigns value to the fact that Melchizedek was a priest without genealogy—a fact that set him apart from the Jewish priesthood. Paul condemned a distorted use of genealogies in his later writings (1 Tim. 1:4; Titus 3:9).

GENERATION

Period of time and its significant events comprising lifespan of a person but also used to talk of a more indefinite timespan. Hebrew *toledoth* gives structure to Book of Genesis (2:4; 5:1; 6:9; 10:1,32; 11:10,27; 25:12-13,19; 36:1,9; 37:2). Thus creation, Adam, Noah, Noah's sons, Shem, Terah, Ishmael, the sons of Ishmael, Isaac, Esau, and Jacob each provide a generation and a structural unit in the Genesis narrative. Israel thus modified a pattern long used by Near Eastern neighbors, that of describing creation as a series of births. Israel's neighbors spoke of the birth of gods, such births representing at the same time a part of the universe, since the sun, moon, and the stars were all looked on as gods. Israel simply spoke of the birth of creation by God's words and actions. This started a process by which human generations would endure as long as the first generation—creation—endured. Each human generation lasts from the death of the father through the death of the son. Human history in its simplest form of family history, the continuing series of human births and deaths, is the way God tells His story of working with human beings to bless them and to accomplish His purposes for them.

Hebrew *dor* refers to life circle of an individual, either from birth to death or from birth to the birth of the first child. Genesis 15:13-16 apparently equates 400 years with four generations, thus 100 years per generation. Numbers 32:11-13 may reckon a generation as 60 years, including people 20 and above and giving them 40 more years to live. One may interpret this to mean a generation is the 40 years of adulthood between ages 20 and 60. God promised Jehu his sons would rule to the fourth generation, apparently meaning four sons (2 Kings 10:30; 15:12). Jehu began ruling about 841 B.C., his first son Jehoahaz about 814 B.C., and the fourth generation's Zechariah died about 752 B.C. The five generations ruled less than 90 years, while the four sons' generations ruled about 60 years. This is reducing a generation to a quite small number. After his tragedies, Job lived 140 years and saw four generations (Job 42:16). This would make a generation about 35 years. Basically, generation is not a specific number of years but a more or less specific period of time. (See Job 8:8; Isa. 51:9.)

The generations come and go (Eccl. 1:4). This should establish wisdom on which a present generation can draw (Deut. 32:7). A generation also represents those who can gather for worship, so that the gathered worship community forms a generation (Pss. 14:5; 24:6; 73:15). The generations of people change, but God has given His name Yahweh to be remembered through all generations (Ex. 3:15). He is the refuge for all generations (Ps. 90:1). The danger is that a generation will arise that does not know Yahweh (Judg. 2:10; compare Ps. 12). Thus, one generation must tell God's acts and write them down for the next generation (Pss. 22:30-31; 102:18, NRSV; compare Ps. 79:13). God is faithful to a thousand generations by His very nature (Deut. 7:9). His salvation is available through the generations: that is forever (Isa. 51:8). Jesus often used "generation" to describe the evil nature of the people He addressed (Matt. 11:16; 12:39; Luke 17:25). The message of the NT can be summarized: "Unto him be glory in the church by Christ Jesus throughout all ages, world without end" (Eph. 3:21).

GENESIS, BOOK OF

First book of the Bible, providing a universal setting for God's revelation and introducing basic biblical teachings. Genesis moves in two parts:

(1) universal creation, rebellion, punishment, and restoration;

(2) God's choice of a particular family through whom He promises to bless the nations.

Genesis 1–11 provides the universal setting for Israel's story. Taking up themes and motifs prominent in the literature of their neighbors, the inspired writer showed how only one God participated in creation of the whole world and in directing the fortunes of all its nations. The focus narrows from creation of the universe to creation of the first family (1:1–2:25). Trust in a wily serpent rather than in God brought sin into the world and shows God's judgment on sin. Thus human life is lived out in the suffering, pain, and frustration of the world we know (ch. 3). In that world God continues to condemn sin, bless faithfulness, and yet show grace to sinners (4:1-15). From the human perspective, great cultural achievements appear, but so does overwhelming human pride (4:16-24). Thus humans multiply their race as God commanded; they also look for a better life than that of pain and toil (4:25–5:32). Help does come, but only after further punishment. Through the flood, God eliminated all humanity except the family of Noah, then made a covenant with that family never again to bring such punishment (6:1–9:17), but human sin continued at the individual and the societal levels, bringing necessary divine punishment of the nations at the tower of Babel (9:18–11:9).

God thus established a plan to redeem and bless the humanity that persists in sin. He called one man of faith, Abraham, and led him to a new beginning in a new land. He gave His promises of land, nation, fame, and a mission of blessing for the nations. This worked itself out in blessing nations that helped Abraham and punishing those who did not. It climaxed in God's covenant with Abraham in which Abraham showed faithfulness in the sign of circumcision, and God renewed His promises.

New generations led by Isaac and Jacob find God continuing to lead them, to call them to be His people, and to renew His promises to them. Human trickery and deception personified in Jacob did not alter God's determination to carry out His redemptive plan. Thus is established the heritage of God's people in the triad of patriarchal fathers—Abraham, Isaac, and Jacob. God's promises and revelation to them became the foundation of Israel's religious experience and hope. See *Creation; Flood; Sin; Humanity; Anthropology; Earth; Image of God; Abraham; Isaac; Jacob; Joseph; Adam and Eve; Noah; Names of God.*

GENNESARET See *Galilee, Sea of.*

GENTILES

People of the nations who are not part of God's chosen family at birth and thus can be considered "pagans." As covenant people, Israel knew themselves to be different from the nations (Ex. 19:16; Lev. 19:2; Deut. 7:3,6,16; Ezra 6:21; 2 Kings 16:3).

Affliction by other nations increased tension between Israel and the nations, which gave rise to invoking curses on the nations (Pss. 9; 59; 137). The ultimate punishment of Israel for disobedience was being scattered among the nations with all their differences. The nations were under God's control and were unconsciously being used (Isa. 10:5-7; compare 45:22-24) but would be punished (Isa. 10:12-16; compare Joel 3:12-16).

The door was never closed to the foreigner who wished to serve the Lord (1 Kings 8:41-43). God looked for the day when the nations would gather to worship the God of Jacob (Pss. 86:9; 102:15-17; Isa. 2:2-4; Zeph. 3:9-10). Israel's mission was to bring justice (Isa. 42:1) and light to the nations (Isa. 49:6).

Jesus' ministry related to OT expectations for the Gentiles. Though He directed His work to Jews (Matt. 15:24) and at first limited His disciples to them (Matt. 10:5), Jesus was a light to the Gentiles (Matt. 4:16-17; Luke 2:32). He threatened that the kingdom would be taken from the Jews and given to a nation bringing its fruits (Matt. 21:43). Though Jesus was crucified by Gentiles (Matt. 20:19), equal blame is placed on both Gentiles and Jews (Acts 4:27).

Following the resurrection of Jesus, the commission included "all nations" (Matt. 28:19; compare 25:31-32; Acts 2:39). At the house of Cornelius, the Spirit was poured out on the Gentiles (Acts 10:45; 11:1,18; 15:7). The apostolic gathering in Jerusalem freed Gentiles from obedience to the law (Acts 15:19; compare 21:19,21,25).

In apostolic preaching, the promise to Abraham (Gen. 12:3; 18:18) found fulfillment (Gal. 3:8). Though in times past the Gentiles had been without God (Eph. 2:12-22), God in Christ broke through all boundaries (see 1 Pet. 2:9). Paul, sent to preach among the Gentiles (Acts 9:15; 22:21; 26:17; Gal. 1:16; 2:9), was in peril (2 Cor. 11:26). When rejected in the synagogues, he turned to the Gentiles (Acts 13:46; 18:6; 28:28), understanding his work in the light of OT predictions (Acts 13:47-48; Rom.

15:9-12). As the apostle to the Gentiles (Gal. 2:8-9), claiming that in Christ racial distinctions were obliterated (Gal. 3:28), Paul proclaimed an equal opportunity of salvation (Rom. 1:16; 9:24; Col. 3:11; compare Acts 26:20,23; Rom. 11:16-25). Paul experienced great resentment among the Jews because of the opportunity he was offering the Gentiles (2:15-16).

The apocalypse depicts a redeemed multitude of all nations (Rev. 5:9; 7:9), and the One who overcomes has power over the nations (Rev. 2:26). All nations come to worship (Rev. 15:4) One born to rule with a rod of iron (Rev. 12:5; compare 21:23-24,26; 22:2).

GERAR (*drag away*)

City between Gaza and Beersheba (Gen. 20; 26) on border of Canaanite territory (Gen. 10; 19); possibly tell Abu Hureirah on northwest side of Wadi Esh-Sheriah. See 2 Chron. 14:13-14. TEV reads "Gerar" with the earliest Greek translation of 1 Chron. 4:39-40.

GERASA, GERASENES

(1) See *Gadara*.

(2) Town located 26 miles north of present-day Amman in Jordan. See *Arabia*.

GERGESENES See *Gadara*.

GERIZIM AND EBAL (*cut off ones* and *stripped one* or *baldy*)

Two mountains that form the sides of important east-west pass—the Valley of Shechem—that controls all roads through the central hill country of Israel. Ancient Shechem lies at the east entrance, and modern Nablus stands in the narrow valley between the two mountains.

Gerizim (Jebel et-Tor) stands 2,849 feet above the Mediterranean and 700 feet above the valley. Ebal (Jebel Eslamiyeh), directly opposite Gerizim, is 2,950 feet above sea level. Joshua obeyed Moses and placed half the tribes on Mount Gerizim to pronounce the blessing (Deut. 27:12)

and the other half on Mount Ebal to pronounce the curses (Deut. 11:29; Josh. 8:30-35). Joshua built an altar on Ebal (Josh. 8:30). See Judg. 9:7; 2 Kings 17:33.

Josephus reported that Alexander the Great gave the Samaritans permission to build a temple on Mount Gerizim. Josephus also reported that John Hyrcanus destroyed the temple in 128 B.C. The small Samaritan community continues to worship on Gerizim today, just as they did in Jesus' lifetime when He met the Samaritan woman drawing water from Jacob's well (John 4:20). See *Samaritans*.

GERSHOM (*sojourner there, expelled one*, or *protected of the god Shom*)

(1) First son of Moses and Zipporah (Ex. 2:22). Apparently Gershom was the son circumcised in the unusual ritual of Ex. 4:24-26.

(2) Son of Levi and head of a clan of Levitic priests (1 Chron. 6:16-20, 43, 62, 71; 15:7). 1 Chron. 23:14 shows that Moses' sons had been incorporated into the line of Levites. Compare 1 Chron. 26:24.

(3) Man who accompanied Ezra on return from Babylon to Jerusalem (Ezra 8:2).

GERSHON

Eldest son of Levi (Gen. 46:11); progenitor of Gershonites who were responsible for transporting the tabernacle in the wilderness. Compare Ex. 6:16-17; Num. 3:17-25; 4:22-41; 7:7; 10:17; 26:57; Josh. 21:6,27. First Chronicles often spells the name "Gershom."

GESHEM (*rain*)

Arabian ruler of Kedar who joined Sanballat and Tobiah in opposing Nehemiah's efforts to rebuild the wall of Jerusalem (Neh. 2:19; 6:1-19). In name, he was a vassal of Persia but apparently wielded great personal power with tribes in the Syrian desert, southern Palestine, the delta of Egypt, and northern Arabia.

GESHUR (bridge), GESHURI or GESHURITE

Small Aramean city-state between Bashan and Hermon; served as buffer between Israel and Aram. See 2 Sam. 3:3; 13:37-38. Many scholars think Josh. 13:2 and 1 Sam. 27:8 refer to a group of southern Philistine cities about which nothing else is known.

GESTURES

Movements of either a part or all of the body to communicate one's thoughts and feelings. Gestures often may involve external objects such as the tearing of one's clothing (Joel 2:13) or the casting down of one's crown before God (Rev. 4:10).

Whole Body Gestures

(1) Standing to pray indicates respect to God (1 Sam. 1:26; 1 Kings 8:22; Mark 11:25).

(2) Sitting before the Lord indicates reverence, humility, and submission (2 Sam. 7:18), while Jesus sitting down at the right hand of God indicates finality and completion as well as power and authority (Heb. 10:12).

(3) Kneeling and bowing express honor, devotion, and submission in worship (1 Kings 19:18; Isa. 45:23; Rev. 4:10; 5:8) and reverence in prayer (1 Kings 8:54; 18:42; Dan. 6:10; Luke 22:41).

(4) Weeping can be a sign of both sorrow (Job 16:16; Jer. 9:10; Luke 22:62; John 11:35) and happiness (Gen. 46:29).

(5) Dancing shows joy (Ex. 15:20; Judg. 11:34) and celebration in praise (2 Sam. 6:16; Ps. 149:3).

(6) Tearing of one's clothes and heaping of ashes upon one's head signify deep grief (2 Sam. 1:11; 13:19), shocking horror (Num. 14:6; Josh. 7:6), and sudden alarm (Matt. 26:65; Acts 14:14).

Head Gestures

(1) Shaking one's head communicates scorn and reproach (Ps. 22:7; Lam. 2:15; Matt. 27:39; Mark 15:29).

(2) Lifting one's head can indicate exaltation (Ps. 27:6), contempt (Ps. 83:2), and freedom (2 Kings 25:27).

(3) Bowing one's head shows reverence in worship and prayer (Gen. 24:26; Neh. 8:6).

Face Gestures

(1) Winking the eye may show mischief and deceit (Prov. 6:13), which also can lead to sorrow (Prov. 10:10). Wanton eyes are sensual eyes that deserve condemnation (Isa. 3:16). Jesus' looking at Peter at the point of his denial is an example of eyes showing both hurt and condemnation (Luke 22:61). The lifting of one's eyelids expresses haughtiness and pride (Prov. 30:13). One's eyes can show anger (Mark 3:5). The eyes, when uplifted in prayer, signify both respectful acknowledgment of God and devotion to Him (Mark 6:41; Luke 9:16). To fail to lift one's eyes up to God while praying indicates one's sense of unworthiness (Luke 18:13). Jesus' lifting up of His eyes upon the disciples shows His personal regard for them (Luke 6:20).

(2) To smile and laugh can mean happiness and joy and show goodwill (Job 29:24), scorn (Ps. 22:7; Mark 5:40; Luke 8:53), or even rebuke (Ps. 2:4). The shooting out of the lip communicates contempt (Ps. 22:7). Kissing is an act that expresses the warmth of a friendly greeting (Rom. 16:16; 1 Cor. 16:20), the affection of one for another (Song of Sol. 8:1), the sorrow of one who dearly cares for another (Ruth 1:14; Acts 20:37), the deceit of one who hides true intentions (Prov. 27:6; Matt. 26:48), the submission of the weak to the strong (Ps. 2:12), and the seduction of a foolish man by a loose woman (Prov. 7:5-23). Spitting is an emphatic way of showing contempt to shame another (Deut. 25:9; Isa. 50:6; Matt. 26:67; 27:30).

(3) To incline one's ear is to give attention to another (Ps. 45:10; Jer. 7:26).

(4) Putting a branch to the nose, a pagan gesture, is an offense to God and possibly has obscene connotations (Ezek. 8:17).

(5) A hardened neck indicates stubbornness (Neh. 9:16; Prov. 29:1; Jer. 7:26), while an outstretched neck reveals haughtiness (Isa. 3:16).

Hand Gestures

(1) The raising of hands in prayer is a gesture signifying one's request is unto God (Ps. 141:2; 1 Tim. 2:8). The raising of one's hands can also be a symbol of blessing (Lev. 9:22; Neh. 8:6; Luke 24:50), or it can be an act that gives emphasis to an oath (Deut. 32:40; Ezek. 20:5,15,23,28).

(2) Covering one's mouth with the hand signifies silence (Job 29:9).

(3) Lifting one's hand or shaking one's fist means defiance (2 Sam. 18:28; Isa. 10:32; Zeph. 2:15).

(4) Laying a hand or hands on someone can mean violence (Gen. 37:22), or it can mean favor and blessing as on a son (Gen. 48:14) or in healing (Luke 4:40; Acts 28:8). The placing of hands on someone's head shows favor and blessing as in the acknowledgment of an office (Acts 6:6) or in the coming of the Holy Spirit (Acts 8:17). Striking or shaking of hands indicates a guarantee or confirmation (Prov. 6:1; 17:18; 22:26), while the giving of one's hand to another is a sign of fellowship (2 Kings 10:15; Prov. 11:21).

(5) To clap one's hands can mean either contempt (Job 27:23; Lam. 2:15; Nah. 3:19) or joy and celebration (2 Kings 11:12; Pss. 47:1; 98:8; Isa. 55:12).

(6) Waving one's hand can mean to beckon (Luke 5:7; John 13:24), to call for silence in order to speak (Acts 12:17; 13:16; 19:33), or to call on God for healing (2 Kings 5:11).

(7) Dropping hands shows weakness and despair (Isa. 35:3; Heb. 12:12).

(8) A hand on one's head communicates grief (2 Sam. 13:19; Esth. 6:12; Jer. 2:37).

(9) Washing one's hands in public declares one's innocence (Deut. 21:6-7; Matt. 27:24).

(10) Pointing a finger can show ill favor (Prov. 6:13) or accusation (Isa. 58:9).

(11) The hand or arm outstretched is a sign of power and authority (Ex. 6:6).

(12) To hug or embrace is to show warmth in greeting another (Gen. 33:4).

Feet Gestures

(1) Placing a foot on one's enemy shows victory and dominance for the one standing, defeat and submission for the one downfallen and vanquished (Josh. 10:24; Ps. 110:1; 1 Cor. 15:25).

(2) To shake the dust off one's feet is a sign of contempt and separation (Matt. 10:14; Acts 13:51).

(3) To wash the feet of another is to humble oneself as a servant (John 13:5-12).

(4) Lifting one's heel against another shows opposition (Ps. 41:9; John 13:18).

(5) To cover one's feet is to relieve oneself with some degree of privacy (Judg. 3:24; 1 Sam. 24:3).

(6) To uncover one's feet or to walk barefooted indicates grief or repentance (2 Sam. 15:30; Isa. 20:2).

(7) Uncovering one's feet as in the case of Ruth with Boaz (Ruth 3:4) was an established practice, indicating not only one's willingness to marry but also the protection of the husband over his wife.

Old Testament Sacrificial Gestures

(1) Eating with loins girded, shoes on your feet, and staff in your hand (Ex. 12:11) symbolizes urgency and readiness (Ex. 12:14).

(2) Putting a hand on the head of the burnt offering and killing it let the sinner identify with the animal to be killed and sacrificed.

New Testament Sacrificial Gestures

(1) Baptism is a whole body gesture that expresses one's identification with Christ's atoning work.

(2) The Lord's Supper (Matt. 26:26-30; 1 Cor. 11:23-29) emphasizes one's identification with the sacrificial death of Christ and a willingness to deny oneself and take up the cross (Matt. 16:24) to follow Christ.

Prophetic Symbolic Gestures

(1) Prophets dramatized their message with symbolic gestures. Ezekiel's mock attack against a clay model of Jerusalem symbolized of God's impending judgment on the city (Ezek. 4:1-3).

(2) Jeremiah's purchase of a field (Jer. 32:1-44) symbolized God's future restoration of the Southern Kingdom as its Kinsman Redeemer.

(3) Walking naked and barefoot symbolized the humiliation Egypt and Ethiopia were to know when Assyria conquered them (Isa. 20:3).

(4) Wearing a yoke of wood around his neck symbolized the Babylonians' domination over Judah and her neighbors (Jer. 27:1-7). Laying on your side for many days (Ezek. 4:4-8) indicated bearing the people's sin, a year for each day of their iniquity and of their impending siege. Eating scant rations (Ezek. 4:9-17), cutting his hair and its various consequences (Ezek. 5:1-17), and the setting of his face toward the mountains of Israel (Ezek. 6:1-7)—all symbolized the judgment of God was soon to come upon his people. (See Ezek. 12:1-28 for additional examples.)

GETHSEMANE (*olive press*)

Place Jesus went to pray after Last Supper; garden outside city, across the Kidron on the Mount of Olives (Matt. 26:36-56; Mark 14:32-52; Luke 22:39-53; John 18:1-14). Judas led the enemies of Jesus to Gethsemane where Jesus was arrested and taken away for trial.

GEZER (*isolated area*)

One of largest and most important cities in Palestine, Levitic city in Ephraim (Josh. 16:3; 21:21); 19 miles northwest of Jerusalem at tell Gezer on edge of Judah's foothills near Shephelah, 7 miles southeast of Ramleh; military post for highway junction of the Via Maris and the road leading through the valley of Ajalon to Jerusalem, Jericho, and over the Jordan. Archaeologists have found important inscriptions here such as

the Gezer calendar, perhaps the earliest (before 900 B.C.) example of Hebrew writing known. A high place or sanctuary with 10 stone stele or masseboth demonstrates Canaanite worship practices about 1600 B.C. Some of these tower over 9 feet high. Merneptah's stele from about 1200 B.C. claims the pharaoh captured Gezer. Tiglath-pileser III of Assyria pictured the capture of Gezer about 734 B.C. in his palace at Nimrud. See Josh. 10:33; 16:10; Judg. 1:29; 2 Sam. 5:25; 1 Kings 9:15-17; 1 Chron. 20:4. Between the Testaments, Gezer became known as Gazara.

GHOST

KJV for human life force given up at death (Gen. 25:8; 35:29; Matt. 27:50; Acts 5:5; 12:23) and for God's Holy Spirit; never for the disembodied spirits of the dead. Jesus' disciples mistook Him for a ghost as He walked on water (Matt. 14:26; Mark 6:49) and when He appeared after the resurrection (Luke 24:37, 39).

GIANTS

Persons of unusual stature often reputed to possess great strength and power. Nephilim born to the "daughters of men" and the "sons of God" (Gen. 6:1-4) were giants. Some interpreters understand the "sons of God" to be angelic beings who intermarried with human women (see Jude 6). Others view them as descendants of Seth who intermarried with the ungodly. Later descendants of the nephilim were called "the sons of Anak" (Num. 13:33) or Anakim (Deut. 2:11; 9:2). Egyptian records testify to their presence as early as 2000 B.C. Similar races of giants had also inhabited Moab (Deut. 2:9-10) and Ammon (Deut. 2:19-20).

Og, king of Bashan, was the last survivor of the rephaim (Deut. 3:11, 13; compare Josh. 15:8; 17:15; 18:16). Goliath (1 Sam. 17) was a Philistine champion. A family of giants from Gath were among the Philistine enemies David and his followers killed (2 Sam. 21:16-22; 1 Chron. 20:4-8).

GIBBETHON (arched, hill, or mound)

Levitic city in Dan (Josh. 19:44; 21:23); variously identified as tell el-Melat north of Ekron, and as Agir, two-and-a-half miles west of tell el-Melat. During the monarchy, the Philistines controlled Gibbethon. See 1 Kings 15:25-28; 1 Kings 16:15-17.

GIBEAH (a hill) or GIBEATH

Closely related to names of Geba and Gibeon.

(1) City in hill country of Judah (Josh. 15:57); may be home of King Abijah's mother Maacah (2 Chron. 13:2) and could be same as place name presupposed in list of Caleb's descendants (1 Chron. 2:49).

(2) City closely connected with Phinehas, high priest and grandson of Aaron; his father Eleazar was buried there (Josh. 24:33); some identify it with levitical city of Geba (Josh. 21:17) in Benjamin.

(3) The ark was lodged on a hill (Hebrew, Gibeah) between its return by the Philistines and David's initial effort to move it to Jerusalem (2 Sam. 6:4, KJV); Hebrew word is probably not a proper noun ("hill," NASB, NIV, NRSV, REB; compare 1 Sam. 7:1-2; Josh. 15:9-11).

(4) Most significant Gibeah was a city in Benjamin (Josh. 18:28). See Judg. 19:1–21:25; tell el-Ful on a high ridge three-and-a-half miles north of Jerusalem. Saul had family connections to the city (also connected with the nearby and similar-sounding Gibeon; see Gibeon, 1 Chron. 8:29-33) and made it his capital after he became king (1 Sam. 10:5,26; 15:34; 23:19). If the "hill of God" (1 Sam. 10:5 KJV, NASB, REB) or "Gibeath-elohim" (NRSV) should be translated "Gibeah of God" (NIV) and equated with Gibeah of Saul, then the Philistines controlled the city prior to Saul gaining control. See Isa. 10:29; Hos. 5:8; 9:9; 10:9.

GIBEON (hill place), GIBEONITE

Canaanite industrial, wine-growing area that became Levitic city in Benjamin (Josh. 18:25; 21:17); el-Jib, eight miles northwest of Jerusalem; settled about 3000 B.C. Its 2,400 foot elevation made it easily defended, so it served as the fortress city at the head of the Valley of Ajalon, which provided the principal access from the coastal plain into the hill country.

The people of Gibeon concocted a deceptive strategy to protect themselves from the Israelites (Josh. 9). When Joshua later discovered the truth, he forced the Gibeonites to become water carriers and woodcutters for Israel.

Saul's family seems to have had some connections to Gibeon (1 Chron. 8:29-33; 9:35-39). See Gibeah. Following Saul's death a crucial meeting occurred in Gibeon involving Abner and Joab, the respective generals of Saul and David (2 Sam. 2:12-17). See 2 Sam. 20:8-13; 21:1-9. During one of the sacrifices Solomon made in Gibeon, the Lord appeared and granted the new king's request for wisdom (1 Kings 3:3-14; compare 9:2). Apparently, Gibeon was Israel's major place of worship before Solomon built the temple. See Jer. 28; 41; Neh. 3:7; compare 7:25.

GIDEON (one who cuts to pieces)

Fifth major judge of Israel; also called Jerubbaal; from Manasseh (Judg. 6:11–8:35). God called Gideon to deliver Israel from the Midianites and Amalekites, desert nomads who repeatedly raided the country. Twice he laid out the fleece, apparently trying to avoid the will of God by imposing impossible conditions. God met his conditions both times and then set out the strategy that would guarantee victory for Israel.

He angrily punished Succoth and Penuel for not helping in his war against the Midianite kings (Judg. 8:1-17). He refused the people's offer to crown him king, testifying that only God was King (Judg. 8:22-23), but he ordered the people to give him their golden earrings, taken as war spoil from the Ishmaelites. He made a worship symbol, an ephod, out of it and led his people astray with it (Judg. 8:24-27). His family did not follow his God (Judg. 8:33).

GIFT, GIVING

A favor or item bestowed on someone as dowry for a wife (Gen. 34:12); tribute to a military conqueror (2 Sam. 8:2); bribes (Ex. 23:8; Prov. 17:8; Isa. 1:23); rewards for faithful service and to ensure future loyalty (Dan. 2:48); and relief for the poor (Esth. 9:22). Since gifts might be required by custom, law, or force, modifiers are sometimes used to specify gifts given voluntarily: "willing" or freewill offerings or gifts (Ex. 35:29); free gift or "gift by grace" (Rom. 5:15-17; 6:23); bountiful gift not motivated by covetousness (2 Cor. 9:5).

God is the giver of every good gift (1 Chron. 29:14; Jas. 1:17; see Gen. 1:29; 2:18-24; 3:12; 17:16; 28:20; Ex. 31:6; Lev. 26:4; Num. 21:16; Deut. 8:18; 11:15; Ps. 127:2; Dan. 1:17; Job 1:21). These gifts demonstrate God's general providence.

Scripture also witnesses to God's gifts as evidence of a special providence. In the OT such gifts include: the Promised Land (Gen. 12:7), including its successful conquest (Deut. 2:36), possessing its cities (Deut. 6:10), and its spoils (Deut. 20:14); the sabbath (Ex. 16:29); the promises (1 Kings 8:56); the covenants (2 Kings 17:15); the law (Ex. 24:12); and peace (Lev. 26:6). In the NT, God's special providence is especially evident in the gift of God's Son (John 3:16) and of God's Holy Spirit (Luke 11:13).

God makes relationship with Himself possible by giving His people wisdom (1 Kings 4:29), understanding (1 Kings 3:9), a new heart (1 Sam. 10:9), and a good Spirit to teach them (Neh. 9:20). The NT expresses these gifts as the power to become children of God (John 1:12), justification from sin (Rom. 3:24; 5:15-17); and eternal life (John 10:28; Rom. 6:23).

Both Testaments witness to God's gift of leadership to God's people as: priests (Num. 8:19; Zech. 3:7); Davidic kings (2 Chron. 13:5); deliverers (2 Kings 13:5); shepherds with Godlike hearts (Jer. 3:15); apostles, prophets, evangelists, and pastor-teachers (Eph. 4:11-12). Paul spoke of God's giving the ministry of reconciliation (2 Cor. 5:18), authority for building up the church (2 Cor. 10:8), and grace for sharing the gospel with the Gentiles (Eph. 3:8). The NT also stresses God's gift of spiritual abilities to every believer (Rom. 12:6; 1 Cor. 12:4; 1 Pet. 4:10).

God's gifts should prompt the proper response from the recipients. This response includes not boasting (1 Cor. 4:7; Eph. 2:8) but amazement at God's inexpressible goodness (2 Cor. 9:15); the using of gifts for the furtherance of Christ's kingdom (1 Tim. 4:14; 2 Tim. 1:6-11); and a life of good works (Eph. 2:10).

GIFTS, SPIRITUAL See *Spiritual Gifts.*

GIHON (*gushing fountain*)

Primary water supply for Jerusalem from spring in Kidron Valley and one of four rivers into which river of Eden divided (Gen. 2:13). The river cannot be identified with any contemporary river.

GILBOA

Israelite encampment (1 Sam. 28:4) where Saul and three of his sons died in battle against Philistines (1 Sam. 31:8; compare 2 Sam. 1:17-27); modern Jebel Fuqus, on eastern side of the Plain of Esdraelon.

GILEAD (*raw* or *rugged*), **GILEADITE**

(1) North-central section of Transjordanian highlands northeast of the Dead Sea with peaks over 3,500 feet; famous for flocks and herds; bisected by Jabbok River; kingdom of Ammon occupied its eastern fringe; applied to different areas in different contexts depending on political situations. Compare Judg. 10:17; Hos. 6:8; Amos

1:3. Gilead extends about 50 miles from southern Heshbon not quite to the Yarmuk River in the north. Its east-west extent is about 20 miles. The King's Highway, an important international trade route, passed through Gilead. Gilead was also known for the balm of Gilead, an aromatic and medicinal preparation. See Gen. 31:22-23; 32:30; Judg. 11:1; 2 Sam. 17:24. Old Testament cities of importance were Heshbon in the south, Rabboth-ammon on the eastern desert fringe, Jabesh-gilead, and Ramoth-gilead. Rabboth-ammon is the NT Philadelphia; Pella and Jerash (Gerasa) are other important NT cities.

(2) Great grandson of Joseph and original clan leader in tribe of Manasseh (Num. 26:28-32; 36:1). The clan was so strong it could be listed with Israel's tribes in Deborah's song (Judg. 5:17). They fought for recognition among other tribes (Judg. 12:4-7).

GILGAL (*circle*)

City featuring circle of stones or circular altar; several different Gilgals may well have existed.

(1) Joshua's first camp (Josh. 4:19) and Israel's first worship place, where they were circumcised and observed the Passover (Josh. 5). This Gilgal apparently became Israel's military base of operations (Josh. 9:6; 10:6; 14:6), though some scholars would identify this with a Gilgal farther north near Shechem. Joshua set up Gilgal as the border between Judah and Benjamin (Josh. 15:7; compare 18:17), though many Bible students think the border town must be south of the original camp. (See Judg. 3:19,26; 1 Sam. 7:16; 11:14-15; 13:14-15; 2 Sam. 19:15,40.) Saul was both crowned and rejected as king at Gilgal. Gilgal permitted worship associated with other gods and became the object of prophetic judgment (Hos. 4:15; Amos 4:4; 5:5).

(2) Tell Jiljulieh about three miles southeast of Shiloh or Joshua's original Gilgal. Elijah and Elisha were

associated closely with Gilgal (2 Kings 2:1; 4:38).

(3) Gilgal of the nations, royal city near Dor (Josh. 12:23). Septuagint reads this as "kings of the nations in Galilee," which many scholars think is the original reading.

GIRGASHITE (*sojourner with a deity*) or **GIRGASITE**

Original tribal group inhabiting Canaan, traced back to Canaan, son of Ham and grandson of Noah (Gen. 10:16). Ugaritic texts also apparently mention them.

GLASS

Amorphous substance, usually transparent or translucent formed by fusion of silicates without crystallization; known in Egypt from about 2600 B.C.; value equated with that of gold and used in parallel with jewels (Job 28:17). Transparent glass was not made until NT times when Alexandria, Egypt, became world famous as center for glassware production. Beakers, bowls, flasks, goblets, and bottles were made from the transparent glass.

John probably had transparent glass in mind when he wrote Revelation (Rev. 21:18,21). John also described the sea as being like glass (Rev. 4:6; 15:2).

KJV uses glass for a polished metal mirror (Job 37:18; Isa. 3:23; 1 Cor. 13:12; 2 Cor. 3:18; Jas. 1:23). Glass was not used to make mirrors in biblical times.

GLEANING

Process of gathering grain or produce left in a field by reapers or on a vine or tree by pickers. Mosaic law required leaving this portion so that the poor and aliens might have a means of earning a living (Lev. 19:9-10; 23:22; Deut. 24:19-21; compare Ruth 2). Isaiah compared the few grapes or olives left for gleaners to the small remnant of Israel God would leave when He judged them (Isa. 17:5-9). One day, however, God would again gather or glean His remnant one by one and return them to worship in Jerusalem (Isa. 27:12).

GLORY

Weighty importance and shining majesty accompanying God's presence; basic meaning of Hebrew *kabod* is heavy in weight. (See 1 Sam. 4:18; Prov. 27:3.) Thus, it can refer to a heavy burden (Ex. 18:18; Ps. 38:4; compare more idiomatic uses in Gen. 12:10; 47:4; Ex. 4:10; 7:14). On the other side, it can describe extreme good fortune or mass numbers, a use with many different English translations (see Gen. 13:2; Ex. 12:38; Num. 20:20; 1 Kings 10:2).

The verb thus often comes to mean "give weight to, honor" (Ex. 20:12; 1 Sam. 15:30; Ps. 15:4; Prov. 4:8; Isa. 3:5). Such honor is a recognition of the place of the honored person in the human community. A nation can have such honor or glory (Isa. 16:14; 17:3). This is not something someone bestows on another but a quality of importance that a person, group, or nation has and another recognizes.

"To give glory" is to praise, to recognize the importance of another, the weight the other carries in the community. In the psalms, people give such glory to God; that is, they recognize the essential nature of His Godness that gives Him importance and weight in relationship to the worshiping community. (See Pss. 22:23; 86:12; Isa. 24:15.) Human praise to God can be false, not truly recognizing His importance (Isa. 29:13; compare 1 Sam. 2:30). At times God creates glory for Himself (Ex. 14:4,17; Ezek. 28:22). As one confesses guilt and accepts rightful punishment, one is called on to recognize the righteousness and justice of God and give Him glory (Josh. 7:19; 1 Sam. 6:5). God thus reveals His glory in His just dealings with humans. He also reveals it in the storms and events of nature (Ps. 29; compare Isa. 6). Glory is, thus, that side of God that humans recognize and to which humans respond in confession, worship, and praise. (See Isa. 58:8; 60:1.) In the OT, the greatest revelation of divine glory came on

Sinai (Deut. 5:24). Such experiences are awesome and fearful (Deut. 5:25). Such revelation does not, however, reveal all of God (Ex. 33:17-23).

The NT uses *doxa* to express glory and limits the meaning to God's glory. New Testament carries forward the OT meaning of divine power and majesty (Acts 7:2; Eph. 1:17; 2 Pet. 1:17) and extends this to Christ as having divine glory (Luke 9:32; John 1:14; 1 Cor. 2:8; 2 Thess. 2:14). Divine glory means humans do not seek glory for themselves (Matt. 6:2; John 5:44; 1 Thess. 2:6). They look to receive praise and honor from Christ (Rom. 2:7; 5:2; 1 Thess. 2:19; Phil. 2:16).

GLOSSOLALIA

Technical term for speaking in tongues (Greek *glossa*, "tongue").

GLUTTON

One habitually given to greedy and voracious eating; associated with stubbornness, rebellion, disobedience, drunkenness, and wastefulness (Deut. 21:20). A more general meaning for the Hebrew term as a "good-for-nothing" (Prov. 28:7, TEV) is reflected in some translations: "wastrel" (Deut. 21:20, REB); "profligate" (Deut. 21:20, NIV; Prov. 28:7, REB); "riotous" (Prov. 28:7, KJV). Jesus was accused of being a "gluttonous man, and a winebibber" (Matt. 11:19; Luke 7:34) in this expanded sense of being one given to loose and excessive living. The Bible shows gluttony makes one sleepy, leading to not working and poverty (Prov. 23:21).

GNASHING OF TEETH

Grating one's teeth together; an expression of anger reserved for the wicked and for one's enemies (Job 16:9; Pss. 35:16; 37:12; Lam. 2:16); associated with the place of future punishment (see Matt. 8:12; 13:42,50). There the gnashing of teeth is perhaps an expression of the futility of the wicked before God's judgment or else a demonstration of their continuing refusal to repent and acknowledge the justness of God's judgment. (Compare Rev. 16:9,11.) See *Hell.*

GNAT See *Insects.*

GNOSTICISM

Modern designation (from Greek *gnosis,* "knowledge") for certain religious and philosophical perspectives that existed prior to the establishment of Christianity and for specific systems of belief, characterized by these ideas, which emerged after A.D. 100. Gnosticism established itself as a way of understanding Christianity in all of the church's principal centers. The church was torn by the heated debates over the issues Gnosticism posed. By the end of the second century many of the Gnostics belonged to separate, alternative churches or belief systems viewed by the church as heretical.

Understanding Gnosticism aids in interpreting certain features of the NT. Irenaeus reported that one reason John wrote his Gospel was to refute the views of Cerinthus, an early Gnostic. Over against the Gnostic assertion that the true God would not enter our world, John stressed in his Gospel that Jesus was God's incarnate Son. Wide variations existed among the many Gnostic sects, but certain major features were common to most of them—the separation of the god of creation from the god of redemption; the division of Christians into categories with one group being superior; the stress on secret teachings that only divine persons could comprehend; and the exaltation of knowledge over faith.

Some Gnostics sought to withdraw from the world to asceticism. Other Gnostic systems took an opposite turn into antinomianism (belief that moral law is not valid for a person or group). They claimed that spiritual Christians were not responsible for what they did and could not really sin. They could act any way they pleased without fear of discipline.

Gnostics placed great stress on secret teachings or traditions given by Jesus either in special revelation or through His apostles. The secret knowledge was superior to the revelation recorded in the NT and was an essential supplement to it because only this secret knowledge could awaken or bring to life the divine spark or seed within the elect. Salvation came through knowledge rather than faith. This precise knowledge was a self-discovery each Gnostic had to experience.

The early Christian preachers and writers, seeking to speak and write to be understood, used terms current in the first- century world in the vague context of Gnostic religious longings and gave them new meaning in the context of the incarnation, death, and resurrection of Jesus.

GOAT See *Animals.*

GOD

Personal Creator worthy of human worship because of His holy nature and His perfect love revealed in creating the universe, electing and redeeming His people, and providing eternal salvation through His Son Jesus Christ.

God is unique in nature. No person, object, or idea can be compared to God. The reality of God is always much greater than human minds can understand or express. Anything said about God must be based on His revelation of Himself to us.

The Bible and history begin with God (Gen. 1:1; Rev. 22:13). As spirit, God has the perfect capability of being present everywhere in the world at once. Moses experienced that presence on a wilderness mountain (Ex. 3); Isaiah, in the Jerusalem temple (Isa. 6); and Paul, on an international highway (Acts 9). Most often the Bible speaks in terms of God being present in relationships. He called Israel to be His people (Ex. 19:3-6). He appeared to Elijah in a "still, small voice" (1 Kings 19:12). Most of all, God appeared Person to person in the human flesh of His Son Jesus.

The personal presence of God in Jesus Christ is the central and normative source of knowledge about God. Christ is known today through the witness of inspired Scripture and through the personal witness of the Holy Spirit. Even as it is revealed, God's revelation in Jesus Christ remains mysterious (Rom. 16:25-26; Eph. 3:1-10; Col. 1:24-27; 4:2-4). Faith believes that what remains hidden in mystery is totally consistent with what is revealed in Christ.

Perhaps the closest we can come to a definition is that God is the holy Being who is Love in servant form. See Ps. 99:9; 1 John 4:8,16. The norm for a definition comes in Jesus, who said, "I am among you as he that serveth" (Luke 22:27; 2 Cor. 4:5).

God is the only God. God is the living God. This separates Him from all other gods and idols, which are merely forms humans have created in the image of things God created (Isa. 41:22-24; 44:9-20; 46:1-2,6-7; Jer. 10:10; compare 1 Thess. 1:9). Christians join Peter in confessing, "Thou art the Christ, the Son of the living God" (Matt. 16:16).

The living God is also Lord and Master. God is sovereign Ruler over all the earth, the Creator and Judge of all persons. He is "Lord of lords" (Deut. 10:17). Jesus the crucified is both Lord and Christ (Acts 2:36). Jesus receives the same titles as the Father, leading to a doctrine of the Trinity.

God is holy. This is the unique quality of God's existence that marks Him off as separate and distinct from all else. Holiness belongs to God alone. It sets Him above us in majesty, power, authority, righteousness, moral purity, and love. Persons or objects can be said to be holy only by virtue of being drawn into relationship with God (Lev. 11:44; 19:2; Isa. 5:16; 6:3; 1 Pet. 1:15-16).

God is eternal. He has no beginning and no ending. God has always existed and will always continue to exist. God is spirit. He is not material or physical as we are. As Spirit, He does not have the limitations of material form. Spirit enables God to be with His people everywhere simultaneously. As Spirit, God chose to hum-

ble Himself and take on the form of human flesh (Phil. 2:6-11).

God is love (1 John 4:8,16). God's love is always righteous, and His righteousness is always marked by love. Love is the primary motivation behind revelation (John 3:16). God's love is expressed as His mercy in forgiving sinners and in rescuing or blessing those who do not deserve His attention.

God is Father. The love of God finds supreme expression as Father. God is Father in three separate senses that must not be confused:

(1) He is Father of Jesus Christ in a unique sense—by incarnation (Matt. 11:25-27; Mark 14:36; Rom. 8:15; Gal. 4:6; 2 Pet. 1:17);

(2) He is Father of believers—by adoption or redemption (Matt. 5:43-48; Luke 11:2, 13; Gal. 3:26);

(3) He is Father of all persons—by creation (Ps. 68:5; Isa. 64:8; Mal. 2:10; Matt. 5:45; 1 Pet. 1:17).

God is intimate. He is not an impersonal force like gravity, exerting influence in some mechanical, automatic way. He has personal characteristics, just as we do. He forms relationships and has purpose and will. He is a jealous God, taking Himself seriously and insisting that others take Him seriously (Ex. 34:14; Nah. 1:2; 1 Cor. 10:22).

God's glory refers to the weight or influence He carries in the universe and to the overwhelming brilliance when He appears to people (Ex. 16:7-10; Isa. 6:3; Eph. 1:12-17; Heb. 1:3). It is His presence in all His sovereign power, righteousness, and love. We see the glory of God when we are deeply impressed with a sense of His presence and power.

God's wisdom is His perfect awareness of what is happening in all of His creation in any given moment. This includes His knowledge of the final outcome of His creation and of how He will work from beginning to ending of human history (Job 11:4-12; 28:1-28; Ps. 139; Rom. 11). It also includes His ability to know what is best for each and every one of His creatures.

God's *power* is His ability to accomplish His purposes and carry out His will in the world. He can do what needs to be done in any circumstance (Job 36:22-33; Isa. 40:10-31; Dan. 3:1-30; Matt. 19:16-26; 1 Cor. 1:18-25).

God's *righteousness* expresses itself in many ways (Ex. 2:23-25; Josh. 23:1-16; Ps. 71:14-21; Isa. 51:5-8; Acts 10:34-35; Rom. 3:5-26). He is the ultimate standard of right and wrong. He is faithful, constant, and unchanging in His character. He works for the right, seeking to extend righteousness and justice throughout the world. He defends the defenseless, helpless, victimized, and oppressed. He opposes evil through personal expressions of His wrath, anger, judgment, punishment, and jealousy. He sits in present and eternal judgment on those who do evil.

God's *grace* is apparent as He works in love as Redeemer to save the sinful, rebellious human creatures and to renew His fallen creation. He makes salvation possible. He redeemed Israel in the exodus from Egypt (Ex. 1–15); through the prophets He promised a Messiah who would save His people, and in Jesus Christ He provided that salvation (John 3:16). Redemption in Christ completes creation, carrying out the purposes of God and making final, complete salvation possible.

God works in history. The sovereign God exercises His lordship or ownership of the world by continuing to work in His world and through His people. God allows people the freedom to be themselves and make their own free choices, but works within those choices to accomplish His eternal purposes. This is called God's *providence.* God has not predetermined all the events of human history; yet He continues to work in that history in ways we do not necessarily see or understand. God will one day bring His purposes to fulfillment, bringing history to a close and ushering in eternity.

God is Triune. God has revealed Himself as Father and Creator, as Son and Savior, and as Holy Spirit

and Comforter. This has led the church to formulate the uniquely Christian doctrine of the Trinity. New Testament passages make statements about the work and person of each member of the Trinity to show that each is God; yet the Bible strongly affirms that God is one, not three (Matt. 28:19; John 16:5-11; Rom. 1:1-4; 1 Cor. 12:4-6; 2 Cor. 13:14; Eph. 4:4-6). The doctrine of the Trinity is a human attempt to explain this biblical evidence and revelation in harmony with the early Christian message that "God was in Christ, reconciling the world unto himself" (2 Cor. 5:19). It expresses the diversity of God the Father, God the Son, and God the Holy Spirit in the midst of the *unity* of God's being. See *Christ; Holy Spirit; Trinity.*

GODLESSNESS

An attitude and style of life that excludes God from thought and ignores or deliberately violates God's laws. The godless refuse to acknowledge God in spite of the evidence of creation (Rom. 1:22), engage in willful idolatry (1:25), and practice a lifestyle unconstrained by divine limits (1:26-31). The godless show no fear of God's judgment and also seek to involve others in their wickedness (1:32). See 1 Tim. 4:7; compare 6:20; 2 Tim. 2:16.

GODLINESS

An attitude and style of life that acknowledges God's claims on human life and seeks to live in accordance with God's will.

Individuals can be trained in godliness (1 Tim. 4:7). Godly teaching (1 Tim. 6:3) is that which results in godly lives (Titus 1:1). False teachers sought to make their godliness a source of financial gain (1 Tim. 6:5). In lists with other virtues, "godliness" perhaps retains its earlier sense of respect for God and divinely ordained institutions (1 Tim. 6:11; Titus 2:12; 2 Pet. 1:3-7). The form of godliness lacking godly power (2 Tim. 3:5) likely refers to professed godliness that failed to shape moral lives since the profession was not accompanied by a vital relationship with God.

GODS, PAGAN

Objects of false worship in the Bible who had no independent existence or power, since only one God created and rules the universe. Many pagan gods had their origin as gods of certain places such as cities or regions. Such gods or a combination of gods became nationalistic symbols as their cities or regions struggled for political dominance. The names of Near Eastern kings thus frequently contained a national god's name. A by-product of the connection between gods and certain locales was the belief that a god's power was limited to certain regions. Thus, officials of the Syrian king advised a battle with Israel on the plains, observing, "their gods are gods of the hills" (1 Kings 20:23). Israel, against the background of this common belief, struggled with the concept that God was the Lord over all aspects of creation. See *Egypt; Canaan; Assyria; Babylon.*

The gods were thought of as present in their image, or idol, and living in their temples as a king in his palace. The gilded wooden images were in human form, clothed in a variety of ritual garments, and provided with meals. On occasion the images were carried in ceremonial processions or to "visit" one another in different sanctuaries.

The Arameans of Damascus (Syria) worshiped the generic Semitic storm god Hadad, frequently referred to by the epithet Rimmon (2 Kings 5:18; see Zech. 12:11), meaning "thunder." The god Dagon, of the Philistines (Judg. 16:23), was apparently a Semitic god of grain mentioned in the Ugaritic texts as Dagan, the father of Baal. The Philistines worshiped Dagon in temples at Ashdod (1 Sam. 5:1-5) and Beth-Shean (1 Chron. 10:10). The national god of the Ammonites was called Molech (1 Kings 11:7). See *Molech; Milcom.* Molech may have served as a title ("the king"; compare Amos 1:15) for

the Ammonite god much as Baal served as a title for the storm god. Worship of Molech involved human sacrifice, especially making one's children "pass through the fire" (Lev. 18:21; 20:2-5; 2 Kings 23:10; Jer. 32:35). Judges 11:24 refers to Chemosh as the Ammonite god. Chemosh, the national god of the Moabites (Num. 21:29; Jer. 48:46), thus may be identical to Molech although they are listed separately as abominations brought to Jerusalem by Solomon (1 Kings 11:7). Chemosh is mentioned prominently in the famous Moabite Stone. Mesha, king of Moab, probably offered up his son to Chemosh (2 Kings 3:27). (See *Chemosh.*) The Canaanite god Horon was evidently worshiped in the two cities of Beth-horon ("house of Horon"). Resheph (Hebrew for "flame" or "pestilence" Hab. 3:5) was a god of plague, equivalent to the Nergal of Mesopotamia.

The pagan gods of the NT world were the deities of the Greco-Roman pantheon and certain eastern gods whose myths gave rise to the mystery religions. The conquests of Alexander the Great of Macedon took the Greek culture throughout the Near East.

A few of the Greco-Roman gods are mentioned in the NT. At the head of the Greek pantheon was Zeus, the Roman Jupiter, god of the sky, originally the weather or storm god. Zeus was equated with the Semitic storm god Hadad. When Antiochus IV attempted to force Hellenism on the Jews in 167 B.C., he transformed the Jewish temple into a temple to Zeus. A huge altar to Zeus at Pergamum is probably the "Satan's throne" of Rev. 2:13. The messenger of the Greek gods was Hermes (Roman Mercury). When the people of Lystra assumed Barnabas and Paul to be gods (Acts 14:8-18), they called Paul Hermes because he was the spokesman; and they identified Barnabas with Zeus or Jupiter. The oxen and garlands they brought forward were appropriate offerings for Zeus. Hermes was also the god of merchants and travelers. Artemis was the Greek goddess of the wildwood, of childbirth, and, consequently, of fertility. The great mother goddess of Asia Minor worshiped at Ephesus was identified with Artemis, the Roman Diana. Her temple at Ephesus was one of the seven wonders of the ancient world and an object of pilgrimages. Paul's work in Ephesus resulted in an uproar incited by the silversmiths who sold souvenirs to religious pilgrims (Acts 19:23-41).

Other Greco-Roman gods are not mentioned in the NT but formed an important part of Hellenistic culture. These included Apollo, the epitome of youthful, manly beauty and god of medicine, law, and shepherds; Aphrodite, goddess of sexual love and beauty, identified with Semitic goddess Ishtar/Astarte and with Roman Venus; Athena (Roman Minerva), was virgin goddess patron of the city of Athens, connected with arts and crafts, fertility, and war; Hera (Roman Juno) was the wife of Zeus and goddess of marriage, women, and motherhood; Poseidon (Roman Neptune) was god of the sea, earthquakes, and horses; Ares (Roman Mars) the war god; Hephaistos (Roman Vulcan) was god of fire and the patron of smiths; Hades (Roman Pluto) was the Greek god of the underworld. See *Fertility Cult; Mystery, Mystery Religions.*

GOG AND MAGOG

(1) Gog of the land of Magog is the leader of the forces of evil in an apocalyptic conflict against Yahweh (Ezek. 38–39). In Rev. 20:8, Gog and Magog appear together in parallel construction as forces fighting for Satan after his 1,000 year bondage. Ezekiel's prophecy is apparently built on Jeremiah's sermons against a foe from the north (Jer. 4–6). Ezekiel's historical reference may have been Gyges, king of Lydia, who asked Ashurbanipal, king of Assyria, for help in 676 B.C. but then joined an Egyptian-led rebellion against Assyria about 665 B.C. His name became a symbol for the powerful, feared king of the north. Magog is apparently a

Hebrew construction meaning "place of Gog."

(2) Descendant of the tribe of Reuben (1 Chron. 5:4-6).

GOLAN (*circle* or *enclosure*)

City of refuge and Levitic city in Bashan for Manasseh east of the Jordan River (Deut. 4:43; Josh. 21:27); modern Sahem el-Jolan on the east bank of the River el-Allan. See *Cities of Refuge; Levitical Cities.*

GOLD See *Minerals and Metals.*

GOLDEN CALF

Image of young bull, probably constructed of wood and overlaid with gold, which the Hebrews worshiped in the wilderness (Ex. 32:1-8) and in the Northern Kingdom of Israel (1 Kings 12:25-33). See *Aaron; Bethel; Bull; Dan; Exodus; Jeroboam; Moses; YHWH.*

GOLDEN RULE

Command of Jesus (Matt. 7:12; Luke 6:31): Do to others as you would like them to do to you.

GOLGOTHA (*skull*)

Hebrew name for place where Jesus was crucified (Mark 15:22). See *Cross, Crucifixion; Calvary.*

GOLIATH

Huge Philistine champion who baited the Israelite army under Saul in the Valley of Elah for 40 days (1 Sam. 17:4); slain by youthful David. See *El-hanan.*

GOMER (*complete, enough,* or *burning coal*)

(1) Wife of Hosea (Hos. 1:3); "a wife of whoredoms" (Hos. 1:2). She may have been a common prostitute, a cultic prostitute in the service of Baal, a symbol of Israel's worship of many gods, or an ordinary woman who became unfaithful after her marriage to Hosea. Her unfaithfulness to her husband became a sort of living par-

able of Israel's unfaithfulness to Yahweh. See *Hosea.*

(2) Son of Japheth and grandson of Noah in the Table of Nations (Gen. 10:2); apparently seen as representing the Cimmerians, an Indo-European people from southern Russia who settled in Cappadocia in Asia Minor; father of Ashkenaz or the Scythians of Jer. 51:27 who displaced the Cimmerians from their home in Russia.

GOMORRAH See *Sodom and Gomorrah.*

GOOD

Concrete experiences of what God has done and is doing in the lives of God's people. God is and does good (1 Chron. 16:34; Ps. 119:68). See Gen. 50:20; Josh. 21:45; Pss. 14:1,3; 52:9; Mark 8:28; Jas. 1:17. His goodness is experienced in the goodness of His creative work (Gen. 1:31) and saving acts (Ex. 18:9; Ezra 7:9; Ps. 34:8; Phil. 1:6). Persons who seek to live in accordance with God's will are called good. Christians have been saved to do good (Eph. 2:10; Col. 1:10) with the Holy Spirit's help.

GOPHER WOOD

Noah's building material for ark (Gen. 6:14); no certainty as to the type of wood to which it refers. See *Ark.*

GOSHEN, LAND OF

(1) Apparently hill country between Hebron and the Negev (Josh. 10:41; 11:16); some refer it to a country.

(2) Area near city of Goshen in district of Debir (Josh. 15:51); city was either located at Tell el Dhahiriyeh, 12 miles southwest of Hebron or further east.

(3) Area in northeast sector of Nile Delta occupied by the Hebrews from time of Joseph until the exodus (Ex. 8:22; 9:26; compare 12:37; Num. 33:3); "best of the land" (Gen. 47:6,11); equated with "land of Rameses," which was probably identical with or near to the "field of Zoan"; wadi Tumilat, from eastern arm of the Nile to Great Bitter Lakes; 35 miles long and covers 900 square miles. See *Rameses; Zoan.*

GOSPEL

Message and story of God's saving activity through the life, ministry, death, and resurrection of His unique Son Jesus; originally used to describe reports of victory in battle (2 Sam. 4:10); to proclaim God's triumph over God's enemies; good news when God delivered from personal distress (Ps. 40:10); anticipated deliverance and salvation that would come from the hand of God when the long-awaited Messiah appeared to deliver Israel (Isa. 52:7). In NT, "gospel" is actual message on the lips of Jesus about the reign of God (Mark 1:14) and the story told about Jesus after His death and resurrection (Gal. 1:11-12). There is only one gospel (Heb. 1:1-2) with God as its Author (1 Thess. 2:13; compare Rom. 10:14-15; 1 John 1:5).

GOSPELS

First four books of NT giving interpretation of life, teaching, death, and resurrection of Jesus the Messiah. In the NT, "gospel" always refers to oral communication, never to a document or piece of literature. After A.D. 100, the church fathers referred to "gospels" in the plural, indicating written documents. For many years the stories and teachings of Jesus were communicated primarily by word of mouth. About 30 years after Jesus' ascension, three interrelated crises began to impinge upon the church and led to writing "Gospels": persecution, death of eyewitnesses of Jesus, delay of Christ's return.

From approximately A.D. 60 until A.D. 90, four individuals responded to the inspiration of God by writing down the message of, and about, Jesus. They wanted to preserve the gospel message in an accurate form for believers who would follow in future generations and to use a written form of the gospel as an additional tool for evangelism (John 20:30-31).

Each Gospel was written from a slightly different perspective; each one had a different audience in mind; each one was designed to highlight the elements of the gospel that the author felt most important. The four Gospels witness both the divine inspiration of God and the individual, human personalities of their authors. God led the early church to choose four that He had inspired. See *Matthew; Mark; Luke; John.* Other "gospels" were either inadequate Jewish interpretations of Jesus or works heavily influenced by Gnostic heretics. See *Apocrypha, New Testament.*

GOVERNMENT

Sovereign authority over a body of people; customs, mores, laws, and institutions of a people. The rise of the first empires at the beginning of the Early Bronze Age is related in part to the rise of centralized governments. Centralized government was necessary for building and maintaining of canals used for irrigation in Mesopotamia, the development of a standing army, and control over the economic institutions for international trade.

In the Patriarchal period, the Hebrews had no centralized government. The major unit was the extended family or, on a larger basis, the tribe. The oldest male was chief official of family and government. The next level of social organization was the clan, composed of several related extended families. One individual might be designated as chief or head of each clan. The next larger social level was the tribe composed of several clans. A tribe might have a chief or even a prince as its leader. A group of tribes could be known as a people. The tribe was a rather small and isolated group. A clan might be formed by two or three villages banding together, and a tribe by two or three of the clan units.

We assume patriarchal society was nomadic or seminomadic and probably democratic. Tribal decisions would be made on the basis of discussion by all the adult men. The elders held a major source of author-

ity. The elders for a clan were probably the heads of the households that comprised the clan. For a tribe, the elders would have been all the household heads, or selected elders from each clan. Elders had the responsibility to decide many of the everyday matters, religious and judicial, and to represent the community in religious and military matters. They could conclude a covenant (2 Sam. 5:3) or treaty on behalf of the people. The elders regularly dispensed justice at the city gate (Deut. 21:19). See *Elder; Tribes of Israel.*

Israel was a theocracy, having God as King and Ruler (Judg. 8:22-23; 1 Sam. 8:7-9; Pss. 93–99; Rom. 13:1-4). Human government is always limited, intended to be in the framework of God's will. The best ruler will be the one who best carries out God's design for just rule.

With the exodus, Israel became a confederation of tribes with one leader: Moses, then Joshua, then the judges, but with no centralized government. The judge decided cases (Deut. 1:16; 16:18-20; 17:8-9) but was primarily a charismatic military leader (Judg. 3:7-11,12-30; etc.). With Eli and Samuel, the judge became a priestly official. Some judges like Eli and Samuel attempted to have a son assume the office, but it was not hereditary (compare the problems of Abimelech, Judg. 8:22–9:56). The judge was just a tribal chief or leader for several combined tribes. The judge seldom played a strong role in maintaining the people's religious traditions (Judg. 2:10; 17:6; 21:25).

With the monarchy, the king stood as a single ruler for all the people, a sort of chief raised to a national level but with a royal court to carry out his mandate. A new cadre of officials included military officers and a professional army alongside the old militia from the tribes and administrators over administrative districts alongside the old system of elders. A taxation system was developed with its attendant officials. The Samaria ostraca record the receipt of taxes paid from various estates to the government. "*Lamelek*" jar handles (inscribed with "for the king") indicate either taxation or produce of royal farms. Building projects required massive labor, so the corvee or forced-labor contingents were organized. International involvement required officials to conduct warfare against international as well as local nations, negotiate treaties and alliances, make trade and commercial agreements, and arrange royal marriages.

Specific officials included "the one who is over the house," a sort of Secretary of State or Prime Minister; the recorder, a herald, press secretary, and chief of protocol combined; the chief scribe, counselors, priests, and prophets (1 Kings 4). In addition, many attendants would minister to the king.

With the collapse of the monarchy, self-government and independence were lost. Elders continued to function as local leaders, but royal officials were replaced by new imperial and military officials of the conquering power—first Assyria, then Babylon, Persia, and Hellenistic and Roman states. Tax revenues went to the foreign state, and a new legal system had to be obeyed alongside Hebrew law. As seen in the trial of Jesus, that involved hearings before the religious court (at that time the highest Jewish court) and the Roman authorities. The chief ruler was a local governor (such as Nehemiah) appointed by the foreign power or a foreigner (like Pilate) as the Roman procurators. Local kings were allowed to rule only at the pleasure of the foreign power and under the watchful eye of foreign military.

After the exile, Jewish government fell more and more into priestly hands. Even the elders came to have an especially religious role as judicial officers.

In the NT we find Judea governed by a Herodian king appointed by the Roman government. Later direct Roman rule replaced the king. The high priest and the priesthood exercised considerable authority, though it remained in name "religious" authority. The elders belonged to a formal body, the Sanhedrin, as also did certain priests. Civil government now belonged basically to the foreign overlord, but religious power rested in the hands of the priests and Sanhedrin.

GOVERNOR

Appointed civil official charged with the oversight of a designated territory. KJV uses "governor" to translate a variety of terms encompassing almost every form of leadership or oversight: of city and tribal leaders (Judg. 5:9; 1 Kings 22:26), rulers (Ps. 22:28), temple officials (Jer. 20:1), managers of households (John 2:8; Gal. 4:2), and even pilots of ships (Jas. 3:4). Recent versions translate more specifically: ruler, leader, prince, commander, chief officer, master, manager, trustee, and ethnarch, using governor for officials who have administrative responsibility for assigned territories or projects. Generally, the governor exercised both law enforcement and judicial functions as a representative of his superior. See 2 Kings 18:24; 20:24; Ezra 5:3,14; 6:7,13; Neh. 5:14; Isa. 36:9; Hag. 1:1.

Roman "governors" exercised tax and military authority of the emperor. Quirinius (Luke 2:2), Pontius Pilate (Luke 3:1; Matt. 27:2), Felix (Acts 23:24), and Porcius Festus (Acts 24:27) are specifically named.

Because governors are sent by the king "to punish evildoers and for the praise of them that do well" (1 Pet. 2:13-14), believers are to submit to their authority (Rom. 13:1-7). Sent out by Christ, however, Christians will be brought before governors and kings for judgment. Faithfulness in such situations will bear witness for His sake (Matt. 10:18).

GOZAN

Syrian city-state to which the Assyrians exiled many of the people from Israel in 732 (1 Chron. 5:26) and 722 B.C. (2 Kings 17:6; 18:11; see 2 Kings 19:12); probably tel Halaf in northwestern Mesopotamia on southern bank of the River Khabur.

GRACE

Undeserved acceptance and love received from another, especially the characteristic attitude of God in providing salvation for sinners. In secular Greek, "grace" referred to something delightful or attractive in a person, something that brought pleasure to others and came to mean a favor or kindness done to another or of a gift that brought pleasure to another. Viewed by the recipient, "grace" referred to the thankfulness felt for a gift or favor.

The OT refers to the kind turning of one person to another in an act of assistance, such as aid to the poor (Prov. 14:31) and calls upon the gracious assistance of God in times of need (Pss. 4:1; 6:2; 25:16; 31:9; 86:3; 86:16; 123:3). God is said to make one attractive or favorable in the eyes of another (Gen. 39:21; Ex. 3:21; 11:3; 12:36). Persons seek or obtain the favor of another (Gen. 32:5; 33:8; 39:14; Ruth 2:2,10; Esth. 2:17). More rarely it refers to a person receiving God's special favor (Gen. 6:8; Ex. 33:12-19; Judg. 6:17). The OT does not emphasize the recipient's lack of merit as in NT "grace." Closest to this idea are the few passages about God's gracious favor in delivering Israel from captivity (Jer. 31:2; Zech. 4:7; 12:10).

Other Hebrew words refer to the one merciful, loving, gracious God (Ex. 34:6; Neh. 9:17; Pss. 86:15; 103:8; 145:8; Joel 2:13; Jonah 4:2). The idea that Israel did not deserve God's mercy and love is found in the OT (Deut. 7:7-10; 9:4-6; 2 Sam. 7:14-16). Jonah deals with God's merciful concern to save the wicked Ninevites, and Hosea powerfully conveys God's undeserved mercy and grace with the image of the prophet's love for the faithless Gomer. God's grace shines forth clearly in the exodus, where God delivered an undeserving people before they entered into His covenant.

The NT sometimes used "grace" in its more secular meanings: credit or benefit (Luke 6:32-34; 1 Pet. 2:19-20); "gracious" or "attractive" speech (Luke 4:22; Col. 4:6; Eph. 4:29); a visit as "grace" that would bring them pleasure (2 Cor. 1:15, NASB text note); gift in reference to the collection for the Jerusalem saints (1 Cor. 16:3; 2 Cor. 8:1,4,6,7,19); favor of one human to another (Luke 2:52; Acts 2:47; 7:10; 24:27; 25:3,9); God's favor for individuals (Luke 1:28,30; 2:40; Acts 7:46); thanks (Luke 17:9; Heb. 12:28), as in the thanksgiving over a meal (1 Cor. 10:30) or in songs of praise (Col. 3:16). Frequently, Paul employed the set expression, "Thanks be to God" (Rom. 6:17, 7:25; 1 Cor. 15:57; 2 Cor. 2:14; 8:16; 9:15; 1 Tim. 1:12; 2 Tim. 1:3). One wonders if for Paul this common Greek idiom did not carry a deeper nuance, his experience of God's grace leading to his profound sense of thanksgiving.

Paul's profound sense of sin convinced him no person could earn God's acceptance (Rom. 3:23). A person had to accept God's acceptance through Jesus Christ. Law is the way of self-help, of earning one's own salvation. Grace is God's way of salvation, totally unearned (Rom. 3:24; 4:4; 11:6; Eph. 2:8; see John 1:17; 1 Pet. 1:10,13; 5:10). Grace is appropriated by faith in what God has done in Christ on the cross (Rom. 4:16; 1 Cor. 1:4; Eph. 1:6-7; compare 2 Cor. 8:9; 2 Tim. 1:9; 2:1; Heb. 2:9), setting us free from the bondage of sin (Rom. 3:24-31). God's grace comes to sinners, not to those who merit God's acceptance (Rom. 5:20-21).

Grace brings salvation (Acts 11:23; 13:43; 15:11; 18:27; 20:24, 32; Eph. 2:5,8) and eternal life (Rom. 5:21; Titus 3:7). To share in the gospel is to be a partaker of grace (Phil. 1:7; Col. 1:6). In Christ Jesus, God's grace is open to all people (Titus 2:11; compare John 1:14,16; 2 Cor. 4:15). It can be rejected or accepted (2 Cor. 6:1; Gal. 1:6; 5:4; Heb. 10:29; 12:14-15; compare Jude 4). Grace never gives freedom to sin (Rom. 6:1,14-15). All who experience God's grace have gifts of that grace for ministry and service (Acts 4:33; 6:8; 14:26; 15:40; Rom. 12:6; Eph. 4:7; 1 Pet. 4:10). See *Mercy; Love; Justification.*

GRAIN

General term for edible seed of cultivated grasses: "wheat" (Gen. 30:14), "spelt" or emmer (Ex. 9:32, REB "vetches"), "barley" (Ex. 9:31), and "millet" (Ezek. 4:9). KJV normally translates "corn" that means not maize (as in American usage) but any grain.

GRASS

Herbage suitable for consumption by grazing animals (Job 6:5); translation of several words:

(1) Things that sprout and turn green (Gen. 1:11); vegetation to be grazed in the field (Dan. 4:15,23). With rain it forms green pastures (Ps. 23:2). See Isa. 66:14; 2 Kings 19:26.

(2) Pale yellow, green, or gold plants (2 Kings 19:26; Ps. 37:2; Isa. 37:2); green herbs animals eat (Gen. 1:30; 9:3; Num. 22:4); green sprouts of trees (Ex. 10:15); God's judgment destroys the green things (Isa. 15:6); garden vegetables (Deut. 11:10; 1 Kings 21:2; Prov. 15:17).

(3) Annuals the early rains bring forth (Gen. 1:11,29) as contrasted with the perennials; thus herbs of the field (Gen. 1:30; 2:5; 9:3). Humans depend on God to make grass grow (Ps. 104:14; Mic. 5:7; Zech. 10:1). Grass illustrates the brevity of human life (Ps. 102:4,11) but also rich, flourishing growth (Pss. 72:16; 92:7) and the king's enriching favor (Prov. 19:12).

(4) Wild grass growing on roofs (2 Kings 19:26), mountains (Ps. 147:8), and even resistantly hanging on by watering places during drought (1 Kings 18:5). Humans in their mortality can be compared to grass in contrast to God's Word (Isa. 40:6-8; compare 51:12; Pss. 90:5; 103:15). The lily (Matt. 6:28) is later referred to as grass (v. 30).

GRASSHOPPER See *Insects.*

GRAVE

Pit or cave in which a dead body is buried. The most normal grave was the shaft or trench. Caves were often chosen as a convenient alternative to the cost and time involved in cutting a rock tomb. The tomb cut out of rock was sometimes fashioned to serve as a multiple grave with separate chambers. Ledges were often constructed to hold individual family members; and when the tomb was full, the bones from previous burials were set aside to make more room. Bones were placed in jars or stone boxes called ossuaries. Ossuaries sometimes held the bones of more than one person and were frequently marked with decorative or identifying designs. The entrances to tombs were secured either by hinged doorways or large flat stones that could be moved by rolling.

The most desirable grave site was the family tomb to which ample reference is made in the patriarchal narratives of Genesis. The Hebrews apparently envisioned a "shade" existence in death and preferred proximity to ancestors over solitude for the placement of their loved ones' remains.

While most graves were left unmarked, some were marked with trees (Gen. 35:8) or stone pillars (2 Sam. 18:18). The graves of the infamous dead were often marked with a pile of stones (Josh. 7:26; 2 Sam. 18:17; Josh. 8:29; 10:27). In NT times graves were whitewashed each spring so people could easily see and avoid touching them to prevent ritual defilement during the Passover and Pentecost pilgrimages (Matt. 23:27; compare Luke 11:44).

In Hebrew thought, graves were not simply places to deposit human remains. They were in a sense extensions of Sheol, the place of the dead. Since the realm of Sheol was threatening and since each grave was an individual expression of Sheol, the Israelites avoided burial sites when possible and treated them with circumspection. They performed purification rites when contact was unavoidable. See *Death; Eternal Life; Sheol.*

GRAVEN IMAGE See *Idol.*

GREAT SEA See *Mediterranean Sea.*

GRECIA See *Greece.*

GREECE

International power and origin of much Western culture; peninsula between Italian Peninsula and Asia Minor with Adriatic and Ionian Seas on west and Aegean Sea on east; southern end of central European mountain range; southernmost area, the Peloponnesus, virtually an island, connected to mainland by only a narrow neck of land known as Isthmus of Corinth; unusually long shoreline gives it many natural harbors. Since its mountains were heavily forested in earlier times, shipbuilding and the sea trade developed.

Rough terrain discouraged a sense of unity among its people since communication between them was not easy. The land for agriculture was fertile but limited so that what was produced could not sustain a large population. Small grains, grapes, and olives were the main agricultural products while the mountains provided pastures for sheep and goats.

After 800 B.C., city-states began to develop in Greece. Limited food supplies forced Greeks to leave the homeland and establish colonies on Mediterranean islands, Asia Minor, Sicily, Italy, and in the Black Sea area. Colonies provided the basis for trade that encouraged growth of cities since the economy was not tied to agriculture.

The high-water mark for city-states was 500–404 B.C. Athens and Sparta dominated. About 500–475 B.C. Athens beat off a threat from the Persians, and "the Golden Age of Athens" followed. Under its great leader Pericles, Grecian architecture, art, and drama flourished. Peloponnesian city-states feared the power of Athens, however, and united under the leadership of Sparta to war against Athens. The defeat of Athens in 404 B.C. began a period of decline for city-states.

About 350 B.C., Philip II came to the throne of Macedonia, a territory in what is now largely northern Greece, and gradually brought all the Greek peninsula under his control— only to be assassinated in 336 B.C. He was succeeded by his twenty-year-old son, Alexander, whose schoolmaster had been the great philosopher Aristotle. Note Dan. 8:21; 10:20; 11:2; Zech. 9:13. See *Alexander the Great.*

When the Romans took over much of Alexander's empire two centuries later, they imposed their legal and military system but were conquered by Greek culture.

Some of Paul's most fruitful work was done in Greek cities: Philippi (Acts 16); Thessalonica, and Berea (Acts 17:1-14); Athens (Acts 17:16-33).

GREED

Excessive or reprehensible desire to acquire; covetousness (1 Sam. 2:29; Hos. 4:8). Jesus warned against all types of greed (Luke 12:15). The Pauline standard for Christian ministry gave no pretext for greed (1 Thess. 2:5; 1 Tim 3:3,8). Greed marked the Gentile or pagan way of life (Eph. 4:19).

GREEK LANGUAGE

Highly inflected Indo-European language used by NT authors and classical philosophers and writers.

The literary style of the writers of the NT falls somewhere between the extremes of semiliterate to highly stylized. Consequently, the average citizen who lived in Alexandria (Egypt), in Jerusalem, or in Rome could have easily understood the writings found in the Greek of the NT.

GREEN See *Colors.*

GREETING

A salutation on meeting; an expression of good wishes at the opening (or in Hellenistic times also the close) of a letter. Among Semitic peoples the usual greeting was and is peace (*shalom*): "Peace be both to thee, and peace be to thine house, and peace be unto all that thou hast" (1 Sam. 25:5-6; compare Luke 10:5).The usual Greek greeting on meeting is *charein*, translated "hail" or "greeting" (Luke 1:28; Matt. 28:9). A kiss was frequently a part of such greeting (Gen. 29:13; Rom. 16:16; 1 Cor. 16:20; 2 Cor. 13:12; 1 Thess. 5:26; 1 Pet. 5:14). The command not to stop to exchange greetings (2 Kings 4:29; Luke 10:4) underlines the urgency of the commission given.

James is the only NT book to begin with the normal Greek greeting *charein*. Paul transformed the customary greeting into an opportunity for sharing the faith, substituting "Grace [*charis*] to you and peace from God our Father, and the Lord Jesus Christ" (Rom. 1:7; 1 Cor. 1:3; 2 Cor. 1:2; Gal. 1:3; Eph. 1:2; Phil. 1:2; Titus 1:4). See *Letter.*

Hellenistic letters frequently included closing greetings. Most often these are "third person" greetings of the form *X sends you greetings (by me)* (1 Cor. 16:19-20; Col. 4:10-14) or *send my greetings to Y* (who is not directly addressed; see Col. 4:15). Closing greetings often included a prayer or benediction.The simplest is, "Grace be with you" (Col. 4:18; 1 Tim. 6:21; Titus 3:15; Heb. 13:25). Elsewhere the benediction is expanded (Rom. 16:25-27; 1 Cor. 16:23-24; Gal. 6:16; Eph. 6:23-24; Phil. 4:23). Some of the most familiar benedictions used in Christian worship come from such closing greetings (2 Cor. 13:14; Heb. 13:20-21; Jude 24-25).

GRIEF AND MOURNING

Practices and emotions associated with the experience of the death of a loved one or of another catastrophe or tragedy. Jacob mourned for Joseph, thinking he was dead (Gen. 37:34-35; compare 23:2; 50:3). Leaders were mourned, often for 30 days: Aaron (Num. 20:29), Moses (Deut. 34:8), and Samuel (1 Sam. 25:1).

Weeping was the primary indication of grief (John 11:31,35; compare Ps. 42:3a). Loud lamentation was also a feature of mourning (Ex. 12:30),

often with professional mourners (Eccl. 12:5b; compare Matt. 9:23; Jer. 9:17, where "cunning women" suggests professional women mourners practiced certain techniques with unusual skill).

Mourning often involved personal disfigurement, probably to convince onlookers the person was really grieving. Sometimes they tore their garments (Gen. 37:29), wore sackcloth (2 Sam. 3:31), wore black or somber material (2 Sam. 14:2), and covered their heads (2 Sam. 15:30). Job's friends came to help him in silence (Job 2:13).

GUARD

Individual or body of troops assigned to protect a person or thing; officers of foreign kings (Gen. 37:36; 39:1; 2 Kings 25:8-20; Jer. 39:9-13); "watch" (Neh. 4:9; 7:3); "runners" escorting the king's chariot (1 Sam. 22:17; 1 Kings 1:5; 14:27-28); defenders and protectors of king (2 Chron. 23:10); guards of the high priest's quarters (Matt. 26:58; Mark 14:54; composed of Roman soldiers, Matt. 27:66; 28:11). Modern translations frequently use "court of the guard" where KJV used "court of the prison" (Neh. 3:25; Jer. 32:2). God is the guard of His people (Zech. 9:8). Guards had posts or stations (Acts 12:10).

GUILE

Crafty or deceitful cunning; treachery; duplicity; deceit. Jacob dressed in his brother's clothes with the goatskins on his arms and neck is Scripture's best-known illustration of guile (Gen. 27:35; compare John 1:47). Christ was without guile in His mouth (1 Pet. 2:22). Christians are to be "guileless as to what is evil" (Rom. 16:19, NRSV; compare 1 Pet. 2:1), that is, innocent or naïve, or simple (KJV) when it comes to evil.

GUILT

Sense of shame at personal wrongdoing; either a fact or a feeling; implies being responsible for offense or wrongdoing; contrasted with righteousness or just behavior (Job 27:1-6; compare 22:5; 35:1-8); situation that exists because one has done something forbidden or failed to do something required. The source of the forbidden thing or omitted thing may be religious, legal, social, or personal. It may be wrongdoing against something written or unwritten.

To be guilty can mean to be wicked. Psalm 1 assumes the wicked, sinners, and scoffers are guilty of sin and will ultimately perish. No guilt means to be innocent of charges brought against you (compare Luke 23:14; John 19:4,6). Guilt is both corporate (2 Chron. 24:18; Ezra 9:3-6) and individual (Ps. 32; Jer. 31:30).

Bible generally does not distinguish between the act of sin and the guilt that came from the act. To sin is to become guilty (Lev. 5:1-5; Jer. 2:3; Hos. 5:15; 10:2). All humankind is guilty before God (Rom. 1:18-20; Rom. 3:23). Something must be done to remove the guilt.

To remove guilt, sinners could confess their sins and make restitution for the wrongs they had committed (Num. 5:6-10) and/or bring sacrifices to the priests for a guilt offering (Lev. 5:6–7:38). A righteous one can suffer for the guilt of others, bear the sin of many and intercede for their transgressions (Isa. 53:12). Jesus fulfilled the role of the one suffering for the sins of many—"Christ died for the ungodly"—and we are reconciled to God (Rom. 5:6-11; compare Eph. 1:7; Col. 1:19-20; Heb. 2:17; compare 1 John 2:2; 4:10). Human guilt requires the sacrifice of the Son of God. See *Expiation, Propitiation.*

As a feeling, "guilt" refers to the emotional aspects of a person's experience. One may feel guilty when there is no evidence to suggest a reason for guilt. Feeling is often a legitimate expression of guilt (Pss. 38; 51). Guilt is a burden (Ps. 38:4) that creates anxiety (Ps. 38:18).

Unresolved guilt can have a paralyzing effect on a person. Asking for and receiving forgiveness is one of the major ways that we can be absolved from guilt. God in His faithfulness has promised to forgive us from all iniquity (1 John 1:9). See *Atonement; Christ; Forgiveness; Reconciliation; Sin.*

GUN CONTROL

A biblical analogy to gun control is recorded in 1 Sam. 13:19-22. The Philistines, who held a monopoly on the manufacture of iron implements, refused to allow the Israelites access to swords or spears. In spite of the Philistine attempt at armament control, the Israelites were able to defeat both the Philistines (1 Sam. 14) and Amalakites (1 Sam. 15) in battle.

More pointedly, David "prevailed over [Goliath] with a sling and with a stone . . . [even though] there was no sword in the hand of David" (1 Sam. 17:50; compare vv. 31-40). The theological lesson of David's victory is that trust in God is more powerful than human attempts at armament, a lesson which Isaiah found necessary to repeat to Hezekiah in the face of the Assyrian invasion of 701 B.C. (Isa. 22:8b-11).

H

HABAKKUK (embrace)

Prophet just before 600 B.C.; contemporary to Jeremiah. Other than his work as a prophet, nothing for certain of a personal nature is known about Habakkuk. Tradition makes him a priest of the tribe of Levi. The apocryphal work Bel and the Dragon (vv. 33-39) tells a story about Habakkuk being taken to Babylon by an angel to feed Daniel while he was in the lions' den.

HABAKKUK, BOOK OF

Eighth book of Minor Prophets. Habakkuk spoke to the Lord for the people (1:2–2:5) instead of to the people for the Lord. He asked two questions: Why does violence rule where there should be justice? (1:2-5); Lord, how can you use someone more sinful than we are to punish us? (1:12-17). The first expressed the prophet's sense of dismay about conditions within his own land caused by King Jehoiakim. The Lord told the prophet He was at work sending the Chaldeans as the instrument of His judgment (1:5-11). When an answer to the second question was not forthcoming immediately, Habakkuk took his stand in the watchtower to wait. God told him: "Behold, his soul which is lifted up is not upright in him: but the just shall live by his faith" (2:4). The term "faith" has more of the sense of faithfulness or conviction that results in action.

The woes (2:6-20) are the only part of the book that fits the traditional pattern of the prophets. They denounce various kinds of tyranny: plunder (2:6-8); becoming rich and famous by unjust means (2:9-11); building towns with blood (2:12-14); degrading one's neighbor (2:15-17); and idol worship (2:18-19). This section ends with a ringing affirmation of the sovereignty of the Lord.

The final section (3:1-19) is a psalm, not unlike those in the Book of Psalms, extolling the Lord's triumph over His and His people's foes.

This book was a favorite of the people of the Dead Sea Scrolls. They interpreted the first two chapters as prophecy of their triumph over the Romans. Habakkuk's declaration that "the just [righteous] shall live by his faith" (2:4) was taken by Paul as a central element in his theology (Rom. 1:17; Gal. 3:11). Through Paul, this passage came alive for Martin Luther, setting off the Protestant Reformation.

HABOR

Major tributary of Euphrates River. Assyrians resettled many exiles from Israel there near Gozan when they captured Northern Kingdom in 722 B.C. (2 Kings 17:6). See Gozan.

HADAD (mighty)

(1) Edomite king (Gen. 36:35); name borne by several members of royal household of Edom.

(2) Chief deity, storm-god of Ugaritic pantheon. See Canaan; Ugarit.

HADAD-EZER (Hadad [god] helps)

Syrian royal name; king of Zobah whom David defeated to establish his control over Syria (2 Sam. 8:3-13; compare 2 Sam. 10:6-19). Rezon (1 Kings 11:23) revolted against Hadad-ezer (possibly son of the one in 1 Sam. 8; or the same king) and established a kingdom in Damascus. See Syria.

HADAD-RIMMON

Two Syrian gods combined into one word (Zech. 12:11); mourning on the day of the Lord could be compared only to "mourning of Hadad-rimmon," apparently a reference to pagan worship ceremonies, perhaps for a dying and rising god.

HADASSAH (myrtle or bride)

Name or title for Esther (Esther 2:7).

HADES

Abode of the dead; KJV, usually, "hell." See Hell.

HADRACH

Syrian city-state (Zech. 9:1); apparently the large mound tell Afis, 28 miles southwest of Aleppo; capital of Luhuti, ally of Hamath from 854 to 773 B.C.

HAGAR (stranger)

Personal servant of Sarah; given as concubine to Abraham; mother of Ishmael (Gen. 16:1-16; 21:8-21; 25:12; Gal. 4:24-25). Paul (Gal. 4) used Hagar's story to stand for slavery under Old Covenant in contrast to freedom of the New Covenant symbolized by Isaac.

HAGGAI (festive)

Prophet who led Jews to rebuild temple in 520 B.C.

HAGGAI, BOOK OF

Tenth book of Minor Prophets; series of Haggai's addresses together with results of his work between sixth and ninth months of 520 B.C.

Returning exiles found rebuilding their own homes and the temple at the same time put a strain on their resources. They despaired of ever restoring the temple to its former glory. Work on the temple ceased. Haggai, along with Zechariah, helped Zerubbabel gain the support he needed to rebuild the temple. Haggai may have viewed the restoration of order by Darius and his appointment of Zerubbabel as a sign of the end of Gentile rule and preparation for the messianic kingdom.

The Book of Haggai linked worship and work, a characteristic feature of Jesus' teaching and of the NT. It revived hope for the future in a dejected community.

The book consists of five short addresses and a description of the results of Haggai's efforts to persuade his people to resume work on the temple. The recipients of Haggai's message included Zerubbabel and Joshua, the high priest. Haggai suggested how they should respond to the excuses people were making for not resuming work on the temple

(1:2). If it was right to rebuild their own houses, it was also right to rebuild the temple (1:3-4). They resumed work on the temple.

In the second speech, Haggai assured them of the Lord's presence and approval (1:13). The Lord stirred the spirit of both leaders and people as they worked together (1:14-15). In the third address (2:1-2), Haggai asked the older members of the community to recall the glory of the former temple and thus to stir the new generation to new enthusiasm. God would bring treasures from other nations to make the splendor of the new temple even greater than the former one (2:6-9).

The fourth address (2:10-19) claimed carelessness in observing accepted rules reflected a lack of seriousness in their purpose. They robbed themselves of the full measure of God's blessing.

The final speech (2:20-23), addressed only to Zerubbabel, announced the imminent overthrow of the kingdoms of the world and the role that Zerubbabel would play in the triumphant victory of God's kingdom on earth.

HAIR

Covering of human head (Num. 6:5) and of animals (Matt. 3:4). Beautiful hair has always been desirable for both women and men (Song of Sol. 5:11). In OT times both men and women wore their hair long (Judg. 16:13; 2 Sam. 14:25-26). In the NT era, men wore their hair much shorter than women did (1 Cor. 11:14-15).

Gray or white hair was a respected sign of age (Prov. 20:29). See Baldness. In Lev. 13, the color of the hairs in an infected area of skin indicated whether "leprosy" was present or had been cured. A cured leper was required to shave his entire body (Lev. 14:8-9). See Leprosy.

Women usually wore their hair loose, but sometimes they braided it (2 Kings 9:30). NT writers cautioned against ostentation in women's hairstyles (1 Tim. 2:9; 1 Pet. 3:3). Hair that was anointed with oil symbolized blessing and joy (Ps. 23:5; Heb. 1:9;

compare Luke 7:46). Mourning was indicated by disheveled, unkempt hair (Josh. 7:6; 2 Sam. 14:2). Jesus told His followers not to follow the custom of the Pharisees, who refused to care for their hair while they were fasting (Matt. 6:17).

Israelite men trimmed their hair, but the law prohibited them from cutting off the hair above their ears (Lev. 19:27; compare Deut. 14:1-2); orthodox Jews still wear long sidecurls. Those who took a Nazirite vow were forbidden from cutting their hair during the course of their vows; afterward, their entire heads were to be shaved (Num. 6:1-21; Acts 18:18; 21:24).

Hairs may symbolize the concept of being innumerable (Ps. 40:12) or stand for insignificant things (Luke 21:18).

HALAH

City-state or region in northern Mesopotamia where Assyrians exiled some leaders of the Northern Kingdom after capturing Samaria in 722 B.C. (2 Kings 17:6); may have been Hallahhu, northeast of Nineveh.

HALAK (*barren* or *naked*)

Mountain marking southern extent of Joshua's conquests (Josh. 11:17; 12:7); jebel Halak, about 40 miles southwest of Dead Sea in Edom.

HALLEL

Song of praise from Hebrew, "Praise Thou." Singing psalms of praise was a special duty of the Levites (2 Chron. 7:6; Ezra 3:11). "Egyptian" Hallel (Pss. 113–118) was recited in homes as part of the Passover celebration (compare Ps. 114:1; Matt. 26:30). The "Great Hallel" was recited in the temple as Passover lambs were being slain and at Pentecost, Tabernacles, and Dedication. Some limit "Great Hallel" to Ps. 136; some include Ps. 135; others include "Songs of Ascents" (Pss. 120–134).

HALLELUJAH

Exclamation meaning "Praise Yahweh!" that recurs frequently in psalms. Psalms 146–150 sometimes are designated the Hallelujah psalms. See *Psalms.*

HAM (*hot*)

Second of Noah's three sons (Gen 5:32). Following flood, he discovered his father naked and drunken and reported it to Shem and Japheth (Gen. 9:20-29). Noah put a curse on Canaan, Ham's son. Ham became original ancestor of Cushites, Egyptians, and Canaanites (Gen. 10:6).

HAMAN (*magnificent*)

Agagite who became prime minister under Persian king Ahasuerus (Esther 3:1); fierce enemy of the Jews who devised plot to exterminate them. Through intervention of Esther, his scheme was unmasked. He was hanged on gallows he had designed for Mordecai. See *Esther.*

HAMATH (*fortress* or *citadel*)

City-state in valley of Orontes River, about 120 miles north of Damascus; occupied as early as Neolithic times.

HAMOR (*donkey* or *ass*)

Father of Shechem (Gen. 33:19; Judg. 9:28) from whose children Jacob purchased land for an altar. Joseph was buried there (Josh. 24:32). Simeon and Levi killed Hamor and Shechem in revenge for the outrage committed against Dinah (Gen. 34:25-26).

HANANIAH (*Yah is gracious*)

Name of 15 men including:
(1) Prophet from Gibeon who opposed Jeremiah by promising immediate deliverance from Babylon. Jeremiah could combat this false prophecy only by telling the people to wait until they saw it fulfilled in history (Jer. 28:8-9). Jeremiah did not even oppose Hannaniah when he tried to embarrass Jeremiah by breaking the symbolic yoke Jeremiah was wearing (vv. 10-11). Only later did Jeremiah receive a counter-

ing word from God to oppose Hananiah (vv. 12-17).

(2) Son of Zerubbabel in the royal line of David (1 Chron. 3:19).

(3) Ruler of the temple fortress under Nehemiah (Neh. 7:2, NASB). Nehemiah set him up as one of two administrators of Jerusalem because he was trustworthy and reverenced God more than other men.

HAND

Part of human body, namely the terminal part of the arm that enables a person to make and use tools and perform functions; used for parts of hand: finger (Gen. 41:42); wrists (Ezek. 23:42).

The "hand of God" or "in thine hand" refers to supreme power and authority of God (1 Chron. 29:12; compare Isa. 59:1; Ex. 13:3-16; Pss. 8:6; 37:24; 95:5; 139:10). Punishment and affliction come from the hand of God (Ex. 9:3; Deut. 2:15; Judg. 2:15; 1 Sam. 7:13; 12:15; Ruth 1:13; compare Amos 1:8).

"To give the hand" meant that one had pledged or submitted to another (2 Kings 10:15; Ezra 10:19). "To stretch the hand" conveyed two thoughts: attacking the enemy in battle (Josh. 8:19,26) and an intense desire for communion with God (Ps. 143:6). "High hand" indicated willful rebellion against God (Num. 15:30; see Deut. 32:27) but also military power (Ex. 14:8; Mic. 5:9). "To fill the hand" expressed the consecration of a priest (Judg. 17:5) or a congregation's dedication (2 Chron. 29:31).

"Hand" came to mean *side*, perhaps because of the location of the hands and arms on the body, and *monument* (1 Sam. 15:12). See *Work, Theology of; Worship; Laying on of Hands.*

HANDKERCHIEF

Cloth for wiping sweat or a sweatband (Acts 19:12); cloth in which money was buried (Luke 19:20); cloth to cover face of the dead (John 11:44; 20:7).

HANES

Egyptian city to which Israel sent ambassadors to seek military and economic help (Isa. 30:4), action Isaiah condemned as not trusting Yahweh; often located at Heracleopolis Magna in southern Egypt just north of the Nile Delta, modern Ahnas; more likely Heracleopolis Parva, modern Hanes, almost directly east of Tanis.

HANGING

Method of ridiculing, shaming, and desecrating the corpse of an enemy—not a means of capital punishment in biblical law, although practiced by Egyptians (Gen. 40:19, 22) and the Persians (Esther 7:9). Israelites, after putting enemy or criminal to death, might hang them on a gibbet or tree for public scorn as added degradation and warning (Gen. 40:19; Deut. 21:22; Josh. 8:29; 2 Sam. 4:12), but biblical law demanded that corpses be taken down and buried the same day (Deut. 21:22-23; compare Gen. 40:19; Josh. 8:29; 10:26-27; 1 Sam. 31:10; 2 Sam. 21:8-10).

HANNAH (*grace*)

Mother of Samuel (1 Sam. 1:2).

HANUKKAH

Eight-day festival that commemorated the cleansing and rededication of the temple following the victories of Judas Maccabeus in 167/165 B.C. See *Festivals.*

HARA

City or region in northern Mesopotamia where Assyrians under Tiglath-pileser settled some of the exiles from east of the Jordan in 734 B.C. (1 Chron. 5:26); not in parallel passages (2 Kings 17:6; 18:11).

HARAN (*mountaineer* or *caravan route*)

Three men (Gen. 11:26-29,31; 1 Chron. 2:46; 23:9) and important city of northern Mesopotamia on Balik River. The city became Abraham's home (Gen. 11:31-32; 12:4-5) and remained home for his relatives like Laban (Gen. 27:43). Jacob went there and married (Gen. 28:10; 29:4). In the eighth century, Assyria conquered it (2 Kings 19:12; Isa. 37:12). It was a trade partner of Tyre (Ezek. 27:23) and major center of worship for the moon god Sin.

HARAR (Mountaineer), HARARITE

Town, region, tribe, or general reference to mountain country (2 Sam. 23:11,33; 1 Chron. 11:34-35).

HARD SAYING

Teaching difficult to understand or accept (John 6:60).

HARDNESS OF THE HEART

Stubborn attitude that leads a person to reject God's will; stems from human heart and from God's action (Ex. 8:32; 9:12). Humans can resist God who respects the free human will. One of the most important ways of resisting God is for a person to "harden his heart" so that the individual has no feeling and is like a piece of stone.

For Pharaoh, punishment came as the consequence of his own initial self-hardening. Pharaoh hardened his own heart and then became confirmed in his obstinacy. Sin became its own punishment. We are warned, "Harden not your heart" (Ps. 95:8). Jesus asked His disciples, "Have ye your heart yet hardened?" (Mark 8:17). Hardening the heart was evidence of skepticism (Mark 6:52). God's people can have hardened hearts and begin to complain when God's ethical standards seem too high (Mark 10:5-6; compare Deut. 24:1). Failure to hear the voice of God may come from a hardened heart (Prov. 28:14; 29:1; see Heb. 4:7).

HARLOT

A prostitute such as Rahab of Jericho, who saved the Israelite spies sent by Joshua to scout out the Promised Land (Josh. 2; 6:23-25; Matt. 1:5; Heb. 11:31; compare Jas. 2:25).

See Fornication; Prostitution.

HARMONY OF THE GOSPELS

Arrangement of four Gospels in parallel columns to study their similarities and differences; also called synopsis or parallel of Gospels.

After A.D. 100, Tatian, a Christian from Syria, compiled the four Gospels into a paraphrased narrative called the Diatessaron. His approach weaves together material from the Gospels to present one continuous narrative of Jesus' life. Contemporary scholars compare the variations between the Gospels and use their findings as an aid for interpretation. To do this they place the text of each Gospel in a parallel column. Such a study of Matthew, Mark, and Luke shows:

(1) Some material in one Gospel is repeated almost word for word in one or both of the other Gospels (Mark 2:23-27; Matt. 12:1-8; Luke 6:1-5).

(2) Some material is included in only one Gospel (the parable of the prodigal son, Luke 15:11-32).

(3) In the three "Synoptic Gospels": the appearance of John the Baptist, Jesus' baptism and temptation, and the initiation of Jesus' public ministry are linked together; Jesus' ministry was confined to Galilee until He attended the Passover celebration in Jerusalem where He was crucified; the story ends with His crucifixion and resurrection.

Luke contains 50 percent of the substance of Mark's verses, while Matthew contains a full 90 percent of Mark. Yet the three Gospels also possess significant differences. Explanations of this include:

(1) An Early Solution. Augustine (A.D. 354–430) decided Matthew wrote first; Mark abridged Matthew; and Luke was dependent on both of them.

(2) Later Solutions after 1800. A single, original Gospel is now lost to us, perhaps an orally transmitted Gospel formalized through constant repetition or an actual document. Matthew, Mark, and Luke individually selected material from this Gospel as they wrote their accounts.

Gospel writers used two documents: Mark and a collection of Jesus' teachings now appearing in both Matthew and Luke.

(3) *The Four-Document Hypothesis.* Shortly after 1900, B. H. Streeter said the Synoptic writers used four documents:

(a) Mark, whose order, vocabulary, and sentence structure is followed by both Matthew and Luke;

(b) "Q" (from German *Quelle*, "source"), the common teachings source Matthew and Luke used, Q's most significant contribution being the Sermon on the Mount (Matt. 5–7 and Luke 6:20-49);

(c) "M," Matthew's body of material unknown to (or at least unused by) Mark and Luke, including Matthew's infancy story and OT proof texts related to Jesus' role as Messiah;

(d) "L," material exclusive to Luke containing at least an infancy story and many parables such as good Samaritan and prodigal son.

While most contemporary scholars hold that Matthew and Luke used Mark and "Q" but no other written sources, one must recognize any solution to the synoptic problem is a theory and not a proven fact. Many Bible students today are returning to the view Matthew was written first.

HAROD (*quake, terror,* or *intermittent spring*), **HARODITE** or **HARORITE**

Place where God led Gideon to test his troops to reduce their numbers before fighting Midian (Judg. 7:1); modern ain Jalud near Gilboa, half way between Affulah and Beth-Shean; about two miles east southeast of Jezreel. See 2 Sam. 23:25; compare 1 Chron. 11:27. The "fountain" of 1 Sam. 29:1 was probably Harod. Some Bible students see a reference to Judg. 7:1 in Ps. 83:10 and change the Hebrew text slightly to read "Harod" instead of "En-dor." Compare REB.

HAROSHETH (*forest land*) or **HAROSHETH HAGGOYIM** (*Harosheth of the nations*) or **HAROSHETH-HAGOYIM**

Home of Sisera, captain of the army of Jabin of Hazor (Judg. 4:2,13-16); may be same as Muhrashti of the Amarna letters; perhaps tell el-Ama at the foot of Mount Carmel about nine miles south of Haifa near the Arab village of Haritiyeh or common noun meaning "woods" or forests of Galilee. This view would read Josh. 12:23, "king of Goiim in Galilee" (TEV, NRSV) and equate the king with the ruler of the Galilean forests.

HARP See *Music, Instruments, Dancing.*

HARROW

To pulverize and smooth the soil by means of a cultivating implement with spikes, spring teeth, or disks; breaking clods (Job. 39:10; Isa. 28:24; Hos. 10:11) in distinct process from plowing; perhaps dragging branches to smooth the soil over seed; See *Agriculture; Tools.*

HART

Adult male deer (Ps. 42:1; Isa. 35:6). See *Animals.*

HASIDEANS (*saints* or *faithful*)

Militant, religious community active in the Maccabean revolt (begun 168 B.C.). Pharisees and Essenes likely derived from different streams of the Hasidean movement. See *Intertestamental History and Literature; Jewish Parties in the New Testament.*

HATE, HATRED

Strong negative reaction, feeling toward someone considered an enemy as well as loving someone less than another. Conflict, jealousy, and envy often result in animosity, separation, revenge, and even murder (Gen. 26:27; 27:41; Judg. 11:7; 2 Sam. 13:15,22). Some Hebrew laws explicitly deal with hatred or favoritism (Deut. 19:11-13; 21:15-17; 22:13-21).

Hatred of other people is condemned, and love toward enemies is encouraged (Lev. 19:17; Matt. 5:43-44). Hatred characterizes the sinful life (Gal. 5:19-21; Titus 3:3; 1 John 2:9, 11). Jesus knew of a tradition commanding hatred of enemies (Matt. 5:43). Dead Sea Scrolls indicate the Essenes at Qumran cultivated hatred for enemies, but they discouraged retaliation. Jesus stressed loving enemies and doing good to those who hate us (Luke 6:27). Believers are to hate whatever opposes God, reflecting agreement with God's opposition to evil (Pss. 97:10; 139:19-22; Prov. 8:13; 13:5; Amos 5:15).

Jesus' disciples would have to hate their families to follow Him (Luke 14:26), that is, consciously establish priorities of kingdom over family, loving family less than one loves Jesus (Matt. 10:37). Similarly, one should hate personal life to gain eternal life (John 12:25). Disciples can expect to be hated, just as the world hated Jesus (John 15:18-24; 17:14; 1 John 3:13). Hatred and persecution will occur near the end of time (Matt. 24:9). Jesus encouraged His disciples to rejoice at this opposition (Luke 6:22-23).

People sometimes hate God (Pss. 68:1; 81:15) and His people. These enemies of God will be punished. God is love (1 John 4:8), but a holy, jealous God also hates human sin (Prov. 6:16-19; 8:13; Mal. 2:16). God hates pagan idolatry (Deut. 12:31) as well as hypocritical Hebrew worship (Isa. 1:14; Amos 5:21). He desires the sinner's repentance (Ezek. 18:32). Some texts imply God's hate is directed primarily to sinful actions rather than to sinful persons (Heb. 1:9; Rev. 2:6).

God's hate is a strong moral reaction against sin, closer to the sense of loving less. God's hating Esau (Mal. 1:2-5; Rom. 9:13) stresses divine freedom in election, not an emotional reaction. See *Enemy; Love; Wrath, Wrath of God.*

HAVILAH (*sandy stretch*)

Sand-dominated region covering what we call Arabia without necessarily designating a particular geographical or political area. A river flowed from Eden "to water the garden; and from thence it was parted, and became into four heads. The name of the first is Pison: that is it which compasseth the whole land of Havilah" (Gen. 2:10-11), a land noted for gold and other precious stones. The Table of Nations lists Havilah as son of Cush, showing Havilah's political ties (Gen. 10:7; compare v. 29; 25:18; 1 Sam. 15:7).

HAVOTH-JAIR (*tents of Jair*) or **HAVVOTH-JAIR**

Villages in Gilead east of the Jordan that Jair, son of Manasseh, captured (Num. 32:41; compare Deut. 3:14; Josh. 13:30; Judg. 10:3-4; 1 Kings 4:13; 1 Chron. 2:18-23).

HAZAEL (*El* [a god] *is seeing*)

Powerful and ruthless king of Damascus. See 1 Kings 19:15-17; 2 Kings 8:7-15. Elijah and Elisha prophesied Hazael's future kingship and his cruel treatment of Israel. Hazael returned to his master, murdered him, and became king of Syria in 841 B.C. Hazael joined in combat against both Ahaziah, king of Judah, and Joram, king of Israel (2 Kings 8:28-29; 9:14-15). He eventually extended his rule into both the Northern Kingdom of Israel (2 Kings 10:32-33; 13:1-9,22) and the Southern Kingdom of Judah (2 Kings 12:17-18; 2 Chron. 24:23-24). Half a century later, Amos used his name as a symbol of Syria's oppression that would be judged by God (Amos 1:4). See *Damascus; Syria.*

HAZAR-MAVETH (*encampment of death*)

Son of Joktan in line of Eber and Shem (Gen. 10:26); region of Hadramaut east of Yemen.

HAZEROTH (villages or encampments)

Wilderness station on Israel's journey from Egypt (Num. 11:35). See Num. 12; Deut. 1:1. Some would locate it at ain Khadra, south of Ezion-geber.

HAZOR (enclosed settlement)

(1) City in upper Galilee at tell el-Qedah, 10 miles north of Sea of Galilee and five miles southwest of Lake Huleh; 30-acre upper tell or mound rising 40 meters above the surrounding plain and 175-acre lower enclosure that was well fortified; largest city in ancient Canaan. Estimates set the population at its height well over 40,000.

The upper tell was occupied between 2750 and 200 B.C. Canaanites occupied Hazor until Joshua destroyed it. The Israelites controlled it until 732 B.C. when the Assyrians captured the city. Hazor then served as a fortress for the various occupying powers until the time of the Maccabees. The lower enclosure was occupied from 1750 B.C. until Joshua destroyed it. It was never rebuilt.

Hazor overlooked the Via Maris and thus became a major trading center. Hazor also overlooked the Huleh Valley, a critical defense point against armies invading from the north. See Josh. 11:1-15; 12:19; 19:36; Judg. 4; 1 Kings 9:15; 2 Kings 15:29.

(2) Town in Judah (Josh. 15:23), probably to be read with Septuagint as Hazor-Ithnan; may be el-Jebariyeh.

(3) Town in southern Judah, probably to be read as Hazor-Hadattah (Josh. 15:25) with most modern translations; may be el-Hudeira near Dead Sea's southern end.

(4) Town identified with Hezron (Josh. 15:25).

(5) Town where part of Benjamin lived (Neh. 11:33); may be khirbet Hazzur four miles north northwest of Jerusalem.

(6) Name of "kingdoms" that Nebuchadnezzar of Babylon threatened (Jer. 49:28-33). Apparently, small nomadic settlements of Arab tribes are meant.

HEAD

Uppermost part of body considered to be seat of life, but not the intellect; figuratively, first, top, or chief. Jews believed the heart was center or seat of intellect. "Head" meant the physical head of a person (Gen. 48:18; Mark 6:24) or of animals (Lev. 1:4). It was often used to represent the whole person (Acts 18:6).

"Head" can mean leader, chief, or prince (Isa. 9:15) and can have idea of first in a series (1 Chron. 12:9). Israel was the "head" (translated "chief") nation, God's firstborn (Jer. 31:7). Damascus was the "head" (capital) of Syria (Isa. 7:8). A husband is the "head of the wife" (Eph. 5:23).

Christ is the "head" of His body, the church; the church is His "bride" (Eph. 5:23-33). Christ enables church to grow (Eph. 4:15-16). Christ is also "head" of the universe as a whole (Eph. 1:22) and of every might and power (Col. 2:10). The divine influences on the world result in a series: God is the "head" of Christ; Christ is the "head" of man; man is the "head" of the woman, and as such he is to love and care for his wife as Christ does His bride (1 Cor. 11:3).

Blessing comes upon the head (Gen. 49:26); and, therefore, hands are laid on it (Gen. 48:17). Anointing the head with oil symbolized prosperity and joy (Ps. 23:5; Heb. 1:9). In ordination the head of the high priest was anointed with oil (Ex. 29:7; Lev. 16:32). Human sins were transferred to the animal for the sin offering by laying hands on its head (Ex. 29:10,15,19).

HEALING, DIVINE

God's work through instruments He chooses to bring health to persons sick physically, emotionally, and spiritually. Jesus commissioned His disciples to continue His basic ministry, including healing (Matt. 10:5-10; Mark 6:7-13; Luke 9:1-6) which they did in Acts.

Jesus spoke of doctors in a positive way (Matt. 9:12; Mark 2:17; Luke 5:31). Jesus healed through prayer, laying on of hands, anointing with oil, and assurance of forgiveness of sins. The church continued to use these methods (Jas. 5:14-16).

HEART

Center of physical, mental, and spiritual life of humans; physical organ considered center of physical life (Gen. 18:5; Judg. 19:5; Acts 14:17). The heart became the focus for all the vital functions of the body, including both intellectual (Prov. 23:7; Matt. 13:15; Luke 1:66; 2:19) and spiritual life.

The heart is closely connected to the feelings and affections of a person: joy (Ps. 4:7; Isa 65:14); fear, described as "his heart died within him" (1 Sam. 25:37; compare Ps. 143:4); discouragement or despair described as "heaviness in the heart" that makes it stoop (Prov. 12:25; compare Eccl. 2:20); sorrow (Prov. 25:20; John 16:6); love and hate (Lev. 19:17; Mark 12:30; compare Deut. 6:5; 1 Tim. 1:5); and bitter jealousy (Jas. 3:14).

The heart is center of the moral and spiritual life. The conscience is associated with the heart (1 Sam. 25:31; Job 27:6; 1 John 3:19-21). Depravity issues from the heart (Jer. 17:9; Matt. 15:19).

The heart is where God does His work in the individual. The work of the law is "written in their hearts," and conscience is the proof of this (Rom. 2:15). The heart is the field where the Word of God is sown (Matt. 13:19; Luke 8:15). The heart is the place of renewal (1 Sam. 10:9; Ezek. 11:19). Paul said that a person must believe in the heart to be saved (Rom. 10:10). See also Mark 11:23; Heb. 3:12.

The heart is the dwelling place of God. See Rom. 5:5; 2 Cor. 1:22; Eph. 3:17.

HEAVE OFFERING

Portion of offering or sacrifice set apart and reserved for Yahweh and priests (Ex. 29:27-28). See *Sacrifice and Offering.*

HEAVEN

Part of God's creation above the earth and the waters, including "air" and "space" and serving as home for God and His heavenly creatures. Heaven could be described as a partition God "stretched out" (Isa. 42:5; 44:24; Ps. 136:6; compare Ezek. 1:22-26; 10:1) to separate rain-producing heavenly waters from the rivers, seas, and oceans below (Gen. 1:6-8). The heavenly lights—sun, moon, and stars—were installed into this partition (Gen. 1:14-18) that has windows or sluice gates with which God sends rain to irrigate or water the earth (Gen. 7:11). Clouds serve a similar rain-producing function, so the KJV often translates Hebrew "clouds" as "sky" (Deut. 33:26; Ps. 57:10; Isa. 45:8; Jer. 51:9; compare Pss. 36:6; 108:4).

Just as He built the partition, so God can "rend" it or tear it apart (Isa. 64:1). It does not seal God off from His creation and His people. English translations use "firmament" (KJV), "expanse" (NASB, NIV), "dome" (TEV, NRSV, CEV), "space" (NLT), "air" (NCV), or "vault" (REB) to translate the special Hebrew word describing what God created and named "Heaven" (Gen. 1:8). Hebrew does not employ a term for "air" or "space" between heaven and earth. This is all part of heaven. Thus the Bible speaks of "birds of the heavens," though English translations often use "air" or "sky" (Deut. 4:17; Jer. 8:7; Lam. 4:19). Even Absalom hanging by his hair from a tree limb was "between heaven and earth" (2 Sam. 18:9; compare 1 Chron. 21:16; Ezek. 8:3). Heaven is God's treasure chest, storing treasures such as rain (Deut. 28:12), wind and lightning (Jer. 10:13), and snow or hail (Job 38:22). The miraculous manna came from God's heavenly storehouses for Israel in the wilderness (Ex. 16:11-15).

Heaven is a channel of communication between God and humans (Gen. 28:12; 2 Sam. 22:10; Neh. 9:13;

Ps. 144:5). Unlike neighboring nations, Israel knew heaven and the heavenly bodies were not gods and did not deserve worship (Ex. 20:4). Heaven is not eternal (Job 14:12; Isa. 34:4; 51:6). A new heaven and new earth will appear (Isa. 65:17; 66:22).

Other than Paul's reference to the three heavens (2 Cor. 12:2-4), biblical writers spoke of only one heaven. Jesus preached that the kingdom of heaven/God had dawned through His presence and ministry (Mark 1:15). Jesus promised a heavenly home for His followers (John 14:2-3; compare 2 Cor. 5:1-2). Heaven is the hope of glory (Col. 1:27). The Holy Spirit is the pledge of the believer's participation in heaven (2 Cor. 5:5). The image of a messianic banquet reveals heavenly life as a time of joy, celebration, and fellowship with God (Matt. 26:29). There will be no marrying or giving in marriage in heaven (Luke 20:34-36). Christians should rejoice because their names are written in heaven (Luke 10:20). Christ is seated in heaven at the right hand of God (Eph. 1:20). Heaven is where the believer's inheritance is kept with care until the revelation of the Messiah (1 Pet. 1:4).

In Rev. 21:1-22:5, heaven is portrayed as: (1) the tabernacle (21:1-8), (2) the city (21:9-27), and (3) the garden (22:1-5), that is, as perfect fellowship with God, perfect protection, and perfect provision.

HEAVENLY CITY, THE

Fulfillment of hopes of God's people for final salvation representing ordered life, security from enemies, and material prosperity (Heb. 11:10,16; 12:22). See *Cities and Urban Life*. Believers have already come (12:22) to the heavenly Jerusalem, at least in part. The experience of the patriarchs whose hope lay beyond their earthly lives (Heb. 11:13-16) points to a final fulfillment of salvation in heaven. See *Heaven*.

HEAVENS, NEW

Technical, eschatological term (Isa. 65:17; 66:22; 2 Pet. 3:13; Rev. 21:1) for

final perfected state of the created universe. The promise of a re-creation of the heavens and earth arose because of human sin and God's subsequent curse (Gen. 3:17). Persons cannot be completely set free from the power of sin apart from the redemption of the created order — earth as well as the heavens (Isa. 51:16; Matt. 19:28; 24:29-31; 26:29; Mark 13:24-27, 31; Acts 3:20-21; Rom. 8:19-23; 2 Cor. 5:17; Heb. 12:26-28; 2 Pet. 3:10-13). God is the cause of this new creation (Isa. 65:17; 66:22; Rev. 21:22; compare Isa. 66:28; Heb. 12:28; 2 Pet. 3:13). Purity (Rev. 21:27), freedom from the wrath of God (Rev. 22:3), and perfect fellowship of the saints with one another and with God (21:1,3) are marks of the new heaven and earth.

HEBREW

Descendant of Eber; early Israelites distinguished from foreigners. The designation apparently begins with Abraham (Gen. 14:13), showing that he belonged to an ethnic group distinct from the Amorites. It distinguished Joseph from the Egyptians and slaves of other ethnic identity (Gen. 39:14,17; 41:12; 43:32). Abraham's land became the land of the Hebrews (Gen. 40:15), and his God, the God of the Hebrews (Ex. 5:3). Special laws protected Hebrew slaves (Ex. 21:2; Deut. 15:12; compare Lev. 25:40-41; Jer. 34:8-22). After the death of Saul (1 Sam. 29), the term *Hebrew* does not appear in the historical books, pointing possibly to a distinction between Hebrew as an ethnic term and Israel and/or Judah as a religious and political term for the people of the covenant and of God's nation.

HEBREW LANGUAGE

Language in which canonical books of OT were written, except for Aramaic sections in Ezra 4:8–6:18; 7:12-26; Dan. 2:4b–7:28; Jer. 10:11, and a few other words and phrases from Aramaic and other languages; known as "the language [literally, lip] of Canaan" (Isa. 19:18) or as "Judean" (NASB) (Neh. 13:24; Isa. 36:11). NT references to the "Hebrew dialect" seem to refer to Aramaic. Biblical or classical Hebrew belongs to the Northwest branch of Semitic languages that includes Ugaritic, Phoenician, Moabite, Edomite, and Ammonite.

Hebrew has an alphabet of 22 consonants written right to left.

The growing number of Hebrew inscriptions dating from the preexilic age provides an important supplement to the study of classical Hebrew. These inscriptions were chiseled into stone, written on ostraca (broken pieces of pottery), cut into seals, or inscribed on jar handles and weights. Some of the most important inscriptional evidence includes the Gezer calendar (after 1000 B.C.), the Hazor ostraca (after 900), the Samaria ostraca (shortly after 800), the Siloam inscription (shortly before 700), Yavneh-yam ostracon (shortly before 600), jar handles from Gibeon (shortly before 600), the Lachish ostracon (shortly after 600), and the Arad ostraca (around 600). To these may be added the Moabite Stone (Stele of Mesha, after 900) and the Ammonite stele (after 900) that contain inscriptions in languages very similar to classical Hebrew.

HEBREWS, LETTER TO THE

Nineteenth book of NT, calling for faithfulness to Jesus, the perfect fulfillment of OT institutions and hope. The author describes himself as belonging to second generation of Christians dependent on the eyewitnesses of the apostles (Heb. 2:3). Paul, who considered himself an eyewitness of the resurrection of Jesus (1 Cor. 15:8-11), would not describe himself in this way. Luke, Clement of Rome, Priscilla, Barnabas, Apollos, or a Hellenist like Stephen have all been suggested as the author. The early Church Father, Origen, was probably more correct when he said that only God knew who wrote Hebrews. Hebrews was not accepted as part of the NT canon in the Western church until after A.D. 367 when the Western church finally accepted

the Eastern church's theory of Pauline authorship.

Hebrews does not have the normal opening that the letters of Paul have. (compare, for example, Rom. 1:1-7; 1 Cor. 1:1-3; 2 Cor. 1:1-2). It does conclude like a normal letter (Heb. 13:20-25; see *Letter Form and Function*). Many have speculated that Hebrews was originally a sermon preached to a church in Rome (notice the reference to "hearing" and "teaching" in Heb. 5:11) and later sent to a church outside of Rome (Heb. 13:24), perhaps experiencing similar circumstances. In this case, Heb. 1-12 would represent the original sermon, and Heb. 13 would represent the brief note (Heb. 13:22) attached for the second congregation.

Some evidence points to a time of writing before destruction of the temple. Hebrews 10:32-34 describes persecution the original recipients endured. The persecution seems to have only included the loss of property. These circumstances would fit the edict of Claudius in A.D. 49 banning Christians from the city of Rome. The author then warned of greater tests ahead, probably referring to the persecutions underway during the reign of Nero in A.D. 64. The writing of Hebrews is probably during or just after A.D. 64. Others see Heb. 10:32-34 as a reference to persecutions by Nero and place the writing during a persecution assumed to have taken place during Domitian's reign (A.D. 81–96). This seems less likely, as the severity of Nero's persecutions does not seem to be reflected in Hebrews.

The recipients of Hebrews were tempted to deny being Christians so as to avoid persecution. Some scholars think the recipients had been converted to Christianity from Judaism and were tempted to return to their Jewish faith and the relative safety from persecution that being Jewish brought. The writer of Hebrews went to great length to demonstrate that Jesus and the Christian faith were superior to the Jewish faith.

Jesus is God's superior revelation (1:1-4): superior to the angels (1:5–2:18) and to Moses (3:1–4:13), to the earthly high priest with His superior ministry that establishes a superior covenant able to bring to maturity those who have faith (4:14–10:31). As the author and finisher of faith, Jesus is the superior Model of faith (12:1-2).

The superiority of Jesus called the readers not to neglect such a great salvation (2:3). The readers should enter God's rest while it is still available (4:1-13); they should go on to maturity (6:1-8). They should draw near God's throne in confidence (10:19-25). God's children suffer because they are His children (12:7-8). Suffering functions as a discipline that leads God's children to maturity or perfection. Jesus was perfected in this way (2:10; 5:8) and is qualified to stand in God's presence in the heavenly sanctuary as High Priest (2:17-18; 5:9-10). The readers could also be qualified to stand in God's presence by means of the discipline of suffering. God disciplines His children for their good, that they might share His holiness (12:10). Without holiness no one will see God, that is, stand in His presence (12:14). Suffering may seem harsh at the time, but "afterward it yieldeth the peaceable fruit of righteousness unto them which are exercised thereby" (12:11). Therefore, the writer exhorted the recipients to go to Jesus outside the camp, "bearing his reproach" (13:13).

Because Jesus has suffered as they were about to suffer and was tempted as they were being tempted, Jesus was able to help them (2:18; 4:15). Jesus could "sympathize" with the weakness that the recipients experienced when facing the prospects of suffering (4:15 NASB). Just as Jesus learned what it meant to be obedient to God through suffering (5:8), the readers were exhorted to exhibit the same kind of obedience in their suffering (10:36-39). "Shrinking back" from God in the face of suffering is a sin that God detests (3:12-19; 10:26-31). Jesus was tempted (2:18; 5:7) but did not sin (4:15). Because Jesus remained faithful and did not sin during the hour of His suffering,

He became the "author of eternal salvation unto all them that obey him" (5:9).

The writer encouraged the recipients to remain faithful in the midst of suffering by giving them examples of others who were able to remain faithful (11:1-39). The writer reminded them of their own past faithfulness in suffering (10:32-39) and of the example of their former leaders (13:7). Those who remain obedient to God in the midst of suffering are able to do so by means of their faith, because "faith is the substance of things hoped for, the evidence of things not seen" (11:1).

Entrance before the throne of grace is permitted on the basis of the obedience and offering of Christ. Jesus is the one who sanctifies those who follow Him (2:11; 10:19-20; 13:12).

HEBRON (*association* or *league*), **HEBRONITE**

Two men and major city in hill country of Judah about 19 miles south of Jerusalem and 15 miles west of Dead Sea; over 3,000 feet above sea level; occupied almost continuously since about 3300 B.C. After his separation from Lot, Abraham moved to Hebron, known as Mamre, and associated with the Amorites (Gen. 13:18; 14:13; 23:19). When Sarah died, the place was called Kirjath-arba; and the population was predominantly Hittite (Gen. 23:2; Josh. 14:15; 15:54; Judg. 1:10). From them Abraham purchased a field with a burial plot inside a nearby cave. Abraham and Sarah, Isaac and Rebekah, and Jacob and Leah were buried there (Gen. 23:19; 25:9; 35:29; 49:31; 50:13).

Hebron was "built" seven years prior to Zoan, the Egyptian city of Tanis (Num. 13:22). Archaeological evidence suggests the reference was to Tanis's establishment as the Hyksos capital around 1725 B.C. and not its beginning. After the Israelite conquest of Canaan, Hebron was given to Caleb (Josh. 14:9-13) and became a city of refuge (Josh. 20:7; see Judg. 16:3).

After the death of Saul, David settled in the city (2 Sam. 2:3) and made it his capital during the seven years he ruled only Judah (1 Kings 2:11). His son, Absalom, launched an abortive revolt against David from Hebron (2 Sam. 15:10). Between 922 and 915 B.C. Rehoboam fortified the city as a part of Judah's defense network (2 Chron. 11:5-10). When the Babylonians destroyed Jerusalem in 587 B.C., the Edomites captured Hebron. It was not recaptured until Judas Maccabeus sacked the city in 164 B.C.

HELBON *(forest)*

City known for its trade in wine (Ezek. 27:18); Halbun about 11 miles north of Damascus.

HELKATH-HAZZURIM *(field of flint stones* or *field of battle)*

Site of "play" (2 Sam. 2:14) battle between young warriors of Saul and those of David leading to defeat of Ish-bosheth's army (2 Sam. 2:12-17).

HELL

Abode of the dead, especially as a place of eternal punishment for unbelievers; KJV often translates Hebrew *Sheol.* See *Sheol.*

Three Greek words often translated "hell" are *hades, gehenna,* and *tartaroo.* Hades was the Greek god of the underworld and the underworld itself. The Septuagint used "hades" to translate the Hebrew *Sheol.* Whereas in the OT, distinction in the fates of the righteous and wicked was not always clear, in the NT "hades" refers to a place of torment opposed to heaven as the place of Abraham's bosom (Luke 16:23; Acts 2:27,31). In Matt. 16:18, "hades" is not simply a place of the dead but represents the power of the underworld.

"Gehenna" is the Greek form of two Hebrew words *ge hinnom* meaning "valley of Hinnom," a ravine on the south side of Jerusalem where pagan deities were worshiped (2 Kings 23:10; Jer. 7:32; 2 Chron. 28:3; 33:6). It became a garbage dump and a place

of abomination where fire burned continuously (2 Kings 23;10; compare Matt. 18:9; Mark 9:43,45,47; Jas. 3:6).

Tartaroo ("cast into hell," 2 Pet. 2:4) referred in classical Greek to a subterranean region, doleful and dark, regarded by the ancient Greeks as the abode of the wicked dead, a place of punishment. Peter referred to the place of punishment for rebellious angels.

Language about hell seeks to describe for humans the most awful punishment human language can describe to warn unbelievers before it is too late (Matt. 8:12; 22:13; 25:30). Earthly experience would lead us to believe that the nature of punishment will fit the nature of the sin. Certainly, no one wants to suffer the punishment of hell, and through God's grace the way for all is open to avoid hell and know the blessings of eternal life through Christ. See *Gehenna; Hades; Heaven; Salvation; Sheol.*

HELLENISM See *Intertestamental History and Literature.*

HELLENISTIC, HELLENISTS *(Greeks)*

Customs or features of the Greek culture and those promoting Greek culture whether racially Greek or not. Differences arose in the early church between those Christians more closely tied to Hebrew and Jewish practices and culture and those identifying themselves more closely with Greek language and culture (Acts 6:1; 9:29).

HELMET See *Arms and Armor.*

HELP, HELPS

Assistance; in KJV, two technical senses: equipment used to secure a ship in storm (Acts 27:17) and a gift of ministry (1 Cor. 12:28).

HELPER

Translation of *parakletos,* distinctive title for the Holy Spirit in the Gospel of John (14:16,26; 15:26; 16:7, NASB, NKJV, TEV, NCV). See *Advocate.*

HEMAN (*faithful*)

(1) Descendant of Esau (Gen. 36:22);

(2) Sage to whose wisdom Solomon's is compared (1 Kings 4:31);

(3) Kohathite temple singer under David and Solomon (1 Chron. 6:33);

(4) Seer who used musical instruments (1 Chron. 25:5); may be same as 2 above;

(5) Author of Ps. 88.

HEN (FOWL) See *Birds*.

HEN (PERSON) (*grace, favor*)

Proper name or a title, "favored one," of Josiah (Zech. 6:14; compare 6:10) if present Hebrew text is original. Syriac (see NRSV, REB, TEV, NCV, CEV, NLT) has name Josiah in place of Hen in 6:14; Septuagint understood name as a title.

HENA

City Sennacherib of Assyria captured prior to threatening Hezekiah and Jerusalem in 701 B.C. (2 Kings 18:34); may be Ana or Anat at middle of Euphrates River.

HERBS See *Plants*.

HERESY

Opinion or doctrine not in line with the accepted teaching of a church; the opposite of orthodoxy. In the NT, the concept of heresy had more to do with fellowship within the church than with doctrinal teachings. The word in the NT never has the technical sense of "heresy" as we understand it today:

(1) Most frequently, party or sect referring to Pharisees and Sadducees (Acts 5:17; 15:5; 26:5).

(2) Slightly derogatory sense referring to Christians viewed as separatists or sectarians by the Jews (Acts 24:14; 28:22).

(3) Groups that threatened the harmonious relations of the church: 1 Cor. 11:18-19, disgraceful way in which the Corinthians were observing the Lord's Supper; Gal. 5:20,

works of the flesh including strife, seditions, envyings, and also people who choose to place their own desires above the fellowship of the church; Titus 3:10, a fractious person.

(4) False prophets who have denied true teaching about Christ (2 Pet. 2:1 and perhaps Titus 3:10) with reference to their decadent living. See *Christ, Christology; Gnosticism*.

HERMAS

Christian to whom Paul sent greetings (Rom. 16:14). Some have tried to identify him with author of "The Shepherd of Hermas," which is unlikely. See *Apostolic Fathers*.

HERMENEUTICS See *Bible, Hermeneutics*.

HERMES

Greek deity for whom superstitious people at Lystra took Paul (Acts 14:12); messenger of the gods associated with eloquence. KJV uses Latin name, "Mercurius."

HERMETIC LITERATURE

Diverse collection of writings composed in Greek in Egypt between A.D. 100 and 300 associated with the name Hermes Trimegistos (Thrice-great Hermes). Some texts are primarily astrological, magical, or alchemical. Others are primarily religious and philosophical texts. Some texts are monistic (viewing all reality as a unity) and pantheistic (seeing God present in everything that is). Others are dualistic (seeing God and the creation as separate).

Some scholars have seen the influence of Hermetic doctrine in the Gospel of John (creation by the *logos*, rebirth). More likely, both John and the later Hermetics developed earlier Jewish and Greek ideas independently. See *Gnosticism; John*.

HERMOGENES (*born of Hermes*)

Follower who deserted Paul, apparently while he was in prison in Ephesus (2 Tim. 1:15).

HERMON, MOUNT (devoted mountain); HERMONITE

Highest mountain in Syria (9,100 feet); site of sanctuary of Baal and northern boundary of Israel; called Sarion (Sirion) by Sidonians Phoenicians (Deut. 3:9; Ps. 29:6) and Sanir (Senir) by Amorites (Deut. 3:9). Both appellations signify "breastplate," evidently because of the mountain's rounded snow-covered tip that gleamed and shone in the sunlight. Water from its melting snow flows into the rivers of the Hauran and provides the principal source for the Jordan River. Senir seemingly is the name of a peak adjacent to Hermon (1 Chron. 5:23; Song of Sol. 4:8), also called Sion (Deut. 4:48), probably on account of its height. Once it is called "Hermons" (KJV mistakenly renders this as "the Hermonites," Ps. 42:6), probably a reference to the triple summits of the mountain. The biblical record praises: the dew of Hermon (Ps. 133:3), its lions (Song of Sol. 4:8), and its cypresses (Ezek. 27:5).

The mount is significant for four reasons:

(1) northern border of the Amorite kingdom (Deut. 3:8; 4:48);

(2) northern limits of Joshua's victorious campaigns (Josh. 11:17; 12:1; 13:5);

(3) always regarded as a sacred mountain;

(4) transfiguration of Jesus may have occurred there.

HEROD

Family ruling Palestine immediately before and to some degree immediately after Christ's birth.

The most prominent family member and ruler was Herod, son of Antipater. He was appointed governor of Idumea by Alexandra Salome, the Maccabean queen who ruled Palestine 78–69 B.C. With the permission of the Romans, Antipater left his son Phasael as Prefect of Jerusalem and his second son, Herod, as governor of Galilee. See Intertestamental History.

Herod was a paradox—one of the most cruel rulers of all history who seemed fiercely loyal to what he did believe in. Because of his effective administration, he virtually made Palestine what it was in the first Christian century. He has gone down in history as "the Great," yet that epithet can only be applied to him as his personality and accomplishments are compared to others of his family.

Other Herods named in the NT include the following:

(1) Agrippa I, son of Aristobulus and grandson of Herod. He ruled with the title of king from A.D. 41–44. Agrippa I ordered James the son of Zebedee killed with the sword and imprisoned Peter (Acts 12:1-23).

(2) Agrippa II, son of Agrippa I, heard Paul's defense (Acts 25:13-27; compare Acts 26:32). With his death, the Herodian dynasty came to an end.

(3) Drusilla (Acts 24:24), third and youngest daughter of Agrippa I, had been married briefly at age 14 to Azizus, king of Emessa, probably in the year 52. In 53 or 54, she was married to Felix, the Roman procurator.

(4) Bernice was the sister of Drusilla and Agrippa II, and also became Agrippa's wife. Paul appeared before Agrippa II and Bernice in Acts 25.

(5) Herod Philip, son of Herod the Great and Cleopatra of Jerusalem (Luke 3:1), built Caesarea Philippi and was governor of the northeastern districts of Iturea, Gaulinitis, Trachonitis, and Decapolis. He was married to Salome, daughter of Herodias.

(6) A Herod Philip is mentioned in Mark 6:17 as the first husband of Herodias. In some places he is mentioned simply as Herod, or Herod II. Most scholars do not believe that he was the same person as the governor of the northeastern districts.

(7) Herodias (Matt. 14:3) was the daughter of Aristobulus (son of Herod and Mariamne I) and Bernice. She was first married to the half brother of her father, identified in Mark 6:17 as Philip. By Philip she bore a daughter named Salome. Antipas, Philip's brother, divorced his own wife and wooed Herodias

away from Philip. She called for the head of John the Baptist (Matt. 14:3-12; Mark 6:17-29; compare Luke 3:19-20) when he denounced this gross marital misconduct.

(8) *Salome,* daughter of Herodias, was married to Philip. After his death in 34, she married a relative—Aristobulus, prince of Chalcis—and had three children (Matt. 14:6-12; Mark 6:22-29).

HERODIAN See *Herod; Jewish Parties in the New Testament.*

HERODIAS See *Herod; John 2.*

HESHBON (*reckoning*)

City in Moab ruled by Sihon and captured by Moses (Num. 21:21-30); tell Hesban, east of the Dead Sea and north of the Arnon River. Generally it was regarded as part of Moab (Isa. 15–16; Jer. 48; see Judg. 11:12-28); at times, at least partially occupied and claimed by Israel (Num. 21:21-31; 32:3,37), assigned Gad as a Levitical city (Josh. 13:27-28; 21:38-39).

Herod the Great fortified the site, and it became a flourishing city (called Esbus) during late Roman times. See *Gad; Moab; Sihon.*

HETH

Son of Canaan; great-grandson of Noah; original ancestor of Hittites, some of original inhabitants of Palestine (Gen. 10:15; compare ch. 23). See *Hittites.*

HEZEKIAH (*Yahweh is my strength*)

Son and successor of Ahaz as king of Judah (716/15–687/86 B.C.). Unwilling to court the favor of Assyrian kings, Hezekiah reopened the temple in Jerusalem, removed idols from it, sanctified temple vessels desecrated during Ahaz's reign, and initiated sacrifices. Hezekiah invited Israelites from the north ruled by Assyria to join in the Passover in Jerusalem. Places of idol worship were destroyed. Hezekiah even destroyed the bronze serpent Moses had erected in the wilderness (Num.

21:4-9) so the people would not view the bronze serpent as an object of worship. Hezekiah organized the priests and Levites for conducting religious services. The tithe was reinstituted. Plans were made to observe the religious feasts called for in the law.

In 711 B.C. Sargon II of Assyria captured Ashdod. Hezekiah anticipated the time when he would have to confront Assyrian armies, so he fortified Jerusalem and organized an army. Hezekiah constructed a tunnel through solid rock from the spring of Gihon to the Siloam pool and extended the city wall to enclose this important water source.

Isaiah warned Hezekiah not to become involved with Assyria (Isa. 20:1-6). The critical time came in 705 B.C. when Sennacherib became king of Assyria. Hezekiah gave him a heavy tribute of silver and gold. In 701 B.C., Hezekiah became seriously ill (Isa. 38:1-21). Isaiah warned the king to prepare for his approaching death, but Hezekiah prayed that God would intervene. God answered by promising Hezekiah 15 more years and deliverance of Jerusalem from Assyria (Isa. 38:4-6).

Sennacherib besieged Lachish and sent messengers to the Jerusalem wall to urge the people to surrender. Hezekiah, dressed in sackcloth and ashes, went to the temple to pray. He called for Isaiah, who announced that Sennacherib would "hear a rumor" and return to his own land where he would die by the sword (2 Kings 19:7).

Hezekiah's faith and physical recovery brought him recognition from the surrounding nations (2 Chron. 32:33). The Babylonian leader Merodachbaladan congratulated Hezekiah on his recovery and hosted a reception for Hezekiah, but Isaiah warned that succeeding generations would be subjected to Babylonian captivity (Isa. 39:1-8). Sennacherib destroyed Babylon in 689 B.C. He then marched toward Egypt. Hoping to ward off any interference from Judah, Sennacherib sent letters to Hezekiah ordering him to surrender

(Isa. 37:9-38). Hezekiah took the letters to the temple and prayed for God's help. Isaiah promised Sennacherib would not prevail, and his army would be miraculously destroyed (2 Kings 19:35-37). In 681 B.C., Sennacherib was killed by two of his sons.

HIDDEKEL

Third river flowing from the Garden of Eden (Gen. 2:14); Tigris in modern translations. KJV (Dan. 10:4) retains transliteration for Tigris. See *Euphrates and Tigris Rivers.*

HIERAPOLIS (*sacred city*)

Site of early church where Epaphras worked (Col. 4:13); Pambuck Kulasi 12 miles northwest of Colossae and 6 miles north of Laodicea on Lycus River a short way above its junction with Meander River. Its fame rested on textile and cloth dyeing industries.

HIGH PLACE

Elevated site, usually on top of mountain or hill; most were Canaanite places of pagan worship. The average high place would have an altar (2 Kings 21:3; 2 Chron. 14:3), a carved wooden pole that depicted the female goddess of fertility (Asherah), a stone pillar symbolizing the male deity (2 Kings 3:2), other idols (2 Kings 17:29; 2 Chron. 33:19), and some type of building (1 Kings 12:31; 13:32; 16:32-33). The people sacrificed animals (and at some high places even children, according to Jer. 7:31), burned incense to their gods, prayed, ate sacrificial meals, and were involved with male or female cultic prostitutes (2 Kings 17:8-12; 21:3-7; Hos. 4:11-14). Although most high places were part of the worship of Baal, the Ammonite god Molech and the Moabite god Chemosh were also worshiped at similar high places (1 Kings 11:5-8; 2 Kings 23:10).

God ordered Israel to destroy the high places (Ex. 23:24; 34:13; Num. 33:52; Deut. 7:5; 12:3) lest the Israelites be tempted to worship Canaanite false gods and accept their immoral behavior. David and Solomon wor-

shiped the God of Israel at the high place at Gibeon where the tabernacle and the altar of burnt offering were located (1 Chron. 16:1-4,37-40; 21:29; 2 Chron. 1:3-4,13).

After the temple was constructed, the people were to worship God at this place that He had chosen (Deut. 12:1-14), but Solomon built high places for the gods of his foreign wives and even worshiped there himself (1 Kings 11:1-8). Each new king of Judah and of Israel was evaluated in the Books of Kings and Chronicles according to what he did with the high places where false gods were worshiped. When Jeroboam created the new kingdom of Israel after the death of Solomon, he put two golden calves at high places in Dan and Bethel (1 Kings 12:28-32; compare 13:1-3). Following kings of Israel did not remove the high places where the false gods were worshiped.

The Israelite prophets condemned the high places of Moab (Isa. 15:2; 16:12), Judah (Jer. 7:30-31; 17:1-3; 19:3-5; 32:35), and Israel (Ezek. 6:3, 6; 20:29-31; Hos. 10:8; Amos 7:9) because they were places of sin where false gods were worshiped. See *Asherah; Gods, Pagan; Golden Calf; Prostitution.*

HIGH PRIEST

Priest in charge of temple (or tabernacle) worship: the priest (Ex. 31:10), the anointed priest (Lev. 4:3), the priest who is chief among his brethren (Lev. 21:10), chief priest (2 Chron. 26:20), and high priest (2 Kings 12:10).

The high priesthood was a hereditary office based on descent from Aaron (Ex. 29:29-30; Lev. 16:32). Normally, the high priest served for life (Num. 18:7; 25:11-13; 35:25,28; Neh. 12:10-11), though as early as Solomon's reign a high priest was dismissed for political reasons (1 Kings 2:27).

A special degree of holiness was required of the high priest (Lev. 10:6,9; 21:10-15). If the high priest sinned, he brought guilt upon the whole people (Lev. 4:3). The sin offering for the high priest (Lev. 4:3-12) was identical to that required "if the whole congregation of Israel commits a sin" (4:13-21).

The consecration of the high priest was an elaborate seven-day ritual involving special baths, putting on special garments, and anointing with oil and with blood (Ex. 29:1-37; Lev. 6:19-22; 8:5-35). The high priest kept the sacred lots, the Urim and Thummim, used to inquire of the Lord (Ex. 28:29-30; Num. 27:21). See *Breastpiece; Ephod; Urim and Thummim.*

Only the high priest was allowed to enter the holy of holies and then only on the Day of Atonement (Lev. 16:1-25; see *Day of Atonement*). One guilty of involuntary manslaughter was required to remain in a city of refuge until the death of the high priest (Num. 35:25,28,32; Josh. 20:6). The expiatory death of the high priest removed blood guilt that would pollute the land (compare Num. 35:33).

Eleazar was charged with supervision of the Levites (Num. 3:32; compare 1 Chron. 9:20) and of the sanctuary apparatus (Num. 4:16). As chief priest, Eleazar assisted Moses with the census (Num. 26). Eleazar served as an advisor to Moses (Num. 27:1) and to Joshua, consulting the Lord by means of the sacred lots. Such counsel formed the basis for the apportionment of the Promised Land among the tribes (Num. 34:17; Josh. 14:1; 17:4; 19:51; 21:1). One indication of the significance of Eleazar is that the Book of Joshua concludes with the death of this chief priest (24:33).

Phinehas, son of Eleazar, is best known for his zealous opposition to intermarriage with the Moabites and the concomitant idolatry (Num. 25:6-13). For his zeal, Phinehas was granted a covenant of perpetual priesthood (Num. 25:13) and reckoned as righteous (Ps. 106:30). Part of his ministry before the ark involved consulting the Lord for battle counsel (Judg. 20:27-28). Phinehas served as the major figure in the resolution of the conflict over the "commemorative" altar the tribes east of the Jordan built (Josh. 22:13,31-32).

Until Eli's appearance at end of the judges, a puzzling silence surrounds the high priesthood. First Chronicles 6:1-15 offers a (partial?) list of seven high priests between Phinehas and Zadok, a contemporary of David and Solomon. Of these, nothing is known except their names. Nor is Eli included among this list, though he functioned as the chief priest of the Shiloh sanctuary.

Eli is best known for his rearing of Samuel (1 Sam. 1:25-28) and for his inability to control his own sons (1 Sam. 2:12-17,22-25; 3:13), resulting in the forfeiture of the high priesthood (1 Sam. 2:27-35). Following the death of Eli, the Shiloh priesthood apparently relocated to Nob. Saul suspected the priesthood of conspiracy with David and exterminated the priestly family of Ahimelech (1 Sam. 22:9-19). Only Abiathar escaped (22:20). When David moved the ark to Jerusalem, Abiathar and Zadok apparently officiated jointly as chief priests (2 Sam. 8:17; 15:24-29, 35; 19:11), though Zadok already appears as the dominant figure in 2 Samuel. Solomon suspected Abiathar of conspiracy with his brother Adonijah and exiled him to his ancestral home (1 Kings 2:26-27). The high priesthood remained in the family of Zadok from the beginning of Solomon's reign (about 964 B.C.) until Menelaus bought the high priesthood (171 B.C.) in the days of Antiochus Epiphanes.

The high priest Hilkiah discovered the "Book of the law" that provided the incentive for King Josiah's reforms (2 Kings 22:8). Hilkiah removed all traces of Baal worship from the Jerusalem temple (2 Kings 23:4).

In the early postexilic period, the high priest Joshua is presented as the equal of the Davidic governor Zerubbabel (Hag. 1:1, 12, 14; 2:2, 4). Both high priest and governor shared in the rebuilding of the temple (Ezra 3; 6:9-15; Hag. 1–2). Both are recognized as anointed leaders (Zech. 4:14; 6:9-15). A further indication of the high priesthood's heightened importance in the postexilic period is an interest in succession lists of high priests (1 Chron. 6:1-15,50-53; 9:11; Ezra 7:1-5; Neh. 12:10-11), a new development in biblical literature.

In the period before the Maccabean revolt, the high priesthood became increasingly political. Jason, a Hellenistic sympathizer, ousted his more conservative brother Onias III (2 Macc. 4:7-10,18-20). Jason was, in turn, ousted by the more radically Hellenistic Menelaus who offered the Seleucid rulers an even larger bribe to secure the office (2 Macc. 4:23-26). With Menelaus, the high priesthood passed out of the legitimate Zadokite line.

The Maccabees combined the office of high priest with that of military commander or political leader. Alexander Balas, a contender for the Seleucid throne, appointed Jonathan Maccabee "high priest" and "king's friend" (1 Macc. 10:20). Simon Maccabee was, likewise, confirmed in his high priesthood and made a "friend" of the Seleucid King Demetrius II (1 Macc. 14:38). Temple and state were combined in the person of Simon who was both high priest and *ethnarch* (1 Macc. 15:1-2).

During the Roman period, Annas (high priest A.D. 6–15) was clearly the most powerful priestly figure. Even when deposed by the Romans, Annas succeeded in having five of his sons and a son-in-law, Joseph Caiaphas (high priest A.D. 18–36/37) appointed high priests. Ananias, one of Annas's sons, was the high priest to whom Paul was brought in Acts 23:2; 24:1.

HILKIAH *(Yah's portion)*

Eight Old Testament men including:

(1) Father of Jeremiah (Jer. 1:1);

(2) High priest who aided in Josiah's reform movement (2 Kings 22:4).

HILL, HILL COUNTRY

Elevated land, usually distinguished as lower than a mountain or with a less distinct peak; hills the length of Palestine separating Mediterranean coastal plain from Jordan Valley; area east of Jordan and Dead Sea is likewise hill country.

HINNOM, VALLEY OF, or VALLEY OF THE SON(S) OF HINNOM

Valley just south of ancient Jerusalem (Josh. 15:8; 2 Kings 23:10). Worshipers of pagan deities, Baal and Molech, practiced child sacrifice in the Valley of Hinnom (2 Kings 23:10; compare 2 Kings 16:3; 2 Kings 17:17; 2 Chron. 28:3). See *Baal; Gehenna; Hell; Jerusalem; Molech.*

HIRAM *(brother of the lofty one)*

(1) King of Tyre, associated with David and Solomon in building the temple; called Huram in Chronicles; son of Abibaal; 19 years old when he succeeded his father as king of Tyre. When David became king of Israel, Hiram sent congratulatory gifts to him, including men and materials to build a palace (2 Sam. 5:11). The friendship between the men grew, evidenced by commerce that developed between their two nations. The close relationship continued into Solomon's reign, and the two men made a mutually beneficial agreement that resulted in construction of the temple in Jerusalem (1 Kings 5:1-12). Jerusalem was inland and had the advantages of overland trade routes. Tyre, as a major seaport, offered the advantages of sea trade. See *David; Phoenicia; Solomon; Tyre.*

(2) Craftsman who did artistic metal work for Solomon's temple (1 Kings 7:13-45). He lived in Tyre, his father's hometown, but had a widowed Jewish mother from Naphtali.

HIRELING

Worker paid wages; laborer; hired hand. The work of hired laborers was generally difficult (Job 7:1-2). Mosaic law required paying workers at the close of the day so that they might provide for their families (Deut. 24:14-15). Workers were frequently exploited (Mal. 3:5; Jas. 5:4). John 10:12-13 contrasts the cowardice of a hired shepherd with an owner's self-sacrificing concern for his sheep.

HITTITES AND HIVITES

Non-Semitic minorities within the population of Canaan who frequently became involved in the affairs of the Israelites. Hittite and Hivite peoples were as "sons" of Canaan in the Table of Nations (Gen. 10:15,17), and seemingly infiltrated Palestine from their cultural and political centers in the north.

Hivites are of unknown origin without any extrabiblical references. That they were uncircumcised (Gen. 34:2,14) would suggest an Indo-European rather than Semitic origin. The more acceptable identification, therefore, would be with the biblical Horites (Hurrians) whose history and character are well known from extrabiblical sources and consistent with the role attributed to them in the biblical text.

Hittites appear among the ethnic groups living in urban enclaves or as individuals in Canaan interacting with the Israelites from patriarchal times to the end of the monarchy (Gen. 15:20; Deut. 7:1; Judg. 3:5). In patriarchal times, the reference to King Tidal (in Hittite Tudhaliya II) in Gen. 14:1 is a possible link to early imperial Hatti. In Canaan, the Hittites established a claim on the southern hill country, especially the Hebron area, where Abraham purchased the Cave of Machpelah from Ephron the Hittite as a family tomb (Gen. 23). Esau's marriage to two Hittite women greatly grieved and displeased his parents (Gen. 26:34-35; 27:46).

"All the land of the Hittites" (Josh. 1:4; compare Ex. 3:8,17; 13:5; 23:23; 33:2; Num. 13:29; Josh. 11:3) on the northern frontier of the Promised Land may indicate a recognition of the Hittite/Egyptian border treaty established by Rameses II and the Hittites under King Hattusilis III of about 1270 B.C. Devastation and pressures from the west by the Phrygians and the Sea Peoples brought another Hittite population to Canaan about 1200 B.C. Ezekiel recalled that Jerusalem had Amorite and Hittite origins (Ezek. 16:3,45; compare 2 Sam.

24:16-25). (See *Araunah*). Uriah and possibly other Hittites were serving as mercenaries in David's army (2 Sam. 11:3,6; 23:39). The Hittite woman among Solomon's foreign wives was probably the result of a foreign alliance with a neo-Hittite king of north Syria (1 Kings 10:29-11:2; 2 Chron. 1:17). Hittites together with other foreign elements may have been conscripted to forced labor during Solomon's reign (1 Kings 9:20-21).

Following the end of the Hittite Empire, a large number of Hittite principalities were established in northern Syria, Cilicia, and the regions of the Taurus and Anti-Taurus. They maintained a distinct identity as a minority within a predominantly Semitic environment for over 400 years. By the end of 700 B.C,. the Hittites had been absorbed into the Assyrian Empire.

HOBAB (*beloved* or *cunning*)

Father-in-law of Moses (Num. 10:29; Judg. 4:11); also called Jethro (Ex. 3:1; 18:2) and Reuel (Ex. 2:18). See *Moses; Jethro; Reuel.*

HOLY

Characteristic unique to God's nature that becomes the goal for human moral character, based in God's transcendent otherness and moral perfection. On earthly level the holy is something set apat for God. The holy evokes veneration or awe, causing a person to be frightened beyond belief. The holy is filled with superhuman and potential fatal power. A saint is a holy person. To be sanctified is to be made holy.

God's name is Holy. Holiness comes to imply the fullness and completeness of God and godliness in all its facets and meanings. God as holy is separated from humans, but God as person is related in love to people. Both characteristics must be included in a fully-developed portrait of God.

Leviticus 17–25 presents laws to be kept so that persons may be holy as God is holy. Holiness in believing Christians was attained through the cross and is to be preserved in clean and moral living.

"Holy" defines the godness of God. For the holy God to be present among His people, special holy places were set apart where God and people could safely come together. Special restrictions on access were established for the safety of the worshipers. Rules of sacrifice and cleanliness helped them prepare for this contact. A special place, the holy of holies, was completely cut off from common access. Only the high priest could enter there, and then only once a year after special preparation.

"Holy" also applied to persons who were to meet God. The priests had to undergo special rites that sanctified and purified them for service in the temple.

Christians are called to holy living (1 Cor. 1:2; 3:17). Being sanctified, or made holy, is a work of the Holy Spirit (Acts 1:8; 2:4; 5:32; 13:2-4) on the basis of Christ's atonement that calls for obedient submission from those who have been saved. Christians are holy because of their calling in Christ, because of His atonement for their sins, and because of the continual ministrations of the Holy Spirit who keeps the church pure (Acts 5:1-11) and promotes holiness in its members (1 Cor. 6:19; 1 Thess. 4:7).

HOLY GHOST See *Holy Spirit.*

HOLY OF HOLIES

Innermost sanctuary of the temple separated from other parts of the temple by thick curtain; specially associated with the presence of Yahweh; contained the ark of the covenant. See *Temple.*

HOLY SPIRIT

Mysterious third Person of the Trinity through whom God acts, reveals His will, empowers individuals, and discloses His personal presence; term appearing in OT only in Ps. 51:11; Isa. 63:10-11. The Spirit of God is depicted as a mighty wind, Hebrew using the same word *ruach* for wind, breath, and spirit. God deployed this wind to

part the sea, thus enabling the Israelites to pass through safely and elude Pharaoh and his army (Ex. 14:21). God used this agent as a destructive force that dried up the waters (Hos. 13:15) and as power of God in gathering clouds to bring the refreshing rain (1 Kings 18:45). The Spirit exercised control over the chaotic waters at the beginning of creation (Gen. 1:2; 8:1; compare Ps. 33:6; Job 26:13). This mysterious power (Ps. 104:3) is able to transport God on its wings to the outer limits of the earth. No one can tell where He has been or where He is going.

God inspired the prophets indirectly by the Spirit (Gen. 41:38; Judg. 3:10; 14:6; 2 Sam. 23:2; Zech. 4:6). See 1 Sam. 10:16; 19:23-24.

The Spirit is also the ultimate origin of all mental and spiritual gifts (Ex. 31:1-6; Isa. 11:2; Job 4:15; 32:8). The Spirit will be shed upon the people of God (Isa. 44:3; compare Joel 2:28). The reception of the new Spirit, prophesied in Ezekiel and Jeremiah, is dependent on repentance (Ezek. 18:31) and associated with the creation of a new heart (Jer. 31:31-34). This prophetic foreshadowing looked forward to a time when the Spirit of God would revitalize His chosen people, empower the Messiah, and be lavishly poured out on all humankind.

With John the Baptist, the spirit-inspired prophetic voice returned after a 400-year absence (Luke 1:15). The Spirit came upon Mary, leading to the virgin birth of Jesus (1:35). At baptism, Jesus was anointed by the Spirit of God (3:22), who thrust Jesus into the wilderness to undergo temptation (4:1-13). Paul offers the most theological reflections on the Spirit (see Rom. 8; 1 Cor. 2; 12-14; 2 Cor. 3; Gal. 5).

In the Gospel of John, the Spirit possesses Christ (1:32-33); is indicative of the new birth (3:1-16); will come following Jesus' departure (16:7-11); and will endow the believer after the resurrection (20:22). The Christian community is anointed by the Spirit (1 John 2:20); and the Spirit assures the believer of the indwelling presence of Jesus (1 John 3:24). See *God.*

HOLY SPIRIT, SIN AGAINST THE

Attributing the work of the Holy Spirit to the devil (Matt. 12:32; Mark 3:29; Luke 12:10). See *Unpardonable Sin.*

HOLY WEEK

Week climaxing with Easter Sunday in which the church remembers the death and resurrection of Christ. In the early centuries, Easter Sunday celebrations included remembrance of both the crucifixion and the resurrection. By about 500, Good Friday came to be the focus of the remembrance of the crucifixion. Christians began to regard Thursday of Holy Week ("Maundy Thursday," a reference to Christ's giving a "new commandment," John 13:34) as a special time for participating in the Lord's Supper. Early Maundy Thursday observances included a ceremonial footwashing, an imitation of Christ's washing the feet of the disciples (John 13:5-11). See *Church Year.*

HOMELESSNESS

In a sense, all Christians, like Abraham, are "homeless" in that they are but sojourners in this world (Heb. 11:13). This reality, however, must not lessen the impact of the responsibility of Christians who are able to own a house or pay rent on an apartment toward persons who, for a variety of reasons, are unable to do either.

The biblical term "sojourner" includes a variety of persons, native and non-native, who did not have permanent homes of their own in the land in which they were living. While some sojourners were attached to a household (1 Kings 17:20; Job 19:15), others were transient (eg. 2 Sam. 4:3; 2 Chron. 15:9), "like a bird that strays from its nest" (Prov. 27:8). The rights of all were vulnerable. For this reason, sojourners, like the poor, orphans and widows, fell under the special protection of God (Deut. 10:17-18; Ps. 146:9; compare Rom. 8:38-39) and were to be treated as equals under the Mosaic

law (Lev. 24:22; Deut. 24:17). Both the Old and New Testaments declare that God's people are to provide for the homeless (Lev. 19:10; Deut. 10:18-19; Job 31:32; Isa. 58:7; Zech. 7:9-10; Matt. 25:31-46).

Other biblical examples of homelessness include Absolom, who fled home as a fugitive (2 Sam. 14:13-14), various OT saints (Heb. 11:37-38), Jesus (Matt. 8:20) the prodigal son (Luke 15:13-16) and Paul (1 Cor. 4:11). The people of Israel considered themselves homeless when they were uprooted from their land in exile (Jer. 12:7; Lam. 4:14-15; 5:2; Hos. 9:17; Amos 7:17).

HOMOSEXUALITY

Sexual preference for and sexual behavior between members of the same sex, considered to be an immoral lifestyle and behavior pattern throughout the biblical revelation. The Bible makes no distinction between what some today refer to as "homosexual orientation" and homosexual behavior. Homosexual desires or feelings are never mentioned as such in Scripture, but homosexual behavior is strongly condemned as a deviation from God's will for human beings (see Lev. 18:22) even punishable by death (20:13). Therefore, it stands to reason that any homosexual inclination, feeling, or desire must be seriously dealt with as a potentially dangerous temptation much like those temptations of a heterosexual nature such as the desire to commit fornication or adultery.

Genesis 19:1-11 tells the story of an attempted homosexual gang rape at the house of Lot by the wicked men of Sodom. Lot considered this behavior wicked (v. 7); raping his daughters was considered the lesser of two evils (v. 8). This evil of Sodom is mentioned elsewhere (Jer. 23:14; Ezek. 16:49-50; 2 Pet. 2:6-10; Jude 7) in the strongest terms of condemnation. The term *sodomy* has its roots here. A similar story is found in Judg. 19:22-30.

Male homosexuality was forbidden by Mosiac Law (Lev. 18:22; 20:13).

The early church also considered homosexuality contrary to "sound doctrine" (1 Tim. 1:10), a sign of God's wrath upon blind sinfulness (Rom. 1:26-27). Such behavior is considered a degrading passion, unnatural, an indecent act, and an error, even worthy of death (Rom. 1:32). Some of the Corinthian Christians apparently had been homosexuals (1 Cor. 6:9-11). Through faith in Christ they had been "washed," "sanctified," and "justified" (v. 11). Paul implied here that homosexual behavior is forgivable through the gospel and that any homosexual temptations should be resisted as seriously as those toward fornication or adultery.

The Bible links homosexuality to the sinful nature of humanity—a psychosocial, learned behavior, expressing rebellion against God and calling for redemption. Homosexuals are responsible for their behavior. This is a very complex psychological problem with many possible roots or causes, calling for Christian compassion on the part of God's people as well as God's redemptive power through the gospel. The ministry of the church to homosexuals should include conversion, counseling, education, and support-group relationships.

HONESTY

Fairness and straightforwardness of conduct; in modern translations: honorable/honorably (Rom. 13:13; Phil. 4:8; Heb. 13:18; 1 Pet. 2:12); noble (Luke 8:15; Rom. 12:17); dignity (1 Tim. 2:2); properly (1 Thess. 4:12). Men of "honest report" (Acts 6:3) are men of good standing (NRSV).

Jacob claimed honesty (Gen. 30:33), but manipulated the breeding of Laban's flocks (30:37-43). Jacob's sons repeatedly assured Joseph of their honesty (Gen. 42:11,19,31,33-34), never guessing that their brother knew their deceptive natures all too well (37:31-33).

HONEY

Nectar produced by bees providing a sweet food stuff for people to eat. During Bible times, honey appeared in three forms:

(1) honey deposited from wild bees (Deut. 32:13),

(2) honey from domesticated bees (one of the products "of the field," 2 Chron. 31:5);

(3) a syrup made from dates and grape juice (2 Kings 18:32). Honey served as a food stuff (Gen. 43:11) and as an item of trade (Ezek. 27:17).

HOOK

Curved or bent device for catching, holding, or pulling; used for hanging curtains (Ex. 26:32; 27:10), fishing (Isa. 19:8; Job. 40:24; Hab. 1:15; Matt. 17:27), and leading war captives by means of hooks or thongs put through their noses or jaws (2 Chron. 33:11; Ezek. 38:4; Amos 4:2).

HOPE

Trustful expectation, particularly with reference to the fulfillment of God's promises; anticipation of a favorable outcome under God's guidance; confidence that what God has done for us in the past guarantees our participation in what God will do in the future. This contrasts to the world's definition of hope as "a feeling that what is wanted will happen."

God is the ultimate ground and object of hope. Even when Israel was unfaithful, hope was not lost because of God's faithfulness and mercy (Mal. 3:6-7; compare 2 Chron. 7:14; Ps. 86:5). God is the "hope of Israel, the saviour thereof in time of trouble" (Jer. 14:8; compare 14:22; 17:13).

It is futile to vest ultimate hope in wealth (Pss. 49:6-12; 52:7; Prov. 11:28), houses (Isa. 32:17-18), princes (Ps. 146:3), empires and armies (Isa. 31:1-3; 2 Kings 18:19-24), or even the Jerusalem temple (Jer. 7:1-7). God, and God only, is a rock that cannot be moved (Deut. 32:4,15,18; Pss. 18:2; 62:2; Isa. 26:4) and a refuge or fortress who provides ultimate security (Pss. 14:6; 61:3; 73:28; 91:9).

God's promise that He would establish the throne of David forever (2 Sam. 7:14) led to Israel's expectation of a Messiah, an anointed ruler from David's line to restore Israel's glory and rule the nations in peace and righteousness.

NT hope rests in the "God which raiseth the dead" on whom "we have set our hope" (2 Cor. 1:9-10 NIV; compare 1 Tim. 4:10; 1 Pet. 1:21; Rom. 15:13). Hope is also focused in Christ— "our hope" (1 Tim. 1:1). The hope of glory is identified with "Christ in you" (Col. 1:27; compare Luke 2:11; John 6:35; Acts 13:23; Titus 1:4; 3:6; 1 Pet. 2:4-7; Rev. 1:17; 22:5). Christ is the object and ground of hope for two reasons: (1) The Messiah has brought salvation by His life, death, and resurrection (Luke 24:46). God's promises are fulfilled in Him (2 Cor. 1:20). (2) A unity exists between Father and Son, a unity of nature (John 1:1; Col. 1:19) as well as a unity in the work of redemption. Because "God was in Christ, reconciling the world unto himself" (2 Cor. 5:19), hope in the Son is one with hope in the Father.

NT hope centers on the second coming of Christ. The "blessed hope" of the church is nothing less than "the glorious appearing of the great God and our Saviour Jesus Christ" (Titus 2:13). See *Eschatology.*

Christians live in hope because of what God has done in Christ through the resurrection (1 Pet. 1:3) and because of the indwelling of the Holy Spirit (Rom. 8:16). Christians live in the present with confidence and face the future with courage. They meet trials triumphantly because they know that tribulation "worketh patience; and patience, experience; and experience, hope" (Rom. 5:3-4). Christian hope is the gift of God: "Which hope we have as an anchor of the soul, both sure and steadfast" (Heb. 6:19).

HOPHNI AND PHINEHAS
(tadpole and *dark-skinned one)*

Sons of Eli and priests at Shiloh (1 Sam. 1:30); disreputable men con-temptuous of sacred matters; slain in battle against the Philistines (1 Sam. 4:4). The news of their deaths precipitated the death of their father Eli (1 Sam. 4:18). See *Eli; Samuel.*

HOPHRA *(the heart of Re endures)*

Egyptian pharaoh (589–569 B.C.) who tried to drive the Babylonian army away from its siege of Jerusalem (Jer. 37:5). Jeremiah mocked the Pharaoh, making a pun on his name, calling him a loud-voiced boaster ("King Bombast, the man who missed his opportunity" Jer. 46:17, REB). Jeremiah warned that the pharaoh would be handed over to his enemies; at the same time he warned Jews living in Egypt that salvation history was reversed, and they would be destroyed (Jer. 44:26-30). Hophra eventually lost his power in a revolt by his general Amasis in 569 B.C.

HOR *(perhaps mountain)*

(1) Place where Aaron, the high priest, died, fulfilling God's Word that he would be punished for rebelling at the water of Meribah (Num. 20:22-29; 21:4; 33:38-41; compare Deut. 10:6); possibly Jebel Madurah northeast of Kadesh on Edom's border.

(2) Mountain marking northern boundary of Promised Land (Num. 34:7-8), possibly a variant name for Mount Hermon.

HOREB

Alternative name for Mount Sinai (Ex. 3:1-12; 17:6-7; Deut. 1:19; 5:2; 1 Kings 19:8). See *Mount Sinai.*

HORESH *(forest)*

Place where David hid from Saul and where Jonathan, Saul's son, came out to help him and made a covenant of mutual help (1 Sam. 23:15-18); perhaps khirbet Khoreisa, 2 miles south of Ziph and 6 miles south of Hebron. KJV interprets as common noun.

HORIM or HORITES

Pre-Edomite inhabitants of Mount Seir in the southern Transjordan (see Gen. 34:2; 36: 2,20; Josh. 9:7). Hebrew corresponds to extrabiblical Hurrians, a non-Semitic people who migrated into the Fertile Crescent about 2000 B.C. The Hurrians created the Mitannian Empire in Mesopotamia about 1500 B.C. and later became an important element in the Canaanite population of Palestine. In locations where there is extrabiblical evidence for Hurrians, the Hebrew term "Hivites" appears (Gen. 34:2; Josh. 9:7; 11:3,19) as a designation for certain elements of the Canaanite population. Many scholars equate both Horites and Hivites with the extrabiblical Hurrians.

Hebrew text only mentions Horites in Mt. Seir where there is no record of Hurrians. Thus some think biblical Horites were not Hurrians, but simply the original cave-dwelling (the Hebrew hor means "cave") population of Edom (Mt. Seir). The Hivites, according to this theory, should be identified with the extrabiblical Hurrians. See *Hittites and Hivites.*

HORMAH (*split rock* or *cursed for destruction*)

Simeonite city (Josh. 15:30; 19:4; 1 Chron. 4:30) marking limits of Canaanite route the Israelites took after a failed attempt to invade Canaan (Num. 14:45; Deut. 1:44; compare Num. 21:1-3; Judg. 1:17); possibly tell Masos about seven miles east of Beersheba. The site controlled the east-west road in the Beersheba Valley and the north-south road to Hebron.

HORN

Curved bonelike structures growing from the heads of animals such as deer or goats (Gen. 22:13; Deut. 33:17; Dan. 8:5) and vessels, features, or instruments made from or shaped like such horns: trumpets (Josh. 6:5), vessels (1 Sam. 16:1), topographical features, and figurative symbols.

The basic meaning of horns relate to animal horns. Elephant tusks were also called horns (Ezek. 27:15). (See *Music, Instruments, Dancing.*) Hornlike projections were built onto the corners of the altar of burnt offerings in the temple and in tabernacles (Ex. 27:2). The horns were smeared with the blood of the sacrifice, served as binding posts for the sacrifice, and were clung to for safety from punishment (1 Kings 2:28). Peaks or summits of Palestinian hills were called horns (Isa. 51:1).

Christ is called "an horn of salvation" (Luke 1:69), signifying strength. Powers opposing God are pictured as horned animals (Dan. 7:7; Rev. 5:6; 13:1; 17:3,7).

HORONAIM (*twin caves*)

Prominent town in Moab which Isaiah (15:5) and Jeremiah (48:3,5,34) warned of coming destruction; apparently in southwestern part of Moab.

HORSE See *Animals; Megiddo.*

HOSANNA (*Save now* or *Save, we beseech Thee*)

Cry with which crowds greeted Jesus on His triumphal entrance into Jerusalem (Mark 11:9); drawn from Ps. 118:25-26; a plea for salvation.

HOSEA (*salvation*)

(1) Prophet (Hos. 1:1-2; Rom. 9:25) from Northern Kingdom to the Northern Kingdom (approximately 750–725 B.C.) with same Hebrew name as Joshua's original name (Num. 13:16; Deut. 32:44); contemporary of Amos, southern prophet who came north, and Isaiah, prophet of Jerusalem. Hosea's name symbolized the pressing need for national deliverance. His message pointed the nation to the Deliverer (Hos. 13:4). Not only are Hosea's oracles (Hos. 4–14) the word of the Lord to Israel, but so also are the materials dealing with his domestic problems (Hos. 1–3).

Hosea witnessed the political chaos in Israel following the death of Jeroboam II. He rebuked efforts at alliance with Assyria and Egypt as the means to national security. Hosea had the unenviable task of presiding over the death of his beloved nation, but he held out hope of national revival based on radical repentance (Hos. 14).

(2) Last king of Israel (2 Kings 17:1), who lived at the same time as the prophet.

(3) One of David's officers (1 Chron. 27:20).

(4) Clan chief (Neh. 10:23). English translators spell prophet's name "Hosea" to distinguish him from others, whose names they spell "Hoshea."

HOSEA, BOOK OF

First in the Books of the Twelve or Minor Prophets with two divisions: (1) Hosea's Marriage, 1–3; and (2) Hosea's Messages, 4–14. A pattern of judgment followed by hope recurs in each of the first three chapters. A similar pattern is discernible in the oracles of Hosea (Hos. 4–14) but most oracles are judgmental. The dominant theme is love (covenant fidelity), God's unrelenting love for His wayward people and Israel's unreliable love for God.

Hosea's marriage and family life dominate chapters 1–3 and surface from time to time in the remainder of the book. References to Hosea's family serve as prophetic symbolism of God and His family Israel. God ordered Hosea to take a wife of harlotry and have children of harlotry, "for the land hath committed great whoredom, departing from the Lord" (Hos. 1:2). Primary interest is not in Hosea and his family, but in God and His family.

At the heart of Hosea's theology was the relationship between God and Israel. Yahweh alone was Israel's God. Israel was Yahweh's elect people. Hosea presented Yahweh as a faithful husband and Israel as an unfaithful wife. Hosea stressed the knowledge of God and loyal love. God's love for Israel would not permit Him to give up on them in spite of their lack of knowledge and infidelity. Hope for Israel's future lay in their repentance and God's forgiveness and love that made Him willing to restore their relationship.

HOSHEA See *Hosea.*

HOSPITALITY

To entertain or receive a stranger (sojourner) into one's home as an honored guest and to provide the guest with food, shelter, and protection; not merely an oriental custom or good manners but a sacred duty that everyone was expected to observe. Since public inns were rare, a traveler had to depend on the kindness of others and had a right to expect it. This practice was extended to every sojourner, even a runaway slave (Deut. 23:16-17) or one's arch enemy.

Israelites were to love strangers as themselves (Lev. 19:33-34; Deut. 10:18-19) and to look after their welfare (Deut. 24:17-22) because Israel themselves were once strangers in Egypt. Some acts of hospitality were rewarded (Josh. 6:22-25; Heb. 11:31; Jas. 2:25). Breaches of hospitality were condemned and punished (Gen. 19:1-11; Judg. 19:10-25). The only exception was Jael who was praised for killing Sisera (Judg. 4:18-24).

Hospitality formed the background of many details in the life of Jesus and the early church (Matt. 8:20; Luke 7:36; 9:2-5; 10:4-11). It was to be a characteristic of bishops and widows (1 Tim. 3:2; 5:10; Titus 1:8) and a duty of Christians (Rom. 12:13; 1 Pet. 4:9). It was a natural expression of brotherly love (Heb. 13:1-2; 1 Pet. 4:8-9) and a necessary tool of evangelism. One might even entertain angels or the Lord unawares (Heb. 13:2; Matt. 25:31-46).

HOST OF HEAVEN

The army at God's command, composed of either heavenly bodies such as sun, moon, stars, or angels. "Host" is a military term frequently used to designate a group of men organized for war: a human army (Gen. 21:22,32; Judg. 4:2,7; 9:29; 1 Sam. 12:9; 2 Sam. 3:23; Isa. 34:2; Jer. 51:3). The term can refer to an act of war (Num. 1:3,20; Deut. 24:5; Josh. 22:12). "Hosts" can designate a length of time of hard service (Job 7:1; Isa. 40:2;

Dan. 10:1) or the service of the Levites in the sanctuary as in Numbers.

The celestial bodies were thought to be organized as were earthly military bodies. The sun, moon, and stars were the "host of heaven" (Gen. 2:1). God created this host by His breath (Ps. 33:6) and preserved their existence (Isa. 40:26). God warned Israel about the danger of worshiping the heavenly bodies (Deut. 4:19) and prescribed the death penalty for the crime of worshiping the sun, or the moon, or any of the "host of heaven" (Deut. 17:2-7). Unfortunately, Israel and Judah yielded to the temptation, especially during the period of Assyrian and Babylonian influence (2 Kings 17:16-23; 21:3,5).

Manasseh, king of Judah (697–642 B.C.), built altars in Jerusalem for all the "host of heaven" (2 Kings 21:5), an effort Josiah reversed (2 Kings 23:7).

Israel drew comparisons between their God and the gods of Canaan and Babylonia. Yahweh came to be understood as a king who presided over a heavenly council, composed of angelic servants, sometimes called "sons of God" (1 Kings 22:19; compare Job 1–2). See *Angel; Sons of God.*

HOUR

Appointed time for meeting or for religious festival (1 Sam. 9:24 RSV); brief moment of time (Matt. 14:15; Rev. 18:17; compare John 5:35); time of an expected momentous event (Matt. 8:13; Mark 13:11); one twelfth of the day or of the night; in Gospel of John, the significant period of Jesus' saving mission on earth from His triumphal entry until His death and resurrection (12:23).

Biblical Hebrew has no word for hour, only an expression for an appointed meeting time. In NT times, a day was divided into two twelve-hour periods (or watches) of light and darkness beginning at sunrise, making the seventh hour (John 4:52) about 1:00 P.M.

The Gospel of John presents Jesus' suffering and death as the "hour" of Jesus' "glory," the time of His "exaltation/lifting up." Jesus' death is the means by which eternal life is provided for the world (John 3:14-15; 6:51-53). From that hour on, human distinctions no longer apply (4:21-24; 11:51-53; 12:20-23). The glory of Jesus' death is found both in what it enabled Him to offer the world (6:51-53; 7:37-39) and in its being the means by which He returned to the Father (13:1). See *Glory; John, the Gospel of; Time.*

HOUSE

Place where people live, usually in an extended family unit that can also be called a house. Abraham left Mesopotamia where he lived in houses made of mud brick (compare Gen. 11:3) and became a tent dweller (Heb. 11:9). Tents were made of goat hair and were suitable to nomadic life. When Joshua captured Canaan, Israel began to build houses like the Canaanites.

In the lowlands of the Jordan Valley, the houses were built of mud brick because stone was not readily available. In the hill country field stones were used. The homes of the poor were small and modest, consisting of one to four rooms, usually, and almost always including a courtyard on the east of the house so that the prevailing westerly winds would blow the smoke away from the house. In this courtyard the family prepared food in an oven built of clay, kept storage jars, made clothing and pottery, and housed their animals.

Because of heat in summer and cold in the winter, houses were built with few, if any, windows. This also provided more protection from intruders, but it meant that the houses were dark and uninviting. The only escape from the dim, cramped interior of the house was the courtyard and, especially, the flat roof. Here, the women of the house could do many of their daily chores—washing, weaving, drying of figs and dates, and even cooking. They could enjoy the cool breezes in the heat of the day and sleep in summer (Acts 10:9; compare 2 Kings 4:10). The poor had neither the space nor money for furniture. They ate and slept on floor mats that could be rolled out for that purpose. Most floors consisted of beaten earth, although some were made of mud or lime plaster and, occasionally, even limestone slabs. The roof was supported by beams laid across the tops of narrow rooms, which were then covered by brush and mud packed to a firm, smooth surface. The paralytic at Capernaum was let down to Jesus through a hole "dug out" of such a roof (Mark 2:4; it was covered with clay tiles, Luke 5:19). Israelites were required to build a bannister around the roof to prevent falling off (Deut. 22:8).

Wealthy families built larger houses that sometimes utilized cut stone. They furnished them with chairs, tables, and couches that could double as beds. In NT times, the wealthy were able to cover their floors with beautiful mosaics and adorn their plastered walls with lovely frescoes. By this time, many of the better homes under Roman influence included atria, adding to the concept of outdoor living already experienced in the courtyards and on the roofs. Two story houses were built throughout biblical times, the upper floor being reached by outside stairs or ladders.

HOUSEHOLD

Kinfolk, members of one's own family (Gen. 7:1), including those employed in the service of that family (Matt. 13:57; 24:45; John 4:53; Acts 16:31); family's descendants as an organized body (Gen. 18:19; Deut. 25:9; 1 Kings 11:38); Hebrew people as a nation or any of its tribes or clans (Ex. 19:3; 40:38; Isa. 8:17; Amos 3:13; 7:16); descendants of a particular nation (Matt. 10:6; Luke 1:27,69); paternal ancestry (Ex. 6:14; 12:3; Num. 1:2; Josh. 22:14); household affairs: persons, property, belongings, etc. (Gen. 39:4; 1 Kings 4:6; 2 Kings 15:5; Isa. 22:15; 36:3; Acts 7:10).

Next to the state, the household was the most important unit in the Greco-Roman world, largely because of its role as a guarantor of stability in society. If order prevailed in the household, so it would in the state. Just as the household was basic to Jewish society, so it was to early Christianity. Household groups were the basic units that made up the church in any given locale (Acts 2:2,46; 12:12; Rom. 16:5,23; 1 Cor. 16:19). The household was often the focus of the church's evangelistic activity (Acts 11:14; 16:15,31-34; 18:8). The faith of the head of the household was the faith of the entire household. In baptism each household member confessed Christ as Lord and showed forth His death and resurrection.

The church is the "household" of faith or of God (Gal. 6:10; Eph. 2:19). Christians are "servants" of God, and their leaders are "stewards" (1 Cor. 4:1; Titus 1:7; 1 Pet. 4:10). Standardized rules for behavior or domestic codes were developed in society, and these were adapted for use in the early church (Col. 3:18–4:1; Eph. 5:21–6:9; 1 Pet. 2:13–3:7).

HULDAH (*mole*)

Prophetess (2 Kings 22:14) Josiah consulted after a copy of the book of the law was found as preparations were being made to restore the temple. She prophesied judgment for the nation but a peaceful death for Josiah the king. See *Josiah.*

HUMAN SACRIFICE

Ritual slaying of one or more human beings to please a god. Before 2000 B.C. both Egyptians and Sumerians killed servants and possibly family members to bury them with deceased kings to accompany them to the realm of the dead. In Mesopotamia, and perhaps elsewhere, the remains of animals and humans offered as sacrifice were deposited within foundations to protect the building from evil powers (compare 1 Kings 16:34).

Jephthah sacrificed his daughter as a fulfillment of a vow (Judg. 11:30-40). Mesha, king of Moab, offered his son as a burnt offering — presumably to Chemosh, national god of Moab—upon the walls of his capital while under siege by Israel and Judah (2 Kings 3:27). The event was so shocking the siege was terminated. Although Israelite law specifically forbade human sacrifice (Lev. 18:21; 20:2-5), persistent references to the practice occur, especially between 800 and 500 B.C. Both Ahaz and Manasseh burned their sons as an offering in times of national peril (2 Kings 16:3; 21:6; compare 1 Kings 11:7; Jer. 7:31-32; 19:5-6; Ezek. 16:20-21; 20:31). See *Hinnom, Valley of; Molech.* Josiah defiled Topheth as a part of his reformation so that "no man might make his son or his daughter to pass through the fire to Molech" (2 Kings 23:10). These practices, foreign to the worship of Yahweh, must have been adopted by Israel from the surrounding peoples. Sepharvites, people deported to Palestine in 721 B.C. by Sargon II from an area dominated by Arameans, burned their children as offerings to Adrammelech and Anammelech (2 Kings 17:31). Yet the abomination of human sacrifice never entered the mind of Yahweh (Jer. 19:5).

HUMANITY

Characteristics that unite all persons despite their many individual differences and constitute them as God's "image" (Gen. 1:27). The suggestion that the image consists in humankind's lordship over and stewardship of creation, the theme of the following verses (Gen. 1:28-31). See *Image of God.*

HUMILITY

Personal quality in which an individual shows dependence on God and respect for other persons. The OT connects humility with Israel's lowly experience as slaves in Egypt—a poor, afflicted, and suffering people (Deut. 26:6). Humility was closely associated with individuals who were poor and afflicted (2 Sam. 22:28).

What God desires most is not outward sacrifices but a humble spirit (Ps. 51:17; Mic. 6:8). Such a humble

spirit shows itself in several ways: (1) a recognition of one's sinfulness before a holy God (Isa. 6:5); (2) obedience to God (Deut. 8:2); and (3) submission to God (2 Kings 22:19; 2 Chron. 34:37). The OT promised blessings to those who were humble (Prov. 11:2; 15:33; Isa. 61:1).

Those who humble themselves before God will be exalted (1 Kings 21:29; 2 Kings 22:19; 2 Chron. 32:26; 33:12-19; Luke 1:52; Jas. 4:10; 1 Pet. 5:6). Those who do not humble themselves before God will be afflicted (2 Chron. 33:23; 36:12). The pathway to revival is the way of humility (2 Chron. 7:14).

Jesus Christ's life provides the best example of humility (Matt. 11:29; 1 Cor. 4:21; Phil. 2:1-11). Jesus preached and taught often about the need for humility (Matt. 18:1; 23:12; Mark 9:35; Luke 14:11; 18:14). The person with humility does not look down on others (Matt. 18:4; Luke 14:11). While God resists those who are proud, He provides grace for the humble (Jas. 4:6). One who has humility will not be overly concerned about his or her prestige (Matt. 18:4; 23:12; Rom. 12:16). Quality relationships with other people, especially those who had erred spiritually, hinged on the presence of meekness or humility (1 Cor. 4:21; Gal. 6:1; 2 Tim. 2:25).

HUNDRED, TOWER OF

(KJV, "Tower of Meah") Tower located on the north wall of Jerusalem that was restored by Nehemiah (Neh. 3:1; 12:39). It may have been part of the temple fortress (Neh. 2:8).

HUNT, HUNTER

To pursue game for food or pleasure. Hunting was an important supplementary food source, especially in the seminomadic stage of civilization: Nimrod, Gen. 10:9; Ishmael, 21:20; Esau, 25:27. The blood of captured game was to be poured out on the ground (Lev. 17:13; compare Deut. 14:3).

The tools of the hunter include bows and arrows (Gen. 21:20; 27:3), nets (Job 18:8; Ezek. 12:13), snares or pitfalls (Job 18:8), if the term does not refer to part of the net (NASB, NIV, REB); traps, snares, and ropes (Job 18:9-10).Terror, the pit, and the trap of Isa. 24:17-18 (also Jer. 48:43-44) perhaps allude to the Battue method of hunting whereby a group forms a cordon and beats over the earth, driving game into a confined area, pit, or net. Ancient Egyptian carvings depict such methods of hunting.

Jeremiah pictured God hunting the scattered exiles to return them to Israel (Jer. 16:16). Saul hunted David (1 Sam. 24:11). Pharisees plotted "to entrap" Jesus (Matt. 22:15), "lying in wait" for Him (Luke 11:54).The devil has a snare for us (1 Tim. 3:7; 2 Tim. 2:26).Women practicing magical arts were fowlers ensnaring the people (Ezek. 13:17-23). Micah 7:2 portrays the unfaithful as hunting each other with nets. Proverbs 6:5 warns to save oneself (from evil) like the gazelle or roe flees the hunter.

HUR (perhaps *white one, Horite* or perhaps derived from name of the Egyptian god *Horus*)

(1) Israelite leader who accompanied Moses and Aaron to top of the mountain in fight against Amalekites. Hur helped Aaron hold Moses' hands up so Israel could prevail (Ex. 17:10-12). Hur and Aaron also represented Moses and settled any problems among the people while Moses ascended the mountain to receive God's instructions (Ex. 24:14; compare 31:2; 1 Chron. 2:19).

(2) King of Midian whom Israel slew as they moved toward the Promised Land (Num. 31:8; see Josh. 13:21).

(3) District governor under Solomon over Mount Ephraim (1 Kings 4:8). His name may also be translated Ben-hur.

(4) Administrator over half the district of Jerusalem under Nehemiah or father of the administrator (Neh. 3:9).

HUSHAI (*quick*, from *Hushah*, or *gift of brotherhood*)

"David's friend" (2 Sam. 15:37), probably referring to an official government post as in Egypt, a close personal adviser somewhat like the secretary of state (see 2 Sam. 15:32,34; 16:16-19; 17). Solomon's commissioner in charge of collecting royal provisions in Asher was the son of Hushai, perhaps the same as "David's friend" (1 Kings 4:16).

HYKSOS (*rulers of foreign lands*)

Kings of Fifteenth and Sixteenth Dynasties of Egypt; later misinterpreted by Josephus as "shepherd kings." With the decline of the Middle Kingdom of Egypt (about 2000–1786 B.C.), large numbers of Asiatics, mostly Semites like the Hebrew patriarchs, migrated into the Nile Delta of northern Egypt from Canaan. These probably came initially for reasons of economic distress, such as famine, as did Abraham (Gen. 12:10). Under the weak Thirteenth Dynasty, some Asiatics established local independent chiefdoms in the eastern Delta region. Eventually, one of these local rulers managed to consolidate the rule of northern Egypt as pharaoh, thus beginning the Fifteenth Dynasty.The Sixteenth Dynasty, perhaps contemporary with the Fifteenth, consisted of minor Asiatic kings. As these dynasties of pharaohs were not ethnic Egyptians, they were remembered by the native population as "Hyksos."

While the Hyksos pharaohs ruled northern Egypt from Avaris in the eastern Delta, the native Egyptian Seventeenth Dynasty ruled southern Egypt from Thebes. This period is known as the Second Intermediate or Hyksos Period (about 1786–1540 B.C.). About 1540 B.C., Ahmose I sacked Avaris, expelled the Hyksos, reunited Egypt, and established the Eighteenth Dynasty.

Some think Joseph's rise to power as pharaoh's second-in-command (Gen. 41:39-45) likely occurred under a Hyksos king and that Ahmose I was the pharaoh "who had not known Joseph" (Ex. 1:8).

HYMENAEUS or HYMENEUS

Greek god of marriage; name of fellow worker of Paul whose faith weakened and whose lifestyle changed, leading Paul to deliver him to Satan (1 Tim. 1:20). That probably means Paul led the church to dismiss Hymenaeus from membership to purify the church, remove further temptation from the church, and to lead Hymenaeus to restored faith, repentance, and renewed church membership. Along with Philetus, Hymenaeus taught that the resurrection had already occurred (2 Tim. 2:17-18; compare 1 Cor. 5). See *Gnosticism.*

HYMN

Generic term given to vocal praise in the Bible especially in response to important events such as the Hebrews' passage through the Red Sea (Ex. 15:1-21), Deborah and Barak's triumph over the forces of Jabin, king of Hazor (Judg. 5:1-31), and David's victorious return from battle with the Philistines (1 Sam. 18:6-7). Moses gave the Israelites some of his last warnings in a great song (Deut. 32:1-43). The Book of Psalms is a hymnbook with hymns by different authors composed over long periods of time and used by the people of Israel in their worship. Hymn singing in the Jerusalem temple was led by trained choirs, sometimes using instrumental accompaniment (2 Chron. 29:25-28). The people joined the choir in singing hymns in unison, responsively, and antiphonally.

Singing of spiritual songs was a part of the early Christian church: Luke 1:46-55, Mary's song: "The Magnificat"; Luke 1:68-79, Zacharias's prophetic song: "The Benedictus"; and Luke 2:29-32, Simeon's blessing of the infant Jesus and farewell: "The Nunc Dimittis." Numerous doxolo-

gies (Luke 2:14; 1 Tim. 1:17; 6:15-16; Rev. 4:8, for example) were used in corporate worship. Other passages in the NT give evidence of being quotations of hymns or fragments of hymns (Rom. 8:31-39; 1 Cor. 13; Eph. 1:3-14; Eph. 5:14; Phil. 2:5-11; 1 Tim. 3:16; 2 Tim. 2:11-13; Titus 3:4-7). Jesus and His disciples sang a hymn at the end of the Last Supper (Matt. 26:30; Mark 14:26). Christian songs were used in worship, to instruct in the faith, and to express joy. Paul and Silas sang hymns in prison (Acts 16:25). Hebrews 2:12 (a quotation of the messianic Ps. 22:22) stressed that Jesus will declare His name to the church, that He will "sing praise," or hymns.

HYPOCRISY

Pretense to being what one really is not, especially the pretense of being a better person than one really is; in classical Greek, a neutral term—an interpreter of dreams, an orator, a reciter of poetry, or an actor—that gained negative connotation of pretense, duplicity, or insincerity.

Hypocrisy in sense of playing a role is highlighted in the NT. Jesus criticized hypocrites for being pious in public (Matt. 6:2,5,16); and interested in human praise when they gave alms, prayed, and fasted than in God's reward.

Hypocrisy was part of the sin of Ananias and Sapphira (Acts 5:1-11). Paul accused Peter of hypocrisy for refusing to eat with Gentile Christians in Antioch (Gal. 2:12-13). Paul warned Timothy about hypocritical false teachers (1 Tim. 4:2). Peter included hypocrisy as one of the attitudes Christians should avoid (1 Pet. 2:1). Sincerity (without hypocrisy) should characterize the Christian: love (Rom. 12:9; 2 Cor. 6:6; 1 Pet. 1:22), faith (1 Tim. 1:5; 2 Tim. 1:5), and wisdom (Jas. 3:17) should be sincere.

HYSSOP See *Plants.*

ICHABOD (*Where is the glory?*)
Son of Phinehas, Eli's son (1 Sam. 4:21). See *Eli.*

ICONIUM See *Asia Minor, Cities of.*

IDDO

Six men with four different Hebrew names including:
(1) person with authority in exilic community to whom Ezra sent messengers to secure Levites (Ezra 8:17);
(2) leader of eastern half of tribe of Manasseh under David (1 Chron. 27:21);
(3) prophet whose records the chronicler refers to for more information about Solomon and Jeroboam (2 Chron. 9:29), Rehoboam (2 Chron. 12:15), and Abijah (2 Chron. 13:22);
(4) grandfather of Zechariah, the prophet (Zech. 1:1,7; compare Ezra 5:1; 6:14 using "son" to mean descendant). See Neh. 12:4,16.

IDOL

Physical or material image or form representing a reality or being considered divine and thus an object of worship: "image," either graven (carved) or cast; "statue," "abomination." Biblical religion uniquely demands imageless worship (Ex. 20:4,5).

The Hebrews' first rebellion centered on the golden calf (Ex. 32). The bronze serpent illustrates the Hebrews' propensity for idol worship. Moses set it up in the wilderness to allay a plague of serpents (Num. 21), but Israel retained it and made it an object of worship (2 Kings 18:4). Joshua called on the people to put away the gods their fathers had served in Mesopotamia and in Egypt (Josh. 24:14). Perhaps a misguided King Jeroboam intended to represent Yahweh by the golden calves set up in his temples at Bethel and Dan (1 Kings 12:28-33).

Isaiah 44:9-20 devastatingly denounced idolatry. The idol made by a workman was powerless even to sustain the workman in completing his task. The idol began as a leftover piece of tree from which a person made a god. He then worshiped no more than a block of wood.

The most noted problem in the NT concerns the propriety of eating meat that has previously been offered to an idol (1 Cor. 8–10). Paul seemingly broadened the Christian concept of idolatry when he identified covetousness with idolatry (Col. 3:5). See *Food Offered to Idols; Gods, Pagan.*

IDUMEA

Nation destined for judgment (Isa. 34:5); term used in Septuagint and by Josephus for Edom, the region southeast of the Dead Sea. The Herods came originally from Idumea. Crowds from Idumea followed Jesus early in His ministry (Mark 3:8). See *Edom.*

IGNORANCE

Lack of knowledge or comprehension. OT law distinguished between sins of ignorance or unintentional sin (Lev. 4:2,13-14; Num. 15:24-29) and premeditated sins ("to sin presumptuously" or with a high hand, Num. 15:30-31). Sins committed in ignorance incur guilt (Lev. 4:13,22,27); however, the sacrificial system provided atonement for such sins (Lev. 4; 5:5-6). In contrast, "high-handed" or "presumptuous" sin is an affront to the Lord punishable by exclusion from the people of God. The law provided no ritual cleansing for such sin (Num. 15:30-31).

The NT speaks of past ignorance that God excuses. Such was the ignorance of those Jews who participated in crucifying Jesus (Acts 3:17; 13:27), of Paul who persecuted Christians (1 Tim. 1:13), and of Gentiles who did not recognize the true God (Acts 17:30). God still requires repentance (Acts 3:19; 17:30). Obedience characterizes lives of the converted just as ignorant desires characterize those without Christ (1 Pet. 1:14). Deliberate ignorance involves the stubborn refusal to acknowledge nature's witness to the powerful existence of God (Rom. 1:18-21; Eph. 4:18; 2 Pet. 3:5).

IJON *(ruin)*

Place in Naphtali; near Marj Uyun between the rivers Litani and Hesbani at tell Dibbin (1 Kings 15:20-22). Tiglath-pileser conquered the city and carried many Israelites into captivity about 734 B.C. (2 Kings 15:29).

ILLYRICUM

District in Roman Empire between Danube River and Adriatic Sea including modern Yugoslavia and Albania. The Romans divided it into Dalmatia and Panhynonia. Illyricum represented the northeastern limits of Paul's missionary work (Rom. 15:19).

IMAGE OF GOD

Unique nature of human beings in their relationship to the Creator God (Gen. 1:26-27). Humans are not an evolutionary accident, but a special creation purposefully produced by God to fulfill a preordained role in His world. They have peculiar qualities that somehow reflect the nature of God Himself and set them apart and above all other created beings.

Attempts at distinguishing the meaning of "image" and "likeness" fail to recognize Hebrew parallelism and the narrative description of one act, not two, in creating humans. The Hebrew *selem* ("image") refers to a hewn or carved image (1 Sam. 6:5; 2 Kings 11:18) like a statue, bearing a strong physical resemblance to the person or thing it represents. Likeness *(demuth)* means a facsimile. Compare 2 Kings 16:10, "fashion" or "pattern" (NASB), "sketch" (NIV, REB), "exact model" (TEV). Neither of the words implies that persons are divine. They were endowed with some of the characteristics of God. There is a likeness, but not a sameness.

God made each male and female a person in the likeness of His own personhood. Personhood encompasses individuals in their entirety—body and spirit — as rational, loving, responsible, moral creatures with self-awareness and God-awareness. Humans created in God's image share His rational nature with the power to think, analyze, and reflect even on abstract matters. As God is spiritual (John 4:24), persons are spiritual and so can communicate with God.

Human beings have purpose, an instinctive need to be something and to do something, a unique sense of "oughtness." Humans are moral creatures. They can and do make moral judgments (Gen. 2:16-27). Persons have a censoring conscience that they may defy. They are choice makers; they can obey their highest instincts or follow their most morbid urges. A human is the only creature who can say no to God. Humans have freedom to govern their own lives and to choose to have fellowship with God. God created "man" in His own image because He wanted a relationship with another sovereign person. As an image of God, humans represent God on earth, taking care of His creation for Him and revealing God to other humans. See *Humanity.*

IMAGE WORSHIP See *Idol.*

IMMANUEL *(God with us)*

Name of son to be born in Isaiah's prophecy to King Ahaz (Isa. 7:14) and fulfilled in birth of Jesus (Matt. 1:22-23). When King Ahaz refused to show his faith by asking God for a sign (Isa. 7:10-12), Isaiah gave him a sign of the birth of Immanuel, using the traditional form of a birth announcement (7:14; compare Gen. 16:11; Judg. 13:3,5). The Hebrew language apparently indicates the prophet and king expected an immediate fulfillment. Recent study has pointed to Ahaz's wife as the woman expected to bear the child, showing that God was still with the Davidic royal dynasty even in the midst of severe threats from Assyria. Such a sign would give hope to a king who trusted God but would have been a constant threat to one who followed his own strategy. The double meaning of the Immanuel sign appears again in Isa. 8:8. The Assyrian army was to flood the land until Judah was up to its neck in trouble and could only cry out, "O Immanuel," a cry confessing that God is with us in His destructive rage but at the same time a prayer, hoping for divine intervention. Isaiah followed this with a call to the nations to lose in battle because of Immanuel: God with us (8:10).

The Bible announces the great fulfillment in Jesus Christ (Matt. 1:22-23). Jesus was not just a sign of God with us: Jesus was God become flesh, God incarnate, God with us in Person. See *Incarnation.*

IMMORALITY

Any illicit sexual activity outside of marriage; figuratively, idolatry or unfaithfulness to God. The OT *zanah* regularly refers to wrongful heterosexual intercourse, primarily in regard to women (Judg. 19:2; Jer. 3:1; Hos. 4:13). The noun "harlot" or "whore" is derived from the same stem (Gen. 34:31; Josh. 2:1-3; Prov. 23:27; Hos. 4:13-14). In a figurative sense, *zanah* refers to Israel's unfaithfulness to God (2 Chron. 21:11; Isa. 1:21; Jer. 3:1-5; Ezek. 16:26-28). In addition, the sinfulness of Tyre (Isa. 23:17) and Nineveh (Nah. 3:4) are portrayed in this manner.

Porneia and/or related words refer to an incestuous relationship (1 Cor. 5:1), sexual relations with a prostitute (1 Cor. 6:12-20; compare Rev. 2:14,20), various forms of unchastity both heterosexual and homosexual (Rom. 1:29; 1 Cor. 5:9-11; 6:9-11; 7:2; 2 Cor. 12:21; Eph. 5:3; 1 Thess. 4:3), and adultery (Matt. 5:32; 19:9). The word *harlot* or "whore" is derived from the same root word (Rev. 19:2). Immorality is a sin against God (1 Cor. 3:16-17; 6:15-20; 1 Thess. 4:3-8). The Apostolic Council required that Gentiles avoid *porneia* (Acts 15:20,29). *Porneia* and related words also have a figurative meaning of unfaithfulness to God (Matt. 12:39; John 8:41; Rev. 2:21; 9:21; 14:8; 19:2). See *Adultery; Sex, Biblical Teaching on.*

IMMORTALITY

Quality or state of being exempt from death. Only God is immortal (1 Tim. 6:16; see 1 Tim. 1:17; 2 Tim. 1:10), for only God is living in the true sense of the word. See *Life.* Humans may be considered immortal only insofar as immortality is the gift of God (Rom. 2:7; 1 Cor. 15:53-55; see Isa. 25:8; Hos. 13:14). Humans in their earthly life are mortal, subject to death. They receive eternal life as a gift of redemption. Those who did escape death—Enoch (Gen. 5:24) and Elijah (2 Kings 2:10-11)—did so only by the power of God and not by some inherent power they had to live forever. See *Eternal Life.*

IMPUTE, IMPUTATION

Setting to someone's account or reckoning something to another person. God reckoned righteousness to believing Abraham (Gen. 15:16). He credited to Abraham that which the man did not have in himself (Rom. 4:3-5). This does not mean God accepted Abraham's faith instead of righteousness as an accomplishment meriting justification. Rather, it means that God accepted Abraham because he trusted in God rather than trusting in something he could do.

Only God can forgive sin. Those who are forgiven are not regarded as wicked since the Lord does not impute to them their iniquity. Instead, these are considered or reckoned as children of God (Rom. 4:7-8,11,23-24; compare Ps. 32:1-3). God grants righteousness to those who have faith in Christ (Rom. 1:17; 3:21-26; 10:3; 2 Cor. 5:21; Phil. 3:9). This righteousness imputed or reckoned to believers is, strictly speaking, an alien righteousness. It is not the believer's own righteousness, but God's righteousness imputed to the believer. So, as Luther said, believers are simultaneously righteous and sinful.

The Bible in some sense implies that Adam's sin was imputed to humankind (Rom. 5:12-21; 1 Cor. 15:21-22), and the sins of humanity were imputed to Jesus Christ (2 Cor.

5:21), although the exact nature of this divine imputation remains a mystery. In Adam God judged the whole human race guilty. Yet humankind has not merely been declared guilty; each human has acted out his or her guilt. It is impossible for sinners to be righteous in God's sight apart from the gift of righteousness graciously granted to them in Christ through faith.

INCARNATION

God's becoming human; the union of divinity and humanity in Jesus of Nazareth. Incarnation refers to the affirmation that God without in any way ceasing to be the one God has revealed Himself to humanity for its salvation by becoming human (John 1:14). Jesus, the Man from Nazareth, is the incarnate Word or Son of God. As the God-Man, He mediates God to humans; as the Man-God, He represents humans to God. By faith-union with Him, men and women—as adopted children of God—participate in His filial relation to God as Father.

Jesus referred to Himself as a man (John 8:40; compare Acts 2:22). The respective genealogies of Jesus serve as testimonies to His natural human descent (Matt. 1:1-17; Luke 3:23-37). Jesus attributed to Himself such normal human elements as body and soul (Matt. 26:26,28,38). He grew and developed along the lines of normal human development (Luke 2:40). During His earthly ministry, Jesus displayed common physiological needs: fatigue (John 4:6), sleep (Matt. 8:24), food (Matt. 4:2; 21:18), and water (John 19:28). Human emotional characteristics accompanied the physical ones: joy (John 15:11) and sorrow (Matt. 26:37); compassion (Matt. 9:36) and love (John 11:5); and righteous indignation (Mark 3:5). In the garden, He prayed for emotional and physical strength to face the critical hours that lay ahead. He perspired as one under great physical strain (Luke 22:43-44). He died a real death (Mark 15:37; John 19:30). When a spear was thrust into His side, both blood and water poured from His body (John 19:34). Jesus thought of Himself as human, and those who witnessed His birth, maturation, ministry, and death experienced Him as fully human.

His was perfect humanity—distinct and unique. Jesus was supernaturally conceived, being born of a virgin (Luke 1:26-35). Jesus was sinless (John 8:46; compare 2 Cor. 5:21; 4:15). Jesus was God (John 6:51; 10:7,11; 11:25; 14:6; 15:1; esp. 8:58). In Him lived the fullness of God (Col. 1:19; compare John 20:28; Titus 2:13). Jesus was aware of His divine status (John 10:30; 12:44-45; 14:9). With the "I am" sayings, He equated Himself with the God who appeared to Moses in the burning bush (Ex. 3:14). He was preexistent (John 1:1-2; see also John 1:15; 8:58; 17:5; Phil. 2:5-11). Jesus realized accomplishments and claimed authority ascribed only to divinity. He forgave sins (Matt. 9:6) and sent others to do His bidding, claiming all authority "in heaven and in earth" (Matt. 28:18-20). Jesus is the only way to eternal life, a status held by deity alone (John 3:36; 14:6; compare Acts 4:12; Rom. 10:9). He is worthy of honor and worship due only to deity (John 5:23; Heb. 1:6; Phil. 2:10-11; Rev. 5:12). He is the Agent of creation (John 1:3) and the Mediator of providence (Col. 1:17; Heb. 1:3). He raised the dead (John 11:43-44), healed the sick (John 9:6), and vanquished demons (Mark 5:13). He will effect the final resurrection of humanity either to judgment or to life (Matt. 25:31-32; John 5:27-29).

The titles ascribed to Jesus provide conclusive evidence for the New Testament's estimate of His person as God. Jesus is "Lord" (Phil. 2:11), "Lord of lords" (1 Tim. 6:15), "the Lord of glory" (1 Cor. 2:8), "the mediator" (Heb. 12:24), and "who is over all, God blessed for ever" (Rom. 9:5). In addition, the NT repeatedly couples the name "God" with Jesus (John 1:18; 20:28; Acts 20:28; Rom. 9:5; 2 Thess. 1:12; Titus 2:13; Heb. 1:8; 2 Pet. 1:1; 1 John 5:20).

After centuries of debate the Council of Chalcedon (A.D. 451) declared Jesus was one person with two natures—human and divine. See *Christ, Christology.*

INCENSE

Mixture of aromatic spices prepared to be burned in connection with sacrifices (Ex. 25:6); smoke produced by the burning. Zacharias was burning incense in the temple when the angel Gabriel visited him (Luke 1:8-20). See *Sacrifice and Offerings.*

INCEST

Sexual intercourse between persons too closely related for normal marriage, practiced among Egyptians and Canaanites whom God judged (Lev. 18:3,24-25). Leviticus 18:6-19 prohibited unions between a man and his mother, stepmother, sister, half-sister, daughter-in-law, granddaughter, aunt (by blood or marriage), or sister-in-law; it prohibited a man's involvement with a woman and her daughter or granddaughter and the taking of sisters as rival wives. Penalties for various forms of incest included childlessness (Lev. 20:20-21), exclusion from the covenant people (Lev. 18:29; 20:17-18; compare 1 Cor. 5:2, 5), and death (Lev. 20:11,12,14). In patriarchal times, marriage to a half sister (Gen. 20:12) and marriage to rival sisters (Gen. 29:21-30) were permissible, though such marriages proved troublesome to both Abraham and Jacob. Scriptural accounts of incest include Gen. 19:31-35; 35:22; and 2 Sam. 13.

INCREASE

Multiplication or growth; reproduction of livestock; harvest (Lev. 26:3-4; Deut. 7:12-13). The promise of increase is contingent on Israel's fulfilling its covenant commitments. Increase is used figuratively for Israel as the firstfruits of God's increase (KJV) or harvest. See Isa. 9:7; 29:19; 40:29; Acts 6:7; 16:5; Eph. 4:16; Col. 2:19; 1 Thess. 3:12; 4:10. Boasting in the results of one's work for God is without basis since God gives increase (1 Cor. 3:6; Col. 2:19).

INCLUSIVENESS

God chose Abraham from among the families of the earth to be the father of a great nation which would then convey God's blessing to others (Gen. 12:3; Gal. 3:6-9). God's special relationship with Israel (Ex. 19:5-6) was never intended to be exclusive, however. Numerous non-Israelites (during the OT period) and non-Jews (during the intertestamental and NT periods) participated in the covenantal blessings of Abraham. These include the mixed multitude who left Egypt with Moses (Ex. 12:38), Rahab (Josh. 6:25; Matt. 1:5), Ruth (Ruth 1:4; Matt. 1:5), various Syrophoenician women (2 Kings 17:8-24; Luke 4:25-26), Naaman (2 Kings 5:1-19; Luke 4:27), the Ninevites (Jonah 3:5-10; 4:11), a Roman centurion (Matt. 8:5-13), the Samaritan woman (John 4:1-42), Simon of Cyrene (Mark 15:21), Cornelius (Acts 10:9-48), Timothy (Acts 16:1), and a host of Gentile converts throughout the history of the church. The population of heaven will include persons "from every nation, tribe, people and language" (Rev. 7:9).

With one exception, God shows no partiality in matters of judgment or salvation (Acts 10:34; Rom. 2:9-11; Eph. 2:11-14). The exception is that salvation is found in the work of Jesus Christ alone (John 14:6; Acts 4:12). The language which God used of Israel at Mount Sinai ("ye shall be unto me a kingdom of priests, and an holy nation"—Ex. 19:6) was adopted by Peter to refer to Gentiles (1 Pet. 2:9) who, because of Christ, became fellow heirs with the believing descendants of Abraham (Gal. 3:29; 4:7).

All barriers between people based on gender, ethnicity, or socio-economic status are removed in Christ (Gal. 3:28-29).

INDIA

Eastern boundary of the Persian Empire of Ahasuerus (Xerxes) (Esther 1:1; 8:9); possibly port of call for Solomon's fleet (1 Kings 10:22); Persian satrapy or province. Biblical references refer to the Punjab, area of Pakistan and northwest India drained by the Indus River and its tributaries. Trade between India and the biblical lands began before 2000 B.C.

INERRANCY

Inerrancy refers to the truth of Scripture. Belief in the Bible as the infallible, authoritative, and reliable Word of God has always been a firm and crucial doctrine of the church, having as its base the very nature of God and character of the Bible itself.

The Bible's witness to itself testifies to a record of truth spoken by God and the Holy Spirit (e.g., Ex. 20:1; Isa. 1:2; Acts 1:16; Heb. 1:1-2; 3:7; 2 Pet. 1:21). The word "inspired" (Gk *theopneustos*), used to describe the origin and nature of Scripture in 2 Tim. 3:16, literally means "God-inspired" or "God breathed-out." Although God used many people to physically write the words of Scripture (e.g., Eccl. 1:1; Jer. 36:2-4), the Bible is clear that the words written issued from divine initiative: "For the prophecy came not in old time by the will of man: but holy men of God spake as they were moved by the Holy Ghost" (2 Pet. 1:21).

Because God is truth (Num. 23:19; Jer. 10:10; John 15:26; 17:3; Titus 1:2), His revelation in Scripture is true and entirely trustworthy (Ps. 19:7; Prov. 30:5-6; John 10:35; 1 Tim. 1:15; 2 Tim. 3:16). For this reason, the Word of God alone stands forever (Isa. 40:6-8).

INFANT BAPTISM

Christening a baby by the church. Christian groups take varying stances on the practice and meaning of infant baptism. Those who emphasize a conscious faith response in the salvation process limit baptism to believers. Those who interpret baptism as the sign of God's New Covenant reserve the rite for the children of believers (compare 1 Cor. 7:14). Those viewing baptism as a means by which God's grace becomes effective for salvation welcome all children.

Those favoring infant baptism raise the following arguments:

(1) Household baptisms likely included some infants (Acts 16:5,33; 18:8; 1 Cor. 1:16).

(2) Jesus' welcome and blessing of children is a mandate to baptize infants (Mark 10:13-16); "hinder" is a technical term associated with baptism (Acts 8:36).

(3) Circumcision that prefigured baptism (Col. 2:11) included children (Gen. 17:12).

(4) Children participated in OT ceremonies of covenant renewal (Deut. 29:10-13; Josh. 8:35; Joel 2:16).

Adherents of believer's baptism counter:

(1) The NT prerequisite of baptism is faith (Acts 18:8) that is evidenced by confession (Rom. 10:9-10) and repentance (Acts 2:38).

(2) Infant baptism rests ultimately on the fear that infants are held accountable for organic sin. Baptists counter with a doctrine of an age of accountability where conscious sin occurs (Gen. 8:21; Ps. 25:7; Jer. 3:25) and at which a conscious response to God is possible (1 Kings 18:12; Ps. 71:5,17).

(3) Household baptisms need not have included children; baptism is prefigured in the salvation of Noah and his exclusively adult household in the ark (1 Pet. 3:20-21).

(4) Jesus' blessing of the children demonstrates Christ's love for children. Children are presented as an example to disciples rather than as disciples themselves (Matt. 18:2-4).

(5) Circumcision is an imperfect analogy to baptism; only males participated in circumcision, whereas in baptism there is "neither male nor female" (Gal. 3:28). The witness of the NT is: "What is born of the flesh is flesh," and a spiritual birth is necessary to enter God's kingdom (John 3:5-6). It is not Israel of the flesh that inherits the promises of God but those who are the spiritual Israel by a faith commitment (Rom. 6–8; Gal. 6:16).

(6) The responsibility of the faith community to its children is instruction in the way of the Lord (Deut. 4:9-10; 11:19; Prov. 22:6); participation in covenant renewal is educational for children. See *Accountability, Age of; Baptism.*

INHERITANCE

Legal transmission of property after death. In ancient Israel possessions were passed on to the living sons of a father, but the eldest son received a double portion (Deut. 21:17). Reuben lost preeminence because of incest with Bilhah (Gen. 35:22; 49:4; 1 Chron. 5:1), and Esau surrendered his birthright to Jacob (Gen. 25:29-34). Sons of concubines did not inherit unless adopted (Gen. 30:3-13; 49). Women were not to inherit from their fathers except in the absence of a son (Num. 27:1-11).

God granted the land as an inheritance to Israel (Josh. 1:15; Num. 36:2-4). Levites had no share of the land; the Lord was their"inheritance" (Num. 18:20-24; Deut. 10:9; 18:2; Josh. 13:33). Jeremiah used the concept of "inheritance"to refer to Israel's restoration to the land from "the north" after the time of punishment (Jer. 3:18-19).

Israel (Jer. 10:16), as well as Jerusalem and the temple, is the "inheritance" of the Lord (Ps. 79:1). In a broader sense, God can be said to "inherit" all nations (Ps. 82:8). Anything given by God can be called an "inheritance": pleasant conditions of the psalmist's life (Ps. 16:5); God's testimonies (Ps. 119:111); God's punishment of the wicked (Job 27:13); honor to the wise (Prov. 3:35).

In the NT "inheritance" can refer to property (Luke 12:13), but it most often refers to the rewards of discipleship: eternal life (Matt. 5:5; 19:29; Mark 10:29-30; Titus 3:7), the Kingdom (Matt. 25:34; Jas. 2:5; negatively, 1 Cor. 6:9-10; 15:50), salvation (Acts 20:32; Eph. 1:14,18; Rev. 21:7). Christ is the Heir par excellence (Matt. 21:38; Heb. 1:2). Through Christ Christians can be heirs of God and "fellow heirs"with Christ (Rom. 8:17;

compare Eph. 3:6). Only Hebrews makes explicit use of the idea of "inheritance" as requiring the death of the testator, Christ. A "will" requires a death to come into effect, so the death of Christ brings the New "Covenant"/"Will" into effect (Heb. 9:16-17). See *Covenant.*

INN

Different kinds of shelters or dwellings; camping place for an individual (Jer. 9:2), a family on a journey (Ex. 4:24), an entire caravan (Gen. 42:27; 43:21), or an army (Josh. 4:3,8). Presence of a building is not implied; often only a convenient piece of ground near a spring. Unlike OT period, public inns existed in Greek times and throughout the Roman period. Such an inn consisted primarily of a walled-in area with a well. A larger inn might have small rooms surrounding the court. People and animals stayed together.

Inns generally had a bad reputation. Travelers were subjected to discomfort and at times robbery or even death. The primary services that could be depended on were water for the family and animals and a place to spread a pallet.The same Greek word can refer to a guest room in a private home (Mark 14:14; Luke 22:11). In Bethlehem, Joseph and Mary could find no room at the inn (Luke 2:7). This may have been a guest room in a home or some kind of public inn. Luke 10:34 clearly refers to a public place where wounded could be fed and cared for by the innkeeper. See *Hospitality; House.*

INNER MAN; INWARD MAN

Component of human personality responsive to the requirements of the law. Human personality has three components (Rom. 7:22-23):

(1) the inmost self where the law dwells: reason (*nous*, v. 23); the inmost self approximates the rabbinic *yeser hatob* (inclination to good);

(2) the flesh or its members that are responsive to desire; the flesh

approximates the rabbinic *yeser harah* (inclination to evil); and (3) the conscience that is aware of both reason and desire. In rabbinic thought, the law served to tip the balance in favor of the good inclination. Paul rejected this optimistic view of the law. Only the Spirit dwelling in the inner self can free the individual from the power of sin (Rom. 8:2; Eph. 3:16).

INSANITY

Mental illness. See *Diseases*.

INSCRIPTION

Words or letters carved, engraved, or printed on a surface (Mark 15:26; Luke 23:38; "superscription," KJV). Pilate likely intended the inscription above the cross in a derogatory sense: "See the defeated King of the Jews." The Jewish leadership found the inscription offensive (John 19:21). Pilate's mockery told the truth about Jesus who in His suffering and death fulfilled His messianic role.

INSECTS

Air-breathing arthropods on land and in water that make up the class *Hexapoda*, having three distinct body parts: head, thorax, and abdomen, as well as three pair of legs, one pair of antennae, and usually one or two pairs of wings. Their primary food is green plants.

Insects are mobile and migratory. Migration is usually a seasonal phenomenon. Insects lay enormous numbers of eggs. Insects ravage: agricultural products, humans and other animals, woodwork, wool, and clothing. Insects also transmit diseases such as malaria, the plague, and typhoid. Some insects are beneficial, producing honey, wax, silk, pigments, and tannins while pollinating plants. They are also a substantial food source for other animals, including people. Other insects are scavengers, helping to dispose of decaying flesh. The Bible names at least six orders:

Hymenoptera: Ants, Bees, and Wasps (with four wings)

Female usually has a stinger as well as an ovipositor, or egg-laying organ, at the tip of the abdomen. Many of the species are social creatures:

(1) *Ants* live in communities, sometimes as large as one-half million individuals. The workers are female, having neither wings nor the ability to reproduce. The queen and males have wings. Ants are known to domesticate and enslave other insects, such as aphids and other ants. Proverbs 6:6-8 praises her as the supreme example of industry (compare 30:25).

(2) *Bees* have been domesticated for centuries. A beehive may contain 50,000 or more bees. Bees eat pollen and produce a wax used to build their combs and nests.

Bees are noted for their antagonism, and armies were compared to swarms of bees (Deut. 1:44). Samson ate honey from the carcass of a lion and later tested the Philistines with a riddle concerning the incident (Judg. 14:5-18). See Ps. 118:12; Isa. 7:18.

(3) *Wasps and hornets* (Ex. 23:28; Deut. 7:20; and Josh. 24:12) construct nests by scraping dead wood and making a pulp used to form paper. Hornets (or perhaps wasps and yellow jackets) are recognized for their venomous stings.

Lepidoptera: Butterflies and Moths

Moths generally fly at night; butterflies are day fliers. Moths usually have feathery antennae, while butterflies have hairlike or "clubbed" ones. Adults feed primarily on nectar. They have a proboscis or tongue, which may be more than twice the length of the rest of the body. Some moths have mouthparts specialized for piercing fruit and even other animals.

Moths and their larvae were known for their destructive ability (Job 4:19; 13:28; 27:18; Ps. 39:11; Isa. 50:9; 51:8; Hos. 5:12; Matt. 6:19,20; Luke 12:33; Jas. 5:2). For people who had few possessions and no safe places for storage, moth infestation could be devastating.

Diptera: Flies and Gnats (with one pair of wings)

Adults feed on plant and animal juices. Many species are considered injurious, both to animals and plants. Some of these creatures suck blood, transmitting diseases in the process. Many species are beneficial.

(1) *Flies* are household pests, but they are primarily associated with livestock stables. Eggs hatch in 24 hours, producing larvae known as maggots that are active for two to three weeks, feeding on decaying matter. During a resting stage, transformation into an adult occurs. An egg becomes an adult within 12 to 14 days. Adults may live one or two months during the summer, and longer in the winter. When combined with poor sanitation and inadequate medical knowledge, flies could be a serious threat to health. See Eccl. 10:1; Isa. 7:18. The "swarms" of Ex. 8:21-31 may have been flies (compare Pss. 78:45; 105:31). Second Kings 1 names the god of Ekron Baal-zebub, perhaps meaning "lord of the flies." This may mean flies were feared to the extent that people worshiped a "fly-god," hoping to prevent infestation by the insects. A cattle-biting fly (also seen as a mosquito or "destruction"), perhaps the gadfly (NRSV, NIV), is found in Jer. 46:20.

(2) *Gnats* are scarcely visible to the naked eye and leave bites that sting and burn. Some gnats do not bite, but swarm in dense clouds numbering perhaps a million. The larvae of some species live in water and provide a source of food for aquatic life. They were known to be fragile creatures (Isa. 51:6). Jesus highlighted the small size of the gnat to teach the scribes and Pharisees a lesson (Matt. 23:24). The Egyptian plague of Ex. 8:16-18 perhaps should be understood as a plague of gnats or mosquitoes rather than lice. The same is true of Ps. 105:31.

Siphonaptera: Fleas

Small, wingless parasites that are particularly fond of birds and mammals as hosts. They have a tall and thin body. The adult female lays eggs on the host or in its nest or bed. Adults suck blood, while the larvae live on decaying animal and vegetable material.

Fleas were recognized both for their bite and for their size. Their small and insignificant nature even led to the formulation of proverbs of jest (1 Sam. 24:14; 26:20). Some scholars interpret the plague that fell on the Assyrians as one caused by fleas, similar to the Bubonic plague (Isa. 37:36-37).

Anoplura: Lice

At least two varieties are known: chewing and sucking lice. The lice of the Bible are almost certainly sucking lice. Small, wingless insects, they are noted for short legs and antennae, laterally flattened body, and specialized mouthparts. They have claws and are parasitic upon mammals. Both adults and larvae feed on blood. They attach themselves to clothing, body hair, and bedding. Lice are carriers of some serious diseases, such as typhus and trench fever. The Egyptian plague of Ex. 8:16-18 is one of dust becoming lice. Psalm 105:31 reminds the reader of the plagues upon Egypt. Both these occurrences of lice could be understood as gnats or another biting insect.

Orthoptera: Grasshoppers and Locusts

Flying members of this order (grasshoppers, locusts, katydids, crickets, roaches, and mantids) normally have two pairs of wings. Locusts and grasshoppers were so prolific that the Bible contains approximately a dozen words that describe them, perhaps indicating different species or even different stages of development. The migratory locust, or desert locust, is the locust of the plague (Ex. 10:4-5). This type of locust invaded agricultural areas in immense numbers, so that they were said to "cover the face of the earth, that one cannot be able to see the earth" and would "eat every tree which groweth for you"(Ex. 10:5; compare Deut. 28:38; 1 Kings 8:37; 2 Chron. 6:28; Pss. 78:46; 105:34; Joel 1:4; 2:25). Many references point to the great numbers in which the swarms would come (Judg. 6:5; 7:12; Jer. 46:23; Nah. 3:15). Though the locust was a formidable enemy, it was not mighty in strength (Job 39:20; Ps. 109:23; Nah. 3:17). In Prov. 30:27 the locust is praised for its ability to work in orderly fashion while having no leader. Israelites could eat locusts (Lev. 11:22).

The palmerworm, caterpillar stage of one locust species (Joel 1:4; 2:25; Amos 4:9), was known for its destructive nature. A specific type of "grasshopper" or locust (2 Chron. 7:13) was edible (Lev. 11:22), a "burden" (Eccl. 12:5), and small in stature (Num. 13:33; Isa. 40:22). The second stage after hatching of the locust egg, or perhaps a cockroach, was known for its voracious appetite (1 Kings 8:37; 2 Chron. 6:28; Ps. 78:46; Isa. 33:4; Joel 1:4; 2:25).

A beetle (KJV) or katydid was one of the edible varieties (Lev. 11:22). "The bald locust" (Lev. 11:22) was also allowed for food. A type called a katydid, cricket, mole cricket, or even a cicada (Deut. 28:42; KJV, "locust") is one of the curses for disobedience. The great numbers of an infestation of this insect may be reflected in Isa. 18:1, where the land "shadowing with wings" reflects a group of Ethiopian ambassadors arriving in Jerusalem to enlist Judah's support in an anti-Assyrian alliance.

The cankerworm (Joel 1:4; 2:25; Nah. 3:15-16), caterpillar (Ps. 105:34; Jer. 51:14), or rough caterpillar (Jer. 51:27) evidently was some form of locust larvae known to plague crops.

The locust was food for John the Baptist (Matt. 3:4; Mark 1:6) and an instrument of judgment (Rev. 9:3,7).

Miscellaneous Insects

Vague Hebrew terms make identity of types of worms impossible. Maggotlike worms (Ex. 16:20; Isa. 14:11) or moth larvae (Deut. 28:39; Jonah 4:7) produced a scarlet dye (Ex. 25:4; Lev. 14:4). See Job 25:6; Ps. 22:6; Isa. 41:14; 66:24 (compare Mark 9:44, 46,48). A related maggot appears in Ex. 16:24; Job 7:5; 17:14; 21:26; 24:20; Isa. 14:11 and in a more

general sense in Job 25:6. KJV's "worm" (Mic. 7:17) is a serpent (compare Deut. 32:24). Worms ate the corpse of Herod (Acts 12:23).

Scale insects appear in the Bible only in connection with the crimson dye extracted from them or from their eggs. A coloring material was manufactured from a member of the order *Rhynchota* known for its red scales. These insects, of the genus *Kermes*, are pea-sized and of various colors. They generally are found on oak trees. At death eggs are gathered from the females for the extraction of dye. See 2 Chron. 2:7,14; 3:14. Some scholars identify the manna of Ex. 16; Num. 11 as an excretion of scale insects, miraculously provided by God.

God's sovereignty is reflected in His use of hornets to accomplish His divine purpose of driving Israel's enemies out of Canaan. He also could chasten the chosen people with locusts if they should disobey. The absence of advanced methods of insect control reminds us of Israel's utter dependence on God. The Lord would inspire His servants to use the lowly ant and locust as examples for humankind to follow. The wisdom writers would use even the disgusting fly larva to remind humanity of its mortal nature.

INSPIRATION OF SCRIPTURE

Actions of God leading to the writing, preservation, and collection of His words to His people into the Bible; the influence of the Holy Spirit on individuals for the purpose of producing an authoritative record of persons, teaching, and events.

"The word of the Lord came" was the formula Jeremiah used (Jer. 1:2; compare 1:9; Isa. 51:15-16; Ezek. 2:7) to emphasize his experience of inspiration. "All scripture is given by inspiration of God" (2 Tim. 3:16). Often the inspiration is a revelation of that which goes beyond normal human cognitive and experiential knowledge: "For the prophecy came not in old time by the will of man: but holy men of God spake as they were moved by the Holy Ghost" (2 Pet. 1:21).

Inspiration is a divine-human encounter whereby God reveals truth. The Bible is a record of God's self-disclosure as Truth and as the source of all truth that humans could not comprehend through ordinary thought processes. Persons God chose declared God's attitude toward, His relations with, and His purposes for His people and His world. A climax to that divine-human encounter is the focus of the Scripture on the divine-human person of Jesus Christ.

Although the Bible is a collection of books written by at least 40 writers over a period of about 1,400 or more years, it has a unity of subject, structure, and spirit. It contains a consistent system of doctrinal and moral utterances. Its unparalleled treatment of certain themes such as the holy, the true, the good, and the future, are mysterious, authoritative, and practical. This witness of its inspiration is attested by countless thousands of testimonies from individuals who have been transformed by the reading of this Book.

Luke affirmed his inspiration was tied to his experience of researching the facts about Christ (Luke 1:3). Paul identified his inspiration as a strong inner impression (1 Cor. 7:25). On other occasions, inspiration came through dreams (Matt. 1:20) or visions (Gen. 15:1; Num. 12:6; 1 Sam. 3:1, Isa. 1:1; Ezek. 1:1; Dan. 2:19; Obad. 1; Nah. 1:1; Hab. 2:2). Inspiration also came through historical situations (1 Cor. 7:1).

The Bible has no theory of inspiration. It simply affirms that the Bible is the inspired Word of God. The Bible, like Jesus, must be accepted by faith. Humans develop theories seeking to understand divine inspiration.

Natural intuition theory sees inspiration as a higher development of that natural insight into truth that all persons possess to some degree and geniuses to a greater degree. This view makes all works equally inspired, in spite of the fact that they may be contradictory. It makes the Bible a human, or natural, book, rather than a supernatural Book.

Mechanical dictation theory claims God literally dictated the words of the Bible to the biblical writers. This view is not consistent with God's way of relating to persons and implies that all of the Bible should have the same literary style.

The general Christian theory of inspiration says the illumination of the Holy Spirit is experienced by all believers. This overlooks the problem of opposing viewpoints among believers and reduces biblical writers to the level of all Christian interpretation and proclamation.

Partial inspiration theory says inspiration is limited to certain parts of the Bible. What the writers would have known naturally and incidental matters are not necessarily inspired. This contradicts the statements of Scripture that all Scripture is inspired.

Levels of inspiration theory claims that God used different levels of control at different times in the process of inspiration. Assigning such levels of inspiration is arbitrary, based on human judgment, not divine actions.

Infallible theory states that the Bible as a whole is without any errors because it is in its entirety the Word of God. Usually those who hold this view are careful to distinguish between the original manuscripts and the present form of the Bible. Each of the differences that may be found in parallel passages are harmonized by some type of explanation.

Verbal inspiration theory states that the Holy Spirit inspired the biblical writers to choose the exact words to convey the message of God. Many passages of Scripture support the idea of verbal inspiration. Some have discredited this view because it does not relate to the differences in the personalities of biblical writers.

Dynamic inspiration theory suggests that the Holy Spirit had control over the process of inspiration, but He allowed the individuals to express their personalities in communicating God's message. Those who criticize this view do so on the basis that the view does not guarantee inerrancy.

Phrasing a theory is really secondary to the more important fact that the Bible is the authoritative Word of God and to the calling of obeying that Word. See *Bible, Theology of; Revelation of God.*

INSTRUCTION

Teaching or exhortation on aspects of Christian life and thought directed to persons who have already made a faith commitment. Instruction (*didache*) is frequently distinguished from missionary preaching (*kerygma*). Jesus "taught them as one having authority" (Matt. 7:29). The Sermon on the Mount (Matt. 5–7) is foundational teaching for Christian living (Matt. 7:24-27). Jesus admonished His disciples to make disciples and baptize them, "teaching them to observe all things whatsoever I have commanded" (Matt. 28:20). One office of the church was the pastor/teacher who works "to equip God's people for work in his service, for the building up of the body of Christ" (Eph. 4:12, REB). The church's teaching ministry has numerous dimensions:

The church teaches about Jesus: His death, burial, and resurrection. See *Gospel; Jesus, Life and Ministry of.*

The church teaches Christian spirituality, the process of growing in faith through prayer, Bible study, meditation, and spiritual reflection (1 Cor. 3:1-3; Heb. 5:13; 2 Pet. 3:18).

The church teaches Christian ethics. Those who follow Christ must be conformed to His image. Ethical instruction fleshes out Christ's new commandment to love one another (John 13:34-35). See *Ethics.*

The church instructs in Christian doctrine, guiding faithful Christians to maturity so its members may not be "tossed to and fro, and carried about with every wind of doctrine, by the sleight of men, and cunning craftiness" (Eph. 4:14). See *Doctrine; Bible, Theology of.*

The church instructs to evangelize. The teaching ministry of the church is another way in which the people of God declare their faith that others may know Christ and grow up in Him. See *Evangelism.*

INTEGRITY

State of being complete or undivided: "righteousness" (Ps. 7:8); "uprightness" (Ps. 25:21); "without wavering" (Ps. 26:1, NRSV, NASB, NIV); "blameless" (Ps. 101:2, NRSV). Several OT characters are designated persons of integrity: Noah (Gen. 6:9); Abraham (Gen. 17:1); Jacob (Gen. 25:27); Job (Job 1:1,8; 2:3); and David (1 Kings 9:4). English translations frequently render the underlying Hebrew as "perfect" or "blameless." Inclusion of Jacob is surprising since he is better known for his deceit (Gen. 27:5-27; 30:37-43; 33:13-17). English translators describe Jacob as a "plain" (KJV), "peaceful" (NASB), or "quiet man" (NRSV, NIV, REB).

In the NT, integrity occurs only at Titus 2:7 (NRSV, NIV, REB) in reference to teaching. The idea of singleness of heart or mind is frequent (Matt. 5:8; 6:22; Jas. 1:7-8; 4:8).

INTERCESSION

Act of intervening or mediating between differing parties; particularly the act of praying to God on behalf of another person.

Intercession is expected of all believers (1 Tim. 2:1-3). Intercession for the sick is particularly important (Jas. 5:14). Paul constantly referred to his prayers for the readers, and Jesus set forth the supreme example of intercession (Luke 22:32; 23:34; John 17).

Intercession is performed by the Holy Spirit, Christ, and Christians. The Holy Spirit works to sustain the burdened believer, interceding to carry even inexpressible prayers to God (Rom. 8:26-27). The risen Christ will maintain His intercession for the believer, being the Mediator between God and humanity (Rom. 8:34). Christ is ever present in heaven to intercede for those who come to Him (Heb. 7:25). See *Prayer.*

INTERMEDIATE STATE

Condition in which the deceased exists between death and the resurrection or final judgment. Some Bible students have understood "sleep in Jesus" (1 Thess. 4:14) as suggesting that the soul is unconscious during this time. Jesus awakens the person at the resurrection. This seems to contradict Paul's conviction that after death he anticipated conscious fellowship with Christ (Phil. 1:23).

Others have interpreted 1 Pet. 4:6 as giving a second opportunity for receiving the gospel message during this intermediate period, but the "dead" in 1 Pet. 4:6 might be believers who had responded to the gospel while they were living.

Believers appear in a state of rest. This rest does not refer to inactivity but to the joy of achievement and accomplishment (Heb. 4:10; Rev. 14:13). Believers are alive and conscious in the presence of God (Matt. 22:32; John 11:26; compare Phil. 1:23; 2 Cor. 5:8). Jesus assured the repentant thief he would be with Him in paradise (Luke 23:43). See *Paradise*. Even though the believer enjoys life, rest, and the presence of God, there is still a sense of incompleteness. Paul centered his hope on the resurrection (Phil. 3:10-11).

The unbeliever is pictured as alive and conscious but separated from God during the intermediate state (Luke 16:19-31). God keeps the wicked in a state of punishment until the final judgment (2 Pet. 2:9).

"Hades" is a general reference to the location of the dead between the time of physical death and resurrection. The KJV has translated this term as "hell" or "grave." Sometimes the term is a general reference to the grave and may allow for the presence of even the righteous (Acts 2:27,31; 1 Cor. 15:55). On other occasions, Hades refers to the place of the wicked dead (Luke 16:23; Rev. 20:14). See *Hades; Hell; Resurrection*.

INTERTESTAMENTAL HISTORY

Events and writings originating between the final prophet mentioned in the OT (Malachi, about 450 B.C.) and the birth of Christ (about 4 B.C.).

In 586 B.C., the Babylonians captured Jerusalem, destroyed the temple, and took away many of the people as captives. After Cyrus overcame the Babylonian Empire (539), the Jews who desired were allowed to return. The temple was rebuilt (515). Under the leadership of Nehemiah and Ezra (458–432), the Jewish religious community established itself. Here OT history ends, and the Intertestamental Period begins.

The Greek Period, 323–167 B.C.

Philip of Macedon sought to consolidate Greece so as to resist attack by the Persian Empire. When he was murdered in 336 B.C., his young son Alexander at age 19 took up the task. In two years he gained control of the territory from Asia Minor to Egypt, including Palestine and the Jews. In 331 B.C., Alexander gained full control over the Persian Empire. Alexander treated the Jews well. When he founded the new city of Alexandria in Egypt, he moved many Jews from Palestine to populate one part of that city.

Alexander's conquest had three major results:

(1) Hellenization—introduction of Greek ideas and culture into the conquered territory, creating a common way of life. He did not seek to change the religious practices of the Jews;

(2) establishing Greek cities and colonies throughout the conquered territory;

(3) making Greek a universal language.

When Alexander died in 323 B.C., chaos resulted. Five of his prominent generals established themselves over different parts of his empire: Ptolemy in Egypt; Seleucus, Babylonia; Antigonus, Asia Minor and northern Syria. The other two ruled in Europe and did not have direct influence over events in Palestine.

Ptolemy and Antigonus struggled over Palestine. In the battle of Ipsus (301 B.C.), the other four generals killed Antigonus. Seleucus received his territory, including Palestine. Ptolemy did not take part in the battle. Instead, he took over Palestine, which continued to be a point of contention between Ptolemies and Seleucids.

The Jews fared well under the Ptolemies. They had much self-rule. Their religious practices were not hampered. Greek customs gradually became more common among the people. The translation of the OT into Greek (Septuagint) began during the reign of Ptolemy Philadelphus, 285–246 B.C. The early Christians used it, and NT writers often quoted it.

Antiochus III (the Great, 223–187 B.C.) attempted to take Palestine from the Ptolemies in 217 B.C. without success. At the battle of Panium in 198 B.C., he defeated Ptolemy IV. He and his successors ruled Palestine until 167 B.C. The Jews' situation changed after the Romans defeated Antiochus in the battle of Magnesia (190 B.C.). Antiochus had supported Hannibal of North Africa, Rome's hated enemy, and had to give up all his territory except the province of Cilicia. He had to pay a large sum of money to the Romans for a period of years, and he had to surrender his navy and elephants. The tax burden of the Jews increased, as did pressure to adopt Greek practices.

Antiochus was succeeded by his son Seleucus IV (187–175 B.C.). When he was murdered, his younger brother became ruler. Antiochus IV, 175–163 B.C., was called Epiphanes ("manifest" or "splendid"), although some called him Epimenes ("mad"). During the early years of his reign, the situation of the Jews became worse. Part of it was due to their being divided. Some of their leaders, especially the priests, encouraged Hellenism. The office of high priest had been hereditary and was held for life. Jason, the brother of the high priest, offered Antiochus a large sum of money to be appointed high priest and an additional sum to receive permission to build a gymnasium near the temple. This shows the pressure toward Hellenism. Within a few years, Menelaus, a priest but not of the high priestly line, offered the king more money to be named high priest in place of Jason. He stole vessels from the temple to pay what he had promised.

Antiochus sought to add Egypt to his territory. He was proclaimed king of Egypt; but when Antiochus returned the following year to take control of the land, the Romans confronted him and told him to leave Egypt. When he reached Jerusalem, he found Jason had driven Menelaus out of the city. He saw this as full revolt. He allowed his troops to kill many of the Jews and determined to put an end to the Jewish religion. He sacrificed a pig on the altar of the temple. Parents were forbidden to circumcise their children, the sabbath was not to be observed, and all copies of the law were to be burned. To be found with a copy of the law was a capital offense.

Jewish Independence, 167–63 B.C.

Resistance was passive at first; but when the Seleucids sent officers throughout the land to compel leading citizens to offer sacrifice to Zeus, open conflict flared, first at the village of Modein, about halfway between Jerusalem and Joppa. An aged priest named Mattathias was chosen to offer the sacrifice. He refused, but a young Jew volunteered to do it. This angered Mattathias, and he killed both the Jew and the officer. Then he fled to the hills with his five sons and others who supported his action.

Leadership fell to Judas, the third son of Mattathias. He was nicknamed Maccabeus, the hammerer. He fought successful battles against much larger forces. A group devoutly committed to religious freedom called the Hasidim made up the major part of his army.

Antiochus IV was more concerned with affairs in the eastern part of his empire than with what was taking place in Palestine. He did not commit many troops to the revolt at first. Judas was able to gain control of Jerusalem within three years. The temple was cleansed and rededicated exactly three years after it had been polluted by the king (164 B.C.). (Dates through this period are uncertain and may be a year earlier than indicated.) This is still commemorated by the Jewish feast of Hannukah. The Hasidim had gained what they were seeking and left the army, but Judas wanted political freedom. He rescued mistreated Jews from Galilee and Gilead and made a treaty of friendship and mutual support with Rome. In 160 B.C. at Elasa, with a force of 800 men, he fought a vastly superior Seleucid army and was killed.

Jonathan, another son of Mattathias, took the lead. He was weak militarily. He was driven out of the cities and only gradually established himself in the countryside. Constant struggles engaged those seeking the Seleucid throne; rivals offered Jonathan gifts to gain his support. In 152 B.C. he gave his support to Alexander Balas, who claimed to be the son of Antiochus IV. In return Jonathan was appointed high priest. For the first time Jewish religious and civil rule were centered in one person. Jonathan was taken prisoner and killed in 143 B.C.

Simon, the last surviving son of Mattathias, ruled until he was murdered by his son-in-law in 134 B.C. He secured freedom from taxation for the Jews by 141 B.C. At last they had achieved political freedom. Simon was acclaimed by the people as their leader and high priest forever. The high priesthood was made hereditary with Simon and his descendants. The Hasmonean Dynasty, named after an ancestor of Mattathias, had its beginning.

When Simon was murdered, his son John Hyrcanus became the high priest and civil ruler (134–104 B.C.). For a brief time the Seleucids exercised some power over the Jews, but Hyrcanus broke free and began to expand the territory of the Jews. He destroyed the temple of the Samaritans on Mount Gerizim and conquered the land of the Idumeans, the ancient kingdom of Edom. The residents were forced to emigrate or convert to Judaism. From this people came Herod the Great.

The oldest son of Hyrcanus, Aristobulus I (104–103 B.C.), succeeded him. He had his own mother and three brothers put in prison. One brother was allowed to remain free, but he was later murdered. He allowed his mother to starve to death in prison. He extended his rule to include part of the territory of Iturea, north of Galilee. He was the first to take the title of king.

Salome Alexandra was the wife of Aristobulus. When he died, she released his brothers from prison and married the oldest of them, Alexander Jannaeus. He became high priest and king (103–76 B.C.). He made many enemies by marrying the widow of his brother. The OT stated that a high priest must marry a virgin (Lev. 21:14). Alexander enlarged his kingdom to about the size of the kingdom of David. He used foreign soldiers because he could not trust Jews in his army. As high priest, he did not always follow prescribed ritual. On one occasion the people reacted to his improper actions by throwing citrons at him. He allowed his soldiers to kill 6,000 of them. At another time, he crucified 800 of his enemies. As they hung on the crosses, he had their wives and children brought out and slain before their eyes.

Salome Alexandra succeeded her husband as ruler (76–67 B.C.). Her oldest son, Hyrcanus II, became high priest. When Salome died, civil war broke out and lasted until 63 B.C. Aristobulus II easily defeated Hyrcanus, who was content to retire. Antipater, an Idumean, persuaded Hyrcanus to seek help from the king of Nabatea to regain his position. Aristobulus was driven back to Jerusalem. Then Rome arrived on the scene. Both Aristobulus and Hyrcanus appealed to Scaurus, the Roman general charged with administration of Palestine. He sided with Aristobulus. When the Roman commander Pompey arrived later, both appealed to him. Aristobulus fought the Romans, was defeated, and taken prisoner to Rome. Then the Romans took control over Palestine.

The Roman Period, 63 B.C.–A.D. 70

Under the Romans, the Jews paid heavy taxes; but their religious practices were not changed. Roman power was exercised through Antipater, who was named governor of Palestine. Hyrcanus was made high priest. Aristobulus and his sons continued to lead revolts against Rome.

Antipater was the stabilizing force. His son Phasael was named governor of Judea; a second son, Herod, was made governor of Galilee. Herod sought to bring order to his area. He arrested Hezekiah, a Jewish robber or rebel, and executed him. The Sanhedrin in Jerusalem summoned Herod to give an account of his action. He went, dressed in royal purple and with a bodyguard. The Sanhedrin could do nothing.

Antipater was murdered in 43 B.C. Antony became the Roman commander in the East in 42 B.C. In 40 B.C. the Parthians invaded Palestine and made Antigonus, the last surviving son of Aristobulus, king of Palestine. Hyrcanus was mutilated by having his ears cut or bitten off so he could not serve as high priest again. Phasael was captured and committed suicide in prison. Herod barely escaped with his family. He went to Rome to have his future brother-in-law — Aristobulus — made king, hoping to rule through him as his father had ruled through Antipater. The Roman Senate, at the urging of Antony and Octavian (Augustus), made Herod king (40 B.C.). It took him three years to drive the Parthians out of the country and establish his rule. He was king until his death in 4 B.C.

Herod's rule was a time of turmoil for the Jewish people. An Idumean whose ancestors had been forced to convert to Judaism, the people saw him as the representative of a foreign power and never accepted him. Even his marriage to Mariamne, the granddaughter of Aristobulus II, gave no legitimacy to his rule in their sight. The most spectacular of his building achievements, the rebuilding of the Jerusalem temple, did not win the loyalty of the Jews.

Jealousy and fears overwhelmed Herod. He had Aristobulus, his brother-in-law, executed. Later Mariamne, her mother, and her two sons were killed. Just five days before his own death, Herod put his oldest son Antipater to death. His relations with Rome were sometimes troubled due to unsettled conditions in the empire. Herod was a strong supporter of Antony even though he could not tolerate Cleopatra with whom Antony had become enamored. When Octavian defeated Antony in 31 B.C., Herod went to Octavian and pledged his full support. This support was accepted. Herod proved himself an efficient administrator on behalf of Rome. He kept the peace among a people who were hard to rule. A cruel and merciless man, still he was generous, using his own funds to feed the people during a time of famine. He never got over the execution of Mariamne, the wife he loved above all others. His grief led to mental and emotional problems. During Herod's reign Jesus was born (Matt. 2:1-18; Luke 1:5). Herod ordered the execution of the male babies in Bethlehem (Matt. 2:16-18).

Herod willed his kingdom to three of his sons. Antipas was to be tetrarch ("ruler of a fourth") of Galilee and Perea (4 B.C.–A.D. 39); Philip, tetrarch of Gentile regions to the northeast of the Sea of Galilee (4 B.C.–A.D. 34); Archelaus, king of Judea and Samaria. Rome honored the will except that Archelaus received the title of ethnarch ("ruler of the people"), not king. He proved to be a poor ruler and was deposed in A.D. 6. His territories were placed under the direct rule of Roman procurators under the control of the governor of Syria.

The Jews produced many writings during the Intertestamental Period. The Apocrypha are writings included, for the most part, in the Septuagint. They were translated into Latin and became a part of the Latin Vulgate, the authoritative Latin Bible. First

Maccabees is our chief source for the history of the period from Antiochus Epiphanes to John Hyrcanus. See *Apocrypha.*

A second group of writings is the Pseudepigrapha, a larger collection than the Apocrypha, but there is no final agreement as to which writings should be included in it. Fifty-two writings are included in two volumes: *The Old Testament Pseudepigrapha,* edited by James H. Charlesworth. They are attributed to noted people of ancient times such as Adam, Abraham, Enoch, Ezra, and Baruch. For the most part they were written in the last centuries before the birth of Jesus, although some of them are from the first century A.D. See *Pseudepigrapha.*

The final group of writings are the Qumran scrolls, popularly known as the Dead Sea Scrolls. These writings include OT manuscripts, writings of the Qumran sect, and writings copied from other sources and used by the sect. These writings show us something of the life and beliefs of one group of Jews in the last two centuries before Jesus. See *Dead Sea Scrolls.*

IOTA See *Dot.*

IRON

Metal that was basic material for weapons and tools in biblical period. The Iron Age began in Israel about 1200 B.C., though introduction of the metal into daily life occurred slowly. The availability of iron was a sign of the richness of the Promised Land (Deut. 8:9), and articles of iron were indications of wealth (Deut. 3:11; Josh. 6:19). Excavations of Israelite sites dating from the eleventh and twelfth centuries have uncovered rings, bracelets, and decorative daggers made of iron.

In early forging techniques, iron was not much harder than other known metals and, unlike bronze and copper, it had to be worked while hot. As improved metalworking techniques became known, however, iron gradually became the preferred

metal for tools such as plows, axes, and picks as well as for weapons like spears and daggers. Iron chariots were a sign of great power in warfare (Josh. 17:18; Judg. 1:19; 4:3).

The Book of First Samuel records that the Philistines prevented smiths from working in Israel (1 Sam. 13:19-21). The prohibition of smiths in Israel may refer to workers in bronze rather than iron, or the Philistines may have had an economic and perhaps technological advantage, being able to control the iron industry for a period of history.

After 1000 B.C. iron became widely used. David used stockpiles of iron and bronze in preparation for building the temple (1 Chron. 22:3).

Iron is frequently used symbolically in the Bible as a threat of judgment (Ps. 2:9; Rev. 2:27) or as a sign of strength (Isa. 48:4; Dan. 2:40). The furnace was a symbol of oppression (1 Kings 8:51), and the cauterizing effect of hot iron described those with no conscience (1 Tim. 4:2). See *Arms and Armor; Minerals and Metals; Mines and Mining; Philistines.*

ISAAC *(laughter)*

Only son of Abraham by Sarah and a patriarch of the nation of Israel; the child of promise from God, born when Abraham was 100 years old and Sarah was 90 (Gen. 17:17; 21:5). His name reflects his parents' unbelieving laughter regarding the promise (Gen. 17:17-19; 18:11-15) as well as their joy in its fulfillment (Gen. 21:1-7). Sarah wanted Hagar and Ishmael banished. God directed Abraham to comply, saying that his descendants would be reckoned through Isaac (Gen. 21:8-13; compare Rom. 9:7). Abraham's test of faith was God's command to sacrifice Isaac (Gen. 22:1-19).

Isaac married Rebekah (Gen. 24), who bore him twin sons, Esau and Jacob (Gen. 25:21-28). Isaac passed her off as a sister at Gerar (as Abraham had done). He became quite prosperous, later moving to Beersheba (Gen. 26). Isaac was deceived into giving Jacob his blessing and priority over Esau (Gen. 27). Isaac died at Mamre near Hebron at the age of 180 and was buried by his sons (Gen. 35:27-29). Isaac was revered as one of the Israelite patriarchs (Ex. 3:6; 1 Kings 18:36; Jer. 33:26). Amos used the name "Isaac" as a poetic expression for the nation of Israel (Amos 7:9,16).

In the NT, Isaac appears in the genealogies of Jesus (Matt. 1:2; Luke 3:34), as one of three great patriarchs (Matt. 8:11; Luke 13:28; Acts 3:13), and an example of faith (Heb. 11:20). Isaac's sacrifice by Abraham (Heb. 11:17-18; Jas. 2:21), in which he was obedient to the point of death, serves as a type looking forward to Christ and as an example for Christians. Paul reminded believers that "we, brethren, as Isaac, are the children of promise" (Gal. 4:28).

ISAIAH (*Yahweh saves*)

Prophet in Judah from his call vision (about 740 B.C.) until last years of Hezekiah (716–687) or early years of Manasseh (687–642). During Isaiah's ministry, Tiglath-pileser III (745–727) founded the mighty Assyrian Empire; Samaria fell to Assyria in 722 B.C.; Egypt, resurging to power in the Twenty-Fifth Dynasty (about 716–663), occasioned international intrigue among the Palestinian states to overthrow Assyria. See *Israel, History of*; *Assyria, History and Religion of*; *Egypt.*

Isaiah, the son of Amoz, was born in Judah, no doubt in Jerusalem, about 760 B.C. He enjoyed a significant position in the contemporary society and had a close relationship with the reigning monarchs. His superb writing has gained him an eminence in Hebrew literature hardly surpassed by any other. His knowledge of the religious heritage of Israel and his unique theological contributions inspire awe. He was aware of what was transpiring in the court, in the marketplace, in high society with its shallowness, and in the political frustrations of the nation.

Isaiah was called to be a prophet of Yahweh in a striking vision in the temple about 740 B.C., the year that the aged Judean king Uzziah died (Isa. 6). Isaiah met the Holy One of Israel. God warned Isaiah that his ministry would meet with disappointment and meager results, but also assured him that forgiveness would ever attend the penitent (Isa. 6:5-7; 1:19-20), and the ultimate promises of God would be realized (Isa. 6:13d).

The prophet was married and the father of two sons whose names symbolized Isaiah's public preaching: Mahershalalhashbaz ("the spoil speeds; the prey hastes"), a conviction that Assyria would invade Syria and Israel about 734 B.C., and Shearjashub ("a remnant shall return"), a name that publicized his belief in the survival and conversion of a faithful remnant in Israel (Isa. 1:9; 7:3; 8:1,4; 10:20-23).

Isaiah firmly contended that the Judean monarchs ought to remain as neutral as possible, to refrain from rebellious acts, and to pay tribute. When the Israelites and Syrians jointly attacked Judah for refusing to join the anti-Assyrian coalition (Isa. 7:1-9; 8:1-15), he deplored the dangerous policy of purchasing protection from the Assyrians. In 711 B.C. when the city of Ashdod rebelled against Assyria, Isaiah assumed the garb of a captive for three years—calling on Hezekiah not to take the fatal step of joining the rebellion. No doubt he was instrumental in influencing Hezekiah to reject the seditious plot (Isa. 20:1-6). That same resolute policy assured Isaiah that Jerusalem would not fall to Sennacherib in 701 B.C., despite the ominous outlook the Assyrian envoys forecast (Isa. 36–37). Isaiah soundly castigated Hezekiah for entertaining the seditious Babylonian princelet whose real purpose was to secure military aid for a rebellion and overthrow Sennacherib in south Babylonia (Isa. 39).

ISAIAH, BOOK OF

First book in OT prophetic collection, representing collection of prophetic sermons and narratives outlining God's plans and purposes for Israel from 740 B.C. to the return from the exile after 538 B.C. and into God's promised messianic future. Three sections speak to three periods of Israel's history: 1–39, about 740 to 687 B.C.; 40–55, about 586 to 540 B.C.; 56–66, after 538 B.C.

In Isaiah's time Assyria was the great military power that threatened the Palestinian states. In much of the Book of Isaiah, the reigning power was Babylon, which did not rise to power until after 625 B.C., over 50 years after Isaiah's death. Some Bible students think the writings reflecting the Babylonian period may be the work of disciples of Isaiah, who projected his thought into the new and changed situation of the Babylonian world. Others would say the Spirit projected Isaiah supernaturally into the future, thus making him able to know even the name of Cyrus, king of Persia (44:28; 45:1).

Isaiah 1–39

Isaiah inveighed against the errant nation of Judah (Isa. 1:2-9; 2:6-22; 3:1–4:1), even using the guise of a love song (5:1-7). He pronounced six "woes" on the immoral nation. His wrath also attacked Israel (Isa. 9:8-21; 28:1-29). True religion was absent; they needed to desist from evil, to learn to do good, to seek justice, correct oppression, defend the fatherless, plead for the widow (Isa. 1:17).

Isaiah still held out the hope of forgiveness to the penitent (Isa. 1:18-31) and pointed to days coming when God would establish peace (Isa. 2.1-4; 4:2-6). He promised the Messiah, the son of David, who would assume the chief role in the fulfillment of the Abrahamic-Davidic covenantal promises (Isa. 9:2-7; 11:1-9).

Isaiah is remembered for his magnificent conception of the holy God (6:3). Yahweh is Lord of all, King of the universe, the Lord of history who exhibits His character in righteousness (Isa. 5:16). The prophet demanded social and religious righteousness

practiced in humility and faith. He strongly affirmed God's plans would be fulfilled and announced that the Assyrian king was but the instrument of God and accountable to Him. He stressed the Day of Yahweh, a time when the presence of God would be readily discoverable in human history. Isaiah was certain that a faithful remnant would always carry on the divine mission (Isa.1:9; 7:3,"Shearjashub").

When the Judeans discounted his stern warnings, Isaiah ordered that his "testimony" and "teaching" be bound and sealed—no doubt in a scroll—and committed to his disciples until history proved his words true (Isa. 8:16).

Israel's prophecies devoted considerable attention to political pronouncements regarding foreign nations: Babylon (Isa. 13–14), Moab (Isa. 15–16), Damascus (Isa. 17:1-14), Ethiopia (Isa. 18), Egypt (Isa. 19–20), and Tyre (Isa. 23).The speeches of Isaiah or his disciples would be relayed to the foreign capitals as a significant utterance on foreign affairs. They also informed God's people of His world plans, giving encouragement of final victory.

Midway between prophetic prediction and apocalypticism are four chapters called the "Little Apocalypse" (Isa. 24–27). See Apocalyptic. Two opposing forces were presented as two cities. When the city of chaos triumphs, the city of God laments; when it suffers defeat, the city of God breaks forth into song. Isaiah 24–27 thus contains four hymns. Ultimately, the kingdom of God is victorious with such blessings as the removal of national hatred, the overcoming of sorrow and death, and the resurrection, in short, the resolution of history as the kingdom of God.

Five prophecies in Isa. 28–35 commence with an introductory "woe." The inebriated aristocracy of Israel failed to discern the fading flower of their nation; they were supported in their dereliction by the priests and prophets. They mimicked sarcastically Isaiah's plain speech as childish prattle, to which he retorted that if they did not understand simple Hebrew, Yahweh would speak to them in Assyrian! Yet, those who trusted in God stood on a firm foundation, a foundation laid in righteousness and justice. It alone would stand (Isa. 28:16-22).

In Isaiah 29–35 the Judeans were reproved for their rejection of the authentic voice of prophecy, their defiant atheism, their meaningless parade of religion, their rebellious plotting with the Egyptians, and their buildup of the military. Passages such as Isa. 28:5-6; 29:5-8, 17-24; 30:18-33; 31:4-9; 32:1-5,8,15-20; 33:2-6,17-24 offer comfort. The conclusion of this segment forecasts the ultimate fulfillment of divine purposes in history.

With the exception of Isa. 38:9-21, an original thanksgiving song of Hezekiah after a severe illness, Isa. 36-39 duplicates 2 Kings 18:13-20:19; compare 2 Kings 24:18-25:30; with Jer. 52. This narrative provides the reader of the prophet with a historical background for the understanding of the book.

Isaiah 40–55

The Book of Consolation (Isa. 40–55) is set in the later years of Babylonian exile when Cyrus (Isa. 44:28; 45:1) was beginning his conquests that would ultimately overthrow the Babylonian power. See *Israel, History of.* The prophet hailed Cyrus as the shepherd of Yahweh who would build Jerusalem and set the exiles free (Isa. 44:26-45:1). The prophetic voice assured the exiles God would prepare a level highway for their journey home through the desert (Isa. 40). He would restore Zion and its temple. Arising from the messages of comfort and dialogue are four so-called Servant Songs (Isa. 42:1-4; 49:1-6; 50:4-9; and 52:13–53:12). They reiterate the role of Israel as the chosen servant of God, the nation that would evangelize all nations. Endowment by the Spirit would provide the enablement for that mission. The Servant would suffer for the people of God, and that suffering would take away their sins. Authentic Israel was the servant the prophet had in mind (Isa. 49:3), but the Suffering Servant finds ultimate fulfillment in the life, death, and resurrection of the Lord Jesus Christ, the Savior of the world. The cross-bearing Christian church (Gal. 6:14-16) carries on the Servant's mission.

The prophetic announcement disclosed the movement of God in history—the exile was over. The Persians were about to take over Babylonian power; they would be trustworthy and friendly to the exiles. God would duplicate the exodus by releasing the exiles from Babylonian tyranny. Yahweh had stirred up Cyrus, and through him His purpose would be secured. Assured of divine forgiveness and comforted in their grief, the exiles were exhorted to identify with their ancient role in the blessing of the earth's population through the dissemination of the religion in which the world would be blessed (Gen. 12:3). The Servant Songs were the blueprints for Israel's devotion and adherence—to love, to serve, to suffer, and to teach the knowledge of God for the salvation of humankind.

Isaiah 56–66

The concluding oracles (Isa. 56–66) change venue again. No longer was Babylon the focus; Palestine was, with the temple restored and sacrifice and worship being conducted.

Chapters 56–66 include an oracle on sabbath keeping (Isa. 56:1-8), censure of civil and religious leaders (56:9–57:12), an analysis of the meaning of fasting (ch. 58), the dilemma of the unfulfilled divine promises (ch. 59), hopeful encouragement (chs. 60–64), the grievous sin of Judah and the blessedness of the righteous remnant (ch. 65), and brief fragments on a number of subjects (ch. 66).

This portion of inspired Scripture places the reader in the midst of a discordant community where the righteous struggle against their powerful opponents. It censures the moral depravity of rulers, of those who succumb to pagan practices, of those who practice external rites without true identification with their meaning. Foreigners and eunuchs (56:3-7) would no longer be excluded from the temple worship. This injected grace and hope into the law of Deut. 23:1. Other verses praise humility (Isa. 66:1-2), announce the new heaven and the new earth (Isa. 66:22), and report the anointing by the Spirit (Isa. 61:1-4).

ISCARIOT (*man of Kerioth or assassin or bandit*)

Surname of both the disciple Judas who betrayed Jesus (Mark 3:19) and of his father Simon (John 6:71). Judas and his father may have been members of the Zealots, a patriotic party. "Man of Kerioth" is probably the meaning of the surname, referring to town of Kerioth. See *Judas*.

ISH-BOSHETH (*man of shame*)

Son of Saul and his successor for two years as king of Israel (2 Sam. 2:8; 4:1-7). Originally his name was Ish-baal (1 Chron. 8:33), which means "man of Baal." The repugnance of Baal worship led to the substitution of the word for *shame* in the place of the name of the Canaanite deity. See *Saul*.

ISHMAEL (*God hears*)

Son of Abraham by Egyptian concubine Hagar (Gen. 16:11); progenitor of the Ishmaelite peoples. Ishmael was near death in the wilderness when the angel of God directed Hagar to a well. Genesis 21:20 explains that God was with Ishmael, and he became an archer. See *Abraham; Patriarchs, The*.

ISHMAELITE

Tribal name for descendants of Ishmael, nomadic tribes of northern Arabia (Gen. 25:12-16; compare 37:25). See *Ishmael; Abraham*.

ISRAEL (*God strives, God rules, God heals*, or *he strives against God*)

(1) Name God gave Jacob after he wrestled with the divine messenger (Gen. 32:28). His 12 sons became known as the "sons of Israel," and the resulting nation became the nation of Israel.

(2) Name of the Northern Kingdom after Jeroboam led the northern tribes to separate from the southern tribes (1 Kings 12).

ISRAEL, HISTORY OF

Chronological Outline

THE PREEXILIC PERIOD
    The Patriarchal Period 2000–1720*
    The Egyptian Period 1720–1290
    The Exodus and the Wilderness Sojourn 1290–1250
    The Settlement 1250–1020
    The United Monarchy 1020–922
    The Divided Monarchy 922–587
    The Kingdom of Israel 922–721
    The Kingdom of Judah 922–587

THE BABYLONIAN EXILE
597/587–539/538

THE POSTEXILIC PERIOD
    The Persian Period 539–331
    The Hellenistic Period 331–168
    The Maccabean Period 168–63
    The Roman Period 63–A.D. 400

*All dates will be assumed to be B.C. unless otherwise designated.

See *Chronology of Biblical Periods* for dating alternatives to those used in this article.

The Preexilic Period

(1) *The Patriarchal and Egyptian Periods (Gen. 12–50)*. Israel's roots derive from the Mesopotamian Valley, where Abraham started. About 2000, responding to a divine command, he began a journey with his tribe that took him to Haran. There Abraham's father, Terah, died, and a brother, Nahor, decided to settle. Abraham and his wife, Sarah, traveled onward to Canaan where, ultimately, they established their home. To them was born Isaac, the son of promise, who married Rebekah — granddaughter of Nahor. To Isaac and Rebekah were born Jacob and Esau. Jacob, having made his way back to the region of Haran to Laban, the brother of Rebekah, married both Leah and Rachel, Laban's daughters.

To Jacob and his wives were born 12 sons, who, having migrated to Egypt, became the foundation for the 12 tribes and fulfillment of the promises originally made to Abraham. Moses led these tribal descendents in the exodus from Egypt in 1290.

(2) *The Exodus and the Wilderness Sojourn (Ex. 1–24; 32–34; Num. 10–14)*. Israel is a product of the Sinaitic experience, begun when God called the "renegade" Moses to return to Egypt and deliver His people. Moving from Goshen in Egypt through God's leadership in the miracle at the sea to the Sinai peninsula under Moses' leadership, the Hebrews at Sinai ratified a covenant with the God Yahweh (Ex. 24); thus Israel as a landless people came into being. For 11 months they remained at Sinai; Israel departed Sinai as a covenant people who would continually struggle with God. The generation that departed Egypt died: Yahweh's judgment on them because they refused to believe the God of deliverance could lead them into Canaan.

(3) *The Settlement (Josh. 1–24; Judg. 1–16)*. Eventually, however, they entered Canaan via the Tranjordanian area. Under the leadership of Joshua, they crossed the Jordan River and entered the "Promised Land" at Jericho. The Book of Joshua records the settlement of the Israelites into Canaan, first in mid-country, then in the south, and finally in the north. Joshua distributed the land among the tribes (Josh. 13–21) and renewed the Covenant (Josh. 24).

For approximately 200 years, the Israelites were joined as autonomous tribes around the ark of the covenant, a loose relationship centering in common worship commitments. Divinely designated judges led them in battle, men like Gideon and Samson, and one woman, Deborah. Gradually, any sense of unity broke down until "every man did that which was right in his own eyes" (Judg. 21:25).

(4) *The United Monarchy (1 Sam. 1–3; 8–15; 2 Sam. 1–6; 9–20; 1 Kings 1–4; 6–8; 11)*. Under the judges, Israel could not assert centralized economic, political, or military strength.

This situation, plus other factors such as the emergence of the Philistine threat, caused a clamoring for kingship. Thus, about 1020, the Israelites moved politically into a monarchy.

Saul (1020–1000) was Israel's first king, although he often acted more as a judge. He understood himself designated by God to rule because of having received the Spirit of God. He fought valiantly against the Philistines, dying ultimately in the struggle.

David (1000–965) united the people, however tenuous that relationship (2 Sam. 5:4-5), and established Jerusalem as the capital, contained the Philistines, expanded Israel's borders and her trade, and established a monarchical line that ruled in uninterrupted fashion, save one exception (Athaliah, 842–837), until the fall of Judah to Babylonia in 587.

Solomon (965–922), David's son and successor, inherited all David had amassed, but he was able neither to build upon nor to maintain David's kingdom. He did temporarily intensify trade, but he is remembered primarily for building the temple in Jerusalem. Solomon's legacy was a division in the kingdom, so that, henceforth, we speak of Israel in the north and Judah in the south.

(5) *The Divided Monarchy (1 & 2 Kings; Amos; Hosea; Isa. 1–39; Micah; Jeremiah)*. The north was contextually tied into international politics more than the south, in part because the primary east-west trade route traversed Israel at the Valley of Jezreel. Israel was both the larger country and the more populous area. Her involvement in the larger world of nations meant that Israel was destined to fall politically more quickly than Judah. Israel fell to Assyria in 721, while Judah was conquered by Babylonia initially in 597.

Israel emerged as a separate power under Jeroboam I (922–901 B.C.). Nineteen kings ruled during the country's two centuries of existence, and coup attempts brought eight succession crises. Jeroboam is most remembered, however, for his establishment of rival shrines at Dan and

Bethel (1 Kings 12) with bull images to compete with Solomon's temple in Jerusalem. The Omride Dynasty was established in Israel, beginning with Omri (876–869) and concluding with Jehoram (849–842). Overt Baalism gained support from the royal house under Ahab (869–850) and Jezebel, his queen from Sidon. Elijah (1 Kings 18–19) showed that Yahwism could not coexist with Baalism. Jehu (842–815) took up the struggle against Baalism. He successfully overthrew King Jehoram (ending the Omride dynasty) and instigated a violent anti-Baalistic purge in Israel. Jehoram, Jezebel, many of the Baal worshipers, and King Ahaziah of Judah died.

This struggle against Baalism was a key factor in the emergence of Israel and Judah's prophetic movement after 750 B.C. Isaiah (742–701) and Micah (724–701) spoke in the south, while Amos (about 750) and Hosea (about 745) spoke in the north. Amos emphasized social justice (Amos 5:24), particularly concerned that Israel recognize her covenantal responsibility before God (Amos 3:1-2). He was convinced that judgment was inevitable for Israel. (See especially the five visions recorded in Amos 7–9.)

Hosea was Israel's proponent of *hesed* ("covenant fidelity") theology. On the analogy of his relationship with his wife Gomer (Hos. 1–3), he exhorted Israel to be faithful to Yahweh. Assuring Israel of Yahweh's love, Hosea warned her of impending judgment resulting from her abuse of the covenant relationship.

The dangers the prophets saw materialized for Israel after 725. King Hoshea (732–721) of Israel staged an anti-Assyrian revolt in anticipation of Egypt's coming to Israel's defense. Instead, the Assyrian troops under Shalmaneser V came to Israel and took the area around Samaria quickly. A siege of Samaria lasted for three years. During the siege, Shalmaneser V died. Sargon II assumed the Assyrian throne and felled Samaria in 721. As per Assyrian policy, large numbers of the people of Samaria were deported to an unknown area, while peoples from another conquered area were imported into Samaria (2 Kings 17). This policy was intended to break down nationalism and to prevent political uprisings. In Israel's case it ultimately precipitated the emergence of the hybrid people despised by the "pure" Jew. Later history designated these people as "Samaritans." The fall of Samaria in 721 marked the end of Israel as a part of the Divided Monarchy.

Solomon left the throne in Judah to his son, Rehoboam (922–915). Jehu's revolt in Israel in 842 brought the death of Ahaziah (842) of Judah. The Queen Mother, Athaliah (842–837), then usurped Judah's throne. Her five-year rule is the only non-Davidic break in Judah's royal succession. During this period a systematic attempt was made to establish Baalism in Judah. The Southern Kingdom, in part because the Jerusalem temple was the focus of Yahwism, did not embrace Baalism in the fashion of the north. When Yahwistic priests placed young Jehoash (837–800) on the throne, progress made by Baalism in displacing Yahwism was rapidly reversed.

Isaiah of Jerusalem experienced his commission (see Isa. 6) to be Yahweh's prophet at the death of King Uzziah (742). He delivered God's word during three political crises: Syro-Israelite crisis (Isa. 7) under King Ahaz (735–715) in 735 B.C.; Egyptian-led revolt against Assyria (Isa. 20) in 711 B.C. under Hezekiah (715–687); and Sennacherib of Assyria's siege of Jerusalem (Isa. 36–37; see also 2 Kings 18–19) in 701 B.C. Isaiah called the kings to faith in Yahweh, letting Yahweh struggle against those who would oppress rather than depending on military and political alliances and processes. He pointed to the holy God, not a mighty earthly king.

Micah of Moresheth (724–701) was Isaiah's younger contemporary. Micah 6:1-8 describes a courtroom scene where Yahweh's people are brought to trial for their constant rejection and transgression of the covenant. Verse 8 is perhaps the best definition of prophetic religion:"to do justly, and to love mercy, and to walk humbly with thy God."

In the lengthy rule of Manasseh (687– 642), Judah jettisoned much of the concern for exclusive Yahwism. Yahwistic prophets were persecuted, Baalism encouraged, activities associated with Assyrian astrological rites were incorporated, and the practice of human sacrifice was revived.

King Josiah (640–609) reversed the decline Manasseh had set in motion. At least by 621, the Deuteronomic Reformation was instituted. This reform sought to take advantage of the weakened conditions of both Mesopotamian and Egyptian powers to unite anew the Northern and Southern Kingdoms. This political aspiration was coupled with a religious fervor for combating Baalism. The primary impetus for the reform was removed with Josiah's death in 609 as he fought against Pharaoh Necho of Egypt at Megiddo (2 Kings 23:29).

The nation no longer had the leadership to sustain an effective reformation. Jehoiakim (609–598) waged a revolt against the nation's Babylonian overlordship. Before Nebuchadrezzar of Babylon arrived, Jehoiakim died, bringing his son Jehoiachin (598–597) to the throne. Jehoiachin was taken into exile in 597 when Nebuchadrezzar conquered Jerusalem. In his place, Nebuchadrezzar set Zedekiah (597–587). His revolt against Babylon in 588 led to the ultimate fall of Jerusalem, including the razing of the Jerusalem temple by Nebuchadrezzar in 587. Thus the kingdom of Judah was ended, and the Babylonian exile (597/587–539/538) initiated.

The Babylonian Exile (Ezek., Isa. 40–55)

The Babylonian exile was initiated in 597 by the initial deportation of Jerusalemites to Babylon, with additional deportations in 587 and 582 (Jer. 52:15,30). Life in exile was not completely unacceptable because the people enjoyed a degree of social and economic freedom. Nonetheless, they were secluded from Jerusalem and the temple and hardly desired to sing Yahweh's song in this strange land (Ps. 137).

The Babylonian exile was the benchmark in the religious development of the people. The Torah provided the basis for the emergence of what authentically is Judaism and the Jews, "the people of the book." Other literary products were formulated, including most of the written record associated with the preexilic prophets, the final editorial work on the Deuteronomic History (Joshua, Judges, Samuel, and Kings), and the prophetic contributions of Ezekiel. Isaiah 40–55 speaks to the last part of the exilic period with Cyrus on the horizon.

Ezekiel increased awareness that Yahweh has absolute mobility; that is, He was not geographically confined to Jerusalem (Ezek. 1–3). His often cryptic message encouraged hope in the future (Ezek. 33–39). He laid out "faith's" blueprint for a restored Jerusalem (Ezek. 40–48).

The prophecies of Isa. 40–55 prepared the people for a second exodus (Isa. 40), impressing upon them their role as the servant people of Yahweh (Isa. 42:1-4; 49:1-6; 50:4-9; 52:13–53:12). These chapters deride pagan idols and clearly teach monotheism (Isa. 44:6; 45:5), a concept inevitably coupled with Yahweh's universality (Isa. 42:6; 45:22).

The synagogue arose during exile and came to be the defining institution of Judaism—a social, educational, and religious center for the community but without sacrificial worship. Once Rome destroyed the rebuilt temple in Jerusalem in A.D. 70, the synagogues preserved Judaism wherever Jews were settled.

The Postexilic Period

(1) *The Persian Period (Ezra 1; 5–6; 9–10; Neh.1–6; 8–9; 13; Haggai; Zechariah; Obadiah; Malachi; Jonah).* Judah's postexilic era began in late

539 with the entrance of the troops of Cyrus of Persia into Babylon. In early 538 Cyrus issued a decree (Ezra 1:2-4; 6:3-5) permitting the exiles to return home. Many did return under the leadership of Zerubbabel, a descendant of King Jehoiachin. Unfortunately, Zerubbabel mysteriously disappeared, probably because the Persians recognized the inherent dangers associated with some of the Jews thinking Zerubbabel to be the anticipated messiah (Hag. 2:20-23). Work began immediately on rebuilding the temple. For various reasons, they accomplished little. Under the influence of Haggai and Zechariah, the temple was rebuilt from 520 to 515; temple worship was reinstituted.

The city remained defenseless until Nehemiah (appointed twice in 445 and 432 to be Persia's governor in Judea) rebuilt and repaired the walls around the city. About the same time, Ezra came to Jerusalem and impressed upon the people the importance of placing Torah at the center of community life, giving birth to the modern phenomenon of Judaism. In the interval between completion of the temple (515) and Nehemiah's first visit (445), several prophets spoke. Obadiah's brief message was a hymn of hate against the Edomites, who had assumed Judah's lands and homes when the people were taken into exile. Joel emphasized the day of Yahweh as a day of Judah's preservation coupled with the destruction of Edom and Egypt. Malachi addressed the need for reformation in worship, condemned the activities of the priesthood, denounced the intermarriage of Jews with non-Jews, and criticized the popular piety of his day.

Wisdom Literature including Job, Ecclesiastes, and Proverbs plus some of the psalms (1; 32; 34; 37; 49; 91; 112; 119; 128) began under Solomon and received its literary fixation in this period. This literature borrowed heavily from Israel's neighbors (see Prov. 22:17-23:1) and directed itself predominately to the youth (note the allegory on old age in Eccl. 12:1-8); it basically sought to enhance one's ability to live a healthy and productive life, recognizing that the fear of God served as the basis for such a life. See Job, Book of; Ecclesiastes, Book of; Proverbs, Book of; Wisdom and Wise Men.

As Judaism developed, inevitably, debate rose as regards Yahweh's availability to the non-Jew. Literarily, the Books of Ruth and Jonah encouraged the Jews to embrace all humankind within the umbrella of their faith, while the Book of Esther, which supports the highly nationalistic festival of Purim, encouraged a patriotism affirming Yahweh to be God for the Jews by protecting them from foreign enemies.

(2) The Hellenistic Period. Philip of Macedon was murdered in 336. This brought Alexander, his 19-year-old son and student of Aristotle to Philip's throne. After two years consolidating his power, Alexander crossed the Hellespont, beginning his bid for a unified Hellenistic Empire. Alexander was not quite 33 when he died unexpectedly in 323. By the time of his death, however, an indelible Hellenistic imprint had been left on the massive area he had conquered. See Intertestamental History and Literature.

Partly as a result of this Hellenization process, approximately 300, the chronicler's history composed of Chronicles, Ezra, and Nehemiah was formulated. The chronicler's work emphasized the accomplishments of Judah and its Davidic kings and encouraged purity within Jewish worship practices in the face of Alexander's Hellenization. See Chronicles, Books of; Ezra, Book of; Nehemiah, Book of.

(3) The Maccabean Period. The apocalyptic era is usually understood to encompass the period 200 B.C.–A.D. 200. During this period, the Jews were religiously and politically persecuted. To address this circumstance a highly symbolic, cryptic literature developed that promised the faithful community the hope of Yahweh's imminent intervention.

When Alexander died in 323, his massive kingdom was thrown into turmoil. The control of Canaan was contested between two of his successor rulers, Seleucus and Ptolemy. Resultant to battles waged between 200 and 198, the Seleucid ruler, Antiochus III (223–187), gained control of Canaan. Antiochus IV (175–163) attempted a systematic destruction of Judaism and precipitated an uprising led by a priest, Mattathias, and his four sons. One of these sons, Judas Maccabeus, was the military architect of the revolt and the individual whose name the revolt bears, the Maccabean Revolt. See *Intertestamental History and Literature*. On the twenty-fifth of Chislev, 165, Judas Maccabeus captured the Jerusalem temple, purified it, and reinstituted the worship of Yahweh (the basis for the festival of Hanukkah). The Book of Daniel, clearly an apocalyptic book, focused on this era. See *Daniel, Book of.* By 142 the Jews were exempted from all Seleucid taxation, and in 129 all Seleucid soldiers were removed from the country. Jews were totally free in their own country.

The Psalter was finally completed in this era, though many of the 150 poems are preexilic (as Ps. 29). Some are exilic (as Ps. 137); some, postexilic (as Ps. 119). See *Psalms, Book of.* The Psalter, as the hymnbook of the second temple, is particularly important for portraying the people as a worshiping community through her diverse historical eras and for enlightening the multitude of problems and situations she encountered.

(4) *The Roman Period.* True freedom had been achieved through the Maccabean Revolt, but unfortunately the Hasmonean rule was constantly beset by internal dissension. Intermarriage of Jews with non-Jews in surrounding countries precipitated conflict. This unrest came to a climax in 63 B.C. when the constant turmoil, which now involved the governor of Idumaea and the Nabataean king, brought Pompey, the Roman general to Judea. Jerusalem fell; and the country, henceforth designated as the Roman province of Palestine,

continued under Roman control until the fourth Christian century.

ISRAEL, SPIRITUAL

The church; one gathering of all believers under the lordship of Christ as the continuation of God's work with OT Israel; contrasted to religious or political assemblies or a local church.

ISSACHAR (*man for hire* or *hireling*)

Ninth son of Jacob, fifth borne by Leah (Gen. 30:18); progenitor of the tribe of Issachar. Tola, one of "minor judges," was from Issachar (Judg. 10:1-2). So was King Baasha of Israel (1 Kings 15:27). Jezreel, an Israelite royal residence, was in Issachar. See *Tribes of Israel; Chronology of Biblical Periods.*

ISSUE OF BLOOD

KJV for hemorrhage (Matt. 9:20).

ITALY

Boot-shaped peninsula between Greece and Spain that extends from the Alps on north to Mediterranean Sea on south. Through the Punic Wars with Carthage (264-146 B.C.), the city of Rome extended its control over the whole country and eventually conquered the entire Mediterranean. Compare Acts 18:2; 27:1, 6; Heb. 13:24. See *Rome and the Roman Empire.*

ITHAMAR (perhaps, *island of palms,* or *where is Tamar,* or shortened form of *father of Tamar* [palms])

Fourth son of Aaron (Ex. 6:23). After the death of Nadab and Abihu, Ithamar and his surviving brother Eleazar rose to prominence. During wilderness years, Ithamar apparently was in charge of all the Levites (Ex. 38:21). Moses became angry when Ithamar and his brother did not eat part of an offering as commanded (Lev. 10:16). House of Eli evidently was descended from Ithamar. See *Aaron; Priests; Levites.*

ITHIEL (*with me is God*)

(1) Benjaminite after return from exile (Neh. 11:7).

(2) Person to whom Prov. 30 is addressed, following standard Hebrew text (KJV, NASB, NIV). Many Bible students put spaces between different letters of the Hebrew text assuming an early copying change and read, "God is not with me, God is not with me, and I am helpless" (TEV), or "I am weary, O God, I am weary, O God. How can I prevail?" (NRSV; compare REB).

ITTAI (*with God*)

(1) Gittite (from Gath) soldier who demonstrated loyalty to David by accompanying the latter in flight from Jerusalem after the outbreak of Absalom's rebellion (2 Sam. 15:19-22); Philistine who had cast his lot with the Israelite David; shared command of David's army with Joab and Abishai (2 Sam. 18:2). See *David*.

(2) One of the "Thirty" of David's army (2 Sam. 23:29).

ITURAEA (*related to Jetur*) or **ITUREA**

Region over which Herod Philip was governor when John the Baptist began his public ministry (Luke 3:1); northeast of Galilee between Lebanon and Anti-Lebanon mountains. Ituraeans were of Ishmaelite stock (Gen. 25:15). Pompey conquered territory for Rome about 50 B.C. Ituraea was eventually absorbed into other political districts, losing its distinct identity by A.D. 100. See *Herod*.

IVORY

English translation of Hebrew for "tooth"; used for decorations on thrones, beds, houses, and the decks of ships (1 Kings 10:18; 22:39; 2 Chron. 9:17; Ps. 45:8; Ezek. 27:6,15; Amos 3:15; 6:4). Archaeologists in Palestine have unearthed numerous articles made of ivory: boxes, gaming boards, figurines, spoons, and combs. Apparently, Solomon's ships returned with ivory as a part of their cargo (1 Kings 10:22). Elephants were hunted into extinction in northern Syria by 800 B.C. Amos mentioned ivory as a token of luxury and wealth (Amos 3:15; 6:4).

JAAR (*forest*)

Modern versions' transliteration of Hebrew in Ps. 132:6 (TEV reads Jearim, a plural form; KJV translates "wood"); probably poetic abbreviation for Kiriath-jearim. See *Kiriath-jearim*.

JAAZANIAH (*Yahweh hears*)

Four OT men including:

(1) member of party led by Ishmael who opposed Gedaliah after the Babylonians made him governor over Judah in 587 B.C. Jaazaniah may also have been in Ishmael's party that assassinated Gedaliah (2 Kings 25:23-25). His name has a slightly different spelling in Jer. 40:8. See *Jezaniah*.

(2) one of elders of Israel Ezekiel found worshiping idols in temple (Ezek. 8:11). His father Shaphan may have been the counselor of Josiah (2 Kings 22).

JABBOK (*flowing*)

A 50-mile-long river near which Jacob wrestled through the night with God (Gen. 32:22); modern Nahr ez-Zerqa; tributary of Jordan, joining the larger river from the east about 15 miles north of the Dead Sea; western boundary of Ammon; boundary between kingdoms of Sihon and Og, and a division in Gilead. See *Jacob*.

JABESH (*dry*)

Shortened form of Jabesh-gilead (1 Sam. 11; 1 Sam. 31; 2 Kings 15:10,13). See *Jabesh-gilead*.

JABESH-GILEAD (*dry, rugged* or *dry place of Gilead*)

City whose residents, with the exception of 400 virgins, were put to death by an army of Israelites (Judg. 21:8-12); women became wives for Benjaminites; probably east of the Jordan River about 20 miles south of Sea of Galilee.

Saul's rescue of people of Jabesh-gilead from Nahash the Ammonite marked the effective beginning of Israelite monarchy (1 Sam. 11:1-11; see 1 Sam. 31:11-13; 2 Sam. 2:4-7; 21:12).

JABIN (*he understands*)

(1) King of Hazor (Josh. 11:1); leader of northern coalition of kings who attacked Joshua at the water of Merom and met their death (compare Josh. 12:19-24).

(2) King of Hazor; controlled Israelites when they turned away from God at Ehud's death (Judg. 4:1-2; compare Ps. 83:9).

JABNEEL (*God builds*) or **JABNEH**

(1) Town marking northwestern boundary of Judah in land of Philistines (Josh. 15:11); modern Yibna. Uzziah took the town, called by the shortened Hebrew form Jabneh, from the Philistines (2 Chron. 26:6). Later the city was called Jamnia and became a center of scribal activity for the Jews. See *Bible, Formation and Canon of, Old Testament.*

(2) Town in Naphtali (Josh. 19:33); tell en-Naam or Khirbet Yemma, west-southwest of the Sea of Galilee and northeast of Mount Tabor.

JACHIN and BOAZ (*he establishes and agile*)

Two bronze pillars (1 Kings 7:21) on either side of entrance to Solomon's temple; may have been 27 feet high and 6 feet in diameter with a 10-foot capital on top. Perhaps each word was the beginning of an inscription that was engraved on the respective pillars. Their function appears to have been primarily ornamental, though some have suggested they may have been giant incense stands. See *Temple of Jerusalem.*

JACOB (*he grasps the heel* or *he cheats, supplants*)

(1) Original ancestor of nation of Israel; father of 12 ancestors of the 12 tribes of Israel (Gen. 25:1–Ex. 1:5);

son of Isaac and Rebekah; younger twin brother of Esau; husband of Leah and Rachel (Gen. 25:21-26; 29:21-30). God changed his name to Israel (Gen. 32:28; 49:2).

Jacob's story occupies half the Book of Genesis. Jacob bargained for Esau's birthright. See *Birthright*. Parental partiality fostered continuing hostility between Esau, the hunter beloved of his father, and Jacob, the quiet, settled, integrated person favored by his mother. Tensions seemed to threaten fulfillment of divine promise. Jacob and his mother deceived his father and gained the blessing for the younger brother. The blessing apparently conveyed the status of head of family apart from the status of heir. Rebekah had to arrange for Jacob to flee to her home in Paddan-aram to escape Esau's wrath (27:46-28:1).

At 40, a lonely night in Bethel — interrupted by a vision from God — brought reality home. Life had to include wrestling with God and assuming responsibility as the heir of God's promises to Abraham (28:10-22). Jacob made an oath, binding himself to God. In Aram Laban tricked him into marrying Leah, the elder daughter, before he got his beloved Rachel, the younger (29:1-30). Jacob returned the deception and gained wealth at the expense of his father-in-law, who continued his deception, changing Jacob's wages ten times (31:7,41) Eventually Jacob had 12 children from four women (29:31-30:24). Jacob departed while Laban and his sons were away in the hills shearing sheep. Laban complained that he had not had an opportunity to bid farewell to his daughters with the accustomed feast. More importantly, he wanted to recover his stolen gods (31:30, 32). See *Teraphim*. Laban proposed the terms of a covenant of friendship: (a) never ill-treating his daughters, (b) never marrying any other women, and (c) establishing the site of the covenant as a boundary neither would cross with evil intent.

A band of angels met Jacob at Mahanaim (32:1-2). Esau's seem-ingly hostile advance led Jacob to send an enormous gift to his brother. When all had crossed the Jabbok River, Jacob met One who wrestled with him until daybreak (ch. 32) and dislocated his hip. The Opponent renamed the patriarch Israel, the one on whose behalf God strives (32:30).

Jacob's fear of meeting Esau proved groundless. Jacob turned westward to the Promised Land. Esau headed to Seir to become the father of the Edomites. The twins did not meet again until their father's death (35:27-29).

Jacob returned to Bethel and again received the patriarchal promises. His mother's nurse died (35:8; 24:59), and then his beloved wife Rachel died giving birth to Benjamin at Ephrath (35:19; 48:7). Reuben forfeited the honor of being the eldest son by sexual misconduct (35:22). The death of Jacob's father brought Jacob and Esau together again at the family burial site in Hebron.

Severe famine gripped Canaan and finally forced Jacob and his sons to move to Egypt. At Beer-sheba Jacob received further assurance of God's favor (46:1-4). Jacob dwelt in the land of Goshen until his death. He bestowed the blessing not only on his favorite son Joseph but also on Joseph's two oldest sons, Ephraim and Manasseh. He was finally laid to rest at Hebron in the cave Abraham had purchased (50:12-14).

God did not choose Jacob because of what he was but because of what he could become. See John 4:12; Acts 7:8-16; Rom. 9:10-13; Heb. 11:9,20-22. His life is a long history of discipline, chastisement, and purification by affliction. In the midst of the all-too-human quarrels over family and fortune, God was at work protecting and prospering His blessed.

(2) Father of Joseph and earthly grandfather of Jesus (Matt. 1:16).

JACOB'S WELL See *Jacob*.

JAEL (*mountain goat*)

Wife of Heber the Kenite (Judg. 4:17), who assassinated Sisera, an action celebrated in Song of Deborah (Judg. 5:24-27). See *Deborah.*

JAHAZ (perhaps *landsite*)

Moabite place name; assigned to Reuben (Josh. 13:18) as Levitic city (Josh. 21:36; compare 1 Chron. 6:78). Israel defeated King Sihon there (Num. 21:23-24; Deut. 2:32-33; Judg. 11:20-21; see Isa. 15:4; 48:21,34; compare v. 21).

JAHWEH See *YHWH.*

JAIR (*Jah shines forth*), **JAIRITE**

Four OT men including:

(1) son of Manasseh who took possession of a number of villages in Gilead (Num. 32:41);

(2) Gileadite who judged Israel for 22 years (Judg. 10:3-5). See *Judges, Book of.*

JAIRUS (*Jah will enlighten*)

Synagogue official who came to Jesus seeking healing for his 12-year-old daughter (Mark 5:22). Before Jesus arrived at Jairus's house, the little girl died. Jesus restored her to life, showing His power over death.

JAMES

English form of Jacob, and the name of five men mentioned in the NT:

(1) *James, son of Zebedee and brother of John* (Matt. 4:21; 10:2; Mark 1:19; 3:17; Luke 5:10); one of 12 disciples (Acts 1:13), he, with Peter and John, formed Jesus' innermost circle of associates (Matt. 17:1; 26:36-37; Mark 5:37; 9:2; 14:32-34; Luke 8:51; 9:28). Perhaps James's and John's fiery fanaticism, they sought to call down fire from heaven on the Samaritan village refusing to receive Jesus and the disciples (Luke 9:52-54). Jesus called the brothers "Boanerges" or "sons of thunder" (Mark 3:17). James's zeal was revealed in a more selfish manner as he and John (their mother, on their behalf, in Matt. 20:20-21) sought special positions of honor for the time of Christ's glory (Mark 10:35-40).

They were promised, however, only a share in His suffering. James was the first (about A.D. 44) of the Twelve to be martyred (Acts 12:2).

(2) *James, son of Alphaeus;* one of 12 disciples (Matt. 10:3; Mark 3:18; Luke 6:15; Acts 1:13).

(3) *"James the younger,"* whose mother, Mary, was among the women at Jesus' crucifixion and tomb (Matt. 27:56; Mark 15:40; 16:1; Luke 24:10); may be the same as son of Alphaeus. In John 19:25, this Mary is called the wife of Clopas, perhaps to be identified with Alphaeus. See *Clopas; Mary.*

(4) *Father of Judas (not Iscariot)* (Luke 6:16; Acts 1:13).

(5) *James, brother of Jesus* (Gal. 1:19). During the Lord's ministry, the brothers of Jesus (Matt. 13:55; Mark 6:3; 1 Cor. 9:5) were not believers (John 7:3-5; compare Matt. 12:46-50; Mark 3:31-35; Luke 8:19-21). The resurrected Jesus appeared to James (1 Cor. 15:7). After the resurrection and ascension, the brothers were with the Twelve and other believers in Jerusalem (Acts 1:14). After his conversion, only James remained among the apostles (Gal. 1:19) and assumed leadership of the Jerusalem church, originally held by Peter. Evidently, such was achieved by James's constancy with the church while Peter and other apostles traveled. James presided as spokesman for the Jerusalem church at the Apostolic Council (Acts 15). See *Apostolic Council; Jacob.*

JAMES, LETTER FROM

New Testament general epistle exhorting readers to practical Christianity. The author stated principles of conduct and then frequently provided poignant illustrations.

James the "servant of God" (1:1) may have been

(1) James the brother of John and the son of Zebedee,

(2) James the son of Alphaeus, one of the Twelve, or

(3) James the half brother of Jesus, a younger son of Mary and of Joseph.

Of the three, James, the brother of the Lord, is the most likely choice. See James 5. Tradition of the early church fathers universally ascribes the letter to James, the pastor of the church in Jerusalem.

The author of the epistle was also steeped in the OT outlook in general and in Judaism in particular. The letter is addressed to "the twelve tribes which are scattered abroad" (1:1), suggesting the recipients were Jews. Apparently, James had in mind "Christian" Jews of dispersion (1:1; 2:1).

James's martyrdom by A.D. 66 provides us with the latest possible date of writing. Evidences of a very early date, such as the mention of those coming into the "assembly" (Greek, *sunagoge*), point to a time very early in Christian history, perhaps prior to the Jerusalem Conference in A.D. 49–50. Though some Bible students date James after A.D. 60, many scholars are convinced that James is the first book of the NT to be written, some dating it as early as A.D. 48.

The letter voiced concerns of early pastoral leadership about the ethical standards of early Christians. The author deals with how to respond to temptation and trial (1:1-18), the necessity of "doing" the Word as well as "hearing" the Word (1:19-27), treatment of the poor and the appropriate management of wealth (2:1-13; 5:1-6), the waywardness of the tongue and the necessity of taming it (3:1-18), conflicts and attitudes to other Christians (4:1-17), and appropriate responses to life's demands and pressures (5:1-20).

The theme of the book is that practical religion must manifest itself in works that are superior to those of the world. Such works include personal holiness and service to others, such as visiting "the fatherless and widows," and keeping oneself "unspotted from the world" (1:27). These "works" further demand active resistance to the devil (4:7), submis-

sion to God (4:7), and even brokenhearted repentance for sins (4:9).

Patience in the wake of trials and temptations is the subject both of the introduction and of the conclusion. Readers are to "count it all joy" when trials come (1:2) and expect reward for endurance of those trials (1:12). Job and the prophets are appropriate examples of patience in the midst of tribulation (5:7-11).

In 2:14-26, James argued that "faith if it hath not works is dead" (2:17). This apparent contradiction to the teaching of the apostle Paul has caused much consternation among some theologians. The contradiction is apparent rather than real. James argued that a faith that is only a "confessing faith," such as that of the demons (2:19), is not a saving faith at all. Orthodoxy of doctrine that does not produce a sanctified lifestyle is worthless.

In 5:13-18, James spoke of healing and its means. The purpose of the discussion is to stress the effectiveness of the earnest prayer of a righteous man (5:15-16). This is illustrated by a reference to Elijah, whose prayers were sufficient alternately to shut up the heavens and then to open them (5:17-18). The prayer of faith "saves the sick." The anointing oil, whether medicinal, as some have argued, or symbolic, as others have held, is not the healing agent. God heals, when He chooses to heal (4:14), as a response to the fervent prayers of righteous men.

JANNES AND JAMBRES

Two opposers of Moses and Aaron (2 Tim. 3:8). Though the names do not appear in the OT, rabbinic tradition identified Jannes and Jambres as being among those Egyptian magicians who sought to duplicate for Pharaoh the miracles performed by Moses (Ex. 7:11).

JANOAH (*he rests*) or **JANOHAH**

(1) Town in Ephraim (Josh. 16:6-7); probably Khirbet Janun about seven miles south of Nablus.

(2) City in northern Israel that Tiglath-pileser, king of Assyria (744–727 B.C.), captured from Pekah, king of Israel (752–732 B.C.), about 733 B.C.

JAPHETH (*may he have space*)

One of Noah's three sons (Gen. 5:32). Progenitor of Indo-European peoples who lived to the north and west of Israel, farthest from Israel (Gen. 10:2). Genesis 9:27 pronounces God's blessing on Japheth and his descendants. Here is an early indication of non-Israelites having a share with God's people. See *Noah; Table of Nations.*

JARMUTH (*height or swelling in the ground*)

(1) City in western "lowlands,'"'foothills" (NIV), or Shephelah (REB) of Judah (Josh. 15:33,35); tell Jarmuth three miles southwest of Beth Shemesh and 15 miles southwest of Jerusalem; its king joined southern coalition against Joshua and Gibeon (Josh. 10). Joshua "stored" the king in the cave of Makkedah before shaming him and slaying him (compare 12:11). In Nehemiah's time, Jewish settlers lived there (Neh. 11:29).

(2) Levitic city in Issachar (Josh. 21:29; compare 19:21; 1 Chron. 6:73, both spelled differently and differing from *1* above; thus spelling of Remeth, Ramoth). This city may be located at modern Kaukab el-Hawa.

JASHAR, BOOK OF

Ancient written collection of poetry quoted by Bible authors. See *Book(s).*

JASHOBEAM (*the uncle* [or people] *will return*)

Warrior of Saul's tribe of Benjamin who supported David at Ziklag as he fled from Saul (1 Chron. 12:6); listed first among "the mighty men whom David had" (1 Chron. 11:11).

JASON

Personal name often used by Jews as a substitute for Hebrew Joshua or Joseph and also used by Gentiles.

(1) In Acts 17:5, Paul's host in Thessalonica brought on charges before the city officials when the angry Jewish mob was unable to find Paul (Acts 17:6-7); Jason in Rom. 16:21 may have been same person.

(2) Jewish high priest during final years of Seleucid control of Palestine. See *Inter- testamental History and Literature.*

JASPER

Green chalcedony; sixth stone in headdress of king of Tyre (Ezek. 28:13); stone in the high priest's breastplate (Ex. 28:20; 39:13), rendered "onyx" at Ezek. 28:13; face of the One seated on the throne (Rev. 4:3) and the glory of the new Jerusalem (Rev. 21:11,18-19). The NIV used "jasper" to translate an obscure Hebrew term at Job 28:18. Other translation options include: "alabaster" (REB), "crystal" (NASB, NRSV, TEV), and "pearls" (KJV). See *Minerals and Metals.*

JATTIR (*the remainder*)

Levitic town (Josh. 20:14) in the hills of Judah (Josh. 15:48); modern Khirbet Attir about 13 miles south southwest of Hebron and 14 miles northeast of Beersheba. David gave some of his war booty from victory over Amalekites to Jattir (1 Sam. 30:27).

JAVAN (*Greece*)

Son of Japheth (Gen. 10:2), original ancestor of Greek peoples (Gen. 10:4.) See *Greece; Table of Nations.*

JAZER (*may He help*)

Amorite city state Israel conquered while marching across the land east of the Jordan towards the Promised Land (Num. 21:32). The tribe of Gad rebuilt and settled Jazer (Num. 32:35; compare Josh. 13:25). Joshua assigned it to the Levites (Josh. 21:39). See

1 Chron. 26:32; Isa. 16:8-9; Jer. 48:32; compare 1 Macc. 5:8.

JEALOUSY

Intolerance of rivalry or unfaithfulness; disposition suspicious of rivalry or unfaithfulness; and hostility or envy towards a rival or one believed to enjoy an advantage. God is jealous for His people Israel; that is, God is intolerant of rival gods (Ex. 20:5; 34:14; Deut. 4:24; 5:9). One expression of God's jealousy for Israel is God's protection of His people from enemies. Thus, God's jealousy includes avenging Israel (Ezek. 36:6; 39:25; Nah. 1:2; Zech. 1:14; 8:2). Phineas is described as jealous with God's jealousy (Num. 25:11,13, sometimes translated "zealous for God"). Elijah is similarly characterized as jealous (or zealous) for God (1 Kings 19:10,14). In the NT, Paul speaks of his divine jealousy for the Christians at Corinth (2 Cor. 11:2).

Numbers 5:11-30 concerns the process by which a husband suspicious of his wife's unfaithfulness might test her. Joseph's brothers were jealous (Gen. 37:11) and sold their brother into slavery (Acts 7:9). A jealous group among the Jews incited the crowd against Paul (Acts 17:5). Jealousy, like envy, is common in vice lists (Rom. 13:13; 2 Cor. 12:20; Gal. 5:20-21). Jealousy is regarded as worse than wrath or anger (Prov. 27:4). James regarded jealousy (or bitter envy) as characteristic of earthy, demonic wisdom (3:14) and as the source of all disorder and wickedness (3:16). See *Envy*.

JEBUSI or JEBUSITES

Clan who originally controlled Jerusalem before David conquered the city (see Gen. 10 connecting to Canaanites). Jerusalem was attacked and burned by the men of Judah (Judg. 1:8), but the Jebusites were not expelled. David captured the city and made it his capital. David purchased a stone threshing-floor from a Jebusite named Araunah (2 Sam. 24:16-24), and this later became the site of Solomon's temple. The remnants of the Jebusites became bondservants during Solomon's reign (1 Kings 9:20-21). Jebusite names appear to be Hurrian rather than Semitic. See *Jerusalem*.

JEDUTHUN (*praise*)

Prophetic musician and Levite in service of King David (1 Chron. 16:37-42; 25:1,3; 2 Chron. 35:15); original ancestor of temple musicians. Compare 1 Chron. 15:17. Ethan and Jeduthun may be different names for the same person. Three psalms (39; 62; 77) include his name in their titles. The exact nature of Jeduthun's relationship to these psalms is uncertain. See *Priests; Levites; Music; Psalms, Book of*.

JEHOAHAZ (*Yahweh grasps hold*)

(1) In 2 Chron. 21:17, son and successor of Jehoram as king of Judah (841 B.C.); more frequently referred to as Ahaziah.

(2) In 2 Kings 10:35, son and successor of Jehu as king of Israel (814–798 B.C.). See 2 Kings 13.

(3) In 2 Kings 23:30, son and successor of Josiah as king of Judah (609 B.C.); also known as Shallum. See *Israel; Chronology of Biblical Periods*.

JEHOASH (*Yahweh gave*)

Variant spelling of Joash. See *Joash*.

JEHOHANAN (*Yahweh is gracious*)

Eight OT men including:

(1) priest in whose temple quarters Ezra refreshed himself and mourned for the sin of the people in taking foreign wives (Ezra 10:6).

(2) Son of Tobiah, who opposed Nehemiah's work in Jerusalem (Neh. 6:18); marriage to a prominent Jerusalem family gave Tobiah an information system concerning Jerusalem happenings. See *Tobiah*.

JEHOIACHIN (*Yahweh establishes*)

Son and successor of Jehoiakim as king of Judah (2 Kings 24:6); 18 years old when he came to throne late in

598 B.C.; reigned for three months in Jerusalem before being taken into captivity by Nebuchadnezzar of Babylon; throne name for original Jeconiah or Coniah; ultimately released from prison by Evil-merodach of Babylon and accorded some honor in the land of his captivity (2 Kings 25:27-30). See *Israel; Chronology of Biblical Periods.*

JEHOIADA (*Yahweh knows or Yahweh concerns Himself for*)

Three OT men including priest who led coup in which Queen Athaliah, who had usurped the throne of Judah, was slain. Seven-year-old Joash (Jehoash), the legitimate heir to the monarchy, was then enthroned (2 Kings 11:4). Jehoiada evidently acted as regent for a number of years and influenced young king to restore the temple. The death of Jehoiada marked a precipitous decline in the king's goodness and faithfulness to the Lord (2 Chron. 22–24). See *Joash; Athaliah; Priests; Levites.*

JEHOIAKIM (*Yahweh has caused to stand*)

Son of Josiah who succeeded Jehoahaz as king of Judah (609–597); throne name given him by Pharaoh Neco of Egypt, who deposed his brother Jehoahaz; original name was Eliakim (2 Kings 23:34). At the beginning of reign, Judah was subject to Egypt. Probably in 605 B.C., Babylon defeated Egypt. Jehoiakim, who apparently had been content to be a vassal of Egypt, transferred his allegiance to Babylon but rebelled after three years. See *Israel; Chronology of Biblical Periods.*

JEHONADAB (*Yahweh incites or Yahweh offers Himself freely*)

Son of Rechab who supported Jehu in the latter's bloody purge of the house of Ahab (2 Kings 10:15); a representative of austere ultraconservatives known as Rechabites. Rechabites meeting with Jeremiah cited the teaching of their ancestor Jehonadab (in Jer. called "Jonadab"; see Jer. 35). See *Rechabites; Jehu.*

JEHORAM (*Yahweh is exalted*)

Alternate form of Joram. See *Joram.*

JEHOSHAPHAT (*Yahweh judged or Yahweh established the right*)

Name of four OT men including son and successor of Asa as king of Judah (1 Kings 15:24; see ch. 22; 2 Chron. 17–20) for 25 years (873–848 B.C.); able ruler and faithful worshiper of Yahweh (1 Kings 22:43); made disastrous alliance with Ahab, king of Israel, ending years of conflict by marriage between Jehoshaphat's son Jehoram and Ahab's daughter Athaliah. Athaliah's influence in Judah finally proved to be horrific. See *Athaliah; Israel; Chronology of Biblical Periods; Micaiah.*

JEHOSHAPHAT, VALLEY OF (*valley where Yahweh judged*)

Place to which the Lord summons the nations for judgment (Joel 3:2). The reference in Joel probably was meant to be symbolic. Through Joel, God promised all nations will ultimately be called to God's place of judgment. See *Joel.*

JEHOVAH

English transliteration of Hebrew text's current reading of divine name: Yahweh. Hebrew text, however, represents scribe's efforts to prevent people from pronouncing the divine name by combining consonants of Yahweh and vowels of Hebrew word *adonai* ("Lord"). Readers would pronounce *adonai* rather than risking blasphemy by improperly pronouncing divine name. See *God; Lord; YHWH; Names of God.*

JEHOVAH-JIREH (*Yahweh will provide*) See *Jehovah; YHWH; Names of God.*

JEHU (*Yah is He*)

Name of four OT men including:

(1) Son of Jehoshaphat and king of Israel (841–814 B.C.); commander of army when Elisha sent one of the sons of the prophets to Ramoth-gilead to anoint him as king (2 Kings

9:1-10). Jehu was responsible for the deaths of Joram, king of Israel; Ahaziah, king of Judah; Jezebel, still powerful former queen of Israel, and some 70 surviving members of the household of Israel's late King Ahab. He used trickery to gather and destroy the worshipers of Baal, so Baal was destroyed out of Israel (2 Kings 10:28). See *Israel; Chronology of Biblical Periods; Elijah.*

(2) Prophet who proclaimed God's judgment on King Baasha of Israel (1 Kings 16:1-12) warned King Jehoshaphat of Judah (2 Chron. 19:2); he recorded acts of Jehoshaphat in source in which Chronicler referred his readers (2 Chron. 20:34).

JEHUDI (*Judean or Jewish*)

Messenger for Jewish leaders calling Baruch to read Jeremiah's preaching to them and then messenger of the king to get the scroll so the king could read it. Jehudi read the scroll to King Jehoiakim, then cut it up and threw it into the fire about 604 B.C. Still, God preserved his prophetic word (Jer. 36:11-32).

JEPHTHAH (*he will open*)

One of Israel's judges (Judg. 11:1–12:7); "chief" deliverer of his people (1 Sam. 12:11); hero of faith (Heb. 11:32); Gileadite driven from home as "son of an harlot" (Judg. 11:1); raided in land of Tob with band of outlaws as "mighty warrior." When Ammonites moved against Israel, the people asked Jephthah to return and lead them. His victory came about after he vowed to offer as a burnt offering the first living thing he saw on return from battle. When his daughter greeted him, Jephthah still fulfilled his vow.

JERAHMEELITE (*God shows compassion*)

Member of clan of Jerahmeel; lived south of Beersheba in Negeb (see 1 Sam. 27:10; 30:29).

JEREMIAH (*may Yahweh lift up, throw, or found*)

Ten OT men and others named in inscriptions from Lachish and Arad about 700 B.C. and in Jewish seals including:

(1) father-in-law of King Josiah of Judah (640–609 B.C.); grandfather of Kings Jehoahaz (609 B.C.) (2 Kings 23:31) and Zedekiah (597–586 B.C.) (2 Kings 24:18; Jer. 52:1).

(2) prophet in Jerusalem 727 B.C. until after 586 B.C.; son of Hilkiah, priest from Anathoth (Jer. 1:1); after Jerusalem was destroyed in 586 B.C., moved to Mizpah, the capital of Gedaliah, newly appointed Jewish governor of Babylonian province of Judah (40:5). When Gedaliah was assassinated (41:1), Jeremiah was deported to Egypt against his will by Jewish officers (42:1–43:7) and continued to preach oracles against the Egyptians (43:8-13) and his compatriots (44:1-30).

Jeremiah's call came in thirteenth year of King Josiah, about 627/626 B.C. (1:2; 25:3; compare 36:2), but no word is spoken in the whole book about Josiah and his dramatic reforms (2 Kings 22:1–23:30). Some scholars suggest his call and birth were at same time (see 1:5), prophetic activity beginning many years later. Jeremiah lived in constant friction with authorities: religious (priests 20:1-6; prophets 28:1; or both 26:1), political (ch. 21–22; 36–38), and all together (1:18-19; 2:26; 8:1), including Jewish leaders after Babylonian invasion (42:1–43:13). His preaching emphasized a high respect for prophets whose warning words could have saved the people if they had listened (7:25; 26:4; 29:17-19; 35:13). He trusted in the promise of ideal future kings (23:5; 33:14-17). He recommended national surrender to Babylonian Empire and called Nebuchadnezzar, Judah's most hated enemy, the "servant of the Lord" (25:9; 27:6). He even incited his compatriots to desert to the enemy (21:9). He was accused of treason and convicted (37:11; 38:1-6), and yet the most aggressive oracles against Babylon are attributed to him (50–51). Enemies challenged his prophetic honesty and the inspiration of his message (43:1-3; 28:1; 29:24), still kings and nobles sought his advice (21:1; 37:3; 38:14; 42:1).

Jeremiah constantly proclaimed God's judgment on Judah and Jerusalem; yet he was also a prophet of hope, proclaiming oracles of salvation, conditioned (3:22–4:2) or unconditioned (30–31; 32:36; 33:6; 34:4). God forbade him to intercede for his people (7:16; 11:14; 14:11; compare 15:1); yet he interceded (14:7-9,19-22). God ordered him to live without marriage and family (16:2). He had to stay away from the company of merrymakers (15:17) and the houses of feasting (16:8). He complained to and argued with God (12:1-17), complaining about the misery of his office (20:7-18). At the same time he sang hymns of praise to his God (20:13).

JEREMIAH, BOOK OF

Second longest book of Bible, next to Psalms; first version dictated to Baruch (36:1-26); read first in public, and then again for state officials and King Jehoiakim, who burned it piece by piece. Jeremiah dictated a second and enlarged edition (36:32), later adding to it (30:2; 51:60; compare 25:13). The book may be subdivided into the following main sections:

(1) call narrative and visions (1:1-19),

(2) prophecies and visions (2:1–25:14),

(3) stories about Jeremiah (26:1–45:5),

(4) oracles against foreign nations (25:15-38; 46:1–51:64),

(5) historical epilogue (52:1-34),

(6) oracles on the restoration of Israel (30:1–31:40).

Structure is not based on chronology or form. Confessions of Jeremiah (11:18-23; 12:1-6; 15:10-21; 17:14-18; 18:19-23; 20:7-13,14-18) are scattered through chapters 11–20. Oracles of hope (chs. 30–31) interrupt stories about Jeremiah (chs. 26–45). Words against kings (21:11–22:30) and against prophets (23:9-40) appear to be independent collections. The Greek Septuagint is more complex, 12.5 percent shorter than the Hebrew text; and places oracles against foreign nations in different order and imme-

diately after 25:13 rather than at 46:1. Fragments of Hebrew manuscripts from Qumran show that a longer and a shorter Hebrew text existed side by side in the time of Jesus. This suggests a long and complicated process of collection through which God led these to produce His inspired Book.

Theologically, the Book of Jeremiah stimulates the search for the will of God in moments when all institutions and religious representatives normally in charge of administrating His will are discredited. Neither the Davidic monarchy (Jer. 21:1–22:30), nor prophets and priests (Jer. 23:9-40), nor the cultic institutions of the temple (Jer. 7:1-34; 26:1-9) could help the people to prevent impending calamities; nor could they detect that inconspicuous apostasy that mixes up the little aims of personal egoism (Jer. 2:29-37; 7:21-26; 28:1-17) with God's commission (Jer. 4:3). God's justice and righteousness cannot be usurped by His People. He can be a stumbling block even for His prophet (Jer. 12:1-6; 20:7-12). Execution of judgment and destruction is not God's delight. God Himself suffers pain because of the alienation between Himself and His people (2:1-37). God continued to be their Father, and His anger would not last forever (3:4,12-13). Conversion is possible (3:14,22; 4:1-2), but this is no consolation for the apostate generation. Judah and Jerusalem would meet with cruel catastrophe. Still, God's faithfulness prevails and creates new hope where all hope is lost (chs. 30–33).

JERICHO (moon)

Apparently oldest city in the world dating at least to 9250 B.C. with world's earliest wall by 8000; first city Israel conquered under Joshua; called "city of palms" (Deut. 34:3; Judg. 1:16; 3:3; 2 Chron. 28:15); tell es-Sultan near one of Palestine's strongest springs. New Testament Jericho, founded by Herod the Great as his winter capital, was about one and one-half miles southward in magnificent wadi Qelt.

In NT times, Jericho was a wealthy city, famous for its balm and valuable sycamore trees. Zacchaeus probably hosted Jesus (Luke 19:1-10) in one of Jericho's finest houses. In stark contrast stood its beggars (Matt. 20:29-34; Mark 10:46-52; Luke 18:35-43).

From about 1400 to possibly slightly after 1300 B.C., Jericho was a small settlement. The town at Joshua's time was small and may have used some of its earlier walls for defenses. More critical scholars underline conflict between archaeological data and biblical conquest narrative. More conservative scholars have tried to redate the archaeological evidence or deny that tell es-Sultan is biblical Jericho.

JEROBOAM (possibly *he who contends for justice for the people* or *may the people multiply*)

(1) First king of Northern Kingdom, Israel, about 926–909 B.C.; managed the laborers Solomon had conscripted for his huge building projects (1 Kings 11:28) when Ahijah, prophet from Shiloh, tore his coat into 12 pieces, giving ten to Jeroboam (1 Kings 11:29-39) as God's pledge that Jeroboam would become king over ten tribes. Upon Solomon's death, Jeroboam led ten tribes to revolt against the house of David. They crowned him king.

Jeroboam became the example of evil kings in Israel because he built temples in Dan and Bethel with golden calves representing God's presence. All the following northern kings suffered the biblical writers' condemnation because they walked in "the ways of Jeroboam," encouraging worship at Dan and Bethel (see 1 Kings 15:26, 34; 16:19,31). Jeroboam (1 Kings 12:25-33) made Israelite worship different from that in Jerusalem, though claiming to worship the same God with the same worship traditions. Prophetic warnings failed to move Jeroboam (1 Kings 13:1–14:20).

(2) Powerful king of Israel in dynasty of Jehu about 793–753 B.C. (2 Kings 14:23-29); restored prosperity and territory to a weak nation but continued the religious practices of Jeroboam I and thus met condemnation from the biblical writers. Jonah, Amos, and Hosea prophesied during his reign. Jeroboam restored boundaries of David's empire, reaching even into Syria.

JERUSALEM (*founded by* [god] *Shalem*)

Also known as Beth-Shalem or "House of Shalem"; chief city of Palestine, 2,500 feet above sea level and 18 miles west of northern end of Dead Sea; Amarna Letters refer to Beth-Shalem about 1400 B.C.; first mentioned in Bible as Salem (Gen. 14:18), which Hebrews (7:2) interpreted to mean "peace" because of its similarity to *shalom;* on the border between the northern and southern tribes; also called Zion, Jebus, Mount Moriah, and the city of David. See *City of David.*

Jerusalem is built on mountain plateau and surrounded by mountains related to three valleys—the Kidron on the east, the Hinnom on west and south, and the Tyropoeon that cuts into lower part of city, dividing it into two unequal parts. Its main water source was Gihon Spring at foot of the hill of Zion. The lower portion of the eastern part was the original fortress, built by prehistoric inhabitants.

Jerusalem seems to have been inhabited by 3500 B.C. Written mention of Jerusalem may occur in the Ebla tablets (about 2500 B.C.) and certainly in Egyptian sources (Execration Texts about 1900 B.C. and Amarna Letters). Archaeologists have discovered walls, a sanctuary, a royal palace, and a cemetery dated about 1750 B.C. About this time Abraham, returning from a victory, met Melchizedek, the king of Salem, who received gifts from him, and blessed him (Gen. 14). Later Abraham was commanded to offer Isaac on one of the mountains in the land of Moriah (Gen. 22:2). Second Chron. 3:1 points to Moriah as the place where Solomon built the temple (2 Chron. 3:1) on the threshing floor of Araunah. David had purchased it for an altar to God (2 Sam. 24:18). The Muslim mosque, Dome of the Rock, stands in this area today.

Joshua defeated Adoni-zedek, king of Jerusalem (Josh. 10), but Jerusalem was not taken (compare Judg. 1:8,21). Apparently, Jebusites reclaimed it, calling it Jebus (Judg. 19:10; 1 Chron. 11:4). See *Jebusi.* David led his private forces to capture Jerusalem (2 Sam. 5:1-10) and made it his capital. Zion, the name of the original fortress, now became synonymous with the city of David. The moving of the ark (2 Sam. 6) made Jerusalem the religious center of the nation. God made an everlasting covenant with house of David (2 Sam. 7:16). Solomon built the temple as a dwelling place for God (1 Kings 8:13), and the sacred ark, symbolizing His presence, was placed in the holy of holies.

To the temple came the tribes three times a year for its religious festivals. One group of psalms came to be known as "Psalms of Zion" (Pss. 46; 48; 76; 84; 87; 122; 132). The physical beauty of the city was extolled (Ps. 48), and its glorious buildings and walls were described (Ps. 87). To be a part of the festival processions there (Ps. 68:24-27) was a source of great joy (Ps. 149:3). Jerusalem, the dwelling place of both the earthly (Ps. 132) and the divine king (Pss. 5:2; 24:7), was where Israel came to appreciate and celebrate the kingship of God (Pss. 47; 93; 96–99).

When the kingdom split at the death of Solomon, Jerusalem continued to be the capital of the Southern Kingdom. Egypt attacked it (1 Kings 14:25-26), as did Syria (2 Kings 12:17), and northern Israel (2 Kings 15:29; Isa. 7:1). Hezekiah (715–686 B.C.) dug a 1,750-foot tunnel out of solid rock to provide water from the Gihon Spring in time of siege (2 Kings 20:20). In 701 B.C., the Assyrian general Sennacherib destroyed most of the cities of Judah and shut up King Hezekiah "like a bird in a cage." The Assyrians would have destroyed Jerusalem had it not been

miraculously spared (2 Kings 19:35). This deliverance, linked to God's covenant with house of David, led some to mistaken belief that Jerusalem could never be destroyed (see Jer. 7:1-15). Both Micah (3:12) and Jeremiah (7:14) prophesied the destruction of Jerusalem for her unfaithfulness to God's covenant. The prophets also spoke of Jerusalem's exaltation in the "latter days" (Isa. 2:2-4; compare 24:23; 60:19).

Babylonians conquered Jerusalem in 598 B.C., taking 10,000 of the leading people into captivity. A further uprising led to the destruction of the city in 586 B.C. The exiles kept memory of Zion alive (Ps. 137:1-6) and centered hopes for the future on it.

When Cyrus of Persia overran the Babylonians (539 B.C.), he encouraged the Jews to return to Jerusalem and rebuild the temple (Ezra 1:1-4). Haggai and Zechariah finally motivated the people to complete it in 516 B.C. (Ezra 6:15). Nehemiah came in 445 to rebuild the walls.

The restoration of Jerusalem spoken of by the preexilic prophets had taken place (Jer. 29:10; 33:7-11), but only in part. The glorious vision of the exaltation of Zion (Mic. 4:1-8) and the transformation of Jerusalem (Ezek. 40–48) had not yet been fulfilled. Prophets painted new images of Jerusalem's future (Zech. 14).

Herod the Great remodeled Jerusalem with a theater, amphitheater, hippodrome, a new palace, fortified towers, and an aqueduct to bring water from the Bethlehem area. He doubled the temple area, constructing a magnificent building of huge white stones, richly ornamented. Here Jews from all the world came for religious festivals, and here Jesus from Nazareth came to bring His message to the leaders of the Jewish nation. See *Temple.* The Roman general Titus destoyed the city in A.D. 70 after zealous Jews revolted against Rome. A second revolt in A.D. 135 (the Bar-Kochba Rebellion) resulted in Jews being excluded from the city.

The central events of the Christian faith—the crucifixion and resurrection of Jesus—took place in Jerusalem. The prophecy of Jerusalem's destruction (Matt. 24; Mark 13; Luke 21) is mixed with prophecies concerning the Son of man's coming at the end of the age when forsaken and desolated Jerusalem will welcome the returning Messiah (Matt. 23:39).

Jerusalem was the center of the missionary activity of the church, which must extend to the end of the earth (Acts 1:8). Paul kept in contact with the Jerusalem church and brought them a significant offering toward the close of his ministry. The "man of sin" would appear in Jerusalem before the Day of the Lord (2 Thess. 2:3-4). "Out of Zion" would come the deliverer who would enable "all Israel" to be saved after the full number of Gentiles had come in (Rom. 11:25-27; compare Gal. 4:24-31; Heb. 11:10; 12:22).

In Revelation, earthly Jerusalem appears for the last time after the thousand-year reign of Christ when the deceived nations, led by the temporarily loosed Satan, come against the beloved city and are destroyed by fire from heaven (Rev. 20:7-9). The new Jerusalem will descend from heaven to the new earth. The goal of the whole sweep of biblical revelation is fulfilled, and God reigns with His people forever and ever (Rev. 21–22:5). See *Revelation, the Book of.*

JERUSALEM COUNCIL See *Apostolic Council.*

JESHUA (*Yahweh is salvation*)

Eight men and village whose names are spelled in Hebrew the same as Joshua. These include:

(1) high priest taken into exile by Nebuchadnezzar of Babylon in 586 B.C.; returned to Jerusalem with Zerubbabel about 537 B.C. (Ezra 2:2); led in rebuilding altar and restoring sacrifice in Jerusalem (Ezra 3:2-6); followed prophetic preaching of Zechariah and Haggai and rebuilt the temple (Ezra 5:2–6:15; Hag. 1:1, 12-14; 2:4), finishing in 515 B.C. Still, some of his sons married foreign

women and had to follow Ezra's teaching by divorcing them (Ezra 10:18-19). Zechariah had a vision featuring Jeshua in which God announced the cleansing of the high priest, preparing him to lead in atonement rites for people and pointing to a day when Messiah would come and provide complete and eternal atonement for God's people (Zech. 3). Jeshua was apparently one of the two anointed ones of Zechariah's vision (4:14; compare 6:12-13).

(2) name for conquest hero Joshua, son of Nun (Neh. 8:17). See *Joshua.*

JESHURUN (*upright* or *straight*)

Poetic name for Israel (Deut. 32:15; 33:5,26; Isa. 44:2; compare Eccl. 37:25); may represent play on "Jacob," the original Israel, known for deception.

JESSE (*man* or *manly*)

Father of David (1 Sam. 16:1); Judahite who lived in Bethlehem (1 Sam. 16:1; Ruth 4:17). See *David.*

JESUS, LIFE AND MINISTRY OF

Earthly life of the main character of the Bible, the Son of God and Savior of the world "Jesus of Nazareth" (Mark 1:9; John 19:19).

He was born—as Jewish messiah must be (Mic. 5:2)—in Bethlehem, the "city of David," as a descendant of David's royal line (Matt. 1:1-17; 2:1-6). A Roman census led Joseph and Mary to the ancestral city of Bethlehem just before Jesus' birth (Luke 2:1-7). Luke provided glimpses of Jesus as an eight-day-old infant (2:21-39), a boy of 12 years (2:40-52), and a man of 30 beginning His ministry (3:21-23). Jesus identifed with the entire human race in its descent from "Adam," but He was more—"the son of God" (Luke 3:38). John thus traced Jesus' existence to the creation of the world and before (John 1:1-5). Still, when He taught in Nazareth, He was known only as "the carpenter, the son of Mary, the brother of James, and Joses, and of Juda, and Simon" (Mark 6:3; compare Luke 4:22; John

6:42). Matthew and Luke explained His special nature through His virgin birth (Luke 1:34-35; Matt. 1:18-23).

Identifying with people called to repentance, Jesus was baptized in the Jordan River. God's Spirit descended on Him like a dove, and the voice from heaven announced, "Thou art my beloved Son, in whom I am well pleased" (Mark 1:10-11). Still, His identity as Son of God remained hidden from those around Him, but not from Satan: in temptations he tried to get Jesus to do what only the Son of God could do (Luke 4:3,9).

Jesus made no attempt to defend or make use of His divine sonship but appealed instead to an authority to which any devout Jew of His day might have appealed — the holy Scriptures—and through them to the God of Israel. Jesus called attention —not to Himself—but to "the Lord thy God" (Luke 4:8; compare Mark 10:18; 12:29-30). Thus He could teach His disciples that they, too, must "live ... by every word that proceedeth out of the mouth of God" (Matt. 4:4); they must "not tempt the Lord their God" (Luke 4:12), humbly "worship the Lord their God, and him only [should they] serve" (Luke 4:8).

In His ministry, Jesus maintained the God-centered character of His message: "The time is fulfilled, and the kingdom of God is at hand; repent ye, and believe the gospel" (Mark 1;15; compare Matt. 4:17; Mark 1:14). He had come not to glorify or proclaim Himself; He came solely to make known "the Father," or "the One who sent" Him (John 4:34; 5:19,30; 6:38; 7:16-18,28; 8:28,42,50; 14:10,28). Throughout His ministry, the issue of Jesus' identity continued to be raised—first by the powers of evil (Mark 1:24; 5:7). Jesus seemed not to want the question of His identity raised prematurely. He silenced the demons (Mark 1:25,34; 3:12). When He healed the sick, He frequently told the cured not to speak of it to anyone (Mark 1:43-44; 7:36a). The more He urged silence, however, the faster the word of His healing power spread (Mark 1:45; 7:36b).

The crowds appear to have concluded that He must be the Messiah expected to come and deliver the Jews from Roman rule. The Gospels present Him as a strangely reluctant Messiah (John 6:15). Seldom, if ever, did He apply to Himself the customary terms "Messiah" or "Son of God." He had instead a way of using the emphatic *I* when it was not grammatically necessary and a habit sometimes of referring to Himself indirectly and mysteriously as "Son of man." Even so, Jesus spoke and acted with the authority of God Himself. He gave sight to the blind and hearing to the deaf; He enabled the lame to walk. His touch made the unclean clean. He even raised the dead to life and forgave sinners. In teaching the crowds He did not hesitate to say boldly, "Ye have heard that it was said ... but I say unto you" (Matt. 5:21-22, 27-28, 31-32, 33-34, 38-39, 43-44).

So radical was He toward the accepted traditions that He found it necessary to state at the outset: "Think not that I am come to destroy the law, or the prophets: I am not come to destroy, but to fulfil" (Matt. 5:17). The crowds who heard Him "were astonished at his doctrine: for he taught them as one having authority, and not as the scribes" (Matt. 7:28-29). He had to get up before daylight to find time and a place for private prayer (Mark 1:35; compare 2:4; 4:1 for crowd reaction).

Who were "the lost sheep" to whom Jesus was called to be the Shepherd? The apparent answer is that they were those who were not expected to benefit from the coming of the Messiah. Through their carelessness about the law, they had become the enemies of God; but God loved His enemies. Jesus' conviction was that both He and His disciples must love them too (Matt. 5:38-48; compare Mark 2:17). He claimed that God's joy at the recovery of all such sinners (tax collectors, prostitutes, shepherds, soldiers, and others despised by the pious in Israel) was greater than any joy "over ninety and nine just persons, which need no repentance" (Luke 15:7; compare vv. 3-32). Such an exuberant celebration of divine mercy seemed to religious leaders a serious lowering of ancient ethical standards and a damaging compromise of the holiness of God.

Jesus explicitly denied that He was sent to Gentiles or Samaritans (Matt. 15:24; see 10:5-6). Yet the principle—"not to the righteous, but to sinners"—made extension of gospel of the kingdom of God to the Gentiles after Jesus' resurrection a natural one (compare Luke 4:25-27). Even during Jesus' lifetime, He responded to the initiatives of Gentiles seeking His help (Matt. 8:5-13; 15:21-28; Luke 7:1-10; Mark 7:24-30), sometimes in such a way as to put Israel to shame (Matt. 8:10). Twice He traveled through Samaria (Luke 9:51-56; John 4:4); once He stayed in a Samaritan village for two days, calling a Samaritan woman and a number of other townspeople to faith (John 4:5-42), and once He made a Samaritan the hero of a parable (Luke 10:29-37; compare Matt. 8:11-12). He predicted that twelve uneducated Galileans would one day "sit upon twelve thrones, judging the twelve tribes of Israel" (Matt. 19:28; compare Luke 22:28-29). He warned the religious leaders sternly that they were in danger of "blasphemy against the Spirit" by attributing the Spirit's ministry through Him to the power of the devil (Matt. 12:31). He met his family's concern over His safety and sanity (Mark 3:21) by His affirming His disciples as a new family based on obedience to the will of God (Mark 3:31-35).

The so-called Beel-zebub controversy set a grim precedent for Jesus' relationship with the Jerusalem authorities and made His eventual arrest, trial, and execution almost inevitable (Mark 3:20-35). From that time on, Jesus began speaking in parables to make the truth about God's kingdom clear to His followers while hiding it from those blind to its beauty and deaf to its call (Mark 4:10-12; compare Mark 3:23). He also began to intimate, sometimes in analogy or parable (Mark 10:38; Luke 12:49-50; John 3:14; 12:24,32) and

sometimes in explicit language (Mark 8:31; 9:31; 10:33-34), that He would be arrested and tried by the religious leadership in Jerusalem, die on the cross, and rise from the dead after three days. From the start He had defined His mission, at least in part, as that of the "Servant of the Lord" described in Isa. 40-66 (for example, the citation of Isa. 61:1-2 in Luke 4:18-19; see Mark 10:45; 12:24). He also saw Himself as the stricken Shepherd of Zech. 13:7 (Mark 14:27) and in the role of the righteous Sufferer of the biblical Psalms (Mark 15:34; Luke 23:46; John 19:28).

Before His arrest, Jesus dramatized for the disciples His impending death by sharing with them in the bread and the cup of the Passover with the explanation that the bread was His body to be broken for them, and the cup of wine was His blood to be shed for their salvation. Only His death could guarantee the coming of the Kingdom He had proclaimed (Matt. 26:26-29; Mark 14:22-25; Luke 22:14-20; compare 1 Cor. 11:23-26).

He seems to have come to Jerusalem for the last time knowing He would die there. Though He received a royal welcome from crowds who looked to Him as the long-expected Messiah (see Matt. 21:9-11; Mark 11:9-10; John 12:13), no evidence points to this as the reason for His arrest. Rather, His action in driving the money changers out of the Jerusalem temple (Matt. 21:12-16; Mark 11:15-17; compare John 2:13-22), as well as certain of His pronouncements about the temple, aroused the authorities to act decisively against Him.

During His last week in Jerusalem, Jesus had predicted the Temple's destruction (Matt. 24:1-2; 26:61; Mark 13:1-2; 14:58; Luke 21:5-6). Jesus' intention to establish a new community as a "temple," or dwelling place of God (see Matt. 16:18; John 2:19; 1 Cor. 3:16-17) was perceived as a very real threat to the old community of Judaism and to the temple that stood as its embodiment. On this basis He was arrested and charged as a deceiver of the people.

During a hearing before the Sanhedrin, Jesus spoke of Himself as "Son of man sitting on the right hand of power, and coming in the clouds of heaven" (Mark 14:62; compare Matt. 26:64, Luke 22:69). Though the high priest called this blasphemy and the Sanhedrin agreed that such behavior deserved death, the results of the hearing seem to have been inconclusive. If Jesus had been formally tried and convicted by the Sanhedrin, He would have been stoned to death like Stephen in Acts 7, or like the attempted stoning of the woman caught in adultery in a story reported in some manuscripts of John 8:1-11. For whatever reason, the high priest and his cohorts apparently found no formal charges they could make stick. If Jesus were stoned to death without a formal conviction, it would be murder: a sin the Ten Commandments forbad.

The Sanhedrin decided, therefore, to send Jesus to Pontius Pilate, the Roman governor, with charges against Him that the Romans would take seriously: "We found this fellow perverting the nation, and forbidding to give tribute to Caesar, saying that he himself is Christ a King" (Luke 23:2). Jesus' execution is attributable to a small group of priests who manipulated the Romans into doing what they were not able to accomplish within the framework of their law. Though Pilate pronounced Jesus innocent three times (Luke 23:4,14,22; compare John 18:38; 19:4,6), he was maneuvered into sentencing Jesus with the thinly veiled threat (John 19:12). Consequently, Jesus was crucified between two thieves, fulfilling His own prediction that "as Moses lifted up the serpent in the wilderness, even so must the Son of man be lifted up" (John 3:14). Most of His disciples fled at His arrest; only a group of women and one disciple, called the disciple whom Jesus loved, were present at the cross when He died (John 19:25-27; compare Matt. 27:55-56; Mark 15:40; Luke 23:49).

The story did not end with the death of Jesus. His body was placed in a new tomb (Luke 23:50-56; John 19:38-42). Two days later, some of the women discovered the stone over the entrance to the tomb rolled away and the body of Jesus gone. A young man was there (Mark 16:5); he told the women to send word to the rest of the disciples to go and meet Jesus in Galilee, just as He had promised them (Mark 16:7; see 14:28). When they brought word, the disciples went to a mountain in Galilee, where the risen Jesus appeared to them as a group. He commanded them to make more disciples, teaching and baptizing among the Gentiles (Matt. 28:16-20). The risen Jesus appeared to the gathered disciples already in Jerusalem on the same day He was raised, and before that to two disciples walking to the neighboring town of Emmaus (Luke 24:13-48; compare John 20:10–21:23). By the Sea of Tiberius Jesus reenacted the initial call of the disciples by providing them miraculously with an enormous catch of fish. The appearances of the risen Jesus went on over a period of 40 days in which He continued to instruct them about the kingdom of God (Acts 1:3). The disciples' experience of the living Jesus transformed them from a scattered and cowardly band of disillusioned visionaries into the nucleus of a coherent movement able to challenge and change forever the Roman Empire within a few short decades.

The story of Jesus is not over; He continues to fulfill His mission wherever His name is confessed and His teaching is obeyed, and the faith of Christians is that He will do so until He comes again.

JETHRO (*excess* or *superiority*)

Priest of Midian and father-in-law of Moses (Ex. 3:1); declared Yahweh to be greater than all gods (Ex. 18:11); advised Moses on how to organize people (Ex. 18); also called Reuel (Ex. 2:18) and Hobab (Num. 10:29). See *Moses*.

JEWELS, JEWELRY

Stones valued for their beauty or scarcity; often they were cut and polished to enhance their appearance. Israel had no natural deposits of precious stones. Jewels (sometimes in the form of jewelry) were taken as booty during war (Num. 31:50), brought as gifts to the king (1 Kings 10:2,10; 2 Chron. 9:1,9; compare 2 Sam. 12:30; Ezek. 28:13); or purchased from merchants (1 Kings 10:11; compare Rev. 18:11-12). Jewels functioned as medium of exchange in Ancient Near East before invention of money. Accumulation of jewels and other wealth was a great vanity (Eccl. 2:4-11).

Jewels were a fitting contribution for a special offering (Ex. 35:22). The high priest was garbed in fine clothing decorated with jewels (Ex. 28; 39).

Since the ancients had no way to cut *diamonds,* they were not yet precious stones. "Diamond" in Ex. 28:18; 39:11 is probably not what we call a diamond (NIV, "emerald"; REB, "jade"; NRSV, "moonstone").

Men and women have adorned themselves with various kinds of jewelry almost from the earliest known times. Abraham's servant put a nose ring and bracelets on Rebekah (Gen. 24:47) and gave her other gold and silver jewelry. The Israelites "despoiled" the Egyptians by begging gold and silver jewelry of their neighbors in preparation for the exodus (Ex. 3:22; 11:2-3). At least 15 precious stones were mined in ancient Egypt. Egyptian metal workers were especially skilled in the art of making gold jewelry.

During the monarchy, an ordinary man or woman might have had a few pieces of jewelry—something made of bronze or, if they could afford it, gold. Gold was relatively plentiful and could be made into a necklace, bracelet, or ring by a local craftsman. Royalty, of course, could wear more expensive jewelry set with precious stones.

Many kinds of jewelry are mentioned in the OT: bracelets for women (Gen. 24:47); and men (2 Sam. 1:10), ankle bracelets (Isa. 3:16,18), necklaces and pendants (Song of Sol. 1:10). A certain kind of gold necklace probably functioned as a symbol of authority (Gen. 41:42; Dan. 5:7,29). The "crescents" mentioned in Isa. 3:18, like those of Judg. 8:21,26, were probably moon-shaped pendants worn on chains. The crescent may have functioned as a royal insignia. Chains, collars, or "pendants" (NRSV), Isa. 3:19; Judg. 8:26) were probably also worn around the neck, perhaps on cords.

Earrings may have had some religious significance (Gen. 35:4). "Nose rings" are mentioned in Gen. 24:22, 30, 47 (NIV) and Isa. 3:21 (NIV). The same term, *nezem,* is used for both, so the references are often ambiguous (Num. 31:50; Prov. 25:12).

Good luck "amulets" are not mentioned often in the Bible but have been widely found throughout Palestine from all periods. Some represented gods and goddesses. Isaiah 3:20 may include a reference to amulets (see NRSV). The earrings Jacob buried under the oak near Schechem may have been amulets (Gen. 35:4). Such amulets were violations of the commandment not to make graven images (Ex. 20:4).

The most important item of jewelry mentioned in the OT is the signet ring (Gen. 41:42; Esther 3:10; 8:2) used to make an impression on clay or wax and thus to seal and authenticate documents. Generally the signet was a finely engraved semiprecious stone. A hole could be bored through the signet, and it could be hung from a cord around the neck (Gen. 38:18), or it could be used as a setting for a ring or more elaborate necklace.

Jewelry was also used to decorate animals, at least by the wealthy (Judg. 8:21,26). Isaiah 3:18-23 condemns the misuse of wealth and power at the expense of the poor (compare Jas. 2:1-7; 1 Tim. 2:9-10). In Ezek. 16:8-13, the Lord is portrayed as a Bridegroom decking His bride, Jerusalem, with fine clothing and jewelry, including a nose ring, earrings, and a crown (compare Rev. 21:2). Pearls were highly valued in NT times and, thus, a fitting metaphor for the kingdom of God (Matt. 13:45-46).

The idea of rebuilding Jerusalem with jewels as building materials (Rev. 21) reflect Isa. 54:11-12. Unlike the old Jerusalem, the new Jerusalem—associated with the completion of the kingdom of God—will not be unfaithful. See *Minerals and Metals*.

JEWISH PARTIES, NEW TESTAMENT

Judaism in NT times was diverse with Pharisees, Sadducees, and Herodians. One man was called a Zealot. Other sources point to the Essenes.

The *Pharisees* constituted the most important group. They appear in the Gospels as the opponents of Jesus. Paul was a Pharisee before becoming a Christian (Phil. 3:5). They were the most numerous of the groups, although Josephus stated that they numbered only about 6,000. They controlled the synagogues and exercised great control over the general population. The earliest reference to them is dated in the time of Jonathan (160–143 B.C.), where Josephus refers to Pharisees, Sadducees, and Essenes. Their good relations with the rulers ended in the time of John Hyrcanus (134–104 B.C.). They came to power again when Salome Alexandra became queen (76 B.C.).

"Pharisee" means "the separated ones." It may mean they separated themselves from the masses of the people, or they separated themselves to the study and interpretation of the law. Apparently, they were spiritual descendants of the Hasidim, the loyal fighters for religious freedom in the time of Judas Maccabeus. They appear to be responsible for the transformation of Judaism from a religion of sacrifice to one of law. They were the progressives of the day, willing to adopt new ideas and adapt the law to new situations.

The Pharisees were strongly monotheistic. They accepted all the OT as authoritative. They affirmed the reality of angels and demons. They had a firm belief in life beyond the grave and a resurrection of the body. They were missionary, seeking the conversion of Gentiles (Matt. 23:15). They saw God as concerned with the life of a person without denying that the individual was responsible for how he or she lived. They had little interest in politics. The Pharisees opposed Jesus because He refused to accept the teachings of the oral law.

The *Sadducees* were the aristocrats of the time, the party of the rich and the high priestly families. They were in charge of the temple and its services. They claimed to be descendants of Zadok, high priest in the time of Solomon. They opposed the Pharisees; they sought to conserve the beliefs and practices of the past. They opposed the oral law, accepting only the Pentateuch as the ultimate authority. Materialistic in outlook, they did not believe in life after death or any reward or punishment beyond this life. They denied the existence of angels and demons. They did not believe that God was concerned with what people did; rather, people were totally free. They were politically oriented, supporters of ruling powers, whether Seleucids or Romans. They wanted nothing to threaten their position and wealth, so they strongly opposed Jesus.

The *Zealots* receive only brief mention in the NT. Simon, one of the disciples, is called a Zealot (Luke 6:15). John 18:40 uses a word for Barabbas that Josephus used for "Zealot." Josephus states that the Zealots began with Judas the Galilean seeking to lead a revolt over a census for taxation purposes (A.D. 6). He did not use the name "Zealot" until referring to events in A.D. 66, the beginning of the Jewish revolt against Rome. The Zealots were the extreme wing of the Pharisees. In contrast with the Pharisees, they believed that only God had the right to rule over the Jews. They were willing to fight and die for that belief. For them patriotism and religion were inseparable.

The *Herodians* joined with the Pharisees in a plot to kill Jesus (Matt. 22:16; Mark 3:6; 12:13). They were perhaps Jews who supported Herod

Antipas or sought to have a descendant of Herod the Great given authority over Palestine. Apparently they lived in Galilee, where Antipas ruled, and joined the Jerusalem religious authorities in opposing Jesus. They tried to trap Jesus into denying responsibility for Roman taxes (Matt. 22:15-22; Mark 12:13-17). Their plots began the road to Jesus' crucifixion (Mark 3:6).

The *Essenes* are not mentioned in the NT. We know of them from Josephus, Philo, and the Dead Sea Scrolls. Apparently, the people of the Scrolls were closely related to the Essenes. Essenes may have begun about the same time as the Pharisees and Sadducees. They were an ascetic group, many of whom lived in the desert region of Qumran, near the Dead Sea. They took vows of celibacy and perpetuated their community by adopting male children. Some did marry. When one joined the Essenes, he gave all his possessions to the community. A three-year period of probation was required before full membership was granted. The Essenes devoted themselves to the study of the law. They went beyond the Pharisees in their rigid understanding of it. There is no evidence that either Jesus or John the Baptist ever had any relation to Qumran. Jesus would have strongly opposed their understanding of the law. The vast majority of the people were not members of any of these parties, although they would have been most influenced by the Pharisees.

JEWS IN THE NEW TESTAMENT

Originally descendants of the tribe of Judah and then those who inhabited the territories claimed by them (2 Kings 16:6; 25:25; Jer. 32:12). With deportation and subsequent assimilation of the "Ten Lost Tribes" from the Northern Kingdom after 722 B.C., the only Israelites to survive into the exilic period were a few from the tribe of Benjamin and the tribe of Judah, hence the name "Jews" (Neh. 1:2; Dan. 3:8,12).

Jews can be described in quite positive terms (John 4). Jesus said, "Salvation is of the Jews" (John 4:22). Many of the Jews believed in Jesus (8:31; 11:45; 12:11). Other references are neutral (John 3:1).

The Gospel of John uses "Jews" rather than scribes, Sadducees, and Pharisees for Jesus' opponents, often implying Jewish authorities (7:13; 9:22; 19:38; 20:19). The Jews impugned Jesus' birth and His sanity (8:48); they even alleged He was demon possessed (8:52). They questioned His statements about the temple (2:20) and were scandalized at His claim to be the bread from heaven (6:41). They regarded His affirmations of equality with the Father as blasphemous and picked up stones to kill Him (5:18; 7:1; 10:31,33; 11:8).

Paul was a Jew from Tarsus (Acts 21:39; 22:3). After his dramatic conversion on the road to Damascus, his fellow Jews sought to kill him (9:23). King Herod Agrippa I arrested Peter and killed the apostle James, believing this would please the Jews (12:1-3).

Following his conviction that the gospel should be preached first to the Jews (Rom. 1:16), Paul, on his missionary journeys, began his preaching in Jewish synagogues: Salamis on Cyprus (Acts 13:5), Iconium (14:1), Thessalonica (17:1), Athens (17:15-17), and Corinth (18:1). He made some converts among the Jews, even converting the synagogue ruler at Corinth (18:8), and no doubt had success among the "god fearers" or proselytes who were interested in converting to Judaism (13:43; 17:4). The majority of the Jews reacted violently against Paul's message (13:50; 14:2; 17:5; 18:12). Paul, therefore, turned his efforts increasingly toward the Gentiles, the non-Jews.

Paul argued against "Judaizers" that Gentile converts did not have to be circumcised—become Jews first—before they became Christians (Acts 15:1-5). His arguments were accepted by James and the church council at Jerusalem held about A.D. 49. Paul came to the radical conclusion that a true Jew is not one who physically descended from Abraham (compare John 8:31-41), adhered to the Torah or law of Moses (Rom. 2:17,28), and was circumcized. A true Jew believes that Jesus is the Messiah or Christ (Gal. 3:26-29), relies on God's grace rather than "works" of the law (Eph. 2:8-9), and has been circumcised in his or her heart by the Holy Spirit (Gal. 2:2-9; 5:6). Paul did not teach that God had abandoned the Jews; he believed that God still had a plan for them (Rom. 9–11). Revelation 2:9 and 3:9 refers to those claiming to be Jews but who were denounced as the "synagogue of Satan" because they opposed Christians.

JEZANIAH (*Yahweh gave ear*)

Army captain loyal to Gedaliah, the governor Babylon appointed over Judah immediately after destroying Jerusalem (Jer. 40:8); called Azariah in 43:2.

JEZEBEL (*Where is the prince?* or perhaps Phoenician, *Baal is the prince*)

Wife of King Ahab of Israel (874–853 B.C.), who brought Baal worship from Sidon, where her father Ethbaal was king (1 Kings 16:31); tried to destroy all God's prophets in Israel (1 Kings 18:4) while installing prophets of Baal and Asherah (1 Kings 18:19, modern translations) as part of the royal household. Elijah proved these prophets to be false on Mount Carmel (1 Kings 18), bringing Jezebel's threat to kill Elijah (1 Kings 19:2). Elijah ran for his life to Beer-sheba.

When Ahab wanted Naboth's vineyard, Jezebel connived with the leaders of the city who falsely accused and convicted Naboth, stoning him to death. Elijah then prophesied Jezebel's death, she being the one who had "stirred up" Ahab to wickedness (1 Kings 21). She continued her evil influence as her son Joram ruled (2 Kings 9:22). Elisha anointed Jehu to replace Joram. Jehu assassinated Joram and then went to Jezreel after Jezebel. She tried to adorn herself and entice him, but her

servants obeyed Jehu's call to throw her from the window to the street, where horses trod her in the ground (2 Kings 9:30-37). Jezebel's name became so associated with wickedness that the false prophetess in church at Thyatira was labeled "Jezebel" (Rev. 2:20).

JEZREEL *(God sows)*, **JEZREELITE**

(1) Entire valley of Jezreel that separates Galilee from Samaria, including the valley of Esdraelon; important militarily as battle site for Deborah (Judg. 4–5), Gideon (Judg. 6–7), Saul (2 Sam. 4), Jehu (2 Kings 9–10), and Josiah (2 Kings 22); major route for travel from north to south and from east to west.

(2) Northern city that guarded corridor to Beth-shan; site of royal residence of Omri and Ahab where the incident of Naboth's vineyard occurred (1 Kings 21).

(3) Southern city in vicinity of Ziph (1 Sam. 25:43-44; compare Josh. 15:56).

(4) Symbolic name of Hosea's son; indicates evil nature of the dynasty of Jehu that began with much bloodshed in Jezreel; also symbolized that God will sow seeds of prosperity after the destruction (Hos. 1:4,5; 1:10–2:1).

JOAB (*Yahweh is father*)

Military commander during most of David's reign; oldest son of Zeruiah, David's sister (2 Sam. 2:13; 1 Chron. 2:16); loyal to David and ruthless in achieving his objectives. After Saul's death, David was negotiating with Abner, Saul's military commander. Joab, whose brother Abner had slain in battle, deceived Abner and murdered him. David publicly lamented this assassination (2 Sam. 2–3).

Joab's exploits in the capture of Jerusalem led David to name him commander (1 Chron. 11:4-8). Joab successfully led David's armies against the Ammonites (2 Sam. 10–11). Joab was instrumental in reconciliation of David and Absalom (2 Sam. 14). When Absalom led a rebellion, Joab remained loyal to David. Joab killed Absalom against the clear orders of David (2 Sam. 18:14). He also convinced David to end his obsessive grieving for Absalom (2 Sam. 19:4-8). Joab murdered Amasa, whom David had named commander (2 Sam. 20:10). He opposed David's plan for a census, but carried it out when ordered to do so (2 Sam. 24:1-9).

When David was dying, Joab supported Adonijah's claim to the throne (1 Kings 1). David named Solomon king and told him to avenge Abner and Amasa by killing Joab (1 Kings 2).

JOANNA (*Yahweh's gift*)

Woman whom Jesus had healed and who ministered to Him out of private means (Luke 8:3; compare 24:10) wife of Herod's steward Chuza.

JOASH (*Yahweh gives*)

Eight men in OT including:

(1) infant son of King Ahaziah of Judah (2 Kings 11:2) who survived bloodbath carried out by Athaliah, the queen mother; following Ahaziah's murder took throne at age of seven; assassinated in palace conspiracy. See *Israel; Chronology of Biblical Periods; Athaliah; Jehoiada.*

(2) son and successor of Jehoahaz (800–785) as king of Israel (2 Kings 13:10); visited dying prophet Elisha (2 Kings 13:14-19) who promised king three victories over Syria; enjoyed military success against Syria and Judah; defeated Amaziah of Judah in battle at Beth-shemesh; actually entered Jerusalem and plundered the temple. See *Israel; Chronology of Biblical Periods.*

JOB (*the persecuted one*)

Hero of faith who dialogued with God and three friends concerning suffering and losses he endured but did not deserve; apparently lived in the patriarchal or prepatriarchal days, for he does not mention the law or the exodus, he is pictured as a wealthy nomad (Job 1:3; 42:12) still offering sacrifices himself (Job 1:5; 42:8). Undoubtedly, Job was a most

respected man; not only did the prophet Ezekiel refer to him as one of Israel's greatest ancestors (Ezek. 14:14), but James uses him as an excellent example of patient and persistent faith (Jas. 5:11).

JOB, BOOK OF

Anonymous wisdom book in OT that deals with sovereignty of God, human suffering, and loss. The text never speaks of Job as its author, just its subject. Though most will agree the character Job lived in patriarchal times, many believe the book was written many years later, possibly in postexilic period.

The book of Job is most frequently pictured as a drama with prologue (chs. 1–2) and epilogue (42:7-17) enclosing three cycles of poetic speeches between Job and his three friends (chs. 3–27), a beautiful wisdom poem from Job (ch. 28), Job's concluding remarks (chs. 29–31), the mysterious Elihu speeches (chs. 32–37), and God's whirlwind speeches (38:1–42:6).

The book of Job wrestles with issues all people eventually face. Two important issues are the cause and effect of suffering and the justice and care of God. Job begins by accepting suffering as part of human life to be endured through trust in God in good and bad times. He moves to human frustration with problems for which we cannot find answers. Yet, he refuses to accept his wife's perspective of giving up on God and life. Rather, he constantly confronts God with cries for help and for answers. He shows faith can be struggling in the dark for answers—struggling with God, not with other people.

His friends note that suffering will not last forever, punishment is not as bad as it could have been, sin is forgivable, suffering can be endured, and God's Word should be heeded. Job's complaint is that he cannot find God to present his case to Him, get his name cleared and his body healed.

God's speaking to Job shows that God cares and that He still controls the world, even a world with unexplainable suffering. His creative acts and the mysterious creatures He has created only prove that humans must live under God's control. People must be content with a God who speaks to them. They cannot demand that God give all the answers we might want. God can be trusted in the worst of circumstances as well as in the best. See *Wisdom and Wise Men; Suffering; Faith.*

JOCHEBED (*Yahweh's glory*)

Mother of Miriam, Aaron, and Moses (Ex. 6:20); member of tribe of Levi; name includes divine name Yahweh, evidence the name Yahweh was known before Moses' birth. See *Moses.*

JOEL (*Yah is God*)

Name of at least 13 OT men including:

(1) son of Samuel who became an evil judge, leading Israel's leaders to ask Samuel to give them a king (1 Sam. 8; compare 1 Chron. 6:33);

(2) prophet whose preaching ministry produced the Book of Joel; son of Pethuel, probably lived in Jerusalem; dated anywhere between 800 and 400 B.C.

JOEL, BOOK OF

Second book in Book of the Twelve or Minor Prophets; contains only 70 verses with description of terrible locust plague concluding with plea for confession of sins (1:1–2:17); and first-person response from God proclaims hope for the repentant people coupled with judgment upon their enemies (2:18–3:21). An unprecedented locust plague symbolized the coming day of the Lord. Drought and famine followed the locust infiltration. All God's creation suffered because of the sinfulness of His people. Priests were urged to call for fasting and prayer (2:15-17). Only God's grace could avert annihilation. Then, on the basis of their repentance, God answered that He would show pity and remove their plague (2:18-27).

As a result of their return to God, His people were promised the presence of God's Spirit among them. Locusts were used to tell about a greater day of the Lord in the future. Judgment was pronounced against Phoenicia and Philistia (3:4) and eventually upon all nations as they were judged by God in the Valley of Jehoshaphat (3:2,12). Judah faced unparalleled prosperity, but Egypt and Edom could look for terrible punishment (3:18-19). The Lord triumphed over His enemies in order that all should "know that I am the Lord Your God" (3:17; compare 2:27).

Dating the book is difficult. Theories range from before 800 B.C. to after 400. Its position immediately after Hosea points to an early date. Its silence on world empires, northern Israel, and apocalyptic tones points to a late date. No conclusive evidence is available.

Joel teaches:

(1) The Creator and Redeemer God of all the universe is in complete control of nature and can use calamities to bring His people to repentance.

(2) All of God's creation is interdependent. People, animals, and vegetation all suffer when people sin.

(3) The day of the Lord can punish God's people as well as their enemies.

(4) The God of judgment also is a God of mercy who stands ready to redeem and restore when His people come before Him in repentance.

(5) The Spirit of God will come on all people (see Acts 2:17-21).

JOGBEHAH (*height, little hill*)

City east of Jordan where Gideon defeated the kings of Midian (Judg. 8:11; compare Num. 32:35); Khirbet el-Jubeihat 20 miles southeast of Jordan and seven miles northwest of Amman.

JOHANAN (*Yah is merciful*) or **JOHANNAN**

Nine OT men including:

(1) Jewish military leader in Judah immediately after exile in 586 B.C. (2 Kings 25:23; compare Jer. 40–43).

(2) high priest about 411 B.C. known in the Elephantine papyri as Jehohanan but in Neh. 12:22-23 as Johanan.

JOHN (*Yahweh has been gracious*)

(1) Apostle; son of Zebedee; brother of James; mother may be Salome with John being Jesus' first cousin (compare Matt. 27:56 with Mark 15:40; John 19:25); among first disciples called (Matt. 4:21-22; Mark 1:19-20); fisherman on Sea of Galilee; probably lived in Capernaum; "partners with Simon" Peter (Luke 5:10); pillar of early church (Gal. 2:9). Their father was sufficiently prosperous to have "hired servants" (Mark 1:20).

John is among the "inner three" with Jesus on special occasions: raising of Jairus's daughter (Mark 5:37), transfiguration (Mark 9:2), and Garden of Gethsemane (Mark 14:32-33). Andrew joined these three when they asked Jesus about the signs of the coming destruction of Jerusalem (Mark 13:3).

The sons of Zebedee were given the surname Boanerges, "sons of thunder" (Mark 3:17; compare Luke 9:54). See Mark 9:38; Luke 9:49. The two brothers asked to sit in places of honor in Jesus' glory (Mark 10:35-41; compare Matt. 20:20-24; Luke 22:8). See Acts 1:13; 3:1-11; 4:13, 20; 8:14. John is apparently the "beloved disciple" in John's Gospel (13:23-26; 19:25-27; 20:2-10; 21:7; 21:20-23; 21:24-25; compare 1:35; 18:15-16; 21:1).

Five books of the NT have been attributed to John the Apostle: the Gospel, three Epistles, and Revelation. See *John, The Gospel of; John, The Letters of; Revelation, The Book of.*

(2) John the Baptist, prophet from priestly family, preached message of repentance, announced the coming of the Messiah, baptized Jesus, and was beheaded by Herod Antipas. Destined before birth not to drink wine or strong drink, he would be filled with the Holy Spirit, and as a prophet would have spirit and power of Elijah. His role would be to prepare the Lord's people for the coming of the Messiah. See Luke 1:5-80.

John began his ministry around Jordan River in fifteenth year of Tiberius Caesar (Luke 3:1-3), probably A.D. 26 or 27. John's preaching emphasized the coming judgment, the need for repentance issuing into radical actions, and the coming of the Messiah (Luke 3:4-14).

Jesus was baptized by John "to fulfill all righteousness" (Matt. 3:15; compare Luke 3:20-21). John's disciples practiced fasting (Mark 2:18), and he taught them to pray (Luke 11:1). John was vigorous in his attacks on Herod. Some criticized John for his ascetic lifestyle (Matt. 11:16-19), but Jesus praised John as the greatest of the prophets (Matt. 11:11). He was popular with the people (Matt. 21:31-32; Mark 11:27-32; Luke 7:29-30; John 10:41). While in prison, John sent two disciples to inquire whether Jesus was the coming One (Matt. 11:2-3; Luke 7:18-23). Herod beheaded him (Mark 6:14-29). Jesus even identified John with the eschatological role of Elijah (Matt. 17:12-13; Mark 9:12-13).

Years later, a group of John's followers were found around Ephesus, among them the eloquent Apollos (Acts 18:24–19:7). See *Baptism.*

(3) Relative of Annas, the high priest (Acts 4:6), unless manuscripts reading Jonathan are right.

(4) John Mark. See *Mark, John.*

JOHN, GOSPEL OF

Fourth Gospel traditionally attributed to John the apostle in Ephesus, toward the end of his life. Gospel says only that it was written by the beloved disciple (21:20-24). See *Beloved Disciple.* Part of the enigma of John is its distinctiveness from the other three canonical Gospels. John does not tell of Jesus' birth in Bethlehem; scarcely mentions kingdom of

God; has no parables; has no list of the twelve disciples; has nothing like Sermon on the Mount; has no healing of lepers; has no bread and wine at the last supper; and never mentions demons. John reports Jesus' extended discourses rather than the Synoptics' short, pithy sayings. In the Synoptics, Jesus spends His entire ministry in and around Galilee and makes one trip to Jerusalem, just a week before His death. According to John, however, Jesus made four trips to Jerusalem (John 2:13; 5:1; 7:10; 12:12) and spent a significant part of His ministry in Judea.

The Gospel of John gives a distinctive account of Jesus' "signs," His words, and His ministry. A widely accepted theory holds that the Gospel makes use of an account of the signs Jesus performed. The first two of these are numbered (John 2:1-11; 4:46-54). Whatever the sources of the Gospel, the purpose is clear: "that ye might believe that Jesus is the Christ, the Son of God; and that believing ye might have life through his name" (20:31).

The Gospel of John features episodes in which individuals are caught between Jesus' call for faith and the Jewish authorities' rejection of His claims (Nicodemus, John 3; the man at the pool of Bethesda, John 5; the crowds in Galilee, John 6; and the man born blind, John 9). The purpose of the Gospel, therefore, was twofold:

(1) to call believers to reaffirm their faith and move on to a more mature faith, and

(2) to call the "secret believers" (12:42; 19:38) to confess Jesus as the Christ and join the Christian community.

Eventually a dangerous belief that either denied or diminished the significance of the incarnation began to develop. False teachers said Jesus was certainly the Christ, but they denied that the Christ had come "in the flesh" (see 1 John 4:2-3; 2 John 7). See *John, The Letters of.*

The roots of the Johannine tradition reach back to the ministry of Jesus, and the Gospel stands on eyewitness testimony (19:34-35; 21:24-25).

The Gospel reached its present form around A.D. 90-100. Its place in the NT, following the other three Gospels, may reflect the memory that it was the last of the four Gospels.

The Gospel of John draws a portrait of Jesus as the divine Logos, the Christ, the Son of God. Its message is thoroughly Christological. Jesus has a dual role as Revealer and Redeemer. He came to reveal the Father and to take away "the sin of the world" (1:18,29). As the Logos, Jesus continued God's creative and redemptive work, turning water into wine, creating eyes for a blind man, and breathing the Holy Spirit into His disciples. As the Revealer, Jesus revealed that He and the Father were one (10:30), so those who saw Him (that is, received Him in faith) saw the Father (14:9). All that Jesus does and says points beyond and above to the knowledge of God. Through Jesus' revelation of the Father, which reaches its fulfillment in His death on the cross, Jesus delivers the world from sin. Sin is understood in the Gospel of John primarily as unbelief (16:9).

John contains a profound analysis of the experience of faith. The human condition apart from God is characterized in John as "the world," which is under the power of sin. Some never believe because they love the darkness and the glory of men rather than the glory of God. All who believe are called, drawn, and chosen by the Father (6:37, 44; 10:3, 27; 17:6). Some believed only because of Jesus' signs. The Gospel accepts this response as faith but calls believers to a faith that is based on Jesus' words and on the knowledge of God as revealed in Jesus.

Those who believe in His name are born "from above" (3:3, NRSV). They are the "children of God" (1:12), whose life is sustained by living water and the bread of life. They live in community as His sheep (John 10), the branches of the true Vine (John 15). Jesus' disciples are to live "just as" He lived. The twin commands of the Johannine community were to have faith and to love one another

(14:1; 13:34; 1 John 3:23). Those who believe already have eternal life, here and now (John 17:3). They have already crossed from death into life (5:24), and the judgment occurs in one's response to Jesus (3:19). John emphasized the present fulfillment of future expectations. Believers, however, will also be raised "at the last day" (6:39-40,44,54).

JOHN, LETTERS OF

Three NT books attributed to the apostle John. The Johannine character of the three letters is universally recognized, but debate over their authorship continues. Some scholars regard the apostle John as the author of all three letters. Others, citing stylistic and theological differences, between the Gospel and the Letters, contend that they were written by an elder in the Johannine community, who was not the evangelist.

Most scholars agree that the three Letters were written by the same author and that they were written after the Gospel. A date of about A.D. 100 seems to be indicated, but both earlier and later dates have been proposed. The Letters are concerned with correcting a false belief about Christ that was spreading in the churches. We may assume that the opponents held to the divinity of Christ but either denied or diminished the significance of His humanity. This false belief had already led to schism (1 John 2:19; 4:1). These "opponents" of the author's group are charged with not following the command to love one's fellow Christians. They apparently also claimed that they were free from sin (1 John 1:8,10). Both groups held that believers have "passed from death unto life" (1 John 3:14), but the author recognized the potential danger in this teaching and contended that the future coming of the Lord (1 John 3:2) requires believers to purify themselves and be righteous (1 John 3:3-7).

First John

The statement "God is" appears three times: "God is light" (1:5), "He is righteous" (2:29), and "God is love" (4:8). First John demands that these qualities must dominate the lives of believers. As a way of refuting false teaching that threatened the community, the author quoted tenets of the opponents in 1 John 1:6,8,10; 2:4,6,9, and answered each point. He called those who remained to practice the command of love (2:3-11). He gave assurance to the community and warned the believers that they cannot practice love for one another and love for the world at the same time (2:15-17). "The world" here means all that is opposed to Christ.

One of the tests of faithfulness is righteousness (2:29). The opponents may have claimed the judgment was already past and Christians had already passed from death into life. The author reasserted a more traditional eschatology (see 3:2). Hope for the future, however, carries with it the imperative of righteous, pure living. Christians cannot make sin a way of life (compare 3:6,9 with 1:8-10).

Another test of faithfulness is living by the command to love one another; this means sharing with those in need (3:11-24, especially v. 17). The false prophets, who had gone out from the community, denied the incarnation (4:1-6). The incarnation is crucial for Christian doctrine, however, because in Christ we find the love of God revealed (4:7-21). Love of God requires that we love one another.

Those who have faith in Christ and love God keep His commands, and to them God gives eternal life (5:1-12). The water, the blood, and the Spirit all bear witness to Christ, His incarnation, and His death. Christians are to pray for one another, but there is sin that is "mortal" (5:16). By this the elder probably meant denying Christ, the one through whom sin is forgiven. Christ also keeps those who are "born of God." He is the only source of eternal life.

Second John

Second John was written to a sister community to warn the church about the dangers of the false teaching already threatening the author's church. The writer praised the sister church for following the truth and appealed for her to continue to show love. He apparently wanted to be sure the sister church would continue in fellowship with his church. His real concern, however, was to warn "the elect lady"(v. 1) about those"who confess not that Jesus Christ is come in the flesh"(v. 7). Such deceivers and antichrists are not to be received by the church. These were apparently members of the same group referred to in 1 John 2:19 and 4:1-2.

Third John

Third John is a personal letter to Gaius, who had been providing hospitality to fellow Christians and to messengers from the writer's community. Diotrephes, however, refused to receive those sent by the elder. The elder charged that Diotrephes "loveth to have the preeminence among them" (v. 9). Some interpreters suggest Diotrephes was an appointed leader or bishop of the church. Others conclude that Diotrephes had rejected the authority of the church's leaders, ambitiously asserting his own leadership. It may be that in an effort to prevent outsiders from spreading false teachings and dissension in the church he refused to receive any traveling prophets or teachers.

Gaius may or may not have been a member of Diotrephes's church. The elder praised Gaius and commended Demetrius (who may have carried the letter) as a faithful witness. The letter closes with greetings from fellow Christians, who are called "the friends" (v. 14; see John 3:29; 11:11; 15:13-15).

JOKMEAM (*He establishes the people or the Kinsman establishes or delivers*) or **JOKNEAM**

(1) Border city of fifth district of Solomon's kingdom (1 Kings 4:12; probably tell Qaimun about 18 miles south of Haifa on northwestern corner of JezreelValley; fortress city protecting pass into Plain of Sharon; on border belonging to Zebulun (Josh. 19:11, assigned to Levites (Josh. 21:34). Joshua defeated its king whose kingdom was near Mount Carmel (Josh. 12:22).

(2) Levitic city of Ephraim (1 Chron. 6:68), either omitted in the list in Josh. 21:22 or to be equated with Kibzaim there; may be tell es-Simadi or Qusen west of Shechem.

JOKSHAN (*trap, snare*)

Son of Abraham by Keturah and ancestor of Arabian tribes in wilderness east of Jordan (Gen. 25:2-3).

JOKTAN (*watchful* or *he is small*)

Son of Eber in line from Shem in Table of Nations (Gen. 10:25-26); original ancestor of several tribes in the Arabian desert, particularly in Jemin. See *Mesha*.

JONAH (*dove*)

Prophet (2 Kings 14:23-29) active in Israel in the reign of Jeroboam II (about 785–745 B.C.). His prediction of national expansion for the Northern Kingdom, evidently made early in the reign, expressed God's longing to save His people, wicked though they were.

JONAH, BOOK OF

The book of Jonah is unique among the prophets in that it is almost entirely narrative. It recounts how Jonah learned that God was much bigger than he had thought, especially in the extent of His power and His compassion.

Jonah was not pleased when God commanded him to go to Nineveh and preach repentance. The Assyrians worshipped the vicious god Ashur and a multitude of other gods and goddesses. Assyrian brutality and cruelty were legendary. Jonah decided that he would rather quit the prophetic ministry than preach to such people. Nineveh was about 500 miles to the east, so he headed for Tarshish, probably what is now Spain, the farthest western location he knew, about 2,000 miles.

Many since the 19th century A.D. have regarded Jonah as a parable or didactic fiction, as if factual history were ruled out by literary artistry or the recounting of miraculous events. If this narrative, however, whose form bears at every point the mark of a historical account, was judged unhistorical on either of these bases, then most of the Bible would follow easily along.

The book has been called "a masterpiece of rhetoric" and a "model of literary artistry, marked by symmetry and balance." No indication of the book's author is given, only that it gives an account of an incident in the life of a prophet of Yahweh. On the other hand, there is no indication that Jonah was not or could not have been the book's author.

Jonah is the story of how God teaches a lesson to a narrow-minded, sinful prophet, who represents all God's people who think we have a monopoly on God's grace. When Jonah refuses to go preach in Nineveh and God retrieves him and mercifully delivers him, Jonah is thankful. Yet when Jonah preaches in Nineveh and the people repent and are mercifully spared, Jonah is angry. The book of Jonah ends with an unanswered divine question regarding compassion, suggesting to the reader that Jonah repented, and inviting the reader to do the same. This must be regarded as the key to Jonah's overall purpose, to stir up compassion in God's people. The message of the book is that whether God's people like it or not, God desires all nations to worship Him.

JONATHAN (*Yahweh gave*)

Fifteen OT men including:

(1) Levite who served as priest of Micah in Ephraim and later with tribe of Dan (Judg. 17–18).

(2) Eldest son of King Saul; father of Mephibosheth (Meribbaal). Jonathan possessed courage, fidelity, and friendship. He led 1,000 soldiers to defeat the Philistines at Geba (Gibeah) (1 Sam. 13:2-3). Then he took only his armor bearer to the rocky crags at Michmash and brought panic to the Philistines by killing 20 of them (1 Sam. 14:1-16). Saul discovered that Jonathan was missing, called for the ark of God, went to battle, and defeated the Philistines; however, Jonathan had eaten honey, unaware that Saul had forbidden the people to eat that day. Saul would have put Jonathan to death, but the people spoke in praise of Jonathan and ransomed him from death (1 Sam. 14:27-46).

Jonathan formed a close friendship with David by giving him his robe, armor, sword, bow, and girdle (18:1-5). He pleaded successfully with Saul to reinstate David (19:1-7), but he left Saul's table angrily to inform David later that the king would never receive David again (20:1-42). Jonathan made covenant with David, acknowledging David as next king (23:16-18). He died with his father in battle (1 Sam. 31:1-13; compare 2 Sam. 21:12-14). See *Saul; David; Mephibosheth.*

JOPPA (*beautiful*)

Only natural harbor on Mediterranean between ancient Ptolemais and Egypt; 35 miles northwest of Jerusalem. Reefs forming a roughly semicircular breakwater approximately 300 feet offshore made entrance from the south impossible. Entrance from the north was shallow and treacherous, but small vessels could navigate it. Dan received Joppa; but it never came firmly into Hebrew hands. The Philistines took the city, but David recaptured it. Solomon developed it into the major port serving Jerusalem. To Joppa rafts of cedar logs were floated to be transported to Jerusalem for Solomon's splendid temple (2 Chron. 2:16).

Phoenicia gained control of Joppa by the time of Jonah (Jonah 1:3). Joppa was the home of Dorcas, a Christian woman known for her gracious and generous deeds (Acts 9:36-41). Peter received his Gentile-accepting vision here (Acts 10:9-16).

JORAM (*Yahweh is exalted*)

King (2 Kings 3) of Israel (849–843 B.C.) and a contemporary king (2 Kings 8) of Judah (850–843 B.C.). The Israelite king led a coalition with Judah and Edom, advised by Elisha, to defeat Moab. Joram of Judah married the daughter of Ahab of Israel and brought Baal worship to Judah. Edom and Libnah gained independence from Judah in his reign.

JORDAN RIVER (*the descender*)

River forming geographical division separating eastern and western tribes of Israel; longest and most important river of Palestine. It rises from the foot of Mount Hermon and flows into the Dead Sea. Four sources from the foothills of Mount Hermon come together to form the Jordan River: Banias, el-Leddan, Hasbani, and Bareighit rivers.

Several major tributaries (including Yarmuk and Jabbok), flow into the Jordan, emptying almost as great an amount of water as the Jordan itself. See *Palestine*.

Under the leadership of Joshua, Israel crossed the Jordan "on dry ground" (Josh. 3:15-17). During the period of the judges and the early monarchy, the possession of the fords of the Jordan more than once meant the difference between defeat and victory. The Jordan was a strong line of defense, not to be easily forded. The essential story of the Gospels begins at the Jordan River where John the Baptist came preaching the coming kingdom of heaven and baptized Jesus (Mark 1:9).

JOSEPH (*adding*)

Name of about 12 men including:

(1) Patriarch, favorite son of Israel whose mother was Rachel (Gen. 30:24); received "coat of many colors" (Gen. 37:3; "long robe with sleeves," NRSV, NEB; "richly ornamented robe," NIV) from his father; dreamed about his rule over his family, inspiring envy of his brothers, who sold Joseph to caravan of Ishmaelites (Gen. 37). Rejecting temptations of master's wife led to prison, where dream interpretations brought him to Pharaoh's attention and eventually to second in command in Egypt. He provided food for his family while hiding his identity from them. Under Joseph's patronage, Jacob moved to Egypt (Gen. 46:1–47:12). Joseph died in Egypt, was embalmed and later buried in Shechem (Gen. 50:26; Ex. 13:19; Josh. 24:32). His two sons, Manasseh and Ephraim (Gen. 41:50-52), were counted as sons of Jacob (48:5-6). Their tribes dominated the northern nation of Israel. Joseph is used in the OT as a reference to tribes of Ephraim and Manasseh (Num. 1:32; 36:1,5; 1 Kings 11:28) or as a designation for the whole Northern Kingdom (Ps. 78:67; Ezek. 37:16,19; Amos 5:6,15; 6:6; Obad. 18; Zech. 10:6).

(2) Husband of Mary, mother of Jesus; legal or foster father of Jesus (Matt. 1:16,20; Luke 2:4; 3:23; 4:22; John 1:45; 6:42); descendant of David; carpenter (Matt. 13:55); righteous man of piety and character (Matt. 1:18-25). He probably died prior to Jesus' public ministry.

(3) Joseph of Arimathea, rich member of Sanhedrin and a righteous man (Matt. 27:57; Mark 15:43; Luke 23:50). After the crucifixion, Joseph, a secret disciple of Jesus, requested the body from Pilate and laid it in his own unused tomb (Matt. 27:57-60; Mark 15:43-46; Luke 23:50-53; John 19:38-42).

JOSEPHUS, FLAVIUS

Early historian of Jewish life and our most important source for the history of the Jews in the Roman period. His four surviving works are *The Jewish War* (composed about A.D. 73), *The Antiquities of the Jews* (about A.D. 93), *Life* (an autobiographical appendix to *The Antiquities*), and *Against Apion*, penned shortly after *The Antiquities*. The date of Josephus's death was probably after A.D. 100. Josephus came to Rome in 73 and lived in a house provided by Vespasian, who also gave him a yearly pension. *The Antiquities, Life,* and

Against Apion were all written in Rome. He was commander of Jewish forces in Galilee and refuted the charge made by Justus of Tiberias that Josephus had organized the revolt in Galilee.

JOSHUA (*Yahweh delivered*)

(1) Leader of Israelites who led Israel to conquer Canaan. Joshua was born in Egypt during the period of slavery and was Moses' general who led the troops while Aaron and Hur held up Moses' hands (Ex. 17:8-13). As Moses' servant (Ex. 24:13), he was on the mountain when Moses received the law (Ex. 32:17); and was one of spies Moses sent to investigate Canaan (Num. 13:8). He and Caleb returned with a positive, minority report (Num. 14:28-30,38).

The Lord selected Joshua to be Moses' successor long before Moses' death (Num. 27:15-23; Deut. 31:14-15,23; 34:9). Joshua distributed the land among the tribes (Josh. 13-21) and led in the covenant renewal at Shechem (Josh. 8:30-35; 24:1-28).

(2) High priest of the community who returned from Babylonian exile in 538 B.C. See *Jeshua 1.*

JOSHUA, BOOK OF

Sixth book of OT; first book of Former Prophets or Historical Books. No author is mentioned in the book. Some Bible students think Joshua wrote the book except for the death reports (24:29-33). Joshua did at least write the laws on which the covenant renewal was based (Josh. 24:26).

Some Bible students suggest a date of writing about 100 years after Joshua's death, or at least by the time of the beginning of the monarchy. Other Bible students think the Book of Joshua only reached its present form when the Former Prophets were collected together during the exile. The date of the events recorded in the book depends on the date of the exodus. If this was in 1446 B.C., the conquest occurred about 1400 B.C.

The Book of Joshua tells the story of the conquest of the land of Canaan in light of theological themes of Deu-teronomy; thus, the historical Books of Joshua, Judges, Samuel, and Kings are often spoken of as the Deuteronomic History. The book has only two main parts and an appendix:

(1) the conquest of the land, 1-12;
(2) the settlement of the land, 13-22;
(3) Joshua's farewell addresses, 23-24.

Numerous passages (13:13; 15:63; 16:10; 17:12-13,16-18) agree with the Book of Judges that individual clans had to root out the many pockets of Canaanite resistance still scattered throughout the land. The difference is between occupation and subjugation. The book emphasizes the Lord's mighty acts. The glory goes to God alone (3:10; 4:23-24; 6:16).

The Lord's covenant with His people was open to anyone of faith. Rahab, the Canaanite prostitute, was accepted, along with her family, as a part of the covenant community (2:9-13; 6:22-23,25). It may well be that people related to the Hebrews who lived in the Shechem area voluntarily joined in their fellowship of faith (8:30-35). The people of Gibeon and its four-city league of cities were accepted, and even became associated with temple service (9:3-27).

The Hebrews did not divide life up into sacred and secular spheres. The soldiers were holy. Religious ceremonies prepared them for battle (5:2-11). All of the spoils of battle belonged to Him (6:18-19). None was to be taken for personal use. A certain city, for instance Jericho (ch. 6), was placed under the ban, devoted to destruction in the name of the Lord. Everything in it was to either be destroyed or else placed in the Lord's service in the tabernacle. Holy war became God's method in that setting to eradicate the spiritual contagion of pagan religion. Holy war was not set up as an eternal example (compare Deut. 20:16). One element in the explanation for the holy wars of Joshua is judgment on sin. The iniquity of the Amorites (Canaanites) was at last full (Gen. 15:16). The catch to this arrangement is that if the other nations could be judged for their sins, the Hebrew people could, too, and later were.

JOSIAH (*Yahweh heals*) or **JOSIAS** Judah's king from about 640–609 B.C.; became king at age eight due to wishes of "the people of the land" who put his father's assassins to death (2 Kings 21:19–22:1; 2 Chron. 33:21–34:1). In his eighth year as king, he began to seek the God of David (2 Chron. 34:3). He initiated a religious purge of Jerusalem, Judah, and surrounding areas during his twelfth year on the throne (34:3-7), tearing down high places, Asherah, and altars to Baal. See *Canaan, History and Religion of*.

In his eighteenth year during repair of the temple Hilkiah, the high priest, found a "Book of the Law." This book prompted Josiah to instigate the most far-reaching religious reforms in Israel's history. Most scholars believe that this book included at least the core of our present Book of Deuteronomy.

Pharoah Neco's troops were passing through territory north of Judah to join forces with Assyria. Josiah's army blocked the movement of Egyptian troups at Megiddo. In the battle that followed, Josiah was mortally wounded (2 Kings 23:29). Josiah was remembered as Judah's greatest king (2 Kings 23:25).

JOT See *Dot.*

JOTBAH (*it is good*)

Home of Meshullemeth, queen mother of King Amon of Judah about 642–640 B.C. (2 Kings 21:19); Khirbet Gefat about nine miles north of Nazareth or identical with Jotbathah (Num. 33:34) at et-Taba 20 miles north of Akaba.

JOTHAM (*Yahweh has shown Himself to be perfect*)

(1) Youngest of Gideon's 70 sons (Judg. 9:5); survived mass killing of Gideon's sons by Abimelech, their half brother; addressed fable to peo-

ple of Shechem mocking idea of Abimelech acting as a king.

(2) Son and successor of Uzziah as king (2 Kings 15:32) of Judah (750–732 B.C.); reign marked by building projects, material prosperity, and military successes.

JOY

Happy state that results from knowing and serving God; fruit of right relation with God, not of self-indulgent pleasure seeking (Prov. 14:13; Eccl. 2:1-11; Luke 8:14; 1 Tim. 5:6; Titus 3:3). God knows joy and wants His people to know joy (Ps. 104:31; Isa. 65:18; Luke 15).

The joy of God came to focus in human history in Jesus Christ. (Luke 1:14,44; Matt. 2:10). His birth brought "good tidings of great joy, which shall be to all people" (Luke 2:10). Jesus spoke of His own joy and of the full joy He had come to bring to others (John 15:11; 17:13). He illustrated the kingdom of heaven by telling of the joy of a man who found treasure (Matt. 13:44; compare Luke 19:6).

As Jesus' death approached, He told His followers that soon they would be like a woman in labor, whose sorrow would be turned into joy (John 16:20-22). Later they understood, when the dark sorrow of the cross gave way to the joy of the resurrection (Luke 24:41; compare 24:52; Heb. 12:2).

After Philip preached in Samaria, the people believed, and "there was great joy in that city" (Acts 8:8; compare Acts 13:52; 15:3; 16:34). Believers can rejoice because they walk with the Lord (Phil. 4:4). Joy is a fruit of a Spirit-led life (Gal. 5:22). Sin in a believer's life robs the person of joy (Ps. 51:8,12). A Christian can continue to rejoice even when troubles come (Matt. 5:12; Rom. 5:3-5; Jas. 1:2; 1 Pet. 1:6-8).

Joy in the Lord enables people to enjoy all that God has given. They rejoice in family (Prov. 5:18), food (1 Tim. 4:4-5), celebrations (Deut. 16:13-15), fellowship (Phil. 4:1). They share with other believers the joys and sorrows of life: "Rejoice with them that do rejoice, weep with them that weep" (Rom. 12:15).

JUBAL (*a ram*)

Son of Lamech associated with invention of musical instruments (Gen. 4:19-21).

JUBILEE, YEAR OF See *Year of Jubilee.*

JUDAH (*Praise Yahweh*)

Four postexilic men and:

(1) fourth son of Jacob; progenitor of tribe of Judah (Gen. 29:35); mother was Leah; seduced by daughter-in-law Tamar for not fulfilling Levirate marriage promises (Gen. 38).

(2) Tribe of Judah occupied strategically important territory just west of the Dead Sea. Jerusalem was on the border between Judah and Benjamin. David was from the tribe of Judah. See *Tribes of Israel.*

(3) Southern Kingdom after the nation was divided. See *Israel, History of.*

(4) province set up by the Persian government to rule a conquered Judean kingdom (Neh. 5:14; Hag. 1:1) alongside provinces of Samaria, Galilee, and Idumea. All these reported to Satrap of the Persian satrapy of Abarnaharah that encompassed the land west of the Euphrates River with its center in Damascus (Ezra 5:3,6; 6:6,13). The satrap reported to a higher official over Babylon and Abarnaharah with headquarters in Babylon. When Judah's exiles returned from Babylon, Zerubbabel was governor of Judah; Tattenai, satrap of Abarnaharah or Beyond the River; and Ushtannu, satrap of Babylon and Abarnaharah.

(5) obscure geographical reference in tribal borders of Naphtali (Josh. 19:34).

JUDAISM

Religion and way of life of the people of Judah, the Jews. Paul contrasted his Christian calling with his previous life in Judaism (Gal. 1:13-14). For-

eigners could convert to Judaism. See *Proselytes; Jewish Parties in the New Testament.*

JUDAS (*Praise Yahweh*)

Seven NT men including:

(1) brother of the Lord (Matt. 13:55; Mark 6:3).

(2) leader of revolt against Romans about A.D. 6 (Acts 5:37).

(3) Jesus' disciple always listed after James the son of Alphaeus; called brother of James (Luke 6:16; Acts 1:13); also appears to have been known as Lebbaeus Thaddaeus (Matt. 10:3; Mark 3:18). See John 14:22.

(4) Judas Iscariot, the betrayer; treasurer for disciples; known as miser and thief (John 12:5-6); present at Last Supper, where Jesus predicted his betrayal (Luke 22:21; Matt. 26:20-21). The price of the betrayal was 30 pieces of silver, which Judas returned to Jewish leaders; then he went out and hanged himself. Because it was blood money, the money could not be returned to the treasury and was used to buy a potter's field in Judas's name (Matt. 27:3-10; compare Acts 1:18-19). See *Iscariot.*

JUDE, LETTER FROM

Letter of exhortation to those who are "called" (v. 1) and "beloved" (vv. 3,17,20) to "contend for the faith that was once delivered unto the saints" (v. 3); direct attack against the opponents of the gospel. Jude concluded the letter by urging his readers to have attitudes and lifestyles different from the opponents. Then he committed them to the Lord's safekeeping in a benediction (vv. 24-25).

Authorship has traditionally been ascribed to Jude, half brother of Jesus (Mark 6:3) and dated later than A.D. 60 and earlier than A.D. 100. The content of faith is clearly fixed (v. 3), and the congregation was comprised of second-generation Christians (v. 17). The recipients were most likely Jewish Christians in Syria.

The hard-hitting attack denounces the demoralizing faction that had slipped into the congregation (vv. 4,12). They were arrogant in theology; they boasted of visions and reviled angelic beings (vv. 8-10). They were self-centered (vv. 4,8,15); they created divisions (vv. 16-19) and left disappointment behind (v. 12).

Jude, by use of a creative interpretation of OT examples (some found in noncanonical sources), responded with two sets of three exhortations. His first set of examples appealed to the murmuring Israelites, the fallen angels, and those in Sodom and Gomorrah. The second set appealed to Cain, Balaam (who in Rabbinic tradition is the father of the libertines), and Korah (who challenged Moses' authority).

Jude told the believers to pray in the Spirit, keep themselves in the love of God, and await the coming of the Lord Jesus Christ. Then he concluded by exhorting them to show mercy, snatch others from the brink of disaster, and avoid those who had fallen under false teaching. Jude reminds us that God alone can safely bring believers through the hazardous environment. While false teachers may reject Christ's authority, Jesus is our Savior and Lord now and forevermore.

JUDEA (*Jewish*)

Aramaic designation (Ezra 5:8) of province that varied in size with changing political circumstances, but always included the city of Jerusalem and the territory immediately surrounding it. During Persian period, Judea occupied a very small area. Under the Maccabees the territory expanded in size and enjoyed a period of political independence. Herod the Great, appointed over roughly the same territory by Rome, had the title: king of Judea. Judea, Samaria, and Galilee were generally considered, in Roman times, to be the three main geographical divisions of Palestine. See *Rome and the Roman Empire*.

JUDEAN

Resident or citizen of Judah in one of its several national and geographical meanings. See *Judah*.

JUDGE (OFFICE)

(1) Official with authority to administer justice by trying cases;

(2) One who usurps the perogative of a judge;

(3) A military deliverer in the period between Joshua and David (for this sense, see *Judges, Book of*). Moses served as the judge of Israel, both deciding between persons and teaching Israel God's statutes (Ex. 18:16). At Jethro's suggestion, Moses himself served as the people's advocate before God and their instructor in the law (18:19-20) and appointed subordinate judges to decide minor cases (18:21-23; Num. 11:16-17; Deut. 1:12-17; 16:18-20). Elders of a community frequently served as judges at the city gate (Deut. 22:15; 25:7; Ruth 4:1-9; Job 29:7-8). Difficult cases were referred to the priests or to the supreme judge (Deut. 17:8-13; compare Num. 5:12-31 for a case involving no witnesses). During the monarchy, the king served as the supreme judge (2 Sam. 15:2-3) and appointed local judges (1 Chron. 23:4; 2 Chron. 19:5), along with an appeals process (2 Chron. 19:8-11). Following the exile, Artaxerxes gave the priest Ezra the authority to appoint judges in Judea (Ezra 7:25).

Absalom took advantage of discontent with the legal system to instigate revolt (2 Sam. 15:4). Judges were accused of showing partiality (Prov. 24:23); of taking bribes (Isa. 61:8; Mic. 7:3; compare Ex. 23:2-9); of failing to defend the interest of the powerless (Isa. 10:2; Jer. 5:28). Zephaniah described the judges of Jerusalem as wolves on the prowl (3:3).

God is the ultimate Judge of all the earth (Gen. 18:25; Isa. 33:22; Jas. 4:12). As God's representative, Christ functions as Judge as well (John 8:16; Jas. 5:9; 1 Pet. 4:5).

The Christian's role in exercising judgment on others is found in a tension between warnings to avoid judging others and admonitions concerning how best to judge others. Christians are forbidden to judge others when such judgment entails intolerance of another's sin coupled with blindness of one's own sin (Matt. 7:1-5; Luke 6:37; John 8:7; Rom. 2:1-4) or when human judgment impinges on God's prerogative as Judge (Rom. 14:4; 1 Cor. 4:5; Jas. 4:11-12). Instructions on proper exercise of judgment include: the call to judge reputed prophets by their fruits (Matt. 7:5-17); encouragement for Christians to judge what is right for themselves and thus avoid pagan law courts (Luke 12:57-59; 1 Cor. 6:1-6); and instructions regarding church cases (Matt. 18:15-20). First Corinthians 5:3-5 illustrates the function of a church court.

JUDGES, BOOK OF

Second book of Former Prophets or Historical Books in OT; relates important episodes between death of Joshua and advent of Samuel.

Judges shows the cyclical nature of Israel's obedience to God (2:16-19). Israel would forsake Yahweh and follow after other gods, and Yahweh would give them into the hand of an oppressor. Israel would cry out for deliverance; Yahweh would send a deliverer; Israel would be obedient to Yahweh until the death of the deliverer, when the cycle would begin again. The deliverers were called *shophetim,* "Judges." A *shophet,* or judge, was a military leader, civil administrator, and decider of cases at law, very likely acting as an appellate court.

The Book of Judges tells of Judah's conquests and the land yet unconquered (1:1-36), Israel's cycles of apostasy (2:1–3:6), the individual judges (Ehud, Deborah, Gideon, Jepthah, and Samson 3:7–16:31), and illustrative incidents (17:1–21:25). Minor judges who receive only minimal notice are: Othniel, Shamgar, Tola, Jair, Ibzan, Elon, and Abdon.

Abimelech, the son of Gideon, attempted to establish the dynastic principle in Israel on the strength of his father's accomplishments, but was unsuccessful.

Apparently no single judge led all the tribes of Israel at once. Several of the narratives make a point of noting the absence of one or more tribes from the fighting forces under a judge (5:15-17; 8:1; 12:1). Some of the judges may have been contemporaries. The last five chapters (17–21) record two separate incidents unrelated to any individual judge. The first is the setting up of an illegitimate priesthood by an individual Ephraimite named Micah, followed by the theft of Micah's priest and his "gods" by part of the tribe of Dan migrating from their territory (on the west of Judah) to the northern part of the Hula Valley in the extreme north of Israel. The second episode concerns the rape and murder at Gibeah in Benjamin of the concubine of a nameless Levite. The 11 tribes rallied to the Levite's call for justice; Benjamin defended the town of Gibeah, and civil war followed. Benjamin was annihilated, except for 600 warriors. The eleven tribes devised a dubious way around their oath not to allow any of their daughters to marry into the tribe of Benjamin. The book closes with the author's assessment of the period, which has been illustrated particularly well by these two episodes, "In those days there was no king in Israel; every man did that which was right in his own eyes" (Judg. 21:25).

JUDGMENT DAY

Time of God's punishment and refining of the evil in the world, especially of the final, history-ending time of eternal judgment; frightful day of dread (Heb. 10:27) connected with the wrath of God (Heb. 12:29) and overcome only through mature faith in Christ (1 John 4:17-18; compare Rom. 8:33-34; 2 Tim. 4:8); closely connected with second coming of Christ (2 Thess. 1:7-10). The idea of judgment day reaches back into the OT concepts of divine judgment and the day of the Lord. See *Day of the Lord.* The wrath of God is poured out in judgment on the nation of Israel (1 Chron. 27:24; 2 Chron. 24:18; 29:8; Amos 3:2; 5:18; Hos. 13:9-11), her wicked rulers (1 Sam. 15; 2 Kings 23:26-27; 1 Chron. 13:10; 2 Chron. 19:2), Moses (Ex. 4:14,24; Deut. 1:37), Aaron (Deut. 9:20), Miriam (Num. 12:9), Nadab and Abihu (Lev. 10:1-2), surrounding nations and their rulers (Pss. 2:5, 11; 110:5; Isa. 13:3,5,9,13; Jer. 50:13,15; 51:45; Ezek. 25:14; 30:15).

His wrath is fierce (Ex. 32:12; Ezra 10:14), kindled like a fire (Ps. 106:40), and waxes hot like molten wax (Ex. 22:24; 32:10). A day of wrath was spoken of as a specific time in which God would act in temporal judgment (Job 21:30; Prov. 11:4; Ezek. 7:12; Zeph. 1:15,18).

This orientation became more prominent in Jewish writings in the interbiblical period (Enoch 47:3; 90:2-27; 4 Ezra 7:33; 12; Baruch 24; Testament of Benjamin 10:6-8; Judith 16:17). Judgment Day follows the resurrection of the dead and determines the eternal destiny of the righteous (either paradise in heaven or on a renewed earth) and of the wicked (Gehenna or some other place of eternal punishment) based on their obedience/disobedience to the law of God. Both Jews and Gentiles are included.

The NT presents divine judgment as both a present and a future reality. Jesus' first coming represents a divine judgment (John 3:19; 9:39; 12:31). Sinful humanity presently stands under divine condemnation (John 3:36) and experiences in part now the wrath of God (Rom. 1:18-32). The people of God are chastised for their waywardness (Heb. 12:4-11; Prov. 3:11-12), but that final divine verdict of judgment is yet to be carried out in a future day (1 John 4:17; John 5:24-29) by the Son of Man Himself (John 12:48; 5:22). Human activity in this life basically determines the verdict rendered in this future judgment.

In the great white throne judgment scene (Rev. 20:11-15), the basis of judgment is first from the book of life (vv. 12a,15) and then from books of works (vv. 12b-14). One's relationship with Christ is that determiner of eternal destiny (John 3:36), but one's faithfulness to Christ is crucial to a genuine relationship with Christ (Jas. 2:14-26; Matt. 7:21-23; 1 John 2:3-6). Very similar in emphasis is the parable of the sheep and goats (Matt. 25:31-56). Pious deeds of devotion done to those in need stands as the distinguishing criterion between the sheep and the goats and settles their eternal destiny (v. 46). Paul (Rom. 2:1-16) underscores that demand for obedient commitment to Christ as well. The concept of retribution for good and bad is also applied to believers (1 Cor. 3:12-15; 2 Cor. 5:10), but the specifics of rewards and punishments are not stated. No one will escape Judgment Day (Acts 17:30-31). Thus comes the apostolic call to repentance and faith. See *Day of the Lord; Day of Christ; Second Coming; Hell; Heaven.*

JUDGMENT SEAT

Raised platform or bench Pontius Pilate occupied while he was deliberating the accusations made against Jesus (Matt. 27:19; compare Acts 18:12). In Rom. 14:10 and 2 Cor. 5:10, the judgment seat of Christ is a theological concept, stressing that individuals are accountable to the Lord for their lives and must one day face Him in judgment.

JUDITH (*Jewess*)

(1) One of Esau's Hittite wives (Gen. 26:33-34).

(2) Heroine of Book of Judith in the Apocrypha. See *Apocrypha.*

JULIUS CAESAR See *Rome and the Roman Empire.*

JUSTICE

Order God seeks to reestablish in His creation where all people receive the benefits of life with Him; central ethical idea of the OT. Justice has two major aspects: the standard by which penalties are assigned for breaking the obligations of the society and the standard by which the advantages of social life are handed out, including material goods, rights of participation, opportunities, and liberties.

Justice in the Bible involves God's wrath on evil (John 3:19; Rom. 1:18). The Bible wants benefits distributed according to need. Justice then is very close to love and grace (Deut. 10:18, NRSV; compare Hos. 10:12; Isa: 30.18).

Various needy groups are the recipients of justice: widows, orphans, resident aliens (also called "sojourners" or "strangers"), wage earners, the poor, and prisoners, slaves, and the sick (Job 29:12-17; Ps. 146:7-9; Mal. 3:5). The forces that deprive people of what is basic for community life are condemned as oppression (Mic. 2:2; Eccl. 4:1; see Mark 12:40; compare Jer. 5:28; Job 29:12-17). To do justice is to correct that abuse and to meet those needs (Isa. 1:17).

The content of justice, the benefits that are to be distributed as basic rights include land (Ezek. 45:6-9; compare Mic. 2:2; 4:4), the means to produce from the land, such as draft animals and millstones (Deut. 22:1-4; 24:6) food (Deut. 10:18; Ps. 146:7), clothing (Deut. 24:13), and shelter (Ps. 68:6; Job 8:6). Job 22:5-9,23; 24:1-12 decries the injustice of depriving people of each one of these needs, which are material and economic. The equal protection of each person in civil and judicial procedures is represented in the demand for due process (Deut. 16:18-20; compare 28:48).

Justice presupposes God's intention for people to be in community. Biblical justice restores people to community (Lev. 25:35-36). The year of Jubilee (Lev. 25) helped those who had lost family land through sale or foreclosure of debts (v. 28) to regain economic power. Similarly, interest on loans was prohibited (v. 36) as a process that pulled people down, endangering their position in the community. See Year of Jubilee. Helping the needy means setting them back on their feet, giving a home, leading to prosperity, restoration, ending the oppression (Pss. 68:5-10; 10:15-16; compare 107; 113:7-9). In the act of restoration, those who were victims of justice receive benefits while their exploiters are punished (1 Sam 2:7-10; compare Luke 1:51-53; 6:20-26).

As the sovereign Creator of the universe, God is just (Ps. 99:1-4; Gen. 18:25; Deut. 32:4; Jer. 9:24), particularly as the Defender of all the oppressed of the earth (Pss. 76:9; 103:6; Jer. 49:11). Justice, thus is, universal (Ps. 9:7-9) and applies to each covenant or dispensation. Jesus affirmed for His day the centrality of the OT demand for justice (Matt. 23:23). Justice is the work of the NT people of God (Jas. 1:27). God's justice is the source of all human justice (Prov. 29:26; 2 Chron. 19:6,9). Justice is grace received and grace shared (2 Cor. 9:8-10).

The most prominent human agent of justice is the ruler. The king receives God's justice and is a channel for it (Ps. 72:1; compare Rom. 13:1-2,4). The same caring for the needy groups of society is demanded of the ruler (Ps. 72:4; Ezek. 34:4; Jer. 22:15-16), even of pagan rulers (Dan. 4:27; Prov. 31:8-9).

Justice is also a central demand on all people who bear the name of God. Justice is required to be present with the sacrificial system (Amos 5:21-24; Mic. 6:6-8; Isa. 1:11-17; Matt. 5:23-24), fasting (Isa. 58:1-10), tithing (Matt. 23:23), obedience to the other commandments (Matt. 19:16-21), or the presence of the temple of God (Jer. 7:1-7). "The righteousness of God" represents God in grace bringing into the community of God through faith in Christ those who had been outside of the people of God (particularly in Romans but compare also Eph. 2:12-13).

JUSTIFICATION

Process by which an individual is brought into an unmerited, right relationship with a person, whether that relationship is established between people or with God; cardinal theme of Scripture is justification, how an individual enters into and lives out relationship with God. Justification is the remedy for the sin that separates God and sinners.

God called Abraham and promised to make him into a great people (Gen. 12:1-3). Advanced in years, Abraham was promised a child, Isaac, through whom innumerable descendants would emerge. Abraham's response to this promise is the crux of the whole idea of justification: "And he [Abraham] believed in the LORD; and he counted it to him for righteousness" (Gen. 15:6). To act righteously is to act in compliance with the covenant. God accepted the response of Abraham's faith.

Justification is something God does (see Job 11:2; 13:18; 25:4; Pss. 51:4; 143:2; Isa. 43:9,26; 45:25). Hebrew prophets strongly decried Israel's proclivity to prostitute themselves with foreign gods, causing Him to act "justly." He had to render a judgment, or He would be characterized as a bad judge. God's actions resulted directly from a major disruption in the covenantal bond. The Hebrew conception of justice included an important redemptive element: "How shall I give thee up, Ephraim? how shall I deliver thee, Israel?" (Hos. 11:8). Justification requires obedience on the part of God's people, but justification also always requires judgment and restoration on the part of God.

In the NT, God dealt with the sin of humankind by the highest and most intimate form of revelation, His Son Jesus Christ. Christians are "made right" with God through the death and resurrection of Jesus Christ (Rom. 3:21-26; 4:18-25; 1 Cor. 1:30; 6:11; 1 Tim. 3:16; 1 Pet. 3:18). Sin created a massive gulf between God and people, requiring a bridge to bring all humanity into a right relationship with God. God's bridge building is "reconciliation." Reconciliation functions to bring humans "justification." Jesus' death on the cross made it possible for God and people to be recon-

ciled (Rom. 5:10) and thus for humans to be justified.

Justification does not encompass the whole salvation process; it marks the instantaneous point of entry or transformation that makes one right with God. Christians are justified in the same way Abraham was — by faith (Rom. 4:16; 5:1; Gal. 2:16; Titus 3:7). God in the present moment announces the verdict He will pronounce on the day of final judgment. Trusting faith in Jesus Christ puts people in the right with God, bringing eternal life now and forever.

JUVENILE DELINQUENCY

Juvenile delinquency was treated very seriously by the writers of the Bible because rebellion among children, in disrupting the authority structure of the family, tore at the very fabric of society. A well-ordered family prevented trouble outside the home which in turn ensured a stable society (compare Eph. 6:2-3).

God expects parents to control their children and children to obey their parents (Ex. 20:12; Eph. 6:1-4; 1 Tim. 3:4), yet realizes that this is not always the case (Isa. 3:5; Ezek. 22:7). The sons of Eli (1 Sam. 2:22-25; compare 8:3), the boys who jeered at Elisha (2 Kings 2:23-25) and the prodigal son (Luke 15:12-13) are all examples of juvenile delinquency. The Mosaic law categorized striking (Ex. 21:15), cursing (Ex. 21:17) and dishonoring (Deut. 27:16) one's parents as acts of familial rebellion and mandated that a son who refused correction should be stoned in public (Deut. 21:18-21).

In spite of the responsibility placed on parents for child rearing (Deut. 6:7; Prov. 13:24; 19:18; 22:6; Eph. 6:1-4), the Bible recognizes that, ultimately, children are responsible for their own actions (Ezek. 18:10-13). Jesus used the example of the prodigal son to teach that everyone stands delinquent before God and must come to him for forgiveness (Luke 15:11-32).

KAB See *Weights and Measures.*

KABZEEL (*may God gather*)

Town in southeast Judah near Edom (Josh. 15:21). See 2 Sam. 23:20; 1 Chron. 11:22; Neh. 11:25.

KADESH See *Kadesh-Barnea.*

KADESH-BARNEA (*consecrated*)

Site where Hebrews stayed most of 38 years after leaving Mt. Sinai before entering Promised Land; southern border of Judah (Josh. 15:3); near Ein el-Qudeirat on major crossroads —road from Edom to Egypt and the road from Red Sea to Negev and southern Canaan, later southern Judah. Moses sent out 12 spies from Kadesh-Barnea (Num. 13:3-21,26). Hebrews attempted abortive southern penetration into Canaan from there (Num. 14:40-45). See Gen. 14:7.

KADMONITE (*easterners*)

Tribe God promised (Gen. 15:19) Israel would dispossess; probably inhabited Syro-Arabian desert between Palestine-Syria and the Euphrates; may be related to "children of the east" (Judg. 6:33; compare Gen. 25:6; Judg. 8:10-12,21,26; 1 Kings 4:30-31; Job 1:3).

KAIWAN See *Chiun; Sakkuth.*

KANAH (*place of reeds*)

(1) Brook that forms part of boundary between Ephraim and Manasseh (Josh. 16:8; 17:9); wadi Qanah.

(2) City on northern border of Asher (Josh. 19:28); Qana, about six miles southeast of Tyre; not to be confused with Cana of the NT.

KEBAR See *Chebar.*

KEDAR (*mighty* or *swarthy* or *black*)

(1) Second son of Ishmael and grandson of Abraham (Gen. 25:13; 1 Chron. 1:29).

(2) Arabic tribe descended from Kedar; lived south of Palestine and east of Egypt (Gen. 25:18); nomadic; lived in tents (Ps. 120:5; Song of Sol. 1:5); raised sheep and goats (Isa. 60:7; Jer. 49:28-29,32), as well as camels, which they sold as far away as Tyre (Ezek. 27:21); led by princes (Ezek. 27:21); famous warriors, particularly archers (Isa. 21:16-17).

KEDEMOTH (*ancient places* or *eastern places*)

Levitical city in Reuben (Josh. 13:18; 21:37; 1 Chron. 6:79). Compare Deut. 2:26.

KEDESH (*sacred place* or *sanctuary*)

(1) City in southern Judah (Josh. 15:23). Probably same as Kadesh-Barnea. See *Kadesh-Barnea.*

(2) Canaanite town in eastern Galilee defeated by Joshua (Josh. 12:22); allotted to Naphtali (Josh. 19:32,37; compare Judg. 4:6) for Levites (Josh. 20:7; 21:32); also called Kedesh in Galilee; Khirbet Qedish, about two miles south of Tiberias. Kedesh in Naphtali was the home of Barak (Judg. 4:6) and place where Deborah and Barak gathered their forces for battle (Judg. 4:1-10; compare 4:21; 5:24-27). Tiglath-pileser III captured Kedesh in Naphtali during reign of Pekah of Israel. The inhabitants were exiled to Assyria (2 Kings 15:29).

(3) Levitic City in Issachar (1 Chron. 6:72), also called "Kishon" (Josh. 21:28, KJV; Kishion in other versions); perhaps tell Abu Qudeis, about two miles southeast of Megiddo.

KEILAH (perhaps *fortress*)

(1) Descendant of Caleb (1 Chron. 4:19).

(2) Fortified city in the lowland plain (Shephelah) of Judah; Khirbet Qila, about eight miles northwest of Hebron and 18 miles southwest of Jerusalem. (See 1 Sam. 23:1-13; Neh. 3:17-18).

KENATH (*possession*)

City in eastern Gilead taken by Nobah and given his name (Num. 32:42; compare 1 Chron. 2:23); easternmost city of Decapolis Qanawat in el-Hauran. See *Decapolis.*

KENAZ

(1) Grandson of Esau; clan chieftain of Edomites (Gen. 36:11,15).

(2) Father of Othniel (Josh. 15:17; Judg. 1:3); brother to Caleb (1 Chron. 4:13).

(3) Grandson of Caleb and son of Elah (1 Chron. 4:15).

KENITES (*smith*)

Nomadic tribe from southeastern hill country of Judah, probably blacksmiths, whose land God promised to Abraham (Gen. 15:19). Balaam pronounced doom and captivity for them (Num. 24:21-22). Moses' father-in-law, Jethro, is called a "priest of Midian" (Ex. 3:1) and described as a Kenite (Judg. 1:16). See 1 Sam. 15:6; 1 Chron. 2:55.

KENIZZITE

Clan God promised Abraham the Israelites would dispossess (Gen. 15:19); lived in Negev before the conquest. The tribe of Judah absorbed some of the Kenizzites while Edom absorbed others.

KENOSIS

Act of Christ in emptying Himself of the form of God, taking on the form of a servant, and suffering death on a cross (Phil. 2:6-11).

KERIOTH (*cities*)

Fortified city of Moab (Jer. 48:24,41; Amos 2:2, KJV has "Kirioth"); may be identical to Ar, ancient capital of Moab (see Amos 2:2). See *Iscariot.*

KETURAH (*incense* or *the perfumed one*)

Abraham's wife (Gen. 25:1) or concubine (1 Chron. 1:32); mother of tribes east and southeast of Palestine.

KEYS

Holder of keys had power to admit or deny entrance to the house of God (1 Chron. 9:22-27; Isa. 22:22). In late Judaism this key imagery was extended to angelic beings and to God as keepers of the keys of heaven and hell. In the NT, keys are used only figuratively as a symbol of authority, particularly the authority of Christ over the final destiny of persons (Rev. 1:18; 3:7). See *Keys of the Kingdom.*

KEYS OF THE KINGDOM

What Jesus entrusted to Peter in Matt. 16:19. "Keys of the kingdom" relate to the authority given to Peter as a representative of the apostles, to "bind" and "loose" (compare Eph. 2:20). The authority given Peter and the apostles cannot be separated from the heavenly insight and confession that Jesus is the Christ, the Son of God. The revelation given to (and confessed by) Peter called forth our Lord's blessing. Paul (like Jesus, Matt. 16:23) certainly felt free to criticize Peter when his theology / behavior warranted correction (Gal. 2:6-14). Moreover, the authority to "bind" and "loose," the result of receiving "the keys of the kingdom," is a stewardship, a delegated authority from Christ (compare Matt. 16:19 with John 20:21-23 and Rev. 1:18; 3:7-8).

Scripture nowhere suggests that the "power of the keys" was either a personal privilege or an ecclesiastical office that could be handed on by Peter or anyone else. Rather, it refers to the stewardship of the gospel (1 Cor. 3:10–4:1) entrusted to those historically unique eyewitnesses who as Christ's apostles could give authoritative testimony to the salvation that is found only in Him, a hope that could be confidently offered and promised ("on earth") as an already present gift ("in heaven") to those who confess Him. See *Disciples, Apostles; Binding and Loosing.*

KIBROTH-HATTAAVAH (graves of craving, lust, gluttony)

First stopping place of the Israelites after they left Sinai (Num. 33:16). Israelites craved meat, which Lord gave them (Num. 11:31). Because they overindulged, an epidemic broke out, and many died (Num. 11:34; Deut. 9:22; Ps. 78:30-31).

KIDNAPPING

Act of capturing and holding a person using unlawful force and fraud, usually to use or sell the person into slavery (see Gen. 37:28; 40:15). NIV, NRSV translate the corresponding Greek term, as "slave traders" (1 Tim. 1:10). Kidnapping freeborn Israelites either to treat them as slaves or to sell them into slavery was punishable by death (Ex. 21:16; Deut. 24:7).

KIDNEY

One of pair of vertebrate organs lying in a mass of fatty tissue that excrete the waste products of metabolism. Used figuratively of humans, the term is translated "reins" (KJV Jer. 12:2; Rev. 2:23); "mind" (NRSV Rev. 2:23); "heart" (Job 19:27; Pss. 7:9; 16:7, 73:21; Jer. 12:2), "vitals" (Lam. 3:13), "soul" (Prov. 23:16), or "inward parts" (Ps. 139:13; but see Job 16:13). The kidneys are often associated with the heart as constituting the center of human personality (Pss. 7:9; 26:2; Jer. 11:20; 17:10; 20:12; Rev. 2:23). Because the areas around the kidneys are sensitive, the Hebrews believed the kidneys were the seat of the emotions (see Job 19:27; Ps. 73:21; Prov. 23:16). The kidneys were also used figuratively as the source of the knowledge and understanding of the moral life (Ps. 16:7; Jer. 12:2).

The kidney, along with the fat surrounding it, was reserved for God as among the choicest parts of the animal (Ex. 29:13,22). Deuteronomy 32:14 (KJV) speaks of the best wheat as the "fat of kidneys" (see NRSV).

KIDRON VALLEY (turbid, dusky, gloomy)

Deep ravine beside Jerusalem separating temple mount and city of David on west from Mount of Olives on east; Spring of Gihon lies on the western slope. The Garden of Gethsemane would have been above the valley on the eastern side. Cemeteries have been located in this area since the Middle Bronze Age (before 1500 B.C.). See 2 Sam. 15:23; 1 Kings 2:37; 15:13; 2 Kings 23:4,6,12; 2 Chron. 29:16; 30:14. After the Last Supper, Jesus went through the Kidron Valley on His way to the Mount of Olives (John 18:1).

KINDNESS

Steadfast love that maintains relationships through gracious aid in times of need. Hebrew *chesed* bears the connotation of a loyal love that manifests itself not in emotions but in actions. Originally, this loving-kindness was considered an integral part of covenant relations.

KING'S HIGHWAY

Major transportation route east of the Jordan River in continuous use for over 3,000 years from Damascus to the Gulf of Aqabah; main caravan route for the Transjordan (Num. 20:17; 21:22). The Romans upgraded it during the reign of Trajan and renamed it Trajan's Road.

KING, CHRIST AS

The biblical teaching that Jesus of Nazareth fulfilled the OT promises of a perfect King and reigns over His people and the universe. Old Testament hope for the future included a vision of a new king like David, called the anointed one, or the Messiah (2 Sam. 7:16). Isaiah intensified the promises (chs. 9 and 11) and pointed to the Messiah yet to come (see Pss. 45; 110). Daniel contains a vision of one to whom was given dominion, glory, and kingdom, one whom all peoples, nations, and languages would serve. His dominion is everlasting and shall never pass away. His kingdom shall never be destroyed (Dan. 7:13-14).

When Jesus Christ was born, His birth was announced in these categories. His earthly ministry then amplified these themes (Matt. 4:17; Luke 1:32-33). Similarly, John the Baptist proclaimed the presence of God's kingdom in the coming of Jesus (Matt. 3). The theme of Jesus as King, Ruler, or Lord dominates the NT from beginning to end. We find the culmination of this theme with the Lord seated on a throne, His enemies being made subject to Him and a new name given: "On his vesture and on his thigh a name written, KING OF KINGS, AND LORD OF LORDS" (Rev. 19:16).

Christ said the kingdom of God is "in your midst" (Luke 17:21, NASB), "among you" (NRSV), or "within you" (KJV, NIV). Christ's kingship is thus both present yet still future, already here and still yet to come, spiritual and universal. The present kingship of Christ is His royal rule over His people (Col. 1:13,18), a spiritual realm (John 18:36) established in the hearts and lives of believers. He administers His kingdom by spiritual means—the Word and the Spirit. Whenever believers follow the lordship of Christ, the Savior is exercising His ruling or kingly function. When we pray "Your kingdom come" (Matt. 6:10), we have in mind this present rule of Christ the King.

Christ's kingship is also present today in the natural world (see John 1:3; Col. 1:17). He is in control of the natural universe as He demonstrated during His earthly ministry (Mark 4:35-41).

His kingship will become fully evident in the future (Matt. 19:28). In the future Kingdom, His rule will be perfect and visible and endure forever (1 Cor. 15:24-28). God the Father will exalt Jesus, His Son, to the highest place of authority and honor (Phil. 2:9-11).

Jesus established His kingship through His sacrificial death. Pilate recognized more than he knew when he created the sign, King of the Jews, for the charge against Jesus. Jesus'

kingship finds its highest exercise as He gives the blessings He secured for His people through His atoning work (Rom. 8:32; Eph. 1:3-11,20-22). Jesus will forever exercise His power for the benefit of the redeemed and for the glory of His Kingdom.

KING, KINGSHIP

Male monarch of a major territorial unit; especially one whose position is hereditary and who rules for life.

As Israel became more settled in Canaan, old tribal institutions of leadership began to dissolve (see, for example, 1 Sam. 8:3). Coupled with the threat of the Philistines, this threatened the existence of Israel itself. Many in Israel began to feel a need for a permanent and national leadership as a way of dealing with the threat (see 1 Sam. 8:20; 10:1).

The first national leader was Saul. Saul was anointed as the *nagid* over Israel—that is, as a national military leader—and not king, a term never used of Saul, in the technical sense. For the first time after settlement in Canaan, Israel had a permanent national military leader. Saul established no central government or bureaucracy, had no court or standing army, and his seat at Gibeah was a fortress—not a palace.

David was also a figure much in the likeness of the judges with a charismatic personality. A prophet designated him king just as the judges and Saul had been designated before him. Unlike Saul, David was able to fuse the tribes of Israel together into a nation who owed allegiance to the crown, to establish and maintain a court, and to establish a standing army. A loose union of 12 tribes became a complex empire centered around the person of David. David captured Jerusalem and made it the religious and political center of Israel. The Canaanite population of Palestine was subject to the king. The foreign empire of Israel was won and held primarily by David's professional army. The subjugated lands paid tribute to David and not to the individual tribes. When David passed the power of the kingship along to his son Solomon, the transition from the system of judges to that of hereditary monarchy was complete. The king functioned as military leader (1 Sam. 8:20; 15:4-5; 1 Kings 22:29-36; 2 Kings 3:6-12), supreme judge (2 Sam. 12:1-6; 14:4-8; 15:2; 1 Kings 3:16-28), and priest (1 Sam. 13:10; 14:35; 2 Sam. 6:13; 24:25; 1 Kings 3:4; 8:62-63; 9:25; 12:32; 13:1; 2 Kings 16:10-18).

Israel, unlike some neighboring nations, placed limitations on the power of its kings. Some Israelites opposed having a king because of the excesses to which a king might go (1 Sam. 8:10-18). It was normal for the elders of the nation to make a covenant with the king (2 Sam. 5:3; 2 Kings 11:17) where the rights and duties of the king were recorded and deposited in the sanctuary—possibly at the time of the anointment ceremony (1 Sam. 10:25). The king was not exempt from observing civil laws (see 1 Kings 21:4), nor was the king the absolute lord of life and death, a power David assumed in his murder of Uriah (2 Sam. 11; compare Ahab's murder of Naboth, 1 Kings 21:14-18; see also 2 Kings 5:7; 6:26-33). The prophetic denunciation of certain kings demonstrates that they were subject to the law (2 Sam. 12:1-15; 1 Kings 21:17-24; compare Deut. 17:14-20).

Saul's court was simple and did not require extensive financial support (1 Sam. 22:6), while David depended on spoils of war (2 Sam. 8:1-14). Solomon divided the nation into 12 districts, each of which would be responsible to support the court for one month out of the year (1 Kings 4:7-19,27-28). Other revenue for the king's court included royal property (1 Chron. 27:25-31; 2 Chron. 26:10; 32:27-29) and forced labor (2 Sam. 20:24; 1 Kings 4:6; 11:28). Solomon also received revenue from a road toll on trade routes through Israel (1 Kings 10:15), trade in horses and chariots (1 Kings 10:28-29), a merchant fleet (1 Kings 9:26-28), and possibly from copper mines.

Israel's faith included the confession that God was its ultimate King (Judg. 8:22). Because God was seen as King, some in Israel saw the desire for an earthly king as a turning away from God (1 Sam. 8:7; Hos. 8:4). The earthly king derived his authority from God as the Lord's anointed (1 Sam. 16:6; 2 Sam. 1:14) or the Lord's captain or prince (1 Sam. 9:16; 10:1; 13:14). Many of the psalms speak of God as King (e.g., Pss. 24; 93; 95-98). See Kingdom of God.

KINGDOM OF GOD

God's kingly rule or sovereignty. In the OT God is spoken of as ruling (e.g., Pss. 47:2; 103:19; Dan. 4:17,25-37). The kingdom of God was the central image in Jesus' preaching (Mark 1:14-15).

In His parables Jesus said the Kingdom is like a farmer (Matt. 13:24), a seed (Matt. 13:31), yeast (Matt. 13:33), a treasure (Matt. 13:44), a pearl merchant (Matt. 13:45), a fishnet (Matt. 13:47), an employer (Matt. 20:1), a king inviting people to a marriage feast (Matt. 22:2), and ten young women (Matt. 25:1). He spoke also of the glad tidings of the Kingdom (Luke 8:1) and of the mystery of the kingdom of God (Mark 4:11). The kingdom of God is God's ruling, the sovereign reign of God.

The kingdom of God looks unimpressive, but it is going to grow into something tremendous like a tiny mustard seed that grows into a bush large enough to provide shelter for God's creatures (Mark 4:30-32).

In one sense, the Kingdom will not come until some unspecified time in the future (see, for example, Matt. 25:1-46). Jesus also said that there is a sense in which the kingdom of God had come in His own time: "The time is fulfilled, and the kingdom of God is at hand"(Mark 1:15); "But if I with the finger of God cast out devils, no doubt the kingdom of God is come upon you"(Luke 11:20).

People can make the Kingdom their priority and seek it ahead of everything else (Matt. 6:33). It is a pearl of such value that they should sell everything they have to be able to purchase it (Matt. 13:44-46). They can repent and believe the good news of the Kingdom (Mark 1:14-15) and so enter the Kingdom like little children (Mark 10:14). They can pray for the rule of God to come soon (Matt. 6:10; compare 1 Cor. 16:22). They can be ready when the Kingdom does come (Matt. 25:1-46).

Jesus regularly invited people to enter the kingdom of God, that is, to open their lives to the ruling of God. He invited everyone. He spoke of God sending His servants out to highways and hedges to urge people to come in to the Kingdom. He said that it is more difficult for the rich to enter the Kingdom than for a camel to go through the eye of a needle (Matt. 19:24). Tax-collectors and prostitutes would go into the Kingdom before moral and religious people (Matt. 21:31).

The apostles began to speak of eternal life, salvation, forgiveness, and other themes. To speak of salvation is to speak of the Kingdom. The kingdom of God is righteousness and peace and joy in the Holy Spirit (Rom. 14:17).

KINGS, BOOKS OF

Eleventh and twelfth books of Christian Bible interpreting God's direction of the kingdoms of Israel and Judah. Originally, 1 and 2 Kings were one book. The first record of the division into two parts is in the Septuagint where 1 and 2 Kings were known as 3 and 4 Kings (1 and 2 Samuel were known as 1 and 2 Kings). The Books of Kings do not indicate who the author was.

Using the principles of Deuteronomy, the author sought to explain why the nation divided after the reign of Solomon and why both nations eventually fell victim to foreign invaders. Deuteronomy 28:1-14 describes the blessings that will belong to Israel if they obey God's commandments. This word of God's blessing was fulfilled in Israel's history. Deuteronomy 28:15-68 describes in graphic detail what would happen to Israel should they turn from obeying the commandment of the Lord. God

faithfully fulfilled the word of warning as well. When the people of Israel departed from God's commandment, they suffered defeat, reduction of their population, severe suffering, and exile.

The Northern Kingdom of Israel suffered defeat and exile at the hands of the Assyrians in 722 B.C. (2 Kings 17:1-41). Judah suffered a similar fate at the hands of the Babylonians between 597 and 586 B.C. (2 Kings 24:1-25:21). God's prophets continually proclaimed God's promises to the people: Elijah (1 Kings 17-19; 21; 2 Kings 1), Elisha (2 Kings 2:1-25; 3:9-20; 4:1-8:15; 9:1-3; 13:14-21), Isaiah (2 Kings 19:1-20:19) and others. The people were without excuse. They had heard God's commandment to be faithful and His warnings of the accompanying blessings and curses.

The author was especially concerned with the commands that only God be worshiped and that God be worshiped in Jerusalem alone (Deut. 12-13). The reigns of the kings of Judah and Israel were evaluated on the basis of their adherence to these two commands. In Judah, only Hezekiah (2 Kings 18:3-7) and Josiah (2 Kings 22:2) were praised without reservation because they adhered to these two principles. Asa (1 Kings 15:11-14), Jehoshaphat (1 Kings 22:41-43), Jehoash (2 Kings 12:2-3), Azariah (2 Kings 15:3-4), and Jotham (2 Kings 15:34-35) were praised as having done what was right in the eyes of the Lord, but their praise is qualified with the addition that they allowed the worship of foreign gods to continue in Judah. All other kings of Judah are condemned as having done what was evil in the sight of the Lord. Even Solomon was criticized. Although Solomon built the temple where God was worshiped, he departed from the command of the Lord and worshiped foreign gods. This sin led to the empire built by David being split in two at the death of Solomon (1 Kings 11:1-12:25; see 3:2-3).

The most notorious king of Judah was Manasseh (2 Kings 21:1-18). He negated the reforms of his father, Hezekiah, and actively promoted the worship of foreign gods. He sacrificed his own son, practiced soothsaying or augury, and dealt with mediums and wizards. Because of Manasseh's sins Judah's history ended (2 Kings 21:12-15; 23:26-27; 24:1-7; compare 17:19-20).

All the kings of Israel are condemned as having done what was evil in the sight of the Lord. Most of the responsibility is placed on Jeroboam, the first king of Israel (2 Kings 17:21-23; see 1 Kings 15:30) who instituted worship in a place other than Jerusalem, (1 Kings 12:26-29) and made two golden calves for the people to worship (1 Kings 12:28). Subsequent kings of Israel are condemned because they did not depart from the sins of Jeroboam (1 Kings 15:34; 16:2,19,26,31; 22:52; 2 Kings 3:3; 10:29,31; 13:2,6,11; 14:24; 15:9,18,24).

The writer saw that Israel could see in Israel's distress evidence of God's continual desire that Israel turn from their sins and return to God as God's people. The blessings of Deut. 28:1-14 could still be theirs. This hope is illustrated in 2 Kings 25:27-30 with the release of Jehoiachin from prison. Perhaps the writer was encouraging the exiles with the possibility that God would bless them again and raise Israel above all peoples (Deut. 28:1) just as Jehoiachin was given preference above other prisoners in captivity (2 Kings 25:28).

KINSMAN

Usually refers to blood relative based on Israel's tribal nature. The most important relationship was that of the father to the oldest son. Certain obligations were laid on the kinsman. In the case of an untimely death of a husband without a son, the law of levirate marriage becomes operative —that is, the husband's brother was obligated to raise up a male descendant for his deceased brother and thus perpetuate the deceased's name and inheritance. The living brother was the dead brother's *goel*—his

redeemer (Gen. 38:8; Deut. 25:5-10; Ruth 3:9-12).

The kinsman was also the blood avenger. A wrong done to a single member of the family was considered a crime against the entire tribe or clan. The clan had an obligation, therefore, to punish the wrongdoer. In the case of a murder committed, the kinsman should seek vengeance. See *Avenger*.

The kinsman was also responsible to redeem the estate which his nearest relative might have sold because of poverty (Lev. 25:25; Ruth 4:4). It was the kinsman's responsibility also to ransom a kinsman who may have sold himself (Lev. 25:47-48).

The Book of Ruth is the most striking example of a kinsman who used his power and Jewish law to redeem. Boaz demonstrated one of the duties of the kinsman— that of marrying the widow of a deceased kinsman. See *Cities of Refuge; Redeem*.

KIR (*wall*)

(1) Moabite city mentioned in connection with Ar (Isa. 15:1); may be same as Kir-Hareseth, ancient capital of Moab along with Ar; Kerak about 17 miles south of the Arnon and 11 miles east of the Dead Sea.

(2) Mesopotamian city east of the lower Tigris River on main road from Elam (Persia) to Babylon; capital of Babylonian province of Gutium (605–539 B.C.), whose governor joined Cyrus the Persian in overthrowing Babylonian Empire in 539 B.C. See 2 Kings 16:9; Isa. 22:6; Amos 1:5; 9:7.

KIR-HARESETH (*city of pottery*)

Known by various names in various texts and versions of OT: "Kir-Hareseth" (2 Kings 3:25; Isa. 16:7), "Kir-Haraseth" (2 Kings 3:25, KJV), "Kir-Heres" (Isa. 16:11; Jer. 48:31,36), and "Kirharesh" (Isa. 16:11, KJV); perhaps same as Kir of Moab (Isa. 15:1); Khirbet Karnak, about 50 miles southeast of Jerusalem and 11 miles east of Dead Sea. See *Kir 1*. See

2 Kings 3:4-27; Isa. 15:1; 16:7,11; Jer. 48:31,36.

KIRIATH (city) See Kiriath-Jearim.

KIRIATH-ARBA (city of Arba or city of four)

Ancient name for Hebron (Josh. 15:54). See Hebron.

KIRIATH-JEARIM (city of forests)

Border city of Dan, Benjamin, and Judah (Josh. 15:9,60; 18:14-15); Deir al-Azhar eight miles north of Jerusalem or Abu Gosh nine miles north of Jerusalem. See Judg. 18:12; 1 Sam. 6:21–7:2; 2 Sam. 6:1-8; Jer. 26:20-24.

KIRIATH-SANNAH (perhaps city of bronze) (Josh. 15:15-16,49). See Debir (2).

KIRIATH-SEPHER (city of book) See Debir (2).

KIRIATHAIM (double city or two cities)

(1) Levitical city and city of refuge in Naphtali (1 Chron. 6:76; KJV has "Kirjathaim"). See Cities of Refuge.

(2) City in Reuben (Gen. 14:5; Num. 32:37; Josh. 13:19; Jer. 48:1,23; Ezek. 25:9).

KISH (perhaps gift)

Five OT men including: Father of Saul (1 Sam. 9:2); man Benjaminite from Gibeah (1 Sam. 9:1-3,21; 2 Sam. 21:14; 1 Chron. 8:33).

KISHON (curving, winding)

Small river that flows from east to west through Valley of Jezreel. In spring, it achieves a width of about 65 feet with a length of 23 miles. See Judg. 4:7,13; 5:21; 1 Kings 18:40; Ps. 83:9.

KISS

Touching of lips to another person's lips, cheeks, shoulders, hands, or feet as a gesture of friendship, acceptance, respect, and reverence. The location of the kiss carried different meanings as Jesus made clear in the episode of the woman kissing His feet (Luke 7:36-50). With the exception of three occurrences (Prov. 7:13; Song of Sol. 1:2; 8:1), the term is used without any erotic overtones.

The holy kiss (1 Thess. 5:26; 1 Cor. 16:20; 2 Cor. 13:12; Rom. 16:16) was widely practiced among the early Christians as a manner of greeting, a sign of acceptance, and an impartation of blessing. The substitute kiss involved kissing the hand and waving it in the direction of the object to be kissed (Job 31:27).

KITTIM

Tribal name for island of Cyprus, sometimes spelled Chittim; derived from Kition, a city-state on the southeastern side of the island. The writer of Daniel understood it to be a part of the Roman Empire (11:30) used to threaten Antiochus Epiphanes. See Cyprus.

KNEAD, KNEADING BOWL

Process of making bread dough by mixing flour, water, and oil along with a piece of the previous day's dough with the hands in a kneading bowl or trough. The mixture was allowed to stand in the bowl to rise and ferment (Ex. 12:34). Kneading the dough was usually the work of the woman (Gen. 18:6; 1 Sam. 28:24) but was performed on occasion by men (Hos. 7:4). The bowls could be made of wood, earthenware, or bronze and were the objects of either God's blessing or curse (Deut. 28:5,17; see Ex. 8:3).

KNEEL

Common posture when requesting a blessing from one believed able to bestow the blessing; comes from same root as word for "bless." Kneeling is also considered a sign of reverence, obedience, or respect. Kneeling was the posture of prayer (Dan. 6:10; Acts 7:60; 9:40; 20:36; Eph. 3:14; compare 1 Kings 18:42), acknowledging a superior (2 Kings 1:13; Matt. 17:14; 27:29; Mark 1:40; 10:17; Luke 5:8), or worship of God (1 Kings 8:54), Jesus

(Phil. 2:10), or idols (1 Kings 19:18; Isa. 66:3 where blessing an idol refers to kneeling before an idol). See *Blessing and Cursing.*

KNIFE

Small instrument made of flint, copper, bronze, or iron used mainly for domestic purposes. Joshua was ordered to make flint knives for the circumcision of Israelite males (Josh. 5:2-3), probably reflecting a very ancient practice of circumcision (compare Gen. 17:11; see *Circumcision*). Knives were used most commonly for killing and skinning animals and for killing sacrificial animals (see Lev. 7:2; 8:15,20,25; 9:8-15; 1 Sam. 9:24).

KNOWLEDGE

Intellectual understanding; personal experience; emotion; personal relationship, attributed both to God and to human beings (including sexual intercourse, Gen. 4:1). God knows all things (Job 21:22; Ps. 139:1-18); His understanding is beyond measure (Ps. 147:5; compare Gen. 30:22; Job 31:4; Pss. 44:21; 94:11; Zech. 13:1; Luke 1:33). God knowing a person can mean God choosing a person for His purposes (Jer. 1:5; Amos 3:2; Gal. 4:9).

Knowledge of God is the greatest knowledge (Prov. 9:10) and the chief duty of humankind (Hos. 6:6). Israelites knew God through what He did for His people (Ex. 9:29; Lev. 23:43; Deut. 4:32-39; Pss. 9:10; 59:13; 78:16; Hos. 2:19-20). This knowledge includes experiencing the reality of God in one's life (compare Phil. 3:10) and living one's life in a manner that shows a respect for the power and majesty of God (compare Jer. 22:15-16). One knows God finally through a knowledge of Jesus Christ (John 8:19; Col. 2:2-3). Knowledge gives direction, conviction, and assurance to faith (2 Cor. 4:14). Knowledge is a spiritual gift (1 Cor. 12:8) that can grow, increase, be filled, and abound (Phil. 1:9; Col. 1:9-10; 2 Cor. 8:7). It consists in having a better understanding of God's will in the ethical sense (Col. 1:9-10; Phil. 1:9), of knowing that God desires to save people (Eph. 1:8-9), and of having a deeper insight into God's will given in Christ (Eph. 1:17; 3:18-19).

Knowledge can be a divisive factor in churches when some Christians claim to be more spiritual because of their knowledge of spiritual matters (Rom. 14:1–15:6; 1 Cor. 8:1-13). Knowledge exercised by the "strong" in faith can cause the "weak" in faith to go against their Christian conscience and lead to their spiritual ruin. Love is more important than knowledge (1 Cor. 13), yet knowledge is still a gift, necessary for Christian teaching (1 Cor. 14:6) and for Christian growth toward a mature faith (1 Cor. 8:7; 2 Pet. 1:5-6; 3:18).

Jesus and the Father have a mutual knowledge (John 10:14-15), and Jesus' knowledge of God is perfect (John 3:11; 4:22; 7:28-29). Jesus brings to lost humankind the knowledge of God, which is necessary for salvation (John 7:28-29; 8:19) but which humankind has distorted through sin (John 1:10). God's knowledge of Jesus consists of giving Jesus His mission and the power to perform it (John 10:18). Jesus' knowledge of the Father consists of His hearing God's word and obediently expressing it to the world. Full knowledge is possible only after Jesus' glorification, since the disciples sometimes failed to understand Jesus (John 4:32; 10:6; 12:16). Knowledge is expressed in Christian witness that may evoke belief in Jesus (John 1:7; 4:39; 12:17-18) and in love (John 17:26).

KOA

Nation God will bring against Israel (Ezek. 23:23); not identified satisfactorily. Some identify Koa with Guti people of Babylon, but this is disputed.

KOHATH, KOHATHITES

Second son of Levi (Gen. 46:11; Ex. 6:16-20); head of Kohathite branch of the Levitical priesthood (Num. 3:19,29-31; 4:15,17-20; 7:9; 26:59; Josh.

21:4-5,9-26; 1 Sam. 5–6; 2 Sam. 6:6-11; 1 Chron. 6:1-3,16,18,33,38,54-61,66-70; 9:32; 15:5; 23:6,12-13,18-20; 26:23; 2 Chron. 20:19; 29:12; 34:12).

KOHELETH

English transliteration of Hebrew title (Eccl. 1:1) of Ecclesiastes (also spelled Qoheleth) meaning: "preacher" (KJV, RSV, NASB), "teacher" (NIV, NRSV), "speaker" (REB), or "philosopher" (TEV).

KOPH

Nineteenth letter of Hebrew alphabet.

KOR See *Weights and Measures.*

KORAH *(bald)*

Five OT men including:

(1) Son of Esau (Gen. 36:5,14; 1 Chron. 1:35) who became chief of a clan of Edom (Gen. 36:18).

(2) Priestly leader of rebellion against Moses and Aaron in wilderness of Paran (Num. 16) contending entire congregation was sanctified and therefore qualified for priestly functions. God punished them with death.

(3) Head of one of two most prominent groups of temple singers (Ex. 6:21; 1 Chron. 6:22,37; 9:19,31; 26:1,19; compare 1 Chron. 6:33-48; 2 Chron. 20:19; Pss. 42; 44–49; 84–85; 87–88).

LABAN (*white* or *moon god*)

Rebekah's brother and father of Leah and Rachel (Gen. 29:16; see chs. 24; 29–31) from Nahor near Haran; directly responsible for the betrothal of Rebekah to Isaac; known for deceiving Jacob. See *Jacob.*

LACHISH (*obstinate*)

City in Shephelah ("lowlands") southwest of Jerusalem; belonged to Judah (Josh. 15:39) tell ed-Duweir, site more recently called tel Lachish; mentioned in ancient Egyptian, Assyrian, and Babylonian records. Amarna letters (about 1400 B.C.) show it was important Canaanite city. Hebrew army under Joshua defeated king of Lachish (Josh. 10:5, 23,32-33). See 2 Chron. 11:9; 2 Kings 14:19; 2 Chron. 25:27. Sennacherib of Assyria besieged and conquered Lachish in 701 B.C. (2 Kings 18; 2 Chron. 32; Isa. 36). See Jer. 34:7; Neh. 11:30. Assyrian records amplify biblical account of Sennacherib's conquest.

The "Lachish Letters"—a group of messages in ancient Hebrew inscribed with ink on pottery sherds dating about 590 B.C. — provide important linguistic and historical information about this period.

LAMB OF GOD

Title John the Baptist gave Jesus as One who takes away sin of the world (John 1:29,36); could be understood from Aramaic as "servant of God." John's testimony probably should be seen as a combination of both concepts (see Acts 8:32-35; compare Isa. 53:7,10,12). The law for guilt offerings (Lev. 5:1–6:7) prescribed a lamb for atonement to be made before the Lord. Peter stressed this sacrificial motif (1 Pet. 1:18). John's identification might also entail a reference to Jesus as the scapegoat sent into the wilderness on the Day of Atonement to bear the iniquities of the Israelites (Lev. 16) or to the Passover lamb (Ex. 12; compare 1 Cor. 5:7). John 1:29,

therefore, signifies the substitutionary, sacrificial suffering and death of Jesus, the Servant of God, by which redemption and forgiveness of sin are accomplished. See *Atonement; Christ, Christology; Passover; Redeem, Redemption, Redeemer; Sacrifice and Offering; Servant of the Lord.*

LAMECH (*powerful*)

Son of Methuselah and father of Noah (Gen. 4:18; 5:25,29); his sons are credited with rise of nomadic way of life, music, and metalworking. Lamech is blamed with beginning polygamy (or bigamy) and increase of sinful pride in the earth. The Song of Lamech (Gen. 4:23-24) is an ancient poem supporting unlimited revenge.

LAMED

Twelfth letter of Hebrew alphabet used as heading for Ps. 119:89-96. Each verse in this section begins with *lamed.*

LAMENT See *Grief and Mourning; Psalms, Book of.*

LAMENTATIONS, BOOK OF

Twenty-fifth book of Bible preserving five elegies used in mourning the fall of Jerusalem in 587 B.C. The first four chapters are in acrostic form, where successive verses begin with successive letters of the Hebrew alphabet with slight variations.

An ancient tradition in the Septuagint (about 250 B.C.) claims Jeremiah as author. Favoring authorship by Jeremiah are the antiquity of the tradition, similarity in tone between Lamentations and portions of Jeremiah's book (Jer. 8–9; 14–15), and a similar perspective in Lamentations and Jeremiah as to the cause of the fall of Jerusalem (for example, Lam. 1:2-18; 2:14; 4:13-17; Jer. 2:18; 14:7; 16:10-12; 23:11-40; 37:5-10).

Factors against Jeremianic authorship are differences in phraseology between the two books and differences in viewpoints on several issues. Lamentations 1:21-22 and 3:59-66 appear to be incongruent with Jeremiah's conviction that the Babylonians were functioning as God's instrument of judgment (Jer. 20:4-5). Lamentations 4:17 suggests that the author was expecting help from the Egyptians, a perspective that Jeremiah strongly opposed (Jer. 37:5-10). The view of Zedekiah, Judah's last king, in Lam. 4:20 is also quite different from that found regarding him in Jer. 24:8-10. The author was surely an eyewitness of the fall of Jerusalem.

Lamentations 1 mourns the misery resulting from the destruction of Jerusalem and explains that the desolation was God's judgment for the nation's sin. Lamentations 2 laments the ruin wrought by divine anger and calls the people to prayer. Lamentations 3 extends mourning over Jerusalem's destruction and calls for repentance because God's steadfast love gives reason to hope that He will extend mercy in the future. Lamentations 4 vividly pictures the horrors of the siege and fall of Jerusalem and places part of the blame for the judgment on the immoral prophets and priests of the city. Lamentations 5 summarizes the calamitous situation and closes with a prayer for restoration.

Lamentations served the Judeans as an expression of their grief, an explanation for the destruction, and a call for repentance and hope. The book warns modern readers that an immoral nation stands in danger of God's awesome judgment and that the only hope for survival is submission to God.

LAMPS, LIGHTING, LAMPSTAND

System and articles used to illuminate homes in biblical times. Archaeological excavations have provided numerous examples of these lighting implements dating from before Abraham to after Christ. Lamps of OT period were made exclusively of pottery with an open-bowl design using a pinched spout to support the wick.

Wicks were made generally of twisted flax (Isa. 42:3). Lamps burned olive oil (Ex. 25:6), though in later times oil from nuts, fish, and other sources were used. Lamps from the Bronze Age to the Hellenistic times were made on the pottery wheel, after which molds were made for the enclosed forms of the Greek and Roman periods (about 500 B.C. onward). For outdoor lighting, the torch (KJV, lantern) was used (Judg. 7:16; John 18:3).

A golden lampstand with three branches extending from either side of the central tier was placed in the tabernacle (Ex. 25:31-40). Each branch may have had a seven-spouted lamp (Zech. 4:2), as do some individual lamps found in Palestine. This seven-branched candelabra (menorah), supporting seven lamps, continued in prominence through the first and second temple periods, and later became symbolic of the nation of Israel. Surrounding nations also employed multitiered and multilegged lamps and lampstands.

Lamps (lights) depicted life in abundance, divine presence, or life's direction versus death in darkness (compare Ps. 119:105; 1 John 1:5 with Job 18:5; Prov. 13:9). Jesus is depicted as the light of the world (John 1:4-5,7-9; 3:19; 8:12; 9:5; 11:9-10; 12:35-36,46). Jesus' disciples are also described as the light of the world (Matt. 5:14-16).

LANDMARK

Pillar or heap of stones serving as a boundary marker (Gen. 31:51-52). Many ancient law codes (Babylonian, Egyptian, Greek, Roman) prohibited the removal of a landmark (Deut. 19:14; compare 27:17; Job 24:2; Prov. 22:28; 23:10). Hosea 5:10 condemns the ruthless rulers of Judah as like those who remove landmarks, that is, those who have no regard for justice or for the traditional law. Moving the landmark meant changing the traditional land allotments (compare Josh. 13–19) and cheating a poor landowner of what little land he owned.

LANGUAGES OF THE BIBLE

Hebrew; Aramaic; Greek. The OT was first written in Hebrew, with the exceptions of much of Ezra 4–7 and Dan. 2:4b–7:28, which appear in Aramaic. The NT was written in Greek, though Jesus and the early believers may have spoken Aramaic.

Hebrew is a Semitic language related to Phoenician and the dialects of ancient Canaan. Importance rests on the verb, which generally comes first in the sentence.

Aramaic is akin to Hebrew and shares a considerable vocabulary with it. It began as the language of Syria and was gradually adopted as the language of international communication. After about 600 B.C., it replaced Hebrew as the spoken language of Palestine. Hebrew then continued as the religious language of the Jews, but the Aramaic alphabet was borrowed for writing it.

Greek belongs to the Indo-European language group. It spread throughout the Mediterranean world after about 335 B.C. with Alexander's conquests. The NT is written in a dialect called *koine* ("common"), the dialect of the common person. New Testament Greek is heavily infused with Semitic thought modes, and many Aramaic words are found rendered with Greek letters (for example, *talitha cumi*, Mark 5:41; *ephphatha*, Mark 7:34; *Eli, Eli, lama sabachthani*, Mark 15:34; *marana-tha*, 1 Cor. 16:22). Some Latin appears: *"kenturion"* (centurion) and *"denarion"* (denarius). Greek's accurateness of expression and widespread usage made it the ideal tongue for the early communication of the gospel.

LAODICEA, LAODICEAN

City in southwest Asia Minor on an ancient highway running from Ephesus to Syria ten miles west of Colossae and six miles south of Hierapolis. See *Asia Minor, Cities of.*

LAODICEANS, EPISTLE TO THE

A short letter claiming Paul as its author; doubtless composed to fill gap suggested by Col. 4:16. The date of writing is unknown. About one half of the Latin manuscripts of the Pauline Epistles produced between 500 and 1600 contain the Epistle to the Laodiceans.

LAPIDOTH, LAPPIDOTH
(lightnings)

Deborah's husband (Judg. 4:4).

LASEA

City on south coast of Crete (Acts 27:8).

LASHA

A point on the original border of Canaan (Gen. 10:19).

LASHARON *(belonging to Sharon)*

Town whose king Joshua killed in conquering Canaan (Josh. 12:18). Sharon is plain in which the preceding town Aphek is located. Original text may have read, "Aphek in Sharon." See *Aphek.*

LAST SUPPER   See *Lord's Supper; Ordinances.*

LATIN

Language of ancient Italy and the Roman Empire; used in inscription over Christ's cross (John 19:20) and in Vulgate. See *Bible, Texts and Versions.*

LAW, TEN COMMANDMENTS, TORAH

Revelation of will of God in OT and later elaboration on law referred to as "traditions of the elders" in NT (Matt. 15:2; Mark 7:5; Gal. 1:14). *Law* may be used for a commandment, a word, a decree, a judgment, a custom, or a prohibition. The first five books of the Bible (the Pentateuch) are known as books of the law (Hebrew Torah, teaching) because they are based on the Commandments that God revealed to Moses.

The covenant agreement between God and His people at Mount Sinai provided the foundation for all of Israel's laws. They were to obey God's laws because of what He had done for them in saving them from Egypt (Ex. 20:2). The laws cover all areas of community life. The Torah is a gift of God to His people. Obeying the Torah would result in His blessing (Ex. 19:5-6) and provide for the health and wholeness of the covenant community. The Ten Commandments are a summary of the law (Ex. 20:2-17; Deut. 5:6-21). By NT times, *torah* meant not only the OT Scriptures (the written law), but also the oral law (unwritten law) of Israel as well.

Two kinds of laws can be found in the OT. Broad categorical laws such as the Ten Commandments set forth general principles for life in a covenant community with God. They do not specify how they are to be enforced or what penalties are to be invoked.

Case laws often begin with an "if" or a "when" and usually deal with very specific situations. Many times they indicate a punishment for breaking the law (Ex. 21:2-4; 22:1-2,4-5,25).

The Ten Commandments are prohibitions (except for Commandments 4 and 5 in Ex. 20:8-11,12). They define negatively the heart of the covenant relationship between God and Israel. The first four Commandments are related to one's relationship with God. The next six have to do with human relationships. Being rightly related to God compels one toward right relationships to one's neighbors.

On several occasions Jesus set His own teachings over against those of the elders (Matt. 5:21-6:48). The Pharisees accused Jesus and His disciples of not following the law with regard to "unclean" things (Matt. 15:1-20) and of eating with tax-gatherers and sinners (Matt. 9:11). Jesus' greatest conflict came because He rejected their interpretation of the sabbath law and said that the Son of man is Lord of the sabbath (Matt. 12:8) and that the sabbath was made for man and not man for the sabbath (Mark 2:27).

Jesus inaugurated a new era. Jesus claimed not to have come to destroy the law, but to fulfill it (Matt. 5:17-20). Law would no longer be the guiding principle for God's Kingdom (Luke 16:16). Jesus moved the understanding of the law from its external, legalistic meaning to its spiritual one (Matt. 5:21-22,27-28). Jesus summed up the whole law and the teaching of the prophets with two great principles of love for God and neighbor (Matt. 22:36-40; compare Rom. 13:8; Gal. 5:13). Such love can be seen in the life, death, and resurrection of our Lord. Only with the aid of the Spirit of God can we meet the requirement to love that fulfills the law (Gal. 5:16; Rom. 8).

Paul had a lifelong struggle with the law. By the term "law," Paul meant the law of God as contained in the OT. He also spoke of a kind of natural law that existed in human beings (Rom. 7:23,25). The "law of sin" meant conduct determined by sin. Paul also used law in this sense when he referred to the "law of faith"—that is, conduct determined by faith in God (Rom. 3:27-28). Paul recognized that the law had been given for a good purpose (Rom. 7:12,14; 1 Tim. 1:8). The demands of the law pointed out the sin of human beings (Rom. 7:7). Because of humanity's sinfulness, the law became a curse instead of a blessing (Gal. 3:10-13).

Paul believed the law could not save (Gal. 3:11; Rom. 3:20). Christ freed us from the requirements of the law by His death and resurrection (Rom. 8:3-4). Therefore, Christ has become the end of the law for Christians (Rom. 10:4), and it is faith that saves and not law (Eph. 2:8-9). The law remains the revelation of God, and helps us understand the nature of our life in Christ (Rom. 8:3; 13:8-10; Gal. 3:24).

LAWYER

Authoritative interpreter of the Mosaic law. The lawyers or scribes rejected God's purpose for themselves by refusing John's baptism (Luke 7:30); they burdened others without offering any relief (11:45-46); they not only refused God's offer of salvation but hindered others from accepting it (11:52); they refused to answer Jesus' question concerning the legality of sabbath healing (14:3). Lawyer is used in the general sense of a jurist in Titus 3:13.

LAYING ON OF HANDS

Ritual act wherein hands are placed on a person or animal in order to establish some spiritual communion; primarily associated with sacrifices (Lev. 1:4; 3:2-13; 4:4-33; 8:14, 18, 22; 16:21). To lay hands on the sacrificial animal was a means of transferring one's iniquity to the animal (Lev. 16:22). Elders (Lev. 4:15), high priest (Lev. 16:21) or the king and princes (2 Chron. 29:20-24) acted as the people's representatives. (See Num. 8:10.) The sin of blasphemy was viewed as so severe that all who overheard one cursing the name of the Lord laid their hands on his head prior to stoning him to death (Lev. 24:14-16).

Laying on of hands had other meanings: blessing (Gen. 48:13-20; Mark 10:16; Matt. 19:13-15; compare God's act, Ps. 139:5); legal arbitration (Job 9:33); commissioning (Num. 27:18-23; Deut. 34:9; compare Acts 6; 13:3); symbolic prophetic act (2 Kings 13:16), and an act of arrest, capture, or violence (Gen. 27:22; Ex. 22:11; 2 Chron. 23:15; Esther 2:21; Matt. 26:50; Mark 14:46; Luke 21:12; John 7:44; Acts 4:3; 12:1). Miraculous healing accompanied the laying on of hands (Mark 5:23; 6:5; 8:23-25; 16:18; Luke 4:40; 13:11-13; Acts 9:12-17; 28:8).

Peter and John laid hands on baptized believers in Samaria so they might receive the Holy Spirit (Acts 8:14-19; compare 19:6). Timothy received a spiritual gift by prophecy with the laying on of the hands of the assembly of elders (1 Tim. 4:14; compare 2 Tim. 1:6). Paul warned against laying hands on any one hastily (1 Tim. 5:22). Hebrews classified laying on of hands among the elementary teachings that persons of maturity must leave behind (Heb. 6:2).

LAZARUS

(1) A principal character in parable Jesus told to warn the selfish rich that justice eventually will be done (Luke 16:19-31).

(2) Personal friend of Jesus and brother of Mary and Martha (John 11:1-3). Jesus raised him from the dead after he had been in the tomb for four days to show the glory of God.

LEAH (wild cow or gazelle)

Older daughter of Laban (Gen. 29:16) and Jacob's first wife through Laban's trickery seeking to preserve custom of elder marrying first.

LEATHER

Animal skins tanned and prepared for human use (2 Kings 1:8; Matt. 3:4; Mark 1:6). Leather shoes symbolize God's lavish care for His beloved bride Jerusalem (Ezek. 16:10). See Skins.

LEAVEN

Small portion of fermented dough used to ferment other dough; often symbolized corruptive influence; used in common daily bread. Such bread was acceptable as wave offerings for the priests and as loaves to accompany the peace offerings (Lev. 2:11-13; 23:17). Bread made with leaven or honey was never to be used in offerings burned on the altar (Lev. 2:11-12). Unleavened bread was also prepared in times of haste (Ex. 12:39) and was required for the Feast of Unleavened Bread celebrated in conjunction with the Passover festival (Lev. 23:4-8). This unleavened bread, or bread of affliction, reminded Israel of their hasty departure from Egypt and warned them against corruptive influences (Ex. 12:14-20).

Jesus warned His disciples against the leaven of the Pharisees, their teaching and hypocrisy (Matt. 16:5-12; Luke 12:1). Paul urged the Corinthians to remove wickedness from their midst and become fresh dough, unleavened loaves of sincerity and truth (1 Cor. 5:6-13). Jesus also used leaven to illustrate the pervasive growth of the kingdom of God (Matt. 13:33).

LEB-KAMAI, LEB-QAMAI

Transliteration of Hebrew text; code name for Babylon (Jer. 51:1, NASB, NIV, NRSV, REB, RSV, "margin"; "Kambul," NEB). The athbash code replaces each letter of a word with a letter that stands as far from the end of the alphabet as the coded letter stands from the beginning (z=a; y=b). NASB margin, "the heart of those who are against me," arose when Masoretes added vowels to the code.

LEBANON (*white* or perhaps *white mountain*)

Small country at eastern end of Mediterranean Sea and western end of Asia; northern boundry of Palestine (Deut. 1:24; Josh. 1:4); controlled by Canaanites and Phoenicians; proverbially lush land, noted for its magnificent forests (Isa. 60:13), especially the "cedars of Lebanon" (Judg. 9:15; Isa. 2:13); world center of transportation and trade. Sandy beaches lie along its Mediterranean coast. Rugged mountains rise in the interior. The country itself is dominated by two mountain ridges parallel to the coast: Lebanon and Anti-Lebanon mountains about 6,230 feet high with summits reaching more than 11,000 feet.

Cedars and other woods of Lebanon were used in great abundance in David's palace and Solomon's temple and palace buildings (1 Kings 5:10-18; 7:2; compare Ezra 3:7). See *Phoenicia.*

LEES

Solid matter that settles out of wine during the fermentation process. Wine was allowed to remain on the lees to increase its strength and flavor. A banquet of wine on the well-refined lees symbolizes God's people enjoying the best God can offer (Isa. 25:6). Compare Jer. 48:11; Zeph. 1:12. To drink dregs or lees is to endure the bitterness of judgment or punishment (Ps. 75:8).

LEG

The upper leg or thigh was regarded as one of choicest parts of a sacrifice and was reserved for the priests (Lev. 7:32-34). The first term translated "leg" in Isa. 47:2 (KJV) is also translated "robe" (NRSV) or "shirt(s)" (NASB, NIV, REB).

LEGION

Roman military designation for units of best soldiers in army. Collection of demons (Mark 5:9,15; Luke 8:30); host of angels (Matt. 26:53). At different times in Rome's history, the legion numbered between 4,500 and 6,000 soldiers. It was composed of differently skilled men: spearmen, commandos, skirmish specialists, calvary, and reserves. Originally, one had to be a property owner and Roman citizen to belong, but these requirements were waived depending on the need for troops.

LEISURE TIME

The Bible usually speaks of "rest" in terms of cessation from toil, trouble and sin (e.g., Ex. 33:14; Isa. 32:18; Heb. 4:1-11). While at rest, persons occupy themselves by enjoying God and each other's company, a foretaste of the activity of heaven.

The Bible recognizes the need for regularly scheduled breaks from work. The weekly sabbath (Ex. 20:8-11) and several yearly festivals (Lev. 23:1-44; Deut. 16:1-17) were intended to focus on Israel's spiritual needs but also provided breaks from physical labor. The Mosaic law mandated a year-long honeymoon for newlyweds (Deut. 24:5; compare Luke 14:20). Jesus tried to find time to be by himself in order to rest and pray, but the press of the crowds often prevented him from doing so (Matt. 14:13; Mark 3:20; 6:31; John 11:54).

The Bible cautions against the misuse of leisure time which leads either to idleness (Prov. 19:15; 24:33-34; Eccl. 10:18; Amos 6:4-6; 1 Tim. 5:13), excessive partying (Isa. 5:11-12) or troublemaking (2 Chron. 13:7; Prov. 6:10-15).

LEMUEL (*devoted to God*)

King who received words of wisdom from his mother concerning wine, women, and the legal rights of the weak and poor (Prov. 31:1-9). See *Massa*; *Proverbs, Book of.*

LENT

Penitential period preceding Easter. Shortly after A.D. 100, many Christians fasted several days to prepare. See *Church Year.*

LEPROSY

Generic term applied to a variety of skin disorders from psoriasis to true leprosy. Even houses and garments could have "leprosy" and, thus, be unclean (Lev. 14:33-57). Jesus made a leper the hero of one of His parables (Luke 16:19-31). See *Diseases.*

LETTER

Written message sent as a means of communication between persons separated by distance (2 Sam. 11:14-15; 1 Kings 21:8-11; 2 Kings 5:5-6; 10:1-7; 19:8-14; 20:12; 2 Chron. 30:1-6; Acts 9:1-2; 15:22-23; 22:5; compare Ezra 4:17; 5:7; Neh. 2; 6; Esther 3; 8-9; Acts 23:16-35; 28:21; 1 Cor. 16:3; 2 Cor. 3:1-2). Jeremiah 29 is a letter with words of exhortation and encouragement from a far-removed prophet.

Paul expanded his ministry by writing letters to places he had been and to places he hoped to visit. Paul's critics in Corinth accused him of being bolder in his letters than in his personal ministry. Paul denied the charge. He viewed his letters as consistent with what he would have said had he been there in person (2 Cor. 10:9-11). Most of Paul's letters were addressed to churches (note Col. 4:16). Even the letters addressed to individuals were designed to minister to churches. Philemon included the church in its greeting (Philem. 1-2). The Roman Empire had a postal service, but it did not include personal letters. Paul's letters, therefore, were carried by messengers (see Phil. 2:25; Col. 4:7-8). Second Peter 3:15-16 mentions the difficulty some people

had in understanding Paul's letters. Other NT letters include: 1, 2 Peter and Jude. James has a salutation but no other letter element. Hebrews ends like a letter. Clear letter forms appear in 2, 3 John but not so clearly in 1 John. Revelation was sent to churches of Asia (Rev. 1:4). Chapters 2–3 contain letters to these churches from the risen Lord.

LEVI (*a joining*)

(1) Third son of Jacob and Leah (Gen. 29:34); original ancestor of Israel's priests; characterized as savage and merciless, avenging the rape of his sister, Dinah, by annihilating the male population of an entire city (Gen. 34:25-31; compare 49:5-7; Ex. 32:28). See *Levites.*

(2) Two of Jesus' ancestors (Luke 3:24, 29).

(3) Tax collector in Capernaum who followed Jesus (Mark 2:14; also called Matthew (Matt. 9:9).

LEVIATHAN (*coiled one*)

Ancient sea creature created by, subject to (Ps. 104:24-30), and subdued by God (Job 3:8; 41:1-9; Ps. 74:14; Isa. 27:1); in primordial warfare with the gods; representative of chaos.

Apocalyptic literature depicts leviathan as throwing off his fetters at the end of the present age, only to be defeated in a final conflict with the divine. See *Apocalyptic.* Scripture used a name known to Canaanites, Hittites, and others, and removed fear connected with it, showing God easily controlled Leviathan, who thus offered no threat to God's people. See *Rahab.*

LEVITES

Lowest of three orders in Israel's priesthood. Originally, Israel's priests and temple personnel were to be drawn from the firstborn of every family in Israel (Ex. 13:11-15). Later, God chose the tribe of Levi to carry out this responsibility for Israel (Num. 3:11-13) because it was the only tribe that stood with Moses against the people who worshiped the golden calf (Ex. 32:25-29; Deut. 10:6-9). The Levites were not given a tribal inheritance in the Promised Land (God was their inheritance) but were placed in 48 Levitical cities throughout the land (Num. 18:20; 35:1-8; Josh. 13:14,33). The tithe of the rest of the nation was used to provide for the needs of the Levites (Num. 18:24-32; compare Deut. 12:12,18; 16:11,14).

LEVITICUS, BOOK OF (the Levitical book)

Third book of OT containing instructions for priests and worship. Exodus 28–29 recounts the Lord's instructions for ordaining Aaron and his sons as priests. This ordination takes place in Leviticus 8–9. One of the primary tasks of the priests was to offer sacrifice at the tabernacle. Leviticus lists five main types of sacrifice (1:3–6:7). See Sacrifice and Offering.

Leviticus 6–7 provides further instruction on sacrifice for the priests, and Leviticus 8–10 describes the beginning of sacrifice at the tabernacle. Leviticus 11–15 provides instruction on that which is clean and unclean. These chapters describe various causes of uncleanness, including improper diet, childbirth, and various skin diseases. Leviticus 11 presents dietary regulations, and Leviticus 12 describes uncleanness related to childbirth. Leviticus 13 gives instruction in determining uncleanness related to leprosy, and Leviticus 14 describes the way to cleanse leprosy. Leviticus 15 lists bodily discharges that cause one to be unclean. Leviticus 16 describes the ritual of the Day of Atonement, a way of removing the impact of sin and uncleanness. See Day of Atonement.

Leviticus 17–27 is the Holiness Code, named from frequent use of "You shall be holy; for I the Lord Your God am holy." See Holy. These chapters then give instruction in how ancient Israel was to live distinct from other people in the land as people of the holy God.

The NT uses Leviticus to speak of the atoning sacrifice of Christ.

LIBERTY, LIBERATION

Freedom from physical, political, and spiritual oppression. One of God's primary purposes for His people is to free them from physical oppression and hardship and to liberate them from spiritual bondage. Yahweh is the God who liberated the Israelites from their bondage in Egypt. God is the one who liberates people from bondage to sin through Jesus Christ. These purposes extend to all who are oppressed, not just those who call on His name (Luke 4:18-19). See Freedom.

LIBNAH (white or storax tree)

(1) Wilderness station east of the Jordan (Num. 33:20).

(2) Town in Shephelah of Judah that Joshua defeated (Josh. 10:29-30), allotted to Judah (Josh. 15:42), and separated as city for Levites (Josh. 21:13); perhaps tell Bornat just west of Lachish. It illustrated western border rebellion against King Joram of Judah (853–841 B.C.) just as Edom represented rebellion in the east (2 Kings 8:22). It lay on the invasion route to Jerusalem followed by Sennacherib about 701 B.C. (2 Kings 19:8). See 2 Kings 23:31; 24:18.

LIBYA, LIBYAN

Large land area between Egypt and Tunisia with northern border on Mediterranean Sea; by people inhabited referred to variously as "Chub" (Ezek. 30:5), "Put" (1 Chron. 1:8; Nah. 3:9), "Phut" (Gen. 10:6; Ezek. 27:10), and "Libyans" (Ezek. 30:5; 38:5; Acts 2:10). Pharaoh Shishak I (about 950 B.C.) is thought to have been a Libyan.

LIFE

Principle or force considered to underlie the distinctive quality of animate beings, both animals and humans (Gen. 1:20; 2:7; 7:15); much wider application than only to physical, bodily existence (Ex. 1:14; Pss. 17:14; 63:3; Jas. 4:14). What is living has movement; in death, all movement ceases. Living organisms grow and reproduce according to their kinds. Physical, bodily existence is subject to suffering, illness, toil, death, temptations, and sin (Pss. 89:47; 103:14-16; 104:23; John 11:1-4,17-44; Rom. 5:12-21; 6:21-23; 8:18; 1 Cor. 7:5; 10:13; 2 Cor. 1:5-7; 11:23-29; 1 Tim. 6:9; Heb. 9:27; Jas. 5:10).

Only God has life in the absolute sense. He is the living God (Deut. 5:26; Josh. 3:10; 1 Sam. 17:26; Matt. 16:16). All other life depends on God for its creation and maintenance (Gen. 2:7,19,21-22; Ps. 36:9; Acts 17:25; Rom. 4:17). God is spoken of as the God of life or as life giving (Num. 14:28; Deut. 32:40; Judg. 8:19; Ruth 3:13; 1 Sam. 14:39; 19:6; Jer. 5:2). In stark contrast to God, the idols are dead (Pss. 115:3-8; 135:15-18; Isa. 44:9-20; Jer. 10:8-10,14) as are those who depend on them for life (Pss. 115:8; 135:18).

No possibility of life exists when God withholds His breath or spirit (Job 34:14-15; Ps. 104:29). God is Lord of both life and death (2 Cor. 1:9; Jas. 4:15). Life is something that only God can give (Pss. 36:9; 66:9; 139:13-14) and that only God can sustain (Job 33:4; Ps. 119:116; Isa. 38:16). Every life is solely the possession of God. No one has a right to end a life (Ex. 20:13; Deut. 5:17; compare Gen. 4:10,19-24). Since life belongs to God, one must abstain from the consumption of blood, the vehicle of life (Gen. 9:4; Lev. 3:17; 17:10-14; Deut. 12:23-25). Even animal life is valued by God as is evidenced by the fact that animal's blood was sacred to God.

The Bible emphasizes quality of life. The person who finds wisdom is fortunate (Prov. 3:18, NRSV). Life is more than food (Deut. 8:3; Matt. 4:4; Luke 4:4) or possessions (Luke 12:15). Each person must live by God's Word (Matt. 4:4). Jesus healed people and raised some from the dead to relieve the harshness of life (compare Mark 5:23-45).

The proper response to life as the gift of God is to live life in service to God (Isa. 38:10-20) by obeying the law (Lev. 18:5), doing God's will (Matt. 6:10; 7:21), and feeding on God's Word (Deut. 6:1-9; 8:3; 32:46-47;

Matt. 4:4). All Christians are to make the Lord Jesus central and live so as to show that He is their purpose for living (Rom. 14:7-9; compare John 6:35,48; 10:10; 11:25; 14:6; 20:31; compare Pss. 42:8; 27:1; 66:9). The genuine life that comes from Jesus to those who obey God is true or eternal life. See *Eternal Life*.

LIFE, BOOK OF

Heavenly document (Ps. 139:16; Luke 10:20; Rev. 13:8) where God recorded names and deeds of righteous people, showing God's power to know His own.

LIFE, ORIGIN OF

The Bible teaches that all matter (John 1:3), including living matter, was created by God *ex nihilo* (out of nothing —Heb. 11:3) through a series of special, decisive acts, each introduced in Genesis 1 by the phrase "and God said" (Gen. 1:3,6,9,14,20,24,26; compare Ps. 148:5; Rev. 4:11). Plants and animals were created in self-reproducing "kinds" (Gen. 1:11-12,21,24). All of creation was God-directed and purposeful (Isa. 43:7; 45:18; Col. 1:16).

The Bible teaches the special creation of people (Gen. 1:26-28; 2:7; Matt. 19:4). God created people to bring glory to himself (Isa. 43:7; compare Col. 1:16), and made the earth to be their specially prepared home (Isa. 45:18). The psalmist stood in wonder at the intricate design of the human body and saw it as testimony of God's creative power (Ps. 139:13-15).

Each of the Bible's statements about creation is incompatible with the various theories of evolution.

LIFE SPAN

The life expectancy in industrialized Western countries closely approximates the natural life span of mankind according to Psalm 90:10: "the days of our years are threescore years and ten; and if by reason of strength they be fourscore years. . ." (compare 2 Sam. 19:32-35; Luke 2:36-37). While modern medicine, improved health care and a healthy diet can increase this natural limit somewhat, it is unreasonable to assume that people will, or should, live as long as the patriarchs of old.

With the exception of Enoch, who "walked with God, and he was not, for God took him"(Gen. 5:24), each of the antediluvian fathers lived in excess of 595 years (Gen. 5:3-31). The recorded life span of the descendants of Noah gradually decreased after the flood so that the patriarchs each lived only twice today's normal span (Gen. 25:7-8; 35:28-29; 47:28; 50:26). While many scholars accept these year totals as accurate, others calculate them downward based on known or suggested genealogical or mathematical formulae.

The Bible records many tragic instances of human life cut off prematurely (e.g., Gen. 4:8; 1 Sam. 31:2; 2 Chron. 35:23-25; Job 21:21; Ps. 39:5, 11; Luke 12:20). No one knows the day of their death (compare Gen. 27:2). Because the years pass so quickly, the psalmist pleaded, "teach us to number our days, that we may apply our hearts unto wisdom"(Ps. 90:12).

LIFE SUPPORT (ARTIFICIAL)

While the Bible does not speak directly to the issue of life support by artificial means, it does provide principles relevant to the time of one's death. These principles suggest that extreme measures to artificially prolong life encroach upon the prerogative of God to control life and death. For the same reason, any and all forms of euthanasia are contrary to the teaching of Scripture.

The Bible teaches that only God gives life, and that only God should take life away (Ex. 20:13; Job 1:21; compare Rom. 14:7-8). Human life is a sacred and precious gift because each person is created in the image of God (Gen. 1:26-27; Ps. 8:5). The writers of the OT voiced a strong preference for life over death (Deut. 30:19), even in the face of crushing pain and defeat (Job 2:9-10).

Yet there comes a God-appointed time for everyone to die (Eccl. 3:2; Heb. 9:27). Although Christians value

life highly, they need not fear death (1 Cor. 15:54-55; Heb. 2:14-15; compare 2 Cor. 5:8). The apostle Paul, who was torn between life on earth and eternal life in heaven, was willing to follow either path that God desired for him (Phil. 1:19-26).

LIGHT, LIGHT OF THE WORLD

That which penetrates and dispels darkness. God created light (Gen. 1:3). God Himself is light (Ps. 27:1; 104:2; compare John 8:12). God is the ultimate source of all knowing and understanding (Ps. 119:105). People love darkness better than light, because their deeds are evil (John 3:19). The character of light is to reveal and to provide understanding and purity, while darkness is designed to obscure, to deceive, and to harbor impurity.

Jesus, the God-man, is the source of all light (John 8:12). His disciples become reflectors in a darkened world, transmitting through their lives the true light of the eternal Son of God (Matt. 5:14). See *Lamps, Lighting, Lampstand.*

LIGHTNING

Flash of light resulting from a discharge of static electricity in the atmosphere; always associated with God, maker of lightning and thunder (Job 28:26; Jer. 10:13) which reveal God's power and majesty (Pss. 77:18; 97:4; Rev. 4:5; 11:19). Lightning and thunder frequently accompany a revelation of God (Ex. 19:16; 20:18; Ezek. 1:13-14; Jesus: Matt. 24:26-27). Lightning appears as God's weapon where God is portrayed as a warrior ("arrows": 2 Sam. 22:15; Pss. 18:14; 77:17; 144:6;"fire": Ps. 97:3; Job 36:32; compare Rev. 8:5; 16:18).

LIME

White, caustic solid consisting primarily of calcium oxide obtained by heating limestone or shells to a high temperature; used as a plaster when mixed with water (Deut. 27:2,4). Burning someone's bones to lime amounts to complete annihilation

(Isa. 33:12); an especially heinous crime (Amos 2:1).

LINE

(1) Tool used for measuring length or distance (1 Kings 7:23; Ps. 16:6; Isa. 34:17; Jer. 31:39; Zech. 1:16; 2:1-2); image for judgment (Amos 7:17) and restoration (Jer. 31:39; Zech. 1:16; 2:1);

(2) Plumb line (2 Kings 21:13; Isa. 28:17; 34:11; Lam. 2:8);

(3) Cord (Josh. 2:18,21);

(4) Row (2 Sam. 8:2; Isa. 28:10,13).

LINEN

Most common fabric in Ancient Near East; spun from flax and bleached before being woven into clothing (Ex. 28:6), bedding, curtains (Ex. 26:1), and burial shrouds. "Fine linen" is woven so finely it cannot be distinguished from silk without magnification.

LIPS

Fleshy, muscular folds surrounding the mouth; frequently take character of whole person. There are flattering and lying lips (Pss. 12:2; 31:18); joyful lips (Ps. 63:5); righteous lips (Prov. 16:13); fearful lips (Hab. 3:16). Uncircumcised lips (Ex. 6:12) most likely refer to stammering lips or lack of fluency in speech (Ex. 4:10). Mourning is expressed in part by covering the upper lip with one's hand (Lev. 13:45).

LIVER

Large organ that secretes bile. Lobe of the liver was offered to God with other choice parts of burnt offering (Lev. 3:4,10,15, NASB). Only covering of liver was offered according to the NIV (also KJV). NRSV understood the offering to consist of the appendage to the liver, likely the pancreas. The ancients examined livers to discern the future (see king of Babylon, Ezek. 21:21). Liver is likely regarded as seat of emotions (Lam. 2:11, "liver," KJV, NASB margin; "heart," NASB, NIV, RSV;

"bile," NRSV). Several references to "glory" (Gen. 49:6; Pss. 16:9; 57:8) are possibly expansions of an earlier reading "liver" ("glory," NASB; "soul," RSV; "spirit," REB; "tongue," NIV).

LO-DEBAR

Place name variously spelled in Hebrew to mean "no word" or "to him a word" or "to speak." Home town of Mephibosheth after his father Jonathan's death (2 Sam. 9:4-5). See Josh. 13:24-28; 2 Sam. 17:27; Amos 6:13.

LOAN

Grant of temporary use, especially of money; should be act of generosity, not act for profit at the poor's expense (Lev. 25:35-37; compare Ex. 22:21-24; Deut. 10:19; Ps. 82:3-4; Prov. 31:8-9). Because the earth was God's (Lev. 25:23; Deut. 10:14) and human possessions were gifts from God (Deut. 8:1-10), lending was sharing God's gifts. Laws for collateral focused on protecting the debtor. The pledge must not threaten the debtor's dignity (Deut. 24:10-11), livelihood (Deut. 24:6), family (Job 24:1-3,9), or physical necessities (Ex. 22:26-27; Deut. 24:12-13). Compassionate lending was one measure of a righteous person (Ps. 15; Ezek. 18:5-9). Years of release and the jubilee year (Ex. 23:10-11; Deut. 15:1-15; Lev. 25) provided a systematic means for addressing long-term economic hardship by returning family property, freeing slaves, and canceling debts. Deuteronomy 15:7-11 warns against scheming creditors who would refuse loans because a year of release was near. See *Banking; Borrow; Coins; Ethics; Festivals; Justice; Law; Poor, Orphan, Widow; Levites; Sabbatical Year; Slave, Servant.*

LOIS (perhaps *more desirable* or *better*)

Mother of Eunice and grandmother of Timothy (2 Tim. 1:5); model of Christian faith instrumental in nurturing her grandson in the faith.

LORD

One who has power and exercises it responsibly; used in respectful address to father (Matt. 21:29-30) or ruler (Acts 25:26); symbolized the Roman caesar's position as absolute monarch; did not mean caesar was a god and was not used in cults devoted to worship of the caesars. When the early Christians confessed Jesus as Lord, they protested against the religious claims of the state but not against the rulership of the caesar as such. Jewish rebels denied the political authority of the caesar. Being exempt from the cult of the caesar, Jews could easily call the caesar "lord." Christians had to dispute the caesar's claim to be lord when that claim was understood to mean the caesar was divine. See *Emperor Worship.*

Nations around Israel often called their gods "lord."The Greeks did not see themselves in a slave/lord relationship. Their gods were subject to fate.

Marduk, the national god of Babylon, was called Bel, another form of Baal (Isa. 46:1; Jer. 50:2; 51:44). From among humans, the king towered above and beyond all others.The god had transferred the administration of divine law to the king.

In the OT, *Lord* usually describes the essence of Yahweh: His power over His people (Ex. 34:23; Isa. 1:24), over the entire earth (Josh. 3:13; Mic. 4:13), and over all gods (Deut. 10:17; Ps. 135:5). *Lord* could stand parallel to the personal name of God, *Yahweh* (Ex. 15:17). Additional terms such as Sabbaoth (that is, Supreme Head and Commander of all the heavenly forces) underscored the absolute lordship of Yahweh (Isa. 3:1; 10:16,33). *Lord* used in direct address to God attested to the honor of God or His representative (2 Sam. 7:18-22,28-29; Josh. 5:14; Zech. 4:4).

About 300 B.C. *adonai* (*Lord*) became more frequently used than Yahweh. Esther, Ecclesiastes, and Song of Solomon do not use the name Yahweh. The title *Lord* was no longer an adjective modifying the divine name but a substitute for the divine name Yahweh.

In important NT passages, *Lord* appears in the sense of OT *adonai* as Creator of the world and Director of history (Matt. 9:38; 11:25; Acts 17:24; 1 Tim. 6:15; the Book of Revelation). Since the NT and early Christians also called Jesus *Lord*, we have difficulty many times determining whether Jesus or God is meant by *Lord* (Matt. 24:42; Mark 5:19-20; Luke 1:76; Acts 10:14).

The two words, "Lord Jesus," composed the first Christian confession of faith (1 Cor. 12:3; Rom. 10:9). The decisive reason for transferring the divine title *Lord* to Jesus was His resurrection from the dead. Before His resurrection, Jesus was addressed with the Jewish title of honor *Rabbi* ("teacher," Mark 9:5; 11:21, for example). Luke always, and Matthew usually, translated this title into Greek as *Lord.* Jesus as the Messiah of Israel (Acts 2:36) was installed as Head of His church and Ruler of the cosmos by His resurrection (Col. 1:17; 2:6,10; Eph. 1:20-23). The resurrection changed the respectful student/teacher relationship of the disciples with Jesus into the believers' servant/Lord relationship. God honored Jesus with the title of *Lord* as His response to Jesus' obedient suffering (Phil. 2:6-11). He has been seated at the right hand of God, which demonstrates the elevation of Jesus to the position of Ruler next to God Himself (Ps. 110:1; see Mark 12:35-37).

The church prays for His return: "Come, our Lord" (or in Aramaic, *maranatha,* 1 Cor. 16:22; 11:26; Rev. 22:20). Jesus will give the judged and redeemed world back to the Father (1 Cor. 15:28).

The lordship of Jesus has ethical consequences. Calling out to Jesus with the title *Lord* is not enough for salvation. Such calling must be accompanied by actions that correspond to the teachings of the resurrected, Crucified One and to His example (Matt. 7:21-22; John 13:14-15). The believer devotes self to serve others, even the ones in power, in voluntary service (Mark 10:42-45).

Jesus Christ either joins people together, or He separates them, when they deny His right to be *Lord* (Rom. 16:18; 1 Cor. 1:2,10-13).

God has fully empowered the resurrected Jesus to send out His Spirit (Acts 2:33). The Lord is the Spirit (1 Cor. 15:45; 2 Cor. 3:17). This does not signify a total identifying of Jesus with the Spirit of God (compare 2 Cor. 13:13), but it testifies to the inseparable unity of the Lordship of God with the sending of Jesus and with the work of the Spirit. See *Christ; God; Holy Spirit; Messiah; Jesus; Rabbi; Resurrection.*

LORD WILL PROVIDE, THE See *Names of God, Yahweh-Jireh.*

LORD'S DAY

Designation for Sunday, the first day of the week (Rev. 1:10). Because the first day of the week was the day on which the early Christians celebrated Lord's Supper, it became known as Lord's Day, the distinctively Christian day of worship. See 1 Cor. 16:1-2; Acts 20:7-12. Evening of the first day could refer to Saturday evening (by Jewish reckoning) or to Sunday evening (by Roman reckoning). Since the incident involved Gentiles on Gentile soil, however, the probable reference is to Sunday night.

Since the earliest collective experiences of the disciples with the risen Lord took place on Easter Sunday evening (Luke 24:36-49; John 20:19-23), one might naturally expect the disciples to gather at that same hour on subsequent Sundays to remember Him in the observance of the Supper. This pattern, perhaps, is reflected in the service at Troas in Acts 20. See *Lord's Supper; Sabbath; Worship.*

LORD'S PRAYER, THE

Words Jesus used to teach His followers to pray. Three forms of the Lord's Prayer exist in early Christian literature—Matt. 6:9-13; Luke 11:2-4 and the noncanonical *Didache* 8:2. See *Apostolic Fathers.*

The Model Prayer for Christians is not praise, thanksgiving, meditation, or contemplation, but petition. It is asking God for something. This prayer of petition seeks two objects. First, one who prays in this way implores God to act so as to achieve His purpose in the world. Second, one who prays in this manner requests God to meet the physical and spiritual needs of the disciples. It is significant that the petitions come in the order they do: first, God's vindication; then, disciples' satisfaction.

Such a prayer of petition assumes a certain view of God. A God to whom one prays in this way is assumed to be in control; He is able to answer. He is also assumed to be good; He wants to answer. The Father to whom Jesus taught His disciples to pray is One who is both in control and good. See *Eschatology; Kingdom of God; Mishnah; Midrash; Rabbi; Talmud; Targum.*

LORD'S SUPPER

A memorial celebrated by the early church to signify Jesus' sacrificial death for humankind's sin. The form of the observance was established by the Lord at the Last Supper when He symbolically offered Himself as the paschal Lamb of atonement. His actual death the next day fulfilled the prophecy. Only Paul uses the phrase "Lord's supper" (1 Cor. 11:20), although implication of it is made in Rev. 19:9 ("marriage supper of the Lamb"). Church fathers began to call the occasion the "Eucharist" (that is, "Thanksgiving") from the blessing pronounced over the bread and wine after about A.D. 100. Church groups celebrate the Lord's Supper regularly as a sign of the new covenant sealed by Christ's death and resurrection. See *Ordinances.*

LOT (concealed)

Son of Haran and nephew of Abraham (Gen. 11:27-28) who traveled with his grandfather to Haran (Gen. 11:31) and with Abraham to Canaan (Gen. 12:5), finally settling between Bethel and Ai (Gen. 13:3). Abraham suggested they separate (Gen. 13:2-7) and allowed Lot to take his choice of the land. Lot chose the well-watered Jordan Valley where the city of Sodom was located (13:8-12). Abraham had to rescue his nephew (Gen. 14:13-16).

After God told Abraham He intended to destroy Sodom and Gomorrah (Gen. 18:20), Abraham interceded (Gen. 18:32). Two angels visited Lot to inspect Sodom (Gen. 19); Lot received them with hospitality. The townsmen wanted to have sexual relations with the two strangers. Lot protected his guests and offered the townsmen his daughters instead. The angels revealed God's desire to destroy Sodom and urged Lot to take his family to the hills to safety. In their flight from Sodom, Lot's nameless wife looked at the destruction and turned to a pillar of salt (Gen. 19:1-29).

Lot's daughters, fearing they would never have offspring, decided to deceive their father into having intercourse with them. They got their father drunk; both conceived a son by him, originating the Moabites and the Ammonites (Gen. 19:30-38). See Luke 17:28-32; 2 Pet. 2:7.

LOVE

Unselfish, loyal, and benevolent concern for the well-being of another; a "more excellent way"than tongues or even preaching (1 Cor. 13); physical love between the sexes, even sexual desire (Judg. 16:14; 2 Sam. 13:1-4); love within a family and among friends (Gen. 22:1-2); love as self-giving appears in the significant commandment that Israelites love the stranger based on God's act of redemption (Lev. 19:33-34).

Faithless Israel's love is "like a morning cloud, and as the early dew it goeth away" (Hos. 6:4). Faithful God desires steadfast love. His own relationship with an adulterous wife allowed Hosea the insight that God had not given up Israel in spite of her faithlessness. Love is the fulfillment of the law (Rom. 13:10; compare Deut. 6:4-6).

Jesus united the Shema of Deuteronomy (the command to love God) with Lev. 19:18 "Thou shalt love thy neighbor as thyself" (Matt. 22:34-40; Mark 12:28-34; Luke 10:25-28). The parable of the good Samaritan illustrates the selfless love that is to be characteristic of Kingdom citizens who fulfill the two commands to love (Luke 10:25-37). Jesus gave the radical command to love one's enemies and to pray for those who persecute (Matt. 5:43-48). Loving only those who love you is, according to Jesus, no better than those who are not His disciples. The love that Jesus' disciples have for others is to be just as complete as God's love (Matt 5:48; compare Rom. 5:8).

Paul associated love with the all-important biblical words of faith and hope (1 Cor. 13, KJV uses "charity"; see 1 Thess. 5:8; Gal. 5:6) and declared love the greatest. Gifts of the Spirit (ecstatic speech, wisdom, faith, and self-sacrifice) are good for nothing without love; only love builds up (1 Cor. 13:1-3). Love is patient and kind, not jealous or boastful, not arrogant or rude. Love is not selfish, irritable, or resentful. Love does not rejoice at wrong but in the right. Love bears, believes, hopes, and endures all things (1Cor. 13:4-7). Love stands in contrast with preaching and knowledge and with faith and hope because only love is forever (1 Cor. 13:8-13).

Christian love is a relationship of self-giving that results from God's activity in Christ. The source of Christian love is God (Rom. 5:8), and the believer's response of faith makes love a human possibility (Rom. 5:5). The Christian is to increase and abound in love (1 Thess. 3:12-13; compare Rom. 14:15; Gal. 5:13-15). Christian love is evidence of and a foretaste of the goal of God's purposes for His children (Rom. 5:2,5; 1 Thess. 3:13).

John 3:16 indicates the relationship of the Father's love to the work of Christ and of both to the life of believers. John emphasizes the ethical dimension of love among Christians based on Jesus' new commandment

(John 13:34-35; compare 14:15, 21,23-24; 15:9,12,17). What is commanded is the disciplined will to seek the welfare of others. Jesus' commandment is based on his life: "as I have loved you." Our love for Jesus Christ is closely related to our fulfillment of the pastoral task (21:15-17). This love is be manifested in deeds (1 John 3:18). Whoever hates his brother is in the darkness (1 John 2:9). Whoever does not do right and love his brother is not of God (1 John 4:20)."He that loveth not knoweth not God; for God is love" (1 John 4:8; compare 2 John 5-6; 3 John 5-6,9-10).

What happens at the final judgment is what happens here and now. Christians love because they have been loved. In such love, God's eternal purposes are being experienced and carried out by His people (Matt. 25:31-46).

LOVE FEAST

Fellowship meal Christian community celebrated in joy in conjunction with its celebration of the Lord's Supper (Jude 12). As a concrete manifestation of obedience to the Lord's command to love one another, it served as a practical expression of the communion that characterized the church's life. See Acts 2:46; 20:7-12; 1 Cor. 11:17-34.

Religious fellowship meals were common practice among first-century Jews. A family or group of friends, banded together for purposes of special devotion, gathered weekly before sundown for a meal in the home or another suitable place. Jesus and His disciples possibly formed just such a fellowship group. The fellowship meals of the early church appear to be a continuation of the table of fellowship that characterized the life of Jesus and His disciples. Such joyous fellowship served as a concrete manifestation of the grace of the kingdom of God that Jesus proclaimed. Jesus' last meal with His disciples may represent one specific example of such a fellowship meal, causing some to trace the ori-

gins of the love feast directly to this event.

LOVING-KINDNESS See *Kindness; Love.*

LUCIFER

Latin translation (followed by KJV) of Hebrew word for "day star" (Isa. 14:12) used as title for king of Babylon, who had exalted himself as a god.The prophet taunted the king by calling him "son of the dawn" (NIV), a play on a Hebrew term that could refer to a pagan god but normally indicated the light that appeared briefly before dawn. A later tradition associated the word with evil, although the Bible does not use it as such.

LUCIUS

(1) Christian prophet and/or teacher from Cyrene who helped lead church at Antioch to set apart Saul and Barnabas for missionary service (Acts 13:1).Thus an African was one of the first Christian evangelists.

(2) Relative of Paul who sent greetings to the church at Rome (Rom. 16:21). He was apparently one of many Jews who adopted Greek names.

LUD, LUDIM (Hebrew plural of Lud) or **LUDITES** (*Persons from Lydia*)

(1) Son of Egypt in Table of Nations (Gen. 10:13); apparently a people living near Egypt or under political influence of Egypt.

(2) Son of Shem and grandson of Noah in Table of Nations (Gen. 10:22) and thus Semites. Apparently groups from two different geographical areas but perhaps with common ancestors from Lydia; may be mercenary troops in Egyptian army; known for skill with bow (Isa. 66:19; Jer. 46:9; Ezek. 27:10; 30:5).

LUHITH (*plateaus*)

Settlement in Moab on road between Areopolis and Zoar; perhaps Khirbet

Medinet er-rash (Isa. 15:5; compare Jer. 48:5).

LUKE

Gentile physician (Col. 4:11,14); author of Third Gospel and Book of Acts; close friend and traveling companion of Paul (compare Acts 16:10-17; 20:5-15; 21:1-18; 27:1–28:16). Many scholars believe Luke wrote his Gospel and Acts while in Rome with Paul during the apostle's first Roman imprisonment. Apparently Luke remained nearby or with Paul also during the apostle's second Roman imprisonment (2 Tim. 4:11).

Luke adopted Philippi as his home, remaining there to superintend the young church while Paul went on to Corinth (Acts 16:40).

LUKE, GOSPEL OF

The NT's third and longest book; first of two-part work dedicated to the "most excellent Theophilus" (Luke 1:3; Acts 1:1); seeking to show "all that Jesus began both to do and teach, until the day in which he was taken up" (Acts 1:1-2; see Acts).

The Book of Acts ends abruptly with Paul in his second year of house imprisonment in Rome. Scholars generally agree that Paul reached Rome around A.D. 60. This makes the Book of Acts written at the earliest around A.D. 61 or 62, with the Gospel written shortly before. Luke 19:41-44 and 21:20-24 records Jesus' prophecy of the destruction of Jerusalem. This cataclysmic event in ancient Judaism occurred in A.D. 70 at the hands of the Romans. It hardly seems likely that Luke would have failed to record this significant event. Assigning a date to the Gospel later than A.D. 70 would ignore this consideration. Many scholars, however, continue to favor a date about A.D. 80.

Many scholars feel Paul was released from the Roman imprisonment he was experiencing as Acts concludes. The apostle was later reimprisoned and martyred under the Neronian persecution that broke out in A.D. 64. Paul was enjoying considerable personal liberty and opportu-

nities to preach the gospel (Acts 28:30-31) even though a prisoner. The optimism of the end of the Book of Acts suggests the Neronian persecution is a future event. Luke seems to have been written between A.D. 61 and 63, probably from Rome. Luke was in Rome when Paul wrote Colossians (4:14) and Philemon (24) during this first Roman imprisonment.

Luke's purpose (Luke 1:1-4) was to confirm for Theophilus the certainty of the things Theophilus had been taught. Luke's target audience were Gentile inquirers and Christians who needed strengthening in the faith. Luke sought to present a historical work "in order" (1:3). Most of his stories fall in chronological sequence. He often gave time indications (1:5,26,36,56,59; 2:42; 3:23; 9:28; 12:1,7). More than any other Gospel writer, Luke connected his story with the larger Jewish and Roman world (see 2:1; 3:1-2).

Some see Luke-Acts as an apology for the Christian faith designed to show Roman authorities that Christianity posed no political threat. Pilate declared Jesus innocent three times (Luke 23:4,14,22). Acts does not present Roman officials as unfriendly (Acts 13:4-12; 16:35-40; 18:12-17; 19:31). Agrippa remarked to Festus that Paul could have been freed if he had not appealed to Caesar (Acts 26:32). Paul is pictured as being proud of his Roman citizenship (Acts 22:28). The apostle is seen preaching and teaching in Rome openly without hindrance as Acts draws to a close.

Most scholars believe Luke (as well as Matthew) relied on Mark's written Gospel and sayings source called Q. (See Harmony of the Gospels.) In addition scholars have identified 500 verses exclusive to Luke, including the 132 verses of Luke 1 and 2. The new material was the result of his own research and literary genius.

Luke stressed the universal redemption available to all through Christ. Samaritans enter the kingdom (9:51-56; 10:30-37; 17:11-19) as well as pagan Gentiles (2:32; 3:6,38; 4:25-27; 7:9; 10:1,47). Publicans, sinners, and outcasts (3:12; 5:27-32; 7:37-50; 19:2-10; 23:43) are welcome along with Jews (1:33; 2:10) and respectable people (7:36; 11:37; 14:1). Both the poor (1:53; 2:7; 6:20; 7:22) and rich (19:2; 23:50) can have redemption.

Luke especially notes Christ's high regard for women. Mary and Elizabeth are central figures in chapters 1 and 2. Anna the prophetess and Joanna the disciple are mentioned only in Luke (2:36-38; 8:3; 24:10). Luke included the story of Christ's kind dealings with the widow of Nain (7:11-18) and the sinful woman who anointed Him (7:36-50). He also related Jesus' parable of the widow who persevered (18:1-8).

LUST

Desire, either positive (desire of the righteous [Prov. 10:24]; Christ's desire to eat the Passover with His disciples [Luke 22:15]; Paul's desire to be with Christ [Phil. 1:23]) or negative (crave/craving [NRSV, Num. 11:34; Ps. 78:18]; "covet" [Rom. 7:7]; "desire" [Ex. 15:9; Prov. 6:25; 1 Cor. 10:6]; "long for" [Rev. 18:14]).

The unregenerate life is governed by deceitful lusts or desires (Eph. 4:22; 2:3; Col. 3:5; Titus 2:12). Following conversion, such fleshly desires compete for control of the individual with spiritual desires (Gal. 5:16-17; 2 Tim. 2:22). Desires of the flesh and eyes (sexual and otherwise) are not from God and will pass away with the sinful world (1 John 2:16-17). Desire is the beginning of all sin and results in death (James 1:14-15). One who lusts has already sinned (Matt. 5:28). Part of God's judgment is to give persons over to their own desires (Rom. 1:24). Only the presence of the Holy Spirit in the life of the believer makes victory over sinful desires possible (Rom. 8:1-2).

LUZ (almond tree)

(1) Original name of Bethel (Gen. 28:19). See Bethel. Joshua 16:2 seems to distinguish the two places, Bethel perhaps being the worship place and Luz the city. Bethel would then be Burj Beitin and Luz Beitin.

(2) City in land of Hittites a man founded after showing the tribe of Joseph how to conquer Bethel (Judg. 1:26). See Hittites.

LXX

Roman numeral 70; symbol for Septuagint, earliest Greek translation of the OT. According to one tradition, the Septuagint was the work of 70 scholars. See Septuagint; Bible, Texts and Versions.

LYCAONIA, LYCAONIAN

Roman province in interior of Asia Minor including Lystra, Iconium, and Derbe. See Acts 14:1-23.

LYCIA

Projection on southern coast of Asia Minor between Caria and Pamphylia. See Acts 27:5.

LYDDA

District captial of Samaria (see Acts 9:32).

LYDIA (from king Lydus), LYDIAN

(1) Country in Asia Minor whose capital was Sardis. Hittites left monuments there. Lydia's most famous ruler was Croessus (560–546 B.C.), a name synonymous with wealth. His kingdom was captured by Cyrus of Persia. Lydians were "men of war" or mercenaries who fought to defend Tyre (Ezek. 27:10) and made an alliance with Egypt (Ezek. 30:5).

(2) First European converted to Christ under the preaching of Paul at Philippi (Acts 16:14). As a "seller of purple," she probably was quite wealthy (Acts 16:12-15,50).

LYE

Substance used for cleansing purposes from earliest times.

LYSANIAS

Roman tetrarch of Abilene about A.D. 25–30 at beginning of John the

Baptist's ministry (Luke 3:1). See *Abilene*.

LYSIAS

Second or birth name of Roman tribune or army captain who helped Paul escape the Jews and appear before Felix, the governor (Acts 23:26). See *Claudius*. His name appears in some Greek manuscripts at Acts 24:7 but not ones followed by many modern translations as earliest; compare 24:22.

LYSTRA

Important Lycaonian center in south central Asia Minor; probably home of Timothy (Acts 16:1). Paul's healing of a crippled man at Lystra (Acts 14:8-10) caused inhabitants to revere him as a god.

M

MAACAH (possibly *dull* or *stupid*) or **MAACATH** or **MAACHAH**

Eight OT persons and a nation including:

(1) Son of Nahor, Abraham's brother (Gen. 22:24); perhaps gave his name to Aramean kingdom west of Bashan and southwest of Mount Hermon whose residents, the Maachathites, Israel could not drive out (Josh. 13:13; compare 2 Sam. 10:6-8); perhaps personified as wife (ally) of Machir (1 Chron. 7:16).

(2) Wife of David and mother of Absalom (2 Sam. 3:3; 1 Chron. 3:2).

(3) Mother of King Abijam (1 Kings 15:2) and ancestress of King Asa (1 Kings 15:10,13).

MAALEH-ACRABBIM

KJV for "ascent" (NASB, NRSV, REB) or "pass" (NIV) of Akrabbim (Josh. 15:3). See *Akrabbim.*

MACCABEES, BOOK OF See *Apocrypha.*

MACCABEES, MACCABEAN WAR

Family of Mattathias, faithful priest who led a revolt against the Hellenizing influences of the Seleucid king Antiochus Epiphanes in about 168 B.C. See *Apocrypha.*

MACEDONIA, MACEDONIANS

Now northernmost province of Greece; in antiquity, fertile plain north and west of Thermaic Gulf from Haliacmon River in southwest to Axios in east ("Lower Macedonia") and mountainous areas to west and north ("Upper Macedonia," today divided between central northern Greece, southeastern Albania, and Macedonia); commercial link between Balkan peninsula to north and Greek mainland and the Mediterranean Sea to south. Macedonia was crossroads for travel and commerce going north and south and east and west.

The Christian message came to Macedonia through the preaching of Paul who followed God's vision there (Acts 16:9-10). Paul and his associates arrived in Neapolis (today Kavalla), the most important port of eastern Macedonia, and went inland to Philippi where, Lydia, a God-fearer from Thyatira, received them (Acts 16:14-15). They founded the first Christian community in Europe, probably in the year A.D. 50. Forced to leave Philippi after an apparently brief stay (Acts 16:16-40), Paul went to the capital Thessalonica via Amphipolis on the Via Egnatia (Acts 17:1). The church he founded in Thessalonica (compare Acts 17:2-12) was the recipient of the oldest Christian writing, First Letter to the Thessalonians, which Paul wrote from Corinth after he had preached in Beroea and in Athens (Acts 17:13-15).

MACHAERUS

Palace-fortress about 15 miles southeast of mouth of the Jordan on a site rising 3,600 feet above the sea. Herod the Great rebuilt the fortress. Josephus gives Machaerus as the site of the imprisonment and execution of John the Baptist.

MACHIR, MACHIRITES

Two men including: oldest son of Manasseh and grandson of Joseph (Josh. 17:1); head of family called Machirites (Num. 26:29; Josh. 13:29-31) with a reputation for being expert warriors (Josh. 17:1).

MACHPELAH (*the double cave*)

Burial place near Hebron for Sarah (Gen. 23:19), Abraham (25:9), Isaac, Rebekah, Jacob, Leah, and probably other members of the family. After Sarah's death, Abraham purchased the field of Machpelah and its cave as a sepulcher from Ephron the Hittite (Gen. 23:1-20; see 49:29; 50:13).

MADMANNAH (dung heap)

City in Negeb assigned to Judah (Josh. 15:31), possibly identical with Beth-marcaboth (Josh. 19:5). The reference to Shaaph as father of Madmannah (1 Chron. 2:49) is open to various interpretations:

(1) Shaaph (re)founded the city;

(2) Shaaph's descendents settled in the city; or

(3) Shaaph had a son named Madmannah.

MADMEN (dung pit)

City of Moab (Jer. 48:2). Dimon (Dibon), the capital city, is perhaps the intended reference. Jeremiah's dirge perhaps refers to Asshurbanipal's suppression of a Moabite revolt in 650 B.C.

MADMENAH (dung hill)

Point on northern invasion route to Jerusalem (Isa. 10:31); possibly Shu'fat.

MADON (site of justice)

Town in Galilee whose king joined in an unsuccessful alliance against Israel (Josh. 11:1; 12:19); summit of Qarn Hattim, northwest of Tiberias.

MAGADAN

Site on the Sea of Galilee (Matt. 15:39). At Mark 8:10, most translations follow other Greek manuscripts reading Dalmanutha. KJV follows received text of its day in reading Magdala.

MAGDALA (tower), **MAGDALENE**

City on western shore of Sea of Galilee on main highway coming from Tiberias; center of prosperous fishing operation. See *Magadan* (home of Mary). See also *Mary*.

MAGI

Eastern Wise men from Persia, Babylon, or Arabian desert—priests, and astrologers expert in interpreting dreams and other "magic arts."

(1) Men whose interpretation of the stars led them to Palestine to find and honor Jesus, the newborn King (Matt. 2). Term has Persian background. Septuagint of Daniel 2:2,10 uses "magi" for astrologer (compare 4:7; 5:7). The magi who greeted Jesus' birth may have been from Babylon, Persia, or the Arabian desert.

(2) Simon practiced sorcery, with a bad connotation (Acts 8:9).

(3) Bar-Jesus or Elymas is designated a sorcerer or one of the magi as well as "a false prophet" (Acts 13:6,8).

MAGOG See *Gog and Magog*.

MAGOR-MISSABIB (terror on every side)

Name Jeremiah gave Pashur the priest after the latter had prophet beaten and put in stocks (Jer. 20:3; compare 6:25; 20:10).

MAHANAIM (two camps)

Levitical city in hill country of Gilead on tribal borders of Gad and eastern Manasseh (Josh. 13:26,30; 21:38); tell edh-Dhabab el Gharbi. See 2 Sam. 2:8-9; 17:24-27. Under Solomon city served as district capital (1 Kings 4:14).

MAHANEH-DAN (camp of Dan)

(1) Site between Zorah and Eshtaol where the Lord's Spirit first stirred Samson (Judg. 13:25).

(2) Site west of Kiriath-jearim where Danites camped on the way to hill country of Ephraim (Judg. 18:12).

MAHER-SHALAL-HASH-BAZ (quick to the plunder, swift to the spoil)

Symbolic name Isaiah gave his son (Isa. 8:1) to warn of impending destruction of Syria and Israel as they threatened Judah and Ahaz, its king. This sign called on Ahaz to have faith or Judah could become part of the spoil.

MAHOL (place of dancing)

Father of three renowned wise men (1 Kings 4:31); alternate interpretation takes the phrase as a title for those who danced as part of the temple ritual (compare Pss. 149:3; 150:4).

The wisdom of the temple dancers may be akin to the prophetic wisdom associated with musicians (1 Sam. 10:5; 2 Kings 3:15; especially 1 Chron. 25:3).

MAIMED

In the theology of ancient Israel, persons who were physically whole were more "complete" and hence "clean" than those whose bodies were deformed or had members missing. For this reason, the Mosaic law prohibited persons with certain physical defects, including missing members, from temple service (Lev. 21:16-24; Deut. 23:1). Because of the sins of the sons of Eli, they and their descendants were banished from serving as priests by the Lord, who declared that they would become as if maimed: "I will cut off thine arm, and the arm of thy father's house" (1 Sam. 2:31).

Maiming was proscribed by the Mosaic law as punishment for certain heinous crimes (Lev. 24:19-20; Deut. 25:11-12). Jesus declared that sin was more serious than even maiming by saying that it would be better to have one's eye, hand or foot cut off than to have that member lead the offender to hell (Matt. 5:29-30; Mark 9:43-49).

The Bible gives several specific examples of persons who were, or became, maimed. The thumbs and great toes of Adonibezek were cut off by the men of Judah and Simeon after they defeated him in battle (Judg. 1:6-7). After killing the men who had murdered Ishbosheth son of Saul, David desecrated their bodies by cutting off their hands and feet (2 Sam. 4:12). Such post-battle mutilation was consistent with warfare practices in the ancient Near East. Malchus, servant of the High Priest, had his ear cut off by Peter during the arrest of Jesus (John 18:10). Jesus referred to "eunuchs who have been made eunuchs by men" (Matt. 19:12), a reference to maiming by castration.

Christ, the Good Shepherd, cared for the maimed in His healing minis-try (Matt. 15:30-31). He expected disciples to invite the maimed who could never repay (Luke 14:13). Jesus taught it is preferable to enter (eternal) life maimed than to go into eternal fire with whatever causes one to sin (Matt. 18:8).

MAKKEDAH (place of shepherds)

Canaanite city; site of Joshua's rout of five Canaanite kings (Josh. 10:10-28); assigned to Shephelah (lowland) district of Judah (Josh. 15:41).

MALACHI (my messenger or my angel)

Personal name or common noun; prophet who ministered after exile (after 538 B.C.). Temple had been rebuilt (1:10; 3:1,10). His preaching was collected in Book of Malachi. Nehemiah's reforms were probably intended to correct some of the social and religious abuses outlined by Malachi (Mal. 3:5; Neh. 5:1-13): tithing (Mal. 3:7-10; Neh. 10:37-39) and divorce and mixed marriages (Mal. 2:10-16; Neh. 10:30; 13:23-28). Nehemiah first returned to Jerusalem from Persia in 445 B.C. (Neh. 1:1; 2:1); therefore, Malachi should be dated after 450 B.C.

MALACHI, BOOK OF

Name of last book in Hebrew Book of Twelve and in English OT; series of six disputations and two appendices. The disputes follow a regular form:

(1) the prophet stated a premise;

(2) the hearers challenged the statement; and

(3) God and the prophet presented the supporting evidence. Malachi tried to rekindle the fires of faith in the hearts of his discouraged people. He sought to assure his people that God still loved them; but He demanded honor, respect, and faithfulness from them. Malachi pointed out religious and social abuses and warned that judgment would come to purge the people of sin unless they repented.

MALCAM or MALCHAM (*their king*)

KJV form for "Malcam" (1 Chron. 8:9) and "Milcom" (Zeph. 1:5).

(1) Benjaminite (1 Chron. 8:9).

(2) Chief god of Ammonites (Zeph. 1:5, KJV); sometimes seen as deliberate scribal misspelling of Milcom (compare Jer. 49:1,3; Zeph. 1:5), common name for Ammonites' god (1 Kings 11:5,33; 2 Kings 23:13). First Kings 11:7 links Milcom with Molech. At Amos 1:15 *malcam* is translated, "their king," though the word choice suggests that the Ammonites' god will go with them into exile. See *Ammon; Milcom; Molech.*

MALCHUS (*king*)

Personal name common among Idumaeans and Palmyrenes, especially for their kings or tribal chiefs. High priest's servant whose ear Peter cut off (Luke 22:5; 1 John 18:10).

MALICE

Vicious intention; desire to hurt someone; characteristic of preconversion life in opposition to God (Rom. 1:29; Eph. 4:31-32; Col. 3:8; Titus 3:3; 1 Pet. 2:1).

MAMMON

Greek form of a Syriac or Aramaic word for "money," "riches," "property," "worldly goods," or "profit"; personification of riches as an evil spirit or deity; used only by Jesus (Matt. 6:24; Luke 16:9,11,13). No one can be a slave of God and worldly wealth at the same time. The undivided concentration of mind to money-getting is incompatible with wholehearted devotion to God and to His service (Col. 3:5). In parable of unjust steward (Luke 16:1-13), Jesus commended the steward's foresight, not his method. His object was to point out how one may best use wealth, tainted or otherwise, with a view to the future. See *Steward.*

MAMRE (*grazing land*)

Main area of habitation for Abraham and his family; apparently named after Amorite (Mamre) who helped Abraham defeat evil king, Chedorlaomer (Gen. 14:1-24); famous for its oak trees. Just east of Mamre Abraham purchased a cave (Machpelah) for a family burial plot.

MAN OF SIN

KJV designation for ultimate opponent of Christ (2 Thess. 2:3). Modern translations follow other manuscripts in reading "man of lawlessness." See *Antichrist.*

MANAEN

Greek form of Menahem ("Comforter"); prophet and teacher in early church at Antioch (Acts 13:1); *syntrophos* ("one who eats with") of Herod the tetrarch (Herod Antipas, reigned 4 B.C. to A.D. 37). Those who shared king's table were persons recognized as valued members of the court (2 Sam. 9:10-13; 19:28; 1 Kings 2:7; 2 Kings 25:29; Neh. 5:17). "Member of court" and "childhood companion" are both possible for Acts 13:1.

MANASSEH (*God has caused me to forget* [*trouble*])

(1) One of at least two sons born to Joseph by Asenath (Gen. 41:50-51); adopted by Jacob as one to receive his blessing; ancestor of tribe of Israel; did not receive blessing of firstborn (Gen. 48:13-20); half of tribe of Manasseh settled on east bank of Jordan and half on west. See *Tribes of Israel.*

(2) King of Judah (696–642 B.C.); son of Hezekiah (2 Kings 20:21). His was longest reign of any Judean king but marked by unfaithfulness to Yahweh. Second Kings blames him for Judah's ultimate destruction and exile (2 Kings 21:10-16).

MANEH

KJV alternate term for "mina" (Ezek. 45:12). See *Weights and Measures.*

MANGER

Feeding trough (Luke 2:16) for cattle, sheep, donkeys, or horses. Stone mangers excavated in horse stables of Ahab at Megiddo were cut out of limestone approximately 3 feet long, 18 inches wide, and 2 feet deep. Other ancient mangers were made of masonry. Mangers were put in cave stables or other stalls. There Jesus was laid to sleep after His birth.

MANNA

Grainlike substance, considered to be food from heaven, which sustained Israelites in wilderness and foreshadowed Christ, true Bread from heaven. Small round grains or flakes appeared around Israelites' camp each morning with the dew and were ground and baked into cakes or boiled (Ex. 16:13-36). Some people identify manna with secretions left on tamarisk bushes by insects feeding on the sap. The Bible emphasizes that God caused manna to appear at the right time and place to meet His people's needs. Jesus assured the Jews that He, and not the wilderness food, was the true Bread from heaven that conferred eternal life on those who partook of it (John 6:30-58).

MANOAH (rest)

Father of Samson (Judg. 13).

MANTLE

Robe, cape, veil, or loose-fitting tunic worn as outer garment by prophets (1 Sam. 15:27; 1 Kings 19:13), women in Jerusalem (Isa. 3:22), and Job (Job 1:20). Transference of the mantle from Elijah to Elisha signified passing of prophetic responsibility and God's accompanying power. See *Cloth, Clothing; Veil.*

MAON (dwelling)

(1) Descendant of Caleb who founded Beth-zur (1 Chron. 2:45).

(2) Village in hill country of Judah (Josh. 15:55); tell Ma'in about eight miles south of Hebron. See 1 Sam. 23:24-25; 25:2).

MAONITES

Oppressors of Israel (Judg. 10:12); perhaps Meunites attacked by Hezekiah (1 Chron. 4:41) and Uzziah (2 Chron. 26:7), a band of marauding Arabs from south of the Dead Sea in the vicinity of Ma'an; Septuagint, "Midianites" (REB).

MARANATHA

Two Aramaic words; either *Marana tha,* "Our Lord, come" or *Maran atha,* "Our Lord has come" (1 Cor. 16:22). Having prayed that those who do not love Christ (compare 1 Cor. 13) would be "anathema" (see *Anathema),* Paul used a formula probably used in celebration of the Lord's Supper to pray that Christ would come, showing the urgency of showing love to Christ. Formula shows that very early the church applied to Jesus the word *Lord* that otherwise belonged only to God.

MARDUK

Chief god of Babylon, sometimes called Merodach or Bel, Babylonian equivalent of Baal: "lord"; credited with creation, a feat reenacted each new year and celebrated with a festival in which Marduk was proclaimed king. The reigning monarch was seen as the son of the god. Marduk was gradually attributed with more powers until he was acknowledged as lord of the heavens. The prophets mocked Marduk and his worshipers as products of human craftsmen who would lead Babylon to defeat and exile (Isa. 46:1; Jer. 50:2,38; 51:47). See *Babylon.*

MARESHAH (place at the top)

(1) Son of Caleb and founder of Hebron (1 Chron. 2:42).

(2) Member of Judah (1 Chron. 4:21).

(3) Canaanite city incorporated into Shephelah district of Judah (Josh. 15:44); tell Sandahannah one mile southeast of Beit Jibrin; fortified by Rehoboam (2 Chron. 11:8); near site of battle between forces of King Asa and the Ethiopian (Cushite) commander Zerah (2 Chron. 14:9-14);

home to prophet Eliezar (2 Chron. 20:37). Micah foretold destruction of the city (Mic. 1:15).

MARK, JOHN

Early missionary and church leader; author of second Gospel; son of Mary in whose home the Jerusalem believers met to pray when Peter was imprisoned by Herod Agrippa I (Acts 12:12); sometimes called by Jewish name, John, and sometimes by Roman name, Mark. John Mark was kin to Barnabas (Col. 4:10). After Barnabas and Saul completed a relief mission to Jerusalem, they took Mark with them when they returned to Antioch (Acts 12:25). When Barnabas and Saul went as missionaries, they took Mark to help (Acts 13:5). They went from Antioch to Cyprus and then on to Pamphylia, where Mark left them and returned to Jerusalem (Acts 13:13). When Paul and Barnabas planned another journey, Barnabas wanted to take Mark. When Paul refused, Barnabas and Mark went together while Paul and Silas went together (Acts 15:36-40).

When Paul wrote Philemon, Mark was one of Paul's fellow workers who sent greetings (Philem. 24). Paul wrote to the Colossians to receive Mark if he came to them (Col. 4:10). Paul asked Timothy to bring Mark with him because Paul considered Mark a useful helper (2 Tim. 4:11). Peter referred to Mark as his "son" (1 Pet. 5:13).

MARK, GOSPEL OF

Second book of NT and shortest account of ministry of Jesus. According to early church tradition, Mark recorded and arranged the "memories" of Peter, thereby producing a Gospel based on apostolic witness. Gospel writer is probably John Mark. See *Mark, John.*

Mark wrote his Gospel for Gentile Christians. Early Christian tradition placed Mark in Rome preserving the words of Peter for Roman Christians shortly before the apostle's death (see 1 Pet. 5:13); this would place the date of Mark's Gospel about A.D. 64

to 68. Such a hostile environment motivated Mark to couch his account of the life of Jesus in terms that would comfort Christians suffering for their faith. The theme of persecution dominates the Gospel of Mark (see Mark 10:30; compare Matt. 19:29; Luke 18:29). Jesus' messianic suffering is emphasized to inspire Christians to follow the same path of servanthood (10:42-45). Roman Christians would be encouraged knowing that Jesus anticipated that "everyone shall be salted with fire" (9:49; see 13:9-13). Dying for the gospel would be equivalent to dying for Jesus (8:35; see Matt. 16:25; Luke 9:24).

Mark has been called the "gospel of action," spurred by his oft-repeated "immediately." Jesus is constantly on the move. Mark apparently had more interest in the work of Jesus than in the words of Jesus. Jesus taught as He moved from region to region, using the circumstances of His travel as valuable lessons for His disciples (8:14-21).

Mark's language is simple, direct, and common. His description of events is replete with vivid images that evoke a variety of emotions (see 5:1-20; compare Matt. 8:28-34).

Mark was careful to relate not only the words of Jesus, but also His gestures, attitudes, and emotions (3:5; 6:34; 7:34; 8:12; 11:16).

After the Baptist fulfilled his role as the forerunner to the Messiah, Jesus began His public ministry in Galilee by preaching the "gospel of God" and collecting a few disciples (1:14-20). Mark presented the life of Jesus by following a simple geographical scheme: from Galilee (chs. 1–9) to Judea (10:31), all a prelude to the approaching passion of Jesus (10:32–15:47). The story ends as abruptly as it began; Mark finished his Gospel account with the angelic announcement of the resurrection of Jesus the Nazarene (the earliest Greek manuscripts of the NT end Mark's Gospel at 16:8).

The stories of the cleansing of the temple and the cursing of the fig tree are interwoven to aid the reader in interpreting the parabolic activity of

Jesus. Along the way to Jerusalem, Jesus indicated to His disciples that He was hungry and approached a fig tree to harvest its fruit. The tree was full of leaves, giving every indication of life; but it possessed no fruit. Mark recorded that Jesus "answered" the tree and announced, may "no man eat fruit of thee hereafter for ever" (11:14). The disciples, who "heard him," must have been puzzled by Jesus' actions, for Mark recorded that "the time of figs was not yet" (11:13). Jesus led His disciples into Jerusalem where he cleansed the temple, where Jesus found no spiritual fruit. Israel, the fig tree, was supposed to provide a "house of prayer for all the nations" (11:17, NIV). Instead, the religious leaders turned the devotion of worshipers into financial profit (11:15,17). Jesus "answered" the fig tree by pronouncing a curse on the Jewish religious leadership. In word and deed, Jesus prophesied that God would no longer use Israel as the vehicle of salvation for humanity. Peter and the disciples thus found the cursed fig tree dead (11:21). By purifying the temple, Jesus marked the death of Judaism, caused His own death (11:18), and gave birth to a religion for all people.

Mark developed the unifying "plot" of the gospel story by unveiling the hidden identity of Jesus. The messianic secret is part of the mystery of the kingdom of God, understood only by insiders (4:11,33-34). Jesus made every attempt to conceal His true identity. Jesus silenced demonic profession because they knew Him (1:34). He ordered those who witnessed miracles not to tell anyone what they saw, although silence was only a remote possibility (7:36). Even when the disciples revealed that they had learned the secret ("Thou art the Christ"), Jesus swore His followers to secrecy (8:29-30). Partly because they failed to understand the full implications of Jesus' messiahship (8:31-38). Mark used the messianic secret to organize his story around the progressive revelation of Christ and the faith pilgrimage of His disciples. Even Gentiles demonstrated that they belonged to the community of faith when they understood Jesus' parables and recognized Him as the Christ.

Mark found irony in pairing the story of the disciples questioning the identity of Jesus after the stilling of the storm, "What manner of man is this?" (4:41) with the account of the demons who are quick to shout, "Jesus, thou son of the most high God" (5:7).

Jesus' favorite self-designation was "Son of Man." Mark portrayed Jesus as a man possessing every human emotion. Moved by compassion, anger, frustration, mercy, and sorrow (1:41; 3:5; 8:17; 14:6,33), Jesus ministered among His own kind. Mark offered the full humanity of Jesus without reservation (see 3:21; 4:38; 6:3-6; 13:32); from the beginning of His earthly ministry (2:20), Jesus lived in the ominous shadow of the cross until the agony of Gethsemane almost overwhelmed Him (14:34). Mark penned a Gospel designed to evoke faith in the deity of Jesus: the divine voice announced it from heaven, demons screamed it in agony, Peter professed it boldly, even a Roman soldier acknowledged, "Truly this man was the Son of God!" (15:39).

MARKETPLACE

Public gathering place featuring small shops. Narrow streets and clustered buildings of most towns and villages in ancient Palestine left little room for a public marketplace. Shops were built into private residences or clustered in the gate area to form bazaars (1 Kings 20:34). Merchants operated booths just inside the city gate or hawked their merchandise outside the gate area in an open space or square. This area also served as a marshaling place for troops (2 Chron. 32:6) and the site for public meetings (Neh. 8:1), victory celebrations (Deut. 13:16), and the display of captives (2 Sam. 21:12).

Herod rebuilt many of the cities of Palestine following the Greek pattern, which included open areas for public gathering (Greek, *agora*). Amidst the shops, children played (Matt. 11:16), day laborers gathered to be hired (Matt. 20:2-3), and Pharisees and other leading citizens wandered, exchanging greetings (Matt. 23:7; Luke 11:43). Paul went to the marketplace (Greek, *agora*) on his visits to Greek cities to speak to the crowd always gathered there (Acts 17:17). He and Silas were also tried by magistrates in the marketplace at Philippi (Acts 16:19).

MARRIAGE

The union of one man and one woman in covenant commitment for a lifetime, second only to their commitment to God (Mark 10:5-9; Matt. 19:4-9; compare Gen. 2:24). In this union God has provided for the man and the woman the framework for intimate companionship, the channel of sexual expression according to biblical standards, and the means for procreation of the human race.

Human sexuality (Gen. 1:27) and sexual union within marriage (Gen. 2:24) were part of God's good creation. Although polygamy was practiced by some OT personalities, monogamy was always God's ideal for humanity (Matt. 19:4-5; compare 1 Cor. 7:2). Adultery is a violation of the covenant inherent in marriage (Ex. 20:14; 1 Thess. 4:2-3; Heb. 13:4). So is any sexual activity that does not express the oneness of marriage (1 Cor. 6:12-20). The biblical condemnation of adultery covers such things as communal marriage, mate swapping, and the so-called open marriage. Singleness—whether involuntary or voluntary—has its own demand, abstinence from sexual union (Matt. 19:10-12). Paul acknowledged that marriage is best for many; but, based on his own experience, he recommended singleness to those who wanted to devote all of their energies to Christian work and could forego sexual relationships (1 Cor. 7:7-9, 32-35). See *Sex, Biblical Teaching On; Divorce; Homosexuality.*

Christians should marry Christians, but Christians are to strive for a godly home even when this is not the case (1 Cor. 7:39; 2 Cor. 6:14). A person's commitment to God takes precedence in those unfortunate situations when the two commitments are in conflict (Matt. 10:37; Luke 9:59-62). A Christian who is married to a non-Christian should seek to maintain the relationship, to raise any children as believers, and to win the unbelieving spouse (1 Cor. 7:12-16; 1 Pet. 3:1-12; compare Acts 16:1; 2 Tim. 1:5; 3:14-15).

Because humans do not live up to the high ideals and standards of God, marriages do fail. Divorce poses a real dilemma for Christians.

Widows are free to remarry, but "only in the Lord" (1 Cor. 7:39; see Rom. 7:2-3). Paul advised single persons and widows to remain unmarried if they could, but he counseled marriage for others (1 Cor. 7:8-9; 1 Tim. 5:10-14). Bible students come to different conclusions on divorced persons marrying someone else after divorce. Those who oppose remarriage of divorced persons cite Mark 10:11-12; Luke 16:18; Rom. 7:3; and 1 Cor. 7:10-11. They interpret the statement by Jesus as teaching that divorced persons who marry again are living in adultery. Another group emphasizes Jesus' exception clause in Matt. 5:31-32 and 19:9 that implies that when a married person commits fornication, the spouse is free to secure divorce and to marry another person. Others believe principles of forgiveness and renewal inherent in the gospel make marriage again a valid option for divorced persons.

Jesus was not a legalist. The emphasis in Mark 10:11, Matt. 19:9, and Luke 16:18 is on the husband who divorces his wife and remarries. This strongly implies that Jesus was talking about a man who divorces his wife to marry someone else. According to this point of view, Paul affirmed Jesus' ideal and cited Jesus as his authority (1 Cor. 7:10-11); however, he acknowledged certain exceptions in trying to apply this ideal (1 Cor. 7:12-16). This interpretation thinks Paul's words imply the possibility of divorce and remarriage.

The husband and wife are of equal worth before God, since both are created in God's image. The marriage relationship models the way God relates to His people. A husband is to love his wife as Christ loved the church. He has the God-given responsibility to provide for, to protect, and to lead his family. A wife is to submit graciously to the servant leadership of her husband even as the church willingly submits to the headship of Christ. She, being in the image of God as is her husband and thus equal to him, has the God-given responsibility to respect her husband and to serve as his helper in managing the household and nurturing the next generation.

From the moment of conception children are a blessing and heritage from the Lord. Parents are to teach their children spiritual and moral values and to lead them, through consistent lifestyle example and loving discipline, to make choices based on biblical truth.

MARS HILL

A prominent rise overlooking the city of Athens where the philosophers of the city gathered to discuss their ideas, some of which revolutionized modern thought. Paul discussed religion with the leading minds of Athens on Mars Hill. He used the altar to an "unknown god" to present Jesus to them (Acts 17:22). See *Greece*.

MARTHA (*lady* [of the house] or *mistress*)

Sister of Mary and Lazarus of Bethany and one of Jesus' best-loved disciples; portrayed as a person in charge. Together with Mary, she sent for Jesus when Lazarus was ill (John 11:3). Luke 10:38-42 contrasts Martha's activist discipleship with Mary's contemplative discipleship (compare John 11:20). Jesus' gentle rebuke serves as a perpetual reminder not to major on minor matters. Jesus led Martha from an inadequate to a lofty confession (John 11:21-27). Faced with the realities of death, Martha later doubted (John 11:39).

MARTYR

Transliteration of Greek "witness"; in particular one who gives his life for a cause; in later usage applied to those who died because of their faith in Christ rather than recant. "Witness" came to be used for those who testified of Christ but were not put to death.

MARY (*rebellious, bitter*)

Greek personal name equivalent to Hebrew Miriam. See *Miriam*.

(1) *Mother of Jesus*, related to Elizabeth, mother of John the Baptist, and wife of Zechariah, the priest. Elizabeth was also of a priestly family. Mary was a person of great faith prepared to be an agent of God in the birth of the Messiah. In later church tradition, two important theological beliefs focus the significance of Mary: "divine maternity" and "virginial conception." Their scriptural orientation is based on Luke 1:34 that details Mary's response to the angel's announcement that she would have a son: "I am not knowing a man." Some have interpreted this as making an eternally valid theological statement that her virginity is an on-going state that equals a "perpetual virginity." Matthew 1:24-25 (including, [Joseph] "knew her not until she had borne a son") would seem to challenge the perpetual virginity belief. In contemporary Christianity, Roman Catholic and Eastern Orthodox churches embrace these doctrines, while most Protestant churches do not. Mary is a revered character in Christian tradition who is believed to represent goodness, innocence, and profound commitment to the ways of God.

Gospel writers attempted to emphasize Jesus' divine origins at the expense of deemphasizing the importance of His mother. In John 2:1-11, Mary's presence at Jesus' first public miracle of changing water to wine at the marriage at Cana underscores, in a profound manner, that Jesus' destiny challenges all norms, including that of immediate family relationships. The recurring Johannine theological theme of Jesus' "hour" being divinely directed is pointedly made by Mary's presence in the episode (compare Mark 3:31-35; Luke 11:27-28). Mary's presence at the foot of the cross (John 19:25-27) highlights the mother's love. Acts 1:14 indicates Mary was present, along with other hero figures of early Christianity, in the upper room scene in Jerusalem.

(2) *Mary Magdalene.* Mark 16:9 and Luke 8:2 indicate this Mary, from Magdala, was exorcised of seven demons and thus quite ill before her encounter with Jesus. Mary eventually became part of an inner circle of supporters of Jesus: witness of His crucifixion (Mark 15:40; Matt. 27:56; John 19:25), burial (Mark 15:47; Matt. 27:61), the empty tomb (Mark 16:18; Matt. 28:1-10; Luke 24:10), and resurrection (Mark 16:9; John 20:1-18).

(3) *Mary (of Bethany)*, sister of Martha and Lazarus, who together formed part of an inner circle of Jesus' associates. Mary from Bethany played a primary role in the episode of Lazarus' rising from the dead (John 11). In John 12, Mary anointed Jesus' feet with precious oil, thus serving an important confessional function of anticipating Jesus' death.

(4) *Mary, mother of James the younger and of Joses and Salome;* appears to have been part of Jesus' following from Galilee who moved with Him during His itinerant public ministry (compare Mark 15:40-41). She witnessed Jesus' crucifixion and encountered the empty tomb (Mark 15:47; 16:1-8; Matt. 27:55-56; 28:1-8; Luke 23:56; 24:1-10).

(5) *Mary, mother of John Mark;* owner of house in Jerusalem where first followers of Jesus met (Acts 12:12). See *Mark, John.*

(6) *Mary, wife of Clopas.* She witnessed Jesus' crucifixion (John 19:25) and may be the same character as Mary, the mother of James, Joses, and Salome, in the Synoptic Gospels accounts.

(7) *Mary, from Rome.* An individual Paul greeted in Rom. 16:6.

MASCHIL

KJV form of Maskil; used in titles of 13 psalms (Pss. 32; 42; 44; 45; 52–55; 74; 78; 88; 89; 142); translated "psalm" (Ps. 47:7). Two of the maskils have clear references to instruction (Pss. 32:8-9; 78:1). Others suggest "maskil" might be a musical notation or an indication that these psalms were performed at festivals (for example, Ps. 78). Though most of the maskils are laments (Pss. 42; 44; 52; 54–55; 74; 88; 142), other form critical types are grouped as maskils as well (Ps. 32, a thanksgiving for healing; Ps. 45, a psalm in celebration of a royal wedding; Ps. 78, a recitation of sacred history).

MASSA *(burden)*

(1) Seventh son of Ishmael (Gen. 25:14; 1 Chron. 1:30).

(2) Arab tribe perhaps descended from *1*; listed among peoples who paid tribute to King Tiglath-pileser III (745–727 B.C.) of Assyria; used in the titles of collections of proverbs (Prov. 30:1; 31:1), probably refers to nationality of the original compiler.

(3) Hebrew term used in special sense of oracle, especially at beginning of prophecies of judgment (for example, Isa. 13:1; Nah. 1:1; Hab. 1:1).

MASSAH *(to test, try)*

Stopping place where people put God to the test during wilderness wandering near base of Mount Horeb (Sinai) (Ex. 17:7); reminder of Israel's disobedience or hardness of heart (Deut. 6:16; 9:22; Ps. 95:8). See Deut. 33:8.

MASTER

(1) One in authority; slaveholders; heads of households (including slaves or servants). See Mark 13:35; Luke 13:25; 14:21; 16:13; Eph. 6:9.

(2) KJV translated Greek terms for teacher as "master" (Matt. 8:19; 9:11; 23:8,10; 26:25; Mark 9:5; John 4:31). Modern translations render terms as "teacher" or "rabbi."

MATTHEW (*the gift of Yahweh*)

Tax collector Jesus called to be an apostle (Matt. 9:9; 10:3); author of first gospel; employee of Herod Antipas; collected "toll" or "transport" taxes from local merchants and farmers carrying their goods to market as well as distant caravans passing through Galilee; same as Levi (Mark 2:14; Luke 5:27), and thus the son of Alphaeus. See *Disciples*. Matthew's office was located on the main highway that ran from Damascus, down the Jordan Valley to Capernaum, then westward to Acre to join the coastal road to Egypt or southward to Jerusalem. Because Matthew had leased his "toll" collecting privileges by paying the annual fee in advance, he was subjected to the criticism of collecting more than enough, growing wealthy on his "profit." Fellow Jews hated him. See *Matthew, Gospel of*.

MATTHEW, GOSPEL OF

Opening book of NT; purpose was to show that Jesus had the power to command His disciples to spread His gospel throughout all the world (Matt. 28:16-20). Knowledge of the resurrection made it evident to them that He had received His authority from God. Jesus said they would make and baptize new disciples as they went away from their meeting with Him. The disciples would pass on to others all that Jesus taught them.

Matthew 1:1–4:25 opens with the royal genealogy and builds to the proclamation of God: "This is my beloved Son" (3:17). The genealogies confirm Jesus' authoritative, kingly lineage and remind the reader of His relation to all nations by mentioning Tamar, Rahab, Ruth, and the wife of a Hittite. The wise men (Gentiles) came seeking the King of the Jews (2:2). The angel affirmed Jesus' divine nature to Joseph. The child received a messianic name (1:18-23). Joseph took the holy family to Gentile territory (Egypt) to escape the threats of Herod. As God's Son, Jesus had the authority and power to confront

Satan and overcome. Jesus then went to Galilee of the Gentiles (4:15) to begin His public ministry. Jesus is clearly designated by God to be the Messiah with authority — for all nations.

Matthew presented Jesus as an authoritative Teacher. The Teaching from the Mount (Matt. 5:1–7:29), gave His essential doctrine in this teaching. He stressed the importance of His commandments (5:19); emphasized the authoritative nature of His teachings by declaring "But I say unto you" (5:22,28, 32,39,44); and was recognized by the crowds as a Teacher with authority (7:28-29). When the disciples went out to teach, they knew what to teach.

Jesus acted out His teachings in displays of power. Matthew 8:1–10:42 opens with 10 miracles demonstrating Jesus' authority over disease, natural catastrophes, demons, and death. His disciples wondered at His power over nature (8:27), and the crowds stood amazed that He had the authority to forgive sins (9:8). Jesus gave authority to His disciples to go out and heal and teach as He had done (10:1), thus preparing them for their final Commission in 28:18-20.

Matthew 11:1–13:52 shows various people reacting to Jesus' authority. When the leaders rejected Jesus' authority (ch. 12), Matthew implied that Jesus would go to the Gentiles by quoting Isaiah (12:18-21). Jesus continued His teaching in parables to those willing to listen (13:10-13).

Matthew 13:53–18:35 opens with the story of Jesus' teaching in the synagogue in Nazareth. The people had the same response to Jesus' teaching as the crowds did at the end of the Sermon on the Mount: astonishment (13:54; compare 7:28). Still His hometown people rejected His authoritative teaching (13:57). His disciples accepted Him (14:33), and so did the Gentile woman (15:22).

Matthew 19:1–25:46 makes the transition from Galilee to Jerusalem. Jesus dramatically presented His kingly authority by His triumphal entry into Jerusalem (21:1-9) and by cleansing the temple (21:10-17). He answered challenges to His authority from chief priests and elders (21:23) with parables and other teachings (21:28–22:46). Jesus warned the people about the examples of the Pharisees and Sadducees (23:1-38). He then concentrated His teaching only on His disciples (24:1–25:46).

Matthew 26:1–28:20 has no teaching situations, but it tells of the conspiracy ending in Jesus' execution. In the midst of the trial scene, Jesus was asked if He were the Messiah. Jesus responded by affirming His authority: "Thou hast said" (26:64). Pilate, a Gentile, recognized Jesus' kingly authority placarding over the cross: "THIS IS JESUS THE KING OF THE JEWS" (27:37). The Gentile centurion proclaimed:"Truly this was the Son of God" (27:54). As in the birth story, so in the end, the author stressed Jesus' divine, kingly authority and emphasized the inclusion of the Gentiles.

Matthew presented Jesus as the "Son of God" 23 times. While the virgin birth story affirms Jesus' sonship, the quotation from Hos. 11:1 (Matt. 2:15) confirms it. Twice God proclaimed Jesus' sonship: at His baptism (3:17) and at the transfiguration (17:5). Peter confessed it (16:16). Jesus attested to His sonship in the Lord's prayer (6:9), His thanksgiving to God (11:25-26), and the Garden of Gethsemane (26:39). The author wanted the reader to be aware that Jesus, the Son of God, is the One crucified on the cross; so Jesus called out to "my God" from the cross (27:46), and a Gentile centurion confessed that the dying One is "truly . . . the Son of God" (27:54).

Forgiveness of sins comes through the death of the divine Son of God (1:21). Jesus assured His disciples His destiny was "to give his life a ransom for many" (20:28). The Lord's Supper is a continuing reminder: "This is my blood of the new testament, which is shed for many for the remission of sins" (26:28).

Some contemporary writers date Matthew as early as A.D. 60; some, as late as A.D. 95. The place of writing was probably some place along the coast of Phoenicia or Syria such as Antioch. Matthew, the tax collector, the son of Alphaeus has been identified as the author since the second century. See *Matthew.*

MATTHIAS (*gift of Yah*)

Disciple who followed Jesus from the time of John's ministry of baptism until Jesus' ascension; chosen by lot and prayer to succeed Judas as an apostle and official witness to the resurrection (Acts 1:20-26). See *Disciples, Apostles; Acts.*

MAUNDY THURSDAY See *Holy Week; Church Year.*

MEADOW

Tract of grassland, especially moist, low- lying pasture; stretches of reed grass or papyrus thickets (Gen. 41:2,18).

MEALS See *Banquet; Food.*

MEAT TO IDOLS

Offerings of animal flesh sacrificed to a pagan god. Since most early Christians had Jewish backgrounds, a problem arose in the church when Gentile converts ate meat that had been offered to idols. The Jerusalem council (Acts 15) decided Christians should abstain from eating meat offered to idols so as not to cause weak believers to stumble. See 1 Cor. 8:13.

MEDAD (*beloved*) See *Eldad.*

MEDEBA (*water of quiet*)

City of Reuben (Josh. 13:9,16) in Transjordan on main north-south road (King's Highway) about 25 miles south of Amman; modern Madeba. Sihon, king of the Amorites, took Medeba from Moab only to have the area pass into Israel's control (Num. 21:24,26,30). Moabite stone says Omri, king of Israel (885-874 B.C.), recaptured Medeba. Mesha, king of Moab, retook the city during the reign of Omri's son. An alliance of Israel, Judah, and Edom recaptured the city but quickly withdrew

(2 Kings 3:25,27). Jeroboam II again secured control of the city of Israel (2 Kings 14:25). Isaiah 15:2 reflects the city's return to Moab.

MEDES, MEDIA

Region south and southwest of Caspian Sea in Zagros Mountains; north of Elam and west of Assyria; traditional capital at Ecbatana; inhabited by Medes, a nomadic Aryan people from north and west of the Caspian Sea.

Before 1500 B.C. the region was part of Mitanni kingdom. Later Elamites controlled the region and its nomadic inhabitants. Medes gradually entered the area between 1400 and 1000 B.C. The Assyrians controlled them or sought to for more than 200 years, though the Medes enjoyed some periods of freedom before the Scythians conquered them in 653 B.C.

The greatest Median king was Cyaxares (625–585 B.C.), who defeated Scythians and attacked Nineveh. Before Nineveh fell in 612 B.C., Cyaxares conquered Asshur, the ancient center of the Assyrian Empire. With aid of Scythians, Babylonians and others, Nineveh was taken. The end of the Assyrian Empire was near.

Babylon and Media divided the Assyrian Empire with Media taking the land east and north of the Tigris River. Nebuchadnezzar II and Cyaxares's grandaughter wed to seal the pact. After a five-year war with Lydia, Cyaxares concluded a peace in 584 B.C., again sealing it with a marriage. His son Astyages married the daughter of the Lydian king. Astyages became king of the Medes when Cyaxares died.

The end of the Median kingdom came with the rise of Cyrus II, founder of the Persian Empire. Cyrus was king of Anshan and a vassal to Astyages. Indeed, Cyrus's mother was Astyages's daughter. About 550 B.C., encouraged by Babylon, Cyrus rebelled against the Medes. His rebellion led to the defeat of Astyages. The kingdom of the Medes was

replaced by the kingdom of the Persians. See *Persia; Cyrus.*

Biblical references frequently combine "the Medes and the Persians" (Dan. 5:28; compare Esther 1:19; 10:2). Kings of the Persian Empire are called "the kings of Media and Persia" (Dan. 8:20). The most famous Mede in Scripture is Darius the Mede (Dan. 5:31; 9:1). See *Darius.* Media is sometimes referred to as the instrument of God, especially against Babylon (Isa. 13:17; 21:2; Jer. 51:11,28); but the Medes also had to drink the cup of God's judgment (Jer. 25:25). Jews or Jewish converts from there were at Pentecost (Acts. 2:9). See *Babylon; Elam; Assyria.*

MEDIA

The Bible offers principles by which media issues might be properly discerned.

Paul commanded the Philippian believers to cultivate pure thoughts (Phil. 4:8). To the Thessalonians he urged that everything be tested so that what is good might be embraced and what is evil could be avoided (1 Thess. 5:21-22). Paul also wrote of the urgency for Christians to use their time wisely in light of the great evil in the world (Eph. 5:16). James noted that Christians ought not to expect anything from God if they plan to use what they receive wrongly, namely, on their own passions (Jas. 4:3).

For these reasons, resources or activities aimed solely at personal pleasure are contrary to biblical teaching. To the extent that the media promote and glamorize activities or attitudes contrary to God's standards, they should be avoided by Christians.

MEDIATOR

Person midway between two parties who establishes an agreement or relationship between the parties and may act as a guarantor of that relationship. Job pleaded for an arbiter to stand between him and God in judgment (Job 9:33). In human relationships, a champion could come between armies and represent his people (1 Sam. 17:4-10), and an interpreter or spokesman helped negotiate agreements. A leader such as Abraham could negotiate with God for the sparing of a city (Gen. 18:22-32), and a father such as Job could intercede with sacrifices for his family (Job 1:5).

The king embodied the people and, at times, represented God to them (Ps. 93:1). Priests were consecrated to offer sacrifices of reconciliation, especially the high priest on the Day of Atonement (Lev. 16:29-34). Israel was to be a kingdom of priests to channel the blessings of God to all people (Ex. 19:6). Prophets had to recall the nation to its vows of obedience and deliver God's words of judgment and hope. The Servant Songs of Isaiah told of one whose sacrifice of Himself would bring pardon to many (Isa. 53).

Moses stood between the people and God, receiving the Commandments on which the covenant was based and beseeching God's mercy when the Commandments and covenant were broken (Ex. 20:18-21; Deut. 9:25-26). The wisdom, word, and Spirit of God were almost personified and used along with angels (messengers) as mediating agents (Prov. 8:22-31; Ps. 104:4).

Mediator in the NT bore several ideas. Primarily meant an umpire or peacemaker who came between two contestants, a negotiator who established a certain relationship, or some neutral person who could guarantee an agreement reached (of Moses in negative sense, Gal. 3:19-28). Christ is the only necessary Mediator (1 Tim. 2:5). Full communion with God comes through faith in the Mediator who gave Himself a ransom for others, mediating a new eternal covenant through His sacrificial death (Heb. 7:22-25; 8:6; 9:15; 12:24).

Christ is the great Intercessor, praying for His disciples while on earth and continuing to do so in heaven (John 17; Rom. 8:34). He is the supreme High Priest who enters once for all into the sanctuary to make a sacrifice of Himself that brings eternal redemption (Heb. 9:11-12).

MEDICINE See *Diseases.*

MEDITATION

Calling to mind some supposition, pondering upon it, and correlating it to one's own life; for God's people, a reverent act of worship leading to spiritual renewal. A wicked individual meditates on violence (Prov. 24:2); a righteous person on God or His great spiritual truths (Pss. 63:6-8; 77:12; 119:15,23,27,48,78,97,148; 143:5). He hopes to please God by meditation (Ps. 19:14). Constant recollection of God's past deeds by hearing Scripture and repetition of thought produce confidence in God (Ps. 104:34).

MEDITERRANEAN SEA, THE

Designated in the Bible simply as "the sea" (Josh. 16:8; Acts 10:6); "Western Sea" (Deut. 11:24, RSV, NIV); and "Sea of the Philistines" (Ex. 23:31); an inland ocean extending about 2,200 miles from Gibraltar to the Lebanon coast and varying in width from 100 to 600 miles. Most of the important nations of ancient times were either on the Mediterranean's shores or operated in its 2,200 miles of water: Israel, Syria, Greece, Rome, Egypt, Philistia, and Phoenicia. Great Sea served as western border for Canaan (Num. 34:6) and the territory of Judah (Josh. 15:12). Paul made three missionary journeys across the Mediterranean. Under Roman arrest, Paul made his final voyage across the Mediterranean Sea and shipwrecked (Acts 27). See *Phoenicia; Tyre; Transportation and Travel; Ships and Boats.*

MEDIUM

One possessed by (Lev. 20:22) or consulting (Deut. 18:11) a ghost or spirit of the dead, especially for information about the future. Acting as a medium was punishable by stoning (Lev. 20:27); consulting a medium, by exclusion from the congregation of Israel (Lev. 20:6). The transformation of Saul from one who expelled mediums (1 Sam. 28:3) to one who consulted a medium at En-dor (28:8-19) graphically illustrates his fall.

MEEKNESS

Personality trait of gentleness and humility; controlled power, the opposite of pride. Meekness or gentleness is exemplified by God (2 Sam. 22:36, Ps. 18:35), Moses (Num. 12:1-13), and Jesus (Zech. 9:9; Matt. 11:29; 12:14-21; 21:5). Meek were often poor and oppressed (Amos 2:7; 8:4; Job 24:4; Ps. 9:18; Prov. 3:34; 16:19).

The meek receive the special concern of God and are called blessed (Ps. 37:11; Matt. 5:5; compare Pss. 10:17; 22:26; 25:9; 147:6; 149:4). The Messiah will have a special ministry to the meek (Isa. 11:4; 61:1; Luke 4:18).

Christians are encouraged to be meek (Eph. 4:1-2; Col. 3:12). Meekness is a fruit of the Spirit (Gal. 5:23) and should mark the Christian's attitude toward sinners (Gal. 6:1). Paul was meek with the Corinthians (1 Cor. 4:21). Pastors should be meek and teach meekness (1 Tim. 6:11; 2 Tim. 2:25; Titus 3:2). Christians should receive God's Word with meekness (Jas. 1:21). Wisdom is expressed with meekness (Jas. 3:13). Christian wives can witness to their unbelieving husbands with their meek spirit (1 Pet. 3:1-4). All Christians should be prepared to give a defense of their faith in meekness (1 Pet. 3:15). See *Humility; Patience; Pride; Poor, Orphan, Widow; Spiritual Gifts.*

MEGIDDO (perhaps *place of troops*)

One of most strategic cities of Canaan; tell el-Mutesellim; in Manasseh (Josh. 17:11; 1 Chron. 17:29); guarded main pass through the Carmel mountain range, an obstacle along the international coastal highway that connected Egypt with Mesopotamia and even further destinations. The city was very active while under Egyptian authority from the time of the patriarchs through to the judges (2000–1100 B.C.), but this golden age came to an end about 1125 B.C. when it was destroyed.

Deborah and Barak fought the Canaanites and their leaders King Jabin and Sisera near the "waters of Megiddo," possibly the wadi Qina running through the surrounding hills (Judg. 5:19). By the time of Solomon, the city was firmly Israelite, since he fortified the city (1 Kings 9:15; compare 4:12).

About 920 B.C. Pharoah Shishak burst into both Israel and Judah, taking control of the coastal highway including Megiddo. Later, the city was the place of death for the Judean king, Ahaziah at the command of Jehu while fleeing from the scene of Jehoram's assassination (843 B.C., 2 Kings 9:27). Over a century later, the conquering Tiglath-pileser III chose Megiddo as the seat of the Magidu administrative district in the Assyrian Empire (733 B.C.).

Josiah attempted to head off Pharoah Neco II as he advanced along the coastal plain on his way to Carchemish (609 B.C.), but Neco archers fatally wounded him (2 Kings 23:29-30; 2 Chron. 35:22-24). Zechariah prophesied that the mourning for the false deities of Hadad and Rimmon (Hadad-rimmon) that took place in the plain below Megiddo would be matched by Israel's mourning for its smitten Lord (Zech. 12:11).

Mount of Megiddo (*har-Megiddon* thus "Armageddon") will be where the kings of the world are gathered for that final battle in the last day of the Lord. Where Israel was initially frustrated during their conquest of Canaan is exactly where they will be victorious with Christ in the end (Rev. 16:16).

MELCHIZEDEK (*Zedek is my king* or *My king is righteousness*)

Priest and king of Salem, city identified with Jerusalem. When Abraham returned from the Valley of Siddim after defeating Chedorlaomer, Melchizedek greeted Abraham with bread and wine. He blessed Abraham in the name of "God Most High." In return, Abraham gave Melchizedek a tithe. Psalm 110:4 refers to one who would be forever a priest in the "order of Melchizedek." Hebrews 5–7 refers to Jesus' eternal priesthood as being of the "order of Melchizedek" as opposed to Levitical in nature, citing Ps. 110:4.

MEMORIAL

Something that serves as a reminder. Memorials to God's saving acts reinforced faith and provided opportunities for teaching. God's covenant name (Yahweh) was to be a "memorial name" (Ex. 3:15, NASB), a reminder of God's liberation of God's people. The Passover served as a similar reminder (Ex. 12:14; 13:9). The 12 stones taken from the Jordan's bed served as a reminder of God's provision of passage across the Jordan (Josh. 4:7). The Lord's Supper serves as a reminder of Christ's sacrificial death and an encouragement of His future coming (Matt. 26:13; Mark 14:9; 1 Cor. 11:25-26).

MENAHEM (consoler)

King of Israel 752–742 B.C.; became king by assassinating Shallum, who had killed King Zechariah only a month earlier (2 Kings 15:10-14). After the death of Jeroboam II in 753 B.C. Shallum and Menahem each led an extremist party that sought the throne. They ruled by force. After becoming king, Menahem attacked and destroyed one of Israel's cities because it resisted his rule (2 Kings 15:16).

MENE, MENE, TEKEL, UPHARSIN

Inscription King Belshazzar of Babylon saw a detached hand write on his palace wall during a drunken party (Dan. 5:1-29). After the wise men of the kingdom could not decipher the writing, Daniel was brought in to give an interpretation.

Scholars have proposed a number of translations, the best of which probably is "mina, shekel, and halves." Daniel interpreted the inscription with a wordplay using Hebrew words that sound similar to each word of the inscription, taking it to mean, "numbered, weighed, and divided." Neb-

uchadnezzar and his kingdom had been weighed in the balance and found wanting. The kingdom would be divided and given to his enemies, the Medes and Persians. The overthrow occurred that very night (Daniel 5:30).

MENORAH

Candelabrum used in Jewish worship, specifically the branched lampstand used in the tabernacle (Ex. 25:31-35; 37:17-20; compare Zech. 4:2,11). See Lamps, Lighting, Lampstand.

MEPHIBOSHETH (shame destroyer or image breaker)

(1) Son of Jonathan; granted special position and privilege in David's court (2 Sam. 9). Fearing that the Philistines would seek the life of the young boy orphaned at five years old, a nurse fled with him, but in her haste she dropped him and crippled him in both feet (2 Sam. 4:4). Mephibosheth may be an intentional change by copyists to avoid writing the pagan god's name "baal." The original name would be Meribaal (1 Chron. 8:34). See 2 Sam. 16; 19.

(2) Son of Saul, who with six other members of Saul's household, was delivered by David to the Gibeonites to be hanged (2 Sam. 21:1-9).

MERAB (to become many)

Eldest daughter of King Saul (1 Sam. 14:49); twice promised to David (1 Sam. 17:25; 18:17-19). Saul reneged on his promise. See 2 Sam. 21:8.

MERARI (bitterness or gall), MERARITES

Third son of Levi (Gen. 46:11; Ex. 6:16; Num. 3:17; 1 Chron. 6:1,16; 23:6); ancestor of a division of priests; with Gershonites, responsible for set up, breakdown, and transport of the tabernacle (Num. 10:17; compare 3:36-37; 4:29-33; 7:8). See Josh. 21:7,34-40; 1 Chron. 6:63,77-81; 15:6,17,19; 1 Chron. 26:10,19; 2 Chron. 29:12; 34:12; Ezra 8:19.

MERCY SEAT

Slab of pure gold measuring about 45 inches by 27 inches that sat atop the ark of the covenant; base for the golden cherubim (Ex. 25:17-19,21); symbolized throne from which God ruled Israel (Lev. 16:2; Num. 7:89). On the Day of Atonement the high priest sprinkled the blood of a sacrificial lamb on the mercy seat as a plea for forgiveness for the sins of the nation (Lev. 16:15). The Hebrew word means literally "to wipe out" or "cover over." This has led modern translators to render the term "cover" (REB, NRSV note), "lid" (TEV, NCV, CEV), or "atonement cover" (NIV; see NLT). "Mercy seat" is based on the earliest Greek and Latin translations. Christ's cross and resurrection showed the perfect presence and accomplished atonement once for all (Heb. 9).

MERCY, MERCIFUL

Personal characteristic of care for the needs of others—from assistance in finding a bride to God's forgiveness of sin. Mercy is closely tied to the compassion and pity of family relationships (Gen. 43:30; 1 Kings 3:26) which provide image for God's mercy (Jer. 31:20; Ps. 103:13; Isa. 54:6-8; 63:15-16; Hos. 2:19; Amos 1:11). God's mercy is even compared to a mother's care for a nursing child (Isa. 49:15). God's mercy is bound up with His covenant with Israel (Ex. 33:19; 2 Kings 13:23; Isa. 54:10; 63:7) and is expressed by His action for Israel (Neh. 9:19; Pss. 64:16-21; 79:8-11; Isa. 30:18; 49:10; Jer. 42:11-12). When Israel turned from God, He showed no pity (Isa. 9:17; 27:11; Jer. 13:14; 16:5; Hos. 1:6-8; 2:4), but He is a forgiving God and shows mercy to a penitent people (Pss. 25:4-7; 40:11-12; 51:1-4; Prov. 28:13-14; Isa. 54:7; 55:7; Lam. 3:31-33; Dan. 9:9; Mic. 7:19; Hab. 3:2). He is merciful in restoring the nation (Ps. 102:13; Isa. 14:1; 49:13; Jer. 12:15; 30:18; 33:26; Ezek. 39:25; Zech. 1:16; 10:6) and renewing His friendship with them (Hos. 2:19,23). God's mercy is the very source of His people's life (Pss. 103:4; 119:77,156).

Israel was to show no mercy to criminals (Deut. 13:8; 19:13,21), but God expected His people to be merciful to their neighbors (1 Kings 8:31-32; Prov. 3:29; 21:13). He especially expected their mercy toward the poor and needy (Zech. 7:9-10).

God expects His people to show covenant mercy to one another because He shows such mercy to them—to individuals such as Abraham (Gen. 24:12-14), Jacob (Gen. 32:10), David (2 Sam. 7:15), and Job (10:12). Above all, He was merciful to His chosen people Israel (Ex. 15:13; Ps. 107:8,15,21,31; Isa. 63:7; Jer. 31:2-6).

Job appealed for "pity" (19:21). The psalmist described one who is generous to the poor (Pss. 37:21; 112:5; compare Prov. 14:21-23; 19:17; 28:8). This type of mercy refers to God's gracious and generous nature. All three Hebrew terms for mercy appear in the recurrent OT liturgy: "God is merciful and gracious, slow to anger, and abounding in steadfast love and faithfulness" (Ex. 34:6; Num. 14:18; Neh. 9:17; Pss. 86:15; 103:8; 145:8; Joel 2:13; Jonah 4:2).

In the NT, mercy expressed strong emotional feelings, particularly of compassion and affection. Jesus showed such compassion—for the multitudes (Matt. 9:36, 14:14, 15:32), for the blind (Matt. 20:34), for a leper (Mark 1:41), for a possessed child (Mark 9:20-127), for a widow's plight (Luke 7:13). His parables use the term to describe the mercy of a master on his indebted servant (Matt. 18:27), the compassion of a father for his prodigal son (Luke 15:20), and a Samaritan's pity for a wounded Jew (Luke 10:33). With this word Paul urged the Corinthians to renew their affection for him (2 Cor. 6:12; compare 7:15), exhorted the Philippians to mutual love and concern (Phil. 2:1-2), and played on the sympathy of Philemon (Philem. 7,12,20). With it, John reminded his readers that one who closes his heart to a brother's need scarcely has God's love (1 John 3:17).

God is "the father of mercies" (2 Cor. 1:3), which should lead us to sacrificial service (Rom. 12:1; compare Luke 6:36). God in His sovereign purposes can withdraw His mercies (Rom. 9:15-16,18,23). Jesus was met by cries and expectations for mercy (Matt. 9:27; 15:22; 17:15; Luke 17:13). His healings testify to the divine mercy (Mark 5:19). Jesus' birth and that of John are testimonies that God is both merciful and faithful to His promises (Luke 1:58,72,78; compare 1 Cor. 7:25; 2 Cor. 4:1; 1 Tim. 1:13,16; Phil. 2:27).

God's mercy is shown in His readiness to forgive the penitent sinner (Luke 8:13) and in the atoning work of Christ (Heb. 2:17; compare Eph. 2:4-5; compare 1 Pet. 1:3; Jude 21) and includes the Gentiles (Rom. 11:30-32). It undergirds the hope of life to come. God's mercy is always available for those who approach His throne (Heb. 4:16). This is why mercy is often an element in NT greetings and benedictions (1 Tim. 1:2; 2 Tim. 1:2; Gal. 6:16; 2 John 3; Jude 2). See *Greeting; Benediction.*

God does not desire the external trappings of religiosity but deeds of mercy to others (Matt. 5:7; 9:13; 12:7; 23:23; Luke 10:36-37; Rom. 12:8). One who shows no mercy to others cannot expect God's mercy (Matt. 18:33-34; Jas. 2:13; 3:17). Jesus Christ is the ultimate manifestation of God's mercy, the assurance of that mercy for believers, and the basis of their own mercy in their relationships with others.

MERIBAH See *Massah.*

MERODACH

Hebrew form of Marduk, chief god of Babylon, also called Bel, corresponding to the Semitic Baal or "Lord" (Jer. 50:2); element in names of the Babylonian kings Merodach-baladan (2 Kings 20:12; Isa. 39:1) and Evil-Merodach (2 Kings 25:27; Jer. 52:31). With a different vocalization, Merodach yields the name Mordecai (Esther 2:5). See *Gods, Pagan.*

MERODACH-BALADAN (*god Marduk gave an heir*)

Ruler of the Bit-Yakin tribe in southern Babylonia; king of Babylon (721–711 B.C.; 704 B.C.); little more than a puppet of Assyria, answering to Sargon. See *Babylon, History and Religion of.*

MEROM (*high place*)

Place in Galilee where Joshua defeated coalition of Canaanite tribes under King Jabin of Hazor in a surprise attack (Josh. 11:1-7); modern Merion. Both Thutmose III and Rameses II of Egypt claimed to have captured the area.

MEROZ

Town condemned in the Song of Deborah for failure to join in the Lord's battle against the oppressive forces of Sisera (Judg. 5:23).

MESHA (*safety*)

Three OT men and city including:

(1) Ruler of Moab who led a rebellion against Israel (2 Kings 3:4-27); "sheep breeder"(2 Kings 3:4, NRSV) is perhaps an honorary title for chief. Mesha seized Israelite border towns and fortified towns on his frontier. An alliance of Israel, Judah, and Edom attacked Mesha from the rear. Mesha retreated to Kir-hareseth from which he attempted, unsuccessfully, to escape to his Aramean allies. Mesha sacrificed his firstborn son to his god Chemosh on the city walls. The Israelites lifted their seige and returned home. The Moabite stone describes Mesha as a builder of cities and highways. Archaeological evidence, however, suggests a decline in Moabite civilization following the revolt. See *Moab.*

(2) City in territory of Joktanites (Gen. 10:30); most likely, Massa (Gen. 25:14; Prov. 31:1), between the head of the gulf of Aqaba and the Persian Gulf.

MESHACH

Friend of Daniel exiled to Babylon 597 B.C. (Dan. 1:6-7); Hebrew name, Mishael ("Who is what God is") was changed to Meshach (perhaps, "Who is what Aku is") to mock Israel's God. Declining the rich food of the king's table, he and his friends proved simple fare of vegetables and water was to be desired to make one wise and strong. After refusing to bow to the king's golden image, he, Shadrach, and Abednego were thrown into a furnace, but were delivered by God (Dan. 3). Thereafter, they were promoted in the king's court.

MESHECH (*sowing* or *possession*)

(1) People of Asia Minor (Gen. 10:2; 1 Chron. 1:5), known for trading in copper vessels (Ezek. 27:13), frequently associated with Tubal (Ezek. 32:26; 38:2-3; 39:1). See Ps. 120:5.

(2) An otherwise unknown Aramaean tribe (1 Chron. 1:17), perhaps identical with Mash (Gen. 10:23).

MESOPOTAMIA (Greek *between the rivers*)

Area between Tigris and Euphrates rivers; more generally, entire Tigris-Euphrates valley. At times culture of Mesopotamia dominated an even larger area, spreading east into Elam and Media, north into Asia Minor, and following the fertile cresent into Canaan and Egypt.

Mesopotamia was homeland of the patriarchs (Gen. 11:31-12:4; 24:10; 28:6). A Mesopotamian king subdued Israel (Judg. 3:8). Mesopotamia supplied mercenary chariots and cavalry for the Ammonites' war with David (1 Chron. 19:6; superscription of Ps. 60). Both the Northern Kingdom of Israel (2 Kings 15:29; 1 Chron. 5:26) and the Southern Kingdom of Judah (2 Kings 24:14-16; 2 Chron. 36:20; Ezra 2:1) went into exile in Mesopotamia.

MESSIAH

Transliteration of Hebrew word for "anointed one"; translated into Greek as *Christos*. See *Christ, Chris-*

tology. Christ has become the proper name of Jesus, the Person whom Christians recognize as the God-given Redeemer of Israel and the church's Lord.

"Anointed" refers to installing a person in an office so person will be regarded as accredited by Yahweh, Israel's God. Even a pagan king such as Cyrus was qualified as the Lord's anointed (Isa. 45:1) to execute a divinely appointed task. Prophets such as Elisha were set apart (1 Kings 19:16). Israel probably saw a close link between the anointed persons and God's spirit (2 Kings 2:9). Israelite kings were particularly hailed as Yahweh's anointed (compare Judg. 9:8), beginning with Saul (1 Sam. 9-10, NIV) and especially referring to David (1 Sam. 16:6,13; see 2 Sam. 2:4; 5:3) and Solomon (1 Kings 1:39). The royal family of David are "anointed ones" (2 Sam. 22:51; compare 2 Kings 11:12; 23:30; Pss. 2:2; 20:6; 28:8; 84:9). The king in Israel thus became a sacred person to whom loyalty and respect were to be accorded (1 Sam. 24:6,10; 26:9, 11,16,23; 2 Sam. 1:14,16). Nathan's oracle (2 Sam. 7:12-16) centers Israel's hope on dynasty of David for succeeding generations. Isaiah 9 and 11 point to a new king.

The king, especially in the Psalms, became idealized as a divine son (Ps. 2:2,7; compare 2 Sam. 7:14) and enjoyed God's protecting favor (Pss. 18:50; 20:6; 28:8). His dynasty would not fail (Ps. 132:17), and the people were encouraged to pray to God on his behalf (Pss. 72:11-15; 84:9). The fall of Jerusalem in 586 B.C. led to great confusion especially when Yahweh's anointed was taken into exile as a prisoner (Lam. 4:20) and his authority as king rejected by the nations (Ps. 89:38,51). Restoration became the pious longing of the Jews both in Babylonian exile (Jer. 33:14-18) and in the later centuries.

After the exile, high priest took on a central role in the community. The rite of anointing was the outward sign of his authority to function as God's representative. This authority was traced back to Aaron and his sons

(Ex. 29:7-9; 30:22-33; compare Ps. 133:2). The high priest was the anointed-priest (Lev. 4:3,5,16) and even, in one place, a "messiah" (Zech. 4:14; compare 6:13; Dan. 9:25).

In the exilic and postexilic ages, the expectation of a coming Messiah came into sharper focus, commencing with Jeremiah's and Ezekiel's vision of a Messiah who would combine the traits of royalty and priestly dignity (Jer. 33:14-18; Ezek. 46:1-8; see, too, Zech. 4:1-14; 6:13). The people in the Dead Sea scrolls were evidently able to combine a dual hope of two Messiahs, one priestly and the second a royal figure.

A question posed in John 4:29 (compare 7:40-43): "Is not this the Christ (Messiah)?" Jesus asked His disciples,"Who do you say that I am?" Peter replied, "Thou art the Christ (Messiah)" (Mark 8:29). Jesus took an attitude of distinct reserve and caution to this title since it carried overtones of political power. Jesus saw His destiny in terms of a suffering Son of man and Servant of God (Mark 8:31-38; 9:31; 10:33-34). Hence He did not permit the demons to greet Him as Messiah (Luke 4:41) and downplayed all claims to privilege and overt majesty linked with the Jewish title. At His Jewish trial (Matt. 26:63-66), He reinterpreted the title "Messiah" and in terms of the Son of man figure, based on Dan. 7:13-14. This confession secured His condemnation. He went to the cross as a crucified Messiah because the Jewish leaders failed to perceive the nature of messiahship as Jesus understood it. Pilate sentenced Him as a messianic pretender who claimed (according to the false charges brought against Him) to be a rival to Caesar (Mark 15:9; Luke 23:2; John 19:14-15). Only after the resurrection did the disciples see how Jesus was truly a king Messiah (see Luke 24:45-46). The national title Messiah took on a broader connotation, a kingly role embracing all peoples (Luke 24:46-47).

From the resurrection onward the first preachers announced that Jesus was the Messiah by divine appointment (Acts 2:36; Rom. 1:3-4) and the royal "Son of David" (Matt. 1:1; Luke 1:32,69; 2:4,11; Acts 2:29-36; 13:22-23; 1 Cor. 5:7-8; Heb. 1:9; 2:2-4; 9:14-15; 1 Pet. 1:11,20; 2:21; 3:18; 4:1,13; 5:1).

METHEG-AMMAH

Phrase in 2 Sam. 8:1. KJV, NIV, NRSV, NCV, REB take it as place name; NASB (see NLT), "the chief city"; CEV, "free from their control." The parallel in 1 Chron. 18:1 has "Gath and its villages." Other suggestions for translation include: "bridle of the water channel,""reins of the forearm,""control of the mother city,""take the common land," or "wrest supremacy from."

METHUSELAH (man of the javelin or worshiper of Selah)

Son of Enoch; grandfather of Noah (Gen. 5:21,26-29); oldest human in Bible, dying at age 969 (Gen. 5:27).

MICAH (Who is like Yahweh?)

Six OT men including:

(1) Ephramite whose home shrine was the source of Dan's idolotrous worship (Judg. 17–18).

(2) Prophet; author of sixth book in Minor Prophets; Micah 1:1 says he came from Moresheth (see Moresheth, Moresheth-Gath), worked under Jotham (750–732 B.C.), Ahaz (735–715 B.C.), and Hezekiah (715–686 B.C.); and addressed Samaria and Jerusalem. Even though Micah ministered in Judah, some of his messages were directed toward Israel. Micah was a contemporary of Isaiah, Hosea, and possibly Amos.

MICAH, BOOK OF

Prophetic book named after the eighth-century B.C. prophet containing some of his messages. See Israel, History of.

Micah constantly renounced the oppression of the poor by the rich who devised ways to cheat the poor out of their land (2:1-5). Fellow Israelites were evicted from their homes and had their possessions stolen (2:6-11). The marketplace was full of deception and injustice (6:9-16). The rulers of the country, responsibile to uphold justice, did the opposite (3:1-4).

Micah also denounced the religious practices of the nation. Other prophets led the people to believe God was residing in the nation and would protect them. Micah contended that the other prophets' message was not from God. God was announcing the imminent devastation of Judah (3:5-12).

The people combined worship of other gods with worship of the God of Judah (5:10-15). The people believed all that religion required of them was to bring their sacrifices and offerings to the temple. Micah argued that God is not just interested in the physical act of making a sacrifice but is supremely concerned with obedience in daily life (6:6-8).

After judgement, God would restore a remnant of the people devoted to Him (4:1-13; 7:14-20). God would bring a ruler who would allow the people to live in peace (5:1-5). Matthew saw a description of Christ in Micah's hope for a new ruler (Matt. 2:6).

MICAIAH *(Who is like Yahweh?)*

Son of Imlah and prophet of Yahweh who predicted the death of Ahab and the scattering of Israel's forces at Ramoth-Gilead (1 Kings 22:7-28). Having witnessed Yahweh's heavenly council, Micaiah was certain Ahab's 400 prophets were possessed by a lying spirit. When accused and imprisoned on a charge of false prophecy, Micaiah replied, "If you return in peace, the LORD has not spoken by me" (22:28, NRSV).

MICHAEL *(Who is like God?)*

Nine OT men and Archangel who served as the guardian of the nation of Israel (Dan. 10:13,21; 12:1). Together with Gabriel, Michael fought for Israel against the prince (angelic patron) of Persia. In Rev. 12:7 Michael commands the forces of God against the forces of the dragon in a war in heaven. Jude 9 refers to a dispute between the devil and Michael over Moses' body. See *Angel.*

MICHAL *(who is like El [God]?)*

King Saul's younger daughter (1 Sam. 14:49) given to David in marriage for the price of 100 dead Philistines (1 Sam. 18:20-29). The king continued to set traps for David. Once Michal helped her husband escape (1 Sam. 19:11-17). For revenge, Saul gave her to Phaltiel (1 Sam. 25:44). Following Saul's death at Gilboa, David made a treaty with Abner, Saul's general. One of the points of the pact was that Michal would be returned to David, much to Phaltiel's regret (2 Sam. 3:14-16). David's dancing before the ark of the covenant as he brought the sacred box to Jerusalem enraged Michal, who criticized the king to his face. As punishment Michal was never allowed to bear children (2 Sam. 6:16-23; compare 2 Sam. 21:8).

MICHMASH *(hidden place)*

City in Benjamin about seven miles northeast of Jerusalem, four and a half miles northeast of Gibeah, rising 1,980 feet above sea level overlooking a pass going from the Jordan River to Ephraim; 4 ½ miles southeast of Bethel, which rises 2,890 feet above sea level; modern Mukhmas. Michmash served as a staging area, first for Saul (1 Sam. 13:2) and then for the Philistine army (13:5-6) as they prepared to fight (see 14:20). It lay on the standard invasion route from the north (Isa. 10:28). See Neh. 11:31; compare 7:31; 1 Macc. 9:73.

MIDIAN, MIDIANITES *(strife)*

Son of Abraham by his concubine Keturah (Gen. 25:2); sent away with his brothers to the east, leading to the assocation of the Midianites with the "children of the east" (Judg. 6:3). Midianites took Joseph to Egypt (Gen. 37:28,36); may be same as or closely related to Ishmaelites. Their main homeland seems to be east of the Jordan and south of Edom. When Moses fled from Pharaoh, he went east to Midian (Ex. 2:15), met Jethro (also called Reuel), the priest of Midian, and married his daughter. During the wandering in the wilderness, Reuel's father-in-law Hobab served as a guide for the Israelites (Num. 10:29-32). The Midianites are associated with the Moabites in seducing Israel into immorality and pagan worship at Baal-peor (Num. 25:1-18). God commanded Moses to execute a war of vengeance against them (Num. 31:3; compare Josh. 13:21). Midianites along with the Amalekites began to raid Israel using camels to strike swiftly over great distances. Gideon drove them out and killed their leaders (Judg. 6–8). See 1 Kings 11:18.

MIDRASH

Jewish term, "to make exposition"; title of body of Jewish literature that gathers together the Jewish scholars' exegesis, exposition, and homiletical interpretations of Scripture in the centuries just before and after Jesus; method to discover deeper meaning of the most minute details contained in the sacred text. A midrash denotes a didactic (teaching) or homilectic (preaching) exposition or an edifying religious story such as that of Tobit. Midrash also includes a religious interpretation of history, as the prophet Iddo's commentary on the acts, ways, and sayings of King Abijam (2 Chron. 13:22) and the Commentary on the Book of the Kings, in which were set forth the burdens laid upon King Joash and his rebuilding of the temple (2 Chron. 24:27). Midrash characteristics:

(1) started with an actual biblical text or texts (often two quite different passages are combined);

(2) designed to edify and instruct;

(3) based on close and detailed scrutiny of actual text, in which it seeks to establish the underlying reasons for each word, phrase, or group of words;

(4) concerned to apply the message to the present age.

Midrash is divided into *halacha* (oral law), midrashic investigation of the legal parts of the OT with the aim of establishing rules of conduct, and *haggadah*, investigation of nonlegal parts with purpose of edifying or instructing. Ezra used Midrash in the public reading of the law (Neh. 8; compare Ezra 7:10). Midrash became the basic work leading to the production of the Targumin (Aramaic paraphrases of Scripture) and of the mainline expression of Judaism (Mishnah, Talmud). See *Targum; Mishnah; Talmud.*

Many Bible students believe numerous examples of midrash appear in the NT: Matt. 2:1-12 on Num. 24:17; Matt. 27:3-10 on Zech. 11:12-13; Jer. 32:6-15. Midrashic elements are also present in Paul (Gal. 3:4; Rom. 4:9-11; 2 Cor. 3) and other areas of the NT.

MIDWIFE

Woman who assists in the delivery of a child (Ex. 1:15-21), cutting umbilical cord, washing and salting the babe, and wrapping the child in cloths (Ezek. 16:4). The civil disobedience of the Hebrew midwives Siphrah and Puah confounded Pharaoh's plan to exterminate male Hebrews for a time (Ex. 1:15-21). Their faithfulness was rewarded with families of their own (Ex. 1:21). See Ruth 4:14-17; 1 Sam. 4:20.

MIGDOL (*tower, watchtower, fortress*)

Transliteration of Hebrew; town or border fortress located in northeast corner of Egypt. Site on or near route of the exodus near Pi-hahiroth and Baal-Zephon (Ex. 14:2; compare Jer. 44:1; 46:13-14); northern extremity of the land paired with Aswan, the southern extremity (Ezek. 29:10; 30:6). Migdol may be common noun, "tower," or could refer to more than one site in Egypt. A papyrus manuscript mentions Migdol of Pharoah Seti I near Tjeku, the location of which is still debated, giving certainty of at least two sites named Migdol: Migdol of Jeremiah and Ezekiel near Pelusium and Migdol on exodus route near Succoth. Both may have been part of a line of border fortresses designed to provide protection for Egypt against invasion from the Sinai.

MILCOM (*king* or *their king*)

A deity; apparently, form created by Hebrew scribes to slander and avoid pronouncing the name of the national god of Ammon (1 Kings 11:5,7), who may have been identified with Chemosh, the god of Moab. See *Chemosh.*

MILE

Roman mile (Matt. 5:41) is about 4,848 feet (or 432 feet shorter than American mile).

MILETUM or **MILETUS** See *Asia Minor, Cities of; Ephesus.*

MILK

Nourishing liquid and its by-products; staple of Hebrew diet; includes sweet milk, soured milk, cheese, butter, symbol of blessing and abundance. Most often milk came from sheep and goats (Prov. 27:27; Deut. 32:14); cow's milk was also known (Isa. 7:21-22). Butter and cheese were known among the ancients (1 Sam. 17:18) as well as curdled, sour milk which still forms, after bread, the chief food of the poorer classes in Arabia and Syria. Soured milk was carried by travelers who mixed it with meat, dried it, and then dissolved it in water to make a refreshing drink such as that Abraham set before the messengers (Gen. 18:8). After setting awhile, the drink would carry an intoxicating effect, leading some to believe that the fermented variety is the drink that Jael gave to Sisera (Judg. 4:19).

The OT's most extensive use of milk is in conjunction with honey to symbolize abundance and blessing (Ex. 3:17; 13:5; 33:3; Lev. 20:24; Num. 13:27; Deut. 6:3; Josh. 5:6). Milk is also used to symbolize whiteness (Lam. 4:7) and marital bliss (Song of Sol. 5:1).

Milk speaks concerning what is basic to the Christian life, but not all that is needed (1 Cor. 3:2; 9:7; Heb.

5:12,13; 1 Pet. 2:2).The ancient bedouins could live on milk for days but eventually had to have meat; so must the Christian. Rabbis interpreted the repeated rule (Ex. 23:19; 34:26; Deut. 14:21) not to boil a kid in its mother's milk to mean that milk and meat should neither be cooked nor eaten together.

MILL

Two circular basalt stones about a foot and a half in diameter and two to four inches thick used to grind grain; usually worked by two women facing each other. One woman fed the grain at the center, and the other guided the products into little piles.To make fine flour, it is reground and sifted. It was forbidden to take millstones as a pledge because they were so important to sustaining life (Deut. 24:6).The manna in the wilderness was tough enough that people ground it in mills before cooking it (Num. 11:7-8). See Matt. 24:41; Rev. 18:21.

MILLENNIUM

Term not found in Scripture but taken from Latin to express the "thousand years" mentioned six times in Rev. 20:1-7. See *Eschatology.*

MILLO (*filling*)

Stone terrace system employed in ancient construction.

(1) Beth Millo (Judg. 9:6,20); probably a suburb of Shechem; most likely Canaanite sanctuary built on an artificial platform or fill.

(2) Extension of Jerusalem beyond original Jebusite city David captured; stretched northward to include Hill of Moriah, site of future temple. Joash's murder by his own men near Beth Millo (2 Kings 12:20) may refer to terraces in this portion of the city.

MIND

Center of intellectual activity and of ethical nature. The mind can be evil. It is described as "reprobate" (Rom. 1:28), "fleshly" (Col. 2:18), "vain" (Eph. 4:17), "corrupt" (1 Tim. 6:5; 2 Tim. 3:8), and "defiled" (Titus 1:15). Israel's "minds were blinded" so that they could not understand the OT (2 Cor. 3:14; see 2 Cor. 4:4; 11:3). We are to love God with "all" our mind (Matt. 22:37; Mark 12:30; Luke 10:27) because the mind can be revived and empowered by the Holy Spirit (Rom. 12:2) and because God's laws under the new covenant are put into our minds (Heb. 8:10; 10:16).

"Mind" is often English translation of "heart" (Num. 16:28; Matt. 13:15) or "soul" (Deut. 18:6; Acts 14:2; Phil. 1:27; Heb. 12:3; compare Gen. 23:8). "Spirit" is rendered "mind" (Gen. 26:35) as are "imagination" (Isa. 26:3), "mouth" (Lev. 24:12), "intent" (1 Pet.4:1), "purpose" (Rev. 17:13), "thought" (Rom. 8:6), and "opinion" (Philem. 14). See *Heart; Soul; Anthropology; Humanity.*

MINERALS AND METALS

Inorganic elements or compounds found naturally in nature.

Precious Stones

Precious stones are desirable because of rarity, hardness, and beauty, the latter expressed in terms of color, transparency, luster, and brilliance. The Bible has three main lists of precious stones: the 12 stones of Aaron's breastplate (Ex. 28:17-20; 39:10-13), the treasures of the king of Tyre (Ezek. 28:13), and the stones on the wall foundation of the New Jerusalem (Rev. 21:18-21). Other lists are found in Job 28:15-19; Isa. 54:11-12; and Ezek. 27:16. The precise identification of some of the terms is unclear, unfortunately.

(1) *Adamant* (Ezek. 3:9; Zech. 7:12, KJV, RSV, REB). Hebrew word is sometimes translated "diamond" (Jer. 17:1, KJV, NRSV, REB, NASB). The stone was "harder than flint" (Ezek. 3:9) and may be emery (Ezek. 3:9, NASB) or an imaginary stone of impenetrable hardness, best translated "the hardest stone" (Ezek. 3:9, NIV, NRSV).

(2) *Agate.* Multicolored and banded form of chalcedony (Ex. 28:19 and Rev. 21:19, NRSV).

(3) *Amethyst* (Ex. 28:19; 39:12; Rev. 21:20). Blue-violet form of quartz.

(4) *Beryl.* Beryllium aluminum silicate (Ex. 28:20; 39:13; REB, "topaz"; NIV, "chrysolite"); (Ezek. 28:13; RSV, NIV, "chrysolite"; NRSV, "beryl"; REB, "topaz"; RSV translates another and NIV a third word as "beryl") (Rev. 21:20).

(5) *Carbuncle* (Ex. 28:17; 39:10; REB, "green feldspar;" NASB, NRSV, "emerald"; TEV, "garnet"; NIV, "beryl"); (Isa. 54:12; REB, "garnet"; NIV, "sparkling jewels").

(6) *Carnelian* (KJV; sometimes RSV, NASB, "sardius"); clear to brownish red variety of chalcedony (Ezek. 28:13; NASB, TEV, NIV, "ruby"; REB, "sardin") (Rev. 21:20; compare 4:3).

(7) *Chalcedony.* Alternate translation for agate (Rev. 21:19, KJV, NASB, REB, NIV); noncrystalline form of quartz, or silicone dioxide, has many varieties including agate, carnelian, chrysoprase, flint, jasper, and onyx.

(8) *Chrysolite.* Various yellowish minerals (Rev. 21:20); replaces KJV "beryl" frequently in RSV (Ezek. 1:16; 10:9; 28:13) and throughout NIV but not in NRSV; REB, "topaz."

(9) *Chrysoprase* or *Chrysoprasus* (KJV). Apple-green variety of chalcedony (Rev. 21:20).

(10) *Coral* (Job 28:18; Ezek. 27:16). Calcium carbonate formed by the action of marine animals. NRSV, REB, NASB translated a second word as coral (Lam. 4:7; KJV, NIV, "rubies").

(11) *Crystal.* Quartz. See Job 28:17-18 (KJV, "pearls"; NIV, "jasper"; REB, "alabaster"). The glassy sea (Rev. 4:6) and river of life (Rev. 22:1) are compared to crystal.

(12) *Diamond.* Not clear if diamonds were known in the Ancient Near East (Ex. 28:18; 39:11; REB, "jade"; NIV, "emerald"); (Ezek. 28:13; NRSV, REB, "jasper"; NIV, "emerald").

(13) *Emerald.* Bright green variety of beryl, readily available to the Israelites (Ex. 28:18; 39:11; Ezek. 28:13; REB, "purple garnet"; NASB, NIV, NRSV, "turquoise" with NRSV

translating another word as "emerald"). Rainbow around the throne is compared to "an emerald" (Rev. 4:3; compare Rev. 21:19).

(14) *Jacinth.* Transparent red to brown form of zirconium silicate (Ex. 28:19; 39:11; KJV, "ligure"; REB, TEV, "turquoise") (Rev. 21:20).

(15) *Jasper.* Red, yellow, brown, or green opaque variety of chalcedony (Ex. 28:20; 39:13; Rev. 21:11,18-19). RSV (Ezek. 28:13) jasper translates word elsewhere rendered "diamond" (REB, "jade"), but NRSV reads "moonstone."

(16) *Lapis Lazuli.* Combination of minerals that yields an azure to green-blue stone popular in Egypt for jewelry; an alternate translation for "sapphire" (NASB in Ezek. 28:13; NIV marginal notes).

(17) *Onyx.* Flat-banded variety of chalcedony (Ex. 25:7,20; 28:9; 35:27; 39:6,13; Ezek. 28:13; provided for settings of temple (1 Chron. 29:2). Sardonyx includes layers of carnelian.

(18) *Pearl.* Formed around foreign matter in some shellfish (Job 28:18; NASB, NRSV; KJV, NIV, "rubies"; REB,"red coral"; Rev. 21:21); simile for kingdom of God (Matt. 13:46), metaphor for truth (Matt. 7:6), and symbol of immodesty (1 Tim. 2:9; Rev. 17:4; 18:16).

(19) *Ruby.* Red variety of corundum, or aluminum oxide (Ex. 28:17; 39:10, NASB, NIV; KJV, RSV, REB, "sardius"; NRSV, "carnelian"; Ezek. 28:13, NASB, NIV; REB, KJV, "sardius"; NRSV, "carnelian").

(20) *Sapphire.* Blue variety of corundum (Ex. 24:10; 28:18; 39:11; Job 28:6,16; Isa. 54:11; Lam. 4:7; Ezek. 1:26; 10:1; 28:13; Rev. 21:19); may refer to lapis lazuli (NIV marginal notes) rather than true sapphire.

(21) *Topaz.* Aluminum floro silicate and quite hard; OT topaz may refer to peridot, a magnesium olivine (Ex. 28:17; 39:10; Job 28:19; Ezek. 28:13; Rev. 21:20). See *Beryl, Chrysolite* above.

(22) *Turquoise.* Sky-blue to bluish-green base phosphate of copper and aluminum; mined in Sinai by Egyptians; highly valued stone in antiquity; sometimes substituted for emerald (Ex. 28:18, NASB, NIV); or "jacinth" (Ex. 28:19; 39:11, REB, TEV).

Common Minerals

(1) *Alabaster.* Fine-grained gypsum; Egyptian alabaster was crystalline calcium carbonate with similar appearance; used for precious ointment containers (Matt. 26:7; Mark 14:3; Luke 7:37). Alabaster may be mentioned (NRSV, NASB Song of Sol. 5:15; KJV, REB, NIV "marble").

(2) *Brimstone.* Sulfur (NRSV, NIV). Burning sulfur deposits created extreme heat, molten flows, and noxious fumes, providing a graphic picture of the destruction and suffering of divine judgment (Deut. 29:23; Job 18:15; Ps. 11:6; Isa. 30:33; Ezek. 38:22; Luke 17:29).

(3) *Salt.* Sodium chloride; an abundant mineral used as seasoning for food (Job 6:6) and offerings (Lev. 2:13; Ezek. 43:24) and as preservative, symbolic of covenants (Num. 18:19; 2 Chron. 13:5). Disciples are to be both seasoning and preservatives (Matt. 5:13). Salt was also symbol of desolation and barrenness, perhaps because of the barrenness of the Dead Sea, biblical Salt Sea."Saltpits" (Zeph. 2:9) were probably located just south of the Dead Sea. Sodium chloride could leech out of the generally impure salt from this area, leaving a tasteless substance (Luke 14:34-35).

(4) *Soda* (Prov. 25:20, NASB, NIV; Jer. 2:22, REB, NIV), nitre (KJV), or lye (Jer. 2:22, NRSV, NASB) is probably sodium or potassium carbonate; possibly "vinegar" in Prov. 25:20 (Septuagint; NRSV, REB).

Metals

Metals occur naturally in compound with other elements as an ore that must be smelted to obtain a usable product (Num. 31:22; Ezek. 22:18,20).

(1) *Brass.* Relatively modern alloy of copper and tin; should be rendered "copper" or "bronze."

(2) *Bronze.* Usual translation of Hebrew word that can indicate either copper or bronze; alloy of copper and

tin, and stronger than both; most common metal used for utensils. Bible mentions "armor" (1 Sam. 17:5-6), "shackles" (2 Kings 25:7), "cymbals" (1 Chron. 15:19), "gates" (Ps. 107:16; Isa. 45:2), and "idols" (Rev. 9:20).

(3) *Copper.* Usually alloyed with tin to make bronze (Lev. 26:19; Deut. 8:9; Job 28:2; Ezek. 24:11; Matt. 10:9; Mark 12:42; Luke 21:2). See *Ezion-Geber.*

(4) *Gold.* Valued and used because of its rarity, beauty, and workability; can be melted without harm; extremely malleable; can be used for cast objects, inlays, or overlays. A number of Israel's worship objects were solid gold or gilded (Ex. 37). Gold occurs in the Bible more frequently than any other metal, being used for jewelry (Ex. 12:35; 1 Tim. 2:9), idols, scepters, worship utensils, and money (Matt. 10:9; Acts 3:6). The New Jerusalem is described as made of gold (Rev. 21:18,21).

(5) *Iron.* More difficult metal to smelt than copper; came into widespread use about the time of Israel's conquest of Canaan, gradually replacing bronze for metal weapons and agricultural tools. The Canaanites'"chariots of iron" (Josh. 17:16,18; Judg. 1:19; 4:3) represent a technological advantage over Israel, while the Philistines may have enjoyed an iron-working monopoly (1 Sam. 17:7; 13:19-21). Iron was more widespread by the time of David (2 Sam. 12:31; 1 Chron. 20:3; 22:14), though it remained valuable (2 Kings 6:5-6). It was used where strength was essential and became a symbol of hardness and strength (Deut. 28:48; Ps. 2:9; Isa. 48:4; Jer. 17:1; Rev. 2:27).

(6) *Lead.* Gray metal of extremely high density (Ex. 15:10) used for weights, heavy covers (Zech. 5:7-8), and plumblines (compare Amos 7:7-8); quite pliable and useful for inlays such as lettering in rock (Job 19:24); used in refining silver (Jer. 6:27-30).

(7) *Silver.* Not occurring often in natural state, but easily extracted from ores; originally more valuable than gold and used as measure of wealth (Gen. 13:2; 24:35; Zeph. 1:18; Hag. 2:8). By Solomon's day it was common in Israel (1 Kings 10:27) and standard monetary unit, being weighed in shekels, talents, and minas (Gen. 23:15-16; 37:28; Ex. 21:32; Neh. 7:72; Isa. 7:23). See *Weights and Measures.* Silver was used for objects in Israel's worship (Ex. 26:19; 36:24; Ezra 8:26,28), idols (Ex. 20:23; Judg. 17:4; Ps. 115:4; Isa. 40:19), and jewelry (Gen. 24:53; Song of Sol. 1:11).

(8) *Tin.* Sometimes confused with lead; articles of pure tin were rare; principally used in making bronze, an alloy of tin and copper (Num. 31:22; Ezek. 22:18,20). See *Mines and Mining.*

MINES AND MINING

The extraction of minerals from the earth. Early mining efforts sought to provide people with stones necessary to make weapons and tools.

(1) *Copper.* The use of mined minerals to form metals began sometime around 6500 B.C. near Catal Huyuk in Asia Minor. Tubal-cain, a descendant of Cain, is called the father of copper forging (Gen. 4:22). Copper ore was taken at first from deposits above the ground. Soon mine shafts and tunnels were cut into areas where surface deposits hinted at the larger ore supplies below. In the Arabah and Sinai, mining settlements were founded. Palestine was relatively poor in copper ore. Copper sheets and ingots were shipped by sea and land thousands of miles to meet the growing needs for metal tools, weapons, and jewelry. Before 3000 B.C. people discovered that copper could be mixed with arsenic to form a stronger alloy.

(2) *Bronze.* Around 3200 B.C. metalsmiths produced bronze, a much stronger metal, by using tin as an alloy. Bronze became the most widely used metal of the period. Bronze tools replaced stone tools for digging the ore. Tin deposits in Mesopotamia gave those countries an advantage in bronze production.

Around 2500 B.C. Phoenicians established colonies in Spain and Portugal to mine the vast local supplies of copper and tin. Roman tin mines in Britain were worked by slave labor and had shafts cutting 350 feet deep into the ground. In Palestine the Timna copper mines came under the control of the Egyptians during the Late Bronze period.

(3) *Iron.* The much higher melting point of iron (400 degrees higher than that of copper) necessitated the development of new smelting methods, with more efficient bellows. Since iron deposits lay close to the surface, they were much easier to mine than those of copper had been. The Hittites were among the earliest people to use iron on a large scale. They traded iron tools and weapons to Egypt. Only after the fall of the Hittite kingdom about 1200 B.C. did iron become more widely used. Israel made little use of it. Iron mines located in the Gilead near 'Ajlun at Magharat Warda probably served as one of the earliest iron sources in Palestine, possibly providing for the iron bedstead of Og, king of Bashan.

The Bible speaks of the Philistines as controlling the ironworking skills in Palestine (1 Sam. 13:19-22). At Beth-Shemesh, a Philistine stronghold in the Jordan Valley, a large industrial area with bronze and ironworking facilities was discovered. For the most part tools in Palestine continued to be made of bronze. Common tools such as sickles were still chipped from flint even after 1000 B.C. Iron chariots, spear points, knives and swords, and common tools such as sickles and plows became more common after 900 B.C.

(4) *Other Minerals.* Other minerals were more difficult to obtain and work. Lapis lazuli, a deep blue stone, was quarried for its beauty and used in jewelry. Egyptian faience was an attempt to produce a synthetic lapis. Lead was mined as early as 3000 B.C., but its soft nature made it unsuitable for tools or jewelry. Lead was later incorporated into bronze and, in the Roman period, was used in glassmaking. Silver was first mined in

northeast Asia Minor and taken from a lead-silver alloy. Electrum, silver mixed with small amounts of gold, was also mined. Raw gold is found in veins in quartzy granite. Gold began to be mined rather late (around 2500 B.C.) because of its more isolated location.

MIRACLES, SIGNS, WONDERS

Events that unmistakably involve an immediate and powerful action of God designed to reveal His character or purposes; called sign, wonder, work, mighty work, portent, power.

"Sign" in the NT is used of miracles taken as evidence of divine authority (Luke 23:8; John 2:11,18,23; 3:2; 4:54; 6:2,14,26; 7:31; 9:16; 10:41; 11:47; 12:18, 37; 20:30; Rev. 12:1,3; 13:13,14; 15:1; 16:14; 19:20; Acts 4:16,22).

"Wonders" in Greek denotes something unusual that causes the beholder to marvel (Acts 2:19,22,43; 6:8). Whereas a sign appeals to the understanding, a wonder appeals to the imagination. "Wonders" are usually presented as God's activity (Acts 2:19; 4:30; 5:12; 6:8; 7:36; 14:3; 15:12), though sometimes they refer to the work of Satan through human instruments (Matt. 24:24; Mark 13:22; 2 Thess. 2:9; Rev. 13:11-13).

New Testament writers also used power or inherent ability to refer to activity of supernatural origin or character (Mark 6:2; Acts 8:13; 19:11; Rom. 15:19; 1 Cor. 12:10,28,29; Gal. 3:5; 2 Thess. 2:9; Heb. 2:4) as well as "work" (Matt. 11:2; John 5:20,36; 7:3; 10:38; 14:11-12; 15:24).

The Bible makes no clear-cut distinction between the natural and supernatural. In the "natural" event the Bible views God as working providentially; whereas, in the miraculous, God works in striking ways to call attention to Himself or His purposes.

MIRIAM (perhaps *bitter, God's gift, beloved,* or *defiant*)

(1) Sister of Moses and Aaron; played key role in rescue of baby Moses (Ex. 2:4-8). After crossing the

Red Sea, she assumed role of prophetess and led women in song of victory (Ex. 15:20-21; compare Mic. 6:4). See *Poetry*. At Hazeroth, Miriam sided with Aaron in rebellion against Moses when he married an Ethiopian woman (Num. 12:1-15). God reminded her of Moses' divinely appointed leadership and chastened her with leprosy (Num. 12:15; compare Deut. 24:9). See *Intercession; Leprosy*. Miriam died at Kadesh (Num. 20:1).

(2) Member of the clan of Caleb (1 Chron. 4:17).

MIRROR

A polished or smooth surface that produces images by reflection; in Bible mirrors were made of polished metal ("bronze," Ex. 38:8; "molten" [metal], Job 37:18). Glass mirrors became available only in the late Roman period. Paul's readers could be expected to appreciate illustration of unclear image of a metal mirror (1 Cor. 13:12). See *Glass*.

MISHNAH

Teaching or learning about oral law (*halakah*) passed on by a particular teacher (rabbi); collected edition of rabbinic discussions of halakah compiled by Judah ha-Nasi (literally "the Prince," or Patriarch) head of the rabbinic academy at Javneh (or Jamnia) about A.D. 220. The Mishnah has six major divisions.

MISSION(S)

Task on which God sends a person He has called, particularly a mission to introduce another group of people to salvation in Christ.

MITYLENE *(Purity)*

Chief city of Aegean island of Lesbos southeast of Asia Minor where Paul stopped on his return trip to Syria from Achaia on third missionary journey (Acts 20:14).

MIZPAH, MIZPEH *(watchtower or lookout)*

Places used to provide security; at least two different sites in Transjordan, one in Gilead, the other in Moab, and at least two sites and one region west of the Jordan:

(1) In Gilead, Laban and Jacob made a covenant (Gen. 31:25-55), set up a pillar, and named it Mizpah (v. 49). Mizpah was also the name of the hometown of Jephthah, the Gileadite (Judg. 11). See *Ramoth-gilead*.

(2) In Moab the site to which David took his parents (1 Sam. 22:3-5) when Saul sought his life.

(3) "Land of Mizpah" (Josh. 11:3) and "valley of Mizpeh" (v. 8) point to region in north Palestine.

(4) City in Judah (Josh. 15:38) probably near Lachish.

(5) Town in Benjamin (Josh. 18:26), most important of the Mizpehs; possibly Nebi Samwil, five miles north of Jerusalem or tell en-Nasbeh, eight miles north of Jerusalem. Mizpah was a rallying point for Israel as they gathered against the tribe of Benjamin (Judg. 20). See 1 Sam. 7. Immediately after Jerusalem fell (586 B.C.) Mizpah became the administrative center of this Babylonian province (Jer. 40).

MOAB, MOABITE

(1) Son of Lot and his daughter (Gen. 19:37).

(2) Nation occupying narrow strip of cultivable land on rolling plateau (averaging approximately 3,300 feet elevation); bounded on west by rugged escarpment that drops to Dead Sea (almost 1,300 feet below sea level); bounded on east by the desert; divided in two by steep Wadi Mujib canyon (the Arnon River of biblical times); bounded on south by Wady el-Hesa, probably the biblical River Zered (Num. 21:12). Moab's agricultural productivity is illustrated by Ruth 1:1-5 and King Mesha's tribute (2 Kings 3:4). The chief cities of northern Moab were Hesbon, Medeba, and Dibon. Ammon (Judg. 11:13), Israel (Josh.13:15-28), and Moab (Isa. 15; Jer. 48; Moabite Stone) all claimed all

territory as far south as the Arnon. See Num. 21:25-30; Jer. 48:45-47.

Moab south of the Arnon was more isolated from the outside world. Its chief cities were Kir-hareseth (present-day Kerak) and Ar Moab (possibly Rabbah approximately nine miles northeast of Kerak). Israel had close relations with Moab, Ruth, ancestress of David, being from Moab. See Judg. 3:12-30; 1 Sam. 14:47; 22:3-4; 2 Sam. 8:2; 1 Kings 11:1-8. King Jehoram of Israel supported by King Jehoshaphat of Judah penetrated Moab and besieged Kir-hareseth. The siege was lifted when King Mesha of Moab sacrificed his oldest son on the city wall (2 Kings 3), probably to Chemosh, the god of Moab. See *Chemosh*.

Our most detailed information about Moabite-Israelite relations comes from about 850 B.C., the time of the Omri dynasty of Israel and King Mesha of Moab (1 Kings 16:15–2 Kings 10:18). The Moabite Stone supplements the biblical record. Omri conquered northern Moab and gained some degree of domination over Moab proper. Ahab continued Omri's policies. Mesha became king of Moab midway during Ahab's reign and, during the turbulent years following Ahab's death (2 Kings 1:1), threw off the Israelite yoke. Ahaziah succeeded Ahab and was unable to respond to Mesha's challenge because of an accident that led to his premature death (2 Kings 1). Jehoram, Ahaziah's successor, attempted unsuccessfully to restore Israelite control over Mesha (2 Kings 3).

By 700 B.C., Moab fell under the shadow of Assyria as did Israel, Judah, Ammon, and other petty Syro-Palestinian Kingdoms. Thus Moab and Moabite kings are mentioned by Tiglath-Pileser III, Sargon II, Sennacherib, and Esarhaddon. Also, prophetic oracles such as Amos 2:1-3; Isa. 15; and Jer. 48 pertain to these last, waning years of the Moabite kingdom.

MOABITE STONE

Monument bearing inscription of King Mesha of Moab; reports major accomplishments of his reign; also called Mesha Inscription. Mesha boasts of having recovered Moabite independence from Israel and of having restored Moabite control over northern Moab.

MOLECH (*king*)

Foreign god or practice related to foreign worship. Molech either denotes a particular type of offering—a votive sacrifice made to confirm or fulfill a vow or is the name of a pagan deity to whom human sacrifices were made. Some Carthaginian-Phoenician (i.e., Punic) inscriptions (400–150 B.C.) imply that the word *mlk* is a general form for "sacrifice" or "offering." Such a meaning is possible in Lev. 18:21; 20:3-5; 2 Kings 23:10; Jer. 32:35.

The divine name often is associated with Ammon (compare 1 Kings 11:7, "the abomination of the children of Ammon"). Leviticus 20:5 condemns those who "commit whoredom with Molech" (see also Lev. 18:21; 20:3-5; 2 Kings 23:10; Jer. 32:35). Some recent archaeological evidence points to child sacrifice in ancient Ammon. Many scholars contend that all the biblical texts referring to Molech can be understood by interpreting it as a divine name. The name may be a deliberate misvocalization of the Hebrew word for king, using vowels from the word for shame (*boshet*) to express contempt for the pagan god.

In times of apostasy some Israelites, apparently in desperation, made their children "go through the fire to Molech" (Lev. 18:21; 20:2-5; 2 Kings 23:10; compare 2 Kings 17:31; Jer. 7:31; 19:5; 32:35), apparently indicating sacrifices of children in the Valley of Hinnom at a site known as Topheth. See *Hinnom*. Others think "passed through Molech" refers to children whose parents gave them to grow up as temple prostitutes. See Lev. 18 (especially vv. 19-23). Another view sees an original fire ceremony dedicating, but not harming children, that later was transformed into a burnt-offering ceremony.

The practice of offering children as human sacrifice was condemned in ancient Israel, but the implication is clear in the OT that child sacrifice was practiced by some in Israel (2 Kings 21:6; 23:10; 2 Chron. 28:3; Ps. 106:38; Jer. 7:31; 19:4-5; Ezek. 16:21; 23:37,39). See *Gods, Pagan; Ashtoreth; Sacrifice and Offering.*

MONEY See *Coins.*

MONEYCHANGERS

Persons whose profession was to sell or exchange Roman or other moneys for Jewish money acceptable in the temple worship. Moneychangers set up tables in the temple court of the Gentiles. Syrian silver coins were the money of Jerusalem then, and worshipers used them to pay their temple tax of a half shekel and to buy sacrifices for the altar. Some exchangers profited greatly and loaned at interest rates that ranged from 20 to 300 percent per year. Jesus turned over the tables of the moneychangers and drove them and the sellers of animals out of the temple court (Matt. 21:12).

MOON

Light in the night sky created by God and controlling the calendar (Gen. 1:14-19). Two of Israel's greatest festivals were celebrated at the beginning of the full moon: the Passover in the spring and the Feast of Booths in the fall. Each month they celebrated the "new moon" with a little more festivity than a regular sabbath (Num. 28:11-15). Still, the OT strongly teaches against worshiping the moon (Deut. 4:19; Job 31:26-28; Isa. 47:13-15) as did Israel's neighbors. The moon was nothing more than an object created by Yahweh and had no power over people. Joel said in the last days the moon would become dark (Joel 2:10; 3:15) or turn to blood (Joel 2:31). The moon will not give its light on the "Day of the Lord," the light of the sun and the moon being replaced by the everlasting light of the Lord (Isa. 13:10; 60:19-20).

MORAL DECLINE

The Bible teaches that in the latter days the world will be gripped by an unprecedented decline in morals. False teaching will allow wickedness to grow, resulting in apathy (Matt. 24:12) and open hostility (Matt. 24:9-11,24; 2 Tim. 3:1-5) toward the things of Christ. Religion will become a pretense for personal gain rather than an expression of true devotion to God (compare 2 Tim. 3:5), and as a result the standards of moral behavior rooted in the Bible will be held to be irrelevant.

The NT lists the characteristics of persons who reject Christ (Gal. 5:19-21; Eph. 5:3-5; Col. 3:5-6; 1 Tim. 1:9-10; Rev. 21:8). These include all thoughts and actions which are less than Christ-like. Today many who speak of morals often limit their discussion to sexual matters. The NT, however, is clear that sexuality is just one of many elements of human behavior to be judged by God's moral code.

Although at their root level the kinds of activities which will become rampant at the end of time will be the same kinds of activities that people have always done in opposition to God, their intensity will be much greater and their effect world-wide in scope.

MORDECAI (*little man*)

(1) Esther's cousin and the mastermind behind her rise to power and subsequent victory over the evil Haman. See *Esther.*

(2) Man who returned to Jerusalem with Zerrubbabel (Ezra 2:2; Neh. 7:7).

MOREH (*instruction* or *archers*)

(1) Abraham's first encampment in Canaan where he entered into covenant (Gen. 12:6-7). Jacob buried there the foreign gods his family had brought from Haran (Gen. 35:4). See Deut. 11:26-30; Josh. 24:26.

(2) Hill in Issachar where Gideon reduced his troops by testing the way they drank water (Judg. 7:1); modern Nebi Dachi opposite Mount Gilboa.

MORESHETH, MORESHETH-GATH *(inheritance of Gath)*

Home of Micah (Mic. 1:1,4); near Philistine Gath; tell ej-Judeideh about 22 miles southwest of Jerusalem and nine miles east of Gath.

MORIAH

Rocky outcropping in Jerusalem just north of the ancient city of David where Abraham placed Isaac on the altar (Gen. 22:2,13); temple site (1 Chron. 28:3-6); may be Khirbet Beth-Lejj.

MORNING

Time before dawn (Mark 1:35; compare Gen. 44:3); dawn (Gen. 19:15; 29:25; Judg. 16:2); some time after sunrise; frequently paired with evening (Gen. 1:5,8) to indicate a complete day. The coming of morning serves as a figure for joy (Ps. 30:5) or vindication (Ps. 49:14) which comes quickly.

MORTAR

(1) Vessel in which substances are crushed with a pestle; frequently fashioned from basalt or limestone; used to grind grain for flour, herbs for medicine, olives for oil (Ex. 27:20). By extension "mortar" designates a hollow place (Josh. 15:19).

(2) District of Jerusalem (Zeph. 1:11).

(3) Building material, usually clay (Ex. 1:14; Isa. 41:25; Nah. 3:14), though sometimes bitumen (Gen. 11:3; KJV, "slime"), used to secure joints in brick or stone. Modern translations use "plaster" (Lev. 14:42,45) or "whitewash" (Ezek. 13:10-11,14-15).

MOSES *(drawn out of the water)*

Leader of Israelites in exodus from Egyptian slavery and oppression, journey through wilderness, and in audience with God at Mount Sinai/ Horeb where the distinctive covenant bonding Israel and God in a special treaty became a reality.

Moses' life began under the Pharoah's judgment of death (Ex. 1:22). A daring plot by mother and daughter saved Moses and placed him in Pharoah's court with his daughter who employed as wet nurse the child's own mother. The mature Moses became concerned about the oppression of his people and killed an Egyptian. Moses fled from Egypt and from his own people to the land of Midian.

Moses saved female shepherds oppressed by male shepherds. The girls' father, Jethro, the priest of Midian, invited him to live and work under the protection of the Midianite's hospitality. One of the Midianite's daughters became Moses' wife. Moses took care of Jethro's sheep, fathered a child, and lived at a distance from his own people. A burning bush caught Moses' attention. There Moses met the God of the fathers who offered Moses a distinctive name as the essential key for Moses' authority —"I am who I am." God sent Moses back to the Pharaoh to secure the release of his people from their oppression.

Moses experienced one failure after the other. Moses posed his demands to the Pharaoh, announced a sign that undergirded the demand, secured some concession from the Pharaoh on the basis of the negotiations, but failed to win the release of the people. Finally, God killed the firstborn of every Egyptian family, passing over the Israelite families. The Egyptians drove the Israelites out of Egypt (Ex. 12:30-36). In leaving Egypt, Israel robbed the most powerful nation of their time of its firstborn sons and of its wealth.

Pursuing Egyptians trapped the Israelites at the Red Sea. God, who had promised divine presence for the people, defeated the enemy at the Sea. He met their needs for food and water in the hostile wilderness. Even the fiery serpents and the Amalekites failed to thwart the wilderness journey of the Israelites under Moses' leadership.

Numbers 12:1-16 shows Moses to be meek, a leader of integrity who fulfilled the duties of his office despite opposition from members of his own family. The law showed Israel how to respond to God's saving act in the exodus. Because of Moses' sin (Num. 20), God denied Moses the privilege of entering the Promised Land. Central to the death report (Deut. 34) is the presence of God with Moses. Moses left his people to climb another mountain. Atop that mountain, away from the people whom he served so long, Moses died. God attended this servant at his death. Only God knows the burial place.

MOTE

Word ("speck," NRSV, NASB, NIV, TEV, REB) Jesus used in Sermon on the Mount (Matt. 7:3-5) to illustrate hypocrisy, equating "mote" with the smallest particle of wood in contrast to a log or beam.

MOTHER

Female parent who carries, gives birth to, and cares for a child; may refer to animals (Ex. 34:26; Lev. 22:27) or even as a metaphor for deity. Biblical wife has two equally important roles: to love, support, and provide companionship and sexual satisfaction for her husband and to bear and rear children. So important was the latter that a stigma was attached to barrenness (Gen. 16:1-2; 18:9-15; 30:1; 1 Sam. 1:1-20; Luke 1:5-25, especially v. 25).

The Bible refers to every aspect of motherhood: conception (Gen. 4:1; Luke 1:24; pregnancy (2 Sam. 11:5; Luke 1:24); pain of childbirth (Gen. 3:16; John 16:21); and nursing (1 Sam. 1:23; Matt. 24:19). A new mother was considered to be ritually unclean, and an offering was prescribed for her purification (Lev. 12; compare Luke 2:22-24). Mothers shared with fathers the responsibility for instructing and disciplining children (Prov. 1:8; 31:1). Mothers have the same right to obedience and

respect as fathers (Ex. 20:12; Lev. 19:3). Death was the fate of those who cursed or assaulted parents (Ex. 21:15,17; Deut. 21:18-21). Jesus enforced the Fifth Commandment and protected it against scribal evasion (Matt. 15:3-6).

Motherly virtues are often extolled: compassion for children (Isa. 49:15), comfort of children (Isa. 66:13), and sorrow for children (Jer. 31:15, quoted in Matt. 2:18). God's use of a human mother to bring His Son into the world has bestowed upon motherhood its greatest honor. Jesus set an example for all to follow by the provision He made for His mother (John 19:25-27). Devotion to God must take precedence to that of a mother (Matt. 12:46-50). A man's devotion to his wife supercedes that to his mother (Gen. 2:24).

Israel is compared to an unfaithful mother (Hos. 2:2-5; Isa. 50:1). Revelation 17:5 calls Babylon (Rome) the mother of harlots (those who are unfaithful to God). A city is the "mother" of her people (2 Sam. 20:19). Deborah was the "mother" (or deliverer) of Israel. Heavenly Jerusalem is the "mother" of Christians (Gal. 4:26). Jesus spoke of His compassion for Jerusalem as being like that of a mother hen for her chicks (Matt. 23:37). Paul compared his ministry to a mother in labor (Gal. 4:19) and a nursing mother (1 Thess. 2:7).

MOUNTAIN

Elevated topographical feature formed by geological faulting and erosion. The geography of Palestine featured high mountains and deep rifts. (See *Palestine.*) Mountain is a natural image for stability (Ps. 30:7), obstacles (Zech. 4:7), and God's power (Ps. 121:1-2). God will remove all obstacles when His redemption is complete, "and every mountain and hill shall be made low" (Isa. 40:4).

MOUTH

Portion of head used to ingest food and to communicate.

(1) Synonymn for lips (1 Kings 19:18; 2 Kings 4:34; Job 31:27; Prov. 30:20; Song of Sol. 1:2);

(2) Organ of eating and drinking (Judg. 7:6; 1 Sam. 14:26-27), sometimes used in figurative expressions such as when "wickedness" (Job 20:12) or God's word (Ps. 19:10) is described as sweet to the mouth. Anthropomorphic descriptions of the earth or Sheol speak of them opening their mouths to drink blood or swallow persons (Gen. 4:11; Num. 16:30,32; Isa. 5:14).

(3) Organ of speech (Gen. 45:12; Deut. 32:1) or laughter (Job 8:21; Ps. 126:2). The phrase "the mouth of the Lord has spoken it" serves as a frequent reminder of the reliability of a prophetic message (Isa. 1:20; 40:5; Jer. 9:12; compare Deut. 8:3; Matt. 4:4). "Fire" (2 Sam. 22:9) or a "sword" (Rev. 1:16) proceeding from the mouth of God pictures the effectiveness of God's word of judgment.

(4) Hebrew term for "mouth" is used for openings of wells, caves, sacks, as well as for the edge of a sword.

MURDER

Intentional taking of human life; unlawful killing of a human being by another (Ex. 20:13; Deut. 5:17) because persons are created in the image of God and human life is viewed as a sacred trust. Deliberately taking the life of a human being ursurps the authority that belongs to God. Murderer should be prepared to forfeit his own life (Gen. 9:6; compare Num. 35:16-31). Jesus removed the concept of murder from a physical act to the intention of one's heart (Matt. 5:21-22). Murder really begins when one loses respect for another human being. "Whosoever hateth his brother is a murderer: and ye know that no murderer hath eternal life abiding in him (1 John 3:15). See *Image of God; Ten Commandments.*

MUSIC, INSTRUMENTS, DANCING

Expression of full range of human emotions vocally or instrumentally.

Jubal "was the father of all those who play the lyre and pipe" (Gen. 4:21, NASB). A farewell might be said "with joy and singing to the music of tambourines and harps" (Gen. 31:27, NIV); a homecoming welcomed "with timbrels and with dances" (Judg. 11:34; compare Luke 15:25). Work tasks of everyday living enjoyed the music evidenced by the songs or chants of the well diggers (Num. 21:17-18), the treaders of grapes (Isa. 16:10; Jer. 48:33), and possibly the watchman (Isa. 21:12).

Singing and dancing around the golden calf (Ex. 32:17-19) symbolized a broken covenant. Isaiah rebuked idle rich who have "lyre and harp, tambourine and flute and wine" at their feasts but failed to notice the deeds of Yahweh (Isa. 5:12, NRSV). Both the scorn of mockers (Job 30:9) and the acclamation of heroes (1 Sam. 18:6-7) were expressed in song.

The song of Miriam celebrated the defeat of Pharoah at the Red Sea (Ex. 15:21). "Song of Deborah" (Judg. 5) celebrated victory over Jabin, the king of Canaan. Chants of victory (Judg. 15:16) or those greeting the one successful in battle (1 Sam. 18:7) establish music as a medium for uncontainable joy. Deepest emotions expressed themselves through the poetry of music as seen in David's lament at the death of Saul and Jonathan (2 Sam. 1:19-27). Women such as Miriam, Deborah, and Jephthah's daughter occupied a special place in musical performance (Ex. 15:1-20; Judg. 5; 11:34).

The establishment of the monarchy about 1025 B.C. brought processional at court (1 Kings 1:34,39-40; 10:12; Eccl. 2:8) and in religious ritual. An Assyrian inscription, praising the victory of the Assyrian king Sennacherib over King Hezekiah of Judah, lists male and female musicians as part of the tribute carried off to Nineveh.

The psalms show the emotional range of music from lament to praise and provide words for some of the songs used in temple worship. Psalm 98 calls for the employment of music, stringed instruments, horns, and trumpets in praise (2 Chron. 29:20-30).

Psalm titles contain musical information (see Pss. 4–5); give liturgical information (see Pss. 92; 100); and designate the "type" of psalm in question (see Ps. 120, "a song of ascents"; Ps. 145, "a song of praise"). The singing of psalms to other tunes popular at the time is suggested by headings such as "Hind of the Dawn" in Ps. 22 (RSV) and "to Lillies" used in Pss. 45; 69; 80 (RSV).

Guilds of musicians, known through reference to their founders in some psalm headings (for example, "the sons of Korah"), were evidently devoted to the discipline of liturgical music. Psalm 137 knows of "songs of Zion" (v. 3). Reestablishment of the temple saw Levitical musicians (compare Ezra 2:40-41) reassume responsibility for liturgical music.

The most frequently named musical instrument is the "Shophar" (ram's horn). Limited to two or three notes, the "Shophar" —often translated "trumpet"—served as a signaling instrument in times of peace and war (Judg. 3:27; 6:34; Neh. 4:18-20). Having as its chief function the making of noise, the "Shophar" announced the new moons and sabbaths, warned of approaching danger, signaled the death of nobility, functioned in national celebration (1 Kings 1:34; 2 Kings 9:13).

The trumpet was a straight metal instrument flared on the end and thought to have had a high, shrill tone. The trumpet was sounded in pairs and known as the instrument of the priests (compare Num. 10:2-10 for a description of usages; see also 2 Chron. 5:12-13 where some 20 trumpeters are mentioned). The sound of the trumpets introduced temple ceremony and sacrifice, the trumpet itself being counted among the sacred temple utensils (2 Kings 12:13; Num. 31:6). Perforated horns of the ram or the wild ox were used to sound ceremonial or military signals. Priests sounded trumpets to call to worship. Trumpets later were made of silver.

As the instrument of David and the Levites, the lyre (KJV, "harp") was employed in both secular and sacred settings (compare Isa. 23:16; 2 Sam. 6:5). The lyre was often used to accompany singing. The number of strings on the lyre could vary; its basic shape was rectangular or trapezoidal. Like the lyre, the harp was often associated with aristocracy, thus being often made from precious woods and metals (see 1 Kings 10:12; 2 Chron. 9:11). A lute was a stringed instrument with a large, pear-shaped body and a neck. NRSV used "lute" to translate two Hebrew terms (Pss. 92:3; 150:3). NASB and NIV translated the first term as "10-stringed lute" and the second as "harp." The KJV translated both terms as "psaltery."

Perhaps better described as a primitive clarinet, the *khalil* (NASB, "flute" or KJV, "pipe") consisted of two separate pipes made of reed, metal, or ivory, each pipe having a mouthpiece with single or double reeds. Used in the expression of joy (1 Kings 1:39-40) or mourning (Jer. 48:36; Matt. 9:23), the *khalil* was primarily a secular instrument that could be played at funerals or feasts.

Other musical instruments mentioned in the biblical texts include the timbrel or tambourine (Gen. 31:27), cymbals, bells (presumably metal jingles without clappers; see Ex. 28:33-34; 39:25-26 where they are attached to the high priest's robe), and a rattle-type noisemaker translated variously as castanets, rattles, sistrums, cymbals, or clappers (2 Sam. 6:5). "Sounding brass" (1 Cor. 13:1) is perhaps understood through rabbinic literature as a characteristic instrument for weddings and joyous celebrations.

As rhythmic movement often performed to music, dancing enjoyed a prominent place in the life and worship of Israel. Hebrew words used to express the idea of dance seem to imply different types of movement: to skip about (Job 21:11), whirling about (2 Sam. 6:14,16), and perhaps twisting or writhing (Ps. 30:11). In women's homecoming welcome of victorious soldiers, dancing could be accompanied by song and instrumental music (1 Sam. 18:6).

Exodus 15:20 celebrates Israel's deliverance at the Sea of Reeds by dancing with singing and musical accompaniment. Judges 21:16-24 accords dancing a role in the celebration of the yearly feast at Shiloh, and David is pictured as dancing before the Lord as the ark was brought to Jerusalem (2 Sam. 6:14). Psalm 150:4 calls God's people to praise Him with the dance. As an idolatrous act, dancing is mentioned in the golden-calf story (Ex. 32:19) and in the worship of Baal at Carmel (1 Kings 18:26).

In the NT, the return of the prodigal son was celebrated with music and dancing (Luke 15:25). The practice of dancers entertaining at royal courts in Hellenistic and Roman times is attested by the dance of Herodias' daughter, Salome, (Matt. 14:6).

MYRA

One of six largest cities of Lysia in southeastern Asia Minor; on River Andracus about 2.5 miles from the sea; modern Dembre; stopping point on Paul's voyage to Rome (Acts 27:5-6).

MYRRH See *Plants.*

MYSTERY, MYSTERY RELIGIONS

Several different cults or societies characterized in part by elaborate initiation rituals and secret rites. Attested in Greece before 600 B.C., the mystery religions flourished during the Hellenistic and Roman periods (after 333 B.C.) before dying out before A.D. 500. Knowledge of the mystery religions is fragmentary due to the strict secrecy imposed on those initiated. Scholars often disagree about the interpretation of the data.

The more important mystery religions were associated with the following deities: the Greek Demeter (the famous Eleusinian mysteries) and Dionysus, the Phyrgian Cybele

(the Magna Mater) and Attis; the Syrian Adonis; the Egyptian Isis and Osiris (Sarapis); and Mithra, originally a Persian deity.

The central feature of each mystery religion was the sacred rites, called mysteries, in which the cultic myth of the god or goddess worshiped in the cult was reenacted. Only those formally initiated into the cult could participate. The rites probably involved a drama based on the cult myth and the dramatic visual presentation of certain sacred objects. References exist to eating and drinking, likely a form of communion. By participating in these rites, the worshiper identified with the deity and shared in the deity's fate. These powerful symbols afforded those initiated the means to overcome the suffering and difficulties of life and promised a share in the life beyond.

Many deities worshiped in the mysteries were originally associated with fertility. Their associated myths often referred to the natural cycle as it waxes and wanes (for instance, Demeter) or to the dying and rising of a god (Attis, Adonis, Osiris). Some concept of immortality seems to be implied.

The spring festival of Cybele (March 15–27) involved processions, sacrifices, music, and frenzied dancing that led to castration. The public revelry, pantomimes, theatric productions, and excesses of drink associated with the worshipers of Dionysus/Bacchus (the Bacchanalia) are well known.

Rites of initiation into the mystery religions included ritual cleansing in the sea, baptisms, and sacrifices. The Taurobolium in the worship of Cybele had a bull slaughtered on a grill placed over a pit in which a priest stood; the person below eagerly covered himself with blood. This was probably a purification ritual affording rebirth for a period of time, perhaps 20 years. The mystery religions dislodged religion from the traditional foundations of state and family and made it a matter of personal choice. Members who met regularly with a designated leader in houses or specially built structures were required to meet certain moral standards; some mention also is made of ascetic requirements.

The mystery of the NT has been described as an "open secret"; matters previously kept secret in God's eternal purposes have now been or are being revealed (Eph. 3:3-5; 1 Cor. 2:7-8). In contrast to the mystery religions, the mystery of the NT appears in the historical activity of the person of Christ (Col. 2:2; Eph. 1:9); the indwelling Christ is the hope of glory (Col. 1:26-27). The mystery is received spiritually (Eph. 3:4-5) and manifested in the proclamation of the gospel (Eph. 6:19). Part of the mystery involves the disclosure that Gentiles share in the blessings of the gospel (Eph. 2:11-13).

NAAMAN (*pleasantness*)

Syrian general cured of leprosy through Elisha (2 Kings 5). Following his cleansing, he professed faith in Israel's God. See *Leprosy*.

NABAL (*fool* or *rude, ill-bred*) See *Abigail*.

NABATEANS

Arabic people of unknown origins who greatly influenced Palestine during intertestamental and NT times. They appear to have infiltrated ancient Edom and Moab from a homeland southeast of Petra—which later became their capital—as far north as Madeba. In 85 B.C. Damascus requested a ruler of the Nabateans. The Arabs responded. Although overrun by Pompey in 63 B.C., they continued to influence Transjordan through a series of governors. Paul narrowly escaped being arrested by the Nabateans in Damascus (2 Cor. 11:32). Paul spent time in Arabia following his conversion, probably preaching the gospel (Gal. 1:17).

NABOTH (perhaps *sprout*)

Owner of a vineyard in Jezreel Valley adjacent to country palace of King Ahab, who desired the property for a vegetable garden. Naboth refused to sell on the grounds that the property was a family inheritance (1 Kings 21:3-4; see Lev. 25:15-23). Jezebel, who had no regard for Israel's laws, plotted Naboth's judicial murder on the charge that he had blasphemed God and the king (1 Kings 21:8-14). Naboth's murder evoked God's judgment on Ahab and his family (1 Kings 21:17-24).

NADAB (*willing* or *liberal*)

Four OT men including:

(1) Aaron's eldest son (Ex. 6:23; Num. 3:2; 1 Chron. 6:3), who participated in the ratification of the covenant (Ex. 24:1,9), served as a priest (Ex. 28:1),

and was consumed by fire along with his brother Abihu for offering unholy fire before the Lord (Lev. 10:1-7; Num. 26:61). Nadab died childless (Num. 3:4; 1 Chron. 24:2).

(2) Son of Jeroboam (1 Kings 14:20) and idolatrous king of Israel (901–900 B.C.). Baasha assassinated him during a seige of the Philistine city of Gibbethon (1 Kings 15:25-28). The extermination of the family of Jeroboam (15:29) was seen as fulfillment of Ahijah's prophesy (14:10-11).

NAG HAMMADI

Modern Egyptian village 300 miles south of Cairo and about 60 miles north of Luxor, or ancient Thebes near which 13 ancient codices containing 51 smaller writings relating to gnosticism were found. These represent first primary gnostic documents written and used by gnostics. The documents are written in Coptic, an ancient language of Egypt, but probably translations of Greek originals. Present documents appear to be from about A.D. 350, but some were probably written before A.D. 200. See *Gnosticism*.

The Nag Hammadi Documents include "gospels" such as *The Gospel of Philip*, *The Gospel of Truth*, and *The Gospel of Thomas*, which purports to be a collection of sayings of Jesus. (See *Apocrypha, New Testament*.) Other documents concern the work and circumstances of the apostles. The *Apocalypse of Paul* relates an account of the heavenly journey of Paul. The *Revelation of Peter* describes special revelations given to Peter by Jesus before Peter's imprisonment. The *Revelation of James* tells of the death of James.

Other documents contain a wide variety of mythological speculations covering creation, redemption, and ultimate destiny. In this category are *On the Origin of the World*, *Secret Book of the Great Invisible Spirit*, *Revelation of Adam*, *The Thought of Our Great Power*, *The Paraphrase of*

Shem, The Second Logos of the Great Seth, and *The Trimorphic Protennoia. The Acts of Peter and the Twelve Apostles,* an apocryphal work about the twelve apostles, does not appear to be gnostic.

These documents prove the existence of gnostic systems independent of the Christian framework, enhance the study of the NT, reflect the diversity of Gnosticism and point to the diversity of early Christianity and the resultant struggle for orthodoxy and reinforces an appreciation for the seriousness of the gnostic threat to early Christianity.

NAHASH (*serpent* or perhaps *magnificence*)

(1) Ammonite ruler whose assault of Jabesh-Gilead set the stage for Saul's consolidation of power as king (1 Sam. 11:1-11). Saul's opponent was likely the Nahash who befriended David (2 Sam. 10:1-2). His son Hanun provoked David's anger (2 Sam. 10:3-5). Another son, Shobi, served as David's ally (2 Sam. 17:27).

(2) Parent of Abigail (2 Sam. 17:25).

NAHOR (*snore, snort*)

(1) Son of Serug, father of Terah, and grandfather of Abraham (Gen. 11:22-26).

(2) Son of Terah and brother of Abraham (Gen. 11:26,29; 22:20-22).

(3) City in Mesopotamia where Abraham's servant sought and found a wife for Isaac (Gen. 24:10); probably southeast of Haran; mentioned in the Mari Texts.

NAHSHON (*serpent*)

Leader of Judah in wilderness (Num. 1:7; 2:3; 7:12,17; 10:14), brother-in-law of Aaron (Ex. 6:23), and ancestor of David (Ruth 4:20-22) and of Jesus (Matt. 1:4; Luke 3:32).

NAHUM (*comfort, encourage*)

Hebrew prophet from Elkosh (Nah. 1:1) between 663 and 612 B.C. Nahum 3:8 refers to the destruction of the Egyptian capital, No-amon or Thebes, in 663 B.C. Chapter 2 looks forward to the destruction of Nineveh (612 B.C.) See *Israel, History of.* Assyrian oppression created a troubling question for Israel. How could God allow such inhumanity to go unanswered? Nahum responded: Assyria's might had been heavy upon Judah, but God would eventually destroy the Assyrians.

NAHUM, BOOK OF

Seventh book of Book of Twelve or Minor Prophets containing messages of Nahum between 663 and 612 B.C. The book opens with an affirmation of God as an avenging God. For over a century, the Assyrians seemed to have had an uncontrolled reign, but now God was responding in fierce wrath. His judgment is likened to an approaching storm, giving Judah no reason to doubt God's justness. Nahum, however, sought to dispel this notion.

The second chapter graphically portrays the future fall of Assyria's capital, Nineveh. Nineveh was a massive city with a defensive wall that measured eight miles in circumference and ranged in height from 25 to 60 feet. A moat surrounded it. Yet, Nahum poetically affirmed the city's fall.

The Book of Nahum closes with more threats against Nineveh. Ironically, as Assyria had destroyed Thebes in 663 B.C., so the same fate would befall Nineveh (3:8-11). No preparations would keep away God's devastating judgment. The Book of Nahum is harsh and deals with the unpleasantness of war, but still gives hope to the people of Judah.

NAIL

(1) Keratinous covering of the top ends of fingers and toes. If an Israelite desired to marry a prisoner of war, she was to cut her nails either as a sign of mourning for her parents or as part of her purification on entering the community of Israel (Deut. 21:12).

(2) Metal fasteners used in construction and for decoration (1 Chron.

22:3; 2 Chron. 3:9; Isa. 41:7; Jer. 10:4). The earliest nails were made of bronze. With the introduction of iron, larger nails were made of iron. Nails were sometimes plaited with precious metal and nail heads decorated with gold foil when used for ornament (compare 2 Chron. 3:9). The nails used in the crucifixion of Jesus were likely iron spikes five to seven inches long (John 20:25).

(3) KJV for peg (Ex. 35:18; Judg. 4:21-22; Zech. 10:4).

NAIN (*pleasant*)

Village overlooking Plain of Esdraelon in southwest Galilee where Jesus raised a widow's son (Luke 7:11-15).

NAMES OF GOD

Designations for Himself that God gives His people as a personal disclosure revealing His relationship with His people. His name is known only because He chooses to make it known. See *Naming*.

The truth of God's character is focused in His name which reveals His power, authority, and holiness. The Ten Commandments prohibited the violation of God's name (Ex. 20:7; Deut. 5:11). Prophets spoke with authority when they uttered God's name. Oaths taken in God's name were considered binding, and battles fought in the name of God were victorious. Other nations would fear Israel because it rallied under the Lord's name. God's name is manifested most clearly in Jesus Christ, "the Word" (John 1:1; compare 17:6).

Before Moses' encounter with God in the Midianite desert, God was known generally as the God of the Fathers. Various names were used for God, most associated with the primitive Semitic word *El*, a generic term for God or deity referring to an awesome power that instills within humankind a mysterious dread or reverence. *El* was the chief God in the Canaanite pantheon. See *Canaan, History and Religion of*.

El in the Bible sometimes refers to deity as opposed to the particular historical revelation associated with the name "Yahweh" (see below). More often it is used as a synonym for Yahweh, the God of Israel, and translated God.

El is used in alliance with other terms to reveal the character of God.

El-Shaddai (*God of the Mountains* or *The Almighty God*) is more closely associated with the patriarchal period (Ex. 6:3) and can be found most frequently in the Books of Genesis and Job. God used it to make His Covenant with Abraham (Gen. 17:1-2).

El-Elyon (*The Most High God* or *The Exalted One*) is name by which Melchizadek blessed Abraham (Gen. 14:19-20), referring to El-Elyon as "Maker of heaven and earth" (compare Num. 24:16; 2 Sam. 22:14; Ps. 18:13). El-Elyon seems to have had close ties to Jerusalem. Canaanites at Ugarit worshiped El-Elyon.

El-Olam (*God of Eternity* or *God the Everlasting One*) shows God's sovereignty extends through the passing of time and beyond our ability to see or understand (Gen. 21:33; Isa. 26:4; Ps. 90:2).

El-Berith (*God of the Covenant*) (Judg. 9:46) transforms the Canaanite Baal Berith (8:33) to show God alone makes and keeps covenant.

El-Roi (*God Who Sees Me* or *God of Vision*) God sees the needs of His people and responds (Gen. 16:13).

Elohim, a plural form for deity, is the most comprehensive of the El combinations. The plural does not hint at polytheism when referring to Israel's God but is a plural of majesty, a revelation of the infinite nature of God (compare Gen. 1:26). This name suggests a mystery to the Creator-God that humankind cannot fully fathom. God is absolute, infinite Lord over creation and history. The Christian sees in this term a pointer to the trinitarian reality of creation.

El is frequently combined with other nouns or adjectives. Some examples are: Isra-el ("one who is ruled by God"), Beth-el ("house of God"), Peni-el ("face of God"). Jesus employed a form of *El* when He cried from the cross (Mark 15:34), *"Eloi, Eloi,"* "my God, my God," quoting Ps. 22.

The covenant name for God was "Yahweh." Israel's faith was a new response to God based on His disclosure. This name was so unique and powerful that God formed a covenant with His people based on His self-revelation (see Ex. 3; 6; 19-24). See *YHWH.*

Yahweh titles appear in English translations as Jehovah.

Yahweh-Jireh (*The Lord Will Provide*) is the name given the location where God provided a ram for Abraham to sacrifice in place of Isaac (Gen. 22:14). This name testifies to God's deliverance.

Yahweh-Mekaddesh (*The Lord Sanctifies*) Holiness is the central revelation of God's character (Ex. 31:13). God calls for a people who are set apart.

Yahweh-Nissi (*The Lord Is My Banner*) Moses acribed this name to God after a victory over the Amalekites (Ex. 17:15). God's name was considered a banner under which Israel could rally for victory.

Yahweh-Rohi (*The Lord Is My Shepherd*) God is the One who provides loving care for His people (Ps. 23:1).

Yahweh-Sabaoth (*The Lord of Hosts* or *The Lord Almighty*) represents God's power over the nations and was closely tied to Shiloh, to the ark of the covenant, and to prophecy (1 Sam. 1:3; Jer. 11:20; compare 1 Sam. 17:45). The title designates God as King and ruler of Israel, its armies, its temple, and of all the universe.

Yahweh-Shalom (*The Lord Is Peace*) was the name of the altar Gideon built at Ophrah, signifying that God brings well-being, not death, to His people (Judg. 6:24).

Yahweh-Shammah (*The Lord Is There*) is the name of God associated with the restoration of Jerusalem, God's dwelling place (Ezek. 48:35).

Yahweh-Tsidkenu (*The Lord Is Our Righteousness*) was the name Jeremiah gave to God, the Righteous King, who would establish a new kingdom of justice and rule over Israel after the return from captivity (Jer. 23:5-6; 33:16).

Baal was the chief god of the Canaanite pantheon. In some ancient religions, Baal and El could be used interchangeably. There were tendencies within Israel to identify Baal with Yahweh, but Baal worship was incompatible with Hebrew monotheism. Prophets, such as Elijah and Hosea, called the people away from these tendencies and back to the covenant.

Adon (or Adonai) This is a title of authority and honor, translated "Lord," and applied to a superior, such as a king or master as well as to God. It ascribes the highest honor and worship to God and became a substitute for Yahweh when Israel refused to pronounce the holy name.

A prominent characteristic of Scripture is its use of figurative language. Many of the names for God are symbolic, illustrative, or figurative.

Ancient of Days pictures an old man who lived for many years (Dan. 7:9,13,22), confessing that God lives forever and His kingdom is everlasting. He gives history meaning and is drawing it to a conclusion (Ps. 90:2).

Rock God is strong and permanent (Deut. 32:18; Ps. 19:14; Isa. 26:4).

Refuge God is a haven from the enemy (Ps. 9:9; Jer. 17:17).

Fortress God is a defense against the foe (Ps. 18:2; Nah. 1:7).

Shield God is protection (Gen. 15:1; Ps. 84:11).

Sun God is the source of light and life (Ps. 84:11).

Refiner God is purifier (Mal. 3:3).

Many descriptions of God came from political life.

King Yahweh's covenant people were to obey Him as a Sovereign. This title is the key to understanding the kingdom of God.

Judge Yahweh is the Judge who arbitrates disputes, sets things right, and intervenes for Israel in its military campaigns.

Shepherd This is a nurturing term to describe the care God gives to His covenant people. It also had political connotations. Yahweh is the Shepherd King (Ezk. 34). The image of God as shepherd appears in parables (Luke 15:4-7) and in John's portrayal of Christ as the Good Shepherd (John 10:1-18).

Father This describes the close kinship God enjoys with His worshipers (Ps. 103:13; Jer. 31:9; compare Ex. 4:22; Hos. 11:1). Father is the distinguishing title for God in the NT. Jesus taught His disciples to use the Aramaic "Abba," to address the heavenly Father. See *Abba*.

Father takes on a richer meaning when it is joined with other designations.

Our Father Jesus taught His disciples to address God in this manner when they prayed (Matt. 6:9).

Father of mercies (2 Cor. 1:3).

Father of lights (Jas. 1:17).

Father of glory (Eph. 1:17).

When the *Father* title is juxtaposed with the word *Son*, the significance of God's name in relation to Jesus Christ is understood. Christ's claim to have come in His Father's name reveals that He was God's unique representative (John 5:43). He shares the Father's essential authority and works done in His Father's name bear witness to this special relationship (John 10:25). Christ has provided a full revelation of God because He has clearly declared His name (John 12:28; 17:6).

NAMING

Giving a child identity by indicating how people will address and know the person. In biblical tradition the task of naming a child generally fell to the mother (Gen. 29:31–30:24; 1 Sam. 1:20) but could be performed by the father (Gen. 16:15; Ex. 2:22) and in exceptional cases by nonparental figures (Ex. 2:10; Ruth 4:17). The last son of Jacob and Rachel

received a name from each parent, Jacob altering the name Rachel gave (Gen. 35:18). Naming could be attributed to God originating through a divine birth announcement (Gen. 17:19; Luke 1:13). Naming took place near birth in the OT and on the eighth day accompanying circumcision in NT narratives (Luke 1:59; 2:21).

To know the name of a person was to know that person's total character and nature. Personal names could express hopes for the child's future. Changing of name could occur at divine or human initiative, revealing a transformation in character or destiny (Gen. 17:5,15; 32:28; Matt. 16:17-18). Knowing a name implied a relationship between parties in which power to do harm or good was in force. That God knew Moses by name occasioned the granting of Moses' request for divine presence (Ex. 33:12, 17). The act of naming implied the power of the namer over the named, evidenced in the naming of the animals in Gen. 2:19-20 or Pharaoh's renaming Joseph (Gen. 41:45; compare Dan. 1:6-7; 2 Kings 24:17).

Proper names conveyed a readily understandable meaning; circumstances of birth (Gen. 35:18; 25:26; see Ex. 2:22; 1 Sam. 4:21-22; Isa. 7:3; 8:3); personal characteristics: (Gen. 25:25; 2 Kings 25:23); animal names such as: Jonah, "dove"; Rachel, "ewe"; plant names such as Tamar, "palm tree"; Susanna, "lily"; epithets such as Nabal, "fool"; Sarah, "princess;" theophoric names employing the divine names El and Yah such as Mattaniah, "gift of Yahweh" and Ezekiel, "may God strengthen." Other names include titles and kinship terms Abimelech, "my father is king."

Giving a child the name of a relative, especially the grandfather (Simon Bar-Jona, "son of Jona") was common by the Christian era. Geographical identities include Goliath of Gath and Jesus of Nazareth. See *Family*.

NAOMI (*my pleasantness*)

Wife of Elimelech and mother-in-law of Orpah and Ruth (Ruth 1:2,4).

Naomi suffered the deaths of her husband and two sons while in Moab. Her matchmaking between Ruth and Boaz was successful, and she became a forebear of David, Israel's greatest king (Ruth 4:21-22). See *Ruth.*

NAPHTALI (*wrestler*) See *Tribes of Israel.*

NAPKIN See *Handkerchief.*

NARCISUS (*daffodil*)

Common name among both slaves and freedmen; head of household, perhaps including slaves and/or associated freedmen and some Christians (Rom. 16:11). The most famous Narcissus was a freedman who advised Emperor Claudius (A.D. 41–54). He committed suicide shortly after Nero's accession to the throne. Paul could have meant this Narcissus.

NARD

Expensive fragrance derived from roots of herb *nardostachys jatamansi* (Song of Sol. 1:12; 4:13-14; Mark 14:3; John 12:3; KJV, "spikenard").

NATHAN (*gift*)

Five OT men, including prophet in royal court of David and early years of Solomon. David consulted Nathan about building a temple. Nathan responded favorably. That night the Lord spoke to Nathan with instructions for David that his successor would build the temple but that David would have a house, a great name, and a kingdom forever. David responded with gratitude to the Lord (2 Sam. 7; 1 Chron. 17).

God sent Nathan to rebuke David for his sins with Bathsheba and her husband, Uriah (2 Sam. 11). Nathan told a story in which a rich man took the only little ewe lamb that belonged to a poor man and prepared a meal for one of his guests. David said the rich man should die. Nathan responded, "Thou art the man." David repented, but his first child born to Bathsheba died (2 Sam. 11–12). Nathan supported Solomon as David's declared suc-

cessor (1 Kings 1:5-53). Nathan wrote chronicles for David (1 Chron. 29:29) and a history of Solomon (2 Chron. 9:29). Nathan advised David in arranging the musical instruments played by the Levites (2 Chron. 29:25).

NATHANAEL (*giver of God*)

Israelite whom Jesus complimented as being guileless (John 1:47) and who, in turn, confessed the Lord as being the Son of God and King of Israel (v. 49); from Cana of Galilee (John 21:2). Some have equated him with Bartholomew. Philip announced to Nathanael that Jesus was the promised Messiah (John 1:45). Nathanael replied, "Can there any good thing come out of Nazareth?" See *Disciples, Apostles.*

NATURAL

According to nature.

(1) Natural use (Rom. 1:26-27, KJV; natural relations, RSV) refers to heterosexual relations, thus "natural intercourse" (NRSV, REB).

(2) Natural affection refers specifically to affection for family members. Those lacking natural affection are unloving to their families or generally inhuman or unsociable (Rom. 1:31; 2 Tim. 3:3).

(3) Natural branches refer to original or native branches as opposed to ingrafted ones (Rom. 11:21,24).

(4) Natural or unspiritual person (1 Cor. 2:14) is not open to receiving gifts from God's Spirit or to discerning spiritual matters (contrast 2:15; compare Jas. 3:15; Jude 19).

(5) Natural face (Jas. 1:23 literally, face of one's birth). To see one's natural face is to see oneself as one actually is.

NAZARETH, NAZARENE (*branch*)

Town in lower Galilee about halfway between Sea of Galilee and Mediterranean Sea where Jesus grew up (Matt. 26:71; Luke 18:37; 24:19; John 1:45; Acts 2:22; 3:6; 10:38); not prominent until associated with Jesus. The city was on the slopes of a natural basin facing east and southeast. Cana was about five miles to the northeast. A Roman road from Capernaum westward to the coast passed near Nazareth. It was a small village in Jesus' day, having only one spring to supply fresh water to its inhabitants. See Luke 1:26-28; Matt. 2:19-23; Luke 2:39-40; 4:16. Nazareth did not possess a good reputation, as reflected in the question of Nathanael, himself a Galilean (John 1:46; compare Acts 24:5). Jesus was rejected by His townspeople, being cast out of the synagogue at Nazareth (Luke 4:16-30; see also Matt. 13:54-58; Mark 6:1-6). See *Galilee.*

NAZIRITE (*consecration, devotion, and separation*)

Member of a class of individuals especially devoted to God. Two traditional forms of the Nazirite are found: a vow by the individual for a specific limited period (Acts 18:18; 21:22-26); a lifelong devotion following the revelatory experience of a parent that announced the impending birth of a child (Judg. 13; 1 Sam. 1; Luke 1:15-17). The Nazirite's outward signs—growth of hair, abstention from wine and other alcoholic products, avoidance of contact with the dead—are illustrative of devotion to God. Violation of these signs resulted in defilement and the need for purification so the vow could be completed (Num. 6:1-21). Amos 2:12 shows an ethical concern for protecting the status of the Nazirite.

NEBO (*height*)

(1) Babylonian god of speech, writing, and water. Worship of Nebo was popular during the Neo-Babylonian era (612–539 B.C.). Isaiah mocked parades featuring the idol of Nebo (Isa. 46:1).

(2) Moabite city southwest of Heshbon. The tribes Reuben and Gad requested the area around Nebo for their flocks (Num. 32:2-3). It was recaptured by King Mesha about 850 B.C.

(3) Town reinhabited by exiles returning from Babylon (Ezra 2:29); identified with Nob.

(4) Mountain about 12 miles east of mouth of Jordan River from which Moses viewed the Promised Land (Deut. 32:49); over 4,000 feet above Dead Sea with excellent view of the southwest, west, and as far north as Mount Hermon. See Num. 22–24; 2 Sam. 8:2.

NEBUCHADNEZZAR (*Nabu protects*)

King of Babylon 602–562 B.C.; son of Nabopolassar under whom he served as a general; brilliant strategist. His victory over the Egyptian forces at Carchemish (605) signaled the completion of Babylon's conquest of Palestine. See *Babylon, History and Religion of.*

NECK

Portion of body connecting head to torso. To put one's feet on the neck of an enemy is a sign of complete victory (Josh. 10:24). A yoke placed on the neck is a frequent emblem of servitude (Gen. 27:40; Deut. 28:48; Isa. 10:27). To fall upon someone's neck with weeping or kissing is a special sign of tenderness (Gen. 33:4; 45:14; compare Luke 15:20). To be stiffnecked or to harden one's neck is a common picture of stubborn disobedience (Ex. 32:9; 33:3,5).

NECO

Second Pharoah (609–594 B.C.) of 26th dynasty of Egypt whose forces killed Josiah in battle (2 Kings 23:29-35; 2 Chron. 35:20-24) and who installed Jehoiakim as king of Judah in his place (2 Kings 23:34-35). The Twenty-Sixth Dynasty was established with Assyrian patronage. The ambitious Neco seized Gaza as a base (Jer. 47:1) to bring Syria under his control and to aid the Assyrian remnant in their struggle with the rising force of Babylon. Josiah met his death in battle with Neco at Megiddo as Neco was on route to Carchemish. Nebuchadrezzar defeated Neco in

605 B.C. (Jer. 46:2). Later Nebucha-drezzar would extend his control as far as the Nile (2 Kings 24:7). See *Assyria; Egypt; Josiah.*

NEEDLE

Small slender sewing instrument with an eye at one end through which thread is passed. Needles were most often made of bronze, though bone and ivory were also used. Jesus' teaching that "it is easier for a camel to go through the eye of a needle than for a rich man to enter into the king-dom of God" (Matt. 19:24; compare Mark 10:25; Luke 18:25) illustrates the impossibility of a rich person's being saved apart from the interven-tion of God who does the impossible (Matt. 19:26).

NEGEB, NEGEV (*dry*)

Arid region in southern Palestine; came to mean "south"; land of the Amalekites during Abraham's day (Gen. 14:7; 21:14). The Israelites wan-dered in the Negeb after a futile attempt to enter Canaan (Num. 14:44-45). David incorporated it into his kingdom, and Solomon estab-lished fortresses in the region. Daniel used the term to refer to Egypt (Dan. 11:15,29). After Judah fell in 586 B.C., Edom took the area into its kingdom. In NT times it was known as Nabatea. See *Directions; Nabateans; Palestine.*

NEHEMIAH (*Yah comforts* or *encourages*)

(1) Jewish leader; cupbearer to Per-sian king (1:11); appointed Persian governor over Judah; led Jews to rebuild walls of Jerusalem. See *Israel, History of.*

(2) Man who returned with Sheshba-zzar (Ezra 2:2; Neh. 7:7).

(3) Helper with rebuilding the walls of Jerusalem (Neh. 3:16).

NEHEMIAH, BOOK OF

Book in OT Writings detailing work of Nehemiah to rebuild Jerusalem and its walls. Nehemiah and Ezra were one book in the ancient Hebrew and Greek OT, and probably were not divided until after the Interbibli-cal Period (see Ezra for more details). Jewish tradition says Ezra or Nehemiah was the author. Because of the close connection between Chronicles and Ezra-Nehemiah, one person might have written or com-piled all three books.

The author/compiler wove Ezra's and Nehemiah's stories together, Ezra being featured in Neh. 8. The book has four major sections: the rebuilding of Jerusalem's walls (chs. 1–7), the Great Revival (chs. 8–10), population and census infor-mation (chs. 11–12), and reforms of Nehemiah (ch. 13). Nehemiah made two visits from King Artaxerxes to Jerusalem (2:1-6; 13:6-7). His first, 445 B.C., was to repair the walls. The second was a problem-solving trip in 432 B.C. (13:6). Nehemiah was a contemporary of Ezra and Malachi.

Nehemiah's memoirs include first person accounts (1:1–7:5; 12:27-47; 13:4-31). Other material uses third person (chs. 8–10). Informed of the dilapidation of Jerusalem's walls, he was so upset he mourned for days (1:4). He confessed Israel's sins (1:5-11). His grief became apparent to Artaxerxes who permitted him to go to Jerusalem. Nehemiah first inspected the walls at night (2:15). He then con-vinced the people of the need for a building program. The work began (ch. 3). Sanballat and his friends tried to stop the work, but without success (ch. 4). Building the walls caused a labor shortage; farms were mort-gaged, and high rates of interest were charged. Nehemiah corrected the problem and even gave financial aid to those in need (ch. 5). Again Sanbal-lat and other non-Jews attempted to lure Nehemiah away from the job. They failed. Nehemiah proved to be a person of strong will and unusual boldness. "So the wall was finished ... in fifty and two days" (6:15).

The theological climax of the Book of Nehemiah and of the life of Ezra is the Great Revival (Neh. 8–10). Ezra read from the book of the law of Moses (8:1), and others helped by giv-ing "the sense, so that the people understood the reading" (8:8, NRSV). This probably included translating the Hebrew scripture into Aramaic, the commonly spoken language.

A great celebration occurred, and they celebrated the Feast of Tabernacles. "They made confession and worshiped the Lord" (9:3 NRSV), divorced their foreign spouses (9:2), prayed a long prayer of confession (9:6-37), made a covenant with God (9:38), and recorded the signers and terms of the covenant (ch. 10).

Nehemiah was dissatisfied with the small size of the population of Jerusalem and so cast lots to bring one in ten people from the towns into Jerusalem (11:1 NRSV). The dedication of the wall is described later in 12:27-43. Nehemiah's last chapter cites his reforms made in 432 B.C. He threw out a Gentile who was permitted to live in the temple; he restored the practice of tithing to support the Levites; he corrected sabbath wrongs by those who bought and sold on the sabbath; and he dealt forthrightly with those who had married foreigners, those not in covenant relation with God.

Nehemiah's theology was very practical; it affected every area of life. Note his practical prayers (1:4-11; 2:4; 4:4-5, 9; 5:19; 6:9, 14; 13:14, 22, 29, 31). He boldly asked, "Remember for my good, O my God, all that I have done for this people" (5:19 NRSV; compare 13:14,31). His faith produced practical results (2:8 NRSV; compare 2:18). He believed "the God of heaven is the one who will give us success" (2:20 NRSV) and that "our God will fight for us" (4:20 NRSV). He had respect for the sabbath, the temple and its institutions, the Levites, and tithing. Nehemiah was the father of Judaism, giving the Jews a fortified city, a purified people, a dedicated and unified nation, renewed economic stability, and a new commitment to God's law.

NEIGHBOR

Person living in same vicinity, engaging in mutual activities, and for whom one takes some responsibility. The Bible's major concern is how we treat our neighbor. Love is the guiding principle (Lev. 19:18). Other references tell what not to do to a neighbor (see Deut. 19:11-14; 27:24; Prov. 14:21; Hab. 2:15). Refusing to respect the rights of a neighbor constituted moral disintegration and provoked punishment on the nation (Isa. 3:5; Jer. 9:4-9; Mic. 7:5-6).

Neighbors were "the children of thy people" (Lev. 19:18), that is, neighbors had to come from your kind. Anyone who believed differently from you could not be your neighbor. By Jesus' day, the rabbis had further restricted the definition of neighbor. For them a neighbor was a Jew who strictly observed the law. Other people were hated as enemies (Matt. 5:43). Jesus sought to broaden the definition of neighbor. Neighbors included your enemies. Love meant doing good for them (Matt. 5:44). His most comprehensive definition of neighbor came in response to a lawyer's question, "Who is my neighbor?" (Luke 10:29). Jesus replied with the story of a man who had been beaten, robbed, and left to die. First, a priest went by and did nothing. Then, a Levite went by and did nothing. Finally, a foreigner (Samaritan) came and compassionately assisted the dying man, saving his life and making provisions for his immediate future (Luke 10:30-35; compare Rom. 13:9-10; Gal. 5:14; James 2:8).

A neighbor, then, is any person we encounter who has any need. That includes every person we encounter. Neighboring is done as we show mercy (Luke 10:37). Loving our neighbor is second in importance only to loving God (Matt. 25:35-39) and means more than all the offerings and sacrifices we could ever give (Mark 12:33).

NEPHILIM (*the fallen ones* or *ones who fall* [violently] *upon others*)

(1) Ancient heroes who, according to most interpreters, are the products of sexual union of heavenly beings ("sons of God"; compare Job 1:6; 2:1; 38:7; Pss. 29:1; 82:6) and human women (Gen. 6:4). The account illustrates

the breakdown of the God-ordained order separating heaven and earth (Gen. 1:6-10) and specifying reproduction "each according to its kind" (1:11-12,21,24-25). God intervened to reestablish limits inherent in creation (6:3; compare 3:22-23).

(2) Nephilim designates a race of giants descended from Anak against whom the Israelites appeared as grasshoppers (Num. 13:33). See *Sons of God; Rephaim.*

NEREUS

(1) Greek sea god who fathered the Nereids (sea nymphs).

(2) Roman Christian, possibly the son of Philogus and Julia (Rom. 16:15).

NERGAL (*Lord of the great city*)

Mesopotamian god of the underworld whose cult was centered in Cuth. In 721 B.C. Assyrians resettled Samaria with Mesopotamian peoples who brought their gods, including Nergal, with them (2 Kings 17:30). The name is an element in the name of Babylonian official Nergal-sharezer (Jer. 39:3,13). See *Assyria.*

NERGAL-SHAREZER (*Nergal, protect the king*)

Officer of Nebuchadnezzar's court who helped destroy Jerusalem in 586 B.C. (Jer. 39:3,13); son-in-law of Nebuchadnezzar; led military campaign across the Taurus Mountains to fight the Medes. He succeeded at first but was bitterly defeated later and soon died, perhaps at the hands of those who placed Nabonidus on the throne. See *Babylon, History and Religion of.*

NERO (*brave*)

Roman emperor A.D. 54–68; became emperor at age 13; succeeded stepfather, Claudius, who was probably murdered at behest of Agrippina, Nero's mother. His early reign was dominated by his mother and his two mentors, Burrus and Seneca. Later he probably was involved in the

death of his half brother, Britannicus, and he had his mother murdered.

Nero could be extremely cruel. His life was marked with debauchery and excess. Yet he was also a poet, an actor, a musician, and an athlete. The Great Fire broke out in Rome (A.D. 64). Nero fiddled while Rome burned.

He could not dispell the rumor that he had the fire set. Nero selected the Christians as his scapegoats, claiming that they had set the fire. A systematic persecution of the Christians followed. Because of his lifestyle and the persecution, many Christians viewed him as the antichrist. Nero lost the loyalty of large segments of the army. Finally, several frontier armies revolted. Nero's support at home melted away. Realizing that the end was inevitable and near, he committed suicide. See *Rome.*

NEST

Hollow container fashioned by a bird to contain its eggs and young; often used as simile or metaphor for human dwelling (Num. 24:21; Job 29:18; Hab. 2:9; Prov. 27:8). The term translated "nest" (Matt. 8:20; Luke 9:58) suggests a leafy "tent" rather than a nest.

NET

(1) Loosely woven mesh of twine or cord used for catching birds, fish, or other prey.

(a) Fishing nets were of two basic types. The first was a cone-shaped net with leads around its wide mouth used for hand casting (Matt. 4:18-21; Mark 1:16-19). The second was the seine net, a large draw with floats at its head and lead sinkers at its foot. Such a net was often hauled ashore to empty (Isa. 19:8; Ezek. 26:5,14; 32:3; 47:10; Matt. 13:47). The seine net is a figure for judgment at the hands of ruthless military forces.

(b) Fowling nets frequently had hinged mouths which could clamp shut when sprung (Prov. 1:17; Hos. 7:11-12).

(c) Nets of unspecified type are frequently used as figures of the Lord's chastisement (Job 19:6; Ps.

66:11; Lam. 1:13; Ezek. 12:13) or of the plots of the wicked (Pss. 9:15; 31:4; 35:7-8).

(2) Netting or network refers to grill-work used as part of the ornament of the altar of burnt offering (Ex. 27:4-5; 38:4) and of the capitals of the temple columns (1 Kings 7:17-20). The grill-work of the altar perhaps functioned as a vent.

NEW AGE

A time when God acts decisively in judgment and salvation; "new age" does not occur in Scripture, but is indicated by parallel expressions, such as "the age to come,'"the close of the age." Many biblical writers con-ceived of history in two periods, the present and a future time when God's salvation and judgment would be manifest. The age to come is associ-ated with the experience of eternal life (Mark 10:30; Luke 18:30), the res-urrection of the dead (Luke 20:35) and the immeasurable riches of God's gracious kindness (Eph. 2:7). The close of the age is associated with final judgment and reward (Matt. 13:39-40,49) and with the com-ing of Christ (Matt. 24:3). The present reality is also God's new age. Christ brought about the end of the age of sin through His sacrificial death (Heb. 9:26). The end of the ages has already come for believers (1 Cor. 10:11). See *Eschatology.*

NEW BIRTH

Term evangelicals use based on John 3:3,6-7; 1 Pet. 1:23 to describe the unique spiritual experience of begin-ning a changed life in Christ. New birth, like the earlier physical birth, is an initiation to a new experience of life. The new birth is an act of God that comes from hearing the word of God (John 1:13; Eph. 2:8; Jas. 1:18,21; 1 Pet. 1:23). Individuals repent (break with a life of sin, Luke 13:3) and com-mit their life to Christ (John 1:12; 3:16). New birth makes one God's child forever. See *Regeneration; Salvation.*

NEW TESTAMENT

Second major division of Christian Bible with 27 separate works (called "books") attributed to at least eight different writers. Four accounts of Jesus' life are at the core. The first three Gospels (called "Synoptic") are very similar in content and order. The fourth Gospel has a completely dif-ferent perspective.

A history of selected events in the early church (Acts) is followed by 20 letters to churches and individuals and one apocalypse. The letters deal mainly with the interpretation of God's act of salvation in Jesus Christ. Matters of discipline, proper Chris-tian behavior, and church polity also are included. The apocalypse is a coded message of hope to the church of the first century that has been rein-terpreted by each succeeding gener-ation of Christians for their own situations.

NICODEMUS (*innocent of blood*)

Pharisee (John 3:1), member of the Sanhedrin, the Jewish ruling council, and "a teacher of Israel," that is, an authority on the interpretation of the Hebrew scriptures (John 3:1,10). Nicodemus's coming at night sug-gests his timidity and his trek from the darkness of his own sin and igno-rance to the light of Jesus (John 3:2). Nicodemus recognized Jesus as a God-sent teacher whose signs bore witness to the presence of God (John 3:2). Jesus replied that Nicodemus could never see the kingdom of God without being "born again" (v. 3) or "born of water and of the Spirit"(v. 5). Nicodemus could only marvel at the impossibility of such a thing (vv. 4,9). Nicodemus defended Christ before his peers (John 7:48-51). They rebuked him. Nicodemus contributed enough aloes and spices to prepare a king for burial (John 19:39-41).

NICOLAITANS

Heretical group in early church who taught immorality and idolatry; con-demned (Rev. 2:6,15) for their prac-tices in Ephesus and Pergamon. Thyatira apparently had resisted the false prophecy they preached (Rev. 2:20-25).

NICOLAS (conqueror of people)

Hellenist "full of the Spirit and wisdom" chosen to administer food to the Greek-speaking widows of the Jerusalem church (Acts 6:5); a proselyte, that is, a Gentile convert to Judaism, from Antioch. See Deacon.

NICOPOLIS (city of victory)

Site in which Paul most likely wintered (Titus 3:12); in Epirus in northwest Greece on north side of the Sinus Ambracicus.

NIGER (black)

Latin nickname; surname of Simeon, teacher-prophet of the early church at Antioch. Simeon's Latin nickname suggests he originated from the Roman province of Africa, west of Cyrenica. His inclusion in Acts 13:1 demonstrates the multiracial and multinational leadership of the church at Antioch. Their concern for missions was likely rooted in their own ethnic diversity.

NIGHT WATCH

Ancient division of time (Pss. 90:4; 119:148; Lam. 2:19; Matt. 14:25). According to later Jewish system, the night was divided into three watches (evening, midnight, and morning). The Greco-Roman system added a fourth (cockcrowing) between midnight and morning (Mark 13:35). The fourth watch (Matt. 14:25; Mark 6:48) designates the time just before dawn.

NILE RIVER (Nile)

Major river considered the "life" of ancient Egypt; formed by union of the White Nile, which flows out of Lake Victoria in Tanzania, and the Blue Nile from Lake Tana in Ethiopia. These join at Khartum in the Sudan and are later fed by the Atbara. Thereafter the Nile flows 1,675 miles northward to the Mediterranean Sea without any further tributary. In antiquity six cataracts or falls prevented navigation at various points.

The first of these, going upstream, is found at Aswan, generally recognized as southern boundary of Egypt. From Aswan northwards, the Nile flows between two lines of cliffs that sometimes come directly down to its edge but in other places are up to nine miles away. The shore land could be cultivated as far as Nile water could be brought. This cultivated area the Egyptians called the Black Land from the color of the rich soil. Beyond lay the Red Land of the low desert stretching to the foot of the cliffs. At the cliff tops was the great inhospitable desert where few Egyptians ventured. Below the modern capital, Cairo, and the nearby ancient capital, Memphis, the Nile forms a huge delta. The eastern edge of the Delta is the site of the land of Goshen where Jacob/Israel and his descendents were settled. See Goshen.

Egypt was unique as an agricultural community in not being dependent on rainfall. The secret was the remarkably fertile black silt deposited on the fields by the Blue Nile's annual flood from winter rains in Ethiopia. Irrigation waters let the Egyptians produce many varieties of crops in large quantities (Num 11:5; Gen 42:1-2). If the winter rains failed, disastrous famine followed (compare Gen. 41). The river was also a natural highway. See Egypt.

NIMRIM (leopards or basins of clear waters)

Stream on which Moab's agricultural productivity depended (Isa. 15:6; Jer. 48:34); either wadi en-Numeirah, which flows east into the Dead Sea about eight miles north of its lower end, or wadi Nimrin, which flows east into the Jordan eight miles north of its mouth.

NIMROD (we shall rebel)

Son of Cush or Ethiopia (Gen. 10:8-10; 1 Chron. 1:10); hunter and builder of kingdom of Babel whom some Bible students have linked to Tukulti-Ninurta, an Assyrian king (about 1246–1206 B.C.). Others think that Amenophis III of Egypt (about

1411–1375 B.C.) or the heroic Gilgamesh might have been the ancient Nimrod. Regardless, extremely popular legends involve Nimrod as a ruler in both Assyrian and Egyptian lore. The prophet Micah called Assyria "the land of Nimrod" (5:6).

NINEVE or NINEVEH

Greatest of capitals of the ancient Assyrian Empire, which flourished from about 800 to 612 B.C.; on left bank of Tigris River in northeastern Mesopotamia (Iraq today); city established by Nimrod (Gen. 10:9-12); enemy city to which God called the reluctant prophet Jonah in eighth century B.C. Nahum prophesied the overthrow of the "bloody city" by the attack of the allied Medes and Chaldeans in 612 B.C.

Sennacherib (704–681 B.C.) built the enormous southwest palace. His reliefs show captive Philistines, Tyrians, Aramaeans, and others working under supervision of the king himself. One relief shows Assyria's capture of Lachish in 701 B.C. Sennacherib's city was enclosed by eight miles of walls with fifteen gates. It had gardens and parks, watered by a thirty-mile long aqueduct.

Ashurbanipal (669–28 B.C.) built the northern palace with its magnificent reliefs of royal lion hunts. He amassed a library of 20,000 tablets, which contained important literary epics, magical and omen collections, royal archives, and letters. See *Assyria.*

NISAN

Foreign term used after the Exile for first month of Hebrew calendar (Neh. 2:1; Esther 3:7) in March and April; formerly called Abib. See *Calendars.*

NISROCH

God worshiped by Assyrian king Sennacherib (2 Kings 19:37; Isa. 37:38); may be (deliberate?) corruption of name Marduk, Nusku (the fire-god), or Ashur.

NOAH (*rest*)

(1) Man who walked with God and stood blameless among the people of that time; chosen by God to be survivor of the flood with his sons Shem, Ham, and Japheth and families (Gen. 6–9). After flood God established rainbow or Noahic covenant with him never again to destroy living creatures as He had done in the flood. Once on dry ground, Noah planted a vineyard, drank of its wine, became drunk, and exposed himself in his tent. Ham informed Shem and Japheth about their father's nakedness. The latter two showed respect for their father and covered him. As a result, they received rich blessings for their descendants from Noah. Ham received a curse for his descendant: Canaan. Hebrews 11:7 affirms Noah's actions of faith in building the ark. The references to Noah in 1 Pet. 3:20 and 2 Pet. 2:5 speak of Noah and those of his family who were saved in the flood. See *Flood.*

(2) One of Zelophehad's five daughters (Num. 26:33).

NOB

City in Benjamin likely situated between Anathoth and Jerusalem (Neh. 11:31-32; Isa. 10:32). Following the destruction of the Shiloh sanctuary about 1,000 B.C. (Jer. 7:14), the priesthood relocated to Nob. Because the priest Ahimelech gave aid to the fugitive David (1 Sam. 21:1-9), Saul exterminated 85 of the priests of Nob (1 Sam. 22:9-23). Only Abiathar escaped. See *Ahimelech.*

NOD (*wandering*)

Site "away from the presence of the LORD" and "east of Eden" (Gen. 4:16) where God exiled Cain after he murdered Abel (Gen. 4:12,14).

NODAB (*nobility*)

Tribe conquered by Reuben, Gad, and the half-tribe of Manasseh (1 Chron. 5:18). The name is preserved by Nudebe in Hauran. The association of Nodab with Jetur and Naphish suggests its identification with Kedemah (Gen. 25:15; 1 Chron. 1:31).

NUCLEAR WEAPONS

The description of the end of the world predicted in 2 Pet. 3:10,12 is interpreted by some as describing the effects of an atomic blast. In modern military arsenals, only nuclear weapons can cause "the elements [to] melt with fervent heat" (2 Pet. 3:10).

Nuclear weapons represent the best in mankind combined with the worst in mankind. People were created with the capacity for great intelligence and creativity. Nothing that people propose to do, said God in response to the Tower of Babel, will be impossible for them (Gen. 11:7). Yet by means of nuclear weapons, people now also hold the capacity to literally destroy creation.

Like all technological advances, nuclear weapons tempt those who control them into thinking that they can control their own lives. For this reason, Isaiah's warning to Hezekiah, who "didst look in that day to the armour of the house of the forest" (Isa. 22:8b) for security, is apropos: without first ordering one's life according to God's principles, even the best of human efforts is futile (Isa. 22:11; compare Isa. 7:9), and quite possibly self-destructive.

NUMBER SYSTEMS AND NUMBER SYMBOLISM

Ways of using numbers in business, daily life, and religion or superstition. Egyptians were already using relatively advanced mathematics by 3000 B.C. as evidenced by construction of pyramids. The Egyptian system was decimal. The Sumerians knew two systems, one based on 10 (a decimal system) and one based on 6 or 12.

The Hebrews did not develop the symbols to represent numbers until the postexilic period (after 539 B.C.). In all preexilic inscriptions, small numbers are represented by individual strokes (for example, //// for four). Larger numbers were either represented with Egyptian symbols, or the name of the number was written out.

Letters of the Hebrew alphabet were first used to represent numbers on coins minted in the Maccabean period (after 167 B.C.).

After 333 B.C. Greek symbols for numbers and later Roman numerals appeared. The Hebrews were well acquainted with the four basic mathematical operations of addition (Num. 1:20-46), subtraction (Gen. 18:28-33), multiplication (Num. 7:84-86), and division (Num. 31:27). The Hebrews also used fractions such as a half (Gen. 24:22), a third (Num. 15:6), and a fourth (Ex. 29:40).

Many numbers came to have a symbolic meaning. Seven symbolized completeness and perfection. God's complete and perfect work of creation was completed in seven days. The seven-day week reflected God's first creative activity. Seven was also important in cultic matters: seventh day sabbath; major festivals such as Passover and Tabernacles lasted seven days as did wedding festivals (Judg. 14:12,17). In Pharaoh's dream, the seven good years followed by seven years of famine (Gen. 41:1-36) represented a complete cycle of plenty and famine. The seven churches (Rev. 2–3) perhaps symbolized all the churches. Jesus taught that we are to forgive, not merely seven times but 70 times seven (limitless forgiveness, beyond keeping count; Matt. 18:21-22). Multiples of seven frequently had symbolic meaning. The year of Jubilee came after the completion of every 49 years (Lev. 25:8-55). Seventy elders are mentioned (Ex. 24:1,9). Jesus sent out the 70 (Luke 10:1-17). Seventy years is specified as the length of the exile (Jer. 25:12, 29:10; Dan. 9:2). The messianic kingdom was to be inaugurated after a period of 70 weeks of years had passed (Dan. 9:24).

The tribes of Israel and Jesus' disciples numbered 12, another symbol of completeness. Twelve seems to have been especially significant in the Book of Revelation. New Jerusalem had 12 gates; its walls had 12 foundations (Rev. 21:12-14). The tree of life yielded 12 kinds of fruit (Rev. 22:2). Multiples of 12 are also important. There were 24 divisions of priests (1 Chron. 24:4), and 24 elders around the heavenly throne (Rev. 4:4). Seventy-two elders, when one includes Eldad and Medad, were given a portion of God's spirit that rested on Moses, and they prophesied (Num. 11:24-26). The 144,000 servants of God (Rev. 7:4), were made up of 12,000 from each of the 12 tribes of Israel.

Three often indicated completeness. The created cosmos had three elements: heaven, earth, and underworld. Three Persons make up the Godhead: Father, Son, and Holy Spirit. Prayer was to be lifted at least three times daily (Dan. 6:10; compare Ps. 55: 17). The sanctuary had three main parts: vestibule, nave, inner sanctuary (1 Kings 6). Three-year-old animals were mature and were, therefore, prized for special sacrifices (1 Sam. 1:24; Gen. 15:9). Jesus said He would be in the grave for three days and three nights (Matt. 12:40), the same time Jonah was in the great fish (Jonah 1:17).

Four was a sacred number: four corners of the earth (Isa. 11:12), four winds (Jer. 49:36), four rivers that flowed out of Eden to water the world (Gen. 2:10-14), and four living creatures surrounding God (Ezek. 1; Rev. 4:6-7). God sent four horsemen of the Apocalypse (Rev. 6:1-8) to bring devastation to the earth.

Forty often represented a large number or a long period of time. Rain flooded the earth for 40 days (Gen. 7:12). For 40 days Jesus withstood Satan's temptations (Mark 1:13). Forty years represented approximately a generation. Thus all the adults who had rebelled against God at Sinai died during the 40 years of the wilderness wandering period. By age 40, a person had reached maturity (Ex. 2:11; Acts 7:23).

NUMBERS, BOOK OF

Fourth book of OT; teaches identity of the people of God, God's provision for authority over His people, and God's plan for their fulfillment as a nation. Most commentators use a geographical outline to summarize the book: 1:1-10:10, what happened at Sinai; 10:11-20:13, what happened in the wilderness; and 20:14-36:13, what happened from Kadesh to Moab.

It seems most productive to consider the contents of the book in the light of the three questions asked above.

Every aspect of life during the wilderness wandering was permeated with the centrality of God. Under God's instructions Israel conscripted an army; God's presence radiated both a sense of awe and well-being in the center of the camp; God's promise of a landed inheritance gave them a goal to strive for and an identity; and God was the ultimate authority and spoke both indirectly through His human representatives and directly through His miraculous power. The rebellion narratives (11:1-12:16; 14; 16; 17; 20; 21:4-9; and 25:1-18), as well as the account of Balaam the wizard (22-24), serve to show how God's plan and provision cannot be thwarted by any rival possibility or power. Israel needed to stay on God's side to find success.

NUN

(1) Father of Joshua (Ex. 33:11; Num. 11:28; 13:8,16);

(2) Fourteenth letter of Hebrew alphabet, which serves as heading for Ps. 119:105-112. Each verse of this section begins with nun.

NUNC DIMITTIS (now lettest thou depart)

First words in Latin of Simeon's psalm of praise (Luke 2:29-32); title of the psalm. See *Benediction*.

NURSE

(1) Woman who breast-feeds an infant (Gen. 21:7; Ex. 2:7; 1 Sam. 1:23); often as long as three years (1 Sam. 1:22-24). Weaning was often a time of celebration (Gen. 21:8). Generally, a mother nursed her own child; though sometimes a wet nurse was employed (Ex. 2:7). A nurse might continue as an honored family member

after the child was grown (Gen. 24:59; 35:8). Paul likened the gentleness of his missionary approach to a mother nursing her children (1 Thess. 2:7).

(2) Woman who cares for a child such as a governess or nanny (Ruth 4:16; 2 Sam. 4:4).

(3) One who cares for the sick (1 Kings 1:2,4 NASB, RSV).

NUTS See *Plants.*

OATHS

Formal appeals to God or some sacred object as a support to fulfill a promise. Lacking means of legal enforcement, binding transactions depended on the power of a person's word. The oath maintained the obligation to speak honestly. Violation of an oath was serious and could not be disregarded (Ezek. 17:13,16,18-19). Parties made oaths to enforce the awareness that a violator of a covenant would suffer the same fate as the sacrificed animal. See *Covenant*. Symbolic acts often accompanied an oath. Oath takers raised their right hands or lifted both hands to heaven (Gen. 14:22; Dan. 12:7; compare Rev. 10:5-6). Even God is pictured swearing by His right hand (Isa. 62:8).

Using the Lord's name in an oath directly appealed to His involvement regarding testimony and established Him as the supreme Enforcer and Judge. To violate the Lord's name was to violate the Lord; therefore, oaths that used God's name carelessly are condemned (Ex. 20:7; Lev. 19:12). The oath reinforced God's promises to His people (Ex. 33:1; Deut. 6:18; 7:8; Ps. 132:11). The oath established boundaries around human speech and set guidelines for human conduct (Num. 30; Deut. 23:21). Israel ratified their treaties by oaths (Josh. 9:15,18,20).

Jesus established a different standard of speech, one based not on oaths but on simple integrity. A clear yes and no would be sufficient for communication (Matt. 5:33-37; 23:16-21; compare Jas. 5:12). At His trial before Caiaphas, He was silent until a binding oath was placed upon Him (Matt. 26:63-65). Jesus did not condemn oaths, only the abuse of God's name in the taking of oaths. An oath accompanied Peter's second denial of Christ. His final denial came in the form of a curse (Matt. 26:69-75). Paul frequently called on God with an oath to witness to his own sincerity (Rom. 1:9; 2 Cor. 1:23; Gal. 1:20). The superiority of Christ's priesthood over the Levitical priesthood was secure because it was promised with an oath whereas the Levitical priesthood was not (7:20-22).

OBADIAH (*Yahweh's servant*)

Twelve OT men including:

(1) Person in charge of Ahab's palace; go-between for Elijah and Ahab (1 Kings 18:3-16). Devoted to Yahweh, he saved Yahweh's prophets from Jezebel's wrath.

(2) Descendant of David through Hananiah (1 Chron. 3:21).

(3) Prophet active sometime after Babylon captured Jerusalem in 586 B.C. who condemned Edom for opposing Judah. His messages make up fourth book of the Book of the Twelve or the Minor Prophets.

OBADIAH, BOOK OF

Fourth and shortest book of the Minor Prophets, preserving the message of Obadiah the prophet shortly before 500 B.C. Its central section, verses 10-14, deals with the fall of Jerusalem to the Babylonians in 586 B.C., concentrating on the part Edom played in that tragic event. Despite treaty ties ("brother," v. 10) the Edomites, along with others, had failed to come to Judah's aid and had even helped Babylon by looting Jerusalem and handing over refugees. Moreover, the Edomites annexed the Negeb to the south of Judah and even its southern territory (compare v. 19).

Obadiah's oracle responded to an underlying impassioned prayer of lament, like Pss. 74, 79, or 137, in which Judah appealed to God to act as providential trial Judge and Savior. Verses 2-9 give the divine verdict. God promised to defeat those supermen and topple their mountain capital, which reflected their lofty self-conceit. Their allies would let them down, and neither their framed wisdom nor their warriors would be able to save them. This seems to look fearfully ahead to the Nabateans' infiltration from the eastern desert and their eventual takeover of Edom's traditional territory.

The catalog of Edom's crimes (vv. 10-14) functions as the accusation that warranted God's verdict of punishment. The underlying thought is that Judah had been the victim of "the day of the LORD" when God intervened in judgment (vv. 15-16; compare Lam. 1:12; 2:21). The day of the Lord embraces not only God's people but their no-less-wicked neighbors. The fall of Edom was to trigger this eschatological event in which order would be restored to an unruly world. Then would come the vindication of God's people, not for their own sakes but as earthly witnesses to His glory; and so "the kingdom shall be the LORD's" (v. 21). The aim of Obadiah is to sustain faith in God's moral government and hope in the eventual triumph of His just will.

OBED-EDOM (*serving Edom*)

Four OT men including the Philistine from Gath who apparently was loyal to David and Israel. At Obed-edom's house, David left the ark of the covenant following the death of Uzzah at the hand of God (2 Sam. 6:6-11). Obed-edom was unusually blessed of God during the three months the ark was at his house.

OBEDIENCE

To hear God's Word and act accordingly. Obedient response to God's Word is a response of trust or faith. To really hear God's Word is to obey God's Word (Ex. 19:5; Jer. 7:23). Disobedience is a failure to hear and do God's Word (Ps. 81:11). Israel's story was one of a nation who failed to hear or to listen to God (Jer. 7:13; Hos. 9:17).

Obedience is essential to worship (1 Sam. 15:22; John 4:23-24). The obedience of faith brings about salvation (Rom. 1:5, 10:16-17; compare Jas. 2:21-26) and secures God's blessings (John 14:23; 1 John 2:17; Rev. 22:14). Spiritual insight is gained through obedience (John 7:17). True obedience means imitating God in holiness, humility, and love (1 Pet. 1:15; John 13:34; Phil. 2:5-8). True disciples do the will of God (Matt. 7:21) rather than obeying other persons (Acts 5:29). Obedience springs from gratitude for grace received (Rom. 12:12), expresses spiritual freedom (Gal. 5:13; 1 Pet. 2:16). Love for God motivates us to obey Him (John 14:21,23-24; 15:10).

Obedience comes from the wife to the husband (Eph. 5:22), from children to their parents (Eph. 6:1), from slaves to masters (Col. 3:22). Obedience with joy should be shown to church leaders (1 Thess. 5:12-13). Obedience is expected from all Christians to persons in authority (1 Pet. 2:13-14). Christ's obedience stands in contrast to Adam's disobedience (Rom. 5:12-21). A desire to obey the will of God motivated Jesus' actions (Luke 4:43; John 5:30; John 3:34). By living a life of obedience, Jesus showed Himself to be the Savior (Heb. 5:7-10). Christ's work on the cross is viewed as a sacrifice of obedience (Rom. 5:19; Heb. 10:7-10).

OBESITY

Because most people in the ancient world constantly lived on the edge of starvation, obesity was neither an option nor, for most, something to be avoided. Only the rich could afford the luxury of being fat, and for this reason fatness became a mark of status and wealth.

Eglon, king of Moab, was "very fat" (Judg. 3:17, 22) and Eli, high priest at Shiloh, was "heavy" (1 Sam. 4:18; compare 1 Sam. 2:29). Both men had attained a social position by which they could be "acceptably fat," yet in both cases their fatness is portrayed as a narrative symbol of extravagance and slothfulness. The Book of Proverbs similarly cautions that excessive eating and drinking is the mark of a fool (Prov. 23:20-21; compare Phil. 3:19), and urges restraint (Prov. 23:1-3; 25:16).

OCCUPATIONS AND PROFESSIONS

Ways persons earned a living and served their country. The development of secular occupations paralleled the settlement of the people into towns and villages, and the evolution of their government from a loose-knit tribal group to a nation involved in international politics. In earliest biblical times, Hebrews followed their herds from pasture land to pasture land and water hole to water hole, though at times they lived for long periods near major cities (Gen. 13:18; 20:1; 26:6; 33:19). Their occupations were centered in the family enterprise.

As a settled people in Canaan, agricultural pursuits became extremely important. Monarchy developed many new occupations, mostly to maintain the royal house. As villages grew larger and commerce between cities and nations expanded, various trades and crafts expanded with them. See *Commerce.*

The earliest occupations and professions

One of the principal duties around the home centered on food preparation:

(1) *Baker* (Gen. 40:5). Member of Egyptian pharaoh's court. Baking bread was a frequent task performed in the Hebrew home long before it evolved into a specialized trade.

(2) *Butler* of pharaoh's palace; also known as a *cupbearer* (Neh. 1:11; compare Gen. 40:21). One who was responsible for providing the king with drink. He, presumably, tasted each cup of wine before it was presented to Pharaoh as a precaution against poisoning.

(3) *Cook.* Person doing majority of food preparation (1 Sam. 9:23-24). Within the home, female family members did the cooking. As cooking became an occupation outside of the home, men entered the trade.

(4) *Grinder* or *miller* (Matt. 24:41). Daily chore of grinding grain; originally in family; later entered the marketplace. See *Mill.* The majority of persons in biblical times were

involved in some form of food gathering or production.

(5) *Fishermen* (Isa. 19:8; Matt. 4:18). Gatherers of fish from bodies of water for personal and commercial use by fishing with hook and line, spears, and nets. Jesus challenged Simon and Andrew to become "fishers of men" (Mark 1:17). See *Fish.*

(6) *Hunter* (Jer. 16:16). Person who sought and killed wild animals for food. Success depended on proficiency in the use of a bow and arrow, spear, traps and snares, and knowledge of the prey. Nimrod (Gen. 10:9) is the Bible's first hunter. See *Hunt/Hunter.*

(7) *Shepherds* (Luke 2:8). Keepers of flocks for their own family or for others. Those persons who have rule over others are often described in terms of the shepherd's duties. They were to care for and feed the people for whom they were responsible. Psalm 23 identifies the Lord as a Shepherd and vividly describes the duties of the keeper of the sheep. Abel is the first to be described as a "keeper of sheep" (Gen. 4:2).

(8) *Herdsman* (Gen. 4:20). Closely akin to the shepherd but kept cattle rather than sheep.

(9) *Farmer* (Ps. 129:3). One who tills the soil to make it produce food crops. Cain was the first farmer (Gen. 4:2). God instructs and works closely with him in producing the crops. See *Agriculture.* Farmwork involved the *gleaner* (Ruth 2:3), *harvestman* (Isa. 17:5), and *reaper* (Ruth 2:3). The harvestman and reaper are, apparently, two names for the same task. A farmer probably served as his own harvester. Gleaners were the poor and landless who obtained food by gleaning what farmers left in the field. See *Gleaning.*

Government became necessary when towns and villages began to form.

(10) *Judges* (Judg. 2:16). Leaders and military deliverers of Israel prior to the monarchy. These and later judges also settled disputes. (Compare Luke 18:2.) See *Judge.*

(11) *King* (1 Sam. 8:5). Head of government. Many kings, among Israel's neighbors, were held to be gods; but in Israel (note, however, the poetic designation in Ps. 45:6) the Israelite king was the spiritual example and leader. His obedience or disobedience to Israel's God determined the fortunes of the nation, but he was never god. See *King*.

(12) *Governor* (Gen. 42:6). Major administrator under the king as Joseph in Egypt (Gen. 41:43).

(13) *President* (Dan. 6:2). Authoritative administrator subject to the king. Daniel was one of three authorities to whom provincial leaders reported.

(14) *Deputy* or *proconsul* (Acts 13:7). Official who oversaw the administrative responsibilities of a province and reported to the Roman government. Deputies were used where the Roman army was unnecessary.

(15) *Governor* (Matt. 27:2) or *procurator*. Roman provincial administrator where a military presence was necessary: Pontius Pilate, Felix, and Festus. See *Rome; Governor*. The army was made up of men of various ranks and responsibilities. Many of the terms designating those in places of leadership are ambiguous and may refer to one and the same rank.

(16) *Armorbearer* (Judg. 9:54). Servant provided to protect a warrior as he went into battle. See *Arms*.

(17) *Commander* (Isa. 55:4). Apparently any leader among the people. *Captain, lieutenant,* and *prince*, which could be included under the umbrella of "commander," were, in the first place, military ranks alone.

(18) *Soldiers* (1 Chron. 7:4). Members of the army. Every adult male (over 20) within the tribes of Israel was expected to serve in the military. The government included a corps of service and judicial personnel, as well.

(19) *Jailer* (Acts 16:23). Person in charge of all prisoners—political or religious. Under Roman rule, jailer was strictly responsible for the safe-keeping of the inmates. If one were to escape, or otherwise be unable to complete his sentence, the jailer was liable to fulfill the sentence of the prisoner.

(20) *Publican* (Matt. 9:10) or *Tax Collector*. Person who extorted as much taxes as possible. The publican may have been able to keep for himself any amount of monies collected beyond that levied by the government.

(21) *Scribe* (Matt. 5:20). Maintainer and interpreter of religious texts or in government of official documents and records. Scribes involved in the copying and interpretation of the law of Moses are known from the time of Ezra (Ezra 7:6).

The Bible lists the organization of David (2 Sam. 8:16-18; 20:23-26) and Solomon (1 Kings 4:1-19). The exact responsibility of each official is difficult to determine as a look at different translations will show.

The marketplace offered numerous opportunities for employment outside the home.

(22) *Carpenter* (2 Sam. 5:11). Craftsman and builder in wood; occupation of Jesus. Usually foreign workers such as workers of Hiram, King of Tyre, who labored on Solomon's temple. Associated with these craftsmen of wood are the *feller* (Isa. 14:8) and *hewers* (Josh. 9:21), both cutters of wood.

(23) *Metalworkers—coppersmith* (2 Tim. 4:14), *goldsmith* (Neh. 3:8), and *silversmith* (Acts 19:24). Craftsmen creating jewelry, tools, and other objects in their respective metals. In more general terms, metalworkers are identified as *founders* (Judg. 17:4) and *smiths* (1 Sam. 13:19). See *Mines and Mining*.

(24) *Merchant* (Gen. 23:16) or *seller* (Isa. 24:2). Person who sold goods to consumers. Their trade developed into one of international proportions. See *Commerce*.

(25) *Potter* (Jer. 18:2; Rom. 9:21). Craftsman in clay producing vessels for business and home use.

(26) *Mason*. Person who cut stone for building purposes (2 Kings 12:12).

(27) *Tanner* (Acts 9:43). Person who prepared skins for use in clothing and as containers.

(28) *Tentmaker* (Acts 18:3). Craftsman who created portable living quarters. Paul, Aquila, and Priscilla made their living by making tents (Acts 18:3).

Many services were offered in biblical times.

(29) *Apothecary* (Neh. 3:8). Person who compounded drugs and ointments for medical purposes. Jewish religious practices suggest that making perfume was also a part of the apothecary's craft (Ex. 30:35).

(30) *Banker* or *lender* (Prov. 22:7). Person who handled money and made it possible to secure money on credit. See *Banking.*

(31) *Fuller* (Mal. 3:2). Ancient laundryman. He worked with soiled clothing and with the material from the loom ready for weaving. His service entailed the cleaning of any fabric.

(32) *Host* (Luke 10:35). Often thought of as an "innkeeper," provided minimal accommodations for travelers, in some cases, little more than provision of space for erecting a tent or a place to lie down to sleep.

(33) *Master* (Jas. 3:1), *instructor,* or *teacher* (Rom. 2:20). Among most respected persons of Scripture; usually referred to religious teaching, but applied to anyone who offered instruction. See *Education.*

Prominent throughout the Bible are various occupations related to musical talents.

(34) *Singers* and *players* (Ps. 68:25) *musicians, harpers, pipers,* and *trumpeters* (Rev. 18:22). Created musical environment for celebration, worship, and entertainment; employed by court and by temple.

While "occupation" is not a technically accurate term when referring to the early church, there were "offices" filled by Christians, normally on a voluntary basis.

The officers of the temple were much more authoritarian.

(35) *Priest* (Ex. 31:10). Intermediary between God and worshipers. In many cases, priests sacrificed the offerings for the people and the nation, taking for themselves a share in the offering. Priests also served as advisers to the king (2 Sam. 20:25).

(36) *Prophet* (Gen. 20:7). Members of temple personnel; "messengers" of their God responsible to mediate "word of God." Others worked apart from temple and even spoke against temple practices. See *Prophecy, Prophets; Priests; High Priest; Levites; Temple.*

OFFERINGS See *Sacrifice and Offering.*

OG

Amorite king of Bashan defeated by the Israelites before they crossed the Jordan (Num. 21:33-35; Deut. 1:4; 3:1-13); last member of Rephaim or giants (Deut. 3:11).

OHOLAH (*tent dweller*)

Woman's name Ezekiel used to portray Samaria (Ezek. 23:1-10). Oholah and her sister, Oholibah (Jerusalem), are shown as whores who consorted with various men (other nations) and thus committed spiritual adultery against God. God declared through the prophet that Samaria would be delivered into the hands of her "lover," Assyria (23:9).

OHOLIAB (*father's tent*)

Danite craftsman, designer, and embroiderer who assisted Bezalel in supervision of the tabernacle construction and its equipment (Ex. 31:6; 35:34; 36:1-2; especially 38:23).

OHOLIBAH (*tent worshiper*)

Younger sister in the allegory of Ezek. 23 identified with Jerusalem (23:4, 11-49). See *Oholah.*

OIL

An indispensable commodity in the Ancient Near East for food, medicine, fuel, and ritual; considered a blessing given by God (Deut. 11:14; compare 8:8).

Domestic oil was prepared from olives. Sometimes oil was combined with perfumes and used as a cosmetic (Esther 2:12). This oil, called "beaten oil," was lighter and considered the best oil. Beaten oil was used in the lamps of the sanctuary (Ex. 27:20; Lev. 24:2) and with the daily sacrifices (Ex. 29:40; Num. 28:5). Solomon also used beaten oil in his trade with Hiram (1 Kings 5:11). After the beaten oil was extracted, another grade of oil was produced by heating the pulp and pressing it again. The third grade of oil was produced by further crushing and pressing the pulp.

Oil was used in the preparation of food, taking the place of animal fat, used with meal to prepare cakes (Num. 11:8; 1 Kings 17:12-16) and used with honey (Ezek. 16:13), flour (Lev. 2:1,4), and wine (Rev. 6:6). Oil was used as fuel for lamps, both in homes (Matt. 25:3) and in the tabernacle (Ex. 25:6).

Oil was used during the offering of purification from leprosy. Oil was used to anoint a body in preparation for burial (Matt. 26:12; Mark 14:8). Several persons were anointed with oil: kings (1 Sam. 10:1; 16:13), priests (Lev. 8:30), and possibly prophets (1 Kings 19:16; Isa. 61:1). Some objects were also anointed in dedication to God: the tabernacle and all its furniture (Ex. 40:9-11), the shields of soldiers (2 Sam. 1:21; Isa. 21:5), altars (Lev. 8:10-11), and pillars (Gen. 35:14).

As medicine, oil or ointment was used in the treatment of wounds (Isa. 1:6; Luke 10:34). James 5:14 may refer either to a symbolic use of oil or to its medicinal use. Oil was used cosmetically as protection against the scorching sun or the dryness of the desert (Ruth 3:3; Eccl. 9:8). See *Cosmetics; Commerce.*

Oil was regarded as a symbol of honor (Judg. 9:9), while virtue was compared to perfumed oil (Song of Sol. 1:3; Eccl. 7:1). As a symbol of affluence, oil was also associated with the arrogance of the rich (Hebrew: "valley of oil"; KJV: "fat valley," Isa. 28:1,4). Oil was a symbol of joy and gladness (Ps. 45:7), so in time of sorrow, anointing with oil was not practiced (2 Sam. 14:2). See *Anoint.*

OINTMENT

Perfumed unguents or salves of various kinds used as cosmetics, medicine, and in religious ceremonies; most common Hebrew word simply means "oil" (Gen. 28:18; Hos. 2:8) with no distinction between oil and ointment. New Testament "ointment" (Matt. 26:7; Mark 14:3-4; Luke 7:37-38) was a perfumed ointment.

One of the most important uses of ointment in the OT was in religious ceremonies (Ex. 30:22-25). Many individuals were anointed with the sacred ointment designating that person to the service of God.

Perfumes were used to counteract bodily odor. The whole body was usually anointed with perfume after bathing (Ruth 3:3; 2 Sam 12:20; Ezek. 16:9). Perfumes were used inside the clothes (Song of Sol. 1:13) and by women who desired to be attractive to men (Esther 2:12).

OLD TESTAMENT

First part of Christian Bible, taken over from Israel. It tells the history of the nation Israel and God's dealings with them to about 400 B.C. For Jews it is the complete Bible, sometimes called Tanak for its three parts (Torah or Law, Nebiim or Prophets, Kethubim or Writings). Christians see its complement in the NT, which reveals Jesus Christ as the fulfillment of OT prophecy. The Law (Genesis-Deuteronomy) begins with the creation of the world and concludes as Israel is about to enter the Promised Land. The Prophets—Joshua, Judges, Samuel, Kings, Isaiah, Jeremiah, Ezekiel, and the Book of the Twelve (Minor Prophets)—continue with the nation in the land of Palestine until the exile and include prophetic messages delivered to the nation. The Writings (all other books) contain the account of the return from exile, collected wisdom and poetic literature throughout the nation's history, and selected stories about God's leading in individual lives. See *Bible, Formation and Canon of, Old Testament.*

OLIVES, MOUNT OF

The 2.5 mile-long mountain ridge that towers over the eastern side of Jerusalem, or more precisely, the middle of the three peaks forming the ridge. Heavily covered with olive trees, the ridge juts out in a north-south direction (like a spur) from the range of mountains running down the center of the region. Both the central Mount of Olives and Mount Scopus, the peak on its northern side, rise over 200 feet above the temple mount across the Kidron Valley. It provided a lookout base and signaling point for armies defending Jerusalem. See 2 Sam. 15:30; Ezek. 11:23; Zech. 14:3-5; Matt. 26:30; Mark 11:1-2; Luke 4:5; 22:39-46; Acts 1:9-12).

OLIVET DISCOURSE

Jesus' major sermon preached on the Mount of Olives giving instructions concerning the end of the age and the destruction of Jerusalem. The discourse (Matt. 24–25; Mark 13) is in part an apocalypse because it uses symbolic, visionary language that makes it a difficult passage to understand. Parts of it appear scattered throughout Luke 12–21.

The opening remarks warn against misplaced belief in deceptive signs that do not in any way signal the end of the world. These signs occurred in Jesus' day and preceded the destruction of Jerusalem, the event uppermost in Jesus' mind and for which He sought to prepare His disciples. Many would say that the reference is to a period of ultimate suffering that is to take place just before the parousia (Christ's return or second coming). Jesus' assertion that the gospel must be preached worldwide seems to strengthen this view. It could also pertain to the end of some other event such as the destruction of Jerusalem.

Jesus spoke in veiled language about His coming. Much of God's plans are mystery, but Jesus disclosed enough. The coming of the Son of Man will be entirely public and completely unexpected. He will come in the clouds with great power (Acts 1:9-11). The sermon is interrupted by the statement, "This generation shall not pass, till all these things be fulfilled" (Matt 24:34). Jesus referred to the destruction of Jerusalem which took place in that generation as a foretaste of the final coming. Concluding parables teach the necessity of remaining watchful. A description of final judgment ends the discourse. Its basic message is a call to be prepared when Jesus does return.

OLYMPAS

Perhaps a shortened form of Olympiodorus (*gift of Olympus*); Christian Paul greeted (Rom. 16:15); apparently a member of a house church including others mentioned in 16:15.

OMEGA See *Alpha and Omega.*

OMNIPOTENCE

State of being all-powerful that theology ascribes to God. See *God.*

OMNIPRESENCE See *God.*

OMNISCIENCE

The state of being all-knowing that theology ascribes to God. See *God.*

OMRI (*pilgrim* or *life*)

(1) King of Israel (885-874 B.C.) and founder of the Omride dynasty, which ruled until 842. Zimri, chariot captain in Israel's army, assassinated King Elah and took control of the palace of Tirzah (1 Kings 16:8-15). Half of the people rebelled and installed Omri ("captain of the host," v. 16) as king. When Zimri realized his situation was hopeless, he burned the palace down upon himself. Omri became king only after successfully opposing another rebellion in the person of Tibni (vv. 21-22). Omri's

greatest accomplishment was to buy the hill of Samaria and build the capital of Israel there. Assyrian sources continued to call Israel, "the land of Omri." See Mic. 6:16.

(2) Officer of tribe of Issachar under David (1 Chron. 27:18).

(3) Grandson of Benjamin (1 Chron. 7:8).

(4) Grandfather of member of tribe of Judah who returned to Jerusalem from exile about 537 B.C.

ON

(1) Egyptian name meaning "city of the pillar," called in Greek Heliopolis or "city of the sun," and in Hebrew as Beth-shemesh, "city of the sun" (Jer. 43:13), and Aven. It was the cult center for sun-god, Re (Atum). Located at Matariyeh about five miles northeast of modern Cairo, the city endured as a cult center until very late. Joseph's Egyptian wife came from On (Gen. 41:45), her father serving as priest in the temple there. See Jer. 43:13; Ezek. 30:17.

(2) Personal name meaning "powerful, rich." Member of tribe of Reuben; leader who challenged authority of Moses (Num. 16:1).

ONAN (power)

Son of Judah and his Canaanite wife, Shuah (Gen. 38:2-8). Onan repeatedly failed to complete Levirate marriage responsibilities, and thus God killed him (38:8-10). See Levites; Marriage.

ONESIMUS (perhaps profitable)

Slave for whom Paul wrote his letter to Philemon. Paul pleaded with Philemon to free the servant because Onesimus had been so helpful to the apostle. Onesimus had robbed his master, escaped, met Paul, and accepted Christ. In sending him back to Philemon, Paul urged the owner to treat the slave as a Christian brother (v. 16). Later, Onesimus accompanied Thychius in bearing Paul's letter to the church at Colossae (Col. 4:7-9). See Philemon.

ONESIPHORUS (profit bearing)

Ephesian Christian praised for his effort to seek out the place of Paul's arrest, his disregard of the shame connected with befriending one in chains, and his past service in Ephesus (2 Tim. 1:16-18; compare 4:19).

ONO (grief)

Benjaminite town about seven miles southeast of Joppa; Kefr' Ana in the wadi Musrara. This broad wadi is called the valley of craftsmen (Neh. 11:35) and the Plain of Ono (Neh. 6:2). The city was rebuilt by Shemed, a descendant of Benjamin (1 Chron. 8:12). Ono was home to some of those who returned from exile (Ezra 2:33; Neh. 7:37; 11:36).

ONYCHA

Spice probably derived from the closing flaps or the shell of a Red Sea mollusk; used in incense reserved for the worship of Yahweh (Ex. 30:34).

OPHIR (dusty)

Place famous in the Ancient Near East for its trade, especially in gold. Solomon's ships with help from Phoenician sailors brought precious goods from Ophir (1 Kings 9:28; 10:11; compare 1 Kings 22:48; Isa. 13:12; Job 22:24; 28:16; Ps. 45:10).

Biblical scholars have suggested three regions as the site of Ophir: India, Arabia, and Africa. See Commerce; Economic Life.

ORACLES

Communications from God; refers both to divine responses to a question asked of God and to pronouncements made by God without His being asked. See Inspiration of Scripture; Priests; Spirit.

ORDINANCES

Baptism and the Lord's Supper were instituted by Christ and should be observed as "ordinances" or "sacraments" by His followers. Some interpreters believe sacrament conveys the concept that God's grace is dispersed almost automatically through participation in the Lord's Supper. Others believe *ordinance* stresses obedience in doing that which Christ explicitly commanded. Extreme dangers involved in the terms range from superstition to legalism.

The "sacraments" varied in number for 1,000 years in the church's early history. Peter Lombard (about A.D. 1150) defended seven, and Thomas Aquinas (about A.D. 1250) argued that all were instituted by Christ. After A.D. 1500, Martin Luther and other Protestant reformers rejected five of these, insisting that only baptism and the Lord's Supper have a biblical basis. Most Protestants agree with their assessment.

Baptism

John the Baptist preached and practiced a baptism of repentance (Matt. 3:11-12; Mark 1:2-8; Luke 3:2-17), looking forward to the coming kingdom (Matt. 3:2). Multitudes confessed their sins and were baptized (Mark 1:5). Apparently, not everyone who came received baptism, for John challenged some to "bring forth therefore fruits meet for repentance" (Matt. 3:8). John regarded his role as a transitional one to prepare the way (Matt. 3:11). The coming One would baptize with the Holy Spirit and with fire.

Jesus was baptized by John (Matt. 3:13-17; Mark 1:9-11; Luke 3:21-22; John 1:32-34). John hesitated to baptize Jesus but finally consented "to fulfill all righteousness" (Matt. 3:15). The identification of Jesus as Messiah followed as the heavens opened, the Spirit descended on Him like a dove, and a voice proclaimed Him the beloved Son. This event inaugurated His public ministry and set the stage for Christian baptism.

Jesus affirmed the ministry of John by submitting to baptism and adopted the rite for His own ministry, giving it new meaning for the new age. Jesus gained and baptized more followers than John the Baptist (John 4:1-2); Jesus referred to His impending death as a baptism (Luke 12:50), linking the meaning of baptism with the cross. The resurrected Lord commissioned His disciples to baptize (Matt. 28:19-20).

At Pentecost after Peter's sermon 3,000 people were baptized (Acts 2:41). They had been exhorted by the apostle, "Repent, and be baptized every one of you in the name of Jesus Christ for the remission of sins, and ye shall receive the gift of the Holy Ghost" (2:38). At other times baptism was "in the name of the Lord Jesus" (8:16; 19:5). Sometimes the gift of the Spirit followed baptism; at other times, the spirit preceded baptism (10:44-48). These were apparently regarded as separate experiences.

Many NT passages stress that forgiveness is based on repentance and trust in what Jesus had done, not on a rite—baptism or otherwise (John 3:16; Acts 16:31). Salvation is provided by Christ and not through baptism. References to Jesus' blessing little children contain no indications of baptism (Mark 10:13-16), and baptism of "households" described in Acts (16:31-33) should not be utilized to defend a later Christian practice.

Paul (Saul) encountered the living Christ on a journey to Damascus to persecute Christians. This led to a meeting in Damascus with Ananias, where Paul's sight was restored and where he was also baptized (Acts 9:17-18). From this time baptism became a part of his missionary message and practice among both Jews and Gentiles. Paul's basic message declared that a right relationship with God is based exclusively on faith in Jesus Christ (Rom. 1:17; 5:2). Christian baptism clearly illustrates one dead to sin lives no longer in it (Rom. 6:3-4).

Paul assumed the universal Christian practice of baptism and a common understanding that it symbolizes death, burial, and resurrection of the believer with Christ. The mode of immersion most clearly preserves this symbolism along with the added emphasis of death to sin and resurrection to a new life in Christ. The stress is on what Christ has done more than what the believer does. Through faith in Him, grace is received and makes baptism meaningful.

Paul in 1 Corinthians related unity in Christ to baptism. "For by one Spirit are we all baptized into one body" (12:13). Galatians 3:26-29 stresses identification with Christ and unity in Him also, using the figure of putting on clothing. For those who belong to Christ, earthly distinctions disappear; and all are one in Christ, heirs according to the promise.

Believers have been buried with Christ in baptism and raised with Him through faith in the power of God, who raised Him from the dead. Consequently, they are to set their hearts on things above and put to death the earthly nature (3:1,5; compare 2:9-12).

Baptism portrays the gospel message of the death and resurrection of Christ, affirms the death of the believer to sin and the rising to walk in newness of life, and signifies a union of the believer with Christ and a unity with other believers. The rite itself does not effect these, for they are based on what Christ has done and is doing. Baptism serves as the effective public symbol and declaration for those who trust in Christ as Savior and Lord.

Lord's Supper

The earliest written account of the institution of the Lord's Supper is in 1 Cor. 11:23-26. The Corinthian church was divided, and many of its members were selfish and self-indulgent. In their fellowship meal, therefore, they did not eat "the Lord's supper" (v. 20); for some overindulged, while others were left hungry and humiliated. Paul reminded them of the tradition that he had received and passed on to them regarding the Supper of the Lord with His disciples the night He was betrayed.

The terms *eucharist* or *thanksgiving* and *communion* or *fellowship* are often applied to the Supper. Each highlights a significant aspect of this ordinance. "The Lord's Supper" appears more satisfactory for the overall designation, reminding Christians that they share the loaf and cup at His table, not their own.

The Gospel accounts of the Last Supper (Matt. 26:26-29; Mark 14:22-26; Luke 22:17-20) join Paul to record the blessing (thanksgiving), breaking of bread, a new covenant in connection with the cup as His blood (see Jer. 31:31-34), and a future emphasis. Mark indicated that Jesus said He would not drink again of the fruit of the vine until He drank it anew in the kingdom of God. Paul related that "whenever you eat this bread and drink this cup, you proclaim the Lord's death until he comes" (1 Cor. 11:26 NIV).

Paul stressed the memorial aspect of the Supper. "This do in remembrance of me" (1 Cor. 11:24). Christians were to remember that the body of Christ was broken and His blood shed for them. As in baptism, sharing the Supper is a proclamation of the gospel in hope, "until he comes." As Passover was a symbol of the old covenant, the Lord's Supper is a symbol of the new.

The Supper shared in remembrance of the past and hope for the future is fulfilled in fellowship for the present. It is a "participation in the blood of Christ" and "in the body of Christ" (1 Cor. 10:16 NIV). Paul was not talking about a repetition of the sacrifice of Christ, but a genuine sharing of fellowship (*koinonia*) with the living Lord. Fellowship in Christ is basic for fellowship in His body (v. 17).

All Christians are unworthy to share the Lord's Supper, but His grace has provided for them in their unworthiness. The tragedy is that some partake in an unworthy manner, not discerning the Lord's body. Paul urged Christians to examine themselves and respect the corporate body of Christ as they share the Supper of the Lord.

Christ instituted both ordinances. Both portray publicly and visibly the essential elements of the gospel, and both symbolize realities involving divine activity and human experience. Baptism is a once-for-all experience, but the Lord's Supper is repeated many times. Baptism follows closely one's profession of faith in Christ and actually in the NT was the declaration of that faith. The Lord's Supper declares one's continuing dependence on the Christ proclaimed in the gospel, who died, was buried, and rose for our salvation.

In observing the ordinances, believers are presenting in a unique way the gospel of Christ and committing themselves fully to its demands. Calling on Christ the Savior and Lord to provide strength and leadership for the people of God individually and collectively, believers will leave the observance of the ordinances to give faithful service in His world.

ORDINATION, ORDAIN

The appointing, consecrating, or commissioning of persons for special service to the Lord and His people. KJV uses "ordain" to translate over 20 Hebrew and Greek words relating to a variety of ideas such as God's work and providence; the appointment to an office or a task; and the establishment of laws, principles, places, or observances. These ideas contain basic concepts of divine purpose, choice, appointment, and institution that undergird the practice of ordination.

Four primary examples provide OT precedents for ordination: the consecration of Aaron and his sons as priests to God (Ex. 28-29; Lev. 8-9), the dedication of the Levites as servants of God (Num. 8:5-13), the appointment of 70 elders to assist Moses (Num. 11:16-17,24-25), and the commissioning of Joshua as Moses' successor (Num. 27:18-23). The variety in these examples helps explain the various contemporary understandings of ordination.

The NT practice of ordination is generally associated with the laying on of hands; but other appointments, consecrations, and commissionings must be considered even if they lack formal investiture.

Jesus' appointment of the Twelve "that they should be with him, and that he might send them forth to preach" (Mark 3:14) involved no formal ordination. The same was true of the 70 (Luke 10:1). The Holy Spirit was given directly without the laying on of hands (John 20:22). Several other NT passages describe appointments without reference to ordination (Acts 1:21-26; 14:23; Titus 1:5).

Several passages describe ordination accompanied by laying on of hands (Acts 6:1-6; 13:1-3; 1 Tim. 4:14; 2 Tim. 1:6). References to laying on of hands in 1 Tim. 5:22 and Heb. 6:2 likely deal with other practices than ordination. See *Laying on of Hands*.

The lack of a consistent biblical pattern raises questions about ordination today. Answers to these questions will vary with the biblical model assumed and continue to be debated in various denominations.

OREB AND ZEEB (*raven* and *wolf*)

Two Midianite princes captured and executed by the Ephraimites following Gideon's rout of their forces (Judg. 7:24-8:3). The Midianite nobles gave their names to the sites of their deaths, the rock of Oreb near Beth Bareh on the Jordan and the winepress of Zeeb. Israel's deliverance from Midian became proverbial for God's deliverance of His people (Ps. 83:11; Isa. 9:4; 10:26).

ORPHANS See *Fatherless*.

OSTIA

Roman city at the mouth of the Tiber about 15 miles from Rome that, following construction of an artificial harbor by Claudius (A.D. 41-54), served as the principle harbor for Rome. Before this construction, silt prohibited seagoing vessels from using the port. Such vessels were forced to use the port of Puteoli about 138 miles to the south of Rome (Acts 28:13).

OTHNIEL (*God is powerful*)

(1) First of Israel's judges or deliverers, Othniel received Caleb's daughter Achsah as his wife in reward for his capture of Kiriath-sepher (Debir)

(Josh. 15:15-19; Judg. 1:11-15). He rescued Israel from the Mesopotamian king Cushan-rishathaim (Judg. 3:7-11). Othniel was the only judge to come from the southern tribes. See *Judges, Book of.*

(2) Clan name associated with a resident of Netophah (1 Chron. 27:15).

OUTER SPACE

The Bible teaches that outer space was created by God (Gen. 1:1, 14-19; Job 9:7-10; 26:7; Pss. 8:3; 136:7-9; Amos 5:8). God made the sun, moon, and stars to provide light for the earth and indicate the passage of time through seasons, days, and years (Gen. 1:14-15).

Long before recorded history, people began to worship the heavenly bodies. The deities of the sun, moon, and stars held prominent places in the pantheons of the ancient Near East. The Babylonians developed a sophisticated system of causation based in part on the movement of the stars. These ideas penetrated ancient Israel (e.g., 2 Kings 23:5; Jer. 8:1-2) where they were roundly condemned as idolatrous by the writers of the Bible (Deut. 4:19; 17:3; Job 31:26-28; Isa. 47:13; Jer. 10:2).

The biblical poets were awestruck by the vastness and mystery of outer space. They often referred to the sun, moon, and stars as witnesses to the power of God and permanence of His work. For instance, Job recognized that the earth "hangs on nothing" (Job 26:7) and that the movements of the constellations were known only to God (Job 38:31-33). The psalmist likened the permanence of the Davidic monarchy to the sun and moon (Pss. 72:5; 89:37). It is only at the end of time, when the creation process will be reversed by the day of the LORD, that the sun, moon, and stars will be darkened (Isa. 13:10; Joel 2:31; Matt. 24:29; Rev. 6:12-13; 8:12).

The Bible gives no indication that there is life on other planets, and strongly supports the uniqueness of life on Earth.

OVERSEER

Superintendent or supervisor; various translations use "overseer" for a variety of secular positions (household manager, Gen. 39:4-5; prime minister, Gen. 41:34; foreman or supervisor, 2 Chron. 2:18) and ecclesiastical (Acts 20:18) offices. NASB, NIV employ "overseer" for the *bishop* of the KJV, NRSV (Phil. 1:1; 1 Tim. 3:1-2; Titus 1:7).

OWNERSHIP

Possession of property. Two general principles guided Israelite laws of ownership:

(1) All things ultimately belong to God, and

(2) land possession is purely a business matter.

After the division of the land among the 12 tribes, individual plots were given to family groups or clans. If the occasion demanded it, the land could be redivided at a later time. Land sales and transfers were recorded by scribes on leather or papyrus scrolls, on clay tablets, or in the presence of witnesses with the symbolic removal of a sandal (Ruth 4:7) or the stepping onto the land by the new owner. Land passed from father to son but could be given to a daughter. Private lands ultimately reverted to the king if not used for several years (2 Kings 8). The law of the kinsman-redeemer (Lev. 25:25) was developed to assure that land belonging to a particular clan did not pass out of its hands despite the death of an heirless husband. The next-of-kin was required to purchase the land and provide an heir to the name of the deceased. The impoverished widow would not be forced to sell her land to outsiders, thus diminishing the tribal area of the clan.

The king did purchase lands from his subjects, but private lands were also subject to seizure by the ruler. Royal land was given as revenue-producing gifts by the ruler to members of his family or men who gained his favor. Often the land was tenant farmed for the king who continued to hold the ultimate right of its disposal.

When economic times were difficult, kings exchanged their lands for other services, such as Solomon's gift of land to Hiram of Tyre for gold and laborers in the building of the temple (1 Kings 9:11). Priestly families and local shrines also owned land, especially that surrounding the levitical cities, where the priests farmed their own fields (Josh. 21). With the consolidation of worship in the Jerusalem temple, many of the priestly lands were sold.

Private ownership continued in much the same fashion during the NT era. Bills of sale and land deeds written on papyrus scrolls from this period have been discovered, attesting to the exchange of private lands. Often the sale of private land was subject to royal approval. The Romans oversaw the control of lands in Palestine, requiring heavy taxes from owners. The early Christian community existed through the generosity of those members who sold many of their possessions to help poorer believers.

P

PADDAN-ARAM (perhaps *way of Syria, field of Syria*, or *plow of Syria*) Land including Haran from where Abraham journeyed to Canaan and to which he sent for a wife for Isaac (Gen. 24:1-9; compare 28:2-5; Hos. 12:13); may be tell Feddan near Carrhae.

PALACE

Residence of a monarch or noble. KJV for a strongly fortified section of the king's residence: "citadel" (1 Kings 16:18; 2 Kings 15:25); "tower" (Ps. 122:7 NRSV; Song of Sol. 8:9 NIV); "stronghold" (Isa. 34:13; Amos 1:4 NRSV); "fortress" (Amos 1:4 NIV); "battlement" (Song of Sol. 8:9 NRSV; "parapet," REB). At Amos 4:3, modern translations replace "palace" with the proper name Harmon. KJV used "palace" for Greek *aule* (Matt. 26:3; Luke 11:21). The crowd in Matt. 26 gathered in the courtyard of the high priest's residence: "palace" (NIV, NRSV, TEV); "court" (NASB); "house" (REB). The strong man of Luke 11 guarded the open courtyard of his home: "castle" (NRSV); "homestead" (NASB); "house" (NIV, TEV); "palace" (REB, RSV). KJV also used "palace" to translate Latin loanword *praetorium* (Phil. 1:13): "praetorian guard" (NASB, RSV) or an equivalent expression ("imperial guard," NRSV, REB; "palace guard," NIV, TEV).

Palaces served as a means of displaying the wealth of a kingdom (Esther 1:6-7). David's palace, built by workers sent by King Hiram of Tyre, featured cedar woodwork (2 Sam. 5:11). Solomon's palace complex required 13 years for completion (1 Kings 7:1). Builders used costly hewn stone and cedar throughout the palace (7:9,11). King Ahab's palace in Samaria was decorated with ivory panels, some of which have been recovered by archaeologists (1 Kings 22:39).

The prophets, particularly Amos, condemned the rich for building palaces at the expense of the poor. Amos's announcements of doom refer to summer and winter residences, ivory furniture and palaces, and great houses of hewn stone (Amos 3:15; 5:11; 6:4,11; Jer. 22:13-15).

PALESTINE

Geographical designation for land of Bible, particularly land west of Jordan River God allotted to Israel for an inheritance (Josh. 13–19). For the purposes of this article, Palestine extends north 10 to 15 miles beyond Dan and NT Caesarea Philippi into the gorges and mountains just south of Mount Hermon; east to the Arabian steppe; south 10 to 15 miles beyond Beer-sheba; west to Mediterranean Sea. Palestine west of the Jordan covers approximately 6,000 square miles. East of the Jordan about 4,000 square miles was included in Israel.

Palestine is naturally divided into four narrow strips of land running north and south.

(1) *Coastal plain.* This very fertile plain begins 10 to 12 miles south of Gaza, just north of the Egyptian border, and stretches northward to the Sidon-Tyre area. Usually it is divided into three sections:

(a) the Plain of Philistia, roughly from south of Gaza to Joppa (Tel Aviv);

(b) the Plain of Sharon, from Joppa north to the promontory of the Carmel chain; and

(c) the detached Plain of Acco, which merges with the Plain of Esdraelon, the historic gateway inland and to the regions to the north and east.

Forming the southwestern end of the Fertile Crescent, the coastal plain has been the highway of commerce and conquest for centuries. The coastal plain lacked an outstanding natural harbor. Joppa had roughly semicircular reefs that formed a breakwater 300 to 400 feet offshore and, consequently, was used as a port. Entrance from the south was impossible, however, and the north entrance was shallow and treacherous. Herod the Great developed Caesarea Maritima into an artificial port of considerable efficiency. See *Caesarea*.

(2) *Central hill country.* The mountainous ridge beginning just north of Beer-sheba and extending through all of Judea and Samaria into upper Galilee is a continuation of the more clearly defined Lebanon Mountains to the north. The only major break in the mountain range is the Plain of Esdraelon, also called the Valley of Jezreel. Three divisions are evident: Judea, Samaria, Galilee.

(a) *Judea.* Rising from the parched Negeb (Negeb means "parched" or "dry land"), the Judean hills reach their highest point, 3,370 feet, near Hebron. See *Negeb*. Jerusalem is located in the Judean hills at an elevation of 2,600 feet. The eastern slopes form the barren and rugged "wilderness of Judea," then fall abruptly to the floor of the Jordan Valley. The wilderness is treeless and waterless.

The western foothills of Judea are called the "Shephelah," meaning "valley" or "lowland," a belt of gently rolling hills between 500 and 1,000 feet in height. Five valleys divide the region, from the Wadi el Hesy in the south to the Valley of Ajalon in northern Judea. The Shephelah formed a military buffer between Judea and their enemies — Philistines, Egyptians, Syrians. Formerly heavily wooded with sycamores, the region served to impede an attack from the west.

(b) *Samaria.* The hills of Samaria descend gently from the Judean mountains, averaging just over 1,000 feet in height. Several notable mountains such as Gerizim (2,890 feet), Ebal (3,083 feet), and Gilboa (1,640 feet) dominate the area. In these wide and fertile valleys the majority of the people lived during the OT era. The openness of Samaria makes movement much easier than in Judea, inviting armies from the north.

From Shechem the main range of mountains sends out an arm to the northwest that reaches the coast at Mount Carmel. Carmel reaches a height of only 1,791 feet, but it seems more lofty because it rises directly from the coastline. It receives abundant rainfall, an average of 28 to 32 inches per year, and consequently is rather densely covered with vegetation. The Carmel range divides the Plain of Sharon from the narrow coastal plain of Phoenicia. It forms the southern side of the Plain of Esdraelon, with the ancient fortress of Megiddo standing as one of its key cities.

(c) *Galilee.* North of the Plain of Esdraelon and south of the Leontes River lies the region called Galilee (Isa. 9:1, "Galilee of the Gentiles," NIV). Asher, Naphtali, and Zebulun were assigned to this area known for mixed population and racial variety from early times. The region is divided into Upper Galilee and Lower Galilee. Most of Lower Galilee is approximately 500 feet above sea level, but mountains like Tabor reach a height of 1,929 feet. Grain, grass, olives, and grapes were abundant. Several major international roads crossed the area.

The terrain of Upper Galilee is much more rugged than Lower Galilee with deeply fissured and roughly eroded tableland marked by high peaks and many wadis. The highest peak is Mount Meron, at 3,963 feet, the highest point in Palestine. In the east, Galilee drops off abruptly to the Jordan, while farther south, near the Sea of Galilee, the slopes become much more gradual and gentle.

(3) *Jordan Rift Valley.* As a result of crustal faulting, the hills of Palestine drop into the deepest split on the surface of the earth. The fault is part of a system that extends north to form the valley between the Lebanon and the Anti-Lebanon chains, also extending south to form the Dead Sea, the dry Arabah Valley, the Gulf of Aqabah, and, eventually, the chain of lakes on the African continent.

The Jordan River has its source in several springs, primarily on the western and southern slopes of Mount Hermon. Several small streams come together near Dan, then flow into shallow, reedy Lake Hula (Huleh).

From its sources to Hula the Jordan drops somewhat less than 1,000 feet over a distance of 12 miles, entering Lake Hula at 230 feet above sea level. Over the 11 miles from Hula to the Sea of Galilee, the Jordan drops 926 feet. From Galilee to the Dead Sea there is an additional drop of 600 feet.

The Sea of Galilee (the Lake of Gennesaret, the Sea of Tiberias, Lake Chinnereth) is formed by a widening of the upper Rift Valley. It is 13 miles long and 7 miles wide. As the Jordan flows south out of the Sea of Galilee, it enters a gorge called the Ghor, or "depression." The meandering Jordan and its periodic overflows have created the Zor, or "jungle," a thick growth of entangled semitropical plants and trees. Although the distance from the lower end of the Sea of Galilee to the upper end of the Dead Sea is only 65 miles, the winding Jordan twists 200 miles to cover that distance.

Seven miles south of Jericho, the Jordan flows into the Dead Sea, one of the world's most unique bodies of water. The surface of the water is 1,296 feet below sea level, the lowest point on the surface of the earth. The Dead Sea is 47 miles long, 8 miles wide and has no outlet. An average of 6.5 million tons of water enter the sea each day. Centuries of evaporation have made 25 percent of the weight of the water mineral salts. Fish cannot live in Dead Sea water.

Thirty miles down the eastern side, the Lisan peninsula, or the "Tongue," juts into the sea. North of it the sea is deep, reaching a maximum depth of 1,319 feet—2,650 feet below sea level. South of the peninsula, the sea is very shallow, with a maximum depth of 13 feet.

(4) *Transjordan Plateau.* Transjordan is divided into sections by several rivers: the Yarmuk, the Jabbok, the Arnon, and the Zered.

(a) Across from Galilee and north of the Yarmuk River is Bashan (Hauron), an area of rich volcanic soil with rainfall in excess of 16 inches per year. The plateau averages 1,500 feet above sea level. To the east of

Bashan lies only desert that begins to slope toward the Euphrates.

(b) South of the Yarmuk, reaching to the Jabbok River, was Gilead. During the Persian rule the boundaries were rather rigid. Both before and after Persian domination, Gilead reached as far south as Rabbah (Philadelphia, modern Amman). Formerly heavily wooded, with many springs and with gently rounded hills, Gilead is one of the most picturesque regions of Palestine.

(c) South of Gilead lies Moab. Originally, its northern border was the Arnon River, but the Moabites pushed north, giving their name to the plains east of the spot where the Jordan enters the Dead Sea. Moab's southern border was the Zered River, Wadi al Hasa.

(d) Still farther south is Edom, with the highest mountains of the region. The area is arid and barren. Fifty miles south of the Dead Sea lies the ancient fortress of Petra.

Palestine lies in the semitropical belt between 30° 15′ and 33° 15′ north latitude. Temperatures are normally high in the summer and mild in the winter, but these generalizations are modified by both elevation and distance from the coast. Along the coastal plain, the daily temperature fluctuation is rather limited because of the Mediterranean breezes. In the mountains and in Rift Valley, daily fluctuation is much greater. Mediterranean influence gives the coastal plain an average annual temperature of 57° at Joppa. Jerusalem, only 35 miles away but 2,500 feet above sea level, has an annual average of 63°. Jericho, 17 miles further east, is 3,400 feet lower (900 feet below sea level), consequently having a tropical climate and very low humidity. Here bitterly cold desert nights offset rather warm desert days. Similarly, much of the area around the Sea of Galilee experiences temperate conditions, while the Dead Sea region is known for its strings of 100° plus summer days.

Palestine is a land of two seasons, a dry season and a rainy season, with intervening transitional periods. The dry season lasts from mid-May to mid-October. From June through August no rain falls except in the extreme north. Moderate, regular winds blow usually from the west or southwest. The breezes reach Jerusalem by noon, Jericho in early afternoon, and Transjordan plateau by midafternoon. The air carries much moisture, but atmospheric conditions are such that precipitation does not occur. Humidity produces extremely heavy dew five nights out of six in July.

With late October, the "early rain" begins to fall. November is punctuated with heavy thunderstorms. The months of December through February are marked by heavy showers. Rainy days alternate with fair days and beautiful sunshine. The cold is not severe, with occasional frost in the higher elevations from December to February. In Jerusalem, snow may fall twice during the course of the winter months.

All of Palestine experiences extremely disagreeable warm conditions occasionally. The sirocco wind (the "east wind" of Gen. 41:6; Ezek. 19:12) blowing from the southeast during the transition months (May–June, September–October) brings dust- laden clouds across the land. It dries vegetation and has a withering effect on people and animals. On occasion the temperature may rise 30°F and the humidity fall to less than 10 percent.

PARABLES

Stories, especially those of Jesus, told to provide a vision of life, especially life in God's kingdom. Parables utilize metaphors or similes and extend them into a brief story to make a point. A parable has only one main point established by a basic comparison or internal juxtaposition. For example, the parable of the mustard seed (Mark 4:30-32; Matt. 13:31-32; Luke 13:18-19) compares a microscopically small seed initially with a large bush eventually. This contrasts to an allegory that makes many comparisons through a kind of coded message. See *Allegory.* Some parables contain subordinated allegorical aspects, such as the parable of the wicked tenants (Mark 12:1-12; Matt. 21:36-46; Luke 20:9-19).

The OT employs the broader category of *mashal,* which refers to all expressions that contain a comparison: proverb (1 Sam. 10:12), taunt (Mic. 2:4), dark riddle (Ps. 78:2), allegory (Ezek. 24:3-4), or parable. The stories of Jesus are linked with the heritage of the prophetic parables in the OT (Isa. 28:23-29; 5:1-7; 1 Kings 20:39-43; Eccl. 9:13-16; 2 Sam. 12:1-4).

Many of the parables grew out of the conflict situations when Jesus answered His religious critics. These answering parables, usually for Pharisees and sinners, simultaneously exposed the self-righteousness of His critics and extolled the kingdom of God (Matt. 11:16-19; Luke 7:31-35; Luke 15:11-32). Jesus interpreted His ministry and its place in salvation history by means of parable. Parables sometimes have a "Christological penetration," that is, Jesus Himself appears indirectly in the story (Mark 3:23-27). The parables proclaim the gospel. The hearer is invited to make a decision about the kingdom and the King.

Jesus uttered:

(1) *Parabolic sayings,* referring to the salt of the earth (Matt. 5:13) or throwing pearls before swine (Matt. 7:6). These incipient parables were generally one-liners with a picturesque appeal to the imagination. The Gospel of John has no parables but 13 parabolic sayings.

(2) *Simple parables* are extended similes that represent a picture elaborated into a story. Examples are the paired parables of the treasure and the pearl (Matt. 13:44-46), the tower builder and the warring king (Luke 14:28-32), and the lost sheep and lost coin (Luke 15:3-10).

(3) *Narrative parables* are dramatic stories composed of one or more scenes, drawn from daily life yet focused on an unusual, decisive circumstance. Included are the parable of the unjust steward (16:1-8), the

compassionate Samaritan (10:30-37), and the rich fool (12:16-21).

To involve His hearers, Jesus constructed many parables that amount to one big question. The parable of the servant and his wages moves by means of two questions (Luke 17:7-10). The parable of the unjust steward (Luke 16:1-8) includes four questions. These interrogatives within parables often define a dilemma (Luke 12:20; Mark 12:9) or call for an agreeing nod in one area of life that carries over to another.

Refusal parables express the intention of a character not to do what is requested. The elder brother refused to enter the festivities in honor of the prodigal son (Luke 15:28), and wedding guests rejected the invitation to attend the festivities of a wedding (Matt. 22:3). Jesus' great thesis centers on the kingdom of God (Mark 1:15). Each parable explores and expands the theme: the nature of the kingdom (Mark 4:26-29), the grace of the kingdom (Luke 18:9-17), the crisis of the kingdom (Luke 12:54-56), and the conditions of the kingdom such as commitment (Luke 14:28-30), forgiveness (Matt. 18:23-35), and compassion (Luke 10:25-37). See *Kingdom of God; Jesus, Life and Ministry of.*

PARACLETE (*One called alongside*) See *Advocate; Comforter; Helper; Counselor; Holy Spirit.*

PARADISE (*enclosure or wooded park*)

Old Persian term used in OT to speak of King Artaxerxes' forest (Neh. 2:8), and twice of orchards (Eccl. 2:5; Song of Sol. 4:13). All three NT occurrences (Luke 23:43; 2 Cor. 12:4; Rev. 2:7) refer to the abode of the righteous dead (heaven). See *Hope; Heaven.*

PARAN

(1) Wilderness area south of Judah, west of Edom, and north of Sinai where Israel camped after leaving Sinai and sent spies to scout out the Promised Land from Kadesh, a location in Paran (Num. 10:11-12; 13:3,26). See Gen. 14:5-7; 21:21; 1 Kings 11:17-18.

(2) Poetic parallel to Mount Sinai (Deut. 33:2; compare Hab. 3:3) as the place of revelation.

PARBAR

Hebrew term; apparently a road, an open area, or a room near the temple (1 Chron. 26:18 KJV, NASB, RSV); sometimes translated: (western) "collonade" (NRSV, REB); "western pavilion" (TEV); "court to the west" (NIV). Suggested renderings of the plural of *parbar* (or a related term) in 2 Kings 23:11 include: "precincts" (NASB, NRSV), "court" (NIV), and "suburbs" (KJV).

PARDON See *Atonement; Forgiveness; Reconciliation.*

PARENTS, PARENTING See *Family.*

PARTHIANS

Tribal people who migrated from Central Asia southeast of the Caspian Sea into what is now Iran. They spoke Aryan dialect close to Persian; worshiped Persian god, Ahura Mazda. The Parthians adopted Greek culture following their fall to Alexander the Great. About 250 B.C. they revolted against the Seleucid rule and reached a height of power under King Mithradates (ruled 171–138 B.C.). In 53 B.C. the Romans invaded but were defeated on several occasions. They did not gain control of Parthia until A.D. 114. On the Day of Pentecost some Parthians heard the gospel in their own language (Acts 2:9-11).

PARVAIM

Source of gold for Solomon's decoration of the temple (2 Chron. 3:6); perhaps el Farwaim (Farwa) in Yemen, or else a general term for the east.

PASCHAL

Relating to the Passover; Paul used the sacrifice of the "paschal lamb" as a picture of the death of Christ (1 Cor. 5:7 NRSV; compare John 1:29; 19:14).

PASHUR (*son of* [the god] *Horus*)

(1) Chief officer in Jerusalem temple in last years before Nebuchadnezzar's victory over the city; had Jeremiah beaten and imprisoned (Jer. 20:1-2). He or another Pashur was father of Gedaliah (Jer. 38:1).

(2) Man in Zedekiah's court (Jer. 21:1) who asked Jeremiah for a word from the Lord as the Babylonian army approached.

(3) Forebear of a priestly family (1 Chron. 9:12) who returned from the exile (Ezra 2:38; 10:22; compare Neh. 10:3; 11:12).

PASSION

(1) Any bodily desire that leads to sin (Rom. 6:12; Gal. 5:24; Eph. 2:3) especially strong sexual desire (Rom. 1:26-27; 1 Cor. 7:9; 1 Thess. 4:5). Unregenerate life is characterized by slavery to passions (Eph. 2:3; Titus 3:3; 1 Pet. 1:14). Those who belong to Christ have crucified fleshly passions (Gal. 5:24; compare Rom. 6:5-14). In their frequent appeals to renounce passions, NT letters likely echo charges to baptismal candidates (Col. 3:5; 2 Tim. 2:22; Titus 2:12).

(2) "Like passions" (Acts 14:15; Jas. 5:17 KJV) means "shared human nature."

(3) Suffering Christ endured from the night of the last supper until His death (Acts 1:3, KJV, RSV).

PASSOVER See *Festivals.*

PASTOR

KJV for "shepherd" (Jer. 2:8; 3:15; 10:21; 12:10; 22:22; 23:1-2; Eph. 4:11), using the biblical image of the people of God as God's flock (Jer. 23:1-4; Ezek. 34:1-16; Luke 12:32; John 10:16). Pastoral ministry is closely associated with teaching (Eph. 4:11) as God's gift to the church. Such ministry trains church members to be mature in faith and equipped for ministry and unifies the church in Christian faith and knowledge (Eph. 4:12-13). In laying down His life for His sheep (John 10:11,15), Christ set the standard for pastoral ministry. Pastoral ministry is an expression of love for Christ (John 21:15-17).

PASTORALS

Designation for First and Second Timothy and Titus, highlights their concern for proper pastoral authority in the face of heresy. See *1 Timothy; 2 Timothy; Titus, Epistle to.*

PATHROS

Hebrew transliteration of Egyptian term for Upper (southern) Egypt (NIV), territory between modern Cairo and Aswan (Isa. 11:11; Jer. 44:1,15; Ezek. 29:14; 30:14).

PATHRUSI or **PATHRUSITES**

Son of Mizraim (Egypt) and ancestor of the inhabitants of Upper (southern) Egypt who bore his name (1 Chron. 1:12).

PATIENCE

Active endurance of opposition, not a passive resignation; steadfastness, long-suffering, and forbearance. God is patient (Rom. 15:5), slow to anger in relation to the Hebrews' sin (Ex. 34:6; Num. 14:18, Neh. 9:17; Ps. 86:15; Isa. 48:9; Hos. 11:8-9; compare Mark 2:1-11). Jesus' parable of the tenants depicted God's patience with His people (Mark 12:1-11). God's patience with sinners allows time for them to repent (Rom. 2:4; 2 Pet. 3:9-10).

God's people are to be patient (Rom. 5:3-5; 2 Cor. 6:6; compare Ps. 37). Patience is a fruit of the Spirit (Gal. 5:22). Christian love is patient (1 Cor. 13:4,7). Hebrews stressed endurance as the alternative to shrinking back during adversity (Heb. 6:9-15; 10:32-39; compare 12:1-3). Perseverance is part of maturity (Jas. 1:2-4; 5:11; Rev. 2:2,19; 3:10; 13:10; 14:12).

PATMOS

Small island (10 miles by 6 miles) in Aegean Sea about 37 miles southwest of Miletus. John was a prisoner, having been sent there for preaching the gospel (Rev. 1:9). See *Revelation, Book of.*

PATRIARCHS, TESTAMENT OF THE TWELVE See *Pseudepigrapha.*

PATRIARCHS, THE

Israel's founding fathers: Abraham, Isaac, Jacob, and the 12 sons of Jacob (Israel). The growth of the Hebrew nation was promised specifically to Abraham in the patriarchal covenant (Gen. 15; 17). See *Covenant; Abraham; Isaac; Jacob; Joseph.*

PAUL

Official Roman name of outstanding missionary apostle; author of NT epistles. Paul's Jewish name was Saul. Tarsus on Turkey's southern shore was Paul's birth place (Acts 22:3). Paul was well trained in the Jewish Scriptures and tradition (Acts 26:4-8; Phil. 3:5-6). He also learned the trade of tentmaking (Acts 18:3).

Paul in his early teen years went to Jerusalem to study under the famous rabbi Gamaliel, best Jewish teacher of that day (Acts 22:3). See *Gamaliel.* Paul became a Pharisee (Phil. 3:5) and was very zealous for the traditions of his people (Gal. 1:14).

Stephen's sermon apparently stimulated Paul's persecution of the church (Acts 8:1-3, 9:1-2; 26:9-11; Phil. 3:6; Gal. 1:13). Three accounts tell of Paul's Damascus road experience (A.D. 35): Acts 9:3-19; 22:6-21; 26:13-23. Paul was traveling to Damascus to arrest Jewish people who had accepted Jesus as the Messiah. A startling light forced him to the ground. The voice asked, "Why persecutest thou me," and identified the speaker as Jesus (compare 1 Cor. 15:8-10; 9:1)—the very one whom Stephen had seen at the right hand of God when Paul witnessed Stephen's stoning. Paul was struck blind and was led into the city. Ananias met Paul and told him that he had been chosen by God as a messenger for the Gentiles (Acts 9:17). After Paul received his sight, he was baptized. The experience was Paul's call to carry the gospel to the Gentile world (Acts 9:15; 22:21; Gal. 1:1; Eph. 3:2-12). The gospel Paul preached had come by revelation (Gal. 1:12). His conversion was like dying and receiving a new life (Gal. 2:20) or being created anew (2 Cor. 5:17-20). See *Conversion.*

The first missionary journey (A.D. 46-48) began at Antioch (Acts 13-14). The church at Antioch chose Paul and Barnabas to be their representatives. John Mark went along as an important assistant. Their itinerary took them from Antioch to Seleucia to Cyprus to Perga on Turkey's southern shore. They came to the province of Galatia, where they concentrated their efforts in the southern cities of Antioch, Iconium, Lystra, and Derbe. Their typical procedure was to enter a new town, seek out the synagogue, and share the gospel on the sabbath day. Usually Paul's message caused a division in the synagogue, and Paul and Barnabas would seek a Gentile audience. In each city, many turned to the new way (Acts 13:44,52; 14:1-4,20-28), and a minimal organization was established in each locality (Acts 14:23). He later addressed an epistle to this district—Galatians. See *Asia Minor, Cities of.*

Paul's second journey (A.D. 49-52) departed from Antioch with Silas as his associate (Acts 15:36-18:18). They traveled through what is now modern Turkey to the Aegean part of Troas. A vision directed Paul to go to Philippi in the province of Macedonia. Paul established a church there as further attested by his letter to the Philippians. From there he traveled to Thessalonica and Berea. His preaching in Athens met with meager results. His work in Corinth (the province of Achaia) was well received and even approved, in an oblique fashion, by the Roman governor, Gallio. From Corinth, Paul returned to Caesarea, visited Jerusalem, and then Antioch (Acts 18:22).

Paul's third missionary venture (A.D. 52-57) centered in Ephesus from which the gospel probably spread into the surrounding cities such as the seven churches in Revelation (Acts 18:23-20:6; Rev. 2-3). From Ephesus he carried on a correspondence with the Corinthian church. While in Corinth at the end of this journey, he wrote the Epistle to the Romans. See *Romans, Book of; 1 Corinthians; 2 Corinthians.*

When Paul returned to Jerusalem for his last visit (21:17–26:32), he was arrested and imprisoned in Jerusalem and then transferred to Caesarea (A.D. 57–59). At first the charges against him were that he had brought a Gentile into the restricted areas of the temple. Later, he was accused of being a pestilent fellow. The real reasons for his arrest are noted: the crowd was enraged at his mentioning his call to the Gentiles (Acts 22:21-22), and he stated to the Sanhedrin that he was arrested because of his belief in the resurrection. See *Resurrection; Sanhedrin.*

Paul was eventually transferred to Rome (A.D. 60–61) as a prisoner of the emperor. The tradition outside the NT that tells of Paul's execution in Rome is reasonable. The tradition that he traveled to Spain is problematic.

Paul's writings are the major source of Christian theology. He taught:

(1) Human beings are alienated from God. They rejected God and established themselves as the ultimate authority. See Rom. 1:18-3:8; *Sin; Humanity.*

(2) Paul's answer to humankind's alienation is the Son God sent (Gal. 4:4; Col. 1:15-20). Christ is the model for all humankind, the image of God (Col. 1:15). The universe's design and purpose center in Christ. He is the appropriate one to reconcile us to God (Col. 1:20; 2 Cor. 5:19). See *Conversion; Reconciliation.*

(3) Christ's death, burial, and resurrection is the focal point of all Paul preached and wrote (1 Cor. 2:2; 1 Cor. 15:14). Paul could think of Christ's death as a Passover sacrifice (1 Cor. 5:7), as a representative sacrifice (2 Cor. 5:14), or as a ransom (1 Tim. 2:5-6). Jesus' resurrection guarantees the hope that the complete resurrection and the new world are sure to come (1 Cor. 15:20-24). See *Jesus, Life and Ministry of; Christ, Christology; Hope.*

(4) Paul used Abraham as the example of persons of faith (Rom. 4:3,21). Faith is simply accepting as certain the promise of salvation God has made through Christ. This response in faith has transforming power and is like creating a new person (Gal. 2:20; 2 Cor. 5:17-19) with a new motivating, energizing force, the Holy Spirit (Rom. 8:9-11). The person of faith is truly "in Christ." See *Faith.*

(5) The believer comes into reconciliation in a community of faith. This believing community is intimately associated with Christ, who holds a position of dignity and authority over the church: He is its Head (Eph. 1:22-23). Christ loves the church and gave Himself for it; the church is subject to Christ in all matters (Eph. 5:21-33). The church nurtures the person of faith so that he or she may mature to be like Christ (Eph. 4:13). The church also witnesses to God's power to reconcile humankind to Himself by its example of Christian fellowship within its walls and by evangelistic outreach beyond itself (Eph. 3:10). See *Church.*

(6) The reconciled person has a new lifestyle without vices (Gal. 5:19-21; Col. 3:5-11; Eph. 4:17-19; 1 Cor. 5; 6:9-10; 2 Cor. 12:20-21) and with worthy qualities (Gal. 5:22-23; Col. 3:12-14; Phil. 4:8). Paul gave advice to Christian households (Col. 3:18-4:1; Eph. 5:21–6:9). He offered guidance in marriage matters (1 Cor. 7). The ultimate standard of Christian conduct is Christ Himself (Phil. 2:1-11). So Christ gives Himself as God's reconciling agent to bring human beings into a right relation with God, living a life motivated by the Spirit. See *Ethics.*

PAVILION

Large, often richly decorated tent; tents used in military campaigns (1 Kings 20:12,16; Jer. 43:10); thick canopy of clouds surrounding God (2 Sam. 22:12; Ps. 18:11), which illustrates the mystery of God; and an image of God's protection (Pss. 27:5; 31:20). NASB used "pavilion" in the literal sense of tent (Dan. 11:45). Elsewhere modern translations use "pavilion" in poetic passages: a "pavilion" for the sun (Ps. 19:5 NIV); God's "pavilion" of clouds (Job 36:29 NASB,

REB, NIV, NRSV); a "pavilion" protecting Jerusalem from heat and rain (Isa. 4:5, RSV).

PEACE OFFERING   See *Sacrifice and Offering.*

PEACE, SPIRITUAL

Sense of well-being and fulfillment that comes from God and depends on His presence; Hebrew *shalom:* "wholeness" or "well-being" (Gen. 28:20-22; Judg. 6:23; 18:6; 1 Kings 2:33). Such peace is the gift of God, for God alone can give peace in all its fullness (Lev. 26:6; 1 Chron. 12:18; 22:9; 1 Kings 2:33; Isa. 26:12; 52:7; Ezek. 34:25; 37:26; Zech. 6:13; Mal. 2:5-6; Job 22:21; 25:2; Pss. 4:8; 29:11; 37:37; 85:8; 122:6-8; 147:14; Prov. 3:17). Spiritual peace may be equated with salvation (Isa. 52:7; Nah. 1:15). Its absence may be equated with judgment (Jer. 12:12; 14:19; 16:5; 25:37; Lam. 3:17; Ezek. 7:15). It is available to all who trust in God (Isa. 26:3) and love His law (Ps. 119:165—note that in vv. 166-168 this love is clearly understood to mean obedience!).This peace is clearly identified with a righteous life apart from which no one is able to find true peace (Isa. 32:17; 48:22; 57:1-2; compare Pss. 72:7; 85:10; Isa. 9:7; 48:18; 60:17).

God is "the God of peace" (Rom. 15:33; Phil. 4:9; 1 Thess. 5:23; Heb. 13:20).The gospel is "the good news of peace" (Eph. 6:15; Acts 10:36) because it announces the reconciliation of believers to God and to one another (Eph. 2:12-18). God has made this peace a reality in Jesus Christ, who is "our peace" (John 14:27; Phil. 4:7; Col. 3:15; Rom. 15:13). Peace is associated with receptiveness to God's salvation (Matt. 10:13), freedom from distress and fear (John 14:27; 16:33), security (1 Thess. 5:9-10), mercy (Gal. 6:16; 1 Tim. 1:2), joy (Rom. 14:17; 15:13), grace (Phil. 1:2; Rev. 1:4), love (2 Cor. 13:11; Jude 2), life (Rom. 8:6), and righteousness (Rom. 14:17; Heb. 12:11; Jas. 3:18). Such peace is a fruit of the Spirit (Gal.

5:22) that forms part of the "whole armor of God" (Eph. 6:11,13), enabling the Christian to withstand the attacks of the forces of evil.

PEACEMAKERS

Those who actively work to bring about peace and reconciliation where there are hatred and enmity. God blesses peacemakers and declares them to be His children (Matt. 5:9).Those who work for peace share in Christ's ministry of bringing peace and reconciliation (2 Cor. 5:18-19; Eph. 2:14-15; Col. 1:20).

PEER PRESSURE

Feeling need to follow course of action because friends and colleagues advise it or follow it; usually works negatively rather than positively (Prov. 18:24; Rom. 12:2; 1 Cor. 15:33; Heb. 3:13; 12:1). Instead of listening to the elder advisors of his father, Rehoboam submitted to pressure from his peers, "the young men who had grown up with him" (1 Kings 12:8; compare 2 Chron. 13:7). In contrast, Solomon asked God for wisdom and knowledge so that he might reign well (2 Chron. 1:10).

PEG

Small, cylindrical or tapered piece of wood (or some other material) used to secure tents (Judg. 4:21-22; 5:26), hang articles (Isa. 22:23, 25; Ezek. 15:3), weave cloth (Judg. 16:14), dig latrines (Deut. 23:13). Isaiah 22:23-25 used the image of a peg, which gives way to picture false security in a leader. Zechariah 10:4 used the peg as one of several images for rulers. In Isaiah 33:22 secure tent pegs symbolize that God keeps Jerusalem secure. The enlarged tent and strengthened tent pegs of Isaiah 54:2 illustrate God's restoration of Jerusalem.

PEKAH   *(open-eyed)*

Officer in Israel's army who became king (752–732 B.C.), in a bloody coup by murdering King Pekahiah (2 Kings 15:25).

PEKAHIAH (*Yah has opened his eyes*)

King of Israel (742–740 B.C.); succeeded his father, Menahem, as vassal of Assyria (2 Kings 15:23); assassinated by army officer, Pekah (15:25). See *Pekah*.

PEKOD (*punishment or judgment*)

Hebrew word that plays on Puqadu, Aramean tribe inhabiting the area east of mouth of Tigris (Jer. 50:21; Ezek. 23:23). Sargon II (722–705 B.C.) incorporated Pekod into the Assyrian Empire.

PELETHITES (*courier*)

Foreign mercenaries King David employed as body guards and special forces (2 Sam. 8:18); probably sea peoples who formed a loyalty to David during his days in the Philistine country while evading Saul. See *Cherethites, Cherethim.*

PENTATEUCH

First five books of OT, known to the Jews as "Torah," meaning "instruction." The Pentateuch is one continuous narrative but had to be divided into five scrolls at least by 200 B.C.

The pivotal event of the Pentateuch is God's revelation of Himself at Sinai. Everything before is prologue, and all that comes after is epilogue. The narrative invites the reader to anticipate the exodus to Sinai by Yahweh's self-identification in Gen. 15:7: "I am Yahweh who brought you up from Ur of the Chaldees," which echoes a phrase appearing dozens of times later,"I am Yahweh, who brought you up out of Egypt" (cp. Lev. 11:45); by citing God's prediction of Israel's enslavement, deliverance, and emergence with wealth (15:13-14), wealth needed to build the tabernacle; by citing Yahweh's promise to give Abraham's descendants the land of Canaan (Gen. 15:18-21), which becomes the expressed reason for the exodus (Exod. 3:7-8; 6:6-8); and by citing God's (El Shaddai's) announcement that He would be God to Abraham and his descendants

after him (Gen. 17:7), with whom He would establish His covenant.

Although the Pentateuch is commonly called "Law," it is dominated by "gospel," good news of God's grace demonstrated through election, salvation, and the providential care of His people. If the Pentateuch were primarily "law," it would scarcely be the psalmist's delight or a source of light and life (Ps. 1:2-3).The gospel element is apparent in Exod. 34:6-7, where Yahweh defines His glory in immanent and gracious terms.

"Law" is present, if by "law" we mean commandments prescribing human behavior. The Pentateuch contains hundreds of such prescriptions. Although prescriptive material is found elsewhere, for the sake of convenience we refer specifically to six prescriptive sections: the Decalogue (Exod. 20:1-17; Deut. 5:6-21); the "Book of the Covenant" (Exod. 21:1–23:33); the Tabernacle Prescriptions (Exod. 25–31); the "Manual on Ritual Worship" (Lev. 1–7); the so-called "Holiness Code" (Lev. 17–25); and the so-called "Deuteronomic Code" (Deut. 12–26). Leviticus and Numbers contain much additional prescriptive material, but the above are commonly recognized as self-contained units.

The problem of the date and authorship of the Pentateuch is one of the major critical problems of OT. Although Jewish and Christian tradition almost unanimously recognize Moses as author of the Pentateuch, from the middle of the 19th century A.D., especially following Julius Wellhausen, most critical scholars have rejected Moses having a significant role in the origin of the Pentateuch.

On the other hand, the internal evidence suggests that Moses kept a record of Israel's experiences in the desert (Exod. 17:14; 24:4,7; 34:27; Num. 33:1-2; Deut. 31:9,11). Furthermore, many statements in the OT credit the Pentateuch to Moses (e.g., Josh. 1:8; 8:31-32; 1 Kings 2:3; 2 Kings 14:6; Ezra 6:18; Neh. 13:1; Dan. 9:11-13; Mal. 4:4), and the NT identifies the Torah very closely with him (Matt. 19:8; John 5:46-47; 7:19; Acts 3:22; Rom. 10:5).

PENTATEUCH, SAMARITAN See *Pentateuch; Bible, Texts and Versions.*

PENTECOST See *Festivals; Holy Spirit.*

PENUEL (*face of God*)

(1) Descendant of Judah and founder (father) of Gedor (1 Chron. 4:4).

(2) Benjaminite (1 Chron. 8:25).

(3) Site on River Jabbok northeast of Succoth where Jacob wrestled with the stranger (Gen. 32:24-32; compare Hos. 12:4). Gideon destroyed the city because its inhabitants refused him provisions while he pursued the Midianites (Judg. 8:8-9,17). Jeroboam I built (perhaps rebuilt or fortified) the city (1 Kings 12:25). The site is identified with the easternmost of two mounds called Tulul edh-Dhahab, which commands the entrance to the Jordan Valley from the Jabbok gorge, about seven miles east of the Jordan.

PEOPLE OF GOD

Group elected by God and committed to be His covenant people; Israel as people God elected by grace in call of Abraham (Gen. 12; Gal. 3:29; Rom 9:7-8) and covenant at Sinai (Ex. 19).

God's covenant promise (Ex. 19:5b-6) involves a God-people and people-God relationship, which is the center of the OT. This promise was inherited by the church as the true Israel or the new Israel (Rom. 9:6-8; 1 Cor. 10:18-21; Gal. 6:16; compare Rom. 9:25-26; 1 Cor. 6:14-17; Titus 2:14; Heb. 8:10; 1 Pet. 2:9-10; Rev. 21:3). See *Church; Covenant; Election; Israel, Spiritual.*

As God disciplined His sinful people, a remnant developed as people of God. To the remnant fell the status and condition of God's long purpose for His people (see Matt. 22:14). The idea of God's people in the OT culminates in the person of the Servant (Isa. 52:12–53:13), who is the idea of the remnant personified as an indi-

vidual. Most of all, Jesus Himself is the remnant, the Suffering Servant, who gave His life as a ransom for many and thereby inaugurated the New Covenant. The call into peoplehood is a call into servanthood.

PEOR (perhaps *opening*)

(1) Mountain in Moab opposite the wilderness of Judah. Balak brought Balaam there to curse the camp of the Israelites, visible from the site (Num. 23:28; 24:2).

(2) Abbreviated form of Baal-Peor (lord of Peor), a god whom the Israelites were led to worship (Num. 25:18; 31:16; Josh. 22:17). See *Baal-Peor.*

(3) Site in Judah identified with modern Khirbet Faghur southwest of Bethlehem (Josh. 15:59 REB, following earliest Greek translation).

PERDITION

Eternal state of death, destruction, annihilation, or ruin; fate of all who do not come to repentance; contrast to the blessing of God; penalty for disobedience (Deut. 22:24; 28:20); sometimes linked to Sheol (2 Sam. 22:5; Ps. 18:4).

"Son of perdition" describes the person who has fallen victim to this destruction (John 17:12). The "man of sin" is doomed to perdition (2 Thess. 2:3). A form of this word is used in Rev. 9:11 to describe the ultimate enemy of God—the Destroyer. See *Death; Devil; Eternal Life; Everlasting Punishment; Hell; Sheol.*

PEREA

Roman district in Transjordan that became a part of Herod the Great's kingdom; "Judea beyond the Jordan" (Matt. 19:1; Mark 10:1 RSV). Capital was Gadara, where KJV says Jesus healed the demoniac (Matt. 8:28; modern translations follow other manuscripts reading "Gerasenes"). Other important sites in the province were the fortress of Machaerus, where John the Baptist was beheaded, and Pella, where Christians from Jerusalem fled just before the Roman destruction of the Holy City in A.D.

66. Perea was the area through which the Jews traveled to avoid going through Samaria. See *Gadara; Machaerus; Transjordan.*

PERFECT, PERFECTION

Reaching an ideal state of spiritual wholeness or completeness; not a quality achieved by human effort alone, nor an end in itself. Christian perfection consists essentially in exercising the divine gift of love (Col. 3:14) for God and for other people (Matt. 22:37-39). The basis of perfection lies in God Himself, whose law (Jas. 1:25), works (Deut. 32:4), and way (Ps. 18:30) are perfect. God is free from incompleteness; He can, therefore, demand from believers, and enable them to receive, completeness (Matt. 5:48).

"Perfect" is ascribed to Noah (Gen. 6:9) and Job (1:1), in response to their wholehearted obedience. In other contexts, corporate perfection and being "upright" belong together (Ps. 37:37; Prov. 2:21). In the NT, through Christ believers can be perfected forever (Heb. 10:14). Christians are to grow from spiritual infancy to maturity so as to share the full stature of Christ, in whose image they may become renewed and perfected (Col. 3:10).

Because on earth sin remains a possibility for all, believers (1 John 1:8) need to become perfect even while attaining a relative perfection (Mic. 6:6-8; Phil. 3:16,12-14). The divine gift of perfection will be fully realized only in eternity (Phil. 3:10-14; 1 John 3:2; compare 2 Cor. 7:1; Eph. 4:13; Heb. 6:1; Jas. 3:2).

Christ is the means of perfection. Through His suffering and exaltation, God made Jesus perfect (Heb. 2:10) and fitted Him to win for the church and the individual believer a completeness that echoes His own (Col. 1:28; Heb. 5:9). See *Holy.*

PERFUME, PERFUMER

Modern translation for "apothecary" (Ex. 30:25,35; 37:29; 2 Chron. 16:14; Neh. 3:8; Eccl. 10:1 KJV). Perfumes mentioned in the Bible include: aloes, balsam (or balm), bdellium, calamus (or sweet or fragrant cane), camel's thorn, cinnamon (or cassia), frankincense, galbanum, gum, henna, myrrh, nard (or spikenard), onycha, saffron, and stacte. See *Confection; Cosmetics; Oil; Ointment; Plants.*

PERGA

Prehistoric city in province of Pamphylia, about eight miles from Mediterranean Sea. A temple to Artemis was one of the prominent buildings. John Mark left Paul and Barnabas there (Acts 13:13).

PERGAMOS or PERGAMUM

(citadel) See *Asia Minor.*

PERIZZITES *(rustic)*

People who opposed Israelite occupation of Canaan (Josh. 9:1-2; compare Gen. 13:7); probably dwelled in open country.

PERJURY

False statement given voluntarily under oath; false witness to past facts or neglect of what has been previously vowed. Mosaic law prohibited false swearing (Lev. 19:12; Ex. 20:7) and giving false witness (Ex. 20:16). False witness was punishable with the sentence that would have gone to the one falsely accused of guilt (Deut. 19:16-21). See *Oaths.*

PERSECUTION

Harassment and suffering that people and institutions inflict on others for being different in their faith, world view, culture, or race. Persecution seeks to intimidate, silence, punish, or even to kill people.

Israel was the agent of persecution of nations (Judg. 2:11-23; Lev. 26:7-8). The Bible gives special attention to Israel's fate in Egypt (Ex. 1–3) and in the exile (Ps. 137). On an individual level, Saul persecuted David (1 Sam. 19:9-12), and Shadrach, Meshach, and Abednego were persecuted because they refused to worship the image of the king (Dan. 3). Jezebel persecuted the prophets of the Lord, and the prophet Elijah persecuted and killed the prophets of Baal (1 Kings 18). Job felt persecuted by God Himself (7:11-21). The prophets—Amos (7:10-12), Jeremiah (Jer. 1:19; 15:15; 37–38), and Urijah (Jer. 26:20-23)—suffered persecution because they fleshed out the will of God in adverse circumstances. The Psalms speak of the righteous sufferer who felt persecuted as a result of faith in God, and who prayed to God for deliverance (7; 35; 37; 79; 119:84-87). Jesus was persecuted and finally killed by the religious and political establishments of His day (Mark 3:6; Luke 4:29; John 5:16; Acts 3:13-15; 7:52; passion stories).

Jesus pronounced God's salvation on those who are persecuted for righteousness' sake (Matt. 5:10-12). In an evil world, disciples are to expect persecution (Matt. 10:16-23; Mark 4:17; 13:9; John 15:20; 16:2), just as was the case with the prophets in the OT (Matt. 5:12; 23:31; Luke 11:47-51; Acts 7:52; Heb. 11:32-38). Paul (1 Cor. 4:11-13; 2 Cor. 4:8-12; 6:4-10; 11:24-27; Gal. 5:11; 1 Thess. 2:2; 3:4; Acts 17:5-10; 18:12-17; 21:30-36; 23:12-35), as well as Stephen (Acts 6:8–7:60), James (Acts 12:2), and Peter (Acts 12:3-5), together with many anonymous martyrs experienced the truth of the Johannine saying:"If they have persecuted me, they will also persecute you" (John 15:20; see Acts 4:3; 5:17-42; 8:1; 12:1; Rev. 2:3,9-10,13,19; 3:8-10; 6:9; 16:6; 17:6; 18:24; 20:4).

First Peter, Hebrews, and Revelation were written to encourage Christians in a situation of persecution (1 Pet. 3:13-18; 4:12-19; 5:6-14; Heb. 10:32-39; 12:3; Rev. 2–3). Something like a theology of persecution emerged, which emphasized patience, endurance, and steadfastness (Rom. 12:12; 1 Thess. 2:14-16; Jas. 5:7-11); prayer (Matt. 5:44; Rom. 12:14; 1 Cor. 4:12); thanksgiving (2 Thess. 1:4); testing (Mark 4:17) and the strengthening of faith (1 Thess. 3:2-3); experiencing the grace of God (Rom. 8:35; 2 Cor. 4:9, 12:10), and being blessed through suffering (Matt. 5:10-12; 1 Pet. 3:14; 4:12-14). For Paul, persecuting Christians could be a living and visible tes-timony to the crucified and risen Christ (2 Cor. 4:7-12).

PERSEVERANCE

Maintaining Christian faith through the trying times of life. The believer was expected faithfully to endure and to remain steadfast in the face of opposition, attack, and discouragement. Believers are to be consistent in prayer (Eph. 6:18; Phil. 4:6) and trained in the ways of God (1 Cor. 9:24-27; Rom. 12:11-12; Heb. 12:1-12). Christians will finish the race because they focus their attention on Jesus, the lead runner and model finisher of their faith (Heb. 2:10; 12:1-2).

Perseverance of the saints is the human side of the salvation equation, and it deals with faithfulness of Christians in matters of God's will (Jas. 1:25). It permits judgment concerning the way people live in this world, but it does not exclude God's abundant graciousness.

Perseverance is a call to faithfulness and also an affirmation that somehow, in spite of our failures, God will bring His committed people through the difficulties and concerns of life to their promised destiny in Christ.

PERSIA

Nation corresponding to modern Iran; empire of states and kingdoms reaching from the shores of Asia Minor in the west to the Indus River valley in the east, northward to southern Russia, and south to Egypt and the regions bordering the Persian Gulf and the Gulf of Oman.

The Persian Empire was the best organized the world had ever seen. By the time of Darius I (522–486 B.C.), the empire was divided into 20 satrapies (political units of varying size and population). Satrapies were subdivided into provinces. Initially, Judah was a province in the satrapy of Babylon. Later, Judah was in one named "Beyond the River." The satrapies were governed by Persians who were directly responsible to the emperor. Instead of imposing an imperial law from above, the emperor and his satraps gave their authority and support to local law. For the Jews, this meant official support for keeping Jewish law in the land of the Jews.

When Cyrus conquered Babylon, he allowed the Jews to return to Judah and encouraged the rebuilding of the temple (Ezra 1:1-4). See *Israel, History of.* Ezra and Nehemiah were official representatives of the Persian government. Ezra was to teach and to appoint judges (Ezra 7). Nehemiah may have been the first governor of the province of Yehud (Judah).

Esther is a story of God's rescue of His people during the rule of the Persian emperor, Ahasuerus (also known as Xerxes I). See *Cyrus; Darius; Daniel; Esther; Ezra; Nehemiah; Temple.*

PESHITTA See *Bible, Texts and Versions.*

PETER (*rock*)

Leader of Jesus' 12 apostles; preacher at Pentecost; took gospel to God-fearing Gentiles; son of Jona or John (Matt. 16:17; John 1:42); author of 1 and 2 Peter; Hebrew name Simeon (Acts 15:14); Greek equivalent, Simon; Cephas (1 Cor. 1:12; 3:22; 9:5; 15:5; Gal. 1:18; 2:9,11,14; John 1:42) and Peter both mean "rock."

He and his brother, Andrew, came from Bethsaida (John 1:44) and were Galilean fishermen (Mark 1:16; Luke 5:2-3; John 21:3), in partnership with the sons of Zebedee, James and John (Luke 5:10). Peter was married (Mark 1:29-31; 1 Cor. 9:5) and maintained a residence in Capernaum (Mark 1:21,29). Peter and Andrew had been influenced by the teaching of John the Baptist (John 1:35-42).

Peter's name always occurs first in the lists of disciples (Mark 3:16; Luke 6:14; Matt. 10:2). He frequently served as their spokesman (compare Mark 8:29) and was usually the one who raised the questions that they all seemed to be asking (Mark 10:28; 11:21; Matt. 15:15; 18:21; Luke 12:41). Jesus often singled out Peter for teachings intended for the entire group of disciples (see especially Mark 8:29-33). As a member of the inner circle, Peter was present with Jesus at the raising of the synagogue ruler's daughter (Mark 5:35-41), at the Transfiguration (Mark 9:2-8), and at the arrest of Jesus in Gethsemene (Mark 14:43-50). As representative disciple, Peter frequently typified the disciple of little faith. His inconsistent behavior (see Matt. 14:27-31) reached a climax with his denial (Mark 14:66-72). Peter was, however, rehabilitated (John 21:15-19; compare Mark 16:7).

He played an influential role in establishing the Jerusalem church (see the early chapters of Acts), and was active in the incipient stages of the Gentile mission (see Acts 10–11) Tradition holds that Peter died as a martyr in Rome in the 60s (1 Clem. 5:1–6:1). See *1 Peter; 2 Peter; Disciples, Apostles.*

PETER, FIRST LETTER FROM

Twenty-first book of NT; written from Rome (called "Babylon" in 5:13) by apostle Peter during Nero's great persecution of believers around A.D. 62–64, though some critics have emphatically rejected Petrine authorship. The address is to churches of the provinces (Pontus, Galatia, Cappadocia, Asia, and Bythynia) in northern Asia Minor (modern Turkey).

The readers were converted Jews and Gentiles, the majority probably Gentiles. The Greek is much more literary in both vocabulary and syntax than one would expect from an ignorant fisherman (Acts 4:13). The place of the amanuensis in early literary work was greater than a modern secretary, and Silvanus (1 Pet. 5:12) could have been responsible for some of the stylistic sophistication.

The persecuted believers in Asia were encouraged to hope in God's ultimate deliverance and hence remain steadfast in their persecutions. The vicarious atonement is stated more clearly in 1 Pet. 3:18 (see also 1:18-19; 2:24) than anywhere else in Scripture. One of the most difficult passages in the Scriptures, 1 Pet. 3:18-22 has the following problems:

(1) the meaning of "preached unto the spirits in prison,"3:19;

(2) the mention of Noah, 3:20; and

(3) "baptism doth also now save us."

Two common positions are held regarding Christ preaching to spirits in prison:

(1) it is a descent of Christ into Hades to announce that He had died for sinners and victory over Satan is assured;

(2) the spirit of Christ was in Noah as he preached to no avail to that hard-hearted generation. Peter was not teaching a second chance for salvation after death. The statement about baptism does not infer that the act of dipping in water accomplishes what Scripture affirms elsewhere is done by grace through faith (Eph. 2:8-9). It is "not the putting away of the filth of the flesh, but the answer of a good conscience toward God" (1 Pet. 3:21).

The appeals to holiness and personal Christian living are everywhere apparent (1:14–2:12; 2:24-25; 3:8-13), but the biblical theology of suffering pervades the book (1:6-9; 2:18-25; 3:9-17; 4:1-6,12-19). His advice to family members is typically Jewish, reflecting his background (2:18 20; 3:1-7). The doctrine of eschatology is often mentioned (1:4,7,11,13; 2:12; 4:7,13). It is the basis for the appeal to holy living and patiently suffering unjustly, knowing that God will finally establish His kingdom with justice. See *Peter; Peter, Second Letter from.*

PETER, SECOND LETTER FROM

Twenty-second book of the NT; claims to be written by the apostle Peter probably shortly after 1 Peter about A.D. 64; Peter's authorship, questioned in ancient times, is still under a cloud of uncertainty in some quarters because of great differences in style and vocabulary from 1 Peter. This may be explained by a change in amanuenses, or by suggesting that Peter used Silas in 1 Peter while 2 Peter reflects his own unedited style. Second Peter is more like 1 Peter than any other NT book. If 2 Pet. 3:1 refers to 1 Peter, then the destination must be the same as the previous letter. See *1 Peter.*The references to Jewishness are not as clear as 1 Peter, but still are inferred in 2 Pet. 1:12; 2:1; 2:4-9; 3:5-8.

A major question is the literary affinity of 2 Pet. 2 with Jude 4-18. There is no way of proving which document relied on the other. Many have assumed Jude is late and that the writer of 2 Peter depended on it, hence 2 Peter is a late document and cannot be apostolic.This is incapable of proof, and, furthermore, may merely show the early date of Jude!

The purpose of the letter was to forestall and defeat the influence of heretics who came in the church to lead the readers into antinomianism or total freedom from the law. This temptation to a sinful lifestyle so affected Peter that shortly after his first letter, he followed with this one.

Practical Christian living is emphasized by the motifs of growth by addition in 1:3-8; judgment in 3:11-14; and exhortation to growth in 3:17-18. It is the Word of God that holds the forefront of this short letter: in chapter 1 by emphasizing knowledge (vv. 3,5-6,8,12,20-21) and its divine origin, in chapter 2 by showing its historicity (vv. 4-8), and in chapter 3 by indicating Paul's letters are equal with "the other Scriptures" (vv. 15-16). Peter strongly supported the influence of Scripture as the most important factor in our faith. One who could rely so much on personal experience did not and only appeals to it to further express the truth of Scripture (1:16-21).

PETHOR (*soothsayer*)

City in upper Mesopotamia; tell Ahmar, 12 miles south of Carchemish near confluence of Sajur and Euphrates rivers; home of Balaam (Num. 22:5; Deut. 23:4).

PETITION See *Prayer.*

PETRA (rock)

Capital city of the Nabatean Arabs located about 60 miles north of the Gulf of Aqabah; sometimes identified with Sela (Judg. 1:36; 2 Kings 14:7; Isa. 16:1; 42:11), because both names mean "rock." Lack of archaeological evidence of Edomite settlement in the basin suggests that Sela is better identified with Um el Bayyarah on the mountain plateau overlooking Petra. The Nabatean king Aretas IV (2 Cor. 11:32-33) reigned from Petra.

PHARAOH (great house)

Title for ancient kings of Egypt. Every ancient pharaoh had five "great names" assumed on the day of accession. Since it was not deemed proper to use such powerful names in direct fashion, a polite circumlocution developed; he came to be called Pharaoh. Egyptians applied "pharaoh" to the royal palace and grounds in the fourth dynasty (about 2500 B.C.) and to the king from about 1500 B.C. until the Persian domination, about 550 B.C.

Egypt's pharaoh was an absolute monarch, supreme commander of the armies, chief justice of the royal court, and high priest of all religion. Justice was defined as "what Pharaoh loves"; wrongdoing as "what Pharaoh hates." He daily conducted "the Rite of the House of the Morning" in which he broke the seal to the statue of the sun god, waking him up with a prayer. This act brought the sun up and started every day. See Gen. 12:10-20; 39–50; Ex. 1; 2:23–15:19; 1 Kings 3–11; 14:25; 2 Kings 18:21; Isa. 36; 2 Kings 23:29; 1 Chron. 4:18; Jer. 44:30 and Ezek. 29:1-16. See *Egypt; Exodus.*

PHARISEES See *Jewish Parties.*

PHILADELPHIA (love of brother)
See *Asia Minor; Revelation of Jesus Christ.*

PHILEMON (affectionate)

Christian convert under Paul (v. 19; compare v. 1) during Paul's extended ministry in Ephesus (Acts 19:10); recipient of Book of Philemon; master of Onesimus. Paul and Philemon became devoted friends.

PHILEMON, LETTER TO

Eighteenth book of NT; Paul's only epistle of a private and personal nature included in the NT; written to Philemon in A.D. 61 about a runaway slave, Onesimus, who had robbed Philemon and escaped to Rome. Onesimus found the apostle Paul who was imprisoned. Paul sent both the epistle and Onesimus, now a Christian, back to Colosse. Paul requested tenderly as a Christian friend that Philemon forgive and receive Onesimus not as a slave but as a brother (vv. 16-17).

Philemon had a judicial right to punish severely or even kill Onesimus. Paul's short epistle of some 355 Greek words challenged Philemon to apply Christian love in dealing with Onesimus. Paul's approach eventually led to the end of slavery. See *Onesimus; Paul; Slave.*

PHILIP (fond of horses)

(1) Respected member of the church at Jerusalem; chosen as one of the seven, first deacons (Acts 6:5). Following Stephen's martyrdom, Philip took the gospel to Samaria (Acts 8:5-13). Subsequently, he was led south to the Jerusalem-Gaza road where he introduced the Ethiopian eunuch to Christ and baptized him (Acts 8:26-38). He was then transported by the Spirit to Azotus (Ashdod) and from there conducted an itinerent ministry until he took up residence in Caesarea (Acts 8:39-40). Nearly 20 years later, Paul lodged in his home on his last journey to Jerusalem (Acts 21:8). He had four unmarried daughters who were prophetesses (Acts 21:9). See *Acts; Deacon; Evangelism.*

(2) One of twelve apostles (Matt. 10:3). From Bethsaida, he led his brother Nathanael to Jesus (John 1:43-51). Jesus tested Philip concerning how to feed the multitude (John 6:5-7). He and Andrew took inquiring Gentiles to Jesus (John 12:21-22).

Philip asked Jesus to show them the Father (John 14:8-9), opening the way for Jesus' teaching that to see Him is to see the Father. See *Disciples, Apostles*.

(3) Tetrarch of Itaraea and Trachonitis (Luke 3:1). See *Herod*.

PHILIPPI

City in Roman province of Macedonia. Paul did missionary work in Philippi (Acts 16:12) and later wrote a letter to the church there (Phil. 1:1). Originally, the site was in a gold-mining area. After 400 B.C., Philip II of Macedon seized the mines, fortified the city, and named it for himself. Philippi, along with the rest of Macedonia, came under Roman control after 200 B.C. In 42 B.C., at Philippi the forces of Octavian (later to be Augustus Caesar, the first emperor) and Antony defeated the army of Brutus and Cassius. In honor of the victory, Antony settled some Roman soldiers there and made Philippi a Roman colony.

Paul first visited Philippi on his second missionary journey in response to his Macedonian vision (Acts 16:9-12). On the sabbath at a prayer meeting on the river bank, Paul spoke, and Lydia and others opened their hearts to the Lord (Acts 16:13-15). Apparently Philippi had no synagogue for Paul to go to.

He healed a possessed slave girl whose owners charged that he troubled the city by teaching customs unlawful for Romans to observe (Acts 16:20-21). The city magistrates ordered Paul and Silas to be beaten and turned over to the jailer (Acts 16:20,22-23). Paul's miraculous deliverance led to the jailer's conversion (Acts 16:35-36). See *Paul; Roman Law; Philippians*.

PHILIPPIANS, LETTER TO THE

Eleventh book of NT written by Paul to the church at Philippi. Paul wrote to thank the church for a gift it had recently sent to Paul in prison and to inform them of his circumstances and of Timothy's and Epaphroditus's travel plans. The underlying theme of the letter is a call for joyous unity in the church.

Paul was in prison. Acts records Pauline imprisonments in Caesarea and in Rome. Some evidence indicates that Paul was also in prison in Ephesus (Acts 19; 2 Cor. 11:23; 1 Cor. 15:30-32). Philippians is traditionally assigned to Rome about A.D. 61/62. An Ephesian origin about A.D. 55 makes sense of Paul's stated intent to visit Philippi upon his release (Phil. 2:24; from Rome Paul intended to go to Spain, Rom. 15:23-24). Philippians 2:25-30 implies that several trips, bearing news, had been made between Paul's locale and Philippi, a fact difficult to fit into a two-year Roman imprisonment. A Caesarean origin about A.D. 58 for Philippians has few supporters.

Philippians is structured much like a typical personal letter. The introduction identifies the sender(s): Paul and Timothy, and the recipients: the saints, overseers, and deacons. The usual secular greeting and wish for good health is transformed into a blessing (v. 2), a thanksgiving for the Philippian church's faithful participation in the work of the gospel (1:3-8), and a prayer that they may be blessed with an ever-growing, enlightened, Christian love (1:9-11). See *Letter*.

The body of the letter begins with Paul explaining his current situation (1:12-26). His primary concern (the proclamation of the gospel) was being accomplished in spite of his difficult circumstances. His captors were being evangelized (vv. 12-13). His compatriots have gained confidence through his bold example (v. 14). Even the brethren who were working with wrong motives were sharing the good news actively. The severity of Paul's imprisonment is reflected in 1:19-26. His death appears to be a real possibility. Death would unite him with Christ. Life would give him the joys of continued productive ministry. He found cause for genuine rejoicing in both.

Philippians 1:27–4:9 is a multifaceted call for unity in the church. The great cause of the proclamation of the gospel calls for them to be united in spirit, in task, and in confidence (1:27-30). Their common Christian experience (2:1) and purpose (2:2) should also rule out a self-centered, self-serving attitude (2:3-4). Those who follow Christ must follow Him in selfless service to others (2:5-11).

Philippians 2:6-11, a pre-Pauline hymn, seeks to teach the believer about the nature and work of Christ—preexistence, incarnation, passion, resurrection, and exaltation. The passage highlights the humility and selfless service Jesus demonstrated, calling on Christians to follow. Paul had sacrificed himself to engender true faith in the Philippians. His desire, for them and for himself, was that he be able to rejoice that his sacrifice was not in vain (2:12-18).

Philippians 2:25-30 explained why Epaphroditus was returning to Philippi. The church had sent him to take a gift to Paul (see Phil. 4:10-20) and minister to him in his imprisonment.

In chapter 3 the encouragement to rejoice (3:1) unexpectedly becomes a stern warning (3:2). Jewish legalism (3:2-11), Christian or gnostic perfectionism (3:12-16), and pagan libertinism (3:17-21) are all attacked. Paul countered the heretical teachings with Christian truths: Jesus Christ is the only avenue to righteousness (3:2-11); the stature of Christ is the goal of Christian maturity (3:12-16); and the nature of Christ and His kingdom is the standard by which the Christian must live (3:17-21).

Chapter 4 returns to more positive instruction and affirmation. Two women, Euodias and Syntyche (4:2-3), were exhorted to end their conflict, for personal disagreements may be as damaging to the unity of the church as false doctrine. General exhortations to rejoice and to remain faithful (4:4-9) led to Paul's expression of gratitude for the Philippians' faithful support of him and of the ministry (4:10-20). The letter closes in typical Pauline fashion, with an exchange of greetings and a prayer for grace.

PHILISTIA

Coastal plain of southwestern Palestine under the control of the Philistines (Ex. 15:14; Pss. 60:8; 87:4; 108:9; Isa. 14:29-31). KJV sometimes referred to Philistia as "Palestina" (Ex. 15:14; Isa. 14:29-31). See *Philistines.*

PHILISTINES

One of rival groups Israel encountered as they settled the land of Canaan; group of people who occupied and gave their name to the southwest part of Palestine. Their homeland was Caphtor (Amos 9:7; Jer. 47:4). Ancient Egyptian records see them as part of a larger movement known as the Sea Peoples, who invaded Egypt about 1188 B.C. by land and by sea, battling the forces of Ramses III, who, according to Egyptian records, defeated them. The Sea Peoples, a massive group that originated in the Aegean area, included the Tjeker, the Skekelesh, the Denyen, the Sherden, and the Weshwesh as well as the biblical Philistines. Moving eastward, the Sea Peoples warred with people in their path, including the Hittites in Anatolia and peoples in North Syria such as those at Ugarit.

Philistines are first mentioned in the patriarchal stories (Gen. 21:32,34), a reference that some suggest is anachronistic and others suggest refers to the migrations of an Aegean colony in the patriarchal period. In the period of the judges, the Philistines were the principal enemy of and major political threat to Israel (Judg. 13–16). They forced Dan to move north (Judg. 18:11,29). In the battle of Ebenezer (1 Sam. 4:1-18), the Israelites were soundly defeated, and the ark of the covenant was captured. The Israelites defeated the Philistines at times (1 Sam. 7:5-11; 14:16-23); their advance against the Israelites continued. Saul lost his life fighting the Philistines at Mount Gilboa (1 Sam. 31:1-13). David finally checked the Philistine advance at Baal-perazim (2 Sam. 5:17-25).

Politically, the Philistines had a highly organized city-state system comprised of five towns in southwest Palestine: Ashdod, Gaza, Ashkelon, Gath, and Ekron (1 Sam. 6:17). Each of the city-states was ruled by a "lord" (1 Sam. 6:18), a kinglike figure. Gath was perhaps the major city of this Philistine pentapolis, and as such, served as the hub of the city-state system.

The Philistines were experts in metallurgy, the skill of processing metals (1 Sam. 13:19-23), putting Israel at a decided disadvantage. (See *Minerals and Metals.*) The Philistines had a highly trained military organization (1 Sam. 13:5; 31:3). The armor of Philistine soldiers included bronze helmets, coats of mail, leg protectors, spears, and shields (1 Sam. 17:5-7). The story of Goliath indicates that at times the Philistines used individual combat (1 Sam. 17). Most likely, the Philistine warrior went through a cursing ritual just prior to the confrontation (1 Sam. 17:43). David, who recognized the military expertise of the Philistines, selected Cherethites (Cretans) and Pelethites (Philistines) (1 Sam. 20:23) for his palace guard or mercenary army. See *Arms.*

The Bible mentions three Philistine gods—Dagon, Ashtoreth, and Baalzebub. Dagon appears to be the chief god of the Philistines. Temples of Dagon were located at Gaza (Judg. 16:21-30) and Ashdod (1 Sam. 5:1-7). Ashtoreth, the fertility goddess of the Canaanites, was most likely adopted by the Philistines. Apparently, the Philistines had Ashtoreth temples at Beth-shan (1 Sam. 31:10 NIV) and, according to Herodotus, at Ashkelon. Baalzebub, the Philistine god whose name means "lord of the flies," was the god of Ekron (2 Kings 1:1-16). Most likely the Philistines worshiped Baalzebub as a god who averted pestilence or plagues.

PHILO JUDAEUS

Early (about 20 B.C. to A.D. 50) Jewish interpreter of Scripture known for use of allegory; also known as Philo of Alexandria; member of wealthy Jewish family in Alexandria, Egypt; well educated in Greek schools and used the Greek OT, the Septuagint, as his Bible.

PHINEHAS (*dark-skinned* or *mouth of brass*)

(1) Grandson of Aaron and high priest who, on several occasions, aided Moses and Joshua. See *High Priest.*

(2) One of Eli, the priest's, worthless sons. He engaged in religious prostitution (1 Sam. 2:22) and led the people to follow. He and Hophni died in a battle with the Philistines while attempting to keep the ark from being captured (4:11). When his pregnant wife heard of his death, she immediately delivered, naming the child Ichabod ("the glory has departed").

PHOEBE (*bright*)

"Servant" (KJV, NIV, NASB), "minister" (REB), "leader" (CEV), "helper" (NCV), "deaconess" (NASB note, NIV note, NCV note), or "deacon" (NRSV, NLT) of church at Cenchrea whom Paul recommended to church at Rome (Rom. 16:1-2). See *Deacon.*

PHOENICIA (*purple* or *crimson*)

Narrow land between Mediterranean Sea and Lebanon Mountains between Tyre in the south and Arvad in the north; NT Phoenicia reached south to Dor. Great forest land enabled the people to build ships and become the dominant seafaring nation. The forests also provided timber for export, Phoenician cedars being the featured material of Solomon's temple (1 Kings 5:8-10).

Phoenician religion was akin to that of the Canaanites, featuring fertility rites of Baal. See *Canaan.* Later, Baal's Greek counterpart Adonis ("my lord") was worshiped in similar fashion to Tammuz. (See *Fertility Cult.*) The Phoenician princess Jezebel imported devotion to Baal to Israel. (See *Jezebel; Elijah.*) Phoenicia introduced the alphabet to the western world, but little of their literature survived.

City-states rather than central government dominated Phoenicia. Leading cities were Tyre, Sidon, Byblos (Gebal), and Berytos (Beirut). An early Neolithic race disappeared about 3000 B.C., being replaced by Semitic colonizers from the east. Invading armies from north (Hittites), east (Amorites and Assyrians), and south (Egyptians) dominated history until 1000 B.C. when King Hiram of Tyre established local rule (981–947 B.C.). (See *Hiram*.) They were able to take advantage of their location on the sea with natural harbors and their forests to establish far-flung trade. Compare Ezek. 27. Their most notable colony was Carthage on the North African coast.

Growth of Assyrian power about 750 B.C. led to Phoenicia's decline. The Persian Empire gave virtual independence to Phoenicia, using the Phoenician fleet against Egypt and Greece. Alexander the Great put an end to Phoenician political power, but the great cities retained economic power.

Jesus' ministry reached Tyre and Sidon (Matt. 15:21). Persecution beginning with Stephen's death led the church to spread into Phoenicia (Acts 11:19; compare 15:3; 21:2-3). See *Sidon* and *Tyre*.

PHOENIX (perhaps *date palm*)

Port on southeast coast of Crete that Paul and the ship's crew hoped to reach for winter harbor (Acts 27:12).

PHRYGIA (*parched*)

Area immediately west of the Hellespont; later, the people migrated into Asia Minor. During Roman times, Phrygia was a subregion of Galatia, and her people often were slaves or servants. The area remained relatively undefined but contained Antioch of Pisidia, Laodicea, and at times, Iconium. Some Phrygians were in Jerusalem on Day of Pentecost (Acts 2:10; compare 16:6; 18:23). See *Asia Minor*.

PHYSICIAN See *Diseases*.

PIBESETH (*house of Bastet*)

Egyptian goddess represented as a cat. Egyptian city located on the shore of the old Tanite branch of the Nile about 45 miles northeast of Cairo; served as capital of the eighteenth nome (administrative district) and, during the Twenty-Second and Twenty-Third Dynasties (940–745 B.C.), as capital of a fragmented Egyptian Empire. The site is tell Basta.

PIETY

(1) NIV: "the fear [or reverence] of the Lord" (Job 4:6; 15:4; 22:4; compare REB). See Acts 3:12 (NASB, NRSV); Heb. 5:7 (NASB).

(2) NRSV: "righteousness" (Matt. 6:1), where the concern was with an external show of religion (Matt. 6:2-6).

(3) Religious duty of caring for physical needs of elderly family members (1 Tim. 5:4 KJV, NASB).

PIHAHIROTH (Egyptian, *house of Hathor*; Hebrew, *mouth of canals*)

Egyptian city in eastern Nile delta east of Baal-zephon where Israelites encamped in early days of exodus (Ex. 14:2,9; Num. 33:7; compare Num. 33:8).

PILATE, PONTIUS

Roman governor of Judea, remembered in history as a notorious anti-Semite and in Christian creeds as the magistrate under whom Jesus Christ "suffered" (1 Tim 6:13). New Testament refers to him as "governor," while other sources call him "procurator" or "prefect" (an inscription found in Caesarea in 1961). Pilate came to power about A.D. 26, close to the time when two of his contemporaries, Sejanus in Rome and Flaccus in Egypt, were pursuing policies apparently aimed at the destruction of the Jewish people. Pilate's procuratorship consisted of one provocation of Jewish sensibilities after another. He broke all precedent by bringing into Jerusalem military insignia bearing the image of Caesar in flagrant defiance of Jewish law. He removed them only when the Jews offered to die at the hands of his soldiers rather than consent to such blasphemy. He brutally suppressed protest by planting armed soldiers, disguised as civilians, among the Jewish crowds. Against such a backdrop, it is not hard to understand the reference in Luke 13:1 to "the Galileans whose blood Pilate had mingled with their sacrifices." Pilate was finally removed from office as the result of a similar outrage against Samaritan worshipers who had gathered on Mount Gerizim, their holy mountain, to view some sacred vessels that they believed Moses had buried there. When the Samaritans complained to Vitellius, the governor of Syria, Pilate was ordered to Rome to account for his actions to the emperor and is not mentioned again in reliable contemporary sources.

Pilate seems to have had no personal inclination to put Jesus to death, and the NT writers are eager to show that he did not (Luke 23:4,14,22; John 18:38; 19:4,6; compare Matt. 17:19). A relatively small group of Jerusalem priests, including the high priest, wanted to forestall any kind of messianic movement by the people because of the repression it would provoke from the Romans (see John 11:47-50,53). They maneuvered Pilate into doing their work for them (compare Luke 23:2). The inscription he insisted on placing over the cross according to all the Gospels was Pilate's last grim joke at Jewish expense: "This is the King of the Jews." Anti-Jewish to the end, Pilate was telling the world,"What a sorry race this is, with such a pitiful figure for their king!" See *Cross, Crucifixion.*

PILGRIMAGE

Journey, especially a religious trek to a site at which God has revealed Himself in the past; KJV for journeys (Ex. 6:4); KJV, NASB, RSV in figurative sense for life journey (Gen. 47:9 KJV, only; Ps. 119:54); NIV for religious "pilgrimage"(Ps. 84:5; compare REB).

In Israel's early history, numerous local shrines were the goals of religious pilgrimage: Bethel (Gen. 28:10-22; 31:13; 35:9-15; Amos 4:4; 5:5); Gilgal (Josh. 4:19-24; Hos. 4:15; Amos 4:4; 5:5); Shiloh (Judg. 20:26-27; 1 Sam. 1:3, 19); Beersheba (Amos 5:5; 8:14); Gibeon (1 Kings 3:3-5); even Horeb (1 Kings 19:8). Jerusalem was not the goal of religious pilgrims until David relocated the ark there (2 Sam. 6:12-19). Hezekiah's and Josiah's reforms attempted to destroy the pagan sites of pilgrimage and idol worship (2 Kings 18:4; 23:8) and make Jerusalem the exclusive focus of pilgrimage. Mosaic law required adult male Israelites to appear before the Lord (where the ark of the covenant rested) three times a year (Ex. 23:14-17; 34:18-23; Deut. 16:16). Crowds of pilgrims (Pss. 42:4; 55:14; Luke 2:44) sang on the way to Jerusalem (Isa. 30:29). The Psalms of Ascent (Pss. 24; 84; 118; 120-134) were likely sung as pilgrims climbed the ascent to the temple mount in Jerusalem.The prophets condemned the celebration of religious pilgrimages and feasts when not accompanied by genuine devotion to the Lord expressed in righteous lives (Isa. 1:12-13; Amos 4:4-5; 5:5-6,21-24).The NT witnessed the continuing popularity of pilgrimage to Jerusalem (Matt. 21:8-11; Luke 2:41; John 2:13; 5:1; 7:2,10; 12:12,20; Acts 2:5-10; 20:16).

PILLAR

Stone monuments or standing architectural structures.

(1) Stones set up as memorials to persons (Gen. 35:20; 2 Sam. 18:18).

(2) Shrines both to the Lord and to false gods. Graven images often were pillars set up as gods. God commanded Israel to break down such "images" (Ex. 23:24). Jacob set up a pillar following his dream (Gen. 28:18) and again when God spoke to him at Bethel (35:9-15)—as memorials of God's revelation. Moses set up 12 pillars to commemorate the giving

of the law to the tribes of Israel (Ex. 24:4).

(3) As structural supports. The tabernacle used pillars for the veil (Ex. 26:31-32), the courts (27:9-15), and the gate (27:16). The temple in Jerusalem used pillars for its support (1 Kings 7:2-3), and the porch had pillars (7:6). Figuratively, pillars were believed to hold up heaven (Job 26:11) and earth (1 Sam. 2:8).

(4) God led Israel through the wilderness with a pillar of cloud by day and a pillar of fire by night (Ex. 13:21; compare 14:19-20). These pillars were symbols of God's presence with Israel as much as signs of where they were to go.

(5) Solomon's temple had two free- standing brass pillars (1 Kings 7:15). See *Jachin and Boaz.*

PINNACLE

Highest point of a structure; term referring to the temple or Jerusalem (Isa. 54:12, NRSV; "battlements," NASB, NIV, REB; "towers," TEV; "windows," KJV): Hebrew suggests a structure catching the sun's rays. The pinnacle (literally, "little wing") of the temple (Matt. 4:5; Luke 4:9) may be southeastern corner of the royal colonnade that overlooked the Kidron valley or a lintel or balcony above one of the temple gates.

PIRATHON, PIRATHONITE

(*princely* or *height, summit*; its inhabitants)

Town in hill country of Ephraim; home of Abdon (Judg. 12:13,15) and Benaiah (2 Sam. 23:30; 1 Chron. 11:31); Far'ata about five miles southwest of Shechem.

PISGAH (perhaps *the divided one*)

Mountain in Abarim range across Jordan River from Jericho; part of Mount Nebo or separate rise, either en-Neba or near modern Khirbet Tsijaga. God allowed Moses to view the Promised Land from the heights of Pisgah (Deut. 34:1). Israel had camped near Pisgah (Num. 21:20). Balak took Balaam to its height so the prophet could see Israel and curse them (Num. 23:14). It was a limit of Sihon's kingdom (Josh. 12:23); and also for the tribe of Reuben (13:20).

PISIDIA

Small area in province of Galatia in southern Asia Minor bounded by Pamphylia, Phrygia, and Lyconia within the Taurus Mountain range; resisted invasion by ancient peoples. Only in 25 B.C. did the Romans gain control over the region through economic diplomacy. Antioch was made the capital, although some historians contend that the city was not actually in Pisidia. Paul and Barnabas came through Antioch (Acts 13:14) after John Mark left them in Perga (v. 13). The NT does not record any missionary activity in Pisidia itself, probably because there were few Jews there with which to start a congregation. See *Asia Minor.*

PIT See *Hell; Everlasting Punishment; Sheol.*

PITHOM (*mansion or estate of Atum* [an Egyptian god])

City Israelites built for Egypt (Ex. 1:11); important clue to the exodus chronology. See *Exodus.*

PLAGUES

Disease interpreted as divine judgment. Ten plagues in Exodus (Ex. 7:1–13:15; compare Deut. 4:34; 7:19; 11:3; Pss. 78; 105; Jer. 32:20) were mighty works of God that gained Israel's release and demonstrated God's sovereignty (Ex. 9:14; 11:1); they were also called "signs" (Ex. 7:13) "wonders" (Ex. 7:3; 11:9). Paul used the plagues to stress the sovereignty of God in the hardening of Pharaoh's heart (Rom. 9:17-18). The plagues of the Revelation reflect OT influence (Rev. 8; 16).

The plagues were the Lord's judgment on the Egyptians and His saving actions for Israel. The plagues depict events of nature that might occur in Egypt. Clearly, the author of Exodus saw them as the product of a purposive, divine will. Since Egypt's magicians duplicated the first two events, the uniqueness of the plagues may rest in their timing, locale, intensity, and theological interpretation. The central purpose was the revelation of God. Pharaoh and the Egyptians, as well as Moses and the Israelites, would come to know the Lord through the events of the plagues (Ex. 7:17; 8:10,22; 9:14,16,29). Paul acknowledged this purpose: "that my name might be declared throughout all the earth"(Rom. 9:17). See *Exodus; Miracles.*

PLAIN See *Palestine.*

PLANTS

All plant life such as wild and cultivated trees, shrubs, and herbs.

Lily and Rose

Red lips of Song of Sol. 5:13 indicate a red-flowered "lily," such as scarlet tulip or anemone. Song of Sol. 2:1-2, may refer to the actual white madonna lily (*Lilium candidum*), now very rare in the area, or wild hyacinth (*Hyacinthus orientalis*), wild crocus (*Croccus* species), the "rose" of Isa. 35:1-2 (see NASB). It is impossible to be sure to which "lilies" Jesus referred (Matt. 6:28; Luke 12:27): it may have been the anemone or any of the conspicuous wild flowers such as crown daisy (*Chrysanthemum coronarium*). The "rose of Sharon" (Song of Sol. 2:1) has been equated with anemone, rockrose, narcissus, tulip, and crocus.

Nettle

Coarse plants with stinging hairs belonging to the family *Urtica;* generally, any prickly or stinging plant (Job 30:7; Prov. 24:31; Isa. 34:13; Hos. 9:6; Zeph. 2:9). NIV frequently replaced nettles with undergrowth, weeds, or briers. The Hebrew term in Job 30:7; Zeph. 2:9 perhaps refers to wild mustard. Nettles are used as a sign of desolation and judgment.

Reeds

Common reed (*Phragmites communis*) forms great stands in shallow water or wet salty sand. The plumed flower head may have been given to

Jesus in mockery (Matt. 27:29). Pens (3 John 13) were made from the bamboolike stems.

Papyrus sedge (*Cyperus papyrus*) also translated "bulrush," also grows in shallow water in hot places such as in Lake Huleh and along the Nile. Its tall, triangular, spongy stems were used for rafts (Isa. 18:1-2) and for making baskets (Ex. 2:3), and papyrus paper—on which much of the Bible may have been written.

Cattail or reed mace (*Typha domingensis*) seems to have been the one among which Moses was hidden (Ex. 2:3). This is often referred to as bulrush, but the tree bulrush (*Scirpus lacustris*) is a sedge with slender stems.

Thorns

Jesus' crown of thorns has led to two shrubs known as christthorn (*Ziziphus spina-christ, Paliurus spina-christi*). The former grows near the Dead Sea not far from Jerusalem (Matt. 27:29; Mark 15:17; John 19:5). Some authors consider the common spiny burnet (*Poterium* or *Sarcopoterium spinosum*) to be the species concerned.

In the Holy Land, the ground is cursed with prickly weeds (Gen. 3:18; Num. 33:55). Thorns are usually woody plants, such as *Acacia, Lycium, Ononis, Prosopis, Rubus, Sarcopoterium;* while thistles are herbaceous, such as *Centaurea, Notobasis, Silybum.* The latter could have been the "thorns" that suffocated the grain in Jesus' parable (Matt. 13:7).

Fragrant Plants

(1) *Cassia and cinnamon* are traditionally identified with the Far Eastern trees *Cinnamomum cassia* and *C. zeylanicum.* The ground bark was used in the holy anointing oil for priests (Ex. 30:24), and cinnamon was used for perfumery (Prov. 7:17; Rev. 18:13).

(2) *Calamus* or *sweet cane* (*Acorus calamus*). Dry rhizome of this water plant imported from temperate Asia and used for perfume (Isa. 43:24 NRSV); ingredient of holy anointing oil (Ezek. 30:23). It was a

good-smelling spice made from an imported reed. It is also translated "fragrant cane" (NIV, NASB) or "aromatic cane" (NRSV).

(3) *Galbanum.* Very strong-smelling resin burnt as incense (Ex. 30:34); obtained from the stem of *Ferula galbaniflua,* a relative of parsley growing on dry hills in Iran.

(4) *Henna (Lawsonia inermis)* leaves were crushed and used both as a perfume (Song of Sol. 1:14 NIV) and as a yellow dye for skin, nails, and hair. It is a subtropical shrub with white flowers.

(5) *Hyssop.* Used for ritual cleansing (Lev. 14:4,49) and sprinkling of blood in the tabernacle (Ex.12:22); white marjoram (*Origanum syriacum* or *Majorana syriacu*) that grows commonly in rocky places and is related to mint.

(6) *Myrtle (Myrtus communis).* Shrub with fragrant leaves and white flowers frequent in bushy places; especially favored for temporary shelters in the fields at the Feast of Tabernacles (Lev. 23:40; Neh. 8:15).

(7) *Rue (Ruta chalepensis)* grows on hills of the Holy Land as a low straggling shrub with pungent smelling leaves. Jesus referred to it being tithed (Luke 11:42).

(8) *Spikenard* or *nard.* Expensive perfumed oil (Song of Sol. 4:13-14; John 12:3) obtained either from the leaves of a desert grass (*Cymbopogon schoenanthus*) or, traditionally, the valerian relative *Nardostachys jatamansi* from the Himalayas.

(9) *Stacte.* Spices (Ex. 30:34) used in incense; may be resin of the balm-of-Gilead (*Commiphora gileadensis*) from southern Arabia.

Culinary Herbs

Bitter herbs for Passover are certain wild plants with sharp-tasting leaves. The desert plant wormwood (*Artemisia*) was also bitter and depicted sorrow and suffering (Prov. 5:4; Lam. 3:15,19).

(1) *Coriander (Coriandrum sativum)* provides both salad leaves and spicy seeds (Ex. 16:31); likened by Israelites to manna in the desert.

(2) *Cummin (Cuminum cyminum)* and *dill (Anethum graveolens).* Like coriander, member of parsley family with spicy seeds (Isa. 28:25-27; Matt. 23:23).

(3) *Fitches* or *black cummin (Nigella sativa).* Annual plant with black oily seeds easily damaged in harvesting (Isa. 28:25-27).

(4) *Mint (Mentha longifolia).* Popular seasoning herb tithed by Jewish leaders (Luke 11:42).

(5) *Mustard (Brassica nigra).* Hot-flavored seeds; small seeds grow into a tree (Matt. 13:31-32).

(6) *Purslane.* Fleshy-leaved, trailing plant used as a pot herb or in salads (Job 6:6 RSV); illustrates tasteless food; also read with Targum, reading "white of an egg" (KJV, NASB, NIV) or find referred to another plant, "the mallow" (NRSV, REB).

(7) *Saffron (Crocus sativus).* Yellow powder prepared from the stigmas; used as subtle flavor (Song of Sol. 4:14) and as food coloring and medicine.

Frankincense and Myrrh

Resins produced by certain trees that grow in dry country in southern Arabia and northern Africa.

(1) *Frankincense.* White or colorless resin yielded by several species of *Boswellia,* chiefly *B. sacra,* a shrub or small tree growing on both sides of the Red Sea. Resin is obtained by cutting the branches and collecting the exuding "tears," which are burnt as incense in religious rites or as a personal fumigant. Frankincense was prescribed for holy incense mixture (Ex. 30:31,34; Luke 1:9) and brought by wise men to baby Jesus (Matt. 2:11).

(2) *Myrrh.* Reddish-colored resin obtained from spiny shrub, *Commiphora myrrha* in a similar manner to frankincense; not usually burnt but dissolved in oil and either eaten or used as medicine and cosmetic (Ps. 45:8; Matt. 2:11).

Medicinal Plants

Many medicinal herbs were gathered from the hills and valleys where the wild plants grew. See *Frankincense and Myrrh* above.

(1) *Aloes* (*Aloe vera*) were succulent plants with long swordlike leaves with serrations and erect flower heads up to three feet high imported from Yemen. The bitter pith was used as a medicine and for embalming (John 19:39). Old Testament aloes meant expensive fragrant timber obtained from a tropical Indian eaglewood tree (*Aquilaria agallocha*).

(2) *Balm* (Gen. 37:25). General term for medicinal ointment prepared from resin-bearing plants such as the rockrose *Cistus laurifolius*, which produces ladanum. The balm of Gilead or opobalsam is yielded by *Commiphora gileadensis*, a non-spiny shrub of dry country in Southern Arabia and said to have been cultivated by Solomon at En-Gedi near the Dead Sea (Song of Sol. 5:1, "spice"). Gum was imported with balm by the Ishmaelites (Gen. 37:25). It is extruded from cut roots of a spiny undershrub (*Astragalus tragacanth*) grown on dry Iranian hillsides.

Some plants, such as the gourd *Citrullus colocynthis*, could be medicinal purges in very small quantities but bitter poisons otherwise (2 Kings 4:39-40).

Cereal Grains for Bread

Well-to-do citizens made bread primarily from wheat, but the poor person had to make do with coarse barley (2 Kings 4:42; John 6:9).

(1) *Wheat* (emmer wheat *Triticum dicoccum*; bread wheat *T. aestivum*). Annual crop that grows about three feet tall, though primitive varieties were taller in rich soil; with bearded ears. Grains of wheat are hard and dry and easily kept in storehouses (Gen. 41:49; KJV, "corn"). It was important to retain seed for sowing (Gen. 47:24), but ancient tomb grain will not germinate. See *Bread.*

(2) *Barley* (*Hordeum vulgare*) Tolerates poorer soil than wheat; is shorter; has bearded ears; and ripens sooner (Ex. 9:31-32); used for brewing beer and as horse and cattle fodder (1 Kings 4:28). Sometimes barley was eaten roasted as parched grain (Ruth 2:14). Wheat and barley straw remaining after threshing was used

for fuel (Isa. 47:14), and the fine chaff for instant heat in the oven.

Fruits

(1) *Olive* trees (*Olea europaea*). Small rounded orchard trees with narrow gray-green leaves and small cream-colored flowers that bloom in May. The stone fruits ripen toward the end of summer and are pickled in brine either unripe as green olives or ripe as black olives. Bulk of the crop was gathered for olive oil. See *Oil.*

(2) *Grape vines* (*Vitis vinifera*). Grown either in vineyards or singly as shady bowers around houses and courtyards; have long flexible stems with tendrils and lobed leaves. Short flower heads grow among the new leaves in early summer, and the numerous tiny flowers develop into a cluster of round sweet grapes that ripen either as green or black fruits. The fruits are eaten fresh as grapes, or dried and stored as raisins (1 Sam. 30:12). Wine was prepared from the fermented juice. See *Wine.*

(3) *Fig* tree (*Ficus carica*). Short stout trunk and thick branches and twigs bearing coarsely lobed rough leaves (Gen. 3:7). Rounded fruits with numerous small seeds in their interior cavity ripen during the summer. Fresh figs were favored as first fruits (Isa. 28:4; Jer. 24:2). Figs dry very well and were stored as cakes for future use (1 Sam. 25:18; 30:12). Jesus referred to figs and fig trees several times (Matt. 7:16; Luke 21:29-31).

(4) *Sycomore* (*Ficus sycomorus*) grew in Egypt and in the warmer areas of the Holy Land; large tree; usually has low-growing branches such as would have enabled the short Zacchaeus to climb up to see Jesus (Luke 19:4).

(5) *Pomegranate* (*Punica granatum*). About size of a tennis ball; full of seeds and sweet pulp; develops from beautiful scarlet flowers that cover the twiggy bush in spring. Pomegranate bushes were often grown in gardens and beside houses (Deut. 8:8; Song of Sol. 6:11). Moses was instructed to embroider pomegranate fruits on the hem of the priests' robes (Ex. 28:33), and their

form ornamented the columns of Solomon's temple in Jerusalem (1 Kings 7:18; 2 Chron. 3:16).

(6) *Date-palm (Phoenix dactylifera)*. Only palm to yield fruit in biblical times; very tall tree with rough unbranched trunk bearing a terminal tuft of huge feather leaves; fruits best in hot conditions of the Dead Sea oases. Jericho was known as the city of palm trees (Judg. 1:16). See Ex. 15:27; Ps. 92:12; Rev. 7:9. When Jesus entered Jerusalem, the people strewed the way with leaves (John 12:13).

(7) *Black mulberry (Morus niger)*. Not present in Holy Land until NT times; originated in the Caspian Sea region. See Luke 17:6; old trees are stout, gnarled, and long-lived.

(8) *"Apple"*(Song of Sol. 2:3,5; 7:8; 8:5; Prov. 25:11; Joel 1:12) or"apricot"; unlikely fine varieties of apples were available so early.

(9) *Caperberry (capparis spinosa)*. Thought to increase sexual powers and used to symbolize the dying physical desire of the aging (Eccl. 12:5 NASB).

Nuts

(1) *Almond (Prunus dulcis)*. Most important biblical nut; small tree with delightful whitish flowers in early spring before leaves have sprouted; kernel is contained in a very hard thick casing. See Gen. 43:11; Num. 17:8; Ex. 25:33; 37:19.

(2) *Walnut tree (Juglans regia)*. Originated in Caspian region and may not have been commonly planted in the Eastern Mediterranean region until after biblical period; possible Solomon grew it in his garden (Song of Sol. 6:11). The tree grows to a considerable size. The leaves are compound, and the oily edible nuts look like a miniature brain—hence the ancient name Jovis glans and the scientific adaptation *Juglans*.

(3) *Pistacio nuts (Pistacia vera)* arrived late; nuts in the Bible (Gen. 43:11 NIV) would be from the native terebinth trees (*Pistachia terebinthus, P. atlantica*) of the hillsides. One is a small shrubby tree, while the other is as large as an oak. Both yield small round edible fruits.

Vegetables

The wandering Israelites longed for vegetables after they left Egypt (Num. 11:5; compare 2 Sam. 17:28; Dan. 1:12).

(1) *Onions (Allium cepa)*. White or purple bulbs; grow quickly from seeds in one season.

(2) *Leeks (Allium porrum)*. Do not form such a distinct bulb; are cooked, or leaves are chopped up.

(3) *Garlic (Allium sativum)*. Strongly flavored onion that produces a bulb composed of separate scales.

(4) *Cucumbers* of biblical Egypt were most likely the snake- or muskmelon *Cucumis melo*, which has longitudinal lines on its exterior.

(5) *Melons* were the *watermelon* (*Citrullus lanatus*) and not the squash or honeydew melon that are of American origin.

(6) *Lentils (Lens culinaris)*. Grew in more arid areas; red pottage or soup made of lentils enabled Jacob to obtain Esau's birthright (Gen. 25:29-34). Lentil plants are small and slender with pealike flowers and small flat pods containing two seeds.

(7) *Broad bean (Vicia faba)* and *chick pea (Cicer arietinum)* may have been vegetables Daniel and his friends ate in Babylon (Dan. 1:12).

Trees of dry and desert areas

(1) *Acacia* (KJV shittim). Several varieties occur in Sinai; timber was used for construction of tabernacle, the tent of meeting (Ex. 25); usually flat-topped trees that possess strong thorns.

(2) *Broom Tree (Retama raetam)*. Bush that often grows large enough to provide shade (1 Kings 19:4-5); foliage and roots were often used as fuel (Job 30:4; Ps. 120:4). Its white flowers with maroon center beautify the Dead Sea area. Rithmah (Num. 33:18-19) was named for this shrub (rothem). KJV, NASB identify the bush as "juniper"; modern scholars agree the bush was the broom tree (NIV, REB, NRSV).

(3) *Tamarisk (Tamarix species)*. Shrub or small tree with fine

branchlets, scale leaves, and pink or white flowers, inhabiting salty places in the desert. Abraham planted one at Beersheba (Gen. 21:33 NIV).

Trees of streams, rivers and lakes

(1) *Plane (Platanus orientalis)*. Large tree with flaking bark and digitate leaves; minute flowers are clustered in several hanging balls; inhabits rocky stream beds; rod Jacob peeled (Gen. 30:37; also Ezek. 31:8, KJV, "chestnut").

(2) *Poplar (Populus euphratica)*. Tree Jacob peeled (Gen. 30:37); grows beside water, especially the rivers Euphrates and Jordan; tall tree with shaking leaves and numerous suckering shoots around its base. The white poplar (P. alba) and the storax *(Styrax officinalis)* were more likely to be the trees upon the mountains (Hos. 4:13).

(3) *Willow (Salix acynophylla)*. Roots easily in wet places; not as tall as poplars; usually have long narrow leaves (Job 40:22; Isa. 44:4; Ezek. 17:5).

Trees of hills and plains

(1) *Balsam* (KJV, *mulberry*). Aromatic, resinous substance imported from Arabia or Abyssinia and used as spice or cosmetic fragrance (2 Sam. 5:23-24; 1 Chron. 14:14-15; REB, "aspens"). Neither balsam nor mulberry tree has been known to grow around Jerusalem, making the identification of the tree uncertain. Poplar and mastic tree have also been suggested as translations. Balsam is also a translation of bosam in the NASB, where other versions have "spice" and "spices" (Song of Sol. 5:1,13; 6:2). See *Cosmetics*.

(2) *Box tree* (Isa. 41:19; 60:13, KJV, REB and NASB). Grows in Asia Minor and Persia; does not occur in Palestine; identified as "pine" (NRSV) or "cypress" (TEV, NIV); "box tree" based on early Greek and Latin translations. Hebrew means "to be straight" and apparently refers to the tall, majestic cypress trees (Isa. 41:20).

(3) *Cypress (Cupressus sempervirens)*. Dense coniferous forest tree typically with spreading branches, although often seen as a tall narrow tree planted beside cemeteries. Cypress is evidently intended in Isa. 40:20; 60:13, among others.

(4) *Cedar (Cedrus libani)*. Cedar of Lebanon; played a still-unknown role in Israel's purification rites (Lev. 14:4; Num. 19:6). Stout flat-topped trees provided excellent timber used for David's house (2 Sam. 5:11) and Solomon's temple (1 Kings 5:6-10; see 6:9-7:12; Ezra 3:7). Cedar signified royal power and wealth (1 Kings 10:27), thus growth and strength (Ps. 92:12; compare Ezek. 17). Majestic cedars could not stand before God's powerful presence (Ps. 29:5). The cedars owed their existence to God, who had planted them (Ps. 104:16).

(5) *Oak (Quercus species)*. Provide excellent timber for ships (Ezek. 27:6) and other construction. Oaks were used to mark graves (Gen. 35:8) or as landmarks (1 Sam. 10:3) or for sacrilegious ceremonies (Hos. 4:13).

(6) *Pine (Pinus halepensis)*. Especially *Aleppo pineis* tall coniferous tree with long needle-leaves and cones containing winged seeds; timber is workable and used for construction; probably referred to in Isa. 44:14 (KJV, "ash"; NRSV, "cedar").

(7) *Terebinth (Pistacia terebinthus, P. atlantica)*. Produced fruits used as nuts, but the timber of the large oaklike *P. atlantica* is also useful. The shade of terebinths was used for pagan sacrifices and offerings (Hos. 4:13 NIV).

Foreign trees

(1) *Almug wood*. Traditionally identified as sandal wood *(Pterocarpus santalinus)*; imported from Ophir to Judah by Hiram's fleet for Solomon (1 Kings 10:10-11). Whether algum and almug are synonymous is matter of dispute, since algum is clearly stated to be from Lebanon (2 Chron. 2:8), in which case it could have been Cilician fir *(Abies cilicia)* or Grecian juniper *(Juniperus excelsa)*.

(2) *Ebony*. Linked with imported ivory tusks (Ezek. 27:15); black-red ebony of ancient Egypt was African leguminous tree *(Dalbergia melanoxylon)*, while later the name was transferred to the tropical Asian

Diospyros ebenum, which has jet-black timber. (3) *Thyine wood.* Timber from North African sanderac tree *(Tetraclinis articulata),* a coniferlike cypress used by Greeks and Romans for cabinetmaking; dark, hard, and fragrant (Rev. 18:12).

PLASTER

Pasty combination usually of water, lime, and sand that hardens on drying and is used for coating walls and ceilings. Mosaic law included regulations for treating homes in which mold or rot appeared in the plaster (Lev. 14:41-48). Writing was easy on a surface of wet plaster (Deut. 27:2-4).

POETRY

Hebrew literature using parallelism, meter, and grouping lines into larger units called stanzas. The distinction in Hebrew between poetry and prose is not so much a difference in kind as a difference in degree. One third of the OT is cast in poetry.

The predominant feature of Hebrew poetry is parallelism. In parallelism, two or three short lines stand in one of three relationships to one another: synonymous, antithetic, or synthetic.

In *synonymous parallelism,* the succeeding line expresses an identical or nearly identical thought:

> My mouth shall speak of wisdom;
>
> the meditation of my heart shall be of understanding.
>
> Ps. 49:3

In *antithetic parallelism,* succeeding lines express opposing thoughts:

> The wicked borrow,
>   and do not pay back,
>
> but the righteous are generous
>   and keep giving.
>
> Ps. 37:21 (NRSV)

In *synthetic parallelism,* succeeding lines display little or no repetition:

> Behold how good and pleasant it is
>
> for brethren to dwell together in unity!
>
> Ps. 133:1

Continuity joins the parallel lines. Synthetic parallel lines may describe an order of events, list characteristics of a person or thing, or simply modify a common theme.

Attempts to establish a classical system of meter (iambic feet, for example) have failed. Other theories use letter counts, vowel counts, stress counts, and word counts. The last mentioned is one of the most effective methods. Individual lines range from two to four words each, even though these "words" may be translated as two or three words in English. Numerous metrical systems are possible. Consequently, Hebrew meter is described in terms of general patterns rather than absolute uniformity.

Stanzas may be set off by identical lines or by parallel lines expressing similar thoughts. These introductions may take the form of a refrain not unlike a musical refrain. Sections separated in this way may be dissimilar in theme, form, and vocabulary. Psalms 42–43 present a good example of clear-cut stanzas. The two chapters together form a single poem. A refrain is repeated three times: 42:5,11; 43:5, subdividing the poem into three sections.

Poetry provides imagery and tone for inspired writers to drum God's word home to His people. Awareness of poetic form alerts the reader to listen for the images and moods of a passage.

POISON

Chemical agent causing ill health or death when in contact with or ingested by an organism; frequent image for wickedness, especially lying speech (Deut. 32:32-33; Job 20:16; Pss. 58:4; 140:3). Poisonous weeds illustrated lawsuits springing up from broken oaths and covenants (Hos. 10:4). In Amos 6:12 poison served as an image of injustice. Poisoned water pictured God's judgment on sin (Jer. 8:14).

POLICE

NASB, NRSV for Roman office of *lictor*, one who enforced the will of a local magistrate (Acts 16:35,38).

POLLUTE See *Clean, Cleanness.*

POLLUTION

Things of an inferior quality (Mal. 1:7, 12) or things fouled by sin (Ezra 6:21; Acts 15:20; Rev. 21:8). In modern parlance, pollution refers to things that befoul the natural environment. As a result of the Fall, the environment, which was created clean and pure, has become subject to all manner of pollution, making the land (Deut. 29:22-28; compare Jer. 4:23), rivers and streams (Ex. 7:20-24; Prov. 25:26; Ezek. 32:2; 34:18-19; Rev. 8:9-10; 16:4), and the sea (Rev. 8:8-9; 16:3) unfit for life as God intended it. The earth and its resources belong to God (Ps. 24:1), yet have been entrusted to people (Gen. 1:28-29; 9:1-4), who have a sacred responsibility to care for the earth with the same diligence that God cares for it (Deut. 11:12).

PONTIUS PILATE See *Pilate, Pontius.*

PONTUS

Province just south of Black Sea in Asia Minor. Mithradates founded the kingdom of Pontus in about 302 B.C. It remained in his dynasty until 63 B.C. when Rome took over. First Peter was addressed to the elect there (1:2-2). Citizens of Pontus were in Jerusalem on Day of Pentecost (Acts 2:9). See *Asia Minor.*

POOL

Collection of water, natural or artificial; commonly seen as place to collect rainwater from the roof to be used for irrigation or drinking; principal pools mentioned in Scripture: pool of Hezekiah (2 Kings 20:20), upper and lower pools of Gihon (Isa. 7:3; 22:9), old pool (Isa. 22:11), King's

pool at Jerusalem (Neh. 2:14), pool of Bethesda (John 5:2,4,7), and pool of Siloam (John 9:7,11). Solomon also made pools to water his nursery (Eccl. 2:6). Most pools near the cities were carved from stone, fed by rainwater channeled into them by channels cut in the rock. Pools were natural meeting places (John 9:7). Pools illustrate God's power to transform the barren into something fruitful (Isa. 41:18), judgment (Isa. 42:15), and the beauty of a woman's eyes (Song of Sol. 7:4). See *Cistern.*

POOR IN SPIRIT

Those who have a humble spirit and thus depend on God (Matt. 5:3; compare Jas. 2:5). Luke's parallel speaks simply of the poor (Luke 6:20).

POOR, ORPHAN, WIDOW

Three groups of people of lower social classes in need of legal protection from the rich and powerful who sometimes abused them (Job 24:3-4). They had been wrongfully oppressed and impoverished (Job 24:14; 29:12; Ps. 10:9; Isa. 3:14); begged for food (Deut. 15:7-11; Job 31:16-21); had no economic or social status (2 Sam. 12:1-4; Prov. 14:20; Eccl. 9:13-18). Ideally, there should be no poor people among the covenant people of God because of the blessings of God and the generosity of the people toward those in need (Deut. 15:7-11). To provide for the poor, God allowed them to glean the remains of the fields and vineyards and harvest the corners (Lev. 19:10; 23:22). The courts were to see that the poor received just, not favorable or unfavorable, treatment (Ex. 23:3,6-7).

God is the refuge and deliverer of the poor (Pss. 12:5; 14:6; 70:5), who are identified as righteous (Ps. 14:5-6). The destruction of Judah and Israel came in part because of their oppression of the poor (Amos 2:6-8; 4:1-3; 5:10-13; 8:4-6; compare Ezek. 16:46-50).

Jesus, a poor man, was particularly concerned to give the poor good news (Matt. 11:5; Luke 4:18). He encouraged generosity toward the poor (Luke 14:13-24). The first Christians provided for the needs of poor widows (Acts 6:1-6; compare 1 Tim. 5:3-16), and Paul exerted great effort to collect funds for the poor in Jerusalem (Rom. 15:26; compare Jas. 2:1-6).

The orphan was a fatherless child (the mother could still be alive), while the widow was husbandless. Biblical (and nonbiblical) legal codes provide for the protection of the rights of the orphan and the widow (Ex. 22:22; Deut. 10:18; 24:17-22; compare Isa. 1:17; Jer. 5:28; Mic. 2:9; Mal. 3:5). God declared He would be a Father to the fatherless and provide justice for the widow (Deut. 10:18; Ps. 68:5). Jesus condemned the Pharisees for devouring widows' houses (Matt. 23:40). The NT measures true religious character by a person's care for the orphan and the widow (Jas. 1:27).

POPLAR See *Plants*.

PORCH

In English, a covered entrance to a building, usually having a separate roof; vast majority of OT references concern the "porch" of the Jerusalem temple (1 Kings 6:3,12,19), reflecting a view of a two-room temple with an attached porch. "Vestibule" (REB; NRSV) reflects a view of a three-room temple. "Porch" (Matt. 26:71; Mark 14:68) can refer to a gateway or forecourt. "Porches" (John 5:2; Acts 3:11) were likely freestanding porticoes or colonnades. See *Arch*.

POTIPHAR (*belonging to the sun*)

Egyptian captain of the guard who purchased Joseph from Midianite traders (Gen. 37:36; 39:1) and appointed him steward over his household. Potiphar had Joseph thrown in prison after his wife's false accusations.

POTIPHERAH

Priest in the Egyptian city of On (Heliopolis) where sun god Re was worshiped. Joseph married his daughter, Asenath, at pharaoh's command (Gen 41:45).

POTTERY

Everyday household utensils whose remains form the basis for modern dating of ancient archaeological remains. The Bible's few statements about preparation of clay, "the potter treads clay" (Isa. 41:25), and the potter's failure and success on the wheel (Jer. 18:3-4) hardly hint at the importance and abundance in antiquity of "earthen vessels" (Lev. 6:21; Num. 5:17; Jer. 32:14), the common collective term for pottery. The work of the potter in shaping the worthless clay provided the imagery the biblical writers and prophets used in describing God's creative relationship to human beings (Job 10:8-9; Isa. 45:9).

The pottery sherds (Job 2:8) have become the key to establishing a firmer chronological framework for other cultural data beginning in Neolithic period before 5000 B.C. when pottery first appeared. See *Archaeology; Vessels and Utensils*.

The Bible specifically identifies only two vessels as pottery: earthen pitchers (Lam. 4:2) and earthen bottles (Jer. 19:1), but many others certainly were.

Clay for the production of pottery may be divided into two types: pure aluminum silicate ("clean" clay) not found in Israel, and aluminum silicate mixed with iron oxides, carbon compounds, and other ingredients (sometimes referred to as "rich" clay). The potter prepared the dry clay by sifting and removing foreign matter, and letting it stand in water to achieve uniform granules. Having achieved the desired texture, the potter mixed it by treading on it or hand-kneading it. Then the potter was ready to shape the vessel. See *Containers and Vessels*.

Each culture produced its own distinctive, durable pottery. That distinctiveness has enabled archaeologists to trace each culture's "fingerprints" through time. The archaeologist can describe the movement of a race from one place to another, the influence of new people in a particular region or area, and the commercial activity of the people.

POWER

Ability to act or produce an effect; possession of authority over others. Because God has revealed His power in creation, He has authority to assign dominion to whomever He wills (Jer. 10:12; 27:5). God revealed His power by miraculously delivering Israel from Egyptian slavery (Ex. 4:21; 9:16; 15:6; 32:11) and in the conquest of Canaan (Ps. 111:6). God's power includes not only the power to judge but also the power to forgive sin (Num. 14:15-19; Jer. 32:17-18). Second Kings 3:15 links the onrush of the power of God with prophecy. Here power approximates God's Spirit (compare Mic. 3:8; Luke 1:35).

Christ's miracles evidenced the power of God at work in His ministry (Matt. 14:2; Mark 5:30; 9:1; Luke 4:36; 5:17). Luke highlighted the role of the Holy Spirit in empowering the ministry of Jesus (Luke 4:14; Acts 10:38) and the ongoing ministry of the church (Acts 1:8; 3:12; 4:7,33; 6:8). Paul stressed the paradox that the cross — what is apparently Jesus' greatest moment of weakness — is the event in which God's power to save is realized (1 Cor. 1:17-18; compare Rom. 1:16). This scandal of God's power revealed in Christ's death continues in God's choice to work through the powerless (1 Cor. 1:26-29; 2:3-4; 2 Cor. 12:9). In some texts, "powers" refers to angelic powers (Rom. 8:38; Eph. 3:10; Col. 2:15; 1 Pet. 3:22).

PRAETORIAN GUARD

Roman imperial bodyguard or troops assigned to a Roman provincial governor (Phil. 1:13 NASB; RSV). In Gospels and Acts the term refers to the palace of a provincial governor. See *Praetorium.*

PRAETORIUM

Barracks where Jesus was taken and mocked by the soldiers before His crucifixion (Mark 15:16); either next to Herod's palace or beside the temple complex; apparently the official residence of the Roman governor. Herod's praetorium in Caesarea

(Acts 23:35 NASB, RSV) served as the residence of the Roman govenor Felix. Paul's confidence that his imprisonment had publicized the Christian cause "in the whole praetorium" (Phil. 1:13) can refer to the whole palace (KJV; NASB and RSV margins) or to the praetorian guard. See *Praetorian Guard.*

PRAISE

Proclaim God's merit or worth; one of humanity's many responses to God's revelation of Himself; men and women may also be the objects of praise, either from other people (Prov. 27:21; 31:30) or from God Himself (Rom. 2:29); angels and the natural world are likewise capable of praising God (Ps. 148).

The modes of praise include offering sacrifices (Lev. 7:13), physical movement (2 Sam. 6:14), silence and meditation (Ps. 77:11-12), testimony (Ps. 66:16), prayer (Phil. 4:6), and a holy life (1 Pet. 1:3-9). Praise is almost invariably linked to music, both instrumental (Ps. 150:3-5) and, especially, vocal. Biblical songs of praise range from personal, more-or-less spontaneous outbursts of thanksgiving for some redemptive act of God (Ex. 15; Judg. 5; 1 Sam. 2; Luke 1:46-55,67-79) to formal psalms and hymns adapted for corporate worship in the temple (2 Chron. 29:30) and church (Col. 3:16).

Praise is to originate in the heart and not become mere outward show (Matt. 15:8). Corporate praise is to be carried on in an orderly manner (1 Cor. 14:40). Praise is also firmly linked to an individual's everyday life (Amos 5:21-24). See *Music; Psalms; Worship.*

PRAYER

Dialogue between God and people, especially His covenant partners. Such dialogue involves cries for help (Ex. 3:7; Judg. 3:9,15; 6:6; 10:10); conversation about God's will (Ex. 3:1–4:17); intercesion (Ex. 32:11-13; Num. 11:11-15; 1 Tim. 2:1; Eph. 1:16; 5:4); sin in the community (Josh. 7:6-9); confession of sin (2 Sam. 12:13;

PREACHING 502

Ps. 51); requests for wisdom (1 Kings 3:5-9); dedication of the temple (1 Kings 8); need for miracles (1 Kings 17:19-22; 18:20-40); reservation and frustration (Jer. 1; 20:7-18). Genuine prayer calls for accompanying moral and social accountability (Hos. 7:14; Amos 4:4-5). Isaiah's call reflected the intense cleansing and commitment involved in prayer (Isa. 6), teaching honesty in prayer. The Psalms teach variety and honesty in prayer are permissible; they proclaim praise, ask pardon, seek such things as communion (63), protection (57), vindication (107), and healing (6). Psalm 86 provides an excellent pattern for prayer. Daily patterned prayer becomes very important to exiles denied access to the temple (Dan. 6:10).

Jesus prayed in crucial moments, including the disciples' appointment (Mark 3:13), their mission (6:30-32), and the transfiguration (9:2). Jesus displayed a regular and intense prayer life (Matt. 6:5; 14:23; Mark 1:35) guided by the Holy Spirit (Luke 3:22; 4:1,14,18; 10:21; Acts 10:38; compare Acts 1:14). Jesus sometimes prayed aloud for benefit of those present (John 11:41-42). Jesus interceded for the first disciples and future believers (John 17). Both prayers display Jesus' unity with the Father and desire to give Him glory (John 11:4; 17:1). See *Lord's Prayer.*

Jesus corrected some abuses and misunderstandings regarding prayer.

(1) Prayer is not to be offered to impress others (Matt. 6:5-6).

(2) Prayer does not involve long-winded attempts to manipulate God.

Jesus' teaching on persistence in prayer is linked to the inbreaking kingdom (Luke 11:5-28; 18:1-8). Children of the kingdom will have their requests heard (Matt. 6:8; 7:7-11; 21:22; John 14:13; 15:7,16; 16:23; compare 1 John 3:22; 5:14; Jas. 1:5), particularly believers gathered in Jesus' name (Matt. 18:19). Prayer in Jesus' name is prayer seeking His will and submitting to His authority (John 14:13; 1 John 5:14).

The early church prayed regarding selection of leaders (Acts 1:24; 6:6; 13:3), during persecution (Acts 4:24-30; 12:5,12), and in preparing to heal (Acts 9:40; 28:8).

The indwelling Spirit enables a believer with the confidence of a child to call God "Abba" (Rom. 8:14-15). Apart from the Spirit, Christians pray without discernment. He takes up our petitions with an earnest pleading beyond words (Rom. 8:26-27; Gal. 4:6).

Not every petition is granted. Job's demand for answers from God was eclipsed by the awesome privilege of encountering Him (Job 38-41). Jesus prayed three times that His cup of suffering might pass, but He was nevertheless submissive to God's will (Matt. 26:38-39,42,45). Paul asked three times for deliverance from his "thorn in the flesh."

Faith is a condition for answered petitions (Mark 11:24). Believers do not receive what they pray for because they pray from selfish motives (Jas. 4:2-3). Prayers are also hindered by corrupted character (Jas. 4:7) or injured relationships (Matt. 5:23-24). Prayer makes a difference in what happens (Jas. 4:2). Prayer will lead to a greater communion with God and a greater understanding of His will.

PREACHING

Human presentation through the Holy Spirit's power of God's acts of salvation through Jesus Christ. True Christian preaching interprets the meaning of God's acts into contemporary contexts.

The prophets heralded God's direct messages against the sins of the people, told of coming judgments, and held out future hope of the great Day of the Lord. During periods of special revival, natural leaders traveled about sharing the revelation in great assemblies (2 Chron. 15:1-2; 17:7-9; 35:3). Ezra and his associates interpreted the "sense" of what was read in such gatherings (Neh. 8:7-9). After the exile, explaining the Scriptures became a regular part of local synagogue worship.

Jesus announced He was the Herald who fulfilled Isaiah's prophecy concerning the preaching of the kingdom and its blessings (Luke 4:16-21). Peter and the other apostles focused on the life, character, death, burial, resurrection, and coming again of Christ. They practiced both *gospel preaching* ("proclaiming salvation in Christ") and *pastoral teaching* ("instructing, admonishing, and exhorting believers in doctrine and lifestyle"; 1 Cor. 15:1-7). Stephen's address (Acts 7:1-53) represents the best of the OT tradition, weaving narrative and historical portions of Scripture together with contemporary interpretation and application to the present situation. Peter's sermon (Acts 2) affirms the atoning nature of Jesus' death and the reality of His resurrection together with a clear call to faith and repentance.

Preaching Christ warns men and women of the need for salvation and helps believers grow towards spiritual maturity (Col. 1:28; compare Acts 20:17-21; Eph. 4:11-16). Paul refused to adopt some of the cunning word craftiness of the secular rhetoricians of his day (2 Cor. 4:2; 1 Thess. 2:3,5); nevertheless, he adapted his preaching well to a variety of audiences and needs (Acts 13:16-41; 17:22-31; 26:2-23).

PRECIOUS STONES See *Minerals and Metals; Jewels, Jewelry.*

PREDESTINATION

God's purposes in grace directed toward those whom He will ultimately save to the uttermost.

The word *predestine* as a verb with God as its subject is used six times in the NT (Acts 4:28; Rom. 8:29,30; 1 Cor. 2:7; Eph. 1:5,11). The Greek word means essentially "to decide upon beforehand."

In both Rom. 8 and Eph. 1 Paul makes strong claims about the priority of God's grace in salvation. "For those He foreknew He also predestined to be conformed to the image of His Son, so that He would be the firstborn among many brothers" (Rom. 8:29 HCSB). To make clear just how this predestination fits into God's overall plan of salvation, Paul then lists a sort of "chain of grace": "And those He predestined, He also called; and those He called, He also justified; and those He justified, He also glorified" (v. 30). In each link in the chain, God is the one acting, and persons are the objects of the action. There is no possibility that someone initially predestined would fail to be finally glorified. In this Paul is in full agreement with Jesus, who in John 6:37-40 makes clear that all of the ones given to Him by the Father (predestination) will believe on Him and will finally be raised up on the last day (glorification). None will fail to be saved to the uttermost.

In Eph. 1:3-6,11 Paul takes up the issue of predestination again. God chose "us" for adoption in love, not when we believed but before the foundation of the world. He chose us not because of something good He saw in us but "according to His favor and will" and "according to the purpose of the One who works out everything in agreement with the decision of His will." God's goals in choosing us was for us "to be holy and blameless in His sight" and to demonstrate "His glorious grace" (v. 6).

In 1 Cor. 2:7 Paul tells his readers that God has predestined Christ and His atoning work as the only hope for salvation. In Acts 4:27-28 the Jerusalem church acknowledged in prayer that Herod, Pontius Pilate, the rest of the Gentiles, and the people of Israel had done to God's anointed Servant Jesus "whatever Your hand and Your plan had predestined to take place" (HCSB). These believers are affirming that wicked men were used by God to carry out His plan of salvation.

God's plans will always be fulfilled (Ps. 33:10-11; Job 9:12; Dan. 4:35). He is in control of all of history so that even minor details are part of His work (Prov. 21:1; 16:1,9,33). Nothing can prevent the fulfillment of His predictions (Isa. 14:24-27; 44:24-45; Prov. 19:21).

Along with these passages that emphasize God's priority in grace, there are many texts that affirm the importance of repentance and faith (Rom. 10:9-14; Acts 2:38), and the need of the sinner to "come" to Christ (Rev. 22:17). Paul says that Christians are predestined by God, and yet he urges, "If you confess with your mouth, 'Jesus is Lord,' and believe in your heart that God raised Him from the dead, you will be saved" because "everyone who calls on the name of the Lord will be saved" (Rom. 10:9-13 HCSB). Paul, who wrote that we are predestined according to the good pleasure of God's will, a few sentences later noted, "For by grace you are saved through faith, and this is not from yourselves; it is God's gift" (Eph. 2:8). For Jesus and Paul the two ideas are complementary, not contradictory (cp. John 10:25-30). It is the church's task to testify to the truth and believe that the Lord will open the hearts of unbelievers (Acts 16:14), so that as those who heard Paul and Barnabas, "all who had been appointed to eternal life believed" (Acts 13:48).

Though Christians today may not be able to understand how all of that works, they can affirm it as true, and they certainly must obey the call of God to the work of ministry. See *Election; Foreknowledge.*

PREEXILIC

Period in Israel's history, before the exile began in Babylon in 586 B.C. See *Israel, History of.*

PREEXISTENCE OF SOULS

Heretical doctrine that souls exist prior to being joined to a body. Disdain for the material body as evil or disregard for the body as inferior to the soul are common corollaries of this doctrine. Scripture affirms the material body as the good creation of God. One does not become a living "soul" apart from the material body (Gen. 2:7; 1 Cor. 15:45). Paul hoped to be clothed in a spiritual body (2 Cor. 5:41; 1 Cor. 15:44).

The consensus of the early church as evidenced by the Apostle's Creed is that the Christian hope is the resurrection of the body, not the inherent immortality of souls. See *Immortality; Resurrection; Soul.*

PREMARITAL SEX

Engaging in sexual intercourse prior to marriage to the sexual partner. The Song of Solomon is an extended poem extolling the virtue of sexuality fidelity between a king and his chosen bride. Sexual desire runs strong throughout the song as the king and his beloved anticipate their union together. At intervals, the poet repeats a refrain counseling sexual restraint: "I adjure you, O daughters of Jerusalem by the gazelles or the hinds of the field that you stir not up nor awaken love until it please" (Song of Sol. 2:7; 3:5; 8:4). To the church in Corinth, a city well known for profligate sexual activity, Paul wrote that Christians must control their sexual desires and that those who cannot do so ought to marry (1 Cor. 7:2, 8-9, 36-37). Paul counseled Timothy to flee youthful passions and pursue instead things that make for pure living (2 Tim. 2:22). Although the temptation to gratify one's passions can be strong, Paul taught that God promises strength to overcome greater than the temptation (1 Cor. 10:12-13).

God chose the marriage relationship as a means to express to people the intimacy He shares with believers (Hos. 1-3; 2 Cor. 11:2; Rev. 21:2). Anything that cheapens or lessens the union of a husband and wife in marriage, such as pre- or extra-marital sex, also tarnishes God's relationship with His people.

PREPARATION DAY

Sixth day of week (6 p.m. on Thursday until beginning of sabbath at 6 p.m. Friday) in which Jews prepared life's necessities to avoid work on the sabbath (compare Ex. 20:8-11; Matt. 12:1-14; John 9:14-16). Preparation of food, completing work, and spiritual purification were included.

The Feast of Passover was immediately followed by the holy convocation of the Feast of Unleavened Bread (Lev. 23:1-7). No one worked on either of these holy days, so a day of preparation was set aside to prepare for the holiday period (John 19:14). John explicitly identified the day of preparation as the day of Jesus' execution (John 19:14,31,42) and placed the Last Supper before Passover (John 13:1). The Synoptic Gospels, however, dated the Last Supper on the day of Passover (Matt. 26: 17; Mark 14:12; Luke 22:7). This apparent contradiction in dating may depend on whether the gospel writers were referring to the preparation day for the sabbath or to the preparation day for the Passover.

PRESBYTER   See *Elder.*

PRESENCE OF GOD

God's initiative in encountering people. During the patriarchal period, God used a variety of means of revelation to communicate with the people (Gen. 15:1; 32:24-30). Moses encountered God in the burning bush and knew God "face to face" (Deut. 34:10). The tabernacle was the place of the Lord's name or glory, a manifestation of God's presence and activity in the world (Ex. 40:34,38). The cloud and fire symbolized the presence of God leading on the journey to Canaan (Ex. 13:21-22).

The ark of the covenant led the people in the journey to Canaan and into battle (Josh. 3:1-6). The ark eventually came to rest in the temple, the place of the presence of God. Here Isaiah had a powerful vision of the holy God (Isa. 6).

God also manifested Himself in fire (1 Kings 18) and in a still small voice (1 Kings 19). Psalms speak of God's presence with the worshiping community (Ps. 139) and of the apparent absence of this present God (Ps. 13). In either case, God is still addressed. Ezekiel spoke of the exile in terms of the glory (presence) of

God leaving ancient Israel but then returning at the end of the exile in Babylon (Ezek. 43:1-5). God is utterly free to be where He wills but constantly chooses to be with His people to give them life.

Jesus Christ is Emmanuel, "God with us" (Matt. 1:23; John 1:14; Heb. 1:1-3). This presence did not end with the death of Christ. The risen Christ appeared to the disciples (John 21:1-14) and to Paul. Through the apostles, Paul, and the disciples, Christ's work continued (Acts 1:8; 26:12-18). The Holy Spirit is an important manifestation of the presence of God and continues the redemptive work of God. The return of Christ will bring permanence to the presence of God with His people. The church is called to be a manifestation of God's presence. That community is fed by the presence of God found in communion between worshiper and God.

PRIDE

Undue confidence in and attention to one's own skills, accomplishments, state, possessions, or position opposite of humility. Pride is rebellion against God because it attributes to self the honor and glory due to God alone. Proud persons do not think it necessary to ask forgiveness because they do not admit their sinful condition. This attitude toward God finds expression in one's attitude toward others, often causing people to have a low estimate of the ability and worth of others and therefore to treat them with either contempt or cruelty. Some have considered pride to be the root and essence of sin. Others consider it to be sin in its final form. In either case, it is a grievous sin.

"Boasting" (1 John 2:16; Jas. 4:16) and "haughtiness" or "arrogance" measure self as above others (Mark 7:23; Luke 1:51; Rom. 1:30; 2 Tim. 3:2; Jas. 4:6; 1 Pet. 5:5).

Jesus denounced pride of race (Luke 3:8). The parable of the Pharisee and the publican was directed at those guilty of spiritual pride, the ones who "trusted in themselves that they were righteous, and despised others" (Luke 18:9). James 1:10 warns the rich against the temptation to be lifted up with pride because of their wealth.

PRIESTHOOD OF CHRIST

Christ's work in offering Himself as the supreme sacrifice for the sins of humankind and interceding on their behalf. See Heb. 4:14-15. This priesthood of Christ is "after the order of Melchizedek" (Heb. 5:6), which means that God appointed Him directly and Jesus did not have to trace His priesthood through the human line of Aaron or Levi. See *Atonement; Christ; Jesus; High Priest.*

PRIESTHOOD OF THE BELIEVER

Christian belief that every person has direct access to God without any mediator other than Christ; believers can respond directly to the personal activity of God in their lives, through the Holy Spirit and through the written word of Scripture. Christians have become a "holy priesthood" (1 Pet. 2:5) and can minister to one another and to the world. No longer does a professional priesthood have an exclusive channel for holy communication. Any believer can be the channel of God's Spirit and mediate the grace of God in prayer, confession, or witness in particular situations. The role of Christ as our only priest means He is the only Mediator between God and the believer (1 Tim. 2:5). Christ's "once for all" sacrifice fulfilled the promise and purpose of the OT priesthood. The priests of the old covenant offered the sacrifice of animals on the altar. Christ, as High Priest, offered His own life on the altar of the cross. Followers of Christ are called on to offer their very bodies as a living sacrifice, a day-by-day commitment and service to God, as the truest form of worship (Rom. 12:1).

PRIESTS

Personnel in charge of sacrifice and offering at worship places, particularly the tabernacle and temple. Priesthood in the OT primarily involved sacrificing at the altar and worship in the shrine. Other functions were blessing the people (Num. 6:22-26), determining the will of God (Ex. 28:30), and instructing the people in the law of God (Deut. 31:9-12). This instruction included the application of the laws of cleanness (Lev. 11-15). Some of these functions, like blessing and teaching, would not be reserved for priests alone, but sacrificing and the use of the Urim and Thummim were theirs exclusively. See *Urim and Thummim.*

Abel, Noah, and Abraham were family priests. Jethro, the priest of Midian, brought sacrifices to God and worshiped with Moses, Aaron, and the elders of Israel (Ex. 18:12). God promised that Israel, if it were faithful, would be a "kingdom of priests, a holy nation" (Ex. 19:6). This may have meant that Israel was called to mediate God's word and work to the world—to be a light to the nations (Isa. 42:6).

On Mount Sinai, God told Moses to appoint Aaron and his four sons to serve as priests, that is, to serve at the altar and in the sanctuary (Ex. 28:1,41). Members of the tribe of Levi not related to Aaron assisted the priests but did not offer sacrifices. Priests were supported by offerings and Levites by tithes (Num. 18:20-24). See *Levites; High Priest; Aaron.*

PRINCE

A ruler; one of noble birth and high position; not just the limited sense of a male heir of a sovereign. (Compare Zeph. 1:8.) KJV used "prince" as a title for Israel's king (1 Sam. 13:14), a leading priest (1 Chron. 12:27), a Midianite tribal chief (Num. 25:18), the leading men of a city or province (Gen. 34:2; 1 Kings 20:15; Jer. 34:19), and for rulers in general (Matt. 20:25; 1 Cor. 2:6,8). By extension, *prince* applies to supernatural beings. "Prince of Peace" (Isa. 9:6), "Prince of life" (Acts 3:15), and "Prince and a Savior" (Acts 5:31) are messianic titles. Daniel 8:25 refers to God as "Prince of princes." Daniel 12:1 gives Michael, the angelic advocate of

Israel, the title "prince." Satan is often described as "the prince of this world" (John 12:31; 14:30; 16:11; compare Matt. 9:34; 12:24; Eph. 2:2).

PRINCIPALITIES

Supernatural spiritual powers, whether good or evil; created by and thus subject to Christ (Col. 1:16). Neither principalities nor any other force can separate a believer from God's love found in Christ (Rom. 8:38).

PRISON, PRISONERS

Any place where persons accused and/or convicted of criminal activity are confined and persons so confined or those captured in war. Imprisonment as a legal punishment is not a feature of ancient law codes. The Mosaic law allowed for a place of custody until the case was decided (Lev. 24:12; Num. 15:34). Only in the Persian period does the Bible mention incarceration as a penalty for breaking the religious law (Ezra 7:26). The Bible gives many examples of political prisoners (Gen. 39:20; 40:3; 2 Chron. 16:10; 1 Kings 22:26-27). The royal prison in which Jeremiah was initially placed was a converted private house (Jer. 37:15). He was confined to an underground dungeon (Jer. 37:16), perhaps a converted cistern, and later in the "court of the guard" (Jer. 37:20-21). There he was available for consultation with the king (Jer. 38:14,28), able to conduct business (Jer. 32:2-3,6-12), and able to speak freely (Jer. 38:1-4).

Prophets were jailed for denouncing royal policy (2 Chron. 16:10), predicting ill of the king (1 Kings 22:26-27), and suspected collaboration with the enemy (Jer. 37:11-15). Political prisoners in Assyrian and Babylonian prisons included former kings of rebellious nations (2 Kings 17:4; 24:15; 25:27; Jer. 52:11). Samson became a prisoner in a Philistine prison (Judg. 16:21). Prisoners of war were usually either killed or enslaved.

Prisoners endured meager rations (1 Kings 22:27) and hard labor (Judg. 16:21). In some cases, prisoners were restrained and tortured by the stocks or collar (2 Chron. 16:10; Jer. 29:26). Prison life became a symbol of oppression and suffering (Ps. 79:11). Release from prison provided a picture of restoration or salvation (Pss. 102:20; 142:7; 146:7; Isa. 61:1; Zech. 9:11-12).

In NT times, persons could be imprisoned for nonpayment of debt (Matt. 5:25-26; Luke 12:58-59), criticizing the king (Luke 3:19-20), political insurrection and criminal acts (Luke 23:19,25), as well as for certain religious practices (Luke 21:12; Acts 5:18-19; 8:3). Peter was held under heavy security, consisting of chains, multiple guards, and iron doors (Acts 12:5-11; compare 16:23-24).

Paul, who imprisoned others (Acts 8:3; 22:4; 26:10), was often in prison himself (Acts 23:16-18,35; 24:23; 2 Cor. 11:23). While awaiting trial in Rome, Paul remained under constant guard in a kind of house arrest (28:16-17,30), met his own expenses, and was free to receive visitors and preach the gospel "openly and unhindered" (28:30). Paul considered his imprisonment as for Christ (Eph. 3:1; 4:1; Phil. 1:13-14; Philem. 1,9).

Concern for prisoners is a virtue expected by Christ of every disciple (Matt. 25:36,39,43-44). It is Satan who will be imprisoned during the millennium (Rev. 20:1-3,7).

PRIVACY

The Bible recognizes the need for personal privacy (Prov. 25:17) while upholding the value of communal living (Acts 2:44-46; 4:32-35; Rom. 14:7-8). The Bible describes privacy as quiet, peaceful living, whether alone ("every man under his vine and under his fig tree" — 1 Kings 4:25; Mic. 4:4) or in community, like the residents of Laish who were "quiet and secure . . . far from the Zidonians and had no business with any man" (Judg. 18:7; see also 18:27-28). Heber the Kenite (Judg. 4:11) and the Israelite tribe of Simeon (1 Chron. 4:39-40) found quiet and peaceful lands in which to settle. Paul admonished the Thessalonian Christians to mind their own affairs (1 Thess. 4:10-11; compare 2 Thess. 3:12). He asked Timothy to pray fervently that persons in positions of authority would allow Christians to lead quiet and peaceable lives (1 Tim. 2:1-2).

Jacob (Gen. 32:23-24) and Jesus (Matt. 26:36) retreated into privacy before undertaking great personal struggles, as did Joshua on the eve of Israel's attack on Ai (Josh. 8:13). Jesus at times withdrew for rest and prayer (Matt. 14:13, 23; Mark 6:31). He said those who truly want to be heard by God should pray by themselves, in private (Matt. 6:6).

PROCLAMATION See *Preaching*.

PROCONSUL

Chief administrative officers for civil and military matters in a Roman province. Proconsuls were responsible to the senate in Rome. The NT refers to two proconsuls: Sergius Paulus in Cyprus (Acts 13:7) and Gallio in Achaia (Acts 18:12). Compare Acts 19:38. See *Rome*.

PROCURATOR

Roman military office with control over entire countries. The procurator could issue death warrants and have coins struck in his name. Three procurators are named in the NT: Pilate (Matt. 27:2; some question whether Pilate was a procurator), Felix (Acts 23:24), and Festus (Acts 24:27). See *Rome*.

PRODIGAL SON

Popular term for Jesus' parable in Luke 15:11-32 told in defense of Jesus' practice of fellowshipping with sinners (15:1). The parable focuses not on the reckless-then-repentant younger son but on the waiting father who rushes to welcome his child home and calls all, elder brother included, to share the joy of homecoming.

PRODUCT SAFETY

Ensuring that goods produced for public use do not contain compo-nents that have potential to injure users. The Bible records several instances of serious injury and even death due to products which broke at importune times. Ahaziah king of Israel was fatally injured when he fell through the lattice of a door or window in an upstairs room of his palace (2 Kings 1:2-4). When the Egyptian army pursued Israel through the Red Sea, their chariots bogged down in the mud so that the wheels came off (Ex. 14:25, NIV). Isaiah compared Egypt to a staff which would splinter and pierce the hand of the man leaning on it (Isa. 36:6).

The Mosaic law had stipulated that all new housing should include a parapet for the roof to prevent persons from falling off (Deut. 22:8), a situation different in detail from that which caused Ahaziah's accident but which nevertheless indicates a legal concern for safety in ancient Israel. The law provided recourse from revenge to a man whose ax head might break loose during use and cause the death of his co-worker (Deut. 19:5; 2 Kings 6:1-7).

PROMISE

God's announcement of His plan of salvation and blessing to His people, one of the unifying themes integrating the message and the deeds of the Old and New Testaments. God's promise covers God's future plan for all the nations of the earth and focuses on the gifts and deeds God will bestow on a few to benefit the many. The gifts include:

(1) He would be their God,

(2) they would be His people, and

(3) He would dwell in their midst.

In Gen. 1–11, the promise of God is represented by the successive "blessings" announced both in the creative order and on the human family—even in spite of their sin. The fathers of Israel (Abraham, Isaac, and Jacob) received a triple promise that included:

(1) the promise of a seed or off-spring (an heir; Gen. 12:7; 15:4; 17:16,19; 21:12; 22:16-18; 26:3-4,24; 28:13-14; 35:11-12; compare Heb. 6:14),

(2) the promise of land (an inheritance; Gen. 12:1,7; 13:17; 15:18; 17:8; 24:7; 26:3-5; 28:13,15; 35:12; 48:4; 50:24;)

(3) the promise of blessing on all the nations (Gen. 12:3; 18:18; 22:17-18; 26:4; 28:14).

God sealed the promise with Abraham in a rite in which only God passed between the pieces (Gen. 15:9-21) thus obligating Himself to fulfill His promises without simultaneously and similarly obligating Abraham and the subsequent beneficiaries of the promise. The promise was eternal. Abraham's descendants had to transmit the promise to subsequent generations until the final Seed, even Jesus the Messiah, came. God expected them to participate personally by faith. Where faith was present, already demands and commands were likewise present. Thus, Abraham obeyed God and left Ur (Gen. 12:1-4) and walked before God in a blameless way (Gen. 17:1; compare 26:5).

The law extended these demands to the entire life of the people with promises as their basis (Ex. 2:23-25; 6:2-8; 19:3-8; 20:2; compare Rom. 3:31). The monarchy received a distinctive role through God's promise (2 Sam. 7; compare Ps. 2:8; 110:1). The new covenant of Jer. 31:31-34 adds several new features. The new promise still contains the law of God, now internalized. It still pledges that God will be their God, and they will be His people. It still declares that He will forgive their sins and remember them no more. It adds that it will no longer be necessary to teach one's neighbor or brother; for everyone, no matter what their station in life, will know the Lord.

The NT compares God's promises of a son to Abraham to Jesus Christ (Rom. 4:13-16,20; 9:7-9; 15:8; Gal. 3:16-22; 4:23; Heb. 6:13-17; 7:6; 11:9,11,17). Promises of David's seed likewise relate to sending Jesus as "a Savior according to promise" (Acts 13:23, 32-33; 26:6; compare Gal. 3:22; 2 Tim. 1:1; Heb. 9:15; 1 John 2:25). The NT also picks up Joel's promise of the

Holy Spirit (2:28-31) and relates it to Pentecost (Luke 24:49; Acts 2:33,38-39).

Other subjects are related to God's promise: rest (Heb. 4:1); the new heavens and new earth (2 Pet. 3:13); the resurrection (Acts 26:6); the emergence of an unshakable kingdom (Heb. 12:28), and Gentiles as recipients of the same promise (Eph. 2:11-13).

PROPERTY See *Inheritance; Ownership.*

PROPHECY, PROPHETS

Reception and declaration of a word from the Lord through a direct prompting of the Holy Spirit and the human instrument thereof. Israel's earliest prophets included Moses (Deut. 34:10; Matt. 17:1-8; Acts 3:21-24); Miriam (Ex. 15:1-18); Deborah (Judg. 4:6-7,9,14); Samuel (1 Sam. 3:11-14, 20; 7:6,15; 12:18); Elijah and Elisha (1 Kings 17–2 Kings 9).

Israel's political turmoil provided the context for the writing prophets. The Assyrian rise to power after 750 B.C. furnished the focus of the ministries of Amos, Hosea, Isaiah, Micah, and Nahum. The Babylonian threat was the background and motive for much of the ministry of Jeremiah, Habakkuk, Zephaniah, Obadiah, and Ezekiel. The advent of the Persian Empire about 540 B.C. set the stage for Haggai, Zechariah, and Malachi. Thus the prophets spoke for God throughout Israel's history.

The prophets were locked up (Jer. 37), ignored (Isa. 6:9-13), and persecuted (1 Kings 19:1-2). They continued to serve Israel's institutions: speaking to judges and kings, criticizing vain worship (Amos 5:23-24) and priestly failures (Amos 7:10; Mal. 2), speaking in public worship (Pss. 50:5; 60:6; 81:6-10; 91:14-16; 95:8-11), and using the law to call to covenant faithfulness (Isa. 58:6-9; Ezek. 18; Mic. 6:6-8; Hos. 6:6; Amos 2:4; 5:21-24). Prophets formed guilds or schools (2 Kings 4:38; 1 Sam. 10:5; 19:20; compare Jer. 23:13-14). These schools or the prophet's friends or aides helped collect and preserve the books of prophecy (Isa. 8:16; Jer. 36:4).

Prophets generally shared several key experiences and characteristics.

(1) A call from God. Attempting to prophesy without such a commission was false prophecy (Jer. 14:14; see Isa. 6:1-7; 1 Kings 22:19-23; Jer. 23:18-22; compare Amos 3:7; Job 1:6-12; 2:1-6; 2 Cor. 12:1-4; Rev. 1:1-3; 22:18-19).

(2) A word from God. This came through many means—direct declarations, visions, dreams, or an appearance of God.

(3) Prophets were primarily spokespersons who called His people to obedience by appealing to Israel's past and future.

(4) Symbolic acts. These served as dramatic, living parables (Isa. 20:1-3; Ezek. 4:1-3; Jer. 19:10-11; Hos. 2:1-13).

(5) Miracles confirmed their message (Ex. 4:1-9; 1 Kings 17; 2 Kings 5; Isa. 38:8; compare Matt. 12:22-29).

(6) Writing God's Word (Isa. 8:1; Ezek. 43:11).

(7) Ministry to their people. Prophets were to test God's peoples' lives (Jer. 6:27) and be watchmen for moral compromise (Ezek. 3:17). They interceded in prayer—sometimes even for the prophet's enemy (1 Kings 13:6; 17:17-24; 2 Kings 4:18-37; Amos 7:2; Jer. 14:17-21; Isa. 59:16).

(8) Ecstatic experiences. These confirmed God's presence and empowered the prophet.

Distinguishing between false and true prophets was very difficult. The true prophet must be loyal to the biblical faith directing one to worship Yahweh alone (Deut. 13:1-3). The words of a true prophet were fulfilled in history (Deut. 18:22; Jer. 42:1-6; Ezek. 33:30-33); but often with long lapses between predictions and fulfillment (Mic. 3:12; Jer. 26:16-19). Some predictions were conditional—based on the hearer's response (Jonah 3:4-5). Furthermore, prophets could behave inappropriately (Num. 12:1-2; 20:1-12; Jer. 15:19-21; 38:24-27). Prophets appeared ambivalent at times when simply delivering the word of God as it was given (2 Kings

20:1-6). Accurate prediction was not a final test. One could predict correctly while not being loyal to Yahweh (Deut. 13:1-3). Other tests included agreement with previous prophets' words (Jer. 28:8), good character (Mic. 3:11), and a willingness to suffer because of faithfulness (1 Kings 22:27-28; Jer. 38:3-13). Similarly, the NT believers had to distinguish true prophecy (1 John 4:1; 1 Cor. 14:29; see Matt. 7:15-20). See *False Prophet*.

Many prophecies have an immediate application to their own situation and are also applicable to another context. Thus the prediction that Christ is born of a virgin (Matt. 1:23) also had a fulfillment in Isaiah's day (Isa. 8:3). Similarly, prophecies of "the day of the Lord" had several fulfillments (partial) that also foreshadowed a final fulfillment (Obad. 15; Joel 1:15; 2:1; Zeph. 1:7,14; Ezek. 30:3; compare 2 Pet. 3:10).

Predictive prophecies can be understood in several ways.

(1) Some prophecies seem to have a direct, literal fulfillment: the Messiah was to be born in Bethlehem (Matt. 2:5-6; Mic. 5:2).

(2) Not all predictions were fulfilled literally. Elijah's return was fulfilled by John the Baptist and not a literal Elijah (Matt. 11:13-15; Mal. 3:1-4). Paul applied prophecies about literal, national Israel to the church (Rom. 9:25-26; Hos. 1:9-10; 2:23). This distinctively Christian reading was thought to be legitimate because of Christ's fulfillment and interpretation of the OT (Luke 4:17-21).

(3) Typological interpretation shows how OT events, persons, or things foreshadowed the later Christian story. Christ can be compared to Adam (1 Cor. 15:22-23; see 10:11). Old Testament expressions may have a divine significance, unforeseen by the OT author, which comes to light only after God's later word or deed. See *Typology*.

The prophets played a foundational role in the early church (1 Cor. 12:28-31; Eph. 4:11; 2:20). The angel's visitation and prediction (Luke 1:11,26-27) provoked Mary and Zecharias to prophesy (1:46-67, 67-79; compare 2:10-12,25, 36-38).

John the Baptist predicted that Jesus would baptize in the Spirit (Matt. 3:11).

Jesus called Himself a prophet (Luke 13:33). His miracles and discernment were prophetic (John 4:19). He taught not by citing expert rabbis, but with His own prophetic authority (Mark 1:22; Luke 4:24). The early believers saw the outpouring of the Spirit (Acts 2:17) as a fulfillment of Joel's prediction that all God's people, young and old, male and female, would prophesy. While any Christian might occasionally receive a prophecy, some seem to have a special gift of prophecy (1 Cor. 12:29; 13:2). Prophets function primarily in the worship of the church (Acts 13:2). They predict (Acts 11:28; 20:23; 27:22-26), announce judgments (Acts 13:11; 28:25-28), act symbolically (Acts 21:10-11), and receive visions (Acts 9:10-11; 2 Cor. 12:1). Prophetic insights led to missionary efforts (Acts 13:1-3; 10:10-17; 15:28,32). Teaching and prophecy can be related (Acts 13:1-2; Rev. 2:20). Some prophets "preached" lengthy messages (Acts 15:32) and gave exposition to biblical texts (Luke 1:67-79; Eph. 3:5; Rom. 11:25-36).

New Testament prophecy was limited (1 Cor. 11:5-7; 13:9); it was to be evaluated by the congregation (1 Cor. 14:26-40; 1 Thess. 5:20-21). One may even respond inappropriately to prophecy (Acts 21:12). The supreme test for prophecy is loyalty to Christ (1 Cor. 12:3; Rev. 19:10). Some Christians have the gift of discernment (1 Cor. 12:10). Prophecy is not a threat to Scripture's special authority (1 Cor. 14:38-39; 2 Tim. 3:16; 2 Pet. 1:20-21).

PROPHETESS

(1) Female prophet, including: Miriam (Ex. 15:20); Deborah (Judg. 4:4); Huldah (2 Kings 22:14); Noadiah, a "false" prophetess (Neh. 6:14); and Anna (Luke 2:36). Jezebel claimed to be a prophetess (Rev. 2:20). The ministries of prophetesses varied greatly. Miriam called on Israel to celebrate God's deliverance. Deborah com-

bined the offices of prophetess and judge, even accompanying Barak into battle. Huldah spoke God's words of judgment (2 Kings 22:16-17) and forgiveness (22:18-20). Anna shared the good news of Jesus' birth with the temple crowds. See Joel 2:28-29; Acts 2:17-18; 21:9; 1 Cor. 14:1,5. First Corinthians 11:5 presumes women were involved in prophesying and prayer in public worship.

(2) The wife of a prophet (Isa. 8:3). See Prophecy, Prophets.

PROPITIATION See Expiation.

PROSELYTES

Converts to a religion; non-Jews who accepted the Jewish faith and completed the rituals to become Jews. The NT attests to the zeal of the first-century Pharisees in proselytizing Gentiles (Matt. 23:15). The success of the Jewish missionary efforts is indicated by synagogue and grave inscriptions referring to proselytes and by Roman and Jewish literary references. Gentiles were impressed by three features of Judaism: concept of one God; lifestyle of moral responsibility; religion of ancient and stable tradition.

Persons attracted to Judaism and keeping the sabbath and food laws were termed fearers or worshipers of God (Acts 10:1-2; 16:14; compare John 12:20; Acts 17:4; 18:4). Many God fearers went on to become proselytes or fully accepted and integrated members of the Jewish community through circumcision (males) (see Gal. 5:3), baptism (males and females) that made one ritually clean, and an offering (males and females) in the Jerusalem temple that atoned for sin.

PROSTITUTION

Trading of sexual services for pay. Hosea criticized the attitude that called for the punishment of prostitutes (and women committing adultery), while tolerating the men with whom these acts were committed (Hos 4:14; compare Prov. 23:27-28;

29:3). The prostitute was tolerated in ancient Israel—as long as she was not married—but her profession was not socially acceptable. The children of harlots suffered from social biases against them (Judg. 11:2). The Holiness Code prohibited Israelite fathers from turning their daughters into prostitutes (Lev. 19:29).

Jesus told religious leaders that harlots would go into the kingdom before they would (Matt. 21:31). Harlots did not have the self-righteousness that kept the religious leaders from repentance. Believers' bodies are the temple of the Holy Spirit; therefore, they should refrain from immorality, including sexual relations with prostitutes (1 Cor. 6:15-20).

The term "cult prostitution" is frequently used to refer to certain practices in Canaanite fertility cults, including the cult of Baal. See *Fertility Cult.* Cult prostitution is outlawed by the Deuteronomic law code (Deut. 23:17-18).

The presence of both "secular" and "cult prostitutes" provided the prophets with a powerful metaphor for the unfaithfulness of the people toward God (Ezek. 16; compare ch. 23; Hos 1:2; Rev. 17:1-6).

PROVERBS, BOOK OF

Book of Hebrew wisdom among Writings in Hebrew Bible; provides a godly worldview. Proverbs 1:7 provides the perspective for understanding all the proverbs: "The fear of the Lord is the beginning of knowledge; but fools despise wisdom and instruction." The phrase "fear of the Lord" is biblical shorthand for an entire life in love, worship, and obedience to God.

The title of Proverbs (1:1) seems to ascribe the entire book to Solomon. Closer inspection reveals that the book is composed of parts formed over several hundred years as titles introducing the book's major subcollections show (1:1; 10:1; 22:17; 24:23; 25:1; 30:1; 31:1). Chapters 25–29 were edited in the court of Hezekiah (25:1), about 700 B.C. The process of compilation probably extended into the postexilic period.

The Book of Proverbs uses a variety of wisdom forms or genres. Different sections of the book utilize characteristic forms. Long wisdom poems, which scholars call "Instructions" after their Egyptian counterpart, dominate 1:8–9:18. These usually begin with a direct address to "son/children" and contain imperatives or prohibitions, motive clauses (reasons for actions), and sometimes narrative development (7:6-23) or public speeches by personified Wisdom (1:20-33; 8:1-36; 9:1-6). The setting of these instructions may be a school for young aristocrats.

Brief "sayings" that express wise insights about reality are the primary forms in 10:1–22:16 and 25:1–29:27. In Hebrew they usually have two lines with only six to eight words. These sayings may simply "tell it like it is," and let readers draw their own conclusions (11:24; 17:27-28; 18:16). They can also make clear value judgments (10:17; 14:31; 15:33; 19:17). "Antithetical sayings" which contrast opposites appear in 10:1–15:33. Mixed in are a few "better than" sayings (12:9; 15:17; compare 16:8,19; 17:1; 19:1; 21:9; 25:24; 27:5,10b; 28:6). The section 25:1-25:27 is especially rich in comparative proverbs that set two things beside one another for comparison: (25:25; compare 25:12-14,26,28; 26:1-3,6-11,14,20).

"Admonitions" and borrowing from Egyptian wisdom characterize 22:17–24:22. Admonitions contain imperatives or prohibitions, usually followed by a motive clause that gives a reason or two for doing that which is being urged (see 23:10-11).

The words of Agur (chap. 30) specialize in numerical sayings (30:15-31). The epilogue of the book (31:10-31) presents an alphabetic poem on wisdom embodied in the "valiant woman."

Proverbs displays a unified, richly complex worldview. The beginning and end of wisdom is to fear God and avoid evil (1:7; 8:13; 9:10; 15:33). The world is a battleground between wisdom and folly, righteousness and wickedness, good and evil. This conflict is personified in Lady Wisdom (1:20-33; 4:5-9; 8; 9:1-6) and Harlot

Folly (5:1-6; 6:24-35; 7; 9:13-18). Both "women" offer love and invite simple young men (like those in the royal school) to their homes to sample their wares. Wisdom's invitation is to life (8:34-36); the seduction of Folly leads to death (5:4-6; 7:22-27; 9:18).

Mysteriously, Lady Wisdom speaks in public places, offering wisdom to everyone who will listen (1:20-22; 8:1-5; 9:3). God has placed in creation a wise order that speaks of good and evil, urging humans toward good and away from evil. The sluggard must learn from the ant because the ant's work is in tune with the order of the seasons (Prov. 6:6-11; compare 10:5). This is not just the "voice of experience," but God's general revelation that speaks to all people with authority (Pss. 19:1-2; 97:6; 145:10; 148; Job 12:7-9; Acts 14:15-17; Rom. 1:18-23; 2:14-15). This perspective eliminates any split between faith and reason, between sacred and secular. Experiences in the world point the person of faith to God. The wise person "fears God" and lives in harmony with God's order for creation.

The short proverbs in chapters 10-29 cover a wealth of topics from wives (11:22; 18:22; 25:24) to friends (14:20; 17:17-18; 18:17; 27:6), strong drink (23:29-35; 31:4-7), wealth and poverty, justice and injustice, table manners and social status (23:1-8; compare 25:6-7; Luke 14:7-11). Proverbs can be misused (Prov. 26:7; compare v. 9). Proverbs are designed to make one wise, but they require wisdom to be used correctly. Proverbs are true, but their truth is realized only when they are fitly applied in the right situation. Wives can be a gift from the Lord (18:22), but sometimes singleness seems better (21:9, 19). Silence can be a sign of wisdom (17:27) or a cover-up (17:28). A "friend" can be trusted (17:17), but not always (17:18)!

Wealth can be a sign of God's blessing (3:9-10), but some saints suffer (3:11-12). Wealth can result from wickedness (13:23; 17:23; 28:11; compare 26:12). It is better to be poor and godly (16:8; compare 15:16-17; 17:1; 19:1; 28:6). In the end God will judge (21:13; compare 3:27-28; 22:16; 24:11-12; 10:2; 11:4). Such dilemmas force us to confront the limits of our wisdom (26:12) and to rely on God (3:5-8).

Proverbs generally operate on the principle that consequences follow acts: you reap what you sow. In a fallen world, however, God's justice is sometimes delayed. The "better than" proverbs in particular show the disorder of the present world, the "exceptions to the rule." The righteous thus works and prays, like the psalmist, for the day when God will make all things right.

PROVIDENCE

God's faithful and effective care and guidance of everything that He has made toward the end that He has chosen. Christian confession says God works everything for my salvation. This biblical doctrine must be distinguished from several distortions:

(1) *Fatalism.* View that all events are determined by an inviolable law of cause and effect, a popular doctrine among the Stoics.

(2) *Deism.* Idea that God created the world but then withdrew from its day-to-day governance.

(3) *Pantheism* virtually identifies God with His creation. God is a kind of World Soul or impersonal force that permeates all the universe.

(4) *Dualism.* View that two opposing forces in the universe are locked in struggle with each other for its control. The ancient religions of Zoroaster and Mani posited two coeternal principles, darkness and light. Modern process theology holds that God is limited by the evolving universe, caught in a struggle with forces over against His control.

The psalms are filled with allusions to God's direction and sustenance of the creation. The heavens declare the glory of God, and the firmament proclaims His handiwork (Ps. 19:1; compare Pss. 65:6; 104:3,19; 107:29; 150:2,6).

Providence may be discussed as general providence related to creation and special providence related to the history of salvation. Nehemiah 9:6-38 brings God's general and special providence together. "Thou, even thou, art Lord alone; thou hast made heaven, . . . the earth, and all things that are therein, . . . and thou preservest them all . . . Thou art the Lord the God, who didst choose Abram, . . . And madest known unto them thy. . . precepts, . . . by the hand of Moses . . . thou art a gracious and merciful God. . . . who keepest covenant."

God is present in the midst of life's stormy tempests, so we need not worry about tomorrow (Matt. 6:25-34). Romans 8:28 does not mean that everything that happens to us is good, nor necessarily the result of a "snap decision" by God. It does mean that nothing can ever happen to us apart from the knowledge, presence, and love of God, and that in the most desperate of circumstances God is always at work toward the good. The sufferings of the present time are not worth comparing with the glory that is to be revealed to us (Rom. 8:18-25).

Often God works through secondary causes such as natural law or special messengers, such as the angels. Sometimes God effects His will directly through miracles or other supernatural happenings. Frequently enough, His ways are mysterious.

The Bible presents no systematic answer to the dilemma of evil. It affirms only the reality of evil, its vicious, demonic power in the present age, and the certainty of Christ's ultimate victory over its every manifestation (1 Cor. 15:24-28). Christians can face the future in the confidence that nothing "in all creation, will be able to separate us from the love of God in Christ Jesus our Lord" (Rom. 8:39 NRSV). See *Election; God; Predestination.*

PSALMS, BOOK OF

Most complete collection of Hebrew poetry and worship material in the Hebrew Bible; theological statements and poetic dialogue with God. The Book of Psalms is found in the third division of the Hebrew canon known as the Writings. The Psalter has five divisions:

(1) Pss. 1–41;
(2) 42–71;
(3) 73–89;
(4) 90–106; and
(5) 107–150. Each concludes with a doxology (41:13; 72:18-19; 89:52; 106:48; 150). Psalm 150 closes off both book five and the collection of psalms; just as Psalm 1 serves as an introduction to the psalter.

Other divisions or collections appear in the Psalms:

(1) The Elohistic Psalter (Pss. 42–83) regularly uses the Hebrew *elohim* for the divine name (compare Pss. 14; 53).

(2) The Songs of Ascent or pilgrimage psalms (Pss. 120–134);

(3) Psalms of the sons of Korah (Pss. 42–49); and Psalms of Asaph (Pss. 73–83). See *Poetry.* Psalms can be classified according to formal types. Clear-cut categorization is not possible for every psalm, nor does every psalm fit a particular category. Psalm types include:

(1) *Lament* expressed both by the community (for example, 44; 74; 79) and by the individual (22; 38; 39; 41; 54). Laments are prayers or cries to God on the occasion of distressful situations. The basic pattern includes an invocation of God, a description of the petitioner's complaint(s), a recalling of past salvation experiences (usually community laments), petitions, a divine response (or oracle), and a concluding vow of praise. Such psalms show prayer as an honest communication with God in life's worst situations. The following psalms are laments: 3–4; 6–7; 12–13; 17; 22; 25–26; 28; 35; 38–44; 51; 54–57; 59–61; 63–64; 69–71; 74; 77; 79; 80; 83; 85–86; 88; 90; 94; 102; 109; 123; 126; 130; 134; 137; 140–144.

(2) *Thanksgiving* or psalms of narrative praise are also spoken by the community (see 124; 129) and the individual (see 9; 18; 30). These psalms are responses to liberation occurring after distress. These expressions of joy are fuller forms of the lament's vow of praise. These psalms show us our need to acknowledge God's work

in our times of trouble and to witness to others of what God has done for us. Thanksgiving psalms are 9–10, 18, 30–32, 34, 66, 92, 107, 116, 118, 120, 124, 129, 138–139.

(3) The *hymn* is closest in form to a modern song of praise. The hymn normally includes a call to praise, reasons for praising God, and a concluding call to praise. Creation hymns include Pss. 8; 19; 104; and 139. These psalms are hymns: 8; 19; 29; 33; 65; 100; 103–105; 111; 113-114; 117; 135–136; 145-150.

(4) The *liturgical psalms* may include antiphonal responses or dialogue and share similarities with the hymns. These psalms include instructions for sacrifice, worship, processionals, or may invoke blessings on the worshipers. They appear in Pss. 67–68; 75; 106; 108; 115; 121.

(5) *Songs of Zion* call for God's protection of the city of God. They praise God indirectly by describing the Holy City where He has chosen to live among His people and be worshiped. They show God lives among His people to protect and direct their lives. These are Pss. 46; 48; 76; 84; 87; 122; 132.

(6) *Royal psalms* are concerned with the earthly king of Israel. They were used to celebrate the king's enthronement. They may have included an oracle for the king. In some cases (such as Ps. 72), prayers were made to intercede on behalf of the king. Royal psalms point ahead to the Messiah, who would inaugurate God's kingdom. From them we learn to pray for and respect the role of government officials as well as praise God's Messiah. Royal Psalms include Pss. 2; 18; 20; 21; 28; 45; 61; 63; 72; 89; 101; 110; 132.

(7) *Enthronement psalms* celebrate Yahweh's kingship. They include Pss. 47; 93; 96–99.

(8) *Entrance ceremonies* (Pss. 15; 24) provide questions and answers to teach the expectations God has of His worshipers.

(9) *Wisdom psalms* have poetic form and style but are distinguished because of content and a tendency toward the proverbial. These psalms

contemplate questions of theodicy (Ps. 73), or celebrate God's Word (Ps. 119), or deal with two different ways of living-the godly and the evil person (Ps. 1). These include Pss. 1; 14; 36–37; 49; 53; 73; 78; 112; 119; 127–128; 133.

(10) *Psalms of confidence* express trust in God's care for and leadership of His people. These appear in Pss. 4; 11; 16; 23; 27; 62; 125; 131.

(11) *Prophetic psalms* announce God's will to His worshiping people. These are 50; 52; 58; 81–82; 91; 95.

PSALTER

(1) Alternate name for book of Psalms.

(2) Any collection of psalms used in worship.

PSEUDEPIGRAPHA (*writings falsely attributed*)

Intertestamental literature not accepted into the Christian or Jewish canon of Scripture and often attributed to an ancient hero of faith. Ongoing discovery and research provide differing lists of contents. A recent publication listed 52 writings.

Pseudepigrapha as a title for these books as falsely attributed is based on those books claiming to be written by Adam, Enoch, Moses, and other famous OT people. Some scholars prefer the name "outside books" for all of these writings, emphasizing that they did not become part of canon. Some ancient Christians and the Roman church have used the term "Apocrypha," since for them what Protestants call Apocrypha is part of their canon. See *Apocrypha.*

Both Palestinian and Hellenistic Jews authored books in the Pseudepigrapha. They used a variety of styles and literary types—legend, poetry, history, philosophy—but *apocalypse* was the dominant type. See *Apocalyptic.*

(1) *First Enoch,* an apocalypse preserved in the Ethiopic language, is a composite work of five sections, written at different times. Chaps. 1–36 tell how Enoch was taken up into heaven and shown its secrets.

Emphasis is placed on judgment and punishment. The realm of the dead is divided into separate places for the righteous and the wicked. Chaps. 37–71 (Parables or Similitudes) refer to the son of man. There is uncertainty about the date of this section. The rest of the book comes from between 200 and 1 B.C., but the Similitudes may have been written shortly before A.D. 100. Chaps. 78–82 deal with heavenly bodies. The author argues for a calendar based on the movement of the sun in distinction to the standard Jewish lunar calendar. Chaps. 83–90 contain two dream visions dealing with the flood and the history of Israel from Adam to the Maccabean revolt. Chaps. 91–108 give religious instruction concerning the end time.

(2) *Second Enoch*, an apocalypse in the Slavonic language, was written between 100 B.C. and A.D. 100. Enoch was taken up into heaven and commanded to write 366 books. He was allowed to return to earth for 30 days to teach his sons. This writing describes the contents of the seven heavens and divides time into seven 1,000 year periods.

(3) *Second Baruch*, written shortly before A.D. 100, is apocalyptic and shows how some Jews responded to the destruction of Jerusalem by the Romans in A.D. 70. Three visions seek to console the people by showing God has prepared something better for them. The Messiah will be revealed to bring in a time of great plenty. Emphasis is placed on obedience to the law.

(4) The *Sibylline Oracles* are popular apocalyptic writings modified from originally pagan writings by inserting ideas about monotheism, Mosaic requirements, and Jewish history. Three of the 15 books are missing. Book 3, from between 200 and 100 B.C., traces Jewish history from Abraham to the building of the second temple. It pronounces God's judgment on pagan nations, but holds out hope that they may turn to God.

(5) The *Testament of Moses* (sometimes called the *Assumption of*

Moses) is also apocalyptic. The manuscripts are incomplete, and the missing portion may have contained an account of Moses' death and his being taken to heaven. Early Christian writers state that Jude 9 was to be found in the Assumption of Moses. This book is a rewriting of Deut. 31–34 tracing the history of the people to the author's own time. The book was probably written shortly after A.D. 1. It emphasized that God has planned all things and keeps them under His control.

(6) The *Testaments of the Twelve Patriarchs* are patterned after Gen. 49. Each of the sons of Jacob addressed his descendants, giving a brief survey of his life, with special attention to some sin or failure and urging their children to live in an upright manner. Special emphasis is given to love for the neighbor and sexual purity. The book refers to two messiahs: one from Levi, one from Judah. The earliest portions of the testaments come from after 200 B.C.

(7) The *Book of Jubilees* is a rewriting of Genesis and the opening chapters of Exodus from after 200 B.C. It traces the history of Israel from creation to the time of Moses, dividing time into jubilee periods, 49 years each. The calendar is based on the sun, not the moon. The writer strongly opposed the Gentile influences he found coming into Judaism, urging Jews to keep separate from the Gentiles. The book shows how a conservative, priestly Jew about 150 B.C. viewed the world.

(8) The *Psalms of Solomon* are a collection of 18 psalms written about 50 B.C. They reflect the situation of the people in Jerusalem following its capture by the Romans under Pompey in 63 B.C. Psalms of Solomon 17 and 18 see the Messiah as a human figure, descendant of David, wise and righteous, and without sin. The titles Son of David and Lord Messiah are used of Him.

(9) *Third Maccabees*, written after 200 B.C., has nothing to do with the Maccabees. It tells about the attempt of Ptolemy IV to kill the Jews in Egypt. God foiled his efforts, result-

ing in the advancement of the Jews. This book shows the vindication of the righteous.

(10) *Fourth Maccabees* is based to some extent on material found in 2 Macc. 6–7. It is a philosophical writing, stressing that pious reason can be the master of the passions. Reason is derived from obedience to the law. The author left out all references to resurrection. The book comes from shortly after A.D. 1.

(11) The *Life of Adam and Eve* has been preserved in Latin and Greek versions different in length and content. Blame for the fall is placed on Eve. This writing refers to Satan being transformed into the brightness of angels (9:1; see 2 Cor. 11:14), and states that paradise is in the third heaven (compare 2 Cor. 12:2-3). The Life of Adam and Eve was written after A.D. 1.

(12) The *Letter of Aristeas* was composed after 200 B.C., telling how the OT law was translated into Greek. It seeks to show that the Jewish law was in conformity with the highest ideals of Greek thought and life. It indicates that it is possible for Jew and Greek to live together in peace. See *Apocalyptic; Apocrypha; Bible, Texts and Versions.*

PSYCHIATRY

Illnesses in the Bible had either physical (e.g., Luke 4:38; John 9:1-3) or spiritual causes, the latter due either to sin (e.g., 2 Kings 5:26-27; Ps. 32:3-4) or an evil spirit (e.g., 1 Sam. 16:14; Matt. 17:14-18; Mark 5:2-4; John 10:20). Some interpreters hold that many of the sicknesses attributed to evil spirits would be classified today as mental illness (e.g., King Saul and Nebuchadnezzar; compare John 10:20).

The Bible recognizes the reality of insanity, describing David feigning madness before King Achish of Gath (1 Sam. 21:13-15). The prophets were sometimes accused of madness because of the strangeness of their prophetic activity (2 Kings 9:11; Jer. 29:26; Hos. 9:7).

Whether present in believers or unbelievers, troubled minds are a result of the Fall. Circumstances often produce depression (Neh. 1:2; Prov. 15:13; 18:14) or anxiety (Deut. 28:65-67; Luke 10:41), and can lead to panic attacks (Prov. 3:25; Zech. 12:4). The minds of unbelievers are described by Paul as "corrupted" (Titus 1:15), and in need of renewal through the saving work of Christ (Eph. 4:23; 2 Cor. 5:17; compare Rom. 12:2). Those who trust in God in the face of trouble are able to find inner peace (Ps. 4:8; Isa. 26:3; Phil. 4:7; 1 Pet. 5:7).

PTOLEMIES

Ruling family in Egypt in the aftermath of the conquests of Alexander the Great.

The Ptolemies made Alexandria a center of learning and commerce. Ptolemy I transported large numbers of Jews from Palestine to Alexandria for settlement, beginning a large and influential Jewish community. (See *Alexandria.*) The Alexandrian Jews imbibed Hellenism much more deeply than their counterparts in Judea as evidenced by their translating the OT into Greek. See *Bible, Texts and Versions.*

PUBLIC RELATIONS

Estabishing a good reputation in the world (Prov. 3:4; 22:1; 31:23, 31; Eccl. 7:1; 2 Cor. 6:3-10; 1 Tim. 3:7). Jesus spoke against those who felt the need to parade their worth before others, and taught instead that God's opinion is of greater value than a person's (Matt. 6:1-4; 23:5; John 12:43; compare Gal. 1:10). While public relations are important, self-congratulatory excesses should be avoided. The Bible provides examples of effective (1 Sam. 25:23-25; 2 Sam. 15:2-6) and ineffective (1 Kings 12:1-15) public relations campaigns.

PUBLICAN

Political office created by the Romans to help collect taxes in the provinces. "Tax collector" is more correct than the older term "publican"in referring to the lowest rank in the structure. Zacchaeus is called a "chief among the publicans" (Luke 19:2), probably indicating one who contracted with the government to collect taxes, and who in turn hired others to do the actual work. In NT times people bid for the job of chief tax collector and then exacted the tax plus a profit from the citizens. Most of the offices were filled by Romans, although some natives got the bids. Publicans were held in the lowest esteem because of their excessive profits, being placed in the same category as harlots (Matt 21:32). Jesus was accused of eating with and befriending them (Matt. 9:11).

PULPIT

KJV, RSV term for raised platform (NRSV, REB, NIV, TEV) on which a speaker stood (Neh. 8:4); not a lectern or high reading desk behind which a reader stands.

PURITY, PURIFICATION See *Clean, Cleanness.*

PUT

Son of Ham (Gen. 10:6; 1 Chron. 1:8) in "Table of Nations" and thus ancestor of inhabitants of Put.

QUEEN

Wife or widow of a monarch; female monarch reigning in her own right. Queen mother refers to mother of reigning monarch. Female regents were known in the Ancient Near East (1 Kings 10:1-13, the queen of Sheba; Acts 8:27, the Ethiopian Candace). No queen ruled Israel or Judah in her own right, though Athaliah usurped power (2 Kings 11:1-3). The wives of monarchs varied in their influence. Since marriages often sealed political alliances (2 Sam. 3:3; 1 Kings 3:1; 16:31; 2 Kings 8:25-27), daughters of more powerful allies such as the Egyptian pharaoh or king of Tyre enjoyed special privileges (1 Kings 7:8) and influence (1 Kings 16:32-33; 18:19; 21:7-14). The mother of the designated heir also enjoyed special status. Nathan enlisted Bathsheba rather than Solomon in his plan to have Solomon confirmed as king (1 Kings 1:11-40). Great care was taken in preserving names of queen mothers, an official position in Israel and Judah (1 Kings 14:21; 15:2,13; 22:42; 2 Kings 8:26). Asa's removal of his mother from the office for idolatry (1 Kings 15:13) points to its official character. On her son's death, Athaliah murdered her own grandsons, the legitimate heirs, in order to retain the power she had enjoyed as queen mother (2 Kings 11:1-2). The queen mother likely served as a trusted counsel for her son (Prov. 31:1). As queen mother, Jezebel continued as a negative force after the death of Ahab (1 Kings 22:52; 2 Kings 3:2,13; 9:22).

QUEEN OF HEAVEN

Goddess women in Judah worshiped to ensure fertility and material stability (Jer. 7:18; 44:17); literally, "stars of heaven" or "heavenly host." Forms of worship included making cakes (possibly in her image as in molds found at Mari), offering drink offerings, and burning incense (Jer. 44:25). The major influence could have been Ishtar, the Mesopotamian goddess called there the queen of heaven (imported to Israel by Manassseh), or the Canaanite Ashtarte. Archaeologists have uncovered many images of nude goddesses from Israelite sites, showing why Jeremiah protested against such worship.

QUIRINIUS

Roman official mentioned in Luke 2:2 as governor of Syria at birth of Jesus; full name was Publius Sulpicius Quirinius. He served as consul of Rome, military leader, tutor to Gaius Caesar, and legate (governor). He died in A.D. 21.

Quirinius was legate in Syria from A.D. 6–9, but this date is far too late for Jesus' birth, which occurred prior to the death of Herod the Great in 4 B.C. Non-biblical sources established either Saturninus (9–7 B.C.) or Varus (6–4 B.C.) as legate of Syria during Christ's birth.

An ancient inscription has shown a legate fitting the description of Quirinius served two different times in Syria. Apparently the nativity occurred during Quirinius's first tenure in Syria as legate with primary responsibilities for military affairs, while Varus was the legate handling civil matters. Quirinius served a second term in A.D. 6–9.

R

RAAMA(H)

Son of Cush (Gen. 10:7); ancestor of Sheba and Dedan—Arab tribes occupying southwest and west-central Arabia (1 Chron. 1:9) and trading partners of Tyre (Ezek. 27:22); likely Nagran in Yemen.

RAAMSES See *Rameses.*

RABBAH *(greatness)*

(1) Village near Jerusalem (Josh. 15:60) assigned to Judah in territory of Benjamin.

(2) Capital of Ammon that Moses apparently did not conquer (Deut. 3:11; Josh. 13:25); 23 miles east of Jordan River. David captured it (2 Sam. 11:1; 12:28-29). It regained its independence shortly after the Israelite division. Rabbah was destroyed during the Babylonian sweep through the area (590–580 B.C.) and not rebuilt for several hundred years. Rabbah was renamed Philadelphia by the Hellenists and later became Amman, the modern capital of Jordan. See *Philadelphia.*

RABBI *(my master)*

Title applied to teachers and others of an exalted and revered position; more narrowly, one learned in law of Moses, without signifying official office; scribes (Matt. 23:7-8); John the Baptist (John 3:26); Jesus (Mark 9:5; 11:21; Mark 14:45, John 1:49; 3:2; 4:31; 6:25; 9:2; 11:8; 20:16). Luke "school-master," for his predominantly Greek readers (Luke 17:13). Jesus and His disciples were forbidden to call each other "rabbi" (Matt. 23:8). Jesus' disciples called Him "Lord."

RABBIT *(Oractolagus cuniculus)*

NASB, NIV, TEV (Lev. 11:6; Deut. 14:7) for "hare." See *Animals.*

RABBONI

Variant spelling of Rabbi.

RAB-MAG

Title of the Babylonian official Nergal-Sharezer (Jer. 39:3,13); meaning unknown; perhaps officer in charge of divination (compare Ezek. 21:21).

RABSARIS *(he who stands by the king)*

Assyrian court position with strong military and diplomatic powers; sent twice to make Israelite kings pay withheld tribute (2 Kings 18:17; Jer. 39:3).

RABSHAKEH *(chief cupbearer)*

Assyrian title of highly influential official who dealt with Hezekiah for Assyrian king (2 Kings 18:17-35).

RACA *(empty or ignorant)*

Word of reproach Hebrew writers borrowed from Aramaic; as a strong term of derision (Matt. 5:22) second only to "fool."

RACHEL *(ewe)*

Younger daughter of Laban; second wife and cousin of Jacob; mother of Joseph and Benjamin. (Gen. 27-35; compare Ruth 4:11; Jer. 31:15; Matt. 2:18). See *Jacob.*

RACIAL TENSION

Unrest and division among people caused by differing racial origins. Personal identity in the ancient world was not primarily based on race, but on family, tribal, city, national, ethnic, or religious ties.

Shepherds (who were typically Semitic) were an abomination to the (non-Semitic) Egyptians (Gen. 46:34). When the Jews lived outside Palestine, racial differences became more significant (Esther 3:1-6; compare Luke 4:25-28). Paul reports a well-accepted Greek maxim stigmatizing the Cretans as always being "liars, evil beasts, slow bellies [lazy gluttons, NIV]" (Titus 1:12-13). Because there is no racial distinction in Christ (Gal. 3:28-29; Eph. 2:19), the church was able to spread rapidly to the Gentile world to encompass persons of all races. Divisions and prejudice based on race are unacceptable for Christians.

RAHAB (*arrogant, raging, turbulent, afflicter*)

(1) Primeval sea monster representing forces of chaos God overcame in creation (Job 9:13; 26:12; Ps. 89:10; Isa. 51:9; compare Ps. 74:12-17).

(2) Symbolic name for Egypt (Ps. 87:4). Isaiah 30:7 includes a compound name *Rahab-hem-shebeth:* "Rahab who sits still" (NRSV); "Rahab who has been exterminated" (NASB); "Rahab the Do-Nothing" (NIV); "Rahab the Subdued" (REB).

(3) Plural (Ps. 40:4) for proud, arrogant enemies.

RAHAB (*broad*)

Harlot in Jericho who hid two Hebrew spies Joshua sent there to determine the strength of the city (Josh. 2:1). Joshua spared her and her clan when the Hebrews destroyed Jericho (Josh. 6:17-25; compare Matt. 1:5; Heb. 11:31).

RAIN

Moisture from heaven providing nourishment for plant and animal life. Palestine depended on yearly rains to ensure an abundant harvest and an ample food supply for the coming year. Presence or absence of rain became a symbol of God's continued blessing or displeasure with the land and its inhabitants. See *Palestine; Fertility Cult.*

RAINBOW

Arch of color caused by reflection and refraction of sunlight by droplets of rain; reminded Israel and her God of His covenant with Noah to never again destroy the earth by flooding (Gen. 9:8-17); symbol of majesty and beauty of God (Ezek. 1:28; compare Hab. 3:9; Rev. 4:3; 10:1).

RAMA or **RAMAH** (*high*)

Name applied to six cities located on heights, especially military strongholds including:

(1) Ramah of Gilead (2 Kings 8:28-29; 2 Chron. 22:6). See *Ramoth-Gilead.*

(2) City in Benjamin (Josh. 18:25); er-Ram five miles north of Jerusalem between rival kingdoms of Israel and Judah (1 Kings 15:16-22; 2 Chron. 16:1,5-6); traditional site of Rachel's tomb (1 Sam. 10:2; Jer. 31:15). Deborah, the prophetess, dwelt and judged Israel from the Ramah vicinity (Judg. 4:4-5). See Jos. 5:8; Isa. 10:29. Babylonians apparently used Ramah as prisoner-of-war camp (Jer. 40:1-6; compare Ezra 2:26; Neh. 7:30).

(3) Birthplace, home, judge's circuit stop, and burial place of Samuel (1 Sam. 1:19; 2:11; 7:17; 8:4; 15:34; 25:1); called Ramathaim-Zophim (1 Sam. 1:1); may be Arimathea, hometown of Joseph, in whose tomb Jesus was buried (Matt. 27:57-60).

RAMATHAIM See *Rama.*

RAMESES

Egyptian capital city and royal residence during the nineteenth and twentieth dynasties (about 1320–1085 B.C.); apparently in Nile delta; may be same as Tanis or Zoan; near where Hebrews settled under Joseph (Gen. 47:11); Israelite slaves forced to help build Rameses and Pithom (Ex. 1:11). See *Egypt; Exodus; Pithom.*

RAMOTH-GILEAD (*heights of Gilead*)

City of refuge (Deut. 4:43; compare Josh. 20:8) and Levitical city (Josh. 21:38); probably in northeastern Gilead. Solomon made Ramoth-gilead a district capital (1 Kings 4:13). About 922 B.C. the city fell to Syria (1 Kings 22:3; compare 22:29-40; 2 Kings 8:29; 9:1-6,14).

RAMPART (*encirclement*)

Outer ring of fortifications, usually earthworks; can be applied to moats and walls (2 Sam. 20:15; Ps. 122:7;

Lam. 2:8). Because Jerusalem was ringed by steep valleys, only its north side had extensive ramparts.

RANGE

KJV for rank or row (of soldiers) (2 Kings 11:8,15; 2 Chron. 23:14).

RANSOM See *Atonement; Expiation, Propitiation; Redeem, Redemption, Redeemer.*

RAPE

Crime of engaging in sexual intercourse with another without consent, by force and/or deception. Mosaic law required a man who had seduced a virgin to pay the bride price and offer to marry her (Ex. 22:16-17). Forcible rape of an engaged woman was a capital offense (Deut. 22:25-27). In other cases of forcible rape, the offender was required to marry his victim and was not permitted to divorce her (Deut. 22:28-29). Rape is a frightful crime with a horrible aftermath, destroying the lives of those involved as well as others (Gen. 34:1-31; 2 Sam. 13:1-39). The soldiers of an invading army expected to rape the women of the conquered towns and villages as part of their spoils of war (Isa. 13:16; Lam. 5:11; Zech. 14:2). The gang rapes at Sodom (Gen. 19:4-11) and Gibeah (Judg. 19:22-30), along with the remedy for the Gibeah crime which involved more rape (Judg. 21:16-23), are included in the biblical story to show the utter depravity of humanity. See *Sex, Biblical Teaching on.*

RAPTURE

Catching up of believers by Christ at the time of His return (1 Thess. 4:17). Premillennialism sees a tribulation period immediately before the second coming of Christ. Pre-tribulationists see the rapture occurring prior to the tribulation with the church in heaven during the tribulation on earth. Mid-tribulationists place the rapture at the mid-point of a seven-year tribulation period, the church on earth for only the first half of the tribulation. The views see the second coming of Christ in two phases: a secret coming in clouds to rapture the church and His return with the church to reign on earth. Posttribulationists hold the church will remain on earth during the tribulation period. The church will be protected from divine wrath although experiencing tribulation. See *Eschatology; Hope; Tribulation.*

RAZORS, SHAVING

Instruments used in and process of removing facial hair. Egyptians shaved the hair of their beard and head except in times of mourning. Pharaohs apparently wore fake beards.

Hebrews, with most Western Asiatics including the Assyrians, considered the beard was as an ornament and point of pride. The dignity of manhood and was only trimmed (2 Sam. 19:24; Ezek. 44:20). Shaving was done with a sharp cutting instrument made from flint, obsidian, or iron (Isa. 7:20; Ezek. 5:1). The razor could be a simple knife or an elaborate instrument, sometimes decorated. Shaving was practiced as a sign of mourning (Job 1:20; Jer. 7:29), as a sign of subservience to a superior (Num. 8:7; Gen. 41:14), and as a treatment for a person with leprosy (Lev. 14:9).

REBEKAH (perhaps *cow*)

Daughter of Bethuel, Abraham's nephew (Gen. 24:15); Isaac's wife (24:67); mother of Jacob and Esau (25:25-26). A beautiful virgin (24:16), willing servant (24:19), and hospitable to strangers (24:25); in obedience to God's will she left her home in Paddan-aram to be Isaac's wife (24:58). Rebekah comforted Isaac after the death of Sarah (24:67). When distressed by her problem pregnancy, she turned to God for counsel (25:22-23). Less favorable is Rebekah's favoritism toward Jacob (25:28; 27:5-17,42-46).

RECHABITES

Three OT men including:

(1) Leader with his brother of band of Benjaminite raiders. They murdered Saul's son Ish-bosheth, thinking to court David's favor. His response was their execution (2 Sam. 4:1-12).

(2) Father or ancestor of J[eh]onadab, supporter of Jehu's purge of the family of Ahab and other worshipers of Baal (2 Kings 10:15,23). His descendants, the Rechabites, about 599 B.C., took refuge from Nebuchadnezazar in Jerusalem (Jer. 35). Jeremiah used them as example of faithfulness to God after they refused to break family vows not to drink wine.

RECONCILATION

Establishment of friendly relations between parties at variance with each other; making peace after an engagement in war; readmission to the presence and favor of a person after rebellion against the person. Deliberate sins could be forgiven only by prayer and repentance. Sacrifices could never bring a sinner into right relationship with God (Heb. 10:1-18). Paul saw the need for reconciliation of humans to oneself, other people, and the environment, but his chief interest was in a person being reconciled to God through Christ (Rom. 5:10-21; 11:15; 1 Cor. 7:11; 2 Cor. 5:18-20; Eph. 2:16; Col. 1:20-21; compare Matt. 5:23-24). Reconciliation for Paul meant that a complete reversal of the relation between God and humans had been accomplished. Through His love manifested to us in the death of Christ on the cross even while we were in the state of being sinners, God delivered us from law, wrath, sin, and death and brought us by faith in Christ into a peaceful relationship with Himself.

The NT also exhorts us to be reconciled to fellow human beings (Matt. 5:23-24). Through the cross Christ reconciled both Gentile and Jew into one new humanity by terminating the hostility that existed between them (Eph. 2:14-18). The church is commissioned to perform a ministry of reconciliation (2 Cor. 5:12-21).

When we are reconciled to God, we have peace (Rom. 5:1; 1 Cor. 7:15; Gal. 5:22; Eph. 4:3; Phil. 4:7; Col. 3:15; 2 Thess. 3:16), freedom (Rom. 6:22; 8:2; Gal. 5:1), and sonship (Rom. 8:15; Gal. 4:5; Eph. 1:5). See *Atonement; Cross; Jesus; Salvation.*

RECYCLING

System of reusing materials to protect the environment. The earth and its resources were created by God to be good (Gen. 1–2) and belong to him (Lev. 25:23; Job 41:11; Pss. 24:1; 89:11). God has entrusted the earth to people (Gen. 1:28-30; 2:15; 9:1-4; compare Deut. 8:7-10) who have a sacred responsibility to care for it with the same diligence that God himself does (Deut. 11:12; Pss. 65:5-13; 104:10-22). The Bible condemns selfish extravagance which takes no thought of the future (compare Job 20:20-22; 21:21; compare Isa. 39:5-8).

The Bible offers as possible parallels of recycling the use of jewelry to make religious objects (Ex. 32:2-4; 35:22; Ezek. 7:20) and the distribution of used clothing to those who were captured in battle (2 Chron. 28:15).

RED SEA (REED SEA)

Body of water God dried up in the exodus; translation of two Hebrew words *yam suph,* the second of which often means "reeds" (Ex. 2:3,5; Isa. 19:6) or "end,'"hinder part" (Joel 2:20; 2 Chron. 20:16; Eccl. 3:11). *Yam suph* could be translated "Sea of Reeds" or "Sea at the end of the world."Red Sea is based on Greek Septuagint (about 200 B.C.) picked up by Jerome's Latin Vulgate (A.D. 400).

Reed Sea goes back to Jewish scholars after A.D. 1000 and to Martin Luther. Many recent attempts have tried to prove "Sea of Reeds" is not a legitimate reading for *yam suph.* The OT uses *yam suph* to refer to more than one location: Gulf of Suez (Ex. 10:19); Gulf of Aqaba (1 Kings 9:26; compare Jer. 49:21); "Way of the Red Sea" is part of the name of a highway out of Egypt (Ex. 13:18; Num. 14:45;

21:4; Deut. 1:40; 2:1; Judg. 11:16)."Red Sea" was name of camp along the way from Egypt (Num. 33:10-11). *Yam suph* marked the ideal southern border of Israel (Ex. 23:31), but the most significant reference of "Red Sea" in the OT was to the place where God delivered Israel from Pharaoh's army (Ex. 15:4,22; Num. 21:14; Deut. 11:4; Josh. 2:10; 4:23; 24:6; Neh. 9:9; Pss. 106:7,9-11,22; 136:13-15). No one knows the exact location where Israel crossed the "Red Sea." Four primary theories have been suggested:

(1) the northern edge of the Gulf of Suez;

(2) center of the isthmus near Lake Timsah;

(3) northern edge of the isthmus and the southern edge of Lake Menzaleh; and

(4) sandy land that separates Lake Sirbonis from Mediterranean Sea. Weight of biblical evidence may be on 2. See *Exodus.*

REDEEM, REDEMPTION, REDEEMER

To pay required price to secure the release of convicted criminal; process therein involved; and person making the payment. Hebrew had legal and commercial uses of the redemptive concept. If a person owned an ox known to be dangerous but did not keep the ox secured and the ox gored the son or daughter of a neighbor, both the ox and the owner would be stoned to death. If the father of the slain person offered to accept an amount of money, the owner could pay the redemption price and live (Ex. 21:29-30; compare v. 32). Numbers 18:15-17 shows how religious practice adopted such language.

Jeremiah demonstrated his confidence in God's promise by acting as next-of-kin to redeem or ransom the family land (Jer. 32:6-15). Such commercial practices easily passed over into religious concepts. God would redeem Israel from her iniquities. See *Kinsman; Atonement; Day of Atonement.*

Religious redemption language grows out of the custom of buying back something that formerly belonged to the purchaser but for some reason had passed into the ownership of another. The basic OT reference is the exodus. At the sea God redeemed His people from slavery in Egypt (for example, Ex. 6:6; 15:13; Deut. 7:8; Ps. 77:15). God similarly redeemed Israel from the Babylonian captivity by giving Egypt, Ethiopia, and Seba to King Cyrus (Isa. 43:3; compare 48:20; 51:11; 62:12). Job knew he had a living Redeemer (Job 19:25). Psalmists prayed for redemption from distress (26:11; 49:15) and testified to God's redeeming work (31:5; 71:23; 107:2). The OT witness is that God is "my strength and my redeemer" (Ps. 19:14).

The NT centers redemption in Jesus Christ. New Testament redemption speaks of substitutionary sacrifice demonstrating divine love and righteousness. This Lamb of God (John 1:29; Rev. 5:8-14) purchased the church with His own blood (Acts 20:28), gave His flesh for the life of the world (John 6:51), as the Good Shepherd laid down His life for His sheep (John 10:11), and demonstrated the greatest love by laying down His life for His friends (John 15:13). Jesus' purpose was to make a deliberate sacrifice of Himself for human sin. As the Suffering Servant, His was a costly sacrifice, the shameful and agonizing death of a Roman cross. See *Christ; Jesus; Atonement; Reconciliation.*

REGENERATION

Radical spiritual change in which God brings an individual from a condition of spiritual defeat and death to a renewed condition of holiness and life when Christ enters the life of an individual; symbolized by baptism (Titus 3:5); new birth or birth from above (John 3:3; compare 1:13; 1 Pet. 1:23; 2:2); new creation (2 Cor. 5:17 NIV); new life (John 5:21; 7:38; 10:10,28) God's "workmanship" made for the purpose of good works (Eph. 2:10). Human beings corrupt God's revelation of Himself and turn to gross forms of disobedience (Rom. 1:18-32).

God demands holiness as a condition for having fellowship with Himself (Heb. 12:14). Human beings must have a radical change in the character of their personality. God promises such a change in the experience of regeneration.

The Holy Spirit takes this truth of Jesus (see Jas. 1:18) and commends it to the understanding of each hearer (John 16:8-11) so in an instantaneous experience the person commits to live the truth. In regeneration each believer has put off the old way of life, become clothed with a new way of life, and is in the process of having one's mind renewed in its thinking, reasoning, and willing (Eph. 4:17-32).

Scriptures present baptism the sign of regeneration (1 Pet. 3:21). The Holy Spirit brings the actual change of regeneration. Regeneration is an inward change, and baptism is the outward sign of that change (Acts 2:38; Col. 2:12; Titus 3:5). Baptism becomes a means of demonstrating publicly and outwardly the nature of this change. See *Baptism.*

REHOBOAM *(he enlarges the people)*

Solomon's son and successor (931–913 B.C.) to throne of united monarchy (1 Kings 11:43); refused (1 Kings 12) northern tribes' request to remove some of the tax burden and labor laws his father had placed on them; decided to increase further the burden. The northern tribes revolted and made Jeroboam their king. Rehoboam was left with only the tribes of Judah and Benjamin. He continued the pagan ways Solomon had allowed (14:21-24) and fought against Jeroboam and Shishak of Egypt.

REHOBOTH *(broad places)*

(1) Rehoboth-Ir likely denotes open space within Nineveh or its suburbs (Gen. 10:11) rather than separate city between Nineveh and Calah.

(2) Site of a well dug and retained by Isaac's men in the valley of Gerar (Gen. 26:22).

(3) Unidentified Edomite city (Gen. 36:37; 1 Chron. 1:48): KJV, NIV, TEV, "Rehoboth by the river"; NASB, NRSV, REB, by the Euphrates; river may be Zered Brook, principal stream in Edom.

RELIGION

Relationship of devotion to or fear of God or gods with outward expressions of piety (Acts 17:22; 25:19). Though a monotheist (believer in one God) would not use "fear of the gods" to describe Judaism, the expression is natural on pagan Roman lips (Acts 25:19). In Acts 26:5; Jas. 1:26-27 religion is "fear of God" as evidenced in religious conduct, particularly ritual practice. The religious observance God cares about is not a cultic matter but an ethical matter, care of the helpless of society. See John 9:31; Acts 13:43; 1 Tim. 2:10; 3:16; 5:4; 2 Tim. 3:5. "Alleged worship" may be meaning in Col. 2:23.

REMISSION

KJV for release, forgiveness from the guilt or penalty of sins; often linked with repentance, both in the preaching of John the Baptist (Mark 1:4; Luke 3:3) and the early church (Luke 24:47; Acts 2:38; 5:31). Remission of sins results from Christ's sacrificial death (Matt. 26:28; compare Heb. 10:17-18) and from Christ's exaltation (Acts 5:31). Remission of sins is available to all who believe in the name of Jesus (Acts 10:43; compare Luke 24:47; Acts 2:38).

REMNANT

Something left over, especially the righteous people of God after divine judgment. Noah and his family were a remnant of a divine judgment in the flood (Gen. 6:5-8; 7:1-23); compare Lot (Gen. 18:17-33; 19:1-29); Jacob's family in Egypt (Gen. 45:7); Elijah and the 7,000 faithful followers (1 Kings 19:17-18); and Israelites going into captivity (Ezek. 12:1-16).

About 750 B.C. Amos found that many people in Israel believed that God would protect all of them and their institutions. He tore down their mistaken ideas (3:12-15; 5:2-3,18-20; 6:1-7; 9:1-6). He corrected the tenet that everyone would live happily and prosper (9:10) with the doctrine that only a few would survive and rebuild the nation (9:8b-9,11-15). This new life could be realized if one and all would repent, turn to the Lord, and be saved (5:4b-6a,14-15).

Hosea shows the Lord's mercy extended to those experiencing judgment (2:14-23; 3:4-5; 6:1-3; 11:8-11; 13:14; 14:1-9). Micah has much the same emphasis. After announcements of judgment, the Lord proclaimed that people would be assembled like sheep and led by the Lord (2:12-13) as their king (4:6-8). The Messiah would give special attention to them (5:2-5,7-9). The climax of the book is an exaltation of God as the one who pardons and removes sin from their lives after the judgment had passed (7:7-20).

The remnant doctrine was so important to Isaiah that he named one of his sons Shear-Jashub, meaning "a remnant shall return" (7:3). The faithful would survive the onslaughts of the Assyrian army (4:2-6; 12:1-6; compare 36-38). Many remnant passages are closely tied with the future king, the Messiah, who would be the majestic ruler of those who seek His mercies (Isa. 9:1-7; 11:1-16; 32:1-8; 33:17-24). The future would have a new people, a new community, a new nation, and a strong faith in one God. An important segment of the remnant would be those who were afflicted (Isa. 14:32; compare Zeph. 2:3; 3:12-13). This remnant would be personified in the Suffering Servant (Isa. 53).

Jeremiah announced that in the exile, those who believed in the one true God would be gathered for a return to the Promised Land. God would create a new community (see chs. 30-33; compare Ezek. 40-48 with new exodus, new settlement, and new temple). Zechariah spoke in glowing terms of how the remnant, the returned exiles to Jerusalem, would prosper (8:6-17; 9:9-17; 14:1-21). Ezra recognized people who had returned to Jerusalem as members of the remnant, but in danger of reenacting the sins of the past (9:7-15).

Paul quoted (Rom 9:25-33) from Hosea and from Isaiah to demonstrate that the saving of a remnant from among the Jewish people was still part of the Lord's method of redeeming His people. There would always be a future for anyone among the covenant people who would truly turn to the Lord for salvation (Rom. 9-11).

REPENTANCE

A feeling of regret, a changing of the mind, or a turning from sin to God. As a feeling of regret the term can apply even to God (Joel 2:13; Jonah 4:2). God was sorry He had created the human race (Gen. 6:6-7). He regretted He had made Saul the king over Israel (1 Sam. 15:11,35). God repented in the sense of changing His mind about announced judgment (Ex. 32:14; Amos 7:1-6; Jonah 3:6-10). One time He changed His mind about good intentions (Jer. 18:10). Referring to people, repentance means a reorientation of the sinner to God. In this sense God does not repent like humans (1 Sam. 15:29).

In ancient Israel, repentance was first expressed corporately. Fasting, wearing sackcloth (the traditional attire for mourning), scattering ashes (Isa. 58:5; Neh. 9:1; Dan. 9:3), and reciting prayers and psalms in a penitential liturgy characterized this collective experience of worship. Prophets attacked feigned worship and called for genuine contrition, introducing the characteristic biblical concept of repentance, making a radical change within the heart (Ezek. 18:31), turning from sin and at the same time turning to God. Such a turning or conversion was openly manifested in justice, kindness, and humility (Mic. 6:8; Amos 5:24; Hos. 2:19-20).

John the Baptist called his generation to this radical kind of turning and baptized those who responded (Mark 1:4-5). He expected people to demonstrate by their actions the change that they had made in their hearts (Luke 3:10-14). His message of repentance was intricately bound up with his expectation of the Messiah (Luke 3:15-17; see also Acts 19:4). The Messiah came preaching a message of repentance, expecting the kingdom (Mark 1:15) for all people (Luke 13:1-5; compare 5:32; 15:11-32). Jesus summoned His followers to turn and become like children (Matt. 18:3). He insisted that the repentant life was obvious by the "fruit" that it bore (Luke 6:20-45). Those who were unrepentant were those who rejected Him (Luke 10:8-15; 11:30-32). In His name repentance and forgiveness were to be proclaimed to all nations (Luke 24:47).

Peter (Acts 2:38; 3:19; 5:31) and Paul (Acts 17:30; 20:21) told Jews and Gentiles alike "that they should repent and turn to God, performing deeds appropriate to repentance" (Acts 26:20 NASB). The apostolic preaching virtually identified repentance with belief in Christ: both resulted in the forgiveness of sins (Acts 2:38; 10:43; compare Acts 20:21; Heb. 6:1; 1 John 1:9).

Judas' repentance was not the type that leads toward salvation (Matt. 27:3). Paul described a change in the Corinthians' attitude about him (2 Cor. 7:8-13) that resulted in their reconciliation with him. Renewal of commitment or reaffirmation of faith seems to be the meaning of repentance in the letters to the seven churches in Revelation (2:5,16,21-22; 3:3,19). See *Confession; Conversion; Faith; Kingdom of God.*

REPHAIM

(1) Residents of Sheol, often translated, "shades" or the "dead" (Job 26:5 NRSV; Ps. 88:10; Prov. 9:18; 21:16; Isa. 14:9; 26:14, 19). See *Sheol.*

(2) Ethnic designation of pre-Israelite inhabitants of Palestine, equivalent to the Anakim, the Moabite term *Emim* (Deut. 2:10-11), and the Ammonite term *Zanzummim* (2:20-21). Despite their reputation for might and height, the Rephaim were defeated by a coalition of eastern kings (Gen. 14:5) and were later displaced by the Israelites (Deut. 3:11,13;

compare Gen. 15:20) and their distant kin, the Moabites (Deut. 2:10-11) and the Ammonites (2:20-21). KJV regularly translated Rephaim as "giants"(except Gen. 14:5; 15:20, and some references to the valley or land of the Rephaim).

REPHAN

Term for foreign, astral deity (Acts 7:43; NASB,"Rompha"). Acts 7 follows Septuagint reading (Amos 5:26), where Hebrew reads "Kaiwan," Babylonian name for Saturn.

REPHIDIM

Wilderness site where Hebrews stopped on their way to Canaan just prior to reaching Sinai (Ex. 17:1; 19:2; compare 18:13-26).

RESTITUTION

Act of returning what has wrongfully been taken or replacing what has been lost or damaged; Divine restoration of all things to their original order. The law required "trespass offerings"to be made for sins against a neighbor (theft, deception, dishonesty, extortion, keeping lost property, or damaging property). Such crimes involved "unfaithfulness" toward God and disrupted fellowship and peace among the people. They were to be atoned for by a guilt offering to God, and "restitution"to the wronged neighbor. Atonement and forgiveness of the sin were received after restitution had been made to the victim. OT law established a principle of "punishment to fit the crime"(life for life, eye for eye, tooth for tooth, wound for wound). Restitution was consistent with this concept of equity. The guidelines for making complete restitution also included a provision for punitive damages (up to five times what had been lost), justice that moved beyond "an eye for an eye." Provisions were made for complications in this process (Ex. 22:3). The principle is illustrated (1 Kings 20:34; 2 Kings 8:6; Neh. 5:10-12; Luke 19:1-10; compare Matt. 5:23-24). God will reestablish all "things" to their pristine order and purpose, universal renewal of the earth (Acts 3:21; compare 1 Cor. 15:25-28).

RESURRECTION

Doctrine, event, and act of persons being brought from death to unending life at the close of the age. Death is the end of human existence, the destruction of life (Gen. 3:19; Job 30:23). In isolated instances revivification occurs (being brought back to life from death but only as a temporary escape from final death; 1 Kings 17:17-22; 2 Kings 4:18-37; 13:21). God took from the earth two OT figures before their deaths: Enoch (Gen. 5:24) and Elijah (2 Kings 2:9-11).

Many Psalms express hope that communion with God, begun on earth, will have no end (Pss. 16:11; 49:15; 73:24). The Song of Moses (Deut. 32) and the Song of Hannah (1 Sam. 2) assert that Yahweh kills and makes alive. These expressions of hope confessing that the living God is able to intervene in life's darkest hours may reflect the beginnings of a doctrine of resurrection.

The prophets proclaimed hope for the future in terms of national renewal (see Hos. 6:1-3; Ezek. 37). New Testament writers sometimes used the language of the prophets to expound the doctrine of resurrection (compare Hos. 13:14; 1 Cor. 15:55). The prophets professed the sovereignty of God over all His subjects, even death. Isaiah 26:19 and Dan. 12:2 decidedly teach a belief in resurrection, a belief that gained full expression in intertestamental literature. See *Eschatology; Hope; Sheol.*

Jesus' preaching presupposed a doctrine of resurrection of the righteous to eternal life and of the wicked to eternal punishment (Matt. 8:11-12; 25:31-34,41-46; John 5:28-29). Opposition by the Sadducees, who denied the resurrection, gave Jesus the opportunity to assert His own thoughts (Mark 12:18-27; Matt. 22:23-33; Luke 20:27-38; compare Deut. 25:5-10). Jesus is the mediator of resurrection who gives to believers the life given Him by His Father (John 6:53-58). Jesus is the resurrection and the life

(11:24-26). In His postresurrection appearances Jesus had a body that was both spiritual (John 20:19,26) and physical (John 20:20, 27; 21:13,15) in nature. Thus, our resurrected body will be a spiritual body, different from the present physical body (1 Cor. 15:35-50); but it will have continuity with the present body because Christ redeems the whole person (Rom. 8:23).

The bedrock of hope for Christian resurrection is the resurrection of Christ, the foundation of gospel preaching (1 Cor. 15:12-20). Christ is the firstfruits of an upcoming harvest (1 Cor. 15:20-23). Destruction awaits those who do not follow Christ (Phil. 3:19). Persons live beyond time not because of any inherent immortality but because God gives them life (2 Cor. 5:1-10). Those united to Christ in faith become not only one with Him in spirit but also one with Him in body (1 Cor. 6:15).

RESURRECTION OF JESUS CHRIST

The bodily, living appearance of Jesus of Nazareth after He died and was buried, providing certain hope for resurrection of believers (1 Cor. 15:3-8; compare Matt. 27:56, 61; 28:1-2,16-20; Mark 16:1-8; Luke 24; Acts 1:6-11; John 20-21).

Jesus taught for 40 days and made various appearances (1 Cor. 15:3-8; Luke 24:34-43; John 20:24-29; Acts 1:9-11; 7:55-56; 9:1-9; 15:13; Rev. 1). He told the disciples to await the Spirit in Jerusalem, repeated His missionary commission, and ascended as they watched and were assured by angels of His return.

Jesus instructed the earliest believers about the prophetic and theological meaning of His death and resurrection. The resurrection of Jesus involved His physical body; but His resurrected life was a new kind of life called into being by God, the Effector of the resurrection (Acts 2:24). Because of the resurrection of Christ, we have assurance of the resurrection of all persons—some to salvation; some to perdition. That is

God's ultimate answer to the problem of death (1 Cor. 15:12-58). See *Ascension; Christ; Jesus; Resurrection.*

REUEL *(friend of God)*

(1) Son of Esau and ancestor of several Edomite clans (Gen. 36:4,10,13,17; 1 Chron. 1:35,37).

(2) Father of Zipporah, Moses' wife (Ex. 2:18). Father of Hobab, Moses' father-in-law (Num. 10:29). See *Jethro.*

(3) A Gadite (Num. 2:14).

(4) A Benjaminite (1 Chron. 9:8).

REVELATION OF GOD

God's manifestation of Himself to humankind in such a way that men and women can know and fellowship with Him. Jesus Christ is God's final revelation. The Bible is the divinely inspired source of knowledge from God about God.

General Revelation

General revelation is God's self-disclosure of Himself in a general way to all people at all times in all places. General revelation occurs through:

(1) nature,

(2) in our experience and in our conscience, and

(3) in history.

To say God reveals Himself through nature means that through the events of the physical world God communicates to us things about Himself that we would otherwise not know. "Ever since God created the world, his invisible qualities both his eternal power and his divine nature, have been clearly seen; they are perceived in the things that God has made. So those people have no excuse at all" (Rom. 1:20 TEV; compare Ps. 19:1). All that can be known about God in a natural sense has been revealed in nature.

God "causes His sun to rise on the evil and the good, and sends rain on the righteous and the unrighteous" (Matt. 5:45 NASB), thus revealing His goodness to all. God makes Himself known in the continuing care and provision for humankind (Acts 14:15-17).

God also reveals Himself in men and women made in the "image" and "likeness" of God (Gen. 1:26-27). Humans, as a direct creation of God, are a mirror or reflection of God evidenced by their place of dominion over the rest of creation; in their capacity to reason, feel, and imagine; in their freedom to act and respond; and in their sense of right and wrong (Gen. 1:28; Rom. 2:14, 15). Especially through this moral sense God reveals Himself in the consciences of men and women. The fact that religious belief and practice is universal confirms the apostle's statements in Romans.

Yet, the creatures who worship, pray, build temples, idols and shrines, and seek after God in diverse ways do not glorify God as God nor give Him thanks (Rom. 1:21-23). Because each person has been given the capacity for receiving God's general revelation, they are responsible for their actions.

All of history, rightly understood, bears the imprint of God's activity. God is revealed in history through the rise and fall of peoples and nations (compare Acts 17:22-31). God's general revelation is plain, whether in nature, in human conscience, or in history. It is often misinterpreted because sinful and finite humans are trying to understand a perfect and infinite God.

General revelation is not sufficient to give the knowledge of God necessary for salvation. For God's power (Rom. 1:20), goodness (Matt. 5:45), and righteousness (Rom. 2:14-15) have been revealed, but not His salvific grace. That is revealed only through special revelation. God in His general revelation reveals Himself so clearly it leaves all without excuse, but because of our sinfulness, humans pervert the reception of His general revelation.

Men and women suppress God's truth because they do not like the God to which the truth leads them so they invent substitute gods and religions instead. The act of suppressing the awareness of God and His demands warps our reason and conscience. Because of this rejection of God, He righteously reveals His wrath against humankind.

Special Revelation

God's special revelation is available to specific people at specific times in specific places; it is available now only through Scripture. Special revelation is first of all particular. God chooses to whom and through whom He will make Himself known. God manifests Himself in a particular manner to His people so they will be a channel of blessing to all others (Gen. 12:3).

Special revelation is also progressive, progressing not from untruth to truth, but from a lesser to a fuller revelation (Heb. 1:1-3). The revelation of the law in the OT is not superseded by the gospel, but is fulfilled in it.

Special revelation is primarily redemptive and personal. Within time and space God has acted and spoken to redeem the human race from its own self-imposed evil. Through calling people, miracles, the exodus, covenant making, and ultimately through Jesus Christ, God has revealed Himself in history. The ultimate point of God's personal revelation is in Jesus Christ. In Him, the Word became flesh (John 1:1,14; 14:9). The redemptive revelation of God is that Jesus Christ has borne the sins of fallen humanity, has died in their place, and has been raised to assure justification. This is the fixed center of special revelation.

Special revelation is also propositional. It made known truths about Him to His people. Knowledge about someone precedes intimate knowledge of someone.

Special revelation has three stages: (1) redemption in history, ultimately centering in the work of the Lord Jesus Christ; (2) the Bible, written revelation interpreting what He has done for the redemption of men and women; (3) the work of the Holy Spirit in the lives of individuals and the corporate life of the church, applying God's revelation to the minds and hearts of His people. As a result, men and women receive Jesus Christ as Lord and Savior and are enabled to follow Him faithfully in a believing, covenant community until life's end.

The content of special revelation is primarily God Himself. God does not fully reveal Himself to any person. God reveals Himself to persons to the degree they can receive it.

God makes Himself known to those who receive His revelation in faith (Heb. 11:1,6). Through the Bible the Spirit witnesses to individuals of God's grace and the need of faith response. Faith is the reception of God's revelation without reservation or hesitation (Rom. 10:17).

God has initiated the revelation of Himself to men and women, making it possible to know God and grow in relationship with Him. For believers today, the Bible is the source of God's revelation. In the written word we can identify God, know and understand something about Him, His will, and His work, and point others to Him.

REVELATION OF JESUS CHRIST

Last book of the Bible, an apocalyptic work pointing to future hope and calling for present faithfulness. To encourage Christian faithfulness, Revelation points to the glorious world to come (21:4; compare 7:16) at the reappearing of the crucified and risen Jesus. This now enthroned Lord will return to conclude world history (and the tribulations of the readers) with the destruction of God's enemies, the final salvation of His own people, and the creation of a new heaven and a new earth. The author used intense personal experience and rich apocalyptic symbolism to warn his readers of the impending disasters and temptations that would require their steadfast allegiance to the risen Lord.

The apostle John, the author, was exiled to the island of Patmos (1:9). A faithful Christian in Pergamum had suffered death (2:13), and the church in Smyrna was warned of a time of impending persecution (2:10); but the persecutions described in the Revelation were still largely anticipated at the time of John's writing.

Scholars have traditionally suggested two dates for the writing of the Revelation based on the repeated references to persecution (1:9; 2:2-3,10,13; 3:9-10; 6:10-11; 7:14-17; 11:7; 12:13–13:17; 14:12-20; 19:2; 21:4). From about A.D. 150, Christian authors usually referred to Domitian's reign (A.D. 81–96) as the time of John's writing, but there is no historical consensus supporting a persecution of Christians under Domitian while hard evidence does exist for a persecution under Nero (A.D. 54–68). In this century, most NT scholars have opted for the later date under Domitian (about A.D. 95), though there has been a resurgence of opinion (including this author's) arguing for a setting just following the reign of Nero (about A.D. 68).

The Revelation has traditionally been called an apocalypse. John called his work a "prophecy" (1:3; 22:10,19), but also gave it some features of an epistle (1:4-7; 22:21).

The introduction (1:1-8) names the recipients "the seven churches" of the Roman province of Asia; the purpose: "revelation" of "the things which must shortly come to pass" (1:1); and theme: the Lord God Himself has guaranteed the final vindication of the crucified Jesus before all the earth. John's vision (1:9-20) was of the risen Lord with instructions to send not only the seven letters, but also a revelation of "the things which must shortly come to pass."

Letters (2:1-3:22) to the seven churches include: recipients; description of the risen Lord using a portion of the visionary description in 1:9-20; an "I know" section of either commendation or criticism; exhortation to repent or (for Smyrna and Philadelphia) to maintain assurance (3:10-13); an exhortation to "hear what the Spirit saith unto the churches"; and a promise of reward to the "overcomer," that is, the one who conquers by persevering in the cause of Christ.

The church at Ephesus (2:1-7) is told to return to their first love; Smyrna (2:8-11) to be faithful unto death; Pergamum (2:12-17) and Thyatira (2:18-29) to beware of false teaching and immoral deeds; Sardis (3:1-6) to wake up and complete their works of obedience; Philadelphia (3:7-13) to be sure faith in Jesus will assure access into the eternal kingdom; and Laodicea (3:14-22) to turn from their self-deception and repent of lukewarmness.

Chapters 4 and 5 tie the risen Lord's opening exhortations to the churches (chaps. 2–3) to the judgments and final triumph of the Lamb (chaps. 6–22). These chapters provide the historical and theological basis of the risen Lord's authority over both the church and the world by depicting His enthronement and empowering to carry out the judging and saving purposes of God. Similar to Dan. 7, Rev. 5 has both a book of judgment and a glorious, redemptive agent of God—the crucified Jesus, the Lamb and Lion of God, now enthroned and therefore worthy to take the book and break the seals.

The Seven Seals (6:1–8:5)

The breaking of the first four seals brings forth four differently colored horsemen (6:1-8), representing God's judgments through the upheavals of war and its devastating social consequences (violence, famine, pestilence, and death). The fifth seal (6:9-11) is the plea of martyred saints for divine justice upon their oppressors. For now, they must wait. The sixth seal brings forth the typical signs of the end: a great earthquake, the blackening of the sun, the ensanguining of the moon, and the falling of the stars of heaven (compare Matt. 24:29). The great day of God's (and the Lamb's) wrath has come, and nothing can save (6:14-17) but the people of God need not despair, for, as the "servants of our God" (7:3), they have the promise of heaven.

Chapter 7 is two visions (7:1-8,9-17), the second both interpreting and concluding the first. The sealing of the 144,000 (7:1-8) employs Jewish symbols to describe those who know God through Jesus Christ. The 144,000 comprise the full number of God's people, God's people now being all (Jew or Gentile) who are followers of Jesus.

In the second vision (7:9-17), the 144,000 have become "a great multitude, which no one could number." They are those "which came out of great tribulation," now to experience the joys of heaven and relief from the tribulations they have endured (compare 7:14-17 with 21:1-6; 22:1-5). They have experienced the tribulations of this evil age, but now in heaven they enjoy the presence of God (7:15; 21:3).

Revelation 8:1-5 gives us the seventh seal and signs of the very end of human history. The prophet starts over, using seven trumpets to declarethat the judgments of God also have a redemptive purpose.

Seven Trumpets (8:6–11:19)

The first four trumpets describe partial judgments ("one-third") upon the earth's vegetation, the oceans, fresh waters, and the heavenly lights (8:6-13). The last three trumpets are described as three "woes" upon the earth, emphasizing God's judgment on humankind. All these judgments have no redemptive effect, for the "rest of the men" who are not killed by these plagues do not repent of their immoralities (9:20-21). Between the sixth and seventh trumpets we are reminded of God's protective hand on His people (10:1–11:14) while the people of God bear a prophetic witness to the world.

In 10:1-8, John's call (after the pattern of Ezek. 2:1–3:11) is reaffirmed. The note of protection and witness is again struck in 11:1-13. Persecutions will last for "forty-two months," but His people cannot be destroyed, for the "two witnesses" (11:3-13) must bear witness to the mercy and judgment of God. The "two witnesses" are the church which must maintain a faithfully prophetic witness to the world even unto death. The temporary triumph of evil ("three-and-a-half days," 11:9,11) will turn to heavenly vindication as the two witnesses are raised from the dead (11:11-12).

With the seventh trumpet (and third woe) the end of history has come, "the time of the dead, that they should be judged" and the saints to be rewarded (11:18). John now unfolds that "42 months" of persecution (and protection/witness).

Dragon's Persecution of the Righteous (12:1–13:18)

The three-and-a-half years or "forty-two months," or "1,260 days," or "a time, times, and half a time" is the period when the powers of evil will do their works. During this time, God will protect His people (12:6,14) while they both bear witness to their faith (11:3) and simultaneously suffer at the hands of these evil powers (11:2,7; 12:13-17; 13:5-7). Chapter 12 unmistakably pinpoints its beginning with the ascension and enthronement of Christ (12:5).

Heaven rejoices because it has been rescued from Satan, but the earth must now mourn, because the devil has been cast down to earth, and his anger is great. He knows that he has been defeated by the enthronement of Christ and has but a short time (12:12). The woman, who (as Israel) brought forth the Christ (12:1-2) and also "other seed, those who have the testimony of Jesus Christ," now receive the brunt of the frustrated dragon's wrath (12:17). The woman is nourished and protected for "1,260 days" (12:6), for a "time, times, and half a time" (12:14).

The dragon brings forth two henchmen (ch. 13) to help him in his pursuit of those who believe in Jesus. Satan is thus embodied in a political ruler, the beast from the sea (13:1), who will speak blasphemies for "forty-two months" (13:5). He will "make war with the saints" (13:7), while the second beast (or false prophet, 19:20), who comes up from the earth (13:11), seeks to deceive the earth so that its inhabitants worship the first beast.

In chapters 12 and 13, the time period is not a literal three-and-a-half years, but the entire time between the ascension and return of Christ that will be permitted the dragon to execute his evil work upon the earth (compare Gal. 1:4; Eph. 2:2). Satan still rages; but his time is short, and his evil will cease at the return of Christ.

Summary of Triumph, Warning, and Judgment (14:1-20)

Chapter 14 employs seven "voices" to relate again the hopes and warnings of heaven. The faithful 144,000 will be rescued and taken to heaven's throne (14:1-5). An angel announces the eternal gospel and warns the earth of coming judgment (14:6-7). The people of God are warned not to follow the beast or else those who follow him suffer separation from God (14:9-12). Finally, two voices call for harvest (14:14-20).

Seven Cups (15:1–16:21)

Similar to the seven trumpets and the seven seals, the cups are also different. The wrath of God is no longer partial or temporary, but complete and everlasting, final and irrevocable. The seven cups have no break between the sixth and seventh outpourings of judgment. Only wrath is left with no more delay. Babylon the Great, the symbol for all who have vaunted themselves against the most high God, will fall. The end has come (16:18).

The Fall of Babylon (17:1–18:24)

Chapter 17 retells the sixth cup, the fall of Babylon the Great, and chapter 18 gives a moving lament for the great city.

Advent of the Bride, the Holy City (19:1–22:25)

All of heaven rejoices over the righteous judgment of God upon evil (19:1-6). The Lamb's bride, the people of God, has made herself ready by her faithfulness to her Lord through the hour of suffering (see 19:7-8). Heaven is opened, and the One whose coming has been faithfully petitioned from ages past appears to battle the enemies of God, a conflict whose outcome is not in doubt (19:11-16). The first beast and the second beast are thrown into the lake of fire from which there is no return (19:20). The dragon—Satan—is cast into a hellish abyss that is shut and sealed for a thousand years (20:1-3).

Since the powers of evil reigned for "three-and-a-half years" (the period of time between the ascension and return of our Lord), Christ will reign for a "thousand years." The dead in Christ are raised to govern with Him (20:4-6), and God's rightful rule over the earth is vindicated.

At the end of Christ's reign, the final disposition of Satan will occur (20:7-10). In one final battle, Satan and his followers are overcome, and the devil joins the beast and the false prophet in the lake of fire where "[they] shall be tormented day and night for ever and ever" (20:10). Then the final judgment takes place, at which whosoever was not found written in the book of life was cast into the lake of fire (20:15).

Chapter 21 is often thought to refer to the period following the 1,000-year reign, but it is more probably a retelling of the return of Christ from the viewpoint of the bride as chapter 17 was a recapitulation of the seventh cup. To be the bride is to be the holy city, the New Jerusalem, to live in the presence of God and the Lamb, and to experience protection, joy, and the everlasting, life-giving light of God (21:9-27). His bond servants shall serve Him and reign with Him forever and ever (21:1-5).

Conclusion (22:6-21)

John concluded his prophecy by declaring the utter faithfulness of his words. Those who heed his prophecy will receive the blessings of God. Those who ignore the warnings will be left outside the gates of God's presence (22:6-15). Solemnly and hopefully praying for the Lord to come, John closed his book (22:17,20). The churches must have ears to hear what the Spirit has said (22:16). The people of God must, by His grace (22:21), persevere in the hour of tribulation, knowing that their enthroned Lord will return in triumph.

REZEPH (*glowing coal*)

Town whose conquest, most likely under Shalmaneser III (about 838 B.C.), Assyrians used as warning to king Hezekiah of Judah in 701 B.C.

against relying on God to deliver him from them (2 Kings 19:12; Isa. 37:12); possibly Rezzafeh about 100 miles southeast of Aleppo.

REZIN

King of Syria about 735 B.C. When Ahaz of Judah refused to join Rezin and Pekah of Israel in fighting against Assyria, Rezin pursuaded Pekah to ally with him against the Judean king (2 Kings 15:37; 16:5). Ahaz appealed for help to Tiglath-pileser of Assyria, who came against Rezin and Pekah and destroyed their kingdoms. Rezin died in 732 B.C. when Damascus fell to the Assyrians.

REZON (prince)

Aramaean leader who led successful revolt against Solomon and established independent state with capital at Damascus (1 Kings 11:23-25). See Damascus.

RHEGIUM (Greek, rent, torn; or Latin, royal).

Port at southwestern tip of Italian boot about seven miles across strait of Messina from Sicily. Paul stopped there en route to Rome (Acts 28:13).

RHODA (rose)

Slave or visitor in John Mark's house who failed to let Peter in (Acts 12:13; compare Luke 24:9-11).

RHODES

Island off southwest coast of Asia Minor in Mediterranean Sea associated with the Dodanim (Gen. 10:4; Ezek. 27:15); founded as Minoan trading colony about 1500 B.C. and came under the control of a single government around 407 B.C. A wealthy shipping center, Rhodes developed navies that controlled the eastern Mediterranean. Standing with one foot on either side of the harbor entrance was the 105-foot-tall brass Colossus, one of the Seven Wonders of the World. Set up in 288 B.C., it fell during an earthquake about 64 years later. Disloyalty to Roman rule met with stiff economic sanctions against the

city. When Paul stopped over on his voyage from Troas to Caesarea (Acts 21:1), Rhodes was only a minor provincial city. See Dodanim.

RIBLAH

(1) Syrian town near Kadesh on Orontes near border with Babylonia. There Pharaoh Neco imprisoned King Jehoahaz of Judah after the young monarch had reigned only three months (2 Kings 23:31-33). Later, when Zedekiah rebelled against Nebuchadnezzar of Babylon, he was taken to Riblah as a prisoner and viewed the execution of his sons before having his eyes put out (25:4-7). See Diblah.

(2) Town on eastern border of Canaan (Num. 34:11). Earliest translations read "Arbelah."

RIGHTEOUSNESS

Actions and positive results of a sound relationship within a local community or between God and a person or His people. Biblical righteousness is rooted in covenants and relationships, fulfillment of the terms of a covenant between God and humanity or between humans in the full range of human relationships. God's righteousness is what He does in fulfillment of the terms of the covenant He established with the chosen people, Israel (2 Chron. 12:6; Ps. 7:9; Jer. 9:24; Dan. 9:14). Characteristic of God experienced by those within the covenantal community as He functioned as the Judge of created order (Ps. 96:13). At times God's righteousness was experienced in God's delivering Israel from enemies and oppressors (Ps. 71); at other times, in God's delivering Israel from the nation's own sinfulness (Ps. 51:19). Such deliverance involved God's righteousness of wrath against the persecutor and the wicked (Ps. 106).

God's chosen nation was responsible to keep God's covenant. God acted to establish the covenant and in so doing bestowed salvation on Israel (Ex. 19). The law was given as an act of divine mercy to provide Israel with guidelines for keeping the nation's own portion of the covenant (Lev. 16; Ps. 40). God expected Israel to keep the law not to earn merit but to maintain the status God had already given the nation. Human righteousness in relation to God was understood as faithful adherence to the law (Lev. 19). The law God gave contained provision for atonement through repentance and appropriate acts of contrition (Lev. 19).

In strictly human terms the person who met the demands of a variety of social relations was thought to be righteous, to have done righteousness, though the requirements of righteousness varied with the covenantal/relational context. Some of the prominent areas were those of family (Gen. 38), friendship (1 Sam. 24), nation (Prov. 14:34), and even in relation to servants and certain foreigners (Job 31).

Human righteousness in the NT is absolute faith in and commitment to God (Matt. 3:15; Rom. 4:5; 1 Pet. 2:24). The one who in faith gives oneself to the doing of God's will is righteous, doing righteousness, and reckoned righteous by God (Jas. 2:23). The focus of faith in God is the saving activity of God in Jesus Christ (Rom. 3:21-26).The human-to-human dimension of righteousness (Phil. 1:3-11), seems less prominent in NT thought perhaps because of the importance of the NT concept of love.

"The righteousness of God" (Matt. 6:33; Acts 17:31; Rom. 1:17; Eph. 4:24; Jas. 1:20) is the key to understanding the salvation of humanity. Interpreters who take "the righteousness of God" to mean "God gives righteousness" see salvation as a God-created human possibility. Righteousness is that which God requires of humanity and which God gives as a gift to the person of faith. In this line of thought, faith is the condition for the reception of the gift of righteousness from God. God acts in Christ, and, in turn, humans react by having faith. Then God gives them righteousness or reckons them, on the basis of their faith, as if they were righteous.

Interpreters who understand "the righteousness of God" to mean "God is righteous" contend that salvation is purely the work of God, God's saving activity in keeping the divine side of the covenant of creation. God acts in Christ, and part of that action is the creation of faith on the part of human beings who otherwise have no faith. Thus "the righteousness of God" is the power of God at work saving humanity (and the whole of creation), through the creation of faith in sinful persons. See *Ethics; Grace; Law; Mercy; Salvation.*

RIMMON (*pomegranate*)

(1) Chief god of Syria, also called Hadad (2 Kings 5:18).

(2) Town of Judah (Josh. 15:32) given to Simeon (19:7; compare 1 Chron. 4:32); modern Khirbet er-Ramamin two miles south of Lahav; southern boundary of God's new exalted kingdom (Zech. 14:10). Early translations and many modern interpreters read En-rimmon in all occurrences. See *En-rimmon.*

(3) Levitical city in Zebulun (Josh. 19:13; 1 Chron. 6:77), probably the original reading for present Dimnah (Josh. 21:35); Rummaneh, six miles northeast of Nazareth.

(4) Rock near Gibeah where the people of Benjamin fled from vengeful Israelites (Judg. 20:45-47), modern Rammun four miles east of Bethel.

(5) Father of Rechab and Baanah, who killed Saul's son Ish-Bosheth (2 Sam. 4:2,9).

RIVERS AND WATERWAYS

(1) *Nile River.*The Nile plays a prominent role in the early events in the life of Moses (Ex. 2:3; 7:15,20). The Nile is alluded to as "the river" (Gen. 41:1), the "river of Egypt" (Gen. 15:18), the "flood of Egypt" (Amos 8:8), Shihor (Josh. 13:3), river of Cush among other names. The "brook of Egypt" mostly is a reference to Wadi el-Arish, the drainage system of the central Sinai. The prophets Amos (8:8; 9:5) and Jeremiah (46:8) used the Nile as the symbol of Egypt. See *Egypt; Nile River.*

(2) *Euphrates* flows 1,700 miles from the mountainous region of northeastern Turkey (Armenia) southward into northern Syria and turns southeasterly to join the Tigris and flows into the Persian Gulf to become the longest river in Western Asia. Two important tributaries, the Belikh and Khabur, flow into the Euphrates from the north. The Lower Euphrates generally formed the western limits of the city-states that made up the early Sumerian civilization. See *Euphrates and Tigris Rivers*.

(3) *Tigris*. From its source in a small lake (Hazar Golu), about 100 miles west of Lake Van, in Armenia, the Tigris flows in a southeasterly direction for about 1,150 miles before joining the Euphrates and emptying into the Persian Gulf. While its upper flow is swift within narrow gorges, from Mosul and Nineveh southward its course was navigable and was extensively used in antiquity for transport. A series of tributaries from the slopes of the Zagros emptied into the Tigris from the east, including the Greater and Lesser Zab and the Diyala. In antiquity its banks were inhabited by a dense population maintained and made prosperous by an excellent irrigation system.

Several rivers water Anatolia, part of modern Turkey. See *Asia Minor, Cities of*.

(4) *Halys River*. From its sources in the Armenian mountains, the Halys begins its 714-mile flow to the southwest only to be diverted by a secondary ridge into a broad loop until its direction is completely reversed in a northeasterly direction through the mountainous regions bordering the southern shore of the Black Sea. Within this loop of the Halys in the northern Anatolian plateau the Hittites established their capital Boghazkoy. The longest river in Anatolia, the Halys, is the result of heavy rainfall in the Pontic zone. Its widening course makes the Halys unnavigable. The course of the Halys generally formed the borders of the district of Pontus.

(5) *Rivers of the Aegean Coast*. The broken Aegean coastline boasted a series of sheltered havens and inlets that prompted Greek colonization and the establishment of the great harbor cities of the later Greek and Roman periods. The mouths of the Aegean rivers, deemed ideal for maritime centers during colonization, ultimately proved disastrous. Constant dredging was required to maintain the harbor's access to the sea and to avoid the formation of malaria-infested swamps. Thus the Hermus (155 miles) was diverted to prevent the destruction of the harbor of Smyrna (Izmir). To the south at Ephesus, the original town site on the disease-ridden marshlands was abandoned about A.D. 400 for the construction of a new harbor on the Cayster River. During the days of Ephesus' prosperity, the constant dredging was adequately maintained. However, with the decline of the Roman Empire after A.D. 200, the silting of the harbor brought the rapid decline of the city. Miletus, on the alluvial plain of the Maeander River (236 miles), was originally established on a deep gulf well sheltered from the prevailing winds. The great Ionian city had possessed four harbors, but the silting of the harbors by the alluvial deposits of the Maeander ultimately brought about the decline and abandonment of the city.

In Syria and Palestine rivers often separated peoples rather than providing economic power.

(6) *Orontes and Litani*. High within the Beqa valley that forms the rift between the Lebanon and Anti-Lebanon mountain ranges, a watershed (about 3,770 feet above sea level) forms the headwaters of the Orontes and Litani Rivers. The rains and snow on the mountain summits at heights of over 11,000 feet course down into the six- to-ten-mile-wide Beqa that is a part of the great Rift ("Valley of Lebanon," Josh. 11:17). From the watershed, the Orontes flows northward and bends westward to empty into the Mediterranean near Antioch. The Litani flows southward and ulti-

mately escapes to the sea north of Tyre. Unfortunately, its lower course has formed such a deep, narrow gorge that it is useless for communication. See *Palestine.*

(7) *Jordan River.* See *Jordan River.*

(8) *Kishon River.* This 23-mile long river drains the Jezreel Plain and the southern portion of the Accho Plain. The Kishon is rarely more than a brook within relatively shallow and narrow banks except during the heavy rains of the winter months, when its course becomes a marshy bog and impassable. From the Jezreel, it passes along the base of Mount Carmel through the narrow pass formed by a spur of the Galilean hills and into the Accho Plain, where some additional tributaries join before it empties into the Mediterranean. Its total length from the springs to the sea is only 23 miles. See *Kishon.*

(9) *Yarkon River* is formed by seasonal runoff from the western slopes of the Samaritan and Judean hills that flows into the Brook Kanah, its major tributary, and the rich springs at the base of Aphek about eight miles inland from the Mediterranean shoreline. Anchorages and small harbors, such as tel Qasile, a Philistine town, were established along its course; cedar timbers from Lebanon were floated inland to Aphek for transport to Jerusalem for the construction of Solomon's palace and temple. Still, the Yarkon historically formed a major barrier to north-south traffic because of the extensive swamps that formed along its course. The Yarkon formed the border between the tribes of Dan and Ephraim to the north. Farther inland, the Brook Kanah formed the boundary between Ephraim and Manasseh (Josh. 16:8; 17:9).

Two major seas heavily influenced Israel's political, economic, and cultural history.

(10) *Mediterranean Sea.* See *Mediterranean Sea.*

(11) *Red Sea.* See *Red Sea.*

RIZPAH (*glowing coals* or *bread heated over coals* or *ashes*)

Saul's concubine whom Abner took as wife in what amounted to a claim to the throne (2 Sam. 3:7; compare 1 Kings 2:22); best known for her faithful vigil over the bodies of her executed sons (2 Sam. 20:10-14).

ROBBERY

Taking another person's property without the person's consent; prohibited by Ten Commandments (Ex. 20:15; Deut. 5:19); irrelevant whether robber acquires property by force, duplicity, or oppression (see Gen. 31:31; Lev. 19:13; Deut. 24:14-15; Mal. 3:5; John 10:1); no specific penalty is prescribed; emphasis on restoration of stolen property to lawful owner (Ex. 22:1,4,7,9; Lev. 6:1-7; Num. 5:5-8). If a thief could not return or replace it, the thief could be sold into slavery until restitution was made (Ex. 22:3).

During NT period, robbery was under jurisdiction of Roman law. Captured robbers, on occasion, were crucified (Matt. 27:38; Mark 15:27). The more militant political groups, such as the Sicarii, resorted to murder and robbery. First-century robbers frequently operated together in bands, attacking travelers (Luke 10:30; compare Matt. 6:19-20; Rev. 3:3).

ROCK

Piece of stone; use of rocky sites as places of refuge (Num. 24:21; Judg. 15:8; 20:47) led to frequent image of God as a rock, a source of protection. Titles of God include: the "Stone of Israel" (Gen. 49:24 NASB); "the Rock" (Deut. 32:4); the Rock of salvation (32:15); the Rock which begat Israel (32:18);"the rock that is higher than I" (Ps. 61:2). Isaiah 8:13-14 pictures the Lord of hosts as a "stone of stumbling" to the unholy people of Israel and Judah. Paul identified Christ as the spiritual Rock that nourished Israel in the wilderness (1 Cor. 10:4). Other texts apply to Christ the Isaiah image of a rock that causes persons to fall (Rom. 9:33; 1 Pet. 2:8). Jesus' teaching is the rock-solid foundation for life (Matt. 7:24-25). The identity of the rock on which Christ promised to build the church (Matt. 16:18) is disputed. Possible identifications include: Peter, whose name means "rock," the larger group of disciples, Christ Himself, and Peter's confession of faith. The different Greek terms employed argue against a quick identification of Peter as the foundation. Both Christ (1 Cor. 3:11) and the larger circle of apostles (Eph. 2:20; Rev. 21:14) are pictured as the foundation of the church elsewhere. It seems unlikely that Matthew presents Christ as both Builder and foundation of the church. Application of the foundation image to evangelistic work (Rom. 15:20; 1 Cor. 3:10) suggests that Peter's God-revealed confession of faith in Jesus as the Christ, the Son of the living God (Matt. 16:16), is the foundation of the church that lays seige to the gates of Hades. See *Keys of the Kingdom; Peter.*

ROD, STAFF

Straight, slender stick growing on (Jer. 1:11) or cut from (Gen. 30:37-41) a tree; "rod" is sometimes used interchangeably with "staff" (Isa. 10:5; Rev. 11:1). Elsewhere, "rod" designates a shorter, clublike stick (Ps. 23:4). Rods and staffs were used as walking sticks (Gen. 32:10), for defense (Ps. 23:4), for punishment (Ex. 21:20; Num. 22:27; Prov. 13:24; 1 Cor. 4:21), and for measurement (Rev. 11:1). Rods and staffs were also used as symbols of prophetic (Ex. 4:2-4; 7:8-24; Judg. 6:21), priestly (Num. 17:1-10), and royal (Gen. 49:10 NRSV; Judg. 5:14 NRSV; Jer. 48:17; Rev. 2:27) office.

ROMAN LAW

System of government and justice developed over a period of 1,000 years, from the publication of the XII Tables in 451–50 B.C. to Emperor Justinian's codification in A.D. 529–34.

Paul was a Roman citizen from birth (Acts 22:27) His citizenship proved advantageous during his missionary travels. Roman citizenship could be obtained by one of several means: inheriting it at birth from parents who were citizens; service to the empire, either civil or military; or purchase (Acts 22:28). False claims to citizenship were punishable by death.

Citizenship bestowed certain rights to: vote for magistrates, be elected as a magistrate, contract a legal marriage, hold property in the Roman community, and appeal to the people, and in later times to the emperor, against the sentences passed by magistrates or other officials of rank. Paul's citizenship surfaced in several details of his missionary activity. Discovering that Paul was a Roman citizen, the lictors or magistrates in Philippi realized that they had punished him without trial—a violation of Roman law (Acts 16:39; compare 22:24-29), moreover his right to appealed to Caesar for a trial at Rome (Acts 25:10-12).

The NT "House Codes" (Eph. 5:21–6:9; Col. 3:18–4:1; and 1 Pet. 2:18–3:7) should be interpreted against the background of the status of the family and the power of the head of the household in Roman society. Roman society, both legally and culturally, looked to the family as the primary unit of society. Traditionally the *paterfamilias* (head of the household) was the only fully legal person in the family. The "family" included the wife, all unmarried sons and daughters, married sons and their families, those persons adopted into the family, and slaves. All of these persons lived under the *patria potestas,* or "absolute power," of the patriarchal head of the household. The father decided whether or not to allow a newborn infant to die. In early Roman times fathers could sell their children just as they could any other property. Persons living under another's *patria potestas* in actuality owned nothing. Upon their marriage, daughters passed into the power of another family's *patria potestas.* Upon the death of the *paterfamilias,* as many new families were created as there had been sons living under his power (or grandsons, in the event their fathers had died). Against such a background, Paul's command to be subject to one another (Eph. 5:21) was a revolutionary word spoken to a society in which all were subject to the *paterfamilias*.

The representative and executor of Roman law was Pontius Pilate, the Roman procurator, or governor, of Judea (A.D. 26–36). Pilate held the *imperium*, the supreme administrative life-or-death power over the subjects in a province. The imperium extended particularly over the *peregrini*, or non-Roman citizens such as Jesus living in an occupied state. Provincial subjects had little to protect them against abuses of the life and death power wielded by proconsuls and lesser governors such as Pilate. In the eyes of his superiors, Pilate's first priority was public order, not the execution of justice. If an innocent Galilean peasant was the focal point of a civil disturbance, the quelling of the disturbance, and not justice for the *peregrinus* involved, was the uppermost concern for Roman officials fearful of revolts in occupied provinces.

The *ordo iudiciorum publicoum*, perhaps best translated as "the list of national courts" contained a list of crimes and punishments with the maximum and minimum penalties that could be exacted against Roman citizens. In the case of a noncitizen like Jesus, Pilate would have been free to proceed based on his *imperium* and his own good judgment. He functioned as prosecuting attorney, judge, and jury. He would have been free to be as harsh and arbitrary as he preferred. A good first-century procurator would, however, have tended more and more to judge a *peregrinus* by the *ordo*.

Roman trial proceedings were public, before the tribune (compare Matt. 27:19). Interested parties brought formal charges, which had to be specific (compare Matt. 27:12). Jesus was charged before Pilate with a political crime. The Romans would never execute someone simply on religious grounds. Roman criminal trials included the *cognitio*, or the questioning of the accused. After A.D.

50 enlightened officials gave accused persons three opportunities to respond to charges made against them (compare John 18:33,35,37), following the most enlightened possible juridical rules of the day. Failure to respond to the charges resulted in conviction by default. When Jesus remained silent and made no defense, under the Roman system, Pilate had no other option but to convict. The governor would render his verdict in the form of a sentence to a particular punishment.

The trial of Jesus conforms in many of its particulars to the fine points of Roman criminal procedure. It was not unknown to transfer jurisdiction to the accused's place of origin (compare Pilate's sending Jesus to Herod in Luke 23:6-7). The trial of Jesus took place early in the day (John 18:28), precisely at the time when ancient Roman officials were the busiest. Roman women normally shared the responsibilities of husbands serving as career diplomats. They often were the husband's best advisor (Matt. 27:19).

The Roman system of criminal justice distinguished between public and private penalties. The private penalty consisted of a sum of money paid to the person wronged as a substitute for private retaliation. Public penalties ranged from light beatings to the infliction of the death penalty: decapitation, gallows or crucifixion, burning, and drowning in a sack. Imprisonment as a penalty for a crime was unknown in Roman times.

Paul's trials accord with Roman trial procedure. Jews made the original charges against Paul, but later disappeared from the case (Acts 24:18-19). Before Felix (Acts 24:19), Paul objected that his accusers ought to be present. Roman law was strongly inclined against persons who made accusations and then abandoned them. Acts closes (28:30) with Paul under "house arrest" in Rome for two years awaiting trial. This could be explained by a congested court list, the failure of his accusers to appear to lodge their charges, or the upheaval that characterized Nero's reign. Acts twice links Paul with Roman proconsuls (Sergius Paulus on Cyprus in 13:6-12 and Annius Gallio at Corinth in 18:12-17). See *Trial of Jesus; Citizen, Citizenship; Marriage; Family; Pilate, Pontius.*

ROMANS, LETTER TO THE

Most significant theological letter ever written; sixth book of NT. Paul had decided to leave Ephesus, travel through Macedonia and Achaia, go to Jerusalem to deliver the offerings for the poor (15:26), and then visit Rome (Acts 19:21). He spent three months in Achaia (Acts 20:2-3). Most scholars would date Romans as written from Corinth between A.D. 54 to 59, probably 55-56.

Paul had desired for a long time to visit Christians in Rome that "we may be mutually encouraged by each other's faith" (Rom. 1:8-13). Paul had run out of room in the eastern empire (15:23), having preached from Jerusalem to Illyricum (15:19). Paul planned to continue his ministry to the western limit of the empire and go to Spain (15:24). Paul wrote to:

(1) request their prayers as he faced the threatening situation in Jerusalem,

(2) alert them to his intended visit,

(3) acquaint them with some of his understanding of what God had done in Christ,

(4) instruct them in areas where the church faced specific problems, and

(5) enlist their support in his planned missionary venture to Spain.

The theme of Romans is the "righteousness of God" (see 1:16-17), but the meaning of this phrase is disputed. Some interpret it to mean the righteousness that God bestows on persons on the basis of Christ's work, understanding "of God" to mean "from God." Other interpreters hold that "the righteousness of God" is the activity of God, understanding the term primarily from its use in the Greek translation of the OT where it refers to God's acting in His saving power. This seems the better alternative—the righteousness of God is God in action, setting things right through the life, death, and resurrection of Jesus. See *Righteousness.*

Justification (God's action in making persons righteous) may refer primarily to one's new status in Christ—justification would thus mean the bestowal of a righteous status before God—or to one's new moral character in Christ—justification would then mean God's action in one's life to enable a person to achieve high ethical standards. The best understanding of justification is one that includes both the new status of a person before God and the new life that this status demands. (See *Justification.*) Salvation is both God's gift of a righteous status before Him in Christ (6:22-23) and God's demand to live the new life that Christ makes possible (6:19). What God has done for us in Christ summons us to what we ought to do for God. See *Ethics; Salvation.*

Paul understood the center of the Christian life to be intense struggle with the power of sin in one's life. God came in Christ to set people free from the enslaving power of sin by enabling guilty sinners to be declared righteous and then to achieve it. Paul used the figures of Adam and Christ as representing the only two possibilities for human existence. Adam, the original transgressor (5:12), was the one through whom sin entered; but sin did not come alone—death is inseparably linked to sin (5:12-14). Sin or death "reigned" (5:14,21). Sin's power demonstrated itself in using the holy law for its own purposes (7:8-12). Sin, death, and law oppose another triad of powers (see 5:18-21) in the realm of Christ: righteousness (against sin), grace (against law), and life (against death).

Flesh, as substance or material, is in itself neutral and has neither evil nor good nature; but a person under sin's control is "in the flesh" (8:9), a contrast to life "in the Spirit" (8:9-11). In this life (in the flesh) believers must rise to the demand of God's gift to us through Christ and walk "according to the Spirit" (8:4-8). The transition from the realm of Adam to the realm of Christ is dying and rising with Christ (6:5-11). This union with Christ in death reveals sin in all its ugliness. Believers follow God as Jesus did, repudiate sin's rule, and realize sin's end is death. Our resurrection with Christ is our rising from death with Him spiritually to live to God. This dying and rising with Christ sets us free from sin in the sense that sin's power is no longer enslaving. The Christian has the resources of God to fight sin victoriously; but intense struggle is necessary (6:11).

Dying and rising with Christ results in a person's being "in Christ" Paul's favorite way of describing salvation. To be "in Christ" is to be in the power field of grace, life, and righteousness; it is to live in the strength of our having been raised with Christ; and it is a life of trust in God that struggles with the power of sin in one's life on the basis of God's powerful presence (Holy Spirit).

Paul's introduction to the letter (1:1-15) sets out the apostolic calling that qualifies him (vv. 1-7) and explains his reason for writing the Romans (vv. 8-15). Paul crisply stated the theme of his letter—the righteousness of God, revealed in the gospel and bringing salvation (1:16-17). Paul then demonstrated that all persons need salvation (1:18–3:20), showing first that the power of sin rules the Gentiles (1:18-32) and, second, that the power of sin rules the Jews as well (2:1–3:8). All humanity stands under the power of sin (3:19-20).

The second major section deals with God's provision of righteousness through Jesus Christ on the basis of faith (3:21–4:25). God has manifested His righteousness apart from the law in the expiating blood of Jesus Christ. God justified (declared righteous) persons on the basis of trust (3:21-26). Justification by faith excludes boasting or exulting in one's goodness achieved by works according to the law. The way God justified Abraham by faith demonstrates that trust as a way of relating to God preceded seeking to relate to Him by the works of the law, meeting the Jewish objection that God requires works for justification (3:27–4:25).

The third section of Romans deals with the impact and implication of what God does for us in Christ and focuses on how salvation results in a victorious new life (5:1–8:39). The immediate result of justification is a realization of peace with God based on the assurance coming from God's love for us and results in one's ability to rejoice in the face of difficulties because Christ has reversed the results of Adam's disobedience (5:1-21). The very heart of salvation is found in the Christian's continuing, but victorious, struggle with sin (6:1–7:25). This victorious struggle is possible because of the power of the risen Christ, experienced as Holy Spirit, who assists us to do what is right (8:1-39).

The fourth section (chs. 9–11) addresses the question among Jewish Christians about the destiny of the Jews who still felt themselves to be God's people even though they had rejected Christ. Paul stressed that the righteousness of God is demonstrated in His faithfulness to all His promises—even those to Israel in the OT. Paul confessed his personal grief over Israel's rejection of Christ (9:1-15) and affirmed that God has, as always, displayed His sovereignty in dealing with Israel (9:6-29). Israel's God-given freedom to choose explains the rejection of Jesus as the Christ (9:30-10:21). Paul reminded his readers that God's righteousness is displayed in His mercy on which all—both Jews and Gentiles—are dependent (11:1-36).

The final section is a summons to practical obedience to God (12:1–15:13). Christians should live transformed lives (12:1-2) and demonstrate this in a good stewardship of their spiritual gifts (12:3-21), in fulfilling their obligations to the state (13:1-7), in making love supreme (13:8-14), and in seeking to nurture others in the fellowship of the church, being particularly careful to bear with and edify the weak (14:1–15:13).

The conclusion to the letter (15:14–16:27) summarized Paul's ministry and his plans for the future, requesting their prayers (15:14-33); commended Phoebe (16:1-2), sent greetings to individual Christians (16:3-24), and ended with praise for God (16:27).

ROME AND THE ROMAN EMPIRE

International rule the government in Rome, Italy, exercised after 27 B.C. when the Republic of Rome died and the Roman Empire was born. Octavian became sole ruler and in 27 B.C. took the name: Augustus Caesar. The republic became the empire, and Octavian became the first emperor of Rome.

Augustus was extremely efficient as an administrator and corrected many of the problems that plagued the old republic. He appointed procurators over these potentially volatile areas, where the Roman legions or armies were stationed. Pontius Pilate was such a procurator or governor over Judea (Luke 3:1).

Jesus was born during the reign of Augustus (27 B.C.–A.D. 14) and conducted His ministry during the reign of Augustus's successor, Tiberius (A.D. 14–37; compare Luke 3:1). The latter's image was stamped on a silver denarius that Jesus referred to in a discussion about taxation (Luke 20:20-26). In about A.D. 18, Herod Antipas, the son of Herod the Great, built his capital on the western shore of the Sea of Galilee and named it Tiberias after the emperor. Tiberius was an extremely able military commander and a good administrator, leaving a large surplus in the treasury when he died. He followed Augustus's example of not expanding the borders of the empire and thus avoiding war. The *pax Romana* (peace of Rome) that Augustus had inaugurated was preserved, providing easy, safe travel throughout the empire. Paul undoubtedly referred to this in Galatians 4:4 when he wrote: "when the *fullness of the time* was come, God sent forth his Son" (author's italics). Tiberius was never popular with

the senate and chose to leave Rome at the first opportunity, choosing after A.D. 26, to rule the empire from his self-imposed seclusion on the Isle of Capri. In this year Pontius Pilate was appointed governor of Judea, a post he held until A.D. 36, just prior to the death of Tiberius in A.D. 37.

Tiberius was succeeded by his mentally unbalanced grandnephew, Gaius (Caligula), who proved to be a disaster. During his reign (A.D. 37–41) and that of his successor, his aging uncle Claudius (A.D. 41–54), most of Paul's ministry took place. Claudius is reported to have expelled Jews from Rome who were creating disturbances at the instigation of Christ (compare Acts 18:2). Initially viewed as inept, Claudius turned out to be one of Rome's more proficient emperors. He was responsible for the conquest of southern Britain in A.D. 43–47, although it took another 30 years to subjugate northern Britain and Wales. His fourth wife, Agrippina poisoned Claudius in A.D. 54 to speed up the succession of Nero, her son by a previous marriage.

Nero (A.D. 54–68) was in some respects worse than Caligula, a man without moral scruples or interest in the Roman populace. Both Paul and Peter seem to have been martyred during Nero's reign, perhaps in connection with the burning of Rome by Nero in A.D. 64, an event he blamed on Christians. The revolt of Galba, one of his generals, led to Nero's suicide.

Galba, Otho, and Vitellius, three successive emperor-generals, died within the year of civil war (A.D. 68-69) that followed Nero's death. Vitellius's successor was Vespasian, one of the commanders who had taken Britain for Claudius and who was in Judea squelching the first Jewish revolt. He was declared emperor by the Syrian and Danube legions and returned to Rome to assume the post, leaving his son Titus to finish the destruction of Jerusalem with its holy temple in the next year (A.D. 70) (note Luke 21:20).

The aristocratic Julio-Claudian dynasties that had reigned until the death of Nero were happily replaced by the Flavian dynasty, which issued from the rural middle class of Italy and reflected a more modest and responsible approach to the use of power. Vespasian's reign (A.D. 69–79) was succeeded by the brief tenure of his son Titus (A.D. 79–81), who at his death gave way to the rule of his brother Domitian (A.D. 81–96). The fourth-century historian Eusebius reported that the apostle John was exiled to Patmos (compare Rev. 1:9) in the reign of Domitian. Eusebius also claimed that in Nerva's reign the senate took away Domitian's honors and freed exiles to return home, thus letting John return to Ephesus.

Nerva's reign was brief, lasting little more than a year (A.D. 96–98). He was succeeded by Trajan (A.D. 98–117), who bathed the empire red in the blood of Christians. His persecution was more severe than that instituted by Domitian. Irenaeus wrote in the second century that John died in Ephesus in the reign of Trajan. The persecution of the church, depicted in the Revelation of John, probably reflects the ones initiated by Trajan and Domitian.

RUHAMAH (pitied)

Name Hosea used to symbolize the change in Israel's status before God following God's judgment (2:1; compare 1:6). First Peter 2:10 applies Hosea's image to Christians who have experienced God's mercy in Christ.

RUTH

Ancestor of David and Jesus. See *Ruth, Book of.*

RUTH, BOOK OF

Book in OT writings that tells the story of the reversal of fortunes for Ruth and her mother-in-law, Naomi; one of five Megilloth (scrolls read for Jewish festivals); read at the Feast of Weeks. See *Festivals.* Set in the period of Israel's judges in the agrarian world of Moab and the environs of Bethlehem, the story begins (1:1-5) by telling why Naomi is in Moab and her plight following the deaths of her husband and sons. Episode A (1:6-22) narrates her return to and reception in Bethlehem, and how Ruth came to be with her. Episode B (2:1-16) finds Ruth and Boaz meeting while she gleans grain during harvest. Episode C (2:17-23) shows Naomi and Ruth discussing Ruth's day in the field and identifies Boaz as a kinsman with a certain role to fulfill. Episode D (3:1-5) finds Naomi pressing Boaz's role as kinsman. Episode E (3:6-13) follows a transition in which Ruth and Boaz encounter each other, and Boaz is confronted by his responsibility as kinsman. Episode F (3:14-18) delays the plot's resolution while Naomi assures Ruth that the matter will be settled. Episode G (4:1-6) tells of Boaz at the gate settling the matters of Elimelech's property and Ruth, with another kinsman. A narrative aside (4:7-8) explains the custom of the sandal. Boaz's actions are witnessed, and he is blessed by the people and the elders for his role as kinsman in Episode H (4:9-12). Episode I (4:13-17a) reverses the fortunes of Naomi and Ruth with Obed's birth, who is declared a child of Naomi. This declaration ensures a name and a future for Naomi's family. A coda (4:18-22) ties up the story with a family genealogy.

Ruth speaks against postexilic particularism by accepting Ruth (a native of Moab) into Israel's genealogical mainstream and the book into the Hebrew canon. See *Moab.* Ruth is concerned with Israelite family and marriage patterns and obligations. Ruth's plot shows levirate marriage (Deut. 25:5-10) as a family obligation at work. Religiously, the book tells the story of the faith of Naomi and Ruth and shows the ways of God in one unique family situation. The text's final form speaks to political concerns by a genealogy (4:17b-22) that details David's family background and serves to legitimate him as king on Saul's throne.

S

SABACHTHANI (*he has forsaken me*) See *Eli, Eli, Lama Sabachthani.*

SABAOTH (*hosts, armies, heavenly bodies*)

Transliteration of Hebrew divine title, "Lord of Hosts," variously interpreted as Lord of Israel's armies (compare 1 Sam. 17:45); the deposed Canaanite nature gods whose title Yahweh assumed; the stars; members of Yahweh's heavenly court or council; a comprehensive title for all beings, heavenly and earthly; an intensive title describing God as all powerful. The title was apparently closely tied to Shiloh and the ark of the covenant (1 Sam. 1:3,11; 4:4; 6:2). Yahweh Sabaoth seems to have emphasized God's place as divine king enthroned on the cherubim with the ark as His footstool ruling over the nation, the earth, and the heavens (Ps. 24:10). He is the God without equal (Ps. 89:8) who is present with His people (Ps. 46:7,11; compare 2 Sam. 5:10).

SABBATH

Day of rest; cessation from all work every seventh day; considered holy to God by His rest on the seventh day after creation and viewed as a sign of the covenant relation between God and His people and of the eternal rest He has promised them. Regulations concerning the sabbath are a main feature of the Ten Commandments. On six days the Israelites should work, but on the seventh, they as well as all slaves, foreigners, and beasts must rest. Two reasons are given. The first is that God rested on the seventh day after creation, thereby making the day holy (Ex. 20:8-11). The second was a reminder of their redemption from slavery in Egypt (Deut. 5:12-15).

The day became a time for sacred assembly and worship (Lev. 23:1-3), a token of their covenant with God (Ex. 31:12-17; Ezek. 20:12-20). Death was the penalty for desecration (Ex. 35:1-3). True observance would lift a person to God's holy mountain and bring spiritual nourishment (Isa. 56:1-7; 58:13), but failure to keep the sabbath would bring destruction to their earthly kingdom (Neh. 13:15-22; Jer. 17:21-27).

Rabbis eventually banned 39 tasks, such as tying or untying a knot. These in turn were extended until ingenious evasions were devised that lost the spirit but satisfied the legal requirement. The habit of Jesus was to observe the sabbath as a day of worship in the synagogues (Luke 4:16), but His failure to comply with the minute restrictions brought conflict (Mark 2:23-28; 3:1-6; Luke 13:10-17; John 5:1-18). At first, Christians also met on the sabbath with the Jews in the synagogues to proclaim Christ (Acts 13:14). Their holy day, the day that belonged especially to the Lord, was the first day of the week, the day of resurrection (Matt. 28:1; Acts 20:7; Rev. 1:10). They viewed the sabbath and other matters of the law as a shadow of the reality that had now been revealed (Col. 2:16-23), and the sabbath became a symbol of the heavenly rest to come (Heb. 4:1-11).

SABBATH DAY'S JOURNEY

Distance a Jew in Jesus' day considered ritually legal to walk on the seventh day; distance from Mount of Olives to Jerusalem (Acts 1:12). While in the wilderness, Israel had been told not to leave home on the sabbath (Ex. 16:29). Rabbis eventually interpreted these commands as limiting sabbath travel to 2,000 cubits (3,000 to 3,600 feet). That was the farthest a loyal Jew should be from his center of worship on the sabbath. Anyone who wanted to "bend" the rule could carry a lunch some time before the sabbath to a place about half mile from his home. Then, by eating it on the sabbath, he could claim that place as a "legal" home and go another sabbath day's journey. See *Sabbath.*

SABBATH YEAR

Every seventh year when farmers rested their land from bearing crops to renew the land and people of Israel (Ex. 23:10-11; Lev. 25:1-7). This not only assured the continued fertility of the land by allowing it to lay fallow, but also protected the rights of the poor. Peasants were allowed to eat from the natural abundance of the untended fields. It may be that only a portion of the land was allowed to rest each seventh year, the remainder farmed as usual. Hebrews sold into slavery were to be released in that year (Ex. 21:2). Loans and debts to Israelites were also to be forgiven (Deut. 15:1-3). Jeremiah reminded the people that their fathers had ignored the observance of the law (Jer. 34:13-14; compare Lev. 26:35). Israel renewed her dedication to practice the sabbath year during Nehemiah's time, but it is unclear whether it was carried out (Neh. 10:31). During the intertestamental period, an attempt was made by Israel to observe the sabbath year despite the political turmoil of the times (1 Macc. 6:49).

SABEAN

Transliteration of two Hebrew national names:

(1) Descendants of Seba, son of Cush (Gen. 10:7a), expected to bring gifts signifying loyalty to Jerusalem (Ps. 72:10; Isa. 45:14; compare Isa. 43:3; Ezek. 23:42). God could use the Sabeans to "pay for" Israel's ransom from captivity (Isa. 43:3). These are often identified with people of Meroe in Upper Egypt between the white and blue Nile, thus the capital of Ethiopia. Other scholars locate it much further south, the territory east and southeast of Cush bordering on the Red Sea. Other scholars would identify at least some references here as identical with 2 below.

(2) Descendants of Sheba, son of Raamah (Gen. 10:7b) or Joktan (Gen. 10:28; compare 25:3). The rich queen of Sheba visited Solomon (1 Kings 10; see Matt. 12:42). Sabeans destroyed Job's flocks and herds and servants (Job 1:15). They were known as "travelling merchants" (Job 6:19, REB; compare Ps. 72:10,15; Isa. 60:6; Jer. 6:20; Ezek. 27:22; 38:13; Joel 3:8). Sheba is usually equated with Marib in Yemen. Some scholars think this is too far south and seek biblical Sheba in northern Arabia near Medina on the wadi esh-Shaba. Sabeans could have become a general term for foreign or nomadic merchants. The Sabeans are credited with domesticating the camel.

SACKBUT

KJV for musical instrument (Dan. 3:5): "zither" (TEV, NCV), "lyre" (NIV, NKJV, NLT), "trigon" (NASB, NRSV), or "triangle" (REB); apparently an instrument of Asian origin, a triangular harp with four or more strings; not used in worship but only in more popular settings, possibly representing a rebuke from the biblical writer for a pagan musical setting for worship.

SACKCLOTH

Garment of coarse material fashioned from goat or camel hair worn as a sign of mourning or anguish (Isa. 58:5; Jonah 3:8); either a loose-fitting sack placed over the shoulders or a loin cloth.

SACRAMENT

Outward and visible sign of an inward and spiritual grace; usually refers to religious ritual that is believed to carry a special healing or saving power. Baptism and the Lord's Supper are the two sacraments almost universally recognized in Christendom, though many evangelical Christians shy away from the word *sacrament* in favor of "ordinances." Later, Christians extended the use of the term to preaching, the Lord's Supper, foot washing, blessing, marriage, ordination, and any other rite seen as a channel of divine grace into the heart and life of the believer. The theological issue that most divided Christians was whether the divine grace was conveyed simply by a correct performance of the rite or whether the recipient must have an active faith and make a personal response to the power of God's spirit.

When Paul wrote of being "buried with Christ" in baptism, he certainly meant that this visible rite demonstrates our spiritual union with Christ in His death and resurrection. It is not, however, an automatic or mechanical transmission of divine grace. It depends on the inward faith and spiritual response of the believer. Since God became flesh in Jesus Christ, it follows that God can use anything He chooses in His created order to convey His truth and saving power to the one who believes in Him. See *Ordinances.*

SACRIFICE AND OFFERING

Physical elements the worshiper brings to the Deity to express devotion, thanksgiving, or the need for forgiveness. For Israel's neighbors, sacrifices and offerings to the gods met physical needs. The sacrifices were the food and drink of the gods.

Cain and Abel brought offerings to the Lord from the produce of the land and from the firstborn of the flock (Gen. 4). Upon leaving the ark, Noah immediately built an altar and offered burnt sacrifices (Gen. 8). Abraham's willingness to sacrifice Isaac stands out among patriachal sacrifices (Gen. 22).

Sacrifices were to be used in the consecration or ordination of the priests (Ex. 29). The sacrifices that constituted much of the worship of Israel were burned on an altar that was made from acacia wood and overlaid with copper (Ex. 27). Incense was burned on a smaller altar (Ex. 30). See *Altar.*

Leviticus 1–7 gives the most detailed description of Israel's sacrificial system, including five types of sacrifices brought by the people as the physical expression of their inward devotion.

(1) *Burnt offering.* Offered both morning and evening, as well as on special days such as the sabbath, the new moon, and the yearly feasts (Num. 28-29; 2 Kings 16:15; 2 Chron. 2:4; 31:3; Ezra 3:3-6). Rituals performed after childbirth (Lev. 12:6-8), for an unclean discharge (Lev. 15:14-15) or hemorrhage (Lev. 15:29-30), or after a person who was keeping a Nazirite vow was defiled (Num. 6:10-11) required a burnt offering, as well as a sin offering. The animal had to be a perfect and complete specimen. The type of animal seems to be dependent on the offerer's financial ability. The one bringing the offering was to lay a hand on the animal so as to identify that the animal was taking the person's place and then to kill it. The entire animal was burned as a sacrifice. The priest received the hide (Lev. 7:8). This sacrifice was made to restore the relationship with God and to atone for some sin (compare 2 Sam. 24:18-25).

(2) *Grain offering* ("meat offering," KJV). Offering from harvest of the land is the only type that required no bloodshed. It was composed of fine flour mixed with oil and frankincense. Sometimes this offering was cooked into cakes without leaven prior to taking it to the priest. Every grain offering had to have salt in it (Lev. 2:13), perhaps as a symbol of the covenant. Only a portion of this offering was burned on the altar, with the remainder going to the priests. It may have symbolized the recognition of God's blessing in the harvest.

(3) *Peace offering* ("well-being," NRSV; "shared," REB; "fellowship," NIV). Consisted of sacrifice of bull, cow, lamb, or goat that had no defect. The individual laid a hand on the animal and killed it. The priests, in turn, sprinkled the blood around the altar. Only certain parts of the internal organs were burned. The priest received the breast and the right thigh (Lev. 7:28-36), but the offerer was given much of the meat to have a meal of celebration (Lev. 7:11-21). As part of the meal, various kinds of bread were offered (and ultimately kept by the priest). The idea of thanksgiving was associated with the peace offering. It often accompanied other sacrifices in celebration of events such as the dedication of the temple (1 Kings 8:63) or spiritual renewal (2 Chron. 29:31-36).

(4) *Sin offering* ("purification,"REB). Designed to deal with sin committed unintentionally. The sacrifice varied according to who committed the sin. If the priest or the congregation of Israel sinned, then a bull was required. A leader of the people had to bring a male goat, while anyone else sacrificed a female goat or a lamb. The poor were allowed to bring two turtledoves or two young pigeons. The one bringing the offering placed a hand on the animal and then slaughtered it. When the priest or the congregation sinned, the blood was sprinkled seven times before the veil in the sanctuary, and some of it was placed on the horns of the incense altar. The rest of the blood was poured out at the base of the sacrificial altar. For others who sinned, the sprinkling of the blood before the veil was omitted. The same internal organs that were designated for burning in the peace offering were likewise designated in this sacrifice. The rest of the animal was taken outside of the camp to the place where the ashes of the sacrifices were disposed, and there it was burned. These disposal procedures were not followed when the sin offering was made on behalf of a nonpriestly person (Lev. 6:24-30). In this case, the priest was allowed to eat some of the meat.

(5) *Guilt offering* ("trespass," KJV; "reparation," REB). Hard to distinguish from sin offering (Lev. 4–5; 5:6-7 calls guilt offering the "sin offering"). The guilt offering was concerned supremely with restitution. Someone who took something illegally was expected to repay it in full plus 20 percent of the value and then bring a ram for the guilt offering. Guilt offerings were also prescribed for cleansing a leper (Lev. 14), having sexual relations with the female slave of another person (Lev. 19:20-22), and for renewing a broken Nazirite vow (Num. 6:11-12).

These sacrifices were carried out on both an individual and a corporate basis. The sacrificial system taught the necessity of dealing with sin and, at the same time, demonstrated that God had provided a way for dealing with sin. The prophets spoke harshly about the people's concept of sacrifice. The people too often tended to ignore faith, confession, and devotion, thinking the mere act of sacrifice ensured forgiveness. Isaiah contended that the sacrifices were worthless when they were not accompanied by repentance and an obedient life (Isa. 1:10-17; compare Mic. 6:4-6). Jeremiah condemned the belief that as long as the temple was in Jerusalem and the people were faithful to perform the sacrifices, then God would protect them (Jer. 7:1-26). Malachi chastised the people for offering the lame and sick animals to God instead of the best (Mal. 1:7-14).

During the NT era, people sacrificed according to the guidelines in the OT. Mary brought the baby Jesus to the temple and offered a sacrifice for her purification. See Leviticus. 12. She sacrificed turtledoves or pigeons, indicating the family's low financial status. When Jesus healed the leper (Luke 5:12-14), He told him to go to the priest and make a sacrifice (compare Lev. 14). The cleansing of the temple (John 2) came about because people were selling animals and birds for the various sacrifices within the temple precincts. These people had allowed the "business" of sacrifice to overwhelm the spiritual nature of the offerings. Jesus chided the Pharisees for neglecting family responsibilities by claiming that something was "corban," or offered to God, and thus unavailable for the care of their parents (Mark 7). *Corban* is a Hebrew word for offering (Lev. 1:2). See *Corban.*

Hebrews portrays Christ as the sinless high priest who offered Himself up as a sacrifice for sinners (7:27). The superiority of Christ's sacrifice over the Levitical sacrificial system is seen in that His sacrifice had to be offered only once. First Peter 2 calls believers a holy and royal priesthood who offer up spiritual sacrifices. Jesus' death was an offering and sacrifice to God and, as such, a fragrant aroma (Eph. 5:2). Jesus was associated with the Passover sacrifice (1 Cor. 5:7). Paul also spoke of himself as a libation poured out (Phil. 2:18). The Philippians' gift was a fragrant aroma and an acceptable sacrifice to God (Phil. 4:18).

When the temple in Jerusalem was destroyed in A.D. 70, the Jews' sacrificial system ceased. By this time, however, the church had begun to distance itself from Judaism. With the death of Christ, physical sacrifice became unnecessary. As the temple and priest of God, the believer now has the responsibility for offering acceptable spiritual sacrifices (Rom. 12:1).

SADDUCEES See *Jewish Parties in the New Testament.*

SAINTS

Holy people; title for all God's people but applied in some contexts to a small group seen as the most dedicated ones. To be holy is to separate oneself from evil and dedicate oneself to God (Ex. 22:31). This separation reflects God's very character, for He is holy (Lev. 19:2). See *Holy; God.* Holiness is more than a one-time separating and uniting activity. It is a way of life: "Ye shall be holy: for I am holy" (Lev. 19:2). Saints are people who try to live holy lives (Dan. 7:18-28).

Dead saints were resurrected at the Lord's crucifixion, the death of the Holy One providing life for those who believe in God (Matt. 27:52). First Ananias and then Peter talked of the saints as simply believers in Christ (Acts 9:13,32,41). Saints are people who name Jesus as Lord. To be a saint is a present reality when a believer seeks to let the Spirit form Christ within (Rom. 8:29; Gal. 4:19; Eph. 4:13). See *Spirit; Witness.*

SAKKUTH

NRSV transliteration of Assyrian divine name applied to god Ninurta (or Ninib), apparently an Assyrian name for Saturn or another astral deity: "shrine" (REB, NIV), "tabernacle" (KJV). Amos condemned Israel for such false worship (Amos 5:26). See *Succoth Benoth.*

SALAMIS

Most important city of Cyprus, located on its east coast and containing more than one Jewish synagogue (Acts 13:5). See *Cyprus.*

SALCAH or **SALCHAH** or **SALECAH**

Territory and/or city on extreme eastern border of Bashan; possibly Salkhad, defensive center of the Jebel el-Druze, 63 miles east of the Jordan (Deut. 3:10; Josh. 12:5). See *Bashan.*

SALEM

Abbreviated form of Jerusalem (Gen. 14:18; Ps. 76:2; Heb. 7:1-2). See *Jerusalem; Melchizedek.*

SALIM (*peace*)

Town near which John the Baptist baptized (John 3:23). See *Aenon; John 2.*

SALMONE

Promontory on northeast coast of Crete; modern Cape Sidero. See Acts 27:7.

SALOME (*pacific*)

Wife of Zebedee and mother of James and John (if one combines Mark 16:1; Matt. 27:56; compare John 19:25); disciple of Jesus; among women at crucifixion who helped prepare the Lord's body for burial. See *Mary.*

SALT See *Minerals and Metals.*

SALT SEA See *Dead Sea.*

SALT, CITY OF See *City of Salt.*

SALT, COVENANT OF See *Covenant; Covenant of Salt.*

SALT, VALLEY OF

Geographical passageway south and east of the Dead Sea. David killed 18,000 Edomites there (2 Sam. 8:13; compare 1 Chron. 18:12; Ps. 60). King

Amaziah (796–767 B.C.) killed 10,000 Edomites (2 Kings 14:7).

SALUTATION

Act of greeting, addressing, blessing, or welcoming by gestures or words; a specific form of words serving as a greeting, especially in the opening and closing of letters.

SALVATION

Acutely dynamic act of snatching others by force from serious peril; saving a life from death or harm; deliverance from the penalty and power of sin.

The primary saving event in the OT is the exodus (Ex. 14:13), which demonstrated both God's power to save and God's concern for His oppressed people (Ex. 34:6-7). Israel recounted God's deliverance from Egyptian slavery in the Passover ritual (Ex. 12:1-13), in sermon (Neh. 9:9-11), and in psalms (Pss. 74:12-13; 78:13,42-54; 105:26-38).

The prophets anticipated God's salvation to be realized in the earth's renewed fruitfulness and the rebuilding of the ruined cities of Israel (Amos 9:13-15). Salvation would extend to all nations who would stream to Zion for instruction in God's ways (Isa. 2:2-4; Mic. 4:1-4; Zech. 8:20-23). The prophets also hinted of salvation outside history (for example, Isa. 51:6). God's salvation embraces abundant life (25:6) and the end of death (25:7), tears, and disgrace (25:8). Throughout most of the OT, salvation is a corporate or community experience. The Psalms, however, are especially concerned with the salvation of the individual from the threat of enemies (Pss. 13:5; 18:2,35; 24:5).

Christ's saving work involves already completed, on-going, and future saving activity. Jesus' earthly ministry made salvation a present reality for His generation. Jesus' healing ministry effected salvation from disease (Mark 5:34; 10:52; Luke 17:19; compare Mark 2:5; Luke 7:50). He assured a repentant Zacchaeus that "This day is salvation come to this house"(Luke 19:9). Through such

encounters, Jesus fulfilled the goal of His ministry:"to seek and to save that which was lost"(Luke 19:10).

The apex of Christ's completed work is His sacrificial death (Mark 10:45; 2 Cor. 5:19; Heb. 9:12). The believer can confess, "I was saved when Jesus died for me." Christ's present saving work primarily concerns Christ's role as mediator (Rom. 8:34; Heb. 7:25; 1 John 2:1). Christ's future saving work chiefly concerns Christ's coming again "unto them that look for him"(Heb. 9:28) and salvation from the wrath of God's final judgment (Rom. 5:9-10). Though Christ's sacrificial death is central, Christ's saving activity extends to the whole of His life, including His birth (Gal. 4:4-5), resurrection (Rom. 4:25; 1 Cor. 15:17), and ascension (Rom. 8:34).

God's saving work involves conviction of sin (John 16:8); repentance (turning) from sin to God (Luke 15:7,10; 2 Cor. 7:10); faith commitment to Christ (John 3:16,36); confession of Christ as Lord (Acts 2:21; Rom. 10:9-10). Scripture describes this act as: new birth (John 3:3; Titus 3:5); new creation (2 Cor. 5:17); adoption (Rom. 8:15; Gal. 4:4-5; Eph. 1:5); empowerment to be God's children (John 1:12); the status of "saints" (1 Cor. 1:2; 2 Cor. 1:1). This initial work in the believer's life is often termed justification. Justification also embraces God's final judgment (Rom. 2:13; 3:20,30).

God's ongoing work in the believer's life concerns the process of maturing in Christ (Heb. 2:3; 1 Pet. 2:2; 2 Pet. 3:18), growing in Christ's service (1 Cor. 7:20-22), and experiencing victory over sin through the power of the Holy Spirit (Rom. 7–8). Here sin remains a reality in the believer's life (Rom. 7; 1 John 1:8–2:1). The believer is caught in between what God has begun and what God is yet to complete (Phil. 1:6; 2:12).

God's yet-to-be-finished work in the lives of all believers is sometimes called"glorification"(Rom. 8:17; Heb. 2:10). Scripture uses a wealth of terms for this future saving work: "adoption"(Rom. 8:23);"redemption"

(Luke 21:28; Rom. 8:23; Eph. 4:30); "salvation" (Rom. 13:11; Heb. 1:14; 9:28; 1 Pet. 1:5; 2:2); and "sanctification"(1 Thess. 5:23). God's future work involves more than the individual; God's future work extends to the renewal of heaven and earth.

Salvation is the free gift of God appropriated through faith (Eph. 2:8-9; Rom. 3:28). No individual merits salvation by fulfillment of God's law (Rom. 3:20). Saving faith is, however, obedient faith (Rom. 1:5; 16:26; 1 Pet. 1:2). We are saved for good works (Eph. 2:10). Faith that does not result in acts of Christian love is not salvific but demonic (Jas. 2:14-26, especially v. 19).

Assurance of salvation is grounded in confidence that God is able to finish the good work begun in us (Phil. 1:6), that God who sacrificed His Son for sinners (Rom. 5:8-9) will not hold back anything necessary to save one of His children (Rom. 8:32), and that nothing can separate us from God's love in Christ (Rom. 8:35-39). Confidence in God's ability to keep those who have entrusted their lives to Christ is not, however, an excuse for any believer's inactivity or moral failure (Rom. 6:12-13; Eph. 2:10). See *Atonement; Conversion; Election; Eschatology; Forgiveness; Grace; Justification; New Birth; Predestination; Reconciliation; Redeem, Redemption, Redeemer; Repentance; Sanctification; Security of the Believer.*

SAMARIA, SAMARITANS (*mountain of watching*)

Mountain, city, region, and Northern Kingdom (1 Kings 13:32; Jer. 31:5); residents thereof; 42 miles north of Jerusalem; nine miles northwest of Nablus in central highlands of Israel; near modern Sebastiya. Samaria was the capital, residence, and burial place of the kings of Israel (1 Kings 16:23-28; 22:37; 2 Kings 6:24-30). Following the Northern Kingdom's fall to Assyria (721 B.C.; 2 Kings 17:5, 18:9-12; compare Isa. 8:4; 9:8-14; 10:9; 28:1-13; 36:19; Jer. 23:13; Ezek. 23:1-4; Hos. 7; 13:16; Amos 3:12; Mic. 1:6), exiles from many nations settled

Samaria (Ezra 4:9-10). Later, the Greeks conquered the region (331 B.C.) and hellenized the area with Greek inhabitants and culture. Then the Hasmoneans, under John Hyrcanus, destroyed the city (119 B.C.). After a long period without inhabitants, Samaria lived again under Pompey and the Romans (63 B.C.). Finally, Herod the Great obtained control of Samaria in 30 B.C. and made it one of the chief cities of his territory. Again, the city was resettled with people from distant places, this time mercenaries from Europe. Herod renamed the city Sebaste, using the Greek word for Augustus, the emperor. By NT times, it became identified with the central region of Palestine, with Galilee to the north and Judea to the south. When the Jews revolted in A.D. 66, the Romans reconquered the city and destroyed it. The Romans later rebuilt Samaria, but the city never regained the prestige it once had.

Samaria is the only major city founded by Israel, the Northern Kingdom. Omri, the sixth king of Israel (885-874 B.C.), purchased the hill of Samaria for his royal residence. When Ahab, Omri's son, became king of Israel, he built an ivory palace at Samaria. Amos denounced him for doing this (Amos 6:1,4; 1 Kings 22:39). Jezebel influenced Ahab, her husband, to make the city the center for Baal worship (1 Kings 16:29-33). Jezebel also had many prophets of Yahweh killed in Samaria (1 Kings 18:2-4). Twice Benhadad, the king of Syria, besieged Samaria unsuccessfully (1 Kings 20; 2 Kings 6; see 2 Kings 1; 5; 10).

"Samaritans" originally were Israelites of the Northern Kingdom (2 Kings 17:29). After the 721 B.C. exile, a "remnant of Israel" remained in the land. Assyrian captives from distant places also settled there (2 Kings 17:24). This led to the intermarriage of some, though not all, Jews with Gentiles and to widespread worship of foreign gods. By the time the Jews returned to Jerusalem to rebuild the temple and the walls of Jerusalem, Ezra and Nehemiah refused to let the Samaritans share in the experience (Ezra 4:1-3; Neh. 4:7). The old antagonism between Israel to the north and Judah to the south intensified the quarrel.

In the days of Christ, the relationship between the Jews and the Samaritans was greatly strained (Luke 9:52-54; 10:25-37; 17:11-19; John 8:48). The animosity was so great that the Jews went an extra distance through the barren land of Perea on the eastern side of the Jordan to avoid going through Samaria. Yet Jesus rebuked His disciples for their hostility to the Samaritans (Luke 9:55-56), healed a Samaritan leper (Luke 17:16), honored a Samaritan for his neighborliness (Luke 10:30-37), praised a Samaritan for his gratitude (Luke 17:11-18), asked a drink of a Samaritan woman (John 4:7), and preached to the Samaritans (John 4:40-42). Then in Acts 1:8, Jesus challenged His disciples to witness in Samaria. Philip, a deacon, opened a mission in Samaria (Acts 8:5). A small Samaritan community continues to this day to follow the traditional worship near Shechem. See *Israel; Sanballat.*

SAMGAR-NEBO or **SAMGAR-NEBU**

Babylonian official who accompanied Nebuchadrezzar of Babylon in capturing Jerusalem in 587 B.C. according to Hebrew text (Jer. 39:3); possibly a city—Simmagir—as home of Nergal-sharezer (REB, compare NIV) or a title Nergal-sharezer held.

SAMOS (*height*)

Small island (only 27 miles long) in Aegean Sea about a mile off coast of Asia Minor near peninsula of Trogyllium. In strait between Samos and mainland, Greeks defeated Persian fleet about 479 B.C. and turned tide of power in the Ancient Near East. Paul's ship either put in at Samos or anchored just offshore (Acts 20:15).

SAMOTHRACE (perhaps *height of Thrace*) or **SAMOTHRACIA**

Mountainous island in northern Aegean Sea 38 miles south of Thrace with peaks rising 5,000 feet above sea level. Paul spent a night there on his second missionary journey as he headed to Philippi (Acts 16:11). A famous mystery cult was practiced there.

SAMSON (*of the sun*)

Last of the major judges over Israel about 1100 B.C. (Judg. 13:1–16:31); son of Manoah; Danite; legendary hero battled Philistines (14:4).Before conception, Samson was dedicated by his parents to be a lifelong Nazirite (13:3-7). Part of the vow included letting the hair grow and abstaining from wine and strong drink. Samson's legendary strength came through the "Spirit of the Lord" who would "come upon" him to enable him to perform amazing feats of physical strength (14:6,19; 15:14; compare 16:28-29). Although a Nazirite, Samson did not live a devoted life. More frequently, he was careless in his vow. He secretly disobeyed the prohibition of approaching a dead body (14:8-9), had immoral relations with a Gaza harlot (16:1), and with Delilah (16:4-20).

Samson never freed Israel from the Philistines. In his death, he killed more Philistines than the total he had killed during his life (16:30). He is listed with the heroes of faith in Hebrews 11:32, because his strength came from God and because in his dying act, he demonstrated his faith. See *Nazirite; Judge; Judges, Book of; Spirit.*

SAMUEL (*the name is God, God is exalted,* or *son of God*)

Last judge, first king-maker, priest, and prophet who linked the period of the judges with the monarchy (about 1066–1000 B.C.). Born in answer to barren Hannah's tearful prayer (1 Sam. 1:10), Samuel was dedicated to the Lord before his birth (1:11) as a "loan" for all his life (1:28; 2:20). Eli raised Samuel at the Shiloh sanctuary (1 Sam. 2:11). Samuel met God and received his first prophetic mission as a young lad (1 Sam. 3:1,11-14).

Samuel was responsible for a revival of the Shiloh sanctuary (1 Sam. 3:19,21; 9:6; compare Ps. 99:6-7). Jeremiah regarded Samuel and Moses as the two great intercessors of Israel (Jer. 15:1). Following the death of Eli and his sons, Israel experienced 20 years (1 Sam. 7:2) of national sin and Philistine oppression. As judge, Samuel called Israel to repentance and delivered them from foreign domination. Samuel administered justice at Bethel, Gilgal, Mizpah, and Ramah (1 Sam. 7:15-17).

The sins of Samuel's sons and the Philistine threat led the elders of Israel to appeal to Samuel for a king "like all the nations" (1 Sam. 8:3,5,20). Samuel rightly understood this call for a king as rejection of God's rule (1 Sam. 8:7; 10:19). Samuel warned Israel of the dangers of a monarchy—forced labor, seizure of property, taxation (1 Sam. 8:10-18)—before anointing Saul as Israel's first king (1 Sam. 10:1). Samuel's recording of the rights and duties of kingship (1 Sam. 10:25; compare 12:17-18) set the stage for later prophets to call their monarchs to task for disobedience to God's commands.

Saul's impatient disobedience (1 Sam. 13:8-15; 15:1-33) led to God rejecting Saul's kingship. Samuel obediently anointed David as king over Israel (1 Sam. 16:13). Later when Saul sought David's life, David took refuge with Samuel and his band of prophets at Ramah (1 Sam. 19:18-24). Finally, Samuel's death brought national mourning (1 Sam. 25:1; 28:3). It also left Saul without access to God's word. In desperation he acknowledged Samuel's power and influence by seeking to commune with Samuel's spirit (1 Sam. 28).

SAMUEL, BOOKS OF

Ninth and tenth books of English Bible following Septuagint order but combined as the eighth book of the Hebrew canon in the "former prophets"; named for major figure of its opening section.

The Bible does not say who wrote these books. Many Bible students think Samuel along with Nathan and Gad had major input, pointing to 1 Chron. 29:29 as evidence. See *Chronicles, Books of.* Others think the books had a long history of composition with various narratives or narrative sources being composed from the time of the events until the time of the exile, when the "former prophets" were gathered into one collection. Such individual narratives would include Shiloh (1 Sam. 1–3), the Ark (1 Sam. 4:1–7:1), the Rise of Kingship (1 Sam. 9:1–11:15), Battles of Saul (1 Sam. 13–15), the History of David's Rise to Power (1 Sam. 16:14–2 Sam. 5:25), and the Succession to the Throne of David (2 Sam. 9–20; 1 Kings 1–2).

The Books of Samuel arose as a reflection on the nature of human kingship in light of Israel's tradition that Yahweh was their king. (See *King, Kingship; Kingdom of God.*) The Books tell the narrative of three major figures: Samuel, Saul, and David. See *David; Samuel; Saul.* The story of each combines tragedy, despair, and direction toward future hope. The dangers of kingship (1 Sam. 8) and the hope for kingship (2 Sam. 7) form the narrative tension for the Books. The final chapter (2 Sam. 24) does not solve the tension. It points further ahead to the building of the temple, where God's presence and Israel's worship can be at the center of life leading the king to be God's humble, forgiven servant.

Leadership is the guiding theme. Can God's people continue with a loosely knit organization as in the days of the judges, or must they have "a king to judge us like all the nations" (1 Sam. 8:5)? Samuel does not explicitly answer the question. God does not wholeheartedly accept kingship as the only alternative. Kingship means the people have rejected God (1 Sam. 8:7; 10:19). Still, kingship can flourish if the people and the king follow God (1 Sam. 12:14-15,20-25). Saul showed God's threats could be soon realized (1 Sam. 13:13-14). A new family from a new tribe would rule. This did not mean eternal war among tribes and families. A covenant could bind the two families together (1 Sam. 20; 23:16-18). Anger on one side does not require anger from the other as David's reactions to Saul continually show, summarized in 1 Sam. 24:17: "Thou art more righteous than I: for thou has rewarded me good, whereas I have rewarded thee evil." David neither planned the demise of Saul and his family nor rewarded those who did (2 Sam. 4:9-12). David established his kingdom and sought to establish a house for God (2 Sam. 7:2). The king, however, gave in to God's plan to establish David's house and let his son build the house for God (2 Sam. 7:13). The king's response shows the nature of true leadership. He expresses praise for God, not pride in personal achievement (2 Sam. 7:18-29).

God worked to establish His own kingdom among His people. He could work through an imperfect king who committed the outlandish sin with Bathsheba (2 Sam. 11) because the king was willing to confess his sin (2 Sam. 12:13). The rule of God's king does not promise perfect peace. Even David's own household revolted against him. Human pride and ego did not determine history. God's promise to David could not be overthrown.

The call for covenant commitment and obedience, the forgiveness and mercy of God, the sovereignty of God in human history, the significance of prayer and praise, the faithfulness of God to fulfill prophecy, the need for faithfulness to human leaders, the holy presence of God among His people, the nature of human friendship, and the importance of family relationships all echo forth from these books.

SANBALLAT (*Sin* [the god] *has healed*)

According to the Elephantine Papyri from reign of Darius I, Sanballat was governor of Samaria around 407 B.C. He had sons whose names included the term Yahweh, for the God of Israel. Although addressed by his Babylonian name (probably acquired during the exile), Sanballat was a practicing Jew. His daughter was married to the grandson of Jerusalem's high priest (Neh. 13:28), indicating harmonious relations between Judah and Samaria at that time. Nehemiah referred to Sanballat as the "Horonite," suggesting a connection with Upper or Lower Beth-horon (Neh. 2:10). Sanballat, in league with Tobiah and Shemiah, opposed Nehemiah's rebuilding of Jerusalem. The struggle appears to have been more political than racial or religious. Papyri from Wadi Daliyeh appear to indicate two later Sanballats also served as governors of Samaria.

SANCTIFICATION

Process of being made holy resulting in a changed lifestyle for the believer. See *Holy.*

The focus of holiness is on God. He is holy (Ps. 99:9); His name is holy (Pss. 99:3; 111:9) and may not be profaned (Lev. 20:3). All that pertains to the holy God must come into that same realm of holiness. This involves time, space, objects, and people.

Certain times are sanctified in that they are set apart especially to the Lord: the sabbath (Gen. 2:3), the various festivals (Lev. 23:4-44), the year of Jubilee (Lev. 25:12). By strictly observing the regulations governing each, Israel sanctified (or treated as holy) these special times of the year. Also the land of Canaan (Ex. 15:13), as well as Jerusalem (Isa. 11:9), was holy to the Lord and was not to be polluted by sinful conduct (Lev. 18:27-28). The tabernacle/temple and all the objects related to it were holy (Ex. 25–Num. 10; Ezek. 40–48; compare Matt. 6:9; 23:17,19; Luke 11:2; 1 Tim. 4:5). The various gifts brought in worship were sanctified. These fall into three groupings: those whose sanctity was inherent (for example, firstborn males of female animals and human beings, Ex. 13:2,11-13; Lev. 27:26); objects whose sanctification was required (for example, tithes of crops and pure animals, Lev. 27:30-33; Deut. 26:13); and gifts whose sanctification was voluntary (see partial list in Lev. 27).The dedication of these objects mostly occurred not at some ritual in the sanctuary but at a prior declaration of dedication (Judg. 17:3; Lev. 27:30-33).

Priests and Levites who functioned in the sanctuary were sanctified to the Lord by the anointing of oil (Ex. 30:30-32; 40:12-15). The Nazirite was consecrated (Num. 6:8), although only for a specified period of time. Finally, the nation of Israel was sanctified to the Lord as a holy people (Ex. 19:6; Deut. 7:6; 14:2,21; 26:19). This holiness was closely identified with obedience to the law of Holiness in Lev. 17–26, which includes both ritual and ethical commands. In the prophets especially, the ethical responsibility of being holy in conduct came to the forefront (Isa. 5–6; Jer. 5–7; Amos 4–5; Hos. 11).

Sanctification is vitally linked to the salvation experience and is concerned with the moral/spiritual obligations assumed in that experience. We were set apart to God in conversion, and we are living out that dedication to God in holiness.

Christ's crucifixion makes possible the moving of the sinner from the profane to the holy (that is, sanctifies, makes holy) so that the believer can become a part of the temple where God dwells and is worshiped (Heb. 13:11-16; 2:9-11; 10:10,14,29). The Holy Spirit's work in conversion is sanctification (Rom. 15:16; 1 Cor. 1:2; 6:11; Eph. 5:26-27; 2 Thess. 2:13; 1 Pet. 1:2), making the believer holy so as to come before God in acceptance. Sanctification/holiness is to be pursued as an essential aspect of the believer's life (Heb. 12:14); the blood of sanctification must not be defiled by sinful conduct (10:26-31). Paul stressed both the individual's commitment to holy living (Rom. 6:19-22; 1 Thess. 4:3-8; 2 Cor. 7:1) and the enabling power of God for it (1 Thess. 3:13; 4:8).The summation of the ethical imperative is seen in Peter's use (1 Pet. 1:15-16) of Lev. 11:44; 19:2; 20:7: "Be ye holy; for I am holy." See *Ethics; Hebrews; Salvation.*

SANHEDRIN

Highest Jewish council in first century; 71 members presided over by high priest; at times *chief priests* seem to refer to the action of the Sanhedrin.The Sanhedrin included both of the main Jewish parties among its membership. Since the high priest presided, the Sadducean priestly party seems to have predominated; but some leading Pharisees also were members (Acts 5:34; 23:1-9).

According to Jewish tradition, the Sanhedrin began with the 70 elders appointed by Moses in Num. 11:16 and was reorganized by Ezra after the exile. However, the OT provides no evidence of a council that functioned like the Sanhedrin of later times. Sanhedrin had its origin sometime during the centuries between the Testaments. See *Intertestamental History; Jewish Parties.*

The Sanhedrin exerted authority under the watchful eye of the Romans.The Sanhedrin, under the leadership of Caiaphas the high priest, plotted to have Jesus killed (John 11:47-53; compare Matt. 26:14-16,59-60; Mark 14:55–15:15; Luke 22:66).The trial of Jesus shows the Sanhedrin did not have the authority to condemn people to death (John 18:31). Stephen was stoned to death after a hearing before the Sanhedrin, but this may have been more a mob action than a legal execution authorized by the Sanhedrin (Acts 6:12-15; 7:54-60).

Peter and John were called before the council and warned not to preach anymore in the name of Jesus (Acts 4:5-21). Later the council had them arrested (Acts 5:21,27, 34-42). Stephen had to appear before the Sanhedrin (Acts 6:12-15). After Paul was arrested in Jerusalem, the Roman commander asked the council to examine Paul to decide what was Paul's crime (Acts 22:30–23:28).

SAPPHIRA (*beautiful* or *sapphire*) See *Ananias 1.*

SARA(H) or **SARAI** (*princess*)

Wife and half sister of Abraham (Gen. 11:29–25:10). See *Abraham.* In her grief over her barrenness, Sarah gave her maid Hagar to Abraham in the hope of an heir; but she expressed resentment when Hagar conceived. When Sarah was almost 90 years old, God changed her name and promised her a son. A year later, she bore Isaac. At the age of 127, Sarah died at Hebron, where she was buried in the cave in the field of Machpelah near Mamre. Sarah's barrenness is seen as evidence of Abraham's faith (Rom. 4:19); her conception of Isaac is an example of God's power in fulfilling a promise (Rom. 9:9). See Gal. 4:21-31; Heb. 11:11; 1 Pet. 3:6.

SARDIS

City of one of churches in Revelation (3:1-6). The church was condemned as being "dead," perhaps a reference to its ineffectiveness in the world. However, some of its members were commended (v. 4). See *Asia Minor.*

SARGON (*the king is legitimate*)

Ancient throne name first taken by the king of Akkad about 2100 B.C. In 722 B.C., Sargon II of Assyria succeeded his brother, Shalmaneser V. See *Assyria; Israel.*

SATAN (*adversary*)

Transliteration of Hebrew word appearing in Num. 22:22,32; 1 Sam. 29:4; 2 Sam. 19:22; 1 Kings 5:4; 11:14,23,25; Ps. 109:6 as adversary or accuser; proper name in Job 1-2; Zech. 3:2; 1 Chron. 21:1. See *Devil, Satan, Evil, Demonic.*

SATRAP(Y)

Political office in the Persian Empire comparable to governor; his territory was a satrapy (KJV, "lieutenants" Ezra 8:36); aided Israel in rebuilding Jerusalem and the temple. At height of Persian rule, there were at least 20 satrapies. See *Persia.*

SATYR

Hairy, demonic figure with appearance of a goat, translating Hebrew term otherwise translated "hairy" or "male goat."

SAUL (*asked for*)

First king of Israel and Hebrew name of Paul. See *Paul.* Four persons in the OT; usually rendered Shaul for king of Edom (Gen. 36:37-38), the last son of Simeon (Gen. 46:10), and a Levite of the Kohathites (1 Chron. 6:24). Saul primarily refers to first king of a united Israel (about 1020-1000 B.C.) from tribe of Benjamin (1 Sam. 9:1-2,21). Chosen by God (1 Sam. 9:15-17) and secretly anointed by Samuel (10:1), Saul was later selected publicly by lot (10:17-24). Despite some people's skepticism (10:27), he proved himself an able leader by delivering the city of Jabesh-gilead and was acclaimed king at Gilgal (11:1-15). He made his capital at "Gibeah of Saul" ("Saul's hill," 1 Sam. 11:4), probably tell el-Ful, three miles north of Jerusalem. From Gibeah, Saul drove the Philistines from the hill country (13:19-14:23) and fought other enemies of Israel (14:47-48).

His presumptuous offering (13:8-14) and violation of a holy war ban led to his break with Samuel and rejection by God (15:7-23). After the Goliath episode, Saul became jealous and fearful of David (18:7,12), eventually making several spontaneous and indirect attempts on David's life (18:10-11,25; 19:1,9-11). His final wretched condition is betrayed by his consultation of the witch at En-dor (28:7-8). The following day, Saul and three sons were killed at the hands of the Philistines on Mount Gilboa (1 Sam. 31). David refused to lift his hand against "the Lord's anointed" (1 Sam. 26:9-11,23) and at Saul's death provided a fitting elegy (2 Sam. 1:17-27).

SAVIOR

One who saves, used with various shades of meaning, ranging from deliverer to healer and benefactor. God Himself and no other is savior (Isa. 43:11; 45:21; Hos. 13:4; Luke 1:47; 1 Tim. 1:1; 2:3; 4:10; Titus 1:3; 2:10; 3:4; Jude 25), though individuals such as Moses and the judges may serve as agents of God's deliverance. God reveals His role as savior primarily through the exodus from Egypt and provision for Israel during the wilderness years (Hos. 13:4-6). The NT reveals God as savior primarily in the Christ event. Christ is savior of the outcasts of Israel (Luke 2:11); Israel (Acts 5:31; 13:23), the church (Eph. 5:23), and the world (John 4:42; 1 John 4:14). Jesus' saving role involves giving "repentance and forgiveness of sins" (Acts 5:31; compare Matt. 1:21). Christ will come again as savior (Phil. 3:20). See *Salvation*.

SCAPEGOAT

Animal that carried away sins of people into the wilderness on Day of Atonement (Lev. 16:8,10,26); said to be "for Azazel," usually interpreted as "goat of removal," or scapegoat; term may refer to rocky place in desert or to demon of the desert. By laying his hands on the goat's head, the priest transferred the sins of the people to it and then had the goat led away into the desert, picturing the removal of the sins. Hebrews 10:3-17 contrasts sanctification through the sacrifice of Christ with the blood of bulls and goats which can never take away sins. See *Day of Atonement*; *Sanctification*.

SCEPTER

Official staff or baton of a king, symbolic of his authority; probably descended from ancient club carried by prehistoric rulers; extended to visitor or dignitary (Esther 5:2) to signal approval of the visit and allow the person to approach the throne.

SCEVA

Jewish "high priest" in Ephesus with seven sons who tried unsuccessfully to exorcise demons in Jesus' name as Paul had done (Acts 19:14). Title may be result of a copyist or title Sceva took upon himself to impress leaders of other religions in Ephesus.

SCORPION

(1) Small invertebrate animal (*buthus*) known for the venom and sting in its narrow segmented tail. God protected Israel from scorpions (Deut. 8:15) and could protect His prophet from them (Ezek. 2:6).

(2) Insidious instrument of punishment with lashes and spikes (1 Kings 12:11,14).

SCOURGE

Severe form of corporal punishment involving whipping and beating, usually done with victim tied to a post or bench and administered by a servant of the synagogue (if for religious reasons), or by a slave or soldier. John 19:1 uses this word for the beating given Jesus before His crucifixion. Matthew and Mark use a word meaning "flog" (a lesser punishment), while Luke says that Pilate offered to have Jesus "chastise[d]" (23:16), which was a still lighter punishment. The number of blows was set in Deut. 25:3 at 40, later reduced to 39, 13 stokes on chest and 26 on back. Often victims died from the beating.

SCRIBE

Person trained in writing skills and used to record events and decisions (Jer. 36:26; 1 Chron. 24:6; Esther 3:12). During the exile in Babylon, educated scribes apparently became the experts in God's written word, copying, preserving, and teaching it (Ezra 7:6). A professional group of such scribes developed by NT times, most being Pharisees (Mark 2:16). They interpreted the law, taught it to disciples, and were experts in cases where people were accused of breaking the law of Moses. They led in plans to kill Jesus (Luke 19:47) and heard His stern rebuke (Matt. 23). See *Government; Sanhedrin; Jewish Parties*.

SCRIPTURE (*a writing*)

Historic Judaeo-Christian name for the specific literature that the church receives as divine instruction, the Bible. See *Inspiration of Scripture*. The purpose of Scripture is to place men and women in a right standing before God and to enable believers to seek God's glory in all of life's activities and efforts. A book of redemptive history, Scripture focuses on the incarnation and redemptive work of Jesus Christ. See *Bible, Theology of.*

SCYTHIANS

Nomadic, Indo-European people, speaking an Iranian dialect, who migrated from central Asia into southern Russia between 800 and 600 B.C.; skilled horsemen who excelled in barbaric attack and plunder; Ashchenaz (Gen. 10:3; Jer. 51:27). Their forces, in pursuit of the Cimmerians, drove south through or around the Caucasus Mountains to the borders of Assyria, forming Scytho-Assyrian alliance about 680–670 B.C.

Herodotus says a Scythian attack forced the Medes to withdraw from an assault against Nineveh (apparently 626–620 B.C.). Later, the Scynthians advanced southward along the Palestinian coast to the Egyptian border (611 B.C.), where Egyptian Pharaoh bought them off. Medes eventually drove them back northward into southern Russia. Scythian power was dominant northwest of Black Sea until about 350 B.C.

Colossians 3:11 uses Scythians to represent the most repugnant barbarian and slave, saying they, too, are accepted in Christ, all social and cultural barriers being abolished in His church.

SEAL

Signet containing a distinctive mark that stood for the individual who owned it; earliest seals found date before 3000 B.C. Seals varied in shapes and sizes. Some were round and worn around the neck. Others were rings for the finger. The mark was made by stamping the seal into soft clay. Tamar asked for Judah's signet as collateral on a pledge he made (Gen. 38:18). Joseph was given pharaoh's ring when he was placed in command of the country (Gen. 41:42), symbolizing Joseph's right to act with the ruler's authority. Jezebel used Ahab's seal to sign letters asking that Naboth be tried and stoned to death (1 Kings 21:8).

SECOND COMING, THE

Biblical teaching on return of Jesus to earth at end of earthly history; blessed hope (Titus 2:13). Jesus told His followers He would be leaving them but would return to the earth (John 14:3; compare Acts 1:11) and warned them to be prepared to welcome Him back (Matt. 24-25; compare Mark 13). Jesus warned of misrepresentations (Matt. 24:4-5,11,23-26) and said His appearance would be bodily and unmistakable (Matt. 24:27,30; compare Acts 1:11).

Believers are to be watchful (Matt. 24:42; 25:1-13; compare Jas. 5:7-8) and faithful (2 Pet. 3:3-4; 1 John 3:3; compare 1 Thess. 3:13; Col. 3:1-17; 1 John 2:28). They are not to attempt to know the time (Matt. 24:36; compare 2 Thess. 2; 2 Pet. 3:4-11). See *Eschatology; Christ, Christology; Jesus; Rapture.*

SECURITY OF THE BELIEVER

Biblical teaching that God protects believers for the completion of their salvation. Salvation does not depend merely upon human effort. God is the author of salvation (2 Cor. 5:18-19; John 3:16). God who has begun the work of salvation in Christians also provides the necessary assurance to bring His work to its completion in the day of Christ (Phil. 1:6). God in Christ protects and keeps Christians (John 10:27-29; 2 Thess. 3:3) just as Jesus took seriously the task of preserving the disciples while He was on earth (John 17:12-15). Jesus promised he would provide a companion Spirit (the Comforter or Paraclete) (John 14:16-18). The Spirit would be their sense of peace and security, their witness concerning Jesus, their attorney with the world, and their guide or teacher into all truth (John 14:25-30; 15:26-27; 16:8-15). See *Advocate; Comforter; Helper.*

Christians are expected to resist temptations and flee ungodly activity (for example, 1 Cor. 10:13-14). The Christian can find in God an enduring security for the soul (Heb. 6:17-20). The Christian is expected to persevere to the end (1 Pet. 1:5;

1 John 5:18; Rev. 3:10). As we identify with the ultimate power of Christ in the resurrection, we, too, shall experience the effective meaning of the security of the believer in the triumph of God (1 Cor. 15:20-28). See *Perseverance.*

SEIR *(hairy; thicket or small forested region)*

Mountain range that runs the length of biblical Edom, leading at times to an equation of Edom and Seir. The highest peak is about 5,600 feet about sea level. The region was home to Esau and his descendants (Gen. 32:3; Josh. 24:4). "Sons of Seir" represent an early Horite clan from the region. See *Edom.*

SELA *(rock)*

Major fortified city in Edom; common noun referring to rocky country or wilderness; see Judg. 1:36; 2 Kings 14:7). Isaiah called for action from Sela, perhaps rocky wilderness bordering Moab rather than more distant town of Sela (Isa. 16:1). Septuagint identified Sela with Petra, capital of Edom. More recent study has placed it at es-Sela, two and a half miles northwest of Bozrah and five miles southwest of Tafileh. Modern translations include Sela in Isa. 42:11.

SELAH

Term of unknown meaning appearing in Psalms and Hab. 3. It is variously seen as pause either for silence or musical interlude, a signal for the congregation to sing, recite, or fall prostrate on the ground, a cue for the cymbals to crash, a word to be shouted by the congregation, a sign to the choir to sing a higher pitch or louder. The earliest Jewish traditions thought it meant "forever."

SELEUCIA

Syrian city founded by Seleucus Nicator, first Seleucid king, in 301 B.C. on Mediterranean coast five miles north of the Orontes River and 15 miles from Antioch. Paul stopped

there on first missionary journey (Acts 13:4). See *Seleucids.*

SELEUCIDS

Members of a Syrian dynasty founded by one of the generals of Alexander the Great. See *Intertestamental History and Literature.*

SELF-CONTROL

Sober, temperate, calm, and dispassionate approach to life, having mastered personal desires and passions. God's people are expected to exercise self-control (Prov. 25:28; 1 Cor. 7:5; 1 Thess. 5:6; 1 Tim. 3:2; 2 Tim. 3:3; Gal. 5:23; 2 Tim. 1:7; Titus 1:8; 2 Pet. 1:6). Freedom in Christ calls for a self-disciplined life following Christ's example of being in the world but not of the world. See *Ethics; Freedom.*

SELF-ESTEEM

Respect for and confident acceptance of oneself as a person created by and useful to God. Self-esteem must be based on an understanding that people are created by God to be highly exalted (Ps. 8:3-8; compare Gen. 1:26-27), yet are miserably fallen sinners (Rom. 3:23; 7:24). Every person, no matter how sinful, is of inestimable value to God (Luke 15:11-32; 1 Cor. 6:20) and supremely loved by him (1 John 4:10; compare Rom. 8:35-39). Christians possess a new nature that allows them to be self-confident, but only through Christ (1 Cor. 9:24; 2 Cor. 3:5; 10:7; Phil. 3:4-7; 4:13). Both self-elation and self-abasement ignore the work of Christ in a believer (2 Cor. 12:7-10; Col. 2:18,23). Paul taught that Christians should strive for a balanced self-esteem that is able to minister to the needs of others (Rom. 12:3; 2 Cor. 10:7-13; Gal. 6:1-3; Phil. 2:3).

SELF-WILLED

To do something arbitrarily without divine permission; to act on one's own decision rather than considering the needs of others and the purpose of God. See Gen. 49:6; Titus 1:7; 2 Pet. 2:10.

SEMITE

Person who claims descent from Noah's son Shem (Gen. 5:32; 10:21-31) or, more precisely as a linguistic term, those peoples speaking one of the Semitic languages. The racial list of Genesis and the list of linguists do not always include the same peoples.

Three major divisions exist in the Semitic family of languages: East Semitic—Akkadian used in ancient Babylon and Assyria; Northwest Semitic—Hebrew, Aramaic, Syriac, Phoenician, Samaritan, Palmyrene, Nabatean, Canaanite, Moabite; South Semitic—Arabic, Sabean, Minean, and Ethiopic. See *Languages of the Bible; Assyria; Babylon; Canaan.*

SENIR (*pointed*)

Amorite name for Mount Hermon (Deut. 3:9). See *Hermon.* Song of Solomon 4:8 may indicate Senir was different peak than Hermon or indicated the entire range (compare 1 Chron. 5:23).

SENNACHERIB (Assyrian, *Sin* [the god] *has replaced my brother*)

King of Assyria (704–681 B.C.). See *Assyria; Israel.*

SENSUAL

Activities or appearances characterized by or motivated by physical lust or luxury (Isa. 47:8); part of the evil of the human heart (Mark 7:22; compare Rom. 13:13), calling for repentance (2 Cor. 12:21). See *Lasciviousness; Sex, Biblical Teaching On.*

SEPHARVAIM, SEPHARVITES

People Assyrians conquered and resettled in Israel in 722 B.C. (2 Kings 17:24); may represent the two Sippars on the Euphrates River or Shabarain in Syria; may be same as Sibraim in Syria (Ezek. 47:16). Despite Assyria's claims, Sepharvaim's gods could not compare with Yahweh (2 Kings 19:12-13; compare 17:31).

SEPTUAGINT (*the 70*)

Oldest Greek translation of the Hebrew OT; contains several apocryphal books. Most NT quotations of OT are from Septuagint. See *Apocrypha; Bible, Texts and Versions.*

SERAPHIM (*the burning ones*)

Winged serpents whose images decorated many of the thrones of Egyptian pharaohs; thought to act as guardians over the king. Israel adopted the symbolism for God's throne. Isaiah envisioned the seraphim as agents of God who prepared him to proclaim the Lord's message to Judah (Isa. 6:2). See *Angel.*

SERMON ON THE MOUNT

Jesus' preaching recorded in Matthew 5–7. The theme is found in Matthew 5:20, "except your righteousness shall exceed the righteousness of the scribes and Pharisees, ye shall in no case enter into the kingdom of heaven." The standard is God's perfection (Matt. 5:48). Our lives can conform to the standards of the sermon only if we allow God through the power of the Holy Spirit to work in us. The sermon pictures what God desires to make of us if we will offer ourselves to Him as living sacrifices (Rom. 12:1-2).

The Sermon on the Mount opens with the beatitudes (5:3-12) and moves on to describe the function of Jesus' disciples (5:13-16). Jesus explained His interpretation of the law (5:17-48) and certain acts of righteousness (6:1-18), described the attitudes required of His disciples (6:19–7:12), and invited the listeners to become and continue as His disciples (7:13-27). See *Beatitudes; Ethics; Jesus, Life and Ministry.*

SERPENT

Snake; symbol for evil and Satan. See *Devil, Evil, Satan, Demonic.* God gave Moses a sign showing His control of the feared serpents (Ex. 4:3; 7:9-10; compare Job 26:13). Jesus accused the Pharisees of being as evil and deadly as serpents (Matt. 23:33). He gave the 70 power over serpents (Luke 10:19; compare Mark 16:18). See *Animals.*

SERPENT OF BRASS; SERPENT, BRONZE See *Bronze Serpent.*

SERVANT OF THE LORD

Title Jesus took from the OT, especially Isaiah 40–55; applied to leaders of God's people: Moses, David, and to Israel as a nation (Isa. 41:8-9b). The ideal Servant of the Lord was to bring God's justice to all the nations (42:1,4). God called attention to the inability of the natural Israelite to fulfill the picture of the ideal Servant (42:19). Still, the Lord says: "Ye are my witnesses, and my servant whom I have chosen" (43:10; compare 44:1-2,21).

Israel had responsibility to do the work of the Servant. Yet not all Israel could be meant, for some were blasphemers and idolaters. Could part of Israel be the real Servant? Or might it really point to One who must come out of Israel—One who could represent Israel in accomplishing the task? Matthew 12:17-21 quotes Isaiah 42:1-4 as fulfilled in Jesus Christ.

Isaiah 49 distinguishes between the One who will fulfill the work of the Servant and the nation of Israel, to which this One belongs and which He represents (vv. 5-6). Not only is He to bring judgment to all the world— He is "to bring Jacob again to him" (v. 5) and "to restore the preserved of Israel" (v. 6). He is to be "a light to the Gentiles" and "my salvation unto the end of the earth" (v. 6). In 50:4-10, we hear of the sufferings to which He will voluntarily submit.

All this leads up to the triumphal picture in Isaiah 52:13–53:12, showing the sufferings of the Servant (52:14; 53:2-5,7-8,10), and their vicarious and redemptive nature (52:15; 53:4-6,8,10-12; compare 1 Pet. 1:1-2). Chapter 54 shows the outreach of the Servant's work, and chapter 55 gives the glorious call to receive the salvation won by the Servant's redemptive work, "without money and without price" (v. 1). After chapter 53, Isaiah never again used "servant" in the singular; rather he spoke of the blessings that the followers of the Servant will receive, calling them "the ser-

vants of the Lord" (54:17); "his servants" (56:6; 65:15; 66:14); and "my servants" (65:8,9,13,14).

Jesus was the Suffering Servant fulfilling the glorious descriptions of Isaiah (Matt. 12:14-21; Luke 4:18-19; 22:37; Acts 3;13; 4:27-28). By washing their feet, Jesus symbolized servanthood for His disciples, calling on them to serve one another and the world (John 13:4-17). This led the early church to pray that as God's servants they would speak with boldness and perform miracles through the name of "your holy child Jesus" (Acts 4:29-30). See *Christ, Christology; Isaiah; Jesus; Slave, Servant; Son of God.*

SETH (*He set or appointed* or *replacement*)

Third son of Adam and Eve born after Cain murdered Abel (Gen. 4:25; 5:3); ancestor of Jesus (Luke 3:38).

SEVEN WORDS FROM THE CROSS

Jesus' statements from the cross as He was crucified for our sin. Jesus' first three statements relate primarily to others between 9:00 A.M. and noon (Mark 15:25). He asked forgiveness for those who were crucifying Him (Luke 23:34), promised to be with the penitent thief in paradise (Luke 23:43), and provided for the care of His mother by John (John 19:26-27).

Jesus' last four statements, spoken between noon and 3:00 P.M., refer to Himself (Matt. 27:45; Mark 15:33; Luke 23:44). He uttered the cry of desolation, quoting Ps. 22:1 in the Aramaic language (Matt. 27:46; Mark 15:34), expressed His thirst, (John 19:28) and issued the cry of victory, "It is finished" (John 19:30). In His final words Jesus quoted Ps. 31:5 as He committed His spirit to God (Luke 23:46). See *Crucifixion.*

SEVEN, SEVENTH

Number of completeness. See *Number Systems and Number Symbolism.*

SEVENTY WEEKS

Time spoken of in Daniel 9:24-27, usually understood as 70 weeks of years or 490 years.The passage groups the weeks in three parts: seven weeks (49 years), 62 weeks (434 years), and one week (7 years).The 49 years are associated with rebuilding Jerusalem in "troublous times" (v. 25). The 434 years relate to the intervening time before a cutting off of the Anointed One (v. 26).The 7 years are connected with the period of a covenant between a ruler and Jerusalem, which is violated in the middle of the 7 years (v. 27). A historical approach relates these years to the period of history between the fall of Jerusalem and the restoration of the temple in 164 B.C. following the atrocities of Antiochus Epiphanes. See *Intertestamental History.* A prophetic approach sees the reference to reach to the birth of Christ, His subsequent crucifixion (the cutting off of the Anointed One), and the destruction of Jerusalem by the Romans in A.D. 70.The same dating without reference to Jesus has been the usual Jewish understanding since Josephus.

The dispensational approach makes the 70 weeks a prophetic framework for end time events, rather than a prophecy of what took place in the work of Christ at His first coming. The 69th week is seen as completed at Christ's death, while the 70th week is yet to be fulfilled at a future Great Tribulation period.The interval between the two is seen as a parenthesis in the prophetic pattern which contains the present church age, a period said not to be revealed in OT prophecy. See *Dispensation; Eschatology; Millennium, Tribulation.*

SEVENTY YEARS

Prophetic and apocalyptic figure pointing to time of Israel's exile in Babylon and to end of tribulation in Daniel's vision. Seventy years represented an even number of the normal human life span (Ps. 90:10). Isaiah 23:15 and the Babylonian Black Stone of Esarhaddon may indicate that 70 years was an expected time of punishment and desolation for a defeated city. Jeremiah predicted that Judah would serve Babylon 70 years (Jer. 25:11; compare 29:10). Second Chronicles 36:21 saw the completion of the 70 years in the coming of Cyrus (538 B.C.). This apparently sees the years as from the first deporting of Judeans into Babylon (about 605 B.C.) until Cyrus came. Zechariah seems to have seen the 70 years ending in his own day with the rebuilding of the temple (Zech. 1:12). This would span the period from the destruction of the temple (586 B.C.) to the dedication in 516 B.C. Some interpreters see in the Chronicler's references to sabbaths an indication of a second meaning for 70 years, that is 70 sabbatical years (Lev. 25:1-7; 26:34-35) or 490 years. By this reckoning Israel had not kept the sabbatical year commandment since the period of the Judges, so God gave the land 70 consecutive sabbatical years during the exile. See *Sabbath Year.* Daniel meditated on Jeremiah's prophecy (Dan. 9:2) and learned that 70 weeks of years were intended (v. 24). See *Seventy Weeks.*

SEX, BIBLICAL TEACHING ON

Physical relations God gave man and wife to express love and to procreate children. God created humans as sexual beings, somehow reflective of His own image (Gen. 1:27), and declared that this reality was "very good" (Gen. 1:31). Some passages truly value sex and celebrate it joyously (Gen. 18:12; 26:8; Song of Sol. 4:1-16); others call for times of abstaining from sexual activity (Ex. 19:15; 1 Sam. 21:4-5); still others raise the life without sex above the normal marital relationship (1 Cor. 7:1-9,37-38; Rev. 14:4). Positively, God blesses sex for both companionship and procreation (Gen. 1:28; 2:18-25). Fertility of women was a blessing, while barrenness was a curse (Gen. 29:30–30:24; 1 Sam. 1:5-20). The sinful nature of humans appears to have corrupted God's good gift. Outside the first garden, a negative attitude toward nudity appears (Gen. 3:7,21; Luke 8:27,35). "Uncovering one's nakedness" refers to a shameful, incestual, or otherwise forbidden sex act (Lev. 18:6-19). Sex can be wasteful of one's strength (Prov. 31:3). Sin has produced a hesitancy and reservation about sex among the biblical characters and writers as compared with the lack of shame in the Garden of Eden (Gen. 2:25).

In the garden Adam and Eve were created equal (Gen. 1:27-28; 2:18-23). Sin produced male dominance and female submissiveness (Gen. 3:16). See *Marriage.* The NT teaches that in Christ this Edenic complementariness is restored (2 Cor. 5:17; Gal. 3:28; Eph. 5:21-33). Mates are equal in possessing one another (1 Cor. 7:4) and are interdependent (1 Cor. 11:11-12). The new creation in Christ makes this possible.

Several deviations of sexual behavior are condemned in the biblical teachings: homosexuality (Lev. 18:22; Rom. 1:26-27; 1 Cor. 6:9-10); bestiality (Ex. 22:19; Lev. 18:23); incest (Lev. 18:6-18; 1 Cor. 5); rape (Ex. 22:16-17; Deut. 22:23-29); adultery (Ex. 20:14; Deut. 22:22); prostitution (Prov. 7:1-27; 29:3;); fornication (1 Cor. 6:9-10; compare Matt. 19:9). These are all declared to be outside the will of God for man and woman who are called to live together in monogamous fidelity within the covenant of marriage. The only other option is the giftedness of celibacy (Matt. 19:12b; 1 Cor. 7:7). The Bible is silent on the subject of masturbation (compare Lev. 15:16), and on physical techniques of sexual intercourse, referring only to marital rights or enjoyment (Ex. 21:10), erotic caresses (Song of Sol. 2:6; 7:1-9), fondling (Gen. 26:8), and pleasure in conceiving (Gen. 18:12). Intimate sexual behavior outside of marriage is considered sexual immorality in the biblical perspective.

God gives humans the gift of sexuality whereby they image God when they join together to complement each other as "one flesh" (Gen. 2:24). God's people are expected to exercise self-control, not by asceticism (Col. 2:23; 1 Tim. 4:1-5), but by the power of the Holy Spirit overcoming sexual impulses (Gal. 5:16-25; 1 Thess.

4:1-8). For the noncelibate, marriage is the only approved outlet for sexual expression (1 Cor. 7:9; Titus 2:5-6). Outside of the limits established by God, sex becomes an evil and destructive force in human life, calling for God's redemptive power to deliver humans trapped therein. Marital sexual love is both a gift and a responsibility from God to be consecrated by the Word and prayer.

SHAALBIM *(place of foxes)*

Amorite stronghold eventually controlled by Manasseh and Ephraim (Judg. 1:35; see 1 Kings 4:9; 2 Sam. 23:32); probably modern Selbit seven miles southeast of Lydda and three miles northwest of Ajalon.

SHADDAI

Transliteration of Hebrew name for God, often translated, "Almighty" following Septuagint. See *Almighty; Names of God.*

SHADOW

Dark image of an object created when the object interrupts rays of light; protection; transitory, short-lived, and changing. The intensive heat, particularly in the summer, made shade and shadows important in Palestine. Travelers sought rest under a tree (Gen. 18:4; compare Job 40:22) or in a house (Gen. 19:8). Especially at midday when shade virtually vanished, people looked for a shadow (Isa. 16:3; compare Gen. 21:15; Jonah 4; Job 7:2). In the afternoon shadows lengthen (Jer. 6:4; compare Neh. 13:19, NIV). In the evening cool, shadows disappear (Song of Sol. 2:17). In the desert wilderness the traveler found little hope for shade but looked for shade or shadow from hills (Judg. 9:36), large rocks (Isa. 32:2), a cave (Ex. 33: 22; 1 Kings 19:9), or a cloud (Isa. 25:5).

Powerful people offer the shadow of protection and security (Song of Sol. 2:3). So does a king (Lam. 4:20; Ezek. 31:6). Still, Israel knew the false claims of kings to provide such protection (Judg. 9:15; compare Isa. 30:2; Ezek. 31). Biblical writers looked to the Messiah for needed shade or shadow (Isa. 32:2; Ezek. 17:23). God was the ultimate shadow of protection for His people (Pss. 36:7; 91:1; 121:5; Isa. 25:4; 49:2; 51:16). Human life itself is only a brief shadow (Job 8:9; 14:2; Pss. 102:11; 144:4; Eccl. 6:12; 8:13).

The Greek *skia* can refer to a literal shadow (Mark 4:32; Acts 5:15). More often it refers to death (Matt. 4:16; Luke 1:79 picking up Isa. 9:2) or to an indication of something to come, a foreshadowing. Dietary laws and religious festivals were only a shadow preparing Israel for the reality made known in Christ (Col. 2:17; Heb. 8:5; 10:1). God is not a fleeting, changing shadow (Jas. 1:17).

SHADRACH (*circuit of the sun*)

Daniel's friend taken to Babylon during the exile (Dan. 1:6-7); Hebrew name, Hananiah. See *Daniel; Meshach.*

SHALLUM (*replacer* or *the replaced*)

Fourteen OT men including King of Israel (752 B.C.) who assassinated Zechariah and was, in turn, assassinated by Menahem a month later (2 Kings 15:10-15).

SHALMAN (*complete, peace*)

Mysterious figure in Hos. 10:14, sometimes identified as an abbreviation of Shalmanezer V of Assyria and sometimes as ruler of Moab listed by Tiglath-Pileser III among kings paying him tribute. His name became synonymous with violence and ruthlessness.

SHALMANESER (*Shalmanu* [the god] *is the highest ranking one*)

(1) Assyrian king (1274–1245 B.C.). Records of his military exploits set precedent succeeding kings followed.

(2) Shalmaneser III ruled Assyria 858–824 B.C.; fought group of small kingdoms, including Israel, in battle of Qarqar in 853 B.C. Despite claiming victory, Shalmaneser proceeded no farther.

(3) Shalmaneser V (726–722 B.C.) completed capture of Samaria begun by his predecessor, Tiglath-pileser III (2 Kings 17:6), ending the Northern Kingdom forever. See *Assyria; Israel.*

SHAME AND HONOR

Humiliation or loss of standing (Jer. 2:26); euphemism for nakedness (Jer. 13:26; Nah. 3:5; Hab. 2:15); and esteem, respect, (high) regard, or (good) reputation. To give honor to private parts is to clothe them (1 Cor. 12:23-24). To honor is to recognize the value of someone or thing and to act accordingly. Honoring parents (Ex. 20:12) involves providing for their material needs (Matt. 15:4-5) so that their poverty would not be a source of shame. To honor can mean to reward with tangible signs of respect (2 Chron. 16:14; Esther 6:8-11). To shame someone is to challenge that one's reputation or to disregard his or her worth. The ancients viewed every human action and interaction as an occasion for either gaining honor, that is, increasing one's value in the public eye, or for being shamed, that is, having one's estimation degraded. The desire to maintain one's honor and to avoid shame or dishonor was a powerful incentive for right action (Job 11:3; Ps. 70:3; Ezek. 43:10). Honor was thought of as a limited good, that is, the amount of available honor was limited. If one lost honor, another had to gain honor (Prov. 5:9).

The naked man and woman (Gen. 2:25) had their honor or respect intact in contrast to the loss of respect they suffered when God made their guilt public (Gen. 3:8-10).

SHAMGAR (Hurrian, *Shimig* [the god] *has given*)

Mysterious warrior who slew 600 Philistines with an oxgoad, a long metal-tipped pole (Judg. 3:31; see 5:6). See *Anath; Judges.*

SHAPHAN (coney)

Scribe and treasurer during King Josiah's reign in Judah (2 Kings 22); delivered the newfound book of the law from Hilkiah the priest to the king's palace; was sent to Huldah the prophetess to confer concerning the book (22:14). Shaphan and his sons befriended Jeremiah on several occasions. See Ahikam; Gedaliah; Jaazaniah.

SHAREZER (may [god's name] protect the king)

(1) Son of Sennacherib who helped murder his father (2 Kings 19:37), 681 B.C. See Assyria.

(2) Name open to several interpretations in Zech. 7:2; full name may be Bethel-sharezer (see REB); may be man sent to the house of God (beth-el in Hebrew) to pray (KJV). The town of Bethel may have sent Sharezer to pray (NASB, NIV, NRSV, TEV). The name probably indicates the person was born in Babylonian exile. He may have come with his questions from Babylon and have come as a representative of the people of Bethel.

SHARON, PLAIN OF (flat land or wetlands), **SHARONITE**

(1) Coastal plain that runs from near Tel Aviv to just south of Mount Carmel (about 50 miles). The area had abundant marshes, forests, and sand dunes, but few settlements during biblical days and was used more by migrant herdsmen than settled farmers. See Isa. 35:2; 65:10. See Palestine.

(2) Area of uncertain location east of Jordan inhabited by Gad (1 Chron. 5:16) and mentioned by Mesha of Moab. See Mesha.

SHEARJASHUB (a remnant shall return)

Symbolic name of first son of Isaiah, born probably around 737 B.C. Name symbolized prophecy that Judah would fall, but a remnant would survive (Isa. 7:3-7). See Isaiah.

SHEATH

Protective holder for sword attached to a belt. See Arms and Armor; Sword.

SHEBA (fullness, completeness)

(1) See Sabean.

(2) Name of Benjaminite who led revolt against David (2 Sam. 20)

(3) Gadite (1 Chron. 5:13).

SHEBNA(H) (He came near)

Royal scribe (2 Kings 18:18,37; 19:2; Isa. 36:3,22; 37:2) and "comptroller of the household" (Isa. 22:15, REB) under King Hezekiah about 715 B.C. See Scribe.

SHECHEM (shoulder, back), **SHECHEMITE**

District and city in hill country of Ephraim in north central Palestine (Josh. 17:7); first capital of Northern Kingdom of Israel; built mainly on slope, or shoulder, between Mount Gerizim and Mount Ebal. Situated where main highways and ancient trade routes converged, Shechem was an important city long before the Israelites occupied Canaan. Compare Gen. 12:6-7; 33–34, where Shechem was the name of the city and also of the prince of the city (37:12; Josh. 24:32).

As the Israelites conquered Canaan, they turned unexpectedly to Shechem. Joshua built an altar on Mount Ebal and led the people in renewing their commitment to the law of Moses (Josh. 8:30-35; compare Deut. 27:12-13). Shechem was a city of refuge (Josh. 20:7) and a Levitical city (21:21). See Cities of Refuge. Joshua led Israel to renew its covenant with God there (Josh. 24:1-17). Gideon's son Abimelech fought the leaders of Shechem (Judg. 8:31–9:49).

Rehoboam, successor to King Solomon, went to Shechem to be crowned king over all Israel (1 Kings 12:1). When the nation divided, Shechem became the first capital of the Northern Kingdom of Israel (1 Kings 12:25; compare Hos. 6:9).

At Shechem (sometimes identified with Sychar), Jesus visited with the Samaritan woman at Jacob's Well (John 4). The Samaritans had built their temple on Mount Gerizim, where they practiced their form of religion.

SHEEP See *Animals; Agriculture; Cattle; Economic Life.*

SHEKINAH (*that which dwells*)

Transliteration of Hebrew word not found in the Bible but used in many of the Jewish writings to speak of God's presence. See *Glory.*

SHEM (*name*)

Noah's oldest son and original ancestor of Semitic peoples including Israel (Gen. 5:32; 6:10; 7:13; 9:18-27; 10:1,21-22,31; 11:10-11). He carried God's blessing (9:26-27).

SHEMA

Transliteration of Hebrew imperative meaning, "Hear" (Deut. 6:4); applied to 6:4-9, as basic statement of Jewish law. The Shema became a confession of faith by which they acknowledged the one true God and His commandments for them. Later worship practice combined Deut. 6:4-9; 11:13-21; Num. 15:37-41 into the larger Shema as the summary of Jewish confession. When Jesus was asked about the "greatest commandment," He answered by quoting the Shema (Mark 12:29).

SHEOL

Place of the dead, or more specifically, the place of the unrighteous dead according to the Hebrew Bible.

The dead are sometimes described as descending to Sheol or of going into a pit (Ps. 88:6,10; Amos 9:2). The dead were buried in graves or tombs, often in family ossuaries, so the language concerning a realm of the dead beneath the earth is figurative and is not simply borrowed from surrounding peoples. Though many other ancient Near Eastern cultures professed belief in some kind of underworld, the OT understanding is

unique both in the language it employs and in the content of its teaching.

Those who dwell in Sheol are said to be separated from Yahweh spiritually and morally (Isa. 38:18; Ps. 6:5-6), though not physically, since there can be no real escape from God, even in Sheol (Ps. 139:8; Amos 9:2). It is a place in which one is captive (Pss. 18:5; 116:3), a place of darkness (Ps. 88:6) and of silence (Ps. 115:17), a place of humiliation, corruption, and despair (Isa. 14; Ezek. 32).

Sheol is the destiny of those who end their lives in impenitence. Some texts seem to indicate that even the righteous will find themselves in Sheol. So Job laments that he is headed for that dread destination (Job 17:13-16), as do Jacob (Gen. 37:35) and Hezekiah (Isa. 38:10). These texts, though, show persons in the depth of sorrowful or tragic circumstances. In these texts Sheol takes on more of a metaphorical meaning, as if a modern person were to say, "I have been deep in a pit these past days."

The fact that in Sheol there is no praise of Yahweh (Pss. 6:5; 115:17) indicates that it is not the abode of the righteous. It is a place of pain and distress (Ps. 116:3), of weakness (Isa. 14:10), helplessness (Ps. 88:4), hopelessness (Isa. 38:10), and destruction (Isa. 38:17).

Sheol in the OT is roughly analogous to hades in the NT, a place of eternal separation from God's righteousness and love.

SHEPHELAH (*lowland*) See *Palestine.*

SHEPHERD

Keeper of sheep. The first keeper of sheep in the Bible was Adam's son Abel (Gen. 4:2). Shepherding was the chief occupation of the Israelites in the early days of the patriarchs: Abraham (Gen. 12:16); Rachel (Gen. 29:9); Jacob (Gen. 30:31-40); Moses (Ex. 3:1). As cultivation of crops increased, shepherding fell from favor and was assigned to younger sons, hirelings, and slaves (compare David in 1 Sam. 16:11-13). Farmers such as in Egypt even hated shepherds (Gen. 46:34). Shepherds led sheep to pasture and water (Ps. 23) and protected them from wild animals (1 Sam. 17:34-35). Shepherds guarded their flocks at night whether in the open (Luke 2:8) or in sheepfolds (Zeph. 2:6) where they counted the sheep as they entered (Jer. 33:13). They even carried weak lambs in their arms (Isa. 40:11). Shepherd came to designate not only persons who herded sheep but also kings (2 Sam. 5:2) and God Himself (Ps. 23; Isa. 40:11). Later prophets referred to Israel's leaders as shepherds (Jer. 23; Ezek. 34). See *Sheep.*

Shepherds were among the first to visit Jesus at His birth (Luke 2:8-20). Jesus is our Shepherd (John 10:7-18; Heb. 13:20). Jesus commissioned Peter to feed His sheep (John 21). Paul likened the church and its leaders to a flock with shepherds (Acts 20:28).

SHESHACH

Code word Jeremiah used to indicate Babylon (25:26; 51:41). The code uses the first word of the alphabet for the last, the second for the next to last, and so on. In English *a* would stand for *z*, *b* for *y*, and so on.

SHESHBAZZAR (probably *may Shamash* [sun god] *protect the father*)

Jewish leader who accompanied the first group of exiles from Babylon to Jerusalem in 538 B.C. (Ezra 1:8). King Cyrus of Persia apparently appointed Sheshbazzar governor of restored Judah. He attempted to rebuild the temple (Ezra 5:16), but got no farther than the foundation when he was replaced by Zerubbabel. Some believe Shenazar of 1 Chron. 3:18 may be Sheshbazzar. If so, he was a son of King Jehoiachin and uncle of Zerubbabel.

SHEWBREAD   See *Bread of the Presence.*

SHIELD   See *Arms and Armor.*

SHIHOR (*pool of Horus* [a god])

Border town of Promised Land (Josh. 13:3), marking widest extent of Israel's territorial claims (1 Chron. 13:5); in Isa. 23:3; Jer. 2:18, apparently refers to branch of the Nile River inside Egypt. This would extend Israel's claim up to the Nile. See *Palestine.*

SHILOAH, WATERS OF (*being sent*)

Waters supplying Jerusalem diverted from the Gihon spring and representing God's supply, making reliance on foreign kings unnecessary (Isa. 8:6). It differs from the Shiloah Tunnel Hezekiah built (2 Kings 20:20). The background may be anointing of kings at the Gihon (1 Kings 1:33-40), thus implying rejection of God's kingship represented through His anointed king.

SHILOH (perhaps *tranquil, secure*)

Israel's religious center for over a century after conquest; home of Israel's tabernacle (Josh. 18:1); about 30 miles north of Jerusalem; 12 miles south of Shechem (see Judg. 21:19). See *Tabernacle.* Shiloh was in a fertile plain at 2,000 feet elevation, apparently modern Seilun was the place where Joshua distributed part of land (Josh. 18); city whose daughters Benjaminites captured for wives (Judg. 21).

Samuel's early years provided another connection with Shiloh (1 Sam. 1-4). Shiloh apparently was destroyed about 1050 B.C. by the Philistines (see 1 Sam. 7:1). See Jer. 7:12; compare 26:6-9; 41:5. See *Joshua; Eli; Samuel.*

SHIMEI (*my being heard*), SHIMEITES

Eighteen OT men including:

(1) Grandson of Levi and head of Levitical family (Ex. 6:17; Num. 3:18; compare 1 Chron. 6:42).

(2) Relative of King Saul who cursed and opposed David as he fled from Absalom (2 Sam. 16; compare ch. 19;

1 Kings 2). Court personality who refused to support Adonijah against Solomon (1 Kings 1:8).

SHINAR, PLAIN OF

Mesopotamia (Gen. 10:10); place name used in various Ancient Near Eastern documents apparently for somewhat different localities. Some evidence points to a Syrian district cited as Sanhara in the Amarna letters. Some scholars equate Shinar in Assyrian texts with modern Sinjar west of Mosul in Iraq. Others think a Kassite tribe was meant originally. See *Mesopotamia.*

The tower of Babel was built in Shinar (Gen. 11:2-9). The King of Shinar opposed Abraham (Gen. 14:1). Isaiah prophesied that God would bring out a remnant of His people from Shinar (11:11). Daniel 1:1-2 and probably Zech. 5:11 equate Babylon and Shinar, thus limiting Shinar to its major city in the writers' day.

SHIPS AND BOATS

Ships and boats are rarely mentioned in the history of Israel. Solomon built a fleet of ships at Ezion Geber (1 Kings 9:26). Jehoshaphat attempted a similar project with disastrous results (1 Kings 22:48). Paul sailed from Caesarea to Rome (Acts 27–28). The ideal sailing season in the Mediterranean was from May 27 to September 14 with an extension to outside limits from March 10 to November 10. Sailing during the late fall and winter was reduced to bare essentials such as carrying of vital dispatches, the transport of essential supplies, and urgent military movement. The severity of winter storms and the poor visibility due to fog and cloudiness made navigation before the compass most difficult. Small vessels operated on the Sea of Galilee but we have no description of them.

SHISHAK

Pharaoh (945–924 B.C.) who founded Twenty-Second Dynasty in Egypt; known also as Sheshonk I. Just after Rehoboam began to reign in Judah, Shishak invaded Jerusalem and carted off the temple treasures (1 Kings 14:25-26). Inscriptions in a temple to the god Amon in Karnak show Shishak captured over 150 towns in Palestine including Megiddo, Taanach, and Gibeon. Some equate him with the pharaoh whose daughter married Solomon (3:1) and who later burned Gezer and gave it to his daughter (9:16). See *Egypt.*

SHITTIM *(acacia trees)*

(1) Large area in Moab directly across the Jordan from Jericho and northeast of the Dead Sea; tell el-Hammam es Samri about eight miles east of the Jordan. Israel camped there before crossing into the Promised Land. See Num. 22–25; compare Deut. 34:9; Josh. 2:1; 3:1; Mic. 6:5.

(2) In Joel 3:18 the symbolic meaning of acacias (note NASB) comes to the fore in the messianic picture of fertility for the Kidron Valley with a stream flowing from the temple.

SHOA *(help!)*

Nation God used to punish His people (Ezek. 23:23); usually identified with Sutu, a nomadic people from the Syrian and Arabian desert known from documents from Mari, Amarna, and Assyria. Some commentators see them mentioned in Isa. 22:5, where most translate "crying."

SHOPHAR

Ceremonial ram's horn used to call the people of Israel together (Ex. 19:16). See *Music.*

SHUAL *(jackal)*

(1) Descendant of Asher (1 Chron. 7:36).

(2) Territory on path Philistines took against Saul (1 Sam. 13:17). Some would identify it with Shaalim (1 Sam. 9:4).

SHULAM(M)ITE

Description of woman (Song of Sol. 6:13); may mean:

(1) as from Shunem through a copying change;

(2) from Shulam, an otherwise unknown town; (3) Solomonite, referring to a relationship to Solomon; (4) or a common noun meaning "the replaced one."

SHUNEM, SHUNAMMITES

Town in Issachar southeast of Mount Carmel; Solem, about eight miles north of Jenin and three miles east of Affulah. The Israelites controlled it under Joshua (Josh. 19:18; compare 1 Sam. 28:4; 1 Kings 2:17; 2 Kings 4). About 920 B.C., the Egyptian pharaoh Shishak captured the town. See *Shishak.*

SHUR, WILDERNESS OF (*wall*)

Region on Egypt's northeastern border, perhaps named after wall Egyptians built to protect their border; may be tell el-Fara; where Moses made first stop after crossing the Red Sea (Ex. 15:22). See Gen. 16:7; 20:1; 1 Sam. 15:7; 27:8.

SHUSHAN (*lily* or *lotus*)

City in southwestern Iran; very rich because of location on caravan routes between Arabia and points north and west; Susa in modern translations; ancient capital of Elam; inhabited as early as 3000 B.C. In Esther 1:2, the city is identified as the throne city of Ahasuerus. The Achaemenean Dynasty between 500 and 300 B.C. took Shushan to its height politically and economically. It served as the king's winter residence; Ecbatana being summer residence. See *Elam; Persia.*

SIBLING RIVALRY

Tensions and fighting among brothers or sisters including Cain and Abel (Gen. 4:1-16); Shem, Ham and Japheth (Gen. 9:20-27); Jacob and Esau (Gen. 25:22–28:9; 32:1–33:17; Mal. 1:2-3); Leah and Rachel (Gen. 29:16–30:24); Joseph and his brothers (Gen. 37; 39–45); Er and Onan (Gen. 38:1-10); Moses, Aaron and Miriam (Num. 12:1-15); Abimelech and Jotham (Judg. 9:1-57); David and Eliab (1 Sam.

17:28-30); Absalom and Amnon (2 Sam. 13:1-39); and Solomon and Adonijah (1 Kings 1:5-53). In each case one, or usually both, of the siblings attempts to gain status or favor over the other.

Families are given by God (Ps. 127:3) and are not, like friends, chosen by their members. The physical and emotional proximity of family members is characteristically quite close. The potential for sibling rivalry is built into the family dynamic, as the writer of Proverbs understood: "A friend loveth at all times, and a brother is born for adversity" (Prov. 17:17; 18:24; Matt. 10:21). The psalmist well praised the goodness and pleasantness of brothers who are able to dwell together in unity (Ps. 133:1-3).

SIBMAH (*cold* or *high*)

City Reuben rebuilt in Transjordan (Num. 32:38; see Josh. 13:19; compare Isa. 16:8-9; Jer. 48:32); may be Khirbet al-Qibsh about three miles east northeast of Mount Nebo and three miles southwest of Hesban. "Sebam" (Num. 32:3) is often seen as a copyist's change from Sibmah.

SIDON AND TYRE

Phoenician cities on coastal plain between the mountains of Lebanon and the Mediterranean Sea (Gen. 10:15). While Sidon seems to have been dominant in early part of their histories, Tyre dominated in latter times. Both cities were centers of trade especially sea trade. One of Tyre's most coveted exports was purple dye. Joshua could not conquer the territory (Josh. 13:3-4). David (2 Sam. 5:11) and Solomon (1 Kings 5) depended heavily on materials and craftsmen from Tyre. About 870 B.C. Ahab married Jezebel, the daughter of the Phoenician king, bringing Baal worship to Israel's court. Ezekiel 28 characterizes the king of Tyre as the ultimate example of pride. Under Roman rule the two cities were important ports of trade, but they did not enjoy the dominance they previously held. Jesus spent time in Tyre and Sidon and contrasted them with the

Jews as examples of faith (Matt. 11:20-22). Paul spent seven days in Tyre after his third missionary journey (Acts 21:3-4). See *Phoenicia.*

SIGN

That which points to something else; an object, occurrence, or person through which one recognizes, remembers, or validates something; military signal (Josh. 2:12); military standard (Num. 2:2; Ps. 74:4). Signs may be classed according to seven somewhat overlapping functions:

(1) *Signs can impart knowledge or give identity.* These signs typically characterize God as Lord of history and champion of oppressed Israel. The goal of the exodus signs is the knowledge that "I am the LORD (in the midst of the earth)" (Ex. 7:5; 8:22; 10:2) and that "the LORD he is God; there is none else beside him" (Deut. 4:34-35; compare Jer. 44:29). These signs encouraged acknowledgment of Yahweh as the only God, obedience to God's covenant, and trust in God's word. John's signs generally impart knowledge about Jesus and His relation to the Father (John 2:1-11; 4:46-54; 5:2-9,17; 6:2-14,35; 9:1-7). The raising of Lazarus (John 11) points to Jesus as the resurrection and the life (11:25). Judas' kiss clearly designated Jesus as the One the mob was seeking (Matt. 26:48). The sign of Jesus' coming and the end of the age is, likewise, an identifying mark (Matt. 24:3; Mark 13:4; Luke 21:7; compare Matt. 24:30).

(2) *Signs protect.* The mark of Cain (Gen. 4:15), blood on the doorposts at Passover (Ex. 12:13) and the seal of God upon the foreheads protected those under the sign (Rev. 9:4).

(3) *Signs motivated faith and worship.* Israel's unbelief in spite of signs is often condemned (Num. 14:11,22; Deut. 1:29-33). The signs fulfill their goal when they inspire obedience (Deut. 11:3,8), worship (Deut. 26:8,10), and loyalty to the Lord (Josh. 24:16-17). The signs in the Fourth Gospel were recounted so "that ye might believe that Jesus is the Christ, the Son of God; and that

believing ye might have life through his name" (John 20:31). John previously noted signs leading to faith (John 2:11; 4:53; 9:38; Acts 4:16,21; 8:6). The signs of pagan prophets similarly serve as a challenge to trust in Yahweh (Deut. 13:1-4). The reality of wonder-working false prophets underscores truth that signs themselves are ambivalent; the function of the sign, either to evoke or challenge faith in Yahweh, is the deciding factor.

(4) *Signs serve as reminders of significant events.* Eating unleavened bread at Passover (Ex. 13:9) and redeeming the first-born (Ex. 13:16) are reminders of God's liberation of Israel. Compare Josh. 4:6-7; Acts 2:19,22; 4:30; 7:36-37; 14:3. The covering of the altar reminded of the danger of usurping the role of God's priests (Num. 17:10). The paired expression "signs and wonders" recalls the foundational saving events of the exodus. The "signs and wonders" which Jesus and the apostles performed designate the inauguration of God's new saving event.

(5) *Other signs serve as reminders of a covenant or established relationship.* Rainbow, covenant with Noah (Gen. 9:12-17); circumcision, covenant with Abraham (Gen. 17:11; Rom. 4:11) sabbath, covenant with Moses (Ex. 31:13,17; Ezek. 20:12). The Lord's Supper points to Jesus' new covenant.

(6) *Signs serve as confirmation.* Signs often authenticated God's special call (of Moses, Ex. 3:12; 4:8; of Gideon, Judg. 6:17; of Saul, 1 Sam. 10:2-9) and confirmed God's word of judgment (1 Sam. 2:34; Jer. 44:29-30) or promise of healing (2 Kings 20:8). The humble circumstances of the Christ-child in the manger confirmed the angel's announcement of a Savior to outcast shepherds (Luke 2:12). Jesus offered the difficult "sign of Jonah" as His authentication (Matt. 12:39-43; Luke 11:29-32).

(7) *Signs take the form of prophetic acts.* The names of Isaiah ("Yahweh is salvation") and his sons Shear-jashub ("A remnant shall return") and Maher-shalal-hash-baz ("The spoil speeds, the prey has-

tens") illustrate Israel's fate (Isa. 7:3; 8:3). Isaiah's walking naked and barefoot for three years illustrated the coming humiliation of Egypt and Ethiopia (Isa. 20:3). Ezekiel illustrated the coming siege of Jerusalem using a brick, earth, and a plate (Ezek. 4:1-3). Agabus' action in binding himself with Paul's belt (Acts 21:11) parallels the acts of the OT prophets.

The NT often rebukes the demand for a sign to confirm God's work (Matt. 16:1; John 2:18; 4:48; 1 Cor. 1:22). A sign may evoke faith in a receptive heart, but no sign will convince the hard-hearted.

SIHON

Amorite king whose capital was Heshbon (Deut. 2:26). He unsuccessfully opposed Israel's passage through his country as they journeyed toward the Promised Land (Num. 21:23).

SILAS, SILVANUS

Leader in early Jerusalem church and evangelist (2 Cor. 1:19); accompanied Paul on missionary journeys (Acts 15:40-41; 16:19-24; 1 Pet. 5:12). One of his first missions was to carry news of the Jerusalem conference to the believers at Antioch (Acts 15:22). In Philippi he and Paul won the jailer and his family to the Lord after God delivered them from prison. He joined Paul in writing the Thessalonians (1 Thess. 1:1; 2 Thess. 1:1). He also served as Peter's scribe, writing 1 Peter. See *Paul; 1 Peter.*

SILK (*something glistening white*)

Cloth made from thread that came from the Chinese silk worm, perhaps via India; may be "fine linen" or "expensive material"(see Ezek. 16:10; Prov. 31:22); rich in Babylon bought silk from merchants (Rev. 18:12).

SILOAM (*sending*)

Place easily confused with the waters of Shiloah (Isa. 8:6); pool on southern end of old Jebusite city of Jerusalem created by Hezekiah's tunnel which diverted the waters of Shiloah from the Siloam Spring to a point less vul-

nerable to the Assyrian enemy. (See *Jerusalem.*) Hezekiah's inscription preserved on the tunnel wall describes the meeting of tunnel builders boring through rock from each end of the tunnel. John 9:7,11 uses play on words to press point that blind man was *sent* to Siloah by one who was Himself the One who was *sent*. Luke 13:4 refers more to an unknown tower at Siloam than to Siloam.

SILVANUS See *Silas, Silvanus.*

SILVER See *Minerals and Metals; Coins.*

SILVERSMITH

Person who refines silver from ore or makes refined silver into finished product. Paul's preaching threatened their livelihood (Acts 19:23-41). See *Occupations and Professions.*

SIMEON (*hearing* or possibly, *little hyena beast*)

(1) See *Jacob; Tribes of Israel.*

(2) Devout Jew who lived in Jerusalem during the time of Jesus' birth and during Jesus' temple purification rites announced to his parents God's plan for the boy (Luke 2:25-34).

(3) Ancestor of Jesus (Luke 3:30).

(4) Prophet and teacher in church at Antioch (Acts 13:1).

(5) Alternate form in Greek for Simon, original Greek name of Peter. See *Peter; Simon.*

SIMON (*flat-nosed*)

Greek alternative for Hebrew "Simeon."

(1) Father of Judas Iscariot (John 6:71).

(2) One of Jesus' disciples; a son of Jonah (Matt. 16:17) and brother of Andrew. After he confessed Jesus as the Christ, the Lord changed his name to Peter (v. 18). See *Peter; Simeon.*

(3) Pharisee who hosted Jesus at a dinner (Luke 7:36-40) and learned about love, courtesy, and forgiveness

after a sinful woman anointed Jesus at this event.

(4) Native of Cyrene who was forced to carry Jesus' cross to Golgotha (Mark 15:21). See *Cyrene.*

(5) Tanner of animal skins from Joppa. Peter stayed at his house (Acts 9:43) and received visionary message declaring all foods fit for consumption (10:9-16).

(6) Jesus' disciple also called "the Canaanite" (Matt. 10:4) or the Zealot (Luke 6:15).

(7) Brother of Jesus (Matt. 13:55).

(8) Leper who hosted Jesus and saw a woman anoint Jesus with costly ointment (Matt. 26:6-13; compare *3* above).

(9) Magician from Samaria who believed Philip's preaching, was baptized, and then tried to buy the power of laying on hands and giving the Holy Spirit to people (Acts 8:9-24).

SIN

Actions by which humans rebel against God, miss His purpose for their lives, and surrender to the power of evil rather than to God, and become estranged from God. Sin is an attitude of rebellion against God. Rebellion was at the root of the problem for Adam and Eve (Gen. 3) and has been at the root of humanity's plight ever since.

Human sin is universal—we all sin (Rom. 3:9-23). God is in no way responsible for sin. Satan introduced sin when he beguiled Eve, but the Bible does not teach that sin had its origin with him either. Sin's origin is to be found in humanity's rebellious nature.

Some passages such as Ps. 51:5; Eph. 2:3 could be interpreted to mean that a person's sinful nature is inherited. Other passages seem to affirm that sin is due to human choice (see Ezek. 18:4,19-20; Rom. 1:18-20; 5:12). Any idea that humanity inherits a sinful nature must be coupled with the corollary that every person is indeed responsible for his/her choice of sin. When Adam rebelled against

God, he incorporated all of his descendants in his action (see Heb. 7:9-10 for a similar analogy). Still, each individual must accept full responsibility for sinful acts. Every person who has lived since has chosen to follow Adam and Eve's example.

God established the law as a standard of righteousness; any violation of this standard is defined as sin (see Deut. 6:24-25). God made a covenant with the nation Israel (Ex. 19; 24; Josh. 24). Any breach of this covenant was viewed as sin (Deut. 29:19-21.)

The righteous and holy God sets forth as a criterion for His people a righteousness like His own. (Lev. 11:45.) Any deviation from God's own righteousness is viewed as sin.

The Bible has a rich vocabulary for sin:

(1) "to miss the mark,"as a person shooting a bow and arrow and missing the target with the arrow. A person sins by missing the mark God has established for the person's life;

(2) "crooked or perverse spirit," seen as persons pervert their spirits and become crooked rather than straight;

(3) "violence" with the connotation of evil breaking out. Sin is the opposite of righteousness or moral straightness. Sin is a lack of fellowship with God. Anything which disturbs or distorts this fellowship is sin. The NT defines sin against the backdrop of Jesus' perfection as the standard for righteousness.

Jesus traced sin directly to inner motives, stating that the sinful thought leading to the overt act is the real sin. The outward deed is actually the fruit of sin. Anger is the same as murder (Matt. 5:21-22). The impure look is tantamount to adultery (Matt. 5:27-28). The real defilement in a person stems from the inner person (heart) which is sinful (Matt. 15:18-20).

The NT interprets sin as unbelief, the rejection of the supreme revelation as it is found in the person of Jesus Christ, producing moral and spiritual blindness. The outcome of such rejection is judgment. The only criterion for judgment is whether or not one has accepted or rejected the revelation of God as found in Jesus Christ (John 3:18-19; 16:8-16). The law of Moses was preparatory. Its function was to point to Christ. The law revealed sin in its true character, but this only aroused in humanity a desire to experience the forbidden fruit of sin. The law offers no means of salvation; rather, it leaves humanity with a deep sense of sin and guilt (Rom. 7).

The Bible looks on sin in any form as the most serious of humanity's problems. Ultimately every sin is against God. Perfect in righteousness, God cannot tolerate that which violates His righteous character. Therefore, sin creates a barrier between God and persons. Since humanity could not extricate itself from the entanglements of sin, God had to intervene if humanity was ever to be freed from these entanglements. See *Salvation*.

Sin so controls a person that one becomes enslaved to sin (Rom. 6). A continuance in sin adds to personal depravity, eventually making it impossible to reject sin. Such depravity pervades society as a whole. Sin blurs the distinction between right and wrong. Each person must accept responsibility for sin and face the guilt associated with it (Rom. 1–3).

One terrible byproduct of sin is death. Continual, consistent sin will bring spiritual death to a person who has not come under the lordship of Christ through repentance and faith (Rom. 6:23; Rev. 20:14.) For those who have trusted Christ Jesus for salvation, death no longer holds this dread. Christ has negated the power of Satan in making death horrible and has freed the person from slavery to this awful fear (Heb. 2:14-15.) See *Death*.

Sin brings separation from God, estrangement, and a lack of fellowship with God. If a person dies not having corrected this problem by trusting Christ, then the separation becomes permanent (Rom. 6:23). See *Hell*. Sin also produces estrangement from other persons. All interpersonal problems have sin as their root cause (Jas. 4:1-3). The only hope for peace to be achieved on either the personal or national level is through the Prince of peace.

SIN, WILDERNESS OF

Barren region somewhere west of the Sinai plateau on the Sinai peninsula. The Hebrew people stopped here on their journey from Egypt to the Promised Land (Ex. 16:1). The place sometimes has been confused with the Wilderness of Zin, which is located on the northwestern side of Sinai. See *Zin*.

SINAI, MOUNT (*shining*)

Mountain of God's revelation in south central part of a peninsula 150 miles long in northwestern end of Arabia bounded on the east by the north end of the Red Sea and on the west by the Gulf of Aqaba with Gaza strip directly north; mountains range from 5,000 to 9,000 feet with oil and manganese deposits; called "the mount" (Ex. 19:2); "the mountain of God" (Ex. 3:1); "the mount of the Lord" (Num. 10:33); modern Jebel Musa (7,500 ft.), one of three granite peaks near southern tip of the peninsula.

Horeb is often used to refer to Sinai in such a way as to make the names synonymous (Ex. 3:1). Horeb appears to be general term for the area and Sinai the specific peak where God manifested Himself to Moses. Many explorers think Ras es-Safsafeh (6,540 feet) is biblical Sinai because it has a plain, er Rahah, on its northwest base, which is two miles long and about two thirds of a mile wide. This plain was certainly large enough to accommodate the camp of the Israelites. Other suggested locations include the top of the Gulf of Aqaba near volcanic action or in the territory of the Amalekites to the north. See *Palestine*.

SINEW

Tendons and connective tissue that connect muscles to bone in the body (Job 10:11; 30:17; Ezek. 37:6,8). Because of Jacob's wrestling with the angel that resulted in the angel's striking the sinew of his thigh, the Jews cut away this sinew and did not eat it (Gen. 32:24-32; compare Isa. 48:4). See *Body*.

SISERA (*mediation*)

Two OT men including military leader of Jabin, king of Canaan (Judg. 4:2) who was killed by Heber's wife, Jael (v. 21). See *Jabin; Judges, Book of; Judge (Office)*.

SLANDER

To speak critically of another person with the intent to hurt (Lev. 19:16). In a court of law it means to falsely accuse another (Ex. 20:16; Deut. 5:20; compare Matt. 12:36; Eph. 4:31; 1 Pet. 2:1). Slander is a mark of the unregenerate world (Jas. 4:11-12; 1 Pet. 2:12; 3:16). Satan is a slanderer (John 8:44). Devil can mean "slanderous" or "the slanderer." See *Devil, Satan, Evil, Demonic; Ethics*.

SLAVE, SERVANT

Person totally responsible to and dependent on another person. Slavery was prevalent and widely accepted in the ancient world. The economies of Egypt, Greece, and Rome were based on slave labor. In the first Christian century, one out of three persons in Italy and one out of five elsewhere was a slave. Huge gangs toiled in the fields and mines and on building projects. Slaves served as domestic and civil servants, temple slaves, craftsmen and gladiators. Some were highly intelligent and held responsible positions. Legally, a slave had no rights; but, except for the gangs, most were treated humanely and were better off than many free persons. Domestics were considered part of the family, and some were greatly loved by their masters. Israel's law protected slaves in various ways. Slavery laws appear in Ex. 12:44-48; 21:1-11, 20-21,26-27; Lev. 25:39-55; and Deut. 15:12-18; 16:11,14; 23:15-16. Most of these concern humane treatment and manumission. See *Jubilee*. Christian preachers called upon masters to be kind, but only the Essenes opposed slavery. See *Jewish Parties in the New Testament*.

A person could become a slave as a result of capture in war, default on a debt, inability to support oneself, "voluntarily" selling oneself, being sold as a child by destitute parents, birth to slave parents, conviction of a crime, or kidnapping and piracy. Slavery cut across races and nationalities.

Manumission or freeing of slaves was possible and common in Roman times. Masters in their wills often freed their slaves, and sometimes they did so during their lifetimes. Industrious slaves could make and save money and purchase their own freedom. See Acts 6:9.

Paul and Peter insisted that Christian slaves be obedient to their masters (Eph. 6:5-8; Col. 3:22-25; 1 Tim. 6:1-2; 1 Pet. 2:18-21) and not seek freedom just because of conversion (1 Cor. 7:20-22). Masters were urged to be kind (Eph. 6:9; Col. 4:1). Slave trading was condemned (1 Tim. 1:10). Paul claimed that in Christ human status was unimportant (Gal. 3:28). Neither Jesus nor the apostles condemned slavery. Jesus and the apostles set forth principles of human dignity and equality which eventually led to abolition. (See *Servant of the Lord*.) A life of sin is spoken of as slavery (John 8:34; Rom. 6:6,16-20; Heb. 2:15). Legalism is a kind of slavery (Gal. 4:24-25; 5:1). Paradoxically, however, there is also a blessed slavery to righteousness (Rom. 6:16-22). See *Freedom*.

SLEEP

Natural state of rest for human beings and animals (Ps. 4:8); God causes "deep sleep" for revelation (Gen. 2:21; 15:12; Job 4:13), and sometimes to prevent prophetic vision (Isa. 29:10; compare 1 Sam. 26:12). It is also used as a sign of laziness (Prov. 19:15). Sleep is a figure of physical death (John 11:11-14; 1 Cor. 15:51). See *Death; Eternal Life*.

SMYRNA See *Asia Minor, Cities of*.

SNARE See *Fowler; Hunt, Hunter.*

SNOW

Frozen percipitation rarely seen in Palestine. Yet Mount Hermon has a snow cap that can be seen throughout much of Palestine. Snow is used in the Bible figuratively: whiteness (Isa. 1:18), cleanness (Job 9:30), refreshing coolness (Prov. 25:13). See *Weather.*

SNUFFERS

Two different instruments. One instrument seems to be a cutting tool used for trimming the wicks of the lamps. The other word is often translated "tongs" (Isa. 6:6), meaning that it consisted of two parts working together. Exodus 25:38 speaks of "tongs" and "snuffdishes."

SOAP

Cleaner made by mixing olive oil and alkali from burning certain salt-producing plants. It was used for washing the body (Jer. 2:22) and washing clothes (Mal. 3:2). People in the Near East use oil for cleansing the body and pound clothes on rocks while wet to cleanse them. See *Fuller.*

SOCOH, SOCO, SHOCHO (*thorns*)

(1) Town in southern Judah hill country used as a fortification against people approaching from the south (Josh. 15:35); Khirbet Abbad. Compare 1 Sam. 17:1; 2 Chron. 11:7).

(2) Town in southern hill country of Judah about ten miles southwest of Hebron (Josh. 15:48) at Khirbet Shuweikeh.

(3) Town belonging to Ben-hesed (1 Kings 4:10, NRSV); as-Shuweikeh west of Nablus and two miles north of Tulkarm.

(4) Native of Judah, the son of Heber (1 Chron. 4:18). Some interpreters feel that this is a place name rather than personal name and may be same as 2.

SODOM AND GOMORRAH

Two cities renowned for their wickedness (Gen. 18:20) at the time of Abraham and so destroyed by God despite Abraham's intercession; among five "cities of the valley" (Gen. 13:12; 19:29; KJV, "plain") of Abraham's time. Exact locations are unknown, but they were probably situated in the Valley of Siddim (Gen. 14:3,8,10-11) near the Dead Sea, perhaps the area now covered by the Sea's shallow southern end. See Gen. 13:10-12; 14:12; 19:1.

The unnatural lusts of the men of Sodom (Gen. 19:4-8; Jude 7) have given us the modern term *sodomy,* but the city was guilty of a full spectrum of sins including pride, oppression of the poor, haughtiness, and "abominable things" (Ezek. 16:49-50). Sodom and Gomorrah provided a point of comparison for the sinfulness of Israel and other nations (Deut. 32:32; Isa. 1:10; Jer. 23:14). The memory of their destruction provided a picture of God's judgment (Isa. 13:19; Jer. 49:18; Matt. 10:14-15; 11:23-24) and made them an example to be avoided (Deut. 29:23-25; 2 Pet. 2:6).

SODOMITE

Originally a citizen of the town of Sodom (Gen 13:12); male who has sexual relations with another male. See *Homosexuality; Sex, Biblical Teaching On.*

SOLDIER

Person trained to fight, usually on active military duty. In early Israelite history every male was called on to fight when the tribes were threatened. David was the first to put together a national army made up of professional soldiers. The NT soldier was usually the Roman soldier. John the Baptist indicated that the average Roman soldier extorted money from civilians by threatening them (Luke 3:14). On the other hand, the centurion (leader of 100 men) is held in esteem in the NT (see Acts 10). See *Army; Centurion.*

SOLEMN ASSEMBLY See *Festivals.*

SOLOMON (*his peace*, [God] *is peace, Salem* [a god], *intact*, or *his replacement*)

Tenth son of David and second son of Bathsheba; third king of Israel; reigned 40 years about 1000 B.C. See 2 Sam. 12:24; 1 Kings 1–2. Solomon is remembered most for his wisdom, his building program, and his wealth generated through trade and administrative reorganization (1 Kings 3:16; 4:32; 5-8; 9:15-19; 10). Proverbs, Ecclesiastes and Song of Solomon in the Bible are attributed to Solomon. (Prov. 1:1; Song of Sol. 1:1) as are several apocryphal and pseudepigraphal books. See *Apocrypha; Pseudepigrapha.*

Solomon divided the country into administrative districts that did not correspond to the old tribal boundaries (1 Kings 4:7-19) and had the districts provide provisions for the central government. This system, combined with control of vital north/south trade routes between the Red Sea and what was later known as Asia Minor, made it possible for Solomon to accumulate vast wealth (1 Kings 9:26-28; 10:26-29). See *Ezion-gaber.*

The "seven hundred wives, princesses, and three hundred concubines" came from many of the kingdoms with which Solomon had treaties (1 Kings 11:1). He apparently allowed his wives to worship their native gods and even had altars to these gods constructed in Jerusalem (1 Kings 11:7-8).

Solomon is mentioned in Jesus' teaching about anxiety (Matt. 6:29; Luke 12:27; compare Matt. 12:42; Luke 11:31; Acts 7:47).

SON OF GOD

Title expressing deity of Jesus of Nazareth as the one, unique Son of God; title for certain men and angels (Gen. 6:1-4; Pss. 29:1; 82:6; 89:6); people of Israel corporately (Ex. 4:22; Jer. 31:20; Hos. 11:1); and for king (Ps. 2:7). The promises in the Davidic covenant (2 Sam. 7:14) are the source for this special filial relationship.

At the center of Jesus' identity in the Fourth Gospel is His divine sonship (John 10:36). Jesus conceived of His divine sonship as unique: "I and my Father are one" (John 10:30); "the Father is in me and I am in him" (John 10:38). He frequently referred to God as "my Father" (John 5:17; 6:32; 8:54; 10:18; 15:15; Matt. 7:21; 10:32-33; 20:23; 26:29,53; Mark 8:38; Luke 2:49; 10:21-22).

At Jesus' baptism and transfiguration, God the Father identified Jesus as His Son, in passages reflecting Ps. 2:7. He was identified as Son of God by an angel prior to His birth (Luke 1:32,35); by Satan at His temptation (Matt. 4:3,6); by John the Baptist (John 1:34); by the centurion at the crucifixion (Matt. 27:54). Several of His followers ascribed to Him this title in various contexts (Matt. 14:33; 16:16; John 1:49; 11:27).

Son of God is closely associated with His royal position as Messiah. Gabriel told Mary that her Son would not only be called the Son of God, but would also reign on the messianic (David's) throne (Luke 1:32-33; compare John 1:49; 11:27; 20:30; Rom. 1:3-4; 1 Cor. 15:28; Col. 1:13; Acts 9:20-22. Primarily, "Son of God" affirms Jesus' deity evidenced by His person and His work.

SON OF MAN

New Testament designation for Jesus as God incarnate in flesh and agent of divine judgment. With the exception of Ezekiel and Daniel, *Son of man* in the OT is a synonym for "man," "humankind" (Isa. 56:2; Jer. 50:40; Pss. 8:4; 80:17; 146:3; Job 25:6).

(1) *Ezekiel.* In Ezekiel, God uses the term 90 times to address the prophet, emphasizing his *humanity.*

(2) *Daniel.* In one of his night visions, the prophet saw "one like the Son of man" (Dan. 7:13) come on the clouds of heaven to appear before the throne of God. He was given dominion over all peoples and an everlasting kingdom. Scholars interpret Son of man here as an angel, as the Messiah, or as all of Israel. Later Jewish

interpretation of Dan. 7:13 is at one in seeing the reference as messianic.

The "Son of man" sayings of Jesus fall into three distinct types.

(1) *Apocalyptic Sayings.* Son of man will descend to earth to gather the elect and to judge. The picture of the Son of man in these passages is strongly reminiscent of Dan. 7:13 (quoted in Matt. 24:30; 26:64; Mark 13:26; 14:62; Luke 21:27; 22:69; compare Matt. 10:23; 13:41; 16:27-28; 19:28; 24:27,38-39; 24:44; 25:31; Luke 12:8; 17:22-27; 18:8; 21:36; John 5:27). Faithful disciples are to join the Son of man in this judgment which perhaps reflects the dual role of the Son of man and saints of the Most High in Dan. 7:13,27. These sayings refer to Jesus and His second coming.

(2) *Passion Sayings.* Three times Jesus predicted the Son of man would be rejected and killed by the priests and scribes but would rise on the third day (Mark 8:31; 9:31; 10:33-34; Luke 24:7; compare Matt. 17:9,12-13; 26:24,45; Mark 9:12-13; Luke 22:48).

John highlighted this dual emphasis on the humiliation of the cross and the glory of the resurrection. "On the cross" is in reality His exaltation, leading to His ascension to the Father (John 3:14; 8:28; 12:34). Jesus' death became His hour of greatest glory (John 12:23-24; 13:31).

Jewish messianic expectation never connected the Son of man with suffering and death, not even the clear description of the Suffering Servant (Isa. 53). That connection (Mark 10:45; Matt. 20:28) of the Son of man, the messianic Judge of the final time with the Suffering Servant of God, is unique to the teaching and ministry of Jesus.

(3) *Sayings Connected with Jesus' Ministry.* Many sayings could be understood in the sense of the Hebrew idiom —"a man, this man, I." Even in these sayings, "Son of man" should be seen as a title pointing to Jesus' special role as the One who has authority to forgive sins (Matt. 9:6; Mark 2:10; Luke 5:24) and to interpret the meaning of the sabbath (Matt. 12:8; Mark 2:28; Luke 6:5). See Matt. 13:37; Luke 6:22; 19:10.

Some of these sayings reflect an incarnational emphasis (Matt. 8:20; 11:19; Luke 7:34; 9:58). One must accept His humanity to find true life (John 6:53). The Son of man is also Son of God, the One who came from above, the Ladder which links all humanity with God (John 1:51).

(4) *The Rest of the New Testament.* Stephen beheld the ascended Son of man standing beside the throne of God to receive him (Acts 7:56). In Rev. 1:13; 14:14-16, the Son of man appears as Judge. Hebrews 2:6 refers Son of man (Ps. 8:4) to Jesus as the unique Son of man and representative of humanity. In the context of Heb. 2, all the Gospel emphases on Son of man coalesce—a strong incarnational emphasis on His real flesh and blood, a vivid depiction of His representative suffering, and the note that by that suffering He acquires His glory and honor and leads many to glory.

SONG OF SOLOMON or SONG OF SONGS

Collection of romantic poetry comprising twenty-second book of the English OT and appearing in Hebrew Writings; Hebrew title, "Solomon's Song of Songs," means best of songs which in some way concern Solomon. That the title means Solomon is the author is debated. An ancient rabbinic tradition (*Baba Bathra 15a*) attributes the Song to Hezekiah and his scribes (compare Prov. 25:1).

Because of its erotic language and the difficulty of its interpretation, the rabbis questioned the place of the Song of Solomon in the canon. Greek views of the body as evil led many interpreters to find in the Song of Solomon an allegory of sacred love between God and Israel, Christ and the church, or Christ and the soul. With few exceptions, allegorical readings of the Song of Solomon have prevailed for most of church history.

In the modern period, most scholars have returned to a literal reading of the Song of Solomon. A recent, promising approach is aware of parallels to Egyptian love poetry but shows that the Song of Solomon itself gives expression to a uniquely biblical perspective on sexual love. Like Gen. 2:23-25, the Song of Solomon celebrates God's gift of bodily love between man and woman. Here the Creator's wisdom and bounty are displayed. Thus, the Song of Solomon is best taken as an example of Israel's wisdom poetry (compare Prov. 5:15-20; 6:24-29; 7:6-27; 30:18-20). The Song of Solomon's *main* purpose is to celebrate rather than to instruct. Yet one can overhear in it biblical wisdom on love. "Love is strong as death.... Many waters cannot quench love.... if a man were to give all the substance of his house for love, it would be utterly contemned" (8:6-7). Love has a right time and place (3:5). Love in all its variety parades before us: moments of union and separation, ecstasy and anguish, longing and fulfillment.

Finally, a certain validity remains in the long history of interpretation, which saw in the pure love of the Song of Solomon a reflection of divine-human love (compare Eph. 5:21-32; Song of Sol. 3:6-11; and the messianic typology of Ps. 45.) Nonetheless, this parallel should not be pushed to the point of allegorizing details of the poem. See also *Allegory; Wisdom and Wise Men.*

SONS OF GOD

Phrase referring to a class of beings in some relationship to God. Its meaning varies with context.

The Hebrew phrase meaning "sons of God" occurs eight times in the OT. In Job 1:6; 2:1 it refers to the assembly of heavenly beings or angels surrounding the divine throne (see also Ps. 89:5-7).

The "sons of God" in Gen. 6:2,4 may refer to heavenly beings. Evidence is found in 1 Pet. 3:19-20; 2 Pet. 2:4; Jude 6. The term may also refer to "godly sons," that is, the godly line of Seth. Israel is referred to as "sons of God" in Deut. 14:1; Hos. 1:10, and Luke 3:23-38 traces Jesus' lineage

back through Seth to Adam, "the son of God."

Israel was the adopted son of God in the OT because of God's sovereign choice and covenant (Exod. 4:22-23; Hos. 11:1). David was God's adopted son in a more intimate sense, representing the messianic King who would come as Savior (2 Sam. 7:14; Ps. 2:7-8; Luke 1:32; Acts 2:29-36; Rom. 1:3-4).

Likewise, Christians are sons of God by adoption and are therefore heirs of God and heirs of the kingdom (Matt. 5:9). They are chosen in Christ, having the Holy Spirit within, and destined to be conformed to Christ's image (Luke 20:36; Rom. 8:14-17,29; Gal. 3:26; 4:4-7; Eph. 1:5). See *Angel; Son of God.*

SONS OF THE PROPHETS

Members of a band or guild of prophets. "Sons of" refers to membership in a group or class and does not imply a family relationship. Elisha is portrayed as the leader of the prophetic guild. He cared for the needs of a prophet's widow (2 Kings 4:1-7), agreed to the building of a common dwelling (2 Kings 6:1-7), and presided at a common meal (2 Kings 4:38-44). The sons of the prophets functioned either as witnesses (2 Kings 2:3,5,7,15) or as agents of Elisha's ministry (2 Kings 9:1-3). See 1 Kings 20:35-42. The "company of prophets" (1 Sam. 10:5,10; 19:20) are groups of prophets whose charismatic spirit involved Saul in prophecy (1 Sam. 10:10; 19:20).

Amos' famous declaration, "I was no prophet, neither was I a prophet's son" (7:14) is probably a declaration of independence from the prophetic guilds of his day. See *Prophecy, Prophets.*

SORCERER See *Divination and Magic.*

SOREK (*red grape*)

Valley on western side of Palestine where Delilah lived (Judg. 16:4); from near Jerusalem toward the Mediterranean Sea. Beth-shemesh guarded the eastern end, while the Philistines controlled the western portion during the era of the judges.

SOUL

The Hebrew term *nephesh*, often rendered "soul," primarily means "life" or that which possesses life, and is used of both animals (Gen. 9:12) and humans (Gen. 2:7). It sometimes indicates the whole person (Gen. 12:5). In Num. 6:6 it is a synonym for the body.

It also refers to the inner life, psychological or spiritual, as in Ps. 42:1; 2 Kgs 4:27. It refers to the source of emotion in Job 30:25, to courage in Ps. 107:26, and even to the source of God's hatred of hypocrisy in Isa. 1:14.

It refers to the physical appetite in Deut. 12:15 and Mic. 7:1. Sometimes it is another way of indicating oneself (1 Sam. 18:1; Ps. 120:6).

The Greek term *psuche* in the NT is very similar in meaning to *nephesh*. Sometimes it refers to the whole person, as in Acts 2:41; Rom. 13:1. It is also used of the emotions (Mark 12:30).

But the NT also speaks of the soul as distinguishable from the physical existence of a person. Jesus makes this distinction in Matt. 10:28, as does James in James 5:20. Whether it is the "immaterial" aspect of the soul that is consciously alive with God after death, awaiting resurrection completeness, or whether believers exist in some kind of physical form, Scripture clearly teaches uninterrupted conscious existence after death (Phil. 1:23; 2 Cor. 5:1-10).

The term *soul* can also be used interchangeably with *spirit* (John 10:17; 19:30). They are not two different parts of a human.

SOVEREIGNTY OF GOD

Biblical teaching that God possesses all power and is the ruler of all things (Ps. 135:6; Dan. 4:34-35). God rules and works according to His eternal purpose, even through events that seem to contradict or oppose His rule.

God rules over His creation (Gen. 1; Mark 4:35-41), including Christ's sustaining and governing of all things (Heb. 1:3, Col. 1:15-17). God rules human history according to His purpose, from ordinary events in the lives of individuals (Judg. 14:1-4; Prov. 16:9,33) to the affairs of nations (Ps. 22:28; Hab. 1:6; Acts 17:26). God also takes the initiative in the provision and application of salvation (2 Thess. 2:13-14; 2 Tim. 1:9-10).

The Bible does not explain the relationship between divine sovereignty and evil. God neither does nor approves of evil (Hab. 1:13; James 1:13). Though He allows it (Lam. 3:37-38), He also restrains it (Job 1:12-2:7), judges it (Rev. 20:11-15), and uses it for good (Gen. 50:20; Rom. 8:28-29).

Man's will is free in that his choices arise from his nature and desires and have actual consequences. Yet without divine grace he chooses freely and consistently to reject God (Eph. 2:1-3). Christ's crucifixion resulted from the free act of sinful men held accountable by God, yet it was also planned by God (Acts 2:23; 4:27-28).

Jesus affirmed the absolute sovereignty of God and in the same context invited sinners to Himself for salvation (Matt. 11:25-30). An affirmation of divine sovereignty is consistent with evangelism, with missionary labors (Rom. 9:1-3; 10:1, 12-13; 2 Tim. 1:12; 2:10), and with desiring and praying for the salvation of any lost person or people.

SPAIN

Country still known by that name in the southwest corner of Europe; opened to Romans just before 200 B.C. Paul wanted to go to Spain (Rom. 15:24,28). See *Tarshish.*

SPICES

Aromatic, pungent substances used in preparation of foods, sacred oils for anointings, incense, perfumes, and ointments used for personal hygiene and for burial of the dead. Expensive and highly prized in antiquity, spices were brought into Palestine from India, Arabia, Persia,

Mesopotamia, and Egypt (see 1 Kings 10:15; 2 Chron. 9:9). See *Ointment*.

Cummin, dill, cinnamon, and mint were used in preparation of foods. Frankincense, stacte, galbanum, and onycha were used in the preparation of the incense to be used in the worship of Israel (Ex. 30:34-35). Balsam, myrrh, cinnamon, cassia, and calamus were used in the preparation of the holy anointing oil (Ex. 30:23-25). Cassia, aloes, and spikenard were some of the spices used in cosmetics (Song of Sol. 4:14; Mark 14:3; John 12:3). Myrrh and aloes were used in ointments for burial (Luke 23:56; John 19:39).

SPINNING AND WEAVING

Major elements involved in making clothes. Threads woven into cloth were produced from raw fibers by spinning (Matt. 6:28; Luke 12:27). Flax, or linen (Lev. 13:47-48; Prov. 31:13; Jer. 13:1; Ezek. 40:3; 44:17; Hos. 2:5), and wool (Lev. 13:47) were the major fibers used in the biblical world.

In spinning, raw fibers were pulled into a loose strand and twisted to form a continuous thread. Sometimes, it was plied or twined, two or three threads being twisted together (Ex. 26:1; 36:8,35). The finished product could then be used for weaving (Ex. 35:25-26).

Weaving is the interlacing of threads to form fabric. Weaving was conducted on looms, devices designed to create openings (sheds) between alternating vertical warp threads through which the horizontal weft threads were passed. After each weft thread was placed, it was beaten against the previous one with a flat stick, thus firming up the fabric.

On a horizontal ground loom, the warp threads were stretched between beams pegged to the ground. This type is apparently referred to in the Samson story (Judg. 16:13-14). In some vertical looms, the warp was stretched between two beams fixed in a rectangular frame. Work proceeded from the bottom of the loom, and the woven cloth could be rolled onto the bottom beam (Isa. 38:12). This permitted the weaver to remain seated and to produce much longer finished products. Another type of vertical loom had the warp threads attached to an upper beam and held taut in groups by a series of stone or clay weights. Weaving was done from the top to the bottom, and the weft beaten upwards.

Stripes or bands of color were made by using dyed threads for portions of the warp or weft threads. Warp weighted looms allowed portions of the shed to be opened at a time, so intricate patterns could be made in the weft by covering small areas with different colors. It was forbidden, however, to wear clothes made of linen and wool woven together (Deut. 22:11). Weavers apparently were professionals who specialized in particular types of work: ordinary weavers, designers, and embroiderers (Ex. 35:35).

SPIRIT

The empowering perspective of human life; based on Hebrew and Greek words meaning, "wind," "breath," or "spirit" depending on the context. Jesus told Nicodemus (John 3) that the Spirit is like the wind in that one cannot see it but one can see its effects. This is true of both the Spirit of God and the spirit of a human being. See *Holy Spirit*.

When used of humans, *spirit* is associated with a wide range of functions including thinking and understanding, emotions, attitudes, and intentions. Elihu told Job it was spirit in a person, the breath of God, which gave understanding (Job 32:8). When Jesus healed the paralytic, He perceived in His "spirit" that the religious leaders present were questioning His forgiving the man's sins (Mark 2:8). "Spirit" is used extensively with human emotions including sorrow (Prov. 15:4,13), anguish (Ex. 6:9; John 13:21), anger (Prov. 14:29; 16:32), vexation (Eccl. 1:14), fear (2 Tim. 1:7), and joy (Luke 1:47).

A variety of attitudes and intentions are associated with spirit. Caleb had a different spirit than most of his contemporaries in that he followed the Lord wholeheartedly (Num. 14:24). The psalmist called persons who have no deceit in their spirits, "blessed" (Ps. 32:2). A person's spirit can be "contrite" (Ps. 34:18), "steadfast" (Ps. 51:10), "willing" (Ps. 51:12), "broken" (Ps. 51:17), "stubborn" (Deut. 2:30), "lying" (1 Kings 22), and "haughty"(Prov. 16:18).

Spirit is used of nonphysical beings, both good and evil. Satan is called the ruler of the kingdom of the air, the spirit who is at work in those who are disobedient (Eph. 2:2). Sadducees and Pharisees debated the existence of angels and spirits. When the risen Christ appeared to the disciples, they were startled and frightened, thinking they were seeing a spirit. Jesus invited them to touch Him. He then reminded them that a spirit does not have flesh and bones (Luke 24:37-39).

SPIRITIST See *Medium.*

SPIRITS IN PRISON

Audience for Jesus' preaching (1 Pet. 3:19-20). This unique event is closely associated with the resurrection of Jesus Christ from the dead (vv. 18,21) and relates to Christ's statement in Luke 17:26 comparing days of Noah and days of Son of Man (compare Matt. 24:37). The immediate focus of the statement in 1 Peter is the situation that necessitated the flood (see Gen. 6:1-8). The disobedient "spirits," accordingly, are not the people who died in the flood, but the evil spirits, or demons, whose influence brought divine judgment on the world. Peter probably viewed these evil spirits as the offspring of the strange union mentioned in Gen. 6:1-4 between the "sons of God" (that is, angelic or superhuman beings of some kind) and the "daughters of men." It is also likely that Peter identified them with the "unclean spirits" over which Jesus had triumphed again and again during His earthly ministry. Jesus' proclamation to these"spirits"must therefore be understood not as redemptive "good news," but as judgment and defeat at the hands of God (see their anxious question in Matt. 8:29).

The outcome of this proclamation was subjection of the disobedient spirits (1 Pet. 3:22; compare Rev. 18:2). Peter's point is not that the disobedient spirits were "imprisoned" but that He came to them in their "haunts" or "havens" to notify them that their power over humanity was finally broken and that now they must surrender to His universal dominion.

SPIRITUAL GIFTS

Skills and abilities that God gives through His Spirit to all Christians, which equip Christians to serve God in the Christian community.

In the OT, the Spirit of the Lord was given to selected leaders rather than to all of God's people. The Spirit brought with Him one or more gifts which equipped the individual to serve God by serving Israel craftsmanship (Ex. 31:2-3); judge (Judg. 3:9-10); military skills (Judg. 6:34); physical strength (Judg. 14:6,19); political skills (1 Sam. 10:6); and prophetic gifts (Mic. 3:8).

The Christian view of spiritual gifts begins with Jesus, the unique bearer of the Spirit (Mark 1:10). The Spirit directed and empowered Him for His ministry (Luke 4:14-18). Jesus promised His disciples that they, too, would receive the Spirit one day and that the Spirit would guide them (see Mark 13:11; Luke 11:13).These promises were fulfilled on the day of Pentecost (Acts 2:1-47).The Spirit was given to all Christians, not just to selected leaders (2:3-4,17-18), and would continue to be given to all who accepted the Christian gospel (v. 38; compare Rom. 8:9).When the Spirit came into a person's life, He brought with Him a gift, or gifts, which that person could use to serve God (1 Pet. 4:10; 1 Cor. 12:4-7). All Christians are given gifts. Paul spoke of gifts in terms of the whole church, the body of Christ, not in terms of individuals only. This leaves no room for arrogance or shame concerning our gifts.

Biblical lists of gifts do not give a comprehensive list of spiritual gifts. The Bible makes no distinction between spiritual gifts and natural abilities (see Rom. 12:6-8). His assumption seems to have been that whatever skills a Christian has are given to him by God and are to be used in God's service. What matters, then, is that Christians discover what their gifts are and then develop them.

The one gift all Christians should have is "love" or "charity" (1 Cor. 12:31–13:1), the ultimate spiritual gift. If we have all other gifts and lack love, we have nothing; if we have love and nothing else, we have everything. Love fulfills the entire law (Rom. 13:10; compare Matt. 22:39-40). Love makes possible the fellowship of the church and guarantees that gifts will be used unselfishly. See *Holy Spirit.*

SPIT, SPITTLE

Spitting at or on someone is the strongest sign of contempt (Deut. 25:7-9). Soldiers mocked Jesus before His crucifixion and spat on Him (Matt. 27:30; compare 26:67). Spittle was used to heal (Mark 8:23; John 9:6). Mixing spittle with clay (John 9:6) may have been to deliberately break the sabbath laws of the Jewish religious leaders.

SPORTS

The Hebrew verb "make sport" is used to indicate ridicule (eg. Gen. 21:9) but also sport in the sense of entertainment (Judg. 16:25,27) or play (Ex. 32:6; Ps. 104:26; Zech. 8:5).

Several games of skill are alluded to in the Bible. Jacob's single-handed combat at Penuel seems to have been a wrestling match between two skilled fighters (Gen. 32:24-32). The fight at the pool of Gibeon between the soldiers of Abner and the soldiers of Joab may have begun as a show of strength through wrestling (2 Sam. 2:12-17). Job 16:12-13 speaks of archery, a sport depicted on Assyrian reliefs. Isaiah 22:18 suggests a game of ball. Foot races are alluded to in Psalm 19:5. Paul mentions Greco-

Roman gladiatorial bouts, surely the most gruesome of all entertainment events, (1 Cor. 4:9 and 15:32).

The NT uses various games as figures of the Christian life. Paul often spoke of his work on behalf of the Gospel as "running" (Gal. 2:2; 5:7; Phil. 2:16, 3:13-14; compare Heb. 12:1) and likened the spiritual discipline required for successful living to that required for winning foot races and boxing matches (1 Cor. 9:24-27; compare 2 Tim. 2:5; 4:7). "Racing" was a natural metaphor for Paul to adopt, not only because of the popularity of foot races in the Greco-Roman world but also because from the earliest days of the OT a believer's relationship with God was described as "walking" or "running" with him (Gen. 3:8; 5:24; Ps. 119:32; Isa. 40:31).

SPOUSAL ABUSE

Physical, emotional, and sexual mistreatment of a marriage partner. Spousal abuse is a particularly serious matter in the eyes of God because it fractures the marriage relationship established as the foundation of society (Gen. 2:24). Biblical stories such as Abraham passing off his wife as his sister in Egypt (Gen. 12:10-20; compare Gen. 20:2-14; 26:6-11) portray the consequences of spousal abuse.

The Bible describes traits which characteristically appear in persons who abuse their spouses. Jealous men act beyond the bounds of control (Prov. 6:34). Sometimes kind and gentle speech, "smoother than butter," masks violence (Ps. 55:20-21). The effects of sins committed by one person are felt in successive generations (Ex. 34:7), a pattern well known in abused families.

Although the husband is head of his wife, his actions toward her must be like those of Christ to the church (1 Cor. 11:3; Eph. 5:23-24). Every husband must love his wife as he loves himself (Eph. 5:25-33), showing her great consideration (1 Pet. 3:7), honor (1 Thess. 4:4), and gentleness (Col. 3:19). A husband must provide for his family, for not to do so would make him worse than an unbeliever (1 Tim. 5:8).

God chose the marriage relationship as a picture of his relationship with both Israel and the church. Any action which tarnishes the marriage relationship, such as spousal abuse, cheapens a believer's relationship with God.

STARS

Constellations, planets, and all heavenly bodies except the sun and the moon. God is acknowledged to be the Creator of all such (Gen. 1:16) as well as the One who knows their names and numbers (Ps. 147:4). Biblical writers knew many of the constellations (Job 38:31; compare Amos 5:26; Acts 7:43). The star of Bethlehem (Matt. 2) is one of many miracles that attest to the power of our God. Jesus is "the bright and morning star" (Rev. 22:16).

STATURE

Height of a person, sometimes used figuratively (Ezek. 17:6; 19:11; Luke 2:52); used to show the weakness of humanity and the need to rely on God (Matt. 6:27; Luke 12:25) and as a measure of the maturity of the Christian (Eph. 4:13).

STEPHANAS (crown)

Believer baptized by Paul (1 Cor. 1:16); lived in Achaia; may be same person who delivered letter from Corinthian church to Paul in Ephesus (1 Cor. 16:17).

STEPHEN (crown)

First Christian martyr; foremost of those chosen to bring peace to the quarreling church (Acts 6:1-7); so mighty in Scriptures that his Jewish opponents in debate could not refute him (Acts 6:10) as he argued that Jesus was the Messiah; led group who saw Christianity as much more than a Jewish sect.

STEWARDSHIP

Utilizing and managing all resources God provides for the glory of God and the betterment of His creation. God created humans to have "dominion" over all of the earth (Gen. 1:26), to be good and gracious managers of God's creation. Early church members saw none of what they possessed as their own (Acts 4:32). All came from the loving heart of God. That is why the sin of selfishness of Ananias and Sapphira was so serious (Acts 5). The source of thanksgiving is not in things but in our relationship to God in Christ (Phil. 3:13-14). Stewardship centers in our commitment to Jesus Christ. When He becomes our Lord, He becomes Lord of our time, talents, finances, and everything. We realize that we are not our own, but we are bought with a price.

STOCKS

Instrument that secured the feet (and sometimes the neck and hands) of a prisoner (Job 13:27; Jer. 29:26; Acts 16:24); usually made of wood with holes to secure the feet; could also be an instrument of torture by stretching the legs apart and causing the prisoner to sit in unnatural positions.

STONE

Hardened mineral matter comprising much of the earth. Palestine is a stony country. Often it was necessary to clear a field of stone preparatory to its cultivation (Isa. 5:2). An enemy's fields were marred by throwing stones on them, and his wells were choked with stones (2 Kings 3:19,25). Stones were used for: city walls (Neh. 4:3), dwellings (Lev. 14:38-40), palaces (1 Kings 7:1,9), temples (1 Kings 6:7; 7:9-12), pavement in courtyards and columns (Esther 1:6), and in Herodian times, at least, for paving streets. The Israelites used unhewn stones for building their altars. They often heaped stones to commemorate some great spiritual event or encounter with God (Gen. 31:46; Josh. 4). They marked the grave of notorious offenders with stones (Josh. 7:26).

Single stones were used to close the mouths of cisterns, wells, and tombs (Gen. 29:2; Matt. 27:60; John 11:38) and to mark boundaries (Deut.

19:14). The Israelites sometimes consecrated a single stone as a memorial to God (Gen. 28:18-22; 1 Sam. 7:12). Stones were lethal weapons (1 Sam. 17:49; Acts 7:58). See *Arms and Armor*. Stones were often used for weights on scales and employed for writing documents like the Ten Commandments.

A stone denotes hardness or insensibility (1 Sam. 25:37; Ezek. 36:26), firmness and strength. The followers of Christ were living stones built up into the spiritual temple of Christ. Christ himself became the chief cornerstone (Eph. 2:20-22; 1 Pet. 2:4-8). See *Minerals and Metals*.

STOREHOUSE, STORAGE CITY

Buildings to protect harvested crops from vermin and extreme weather; rectangular building with a double row of columns which divided the building into three narrow aisles. Large, thick walls supported the roof, and small side rooms led off the main hall. Storerooms at Herod's fortress of Masada had walls 11 feet high constructed of stones weighing over 400 pounds. Community storehouses could also be used as public markets. In large cities, certain sections of the town were designated as storage areas, with several storehouses lining the streets. During the Divided Kingdom period, royal storage facilities were established in regional capitals to collect tax payments made in flour, oil, grain, or wine. Specially marked jars held these royal stores which later could be distributed to the army or royal palaces. The temple complex included special storage areas, both for the utensils of worship and to serve as a sort of bank where valuables might be placed.

STUMBLING BLOCK

Anything that causes a person to stumble or to fall (Lev. 19:14): used of idols (Ezek. 7:19), God's work with faithless people (Jer. 6:21), and God Himself in relation to His people (Isa. 8:14). Christians are not to let their freedom result in a stumbling block to other believers (Rom. 14:13; 1 Cor.

8:9). The disobedient are warned that Jesus Himself could be a stumbling block (Rom. 9:32-33; 1 Cor. 1:23; 1 Pet. 2:8).

SUCCOTH (*booths*)

(1) City east of the Jordan in Gad; perhaps tell Deir Alla. See Gen. 33:17; Judg. 8:5-7,13-16; 1 Kings 7:45-46.

(2) Place where Israelites camped upon leaving Egypt (Ex. 12:37; 13:20; Num. 33:5-6); usually identified with tell el-Maskhutah or tell er-Retabah.

SUCCOTH BENOTH (*booths of daughters*)

Pagan deity people from Babylon brought with them to Israel when it was resettled by the Assyrians after the fall of Samaria in 722 B.C. (2 Kings 17:30); likely Sarpanitu, the consort of Marduk. See *Gods, Pagan; Sakkuth.*

SUFFERING

Enduring undesirable pains and experiences. The Bible accepts evil and suffering as givens in a fallen and sinful world. The Hebrews regarded suffering as punishment for sin against the divine moral order (Pss. 7:15-16; 37:1-3; 73:12-20; 139:19), even though the wicked might prosper for a time (Job 21:28-33). Suffering is interpreted in many cases as a sign of God's wrath and punishment for personal sin, parents' sin (1 Kings 21:20,22,29; compare John 9:2) or for the wickedness of the king (2 Kings 21:10-11).

The suffering of the righteous was explained as a way for God to gain peoples' attention (Job 33:14; 36:15), to correct sin into obedience (2 Chron. 20:9-10; Mal. 3:3), or to develop or refine character (Job 23:10; Ps. 66:10). Ultimately, sufferers trust in God's sometimes hidden wisdom (Job 42:2-3; Ps. 135:6). The prophet gained a vision of a greater purpose in suffering—carrying the sins of others (Isa. 53). The righteous looked forward to the Day of the Lord when they would be vindicated and justice would reign (Dan. 12:1).

God is Himself touched by the suffering of Christ on the cross. The purposefulness and necessity of suffering in the life of the Son of God (Matt. 16:21; Mark 8:31; Luke 9:22) aids in coping with our own. As Christ suffered, so would believers (John 16:33; Acts 14:22; Rom. 8:31-39; 1 Cor. 12:26; 1 Thess. 2:14; 2 Tim. 3:12; 1 Pet. 4:12-13) who continue His mission (Mark 13:12-13; Rev. 17:6; 20:14) because the world hates the disciples as much as it did their Lord (see John 15:18; 1 Cor. 2:8; 1 John 3:11-12). Suffering for His sake was counted a privilege (Acts 5:41; 1 Cor. 11:32; 1 Thess. 1:4-8).

Suffering is to be endured patiently rather than rebelliously (1 Thess. 3:3; Jas. 1:2-4) because God is working His purpose out in His children's lives (Rom. 8:28-29). Satan tempts believers to be defeated in their suffering (2 Cor. 4:8-12; Rev. 2:10). Instead, Christians can grow stronger spiritually through trials (Rom. 6:4-8; 1 Pet. 4:1; Heb. 12:11) and share Christ's ultimate triumph (Mark 13:9; John 16:33; 2 Thess. 1:5; Rev. 5:5; 20:9, 14-15) even now as they experience daily victories (Rom. 8:37; 1 John 2:13-14; 1 Pet. 5:10). Sufferings give rise to hope (Rom. 12:12; 1 Thess. 1:3), for no present suffering compares with the rewards that await the faithful follower of Christ (Rom. 8:17-18).

SUMER

One of two political divisions originally comprising what came to be Babylonia; fertile plain between the Tigris and Euphrates Rivers; referred to as Shinar (Gen. 10:10) or Chaldea (Jer. 50:10); southern part of modern Iraq. Its principal cities were Nippur, Adab, Lagash, Umma, Larsa, Erech, Ur, and Eridu, most of which were on or near the Euphrates.

Sumer developed humanity's first high civilization about 3000 B.C. They invented cuneiform writing. The law code of Ur-nammu, the Sumerian king list, the flood story of Zuisudra, the paradise myth of Enki and Ninhursag, early forms of the Gilgamesh epic, and the descent of Inanna to the underworld.

About 2100 B.C., Sumer was conquered by invading tribesmen from the west and north. Sargon I of Akkad conquered this area and extended his empire from the Persian Gulf to the Mediterranean Sea. He founded a new capital city, Agade, which was, for more than half a century, the richest and most powerful capital in the world. Sumer enjoyed a brief revival at Ur (about 2050 B.C.) only to decline before the rise of the Elamites, a people to their east. Finally, in about 1720 B.C., Hammurabi of Babylon united Sumer (the southern division of ancient Babylon) into one empire.

SUN

Source of light for earth; often viewed as a god: Egyptian, Re; Greek, Helios; Semitic, Shamash. The Canaanite city of Beth- Shemesh probably referred to a temple in the city. The Bible simply views the sun as the "greater light"God created to rule the day (Gen. 1:16). In Israel the new day began with sunset. The Psalms compared the sun's brightness to God's glory by which it will one day be replaced (Ps. 84:11). Zacharias described Christ's coming as a new sunrise for humankind (Luke 1:78). The darkening or eclipse of the sun was often interpreted as a sign of God's displeasure with humans. See *Gods, Pagan.*

SUNDAY   See *Lord's Day.*

SUPH   (*reed*)

(1) Hebrew name for Red Sea. See *Red Sea.*

(2) Place helping locate where Moses delivered speech behind the Book of Deuteronomy (Deut. 1:1); may be Khirbet Safe just southeast of Medeba in mountains of Moab.

SURETY

Person legally responsible for debt of another or the money or thing of value put down to guarantee the debt.

Should there be a default, the "surety" would have to pay the debt or even be enslaved until the debt was paid (Gen. 43:9; 44:32). God was asked by a faithful psalmist to be his surety (119:121-122). Proverbs warns against being surety for someone you do not know well (11:15). Jesus is said to be surety for the faithful under the new covenant (Heb. 7:22). See *Loan; Slave, Servant.*

SYMBOL

Token or sign; objects, gestures, or rituals conveying meaning to rational, emotional, and intuitive dimensions of human beings. The universal and supreme symbol of Christian faith is the cross, an instrument of execution but to Christians a sign of God's love for human beings. Christ's death seen through the resurrection is at the center of the two major symbolic rituals of Christian faith—baptism and the Lord's Supper or the Eucharist. See *Ordinances; Sacrament.*

The sacrificial lamb points to the sacrificial death of Christ. The parables of Jesus are rich in symbols: grain, weeds, various kinds of soil, a lost sheep, a lost coin, and a lost son. Jesus used symbolic language in talking about Himself and His relationship to persons: Bread of life, Light of the world, Good Shepherd, Water of life, and the Door. The apocalyptic writings are rich in symbolic language. See *Apocalyptic.*

SYNAGOGUE

Local meeting place and assembly of the Jewish people during and after exile in Babylon. Even after many of the Jews returned to Jerusalem and rebuilt the temple, places of local worship continued. By the time of Jesus these places and assemblies in and outside Palestine were called "synagogues." During Jesus' time there was even a synagogue within the temple itself. Jewish sources indicate that a synagogue was to be established wherever there were as many as *ten* Jewish men. The principal meeting was on the sabbath. A typical service consisted of the recitation of the Shema (confession of faith in the one God), prayers, Scripture readings from the Law and the Prophets, a sermon, and a benediction (see Luke 4:16-21). See *Shema.*

Local elders had general oversight of the synagogue. They often appointed a ruler of the synagogue, a layman who cared for the building and selected those who participated in the service. The ruler was assisted by an attendant, one of whose duties was to deliver the sacred scrolls to those who read and return them to the special place where they were kept (Luke 4:17,20). Jesus customarily went to the synagogue in His hometown of Nazareth on the sabbath (Luke 4:16). He frequently taught and preached in synagogues throughout the land (Matt. 4:23; 9:35; Mark 1:39; Luke 4:44). He healed a man in the synagogue in Capernaum (Mark 1:21-28; Luke 4:31-37; compare Luke 13:10-16).

Jesus warned against the hypocrisy of those who paraded their righteousness in the synagogue (Matt. 6:2,5; 23:6; Mark 12:39; Luke 11:43; 20:46; compare Matt. 10:17; 23:34; Mark 13:9; Luke 12:11; 21:12). Some Jewish believers continued to worship in the synagogues (Acts 9:2; 22:19; 26:11) until persecution forced them out. Paul preached Christ in the synagogues (Acts 9:20; compare Acts 13:5,14; 14:1; 17:1, 10,17; 18:4; 19:8). He found special interest among the Gentiles who attended the synagogue, but some Jews also believed (Acts 13:42-43). Usually he was forced to leave the synagogue and go elsewhere with the band of believers (Acts 18:6-8; 19:8-10).

SYRACUSE

Major city in Sicily. Paul stayed in the Syracuse harbor three days on his way to Rome (Acts 28:12).

SYRIA

Region or nation directly north of Palestine in the northwest corner of the Mediterranean Sea; modern Syria and Lebanon with small portions of

Turkey and Iraq. Syria, like Palestine, has four basic geographical features as one moves from the Mediterranean eastward: (1) a narrow coastal plain; (2) a line of mountains; (3) the rift valley; and (4) fertile steppe fading into desert. The two main rivers rise near one another in the rift valley. The Orontes flows north before abruptly turning west to the sea in the plain of Antioch, while the Leontes flows south then turns west through a narrow gorge and empties into the sea. See *Palestine; Rivers and Waterways in the Bible.*

The Arameans began to settle in Syria and northern Mesopotamia about 1200 B.C., establishing a number of independent states. The OT mentions the Aramean kingdoms of Beth-eden in north Syria, Zobah in south-central Syria, and Damascus in the south. Saul encountered Zobah (1 Sam. 14:47). David decisively defeated Aram-Zobah (2 Sam. 10:6-19) whose king, Hadadezer, had enlisted help from his Aramean subject states (10:16,19). As a result, Zobah and its vassals, apparently including Damascus, became subject to David (2 Sam. 8:3-8; 10:19). Hamath, a neo-Hittite state in north Syria which had been at war with Zobah, also established friendly relations with David (2 Sam. 8:9-10). Meanwhile, a certain Rezon broke from Hadadezer of Zobah following David's victory and became the leader of a marauding band. Late in Solomon's reign, he

established himself as king in Damascus (1 Kings 11:23-25), taking southern Syria out of Israelite control. Subsequent occurrences of "Aram" or "Arameans" ("Syria" or "Syrians") in the OT refer to this Aramean kingdom of Damascus.

Asa of Judah enticed Ben-hadad the king of Damascus to break his league with Israel and come to Judah's aid (1 Kings 15:18-19). Ben-hadad responded by conquering a number of cities and territory in the north of Israel (v. 20). See *Damascus.*

In NT times, Judea was made part of a procuratorship within the larger Roman province of Syria (Matt. 4:24), the latter being ruled by a governor (Luke 2:2). Paul was converted on the road to Damascus (Acts 9:1-9) and subsequently evangelized in the province (Acts 15:41; Gal. 1:21). Antioch, where believers were first called "Christians" (Acts 11:26), became the base for his missionary journeys (Acts 13:1-3).

SYROPHENICIAN or SYROPHOENICIAN

Combination of Syria and Phoenicia reflecting the joining of the two areas into one district under Roman rule (Mark 7:26).

SYRTIS

Probably Gulf of Sidra, place of shallow water with hidden rocks, sandbanks, and quicksands off African coast west of Cyrene; KJV, "quicksands" (Acts 27:17).

T

TAANACH

Levitical town of Manasseh (Josh. 17:11; 21:25) on northern slope of Carmel range protecting accesses from the Plain of Esdraelon withstood original conquest efforts (Judg. 1:27; compare Josh. 12:21; Judg. 5:19). The Canaanite city originated about 2700 B.C. and was destroyed about 918 B.C. by Pharaoh Shishak.

TABERNACLE, TENT OF MEETING

Sacred tent, a portable and provisional sanctuary, where God revealed Himself to and dwelled among His people (Ex. 33:7-10). Two compound phrases designate this tent: "the tabernacle of the congregation" (Ex. 29:42,44), literally the "tent of meeting" (NRSV, NIV, NASB, REB) and "the tabernacle of witness" (Num. 17:7) or "tent of witness."

The OT mentions three tents or tabernacles. After the sin of the golden calf at Mount Sinai, the "provisional" tabernacle was established outside the camp and called the "tent of meeting" which only Moses entered and Joshua guarded (Ex. 33:7-11; 34:34-35). The "Sinaitic" tabernacle at the center of the camp (Num. 2–3) was built in accordance with directions God gave Moses (Ex. 25–40). The "Davidic" tabernacle was erected in Jerusalem for the reception of the ark (2 Sam. 6:17). The cloud descended on the tent when Moses came to inquire of God; but the cloud stayed on the permanent tabernacle, and the glory of the Lord filled it so Moses could not enter it (Ex. 40:34-35,38; compare 29:43,45).

TABLE

Flat surface supported by legs.

(1) *Dinner tables.* Originally skins spread on the ground. As a piece of furniture, tables go back to about 1300 B.C. (Judg. 1:7). Most references concern a sovereign's table (Judg. 1:7; 2 Sam. 9:7; 1 Kings 2:7; 4:27; 10:5; 18:19; but see 1 Kings 13:20). Tables generally sat on short legs, allowing one to eat sitting or reclined on a rug (Isa. 21:5). Judges 1:7, however, reflects a table high enough for kings to rummage underneath (compare Mark 7:28). In NT times, guests ate while reclining on couches. See *Food; Furniture.*

(2) *Ritual tables.* A table for the bread of the presence formed part of the furnishings for both the tabernacle (Ex. 25:23-30; 26:35; Lev. 24:5-7) and temple (1 Kings 7:48). Other tables were used in the sacrificial cult (1 Chron. 28:14-16; 2 Chron. 4:7-8; Ezek. 40:38-43). Malachi 1:7,12 describes the altar itself as a table. Isaiah 65:11 and 1 Cor. 10:21 refer to idolatrous worship. The "Lord's table" (1 Cor. 10:21) refers to the observance of the Lord's Supper.

(3) *Money tables.* Likely small trays on stands (Matt. 21:12; Mark 11:15; John 2:15).

(4) *Tables of law.* Some translations use table in the sense of a tablet (Ex. 24:12; 31:18; Deut. 9:9).

TABLE OF NATIONS

Gen. 10 (compare 1 Chron. 1:5-23) listing of descendants of Noah's sons to explain the origin of the nations and peoples of the known world, mentioning 70 different ethnic groups.

TABOR (perhaps *height*)

(1) Mountain in valley of Jezreel about six miles east of Nazareth; boundary point for Naphtali, Issachar, and Zebulun (Josh. 19:12,22), where the tribes worshiped early (Deut. 33:18-19). Barak gathered an army at Tabor to defend against Sisera (Judg. 4:6). Apparently, it was site of false worship (Hos. 5:1). Tradition holds that Tabor was the site of Jesus' transfiguration (Mark 9:2).

(2) Levitical city (1 Chron. 6:77), apparently replacing Nahalal in the earlier list (Josh. 21:35). It may be Khirbet Dabura.

(3) "Plain of Tabor" (1 Sam. 10:3) apparently near Gibea.

TABOR, OAK OF

NASB, NRSV designation of site between Rachel's tomb (near Bethlehem) and Gibeah of Saul (1 Sam. 10:3). Other translations read "plain" (KJV), "great tree" (NIV), or "terebinth" (REB) of Tabor.

TADMOR

City Solomon built in northern Palestine (2 Chron. 8:4; compare Tamar, 1 Kings 9:18), probably to control a caravan route; Palmyra, great Arabian city, about 120 miles northeast of Damascus.

TAHPANHES (*fortress of Penhase* or *house of the Nubian*)

City in Nile Delta near eastern border of Egypt (Jer. 2:16); Daphnai (tell Defneh); battle scene between Egypt and Nebuchadrezzar of Babylon (605 B.C.; 601 B.C.). Jeremiah 46:14 perhaps relates to one of these battles. A large group of Jews took Jeremiah with them and fled to Tahpanhes (Jer. 43:7; 44:1; compare 42:19; 46:14).

TAHPENES

Egyptian royal consort (1 Kings 11:19-20).

TALENT See *Weights and Measures.*

TALITHA CUMI (*damsel, arise*)

Transliteration of Aramaic phrase. Jesus' words to Jarius's daughter (Mark 5:41).

TALMAI (*plowman* or Hurrian, *big*)

(1) One of three Anakim (giant, pre-Israelite inhabitants of Canaan) residing in Hebron (Num. 13:22).

(2) King of Geshur, father of David's wife Maacah and grandfather of Absalom (2 Sam. 3:3; 13:37; 1 Chron. 3:2).

TALMUD (*study* or *learning*)

Jewish commentaries; opinions and teachings that disciples learn from their predecessors particularly with regard to the development of oral legal teachings (*halakah*); digest of commentary on the *Mishnah.* The Mishnah (oral legal teachings on the written law of Moses) was probably written down at Javneh in Galilee at about A.D. 220. Between A.D. 220 and 500 the rabbinic schools in Palestine and Babylonia amplified and applied the teachings of the Mishnah for their Jewish communities. Two documents came to embody a large part of this teaching: The Jerusalem Talmud (A.D. 400) and the Babylonian Talmud (A.D. 500), the latter becoming the most authoritative. Scholars represented in Mishnah are known as *Tannaim.* They lived from time of Jesus to A.D. 200. The Talmud gives the opinions of a new generation of scholars referred to as the *Amoraim* (A.D. 200-500).

The importance of the Talmud to Jewish life until the modern period can hardly be overestimated. Some of the halakah in the Talmud may reflect Jewish practice in the time of the writers of the NT or of Jesus. See *Mishnah.*

TAMAR (*date palm*)

(1) Widowed daughter-in-law of Judah, wife of his eldest son, Er (Gen. 38:6); tricked her father-in-law into fathering her child (38:18).

(2) Daughter of David raped by her half brother, Amnon (2 Sam. 13:14); avenged by full brother, Absalom (13:28-29; compare 2 Sam. 12:10).

(3) Absalom's only daughter (2 Sam. 14:27).

(4) See *Tadmor.*

(5) Fortified city at southern end of Dead Sea, marking ideal limit of Israel (Ezek. 47:19; 48:28).

TAMBOURINE See *Music, Instruments, Dancing.*

TAMMUZ

Sumerian god of vegetation (Ezek. 8:14-15); said to be betrayed by his lover, Ishtar, and as a result to die each autumn, leading to great mourning. See *Fertility Cult.*

TAPPUAH (*apple* or *quince*)

(1) Calebite (1 Chron. 2:43).

(2) City in Shephelah of Judah (Josh. 15:34), possibly Beit Nettif about 12 miles west of Bethlehem.

(3) City on north border of Ephraim (Josh. 16:8) whose environs were allotted to Manasseh (17:7-8), likely the Tappuah of Josh. 12:17 and 2 Kings 15:16; perhaps Sheikh Abu Zarod about eight miles southwest of Shechem. Some scholars read, "Tappuah" for "Tiphsah" in 2 Kings 15:16 (REB).

TAR See *Bitumen.*

TARGUM (to *explain,* to *translate*)

Early translations of Bible into Aramaic, native language of Palestine and Babylon in first century A.D.; seem to include large amount of biblical commentary that perhaps reflects sermons in Jewish Palestinian synagogues. See *Aramaic; Bible, Texts and Versions.*

TARSHISH (*yellow jasper* or Akkadian, *smelting plant*)

(1) Son of Javan (Gen. 10:4; 1 Chron. 1:7) and ancestor of an Aegean people.

(2) Benjaminite warrior (1 Chron. 7:10).

(3) One of seven leading officials of King Ahasuerus of Persia (Esther 1:14).

(4) Geographic designation, most likely of Tartessus at the southern tip of Spain but possibly of Tarsus in Cilicia (Jonah 1:3). Compare Isa. 23:1; Jer. 10:9; Ezek. 27:12.

(5) "Ships of Tarshish" may designate seagoing vessels like those of Tarshish or else ships bearing metal cargo like those of Tarshish (compare Isa. 2:16 where ships of Tarshish parallels beautiful crafts) (1 Kings 10:22; 22:48; 2 Chron. 9:21; 20:36).

TARSUS See *Asia Minor, Cities of; Paul.*

TARTAK

Deity worshiped by Arvvites whom the Assyrians settled in Samaria after 722 B.C. (2 Kings 17:31); likely a deliberate scribal corruption of Atargatis, the Syrian high goddess and wife of Hadad.

TARTAN

Title of highest ranking Assyrian officer under the king; commander in chief; supreme commander (2 Kings 18:17; Isa. 20:1).

TATTLING

Revealing secrets or spreading rumors. The Hebrew word *tattler* is sometimes translated "slanderer" or "talebearer" (Lev. 19:16; Jer. 6:28; 9:3; Ezek. 22:9), revealing the usual intent behind the seemingly innocent action of tattling. Tattling destroys friendships (Prov. 16:28) and actually undermines the reputation of the tattler (Prov. 25:9-10). Those who tattle are untrustworthy (Prov. 11:13); tattling is something that fools do (Prov. 20:19). Ecclesiastes cautions against speaking out against the king even in the privacy of one's own bedroom (10:20).

Paul includes gossip in a list of sins characteristic of those who do evil (Rom. 1:29-32; 2 Cor. 12:20). Yet he, too, recognizes reality: young widows "learn to be idle, wandering about from house to house; and not only idle, but tattlers also and busybodies, speaking things which they ought not" (1 Tim. 5:13). Paul's insight is not limited to young widows.

TAX COLLECTOR See *Publican.*

TAXES

Regular payments to rulers and/or government. Early Israel only paid taxes to support the tabernacle and the priests. Tribute had to be paid to invaders such as the Philistines. During David's reign, an army was maintained by tribute paid by conquered tribes. Taxes increased under Solomon's rule. Tradesmen and merchants paid duties; subject peoples paid tribute; farmers paid taxes in kind of oil and wine; and many Israelites did forced labor on the temple. The taxation requirements to fulfill both civil and temple needs increased considerably during the monarchy, and were often deemed to be excessive (1 Sam. 8:10-18; 1 Kings 5:13-17; 12:1-11; Neh. 5:4; Amos 5:11; compare Micah 3:1-3). The most crushing form of taxation was tribute exacted by foreign rulers (1 Kings 14:25-28; 2 Kings 15:19-20; 23:35). Soon, Israel became a vassal state, paying tribute—a compulsory tax—to Assyria, and, eventually, to Rome.

Herod the Great levied a tax on the produce of the field and a tax on items bought and sold. Other duties owed to foreign powers were: a land tax, a poll tax, a kind of progressive income tax (about which the Pharisees tested Jesus, Matt. 22:17), and a tax on personal property. In Jerusalem a house tax was levied. These taxes were paid directly to Roman officials.

Export and import customs paid at seaports and city gates were farmed out to private contractors who paid a sum in advance for the right to collect taxes in a certain area. Such were Zacchaeus (Luke 19) and Matthew (Matt. 9). Rome apparently placed little restriction on how much profit the collector could take. An enrollment for the purposes of taxation under the Roman emperor brought Joseph and Mary to Bethlehem, where Jesus was born (Luke 2:1-7). Jewish people also had to pay temple taxes: *didrachma* or half shekel (Matt. 17:24). Levites collected a tithe, 10 percent of everything the soil produced.

Many zealous Jews considered it treason to God to pay taxes to Rome. In spite of the hardships of taxation, the NT recognizes that being a good citizen involves paying taxes to whom they are due (Matt. 17:24-27; 22:17-21; Rom. 13:1,5-7). At the same time tax collectors are admonished to collect taxes fairly (Luke 3:12-14; compare Luke 19:8).

TEACHING See *Education in Bible Times; Instruction.*

TEKOA (*place of setting up a tent*), **TEKOITE** City in highlands of Judah six miles south of Bethlehem and ten miles south of Jerusalem; home of Amos (Amos 1:1; compare 7:12). See 2 Sam. 23:26; 2 Chron. 11:5-6; 20:20-22; Neh. 3:5). See *Amos.*

TEMA (*south country*)

(1) Son of Ishmael (Gen. 25:15; 1 Chron. 1:30).

(2) Strategic oasis on Arabian penisula 250 miles southeast of Aqaba and 200 miles north-northeast of Medina; caravan stop (Job 6:19); Teima. Isaiah 21:14 likely refers to the campaign of the Assyrian king Tiglath-Pileser III (738 B.C.) when Tema escaped destruction by paying tribute. Jeremiah 25:23 perhaps refers to a campaign of Nebuchadnezzar. Having conquered and rebuilt Tema, Nabonidus, the last king of Babylon, remained there 10 years, leaving his son Belshazzar as vice-regent in Babylon (Dan. 5).

TEMAN (*right side, southern*)

(1) Edomite clan descended from Esau (Gen. 36:11, 15; 1 Chron. 1:36).

(2) City associated with this clan (Jer. 49:7,20; Ezek. 25:13; Amos 1:12; Obad. 1:9; Hab. 3:3); often identified with Tawilan, 50 miles south of the Dead Sea just east of Petra. Others understand Teman to be southern Edom in general or Tema on Arabian peninsula (see Jer. 49:7; Ezek. 25:13).

TEMPERANCE See *Self-control.*

TEMPLE OF JERUSALEM

Place of worship Solomon built in Jerusalem for national worship of Yahweh. David planned the temple and accumulated great wealth and gifts for it after God refused his desire to build it (2 Sam. 7). Previously, a house of Yahweh at Shiloh was called a temple (1 Sam. 1:7,9,24; 3:3; compare 2:22). Jeremiah warned those in the Lord's house in Jerusalem not to trust primarily in the temple (Jer. 7:1-15; 26:1-6). Babylon destroyed the temple in 586 B.C. Zerubbabel with help from Haggai, Zechariah, and Joshua rebuilt it in 515. Herod the Great then spent decades rebuilding it. Both Zerubbabel's and Herod's temples are called the "second temple"by Judaism.

Each temple stood on a prominent hill north of David's capital city (2 Sam. 5:6-7; compare Gen. 22:1-14; 2 Sam. 24:18-25; 2 Chron. 3:1). The temple site is the large rock enshrined within the Dome of the Rock, center of the Muslim enclosure called Haram es-Sharif (the third holiest place in Islam, after Mecca and Medina). Ezekiel's vision of the new Jerusalem temple after the exile (Ezek. 40–43) is idealistic and was perhaps never realized.

The temple with the ark symbolized God's presence in the midst of His people (Ex. 25:21-22). Worshipers could not enter the holy place, reserved only for priests and other worship leaders, much less the holiest place (holy of holies) to be entered by the high priest only once a year (Lev. 16). The worshipers gathered for prayer and sacrifice in the temple courtyard(s) where they could sing psalms as they saw their offerings presented to Yahweh on His great altar.

Solomon's temple was shaped as a "long house" of three successive rooms from east to west, a vestibule of only 15-feet depth, a nave (the holy place) of 60 feet and an inner sanctuary (the most holy place) of 30 feet (1 Kings 6:2-3,16-17). It was approximately 30 feet wide and 45 feet high by its interior measurements, not counting the porch, an open entryway. Around the outside of the house proper were constructed three stories of side chambers for temple storehouses, above which were recessed windows in the walls of the holy place (1 Kings 6:4-6,8-10).

The most holy place, a windowless cube of about 30 feet, housed the

ark of the covenant and was dominated by two guardian cherubim 15-feet tall with outstretched wings spanning 15 feet to touch in the middle and at each side wall (1 Kings 6:15-28). The ark, the mercy-seat lid of which had its own guardian cherubim (Ex. 25:18-20), was Yahweh's "footstool." Beneath these awesome cherubim, God was invisibly enthroned.

The most mysterious creations were two huge free-standing bronze pillars (Jachin, "He shall establish" and Boaz,"In the strength of"), about 35-feet tall (1 Kings 7:15-20). They were nearly six feet in diameter, hollow, with a thickness of bronze about three inches. The bronze altar (2 Chron. 4:1) altar is 30-feet square and 15-feet tall, presumably with steps. The molten sea, which may have had some kind of cosmic symbolism, opposite the bronze altar, was round with a cup-shaped brim, 15 feet in diameter, 7.5-feet tall, with a circumference of 45 feet. It rested on the back of 12 bronze oxen. Since it held about 10,000 gallons of water, it must have supplied water to the lavers by some sort of syphon mechanism.

Ten ornate, rolling stands for lavers, five on either side of the courtyard, were six-feet square and four-and-a-half-feet tall, each containing some 200 gallons of water (2 Chron. 4:6).

Temple treasures of gold were often plundered by foreign invaders like Shishak of Egypt (1 Kings 14:25-26; compare 2 Kings 23:4-6,11-12) and Judah's kings (1 Kings 15:18-19; 14:12-14; 2 Kings 12; 16:8-9,17; 18:13-16). Jehoiakim reversed all Josiah's reforms and filled the temple with pagan abominations (Ezek. 8). The loss of the temple and city were a grievous blow (Ps. 137; Lam. 1–5). Jeremiah and Ezekiel had prepared a remnant in their prophecies of hope for a return and rebuilding. See *Israel, History of.*

Zerubbabel's temple perhaps was mounted on a platform and measured about 100 feet by 100 feet with the interior dimensions being virtually the same as those of Solomon's temple. It was probably not as ornately decorated (Ezra 3:12-13; Hag. 2:3).

The ark of the covenant was never replaced (Jer. 3:16).The holy of holies was separated from the holy place by a veil instead of a door.

Judas Maccabeus rededicated the temple in 167 B.C. after Antiochus had profaned it in December 164 B.C. This joyous event is still remembered in the Jewish celebration of Hannukah. Pompey captured the temple in 63 B.C. but did not plunder it. See *Intertestamental History.*

Herod the Great came to power in 37 B.C. His most notable contribution was the magnificent stonework of the temple platform which was greatly enlarged. Herod surrounded the whole enclosure with magnificent porches, particularly the royal stoa along the southern wall. Worshipers went up through enclosed passageways into the court of the Gentiles. In the southwest corner a monumental staircase ascended into the temple from the main street below. Perhaps this was the "temple pinnacle" from which Satan tempted Jesus to throw Himself.

After the Jewish revolt in A.D. 66, Vespasian and then his son Titus crushed all resistance.The temple was destroyed in A.D. 70. Paul thought of the church and Christians as the new temple (1 Cor. 3:16-17; 6:19-20). For John, the ideal which the temple represented will ultimately be realized in a "new Jerusalem" (Rev. 21:2).

TEMPTATION

KJV for testing, trying, and enticing to evil. God tests the loyalty or disloyalty of persons. God "tested" Abraham's loyalty when He told Abraham to sacrifice Isaac (Gen. 22:1; Hebrews 11:17). God proved what was in wandering Israel's heart (Deut. 8:2; compare Ex. 20:20; Judg. 2:22.) Christ tested Philip's loyalty (John 6:6).

Jesus' enemies tested Him to get something to use against Him (Matt. 16:1; compare Matt. 19:3; 22:18,35; Mark 8:11; 10:2; 12:15; Luke 11:16; 20:23; John 8:6.) Persons are tempted or enticed to sin but not by God (Jas. 1:13). God allows human beings to be tempted by Satan (1 Chron. 21:1;

Matt. 4:1,3; Mark 1:13; Luke 4:2,13; 1 Cor. 7:5; 1 Thess. 3:5; Rev. 2:10). People are also tempted by their own lusts or desires (Jas. 1:14). No person's temptations are unique, and God is faithful not to let you be tempted beyond your ability to resist (1 Cor. 10:13). Jesus taught His disciples to pray: "Lead us not into temptation, but deliver us from evil" (Matt 6:13).

Persons are not to test God (Deut. 6:16; Matt. 4:7) but did (Ex. 17:2,7; Deut. 6:16; 9:22; Num. 14:22; Acts 5:9; 15:10; 1 Cor. 10:9; Heb. 3:8-9; compare Acts 15:6-11). See *Devil, Satan, Evil, Demonic; Adam and Eve; Temptation of Jesus.*

TEMPTATION OF JESUS

Satan's attempts at the beginning of Jesus' ministry to divert Jesus from God's way of accomplishing His mission (Matt. 4:1; Mark 1:12; Luke 4:3). The temptations are based on recognition that Jesus is the Son of God.

The first temptation was to turn into bread the flat stones of the desert, which looked much like the flat round loaves of Middle Eastern bread. Jesus quoted Deuteronomy 8:3 that "man doth not live by bread only, but by every word that proceedeth out of the mouth of the LORD."

Matthew's setting for the second temptation is the pinnacle of the temple in Jerusalem where Jesus was challenged to jump off on the basis of Ps. 91:11-12, promising God's angels would rescue and bear up God's anointed. Jesus responded with Deut. 6:16 that one should not tempt "the Lord your God."

Matthew's third temptation was on a high mountain from which worldly kingdoms could be seen. Satan promised to deliver the kingdoms of this world to Jesus. Jesus quoted Deut. 6:13 and commanded Satan to leave. The devil left, and angels ministered to Jesus.

Satan tempted Jesus to be a bread messiah, a spectacular messiah, and a compromising messiah.When Jesus refused to continue to be a bread messiah, the crowds left Him (John

6:25-68). When Jesus came to the temple, it was not to perform miracles but to cleanse it (Matt. 21:12-17). When the people came to make Him king, He eluded them, choosing instead to be exalted ("lifted up" in Greek) on the cross. Hebrews 4:15 says Jesus was thoroughly and completely tempted. The evil one has nothing in which to find Him guilty (John 14:30). The major temptation of Jesus was to do God's will the devil's way, some other way than the way of suffering God had appointed. Jesus did not yield to this great temptation, nor did He yield to temptation at any point. See *Devil, Satan, Evil, Demonic; Jesus, Life and Ministry.*

TEN COMMANDMENTS See *Law, Ten Commandments, Torah.*

TERAH (perhaps *ibex*)

Father of Abraham, Nahor, and Haran (Gen. 11:26). Terah moved his family, following the Euphrates River to Haran (11:31), where he died at the age of 205 (11:32). Joshua 24:2 apparently points to his family when it claims records that the father worshiped gods other than Yahweh.

TERAPHIM

Idols of indeterminate size and shape used as household gods or for divination (compare Gen. 31; Judg. 17:5; 18:14-20; 1 Sam. 19:13; 15:23; 2 Kings 23:24; Hos. 3:4; Ezek. 21:21; Zech. 10:2). Rachel stole them for unexplained reason. Jacob (Gen. 35:2) disposed of such religious artifacts before returning to Bethel. Teraphim are related to divination. See *Divination and Magic.*

TEREBINTH

Large, spreading tree of uncertain species (compare 2 Sam. 18:9; Isa. 1:30; 6:13); place under which pagan gods were worshiped (Hos. 4:13; Ezek. 6:13); at times taken up in Israel's religion (Gen. 35:4; Josh. 24:26; Judg. 6:11; 1 Kings 13:14).

TETRARCH

Political position in early Roman Empire. Luke 3:1 names one of the tetrarchs who served in the year of Jesus' birth. The position became less powerful with time, and the limits of authority narrowed. When Herod the Great died, his kingdom was divided among his three sons, one of whom was called "ethnarch" while the other two were named tetrarchs. See *Rome and the Roman Law.*

THADDAEUS See *Disciples, Apostles.*

THANKSGIVING

(1) Gratitude directed toward God (except Luke 17:9; Acts 24:3; Rom. 16:4), generally in response to God's concrete acts in history. Sacrifice and offerings were to be made not grudgingly but with thanksgiving (Ps. 54:6; Jonah 2:9). Song of thanksgiving is valued more than sacrifice (Ps. 69:30-31). David employed Levites "to record, to thank, and to praise the Lord" (1 Chron. 16:4; also 23:30; Neh. 12:46). Pilgrimage to the temple and temple worship were characterized by thanksgiving (Pss. 42:4; 95:2; 100:4; 122:4). Thankfulness was expressed: for personal (Ps. 35:18) and national deliverance (Ps. 44:7-8); for God's faithfulness to the covenant (Ps. 100:5); and for forgiveness (Ps. 30:4-5; Isa. 12:1). All creation joins in offering thanks to God (Ps. 145:10). See *Psalms.*

Thanksgiving is a natural element of Christian worship (1 Cor. 14:16-17) and is to characterize all of Christian life (Col. 2:7; 4:2). Early Christians expressed thanks: for Christ's healing ministry (Luke 17:16); for Christ's deliverance of the believer from sin (Rom. 6:17-18; 7:25); for God's indescribable gift of grace in Christ (2 Cor. 9:14-15; 1 Cor. 15:57; compare Rom. 1:21); and for the faith of fellow Christians (Rom. 1:8).

(2) Epistolary thanksgiving. See *Letter, Form and Function.*

THEATER

Apparently unknown in OT Israel, theaters in Palestine were a constant reminder of Greek and Roman control of the Jewish state. Herod I built numerous theaters in the Greek cities during his reign in Palestine (37–4 B.C.). Their presence, especially near the temple in Jerusalem, continually infuriated the Jews. Across the Roman Empire, theaters flourished. Public performances began with a sacrifice to a pagan deity, usually the patron god of the city. Dramas and comedies included historical or political themes and were often lewd and suggestive. Theaters varied in size. Those in small towns held approximately 4,000 persons, while larger theaters, such as that in Ephesus where Paul was denounced (Acts 19:29), were capable of holding 25,000 or more. See *Greece; Rome and the Roman Empire.*

THEBES

Capital of Egypt's Upper Kingdom for most of its history (about 2000–661 B.C.). The city waned only during the brief Hyksos period (about 1750–1550 B.C.). Thebes ("No" in KJV) was center of worship for the god Amon, a chief deity in Egyptian religion. See *Egypt.*

THEBEZ

Likely Tubas, 13 miles northeast of Shechem where roads from Shechem and Dothan converge to lead down to the Jordan Valley (Judg. 9:50-53; 2 Sam. 11:21).

THEOCRACY

Type of government in which Yahweh was king over Israel. Such a rule could be unmediated or mediated through a messianic ruler. Typically, three kinds of theocracy have been outlined:

(1) *A premonarchic form* was based on the Sinaitic covenant (Ex. 19) and on the charismatic leadership of the judges and the prophets. The experience was more religious, less political.

(2) *The monarchic form* brought a compromise between anti- and pro-monarchic forces in Israel. The king was Yahweh's representative and was called Yahweh's anointed or prince.

(3) *A postexilic priestly form* saw both the prince and the priest as Yahweh's representative. Throughout Israel's history, theocracy was often more an ideal God's messengers proclaimed rather than a reality Israel lived out.

THEOPHANY

Physical appearance or personal manifestation of a god to a person. To see God could be fatal (Ex. 33:20; compare Gen. 16:13; Ex. 3:2-6; 19:20-21; Judg. 6:22-23; 13:20-22). People such as Moses and others at Sinai did see God (Ex. 24:9-10; compare Num. 12:4-8; Isa. 6:1,5).

Theophanies are of five types:

(1) *In human form.* Appearance of a human being with a pavement of sapphire "under His feet" (Ex. 24:10; compare Gen. 32:30; Ex. 33:11,18,23). God in His wisdom does not restrict Himself to one method of self-revelation. Compare Num. 12:6-8; Deut. 4:12-15.

(2) *In vision.* Even self-seeking Balaam was allowed to see the Lord in vision (Num. 24:3-4; compare Gen. 28:12-13; Isa. 6; Ezek. 1; Dan. 7:9).

(3) *By the "Angel of the Lord."* Usual form of theophany. The "Angel of the Lord" is identified with Yahweh Himself. He appears only occasionally in human form. See Gen. 16:7-13. See *Angel.*

(4) *Not in human form.* Burning bush (Ex. 3:2–4:17); guidance through the wilderness (13:21; compare Acts 7:30); glory of the Lord; See *Glory.* God's presence is in a cloud (Ex. 16:10; 33:9-10; Ezek. 10:4). God was also manifest in nature and history (Isa. 6:3; Ezek. 1:28; 43:2).

(5) *As the name of the Lord.* God's sacred name represented His presence (Deut. 12:5; 102:15; Isa. 30:27; 59:19).

The NT doctrine of God is final and complete with no need of a theophany. God is always present in the risen Christ and the Holy Spirit.

THEOPHILUS (friend of God)

Person to whom Luke and Acts were written (Luke 1:3; Acts 1:1); exact identity is unknown. Speculation has ranged from generic "friend of God" intended to all Christians to a specific benefactor, perhaps in high social and/or political standing. If the latter is true, the name may be a pseudonym to protect the individual from persecution.

THESSALONIANS, FIRST LETTER TO THE

First letter Paul wrote to church at Thessalonica, largest city in first century Macedonia and capital of the province. See *Macedonia*. Paul, Silas, and Timothy evangelized the city against the strong opposition of the Jews (Acts 17:4).

To help the new church, Paul wrote 1 Thessalonians not long after Timothy came to him at Corinth (1 Thess. 3:6; Acts 18:5), not at Athens (1 Thess. 3:1-2). Paul probably wrote 1 Thessalonians early in A.D. 50, one of Paul's earliest letters and one of earliest Christian documents.

Thessalonian church faced persecution by pagans (2:14) and a temptation for believers to accept pagan sexual standards (4:4-8). Some of the Christians seem to have given up working and to have relied on the others to supply their needs (4:11-12). There was uncertainty about the fate of believers who had died, and some of the Thessalonians appear to have thought that Christ would come back soon and take them all to be with Him. What would happen to those who had died before the great event (4:13-18)? Some of the believers seem to have been concerned about the time of Jesus' return (5:1-11). So Paul wrote this pastoral letter to meet the needs of inexperienced Christians and to bring them closer to Christ. See *Paul.*

THESSALONIANS, SECOND LETTER TO THE

Second letter Paul wrote to church at Thessalonica not long after the first letter. Paul wrote to committed Christians who had not progressed very far in the Christian life. The opening salutation speaks of grace and peace as coming from God the Father and the Lord Jesus Christ (1:2). Throughout the letter, Christ is seen as in the closest relationship to the Father. Sometimes we are uncertain whether *Lord* means the Father or the Son, as in the expression "the Lord of peace" (3:16). The greatness of Christ is seen in the description of His majestic return with the angels when He comes in judgment (1:7-10). The letter briefly mentions the gospel (1:8; 2:14), salvation (2:13), and the "testimony" of the preachers (1:10).

Some had come to believe that "the coming of our Lord" was at hand, or had even begun (2:2). Some of them had given up working for their living (3:6-13), perhaps because they held the view that the Lord's coming was so close that there was no point in it. Paul wrote to settle them down a little, while not restraining their enthusiasm.

Four great teachings mark this letter:

(1) the greatness of God,

(2) the wonder of salvation in Christ,

(3) the second coming, and

(4) the importance of life and work each day.

God loves people like the Thessalonians and has brought them into the church (1:4). He has elected them (2:13), called them (1:11, 2:14), and saved them. His purposes last through to the end when they will be brought to their climax with the return of Christ and judgment of all. His doctrine of justification may appear behind the references to God counting the believers worthy (1:5,11) and in his teaching on faith (1:3; 4:11; 2:13; 3:2).

This great God loves His people and has given them comfort and hope, two important qualities for persecuted people (2:16). The apostle prayed that the hearts of his converts would be directed into "the love of God" (3:5). God has revealed what is necessary and has further revelations for the last days (1:7; 2:6,8).

The second coming is seen in terms of the overthrow of all evil, especially the man of lawlessness. Christ's coming will mean punishment for people who refuse to know God and who reject the gospel and will bring rest and glory to believers (1:7-10).

God will in due course punish those who persecute the believers and will give the believers rest (1:6-7). Those who refuse to know God and those who reject the gospel will receive the consequences of their actions (1:8-9). From 2:2 we see that some converts had misunderstood either a "spirit" (i.e., a prophecy or a revelation) or a "word" (oral communication) or a letter with the result that they thought Christ's return would take place very soon. They thought Christ had already returned. Several things must happen first: "the rebellion" that occurs and the revelation of "the man of lawlessness" (2:3). He did not explain either. He was probably referring to what he had told the Thessalonians while he had been among them. That a rebellion against the faith will precede the Lord's return is a well-known part of Christian teaching (Matt. 24:10ff.; 1 Tim. 4:1-3; 2 Tim. 3:1-9; 4:3-4). *Man of lawlessness* is the same as the one called "antichrist" (1 John 2:18). In the end time one will appear who will do the work of Satan in a special way. He will oppose the true God and claim divine honors for himself (2:4). In due course these things will take place, and God will do away with all the forces of evil (2:8-10).

Paul addressed people he called "disorderly." They appear to be idle, not working at all (3:6-12), perhaps because they thought the Lord's coming was so close there was no point in it, or perhaps they were so "spiritual minded" that they concentrated on higher things and let other people

provide for their needs. Paul counseled all to work for their living (3:12).

THESSALONICA

Largest city of Macedonia founded by Cassander, a general of Alexander the Great, about 315 B.C., naming it after his wife, the daughter of Philip II and half sister of Alexander. Located on the Thermaic Gulf (Gulf of Salonika) with an excellent harbor—and at the termination of a major trade route from the Danube—it became, with Corinth, one of the two most important commercial centers in Greece. See *Macedonia.* Thessalonica was a free city, having no Roman garrison within its walls and maintaining the privilege of minting its own coins. A Jewish synagogue was there (17:1).

THEUDAS (*gift of God*)

Man slain (Acts 5:36) after leading unsuccessful rebellion of 400 men prior to the census (A.D. 6). Josephus knew a Theudas who led an unsuccessful rebellion during the consulate of Cuspius Fadus (about A.D. 44).

THIGH

Side of lower torso and upper part of the leg (Judg. 3:16; Ps. 45:3; Song of Sol. 3:8; 7:1); seat of vital functions, especially procreation (Gen. 46:26; Ex. 1:5; Judg. 8:30). Marital infidelity was punishable by "the falling away of the thigh," that is, by failure of the reproductive system (Num. 5:16-21). In the patriarchal period, oaths were taken by placing a hand "under the thigh," a veiled reference to the reproductive organs. When the "stranger" at Peniel did not prevail against Jacob, he touched Jacob in the hollow of his thigh, leaving him limping (Gen. 32:25-32). Slapping the thigh indicated sorrow, shame, or remorse (Jer. 31:19; Ezek. 21:12). The thigh was among the portions of the sacrifice going to the priests (Lev. 7:32-34; 10:14). Compare 1 Sam. 9:24 where Samuel honored Saul with this portion.

THOMAS (*a twin*) See *Apocrypha, New Testament; Disciples, Apostles.*

THORN IN THE FLESH (*messenger of Satan*)

God gave Paul to ensure his humility following a profound experience of "visions," "revelations," and "ascent into the third heaven" (2 Cor. 12:7). Guesses of its nature range from epilepsy to malaria to eye disease.

Paul's entire apostolic experience of suffering (compare 2 Cor. 1:3-11; 4:7–5:10; 6:1-10; 7:2-7; 11:16-33), abetted by Satan and operative through the evils of this world, was the "messenger of Satan," a "thorn in the flesh," which God gave and used to keep the great apostle humbly obedient.

THUMMIM See *Urim and Thummim.*

THYATIRA

City in Lycus River valley; center of trade guilds. One of Paul's first European converts, Lydia, was a native of Thyatira (Acts 16:14). The church at Thyatira was praised for its works of charity, service, and faith (Rev. 2:19), but criticized for allowing the followers of Jezebel to prosper in its midst (2:20). See *Asia Minor, Cities of; Revelation, Book of.*

TIBERIAS

City on western shore of the Sea of Galilee (John 6:23; compare 6:1; 21:1). About A.D. 18 Herod Antipas (Luke 3:1) built the larger city on a major trade route connecting Egypt with Syria, to replace Sepphoris as the capital of Galilee. It remained the capital until A.D. 61 when it was given to Agrippa II by Nero.

TIBERIUS CAESAR See *Rome and the Roman Empire.*

TIDAL

King in Gen. 14:1,9; name similar to Tud'alia, name of several Hittite kings, suggesting origin in eastern Asia Minor; perhaps Tudhalia I (about 1700–1650 B.C.).

TIGLATH-PILESER (*My trust is the son of Esarra* [the temple of Asshur])

King of Assyria (745–727 B.C.; 2 Kings 16:7), also known as Tilgath-Pilneser (1 Chron. 5:6; 2 Chron. 28:20) and Pul (2 Kings 15:19; 1 Chron. 5:26). See *Assyria, History and Religion of.*

TIGRIS RIVER See *Euphrates and Tigris Rivers; Rivers and Waterways in the Bible.*

TIMBREL

KJV for tambourine. See *Music, Instruments, Dancing.*

TIME, MEANING OF

Chronological sequence of life and its significance in biblical teaching. God is Lord of time, sovereignly present in all the events of time. He offers each new day as an opportunity for judgment or for redemption.

God is eternal from the biblical standpoint means His existence brackets cosmic time. He was there at the beginning of all created things; He will be there when temporal reality ends; and He is present at every moment in between. He actively governs all His creatures, calling each person, to whom He has given the power of free choice, to obey and believe. See Isa. 48:12-13; compare 41:4; 44:6.

People are temporary. Created of dust (Gen. 2:7), humans must sometime die. They cannot seize immortality and become like God (Gen. 3:22; compare Eccl. 11:8; 12).

No evidence indicates the Israelites counted seconds, minutes, or even hours (the Jews of the NT learned to count hours from the Romans). The day was divided into "watches" (compare Ex. 14:24; 1 Sam. 11:11), measured by observation of the sun's position in the sky. They counted years by the cycle of the seasons. Their months were counted from one new moon to the next, making it necessary to add extra "intercalary" days after twelve months to make the new year (365 + days) begin on a new moon = month. Originally the Israelites counted the day from morning till evening, or, counting the night in between, from one morning to the next. Growing importance of the rising moon for festival observances led them to count the day from the evening, the Jewish custom today. Days were identified by their most significant event or experiential quality: "day of rejoicing," "day of trouble," "day of salvation." There was a "day" of Israel's election (Deut. 9:24; compare Ezek. 16:4-5), a "day" when God brought His people out of Egypt (Judg. 19:30; 1 Sam. 8:8; 2 Sam. 7:6; Isa. 11:16; Jer. 7:22,25), but also a "day" of judgment (Lam. 1:11) and a "day" of restoration (Zech. 8:9-12). There was also a final day when God would judge the world; this was "the day of the Lord" (Amos 5:18-19; Isa. 13:6; Zeph. 1:7).

There were good and evil days or times. Ecclesiastes 3:1-8 provides a list of such times while warning that humankind is unable to discern God's intent in sending them. Usually a person's "days" weigh more heavily with evil than with good (compare Gen. 47:9; Job 7:1,16; Ps. 144:4, Eccl. 2:23). Psalm 90 measures mankind's brief life (vv. 9-10) against God's eternity (vv. 2,4) and prays God will do two things:

(1) "teach us to number our days, that we may apply our hearts unto wisdom" (Ps. 90:12) and

(2) "make us glad according to the days wherein thou hast afflicted us, and the years wherein we have seen evil" (Ps. 90:15).

The fullness of time has already appeared (Acts 1:7; 1 Thess. 5:1-11). In His Son God gave mankind the most perfect revelation of Himself (John 14:5-11). Nothing counts but the present moment—the moment of decision for Christ.

Israel's neighbors believed their gods could be contacted at holy places (the shrines) and at holy times (the religious festivals). The biblical God cannot be tied down to special places and special times. Nevertheless, His ancient people obediently built the temple and set aside holy seasons for His worship, not to coerce God but to hallow His holy presence

for prayer and thanksgiving. To keep His sabbaths and holy festivals and to gather in His temple were acts of celebration and recommitment. All time belongs to God (Gen. 1), but sacred times, especially set aside and devoutly observed, serve to show once again our participation in the great events of God's appearance.

TIMNAH (*allotted portion*) or **TIMNATH**

(1) Town assigned to Dan (Josh. 19:43) on southern border with Judah (Josh. 15:10); likely tell el-Batashi about four miles northwest of Bethshemesh in Judah. Philistines occupied the site at the time of Samson (Judg. 14:1-5; compare 2 Chron. 26:6; 28:18). The city fell to the Assyrian king Sennacherib in 701 B.C.

(2) Village in hill country of Judah (Josh. 15:57); likely scene of Judah's encounter with Tamar (Gen. 38:12-14); probably south of Hebron about four miles east of Beit Nettif.

TIMNATH-HERES (*portion of the sun*)

TIMNATH-SERAH (*remaining portion*)

Place of Joshua's inheritance and burial (Judg. 2:9; Josh 19:50; 24:30); dedicated to sun worship (Judg. 2:9); Khirbet Tibneh about 17 miles southwest of Shechem.

TIMOTHY (*honoring God*)

Friend and trusted coworker of Paul (1 Cor. 4:17; 1 Tim. 1:2, 18; 2 Tim. 1:2; 4:9); listed with Paul as author of six letters (2 Cor. 1:1; Phil. 1:1; Col. 1:1; 1 Thess. 1:1; 2 Thess. 1:1; Philem. 1); received two letters from Paul (1 Tim. 1:2; 2 Tim. 1:2); learned Scriptures from mother Eunice and grandmother Lois (2 Tim. 1:5; 3:15) in Lystra; may have been converted on Paul's first missionary journey (Acts 14:6-23; compare 16:1-2). Timothy's father was a Greek, and Timothy had not been circumcised. Because they would be ministering to many Jews and because Timothy's mother was

Jewish, Paul had Timothy circumcised (Acts 16:3). Paul sent Timothy on many crucial missions (Acts 17:14-15; 18:5; 19:22; 20:4; Rom. 16:21; 1 Cor. 4:17; 16:10; 2 Cor. 1:19; Phil. 2:19; 1 Thess. 3:2,6). Paul felt that no one had any more compassion and commitment than Timothy (Phil. 2:20-22). Timothy was imprisoned, but released (Heb. 13:23). See *Paul; 1 Timothy; 2 Timothy.*

TIMOTHY, FIRST LETTER TO

First of two epistles Paul wrote to Timothy about A.D. 63, following Paul's first imprisonment in Rome, perhaps from Macedonia (1 Tim. 1:3). Paul had urged Timothy to remain in Ephesus and lead this important church as its pastor (1:3). Paul wanted Timothy to "know how thou oughtest to behave thyself in the house of God" (3:14-15). The epistle contains instructions concerning order and structure in the church and practical advice for the young pastor. Paul urged Timothy and Titus to confront false teaching by sound or healthy teaching (1 Tim. 1:10; 6:3; 2 Tim. 1:13; 4:3; Titus 1:9,13; 2:1-2).

Some were falsely teaching a mythological treatment of OT genealogies (1:3-4). Timothy was urged to teach "sound doctrine" in its place (1:10-11). Paul consigned two leaders —"Hymenaeus and Alexander to Satan, that they may learn not to blaspheme." The aim of this was that the offenders might be restored (1 Tim. 1:20; compare 1 Cor. 5:5).

Prayer is given priority in the worship services in the church. In 2:5 Paul wrote "there is one God, and one mediator between God and men, the man Christ Jesus." Jesus paid for our redemption with His death on the cross (2:6).

Chapter 3 mentions 15 moral and ethical requirements for church leaders. Paul affirmed that "every creature of God is good, and nothing to be refused, if it be received with thanksgiving" (4:4) though some false teachers maintained marriage and certain foods were wrong. Mankind takes God's good creation and corrupts it.

The apostle reminded Timothy to be a "good minister of Christ Jesus" (4:6) and to "be an example of the believers, in word, in conversation, in charity, in spirit, in faith, in purity" (4:12).

Paul gave practical instructions concerning the ministry of the church to various groups that comprise its membership (ch. 5). The teachers of false doctrine believe that financial gain was godliness (6:5). In light of this false belief Paul warned that "the love of money is the root of all evil" (6:10)

TIMOTHY, SECOND LETTER TO

Second of Paul's Epistles to Timothy, pastor of church in Ephesus; from jail cell during second imprisonment in Rome between A.D. 63-67; last letter we have that Paul wrote. Paul felt he would not be released (4:6); contains Paul's stirring words of encouragement and instruction to his young disciple. Paul longed to see Timothy (1:4) and asked him to come to Rome before winter (4:21) and bring the winter coat Paul left in Troas (4:13). Timothy was also asked to bring the scrolls and the parchments so Paul could read and study (4:13).

Paul had become Timothy's father (1:2) and reminded him that God "hath not given us the spirit of fear; but of power, and of love, and of a sound mind" (1:7). Two men, Phygelus and Hermogenes, deserted Paul (1:15). Onesiphorus was a refreshing friend and not ashamed of Paul's chains (1:16).

Timothy was to "rightly" handle "the word of truth" (2:15) in the face of those like Hymenaeus (1 Tim. 1:20) and Philetus who mishandled it. They were teaching that the resurrection had already taken place and were destroying the faith of some (2:18).

"The last days" are a reference to the second coming of Jesus. The days preceding His return will be "terrible." Paul listed 18 characteristics of evil men (3:2-5). He compared them to Jannes and Jambres who opposed Moses (3:8). See *Jannes and Jambres.* Evil and false teaching is to be overcome by the Holy Scripture (3:16-17).

Paul instructed Timothy to be prepared to "preach the Word" at all times for people will not always adhere to "sound doctrine" (4:3). Paul compared his life to that of a "drink offering" (see Num. 28:24) poured on a sacrifice before it was offered. He was ready to depart this life and go to be with the Lord. He anticipated the "crown of righteousness" that awaited him (4:8).

TIPHSAH (*passage, ford*)

(1) City on west bank of Euphrates about 75 miles south of Carchemish; northeastern limit of Solomon's kingdom (1 Kings 4:24).

(2) Site near Tirzah in Samaria (2 Kings 15:16), possibly corruption of Tappuah, reading of the earliest Greek translation (REB, RSV, TEV).

TIRAS

Division of descendants of Japheth; all seagoing peoples (Gen. 10:2; 1 Chron. 1:5). Traditionally related to Turscha, part of sea peoples Rameses III (1198–1166 B.C.) fought. Some have identified them with Etruscans of Italy.

TIRHAKAH

Egyptian pharaoh of twenty-fifth dynasty (689–664 B.C.); supported Hezekiah's revolt against Assyrian king Sennacherib (2 Kings 19:8-9; Isa. 37:9).

TIRSHATHA

Title of honor designating respect for an official, sometimes translated, "your excellence" (Ezra 2:63; Neh. 7:65,70; 8:9; 10:1).

TIRZAH (*she is friendly*)

(1) Daughter of Zelophehad who inherited part of tribal land allotment of Manasseh since her father had no sons.

(2) Originally a Canaanite city noted for its beauty (Song of Sol. 6:4) but captured in the conquest of the Promised Land (Josh. 12:24); one of early capitals of Israel (1 Kings 14:17;

16:23-24); tell el-Fara, about seven miles northeast of Shechem.

TISHBITE

Resident of unidentified village, Tishbe, used as a title of Elijah (1 Kings 17:1; 21:17,28; 2 Kings 1:3,8; 9:36); possibly a corruption of Jabeshite or a class designation. See *Elijah*.

TITHE

Tenth part, especially as offered to God (Gen. 14:18-20; 28:22). Numbers 18:20-32 provides for support of the Levites and the priests through the tithe. The tithe of agricultural produce was to be used for a family feast at the sanctuary celebrating God's provision (Deut. 14:22-27). The third year's tithe was for care of the Levites, orphans, widows, and foreigners (Deut. 14:28-29). The rabbis of the NT period understood the laws as referring to three separate tithes: a Levitical tithe, a tithe spent celebrating in Jerusalem, and a charity tithe. Malachi 3:8 equates neglect of the tithe with robbing God. Jesus warned that strict tithing must accompany concern for the more important demands of the law—just and merciful living (Matt. 23:23; Luke 11:42).

TITTLE See *Dot.*

TITUS

Gentile companion of Paul (Gal. 2:3; 2 Cor. 8:23) and recipient of the NT letter bearing his name; may have been converted by Paul (Titus 1:4); accompanied Paul and Barnabas to Jerusalem (Gal. 2:1), probably on the famine relief visit (Acts 11:28-30); evidently known to the Galatians (Gal. 2:1,3), possibly from the first missionary journey to that region. He was overseer or bishop of church at Crete (Titus 1:5); Paul sent him to Dalmatia (2 Tim. 4:10). He was entrusted with the delicate task of delivering Paul's severe letter (2 Cor. 2:1-4) to Corinth and correcting problems within the church there (2 Cor. 7:13-15). Titus' genuine concern for and evenhanded dealing with the Corinthians (2 Cor. 8:16-17; 12:18) contributed to his success which he reported in person to Paul, (2 Cor. 2:13; 7:5-6,13-15). Paul responded by writing 2 Corinthians which Titus probably delivered (2 Cor. 8:6,16-18,23).

TITUS, CAESAR

Roman emperor (A.D. 79–81), eldest son of Vespasian; soldier in Germany, Britain, and Middle East. His troops captured the temple in Jerusalem (A.D. 70) and took Masada (A.D. 73); beloved, honest ruler and efficient administrator. See *Jerusalem; Rome and the Roman Empire.*

TITUS, LETTER TO

Paul's letter to Titus, pastor of the church on Crete (1:1,4), after Paul's first imprisonment in Rome about A.D. 63. Paul wrote to encourage and instruct Titus in the face of opposition. Titus was to admonish the people to hold "sound doctrine" and to be "sound in faith" (1:9,13; 2:1-2).

Chapter one says a genuine knowledge of the truth leads to godliness (1:1). Titus' first duty was to appoint elders (vv. 6-9; compare 1 Tim. 3:1-7). False teachers threatened the church. Those "of the circumcision" (1:10) were converts to the Christian faith from Judaism who apparently taught that circumcision was necessary to be a complete Christian. Such teachers were corrupt in their minds and detestable in their actions (1:15-16).

Chapter two urged Titus to teach "sound doctrine" to correct the false teaching. Titus was to be an example to all (2:7). His teaching was to be characterized by "uncorruptness, gravity, sincerity, sound speech" (2:7-8), so that the false teachers could have "no evil thing to say of you" (2:8). The basis of godly living is "the grace of God that bringeth salvation" (2:11). Evidence of receiving God's grace and salvation is a transformation of one's life. The "blessed hope" (2:13) of His return should motivate us to godly living.

Chapter three reminded believers "to be subject to principalities and powers, to obey magistrates" (3:1) because God created government. Believers are to treat all persons with consideration and humility. Our salvation is because of his mercy (3:5). Salvation is likened to "the washing of regeneration, and renewing of the Holy Ghost" (3:5). Rebirth takes place at salvation, and that renewal is a lifetime process. Zenas, the lawyer, and Apollos probably delivered the letter to Titus (3:13). See *Apollos; Circumcision; Holy Spirit; Paul; Salvation.*

TOB (*good*)

Syrian city in southern Hauran to which Jephthah fled from his brothers (Judg. 11:3-5; compare 2 Sam. 10:6-13); perhaps identical with Tabeel (Isa. 7:6); may be et-Taiyibeh about 12 miles east of Ramoth-gilead near source of Yarmuk River.

TOBIAH (*Yah is good*)

(1) Major adversary to Nehemiah's rebuilding efforts at Jerusalem; practicing Jew who lived in a residence chamber in the temple; called an "Ammonite" (Neh. 2:10,19) probably because his family fled to that territory at the destruction of Jerusalem. He opposed the rebuilding of Jerusalem because it would weaken his political authority in the area.

(2) Returned exile who apparently brought a gift of gold from Babylon for the Jerusalem community. Zechariah used him as a witness for his crowning of Joshua, the high priest, and to preserve the crowns in the temple (Zech. 6:9-14).

(3) Ancestor of clan who returned from exile but could not show they were Israelites (Ezra 2:60).

TOGARMAH

Son of Gomer and name of region of Asia Minor (Gen. 10:3; 1 Chron. 1:6; compare Beth-togarmah, Ezek. 38:6) inhabited by his descendants; famed for horses (Ezek. 27:14); likely Gurun 70 miles west of Malatya or an area in Armenia.

TONGUE

Organ of speech (Judg. 7:5; Isa. 41:17); language spoken (Jer. 5:15); people or nation speaking (Isa. 66:18); speech was seen as expression of person's true nature (Pss. 64:2-3; 45:1; Prov. 10:20; 17:20); objects in material world that resemble tongue in shape (Isa. 11:15). The wisdom writings of the OT stressed the practical results of the use of the tongue for the individual's life (Prov. 12:18; 18:21; 21:6,23; 25:23; 26:28; 28:23). The tongue could control the direction of a person's life (Jas. 3:3-8). Since the tongue reveals what is in one's heart, its use had ethical consequences whether for good or bad (Pss. 34:13; 37:30; 109:2; 120:2; 140:2-3; Isa. 59:3; compare Jas. 3:9-10). The tongue could be used to praise God (Pss. 35:28; 51:14; 71:24; Rom. 14:11; Phil. 2:11) or could cause separation from God (Job 15:4-5; Pss. 39:1; 78:35-37). See *Spiritual Gifts.*

TOOLS

Implements or instruments used with the hands for agricultural, construction, commercial, or craft purposes; earliest made of stone, especially flint. An effective cutting surface was achieved by chipping off flakes along the edge of the shaped stone. The first metal tools were of copper, which proved to be too soft for most applications. Harder tools were made from bronze, an alloy of copper and tin that could be melted and poured into molds before final shaping by a smith. The hardest tools were made of iron (Deut. 27:5; 1 Kings 6:5-7), which required much higher temperatures to smelt. Iron only came into use in Canaan around 1200 B.C. Handles and other parts of certain tools were made of wood, leather, bone, or ivory. See *Minerals and Metals.*

Flint knives of earlier periods continued in use even after metal became widespread. The command to use flint knives for circumcision (Josh. 5:2, NIV) may reflect a taboo on using new technology for ancient rites. Blades of bronze and iron knives were cast in a stone mold. The average knife in Palestine was between 6 and 10 inches, but a mold has been found to produce 16-inch blades. These would have been used for general cutting and butchering (Gen. 22:6; Judg. 19:29). A smaller version used by Jehoiakim to cut up Jeremiah's scroll (Jer. 36:23; KJV, NRSV, "penknife"; NIV, "scribe's knife") is represented by a Hebrew word elsewhere used for "razors" (Num. 6:5; Ezek. 5:1). The latter (Judg. 13:5; 16:17; 1 Sam. 1:11) were evidently quite sharp, as they are used as symbols of God's judgment (Isa. 7:20) and the cutting power of the tongue (Ps. 52:2).

Plow handles, crossbar, and other structural parts were of wood, while the plow point, or plowshare, needed to be of harder material to penetrate the ground. The earliest plowshares were of bronze, slowly replaced by iron. Plows were pulled by animals prodded with a goad, a wooden stick fitted with a metal tip (Judg. 3:31; 1 Sam. 13:21; Eccl. 12:11). On difficult to plow hilly or rocky terrain the ground was broken using a hoe (Isa. 7:25, NIV; KJV, "mattock"). A similar tool, the mattock (1 Sam. 13:21), was also used for digging chores. It is probably incorrectly translated as "plowshares" in the famous prophetic passages about the tools of war and peace (Isa. 2:4; Mic. 4:3; Joel 3:10). Philistines, perhaps holding a monopoly on iron technology, forced the Israelites to come to them for sharpening of agricultural tools (1 Sam. 13:19-22). See *Weights and Measures.*

The reaping of standing grain was done with a sickle (Deut. 16:9; 23:25; Jer. 50:16), a small tool with a handle and curved blade. The sickle is used as a symbol of God's judgment (Joel 3:13) and the ingathering of the saints (Mark 4:29; Rev. 14:14-19). A tool which resembled the sickle, but with a broader and shorter blade, was the "pruning hook" (Isa. 2:4; Mic. 4:3; Joel 3:10), a type of knife used for pruning and harvesting grapevines (Isa. 18:5).

The largest ax (Isa. 10:15) was used for felling trees (Deut. 19:5; 20:19) and quarrying stone (1 Kings 6:7). A smaller ax was used for lighter jobs (Judg. 9:48; 1 Sam. 13:20-21; Ps.

74:5; Jer. 46:22). Trimming was done with a different tool (Jer. 10:3 REB; NIV,"chisel"), perhaps an adze with its cutting edge perpendicular to the handle. Small hand axes or hatchets were also known (Ps. 74:6, KJV; NRSV, "hammers"; REB,"pick").The"planes" used in shaping (Isa. 44:13) were probably chisels (as in the NIV). Chisels were used for rough and detail work in both wood and stone. Holes were made with awls (Ex. 21:6; Deut. 15:17) or drills.

Wood and stone were also cut using saws (2 Sam. 12:31; 1 Kings 7:9; 1 Chron. 20:3; Isa. 10:15). Single and double-handled varieties are pictured in Egyptian tomb paintings.

Detail work was marked out using a "line" and "compass" (Isa. 44:13; NIV, "chisels" and "compasses"). Plumb lines were used quite early in Egypt and Palestine for determining verticality and levels in construction (compare 2 Kings 21:13; KJV, "plummet"; Isa. 28:17; Amos 7:7-8).

Hammers (Isa. 44:12; Jer. 10:4) were originally stone pounders, but in the Bronze Age holes were often bored for the insertion of a handle. Egyptian paintings show the use of broad wooden mallets not unlike those still used today in sculpture work.

Early potters used wooden tools to help shape their handmade vessels. A considerable advance came with the invention of the pottery wheel (Jer. 18:3). (See *Pottery*.) Weavers conducted their craft on looms. See *Spinning and Weaving*.

Metalworking required a bellows to bring a fire to the high temperatures required for smelting ore.These were used in small furnaces equipped with nozzles of clay to withstand the extreme heat. Molds were used to shape molten metal into tools, weapons, and other items. Metal smiths also used a variety of tongs, clamps, and hammers (Isa. 44:12).

TOPAZ See *Minerals and Metals*.

TOPHEL

Place near site of Moses' farewell speech to Israel (Deut. 1:1); et-Tafileh

about 15 miles southeast of the Dead Sea between Kerak and Petra; may represent name of a territory rather than a city.

TOPHET or **TOPHETH**

Place in Hinnom Valley outside Jerusalem derived from Aramaic or Hebrew meaning "fireplace," but altered by Hebrew scribes to mean "shameful thing" because of the illicit worship carried on there (Jer. 7:31-32). Child sacrifice was practiced at Tophet, leading the prophet to declare a slaughter of people there when God would come in vengeance (Jer. 19:6-11). See *Hinnom, Valley of*.

TORAH (*instruction, law*)

Teaching or instruction (Job 22:22; Ps. 78:1; Prov. 1:8; 4:2; 13:14; Isa. 30:9); requirements, commands, and decrees (Gen. 26:5; Ex. 18:16); Deuteronomic code (Deut. 4:8; 30:10; 32:46); Jewish title for Pentateuch, first five books of OT given to Moses (Ex. 24:12; compare Josh. 1:8; 8:31-32,34; 2 Kings 14:6; Neh. 8:1; Isa. 5:24; Jer. 32:23; 44:10; Dan. 9:11) and commanded to be kept (Ex. 16:28; Deut. 17:19; Ezek. 44:24). The "book of the law" which fueled Josiah's reforms (2 Kings 22:8-13) is often regarded to be roughly equivalent to the Book of Deuteronomy. In rabbinical Judaism, the scope of Torah is sometimes expanded to include all of the Scriptures or even the entirety of God's revelation. See *Law; Pentateuch*.

TORCH

Long pole with cloths dipped in oil wrapped around one end used as a light (John 18:3; Rev. 4:5; 8:10). The lamps of the wise and foolish virgins (Matt. 25:1-8) were perhaps torches.

TRACHONITIS (*heap of stones*)

Political and geographic district in northern Palestine on east side of Jordan River just south of Damascus; known as "Bashan" in OT (Luke 3:1). Its rugged terrain was best suited to raising sheep and goats. During John the Baptist's ministry, Trachonitis was ruled by Philip, the brother of Herod Antipas. (Amos 4:1). See *Bashan; Herod; Philip.*

TRADE See *Commerce.*

TRAIN

KJV for part of robe that trails behind wearer (Isa. 6:1).

TRANCE (*change of place*)

Mental state of person who experienced an intense emotional reaction to stimuli perceived as originating outside the person and producing visual or auditory sensations; experience in which a person received a revelation by supernatural means (Acts 10:10; 11:5; 22:17). The distinctions among "trance," "dream," and "vision" are not always clear. See *Ecstasy; Prophecy, Prophets.*

TRANSFIGURATION, THE

Transformation of Jesus in His appearance with Moses and Elijah before Peter, James, and John (Matt. 17:1-13; Mark 9:1-13; Luke 9:28-36; compare 2 Pet. 1:16-18). God spoke from the cloud identifying Jesus as His Son (compare the voice at the baptism) and commanding the disciples to hear Him. When the cloud lifted, Jesus was alone with the disciples, who were afraid. Jesus told the disciples to tell no one. The traditional site is Mount Tabor in lower Galilee, but it is not a high mountain (only 1,850 feet) and was probably fortified and inaccessible in Jesus' day. Much more likely is Mount Hermon (9,100 feet) to the north of Caesarea Philippi. See *Hermon.*

Moses and Elijah represented the law and the prophets, which testify to but must give way to Jesus. They were heralds of the Messiah (Deut. 18:15; Mal. 4:5-6). The disciples needed the reassurance of the transfiguration as they contemplated Jesus' death and their future sufferings. See *Jesus, Life and Ministry.*

TRANSGRESSION

Image of sin as overstepping the limits of God's law. See *Evil; Forgiveness; Repentance; Salvation; Sin.*

TRANSJORDAN

Area immediately east of Jordan River settled by Reuben, Gad, half of Manasseh, Edom, Moab, and Amon. By NT times, a cluster of Greco-Roman-oriented cities with primarily Gentile populations (the so-called "Decapolis" cities) had emerged in the northern Transjordan (earlier Bashan, Gilead, and Ammon). The southern Trans- jordan (earlier Moab and Edom) was dominated, on the other hand, by the Nabateans, a people of Arab origin who established a commercial empire along the desert fringe with its capital at Petra. See *Palestine; Ammon; Arnon; Bashan; Decapolis; Edom; Gilead; Jabbok; Moab; Tribes of Israel.*

TRANSPORTATION AND TRAVEL

Means and ways of commercial and private movement among towns and nations in the biblical period. For the most part, transportation and travel in the biblical world was on foot (Judg. 16:3; Josh. 9:3-5; 1 Kings 18:46) following paths animals made through the hills and valleys of Palestine.

International highways and trade routes, like the coastal road, the Via Maris, and the Transjordanian king's highway were developed along with secondary connector roads. These highways promoted the movement of businessmen, religious pilgrims, government officials, and armies between regions of the country and foreign nations.

Travelers and road builders had to overcome the rugged geographical character of Palestine. The desert regions of the Negev and Judean highlands in the south required the identification of wells and pasturage for the draft animals. The hilly spine of central Palestine forced the traveler to zigzag around steep ascents (such as that between Jericho and Jerusalem), or follow ridges along the hill tops (the Beth Horon route northwest of Jerusalem), or go along watersheds (Bethlehem to Mizpah). Numerous streams as well as the Jordan River had to be forded by travelers (2 Sam. 19:18), sometimes at the expense of baggage and animals.

In valleys, such as the Jezreel, roads generally followed the higher ground along the base of the hills so as to bypass marshy areas and stay away from the raging torrents which sometimes filled stream beds in the rainy season. Narrow, twisting valleys, as in the Judean desert, often provided perfect areas for ambushes by bandits. Along the coastal plain, sandy dunes required a detour further inland into the foothills of the Shephelah.

The rough coastline of Palestine lacked a good, deep-water port for shipping. As a result, an additional journey overland was required to transport agricultural and other trade goods to and from the ports of Ezion-geber (1 Kings 9:26-28) on the Red Sea and the Phoenician ports of Tyre and Sidon to the cities of Israel. See *Ships and Boats.*

Roads varied in size from two lane thoroughfares about 10 feet wide to simple tracks through fields barely wide enough for a man and donkey to pass single file. Roadways were probably kept in shape by government-sponsored corvee workers (2 Sam. 20:24; 1 Kings 9:15) or by the army. Since bridges were unknown in the biblical period, fords were identified (Judg. 12:5-6) for general use. Where no river crossing could be found, boats were lashed together to form temporary ferries or large transports.

To help with the constant flow of government travelers, way stations (every 10 to 15 miles in the Persian Empire) and administrative outposts were constructed. In a time before inns, these stations provided supplies to traveling officials and fresh mounts to couriers. The private traveler had to rely on the hospitality of towns or friends along the way (Judg. 19:10-15; 2 Kings 4:8).

The Bible mentions several different types of draft animals: donkeys, mules, camels, and oxen. Donkeys appear to have been the most popular means of transport in the Near East (Gen. 42:26; 1 Sam. 16:20; Neh. 13:15). Mules are less commonly mentioned, perhaps due to a shortage of horses for breeding or to a custom restricting the use of mules to the upper classes (2 Sam. 13:29; compare 2 Sam. 18:9; 1 Kings 1:33). Isaiah 66:20 pictures an extraordinary caravan of returning exiles riding on horses, mules, and dromedaries, as well as in chariots and litters. Camels appear (2 Kings 8:9; Isa. 30:6) carrying huge loads (five times that of a donkey). These beasts were probably used only on the major routes such as the Via Maris, along the coast, or on the smoother valley roads of the Shephelah and the Negev.

Oxen are exclusively associated with travel by wheeled vehicle. Israelite use of horses does not appear before David began to incorporate them into his forces (2 Sam. 8:3-4). They are mentioned primarily in military contexts (Job 39:18-25; 1 Kings 12:18). Official messengers rode horses (2 Kings 9:18-19), as did scouts for the army (2 Kings 7:13-15).

The most commonly mentioned wheeled vehicle is the chariot, used first by Israel's enemies during the conquest period (Judg. 1:19; 4:3). It could not be used effectively in the rough hill country where the tribes first settled (Josh. 17:16). Chariots became an integral part of the kings' battle strategy (1 Kings 10:26; 22:31-34) and a standard means of travel by kings (2 Kings 9:16) and nobles (2 Kings 5:9; compare Isa. 22:18; 8:26-38). A three-man Judean battle chariot with a yoke for four horses is depicted in the Assyrian relief (about 701 B.C.) of Sennacherib's siege of Lachish.

Large two- and four-wheeled carts and wagons were commonly used in biblical times for transporting heavy loads and people (Gen. 45:19-27; Num. 7:1-8). Carts were an everyday aid to farmers who had to transport sheaves of grain to the threshing floor (Amos 2:13; compare 2 Sam. 6:2-17). Several men walked beside the cart to guide the oxen and prevent the cargo from shifting.

The broader roads and heavy wheeled vehicles were used to transport the people into exile. Sennacherib's stone relief of his siege of Lachish includes a picture of Judeans being taken away in two-wheeled carts drawn by a team of oxen. The new exiles sit atop bundles containing their belongings while a man walks alongside the left-hand ox guiding it with a sharpened stick. See *Animals; Economic Life.*

TREASURE, TREASURY

What one values whether silver and gold or something intangible; storage place of what is valuable; in king's palace (2 Kings 20:13) or temple (1 Kings 7:51); 13 trumpet-shaped offering receptacles in the temple court of the women (Mark 12:41). Israel was God's treasure (Ex. 19:5; compare 1 Pet. 2:9). A person's memory is a treasure (Prov. 2:1; 7:1). Fear (awe) of the Lord was Israel's treasure (Isa. 33:6).

Jesus contrasted earthly treasures to those of heaven (Matt. 6:19-20). What a person treasures or values determines one's loyalty and priorities (Matt. 6:21). The treasure of God's revelation of Himself in Christ was deposited in an earthen vessel such as Paul himself (2 Cor. 4:7). See *Temple of Jerusalem.*

TREATY See *Covenant.*

TREE OF KNOWLEDGE

Plant in midst of garden of Eden used to prove the first couple's loyalty to the Creator (Gen. 2–3); eating from the tree brought knowledge of good and evil (Gen. 3:5,22); only tree in garden forbidden to humankind under the penalty of death (Gen. 2:17). The tree of knowledge was Adam and Eve's opportunity to demonstrate obedience and loyalty to God, but the serpent used it to tempt Eve to eat and to become like God "knowing good and evil" (Gen. 3:5). Eating the forbidden fruit resulted in shame, guilt, exclusion from the garden, and separation

from the tree of life and from God. See *Adam and Eve; Eden; Tree of Life.*

TREE OF LIFE

Plant in garden of Eden symbolizing access to eternal life; metaphor used in Proverbs. Adam and Eve's relationship to God changed radically when they sinned; chief of which was that they no longer had access to the tree of life (Gen. 3:22-24; compare Rev. 2:7; 22:2,14).

"A tree of life"is to lay hold on wisdom (Prov. 3:18), "the fruit of the righteous"(11:30), when a desire is fulfilled (13:12), and "a wholesome tongue" (15:4). See *Adam and Eve; Eden; Tree of Knowledge.*

TRIAL OF JESUS

Jewish and Roman legal processes that led to Jesus' crucifixion. Two systems of justice combined to produce a sentence of death for Jesus. Jewish religious leaders accused Jesus of blasphemy, a capital offense under Jewish law (see Lev. 24:16). The Jewish leaders at Jesus' trial manipulated procedures to coerce Jesus into an admission that He was God's Son (see Luke 22:66-71). For them this constituted blasphemy.

The Romans did not give the Jews the right of capital punishment for blasphemy. The Jews had to convince a Roman judge that their demand for capital punishment was justified. Jewish leaders held the Jewish trial at night, hoping Jesus' supporters would be asleep and unable to protest his arrest. The Jewish portion of the trial had three separate phases:

(1) an appearance before Annas;

(2) an informal investigation by Caiaphas in his residence and

(3) a condemnation by the Sanhedrin.

Annas, father-in-law of the high priest Caiaphas and most influential member of the Sanhedrin, had been high priest (A.D. 7–15). The high priest mentioned in John 18:19 may have been Annas. If so, he held a brief interrogation of Jesus and sent Him to his son-in-law Caiaphas (John 18:24).

For the meeting with Caiaphas (Luke 22:54) members of the Sanhedrin worked frantically to locate and train witnesses against Jesus (Matt. 26:59-60). The carefully prepared witnesses could not agree in their testimony (see Mark 14:56; compare Deut. 19:15). Caiaphas put Jesus under oath (Matt. 26:63-64); demanding to know if He were God's Son. Jesus affirmed He was (Mark 14:62). The Sanhedrin condemned Him but did not pronounce a sentence (Mark 14:64). Some began to slap and spit upon Jesus (Mark 14:65).

Shortly after dawn the Sanhedrin met to condemn Jesus formally (Luke 22:66). Jewish law stipulated that a guilty verdict in a capital crime had to be delayed until the next day. No witnesses came forward to accuse Christ. Jesus again claimed that He was God's Son (Luke 22:66-71). The Sanhedrin again approved the death sentence and took Jesus to Pilate for sentencing (Luke 23:1).

The procedures of the Jewish leaders during Jesus' trial were illegal; capital crimes could not be tried at night; judges were to be impartial; could not convict Him.

The Roman trial of Jesus also had three phases:

(1) first appearance before Pilate;

(2) appearance before Herod Antipas;

(3) second appearance before Pilate.

The Jews asked Pilate to accept their verdict against Jesus without investigation (John 18:29-31). Pilate refused this, but he offered to let them carry out the maximum punishment under their law, probably beating with rods or imprisonment. They insisted that they wanted death.

The Jews fabricated three additional charges against Jesus (Luke 23:2). Pilate concerned himself only with the charge of treason that Jesus had claimed to be a king. Pilate decided He was no political rival to Caesar, and hence not deserving of death (John 18:33-38). The Jews responded with vehement accusations against Jesus' actions in Judea and Galilee (Luke 23:5). Learning

Jesus was from Galilee, Pilate sent Him to Herod Antipas of Galilee (Luke 23:6-12). Herod wanted Jesus to entertain him with a miracle. Jesus did not even speak a word to Herod. The king and his soldiers mocked and ridiculed Jesus, finally sending Him back to Pilate.

The Roman governor announced that he still found Jesus innocent of charges of treason. Three times Pilate tried to release Jesus offering:

(1) to chastise or beat Jesus and then release Him (Luke 23:16);

(2) to release either Jesus or Barabbas; the crowd chanted for Barabbas' release (Luke 23:17-19);

(3) to scourge Jesus.

Pilate then presented the bleeding Jesus with a crown of thorns and a mock purple robe to the crowd as their king. He hoped this spectacle would lead them to release Jesus out of pity. Again they chanted for crucifixion (John 19:4-6). The Jews threatened to report his conduct to Caesar (John 19:12). After symbolically washing his hands of the entire affair (Matt. 27:24), he delivered Jesus for crucifixion (John 19:16). See *Annas; Caiaphas; Pontius Pilate; Roman Law; Sanhedrin.*

TRIBES OF ISRAEL

Social and political groups in Israel claiming descent from one of 12 sons of Jacob. The "tribe," a *shebet* or *matteh*, was the major social unit that comprised the makeup of the nation. The tribe was comprised of "clans," a *mishpachah* or family of families or a cluster of households that had a common ancestry. The clan was comprised then of the individual households or families referred to as the "father's house," (Num. 3:24). See *Family.*

The family of Jacob (Israel), from which the tribes came, originated in north Syria during Jacob's stay at Haran with Laban his uncle. Eleven of the 12 sons were born at Haran, while the twelfth, Benjamin was born after Jacob returned to Canaan. The birth of the sons came through Jacob's wives Leah (Reuben, Simeon, Levi, Judah—Gen. 29:31-35—and Issachar and Zebulun, as well as one daughter Dinah—Gen. 30:19-21) and Rachel (Joseph—Gen. 30:22-24—who became the father of Ephraim and Manasseh — Gen. 41:50-52 — and Benjamin—Gen. 35:16-18); and their maids Zilpah (Gad and Asher—Gen. 30:9-13), and Bilhah (Dan and Naphtali—Gen. 30:1-8). Other groups—"a mixed multitude" (Ex. 12:38)—were perhaps incorporated into the nation. Some of the major lists of tribes include that of Jacob's blessing of the 12 (Gen. 49), the review of the households oppressed in Egypt (Ex. 1:1-10), Moses' blessing of the tribes (Deut. 33), and the song of Deborah (Judg. 5). We know few details about the individual tribes:

(1) *Reuben* forfeited his family leadership role because of an illicit affair he had with his father's concubine Bilhah (Gen. 35:22; compare Gen. 49:4). When Jacob's family went to Egypt, Reuben had four sons (Gen. 46:8-9). Reuben occupied the southern region east of the Jordan River extending roughly from the Arnon river to the site of Heshbon (Josh. 13:15-23). Apparently, the tribe was criticized for not taking a more active role in the conquest (Judg. 5:15-16). See *Transjordan.*

(2) *Simeon* played a key role with Levi in seeking vengeance for their sister Dinah's encounter with Shechem (Gen. 34: 1-4,25-26; compare 49:5-7). Simeon was held hostage by Joseph at one point (Gen. 42:24). Simeon seems to be characterized by weakness (Gen. 49:7) and did not receive a separate inheritance (Josh. 19:1-9).

(3) *Levi* was involved with Simeon in the Dinah affair. In the wilderness the sons of Levi slaughtered 3,000 rebellious Hebrew males (Ex. 32:25-29). They became the landless priestly tribe (Josh. 21). See *Levites; Priests.*

(4) *Judah*, a leader and a spokesman among his brothers (Gen. 37:26; 43:3; 44:16; compare 46:28) and was promised preeminence over the other tribes (Gen. 49:8-12; compare Num. 2:9). Judah occupied the southern part of Palestine between Dead Sea and Mediterranean (Josh. 15) north

to the territories of Benjamin and Dan. Judah constituted the major portion of the Southern Kingdom.

(5) *Issachar* faced a variety of hardships (Gen. 49:14-15). Their territory is difficult to outline precisely (Josh. 19:17-23), west of the Jordan just south of the Sea of Galilee stretching down to the Valley of Jezreel. With Zebulun (Deut. 33:19) they may have had a center of worship on Mount Tabor. Issachar may have served as slaves in forced labor projects of their neighbors, the Canaanites.

(6) *Zebulun* lived in southern Galilee bounded by Issachar on the south southeast, Naphtali on the east, and Asher on the west (Josh. 19:10-16), apparently at some time having access to the Mediterranean Sea near Sidon (Gen. 49:13; compare Deut. 33:19). Zebulun apparently went beyond the call of duty in providing support, being the only tribe mentioned twice in the Song of Deborah (Judg. 5:14,18).

(7) *Joseph.* Two of the tribes of Israel came from Joseph, namely his sons, Ephraim and Manasseh (Gen. 41:50-52) whom Jacob adopted (48:8-20). See *Joseph; Machir.* While Manasseh was the older, Jacob gave preference to Ephraim (v. 14; compare Deut. 33:17).

(a) *Ephraim* occupied the region just north of Dan and Benjamin from the Jordan River to the Mediterranean Sea. Joshua (Num. 13:8,16; Josh. 1:1-11); Samuel (1 Sam. 7:15-17); Jeroboam I (1 Kings 12:1-20) came from Ephraim. Ephraim demanded leadership in the period of the judges (Judg. 3:27; 4:5; 7:24; 8:1; 10:1; 12:1-6; 17:1; 18:2,13; 19:1). Shiloh, located in Ephraim, became the major center of worship during the tribal period (Josh. 18:1; 1 Sam. 1:1-18). Hosea used Ephraim as a synonym for Israel as the name of the Northern Kingdom.

(b) *Manasseh* occupied territory both east and west of the Jordan River: in the east, Gilead and Bashan, most likely extending from the Jabbok River to near Mount Hermon (Num. 32:39,41-42; Judg. 5:14); in the west, north of Ephraim. Gideon is the most familiar descendant of Manasseh (Judg. 6–7).

(8) *Benjamin* formed a special group with Ephraim and Manasseh. Benjamin's small territory was sandwiched between Ephraim to the north and Judah to the south (Josh. 18:11-28). The Benjaminites had a reputation as men of war (Gen. 49:27; Judg. 5:14; 20:12-16); responsible for inhumane acts (Judg. 19).The second judge, Ehud (Judg. 3:12-30), and the first king, Saul (1 Sam. 9:15-17; 10:1), came from Benjamin.

(9) *Dan* and his full-blooded brother Naphtali are often mentioned together (Gen. 46:23-24; Ex. 1:4). Dan originally occupied territory just west of Benjamin with Ephraim on the north and Judah and the Philistines on the south (Josh. 19:40-48). Amorites and the Philistines (Judg. 1:34-36; compare Judg. 13–16) forced Dan to migrate north of Lake Hula, to Laish (renamed Dan) and its territory (Judg. 18:14-29). It became a cult center of the Northern Kingdom. See *Dan.*

(10) *Naphtali* occupied the broad strip of land west of the Jordan in the area of Lake Hula and the Sea of Chinnereth (Galilee) running from Issachar and Zebulun in the south to near Dan in the north (Josh. 19:32-39). Naphtali provided forces during the conquest of the land (Judg. 5:18) and during the Midianite threat (Judg. 6:35; 7:23).

(11) *Gad* had territory east of the Jordan River and the Dead Sea, including a part of the region called Gilead (Num. 32:34-36; Josh. 13:24-28), extending from the Jabbok River in the north to the Arnon River in the south, some of the best land in the Transjordan (Deut. 33:20-21). Gad perhaps experienced numerous raids (Gen. 49:19) especially from groups like the Ammonites as reflected in the story of Jephthah (Judg. 11). Apparently the men of Gad achieved great expertise as warriors (1 Chron. 12:8).

(12) *Asher* occupied the choice region (Gen. 49:20) west of Zebulun and Naphtali, the northern coastal region of Palestine from near Mount Carmel in the south to near Tyre in the north (Josh. 19:24-31). Asher is the only tribe not recognized as providing a judge during the tribal period. Asher apparently was reproached and failed to gain the respect of some of the other tribes (Judg. 5:17b).

Tribal ties and traditions continued to be quite strong. Many scholars suggest that tribal jealousies and traditions played a major role in bringing about the division of the kingdom in 922 B.C.

TRIBULATION

Trouble or pressure of a general sort; a particular time of suffering associated with events of the end-time (Matt. 24:21). "The great tribulation" (Rev. 7:14, NIV) is seen by some (amillennialism) to refer historically to persecution faced by Christians after A.D. 90 but also symbolic of tribulation that occurs periodically throughout history. Others (premillennialism) refer the great tribulation to an end-time period. Dispensational premillennialism connects such a seven-year tribulation with the seventieth week of a prophetic framework taken from Dan. 9:24-27. A distinction is usually made between the two halves of the seven years.The last half, often called the Great Tribulation, is measured variously as three and a half years (Dan. 9:27), forty-two months (Rev. 11:2; 13:5), 1,260 days (Rev. 11:3; 12:6), or"a time, and times, and half a time" (Rev. 12:14). Distinctive to this view is the teaching the church will be raptured at the beginning of the tribulation period. Historic premillennialism sees the period as a future time of intense trouble on earth prior to Christ's return, but holds the church will go through the tribulation but not experience God's wrath. See *Dispensation; Eschatology; Millennium; Rapture; Revelation of Jesus Christ; Seventy Weeks.*

TRIBUTE   See *Taxes.*

TRINITY

Theological term used to define God as an undivided unity expressed in the threefold nature of God the Father, God the Son, and God the Holy Spirit. God is manifested through Jesus Christ by means of the Spirit.

Two errors that appear in the doctrine's history: tritheism and unitarianism. In tritheism, error is made in emphasizing the distinctiveness of the Godhead to the point that the Trinity is seen as three separate Gods. Unitarianism excludes the concept of distinctiveness, focusing solely on the unity of God the Father, making Christ and the Holy Spirit less than divine.

The OT (Deut. 6:4; see *Shema*) stressed God's oneness to caution the Israelites against the polytheism and practical atheism of their heathen neighbors. The word of God is recognized as the agent of creation (Ps. 33:6,9; compare Prov. 3:19; 8:27), revelation, and salvation (Ps. 107:20), vocabulary given distinct personality in John's prologue (John 1:1-4) in Jesus Christ. Other vocabulary categories include the wisdom of God (Prov. 8) and the Spirit of God (Gen. 1:2; Ps. 104:30; Zech. 4:6).

New Testament writers unanimously affirm the Hebrew monothestic faith, but they extend it to include the coming of Jesus and the outpouring of the Holy Spirit. The NT evidence for the Trinity can be grouped into four types of passages. The first is the trinitarian formula of Matt. 28:19; 2 Cor. 13:14; 1 Pet. 1:2; Rev. 1:4.

Triadic form (Eph. 4:4-6; 1 Cor. 12:3-6). Emphasis is placed on the administration of gifts by the Godhead.

Mention of the three persons of the Godhead without a clear triadic structure. In the baptism of Jesus (Matt. 3:3-17; Mark 1:9-11; Luke 3:21-22), the Son was baptized, the Spirit descended, and the Father spoke with approval. Paul, in Gal. 4:4-6, outlined the work of the Trinity in the aspect of the sending Father. Other representative passages in this category (2 Thess. 2:13-15; Titus 3:4-6; and Jude 20-21) portray each member of the Trinity in relation to a particular redemptive function.

The farewell discourse of Jesus to His disciples (John 14:16; 15:26; 16:13-15). Jesus explained the work and ministry of the Spirit as the agent of God in the continuing ministry of the Son.

The NT is Christological in its approach, but it involves the fullness of God being made available to the individual believer through Jesus and by the Spirit. In the postbiblical era, discussion shifted from the NT emphasis on the function of the Trinity in redemptive history to an analysis of the unity of essence of the Godhead.

Perhaps four statements can summarize and clarify this study.

(1) *God is One.* The God of the OT is the same God of the NT.

(2) *God has three distinct ways of being in the redemptive event, yet He remains an undivided unity.*

(3) *The primary way of grasping the concept of the Trinity is through the threefold participation in salvation.*

(4) *The doctrine of the Trinity is an absolute mystery.* It is primarily known, not through speculation, but through experiencing the act of grace through personal faith. See *God; Jesus; Holy Spirit.*

TROAS See *Asia Minor, Cities of; Paul.*

TROPHIMUS (*nutritious*)

Gentile Christian from Ephesus who accompanied Paul to Jerusalem for presentation of collection (Acts 20:4-5; 21:29). Paul's free association with Trophimus led to the false charge that Paul had defiled the temple by bringing a Gentile within the Court of Israel (Acts 21:19). The "Trophimus" whom Paul left in Miletus (2 Tim. 4:20) is either another Trophimus or else evidence for a second Roman imprisonment.

TRUTH

That which is reliable and can be trusted; actual fact over against appearance, pretense, or assertion (Zech. 8:16; Mark 5:32-33); correct knowledge or doctrine (1 Tim. 4:3; 2 Tim. 2:18). The essential idea of truth in the Bible is faithfulness or reliability. God is the standard. God's truth (faithfulness or reliability) is basic for all other truth (Deut. 7:9-10). He maintains covenant and steadfast love. He is reliable (Deut. 32:4; 2 Chron. 15:3; Isa. 65:16; Jer. 10:10). God "keepth truth for ever" (Ps. 146:6). The Word of God and His law are true because of God's nature as truth (faithfulness) in what He did in creation, election, redemption, and the giving of the law (Neh. 9:13-14; compare 1 Sam. 12:24; Rom. 3:1-7).

Truth and sincerity are opposed to malice and evil (1 Cor. 5:8). Truth is to be obeyed (Rom. 2:8; Gal. 5:7). The truth of God is revealed not so much in the law as in Christ (Rom. 15:8-9; compare Rom. 1:1-6; 16:25-26; 2 Cor. 4:6; Gal. 2:5,14). One hears and believes the truth and is in Christ (Eph. 1:13).

Christ is the truth (John 1:17-18; 18:37). Since Christ shares in the truth of God, He is full of grace and truth. He is "the way, the truth, and the life" (John 14:6). The activity of the Holy Spirit is associated with the activity of Jesus in so far as truth is concerned (John 15:26-27).

Disciples must appropriate the truth (John 17:17-19). Followers of Christ are of "the truth" (John 18:37). This knowledge of truth is not simply "head knowledge." It is a matter of receiving Christ (John 1:11-13). This acceptance of Jesus and receiving of the truth is accompanied by "walking in the truth" or in the light (2 John 4; 3 John 3-4; 1 John 1:7), doing the truth (John 3:21; 1 John 1:6).

TRYPHAENA; TRYPHOSA (*dainty* and *delicate*)

Two women Paul greeted as "workers in the Lord" (Rom. 16:12).

TUBAL

Son of Jepheth (Gen. 10:2; 1 Chron. 1:5) and ancestor of a people, known for their metalworking ability, likely

of Cappadocia or Cilicia in Asia Minor (Isa. 66:19; Ezek. 27:13; 32:26; 38:2-3; 39:1).

TUBAL-CAIN (*producer* and *smith*)

Son of Lamech, associated with the origin of metalworking (Gen. 4:22).

TUNIC

Loose-fitting, knee-length garment worn next to the skin (Matt. 10:10; Mark 6:9). See *Cloth, Clothing.*

TURBAN

Headdress formed by wrapping long strips of cloth around the head. A distinctive headdress formed part of the garb of the high priest (Ex. 28:4,37,39; 29:6; 39:28,31; Lev. 8:9; 16:4). Removal of one's turban was a sign of mourning or shame (Isa. 3:18-23; Ezek. 24:17, 23). See *Cloth, Clothing.*

TURNING OF THE WALL

KJV for "corner butress" (NASB), "angle" (NRSV), "escarpment" (REB), and "angle of the wall" (NIV). One segment of the Jerusalem ramparts, probably near the palace, fortified by Uzziah (2 Chron. 26:9) and rebuilt by Nehemiah (Neh. 3:19-20,24).

TURQUOISE See *Minerals and Metals.*

TURTLEDOVE See *Birds.*

TWELVE, THE See *Disciples, Apostles.*

TYCHICUS (*fortunate*)

One of Paul's fellow workers on third missionary journey; native of Asia Minor (Acts 20:4). Tychicus and Onesimus carried the Colossian letter from Paul (Col. 4:7-9) and were to relate to the church Paul's condition. Paul also sent Tychicus to Ephesus (2 Tim. 4:12) and possibly to Crete (Titus 3:12).

TYPOLOGY

Method of interpreting some parts of Scripture by seeing a pattern which an earlier statement sets up and by which a later pattern is explained. Typology involves a *correspondence*, usually in *one* particular matter, between a person, event, or thing in the OT with a person, event, or thing, in the NT.

(1) *Old Testament warnings*. Paul (1 Cor. 10:1-11) rehearsed the experiences of the people of Israel in the exodus and in their 40 years in the desert. All the people participated in these experiences, but God was not pleased with most of them who died in the desert (1 Cor. 10:5).The majority were *types* or warning patterns for Christians (1 Cor. 10:6).

(2) *Adam as a type of Christ*. Paul compared Adam and Christ (Rom. 5:12-21). He argued that Christ's deed is much more powerful than Adam's transgression.The one point of correspondence in the passage is *the effect of influence* upon humankind. Adam affected humankind adversely; Christ affects the same humankind for good (vv. 16,18).

(3) *Baptism as a fulfillment of the type*. Peter (1 Pet. 3:20-21) showed baptism is a drama of faith—an acted-out pledge of a good conscience. The flood was a type of baptism because people of faith experienced deliverance.

Typology, a comparison stressing one point of similarity, helps us see the NT person, event, or institution as the fulfillment of that which was only hinted at in the OT.

TYRANNUS *(ruler with absolute authority)*

Either owner of hall or a prominent philosopher associated with hall where Paul preached for two years after he withdrew from the synagogue in Ephesus (Acts 19:9).

TYRE, TYRIAN See *Sidon and Tyre*.

U

UCAL (*I am strong* or *I am consumed*)

Pupil of Agur, wisdom teacher responsible for Prov. 30 (v. 1). REB followed Septuagint in rendering proper names "Ithiel and Ucal" as "I am weary, God, I am weary and worn out" (compare NRSV).

UGARIT

Important city on Mediterranean coast about nine miles north of Latakia in Syria whose excavation has provided tablets giving the closest primary evidence available for reconstructing the Canaanite religion Israel faced; contemporary name is Ras Shamra. Located at the juncture of major trade routes from Anatolia, northwest Mesopotamia, and Egypt and possessing a harbor (modern Minet el-Beida) which accommodated vessels from Cyprus, the Aegean, and Egypt, Ugarit was an important commercial center in most periods. Sea peoples destroyed the city shortly after 1200 B.C.

The Late Bronze city of Ugarit covered about 70 acres and contained temples dedicated to Baal and El. Clay tablets and other inscriptions representing eight languages have come to light. Religious tests include the Bel-Anath cycle, Legend of King Keret, Legend of Aqhat, and others. See *Canaan, History and Religon of; Fertility Cult.*

The Ugaritic texts have provided a welcome resource for clarifying the meanings and nuances of unknown and obscure words and phrases in the OT, understanding poetic and literary structure, identifying names of gods, learning about Canaanite religion and ritual.

ULAI

Canal connecting the Kerkha and Abdizful rivers just north of Susa (Dan. 8:2,16).

UNCIRCUMCISED See *Circumcision.*

UNCTION

KJV for anointing (1 John 2:20,27). See *Anoint.*

UNDEFILED

Ritually clean, frequently used for moral cleanness. See *Clean, Cleanness.*

UNICORN

KJV translation of several related Hebrew terms that modern translations render as "wild ox" (Num. 23:22; 24:8; Deut. 33:17).

UNITY

State of being undivided; oneness. Central to the faith of Israel is the confession of the unity of God: "Hear, O Israel: The Lord Your God is one Lord" (Deut. 6:4). Because God is one, one set of laws was to apply to both Israelites and foreigners (Num. 15:16). Human history is a story of sin's disruption of God's ordained unity. God's ideal for marriage is for husband and wife to experience unity of life, "one flesh" (Gen. 2:24). Stubbornness of will ("hardness" of heart, Mark 10:5) continues to disrupt God's desired unity in marriage (Gen. 3:12). God's ideal for the larger human family is again unity. The primeval unity of humanity ("one language," Gen. 11:1) was likewise disrupted as a result of sinful pride (11:4-8). The prophetic vision of God's future anticipated the day when God will reunite the divided kingdoms of Israel and Judah, bringing back all the scattered exiles (Ezek. 37:15-23). Indeed, the prophetic hope includes the reuniting of all the peoples of the world under the sovereignty of the one Lord (Zech. 14:9).

Jesus prayed that His disciples would experience unity modeled on the unity Jesus experienced with the Father (John 17:11,21-23). The first believers were together in one place; they shared their possessions and were of one heart and soul (Acts 2:1,43; 4:32). The selfishness of Ananias and

Sapphira (Acts 5:1-11), the prejudice of those who neglected the Greek-speaking widows (6:1), the rigidness of those who demanded that Gentiles become Jews before becoming disciples (15:1)—all threatened the unity of the church. The Holy Spirit led the church in working out creative solutions that challenged the church to go beyond dissension to ministry (Acts 6:2-7; 15:6-35). Believers are "one body in Christ" which transcends varieties of giftedness (Rom. 12:5-8; 1 Cor. 12:13,27-30) and human labels (Gal. 3:28; Eph. 2:14-15; 3:6). The unity of the church reflects the unity of the Godhead: one God (1 Cor. 12:6); one Lord (Rom. 10:12; 1 Cor. 12:5; Eph. 4:5); and one Spirit (1 Cor. 12:4,11; also Acts 11:17). Christian unity has various aspects: the shared experience of Christ as Lord and confession of Christ in baptism (Eph. 4:5,13); the shared sense of mission ("one mind," Phil. 2:2); the shared concern for one another (1 Cor. 12:25; "same love," Phil. 2:2; 1 Pet. 3:8); and the shared experience of suffering for Jesus' sake (2 Cor. 1:6; Phil. 1:29-30; 1 Thess. 2:14; 1 Pet. 5:9).

UNLEAVENED BREAD

Bread baked without using leaven; often served to guests (Gen. 19:3; Judg. 6:19; 1 Sam. 28:24). Eating unleavened bread took on special significance through the Feast of Unleavened Bread celebrated in connection with Passover (Ex. 12:8,15,20; 13:3,6-7). See *Exodus; Festivals; Passover.*

UNPARDONABLE SIN, THE

Setting one's mind against the Holy Spirit and crediting Satan with what is obviously God's work (Matt. 12:31-32).

The unpardonable sin is a persistent and deliberate sin maintained in the face of the Holy Spirit. It happens when a person sees a work that is without question God's work and not human work, but says it is Satan's work! The unpardonable sin is committed today when one tells the Spirit that He is trying to do something evil in the person's life by pointing one to

Jesus. See *Blasphemy; Devil; Holy Spirit; Sin.*

UPHARSIN See *Mene, Mene, Tekel, Upharsin.*

UPHAZ

Unidentified source of fine gold (Jer. 10:9; Dan. 10:5) or else term for fine gold; related Hebrew term is translated "best gold" (1 Kings 10:18; Isa. 13:12). Possibly a copyist's change for Ophir at Jer. 10:9 as indicated by early versions.

UPPER CHAMBER, UPPER ROOM

Upstairs room chosen by Jesus for final meal with His disciples before His arrest (Mark 14:14-15).

UR *(fire oven)*

Ancient city in lower Mesopotamia with harbor facilities on the Euphrates River, Abraham's birthplace (Gen. 12:1; Acts 7:2); tell el-Muqayyar some 350 km (220 mi) southeast of Baghdad.

URIAH *(fire of Yah)*

(1) Hittite mercenary, or a native, perhaps noble Israelite of Hittite ancestry, in David's army (2 Sam. 11); member of David's elite warriors (23:39); husband of Bathsheba, the woman with whom David committed adultery, leading to murder of Uriah after the king could cover the affair no longer.

(2) High priest in Jerusalem temple under King Ahaz who followed the king's instructions in setting up an altar in the temple according to a Syrian pattern (2 Kings 16:10-16; compare Isa. 8:2).

(3) Priest in time of Ezra and Nehemiah (Ezra 8:33; Neh. 3:4,21).

(4) Person who helped Ezra in informing the people of God's word (Neh. 8:4).

URIJAH *(flame of Yahweh)*

Variant spelling of Uriah.

(1) See *Uriah 2.*

(2) Prophet who joined Jeremiah in preaching against Jerusalem. When king Jehoiakim ordered his execution, Urijah fled to Egypt. He was captured, returned to Jerusalem, and executed (Jer. 26:20-23).

URIM AND THUMMIM

Objects Israel, and especially the high priest, used to determine God's will; kept by high priest in a "breastplate of judgment" (Ex. 28:15-30; see Num. 27:18-23; 1 Sam. 14:41-45). Later, Moses gave Levi special responsibility for their care (Deut. 33:8). They apparently were two objects that served as sacred lots. They were "given," perhaps drawn or shaken from a bag. One object gave one answer. The other lot gave another answer. Probably, whichever lot came out first was understood to be God's answer. God could refuse to answer (1 Sam. 28:6-25). Expectation continued that someday a priest would arise with Urim and Thummim (Ezra 2:63; Neh. 7:65).

USURY

Sum of money charged for a loan. See *Loan.*

UZZIA(H) (*Yahweh is might*)

(1) Descendant of Levi (1 Chron. 6:24).

(2) Father of one of David's treasurers (1 Chron. 27:25).

(3) Son and successor of King Amaziah of Judah (see 2 Kings 14:21; 15:1,6-8,17,23,27; 2 Chron. 26:1). Uzziah's reign was a time of great material prosperity for Judah (2 Chron. 26:1-23). Uzziah's prideful attempt to usurp the priestly prerogative of offering incense in the temple brought divine punishment. Uzziah became a leper (2 Chron. 26:16-20; compare Num. 16:1-40; 1 Sam. 13:8-15). His son Jotham reigned in his stead, though Uzziah likely remained the power behind the throne (26:21).

(4) Postexilic priest with a foreign wife (Ezra 10:21).

(5) Descendant of Judah and father of a postexilic resident of Jerusalem (Neh. 11:4).

V

VAIN

Self-conceit, usually translation of words meaning "nothingness" or "unreliability." Trying to thwart God's will (Ps. 2:1; see Acts 4:25) or do things without God's help (Ps. 127:1) is vain. You are not to take God's name in vain (as though it were nothing) (Ex. 20: 7; Deut. 5:11). Believers are not to give God vain lip service but obedience from the heart (Mark 7:6-7; see Isa. 1:13; 29:13; Jas. 1:26).

VALLEY

Depression or long, broad sweep between parallel ranges of hills (Num. 14:25; Josh. 8:13; Jer. 21:13); broad plain (Gen. 11:2; Isa. 41:8) or plateau; narrow, deep ravine (Isa. 40:4; Zech. 14:4); wadi or bed of stream that is often dry (Num. 34:5; Ps. 124:4; Ezek. 48:28); low land, plain, or slope sweeping gently down from mountains (Deut. 10:1; Josh. 9:1; Jer. 17:26). God is present with His people, protecting them as they pass through life's valleys (Ps. 23:4). See *Palestine*.

VALLEY OF ZERED See *Zered.*

VASHTI (*the once desired, the beloved*)

Wife of King Ahasuerus and queen of Persia and Media (Esther 1:9) who refused to show off her beauty and was deposed as queen (1:19). See *Ahasuerus; Esther; Persia; Xerxes.*

VEIL

KJV, "vail"; cloth covering.

(1) *Women's veils.* Rebecca veiled herself before meeting Isaac (Gen. 24:65). Her veil was perhaps the sign that she was a marriageable maiden. Tamar used her veil to conceal her identity from Judah (Gen. 38:14,19). Item of finery elite women of Jerusalem would lose in coming siege (Isa. 3:23; same Hebrew term rendered, "shawl," NASB; "cloak," NIV, REB; and "mantle," KJV, NRSV at Song of Sol. 5:7, where removal of shawl was part of humiliat-

ing assault on king's beloved; compare Isa. 47:2). Paul commanded wearing of veils for women praying or preaching ("prophesying") in public (1 Cor. 11:4-16).

(2) *Moses' veil.* Material Moses used to protect people from glow of his face (Ex. 34:33-35). Moses' practice illustrated the superiority of the new covenant (2 Cor. 3:7-11) and the mental barrier preventing Israel from recognizing Christ in the OT (3:12-18).

(3) *Imagery.* The "vail (KJV) that is spread over all nations" (Isa. 25:7) is likely an image for death which is also swallowed up (25:8).

(4) *Temple veil.* This curtain separated the most holy place from the holy place (2 Chron. 3:14; compare Lev. 16:2). At Jesus' death the temple veil was ripped from top to bottom. In Christ God had abolished the barrier separating humanity from the presence of God (Matt. 27:51; Mark 15:38; compare Luke 23:45; Heb. 10:20). See *Temple of Jerusalem.*

VENGEANCE

Demonstration and restoration of solidarity and integrity of community damaged by an offense through deed of retaliation or punishment. See Gen. 4:23-24; Judg. 15:7; Jer. 20:10. Vengeance might be punishment directed toward another who has committed adultery with one's wife (Prov. 6:32-34) or toward a whole ethnic group (1 Sam. 18:25). Enemies of the people of God are described as acting vengefully (Ezek. 25:12,15,17). In the context of loving one's neighbor, human revenge toward fellow Hebrews was forbidden (Lev. 19:17-18; compare Deut. 32:35; Rom. 12:19; 1 Thess. 4:6-7; Heb. 10:30); but it may be used of legitimate punishment for a wrong (Ex. 21:20; compare Ex. 21:23-25; Lev. 24:19; Deut. 19:21).

God's act for His people—retribution and/or deliverance (Deut. 32:35,41,43; Judg. 11:36; compare 2 Sam. 4:48; 22:48; Pss. 18:47; 58:10; 79:10; 94:1; Jer. 11:20; 15:15; 20:12;

Rev. 6:10; 19:2). God exhibited His wrath toward Babylon (Jer. 51:6,11,36; Isa. 47:3; Ezek. 24:7-9) and toward Israel because of their sin (Lev. 26:25). Such divine vengeance against enemies may point to Israel's eschatological deliverance (Isa. 34:8; see "day of vengeance" and "year of my redemption,"61:1-3; 63:4; Luke 21:22; Acts 7:24; 2 Thess. 1:7-8; compare Isa. 66:15; Ps. 79:6).

A widow's persistent request for vindication from her enemy is a worst-case model of God's vindication ("deliverance") of His people (Luke 18:1-8). Paul used vengeance as "punishment" to bring about repentance (2 Cor. 7:10-11; 10:5-6). The ruler of a state is a servant of God, "a revenger to execute wrath upon him who doeth evil" (Rom. 13:4; see 1 Pet. 2:14). See *Avenger; Wrath.*

VENISON

Flesh of wild animal taken by hunting (Gen. 25:28; "game," NASB, NRSV; "wild game," NIV).

VENOM

Poisonous secretion from an animal such as a snake, spider, or scorpion released into its victim by a bite or sting (Deut. 32:33; Job 20:16); also used for dangerous, poisonous plant (Deut. 29:18; Hos. 10:4). See *Poison.*

VESPASIAN See *Rome and the Roman Empire.*

VESSELS AND UTENSILS

Implements or containers ordinarily used in temple service or household activities. Vessels are utensils designed to hold dry or liquid products.

Cups and goblets of precious metals were made by silversmiths and goldsmiths for religious service (Num. 7:13,19; 1 Chron. 28:17; 2 Chron. 4:8; Ezra 1:9-10; 8:27) or for persons of great wealth or authority (Gen. 44:2). Copper and bronze (Ex. 27:3; Lev. 6:28) vessels were also known.

Alabaster was easily carved and polished and especially prized for storage of perfumes (Matt. 26:7; Mark 14:3-4; Luke 7:37). Large stone jars (John 2:6) turned on a lathe. Cups were carved by hand. By NT times, glass was becoming widely used for juglets and bottles. See *Glass.*

Reed baskets were inexpensive containers used for transportation and sometimes storage. Water or wine bottles were frequently made from animal skins (Josh. 9:4,13; Judg. 4:19; 1 Sam. 1:24; 10:3; 2 Sam. 16:1; Neh. 5:18; Job 32:19; Ps. 119:83; Matt. 9:17; Mark 2:22; Luke 5:37).

The most widely used material for vessels was clay (Num. 5:17; Jer. 32:14). See *Pottery.* See Isa. 30:14; 41:25; 45:9; Jer. 18:1-6; 19:1-2,10-11; Rom. 9:20-21.The fragments, or sherds, of a broken pottery vessel are extremely hard (compare Job 41:30) and thus remain forever.

Large mixing and serving bowls or basins (Ex. 24:6, NRSV, "basins"; Song of Sol. 7:2, NIV, "goblet"; Isa. 22:24, NRSV, "cups"), generally had handles in the Israelite period. Similar, perhaps smaller, serving bowls were used (Judg. 5:25; 6:38). Sprinkling bowls (Num. 7:84-85, NRSV,"basins") were usually of metal. Silver bowls were used in the dedication of the altar (Num. 7:84; NASB, "dishes"; NRSV, NIV, "plates"). The main "dish" (2 Kings 21:13; Prov. 19:24, NRSV; 26:15, NRSV; Matt. 26:23) at meals was actually a medium-sized handleless bowl, evidently large enough to use for boiling (2 Chron. 35:13; NRSV, NIV, "pans"). Smaller versions were used for other purposes (2 Kings 2:20). Plates did not become common until NT times. Cups were virtually unknown in OT times, these, too, being small bowls (Gen. 40:11; Isa. 51:17,22; Jer. 35:5; Zech. 12:2). Joseph's silver "cup" (Gen. 44:2,12,16-17) was probably a goblet or chalice. NT cups (Luke 11:39) remained bowl-like and varied in size.

A special bowl-like trough was used for kneading dough in bread making (Ex. 8:3; 12:34; Deut. 28:5,17). Other special bowls served as fireports for holding coals (Zech. 12:6). See *Lamps.*

"Pot" (Ex. 16:3; Num. 11:8; 2 Kings 4:38-41; Job 41:20,31, NIV, "caldron") referred to cooking pots which during the monarchy usually had two handles. NT cooking pots were similar, but smaller and more delicate with thin straplike handles. Pots were produced in graduated sizes much like their modern counterparts.

Storejars were tall, oval or pear-shaped with two or four handles. The tops were closed with an appropriately shaped potsherd or by a clay stopper. A smaller jar was used for storing oil (2 Kings 4:2; KJV,"pot;"NIV, "a little"). Typical storejars had rounded, almost pointed, bases and were placed in stands, holes in wood planks, or pressed into soft ground.

Jugs or pitchers (1 Kings 14:3, KJV, "cruse"; Jer. 19:1,10 KJV, "bottle;" Jer. 35:5, KJV,"pots") generally had a single handle attached to the neck and shoulder. There were wide and narrow-necked varieties. A pilgrim flask, a flattened bottle with twin handles around a thin neck, which functioned like a canteen (1 Sam. 26:11-12, NRSV, "jar"; compare 1 Kings 17:14). Juglets were used for dipping liquids out of large jars and keeping oil (1 Sam. 10:1, NRSV,"vial"; NIV,"flask"; 2 Kings 9:3, NRSV, NIV,"flask"; Matt. 25:4).

A general word for utensils (KJV, "vessels" or "furniture") is often used as a collective term for the gold and bronze articles used in the tabernacle service (Ex. 25:39; 27:3,19; 30:27-28). These included snuffers, trays, shovels, pots, basins, forks, firepans, hooks, and the like. See *Archaeology; Tools.*

VESTIBULE   See *Arch.*

VIA DOLOROSA (*the way of suffering*)

After A.D. 1300 seen as route with 14 stations over which Christ was led to His crucifixion.

VIAL

Vessel that held oil, usually for anointing purposes (1 Sam. 10:1, KJV, NRSV; "flask," NASB, NIV; compare Rev. 5:8; 15:7; 16:1-4,8, 10,12,17; 17:1; 21:9; "bowls," NASB, NIV, NRSV). See *Anoint; Oil; Vessels and Utensils.*

VILLAGE

Residential area with 20 to 30 houses, no city wall, homes usually consisting of one room (Lev. 25:29,31), and little or no organized government. Cattle were kept in the inner open space, where grain was stored. The main job in the villages was farming. Shepherds often gathered around villages. The pastureland was seen as the possession of the village (see 1 Chron. 6:54-60). See *Agriculture; Cities and Urban Life; House.*

VINE

Any plant having a flexible stem supported by creeping along a surface or by climbing a natural or artificial support; usually grapevine or vineyard with some cucumbers and melons (Num. 11:5; Isa. 1:8). Grapevines are used throughout the OT to symbolize fertility of the land (Deut. 6:11; Josh. 24:13; 1 Sam. 8:14; 2 Kings 5:26; Jer. 5:17; 40:10; Hos. 2:12).

The Bible traces the origin of caring for vineyards to Noah (Gen. 9:20-21).

Hillsides are frequently mentioned as the most desirable locations for the vines, especially since they were less suitable for other forms of agriculture (compare Ps. 80:8-10; Jer. 31:5; Amos 9:13). The Hebron area was particularly noted for its grapes (Num. 13:22-24). Stone walls and/or hedges were usually built around the vineyard to protect the grapes from thirsty animals and from thieves (Song of Sol. 2:15; Jer. 49:9). Watchtowers provided further protection. The hewing out of a winepress or vat completed the vineyard installation (Isa. 5:2). Vines were pruned (Lev. 25:4; Isa. 18:5; John 15:1-2) to produce stronger branches and a greater fruit yield.

Harvest of the grapes took place in August or September. A man who had planted a vineyard was exempt from military service (Deut. 20:6). Some of the harvested grapes were eaten fresh (Jer. 31:29), and others dried into raisins (1 Sam. 25:18). Most were squeezed for their juice to make wine. See *Gleaning.* Vineyards were to lie fallow every seventh year (Ex. 23:10-11; Lev. 25:3-5), and other plants could not be sown in them (Deut. 22:9). Vineyards were cultivated by their owners, hired laborers (Matt. 20:1-16), or rented out to others (Song of Sol. 8:11; Matt. 21:33-43).

Israel is said to have been brought out of Egypt and planted as a vine on the land but was forsaken (Ps. 80:8-13; compare Isa. 5:1-7; Jer. 2:21; compare Hos. 10:1; Ezek. 15:1-8; 19:10-14).

Israel was "like grapes in the wilderness" when God found them (Hos. 9:10; compare Isa. 65:8). An abundance of the vine symbolizes the glorious age to come when the treader of the grapes will overtake the one who sows the seed (Amos 9:13-15; compare Gen. 49:10-12).

Jesus often used the vineyard as an analogy for the kingdom of God (Matt. 20:1-16; 21:28-32 and parallels). Ultimately, Jesus Himself is described as the "true vine" and His disciples (Christians) as the branches (John 15:1-11). *See Agriculture; Eschatology; Israel; Wine, Winepress.*

VINEGAR

Drink—either wine or beer from barley—that has soured (Num. 6:3); most commonly produced by pouring water over the skins and stalks of grapes after the juice had been pressed out and allowing the whole to ferment. Any fruit could be used for making wine or vinegar. Vinegar was most commonly used as a seasoning for food or as a condiment on bread (Ruth 2:14). Vinegar in two forms was forbidden to the Nazirite because of its association with strong drink (Num. 6:3). It irritates the teeth (Prov. 10:26) and neutralizes soda (Prov. 25:20). It was an unpleasant drink (Ps. 69:21), though some sopped bread in it (Ruth 2:14). Jesus refused what was apparently a mixture used to deaden the sense of the victim and nullify the pain. He accepted the customary drink of a peasant or soldier called *posca,* a mixture of vinegar, water, and eggs. See *Wine.*

VIOLENCE

Use of force to injure or wrong. God hates violence (Mal. 2:16) and demands an end to it (Jer. 22:3; Ezek. 45:9). The flood was God's response to a world filled and corrupted by violence (Gen. 6:11,13; compare Ezek. 7:23). Those who live lives of violence will meet violent ends (Ps. 7:16; Prov. 1:18-19; 21:7; compare Matt. 26:52). Such violence was especially evidenced in the oppression of the poor by the rich (Ps. 55:9,11; 73:6; Jer. 22:17; Mic. 6:12; Jas. 5:1-6). The servant of the Lord models a nonviolent response to violence (Isa. 53:9; compare 1 Pet. 2:23; Jas. 5:6). Isaiah anticipated the end of violence in the Messianic age (60:18).

Matthew 11:12 is one of the most difficult texts in the NT. Does the kingdom of heaven suffer violence (KJV, NASB, REB, NRSV), or does the kingdom come "forcefully" (NIV)? The violence which John the Baptist (Matt. 14:3-10) and believers (Matt. 5:10-11; 10:17; 23:34) suffer argues for the former. Other "violent" images of the kingdom's coming (Matt. 10:34-36; Luke 14:26-27) support the latter. Candidates for church leadership should be nonviolent persons (1 Tim. 3:3; Titus 1:7).

VIPER

Poisonous snake, possibly *Echis Colorata.* Jesus spoke of the wicked religious leaders as vipers (Matt. 3:7). Paul was bitten by a viper (Acts 28:3) but suffered no ill effect from it.

VIRGIN, VIRGIN BIRTH

One who has not engaged in sexual intercourse (Gen. 24:16; Judg. 11:37-38; 2 Sam. 13:2); nation Israel (Isa. 23:12; 37:22; Jer. 14:17); Jesus' conception in the womb of Mary by miraculous action of God without a human father.

The high priest had to marry a virgin (Lev. 21:13-14). The Hebrew word is often translated "maid" or "maiden" (Pss. 78:63; 148:12; Ezek. 9:6) although the idea of chastity may still be involved. A second Hebrew word is rendered "virgin" four times in KJV

(Gen. 24:43; Song of Sol. 1:3; 6:8; Isa. 7:14). Only one of these is translated "virgin"(Isa 7:14) in NASB, and two in NIV (Song of Sol. 6:8; Isa. 7:14). Some versions like REB do not translate this word as *virgin* in any passage.

The Greek word could refer to unmarried maidens (Matt. 25:1; Acts 21:9; 1 Cor. 7:34,36,37) or to the unmarried in general (1 Cor. 7:25) with the virginity of the unmarried assumed. The word is also used in a spiritual sense (2 Cor. 11:2). The word is used of Mary, the mother of Jesus (Matt. 1:23; Luke 1:27).

Isaiah 7:14 is of special interest because of its use in the Gospel of Matthew. In its context in Isaiah, it seemingly was a message for King Ahaz. The word itself referred to a young woman, usually of marriageable age. God inspired Matthew to interpret Isa. 7:14 for his day and ours in light of God's miraculous new work in Christ.

Belief in the virgin birth is a central doctrine of Christian thought. Mary was a virgin when Jesus was conceived and when He was born. The emphasis is upon the miraculous conception of Jesus. There was no human father. He was the Child of God. God worked in a hidden, secret way which is beyond our ability to understand or explain. Mary and Joseph had several children after the birth of Jesus: James, Joses, Judas, Simon, and sisters (Mark 6:3). The virgin birth is the way that God chose to bring about the incarnation.

VISION

Experience whereby a special revelation from God was received. A vision was given for immediate direction, Abram, Gen. 12:1-3; Lot, Gen. 19:15; Balaam, Num. 22:22-40; Peter, Acts 12:7. Or a vision was given to develop the kingdom of God by revealing the moral and spiritual deficiencies of the people of God in light of God's requirements for maintaining a proper relationship with Him (Isaiah, Amos, Hosea, Micah, Ezekiel, Daniel, John). Vision may involve perception with eyes (Job 27:11-12; Prov. 22:29), the

prophetic function of receiving and delivering the word of God (2 Sam. 7:17; Isa. 22:1,5; Joel 3:1; and Zech. 13:4) or the mysterious revelation of the future (Daniel). See *Prophecy; Revelation of God.*

VOLUNTEERS

Persons who ask God to use them to accomplish His work. The spirit of volunteerism, prompted by devotion to God, arose at crucial times in biblical history, enabling daunting tasks to be accomplished. Moses received voluntary contributions of precious goods from the Israelites sufficient to construct the tabernacle (Ex. 25:1-9). Israelites voluntarily contributed their wealth so Solomon could build the temple (1 Chron. 29:6-9). Under Josiah Israel's leaders again made a voluntarily contribution so that the people of Israel and the priests could have lambs for Passover (2 Chron. 35:7-9). When Sheshbazzar led to returnees from exile in Babylon back to Jerusalem, they carried great wealth voluntarily given by "all who were about them" (Ezra 1:5-6), including the Persian king (Ezra 7:14-15).

In financial giving, the lead in volunteerism was normally taken by persons who had the means by which to give. However, even the widow without means willingly gave (Luke 21:1-4), thus providing an example of selfless giving adopted by the early church (2 Cor. 8:1-4; 9:7).

Others contributed their time and skills. Deborah led vounteer military commanders (Judg. 5:9) and fighters (Judg. 5:2) who delivered Israel Jabin, king of Canaan (Judg. 4:23-25). Those who volunteered to move to Jerusalem during the days of Nehemiah were blessed for doing so (Neh. 11:1-2). Amasiah served as a volunteer in the temple during the reign of Jehoshaphat (2 Chron. 17:16).

VOYEURISM

Seeking sexual stimulation by visual means. In the culture of the Bible, having one's nakedness exposed and viewed publicly was normally done to indicate shame for previous sin not for sexual titillation (e.g., Gen. 9:20-23; Isa. 3:17; 20:2-4; 47:2-3; Jer. 13:22,26; Lam. 1:8; Hos. 1:10; Rev. 3:17-18). Before the Fall, because there was neither shame nor voyeurism, nakedness and sexuality were undefiled (Gen. 2:25).

Voyeurism was the prelude to further sexual sin by David (2 Sam. 11:2) and evidently played a part in the desirous affections of Pharaoh toward Sarah (Gen. 12:14-15) and Potiphar's wife toward Joseph (Gen. 39:6-7). The beauty contest sponsored by Ahasuerus had voyeuristic overtones (Esther 2:2-4).

Job recognized that voyeurism, an act of the heart, breaks God's laws (Job 31:1-4). This was confirmed by Jesus, who equated voyeurism with adultery (Matt. 5:28). Paul's injunctions to avoid youthful lusts (2 Tim. 2:22; compare 1 Thess. 5:22) in favor of pure thoughts (Phil. 4:8) speak against voyeurism.

VOWS

Voluntary expressions of devotion usually fulfilled after some condition had been met. Vows in the OT usually were conditional: "if ... then ..." (Gen. 28:20; Num. 21:2; Judg. 11:30). The one making the religious vow proposed that if God did something (such as give protection or victory), then he or she in return would make some act of devotion. Some vows, such as the Nazirite vow (Num. 6), were made out of devotion to God with no request placed upon God. The Bible emphasis is on keeping the vow. A vow unfulfilled is worse than a vow never made. Paul made a vow that involved shaving his head (Acts 18:18).

VULGATE

Latin translation of the Bible by Jerome about A.D. 400. See *Bible, Texts and Versions.*

VULTURE See *Birds.*

W

WADI

Transliteration of Arabic word for rocky watercourse, dry except during rainy seasons; can become raging torrents when especially heavy rains fall.

WAGES

Terms of employment or compensation for services rendered. In mixed economy of agriculture and pastoralism without coined money, wages often included little more than meals and a place of employment (compare Job 7:2; John 10:12). A skilled shepherd, like Jacob, might receive a portion of the flock and thus begin his own herd (Gen. 30:32-33; 31:8; and legal texts from both Assyria and Babylonia). No fixed wage was set for farm laborers. They may have received a portion of the harvest (John 4:36), or, as in Matt. 20:1-8, an agreed-upon daily wage. By law, these landless workers were to be paid at the end of each day for their efforts (Lev. 19:13; Deut. 24:14-15). This group was often cheated out of their wages (Jer. 22:13; Mal. 3:5; Jas. 5:4).

Kings hired mercenary troops to fight their wars (Judg. 9:4; 2 Sam. 10:6) and employed skilled laborers, along with slaves and unpaid draftees, to build and decorate their palaces and temples (1 Kings 5:6-17; Isa. 46:6; 2 Chron. 24:11-12). The services of priests (Judg. 18:4; Mal. 1:10) and the advice of elders (Ezra 4:5; 1 Tim. 5:17 18) were obtained for gold or silver at fees to match their abilities. The authority of prophets could also be purchased (Num. 22:7; Neh. 6:10-13).

Theological usage of these terms promises God's reward for the faithful (Gen. 15:1) and proper recompense for His people Israel (Isa. 40:10; 62:11). His justice ensured the reward of the unrighteous was equal to their crimes (Ps. 109:20; Rom. 6:23; 2 Pet. 2:15). See *Commerce; Economic Life; Slave,Servant.*

WAGON

Vehicle with two or four wooden wheels pulled by oxen and used to transport people and goods (Gen. 45:17-21); two wheeler was usually called a cart; sometimes used as instruments of war (Ezek. 23:24). See *Transportation and Travel.*

WAIL See *Grief and Mourning; Repentance.*

WALK

A slower pace contrasted with running (Ex. 2:5; Matt. 4:18); a person's conduct or way of life (Gen. 5:24; Rom. 8:4; 1 John 1:6-7).

WALK TO AND FRO

KJV (Zech. 1:10-11) for military term meaning "patrol" (NASB, NRSV) or "go and inspect" (TEV).

WALLS

Outside vertical structures of houses and the fortifications surrounding cities. In ancient times, the walls of cities and houses were constructed of bricks made of clay mixed with reed and hardened in the sun. Archaeologists estimate that the walls of Nineveh were wide enough to drive three chariots abreast and the walls of Babylon were wide enough to drive six chariots abreast on the top. See *Architecture; Fort, Fortifications.*

In scriptural language, a wall is a symbol of salvation (Isa. 26:1; Isa, 60:18), of the protection of God (Zech. 2:5), of those who afford protection (1 Sam. 25:16; Isa. 2:15), and of wealth of the rich in their own conceit (Prov. 18:11). A "brazen wall" is symbolic of prophets and their testimony against the wicked (Jer. 15:20). The "wall of partition" (Eph. 2:14) represented temple worship and Jewish practice separating Jew from Gentile.

WANDERINGS IN THE WILDERNESS

Israel's movements from Egypt to the Promised Land under Moses (Ex. 12:31–Num. 33:49).

WAR CRIMES

Illegal actions by nations, armies, and individuals in time of battle and fighting. Clearly some of the practices of warfare—ancient and modern—exceed all sensibilities (e.g., 2 Sam. 8:2; Ps. 137:9). It may be helpful to label such acts with modern terminology such as "war crimes" or "ethnic cleansing." Amos declared that waging war in order to deport whole populations as slaves, or massacering Israelite women and children in warfare deserved the judgment of God (Amos 1:6,9). Similarly, Moses recognized that Amalek's ambush of the Israelites from behind when they were tired and helpless should not go unpunished (Deut. 25:17-19). More problematic is God's response that Israel similarly wipe out Amalek, including its helpless women and children (1 Sam. 15:1-3; compare Ps. 137:9), or His command to annihilate the Canaanites (Deut. 7:2). In some ways God's election of Israel as a nation (Gen. 12:1-3; Ex. 19:5-6) superseded the right of other nations to harm Israel. The Mosaic law included rules of warfare intended to allow the enemies of Israel room to surrender (Deut. 20:1-20) and to safeguard the rights of captive women (Deut. 21:10-14).

WASHING See *Ablutions; Bathing.*

WASP See *Insects.*

WATCH

Division of time in which soldiers or others were on duty to guard something: "evening," "midnight," "cockcrowing," and "morning" (Mark 13:35, NASB) or simply "beginning of the watches" (Lam. 2:19), "middle watch" (Judg. 7:19), and "morning watch" (Ex. 14:24). See Neh. 4:9; 7:3. See *Time.*

WATCHMAN

One who stands guard. Ancient cities had watchmen stationed on the walls to sound a warning if an enemy approached (2 Kings 9:17; Ezek. 33:2-3). Israel's prophets saw themselves as watchmen warning the nation of God's approaching judgment if the people did not repent. Vineyards and fields had watchmen, especially during harvest, to guard the produce from animals and thieves.

WATCHTOWER

Tower on a high place or built high enough to enable a person to see for some distance (2 Kings 9:17; Isa. 5:2; Mark 12:1). See *Tower.*

WATER

Liquid material resource necessary for life; created by God as part of His good creation; sovereignly controlled by God (Gen. 1–2; Isa. 40:12). He controls the natural processes of precipitation and evaporation, as well as the courses of bodies of water (Job 5:10; 36:27; 37:10; Pss. 33:7; 107:33; Prov. 8:29). God normally assures the provision of water for human needs (Deut. 11:14). Water is sometimes used in punishment for sin, as with the flood of Noah's day (Gen. 6:17) or the drought proclaimed by Elijah (1 Kings 17:1). The divine control of water teaches people obedience to and dependency upon God.

God parted the sea (Ex. 14:21), provided water in the wilderness (Ex. 15:25; 17:6), and divided the Jordan River (Josh. 3:14-17). Water was also involved in several of Jesus' miracles (Matt. 14:25; Luke 8:24-25; John 2:1-11).

Water is a metaphor or simile for fear (Josh. 7:5), death (2 Sam. 14:14), sin (Job 15:16), God's presence (Ps. 72:6), marital fidelity (Prov. 5:15-16), the knowledge of God (Isa. 11:9), salvation (Isa. 12:3), the Spirit (Isa. 44:3-4), God's blessings (Isa. 58:11), God's voice (Ezek. 43:2), God's wrath (Hos. 5:10), justice (Amos 5:24), birth (John 3:5), the Spirit (John 4:10), spiritual training (1 Cor. 3:6), and life (Rev.

7:17). See *Creation; Famine and Drought; Flood; Rain.*

WATERPOT

Vessel made for carrying water, usually made of clay although some were made of stone (John 2:6). Large pots stored water (1 Kings 18:33; John 2:6); smaller pots a woman could carry on her shoulder (John 4:28). Small pitchers were used for pouring water (Luke 22:10; see Jer. 19). Water was also carried in animal skins. See *Pottery; Vessels and Utensils.*

WAW

Sixth letter in Hebrew alphabet. Heading of Ps. 119:41-48 where each verse begins with the letter.

WEALTH AND MATERIALISM

Physical resources God gives humans to control and the human tendency to lift those resources to replace God as the center of life. Wealth is a blessing from God (Gen. 12:1-3; 13:2; 26:12-14; 1 Kings 3:13; 10:23; Job 42:12).

Riches and the pursuit of pleasure may keep some from maturing in the faith (Luke 8:14). Wealth can be destructive (Luke 12:16-21). Life does not consist of one's possessions (Luke 12:15). Money or wealth is a spiritual power (Matt. 6:24) and can become a rival to God. Jesus often asked people to turn away from it (Matt. 19:21; Luke 12:33-34). Giving to the poor and restoring wealth gained by cheating is a sign of desire to follow Christ. (Luke 19:8; compare Acts 20:35). See *Stewardship.*

Members of the Jerusalem church pooled their resources for the common good (Acts 2:44-45; 4:34-35), providing a model for the responsibility Christians have for one another.

A church officer is to be free from the love of money (1 Tim. 3:3,8), "the root of all evil," (1 Tim. 6:10; compare Heb. 13:5). Money can be used to enhance our relationship to God and bless others (2 Cor. 8:1-4; compare 2 Cor. 9:7).

We are not to be anxious over material things, but to trust the Heavenly Father to care for our needs (Matt. 6:25-26), knowing God's kingdom is more important than money (Matt. 6:33). God is the owner of all things. He gives us a portion to use. We will one day give account to God for the use of our wealth.

WEAPONS See *Arms and Armor; Chariots; Animals, Horse.*

WEASEL See *Animals.*

WEATHER

Climatic conditions in Palestine, including geographical factors and seasonal changes. Weather patterns of Palestine result from the clash between the extreme heat of the Arabian desert and the cooler Mediterranean winds from the west. The climate is subtropical with humid, cold winters and hot, dry summers. From October to April the days range from cool and sunny to overcast, cold, and rainy. The rains fill the seasonal brooks and streams, which provide the majority of water for the coming year. The elevation of the land, dropping from 3,900 feet in upper Galilee to 1,296 feet below sea level at the Dead Sea, provides natural barriers which influence the weather. Rain generally diminishes as one travels farther south and inland. Thus, the coastal plain and Galilee receive more rain than the central hill country and Negev desert. Snow covers the higher elevations of Mount Hermon throughout most of the winter and occasionally falls on Jerusalem and the surrounding hills. The Jordan Valley, particularly in the area of the Dead Sea, remains mild in the winter, making it the traditional site of the winter palaces of kings and rulers. The Mediterranean Sea becomes windy and cold, making travel dangerous.

In April and May hot desert winds blow across the land from the east in the early morning hours. The land and seasonal rivers begin to dry, and the vegetation turns brown. Near noon each day, wind turns to the west, bringing with it slightly cooler air from the sea. Still the heat remains intense. The central hill country is cooler than the foothills and coastal areas, but the Judaean wilderness and Negev become fiercely hot. Temperatures along the Dead Sea and Arabah remain above 90 degrees Fahrenheit for weeks on end. Once across the Jordan Valley atop the Transjordan plateau to the east, the temperature moderates once more. Rain is uncommon in the summer months, usually falling in October, November, February, and March.

The winds and rain were considered to be under God's personal direction. Christ's control of the elements demonstrated to the disciples His heavenly calling. The hot east wind was often viewed as the wrath of God, bringing infertility and death. Rain signified the continued blessings of God; its absence, His judgment. See *Fertility Cult; Palestine; Rain; Wind.*

WEAVING See *Cloth, Clothing.*

WEB

(1) A fabric usually woven on a loom (see Judg. 16:13-14).

(2) The weaving of a spider that looks like thread; used figuratively for the impermanent and untrustworthy (Job 8:14). See *Animals; Insects.*

WEDDINGS

The wedding ceremony in biblical times consisted of three elements: the processional, the feast and the consummation.

Normally a wedding began as the groom, prepared in special dress (Isa. 61:10) and with his attendants (John 3:29), walked to the home of the bride. The bride then returned with the bridegroom to his house in joyful procession (Ps. 45:15; Isa. 62:5; compare Jer. 7:34). She, too, wore wedding finery (Ps. 45:13-14a; Isa. 49:18; 61:10; Jer. 2:32; Rev. 19:7-8; 21:2) and was accompanied by her attendants, typically young virgins (Ps. 45:14b).

At the home of the bridegroom the couple, together with their attendants and many guests, feasted with great joy and song (Ps. 78:63; Ezek. 33:32; Matt. 9:15; 25:1-13; John 2:1-10; Rev. 19:9). During the feast the bridegroom spread his cloak over the bride, indicating his commitment to her in marriage (compare Ruth 3:9; Ezek. 16:8).

The marriage was consummated that night (Gen. 29:23-25; Song of Sol. 4:16; compare Deut. 22:13-17). The bride and bridegroom emerged from their chamber the next morning like the rising sun, radiant with warmth and ready for new life (Ps. 19:5).

Building on prophetic image of Israel as God's bride (Hos. 1–3) and on Paul's reference to the church as the bride of Christ (2 Cor. 11:2; Eph. 5:26-27), John foresaw time when the marriage ceremony of Jesus and the church would take place (Rev. 19:7-9).

WEEK

Any seven consecutive days ending with the sabbath (Gen. 2:1-3). Christians moved their day of worship to Sunday, the first day of the week to call attention to the resurrection of Jesus (Luke 24:1-7). See *Calendars; Time.*

WEEPING See *Grief and Mourning.*

WEIGHTS AND MEASURES

Systems of measurement in the Bible. The prophets spoke against merchants who used deceitful weights (Mic. 6:11). Hebrew weights were never an exact system. Not even inscribed weights of the same inscription weighed the same. Weights were used in a balance to weigh out silver and gold, since there was no coinage until the Persian period after 500 B.C.

The *shekel* is the basic unit of weight in the Hebrew as well as the Babylonian and Canaanite systems. The exact weight varied from region to region and sometimes also according to the kind of goods for sale. The Mesopotamian system was sexagesimal, based on sixes and sixties with a *talent* of 60 minas, a *mina* of 60 shekels, and a shekel of 24 *gerahs*. The Hebrew system was decimal like the Egyptian. There seems to have been three kinds of shekel current in Israel: (1) a temple shekel of about 10 grams (0.351 ounces) which depreciated to about 9.8 grams (0.345 ounces); (2) the common shekel of about 11.7 grams (0.408 ounces) which depreciated to about 11.4 grams (0.401 ounces); and (3) the heavy ("royal"?) shekel of about 13 grams (0.457 ounces). The smallest portion of the shekel was the *gerah*, 1/20 of a shekel (Ex. 30:13; Ezek. 45:12), about .571 grams. The *beka* or half shekel (Ex. 38:26), known also from Egypt was over six grams and may have been half of the heavy shekel mentioned above. The *pim*, if it is 2/3 of a shekel as most scholars suppose, is also related to the heavy shekel and weighs about eight grams. It may have been a Philistine weight (1 Sam. 13:19-21).

The sanctuary tax (Ex. 38:25-26) had 3,000 shekels in a talent, probably 60 minas of 50 shekels each. This talent may have been the same as the Assyrian weight, since both 2 Kings 18:14 and Sennacherib's inscriptions mention the tribute of King Hezekiah as 30 talents of silver and of gold. This was 28.38 to 30.27 kilograms (about 70 pounds). The mina was probably 50 shekels (as the Canaanite system), though Ezek. 45:12 calls for a mina of 60 shekels, and the early Greek translation reads, "50." The mina has been estimated at 550 to 600 grams (1.213 to 1.323 lbs.). One table of OT weights, estimated on a shekel of 11.424 grams is as follows:

a talent (3000 shekels)	34.272 kilograms	75.6 lbs.
1 mina (50 shekels)	571.2 grams	1.26 lbs.
1 shekel	11.424 grams	.403 oz.
1 pim (2/3 shekel?)	7.616 grams	.258 oz.
1 beka (1/2 shekel)	5.712 grams	.201 oz.

a talent (3000 shekels)	34.272 kilograms	75.6 lbs.
1 gerah (1/20 shekel)	.571 grams	.02 oz.

OT weights were never so precise as this. The Lord's ideal was *just* weights and measures (Lev. 19:36; Prov. 16:11; Ezek. 45:10); but dishonest manipulations were all too common (Prov. 11:1; 20:23; Hos. 12:7). In the NT, the talent and mina were large sums of money (Matt. 25:15-28; compare Luke 19:13-25), and the *pound* of precious ointment (John 12:3) is probably the Roman standard of 12 ounces.

Measures of capacity were also only approximate and varied from time to time and place to place. The basic unit of dry measure was the *ephah*, which means "basket." The *homer*, "ass's load," was a dry measure, the same size as the *cor*, both a dry and a liquid measure. Each contained 10 ephahs or *baths*, an equivalent liquid measure (Ezek. 45:10-14). The ephah is estimated at 1.52 to 2.42 pecks, about 3/8 to 2/3 of a bushel.

The bath is estimated from two fragments of vessels so labeled from tell Beit Mirsim and Lachish to have contained 2.1 to 2.3 liters or about 1/2 gallon. *Lethech*, which may mean half a homer (or cor), would be five ephahs. *Seah* was a dry measure which may be a third of an ephah. *Hin*, an Egyptian liquid measure, which means "jar," was approximately a sixth of a bath. The *omer*, used only in the manna story (Ex. 16:13-36) was a daily ration and is calculated as a tenth of an ephah (also called *issaron*, "tenth"). A little less than half an omer is the *kab* (only 2 Kings 6:25, NRSV), which was four times the smallest unit, *log* (only Lev. 14:10-20, NRSV) which is variously estimated, according to its Greek or Latin translation as a half pint or 2/3 pint.

Although OT measures of capacity varied as much as the difference between the American and English gallon, the following table at least represents the assumptions of the above discussion:

Dry Measures	
kab	1.16 quarts
omer, issaron 1/10 ephah	2.09 quarts
seah, 1/3 ehpah	2/3 peck
ephah	1/2 bushel
lethech, 1/2 homer	2.58 bushels
homer, cor	5.16 bushels
Liquid Measures	
log	0.67 pint
hin	1 gallon
bath	1/2 gallons
cor, homer	55 gallons

In the NT, measures of capacity are Greek or Roman measures. The *sextarius* or "pot" (Mark 7:4) was about a pint. The measure of John 2:6 (*metretas*) is perhaps ten gallons. The bushel (*modios*) of Matt. 5:15 and parallels is a vessel large enough to cover a light, perhaps about a fourth of an American bushel. The amount of ointment Mary used to anoint Jesus (John 12:3) was a Roman pound of twelve ounces (a measure of both weight and capacity), and Nicodemus brought 100 such pounds of mixed spices to anoint Jesus' body (John 19:39).

In measures of length, all over the Ancient Near East, the standard was the *cubit*, the length of the forearm from the elbow to the tip of the middle finger. Israel knew two different lengths for the cubit just as did Egypt. The common cubit, mentioned in connection with the description of the bed of Og, king of Bashan (Deut. 3:11), was about seventeen and a half inches. Ezekiel (40:5) mentions a long cubit consisting of a common cubit plus a handbreadth which would yield a "royal" cubit of about twenty and a half inches.

Even figuring with the common cubit, Goliath was 9.5 feet tall (1 Sam.

17:4). Figured with the common cubit, Solomon's temple was about ninety-feet long, thirty-feet wide, and forty-five-feet high (1 Kings 6:2). The span is half a cubit (Ezek. 43:13,17), or the distance between the extended thumb and little finger. If it is half the long cubit, the span would be about 10.2 inches; if half, the common cubit was about eight and three-fourths inches.

The *handbreadth* or palm is a sixth of a cubit, consisting of the breadth of the hand at the base of the four fingers. This measure is a little less than three inches. The smallest Israelite measure of length was the finger, a fourth of a handbreadth (Jer. 52:21) and was about three-fourths inch. Larger than a cubit was the *reed*, probably consisting of six common cubits. Summarizing on the basis of the common cubit, linear measurements of the OT were:

Common Cubit		
1 reed	6 cubits	8 ft. 9 in.
1 cubit	6 hand-breadths	17.5 in.
1 hand-breadth	4 fingers	2.9 in.
1 finger		.73 in.
Ezekiel's Cubit		
1 reed	6 cubits	10 ft. 24 in.
1 cubit	7 hand-breadths	20.4 in.

Indefinite measures of great length included a day's journey or three day's journey or seven day's journey, the calculation of which would depend on the mode of transportation and the kind of terrain. Shorter indefinite distances were the bowshot (Gen. 21:16) and the furrow's length (1 Sam. 14:14, NRSV).

In the NT, measures of length were Greek or Roman units. The cubit was probably the same as the common cubit, since the Romans reckoned it as one and a half times the Roman foot. The *fathom* (Acts 27:28) was about six feet of water in depth. The *stadion* or furlong was a Roman measure of 400 cubits or one eighth Roman mile. The Roman mile (Matt. 5:41) was 1,620 yards. Josephus calculated this as six stadia or 1,237.8 yards.

Measures of area were indefinite in the OT. An "acre" was roughly what a yoke of oxen could plow in one day. Land could be measured by the amount of grain required to sow it. In NT times a Roman measure of land was the Latin *jugerum*, related to what a yoke of oxen could plow, figured at 28,000 square feet or five-eighths of an acre. Another was the furrow, 120 Roman feet in length.

WELFARE PROGRAMS

Governmental attempts to assist people in economic need. God expects people to work for a living (Prov. 10:4; 19:5; 20:4; Eph. 4:28; 1 Thess. 4:11; 2 Thess. 3:6-13). Yet the Bible also recognizes that in every society there will be poor people in need of assistance (Deut. 15:11; John 12:8). For this reason, God commands his people to be willing, free, and generous in helping others (Deut. 15:10-14; Acts 11:29; 1 Cor. 16:2-3; 2 Cor. 8:1-4; 9:5-7).

The Mosaic law provided for those who could not adequately care for themselves: sojourners, widows, orphans, and Levites; the latter did not receive a landed tribal inheritance. Each was to receive assistance paid by other Israelites in the form of a tithe (Deut. 14:28-29). These poor were to be allowed to glean in the fields, orchards, and vineyards of those who were able to earn a productive living (Ex. 23:10 11; Lev. 19:9-10; 25:1-7; Deut. 24:19-22; Ruth 2:2-3; 15-17). Every seventh year was a year of release in which all debts were forgiven, thus allowing the poor a fresh start (Deut. 15:1-18). To neglect the poor in ancient Israel was to close oneself to God's blessing (Job 31:16-22; Prov. 25:21-22; 28:27). Yet the prophetic denunciation regarding the lack of social justice in ancient Israel suggests that these welfare programs were not practiced (e.g., Isa. 58:6-7; Ezek. 18:5-9).

Jesus taught the necessary union of true spirituality and personal social responsibility (Matt. 5:42; 19:21; 25:31-46; Mark 9:41; Luke 10:32-37), a connection stressed by James (2:14-17) and the other apostles (Gal. 2:9-10; Eph. 4:28; 1 Tim. 6:18; 1 John 3:17-18). The early church provided for the physical needs of its members (Acts 2:43-47; 4:32-35; 6:1-4; 10:1-2; 11:27-30; Rom. 15:25-27; 2 Cor. 8:1-4; Phil. 4:15-18).

WELL

Source of water created by digging in the earth to find available water. See *Cistern; Fountain; Pit; Water.* The Hebrew word most commonly translated "well" is *beer* (Gen. 21:30-31; Num. 21:16-18). *Beer* also occurs in several place names indicating the location of important wells: Beer (Num. 21:16); Beer-elim (Isa. 15:8); Beeroth (Deut. 10:6); Beer-lahai-roi (Gen. 16:14); Beersheba (Gen. 21:31). The digging of a well could be a time for celebration (Num. 21:17-18), but wells were also fought over as different people tried to control the precious resource (Gen. 21:25-26; 26:15-22; Ex. 2:16-17). Wells were located wherever a water source could be found. This included fields (Gen. 29:2), towns (2 Sam. 23:15), and the wilderness (Gen. 16:7,14).

"Well" is also used figuratively of a harlot (Prov. 23:27, NRSV) and of a wicked city (Jer. 6:7). Elsewhere it is used as a metaphor for sexual pleasure (Prov. 5:15; see Song of Sol. 4:15).

WHALE

KJV translation (Gen. 1:21; Job 7:12; Ezek. 32:2; and in Matt. 12:40 with reference to Jonah) for primeval sea monster or dragon (Isa. 27:1; 51:9), a serpent (Ex. 7:9; Ps. 91:13), or possibly a crocodile (Ezek. 29:3; 32:2). Jonah refers simply to a "great fish" (Jonah 1:17). Matthew used the Greek *ketos*, indicating a great sea monster rather than indicating a particular species.

WHEAT

Staple grain of the Ancient Near East (Num. 18:12); raised in this region since at least neolithic times (8300–4500 B.C.); became major crop after nomads began settling into agrarian societies; used as analogy to speak of God's judgment (Matt. 3:12) and His care (Ps. 81:16). Wheat was used to make bread and was also parched (Lev. 23:14). KJV often translated *wheat* as "corn" (Mark 4:28). Wheat harvest was an ancient time reference (Ex. 34:22) and was celebrated by the Feast of Weeks. Wheat was harvested (1 Sam. 6:13), threshed (Judg. 6:11), and winnowed (Matt. 3:12). See *Agriculture; Bread; Plants.*

WHEEL

Disk or circular object capable of turning on a central axis, probably invented in Mesopotamia before 3000 B.C.; indispensable for transportation—used on wagons, carts, and chariots (Ezek. 23:24; 26:10; Nah. 3:2; compare 1 Kings 7:30-33).

Ezekiel's vision of the great wheel in the sky (1:4-28; 10) was a symbol of God's presence. Perhaps the vision represented the wheels of God's invisible chariot moving across the sky ("chariots of the sun," see 2 Kings 23:11) or the wheels of God's throne (Dan. 7:9). Compare Ps. 77:18; Prov. 20:26; Jer. 18:13). See *Chariots.*

WHELP

Lion's cub (Gen. 49:9; Jer. 51:38; Nah. 2:11). See *Animals.*

WHIRLWIND

Any windstorm that is destructive. Only Ps. 77:18 indicates circular motion. True whirlwinds and tornadoes are rare in Palestine. They usually occur near the coast where the cool breezes of the Mediterranean Sea collide with the hot wind from the desert. Lesser whirlwinds are seen as whirling dust is thrown up into the air. The Lord used the raging wind to take Elijah to heaven (2 Kings 2:1,11) and to talk with Job (38:1; 40:6). The prophets used the storm wind as a figure for judgment (Isa. 5:28; Jer. 4:13; Hos. 8:7; Amos 1:14; Zech. 7:14). God comes to deliver His people riding the storm winds (Zech. 9:14).

WHITE See *Colors.*

WIFE

Female marriage partner. See *Family; Marriage; Woman.*

WILD ASS See *Animals.*

WILD BEASTS

A designation of any wild animal in contrast to domesticated animals; living creatures (Gen. 1:24) including wild animals (Gen. 1:25). The same Hebrew form indicates humans as "living" beings (Gen. 2:7). The context shows the precise type creature meant. See *Animals.*

WILD BEASTS OF THE ISLAND

KJV for hyena or jackal. See *Animals, Hyena.*

WILD DONKEY See *Animals.*

WILD GOAT See *Animals.*

WILD GOURD

A poisonous plant, probably *Citrillus colocynths* (2 Kings 4:39).

WILD OX See *Animals.*

WILDERNESS

Holy Land areas, particularly in the southern part, with little rainfall and few people; desert; rocky, dry wasteland. They can accommodate some nomadic or seminomadic human occupancy. Wilderness could also have the foreboding sense of uninhabitable land (Jer. 2:6), a fearful place in which to get lost (Ps. 107:4-9). The wilderness lay south, east, and southwest of the inhabited land of Israel in the Negeb, Transjordan, and the Sinai. A particular wilderness, closer to home, lay on the eastern slopes of the Judean mountains in the rain shadow leading down to the Dead Sea. This particular wilderness, sometimes called Jeshimon, became a refuge for David when he fled from Saul, and was the locale of the temptation of Jesus.

The wilderness was particularly connected with the wandering of the Hebrews after their miraculous escape from Egypt and just prior to the conquest of Transjordan: "that great and terrible wilderness"(Deut. 1:19; 8:15). The Book of Numbers is called in the Hebrew Bible, *bemidbar,* "in the desert." In the Psalms, the worshiping Israelites confessed these ancient sins (78:40; 106:26), and NT preachers used them as a warning to "wilderness Christians" not to make the same mistakes (1 Cor. 10:1-13; Heb. 3:16-19). Specific wilderness areas included Sin, Shur, Sinai, Paran, and Zin on the way of wilderness wanderings. Specific locales connected with David's outlaw years included the wilderness of En-Gedi, of Judah, of Maon, of Ziph. People in biblical times mostly feared the desert as a place inhabited by beasts of prey, snakes, and scorpions (even demons) to which one might drive out the scapegoat (Lev. 16:10,22,26; Isa. 13:21-22; 34:13-14).

The prophets looked forward to a renewed pilgrimage in the wilderness (Hos. 2:14-15; 9:10; compare Deut. 32:10; Jer. 2:2-3; 31:2-3), a new exodus after the Babylonian exile through the north Syrian desert (Ezek. 20:30-38; Isa. 40:3-5). John the Baptist appeared in the wilderness of Judea as the promised prophetic forerunner (Matt. 3:1-3; Mark 1:2-4; Luke 3:2-6; John 1:23). Jesus fed the 4,000 in a desolate place east of Lake Galilee (Mark 8:1-9). See *Desert; Paran; Shur, Wilderness of; Sin, Wilderness of; Sinai; Wanderings in the Wilderness.*

WILL OF GOD

God's plan and purpose for His creation and for each individual. God does whatever he pleases (Ps. 135:6) and desires that all people do His will. Only people fully mature in Christ are able to do God's will consistently (Col. 4:12; compare Ps. 40:8). God's will is always good, acceptable, and perfect (Rom. 12:2). Doing God's will sustained Jesus for life (John 4:34). Sometimes, however, the will of God

leads to suffering (Rom. 8:28; Jas. 1:2-4; 1 Pet. 3:17), as it did for Jesus (Isa. 53:10; Matt. 26:39,42).

Christians are to strive to know the will of God for their lives (Ps. 143:10; Eph. 5:17; Col. 1:9; compare Rom. 1:10). Christians are to discern God's will through prayer (Col. 1:9), and also pray that God's will for the world be done (Matt. 6:10). Jesus counted those who did God's will as his own family members (Matt. 12:50). They, like Jesus, will live forever (1 John 2:17).

WILLOW   See *Plants.*

WIMPLE

Covering women wore around their head and neck (Isa. 3:22); "cloaks." See *Cloth, Clothing.*

WIND

Natural force that represents in its extended meaning the breath of life in human beings and the creative, infilling power of God and His Spirit. In the OT there is the slight breeze (Ps. 78:39), the storm wind (Isa. 32:2), the whirlwind (2 Kings 2:11), and the scorching wind (Ps. 11:6, NRSV). Winds from the mountains and sea to the north and west brought rain and storm (1 Kings 18:43-45; see Ex. 10:19; Ezek. 1:4); those coming from the deserts of the south and east could at times be balmy but more often would sear the land and dry up the vegetation (Gen. 41:6; Job 37:1-2).

God answered Job out of the whirlwind (Job 38:1), and the four living creatures appeared to Ezekiel in a strong wind from the north (1:4). Wind was a symbol of transience (Ps. 78:39), fruitless striving (Eccl. 1:14, NRSV), and desperateness (Job 6:26). It was a mighty force only God could command (Jer. 10:13; Ps. 104:4). It blows where it will (John 3:8). The wind is His breath which He blew on the sea to cover the chariots of Pharaoh (Ex. 15:10), or by which He froze rivers (Job 37:10) and withered grass (Isa. 40:7).

The wind is also breath in humans as the breath of life (Gen. 6:17; Ezek.

37:5-7). The meaning often expands from the wind to spirit (Isa. 40:13); note Ps. 51:10-12,17. See *Breath; Spirit.*

WINDOW

Holes in a house: as a chimney for smoke to escape (Hos. 13:3); in places were doves live (Isa. 60:8); in heaven through which rain falls (Gen. 7:11; 8:2; Mal. 3:10; compare 2 Kings 7:2); in the wall for air and light (Gen. 8:6; Josh. 2:15; Judg. 5:28). Recessed windows with lattice work marked elaborate public buildings such as the temple (1 Kings 6:4) and the royal palace (2 Kings 9:30). See *Architecture; House.*

WINE

Beverage made from fermented grapes. In NT times wine was kept in skin flasks and often diluted with water. It was also used as a medicine and disinfectant. The harvesting and treading of the grapes was a time of joy and celebration (Isa. 16:10; Jer. 48:33; Deut. 16:13-15); and the image of the abundance of wine is used in the Bible to speak of God's salvation and blessing (Prov. 3:10; Joel 3:18; Amos 9:13). God's judgment is portrayed as the treading of the wine press (Isa. 63:2-3; Rev. 14:19-20). Scripture condemns drunkenness and overindulgence, but pictures wine as a part of the typical ancient meal. See *Vine.*

WINEPRESS

Machine used for making wine from grapes; wine making has always been a major industry in Syria-Palestine. In OT times the presses for making wine were usually cut or hewed out of rock (Isa. 5:2) and were connected by channels to lower rock-cut vats where the juice was allowed to collect and ferment. The juice was squeezed from the grapes by treading over them with the feet (Job 24:11; Amos 9:13). After the juice had fermented, it was collected into jars or wineskins (Matt. 9:17, and parallels). Rock-cut cellars had a storage capacity of 25,000 gallons of wine (see

1 Chron. 27:27; Zech. 14:10). By the NT period, both beam presses and presses with mosaic pavements were in use. See *Agriculture; Vine; Wine.*

WING

Specialized part of bird that allows flight (Gen. 1:21); used figuratively: of God's help (Ruth 2:12), of God's judgment (Jer. 48:40), of strength to return from exile (Isa. 40:31).

WINNOWING

Process of separating grain from the inedible parts. The stalks are thrown into the air, and the wind blows away the chaff and the straw, letting the heavier pure grain fall back to the ground (Isa. 30:24). Winnowing is used as an analogy of God's judgment (Matt. 3:12).

WINNOWING FORK, WINNOWING SHOVEL See *Fan.*

WINTER

Season between fall and spring, usually short and mild in Palestine; rainy season (Song of Sol. 2:11). See *Weather.*

WINTERHOUSE

Part of a palace or a separate home of the rich that is heated and thus warmer than the rest of the house (Jer. 36:22), or built in a warmer part of the country. See Amos 3:15.

WISDOM AND WISE MEN

Educated class of people responsible for preserving and transmitting the culture and learning of the society. Wisdom teaches how to succeed in life living in accordance with that orderliness that appears in the world (Prov. 22:17–24:22). Job and Ecclesiastes seem to deal with issues of the essence of life (see particularly Job 30:29-31). The real essence of wisdom is spiritual and comes from God (Prov. 2:6). It involves observation and instruction, but really begins with God and one's faith in Him (Prov. 1:7; Job 28:28).

At first, such wisdom was probably the responsibility of the patriarch or head of the clan. Every ancient culture developed a distinct class of people—sages—responsible for creating and preserving wisdom: Ahithophel and Hushai (2 Sam. 16:15-17:23); Solomon and his court (1 Kings 4:29-34; 10); Hezekiah's wisdom (Prov. 25:1). Jeremiah's enemies even confronted him regarding his prophecy that the law would perish from the priests, the prophets, and the sages (Jer. 18:18). Magi (or sages) from the east announced the birth of Christ (Matt. 2:1-12) who became the greatest of all wisdom teachers (Matt. 12:42; 13:54; Mark 6:2).

Most of the Ancient Near Eastern wisdom material has been found in some type of poetic structure expressed in parallel patterns. See *Poetry.*

The greatest contribution of Israel's sages has been Job, Proverbs, and Ecclesiastes. Psalms, the Song of Solomon, and Lamentations contain figures of speech and stylized forms reflective of the wisdom tradition. Intertestamental works of Ecclesiasticus and the Wisdom of Solomon continued the tradition and laid an excellent foundation for the ultimate revelation of wisdom in Christ Jesus (Matt. 11:19; Luke 11:49-51; Col. 1:15-20; 1 Cor. 1:24,30; Rev. 5:12). See *Intertestamental History and Literature; Apocrypha; Pseudepigrapha.*

Biblical wisdom like that of other cultures emphasizes the success and well-being of the individual. Some of its major topics are: knowledge, the world, justice, virtue, family, and faith. The greatest of these may be faith which is constantly watching over wisdom and really all of life (Prov. 1:7). See *Ecclesiastes; Job; Proverbs.*

WITCH

Female whose work was in divination and magic. See *Divination and Magic.*

WITNESS, MARTYR

Testimony of a person; something that bears testimony to a person or an event. OT uses Hebrew *moed* to refer to the "meeting" place of God and His people. This meeting is testimony to a particular person or event, such as God or the giving of the covenant, and provides a place of testimony.

One rendered testimony based on observation, testimony was to be true and faithful (Ruth 4:9-11; note trial of Jesus, Matt. 26:65; Mark 14:63; Luke 22:71). Witnesses were also expected to be involved in the judgment (Deut. 17:7). Paul bore witness to the Galatians of their care for him (Gal. 4:15). Timothy was not to act too hastily in accusing an elder without at least two or three witnesses (1 Tim. 5:19). Joshua (24:22) reminded them that the people were witnesses and thus accountable. Joshua set up a memorial as a witness to God's activity for both present and future generations. In Ps. 119, the law is the supreme "testimony" or monument to God.

Jesus is the supreme witness to God and His love. John the Baptist, the Father, and the Scripture all bear witness to Him (John 1; 5; note ch. 8). Jesus is true and faithful, and so is His message. A response is demanded.

Christ challenged believers to be His witnesses throughout the world (Acts 1:8). This witness is informed and empowered by the Holy Spirit (John 15:26-27). A believer's witness is to be true and faithful, reflected both in speech and lifestyle (Acts 4:33; 14:3; Heb. 10:15-17; 1 Thess. 2:10).

Christ's high commitment to witness/testify resulted in His persecution and death. His followers would also suffer persecution for their witness (John 15:20; Acts 7). Stephen was first and foremost a witness, giving testimony even in his death.

WIZARD See *Medium.*

WOLF See *Animals.*

WOMAN

Acknowledged offshoot of the male, having a nature like his but her own unique existence. The woman was received by the man as designed and offered to him by the Creator (Gen. 2:22). When Adam said "she was taken from man" in 2:23, he used a play on words to affirm the physical congruity of this new person. "Man" (Hb. *ish*) is contrasted with "woman" (*ishshah*).

Man and woman are created "in the image of God," and equal dignity prohibits the despising of one by the other; complementary interaction of one with the other requires that differences be honored.

Together man and woman are equipped to continue the generations and to exercise dominion over the earth and its resources. Yet the divine order calls for a reciprocity exhibited in male servant leadership and female submission.

Israelite women managed the household and performed the duties of wives and mothers (Prov. 31:10-31). They had a measure of anonymity in life and were subordinate to their husbands. Women were expected to meet their husbands' sexual needs, but their own needs were also to be met (Song 1:2; 2:3-6,8-10; 8:1-4; 1 Cor. 7:3,5).

The husband was the patriarch of his family or clan, and the wife became part of her husband's family. Women were an integral part of the community and were to be protected therein. Godly women were admired and their contributions greatly valued (e.g., Deborah, Hannah, Abigail, Naomi, Ruth, Esther); widows were to be protected (Deut. 24:19-22; 26:12).

A woman's legal position in Israel was weaker than a man's. Though a husband could divorce his wife for "some uncleanness in her," no law is given suggesting that a wife could divorce her husband (Deut. 24:1-4). Wives could be required to take a jealousy test if they were suspected of unfaithfulness to their husbands, but no law is given permitting a wife to require the same of her husband (Num. 5:11-31).

Although men usually owned property, daughters could receive the inheritance from their fathers if there were no sons in the family (Num. 27:8-11). Since theoretically the dowry belonged to the bride, some have suggested that this gift represented the daughter's share of her father's estate. She received her "inheritance" upon marriage, while her brothers had to wait to receive their shares until the father's death.

Children were to respect both mother and father equally (Exod. 20:12), even though they were the mother's special charge (Exod. 21:15; Prov. 1:8; 6:20; 20:20). To disobey or curse either parent was punishable by stoning (Deut. 21:18-21). If a man and a woman were caught in the act of adultery, both were to be stoned (Deut. 22:22).

The husband exercised his spiritual leadership by presenting the sacrifices and offerings for the family (Lev. 1:2), but only women offered a sacrifice after the birth of a child (Lev. 12:6). Women also participated in worship, but they were not required, as the men, to appear before the Lord (Deut. 29:10; Neh. 8:2; Joel 2:16). This optional participation may have been because of their responsibilities as wives and mothers (1 Sam. 1:3-5,21-22).

Jesus offered women new roles and equal status in His kingdom. A company of women often traveled with Him (Luke 8:1-3), and He often spoke highly of women (Matt. 9:20-22; Luke 21:1-4). He safeguarded the rights of women, especially in His teachings on marriage and divorce (Matt. 5:27-32; 19:3-9).

Jesus treated men and women as equal in spiritual privilege but as different in spiritual activity. No woman was among the 12 disciples nor among the 70 He sent out (Luke 10:1-12); the Lord's Supper was instituted within a group of men (Matt. 26:26-29).

Although in contemporary usage "helper" (Hb. *ezer*) is generally understood as someone in a menial position, "helper" in the OT merely describes the ethical, spiritual, and physical assistance given to one in need. The term *helper* defines a woman's role in the functional difference existing between husband and wife. Whoever helps provides support, walks alongside, offers advice without forcing compliance, and acts in response to a need presented.

A helper is one who provides what is lacking in another, one who can do what another cannot do alone. The Lord comes as a helper to assist the helpless, not because He is inferior and relegated to menial "helping" tasks, but rather because He alone has what is necessary to meet the needs (Exod. 18:4; Deut. 33:7; Hos. 13:9; Ps. 70:5). The nuance of meaning in the term *helper* is not related to worth or personhood but rather concerns role or function, for example, the realm in which help is to be offered. The foundation for the divine institution of marriage is found in the man's need and the woman's ability to meet that need—a reciprocity designed by the Creator.

The Scripture affirms that women functioned in the early church with service, influence, leadership, and teaching. They are encouraged to work within the divinely given framework based upon the natural order of creation and appropriateness of function. Women are admonished to share the gospel; they may pray and prophesy in the church, but they are given boundaries within which to exercise their gifts. Only two restrictions are given: teaching men and ruling over men—and that within two spheres, the home and church (1 Tim. 2:11-15).

WOODWORKER

Person who worked with wood in some sense—cutting trees in a forest (1 Kings 5:6); bringing the logs to where they were needed (v. 9); building the house and the furniture needed for it (2 Kings 22:6); and making beautiful objects of art from wood. See *Occupations and Professions.*

WOOL

Thick hair forming the coat of sheep and some other animals. It was made into thread and used to make clothing, blankets, and other articles. Gideon used a piece of wool to determine God's will for his life (Judg. 6:35-40). Wool was also used as a symbol of whiteness and purity (Isa. 1:18). See *Cloth, Clothing; Sheep.*

WORD

Utterance or saying that may refer to a single work, the entire law, the gospel message, or even Christ. Hebrew *word* can also mean a thing, event, or action (Gen. 18:14). Occasionally, difficulty arises in distinguishing between these meanings (Ps. 35:20, NRSV, "deceitful words"; KJV, "deceitful matters"; REB, "intrigues"; NIV, "false accusations").

The prophets claimed God commissioned them (Isa. 6:8) to deliver the "word of God" (Jer. 1:9). God's word may be visualized as a great salvation (Isa. 2:2-5) or a great judgment (Jer. 26:4-6). In the covenant law God spoke the words of the law to Moses (Ex. 20:1; 24:3-8). The heart of the law is called the ten words (Ex. 34:28; Deut. 4:13). The entire law represents the will of God and so can be called a single "word" (Deut. 4:2, KJV). This word also demands response: faithful obedience will bring God's blessing while disobedience will lead to a curse (Deut. 30:15-20).

God created the world by His word (Gen. 1; Isa. 48:13; Ps. 33:9). This world reveals God's majesty (Ps. 19:1) and thus extends the sphere of His revelation beyond His work with covenant Israel to all people. The word is spoken of as if it were a person who directs the events of nature (Pss. 147:15-18; 148:8), saves (107:20), and gives life (Ezek. 37:1-4).

Jesus' message of the coming kingdom can be called a "word" (Mark 2:2; 4:33; Luke 5:1) as can His individual sayings (Matt. 26:75; Luke 22:61; John 7:36). Jesus' word demanded decision on the part of the hearers (John 8:51; 12:47).

The message concerning Jesus, the gospel, can also be called "a word" (1 Thess. 2:13; compare 1 Cor. 2:2; 15:3-5; Gal. 3:1). Because of His sacrifice and resurrection, the gospel message is a "word of reconciliation" (2 Cor. 5:19) and a "word of life" (Phil. 2:16). The word is witnessed and proclaimed by Jesus' followers (Luke 1:2; Acts 4:2; 6:7). The word revealed through His son (Heb. 1:1-4) brings illumination and judgment.

Jesus Himself is the Word—the living Word. The preexistent Word who was with God "in the beginning" has now become flesh (John 1:1-18). Now the Word dwells among us revealing the glory of God (John 1:14).

Only God's word has irresistible potency (Isa. 55:11) and absolute creative power (Gen. 1:3-31; Luke 1:32-35; compare Isa. 9:8; 31:2; 45:23). A person's word is often powerless (1 Cor. 2:4; 4:19-20) and frequently fails (Matt. 21:28-32).

Words are capable of great good and evil (Matt. 12:36; Jas. 3:5-6,8). Words can deeply injure (Prov. 12:18; 18:14), and revive (Prov. 12:18,25; 16:24). Words from the wicked are like a fire-spreading torch (Prov. 16:27-28); words from the good bring good fruit (Prov. 12:14; 10:11).

WORK, THEOLOGY OF

Meaning and value God places on human labor. God's people work because they are made in His image. God worked to create a universe and continues working to sustain creation. Sin affected the original circumstances of people's work. People after the fall have to labor hard to carve out a living. Nature does not cooperate like it would without the curse. People's physical ability has been limited by the effect of sin. A person's mental capacity has been drastically reduced by the ravages of sin. The primal commission for humanity to subdue the earth remains in force.

Christianity affects the work of employees and the attitude of employers. Christians view their service to their employer as ultimately rendered to God, knowing He is the ultimate judge of their efforts (Eph. 6:5-8). Christian supervisors or employers know they are accountable to God for how they treat those under them (Eph. 5:9).

God's people realize His plan for work also includes a plan for rest (Ex. 20:8-11). God's people see their primary vocation as serving Him.

WORKS

Deeds leading to planned results, both by God and people. God's works are His acts and deeds in creating, saving, and sustaining (Judg. 2:7; Pss. 8:6; 103:22; 104:24; Isa. 64:8; Eph. 2:10; Phil. 1:6). Jesus Christ came to do the work of God (John 4:34; 5:17; 9:4.) The miraculous works of Christ testify to His divine nature and mission (John 5:36; 6:28-29; 10:37-38). Christ calls and enables His followers to continue His works (John 14:12; 1 Cor. 15:58; 16:10). Those who do the works of the devil show that they are of the devil (John 8:34-44; 2 Cor. 11:14-15). Sinners are called to cast off the works of darkness (Rom. 13:12; Gal. 5:19; Eph. 5:11; Col. 1:21). Because sinners cannot save themselves, they must rely on the grace of God: not on their own works (Rom. 3:26–5:2; 9:32; Gal. 2:16; 3:2,5,10; Eph. 2:8-9; Titus 3:4-7).

One evidence of saving faith, however, is the existence of good works in the lives of believers (Matt. 5:16; Acts 9:36; Eph. 2:10; Col. 1:10; 2 Thess. 2:17; 1 Tim. 2:10; 5:10,25; Titus 2:7,14; Heb. 10:24; Jas. 2:14-26; 1 Pet. 2:12). The Lord commends His churches for their good works and rebukes them for the works that are not worthy of His people (Rev. 2:2,5,9,13,19,23,26; 3:1,2,8,15). God does not judge according to outward appearances but according to works (Matt. 7:21-23; 1 Cor. 3:10-15; 1 Pet. 1:17; Rev. 20:12-13; 22:12). See *Faith; Salvation.*

WORLD, THE

The created order in the totality of its space and time; "the heaven and the earth" (Gen. 1:1), "heaven and earth, the sea, and all that in them is" (Ex. 20:11; compare Phil. 2:10), or "heaven, the heaven of heavens, with all their host, the earth, and all things that are therein, the seas, and all that is therein" (Neh. 9:6). The world consisted of an expanse of land ("the earth") surrounded by water and set under the canopy of the heavens.

God created everything above the earth, on the earth, and under it (Gen. 1:1–2:3; Job 38). The Greek concept of the world as an ordered system is absent from Hebrew thought. World in the Bible thus has various nuances:

(1) *The whole created order* (Acts 17:24) witnesses to God's sovereignty (Acts 4:24).

(2) *The earth and its inhabitants* (John 1:9; 12:19; 13:1; 16:28). The meaning of "the world" in John 3:16 should probably be understood in this sense.

(3) *The arena of human activity.* This especially pertains to wealth and material goods. "The cares of this world" can choke out the word (Mark 4:19). Married persons may be especially troubled over worldly affairs (1 Cor. 7:33-34). "Love not the world, neither the things that are in the world" (1 John 2:15; compare 2:16-17).

(4) *All that is hostile, rebellious, and opposed to God* (Rom 8:19-25; compare 2 Pet. 1:4). The world is under the power of "the prince of this world" (John 12:31; 14:30; 16:11; 2 Cor. 4:4; Eph. 2:2; 1 John 5:19). The coming of Jesus brought judgment to the world (9:39; 12:31).

Paul contrasted the wisdom of this world with the wisdom of God (1 Cor. 1:20-21,26-28; 3:19). "The princes of this age" cannot understand God's wisdom hidden in Christ (1 Cor. 2:7-8). Through the cross, Christ triumphed over all the powers of this world (Col. 2:15). Indeed, God was in Christ "reconciling the world unto himself" (2 Cor. 5:19; Col. 1:20; compare 1:29; 3:17; 10:36; 12:47).

The world is not inherently evil being created by God's Word (John 1:3-4). Jesus is "the light of the world" (8:12) and "the Savior of the world" (4:42).

The world will hate the disciples as it hated Jesus (15:18) because they are not of the world (15:19). The disciples are to be in the world but not "of the world" (17:14-16; compare 13:35). Victory over the hostility of the world is assured through the cross of Jesus (16:33) and through faith (1 John 5:4-5). The "world" is already passing away (1 John 2:17). See *Creation; Earth; Heaven.*

WORM

Small, slender, softbodied animal without a backbone, legs, or eyes. Insect larvae are called worms. The earthworm is the most representative of the worms of Palestine, used as a figure of lowliness or weakness (Ps. 22:6; Job 17:14; Isa. 41:14). The place of the ungodly and unbeliever is where the worm is always alive and working (Isa. 66:24: Mark 9:44,48).

WORMWOOD

Nonpoisonous but bitter plant often used in analogy to speak of bitterness and sorrow; opposite of justice and righteousness (Amos 5:7; Jer. 23:15); one of the blazing stars which brings destruction (Rev. 8:10-11).

WORSHIP

Human response to the perceived presence of the divine (Gen. 28:16-17). The response may be private and intensely personal, in the form of prayers, confessions, silence, and meditative experiences of various sorts (Matt. 26:39; Mark 14:32-35; Luke 22:41).

Worship in the Bible moves back and forth between personal experience and corporate experience. Corporate worship is empowered by personal experience, but personal experience needs affirmation and interpretation in corporate worship. Thus, early Christians were warned not to neglect meeting together in worship but to encourage one another in the faith and in the spiritual life (Heb. 10:25). Assembling together in worship is an affirmation of what the worshipers believe and an opportunity for mutual response to the gracious actions of God.

God is present with His people at any time. Still, He has set out times and seasons for worship (Ex. 23:14,17). See *Festivals.* Sharpened awareness of the divine presence may result from intensive exercises of worship during special times and at special places. These occasions and places are also the contexts for religious education and the development and enjoyment of fellowship among the worshipers. The psalms with expressions of lament, confession, thanksgiving, praise, teaching, and celebration show the breadth of OT worship. See *Day of Atonement; Festivals; Sabbath.*

For Christians the whole complex of temple activities, priesthood, sacrifice, and sin-cleansing rituals either became obsolete or were reinterpreted in major ways (for instance, the church itself becomes the temple (1 Cor. 6:19; Eph. 2:21-22; 1 Pet. 2:9). The Lord's Supper, the crucifixion, and the resurrection of Jesus are all closely related to the Passover celebration (1 Cor. 11:23-26; Matt. 26:17, 26-28 and parallels). The Christian Easter is a form of the Passover. Early Christians converted Pentecost (see Acts 2:1-42) into a Christian observance (1 Cor. 16:8; Acts 20:16). Tabernacles/Booths has not been continued in Christian worship except in the related forms of thanksgiving observances and harvest festivals. The Day of Atonement is used theologically to interpret Christ's sacrifice in Heb. 8–9. See *Church Year.*

The early Christians met for worship on the first day of the week (Acts 20:7; compare 1 Cor. 16:2; John 20:19,26). They attended the temple together on a daily basis (Acts 2:46). The early Christian meetings were joyful occasions for teaching, prophesying, singing, praying, reading apostolic letters, and "breaking of bread" in the Lord's Supper (Acts 2:42,46; 1 Cor. 14:26; Eph. 5:19-20; Col. 3:16; 1 Thess. 5:16-18). The first-day-of-the-week meetings of the early Christians were not sabbaths. The first-day celebration became "the Lord's day" (Rev. 1:10) with emphasis on the resurrection.

The heart of Christian worship is the power of Christ's presence in a gathered community of disciples (see Matt. 18:20; John 14:12-14; Acts 2:43-47; 4:9-12,32-37; 1 Cor. 5:3-4; Rev. 2:1). The presence of Christ is especially manifest in the breaking of the bread at the Lord's Supper (compare Luke 24:28-32,35).

WORSHIP STYLES

Differing ways of expressing God's worth to God. All worship performed in spirit and truth is acceptable to God (John 4:23). Styles of worship are as varied as are people who offer themselves to God. The Bible provides numerous examples of worship experiences, both public (1 Chron. 29:20) and private (Gen. 22:5), animated (2 Sam. 6:14-16) and sedate (Dan. 6:10). Typically in worship persons bowed before God as a sign of fear and reverence (Ex. 12:27; 1 Chron. 29:20; Pss. 5:7; 95:6; Matt. 2:11; compare Isa. 6:1-7). At other times singing and dancing before the LORD were more appropriate (Ex. 15:20-21; 2 Sam. 6:14-16).

Psalms were sung or chanted in worship (compare Ps. 57:7-8; 150:1-6). Music also played an important role in the worship experience of the early church (Eph. 5:19-20; Col. 3:16). Animal sacrifices were an important part of worship in the OT (Lev. 1–9). Christians are instructed instead to offer up to God a sacrifice of praise (Heb. 13:15).

WRATH, WRATH OF GOD

The emotional response to perceived wrong and injustice experienced by humans and God. The wrath of God appears as a divine response to human sin and injustice (Num. 11:10; Deut. 9:7; Luke 13:3-5; 15:6; 16:19-31; Matt. 3:7; John 3:36; Rom. 2:5); especially idolatry (Ps. 78:56-66). The wrath of God is consistently directed toward those who do not follow His will (Deut. 1:26-46; Josh. 7:1; Ps. 2:1-6). Historical calamity and disaster were to be expected when God was stirred to anger (1 Sam. 28:18-19). The instruments of God's wrath may be angels (Rev. 15:1,7), nations, kings, and rulers as well as natural catastrophes. The OT often speaks of a "day of wrath" coming in the future (Zeph. 1:14-15; compare Isa. 13:9). See *Day of the Lord.* Repentance turns God's wrath away from the sinner (Ps. 85:1-3).

The grace of God, His unmerited favor, holds the full effect of wrath back at the same time that wrath "rests upon" the sinner. The Christian has no fear of this day, since Jesus "delivers us from the wrath to come" (1 Thess. 1:10).

Human wrath is always suspect. We are not to take revenge (Rom. 12:19), nor to "let the sun go down upon your wrath" (Eph. 4:26). Fathers should not provoke children to wrath (Eph. 6:4). We must rid ourselves of "all these: anger, wrath, malice, blasphemy, filthy communication" (Col. 3:8). The OT psalms of lament such as Pss. 53; 137 show how humans can freely express their anger to God. To realize this freedom from the domination of wrath, the gracious work of the Holy Spirit is needed to sanctify and cleanse the heart of the attitudes and feelings of wrath and anger (Rom. 8:6; compare 6:19). There is no need to continue in the fleshly spirit of wrath for the Holy Spirit provides inner peace (Phil. 4:4-8).

WRITING

Human ability to record and communicate information through etching signs on stone or drawing them on skins or papyrus. Writing began in the Ancient Near East about 3500 B.C. in Mesopotamia. These were business documents used for accounting purposes. The early tablets typically were inscribed with a picture or pictures identifying the commodity, numbers, and personal names. The Sumerians were the first to write different words having the same sound with the same picture. Soon after, the Sumerians began to use stylized pictures composed of wedges impressed in the clay tablet with a stylus, developing the hundreds of wedge- shaped signs of the cuneiform script. The cuneiform script was adopted by the Semitic speaking Akkadians, the Elamites, and Hurrians. Akkadian became the international language of trade and diplomacy for several centuries.

By about 3000 B.C. the Egyptians had developed a hieroglyphic system of writing, the so-called sacred picture writing. Similar to Sumerian,

hieroglyphic signs could be read as signs for words or ideas, as phonetic signs, and as determinatives. The Egyptians developed a cursive script, called hieratic, to meet the needs of everyday life. Hieratic was written with brush and ink on the smooth surfaces of stone and papyrus. About 700 B.C. hieratic was further simplified into another cursive script, demotic.

The Hittites of Anatolia spoke an Indo-European language but adopted the Akkadian cuneiform writing system. Then about 1500 B.C. a hieroglyphic system known as Hittite hieroglyphics, not influenced by the older Egyptian hieroglyphics, began to appear.

The first-known attempts to produce an alphabet were made in Syria-Palestine (Ugarit 1500–1200 B.C.) based on cuneiform. The Sinaitic inscriptions from about 1000 B.C. represent the earliest stage in the development of the Canaanite linear script which is reminiscent of Egyptian hieroglyphics but consists of only about 30 signs.

Hebrew script can be traced beginning with the Gezer Calendar (950 B.C.). After the exile the "square" script of Aramaic origin began to replace the cursive script, as the Elephantine papyri show.

Moses was directed to write down historical events (Ex. 17:14), laws and statutes (Ex. 34:1-9), and the words of the Lord (Ex. 24:4). Joshua wrote the law of Moses (Josh. 8:32) and statutes and ordinances in the book of the law of God (Josh. 24:26; compare Judg. 8:14; 1 Sam. 10:25; 2 Sam. 11:14; 2 Chron. 2:11). Many references to the "chronicles of the kings of Israel" and Judah perhaps indicate court diaries or annals (1 Kings 14:19). The prophets wrote, or dictated, their oracles (Isa. 8:1,16; 30:8; Jer. 30:1-2; 36:27-28). Nehemiah as an official under Persian appointment wrote down the covenant to keep the law of God (Neh. 9:38), to which several men set their seals as witnesses (Neh. 10:1-27). We have no firm evidence the general populace could read or write, or even that they had much need to do so.

Jesus could both read (Luke 4:16-21) and write (John 8:6).

Stone was used in all periods in the Ancient Near East as a writing surface, especially for monumental and memorial inscriptions. In Egypt the walls of temples were covered with historical inscriptions chiseled into the stone. In Mesopotamia and Anatolia inscriptions were cut into the faces of mountains (compare the Behistun Rock) or into stones of various sizes for monuments on public display (compare the Code of Hammurabi and boundary markers) or for small inscriptions to be included in foundation deposits. In the OT the law was written on stone (Ex. 24:12; compare Deut. 27:1-10).

Clay was the main writing medium for cuneiform scripts. Impressions were made on the soft clay by the use of a stylus. Often legal documents and letters would be encased in a clay envelope on which a summary of the text was written and over which cylinder seals would be rolled to identify witnesses. The OT makes no clear reference to clay tablets used by Israelites.

Wooden tablets, covered by clay or wax, were used as writing surfaces in both Egypt and Mesopotamia. The Bible mentions writing on wooden staffs (Num. 17:2-3) and on wooden staves (Ezek. 37:16). Isaiah 30:8 and Hab. 2:2 may refer to writing on wooden tablets. Zechariah wrote on a tablet of wood with a wax surface (Luke 1:63). Inscriptions in a poorly understood syllabic script from Byblos were written on bronze sheets. Especially well known are the two copper scrolls from Qumran which contain a list of the treasures of the community. The potsherd provided a cheap and highly useful surface for letters, economic records, and school copy texts. They were inscribed with pen (or brush) and ink.

Papyrus made from a reed was used very early in Egypt and continued in use through the early centuries of our era. Sheets of papyrus could be glued together to form long scrolls. As Aramaic began to be accepted as the international language, papyrus became more widely used in Mesopotamia and Syria-Palestine. The first edition of Jeremiah's book was likely written on papyrus (Jer. 36). The documents of the Jewish community at Elephantine were written on papyrus. Several works on papyrus were among the literary remains from Qumran. Large collections of papyri from Egypt written in Koine Greek helped to elucidate the NT writings.

Carefully prepared leather was used for most of the biblical scrolls at Qumran. Torah scrolls are still written on leather. Sections of leather would be sewn together to form scrolls of lengths appropriate for the book or work. Horizontal lines were often pressed into the leather to act as guides for the scribe. The codex, or book, was made only from parchment.

Writing implements included the "pen," probably a reference to a reed pen whose end fibers were separated to form a brush (Ps. 45:1) or to an iron pen designed to make inscriptions on rock (Jer. 17:1; Job 19:24), a graving tool (Ex. 32:4) and a stylus (Isa. 8:1).

Ink was made from carbon black and gum resin and could be washed from a writing surface such as papyrus. Writing cases (Ezek. 9:2-3,11), known in both Egyptian and Mesopotamian literature and art work, provided containers for pens, brushes, styluses, and ink. The scribe's knife (Jer. 36:23) was probably used to size and trim papyrus, leather, or parchment. See *Akkadian; Aramaic; Archaeology; Hebrew; Pottery.*

X, Y, Z

XERXES

Persian king (486–464 B.C.), known in Book of Esther as Ahasuerus; son of Darius the Great and grandson of Cyrus the Great; campaigned militarily against the Greeks, avenging the loss at Marathon in 490. His armada suffered a crippling defeat in the Bay of Salamis in 480, and he soon lost interest in attempting to defeat the Greeks. See *Esther; Persia.*

YAH

Shortened form of Yahweh, Hebrew name for God of the covenant. See *God; Jehovah; Lord; YHWH.*

YEAR See *Calendar.*

YEAR OF JUBILEE See *Festivals.*

YELLOW

Two Hebrew words are translated "yellow."

(1) Gold strongly alloyed with silver (Ps. 68:13); sallow color of sick skin (Lev. 13:49).

(2) Bright red or gold; color of hair in a patch of skin that lets priest know it is leprous. (Lev. 13:30,32,36). See *Colors.*

YHWH

Four consonants which make up the divine name in Hebrew (Ex. 3:15); found more than 6,000 times in the OT. The written Hebrew language did not include vowels, thus readers supplied the vowels as they read. Reverence for the divine name led to the practice of avoiding its use lest one run afoul of commandments such as Ex. 20:7 or Lev. 24:16. In time it was thought the divine name was too holy to pronounce at all. Thus, the practice arose of using the word *'adonai:* "Lord." In most English translations YHWH is recognizable where the word LORD appears in small caps following the L. (See *God; Jehovah; Lord.*) The actual pronunciation of YHWH was lost. In the Middle Ages Jewish scholars developed a system of symbols placed under and beside the consonants to indicate the vowels. YHWH appeared with the vowels from *'adonai* as a device to remind them to say "Adonai" when they read the text. A latinized form of this combination of YHWH's consonants and *'adonai's* vowels was pronounced "Jehovah," but it was actually not a real word at all. From the study of the structure of the Hebrew language most scholars today believe that YHWH was probably pronounced "Yahweh."

YOD

Tenth letter of Hebrew alphabet used as title of Ps. 119:73-80 (KJV, "Jod") in which all verses begin with the letter.

YOKE

Wooden frame placed on the backs of draft animals to make them pull in tandem. The simple yokes consisted of a bar with two loops either of rope or wood which went around the animals' necks. More elaborate yokes had shafts connected to the middle with which the animals pulled plows or other implements. The word is used most often in the Bible to speak of slavery, bondage, and hardship (1 Kings 12:4, Jer. 27:8). Positive usages include the yoke of Christ (Matt. 11:29-30) and the joint nature of the church's work (Phil. 4:3).

ZAANAIM

KJV, TEV spelling of Zaanannim (Judg. 4:11) following written Hebrew text rather than scribal note and Josh. 19:33.

ZAANAN (*sheep country* or *outback*)

Unidentified city in southernmost Judah (Mic. 1:11), probably identical with Zenan (Josh. 15:37).

ZAANANNIM

Town on northeastern corner of Naphtali near Kadesh (Josh. 19:33; Judg.

4:11); "plain of Zaanaim" (Judg. 4:11, KJV) is literally, "great tree in Zaanannim" (NIV) or "oak in Zaanannim" (NASB; note transliterations of REB, NRSV). This probably indicates a "sacred tree" associated with a worship center. See Terebinth.

ZAAVAN (tremble or quake)

Son of Ezer (Gen. 36:27; 1 Chron. 1:42).

ZABAD (He has given or gift)

(1) Member of Judah (1 Chron. 2:36-37).

(2) Ephramite (1 Chron. 7:21).

(3) One of David's "thirty" elite warriors (1 Chron. 11:41); first of 21 names the Chronicler appended to list paralleling that of 2 Sam. 23:24-39.

(4) Assassin of King Joash (2 Chron. 24:26), called Jozacar in 2 Kings 12:21.

(5) Three postexilic laymen ordered to divorce their foreign wives (Ezra 10:27,33, 43).

ZABBAI (pure)

(1) Son of Bebai who promised Ezra he would put away his foreign wife (Ezra 10:28).

(2) Father of Baruch who worked on Jerusalem wall (Neh. 3:20). Some say 1 and 2 may be same person. Early scribal note (qere) in Nehemiah writes name, "Zaccai."

ZABBUD (gift)

Descendant of Bigvai who returned to Jerusalem with Ezra (Ezra 8:14). Scribal note (qere) has "Zaccur." See Zabud.

ZABDI (my gift or short form of Yah gives)

(1) Son of Zerah of Judah (Josh. 7:1).

(2) Man of Benjamin (1 Chron. 8:19).

(3) Man in charge of David's wine cellars (1 Chron. 27:27).

(4) Son of Asaph who led in thanksgiving and prayer (Neh. 11:17).

ZABDIEL (God gives gifts or My gift is God)

(1) Descendant of David (1 Chron. 27:2).

(2) Overseer in Jerusalem (Neh. 11:14).

ZABUD (endowed)

Son of Nathan, a priest and Solomon's friend (1 Kings 4:5).

ZABULON

KJV spelling of Zebulun in NT.

ZACCAI (pure or innocent)

Ancestor of returning exiles (Ezra 2:9; Neh. 7:14).

ZACCHEUS (innocent)

Corrupt tax collector in Jericho (Luke 19:2-9). Jesus surprised him by calling him by name to come down from tree and take Jesus home for dinner. His newfound faith led Zaccheus to restore with interest the money he had taken illegally.

ZACC(H)UR (well remembered)

(1) Father of Shammua of Reuben (Num. 13:4).

(2) Descendant of Mishma of Simeon (1 Chron. 4:26).

(3) Descendant of Merari among Levites (1 Chron. 24:27).

(4) Son of Asaph (1 Chron. 25:2; Neh. 12:35).

(5) Son of Imri who helped rebuild walls (Neh. 3:2).

(6) One who sealed covenant of reform (Neh. 10:12).

(7) Father of Hanan, one of the treasurers Nehemiah appointed (13:13). See Zabbud.

ZACHARIAH

KJV alternate spelling of Zechariah.

ZACHARIAS (Greek form of Zechariah, Yah remembered)

Priest in Jerusalem and father of John the Baptist (Luke 1:5-64). Struck dumb for his lack of faith until he confirmed baby's name as John. See Zechariah.

ZACHER

KJV alternate form of Zechariah (1 Chron. 8:31).

ZADOK (righteous, short form of Zedekiah)

(1) Son of Ahitub and father of Ahimaaz, descended from Aaron through Eleazar; priest (2 Sam. 8:17; 1 Chron. 6:3-8; 24:3) loyal to David when Adonijah rebelled in his father's old age (1 Kings 1) and so also served under Solomon when Abiathar was removed from priestly duties (1 Sam. 2:31-33; 1 Kings 2:26-27). See Abiathar. Genealogy of Zadok (1 Chron. 6:3-15) mentions second Zadok seven generations later.

(2) Grandfather of Jotham, king of Judah (2 Kings 15:33).

(3)–(4) Men who helped Nehemiah rebuild Jerusalem wall (Neh. 3:4,29).

(5) Leader who signed Nehemiah's covenant (Neh. 10:21).

(6) Faithful scribe Nehemiah appointed as a treasurer (Neh. 13:13).

ZADOKITES

Descendants of Zadok. Ezekiel reserved service in the ideal future temple to Zadokites (Ezek. 44:9-31). The returning priests, including Joshua son of Jehozadak (1 Chron. 6:15) and Ezra (7:1-7), were Zadokites. See High Priest; Priests; Levites; Zadok.

ZAHAM (fatness or loathing)

Son of King Rehoboam by Abihail (2 Chron. 11:18-19).

ZAHAR

Source of wool traded with Tyre (Ezek. 27:18, NIV, NLT, CEV, NCV; "Sahar," TEV; "Suhar," REB). KJV, NASB, NRSV translate Hebrew as "white wool." If Hebrew refers to place, association with Damascus and Helbon suggests Syrian site, perhaps modern as-Sahra northwest of Damascus.

ZAIR (small)

Place where Joram, king of Judah (853–841 B.C.), fought with Edom

(2 Kings 8:20-21). Some place it south of the Dead Sea near Edom. Others equate it with Zoar (Gen. 13:10) or Zior (Josh. 15:54). Parallel in 2 Chron. 21:9 reads, "with his princes."

ZALAPH (caper plant)

Father of Hanun, who helped repair the walls of Jerusalem (Neh. 3:30).

ZALMON (little dark one or small image)

(1) Mountain near Shechem where Abimelech and his men cut brush with which to burn tower of Shechem (Judg. 9:48-49).

(2) One of David's "thirty" mighty men (2 Sam. 23:28); also known as Ilai (1 Chron. 11:29).

(3) Ps.68:14 mentions a "hill of Bashan" named Zalmon (KJV, "Salmon"). This may refer to the Golan Heights.

ZALMONAH (dark or shady)

Israel's first stop after leaving Mount Hor (Num. 33:41-42).

ZALMUNNA (Protection is withdrawn or Zelem [god] rules)

King of Midian captured and killed by Gideon (Judg. 8:1-21; Ps. 83:11).

ZAMZUMMIM

Name Ammonites gave Rephaim. They lived east of the Jordan River until the Ammonites drove them out (Deut. 2:20). See Rephaim.

ZAMZUMMITES

NIV form of Zamzummim.

ZANOAH (broken district or stinking)

(1) Village in Judah identified with Khirbet Zanu about 3 miles south southeast of Beth-Shemesh (Josh. 15:34; Neh. 3:13; 11:30).

(2) City in highlands of Judah (Josh. 15:56); identification with Khirbet Beit Amra.

ZAPHENATH-PANEAH or ZAPHNATH-PAANEAH (the god has said, "he will live")

Pharaoh's name for Joseph (Gen. 41:45).

ZAPHON (north)

(1) City east of Jordan River in Gad's territory (Josh. 13:27) where Jephthah confronted Ephraim (Judg. 12:1); probably center of worship of god Baalzaphon for Canaanites; identified with tell el-Qos, tell es-Saidiye, or tell el-Mazar. Shophan (Num. 32:35) may be another spelling of same city. See Zephon.

(2) Mountain viewed as home of gods in Canaanite thought, perhaps referred to in Ps. 48:2 (NIV; compare 89:12), Isa. 14:13 (NRSV), and Job 26:7 (NRSV; compare Ezek. 39:2), showing Yahweh controls what Canaan thought their gods possessed. See Directions (Geographical).

ZARA

KJV alternate form of Zerah (Matt. 1:3).

ZAREAH

KJV form of Zorah (Neh. 11:29).

ZAREATHITE

KJV form of Zorathite in 1 Chron. 2:53.

ZARED

KJV form of Zered in Num. 21:12.

ZAREPHATH (smelting, refining)

Town on Mediterranean seacoast 8 miles south of Sidon, 14 miles north of Tyre, and 50 miles north of Mount Carmel near modern Sarafand; where God sent Elijah after prophesying a drought (1 Kings 17:2-9); home of a widow and her son whose supply of meal and oil God miraculously sustained (17:12-16). Elijah restored her son to life (17:17-23). Northern border of Israel in Obadiah's prophecy (v. 20); pottery-making and textile center.

ZARETAN

KJV form of Zarethan in Josh. 3:16.

ZARETH-SHAHAR

KJV form of Zereth-Shahar.

ZARETHAN (cooling)

Place near where Jordan backed up and Israel passed over into Canaan (Josh. 3:16) near Beth-shean (1 Kings 4:12); near where Hiram of Tyre cast bronze temple vessels (1 Kings 7:46; the parallel in 2 Chron. 4:17 reads Zeredah); most often identified with the two mounds of tell es-Saidiyah on east bank of Jordan about 14 miles north of Adam (tell ed-Damiyeh). Alternate sites include tell Umm Hamad, Sleihat, and tell el-Merkbere.

ZARHITE

KJV form of Zerahites.

ZARTANAH

KJV form of Zarethan (1 Kings 4:12).

ZARTHAN

KJV form of Zarethan (1 Kings 7:46).

ZATTHU ZATTU

Head of postexilic family in Jerusalem (Ezra 2:8; 10:27; Neh. 7:13; 10:14).

ZAVAN

KJV form of Zaavan (1 Chron. 1:42).

ZAYIN

Seventh letter of Hebrew alphabet. Title of Ps.119:49-56 where each verse begins with the letter.

ZAZA

Son of Jonathan and descendant of Jerahmeel (1 Chron. 2:33).

ZEALOT See Jewish Parties in the New Testament.

ZEBADIAH (Yahweh has given)

(1) Son of Beriah (1 Chron. 8:15).

(2) Son of Elpaal (1 Chron. 8:17).

(3) Son of Jehoram of Gedor (1 Chron. 12:7).

(4) Gatekeeper (1 Chron. 26:2).

(5) Fourth captain in David's army (1 Chron. 27:7).

(6) Levite Jehoshaphat sent to teach the law (2 Chron. 17:8).

(7) Son of Ishmael who ruled civil cases under Jehoshaphat (2 Chron. 19:11).

(8) Son of Shephatiah who returned to Jerusalem from Babylon (Ezra 8:8).

(9) Priest who put away foreign wife (Ezra 10:20).

ZEBAH (*slaughter* or *sacrifice*)

With Zalmunna, Midianite kings Gideon captured and killed because they had killed Gideon's brothers (Judg. 8:4-21; see Ps. 83:11; Isa. 9:4; 10:26).

ZEBAIM

Home of postexilic children of Pochereth (Ezra 2:57, KJV).

ZEBEDEE (*gift*)

Fisherman on the Sea of Galilee based at Capernaum; father of James and John, two of Jesus' first disciples (Mark 1:19-20). Simon Peter and Andrew worked for him (Luke 5:10). His wife, Mary, followed Jesus and ministered to Him (Mark 27:56). See *Zabdi*.

ZEBIDAH (*gift*)

Wife of Josiah; mother of King Jehoiakim (2 Kings 23:36; "Zebudah," KJV).

ZEBINA (*purchased*)

One who had a foreign wife (Ezra 10:43).

ZEBOIIM (*hyenas*)

City in the valley of Siddim (Gen. 14:2-3) at southern end of the Dead Sea ruled by King Shemeber but under the control of Chedorlaomer, king of Elam; destroyed when God sent fire and brimstone on Sodom and Gomorrah (Deut. 29:23; compare Hos. 11:8).

ZEBOIM (*hyenas* or *wild place*)

(1) Town Benjamites occupied after Exile (Neh. 11:34); may be Khirbet Sabije.

(2) Valley in Benjamin between Michmash and wilderness overlooking Jordan (1 Sam. 13:17-18); may be Wadi Abu Diba.

ZEBUDAH

KJV spelling of Zebidah.

ZEBUL (*prince* or *captain*)

Resident of Shechem and follower of Abimelech, son of Gideon (Judg. 9:30-41).

ZEBULUN (*elevated dwelling*)

Jacob's tenth son, sixth by Leah (Gen. 30:20). See *Tribes of Israel*.

ZECHARIAH (*Yah remembered*)

(1) Son of Jeroboam II, who reigned over Israel for six months in 746 B.C.; assassinated by Shallum (2 Kings 15:8-12). See *Israel*.

(2) Postexilic prophet (520–518 B.C.) who urged people of Judah to rebuild temple.

(3) Grandfather of Hezekiah (2 Kings 18:2).

(4) Priest and prophet whom the people stoned and Joash, the king, killed (2 Chron. 24:20-22).

(5) Postexilic temple gatekeeper of (1 Chron. 9:21).

(6) Gibeonite (1 Chron. 9:37).

(7) Temple musician (1 Chron. 15:20).

(8) Community leader Jehoshaphat the king sent to teach (2 Chron. 17:7).

(9) One of Josiah's overseers in repairing the temple (2 Chron. 34:12).

(10)–(11) Men who accompanied Ezra on return from Babylon (Ezra 8:3,11).

(12) Man Ezra sent to get Levites to return from Babylon (Ezra 8:16).

(13) Israelite with foreign wife (Ezra 10:26).

(14) Man who helped Ezra as he taught the law (Neh. 8:4), perhaps identical with 12 or other above.

(15) Ancestor of postexilic resident of Jerusalem (Neh. 11:4).

(16) Ancestor of postexilic resident of Jerusalem (Neh. 11:5).

(17) Ancestor of priest (Neh. 11:12).

(18) Leading priest in time of Joiakim's high priesthood, possibly the same as the prophet (Neh. 12:16).

(19)–(20) Priestly musicians who helped Nehemiah celebrate (Neh. 12:35,41).

(21) High official Isaiah used as witness, perhaps same as 3 above.

(22) Son of Jehoshaphat whom his brother Jehoram killed upon becoming king (2 Chron. 21:2-4).

(23) Godly advisor of King Uzziah (2 Chron. 26:5).

(24) Descendant of tribe of Reuben (1 Chron. 5:7).

(25) Father of leader of eastern half of tribe of Manasseh (1 Chron. 27:21).

(26)–(34) Levites (1 Chron. 15:18,24; 24:25; 26:2,14,11; 2 Chron. 20:14; 29:13; 35:8). *See Zacharias.*

ZECHARIAH, BOOK OF

Eleventh of so-called Minor Prophets. In 538, Cyrus the Great, Persian emperor issued an edict (Ezra 1:2-4; 6:3-5) allowing Jews in Babylon to return to Jerusalem. Apparently, an effort was made to begin rebuilding the temple under an official named Sheshbazzar (Ezra 5:14-16) and perhaps Zerubbabel (Ezra 3:1-13; Zech. 4:9), but the work stopped due to opposition from persons who had not been in Exile and local officials. Cyrus' son Cambyses (530–521 B.C.) died with no heir. Darius I and Gautama fought for the crown. In the midst of that turmoil, God raised two prophets, Haggai and Zechariah, to urge finishing the temple.

Zechariah 1–6 contains eight visions and two exhortations. God promised Judah and Jerusalem prosperity if they purified themselves from sin. The opening message (1:1-6) reminds the audience that God had warned their forefathers not to sin, but they had not listened or repented. They had brought the Exile upon themselves. The first three visions predict prosperity for Judah and Jerusalem. Four horsemen ride forth (1:7-17) to announce God's return to Zion, a new day when prosperity would come. In the second vision (1:18-21), 4 smiths (agents of God's deliverance) overcome 4 horns (symbols of the nations that ruled over Jerusalem). This reversal of fortunes would bring about the coming prosperity. In the third vision (2:1-13) a man measures Jerusalem, only to find that it is too small to accommodate all those God would return to live there in glory. The visions conclude with a call to Exiles to return home from Babylon.

The last five visions deal with purification. In vision four (3:1-10) the high priest Joshua is symbolically cleansed for his work. The fifth vision (4:1-14) pictures God as a lampstand with two olive trees standing beside Him: Joshua and Zerubbabel. Zerubbabel is named to finish building the temple, worship and sacrifice at which would be the means of purification. Vision six (5:1-4) involves a scroll flying through the air condemning stealing and lying to cover up one's theft. In the seventh vision (5:5-11), Zechariah saw an ephah, a container with a heavy, lead cover. This ephah instead held a woman, who symbolizes impurity. Two women with wings came to take the iniquity back to Babylon, from which it had come. In the last vision (6:1-8), four charioteers head out in all directions to patrol the earth (and presumably to punish evil). Chapters 7 and 8 show that God seeks righteousness and not ritual and will punish his people.

The last six chapters presuppose the temple exists and so at least must have been written after 515, when the temple was finished. In addition, 11:12-13 is quoted in Matt. 27:9-10 as a saying of Jeremaih. The chapters differ in style and contents from both Jeremiah and Zechariah 1–6 and must represent the later work of Zechariah.

Chapters 9 through 11 depict God's victory with His Messiah over the neighboring peoples, including the Greeks (9:1–10:7), the return of the

Exiles (10:6-12), and the punishment of the wicked leaders of Judah (11:4-17). Chapters 12–14 depict an end-time attack upon Jerusalem and the cities of Judah (12:1-3; 14:1-3), an attack in which many people would be killed as God purifies His people (13:7-9). God Himself would rescue His people (12:4-9; 14:4-5,12-15), cleanse the people from idolatry, rid the land of prophecy (which had become synonymous with false prophecy, 13:1-6), and turn Jerusalem into a paradise to which the nations of the world would come to worship. Zechariah 14 envisions the Mount of Olives splitting in two, with fresh water (representing the blessings of God) flowing east and west watering the world. Cold and nighttime, representing threats to God's control, would be eliminated as He came to reign over all the world from Jerusalem.

ZECHER

Form of Zechariah (1 Chron. 9:37) used in 1 Chron. 8:31.

ZEDAD (*sloping place or mountainous*)

Northern border of Canaan (Num. 34:8; Ezek. 47:15); Sadad, 62 miles north of Damascus.

ZEDEKIAH (*Yahweh is my righteousness* or *Yahweh is my salvation*)

(1) False prophet who advised King Ahab, in opposition to Micaiah, to fight against Ramoth-gilead, assuring the king of victory (1 Kings 22). Micaiah stated that God had put a lying spirit in the mouths of Zedekiah and his band of prophets. See *Micaiah; False Prophet*.

(2) Last king of Judah (596–586 B.C.); made king by Nebuchadnezzar (2 Kings 24:17). When he rebelled, Babylonian army besieged Jerusalem and destroyed it. Zedekiah was taken to Riblah along with his family. At Riblah he witnessed the executions of his sons before his own eyes were blinded (25:7). Then Zedekiah

was taken to Babylon. He apparently died in captivity. See *Israel*.

(3) Son either of Jehoiakim or Jeconiah (1 Chron. 3:16), the Hebrew text being unclear at this point.

(4) Signer of Nehemiah's covenant (10:1), KJV, "Zidkijah."

(5) Prophet who promised quick hope to Exiles in Babylon (Jer. 29:21). Jeremiah pronounced God's judgment on him.

(6) Royal official (Jer. 36:12).

ZEEB See *Oreb and Zeeb*.

ZEKER

NIV form of Zecher (1 Chron. 8:31).

ZELA, ZELAH (*rib, side, slope*)

Town allotted to Benjamin (Josh. 18:28), in which the bones of Saul and Jonathan were buried (2 Sam. 21:14); probably Khirbet Salah between Jerusalem and Gibeon.

ZELEK (*cleft, fissure*)

One of David's thirty elite warriors (2 Sam. 23:37; 1 Chron. 11:39).

ZELOPHEHAD (*protection from terror* or *kinsman is my protector*)

Hebrew who wandered in the wilderness with Moses and died without sons (Num. 26:33; 27:1-4). God led Moses to declare the daughters eligible to inherit their father's land (27:6-7; 36:5-9).

ZELOTES

KJV transliteration (Luke 6:15; Acts 1:13) of name for Simon, Jesus' disciple. See *Simon; Zealot*.

ZELZAH

Town near Rachel's tomb in Benjamin; site of first of three signs Samuel promised Saul as confirmation of his kingship (1 Sam. 10:1-2).

ZEMARAIM (*twin peaks*)

(1) Town allotted Benjamin (Josh. 18:22), likely Ras et-Tehuneh.

(2) Mountain in Ephraim where Abijah rebuked Jeroboam (2 Chron. 13:4).

ZEMARITES

Canaanites inhabiting area north of Lebanon between Arvad and Tripolis (Gen. 10:18; 1 Chron. 1:16); possibly gave their name to the town Sumra. NRSV emended the text of Ezek. 27:8 to read "men of Zemer" (KJV, "thy wise men, O Tyrus").

ZEMER (*wool*) See *Zemarites.*

ZEMIRA(H) (*song*)

Descendant of Benjamin (1 Chron. 7:8).

ZENAN (*flocks*)

Village in Shephelah (wilderness) district of Judah (Josh. 15:37), likely identified with 'Araq el-Kharba; perhaps identical to Zaanan (Mic. 1:11).

ZENAS (abbreviated form, *gift of Zeus*)

Christian lawyer whom Paul asked Titus to send, together with Apollos, on his way, lacking nothing (Titus 3:13). Zenas and Apollos perhaps delivered Paul's letter to Titus.

ZEPHANIAH (*Yahweh sheltered* or *stored up* or *Zaphon* [god] *is Yahweh*)

(1) Prophet whose preaching produced thirty-sixth book of the OT.

(2) Priest whom King Zedekiah sent asking Jeremiah to pray for nation threatened by Nebuchadrezzar of Babylon (Jer. 21:1-7; 37:3). He reported false prophecy from Babylon to Jeremiah (29:24-32). When Jerusalem fell, the priest was executed (52:24-27).

(3) Father of Josiah and Hen (Zech. 6:10,14), possibly identical with 2 above.

(4) Levite (1 Chron. 6:36), perhaps the same as Uriel (1 Chron. 6:24).

ZEPHANIAH, BOOK OF

Biblical book among minor prophets looking to punishment of all sinful nations, including Judah, followed by the restoration of Judah and the nations as well.

The first verse tells all we know about the prophet, tracing back four generations to Hezekiah. Some scholars think Hezekiah was the king of Judah (2 Kings 18–20). If so, Zephaniah would have belonged to the royal line. That would perhaps explain why he did not condemn the king in 1:8; 3:3-5, where he blames most of Judah's upper classes for their sins. Other scholars note that Hezekiah was a common name and the text says nothing of a king. Zephaniah's father was Cushi, which could mean "Cushite" or "Ethiopian." Zephaniah's ancestry may have been traced 4 generations to demonstrate he was indeed Israelite.

Zephaniah ministered during Josiah's reign (640–609 B.C.). Most scholars date the book in 630 or between 630 and 621. In 621 King Josiah instituted a sweeping reformation of worship in Judah (see 2 Kings 22:3–23:25) and officially abolished worship of Baal and the stars mentioned in Zeph. 1:4-6. Jeremiah also condemned those practices (Jer. 2:20-28; 8:1-3). Jeremiah 26:1 shows the practices flourished again as early as reign of Jehoiakim (609 B.C.); such worship may have continued secretly between 621 and 609. If that were so, Zephaniah might have prophesied during those years.

Zephaniah predicted punishment on the whole world, including Jerusalem (1:2-6). The punishment is the Day of the Lord (vv. 7-16). Verses 17-18 depict the inability of sinful humanity to escape God's punishment. Punishment would come upon the nobles at the king's court, those who gained materially through violence, the merchants, and those who denied the power of God to reward good or punish evil.

The second chapter contains a series of threats against the Philistines (vv. 4-7), Moabites and Ammonites (vv. 8-11), Ethiopians (v. 12), and Assyrians (vv. 13-15). Zephaniah called all nations to repent and become righteous and meek.

Chapter 3 begins (vv. 1-7) with a woe on Jerusalem for oppression within her walls by princes, prophets, and priests. The final verses (8-20) have a positive word toward Israel. Verses 8 and 14 admonish the people to wait for God to act and to rejoice for what He will do. Verses 8-13 promise that God will punish the nations and convert them from idolatry. What is more, He promises to remove the haughty from Mount Zion, leaving behind a meek and humble people. Verses 14-20 predict the cessation of punishment and oppression and the return of exiles. God Himself is the king of Israel (v. 15). His presence alleviates any reason to fear the nations.

ZEPHATH (*watchtower*) See *Hormah.*

ZEPHATHAH (*watchtower*)

Valley where Asa met Zerah, Ethiopian king, in battle (2 Chron. 14:10). Septuagint translated *Zaphon*, "north," instead of Zephathah. If Zephathah is identified with Safiyah, less than 2 miles northeast of Beit Jibrin, the "valley of Zephathah" is the wadi Safiyah. See *Mareshah.*

ZEPHI (*purity* or *good fortune*), **ZEPHO**

Descendant of Esau (1 Chron. 1:36); called "Zepho" in Gen. 36:11,15.

ZEPHON (*north*)

Eldest son of Gad; ancestor of Zephonites (Num. 26:15). Samaritan Pentateuch and Septuagint support identification with Ziphion (Gen. 46:16).

ZEPHONITE

Member of clan of Zephon.

ZER (*narrow* or *enemy*)

Fortified town in Naphtali (Josh. 19:35), possibly identified with Madon. Commentators often take Zer as copyist's modification, repeating Hebrew for "fenced cities." See *Ziddin.*

ZERAH (*sunrise*)

(1) Twin born to Tamar and her father-in-law, Judah (Gen. 38:30, Zarah, KJV; compare Josh. 7:1,25); included in Matthew's genealogy of Christ, although Perez was the direct ancestor (1:3).

(2) Descendant of Esau and thus clan leader of Edomites (Gen. 36:13,17).

(3) Ancestor of Edomite ruler (Gen. 36:33).

(4) Clan leader in Simeon (Num. 26:13), apparently same as Zohar (Gen. 46:10);

(5) Levite (1 Chron. 6:21,41).

(6) Cushite general God defeated in answer to Asa's prayer (2 Chron. 14:8-13). See *Cush; Ethiopia.*

ZERAHIAH (*Yahweh has dawned*)

(1) Priest descended from Phinehas (1 Chron. 6:6,51; Ezra 7:4).

(2) Descendant of Pahath-Moab ("governor of Moab") and father of Eliehoenai (Ezra 8:4). See *Izrahiah.*

ZERAHITES

Member of clan descended from Zerah; two families, one from Simeon (Num. 26:13), the other from Judah (Num. 26:20; Josh. 7:17; compare 1 Chron. 9:6; Neh. 11:24), descended from men named Zerah. Two of David's thirty elite warriors, Sibbecai and Maharai, were Zerahites (1 Chron. 27:11,13).

ZERED (*white thorn*)

Stream which empties into southern end of Dead Sea; only 38 miles long, it drains a large area of land (Deut. 2:13-14; compare 2 Kings 3:16; Isa. 15:7; Amos 6:14). See *Palestine.*

ZEREDA(H)

(1) Site in Ephraim of home of Jeroboam (1 Kings 11:26), possibly identified as Ain Seridah in wadi Deir Ballut, 15 miles southwest of Shechem.

(2) City in Jordan Valley (2 Chron. 4:17). Parallel text (1 Kings 7:46) reads "Zerethan."

ZEREDATHAH

KJV spelling of Zeredah (2 Chron. 4:17).

ZERERAH

Site on route by which defeated Midianites fled from Gideon (Judg. 7:22; KJV, "Zererath"); possibly variant rendering of "Zarethan" (Josh. 3:16; 1 Kings 4:12; 7:46) or of "Zeredah" (2 Chron. 4:17). See *Zarethan.*

ZERERATH KJV form of Zererah.

ZERESH *(shaggy head, disheveled)*

Haman's wife and counselor (Esther 5:10,14; 6:13).

ZERETH *(splendor)*

Descendant of Judah (1 Chron. 4:7).

ZERETH-SHAHAR *(splendor of the dawn)*

City located "on the hill of the [Dead Sea] valley"; allotted to Reuben (Josh. 13:19); perhaps modern Zarat near Machaerus on the eastern shore of the Dead Sea; others suggest Khirbet el-Libb, 7 miles south of Medeba or Khirbet qurn el-Kibsh, 6 miles northwest of Medeba.

ZERI *(balsam)*

Levitical harpist (1 Chron. 25:3); possibly copying variant of "Izri" (25:11).

ZEROR *(bundle, pouch or particle of stone)*

Ancestor of Saul (1 Sam. 9:1).

ZERUAH *(stricken or leprous)*

Mother of King Jeroboam (1 Kings 11:26).

ZERUBBABEL *(descendant of Babel)*

Grandson of King Jehoiachin (taken to Babylon in the first Exile in 597 B.C. by Nebuchadnezzar, 2 Kings 24:10-17) and son of Shealtiel (Ezra 3:2), second son of Jehoiachin (1 Chron. 3:16-17); led return from Exile in 539 B.C. (Ezra 2:2). According to Ezra 3, Zerubbabel and Jeshua (or Joshua), the high priest, rebuilt the altar and in their second year (538) laid the foundation of the temple, but their work was halted by opposition from persons who had remained in Palestine during the Exile (4:1-6,24). Darius (Persian emperor 522–486 B.C.) granted the Jews permission to continue rebuilding the temple (6:1-12). Under the urging of Haggai (1:1,12-15; 2:1,20) and Zechariah (4:6-10a), Zerubbabel, now governor (Hag. 1:1) in place of

Sheshbazzar (Ezra 5:14), resumed the task (Ezra 5:1-2), completed in 515 B.C. Zechariah 6:9-14 may reflect the wish to crown Zerubbabel king, but his fate remains unknown. See *Babylon; Israel; Zechariah.*

ZERUIAH *(perfumed with mastix or bleed)*

David's (half-)sister (1 Chron. 2:16); mother of three of David's generals—Joab, Abishai, and Asahel (2 Sam. 2:18). According to 2 Sam. 17:25, her sister, Abigail, was the (grand)daughter of Nahash rather than of Jesse, David's father.

ZETHAM *(olive tree)*

Levite who served as temple treasurer (1 Chron. 23:8; 26:22).

ZETHAN *(olive tree or olive merchant)*

Benjaminite (1 Chron. 7:10).

ZETHAR *(slayer, kingdom, or victor)*

Eunuch who served king Ahasuerus of Persia (Esther 1:10).

ZEUS

Greek god of the sky and chief of the pantheon (equivalent to Roman, Jupiter); ruler over all the gods; controlled weather. Barnabas was mistaken for Zeus by the people of Lystra (Acts 14:8-12). See *Gods, Pagan.*

ZIA *(trembling)*

Head of family of Gad (1 Chron. 5:13).

ZIBA (Aramaic, *branch*)

Servant of Saul whom David placed in charge of Mephibosheth's restored property (9:1-13). During Absalom's rebellion, Ziba falsely accused Mephibosheth of treason (2 Sam. 16:1-4). David rewarded Ziba with Mephibosheth's property. Mephibosheth met David on his return to power in Jerusalem and accused Ziba of deception (2 Sam. 19:24-29). David, either uncertain whom to believe or else desiring to leave no strong rivals, divided

Saul's property between Ziba and Mephibosheth.

ZIBEON (*little hyena*)

Horite chieftan (Gen. 36:29) and ancestor of one of Esau's wives (Gen. 36:2; compare Gen. 36:20,24,29; 1 Chron. 1:38,40).

ZIBIA (*gazelle*)

Head of family of Benjaminites (1 Chron. 8:9).

ZIBIAH (*female gazelle*)

Mother of king Jehoash (Joash) of Judah (2 Kings 12:1; 2 Chron. 24:1).

ZICHRI (*remembrance, mindful*)

(1) Levite in Moses' time (Ex. 6:21).

(2) Heads of three families of Benjaminites (1 Chron. 8:19,23,27).

(3) Levite (1 Chron. 9:15), perhaps identical to Zaccur (1 Chron. 25:2,10; Neh. 12:35) and Zabdi (Neh. 11:17).

(4) Descendant of Moses assisting with David's treasury (1 Chron. 26:25).

(5) Reubenite (1 Chron. 27:16).

(6) Father of one of Jehosaphat's army commanders (2 Chron. 17:16).

(7) Father of one of Jehoiada's generals (2 Chron. 23:1).

(8) Ephraimite warrior assisting Pekah in the elimination of Ahaz's family and advisors (2 Chron. 28:7).

(9) Father of leading Benjaminite in postexilic Jerusalem (Neh. 11:9).

(10) Postexilic priest (Neh. 12:17).

ZICRI

NIV form of Zichri.

ZIDDIM (*sides*)

Fortified town in Naphtali (Josh. 19:35), perhaps Hattin el-Qadim about 8 miles west northwest of Tiberias. Some commentators see it as copyist's repetition of "fenced cities." See *Zer.*

ZIDKIJAH

KJV alternate form of Zedekiah (Neh. 10:1).

ZIDON, ZIDONIANS

KJV alternate forms of Sidon, Sidonians.

ZIF KJV form of Ziv.

ZIGGURAT

Stepped building, usually capped by a temple made popular by Babylonians. Many biblical scholars believe tower of Babel was a ziggurat (Gen. 11:3-9).

ZIHA (*the face of Horus* [god] *has spoken*)

(1) Family of temple servants (*nethinim*) (Ezra 2:43; Neh. 7:46).

(2) Overseer of postexilic temple servants (Neh. 11:21).

ZIKLAG

Village in southern Judean plain given to Simeon (Josh. 15:31; 19:5); appears to have belonged to the Philistines; taken during period of rapid expansion in time of Judges (1 Sam. 27:6); variously identified either as tell el-Khuweilifeh, 10 miles north northeast of Beersheba, tell esh-Shariah, 9 miles north northwest of Beersheba, or Khirbet el-Mashash. Achish, king of Gath, gave the town to David during David's "outlaw" period. It became his headquarters as he made raids against the Amalekites. When David found the town had been raided and burned by the Amalekites and his family taken hostage, a daring night raid rescued his people (1 Sam. 30). Jews returning from Babylonian Exile inhabited Ziklag (Neh. 11:28).

ZILLAH (*shadow*)

Second wife of Lamech and mother of Tubal-Cain and Naamah (Gen. 4:19,22-23).

ZILLETHAI (*Yahweh is a shadow, that is, a protector*)

(1) Family of Benjaminites (1 Chron. 8:20).

(2) Manassite supporter of David at Ziklag (1 Chron. 12:20).

ZILPAH (*short-nosed*)

Leah's maid (Gen. 29:24; 46:18), given to Jacob as a concubine (30:9; 37:2); mother of Gad and Asher who were regarded as Leah's sons (30:10,12; 35:26).

ZILTHAI

KJV form of Zillethai.

ZIMMAH (*Yahweh has considered or resolved*)

Levite (1 Chron. 6:20,42; 2 Chron. 29:12).

ZIMNAH

TEV alternate form of Zimmah (2 Chron. 29:12).

ZIMRAN (*celebrated in song, famous* or *mountain goat*)

Son of Abraham and Keturah and ancestor of an Arabian tribe (Gen. 25:2; 1 Chron. 1:32), possibly identified with Zimri (Jer. 25:25).

ZIMRI (*Yah helped, Yah is my protection,* or *Yah is my praise*)

(1) Son of Zerah and grandson of Judah (1 Chron. 2:6).

(2) Chariot captain in Israel who usurped throne by killing Elah (1 Kings 16:9-10); name became a byword for king killers (2 Kings 9:31); shortest reign of Israel's kings, 7 days (16:15).

(3) Leader of Simeon slain by Phinehas for bringing Midianite woman into the wilderness camp (Num. 25).

(4) Descendant of Saul (1 Chron. 8:36).

(5) Difficult name of a nation God judged (Jer. 25:25), often taken as a copying change from the Hebrew for Cimmerians or a coded designation for Elam clarified by the immediate mention of Elam. Nothing is known of a nation of Zimri.

ZIN

Rocky desert area through which Israel passed en route from Egypt to Canaan (Num. 20:1; 27:14; 33:36); stretched from Kadesh-barnea to Dead Sea; formed part of southern border of Canaan and later Judah (Num. 34:3-4; Josh. 15:1,3)."From the wilderness of Zin to Rehob" in Galilee encompasses almost the whole Promised Land (Num. 13:21). Wilderness of Zin should be distinguished from wilderness of Sin which embraces the western Sinai plateau. See *Negeb; Wilderness.*

ZINA

Alternate form of Ziza (1 Chron. 23:10).

ZION

Transliteration of Hebrew and Greek words that originally referred to the fortified hill of pre-Israelite Jerusalem between the Kedron and Tyropean valleys (2 Sam. 5:6-10; 1 Chron. 11:4-9). "Stronghold of Zion" may have referred only to the fortified section of the city. Jerusalem was the name of the city state as a whole and included numerous villages and houses located outside of the fortified area of the city itself. After David captured Zion, he resided there and changed its name to the "city of David." Many psalmists used *Zion* to refer to the temple built by Solomon (2:6; 48:2; 84:7; 132:13). In Isa. 1:27, the idea of "Zion" included the whole nation. Zion also stood for the capital of Judah (Amos 6:1). The most common usage of Zion was to refer to the city of God in the new age (Isa. 1:27; 28:16; 33:5). Zion was understood, also, to refer to the heavenly Jerusalem (Isa. 60:14; Heb. 12:22; Rev. 14:1), the place where the Messiah would appear at the end of time. See *Jerusalem.*

ZIOR (*smallness*)

Village allotted to Judah in hill country near Hebron (Josh. 15:54).

ZIPH (*flowing*), **ZIPHITES**

(1) Son of Mareshah and grandson of Caleb (1 Chron. 2:42); text perhaps means Mareshah was the founder of Ziph near Hebron.

(2) Family of Judah (1 Chron. 4:16).

(3) Town in Judean hill country (Josh. 15:24), likely tell Zif about 3 miles southeast of Hebron. David hid from Saul in the surrounding wilderness

(1 Sam. 23:14-15; 26:2). Residents of Ziph twice revealed David's hideouts to Saul (1 Sam. 23:19; 26:1). Rehoboam fortified the site (2 Chron. 11:8).

(4) Town in Negeb (Josh. 15:24), likely Khirbet ez-Zeifeh southwest of Kurnub.

ZIPHAH (*flowing*)

Family of Judah (1 Chron. 4:16).

ZIPHIMS

KJV alternate form of Ziphites (superscription of Ps. 54).

ZIPHION See *Zephon.*

ZIPHRON (*fragrance*)

Site on northern border of Canaan, near Hazar-enan (Num. 34:9); may be modern Zapherani southeast of Restan between Hamath and Homs.

ZIPPOR ([little] *bird*)

Father of King Balak of Moab (Num. 22:2, 4, 10).

ZIPPORAH (*small bird* or *sparrow*)

Moses' first wife (some believe the woman named in Num. 12:1 may be a reference to Zipporah, too) and mother of his children, Gershom and Eliezer (Ex. 2:21-22; 18:4); daughter of Reuel, priest of Midian. By circumcising Gershom, she saved Moses' life when the Lord sought to kill him (4:24-25). It appears that Zipporah stayed with her father until Moses had led the people out of Egypt (18:2-6).

ZITHER

Stringed instrument composed of 30 to 40 strings placed over a shallow soundboard and played with a pick and fingers (Dan. 3:5,7,10,15, REB, TEV, NLT, NIV, NCV, NASB note). See *Music, Instruments, Dancing.*

ZITHRI

KJV form of Sithri.

ZIV

Second month of Hebrew calendar (1 Kings 6:1). See *Calendar.*

ZIZ (*blossom*)

Pass through steep place where the people of Ammon, Moab, and Mount Seir were going to enter Judah to attack King Jehoshaphat (2 Chron. 20:16); often located at wadi Hasasa, southeast of Tekoa near Dead Sea.

ZIZA (*shining* or *brightness*)

(1) Son of Shiphi; part of the expansion of Simeon into Gedor (1 Chron. 4:37).

(2) Son of Shimei, Levite from Gershon, following some manuscript and early translation evidence (1 Chron. 23:10, NLT, NIV, REB, NCV). "Zina" is the reading of KJV, NASB, TEV, NRSV, CEV following Hebrew text.

(3) One of Rehoboam's sons by Maachah (2 Chron. 11:20).

ZOAN

Hebrew name for Egyptian city of Tanis located at San el-Hagar on the Tanitic arm of the Nile 29 miles south of Mediterranean. Zoan became capital of Egypt about 1070 B.C. under Smendes I and remained so until 655 B.C. Num. 13:22 notes that Hebron was 7 years older than Zoan, but the exact date when either was built is not known. Prophets used Zoan to refer to Egyptian government and its activities (Isa. 19:11,13; 30:4; Ezek. 30:14). The psalmist praised God for Exodus miracles near there (Ps. 78:12,43).

ZOAR (*small*)

City in valley of Siddim, also known as Bela (Gen. 14:2); perhaps Safi on the river Zered. It was attacked by Chedolaomer, but apparently delivered by Abraham (14:17). Lot fled to Zoar with his family just before God destroyed Sodom and Gomorrah (19:23-24). Isaiah prophesied that the citizens of Moab would flee to Zoar when destruction would come upon their nation (Isa. 15:5; compare Jer. 48:34).

ZOBA(H) (*battle*)

Leading Syrian power before the rise of Damascus. See *David*; *Syria*.

ZOBEBAH

Descendant of Judah (1 Chron. 4:8; NIV, "Hazzobebah").

ZOHAR (*witness*)

(1) Hittite (Gen. 23:8; 25:9).

(2) Son of Simeon (Gen. 46:10; Ex. 6:15), also called Zerah (Num. 26:13; 1 Chron. 4:24).

(3) Descendant of Judah according to the traditional marginal correction (*qere*) at 1 Chron. 4:24; Hebrew reads Izhar.

ZOHELETH (*creeping one, sliding, or serpent stone*)

Stone of sacrifice where Adonijah offered sacrifices in light of his coming coronation as king (1 Kings 1:9); near En-rogel, a spring or well near Jerusalem where the Kidron Valley and the Valley of Hinnom meet.

ZOHETH

Son of Ishi (1 Chron. 4:20); head of family in Judah.

ZOPHAH (*jug*)

Family in Asher (1 Chron. 7:35-36).

ZOPHAI (*honeycomb*)

Son of Elkanah (1 Chron. 6:26). See *Zuph*.

ZOPHAR

One of Job's three friends in his misery (2:11); probably the youngest; sharpest critic of the three and more philosophical and dogmatic in his criticism of Job.

ZOPHIM (*watchers* or *the Field of the Watchers* [REB] or *lookout post*)

High place at "top of Pisgah" near northeastern end of Dead Sea. Balak took Baalim there to curse the Israelites (Num. 23:14).

ZORAH (*wasps* or *hornets*)

City of Dan (Josh. 19:41) about 13 miles west of Jerusalem on border with Judah (Josh. 15:33; "Zoreah," KJV); home of Manoah, Samson's father (Judg. 13:2); modern Sarah, one-half mile north of Beth-shemesh. Rehoboam, king of Judah, strengthened Zorah in case of war (2 Chron. 11:5-12).

ZORATHITES

Descendants of Shobal who lived in Zorah (1 Chron. 2:52-53).

ZOREAH

KJV alternate spelling of Zorah.

ZORITES

People from Zorah (1 Chron. 2:54).

ZOROASTER

Ancient Iranian prophet after whom a religion called Zoroastrianism was named. See *Persia*.

ZOROBABEL

KJV alternate form of Zerubbabel (Matt. 1:12-13; Luke 3:27).

ZUAR (*young* or *small*)

Member of Issachar (Num. 1:8; 2:5; 7:18,23; 10:15).

ZUPH (*honeycomb*)

(1) Levitic ancestor of Elkanah and Samuel (1 Sam. 1:1; 1 Chron. 6:16,26,35) from Ephraim.

(2) "Land of Zuph" where Saul was looking for some donkeys (1 Sam. 9:5).

ZUPHITE

NIV term for resident or descendant of Zuph (1 Sam. 1:1).

ZUR (*rock*)

(1) Midianite tribal chief (Num. 25:15) whose daughter, Cozbi, was killed with an Israelite man by Phinehas. Zur

was later killed in a battle Moses led (Num. 31:7-8; Josh. 13:21).

(2) King Saul's uncle (1 Chron. 8:30; 9:36).

ZURIEL (*God is a rock*)

Son of Abihail and head of the Merari family of Levites (Num. 3:35).

ZURISHADDAI (*shaddai is a rock*)

Father of Shelumiel, leader of Simeon, in wilderness (Num. 1:6).

ZUZIM

People who lived in Ham and were defeated by Chedorlaomer (Gen. 14:5); apparently called Zamzummin in Deut. 2:20.

ZUZITE

NIV term for Zuzim (Gen. 14:5).

The Holman Concise Reference Series
Collect the Entire Set!

**3-Volume Set
only $29.97**
0-8054-2837-2

**or Purchase
Each Volume
Separately**